THE CHRISTIAN FAITH

J. NEUNER, S.J. — J. DUPUIS, S.J.

THE CHRISTIAN FAITH

IN THE
DOCTRINAL DOCUMENTS OF THE CATHOLIC CHURCH

EDITED BY

JACQUES DUPUIS

Seventh Revised and Enlarged Edition

ALBA·HOUSE   NEW·YORK

SOCIETY OF ST. PAUL, 2187 VICTORY BLVD., STATEN ISLAND, NEW YORK 10314

Imprint potest
Francisco Egaña, S.J.
Vice-Rector
Pont. Gregorian University,
Rome
7 November 2000

Imprimatur
Most Rev. Dr. Ignatius Pinto
Archbishop of Bangalore
Bangalore, India
16 January 2001

ISBN 0-8189-0893-9

Published in the United States of America by
St. Pauls/Alba House, Division of the Society of St. Paul,
an International Roman Catholic Missionary Religious Congregation
dedicated to spreading the Gospel message via the media of communications,
by special arrangement with Theological Publications of India.
The St. Pauls/Alba House edition is for sale in the U.S.A., Europe,
Canada, Australia, the Philippines and Africa.

Typeset, printed and bound in India at Indira Printers, New Delhi- 110 020

FOREWORD

The origin of this book goes back as far as 1938 to the first publication in German of the Church's doctrinal documents edited by J. Neuner and H. Roos under the title *Der Glaube der Kirche in den Urkunden der Lehrverkündigung*. Later editions of that book were prepared by K. Rahner, the two editors being prevented by circumstances from pursuing their work. An English translation of the sixth edition of the work was brought out by Mercier Press, Cork, Ireland, in 1967, under the title *The Teaching of the Catholic Church*. In 1969 the Mercier Press licensed an Indian edition of the book. This was mostly a reprint of the English edition; except for a few modifications and additions, it innovated only by appending to each chapter a survey of the doctrine of the Second Vatican Council.

The profound changes in theological thinking characteristic of recent years have, however, made it desirable to produce a new edition of the Church's doctrinal documents. Not only was an updating of the material required in order to include some characteristic texts of Vatican II and post-conciliar documents; it seemed also necessary to leave out some texts which have lost their relevance while re-introducing others. The introductions to the chapters had to be re-written in the light of the Council's doctrine; those to the various documents had to be revised in the light of recent scholarship. Translations needed amending and have in many cases been done anew. Most of all, it seemed opportune to introduce new chapters so as to cover some important fields of modern theology.

This work has enlisted the collaboration of professors belonging to the two theological faculties of Vidyajyoti, Institute of Religious Studies, Delhi, and of Jnana-Deepa Vidyapeeth, Institute of Philosophy and Religion, Pune. Individual chapters were prepared by the following authors: Symbols and Professions of Faith, Chapters VI, XI, XII, XIII, XV: J. Dupuis; Chapters I, III, VII, XVI: J. Neuner; Chapter II: R. Van de Walle; Chapters IV, V: P. De Letter; Chapters VIII, IX: J. Lerch; Chapter X: G. Gispert-Sauch; Chapters XIV, XVII, XX: G. Gilleman; Chapters XVIII, XXII: G. Lobo; Chapters XIX, XXIII: A. Bermejo;

Chapter XXI: F. Timmermans. The coordination and unification of the chapters is the work of the two editors. The responsibility for the book in its present form lies therefore with them only.

The editors wish to express their gratitude to the authors for their co-operation.

Since the first edition of the forerunner of this book in 1938 other publications of Church documents have appeared in various languages. It is in the nature of these works that they are all inter-related and mutually dependent as regards the selection and arrangement of texts as well as the evaluation and interpretation of the documents provided in various introductions and notes. As other collections have derived some help from the predecessor of the present book, it has in turn drawn some inspiration from them. Mention may be made of G. Dumeige, *La Foi Catholique*, Paris 1969. Above all, however, it is on the new edition of the *Enchiridion Symbolorum, Definitionum et Declarationum de Rebus Fidei et Morum* first made by A. Schönmetzer in 1962 that every new collection of doctrinal documents necessarily depends as its main source. The editors gratefully acknowledge the help derived by them from these various sources.

J. NEUNER — J. DUPUIS

CONTENTS

CHAPTER XIV: BAPTISM AND CONFIRMATION   575

CHAPTER XVIII: MATRIMONY   763

INTRODUCTION TO THE FIRST EDITION

Catholic theology must be taught "in the light of faith and under the guidance of the Church's teaching authority" *(OT 16)*. It must be solidly anchored in the word of God, "which ought to be, as it were, the soul of all theology" *(ibid.)*. But reflection on divine revelation is not the private pursuit of individuals; it is a task entrusted by Jesus Christ to the Church herself, which she must perform under the vigilance of the teaching office established by him as the custodian of his word. Keeping it faithfully and transmitting it through her living tradition, guided by it as by her ultimate norm, the Church has grown through the centuries in her awareness of the content of the deposit of faith committed to her. The responsibility of her teaching office consists in authentically declaring the divine deposit, in expanding and in interpreting it through the centuries in accordance with the changing conditions of the times and the specific needs of each generation. Thanks to this charism of interpretation, the same message endures through the centuries of Christianity, ever true to itself and capable of reaching out to the contemporary world of every age.

To ensure cotinuity in the task of proclaiming the revealed word to the modern world, this is the function of the doctrinal documents issued by the Church through the centuries; this shows their indispensable place in a study of theology that wishes to be at once creative and faithful to the past. The Church's living tradition today is the sum total of twenty centuries of Christian faith and life, and this no attempt at presenting the Christian message to modern people can afford to ignore. An accurate reading, however, of Church documents requires a keen theological discernment, capable of evaluating their content and of distinguishing in them elements of lasting value from others that time has rendered obsolete.

The deep significance of doctrinal documents lies in the authoritative guidance which they have provided in the past and still provide today for the correct understanding of divine revelation. In the course of history the Church has rejected errors which tended to disfigure the word of God and to evacuate the Christian message; she has done so with a sure instinct for the implications of the deposit entrusted to her. As her consciousness grew, she has unfolded what was latent in the message and, as circumstances required, she has expressed it in more articulate formulations. Her solemn pronouncements of faith give authentic expression to the unchanging word of God; in their deep meaning and intention they remain valid for all times and can never be contradicted by new enunciations.

This is not to say that an absolute value necessarily attaches to the traditional concepts of ancient formulations. For the revealed truth lies beyond human concepts, all of which are essentially inadequate to express it fully. No matter how deeply traditional and founded on authoritative teaching they may be, these concepts are but pointers to a mystery which they can never encompass and whose content they can never exhaust. The definitions even of the early Councils intend no more than to indicate a direction along which the Christian mystery can appropriately be thought. They are not last but first words; not boundaries but signposts. St. Thomas Aquinas knew that "that act of faith is directed not to an enunciation but to the reality" that lies beyond it.[1] Never exhausted by any formulation, this reality remains always open to new and deeper insights.

Human concepts, moreover, fall under the law of historical evolution, and this imposes on them a further unavoidable limitation. As their meaning evolves in the course of time, faithfulness to the intention of ancient formulations may at a later period recommend the use of new concepts. For, as every human discourse, the expression of the Church's faith is subject to the law of change inherent to human language.

Our own times have become more deeply aware of this twofold limitation that affects the discourse of the Church's faith. Under the impulse given it by Pope John XXIII,[2] the Second Vatican Council has reminded theologians that "the deposit of faith, that is the truths contained in it, are one thing, the manner of formulating these truths, while keeping the same sense and meaning, is another" (GS 62). To discern the intention of the faith through the concepts in which it is formulated, to recognise in its various expressions—all of which are conditioned by space and time—the faith of all times and of all places, is the task of the interpreter of doctrine.

---

1. *Summa Theologica*, II, II, 1, 2, ad 2.
2. *Discourse on the opening day of the Second Vatican Council*, cf. *AAS* 54 (1962) 792.

Besides, and more important than, the limitations inherent in human language are those derived from the historical situation of the documents which affects their doctrine. This is in itself historically conditioned. The documents of the Church are occasional pronouncements, usually intended to meet the challenge of definite errors. The historical circumstances in which they were written called for emphasising those elements of the faith which were being threatened. The need for emphasis, however, is by nature little conducive to a harmonious and well-poised formulation of doctrine. The formulation is the more easily selective and one-sided as the documents bear more deeply the stamp of current controversies. In the process full justice is not always done to other facets of the revealed message nor are the truths expressed always properly focussed. Much less do the documents present a complete account of the Christian message. In fact, its most intimate core is rarely touched upon by them; this is taken for granted rather than explicitly stated. And, while the correct conceptual enunciation of the mysteries of the faith is stressed and officially formulated, lilttle is said about knowing the one true God and Jesus Christ whom he has sent (cf. Jn 17:3) as constituting the essence of the Christian life, and about the radical demand made on the Christian to follow Christ in the mystery of his death and resurrection.

In the history of the Church's General Councils Vatican II is, perhaps, the first to be almost entirely free of controversial overtones; this is why, though less doctrinal than pastoral in purpose, it has succeeded better than its predecessors in establishing the balance between complementary aspects of the faith. It is significant to observe that the last Council points to a "hierarchy" of the truths contained in Catholic doctrine, which is based on "their different relationship to the foundation of the Christian faith" (UR 11), and advocates a "fraternal rivalry" by which all Christians "will be spurred on to a deeper knowledge and a clearer expression of the unfathomable riches of Christ" (ibid.). In the same direction, Vatican II also recognises more clearly than did the ancient Councils of union the full legitimacy of differences between East and West in the theological enunciation of doctrine—which "diverse theological formulations are often to be considered as mutually complementary rather than conflicting" (UR 17). By these words the Council states the

principles of legitimate pluralism in the expression of the faith—
a principle which in past centuries has often been overlooked.

What has been said above goes to show that the theological
interpretation of Church documents is a delicate task. Their
doctrinal value must be assessed; this is done in two ways. It
may first be asked what claim the nature of a document makes
to be an expression of the most fundamental data of the Christian
faith. From this point of view the symbols and Professions of
Faith of ancient origin hold a privileged position. Hence the
prominence given to them in this book, where they are treated
in the first place and where an effort is made to follow their
historical development. Distinct from the question of the
relationship of truths to the fundamental data of the Christian
faith is the question of the degree of authority with which any
document pronounces on matters connected with it. It is
important to discern to what extent the teaching authority of the
Church is involved in each text.

All statements in which the legitimate authority of the
Church pronounces on matters pertaining to the divine revelation
demand an inner assent on the part of the members of the
Church. But not all have the same value. Only the universal
authority, including General Councils and Popes, can make final
pronouncements. The criterion by which to recognise them is
the Church's own intention as expressed in each document. The
concrete application of this principle, however, is a delicate
matter, for the Church's precise intention is not always easily
discerned. Modern historical criticism has brought to light the
fact that not every proposition censured with *Anathema* implies
a definition of the truth contradictorily opposed. Not all
documents of General Councils, not even all their canons, are
proposed as infallible definitions. The precise dogmatic value of
documents remains in many cases open to question. In such cases
the irrevocability of propositions is to be ascertained and cannot
be presumed. Other texts, which by themselves make no claim
to infallibility, have through the subsequent approbation of the
Roman Pontiffs or through the general acceptance which they
have received from the Church, acquired a high degree of
authority. Where the need arises, this volume indicates the
doctrinal value of documents in the measure in which it can at
present be prudently assessed.

A note of caution must be added as regards the judicious use that must be made of any collection of doctrinal texts. The danger of using such a collection in too mechanical a manner has been pointed out in recent years. It easily leads to what has been stamped as "Denzinger theology"—a theology in which creativity and personal appropriation of the message are stifled by the repetition of trite formulas. The fact is then overlooked that, while no theology can afford to ignore the heritage of the past, neither can it forego its obligation to contribute to a deeper assimilation of the revealed truth. In this task its main point of reference remains the word of God. Such a theology, moreover, tends to isolate the documents from the ideological context in which they arose and from the life of the Church at the particular period during which they were written. The result is that formulations the precise meaning of which must be discovered against their historical background, tend to be treated as parts of a timeless system of doctrine. In addition, little attention is paid to the fact that a collection is made up of documents hailing from sources of vastly different doctrinal authority, ranging from General Councils to papal encyclicals and decrees of the Roman Congregations. In the process, the Church's teaching office itself is wrongly treated as a uniform, monolithic thing, as a supra-temporal structure disengaged from her socio-historical reality. It is therefore supremely important to counteract the impression that the presentation in one collection of sources of vastly different origin and doctrinal value may easily create, by relating each document to its historical context and ascertaining its precise authority.

In an essay on "The Correct Use of Denzinger".[1] Y. Congar, while recognising the merits of the *Enchiridion* on which every collection of Church documents in modern times has been based, also points to some serious deficiencies. Most important among these is the fact that the *Enchiridion* is sometimes unduly selective. Some texts have been truncated with the result that only one aspect of the truth expressed in particular documents has been preserved, complementary aspects also mentioned in the texts being lost sight of. Such a grievous omission occurs in the declaration of the Roman primacy made by the Council of

---

1. Y. CONGAR, *Situation et tâches de la théologie* (Paris 1967) 111-133.

Florence in its *Decree for the Greeks*, where Denzinger omits the complementary declaration made by the same document of the traditional privileges of the Oriental patriarchates. The same author observes with satisfaction that the recent edition of the *Enchiridion* provided by A. Schönmetzer makes good most of these losses. Yet, even in its present form the *Enchiridion* is not altogether without blemish. The extraordinary magisterium of the General Councils and of papal definitions finds in it its due place; prominence is also rightly given to those particular Councils which in the course of time have acquired much authority through papal confirmation or the broad acceptance mostly of the Western Church. The material representing the Church's ordinary magisterium is, however, too exclusively limited to its Roman expression, with special emphasis on papal encyclicals, while other organs of the same ordinary magisterium are not sufficiently heard. Y. Congar recognises that to supplement this deficiency much work would need to be done, which would require enlisting the collaboration of an international team of scholars. This remains a task for the future.

It was beyond the scope of the present work and beyond the means at the disposal of the editors to improve much on Denzinger-Schönmetzer in this direction. The main novel feature of the work lies elsewhere. In the last decades some areas of theological studies to which in the past little attention had been paid have received new emphasis, and other new fields have emerged. To cope with this broadened theological interest, the scope of the book has been widened beyond the frame-work of traditional treatises and new chapters have been added. These include: "The Church and the World Religions", "The Church and the Missions", "Christian Worship". Moreover, it was also found desirable to cover some areas of Christian morality never included before in collections of Church documents in modern languages. In the vast field of Christian living a strict selection had, however, to be made; some topics have been selected because of the growing importance they have received in recent years. They fall under three chapters: "Principles of Christian Life"; "The Social Doctrine of the Church"; "Sexual Order and Respect for Life". These limitations notwithstanding, the enlarged material and broadened scope of this new book justify its new title. *The Christian Faith* extends here not only to orthodoxy but to orthopraxy as well; it is viewd in all its dimensions and related to the realities of the modern world.

Widening the scope of the book implied enlarging the volume which has grown to a size considerably greater than its predecessor, *The Teaching of the Catholic Church*. Severe limits were therefore imposed on the editors as regards the selection of the material related to the new topics. Only such texts could be included as have played an important role in the development of the doctrine and through which this development can be followed. Texts of a different nature, for instance liturgical texts or other witnesses of the Church's faith and practice, had to be left out of consideration. By and large, the principle of selection remains the same as in the other chapters. Apart from a few significant entries from the ordinary magisterium of local Churches, the stress remains on the Church's central teaching authority.

Other original features of the book have been mentioned in the Foreword. They are all parts of a general up-dating, in approach and content, which the important movement of return to the sources and of new theological reflection, characteristic of recent years, have made necessary. Ten years ago, this movement led to the Second Vatican Council, and the Council itself has given it a new point of departure. Prominence had therefore to be given to the Council's doctrine, in which the great theological themes are solidly based on the universal data of scripture and tradition and presented in relation to the life of the Church. To let the new orientation proper to Vatican II stand out against the background of previous documents, quoting extensive passages was not required in view of the fact that every theological student has access to the complete collection of the conciliar documents. In the case of the Council's ecclesiological doctrine, to make a judicious selection was found impracticable; for other topics important key-passages are explicitly quoted. But the Council's doctrine is in all cases presented by way of synthetic introductions following the order of the various chapters, with ample references to the Council documents.

It is hoped that this new book, with its original features, enlarged material and broadened scope, will provide students of theology with an instrument better fitted to help them perceive all the dimensions of the Christian faith. It is also hoped that it will foster doctrinal clarity and a keen sense of the historical unfolding of Catholic doctrine through the centuries, both of which are of vital importance for our time.

Scripture quotations occurring in the documents are normally given according to the *Revised Standard Version;* this rule is, however, purposely departed from wherever the intention of the documents is clearly to argue from the Vulgate text. The translation of excerpts of some papal encyclicals is borrowed from, or based upon, the text provided by the *Catholic Truth Society,* London; that of the documents of the Second Vatican Council is mostly based on the text published by *The Clergy Monthly.* This dependence on previous translations is herewith gratefully acknowledged. To the introduction to each chapter an analytical table of its main points of doctrine is appended for easy reference to the relevant texts. A chronological table of documents, a biblical index and an analytical and onomastic index are given at the end of the volume. The volume closes with a concordance with the other editions of Church documents mentioned in this introduction.

15 April, 1973   J. NEUNER—J. DUPUIS

KEY TO NUMBERS

Each chapter has its number followed by the numbers of the successive texts. Thus the texts of the first chapter have the numbers 101, 102, etc., those of the second chapter the numbers 201, 202, etc. In this way the number of each text indicates the chapter to which it belongs. The Symbols and Professions of Faith, which are placed at the beginning and form a unit by themselves, have no key number, but only serial numbers: 1, 2, etc. The numbers of the volume are printed in heavy Roman type in the margin. For the sake of easy reference to the original Greek or Latin, the corresponding numbers in Denzinger-Schönmetzer are added for all texts found in that collection; these are printed in italics. For documents which are not found in Denzinger-Schönmetzer the sources are indicated in the introductions to the texts.

Numbers of the volume printed between brackets ( ) indicate either documents which are not quoted but to which an introduction is given or parts of documents which are not quoted but only summarised. For texts quoted elsewhere in the volume cross-references are given. Both in the introductions to the documents and in the texts, cross references indicate the numbers of this volume; *i* following a number refers to the introduction to that number. For documents not quoted in the volume, references are given to their numbers in Denzinger-Schönmetzer *(DS)*. Numbers between square brackets [ ] indicate condemned propositions. A system of sub-numbers has been introduced; these are not always continuous, but indicate, for the sake of easy reference, the serial numbers of the propositions contained in the documents quoted.

ABBREVIATIONS FOR SOURCES

AAS   *Acta Apostolicae Sedis*, Rome, 1909...

ASS   *Acta Sanctae Sedis*, Rome, 1865-1908.

Acta   refers to the Acta of a partilcular Pope.

COD   *Conciliorum Oecumenicorum Decreta*, Freiburg im Breisgau, 1973.

Mansi   J.D. Mansi, *Sacrorum Conciliorum nova et amplissima* collectio, Florence, 1759.....

PG   *Patrologia Graeca*, ed. J.P. Migne, Paris, 1857-1866.

PL   *Patrologia Latina*, ed. J.P. Migne, Paris, 1844-1855.

DS   H. Denzinger-A. Schönmetzer, *Enchridilon Symbolorum, Definitionum et Declarationum de rebus fidei et morum,*

Freiburg im Breisgau, ed. 36, 1976.

D   H. Denzinger, *Enchiridion Symbololrum, Definitionum et Declarationum de rebus fidei et morum*, Freiburg im Breisgau, 1953.

ABBREVIATIONS FOR THE DOCUMENTS OF THE SECOND VATICAN COUNCIL

AA   *Apostolicam Actuositatem*, Decree on the apostolate of the laity.

AG   *Ad Gentes*, Decree on the missionary activity of the Church.

CD   *Christus Dominus*, Decree on the pastoral office of bishops in the Church.

DH   *Dignitatis Humanae*, Declaration on religious freedom.

DV   *Dei Verbum*, Dogmatic Constitution on divine revelation.

GE   *Gravissimum Educationis*, Declaration on Christian education.

GS   *Gaudium et Spes*, Pastoral Constitution on the Church in the modern world.

IM   *Inter Mirifica*, Decree on mass communications media.

LG   *Lumen Gentium*, Dogmatic Constitution on the Church.

NA   *Nostra Aetate*, Declaration on the relationship of the Church to non-Christian religions.

OE   *Orientalium Ecclesiarum*, Decree on the Catholic Oriental Churches.

OT   *Optatam Totius*, Decree on priestly formation.

PC   *Perfectae Caritatis*, Decree on the adaptation and renewal of the religious life.

PO   *Presbyterorum Ordinis*, Decree on the ministry and life of priests.

SC   *Sacrosanctum Concilium*, Constitution on the Sacred Liturgy.

UR   *Unitatis Redintegratio*, Decree on Ecumensim.

OTHER ABBREVIATIONS

CCC   *Catechism of the Catholic Church*

DM   "Dialogue and Mission"

DP   "Dialogue and Proclamation"

EN   *Evangelii Nuntiandi*

ES   *Ecclesiam Suam*

RH   *Redemptor Hominis*

RM   *Redemptoris Missio*

FR   *Fides et Ratio*

INTRODUCTION TO THE SEVENTH REVISED AND ENLARGED EDITION

Nearly thirty years have passed since *The Christian Faith* was first published in 1973. The Foreword and the Introduction to the first edition explained its special features, including chapters on topics of theological interest to which previous collections of doctrinal documents had devoted no special treatment, and the enlarging of the material to include key passages of the documents of the Second Vatican Council as well as of post-conciliar documents. Each edition that followed, at a rhythm of about five years, comprised a further updating till the time of publication. Following this tradition, the present seventh revised and enlarged edition updates the material up to the year 1999, included. The principle of selection of documents among the ever growing material, has remained the same as in previous editions: the stress remains, unavoidably, but not exclusively, on the Church's central teaching authority, though significant documents from episcopal conferences and their federations have also been included.

It is a pleasant duty to thank all the colleagues who through the years have collaborated to the various editions. The names of the contributors to the first edition are mentioned in the Foreword. All belonged to the two Jesuit theological faculties of India. The same team of authors did the updating of the various chapters of the book down to the fifth edition (1991), included. A change intervened for the sixth edition, when circumstances made it imperative to seek the collaboration of professors of the Gregorian University in Rome, who generously took over from the Indian colleagues the responsibility for the further updating. The contributors for the sixth edition (1995) were: J. Wicks (chs. 1,2), G. O'Collins (chs. 3, 6), L. Ladaria (chs. 4, 5, 19, 23), W. Henn (chs. 8, 9), Ch. Pottie (chs. 12, 13, 16, 18), Ph. Rosato (chs. 14, 15, 17), B. Johnstone (chs. 20,22), P. McNellis (ch.21), J. Dupuis, (professions of faith, chs. 7,10,11). For the present seventh edition, the team of scholars remains the same, with some exceptions due to circumstances. We have enrolled the collaboration of some new members, according to their respective specialties, for the updating of some chapters: M. Farrugia (chs. 4,5,16,18,19,23), J. Joblin (ch.21). To all, past and present, goes our gratitude for their willing and competent collaboration.

We also extend our thanks to sister Mary Peter Froelicher, shcj, for updating the indexes of this new edition.

This seventh edition brings the updating of the book down to the end of the second millennium. It is hoped that it may do to teachers and students of the beginning of the third millennium the same service as its predecessors have done for the last thirty years to those that went before them.

30 June 2000,   Jacques Dupuis, S.J.
Gregorian University, Rome

SYMBOLS AND PROFESSIONS OF FAITH

The earliest profession of faith in the apostolic Church is Christological. It is expressed in three concise formulas: 'Jesus is the Christ' (cf. Acts 2:36; 10:36; Col 2:6); 'Jesus is the Lord' (1 Cor 12:3; Rom 10:9; cf. Acts 2:36; Phil 2:11); 'Jesus is the Son of God' (cf. Acts 9:20; 13:33; Rom 1:4; Heb 4:14). Soon it received a more ample development in which the Christ-event, the central event of salvation history, is progressively elaborated upon (1 Cor 15:3-4; Phil 2:6-11; 1 Tim 3:16). A further development in the life of the apostolic Church is the introduction of a Trinitarian profession of faith. This is a natural evolution, for the Trinitarian confession was latent in the Christological (cf. Acts 2:33) and implied in the early kerygma (cf. Acts 2:14-39; 3:12-26; 4:8-12; 5:29-32; 10:34-43; 13:16-41). The Trinitarian profession of faith in the New Testament is best witnessed to by Mt 28:19-20 and 2 Cor 13:13; it corresponds to the Trinitarian teaching of the apostles (cf. Eph 1:3-14).

The post-apostolic Church inherited this double expression of the Christian faith, the Trinitarian and the Christological in its elaborate form. The "Apostles' Creed"—called thus by Rufinus and St. Ambrose in the fourth century—seems to result from the amalgamation of the two; hence the more evolved form of its second article referring to Christ. The legendary tradition according to which the "Apostles' Creed", made up of twelve articles, would have been composed by the apostles themselves, has long been exploded. Yet, though not composed by the apostles, the "Apostles' Creed" can legitimately be considered to represent their faith. Its origin can be reconstituted by having recourse to early documents. Among these only a few are mentioned here; they have been selected because of their historical importance in the development of the symbol of the apostles. A papyrus found at Dêr-Balizeh has preserved a purely Trinitarian profession of faith. The Apostolic Tradition of Hippolytus contains a baptismal profession of faith, Trinitarian in structure but with a more ample Christological development. The Trinitarian formula goes back to 2 Cor 13:13 and Mt 28:19; the Christological development to 1 Cor 15:3-6 and 1 Cor 12:3.

The early professions of faith result, therefore, from the merger of two enunciations, one Trinitarian and one Christological, both of which are based on the New Testament. All the early Creeds have the same structure; all share the same perspective. They are centred not on dogmatic truths, but on the economy of salvation with its Trinitarian rhythm as exposed by St. Paul in Eph 1:3-14. The three articles of the faith correspond to three periods of this history; the three are marked by the work proper to one of the three persons: creation is assigned to the Father, redemption to Christ, sanctification to the Holy Spirit. Initiated by the Father, the history of salvation culminates in the Christ-event; the effects of the Christ-event are operative during the Church era through the working of the Holy Spirit.

To those primitive data, later Creeds have in the course of the centuries added such further precisions as concrete circumstances made necessary to maintain the primitive faith. These later additions are meant to high-light some aspects of the faith; they do not alter it. Nor do they obscure the fundamental vision of the Symbol, which through the centuries remains linked to the history of salvation and bears the mark of its Trinitarian character.

THE DER-BALIZEH PAPYRUS

Discovered in Upper Egypt in the sixth century, this document represents a fourth century liturgy; but the Symbol contained in it goes back to a much earlier date, probably to the end of the second century. Its Trinitarian form expands Mt 28:19; it contains no elaborate Christological development.

Cf. G. ROBERTS—B. CAPELLE, *An Early Euchologion. The Dêr-Balizeh Papyrus* (London 1940) 32.

1   I believe in God, the Father almighty,
2   and in his only-begotten Son, our Lord Jesus Christ,
     and in the Holy Spirit, and in the resurrection of the flesh
[in *(en)* the] Holy Catholic Church.

THE APOSTOLIC TRADITION OF HIPPOLYTUS (c. 215-217)

Written at Rome in the early third century, probably by a Syrian priest, the Apostolic Tradition (21) contains a baptismal liturgy. The sacrament is administered with a threefold profession of faith, accompanied by a threefold immersion. The minister of the sacrament asks three questions, corresponding to the three articles of the faith; to each question the baptizant answers: "I believe". Taken as a unit, this baptismal profession represents a Symbol of faith, the structure of which is Trinitarian. The second article contains an elaborate Christological development.

Cf. B. BOTTE, *La Tradition Apostolique de Saint Hippolyte. Essai de reconstitution* (Münster 1963) 48-50

2   Do you believe in God, the Father almighty?
10   Do you believe in Jesus Christ, the Son of God, who was
     born of the Virgin Mary by the Holy Spirit, has been
crucified under Pontius Pilate, died [and was buried], who on the third day rose again, alive, from the dead, ascended into heaven and took his seat at the right hand of the Father, and shall come to judge the living and the dead?
     Do you believe in the Holy Church and the resurrection of the body in the Holy Spirit?[1]

---

1. "Credis *in* Spiritu et sanctam Ecclesiam et carnis resurrectionem". The object of faith seems to be that the present era in the history of salvation, viz. the Church-era leading to the parousia, is the time of the economy of the Holy Spirit: Do you believe that the Church (lives) *in* the Holy Spirit and that the resurrection of the dead (takes place) *in* him? Cf. P. NAUTIN, *Je crois à l'Esprit Saint dans la Sainte Eglise pour la résurrection de la chair* (Paris 1947) 67. This interpretation is corroborated by another version of the text of Hippolytus: "Do you believe in the Holy Spirit, the source of goodness and life, who makes all things clean in the Holy Church?" (BOTTE, *l. c.* 50).

THE SYMBOL OF ST. AMBROSE (d. 397)

St. Ambrose seems to have been the first to refer to the Symbol of faith as "Symbol of the Apostles". He explains it in an opuscule called Explanation of the Symbol, *the text of which he probably dictated to a scribe. The author refers to it also as the "Symbol of Rome". This is not intended to mean that the text coincides strictly with that in use in Rome (cf. n. 5), but that the content is substantially the same. The text of the Symbol can be reconstituted by joining together the articles interspersed by St. Ambrose's explanations.*

3   I believe in God, the Father almighty,
13   And in Jesus Christ, his only Son, our Lord, who was born
        of the Virgin Mary by the Holy Spirit, who suffered under Pontius Pilate, died and was buried. On the third day he rose again from the dead. He ascended into heaven, and is seated at the right hand of the Father, wherefrom he shall come to judge the living and the dead.

    And in the Holy Spirit, the Holy Church, the forgiveness of sins and the resurrection of the body.

THE SYMBOL OF RUFINUS (c. 404)

Rufinus too makes reference to the "Symbol of the Apostles". While writing c. 404 to explain the text used in Aquilaea, he gives an account of its few divergences from the text accepted in Rome (cf. n. 5). Unlike the Ambrosian text (cf. n. 3), that of Rufinus contains the reference to Christ's descent to the dead.

4   I believe in God, the Father almighty, invisible and
16   impassible,
    And in Jesus Christ, his only Son, our Lord, who was born of the Virgin Mary by the Holy Spirit, was crucified under Pontius Pilate and was buried. He went down to the dead (*ad inferna*). On the third day he rose again from the dead. He ascended into heaven, and is seated at the right hand of the Father. From there he shall come to judge the living and the dead.

    And in the Holy Spirit, the Holy Church, the forgiveness of sins and the resurrection of the body.

THE SYMBOL OF THE ROMAN ORDER OF BAPTISM

This is the form of the "Symbol of the Apostles" accepted in Rome during the tenth century, but already previously recognised throughout the

Western Church. Ninth century codices witness to its being used in Gaul in the local language. Except for accidental variants, this text of the "Symbol of the Apostles" will thereafter remain traditional in the West. It has both the Trinitarian structure and the large Christological development. Numbers in the text indicate the division in twelve articles, on which is based the legendary tradition which attributes it to the twelve apostles. Proper to the West, this Symbol is unknown to the Eastern Churches. These will always refer to the Creed of Nicaea (cf. nn. 7-8) as the first authoritative Symbol of the Christian faith.

5　　I believe in God, the Father almighty, creator of heaven
30　　and earth (1).

And in Jesus Christ, his only Son, our Lord (2), who was conceived by the Holy Spirit, born of the Virgin Mary (3), suffered under Pontius Pilate, was crucified, died and was buried; he went down to the dead *(ad inferna)* (4). On the third day he rose again from the dead (5). He ascended to the heavens, and is seated at the right hand of God, the Father almighty (6), wherefrom he shall come again to judge the living and the dead (7).

I believe in the Holy Spirit (8), the Holy Catholic Church, the communion of saints (9), the forgiveness of sins (10), the resurrection of the body (11), and the life everlasting (12).

THE SYMBOL OF EUSEBIUS

In a letter addressed to his diocese (325), Eusebius, bishop of Caesaraea, refers to the profession of faith with which he had been baptised. This testifies to the use of this Symbol around the middle of the third century. Its historical importance consists mostly in the influence it has exercised on the composition of the Symbol of Nicaea (cf. n. 7). The Trinitarian structure is clear: one God, one Lord, one Spirit, refers to Eph 4:4-6 and 1 Cor 8:6. The Christological development contains dogmatic affirmations unknown to the Symbol of the Apostles; the third article merely mentions the Holy Spirit.

6　　We believe in one God, the Father almighty, the maker
40　　of all things visible and invisible.

And in one Lord Jesus Christ, the Word of God, God from God, Light from Light, Life from Life, the only-begotten Son, first born of all creation, begotten from the Father before all ages, through whom all things were made. For our salvation he became flesh and lived as a man, he suffered and rose again on the third day and ascended to the Father. He shall come again in glory to judge the living and the dead.

We believe also in one Holy Spirit.

THE FIRST GENERAL COUNCIL OF NICAEA
SYMBOL OF NICAEA (325)

Convened by Emperor Constantine to affirm the faith against the Arian crisis, the Council of "318 Fathers", from East and West, was held at Nicaea from June 16 to August 25, 325; a representative sent from Rome by Pope Sylvester attended the Council. Arius, a priest in Alexandria (d. 336) denied the equality of the Son with the Father: the Son was understood to have been created in time by the Father and to have been used by him as his instrument for the creation of the world. In its Creed the Council solemnly proclaimed the oneness in being ("consubstantiality") of the Son with the Father; to the Symbol is appended a clear condemnation of the Arian errors. Eusebius (d. 340) himself testifies to the fact that the Symbol of Caesaraea served as basis for the Nicene Creed. Many formulations have been taken over from it; others have been purposely left out because they could lend themselves to an Arian interpretation; others still were added to provide further precisions necessary in the context of the Arian crisis. Though not directly intended as a baptismal Creed, the Symbol of Nicaea exercised a deep influence on the baptismal Creeds of the fourth century.

Cf. I. Ortiz de Urbina, *Nicée et Constantinople* (Paris 1963) 69-92.

7 We believe in one God, the Father almighty, maker of all
125 things, visible and invisible.

And in one Lord Jesus Christ, the Son of God, the only-begotten generated from the Father, that is, from the being *(ousia)* of the Father, God from God, Light from Light, true God from true God, begotten, not made, one in being *(homoousios)* with the Father, through whom all things were made, those in heaven and those on earth. For us human beings and for our salvation he came down, and became flesh, was made man, suffered, and rose again on the third day. He ascended to the heavens and shall come again to judge the living and the dead.

And in the Holy Spirit.

8 As for those who say: "There was a time when he was
126 not" and "Before being begotten he was not", and

who declare that he was made from nothing *(ex ouk ontôn)*, or that the Son of God is from a different substance *(hupostasis)* or being *(ousia)*, that is, created *(ktistos)* or subject to change and alteration,—[such persons] the Catholic Church condemns.

THE SYMBOL OF CYRIL OF JERUSALEM (c. 348)

It has sometimes been thought that the Symbol of Cyril had served as basis for the Creed of Nicaea. But the closer similarity which exists between some of the expressions of the Eusebian Symbol and the Nicene Creed undermines this assertion. The truth rather seems to be that the Creed of Cyril, in the form in which it has been preserved, has been partly influenced by the Nicene Creed. The term homoousios, *introduced by the Council of Nicaea, is left out because of the Sabellian overtones, which, in the mind of Cyril, could be attached to it. The text of the Creed of Cyril has been reconstituted by gleaning from his various Catechetical Instructions (Cat. Myst. VI-XVIII). As in the text of Eusebius, one God, one Lord, one Spirit, goes back to Eph 4:4-6 and 1 Cor 8:6. Unlike Eusebius and the Council of Nicaea, Cyril develops at length the economy of the Spirit in the third article of his Creed.*

Cf. I ORTIZ DE URBINA, *Nicée et Constantinople* (Paris 1963) 69-73.

9 We believe in one God, the Father almighty, maker of
41 heaven and earth, of all things visible and invisible.

And in one Lord Jesus Christ, the only-begotten Son of God, generated from the Father, true God before all the ages, through whom all things were made. He [came down, became flesh and] was made man, was crucified [and buried]. He rose again [from the dead] on the third day, and ascended to the heavens, and took his seat at the right hand of the Father. He shall come in glory to judge the living and the dead; to his Kingdom there will be no end.

And in one Holy Spirit, the Paraclete, who has spoken in the prophets, and in one baptism of conversion for the forgiveness of sins, and in one Holy and Catholic Church, and in the resurrection of the body, and the life everlasting.

THE SYMBOL OF EPIPHANIUS (374)

This Symbol is a personal composition of Epihanius, bishop of Salamis. It exists under two forms, a short form destined to "these who are to receive holy baptism", and a long form for further catechesis. It depends much on the Symbol of Nicaea, whose condemnation of the Arian error it repeats but to which it adds further precisions. Historically, its importance lies in the influence it will exercise at the Council of Constantinople (cf. nn. 12-13). One of its characteristics is its doctrinal affirmations regarding the Holy Spirit.

Epiphanius (d. 403) writes in the context of the already rising trends which deny the divinity of the Holy Spirit. He thus prepares in advance the doctrine of Constantinople. The short form is quoted here because its more precise formulations as regards the divinity of the Spirit will be adopted by the Council of Constantinople. For the long form, cf. DS 44-45.

10   We believe in one God, the Father almighty, maker of
42   heaven and earth, of all things visible and invisible.

And in one Lord Jesus Christ, the only-begotten Son of God, generated from the Father before all ages, that is, from the being *(ousia)* of the Father, Light from Light, true God from true God, begotten, not made, one in being *(homoousios)* with the Father, through whom all things were made, those in the heavens and those on earth. For us and for our salvation he came down from the heavens, and became flesh from the Holy Spirit and the Virgin Mary, and was made man. For our sake too he was crucified under Pontius Pilate, suffered and was buried. On the third day he rose again according to the Scriptures. He ascended to the heavens and is seated at the right hand of the Father. He shall come again in glory to judge the living and the dead; to his Kingdom there will be no end.

And in the Holy Spirit, the Lord *(to Kurion)* and Giver of life, who proceeds *(ekporeuomenon)* from the Father, who together with the Father and the Son is worshipped and glorified, who has spoken through the prophets. [And] in one Holy, Catholic and apostolic Church. We acknowledge one baptism for the forgiveness of sins. We expect the resurrection of the dead and the life of the world to come. Amen.

11   As for those who say: "There was a time when he was
43   not", and "Before being begotten he was not", or who
declare that he was made from nothing, or that the Son of God is from a different substance or being, or subject to change and alteration,—such persons the Catholic and apostolic Church condemns.

THE FIRST GENERAL COUNCIL OF CONSTANTINOPLE
SYMBOL OF CONSTANTINOPLE (381)

The Council was convened by Emperor Theodosius I to "confirm the faith of Nicaea" and to reaffirm it against the Arian current which had not entirely died out; more particularly the intention was to determine the doctrine of the Holy Spirit—about which Nicaea had remained silent—against various heretical tendencies, notably that of Eunomius and the Macedonians, also called "Pneumatomachs", who denied his divinity. The Council was held from May till July 381. It was composed of "150 Fathers", all from the East. Pope Damasus was not represented. No mention of the Symbol of Constantinople will later be made at Ephesus (431), but Chalcedon (451) will consider it as representing "the faith of the 150 Fathers gathered at Constantinople"; in the West, Constantinople will be regarded as an ecumenical Council only in the sixth century. The post-factum approbation that raises this Byzantine Synod to the rank of General Council extends to its Symbol, and notably to its doctrine of the Holy Spirit. The divinity of the Holy Spirit is proclaimed beyond doubt though in less decisive terms than had been used at Nicaea with regard to the divinity of the Son. The term homoousios *is avoided, probably in an effort to win over the Pneumatomachs. To the Symbol are appended various canons, the first of which condemns various errors against the divinity of the Son and of the Spirit.*

The Symbol of Constantinople, which will only much later (from the 17th century on) be known as the "Nicene-Constantinopolitan Symbol" has not been composed by the Council. It is a revised version of the Symbol of Epiphanius of Salamis, contained in his work Ancoratus *(374); it differs from it in details only. It incorporates many elements of the Symbol of Nicaea and of the apostolic Symbol; some notations seem to be borrowed from the symbol of Cyril of Jerusalem. Though not a new composition made by the Council of Constantinople, the Symbol seems to have been promulgated by the Council. After gaining recognition, it soon acquired greater authority than the Nicene Creed, even in the West. Introduced first in the East in the liturgy of baptism and then in the Mass, it made its way later into the Western liturgy in a slightly different form (cf. DS 150). The original text is given here.*

Cf. I Ortiz de Urbina, *Nicée et Constantinople* (Paris 1963) 182-205.

12 We believe in one God, the Father almighty, maker of
150 heaven and earth, of all things visible and invisible.

And in one Lord Jesus Christ, the only-begotten Son of God, generated from the Father before all ages, Light from Light, true God from true God, begotten, not made, one in being *(homoousios)* with the Father, through whom all things were made. For us and for our salvation he came down from the heavens, and became flesh from the Holy Spirit and the Virgin Mary and was made man. For our sake too he was crucified under Pontius Pilate, suffered and was buried. On the third day he rose again according to the Scriptures, he ascended to the heavens and is seated at the right hand of the Father. He shall come again in glory to judge the living and the dead; to his Kingdom there will be no end.

And in the Holy Spirit, the Lord *(to Kurion)* and Giver of life, who proceeds *(ekporeuomenon)* from the Father,[1] who together with the Father and the Son is worshipped and glorified, who has spoken through the prophets. [And] in one Holy Catholic and apostolic Church. We acknowledge one baptism for the forgiveness of sins. We expect the resurrection of the dead and the life of the world to come. Amen.

Canon I

13   The faith of the 318 Fathers who gathered at Nicaea of
151   Bithinia may not be adulterated. It remains authoritative and all heresy must be condemned, especially that of the Eunomians or 'Anomaeans' *(anomoioi)*, of the Arians or Eudoxians, of the Semi-Arians or Pneumatomachs, of the Sabellians, the Marcellians, the Photinians and the Apollinarists.

THE "FAITH OF DAMASUS"

This profession of faith has sometimes been attributed to Pope Damasus (d. 384) or to St. Jerome. In reality, it belongs to the fifth century and seems to have originated from Southern Gaul rather than from Spain. It reflects the more elaborate enunciation of the faith characteristic of the West during that period. Originally, the addition "and from the Son" (et filio) *concerning the procession of the Holy Spirit, was absent; it has been introduced later (cf. n. 12, note),*

14   We believe in one God, the Father almighty,
71   and in our one Lord Jesus Christ, the Son of God, and in [one] Holy Spirit, God.

---

1. The Latin translation adds "and the Son" *(filioque)*. This addition was first introduced in Spain in the sixth century; it is found in the profession of faith of the third Council of Toledo (589) *(DS 470)*. From Spain, it spread to Gaul and Germany. Under the Carolingian Empire, a Synod of Aachen (809) requested Pope Leo III to have it introduced in the entire Latin Church; the Pope, however, did not acquiesce to this request for fear of imposing a clause added to the traditional text of the Creed. It was introduced in the Roman liturgy of the Mass by Pope Benedict VIII *(d. 1024)*. The Greeks ignored the *filioque* and denied every right to make any addition to the Creed. The question was later to be discussed between Latins and Greeks at the two union Councils: Lyons II (1274) *(cf. n. 321)* and Florence (1439) *(cf. nn. 322 ff)*.

We do not worship and confess three Gods, but one God who is Father and Son and Holy Spirit. He is one God, yet not solitary; he is not at the same time Father to himself and Son, but the Father is he who begets and the Son he who is begotten. As for the Holy Spirit, he is neither begotten nor unbegotten (*ingenitus*), neither created nor made, but he proceeds from the Father and the Son, being equally eternal and fully equal with the Father and the Son and cooperating with them; for it is written: "By the Word of the Lord the heavens were made", that is, by the Son of God, "and all their host by the breath of His mouth" [*Ps 33 (32) 6*]; and elsewhere: "When you send forth your Spirit, they are created, and you renew the face of the earth" [*cf. Ps 104 (103) 30*]. Therefore, in the name of the Father and of the Son and of the Holy Spirit we confess one God, for the term 'God' refers to power, not to personal characteristics (*proprietas*). The proper name for the Father is Father, and the proper name for the Son is Son, and the proper name for the Holy Spirit is Holy Spirit. And in this Trinity we believe that God [is] one because what is of one nature and of one substance and of one power with the Father is from one Father. The Father begets the Son, not by an act of will (*non voluntate*), nor out of necessity, but by nature.

15 In the last times, the Son, who never ceased to be with the
72 Father, came down from the Father to save us and to fulfil the Scriptures. He was conceived from the Holy Spirit and born of the Virgin Mary. He assumed body, soul and sensibility, that is, a complete human nature (*perfectum hominem*): he did not lose what he was, but began to be what he was not, in such a way, however, that he is perfect in his own nature (*in suis*) and truly shares in ours (*in nostris*). For, he who was God has been born as a man, and he who has been born as a man acts as God; and he who acts as God dies as man, and he who dies as man rises again as God. Having conquered the power of death with that body with which he had been born and had suffered and died, he rose again on the third day; he ascended to the Father and is seated at his right hand in the glory which he always has had and always has. We believe that we who have been cleansed in his death and in his blood shall be raised up by him on the last day in this body in which we now live. It is our hope that we shall receive from him eternal life, the reward of good merit,

or else [we shall receive] the penalty of eternal punishment for sins. Read these words, keep them, subject your soul to this faith. From Christ the Lord you will receive both life and reward.

THE PSEUDO-ATHANASIAN SYMBOL *QUICUMQUE*

This Symbol of faith has, since the seventh century, been wrongly attributed to Athanasius of Alexandria (d. 373), who had attended the Council of Nicaea as a deacon and had later become the champion of the Nicene faith in the East. In reality, the content of the Symbol clearly shows that it belongs to another time and another environment. It is a didactic summary of doctrine, characterised by the Latin approach to the mystery of the Trinity. Its antithetic formulations are much in the manner of St. Augustine. It is an original Latin composition belonging to the end of the fifth century, the author of which remains unknown. It has enjoyed great authority in the Latin Church; its rhythmic character has contributed to its widespread diffusion among various Western Liturgies.

Cf. J. N. D. KELLY, *The Athanasian Creed* (London 1964).

16   Whoever wishes to be saved must, first of all, hold the
75   Catholic faith, for, unless he keeps it whole and inviolate, he will undoubtedly perish for ever.

Now this is the Catholic faith: We worship one God in the Trinity and the Trinity in unity, without either confusing the persons or dividing the substance; for the person of the Father is one, the Son's is another, the Holy Spirit's another; but the Godhead of Father, Son and Holy Spirit is one, their glory equal, their majesty equally eternal.

Such as the Father is, such is the Son, such also the Holy Spirit; uncreated is the Father, uncreated the Son, uncreated the Holy Spirit; infinite *(immensus)* is the Father, infinite the Son, infinite the Holy Spirit; eternal is the Father, eternal the Son, eternal the Holy Spirit; yet, they are not three uncreated beings but one eternal, just as they are not three eternal beings or three infinite beings but one uncreated and one infinite. In the same way, almighty is the Father, almighty the Son, almighty the Holy Spirit; yet, they are not three gods but one God. Thus, the Father is Lord, the Son is Lord, the Holy Spirit is Lord; yet, they are not three lords but one Lord. For, as the Christian truth compels us to acknowledge each person distinctly as God and Lord, so too the Catholic religion forbids us to speak of three gods or lords.

The Father has neither been made by anyone, nor is he created or begotten; the Son is from the Father alone, not made nor created but begotten; the Holy Spirit is from the Father and the Son, not made nor created nor begotten, but proceeding. So there is one Father, not three Fathers; one Son, not three Sons; one Holy Spirit, not three Holy Spirits. And in this Trinity there is no before or after, no greater or lesser, but all three persons are equally eternal with each other and fully equal. Thus, in all things, as has already been stated above, both unity in the Trinity and Trinity in the unity must be worshipped. Let him therefore who wishes to be saved think this of the Trinity.

17 For his eternal salvation it is necessary, however, that he
76 should also faithfully believe in the incarnation of our Lord Jesus Christ. Here then is the right faith: We believe and confess that our Lord Jesus Christ, the Son of God, is both and equally God and man. He is God from the substance of the Father, begotten before the ages, and he is man from the substance of a mother, born in time; perfect God and perfect man, composed of a rational soul and a human body; equal to the Father as to his divinity, less than the Father as to his humanity. Although he is God and man, he is nevertheless one Christ, not two; however, not one because the divinity has been changed into a human body, but because the humanity has been assumed into God; entirely one, not by a confusion of substance but by the unity of personhood. For, as a rational soul and a body are a single human person, so God and man are one Christ. He suffered for our salvation, went down to the underworld (*ad infernos*), rose again from the dead on the third day, ascended to the heavens, is seated at the right hand of the Father, wherefrom he shall come to judge the living and the dead. At his coming all human beings are to rise again with their bodies and to render an account of their own deeds; those who have done good will go to eternal life, but those who have done evil to eternal fire.

This is the Catholic faith. Unless one believes it faithfully and firmly, he cannot be saved.

THE ELEVENTH COUNCIL OF TOLEDO
SYMBOL OF FAITH (675)

(18) *Begun on Nov. 7, 675, the provincial Synod of Toledo gathered 17 bishops only. Its Symbol of faith, which formerly was wrongly attributed to Eusebius of Vercelli (d. c. 371), can be considered as the work of the Synod, though its redaction was prepared in advance by the Metropolitan*

Quiricius, and proposed by him to the Fathers of the Synod for their approval.
It borrows from dogmatic statements already formulated in the professions of
faith promulgated by previous local Synods held in the same city, especially
the fourth Council of Toledo (633) (cf. DS 485) and the Sixth Council of
Toledo (638) (cf. DS 490-493). For reference, see also Toledo I (400) (DS 188-
190) and Toledo III (589) (DS 470). It also incorporates data from the Pseudo-
Athanasian Symbol "Quicumque" (cf. nn. 16-17) and from the great Latin
doctors, especially Augustine (354-430). Though never expressly approved by
any general Council or any Pope, it has through the centuries received the
greatest appreciation as an authentic expression of the Church's doctrine, and
remains an important document. Most of its affirmations belong to the doc-
trine of the faith. Later local Councils of Toledo will draw much upon Toledo
XI; such is for instance the case with Toledo XVI (DS 568-575). Just as, and
even more than the Symbol "Quicumque", the Symbol of Toledo XI reflects
the Latin approach to the basic mysteries of the faith, the Trinity and the
incarnation. Its principal merit is that it contains the deepest insights and the
clearest formulations ever proposed by any official document in the West, as
regards these two mysteries. A short paragraph on the fate of the human
person after death is added. The text on the mystery of the Trinity is found in
nn. 308-316; that on the incarnation and the redemption in nn. 628-634; that
on the fate of human persons after death in n. 2302.

THE FOURTH LATERAN GENERAL COUNCIL
SYMBOL OF LATERAN (1215)

Convened by Pope Innocent III, the fourth General Lateran Council, one
of the greatest among the Western Councils, was held in 1215, from Nov. 11
to 30. Its primary task was to meet the challenge of the recent heresies of the
Albigensians and the Cathars, the Amalricians and the Waldensians, in
particular of Abbot Joachim of Fiore. Some of these heretical currents are more
explicitly referred to in subsequent chapters issued by the Council (70 in all);
all however are already taken into account in the profession of the "Catholic
Faith" which constitutes chapter I. This solemn profession of faith was approved
by the Pope. It recalls and on more than one point further explicitates the
contents of the Catholic faith. The faith of Nicaea (cf. n. 7) and Constantinople
(cf. n. 12) are easily recognizable in the text; so too are the doctrine of Ephesus
(cf. nn. 604 ff) and of Chalcedon (cf. nn. 613 ff) as regards the incarnation.
The new Symbol seems also to draw upon more recent and more elaborate
Symbols of faith: for some Christological developments it is inspired by the
Symbol of Toledo XI (cf. nn. 628 ff), from which it also borrows much of its
eschatological doctrine (cf. n. 2302). At the same time it takes up in abridged
form a previous profession of faith already directed against the errors of the
Waldensians (cf. DS 790-797). Its structure remains Trinitarian. One of its
characteristic features is the affirmation that God in his unity is the unique
principle of creation; similarly, the incarnation is said to be the common work
of the entire Trinity. Though in continuity with the ancient tradition, it

*innovates considerably where the formulation of the mystery of the Church is
concerned. Its sacrificial and eucharistic character appears for the first time in
a solemn document; this is based on Christ's own priestly function. The
ecclesiology of this profession of faith is essentially sacramental and eucharistic:
our sharing in the body and blood of Christ is the foundation of the mystery
of communion which is the Church. It also clearly affirms the ministerial
priesthood by the exercise of which the Eucharist is present in the Church.*

Cf. R. FOREVILLE, *Latran, I, II, III, IV* (Paris 1965) 275-286.

Chapter I: On the Catholic Faith

(Definition against the Albigensians and the Cathars)

19 We firmly believe and confess without reservation that
800 there is only one true God, eternal, infinite *(immensus)* and
unchangeable, incomprehensible, almighty and ineffable, the
Father, the Son and the Holy Spirit; three persons indeed but
one essence, substance or nature entirely simple. The Father is
from no one, the Son from the Father only, and the Holy Spirit
equally from both *(pariter ab utroque)*. Without beginning, always
and without end, the Father begets, the Son is born and the Holy
Spirit proceeds. They are of the same substance *(consubstantiales)*
and fully equal, equally almighty and equally eternal. [They are]
the one principle of the universe, the creator of all things, visible
and invisible, spiritual and corporeal, who by his almighty power
from the beginning of time made at once *(simul)* out of nothing
both orders of creatures, the spiritual and the corporeal, that is,
the angelic and the earthly, and then *(deinde)* the human creature,
who as it were shares in both orders, being composed of spirit
and body. For the devil and the other demons were indeed
created by God naturally good, but they became evil by their
own doing. As for the human beings, they sinned at the
suggestion of the devil. This Holy Trinity, undivided according
to its common essence and distinct according to the proper
characteristics of the persons *(secundum personales proprietates)*,
communicated the doctrine of salvation to the human race, first
through Moses, the holy prophets and its other servants,
according to a well ordered disposition of times.

20 Finally, the only-begotten Son of God, Jesus Christ, whose
801 incarnation is the common work of the whole Trinity,
conceived from Mary ever Virgin with the co-operation of
the Holy Spirit, made true man, composed of a rational soul

and a human body, one person in two natures, showed the way of life more clearly. Though immortal and impassible according to his divinity, he, the very same, became passible and mortal according to his humanity. He also suffered and died on the wood of the cross for the salvation of the human race; he went down to the underworld *(ad infernos)*, rose again from the dead and ascended into heaven; but he went down in the soul, rose again in the body and ascended equally in both. He shall come at the end of time to judge the living and the dead and to render to each one according to his works, to the reprobate *(reprobis)* as well as to the elect. All of them will rise again with their own bodies which they now bear, to receive according to their works, whether these have been good or evil, the ones perpetual punishment with the devil and the others everlasting glory with Christ.

21 There is indeed one universal Church of the faithful
802 outside which no one at all is saved,[1] and in which the priest himself, Jesus Christ, is also the sacrifice *(idem ipse sacerdos est sacrificium Jesus Christus)*. His body and blood are truly contained in the sacrament of the altar under the appearances of bread and wine, the bread being transubstantiated into the body by the divine power and the wine into the blood, to the effect that we receive from what is his in what he has received from what is ours *(ut [...] accipiamus ipsi de suo, quod accepit ipse de nostro)* in order that the mystery of unity may be accomplished. Indeed, no one can perform *(conficere)* this sacrament, except the priest duly ordained according to [the power of] the keys of the Church, which Jesus Christ himself conceded to the apostles and their successors. The sacrament of baptism (which is celebrated in water at the invocation of God and of the undivided Trinity, viz. the Father, the Son and the Holy Spirit) conduces to the salvation of children as well as of adults when duly conferred by anyone according to the Church's form. After receiving baptism, anyone who shall have lapsed into sin can always be restored through true penance. Not only virgins and the continent *(continentes)*, but also married persons, by pleasing God through right faith and good work, merit to attain to eternal happiness.

---

1. CYPRIAN OF CARTHAGE, *Letter (73) to Iubaianus*, 21.

THE SECOND GENERAL COUNCIL OF LYONS
"PROFESSION OF FAITH OF MICHAEL PALAEOLOGUS"
(1274)

Convened by Pope Gregory X, the second General Council of Lyons was held in six sessions from May 7 to July 17, 1274. Besides reforming the Church, it aimed at bringing to an end the two century old schism between East and West and to bring about the reunion of the Churches. Invited to be personally present at the Council, emperor Michael VIII Palaeologus sent a delegation to Lyons. At the fourth session held on July 6, 1274, what is usually called the "profession of faith of Michael Palaeologus" was read before the Council Fathers. This document was not written at the Council, nor was it accepted by the Greeks as a basis for a doctrinal agreement with the Latins. It was neither promulgated, nor even discussed by the Council Fathers, but simply read from a letter sent by the Byzantine emperor. In this letter, the emperor merely transcribed, without discussion or modification, the text of a profession of faith proposed to him by Pope Clement IV as early as March 4, 1267. In Clement's mind, this profession contained "the faith of the Holy Roman Church", the acceptance of which by the Greeks was the pre-required condition for union. If the emperor personally subscribed to it, this was due to his desire to establish union with Rome.

The text is therefore pre-conciliar. It is composed of two parts. The first part takes up with a few alterations a Trinitarian and Christological profession of faith submitted by Pope Leo IX to Peter, patriarch of Antioch, two centuries earlier (1053), that is one year before the consummation of the Eastern Schism (1054). For the redaction of this profession (cf. DS nn. 680-686), Leo IX had leaned heavily on the Statuta Ecclesiae Antiqua, a canonical and liturgical compilation made in Southern Gaul towards the end of the fifth century.[1] The second part, written by the theologians of Clement IV, has directly in view the recent discussion with the Greeks; it contrasts abruptly to their "various errors" the current theology of the Latins, mostly as regards the eschatological doctrine, sacramental theology and the primacy of the Roman Church.

In the first part, the Christological doctrine of Chalcedon (cf. nn. 613 ff) is linked to the section of the Trinitarian profession devoted to the second person. The Trinitarian doctrine reflects strongly the Latin approach to the mystery: the unity of nature is the point of departure for the enunciation of the plurality of persons; the procession of the Holy Spirit is conceived after the Latin tradition. Such a one-sided formulation of the mystery was not conducive to establishing union with the Greeks. In the second part, the text of Clement lays stress on the immediate retribution and the nature of purgatory, the two questions raised by the Greeks in the current controversies. But these points are inserted into a complete doctrine of individual eschatology, which will be taken up later by the Council of Florence (cf. nn. 2308 f), and will

---

1. Cf. Ch. MUNIER, Les *"Statuta Ecclesiae Antiqua"* (Paris 1960).

become classical. A clause on the general judgment is added to mark the agreement which existed between Greeks and Latins on this point.

Cf. H. WOLTER-H. HOLSTEIN, *Lyon I et Lyon II* (Paris 1966) 162-171

First Part

22 We believe in the Holy Trinity, Father, Son and Holy Spirit,
851 one almighty God; and that in the Trinity the whole
Godhead is the same essence *(coessentialis)*, the same substance *(consubstantialis)*, equally eternal and equally almighty, of one will, one power and majesty. [This Trinity is] the creator of all things created, from whom, in whom, by whom all things exist in heaven and on earth, the visible and the invisible, the corporeal and the spiritual. We believe that each single person in the Trinity is the one true God, fully and perfectly.

23 We believe in the Son of God, Word of God, eternally born
852 from the Father, of the same substance, equally almighty
and in all things equal to the Father in divinity; born in time, from the Holy Spirit and from Mary ever Virgin, with a rational soul. He has two births, one an eternal birth from the Father, the other a temporal birth from a mother. He is true God and true man, real *(proprium)* and perfect in both natures; neither an adoptive son nor an apparent son, but the one and only son of God, in and from two natures, that is, the divine and the human, in the unity of one person. He is impassible and immortal in his divinity, but in his humanity he suffered for us and for our salvation a true bodily passion; he died, was buried, went down to the dead, and on the third day rose again from the dead by a true bodily resurrection. Forty days after his resurrection he ascended into heaven with his risen body and his soul; he is seated at the right hand of God the Father, wherefrom he shall come to judge the living and the dead and to render to each one according to his works, whether these have been good or evil.

24 We believe also in the Holy Spirit, fully, perfectly and truly
853 God, proceeding from the Father and the Son, fully equal,
of the same substance, equally almighty and equally eternal with the Father and the Son in all things. We believe that this Holy Trinity is not three gods but one only God, almighty, eternal, invisible and immutable.

25 We believe that the Holy Catholic and apostolic Church is
854 the one true Church, in which are given one holy baptism
and the true forgiveness of all sins. We believe also in the
true resurrection of this body which we now bear, and in the
life eternal. We believe also that God, the Lord almighty, is the
one author of the New Testament and the Old, of the Law, the
prophets and the apostles.

855 Such is the true Catholic faith, which in the above
mentioned articles the most Holy Roman Church holds and
preaches.

Second Part

26 But, because of various errors, introduced by some through
855 ignorance and by others out of malice, she says and
preaches: that those who after baptism lapse into sin must
not be rebaptised, but obtain pardon for their sins through true
penance;

856 that, if, being truly repentant, they die in charity before
having satisfied by worthy fruits of penance for their sins
of commission and omission, their souls are cleansed after death
by purgatorial and purifying penalties, as Brother John has
explained to us;[1] and that to alleviate such penalties the acts of
intercession (*suffragia*) of the living faithful benefit them, namely
the sacrifices of the Mass, prayers, alms and other works of piety
which the faithful are wont to do for the other faithful according
to the Church's institutions.

857 As for the souls of those who, after having received holy
baptism, have incurred no stain of sin whatever, and those
souls who, after having contracted the stain of sin, have been
cleansed, either while remaining still in their bodies or after
having been divested of them as stated above, they are received
immediately (*mox*) into heaven.

858 As for the souls of those who die in mortal sin or with
original sin only, they go down immediately (*mox*) to hell
(*in infernum*), to be punished however with different punishments.

---

1. This refers to John Parastron, a Franciscan of Greek origin, who acted as
mediator between Rome and Byzantium, and was entrusted with the task of
conveying to the imperial court and to the patriarchate of Constantinople the
Pope's invitation to the Council.

27 The same most Holy Roman Church firmly believes and
859 firmly asserts that nevertheless on the day of Judgment all
human persons will appear with their bodies before the
judgment-seat of Christ, to render an account of their own deeds
[*cf. Rom 14:10-12*].

28 The same Holy Roman Church also holds and teaches that
860 there are seven sacraments of the Church: one is baptism,
which has been mentioned above; another is the sacrament
of confirmation which bishops confer by the laying on of hands
while they anoint the reborn; then penance, the Eucharist, the
sacrament of order, matrimony and extreme unction which,
according to the doctrine of the Blessed James,[1] is administered
to the sick. The same Roman Church performs *(conficit)* the
sacrament of the Eucharist with unleavened bread; she holds
and teaches that in this sacrament the bread is truly
transubstantiated into the body of our Lord Jesus Christ, and
the wine into his blood. As regards matrimony, she holds that
neither is a man allowed to have several wives at the same time
nor a woman several husbands. But, when a legitimate marriage
is dissolved by the death of one of the spouses, she declares that
a second and afterwards a third wedding are successively
licit, if no other canonical impediment goes against it for any
reason.

29 The Holy Roman Church possesses also the highest and
861 full primacy and authority over the universal Catholic
Church, which she recognises in truth and humility to have
received with fulness of power from the Lord himself in the
person of Blessed Peter, the chief or head of the apostles, of whom
the Roman pontiff is the successor. And, as she is bound above
all to defend the truth of faith, so too, if any questions should
arise regarding the faith, they must be decided by her judgment.
Anyone accused in matters pertaining to the forum of the Church
may appeal to her; and in all causes within the purview of
ecclesiastical enquiry, recourse may be had to her judgment. To
her all the Churches are subject; their prelates give obedience
and reverence to her. Her fulness of power, moreover, is so firm
that she admits the other Churches to a share in her solicitude.

---

1. Cf. *James* 5:14-15

The same Roman Church has honoured many of those Churches, and chiefly the Patriarchal Churches, with various privileges, its own prerogative being, however, always observed and safeguarded both in general Councils and in some other matters.

THE PROFESSION OF FAITH OF PIUS IV
BULL *INIUNCTUM NOBIS* (1564)

The Council of Trent (1545-1563), in its "Decreee on General Reform" (1563), had legislated that all prelates in the Church would have to make a profession of faith and of obedience to the Roman See. Its formulation was promulgated by Pope Pius IV in the Bull Iniunctum Nobis *(13 November 1564), largely under pressure from St. Peter Canisius (d. 1597). It is often called the "Tridentine Profession of Faith", even though the text was not fixed by the Council; it may more adequately be named the "Profession of Faith of Pius IV". Besides repeating the Symbol of Constantinople (cf. n. 12), it sums up the essential doctrinal elements declared by the Council of Trent against the background of the errors of the Reformation. After the First Vatican General Council (1869-1870), a decree of the "Congregation of the Council" (Jan. 20, 1877)[1] introduced in the text of Pius IV the reference to that Council with regard to the primacy of the Roman Pontiff and his infallible teaching office (cf. n. 37). In 1910, Pius X added to it the anti-Modernist oath (cf. n. 143). In 1967, the Sacred Congregation for the Doctrine of the Faith promulgated a new text for the profession of faith to be made by law by various categories of persons.[2] In this new text, the anti-Modernist oath is suppressed, while to the Symbol of Constantinople a single paragraph is added, which replaces the previous summary of Tridentine doctrine. This paragraph merely mentions the Church's doctrine of faith in general; it goes on to refer especially to the mystery of the Church, of the sacraments, especially the Mass, and to the primacy of the Roman Pontiff.*

30   I, N., with firm faith believe and profess each and every
1862   article contained in the Symbol of faith which the Holy
           Roman Church uses:

[There follows the text of the Symbol of Constantinople in its Latin form used in the Roman Liturgy: DS 150 (cf. n. 12)]

31   I most firmly accept and embrace the apostolic and
1863   ecclesiastical traditions, and all other observances and
           constitutions of the same Church. I likewise accept Holy

---

1. *ASS* 1877, 71 ff.
2. *AAS* 59 (1967) 1058.

Scripture according to that sense which Holy Mother Church
has held and does hold, to whom it belongs to judge of the true
meaning and interpretation of the Sacred Scriptures; I shall never
accept or interpret them otherwise than according to the
unanimous consent of the Fathers.

32   I also profess that there are truly and properly speaking
1864   seven sacraments of the New Law, instituted by Jesus
          Christ our Lord and necessary for the salvation of the
human race, though not all are necessary for each individual
person: [they are] baptism, confirmation, the Eucharist, penance,
extreme unction, order and matrimony. And [I profess] that
they confer grace, and that of these, baptism, confirmation and
order cannot be repeated without sacrilege. I also admit
and accept the rites received and approved in the Catholic
Church for the administration of all the sacraments mentioned
above.

33   I embrace and accept each and all the articles defined
1865   and declared by the most Holy Synod of Trent concerning
          original sin and justification.

34   I also profess that in the Mass there is offered to God a
1866   true sacrifice, properly speaking, which is propitiatory
          for the living and the dead, and that in the most Holy
Sacrament of the Eucharist the body and blood together with
the soul and the divinity of our Lord Jesus Christ are truly, really
and substantially present, and that there takes place a change
(conversio) of the whole substance of bread into the body and of
the whole substance of wine into the blood; and this change the
Catholic Church calls transubstantiation. I also confess that under
each species alone *(sub altera tantum specie)* the whole and entire
Christ and the true sacrament is received.

35   I steadfastly hold that there is a purgatory, and that the
1867   souls detained there are helped by the acts of inter-
          cession *(suffragiis)* of the faithful; likewise, that the saints
reigning together with Christ should be venerated and invoked,
that they offer prayers to God for us, and that their relics should
be venerated. I firmly declare that the images of Christ and of
the Mother of God ever Virgin and of the other saints as well
are to be kept and preserved, and that due honour and

veneration should be given to them. I also affirm that the power of indulgences has been left by Christ to the Church, and that their use is very beneficial to the Christian people.

36 I acknowledge the Holy, Catholic and apostolic, Roman
1868 Church as the mother and the teacher of all the Churches, and I promise and swear true obedience to the Roman Pontiff, successor of Blessed Peter, chief of the apostles, and Vicar of Christ.

37 I unhesitantly accept and profess also all other things
1869 transmitted, defined and declared by the sacred canons and the ecumenical Councils, especially by the most Holy Council of Trent [and by the ecumenical Vatican Council, mostly as regards the primacy of the Roman Pontiff and his infallible teaching authority]. At the same time, all contrary propositions and whatever heresies have been condemned, rejected and anathematised by the Church, I too condemn, reject and anathematise.

38 This true Catholic faith, outside of which no one can be
1870 saved, which of my own accord I now profess and truly hold, I, N., do promise, vow and swear that, with the help of God, I shall most faithfully keep and confess entire and inviolate, to my last breath, and that I shall take care, as far as it lies in my power, that it be held, taught and preached by those under me, or those over whom I have charge by virtue of my office. So help me God and these his Holy Gospels.

THE PROFESSION OF FAITH OF PAUL VI (1968)

On the nineteenth centenary of the martyrdom of the apostles Peter and Paul (June 30, 1968), which marked the end of the "year of faith" (1967-1968) called by him one year earlier, Pope Paul VI closed the liturgical celebration with a "solemn profession of faith". Preoccupied by "the disquiet which at the present time agitates certain quarters with regard to the faith", the Pope considered it his duty to "fulfil the mandate entrusted by Christ to Peter", whose successor he is, "to confirm his brothers in the faith". The Pope expressly declared that, "without being properly speaking a dogmatic definition", his profession of faith "repeats in substance the Creed of Nicaea, with some developments called for by the spiritual condition of our times". Besides the clear reference to the Nicene Symbol, it integrates texts from other solemn documents of the Church, in particular the ecclesiological doctrine of the Second Vatican General Council. Some developments are calculated to re-state clearly the Church's faith against the background of recent controversies. The doctrine on original sin and on the Eucharist are cases in point.[1]

39/1   We believe in one God, Father, Son and Holy Spirit, creator of things visible such as this world in which our brief life runs its course—and of things invisible—such as the pure spirits which are also called angels *[cf. n. 412]*—and creator in all human beings of their spiritual and immortal soul *[cf. n. 410]*.

39/2   We believe that this only God is as absolutely one in his infinitely Holy essence as in his other perfections: in his almighty power, his infinite knowledge, his providence, his will and his love. He is 'He who is' as he revealed to Moses *[cf. Ex 3:14 Vulg.]*; He is 'Love', as the apostle John has taught us *[cf. 1 Jn 4;8]*; so that these two names, Being and Love, express ineffably the same divine essence of him who has wished to make himself manifest to us, and who, "dwelling in unapproachable light" *[1 Tim 6:16]*, is in himself above every name and every created thing and every created intellect. God alone can give us right and full knowledge of himself, by revealing himself as Father, Son and Holy Spirit, in whose eternal life we are by grace called to share, here on earth in the obscurity of faith and after death in eternal light. The mutual bonds which from all eternity constitute the three persons, each of whom is one and the same divine Being, constitute the blessed inmost life of the most Holy God, infinitely beyond all that we can humanly understand *[cf. n. 132]*. We give thanks, however, to the divine goodness that very many believers can testify with us before people to the unity of God, even though they know not the mystery of the most Holy Trinity.

39/3   We believe then in God who eternally begets the Son; we believe in the Son, the Word of God, who is eternally begotten; we believe in the Holy Spirit, the uncreated person who proceeds from the Father and the Son as their eternal love. Thus, in the three divine persons who are "equally eternal and fully equal" *[cf. n. 16]* the life and beatitude of God, perfectly one, superabound and are consummated in the supreme

---

1. Cf. *AAS* 60 (1968) 433-445. The "profession of faith" occupies nn. 8-30 of the text *(ibid.* 436-445). References to the documents of the Second Vatican General Council are given between brackets.

excellence and glory proper to the uncreated essence, and always "both unity in the Trinity and Trinity in the unity must be worshipped" [cf. n. 16].

39/4   We believe in our Lord Jesus Christ, the Son of God. He is the eternal Word, born of the Father before all ages and of one same substance with the Father, that is one in being with the Father (homoousios tô Patri) [cf. n. 7]; through him all things were made. He became flesh from the Virgin Mary by the Holy Spirit and was made man. Therefore, he is "equal to the Father as to his divinity, less than the Father as to his humanity" [cf. n. 17], entirely one "not by a confusion of substance" (which is impossible), but by the unity of personhood" [cf. n. 17].

39/5   He dwelled among us, full of grace and truth. He proclaimed and established the Kingdom of God, making the Father manifest to us. He gave us his new commandment to love one another as he himself loved us. He taught us the way of the beatitudes of the Gospel; poverty in spirit, meekness, suffering borne with patience, thirst after justice, mercy, purity of heart, peace-making, persecution suffered for justice sake. He suffered under Pontius Pilate, he, the Lamb of God bearing the sins of the world; he died for us, nailed to the cross, saving us by his redeeming blood. He was buried and, of his own power, rose again on the third day, raising us by his resurrection to that sharing in the divine life which is the life of grace. He ascended into heaven, wherefrom he shall come again, this time in glory, to judge the living and the dead, each according to his merits: those who have responded to the love and goodness of God will go to eternal life, but those who have rejected them to the end will be sentenced to the fire that will never be extinguished. And to his Kingdom there will be no end.

39/6   We believe in the Holy Spirit, the Lord and Giver of life, who together with the Father and the Son is worshipped and glorified. He has spoken through the prophets; he was sent to us by Christ after his resurrection and his ascension to the Father; he enlightens, vivifies, protects and guides the Church; he purifies her members if they do not refuse his grace. His action, which penetrates to the inmost of the soul, enables one to respond to the command of Jesus: "You must be perfect as your heavenly Father is perfect" [Mt 5:48].

39/7 We believe that Mary, who remained ever a Virgin, is the Mother of the Incarnate Word, our God and Saviour Jesus Christ [cf. nn. 605-606/1], and that, by reason of her singular election, "she was, in consideration of the merits of her Son, redeemed in a more eminent manner" [LG 53], "preserved immune from all stain of original sin" [cf. n. 709], and "by an exceptional gift of grace stands far above all other creatures" [LG 53].

39/8 Joined by a close and indissoluble bound to the mysteries of the incarnation and redemption [cf. LG. 53, 58, 61], the Blessed Virgin Mary, the Immaculate, "when the course of her earthly life was finished, was taken up, body and soul, to the glory of heaven" [cf. n. 715] and, likened to her Son who rose again from the dead, she received in anticipation the future lot of all the just. We believe that the Holy Mother of God, the new Eve, "Mother of the Church" [LG 53, 56, 61], "continues in heaven to exercise her maternal role" with regard to Christ's members, "helping to bring forth and to increase the divine life in the souls of all the redeemed" [LG 62].

39/9 We believe that in Adam all have sinned, which means that the original offence committed by him caused the human race, common to all, to fall to a state in which it bears the consequences of that offence. This is no longer the state in which the human nature was at the beginning in our first parents, constituted as they were in holiness and justice, and in which the human being was immune from evil and death. And so, it is human nature so fallen, deprived from the gift of grace with which it had first been adorned, injured in its own natural powers and subjected to the dominion of death, that is communicated to all human persons; it is in this sense that all are born in sin. We therefore hold, with the Council of Trent, that original sin is transmitted with human nature "by propagation, not by imitation" and that it "is in all human beings, proper to each" [cf. n. 510].

39/10 We believe that our Lord Jesus Christ by the sacrifice of the Cross redeemed us from original sin and all the personal sins committed by each one of us, so that the word of the apostle is verified: "Where sin increased, grace abounded all the more" [Rom 5:20].

39/11 We believe in and confess one baptism instituted by our Lord Jesus Christ for the forgiveness of sins. Baptism should be administered even to little children "who of themselves cannot have yet committed any sin", in order that, though born deprived of supernatural grace, they may be reborn "of water and the Holy Spirit" to the divine life in Christ Jesus [cf. n. 511].

39/12 We believe in one, Holy, Catholic and apostolic Church built by Jesus Christ on that rock which is Peter. She is the "Mystical Body of Christ", at once a visible society "provided with hierarchical organs" and a "spiritual community; the Church on earth", the pilgrim People of God here below, and "the Church filled with heavenly blessings"; "the germ and the first fruits of the Kingdom of God", through which the work and the sufferings of redemption are continued throughout human history, and which looks with all its strength for the perfect accomplishment it will obtain beyond time in glory [LG 8, 5]. In the course of time, the Lord Jesus Christ forms his Church by means of the sacraments emanating from his fulness [LG 7, 11]. For, by these the Church makes her members share in the mystery of the death and resurrection of Jesus Christ, through the grace of the Holy Spirit who gives her life and movement [SC 5, 6; LG 7,12,50]. She is therefore holy, though having sinners in her midst, because she herself has no other life but the life of grace. If they live by her life, her members are sanctified; if they move away from her life, they fall into sins and disorders that prevent the radiation of her sanctity. This is why she suffers and does penance for those offences, of which she has the power to free her children through the blood of Christ and the gift of the Holy Spirit.

39/13 Heiress of the divine promise and daughter of Abraham according to the Spirit, through that Israel whose sacred Scriptures she lovingly guards, and whose patriarchs and prophets she venerates; founded upon the apostles and faithfully handing down through the centuries their ever-living word and their powers as pastors in the successor of Peter and the bishops in communion with him; perpetually assisted by the Holy Spirit, the Church has the charge of guarding, teaching, explaining and spreading the truth which God revealed dimly to human beings through the prophets, and then fully in the Lord Jesus. We believe all "that is contained in the word of God, written or handed down, and that the Church proposes for belief as divinely revealed, whether by a solemn decree or by the ordinary and universal teaching office" [cf. n. 121]. We believe in the infallibility enjoyed by the successor of Peter when, as pastor and teacher of all the Christians, "he speaks *ex cathedra*" [cf. n 839] and which "also resides in the episcopal body when it exercises with him the supreme teaching office" (LG 25).

39/14   We believe that the Church founded by Jesus Christ and for which he prayed is indefectibly one in faith, worship and the bond of hierarchical communion [LG 8, 18-23; UR 2]. In the bosom of this Church, the rich variety of liturgical rites and the legitimate diversity of theological and spiritual heritages and of special disciplines, far from "injuring her unity, make it more manifest" [LG 23; OE 2-6].

39/15   Recognising also the existence, "outside the organism" of the Church of Christ of "numerous elements of sanctification and truth which, because they belong to her as her own, call for Catholic unity" [LG 8], and believing in the action of the Holy Spirit who stirs up in the heart of all the disciples of Christ a desire for this unity [LG 15], we entertain the hope that the Christians who do not yet enjoy full communion in one only Church will at last be united in one flock with only one Shepherd.

39/16   We believe that "the Church is necessary for salvation. For, Christ, who is the sole Mediator and the one way to salvation, makes himself present for us in his Body which is the Church" [LG 14]. But the divine design of salvation embraces all human beings; and those "who without fault on their part do not know the Gospel of Christ and his Church but seek God with a sincere heart, and under the influence of grace endeavour to do his will as recognised through the prompting of their conscience", they too in a manner known only to God "can obtain eternal salvation" [LG 16].

39/17   We believe that the Mass, celebrated by the priest representing the person of Christ by virtue of the power received through the sacrament of Order, and offered by him in the name of Christ and of the members of his Mystical Body, is indeed the sacrifice of Calvary rendered sacramentally present on our altars. We believe that, as the bread and wine consecrated by the Lord at the Last Supper were changed into his body and his blood which were soon to be offered for us on the Cross, likewise the bread and wine consecrated by the priest are changed into the body and blood of Christ enthroned gloriously in heaven; and we believe that the mysterious presence of the Lord, under the species which continue to appear to our senses as before, is a true, real and substantial presence [cf. n. 1526].

39/18 Thus, in this sacrament Christ cannot become present otherwise than by the change of the whole substance of bread into his body, and the change of the whole substance of wine into his blood, while only the properties of the bread and wine which our senses perceive remain unchanged. This mysterious change is fittingly and properly named by the Church transubstantiation. Every theological explanation which seeks some understanding of this mystery must, in order to be in accord with Catholic faith, maintain firmly that in the order of reality itself, independently of our mind, the bread and wine have ceased to exist after the consecration, so that it is the adorable body and blood of the Lord Jesus which from then on are really before us under the sacramental species of bread and wine [cf. nn. 1519, 1527, 1577], as the Lord willed it, in order to give himself to us as food and to bind us together in the unity of his Mystical Body.

39/19 The unique and indivisible existence of the Lord glorious in heaven is not multiplied, but is rendered present by the sacrament in the many places on earth where the eucharistic sacrifice is celebrated. And this existence remains present, after the celebration of the sacrifice, in the Blessed Sacrament which is in the tabernacle as the living heart of our churches. Therefore, it is our sweet duty to honour and adore, in the Blessed Host which our eyes see, the Incarnate Word himself whom they cannot see and who, yet without leaving heaven, is made present before us.

39/20 We confess also that the Kingdom of God, begun here on earth in the Church of Christ, is not "of this world" [Jn 18:36] whose "form is passing away" [1 Cor 7:31], and that its proper growth cannot be identified with the progress of civilisation, of science or of human technology, but that it consists in an ever more profound knowledge of the unfathomable riches of Christ, an ever stronger hope of eternal blessings, an ever more ardent response to the love of God, and finally in an ever more abundant diffusion of grace and holiness among human persons. But it is this same love which impels the Church to be also continuously concerned about the true temporal welfare of people. While she never ceases to remind all her children that "they have not" here on earth "a lasting city" [Heb 13:14], she also urges them to contribute, each according to their condition of life and means, to the welfare of their earthly city, to promote justice, peace and fraternal concord among people, to give their help generously to their brothers and sisters, especially to the poorest and most unfortunate. The deep solicitude of the Church, the Spouse of Christ, for the needs of human beings, for their joys and hopes, their griefs and efforts, is therefore nothing other than the desire which strongly urges her to be present to them in order to enlighten them with the light of Christ and to gather and unite them all in him, their only Saviour. This solicitude can never be understood to mean that the Church conforms herself to the things of this world or that the ardour is lessened with which she expects her Lord and the eternal Kingdom.

39/21 We believe in the life eternal. We believe that the souls of all those who die in the grace of Christ—whether they must still be purified in purgatory, or, from the moment they leave their bodies, Jesus takes them to paradise as he did for the good thief—constitute the People of God beyond death; death will be finally vanquished on the day of the resurrection when these souls will be re-united with their bodies.

39/22 We believe that the multitude of those gathered around Jesus and Mary in paradise forms the Church of heaven, where in enjoyment of eternal beatitude they see God as he is [1 Jn 3:2: cf. n. 2305], and where they also, in different ways and degrees, are associated with the holy angels in the divine rule exercised by the glorified Christ, by interceding for us and by providing with their brotherly and sisterly solicitude a powerful help to our infirmity [LG 49].

39/23 We believe in the communion of all the faithful of Christ, those who are pilgrims on earth, the dead who are being purified, and the blessed in heaven, all together forming one Church; and we also believe that in this communion the merciful love of God and his saints is ever turning listening ears to our prayers, as Jesus told us: "Ask and you will receive" *[Jn 16:24]*. Confessing this faith and sustained by this hope, we look forward to the resurrection of the dead and the life of the world to come.

Blessed be God thrice Holy, Amen.

JOHN PAUL II
CONGREGATION FOR THE DOCTRINE OF THE FAITH
NEW FORMULA FOR THE PROFESSION OF FAITH
(9 January 1989)

The Congregation for the Doctrine of the Faith published a revised formula for the profession of faith and a new oath of fidelity. The profession of faith is required of those called to exercise an office in the name of the Church, according to canon 833 of the 1983 Code of Canon Law. The obligation of a special oath of fidelity—previously prescribed only for bishops—has been extended to the categories of people named in canon 833, 5-8. The formula of the profession of faith repeats in its entirety the first part of the text in effect since 1967 which contains the Nicene-Constantinopolitan Creed (cf. AAS 59 (1967) 1058). The second part has been modified and subdivided into three paragraphs so as to distinguish better the type of truth and the corresponding assent that is sought. The text is found in AAS 81 (1989) 104-106.

(Profession of Faith)

40   I, N., with firm faith believe and profess everything *(omnia et singula)* that is contained in the symbol of faith, namely

[*There follows the text of the Symbol of Constantinople as used in the Roman liturgy: DS 150 (cf. n. 12)]*

41   With firm faith I believe as well everything *(ea omnia)* contained in God's word, written or handed down in tradition and proposed by the Church—whether in solemn judgment or in the ordinary and universal Magisterium—as divinely revealed and calling for faith *(tamquam divinitus revelata credenda)*.

I also firmly accept and hold each and every thing *(omnia et singula)* that is proposed by that same Church definitively *(definitive)* with regard to teaching concerning faith and morals.

What is more, I adhere *(adhaereo)* with religious submission of will and intellect *(religioso voluntatis et intellectus obsequio)* to the teachings which either the Roman Pontiff or the college of bishops enunciate when they exercise the authentic magisterium even if they proclaim those teachings in an act that is not definitive.

CHAPTER I

REVELATION AND FAITH

On its first page, Scripture relates that God created human beings in his own image, according to his own likeness. Thus every person can in fact be addressed by God and become a dialogue partner with him. God draws near to us, for personal encounter, and calls all men and women to enter communion of life with himself. Our recurrent sense of dissatisfaction with material and secular values intimates that deeply inscribed in our hearts is an orientation to God and to his word of revelation.

Christian existence rests on the conviction that God has indeed spoken to his human creatures and offered them abundant light on the meaning of their lives. The mysterious source of our being and of all creation has revealed himself as a loving friend and insistent Lord, as Abraham was given to experience, as Israel learned from its prophets, and as Jesus brought home to his disciples. In its culminating expression, revelation is the good news that God is with us to free us from the darkness of sin and raise us up to life eternal (DV 4; n. 151).

The response to revelation is faith, by which one accepts God's invitation to enter his own sphere of truth and to know oneself loved in a radical and unconditional way. Faith is a personal act and attitude, deeply engaging our freedom. But it is also a sharing with others who have answered the same invitation. Communion with the God who reveals himself is as well communion with other believers. A community of faith, the Church, supports our faith and imparts the language of its expression and of our celebration of the good news revealed.

The 19th century documents on revelation and faith show Church authority countering the European Enlightenment's assertion of human autonomy (rationalism). Revelation, especially in the First Vatican Council, was shown not be an arbitrary imposition that degrades human reason and dignity, but instead a much needed instruction that heals and elevates human intelligence.

Other 19th century currents of thought, fideism and traditionalism, were influenced by the Kantian limitation of our minds to empirical *realm. They distrusted human abilities to know the great truths about God and human life that set 'he stage for faith. Against them, Church authority affirmed the fundamental power of human intelligence to reach God and to ascertain the credentials of those through whom God communicates his revelation of himself.*

In a similar vein, late 20th century teaching, especially by Pope John Paul II, has witnessed a remarkable rapprochement between those who speak for the community of faith and men and women dedicated to research in the fields of basic science. But prior to this, the nature of revelation itself was expressed in a fresh way by the Second Vatican Council as a loving call and gift of communion. This culminated in the saving presence of Jesus as one of us, with his revelation of the meaning of our call and the dignity of our lives. Animated by his Spirit, his followers continue in every age to testify to God's revelation as a present blessing and life-giving word that makes present the communion with God that it signifies.

* * *

The main doctrinal points treated in the documents of this chapter are the following:

There are two kinds of religious knowledge, natural by reason and supernatural by faith: 112/8f, 117, 126, 131, 137, 183b, 190a-c.

Human natural knowledge of God

One can come through reason to the knowledge of God: 101, 113, 115, 143/1, 144, (153);
and of other religious truths: 102, 103.
This knowledge, however, is not intuitive: 141f.

Revelation

God can and does reveal himself to humankind: 112/4f, 113, 116f, 131, 149.
Through revelation God confirms naturally known religious truths: 114f, 135, 145, (153);
but primarily calls humanity to participate in his own divine life: 114, 117, 149;
and offers to all the fullness of our human destiny: 106, 149, 190a.
God reveals himself from the beginning of the human race: 150;
in the history of salvation: 150;
and finally in Jesus Christ: 151, (154).

The fact of divine revelation can be shown to be credible mainly through miracles: 104, 110f, 112/7, 119, 127f, 143/2, 146.

Revelation is not a human achievement: 108, 112/4, 190a.

The content of revelation, being God's own life, remains beyond our comprehension: 112/9, 114, 131f, 137;

it cannot be reduced to a philosophical system: 106, 108, 136;

it is entrusted to the Church: 123, 134, 139f, 143/3.9.11, 180 a-d, 188, 836, 859;

which can formulate its content in dogmatic definitions: 121, 160f, 179-180a, 181, 185, 883;

and issue definitive teachings on truths necessarily connected with revelation: 180e, 185, 189.

Though revelation unfolds in history, it remains essentially the same; 112/5, 136, 139, 143/4.7f.11, 161.

Faith

The human response to God's revelation is faith: 110f, 118, 143/5, 152, 181.

It is essentially distinct from a natural assent: 110, 112/8, 118, 126.

It is a free assent involving the whole person: 120, 129, 152;

under the influence of grace: 118, 120, 124, 129, 152, 1930.

It includes the submission of the intellect: 118, 120, 126f, 143/5, 1930.

It is our duty to respond in faith to God's word: 109, 111, 118, 121, 125, 130

Faith is mediated by the ecclesial community: 186-187.

Faith is necessary for salvation: 118, 120, 122, 1935.

Though the content of faith consists in the divine mystery, it can and must be expressed in systematic language: 105, 147f.

Faith is not a leap in the dark but has its certitude and unshakable foundation: 163a.

Faith, while aided by formulae, transcends them: 188.

Atheism

It is understandable in the context of a secular culture: (154), 157-159;

yet, it must be rejected because it destroys the foundations of human life and society: (154), 155f.

Faith and Reason

No real contradiction can exist between faith and reason: 107, 112/6, 133f, 135, 164.

Faith cannot be contradicted by sound philosophy: 107, 133f, 139, 147; *nor by history:* 143/6-12.

Reason is meant to lead to faith and to help penetrating it: 107, 109-111, 132, 135, 183a-b, 190c.

Science cannot propose hypotheses contradicting revelation: 112/10f, 134, 138.

Perpetual questioning can keep a scientific mind on the threshold of faith: 171.

Faith and Science

There is no conflict between faith and science: 164-165, 173, 176a-c, 184c.

The limits of scientific knowledge: 166, 172.

The right use of science: 167-169, 175, 176a-c.

Science needs faith: 170.

Dogma and Theology

Interpretation of dogma: 160-161, 174, 190d.

Dogmatic relativism is excluded: 162.

Theology and Magisterium: 163, 177-182.

CONDEMNATION OF FIDEISM, TRADITIONALISM, RATIONALISM

Two apparently contradictory trends dominate the theology of revelation in the 19th century: fideism with its total reliance on revelation and its distrust of human reason, and rationalism in its various forms which considers natural reason as the only resource of human knowledge, and therefore rejects revelation as hostile to human autonomy and to true human progress. The struggle against these opposite tendencies comes to its climax in the First Vatican Council. Before this Council, however, the Church had already declared her attitude in a series of documents, four of which are mentioned here.

1. The articles subscribed to by L.E. Bautain (1796-1867), professor in Strasbourg, reckoned as the principal representative of fideism. Profoundly impressed by Kant's philosophy and by his own experience in returning to the faith, moved also by pastoral reason, Bautain sought the source of religious and moral knowledge exclusively in divine revelation. He denied the possibility of arriving at a certain knowledge of the existence of God and of the credibility of revelation by purely natural powers. To prove his orthodoxy, he was made to subscribe to six theses by the Bishop of Strasbourg in 1835 and again, with slight modifications, in 1840 (cf. DS 2751-2756). The most precise disavowal of his doctrines is contained in five theses proposed to him by the Roman Congregation for bishops and regulars in 1844, when he intended to found a religious congregation. The first four theses, quoted here, concern the demonstrability of the presuppositions of Christian faith.

2. Closely related to fideism were the representatives of traditionalism: L. de Bonald (d. 1840), F. de Lamennais (d. 1854) and A. Bonnetty (d. 1876). Having the same distrust for human reason, they sought the source of all religious and moral knowledge in human tradition which ultimately goes back to primitive revelation. Bonnetty had to subscribe to four articles proposed to him by the Roman Congregation of the Index (cf. DS 2811-2814). Articles 1 to 3 repeat the articles signed by Bautain and the doctrine of Qui Pluribus *(cf. nn. 106 ff). Only article 4 is quoted here; it defends the scholastic method which was attacked by traditionalism on account of its confident espousal of rational principles and procedures.*

3. Most important among Pius IX's earlier encyclicals is Qui Pluribus, *which is concerned with the controversy over fideism on the one hand, and rationalism in the form of Hermesianism, on the other. The two fundamental errors of Hermes (1775-1831), professor of dogmatic theology in Bonn, were: 1) at the beginning of all theological knowledge there is absolute doubt; 2) the grounds for assent to faith are not different from the grounds for assent to natural knowledge; in both cases it is the inner necessity of the human capacity for knowledge which compels assent; this is held necessary in order to preserve human dignity. Thereby, however, the difference between natural and supernatural knowledge is suppressed. The encyclical rejects rationalism, and positively asserts that there can be no contradiction between faith and reason;*

it then eloquently sets forth the motives of credibility by which reason can reach the threshold of Christian faith.

4. *In view of the critical situation of the Church, not only with regard to the theological disciplines, but in ethical, social, political and other matters as well, Pius IX composed in 1864 a* Syllabus *of 80 propositions containing views already censured in papal discourses and letters (cf. Introduction to DS 2901-2980). We give below only the propositions exalting reason to the detriment of revelation and faith.*

PROMISE SIGNED BY L.E. BAUTAIN (1844)

We promise today and for the future *never to teach:*

101 1. That one cannot give a true proof for the existence of
2765 God by the light of rightly ordained reason only, apart from divine revelation.

102 2. That by reason alone one cannot demonstrate the
2766 spirituality and immortality of the soul or any other purely natural, rational or moral truth.

103 3. That by reason alone one cannot have the knowledge
2767 of principles or metaphysics as well as of the truths that depend on them, a knowledge totally distinct from supernatural theology which is based on divine revelation.

104 4. That reason cannot acquire a true and full knowledge
2768 of the motives of credibility, i.e, of those motives which make divine revelation evidently credible, such as especially the miracles and prophecies, and in particular the resurrection of Jesus Christ.

THE 4TH PROPOSITION SIGNED BY A. BONNETTY (1855)

105 4. The method used by St. Thomas, St. Bonaventure and
2814 after them by other Scholastic theologians does not lead to rationalism, and has not been the cause why modern schools of philosophy move towards naturalism and pantheism. Hence one should not blame these doctors and teachers for using this method, especially as they did so with the approval or at least the tacit consent of the Church.

PIUS IX

ENCYCLICAL LETTER *QUI PLURIBUS* (1846)

(Condemnation of rationalism)

106   [The enemies of Christianity do not hesitate to teach]
2775   that the sacred mysteries of our faith are fictions and
human inventions, that the doctrine of the Catholic
Church is hostile to the good and welfare of human society.
They do not refrain from renouncing even Christ himself and
God. To mislead people more easily and to deceive mainly the
imprudent and the unlearned and to lead them into their own
erroneous ways, they claim to be the only ones who know the
road to prosperity; they do not hesitate to usurp the name of
philosophers as though philosophy, which is totally engaged in
the investigation of natural truth, would have to reject what the
supreme and merciful God, the author of all nature, has deigned
to reveal to us in his singular generosity and mercy so that we
should attain true happiness and salvation.

107   Hence they never cease with absurd and fallacious ways
2776   of argumentation to appeal to the power and excellence
of human reason and to extol it against our holy faith in
Christ; they boldly assert that this faith is contrary to reason.
Surely nothing more foolish, more impious, more opposed
to reason itself can be imagined. For, though faith is above reason,
there can never be found a real contradiction or disagreement
between them, since both of them originate from the same source
of immutable and eternal truth, from the good and great God,
and both so help each other that right reason demonstrates,
safeguards and defends the truth of faith, whereas faith frees
reason from all errors and through the knowledge of divine
things enlightens, strengthens, and perfects it.

108   With similar fallacy these enemies of divine revelation,
2777   while paying supreme homage to human progress,
attempt with arbitrary and sacrilegious means to
introduce this progress into the Catholic religion as though this
religion were a human work, not coming from God, or a
philosophical invention that could be perfected by human means.
To those who so deplorably stray away, one may apply the
verdict with which Tertullian rightly condemned the philosophers
of his age "Who begot a stoic, Platonic, and dialectic [Aristotelian]
Christianity."[1] Indeed, as our holy religion was not invented by
human reason but mercifully revealed by God to human beings,

---

1. TERTULLIAN, *De praescriptione haereticorum*, 7, 11.

everyone can easily see that this religion receives all its strength from the authority of God who speaks to us, and can never be deduced or perfected by human reason.

(Reason leads to faith)

109   It is the duty of human reason with diligence to inquire
2778   into the fact of revelation—lest it be deceived and fall
          into error in such an important matter—in order that it may be assured that God has spoken and that it may offer him "reasonable submission," as the apostle wisely teaches [cf. Rom 12:1 Vulg.]. For who does not know, or could not know, that complete faith must be given to God when he speaks, and that nothing corresponds more to reason than to accept and firmly to adhere to whatever is known to be revealed by God who can neither err nor deceive?

110   But how many, how wonderful, how lucid are the
2779   arguments at hand by which reason ought to be
          thoroughly convinced that Christ's religion is divine and that "our doctrines in their entirety have their origin from above, from the Lord of Heaven",[1] that therefore there is nothing more certain than our faith, nothing safer, nothing more holy, nothing that rests on firmer principles. It is this faith that is the teacher of life, the guide to salvation, the exorcist of all vices, the mother and nurse of virtues. This faith is confirmed through the birth, the life, the death, the resurrection, the wisdom, the miracles and prophecies of him who founded and perfected it, Christ Jesus. Everywhere it shines with the light of its heavenly doctrine; it is enriched through the treasures of celestial riches; through so many predictions of the prophets, through the splendour of so many miracles, through the constancy of so many martyrs and the glory of so many saints it shines forth, clear and sublime. Proclaiming the saving laws of Christ, acquiring ever greater strength from the most cruel persecutions themselves, it has spread over the whole earth, on land and sea, from sunrise to sunset, with only the cross as its standard. It has overthrown the fallacy of idols and dissipated the darkness of errors; it has triumphed over enemies of every kind; it has illumined all peoples, races and nations, however barbarous and crude, and

---

1. John Chrysostom, *Interpretatio in Is.*, 1, 1.

no matter how different in their natural gifts, customs, laws and social structures, with the light of divine knowledge; it has subjected them to the easy yoke of Christ himself [cf. Mt. 11:30], announcing peace and good tidings to all. All this is totally resplendent with such brightness of divine wisdom and power that every thoughtful mind easily understands that the Christian faith is God's work.

111   Thus, human reason clearly and manifestly recognises
2780   from these altogether lucid and firm arguments that God
       is the author of this faith. It can proceed no further, but it has fully to reject and to rid itself of any difficulty and doubt and offer total surrender to this faith, because it is assured that whatever this faith proposes to us to believe and to do, is given by God.

SYLLABUS OF CONDEMNED ERRORS (1864)

(Errors of rationalism condemned)

[112/2]   Any action of God on human beings and the world must
2902   be denied.

[112/3]   Human reason is, without any reference to God, the sole
2903   judge of truth and falsehood, of good and evil; it is
       autonomous, and by its natural powers is sufficient to assure the welfare of peoples and nations.

[112/4]   All religious truths originate from the natural power of
2904   human reason. Hence reason is the principal norm by
       which we can and must reach knowledge of whatever kind of truths.

[112/5]   Divine revelation is imperfect and hence subject to
2905   continual and indefinite progress, which ought to
       correspond to the progress of human reason.

[112/6]   Faith in Christ is detrimental to human reason; and
2906   divine revelation not only is of no use but is even
       harmful to human perfection.

[112/7]   The prophecies and miracles set forth in the accounts
2907   given in Sacred Scripture are poetical fictions; the
       mysteries of the Christian faith are the outcome of philosophical reflections; in the books of both Testaments

mythical tales are contained; Jesus Christ himself is a mythical fiction.

(Errors of semi-rationalism condemned)

[112/8]
2908
Since human reason is on a par with religion itself, theological disciplines have to be handled in the same manner as the philosophical ones.

[112/9]
2909
All dogmas of the Christian religion are, without distinction, the object of natural science or of philosophy; human reason solely as developed in history can, by means of its natural powers and principles, come to a true understanding of all, even the more profound dogmas, provided only that such dogmas be proposed to reason as its object.

[112/10]
2910
As there is a distinction between the philosopher and one's philosophy, one has the right and the duty to submit to the authority acknowledged as legitimate; but philosophy neither can nor must submit to any authority.

[112/11]
2911
The Church must not only abstain from any censure of philosophy; she must also tolerate the errors of philosophy, and leave it to philosophy to correct itself.

THE FIRST VATICAN GENERAL COUNCIL
THIRD SESSION
DOGMATIC CONSTITUTION *DEI FILIUS* ON THE CATHOLIC FAITH (1870)

To meet the numerous problems of the time, Pope Pius IX summoned the 20th General Council. It met in the Vatican from December 1869 to September 1870. From among the many drafts proposed to the Council only two Constitutions were finalised, the first on the Catholic faith, the second on the primacy and infallibility of the Pope (cf. nn. 818 ff).

In the four chapters of the Constitution on the Catholic faith and in the corresponding canons, the Church set forth its doctrine against the current errors of the 19th century: materialism, rationalism, pantheism, and also against the inner-Catholic approaches of fideism and traditionalism. The first chapter deals with God and creation (cf. nn. 412-413); the second with revelation, its relation to human reason, and the channels of Scripture and Tradition through which revelation is communicated; the third chapter treats of faith, its rational and supernatural foundations and its place in the Christian life; the fourth enters into the complex problems of the relation between faith and reason.

The doctrine of the Council is expressed in terms of 19th century theology.

Revelation is presented primarily as the communication of supernatural truth inaccessible to natural reason, and faith as the submissive acceptance of this revealed truth. The Second Vatican Council will later complement this doctrine with a more personalistic approach, according to which God speaks to human beings as to his friends, whom he invites to communion of life with himself, through Christ, in the Holy Spirit. Faith then freely accepts this invitation in a commitment of one's whole self.

Chapter II: Revelation

(Natural knowledge of God and supernatural revelation)

113
3004
The same Holy Mother Church holds and teaches that God, the source and end of all things, can be known with certainty from the things that were created, through the natural light of human reason, for "ever since the creation of the world his invisible nature has been clearly perceived in the things that have been made" *[Rom 1:20]*; but that it pleased his wisdom and bounty to reveal himself and his eternal decrees in another, supernatural way, as the apostle says: "In many and various ways God spoke of old to our fathers by the prophets; but in these last days he has spoken to us by a Son" *[Heb 1:1-2]*.

(The necessity of divine revelation)

114
3005
It is to be ascribed to this divine revelation that such truths about things divine which of themselves are not beyond human reason can, even in the present condition of humankind, be known by everyone with facility, with firm certitude and with no admixture of error. It is, however, not for this reason that revelation is to be judged absolutely necessary, but because God in His infinite goodness has ordained us to a supernatural end, viz., to share in the good things of God which utterly exceed the intelligence of the human mind, for "no eye has seen, nor ear heard, nor the human heart conceived, what God prepared for those who love him" *[1 Cor 2:9]*.

(The rest of the chapter is found in nn. 216f).

Canons on Chapter II

115
3026
1. If anyone says that the One true God, our Creator and Lord, cannot be known with certainty with the natural light of human reason through the things that are created, *anathema sit.*

116   2. If anyone says that it is impossible or useless for
3027   human beings to be taught through divine revelation
           about God and the worship to be rendered to him,
anathema sit.

117   3. If anyone says that human beings cannot be called by
3028   God to a knowledge and perfection that surpasses the
           natural order, but that they can and must by themselves,
through constant progress, finally arrive at the possession of all
that is true and good, *anathema sit.*

Chapter III: Faith

(Definition of faith)

118   Since we are totally dependent upon God, as upon our
3008   Creator and Lord, and since created reason is absolutely
           subject to uncreated truth, we are bound to yield by faith
the full submission of intellect and will to God who reveals
himself. The Catholic Church professes that this faith, which is
the "beginning of human salvation" [*cf. n. 1935*], is a supernatural
virtue whereby, inspired and assisted by the grace of God, we
believe that what he has revealed is true, not because the intrinsic
truth of things is recognised by the natural light of reason, but
because of the authority of God himself who reveals them, who
can neither err nor deceive. For faith, as the apostle testifies, is
"the assurance of things hoped for, the conviction of things not
seen" [*Heb 11:1*].

(The rational basis of faith)

119   However, in order that our submission of faith be
3009   nevertheless in harmony with reason [*cf. Rom 12:1*], God
           willed that exterior proofs of his revelation, viz. divine
facts, especially miracles and prophecies, should be joined to the
interior helps of the Holy Spirit; as they manifestly display the
omnipotence and infinite knowledge of God, they are the most
certain signs of divine revelation, adapted to the intelligence of
all people. Therefore Moses and the prophets, and especially
Christ our Lord himself, performed many manifest miracles and
uttered prophecies; and of the apostles we read: "They went forth
and preached everywhere, while the Lord worked with them
and confirmed the message by the signs that accompanied it"

[Mk 16:20]; and again it is written: "We have the prophetic word made more sure; you will do well to pay attention to this as to a lamp shining in a dark place" *[2 Pet 1:19]*.

(Faith as God's gift)

120   Though the assent of faith is by no means a blind impulse
3010   of the mind, still no one can "assent to the Gospel message", as is necessary to obtain salvation, "without the illumination and inspiration of the Holy Spirit, who gives to all joy in assenting to the truth and believing it" *[cf. n. 1919]*. Wherefore faith itself, even when it is not working through love *[cf. Gal 5:6]*, is in itself a gift of God, and the act of faith is a work appertaining to salvation, by which one yields voluntary obedience to God himself by assenting to and cooperating with his grace, which one could resist.

(The object of faith)

121   Further, all those things are to be believed with divine
3011   and Catholic faith which are contained in the word of God, written or handed down, and which by the Church, either in solemn judgement or through her ordinary and universal teaching office, are proposed for belief as divinely revealed.

(The necessity of faith for salvation)

122   Since "without faith it is impossible to please God" *[Heb
3012   11:6]* and to attain to the fellowship of his children, therefore without faith no one has ever attained justification, nor will anyone obtain eternal life unless he has persevered in it to the end *[cf. Mt 10:22; 24:13]*. However, to enable us to fulfil the obligation to embrace the true faith and persistently to persevere in it, God has instituted the Church through his only-begotten Son and has endowed her with manifest marks of his institution so that she may be recognised by all as the guardian and teacher of the revealed word.

(The Church as guarantor of revelation)

123   To the Catholic Church alone belong all the manifold
3013   and wonderful endowments which by divine disposition are meant to set forth the credibility of the Christian faith. Nay more, the Church by herself, with her marvellous

propagation, eminent holiness and inexhaustible fruitfulness in everything that is good, with her Catholic unity and invincible stability, is a great and perpetual motive of credibility and an irrefutable testimony of her divine mission.

3014   Thus, like a standard lifted up among the nations [cf. Is 11:12], she invites to herself those who do not yet believe, and at the same time gives greater assurance to her children that the faith which they profess rests on a solid foundation.

(Interior grace as guarantee of faith)

124   To this testimony an efficacious help coming from the
3014   power above is added. For the merciful Lord arouses
and aids with his grace those who are wandering astray, so that they be able to "come to the knowledge of the truth" [1 Tim 2:4], and those whom "he has called out of darkness into his admirable light" [1 Pet 2:9] he confirms with his grace so that they may persevere in this light, for he deserts no one who does not desert him [cf. n. 1938]. Therefore, the condition of those who by the heavenly gift of faith have embraced the Catholic truth, and of those who led by human opinions follow a false religion, is by no means the same. For those who have received the faith under the teaching authority of the Church can never have a just reason to change this same faith or to reject it. For this reason, "giving thanks to God the Father who has qualified as to share in the inheritance of the saints in light" [Col 1:12], let us not neglect so great a salvation, but "looking to Jesus the pioneer and perfecter of faith" [Heb 12:2], "let us hold fast to the confession of our hope without wavering" [Heb 10:23].

Canons on Chapter III

125   1. If anyone says that human reason is so independent
3031   that faith cannot be enjoined upon it by God, *anathema sit.*

126   2. If anyone says that divine faith is not distinct from
3032   the natural knowledge of God and of moral truths; that,
therefore, for divine faith it is not necessary that the revealed truth be believed on the authority of God who reveals it, *anathema sit.*

127   3. If anyone says that divine revelation cannot be made
3033   credible by outward signs, and that, therefore, people
           ought to be moved to faith solely by each one's inner
experience or by personal inspiration, *anathema sit.*

128   4. If anyone says that no miracles are possible, and that
3034   therefore all accounts of them, even those contained in
           Holy Scripture, are to be dismissed as fables and myths;
or that miracles can never be recognised with certainty, and that
the divine orgin of the Christian religion cannot be legitimately
proved by them, *anathema sit.*

129   5. If anyone says that the assent to the Christian faith is
3035   not free but is produced with necessity by arguments of
           human reason; or that the grace of God is necessary only
for that living faith which works by love, *anathema sit.*

130   6. If anyone says that the condition of the faithful and
3036   of those who have not yet attained to the only true faith
           is the same, so that Catholics could have a just reason
for suspending their judgement and calling into question the faith
which they have already received under the teaching authority
of the Church, until they have completed a scientific
demonstration of the credibility and truth of their faith, *anathema
sit.*

Chapter IV: Faith and Reason

(The twofold order of religious knowledge)

131   The perpetual common belief of the Catholic Church has
3015   held and holds also this: there is a twofold order of
           knowledge, distinct not only in its source but also in its
object; in its source, because in the one we know by natural
reason, in the other by divine faith; in its object, because apart
from what natural reason can attain, there are proposed to our
belief mysteries that are hidden in God, which can never be
known unless they are revealed by God. Hence the apostle who,
on the one hand, testifies that God is known to the gentiles by
means of the things that have been made [cf. Rom 1:20], on the
other hand, when speaking about the grace and truth that came
through Jesus Christ [cf. Jn 1:17], proclaims: "We speak the
wisdom of God in a mystery, a wisdom which is hidden, which

God ordained before the world unto our glory, which none of the princes of this world knew.[...] But to us God has revealed this by his Spirit. For the Spirit searches everything, even the deep things of God" [1 Cor 2:7-10 Vulg.]. The only-begotten himself praises the Father because he has hidden these things from the wise and understanding and has revealed them to little ones [cf. Mt. 11:25].

(Task and limits of reason)

132 Nevertheless, if reason illumined by faith inquires in an
3016 earnest, pious and sober manner, it attains by God's grace
a certain understanding of the mysteries, which is most fruitful, both from the analogy with the objects of its natural knowledge and from the connection of these mysteries with one another and with our ultimate end. But it never becomes capable of understanding them in the way it does the truths which constitute its proper object. For divine mysteries by their very nature so excel the created intellect that, even when they have been communicated in revelation and received by faith, they remain covered by the veil of faith itself and shrouded as it were in darkness as long as in this mortal life "We are away from the Lord; for we walk by faith, not by sight" [2 Cor 5:6-7].

(Faith and reason cannot contradict each other)

133 However, though faith is above reason, there can never
3017 be a real conflict between faith and reason, since the same
God who reveals mysteries and infuses faith has bestowed the light of reason on the human mind, and God cannot deny himself, nor can truth ever contradict truth. The deceptive appearance of such a contradiction is mainly due to the fact that either the dogmas of faith have not been understood and expounded according to the mind of the Church, or that uncertain theories are taken for verdicts of reason. Thus "we define that every assertion that is opposed to enlightened faith is utterly false" [Lateran V: DS 1441].

134 Further, the Church which, along with the apostolic office
3018 of teaching, received the charge of guarding the deposit
of faith has also from God the right and the duty to proscribe what is falsely called knowledge [cf. 1 Tim 6:20], lest anyone be deceived by philosophy and vain fallacy [cf. Col 2:8].

Hence all believing Christians are not only forbidden to defend as legitimate conclusions of science such opinions which they realise to be contrary to the doctrine of faith, particularly if they have been condemned by the Church, but they are seriously bound to account them as errors which put on the fallacious appearance of truth.

(Mutual support of faith and reason)

135 Not only can there be no conflict between faith and
3019 reason; but they also support each other since right
reason demonstrates the foundations of faith and, illumined by its light, pursues the understanding of divine things, while faith frees and protects reason from errors and provides it with manifold insights. It is therefore far removed from the truth to say that the Church opposes the study of human arts and sciences; on the contrary, she supports and promotes them in many ways. She does not ignore or despise the benefits that human life derives from them. Indeed, she confesses: as they have their origin from God who is the Lord of knowledge *[cf. 1 Sam 2:3]*, so too, if rightly pursued, they lead to God with the help of his grace. Nor does the Church in any way forbid that these sciences, each in its sphere, should make use of their own principles and of the method proper to them. While, however, acknowledging this just freedom, she seriously warns lest they fall into error by going contrary to divine doctrine, or, stepping beyond their own limits, they enter into the sphere of faith and create confusion.

(The development of dogma)

136 For the doctrine of faith which God has revealed has
3020 not been proposed like a philosophical system to be
perfected by human ingenuity, but has been committed to the spouse of Christ as a divine trust to be faithfully kept and infallibly declared. Hence also that meaning of the sacred dogmas is perpetually to be retained which our Holy Mother Church has once declared, and there must never be a deviation from that meaning on the specious ground and title of a more profound understanding. "Therefore, let there be growth and abundant progress in understanding, knowledge and wisdom, in each and all, in individuals and in the whole Church, at all times and in the succession of the ages, but only in its proper

kind, i.e., in the same dogma, the same meaning, the same understanding."[1]

Canons on Chapter IV

137
3041 1. If anyone says that in divine revelation no true and properly so called mysteries are contained but that all dogmas of faith can be understood and demonstrated from natural principles by reason, if it is properly trained, *anathemsa sit.*

138
3042 2. If anyone says that human sciences are to be pursued with such liberty that their assertions, even if opposed to revealed doctrine, may be held as true and cannot be proscribed by the Church, *anathema sit.*

139
3043 3. If anyone says that, as science progresses, at times a sense is to be given to dogmas proposed by the Church, different from the one which the Church has understood and understands, *anathema sit.*

Epilogue

140
3044 Therefore, in fulfilment of our supreme pastoral office, we beseech in the love of Jesus Christ, and we command in the authority of the same God our Saviour, all Christian faithful, and especially those who hold authority or are engaged in teaching, to apply their zeal and effort to removing and eliminating these errors from the holy Church and to spreading the light of pure faith.

3045 It is, however, not enough to avoid the malice of heresy unless those errors more or less near to it are also carefully avoided. We therefore remind all of their duty to observe also the constitutions and decrees by which such perverse opinions, which are not explicitly enumerated here, are proscribed by this Holy See.

LEO XIII
ERRORS OF A. ROSMINI-SERBATI CONDEMNED BY THE HOLY OFFICE (1887)

Though the orthodoxy of Romini (1797-1855) had been questioned during

---

1. VINCENT OF LERINS, *Commonitorium primum*, 23.

his lifetime, his books were declared free from errors by the Congregation of the Index in 1854. yet, after his death renewed doubts were raised, and in 1887 the Holy Office condemned 40 propositions taken mainly from his posthumous works. The following two propositions are taken from his Teosofia *(1859), but are too much isolated from their context. These are reproduced here not so much for their historical interest—whether or not they could be understood in an orthodox sense—but because of their significance for our time. Our natural knowledge of God is not intuitive; it is through the limited experience of created things that we have access to God's transcendent mystery.*

[141]
3201

1. In the order of created things there is immediately manifested to the human intellect something divine in itself, such that it belongs to the divine nature.

[142]
3205

5. The being *(esse)* that we intuit must necessarily be something of the necessary and eternal Being *(entis)*, of the cause that creates, determines, and perfects all contingent beings; and that is God.

PIUS X

OATH AGAINST THE ERRORS OF MODERNISM (1910)

Modernism has become the generic name for the most varied attempts to reconcile the Christian religion with the findings of agnostic philosophy, rationalistic science of history, and in general with all those cultural movements which in their development have progressively become estranged from religion or have set themeselves in hostile opposition to it. In this general sense modernism practically covers all the abortive attempts of the nineteenth century to find a satisfactory solution to the problem of revelation and its rational foundations in the face of modern science and philosophy.

In the technical sense, in which the term is used here, modernism comprises those systems which yielded to the attacks made against the foundations of the Christian faith and, therefore, sought a new basis for religion. This basis would no longer consist in absolute philosophical certitudes about God, creation, etc., and in the historical certitudes concerning the event of Jesus Chist and his work, but solely in human interiority, in religious experience, and in the power with which this experience asserts itself in the Church and throughout the world in all cultures and ages. Through this interiorisation of religion modernism stands against a religious rationalism, but also against Christianity with its insistence on positive revelation.

After repeated individual initiatives, Pius X finally opposed modernism in an official manner in the decree Lamentabili *(1907) which rejects its most important errors (DS 3401-3466), and in the encyclical* Pascendi *(1907) which contains a wide-ranging exposition of its various doctrines and attempts to systematize them (DS 3475-3500).*

In 1910 the entire body of the clergy involved in pastoral work or in the teaching profession was obliged to take an oath rejecting the essential errors of modernism concerning revelation and tradition. On account of the concise form in which it summarises antimodernist positions this oath, apart from its disciplinary importance, has also considerable doctrinal value as a document of the Church's teaching authority. The formula was first replaced in 1967 and then in 1989 by the new formula of profession of faith (cf. nn. 40-41).

143
3537
I firmly embrace and accept each and every teaching that is defined, proposed and declared by the infallible magisterium of the Church, and in particular those principal truths which are directly opposed to the errors of this time.

143/1
3538
First of all, I profess that God, the beginning and the end of all things, can be known with certainty, and that his existence can also be proved through the natural light of reason from the things that were made [cf. Rom 1:20], viz., from the visible works of creation, as the cause is known from its effects.

143/2
3539
Secondly, I recognise the exterior proofs of revelation, that is to say, divine works, mainly miracles and prophecies, as sure signs of the divine origin of the Christian religion, and I hold that they are well adapted to the understanding of all ages and of all people, also those of the present time.

143/3
3540
Thirdly, I hold with equally firm faith that the Church, the guardian and teacher of the revealed word, was personally (*proxime*) and directly instituted by the true historical Christ himself during the life among us, and that it is built upon Peter, the head of the apostolic hierarchy and upon his successors through the ages.

143/4
3541
Fourthly, I sincerely accept the doctrine of the faith which was handed down to us in the same meaning and always with the same purport from the apostles through the orthodox Fathers. I therefore entirely reject the heretical theory of the evolution of the dogmas, viz., that they change from one meaning to another, different from the one which the Church previously held. I also condemn any error which substitutes for the divine trust left to the Spouse of Christ to be faithfully guarded by her, a philosophical system or a creation of human

reflection which gradually developed through human effort and is to be perfected in the future through indefinite progress.

143/5 Fifthly, I hold with certainty and I sincerely confess that
3542 faith is not a blind impulse of religion welling up from the depth of the subconscious under the impulse of the heart and the inclination of a morally conditioned will, but the genuine assent of the intellect to a truth which is received from outside "by hearing". In this assent, given on the authority of the all-truthful God, we hold to be true what has been said, attested to, and revealed by the personal God, our Creator and Lord.

143/6 I also submit myself with due respect and I adhere
3543 whole-heartedly to all the condemnations, declarations, and norms contained in the encyclical *Pascendi* and the decree *Lamentabili*, particularly those referring to the so-called history of dogma.

143/7 I also reject the error of those who maintain that the
3544 faith proposed by the Church can be contrary to history, and that Catholic dogmas in the sense in which they are now understood are irreconcilable with the origins of the Christian religion as they really were.

143/8 I condemn and reject also the conception of those who
3545 say that an educated Christian puts on a double personality, the one of a believer, the other of a historian, as though it were allowed for the historian to hold something contrary to the faith of the believer or to advance premises from which it would follow that the dogmas are false or doubtful, provided only that these are not directly denied.

143/9 Equally I reject any way of judging and interpreting Holy
3546 Scripture which takes no account of the Church's Tradition, of the analogy of faith and the norms laid down by the apostolic See: which adheres to the theories of the rationalists, and presumptuously and rashly accepts textual criticism as the only supreme rule.

143/10 Equally I reject the opinion of those who maintain that
3547 a lecturer or writer on matters of historical theology must first discard all preconceived opinions about the supernatural origin of Catholic Tradition or about the promise

of divine help to preserve for ever all revealed truth; that the writings of the individual Fathers should be interpreted on purely scientific principles to the exclusion of all sacred authority, with the same freedom of judgment with which any profane document is studied.

143/11 Finally, I profess in general that I am completely adverse
3548 to the error of the Modernists who say that there is nothing divine in the sacred Tradition or—what is still worse—who admit it in a pantheistic sense, which would leave us with a bare and simple fact, on a par with the common facts of history, the fact, namely, that a band of individuals continued in subsequent ages through their efforts, their solicitude and ingenuity, the school that was started by Christ and his apostles.

143/12 Thus I firmly hold, and shall continue to hold to my last
3549 breath, the faith of the Fathers, on the basis of the sure charism of truth that is, has been, and always will be in the succession of the bishops from the apostles, for the purpose that not what seems better and more suited according to the culture of each age should be held, but that the absolute and immutable truth, which from the beginning was preached by the apostles, "should never be believed, never be understood, in a different way"[1]

143/13 I promise that I shall keep all this faithfully, wholly, and
3550 sincerely, that I shall keep it inviolate, never deviating from it in teaching or in any way in word or in writing. Thus I promise, thus I swear; so help me God and these holy gospels of God.

PIUS XII

ENCYCLICAL LETTER *HUMANI GENERIS* (1950)

This encyclical issued on 12 August 1950 by Pius XII constituted almost a new Syllabus of errors to be rejected; it was concerned with "certain false opinions which threaten to sap the foundation of Catholic teaching", as the encyclical itself described its theme. It opposed certain theological and philosophical tendencies which had appeared in various places, notably in France (Nouvelle Théologie), without, however, constituting a new system. The encyclical was correspondingly many-sided.

---

1. TERTULLIAN, *De praescriptione haereticorum*, 28.

Two passages are reproduced here. The first refers to the rational foundations of faith. Pius XII maintains the doctrine of Vatican I about the possibility of giving a rational proof for the philosophical and historical foundations of faith, but he admits the possibility of great subjective obstacles which may prevent their acceptance.

The second text deals with the expression of faith through changing philosophical systems. It admits the limitations of human concepts, but it asserts that the terms in which divine revelation has been expressed do contain the word of God in a lasting and binding manner. It deplores the rashness with which the formulations of the faith are abandoned by some theologians.

(The rational basis of faith)

144   Though human reason is, strictly speaking, truly capable
3875   by its own natural power and light of attaining to a true
          and certain knowledge of the one personal God who
watches over and governs the world by his providence, and of
the natural law written in our hearts by the Creator; yet there
are many obstacles which prevent reason from the effective and
fruitful use of this inborn faculty. For the truths that refer to
God and concern the relations between God and our human race
wholly transcend the visible order of things, and, if they are
translated into human action and influence it, they call for self-
surrender and abnegation. The human mind, in its turn, is
hampered in the attaining of such truths, not only by the impact
of the senses and the imagination, but also by disordered
appetites which are the consequences of original sin. So it
happens that people in such matters easily persuade themselves
that what they would not like to be true is false or at least
doubtful.

145   Hence we have to admit that divine revelation is morally
3876   necessary in order that such religious and moral truths
          "which of themselves are not beyond human reason can,
even in the present condition of humankind, be known by
everyone with facility, with firm certitude and with no admixture
of error" [cf. n. 114].

146   Difficulties may occur to the human mind also in
3876   forming a firm judgment concerning the credibility of
          the Catholic faith, though we are provided by God
with such a wealth of wonderful exterior signs by which the
divine origin of the Christian religion can be proved with
certainty even by the natural light of reason alone. But a person

may be guided by prejudices, may be influenced by passions
and ill intentions, and so can turn away from and resist not only
the evidence of the exterior signs which is plain to the eyes, but
also the heavenly inspirations which God conveys to our minds.

(Faith and theological terminology)

147   [Desirous to come as close as possible to the way of
3882   thinking and speaking of modern systems, some
            theologians] hope that the way is made clear for re-
stating dogma in terms of modern philosophy, of immanentism,
idealism, existentialism, or some other system, according to the
needs of the day. As for the bolder spirits, they assert that this is
possible and necessary, because the mysteries of faith can never
be formulated in notions which adequately express the truth,
but only in approximate notions, which, as they say, are always
subject to change, by which the truth is indicated up to a point,
but at the same time is necessarily deformed. Therefore, in their
opinion, it is not absurd, rather it is absolutely necessary, that
theology should constantly exchange old concepts for new ones,
in accordance with various philosophies which it uses as its
instruments in the course of time. So theology would express in
a human way the same divine truths in different, and even to
some extent opposite ways, which, however, they maintain, mean
the same thing. They go on to say that the history of dogma
consists in giving an account of the various successive forms in
which revealed truth has been clothed, in accordance with the
various doctrines and theories which developed in the course of
centuries.

148   It will be clear, from all we have been saying, that the
3883   efforts made by these thinkers not merely lead to what
            is called dogmatic 'relativism' but already contain it. Such
relativism is strongly fostered by the disrespect they show for
the doctrine commonly handed down, and for the terminology
by which it is expressed. Surely, all are agreed that the terms
expressing certain ideas, as they are used in the schools and even
by the teaching authority of the Church itself, are susceptible of
further perfecting and refining: it is also known that the Church
in the use of these terms has not always been consistent. It is
also clear that the Church cannot tie itself to any philosophical
system which flourishes for a short time; but what has been built

up in a common consensus by Catholic teachers in the course of centuries, in their effort to reach a certain understanding of dogma, does certainly not rest on such flimsy grounds. It rests on principles and notions deduced from a true understanding of created things; in the deduction of these insights the divinely revealed truth, like a star, has illumined the human mind through the Church. No wonder, then, that some of these conceptions have not only been used, but even have been sanctioned by ecumenical Councils, so that it is wrong to deviate from them.

THE SECOND VATICAN GENERAL COUNCIL

DOGMATIC CONSTITUTION *DEI VERBUM* (1965)

The Constitution Dei Verbum *is foundational for Vatican II's broad renewal of Catholic doctrine. Early in the deliberations, numerous bishops voiced dissatisfaction over the preparatory schemata on the deposit of faith and the "sources" of revelation. These texts had been cast in the thought-forms of the textbook tradition that established itself after Vatican I and was further strengthened by the anti-modernist measures. But in 1962, many bishops argued that revelation should no longer be explained mainly in terms of its relation to reason, that is, as including transcendent mysteries but at the same time being rationally prepared by arguments for credibility that bring the mind to the threshold of faith.*

The bishops called for an articulation of revelation out of the centre of God's gift of light and life in his Son. Christ is, to be sure, our teacher of supernatural mysteries of salvation, but he is more, for in him revelation itself takes personal form, in the Word who expresses in an incomparable way God's will to save. On revelation, Scripture must furnish the language of exposition, especially the great passages of Paul and John on God's disclosure of his mystery long concealed but unfolding openly in Christ and the Spirit with their abundant gifts of grace and truth.

And so, through four major revisions during the Council, Dei Verbum *grew out of the interventions, both oral and written, of the bishops. Parts of the finished product express fundamental tenets of Christianity in a manner able to create an ecumenical consensus. Moreover, the Constitution relates God's saving word to the larger human family, as stated in its Prologue: "this Synod [...] wants the whole world to hear the summons to salvation, so that through hearing it may believe, through belief it may hope, and through hope it may come to love" (DV 1, adapting St. Augustine,* De catechizandis rudibus, *4, 8).*

The Constitution deals in 6 Chapters: 1) with revelation itself; 2) with its transmission in Tradition; 3) with the inspiration and interpretation of Holy Scripture; 4) with revelation as attested by the Old Testament; 5) with revelation in Jesus Christ as the New Testament proclaims and applies this; 6) with Holy Scripture in the life of the Church.

Chapter 1, 2-5, is quoted here. These paragraphs contain the new perspectives on revelation developed by the Council: the nature of revelation (2), its preparatory stages leading to the coming of Jesus Christ (3), the fulness of revelation in Jesus Christ (4), and the human response to revelation in faith (5)

Chapter I: Revelation Itself

(The nature and object of revelation)

149 2. In his goodness and wisdom God chose to reveal himself and to make known the mystery of his will *[cf. Eph 1:9]*, by which through Christ, the Word made flesh, we have access in the Holy Spirit to the Father, and are made partakers of the divine nature *[cf. Eph 2:18; 2 Pet 1:4]*. Through this revelation, therefore, the invisible God *[cf. Col 1:15; 1 Tim 1:17]*, out of the abundance of his love, speaks to us as friends *[cf. Ex 33:11; Jn 15:14-15]* and dwells among us *[cf. Bar 3:38]*, so that he may invite and receive us into communion with himself. This plan of revelation is realised by deeds and words intrinsically connected: the deeds wrought by God in the history of salvation manifest and confirm the teaching and the realities signified by the words, while the words themselves declare and explain the deeds and the mystery contained in them. The deepest truth thus revealed both about God and about our salvation shines out for us in Christ, who is the mediator and at the same time the fulness of all revelation.

(The preparation of the Gospel)

150 3. God who creates and sustains all things through the Word *[cf. Jn 1:3]* gives men and women permanent testimony to himself in created things *[cf. Rom 1:19-20]*. Moreover, wishing to open the way of supernatural salvation, he revealed himself to our first parents from the very beginning. After their fall he kindled in them the hope of salvation by his promise of redemption *[cf. Gen 3:15]*. He continued to watch over humankind unceasingly so as to grant eternal life to all who seek salvation through the faithful pursuit of good works *[cf. Rom 2:6-7]*. In his own time he called Abraham in order to make of him a great nation *[cf. Gen 12:2]*. After the time of the patriarchs, he taught his people, through Moses and the prophets, to acknowledge him as the one true living God, provident Father and just Judge, and to wait for the promised Saviour. In this way, down through the centuries, God was preparing the way for the Gospel.

(Jesus Christ is in his person the fulness of revelation)

151 4. After God had spoken in many and various ways through the prophets, "in these last days he has spoken to us by a Son" *[Heb 1:1-2]*. For he sent his Son, the eternal Word, who enlightens all human beings, so that he might dwell among them and declare to them the secrets of God *[cf. Jn 1:1-18]*. Jesus Christ, therefore, the Word made flesh, sent as "a man to men",[1] "utters the words of God" *[Jn 3:34]* and accomplishes the work of salvation committed to him by the Father *[cf. Jn 5:36; 17:4]*. To see Jesus is to see also the Father *[cf. Jn 14:9]*. Jesus, therefore, brings revelation to its final perfection by his whole presence and self-manifestation, by his words and deeds, his signs and wonders, particularly by his death and glorious resurrection, and finally by the sending of the Spirit of truth; he confirms with divine testimony the fact of revelation that God is with us to free us from the darkness of sin and death and to raise us up to life eternal.

The Christian dispensation, therefore, being the new and definitive Covenant, will never pass away, and we now await no new public revelation before the glorious manifestation of our Lord Jesus Christ *[cf. 1 Tim 6:14; Tit 2:13]*.

(Revelation is to be received by faith)

152 5. To God who reveals himself must be given "the obedience of faith" *[Rom 16:26; cf. Rom 1:5; 2 Cor 10:5-6]*, by which one freely commits one's whole self to God, offering "the full submission of intellect and will to God who reveals himself" *[cf. n. 118]* and freely assenting to the revelation granted by him. This faith cannot exist without the prevenient and assisting grace of God and the interior succour of the Holy Spirit, who moves the heart and turns it to God, opens the eyes of the mind, and gives "to all joy in assenting to the truth and in believing it" *[cf. n. 120]*. The same Holy Spirit continually perfects faith by his gifts so as to bring about an ever deeper understanding of revelation.

---

1. *Epistola ad Diognetum*, 8, 4.

(The object of revelation)

(153)   6. *(The doctrine of Vatican I is reasserted, concerning reason's natural power to know God, the revelation of divine mysteries, and also the truths which by themselves can be the object of natural knowledge) (cf. n. 114).*

PASTORAL CONSTITUTION *GAUDIUM ET SPES* (1965)

(154)   *It is characteristic of Vatican II that it moves doctrinal questions into the context of actual life. God's revelation and our believing response to it must be realised in our modern age of science, secularism and social transformation.* Gaudium et Spes *analyses the convictions and attitudes toward God and the sphere of human and social values that are characteristic of the modern era.*

The entire document conceives humanity as a community on its "journey to the kingdom of the Father" (1); it answers questions "in the light of Christ, the image of the unseen God" (10). The Constitution vindicates the relevance of revelation and faith for people in their personal lives, in society, and in the various spheres of their activities.

Of special significance is the section about modern atheism, i.e, the refusal to accept God and his revelation. Atheism is considered under the following aspects.

1) The phenomenon of modern atheism: its widespread presence in the modern world with the result that it "must be accounted among the most serious problems of this age"; its various forms, and the reasons for its growing influence (19).

2) Systematic atheism: it claims to liberate the human mind as to make human beings "the sole artisans and creators of their own history"; to lead to "economic and social emancipation"; to guide everyone in the building up of the earthly city (20).

3) The Church's attitude: the significance of faith in God for personal life and for human society (21).

Finally Gaudium et Spes *notably expands the horizon of the teaching on revelation expressed in* Dei Verbum. *What God has uttered to humankind in Christ brilliantly illumines our human history and the mystery of our human existence. In the light of the Word incarnate and of his pashcal mystery, human life is shown to be abundantly significant, even at the most painful and desperate moments of our pilgrimage (cf. nn. 669a-b, 678-680).*

PAUL VI

ENCYCLICAL LETTER *ECCLESIAM SUAM* (1964)

While the Council through its documents inaugurated a new understanding both of the word of God and of the modern world in which it has to be proclaimed, and so prepared a new approach of the Church to human society, Pope Paul VI wrote his first encyclical Ecclesiam Suam *which outlines the renewed attitude of the Church to the world of today.*

Two passages of this encyclical referring to atheism are quoted here. In fact, they are previous to the corresponding Council texts of Gaudium et Spes. *The Pope speaks of the "concentric circles" with which the Church must enter into dialogue. The widest of these circles embraces the whole of humankind. It is in this context that the Pope speaks about atheism. The text is found in* AAS 56 (1964) 650-653.

(The destructive power of modern atheism)

155 We realise, however, that in this limitless circle there are many, very many unfortunately, who profess no religion; not a few also, we know, declare that they deny God in various ways. We are aware that some of them proclaim their godlessness openly and uphold it as a programme of human education and political conduct in the futile and fatal conviction that they are setting people free from obsolete and false opinions about life and the world, and put in their place, as they pretend, conceptions that are scientific and in conformity with the needs of modern progress.

156 This, indeed, is the most serious problem of our time. We are firmly convinced that the principles on which the denial of God is based are by their nature utterly erroneous; they are not in keeping with the ultimate and necessary requirements of thought; they deprive the rational order of the world of its true and effective foundations; they do not provide human life with sound judgment to solve problems but with an empty dogma which degrades and saddens it, and destroys at the root any social order which would base itself on it. Thus it does not bring freedom but is the source of the saddest fall, attempting to quench the light of the living God. We shall therefore resist with all our strength the evil assault of this denial; we do so in the supreme cause of truth, in virtue of our sacred duty faithfully to profess Christ and his Gospel, moved by a burning and unshakable love which inspires in us a concern for the fortunes of the human race. We do it in the invincible hope that people of the modern age may feel again impelled, through those religious ideals which the Catholic faith sets before them, to pursue a civilization that never declines but tends to the natural and supernatural perfection of the human mind, enabled by divine grace to possess temporal goods in peace and honour, and confidently hoping for the attainment of perennial goods.

(The roots of modern atheism)

157 But though we must speak firmly and clearly to preserve and defend religion and the human values it proclaims and fosters, we are moved by our pastoral office to seek in the hearts of modern atheists the reasons for these disturbances and their denial of God. One can easily see that these reasons are many and complex, so that we must examine them carefully and refute them effectively. Some of them arise from the demand that divine things be presented in a worthier and purer way than is the case in certain imperfect forms of language and worship; we ought to do all in our power to improve them and to make them more transparent so that they may express more adequately the sacred reality of which they are the signs. We see people with an earnest and often noble yearning, with hearts moved by zeal, and burning with ideals of the unattainable, who dream of justice and progress and seek in striving for a social order the attainment of values that to them appear the highest and almost divine. Such ideals for them are a substitute for him who is the Absolute and Necessary; they testify to the fact that they are in the grip of the longing for that supreme Source and End that cannot be eradicated from the human heart; it is for us, in the patient and wise exercise of the teaching ministry, to show that all this transcends human nature as well as is immanent in it.

158 Again we see individuals accurately using the tools of human reasoning, at times not without some simplification, for the purpose of building up a notion of the whole universe founded on science. The search is all the less reprehensible as it often follows ways of logical procedure not unlike those received in the classical schools and based on a strict discipline of the mind. But, against the will of those who think that in this way they have found a sure support in defending atheism, this discipline impels them through its innate dynamism to proceed to the renewed and definite acknowledgment of the highest God, to a metaphysical and logical system. The atheistic politico-scientist deliberately stops this cogent process of reasoning at a certain point and so extinguishes the sovereign light through which the universe could become intelligible. Who of us would not effectively assist them to come, ultimately, to the realisation of the objective truth of the universe in which the mind is struck by the divine presence and the lips begin to utter humble words of consoling prayers?

159 At times we also find [atheists] of noble sentiments who are impatient with the mediocrity and the self-seeking of large sections of our present human society; they ingeniously borrow from our gospels ways of speaking and phrases, using them to express solidarity, mutual help and compassion. Shall we not be able to trace these words, which express moral values, back to their true source which is Christian?

DECLARATION *MYSTERIUM ECCLESIAE* OF THE
S. CONGREGATION FOR THE DOCTRINE OF THE FAITH
(11 May 1973)

This document on the mystery of the Church is primarily concerned with the charism of infallibility pertaining to the Church's teaching authority (cf. n. 883). While strongly upholding the traditional doctrine of infallibility, it nevertheless recognizes that dogmatic formulas are historically conditioned, with the result that they always remain incomplete and perfectible. This important section of the Declaration begins by acknowledging the "difficulties of various kinds" to which the transmission of divine Revelation is subject: these arise from the very nature of the mysteries of the faith (cf. n. 132); they "also arise from the historical conditioning that affects the expression of Revelation". With regard to this historical conditioning, the declaration offers considerations—somewhat novel in an official document—by which the unavoidable inadequacy and perfectibility of dogmatic formulas is brought out, all of which "have to be taken into account in order that these pronouncements may be properly interpreted". It goes on to delineate the important consequences deriving from these considerations as regards the interpretation of dogmatic formulas pronounced by the Church's teaching authority. It notes, however, that, incomplete and perfectible as they may be, these formulas remain true in their meaning; this excludes "dogmatic relativism". The text is found in AAS 65 (1973) 402-404.

(The historical conditioning of dogmatic formulas)

160 With regard to this historical conditioning, it must first be observed that the meaning of the pronouncements of faith depends partly upon the expressive power of the language used at a certain point in time and in particular circumstances. Moreover, it sometimes happens that a given dogmatic truth is first expressed incompletely (but not falsely), and at a later date, when considered in a broader context of faith or human knowledge, it receives a fuller and more perfect expression. In addition, when the Church makes new pronouncements, she intends to confirm or clarify what is in some way contained in Sacred Scripture or in previous expressions of Tradition; but at the same time she usually has the intention of solving certain questions or removing certain errors. All these things have to be taken into account in order that these pronouncements may be properly interpreted. Finally, even though the truths which the Church intends to teach through her dogmatic formulas are distinct from the changeable conceptions of the given epoch and can be expressed without them, nevertheless it can sometimes happen that these truths may be enunciated by the Sacred Magisterium in terms that bear traces of such conceptions.

(The interpretaton of dogmatic formulas)

161 In view of the above it must be stated that the dogmatic formulas of the Church's Magisterium were from the beginning suitable for communicating revealed truth, and that as they are they remain perennially suitable for communicating this truth to those who interpret them correctly. It does not however follow that everyone of these formulas has always been or will always be so to the same extent. For this reason theologians seek to define exactly the intention of teaching proper to the various formulas, and in carrying out this work they are of considerable assistance to the living Magisterium of the Church, to which they remain subordinated. For this reason also it often happens that ancient dogmatic formulas and others closely connected with them remain living and fruitful in the habitual usage of the Church, but with suitable expository and explanatory additions that maintain and clarify their original meaning. In addition, it has sometimes happened that in this habitual usage of the Church certain of these formulas gave way to new expressions which, proposed and approved by the Sacred Magisterium, present more clearly or more completely the same meaning.

(Dogmatic relativism is excluded)

162 As for the meaning of dogmatic formulas, this remains ever true and constant in the Church, even when it is expressed with greater clarity or more developed. The faithful, therefore, must shun the opinion, first, that dogmatic formulas (or some category of them) cannot signify truth in a determinate way, but can only offer changeable approximations to it, which to a certain extent distort or alter it; secondly, that these formulas signify the truth only in an indeterminate way, the truth being like a goal that is constantly being sought by means of such approximations. Those who hold such an opinion do not avoid dogmatic relativism and they corrupt the concept of the Church's infallibility relative to the truth to be taught or held in a determinate way.

JOHN PAUL II

APOSTOLIC CONSTITUTION *SAPIENTIA CHRISTIANA* (1979)

The Church's dialogue with modern society, promoted by the Council, necessarily led to an opening of theology towards many spheres of culture and sciences. Theology rightly claims the freedom to investigate new realms in which the message of the Gospel has to be articulated.

Thus the relation of academic freedom in theological research and teaching to the hierarchical magisterium has had to be faced anew. In the Apostolic Constitution which promulgates the new legislation covering ecclesiastical academic studies in Universities and Faculties (29 April 1979), the relationship of academic freedom to ecclesistical authority is carefully formulated: While "just freedom" is recognised both for teaching and research "within the limits of God's Word", teaching must be carried out in accordance with the Church's magisterium. The reason is that theology is taught in the name of the Church, while research may open out towards new avenues, provided it does so in "deference to the Church's Magisterium" and its function of authoritatively interpreting the Word of God.

(Theology and Magisterium)

163 39. 1. Following the norm of the Second Vatican Council, according to the nature of each faculty:

1) just feeedom [GS 59] should be acknowledged in research and teaching so that true progress can be obtained in learning and understanding divine truth;

2) at the same time it is clear that:

a) true freedom in teaching is necessarily contained within the limits of God's Word as this is constantly taught by the Church's Magisterium;

b) likewise, true freedom in research is necessarily based upon firm adherence to God's Word and deference to the Church's Magisterium, whose duty it is to interpret authentically the Word of God.

2. Therefore, in such a weighty matter one must proceed with prudence, with trust and without suspicion, at the same time with judgement and without rashness, especially in teaching, while working to harmonise studiously the necessities of science with the pastoral needs of the People of God.

APOSTOLIC EXHORTATION *CATECHESI TRADENDAE*
(16 October 1979)

In this major document Pope John Paul II takes up the theme of Catechesis in Our Day in response to and on the basis of the 1977 Synod of Bishops which discussed the same topic. The Apostolic Exhortation balances encouragement of the new methods and approaches with repeated insistence that these should not endanger the integrity of content or substitute personal views for teachings revealed through Scripture and developed Christian Tradition. In the eighth chapter entitled "The Joy of Faith in a Troubled World" a section on "Research and Certainty of Faith" emphasizes that faith is not a leap into the dark but has an unshakable foundation. The text is found in AAS 71 (1979) 1277-1340.

(Scientific research and certitude of faith)

163a   A more subtle challenge occasionally comes from the very way of conceiving faith. Certain contemporary philosophical schools [...] like to emphasize that the fundamental human attitude is that of seeking the infinite, a seeking that never attains its object. In theology, this view of things will state very categorically that faith is not certainty but questioning, not clarity but a leap in the dark.

These currents of thought certainly have the advantage of reminding us that faith concerns things not yet in our possession, since they are hoped for; that as yet we see only "in a mirror dimly" *[1 Cor 13:12]*; and that God dwells always in inaccessible light *[cf. 1 Tim 6:16]*. They help us to make the Christian faith not the attitude of one who has already arrived, but a journey forward as with Abraham. For all the more reason one must avoid presenting as certain things which are not.

However, we must not fall into the opposite extreme, as too often happens. [...] Although we are not in full posseession, we do have an assurance and a conviction.[...] Let us not give [...]

too negative an idea of faith—as if it were absolute non-knowing, a kind of blindness, a world of darkness—but let us show [...] that the humble yet courageous seeking of the believer, far from having its starting point in nothingness, in plain self-deception, in fallible opinions or in uncertainty, is based on the word of God who cannot deceive or be deceived, and is unceasingly built on the unmovable rock of this word.

ADDRESS TO SCIENTISTS
(15 November 1980)

On November 15th, 1980, Pope John Paul II addressed a gathering of scientists and university students in the Cathedral of Cologne. It was on the feast of St. Albert the Great, on the 700th anniversary of his death. In fact the invitation of the Pope to Germany was occasioned by this anniversary and Cologne had been the second home of the Saint. The historic importance of Albert the Great lies in the fact that in the first crucial encounter of secular sciences (Aristotelian philosoply) and traditional faith he took up a position which remains programmatic even today. The Pope used the occasion to propose in a systematic way the relation of science to faith in our time; this has radically changed from suspicion and hostility to complementarity and the recognised need, on both sides, of collaboration in a time of crisis of the scientific-technical culture. The text is found in Osservatore Romano *(English Edition), 24 November, 1980, pp. 6-7.*

(The recognition of science according to Albert the Great)

164 2. The claim to truth of a science based on rationalilty is recognised; in fact it is accepted in its contents, completed, corrected and developed in its independent rationality. And precisely in this way it becomes the property of the Christian world. In this way the latter sees its own understanding of the world enormously enriched without having to give up any essential element of its tradition, far less the foundation of its faith. For there can be no fundamental conflict between a reason which, in conformity with its own nature which comes from God, is geared to truth and is qualified to know truth, and a faith which refers to the same divine source of all truth.

(The conflicts of the past are deplored)

165 3. Many people [...] still feel the weight of those notorious conflicts which arose from the interference of religious authorities in the process of the development of scientific knowledge. The Church remembers this with regret, for today we realise the errors and shortcomings of these ways of proceeding. We can say today that they have been overcome, thanks to the power of persuasion of science, and thanks above all to the work of a scientific theology, which has deepened the understanding of faith and freed it from the conditionings of time.

(The crisis of merely functional science)

166 3. Our culture, in all its areas, is imbued with a science which proceeds in a way that is largely functionalistic. This applies also to the area of values and norms, of spiritual orientation in general. Precisely here science comes up against its own limits. There is talk of a crisis of legitimation of science, nay more, of a crisis or orientation of our whole scientific culture. What is its essence? [...]

Science alone is not capable of answering the question of meaning; in fact it cannot even set it in the framework of its starting point. And yet this question of meaning cannot tolerate an indefinite postponement of its answer. If widespread confidence in science is disappointed, then the state of mind easily changes into hostility to science. In this space that has remained empty, ideologies suddenly break in. They sometimes behave as if they were "scientific", but they owe their power of persuasion to the urgent need for an answer to the question of meanings and to the interest in social and political change. Science that is purely functional, without values and alienated from truth, can enter the service of these ideolgies; a reason that is only instrumental runs the risk of losing its freedom.[...]

(The criterion for the right use of science)

167 4. There is no reason to consider technico-scientific culture as opposed to the world of God's creation. It is clear beyond all doubt that technical knowledge can be used for good as well as for evil.[...] Technical science, aimed at the transformation of the world, is justified on the basis of the service it renders to individuals and all humanity [...] Our human personal dignity represents the criterion by which all cultural application of technico-scientific knowledge must be judged.

(Science must safeguard human freedom)

168 4. [Sciences extend also to] the scientific analysis of human existence and of the world in which we live, at the social and cultural level. An absolutely incalculable mass of knowledge has thereby come to light, which has repercussions on both public and private life. The social system of modern states, the health and educational system, economic processes and cultural activities are all marked in many ways by the influence of these sciences. But it is important that science should not keep the human race under its thumb. Also in the culture of technology, human beings, in conformity with their dignity, must remain free; in fact it must be the meaning of this culture to give them greater freedom.

(Science is bound to truth)

169 5. To be able to influence praxis, [science] must first be determined by truth, and therefore be free for truth. A free science, bound only to truth, does not let itself be reduced to the model of functionalism or any other which limits understanding of scientific rationalilty [...].

I do not hesitate at all to see also the science of faith on the horizon of rationality understood in this way. The Church wants independent theological research, which is not identified with the ecclesiastical magisterium, but which knows it is committed with regard to it in common service of the truth of faith and the People of God. It cannot be ignored that tensions and even conflicts may arise. But this cannot be ignored either as regards the relationship between Church and science. The reason is to be sought in the finiteness of our reason, limited in its extension and therefore exposed to error. Nevertheless we can always hope for a solution of reconciliation, if we take our stand on the ability of this same reason to attain truth.

(Science needs faith)

170 5. In the past precursors of modern science fought against the Church with the slogans: reason, freedom and progress. Today, in view of the crisis with regard to the meaning of science, the multiple threats to its freedom and the doubt about progress, the battle-fronts have been inverted. Today it is the Church that takes up the defence:

–for reason and science, which she recognises as having the ability to attain truth, which legitimizes it as a human realisation;

–for the freedom of science, through which the latter possesses its dignity as a human and personal good;

–for progress in the service of a humanity which needs it to safeguard its life and its dignity.

With this task, the Church and all Christians are at the centre of the debate of these times of ours. An adequate solution of the pressing questions about the meaning of human existence, norms of action, and the prospects of a more far-reaching hope, is possible only in the renewed connection between scientific thought and the power of faith in human beings in search of truth. The pursuit of a new humanism on which the future of the third millennium can be based, will be successful only on condition that scientific knowledge again enters upon a living relationship with the truth revealed to us as God's gift. Human reason is a grand instrument for knowledge and structuring of the world. It needs, however, in order to realise the whole wealth of human possibilities, to open to the word of eternal Truth, which became man in Christ.

ADDRESS TO THE SECRETARIAT FOR NON-BELIEVERS
(2 April 1981)

Speaking to the plenary session of the Secretariat for Non-believers John Paul II accepts the legitimate questioning of scientists but points out the risk of a scientific mentality which closes itself to a broader vision of realities beyond pure rationality and so remains on the threshold of faith. The text is found in AAS 73 (1981) 292-296.

(*Science and unbelief*)

171 By reason of the increased rationality which it yields, the development of the sciences [...] appeals to a total vision which it cannot itself provide: it calls for the meaning of meanings.

Science is not the only legitimate form of knowledge. In such radically reductionist perspective faith is nothing but a naive representation of reality [...] bound up with a myth-making mentality.

[...] Proper consideration of the whole reality is a delicate and difficult task. [...] We see a twofold temptation for believers: rationalism and fideism. What is needed is a dialogue between human beings, in which the dynamics of rational thinking are by no means opposed to the specific transcendence of faith but in a sense calls for it. The experience of life reveals the need of moving beyond the interior emptiness created by the collapse of meaning that occurs when all human activities are forced to exist in a closed universe and are no longer seen in a broader and deeper perspective [...], when they are no longer integrated into a supra-rational dimension that far from being non-rational or sub-rational is the foundation and goal of all rationality.

[...] To the extent that the scientific method permeates all thinking and the whole of one's outlook on reality, it can lead in the area of faith to the loss of the certitude proper to this domain in which knowledge is also love.

Thus the spirit of perpetual questioning can lead to doubts about essential points of faith and, while falling short of outright denial, to a suspension of judgment and assent as long as one has not explained for oneself all the reasons for believing and all the aspects of the Christian mystery, as though one were awaiting further discoveries even with regard to the Creed. [...]

[...] Minds imbued with the method of scientific research may find it an embarrassment or an obstacle because they do not understand the specific nature and transcendental character of faith and are in danger of always remaining on the threshold of faith.

ADDRESS TO THE EUROPEAN CONVENTION OF
PAX ROMANA
(13 September 1982)

The convention dealt with the theme "Ethical Responsibility and Christian Faith in a Changing World". In his welcoming address, the Pope urged the participants to distinguish the two orders of knowledge, science and faith, and reminded them of their responsibility to uphold the dignity and the freedom of the human person. The text is found in The Pope Speaks 27 (1982), p. 362.

(Science and faith)

172 You show by your life that faith does not limit the space and freedom of science but rather that the responses of the various scientific disciplines are only partial responses for the person who deeply hungers for the truth. For science neither intends to nor can perceive more than a single sector of reality especially since this perception is again limited by its curtailing methodology, deliberate and necessary.

Faith, on the other hand, can transcend partial visions of reality for such faith sees it as created by God. In this perspective, created things reveal their meaning. Human beings in particular find their dignity in the fact that their origin and ultimate destiny are in God. Scientific progress which injures the inalienable worth of the human person must be denounced and opposed. The philosophico-religious currents which destroy human freedom and promise paradise on earth are mere ideologies.

DISCOURSE TO SCIENTISTS ON THE 350th ANNIVERSARY OF THE PUBLICATION OF GALILEO'S *DIALOGHI* (9 May 1983)

That the Pope should address scientists gathered for a symposium to commemorate the anniversary of the publication of Galileo's Dialoghi, *is in itself a sign of the spirit of dialogue which has replaced the former antagonism between the Church and science. After a dispassionate exposition of the Galileo 'case', the Pope speaks of the responsibility of scientists. He encourages them to open their hearts and minds to the imperatives of today's world in the service of 'the whole truth' but also expresses the gratitude of the Church for the help they give in clarifying some aspects of Christian doctrine. The text is found in AAS 75 (1983) 689-694.*

(Relationship between the Church and science)

173 Divine revelation, of which the Church is the guarantor and witness, does not in itself involve a particular scientific theory and the assistance of the Holy Spirit in no way lends itself to guaranteeing explanations that we would wish to profess concerning the physical constitution of reality.

[...] The Church is always interested in research concerning the knowledge of the universe, whether physical, biological or psychological.

It is only through humble and assiduous study that it learns to dissociate the essentials of faith from scientific systems of a given age, especially when a culturally influenced reading of the Bible seems to be linked to an obligatory cosmology.

The age-old relationships between the Church and science have brought Catholics to a more current understanding of the sphere of their faith, to a sort of intellectual purification and to a conviction that scientific study deserves a commitment to unbiased research which is, in the final analysis, a service to truth and to humanity itself.

We would add that the Church recognises with gratitude all that it owes to research and to science.

[...] Open your mind and heart fully to the imperatives of today's world, which aspires to justice and to dignity founded on truth. You yourselves be ready to seek all that is true, convinced that the realities of the spirit form part of what is real and part of the whole truth.

ADDRESS ON THE CEREMONY OF CONFERRING THE PAUL VI PRIZE ON HANS URS VON BALTHASAR
(23 June 1984)

In honouring the great Swiss scholar, John Paul II acknowledges the service rendered by theological scholars to the better understanding of Christian doctrine, and emphasises the limitations of our human knowledge in its grasp of the divine mysteries. The text is found in The Pope Speaks 26 (1984), pp. 339-340.

174 The service which theology must render to revealed truth is the continuous exploration of it. The aim is to discover and to express, as far as possible in all its aspects, the harmony, the unity and the beauty of it. Exploring will never end, because the truth of God is infinite and because human intelligence cannot approach it except in successive degrees.[...]

Service to revealed truth, then, always postulates a great sense of mystery so that it may accompany authentic theological research. It prevents revealed truth from being reduced, in rationalistic or unnatural terms, to the level of an ideology.

ADDRESS TO THE PLENARY ASSEMBLY OF THE PONTIFICAL ACADEMY OF SCIENCES
(8 October 1986)

On the 50th anniversary of the foundation of the Pontifical Academy of Sciences the Pope received its members in solemn audience. Stressing the Church's esteem for science and her respect of its legitimate autonomy in methodology and research, he exalted the role of scientists in our present age and enumerated the virtues and human values displayed in their professional vocation. The text is found in The Pope Speaks 32 (1987), pp. 51-53.

(Role of scientific research)

175 Christians have been encouraged to read the Bible afresh without seeking in it a scientific cosmological system. Scientists themselves have been invited to remain open to the absoluteness of God and to the awareness of creation. In itself, no field is closed to scientific investigation, provided that this respects the human being; it is rather the methodologies employed that bring the scientists to certain abstractions and definitions.[...]

One must recognise the particular method of each of the sciences. "This is why methodological research, in all the fields of knowledge, will never be truly opposed to faith, if it is carried out in a truly scientific manner and follows the norm of morality: worldly realities and the realities of faith find their origin in the same God" [cf. GS 36,2]. However, it would be false to understand this autonomy of earthly realities to mean that they did not depend on God and that men and women can dispose of them without reference to the Creator.[...]

Today, far from shutting herself up in an apologetic or defensive perspective, the Church rather makes herself the advocate of science, of reason and of the freedom of research for legitimate authentic science.

The Church appreciates not only the scientists' use of intelligence but their professional and moral merit, their intellectual honesty, their objectivity, their search for what is true, their self-discipline, their cooperation in teams, their commitment to serve others, their respect in the presence of the mysteries of the universe. These are human values that display the spiritual vocation of human beings.

LETTER TO THE DIRECTOR OF THE VATICAN OBSERVATORY
(1 June 1988)

In September 1987 a study week was held at Castel Gandolfo, the Pope's summer residence, on the relationships between theology, philosophy, and the natural sciences. In 1988, on the occasion of the publication of the resulting papers, Pope John Paul II wrote to Fr. George V. Coyne, S.J., Director of the Vatican Observatory, on the dialogue that should be promoted between theology and science, for the enrichment of both by the exchange of discoveries and insights. The text is found in Origins *18 (1988-89), pp. 375-378, and in* Physics, Philosophy, and Theology: a Common Quest for Understanding, *ed. R.J. Russell et al. (Vatican City 1988).*

(Science supports faith's perception of unity in the universe)

176a   The scientific disciplines [...] are endowing us with an understanding and appreciation of our universe as a whole and of the incredibly rich variety of intricately related processes and structures which constitute its animate and inanimate components. This knowledge has given us a more thorough understanding of ourselves and of our humble yet unique role within creation. [...]

The unity we perceive in creation on the basis of our faith in Jesus Christ as Lord of the universe, and the correlative unity for which we strive in our human communities, seems to be reflected and even reinforced in what contemporary science is revealing to us. As we behold the incredible development of scientific research, we detect an underlying movement toward the discovery of levels of law and process which unify created reality and which at the same time have given rise to the vast diversity of structures and organisms which constitute the physical and biological, and even the psychological and sociological worlds.[...]

(Science and religion should dialogue in mutual respect)

176b By encouraging openness between the church and the scientific communities, we are not envisioning a disciplinary unity between theology and science like that which exists within a given scientific field or within theology proper. As dialogue and common searching continue, there will be growth toward mutual understanding and a gradual uncovering of common concerns which will provide the basis for further research and discussion.[...]

The unity that we seek [...] is not identity. The church does not propose that science should become religion or religion science. On the contrary, unity always presupposes the diversity and the integrity of its elements. Each of these members should become not less itself but more itself in a dynamic interchange, for a unity in which one of the elements is reduced to the other is destructive, false in its promises of harmony, and ruinous of the integrity of its components. We are asked to become one. We are not asked to become each other.

To be more specific, both religion and science must preserve their autonomy and their distinctiveness. Religion is not founded on science nor is science an extension of religion. Each should possess its own principles, its pattern of procedures, its diversities of interpretation and its own conclusions. Christianity possesses the source of its justification within itself and does not expect

science to constitute its primary apologetic. Science must bear
witness to its own worth. While each can and should support
the other as distinct dimensions of a common human culture,
neither ought to assume that it forms the necessary premise for
the other. The unprecedented opportunity we have today is for
a common interactive relationship in which each discipline retains
its integrity and yet is radically open to the discoveries and
insights of the other.[...]

(Theology should carefully incorporate scientific findings)

176c   Theology [...] must be in vital interchange today with
science just as it always has been with philosophy and
other forms of learning. Theology will have to call on the findings
of science to one degree or another as it pursues its primary
concern for the human person, the reaches of freedom, the
possibilities of Christian community, the nature of belief and the
intelligibility of nature and history. The vitality and significance
of theology for humanity will in a profound way be reflected in
its ability to incorporate these findings.

Now this is a point of delicate importance, and it has to be
carefully qualified. Theology is not to incorporate indifferently
each new philosophical or scientific theory. As these findings
become part of the intellectual culture of the time, however,
theologians must understand them and test their value in
bringing out from Christian belief some of the possibilities that
have not yet been realized.[...]

If the cosmologies of the ancient Near Eastern world could
be purified and assimilated into the first chapters of Genesis,
might contemporary cosmology have something to offer to our
reflections on creation? Does an evolutionary perspective bring
any light to bear upon theological anthropology, the meaning of
the human person as *imago Dei*, the problem of Christology—
and even upon the development of doctrine itself? What, if any,
are the eschatological implications of contemporary cosmology,
especially in light of the vast future of the universe? Can
theological method fruitfully appropriate insights from scientific
methodology and the philosophy of science?

Questions of this kind can be suggested in abundance.
Pursuing them further would require the sort of intense dialogue
with contemporary science that has, on the whole, been lacking
among those engaged in theological research and teaching. It

would entail that some theologians, at least, should be sufficiently well versed in the sciences to make authentic and creative use of the resources that the best-established theories may offer them.

CONGREGATION FOR THE DOCTRINE OF THE FAITH INSTRUCTION ON THE ECCLESIAL VOCATION OF THE THEOLOGIAN (DONUM VERITATIS)
(24 May 1990)

The service rendered by theologians at the Second Vatican Council signalled the opening of a new partnership between the papal-episcopal magisterium and theology. The earlier paradigm of subordination and delegation (cf. nn. 858-859) was giving way to a new pattern of collaboration between these two forms of mediation of God's word. In 1976 the International Theological Commission issued 15 theses on the common elements that connect the magisterial and theological forms of teaching and on the relation of complementarity that should obtain between them.

A more authoritative statement is the Instruction *of 1990 excerpted here, in which the Congregation for the Doctrine of the Faith sets forth the respective roles of the magisterium and theologians and deals with the thorny issue of public dissent from magisterial teaching. Before its treatment of dissent (*Instruction, *nn. 32-41), the congregation describes theology as a needed work of reason in the sphere of revelation and offers a careful analysis of the levels of authoritative teaching and the corresponding responses due to the magisterium's enunciation of the content of faith and related truths.*

The English text of the Instruction *is found in* Origins *20 (1990-91), pp. 118-126.*

(The sources of the vocation of the theologian)

177 6. Among the vocations awakened [...] by the Spirit in the church is that of theologians. Their role is to pursue in a particular way an ever deeper understanding of the word of God found in the inspired Scriptures and handed on by the living tradition of the church. They do this in communion with the magisterium, which has been charged with the responsibility of preserving the deposit of faith.

Revealed truth beckons reason—God's gift fashioned for the assimilation of truth—to enter into its light and thereby to come to understand in a certain measure what it has believed. Theological science responds to the invitation of truth as it seeks to understand the faith. [...]

7. The theologian's work thus responds to a dynamism found in faith itself. Truth, by its nature, seeks to be

communicated since human beings were created for the perception of truth and from the depths of their being desire knowledge of it so that they can discover themselves in the truth and there find their salvation *[cf. 1 Tim 2:4]*. [...]

Theology therefore offers its contribution so that the faith might be communicated. Appealing to the understanding of those who do not yet know Christ, it helps them to seek and find faith. Obedient to the impulse of truth which seeks to be communicated, theology also arises from love and love's dynamism. In the act of faith, one knows God's goodness and begins to love him. Love, however, is ever desirous of a better knowledge of the beloved.[1] From this double origin of theology, inscribed upon the interior life of the people of God and its missionary vocation, derives the method with which it ought to be pursued in order to satisfy the requirements of its nature.

(The resources of theological research)

178 8. Since the object of theology is the truth which is the living God and his plan for salvation in Jesus Christ, theologians are called on to deepen their own life of faith and continuously unite their scholarly research with prayer.[2] In this way they will become more open to the "supernatural sense of faith" on which they depend, and it will appear to them as a sure rule for guiding their reflections and helping them assess the correctness of their conclusions.

10. [...] Theology's proper task is to understand the meaning of revelation and this therefore requires the utilization of philosophical concepts which provide "a solid and correct understanding of humanity, the world, and God" *[OT 15]* and can be employed in a reflection upon revealed doctrine. The historical disciplines are likewise necessary for the theologian's investigations. This is due chiefly to the historical character of revelation itself, which has been communicated to us in salvation history. Finally, a consultation of the human sciences is also necessary, to understand better revealed truth about human beings and the moral norms for their conduct, setting these in relation to the sound findings of such sciences.

---

1. Cf. St. BONAVENTURE, *Proemium in I Sent.*, q. 2, ad 6.
2. Cf. POPE JOHN PAUL II, *Insegnamenti 7/* 1 (1984), p. 1914.

It is the task of theologians in this perspective to draw from the surrounding culture those elements which will allow them to better illumine one or the other aspect of the mysteries of the faith. This is certainly an arduous task that has its risks, but it is legitimate in itself and should be encouraged.

Here it is important to emphasize that when theology employs the elements and conceptual tools of philosophy or other disciplines, discernment is needed. The ultimate normative principle for such discernment is revealed doctrine, which itself must furnish the criteria for the evaluation of these elements and conceptual tools and not vice versa.

(The magisterium's service of Christian truth; cf. LG 25, DV 10)

179 14.[...] It is the mission of the magisterium to affirm the definitive character of the covenant estalished by God through Christ with his people in a way which is consistent with the eschatological nature of the event of Jesus Christ. It must protect God's people from the danger of deviations and confusion, guaranteeing them the objective possibility of professing the authentic faith free from error, at all times and in diverse situations. It follows that the sense and weight of the magisterium's authority are only intelligible in relation to the truth of Christian doctrine and the preaching of the true word.

The function of the magisterium is not, then, something extrinsic to Christian truth nor is it set above the faith. It arises directly from the economy of the faith itself, in as much as the magisterium in its service to the word of God is an institution positively willed by Christ as a constitutive element of his Church. The service to Christian truth which the magisterium renders is thus for the benefit of the whole people of God called to enter the liberty of the truth revealed by God in Christ.

(The highest level of magisterial activity: dogmatic definitions)

180a 15. Jesus Christ promised the assistance of the Holy Spirit to the Church's pastors so that they could fulfil their assigned task of teaching the Gospel and authentically interpreting revelation. In particular he bestowed on them the charism of infallibility in matters of faith and morals. This charism is manifested when the pastors propose a doctrine as contained in revelation and can be exercised in various ways. Thus it is exercised particularly when the bishops in union with their visible head proclaim a doctrine by a collegial act as is the case in an ecumenical council, or when the Roman pontiff, fulfilling his mission as supreme pastor and teacher of all Christians, proclaims a doctrine *ex cathedra*.

(*The level of definitive teaching by the magisterium*)

180b 16. By its nature, the task of religiously guarding and loyally expounding the deposit of divine revelation (in all its integrity and purity), implies that the magisterium can make a pronouncement "in a definitive way" [*cf. n. 41*] on propositions which, even if not contained among the truths of faith, are nonetheless intimately connected with them in such a way that the definitive character of such affirmations derives in the final analysis from revelation itself [*cf. LG 25; Mysterium ecclesiae, 3-5; also n. 41, above*].

(*The magisterium's competency to teach moral norms*)

180c What concerns morality can also be the object of the authentic magisterium because the Gospel, being the word of life, inspires and guides the whole sphere of human behaviour. The magisterium, therefore, has the task of discerning by means of judgments normative for the consciences of believers those acts which in themselves conform to the demands of faith and foster their expression in life, and those which, because intrinsically evil, are incompatible with such demands. By reason of the connection between the orders of creation and redemption, and by reason of the necessity, in view of salvation, of knowing and observing the whole moral law, the competence of the magisterium also extends to that which concerns the natural law.[1]

Revelation also contains moral teachings which *per se* could be known by natural reason. Access to them, however, is made difficult by our sinful condition. It is a doctrine of the faith that these moral norms can be infallibly taught by the magisterium [*cf. n. 114*].

(*Non-definitive teaching by the magisterium*)

180d 17. Divine assistance is also given to the successors of the apostles teaching in communion with the successor

---

1. Cf. Pope Paul VI, *Humanae Vitae*, n. 4; *AAS* 60 (1968) 483.

of Peter, and in a particular way to the Roman pontiff as pastor of the whole church, when exercising their ordinary magisterium, even should this not issue in an infallible definition or in a "definitive" pronouncement, but in the proposal of some teaching which leads to a better understanding of revelation in matters of faith and morals and to moral directives derived from such teaching.

(The different responses due to the different levels of teaching)

181 23. When the magisterium of the Church makes an infallible pronouncement and solemnly declares that a teaching is found in revelation, the assent called for is that of theological faith. This kind of adherence is to be given even to the teaching of the ordinary and universal magisterium when it proposes for belief a teaching of faith as divinely revealed.

When the magisterium proposes "in a definitive way" truths concerning faith and morals, which even if not divinely revealed are nevertheless strictly and intimately connected with revelation, these must be firmly accepted and held [cf. n. 41].

When the magisterium, not intending to act "definitively" teaches a doctrine to aid a better understanding of revelation and make explicit its contents, or to recall how some teaching is in conformity with the truths of faith or finally to guard against ideas that are incompatible with these truths, the response called for is that of the religious submission of will and intellect [LG 25]. This kind of response cannot be simply exterior or disciplinary, but must be understood within the logic of faith and under the impulse of obedience to the faith.

(Magisterial interventions of a prudential and reformable kind)

182 24. Finally, in order to serve the people of God as well as possible, in particular by warning them of dangerous opinions that could lead to error, the magisterium can intervene in questions under discussion which involve, in addition to solid principles, certain contingent and conjectural elements. It often only becomes possible with the passage of time to distinguish between what is necessary and what is contingent.

The willingness to submit loyally to the teaching of the magisterium in matters *per se* not irreformable must be the rule. It can happen, however, that a theologian may, according to the case, raise questions regarding the timeliness, the form, or even the contents of magisterial interventions. Here the theologian will need, first of all, to assess accurately the authoritativeness of the interventions, which becomes clear from the nature of the documents, the insistence with which a teaching is repeated, and the very way in which it is expressed [LG 25, 1].

In the area of interventions in the prudential order, it has happened that some magisterial documents were not free from deficiencies.[1] Bishops and their advisers have not always taken into immediate consideration every aspect or the entire complexity of a question. But it would be contrary to the truth if, proceeding from some particular cases, one were to conclude that the church's magisterium can be habitually mistaken in its prudential judgments or that it does not enjoy divine assistance in the integral exercise of its mission. In fact, theologians, who cannot pursue their discipline without a certain competence in history, are aware of the filtering that occurs with the passage of time. This is not to be understood in the sense of a relativization of the tenets of the faith. Theologians know that some judgments of the magisterium could be justified at the time in which they were made, because while the pronouncements contained true assertions and others which were not sure, both types were inextricably connected. Only time has permitted discernment and, after deeper study, the attainment of true doctrinal progress.

POPE JOHN PAUL II

APOSTOLIC EXHORTATION *PASTORES DABO VOBIS* (7 April 1991)

In October 1990 the Synod of Bishops treated the topic "The Formation of Priests in the Circumstances of the Present Day". Pope John Paul II's post-synodal document weaves together the propositiones *submitted by the Synod into a comprehensive sketch of the priestly vocation, its spirituality, and formation for priestly ministry in the contemporary world. The exhortation interprets and updates Vatican II's decree* Optatam totius *for a world in rapid transition. Priestly formation entails the cultivation of fundamental human qualities, prayerful familiarity with Scripture, preparation for celibate living, a broad intellectual education, and training for pastoral service.*

On the role of philosophy in seminary education, the document brings

---

1. The English text of this sentence has been corrected in the light of the Latin and Italian versions. *Enchiridion Vaticanum* 12 (Bologna 1992), pp. 212-213.

out themes not present in Optatam totius *(cf. n. 15), especially on the relation of the human mind and truth.*
    The full text is given in Origins 21 *(1991-92), pp. 717-759.*

(The present urgency of intellectual formation)

183a   51. Intellectual formation has its own characteristics, but
        it is also deeply connected with, and indeed can be seen
as a necessary expression of both human and spiritual formation.
It is a fundamental demand of human intelligence by which one
"participates in the light of God's mind" and seeks to acquire a
wisdom which in turn opens to and is directed toward knowing
and adhering to God *[GS 15]*.[...]
    The present situation is heavily marked by religious
indifference, by a widespread mistrust regarding the real capacity
of reason to reach objective truth, and by fresh problems brought
on by scientific and technological discoveries.[...] Moreover, there
is the present phenomenon of pluralism, which is very marked
in the field not only of human society but also in the community
of the church itself. It demands special attention to critical
discernment and is a further reason for an extremely rigorous
intellectual formation.[...]

(The contribution of philosophy)

183b   52. A crucial stage of intellectual formation is the study
    .   of philosophy, which leads to a deeper understanding
of the person and of the person's freedom and relationships with
the world and with God. A proper philosophical training is vital,
not only because of the links between the great philosophical
questions and the mysteries of salvation studied in theology
under the guidance of the higher light of faith,[1] but also vis-à-
vis an extremely widespread cultural situation which emphasizes
subjectivism as a criterion and measure of truth. Only a sound
philosophy can help candidates for the priesthood to develop a
reflective awareness of the fundamental relationship that exists
between the human spirit and truth, that truth which is revealed
to us fully in Jesus Christ.
    Nor must one underestimate the importance of philosophy
as a guarantee of that "certainty of truth" which is the only firm

---

1. See Congregation for Catholic Education, *De necessitate philosophiae studia*
[...] *promovendi*, 1972.

basis for a total giving of oneself to Jesus and to the church. It is not difficult to see that some very specific questions, such as that concerning the priest's identity and his apostolic and missionary commitment, are closely linked to the question about the nature of truth, which is anything but an abstract question. For if we are not certain about the truth, how can we put our whole life on the line, and how can we have the strength to challenge others' way of living?

Philosophy greatly helps the candidate to enrich his intellectual formation in the "cult of truth," namely, in a kind of loving veneration of the truth, which leads one to recognize that the truth is not created or measured by human beings but is given to us as a gift by the supreme truth, God; that, albeit in a limited way and often with difficulty, human reason can reach objective and universal truth, even that relating to God and the radical meaning of existence; and that faith itself cannot do without reason and the effort of thinking through its contents.

ADDRESS TO THE PONTIFICAL ACADEMY OF SCIENCES
(31 October 1992)

The year 1992 marked the conclusion of work by the papal commission appointed in 1981 to study the ecclesiastical censure of Galileo Galilei in 1633. At a gathering of the Pontifical Academy of Sciences on October 31, 1992, attended as well by the principal members of the Roman Curia and the heads of diplomatic missions to the Holy See, Pope John Paul II received the findings of the commission and commented on them in an address excerpted below.

The findings were summarized by Cardinal Paul Poupard, president of the Pontifical Council for Culture, in a presentation that underscored the tentative grounds that Galileo had advanced for Copernican heliocentrism, the equivalent revocation of the condemnation in 1741, when Galileo's works received the imprimatur of the Holy Office, and the failure of the theologians who judged Galileo to grasp the nature of biblical statements about the cosmos. Galileo's judges erred in judgment by transposing a question calling for an answer based on observation and reasoning to the realm of revelation and faith.

Pope John Paul took up this theme and developed it in his response, the text of which is found, along with the presentation by Cardinal Poupard, in Origins *22 (1992-93), pp. 369-375.*

(The need to acknowledge complexity)

184a   9. If contemporary culture is marked by a tendency to scientism, the cultural horizon of Galileo's age was uniform and carried the imprint of a particular philosophical formation. This unitary nature of culture, which in itself is positive and desirable even in our own day, was one of the reasons for Galileo's condemnation. The majority of theologians did not recognize the formal distinction between Sacred Scripture and its interpretation, and this led them unduly to transpose into the realm of the doctrine of the faith, a question that in fact pertained to scientific investigations.[...]

(Our transformed understanding of the universe)

184b   11. From the Galileo affair we can learn a lesson that remains valid in relation to similar situations that occur today and that may occur in the future.

In Galileo's time, to depict the world as lacking an absolute physical reference point was, so to speak, inconceivable. And since the cosmos as then known was contained in the solar system alone, this reference point could only be situated in the earth or the sun. Today, after Einstein and within the perspective of contemporary cosmology, neither of these two reference points has the importance they once had. This observation [...] is not directed against the validity of Galileo's position in the debate; it is only meant to show that often beyond two partial and contrasting perceptions there exists a wider perception that includes them and goes beyond both of them.

(Biblical revelation distinct from scientific findings)

184c   12. Another lesson that we can learn is that the different branches of knowledge call for different methods. Thanks to his intuition as a brilliant physicist and by relying on different arguments, Galileo [...] understood why only the sun could function as the centre of the world as it was then known, that is to say, as a planetery system. The error of the theologians of the time when they maintained the centrality of the earth was to think that our understanding of the physical world's structure is in some way imposed by the literal sense of Scripture.[...]

In fact, the Bible does not concern itself with the details of the physical world, the understanding of which is the competence of human experience and reasoning. There exist two realms of knowledge, one that has its source in revelation and one that reason can discover by its own power. To the latter belong especially the experimental sciences and philosophy. The distinction between the two realms of knowledge ought not to be understood as opposition. The two realms are not altogether foreign to each other; they have points of contact. The methodologies proper to each make it possible to bring out different aspects of reality.

CATECHISM OF THE CATHOLIC CHURCH
(7 December 1992)

The 1985 extraordinary synod of bishops, meeting on the twentieth anniversary of the close of the Second Vatican Council, gave voice to the desire of many for a compendious statement of all of Catholic doctrine, to serve as a universal point of reference for teaching, as, for example, in catechisms composed in particular regions of the world.

After six years of preparation, Pope John Paul II approved the text of the new universal catechism on 25 June 1992, and in the Apostolic Constitution Fidei Depositum, *on 11 October, the Pope ordered that the* Catechism of the Catholic Church *be published "as a statement of the Church's faith and of catholic doctrine,... a sure norm for teaching the faith and thus a valid and legitimate instrument for ecclesial communion."*

Part One of the Catechism *(CCC) sets forth the profession of faith in two major sections: first, God's revelation and our response of faith (CCC 26-184); and, second, the articles of the Creed (CCC 185-1065). On revelation, the* Catechism *first explains the human capacity to find God and to speak about him (CCC 27-49) and then sets forth, with selected biblical and patristic texts, the teaching of Vatican II in DV 2-4 (nn. 149-151; CCC 50-73).*

In treating the communication of revelation in Tradition, the Catechism *speaks of the Church's interpretation of revelation in its dogmas, bringing out their spiritual role and inner coherence. Our excerpt from this passage (n. 185) is from the 1997 definitive edition of the* Catechism, *which corrects CCC 88 so as to distinguish revealed truths calling for an assent of faith from other truths taught definitively as necessarily connected with revelation, which call for firm adherence. This brings the* Catechism *into line with the 1990 Instruction on the Ecclesial Vocation of the Theologian (cf. nn. 180a-b, 181). All the 1997 changes are given in* Origins 27 *(1997-98), pp. 257-260.*

The Catechism *devotes a chapter to the response given in faith to God's invitation to communion of life with himself. A first article explains faith as personal adherence to Father, Son and Holy Spirit (CCC 150-152), and offers a resumé of the characteristics of personal faith (CCC 153-165), drawing on Vatican I's* Dei Filius *(nn. 118-139) and DV 5 (n. 152). The account is concretized and deepened by references to Abraham as the model and to the Virgin Mary as the perfect embodiment of faith (CCC 144-149, 165).*

In a second section on faith, the Catechism *moves beyond recent doctrine by setting forth the ecclesial dimension of faith and by adopting St. Thomas's account of the spiritual dynamism by which faith moves beyond formulated propositions to attain to the realities of divine life. Then, in texts not given here, passages from St. Irenaeus of Lyons set in contrast the diversity of those who believe and the oneness of the faith they profess (CCC 172-175).*

(The dogmas of the faith)

185 88. The Church's Magisterium exercises the authority it holds from Christ to the fullest extent when it defines dogmas, that is, when it proposes, in a form obliging the Christian to an irrevocable adherence of faith, truths contained in divine Revelation or also when it proposes, in a definitive way, truths having a necessary connection with these.

89. There is an organic connection between our spiritual life and the dogmas. Dogmas are lights along the path of faith; they illumine it and make it secure. Conversely, if our life is upright, our intellect and heart will be open to the light shed by the dogmas of faith *[cf. Jn 8:31-32]*.

90. The mutual connection between dogmas, and their coherence, can be found in the whole of the Revelation of the mystery of Christ *[cf. n. 132: nexus mysteriorum; LG 25]*. "In Catholic doctrine there exists an order or 'hierarchy' of truths, since they vary in their relation to the foundation of the Christian faith" *[UR 11]*.

(Faith of the individual depends on the faith of others)

186 166. Faith is a personal act—the free response of the human person to the initiative of God who reveals himself. But faith is not an isolated act. No one can believe alone, just as no one can live alone. You have not given yourself faith as you have not given yourself life. The believer has received faith from others and should hand it on to others. Our love for Jesus and for our neighbour impels us to speak to others about our faith. Each believer is thus a link in the great chain of believers. I cannot believe without being carried by the faith of others, and by my faith I help support others in the faith.

167. "I believe" *(Apostles' Creed)* is the faith of the Church professed by each believer, principally during Baptism. "We believe" *(Niceno-Constantinopolitan Creed)* is the faith of the Church confessed by bishops assembled in council or more generally by the liturgical assembly of belivers. "I believe" is also the Church, our mother, responding to God by faith as she teaches us to say both "I believe" and "We believe".

(The church's role in mediating faith)

187 168. It is the Church that believes first, and so bears, nourishes and sustains my faith. Everywhere it is the Church that first confesses the Lord: "Through the world the holy Church acclaims you", as we sing in the hymn *Te Deum*; with her and in her, we are won over and brought to confess: "I believe", "We believe". It is through the church that we receive faith and new life in Christ by Baptism. In the *Rituale Romanum*, the minister of Baptism asks the catechumen: "What do you ask of God's Church?' And the answer is: "Faith." "What does faith offer to you?" "Eternal life."[1]

169. Salvation comes from God alone; but because we receive the life of faith through the Church, she is our mother: "We believe the Church as the mother of our new birth, and not *in* the Church as if she were the author of our salvation."[2] Because she is our mother, she is also our teacher in the faith.

(The language of faith)

188 170. We do not believe in formulae, but in those realities they express, which faith allows us to touch. "The believer's act [of faith] does not terminate in the propositions, but in the realities [which they express].[3] All the same, we do approach these realities with the help of formulations of the faith which permit us to express the faith and to hand it on, to celebrate it in community, to assimilate and live by it more and more.

171. The Church, "pillar and bulwark of the truth" *[1 Tim 3:15]*, faithfully guards "the faith which was once for all delivered to the saints" *[Jude 3]*. She guards the memory of Christ's words; it is she who from generation to generation hands on the apostles' confession of faith. As a mother who teaches her children to speak and so to understand and communicate, the Church our Mother teaches us the language of faith in order to introduce us to the understanding and the life of faith.

MOTU PROPRIO *AD TUENDAM FIDEM*
(18 May 1998)

In the Code of Canon Law *of 1983, Can. 750 declares what is to be*

---

1. *Rite of Baptism of Adults.*
2. FAUSTUS OF RIEZ, *De Spiritu Sancto*, 1, 2; *PL* 62, 11.
3. ST. THOMAS AQUINAS, *STh* II-II, 1, 2 ad 2.

believed with divine and catholic faith in adherence to God's revelation. The
New Formula for the Profession of Faith *of 1989 corresponds to this canon
in the Creed and its first added paragraph (cf. nn. 40-41). After Can. 751
explains the differences between heresy, apostasy, and schism, Can. 752 lays
down those teachings which, while not definitively taught, are to be held "with
religious submission of intellect and will," which corresponds to the third
added paragraph of the* Profession of Faith *(cf. n. 41). Thus, the* Code *had
no canon corresponding to the second added paragraph of the* Profession, *on
firm adherence to truths necessarily connected with revelation and taught
definitively by the Magisterium.*

To remedy this lacuna, Ad tuendam fidem *promulgates a revision of
Can. 750. In its new form, Can. 750 §1 retains the text of Can. 750 published
in 1983. But a new Can. 750 §2 is added as given below. To complete the
revision, a reference to Can. 750 §2 is inserted into Can. 1371, which decrees
a "just penalty" for those obstinately rejecting such definitively taught
doctrines. The same revisions are also decreed in the* Code of the Canons of
the Eastern Churches, *Canons 598 and 1436.*

When Ad tuendam fidem *was released, Cardinal Joseph Ratzinger, of
the Congregation of the Doctrine of the Faith, issued a commentary that
explains and exemplifies the three levels of magisterial teaching present in the*
Profession of Faith *and now in the* Code of Canon Law, *published in*
AAS 90 (1998) 544-551, *in English in* Origins 28 (1998-99) 116-119. *We
cite the new Can. 750 §2 from* Ad tuendam fidem *as given in* Origins 28
(1998-99) 113-116.

189   Can. 750 §2. Each and every proposition stated
definitively by the magisterium of the church concerning
the doctrine of the faith or morals, that is, each and every
proposition required for the sacred preservation and faithful
explanation of the same deposit of faith, must also be firmly
embraced and maintained (*firmiter etiam amplectenda ac ritinenda
sunt*); anyone, therefore, who rejects those propositions which
are to be held definitively is opposed to the doctrine of the
Catholic Church.

ENCYCLICAL LETTER *FIDES ET RATIO*
(14 September 1998)

*The documents of this chapter show the concern of the modern
magisterium to clarify the right relation between faith and human reason,
beginning especially with* Dei Filius *of Vatican I (cf. nn. 113-135) and
intensified in the addresses of Pope John Paul II to scientists (cf. nn. 164-
176c, 184a-c).*

In Fides et Ratio *the Pope takes up this problematic with special attention
to philosophical reflection in relation to revelation and faith. While critical of*

philosophical outlooks alien to the Christian vision of reality (Fides et Ratio, nn. 86-90), the encyclical is appreciative of insights gained by modern philosophy and appeals for new vigour in philosophical investigation (n. 48). But this must go beyond the technical and pragmatic use of reason, not being content with fragments from limited sectors of knowledge, to pursue the ultimate meaning of human existence and the foundation of reality beyond phenomena.

The encyclical underscores the positive impulses given to rational inquiry by revelation, as shown in the Wisdom literature of Israel (nn. 16-22) and by major figures of the Christian tradition from the Fathers through St. Thomas down to Newman and Edith Stein (38-44, 59, 74). In the other direction, a philosophical contribution is essential in dogmatic, fundamental, and moral theology, as well as in the Christian encounter with cultures (65-73).

(Revelation stimulates ever wider rational inquiry)

190a 14. From the teaching of the two Vatican Councils there also emerges a genuinely novel consideration for philosophical learning. Revelation has set within history a point of reference which cannot be ignored if the mystery of human life is to be known. Yet this knowledge refers back constantly to the mystery of God which the human mind cannot exhaust but can only receive and embrace in faith. Between these two poles, reason has its own specific field in which it can inquire and understand, restricted only by its finiteness before the infinite mystery of God.

Revelation therefore introduces into our history a universal and ultimate truth which stirs the human mind to ceaseless effort; indeed, it impels reason continually to extend the range of its knowledge until it senses that it has done all in its power, leaving no stone unturned. [...]

15. The truth of Christian revelation, found in Jesus of Nazareth, enables all men and women to embrace the "mystery" of their own life. An absolute truth, it summons human beings to be open to the transcendent, while respecting both their autonomy as creatures and their freedom. At this point the relationship between freedom and truth is complete, and we understand the full meaning of the Lord's words: "You will know the truth, and the truth will make you free" [Jn 8:32].

Christian revelation is the true lodestar of men and women as they strive to make their way amid the pressures of an immanentist habit of mind and the constrictions of a technocratic logic. It is the ultimate possibility offered by God for the human being to know in all its fullness the seminal plan of love which began with creation. To those wishing to know the truth, if they can look beyond themselves and their own concerns, there is given the possibility of taking full and harmonious possession of their lives, precisely by following the path of truth.[...]

These considerations prompt a first conclusion: the truth made known to us by revelation is neither the product nor the consummation of an argument devised by human reason. It appears instead as something gratuitous, which itself stirs thought and seeks acceptance as an expression of love. This revealed truth is set within our history as an anticipation of that ultimate and definitive vision of God which is reserved for those who believe in him and seek him with a sincere heart. The ultimate purpose of personal existence, then, is the theme of philosophy and theology alike. For all their difference of method and content, both disciplines point to that "path of life" [Ps 16:11], which, as faith tell us, leads in the end to the full and lasting joy of the contemplation of the Triune God.

(Despite philosophical gains in separation, faith and reason need each other)

190b 48. [T]he history of philosophy, then, reveals a growing separation between faith and philosophical reason. Yet closer scrutiny shows that even in the philosophical thinking of those who helped drive faith and reason further apart there are found at times precious and seminal insights which, if pursued and developed with mind and heart rightly tuned, can lead to the discovery of truth's way. Such insights are found, for instance, in penetrating analyses of perception and experience, of the imaginary and the unconscious, of personhood and intersubjectivity, of freedom and values, of time and history. The theme of death as well can become for all thinkers an incisive appeal to seek within themselves the true meaning of their own life.

But this does not mean that the link between faith and reason as it now stands does not need to be carefully examined, because each without the other is impoverished and enfeebled. Deprived of what revelation offers, reason has taken sidetracks which expose it to the danger of losing sight of its final goal. Deprived of reason, faith has stressed feeling and experience, and runs the risk of no longer being a universal proposition. It is an illusion to think that faith, tied to weak reasoning, might be more penetrating; on the contrary, faith then runs the risk of withering into myth or superstition. By the same token, reason which is unrelated to an adult faith is not prompted to turn its gaze to the newness and radicality of being.

This is why I make this strong and insistent appeal—not, I trust, untimely—that faith and philosophy recover the profound unity which allows them to stand in harmony with their nature without compromising their mutual autonomy. The *parrhesia* [joyous confidence] of faith must be matched by the boldness of reason.

(Affirmation of the capabilities of human language and rational inquiry)

190c   84. The importance of metaphysics becomes still more evident if we consider current developments in hermeneutics and the analysis of language. The results of such studies can be very helpful to the understanding of faith, since they bring to light the structure of our thought and speech and the meaning which language bears. However, some scholars working in these fields tend to stop short at the question of how reality is understood and expressed, without going further to see whether reason can discover its essence. How can we fail to see in such a frame of mind the confirmation of our present crisis of confidence in the powers of reason? [...] Faith clearly presupposes that human language is capable of expressing divine and transcendent reality in a universal way—analogically, it is true, but no less meaningfully for that.[1] Were this not so, the word of God, which is always a divine word in human language, would not be capable of saying anything about God. [...]

85. I am well aware that these requirements which the word of God imposes upon philosophy may seem daunting to many people involved in philosophical research today. Yet this is why, taking up what has been taught repeatedly by the Popes for several generations and reaffirmed by the Second Vatican Council itself, I wish to reaffirm strongly the conviction that the human being can come to a unified and organic vision of knowledge [cf. GS 15]. This is one of the tasks which Christian thought will

---

[1]Fourth Lateran Ecumenical Council, *De errore Abbatis Ioachim*, II; *cf. n. 320.*

have to take up through the next millennium of the Christian era. The segmentation of knowledge, with its splintered approach to truth and consequent fragmentation of meaning, keeps people today from coming to an interior unity. How could the Church not be concerned by this? It is the Gospel which imposes this sapiential task directly upon her pastors, and they cannot shrink from their duty to undertake it.

(The meaning of Scripture and dogmas; cf. nn. 147-148, 160-162, 272-274)

190d   94. An initial problem is that of the relationship between meaning and truth. Like every other text, the sources which the theologian interprets primarily transmit a meaning which needs to be grasped and explained. This meaning presents itself as the truth about God which God himself communicates through the sacred text. Human language thus embodies the language of God, who communicates his own truth with that wonderful "condescension" which mirrors the logic of the incarnation.[1] In interpreting the sources of revelation, then, the theologian needs to ask what is the deep and authentic truth which the texts wish to communicate, even within the limits of biblical language.

The truth of the biblical texts, and of the Gospels in particular, is certainly not restricted to the narration of simple historical events or the statement of neutral facts, as historicist positivism would claim.[2] Beyond simple historical occurrence, the truth of the events which these texts relate lies rather in the meaning they have *in* and *for* the history of salvation. This truth is elaborated fully in the Church's constant reading of these texts over the centuries, a reading which preserves intact their original meaning. There is a pressing need, therefore, that the relationship between fact and meaning, a relationship which constitutes the specific sense of history, be examined also from the philosophical point of view.

95. The word of God is not addressed to any one people or any period of history. Similarly, dogmatic statements, while

---

1. Second Vatican Council, Dogmatic Constitution on Divine Revelation *Dei Verbum*, 13; cf. n. 251.

2. Pontifical Biblical Commission, Instruction on the Historical Truth of the Gospels (1964). *AAS 56* (1964), 713; *Enchiridion Biblicum* (1993), n. 646.

reflecting at times the culture of the period in which they were defined, formulate an unchanging and ultimate truth. This prompts the question of how one can reconcile the absoluteness and the universality of truth with the unavoidable historical and cultural conditioning of the formulas which express that truth. The claims of historicism, I noted earlier, are untenable; but the use of a hermeneutic open to the appeal of metaphysics can show how it is possible to move from the historical and contingent circumstances in which the texts developed to the truth which they express, a truth transcending those circumstances.

Human language may be conditioned by history and constricted in other ways, but the human being can still express truths which surpass the phenomenon of language. Truth can never be confined to time and culture; in history it is known, but it also reaches beyond history.

96. [The enduring validity of concepts used in dogmatic definitions] is a complex theme to ponder, since one must reckon seriously with the meaning which words assume in different times and cultures. Nonetheless, the history of thought shows that across the range of cultures and their development certain basic concepts retain their universal epistemological value and thus retain the truth of the propositions in which they are expressed.[1] Were this not the case, philosophy and the sciences could not communicate with each other, nor could they find a place in cultures different from those in which they were conceived and developed. The hermeneutical problem exists, to be sure, but it is not insoluble. More over, the objective value of many concepts does not exclude that their meaning is often imperfect. There is where philosophical speculation is often helpful. We may hope, then, that philosophy will be especially concerned to deepen the understanding of the relationship between conceptual language and truth, and to propose ways which will lead to a right understanding of that relationship.

---

1. Congregation for the Doctrine of the Faith, Declaration *Mysterium Ecclesiae* (1973), n. 5; cf. n. 161.

CHAPTER II

TRADITION AND SCRIPTURE

God has manifested himself as Saviour of all humankind "in deeds and words" (DV 2). In Israel he chose a people, formed them in authentic worship and morality, and engendered in them the hope of future salvation. The Scriptures of Israel tell of the life of this people in a way that gives testimony to God himself and to his design for human salvation. The New Testament centres on the culmination of saving history in the person and work of Jesus of Nazareth. Its books tell of his teaching and healing, his death and exaltation, and his sending of the Holy Spirit to animate the faith of those who confess him as risen Lord and seek to extend his message and presence to all people.

Christian revelation took form once and for all in the gospel announced by Christ's apostles. This gospel, as a source of new life in the Spirit, Tradition and Scripture make present in every age. Tradition, in general, is the collective acceptance of truths and a way of life in community. In Christian parlance, it is first the process of communication by which God's word and the corresponding way of life, coming from Christ through his apostles, becomes continually and freshly present in the Church in every age. Animated by God's Spirit, Tradition develops dynamically as the Church transmits her faith and life, especially in facing the challenges posed by her encounters with cultures. Tradition then also refers to the content of the message and norms of life that the Church receives and transmits.

Scripture is the fixed, textual form of what was vital discourse in Israel and the apostolic Church. In Scripture, chosen ministers of the word speak to their communities about salvation history and its present significance, about prayer and worship in response to the Lord of this history, and about the way of life by which community members are called and encouraged to put their faith into action. Thus Scripture derives from key moments within the dynamic of tradition in Israel and the apostolic Church. In time the Church recognized the biblical writings as "canonical", that is, as normative expressions of God's word in human mediation.

The Scriptures were written in communities abundantly blessed by God's animating Spirit, and so are accepted as "inspired" books, that is, as works of authors in whom God was acting to give truthful and efficacious expression to his saving word and work.

From Scripture's origin in foundational Tradition, it follows that it must be applied and further interpreted in the subsequent tradition of the Church's faith and doctrine, in her worship and life. In such an ambience, Scripture comes alive to engender faith and inspire evangelical living.

The earliest documents stem from eras in which Tradition was more lived than reflected upon, to say nothing of being a topic of debate. A number of early interventions, against gnostic views, defend the ongoing relevance of Israel's Scriptures for Christians and their unity with the apostolic writings of the New Testament. Also at issue was the gradual determination of the canon of books accepted as normative by the Church.

With the Council of Trent, the relation between Scripture and the Church, with its traditions and teaching authority, became a theme of explicit teaching. Against Protestant denials, Trent lays down that both traditions of apostolic origin and Scripture, as interpreted in the Church, are necessary for an integral communication of the Gospel. The Second Vatican Council expresses the global sense of Tradition, with its fecundity for development, and correlates this with Scripture and the magisterium.

The biblical encyclicals of Leo XIII and Benedict XV sought to promote scholarly study of the Bible in order to defend its inerrant witness to revelation. More recent interventions, especially by Pius XII and Vatican II, give guidance toward the exegetical recovery of the meaning of Scripture, both as the discourse of the prophets and apostles in their original situation and as a present message through inspired texts of perennial significance for Christian faith and life.

* * *

The main points of doctrine contained in this chapter fall under the following headings:

Divine Revelation is attested both in Tradition and Scripture: 31, 39/ 13, 121, 209, 210, 216, 219, 246, 247.
Tradition transmits the word of God: 31, 143/11, 204, 205, 210, 215, 216, 219, 265a-b, 266a, 270

Tradition is found in the teaching of the Fathers, in liturgy, in the doctrine of the Councils: 31, 37, 143/12, 204, 205, 209, 219, 222, 266a-b.

Tradition develops dynamically in the Church: 136, 246, 260, 265b, 266b, 268, 270.

The Bible comprises the books of the Old and New Testaments: (201), (202), (203), 208, 210-213, 216, 218, 252-254, 263-264.

The Latin Vulgate is the accepted standard version: 213, 214, 233

The books of the Bible are, with all their parts, inspired and have God as author: 207, 208, 210, 216, 218, 221, 226, 227, 228/9-16, 229, 230, 249.

They contain salvific truth free from error: 128, 216, 226, 227, 228/ 11-16, 230, 231, 240, 249.

Their inerrancy is not limited to their moral and religious doctrine: 226, 230, 238.

The Bible is entrusted to the Church and is to be interpreted by her: 31, 39/13, 143/9, 208, 210, 215, 217, 220, 221, 228/1.4, 238, 248, 259, 271.

Its literal sense must be found: 234; 273-274;

according to the literary genres: 236, 237, 239, 240-245.

The spiritual sense must be ascertained: 235, 250, 263-264, 271, 276-277.

The interpretation must be based on Tradition: 143/9, 215, 217, 220-222, 228/23, 238, 250, 260, 267-268, 271.

Modern sciences are to be used as helps: 223, 232, 234.

There is no ultimate conflict between Scripture and the natural sciences: 224, 226;

nor with history: 225, 228/14.16.24, 231.

The spiritual and theological use of Scripture: 255-257, 267a-b.

The role of Scripture in theology: 256, 258.

THE COUNCIL OF LAODICEA (360?)

(The canon of Scripture)

(201) *(Canon 60 of the Council enumerates the books recognised as Sacred Scripture. Baruch is explicitly mentioned with Jeremiah but Tobit, Judith, Wisdom, Sirach, 1 and 2 Maccabees, and Revelation do not figure on the list).*

INNOCENT I (402-417)
LETTER *CONSULENTI TIBI* TO EXSUPERIUS, BISHOP OF TOULOUSE (405)

(The canon of Scripture)

(202) *(All the deutero-canonical books of the Old Testament are*
213 *listed. Baruch is not explicitly mentioned but is most probably considered as a part of Jeremiah).*

GELASIUS I (492-496)
DECREE OF GELASIUS (time unknown)

This decree is a compilation of documents, the various parts of which pertain to various periods. Its part II on the canon of scriptures goes back in substance to Pope Damasus I (366-384), even though the text as found in the Decree of Gelasius cannot be attributed to the Decree of Damasus (382).

(The canon of Scripture)

(203) *(Judith is placed at times before Esther and Ezra-Nehemiah,*
179 *at times after these, and at times is omitted. Baruch is mentioned with Jeremiah, "cum uno Baruch", or omitted).*

THE SECOND GENERAL COUNCIL OF CONSTANTINOPLE
PROFESSION OF FAITH (553)

The ultimate foundation for the inerrant Christian doctrine is not a proof drawn from Holy Scripture alone; still less is it one that is based on theological reasoning. It is the living Tradition itself, inherited from apostolic times. On this Council, see n. 619i and n. 620i.

(Tradition)

204 We profess that we hold and preach the faith which from the beginning was given to the apostles by our great God and Saviour Jesus Christ, and was proclaimed by them to the whole world. The Holy Fathers professed, explained and handed on this faith to the holy Church, particularly those Fathers who took part in the four holy Councils which we follow and accept entirely for everything.[...]

THE LATERAN COUNCIL (649)

(Tradition)

205
517

Canon 17: Whosoever does not confess, in accordance with the holy Fathers, by word and from the heart, really and in truth, to the last word, all that has been handed down and proclaimed to the holy, catholic and apostolic Church by the holy Fathers and by the five venerable General Councils, *condemnatus sit.*

THE SECOND GENERAL COUNCIL OF NICAEA (787)

(On ecclesiastical Tradition)

206
609

Anyone who does not accept the whole of the Church's Tradition, both written and unwritten, *anathema sit.*

LEO IX

LETTER *CONGRATULAMUR VEHEMENTER* TO PETER, PATRIARCH OF ANTIOCH (1053)

The classic formula 'God is the author of both the Old and New Testaments' is taken from the Statuta Ecclesiae Antiqua. *Since the fifth century, the newly consecrated bishops had to profess their belief in the divine authorship of the Old Testament; Marcion had asserted that the Old Testament was inspired by the Devil.*

The formula occurs in most of the official documents on Biblical inspiration:

—*The Creed of Leo IX (1053)*   (DS 685)
—*The profession of faith for the Waldensians (1208)*   (DS 790)
—*The Council of Lyons (M. Palaeologus) (1274)*   (DS 854)
—*The Council of Florence (Copts) (1441)*   (DS 1334)
—*The Council of Trent (Session IV) (1546)*   (DS 1501)
—*The First Vatican Council (Session III) (1870)*   (DS 3006)
—Providentissimus *Deus, Leo XIII (1893)*   (DS 3293)
—*The Decree* Lamentabili, *Pius X (1907)*   (DS 3409)
—*The Second Vatican Council,* Dei Verbum, *11 (1965)*

The letter of Pope Leo IX, mentioned here, contains a profession of faith.

(God is the author of Scripture)

207   [...] I also believe that God, the Lord almighty, is the
685   only author of both the Old and the New Testaments,
i.e., the Law and the Prophets, and the Apostles.

THE GENERAL COUNCIL OF FLORENCE
DECREE FOR THE COPTS (1442)

This decree reaffirms that God is the author of both Old and New Testaments, against gnostic ideas which were still surviving. The Coptic Church held a number of apocryphal books to be inspired. Hence the list of the canonical books was also included. It will be repeated later by the Council of Trent.

(God is the author of the books of the Old and New Testaments)

208   [The holy Roman Church] professes that one and the
1334   same God is author of the Old and New Testaments, i.e,
of the Law, the Prophets and the Gospel, because
by inspiration of one and the same Holy Spirit, the saints of
both covenants have spoken. She accepts and venerates their
books.[...]

(There follows the list of canonical books: DS 1335; cf. the Council of Trent: nn. 211-212).

THE COUNCIL OF SENS (PARIS) (1528)

The Reformers rejected Tradition and adhered to Scripture only, sola Scriptura. This regional Council condemns this teaching in its fifth decree. The text is found in Enchiridion Biblicum *(1993), n. 55.*

(Some things which are not explicitly contained in Scripture must be firmly adhered to)

209 5. There is no doubt that Scripture covers a vast field of
religious doctrines and expounds them with ineffable
profundity. It is nevertheless a pernicious error to think that
nothing has to be accepted that is not expressed in Scripture;
indeed many things have come from Christ through the apostles
to later generations and have been transmitted from mouth to
mouth by familiar discourse. All these must be held with

unshakable conviction, even though they are not contained explicitly in sacred Scripture.

THE GENERAL COUNCIL OF TRENT
FOURTH SESSION (8 April 1546)

In the initial crossfire of Reformation controversy over purgatory and indulgences, the Catholic apologist Johann Eck appealed to 2 Macc 12, on Judas Maccabeus's offerings and prayer to atone for the sins of his fallen soldiers. Luther responded with an attack on the canonical standing of such a text, which belongs to a deutero-canonical book not found in the Jewish canon. These books were placed in an appendix of the first Protestant bibles, for edifying reading but not as authoritative Scripture, but soon were excluded from printed bibles as apocryphal works.

In the New Testament, Luther's immensely popular translation expressed his reservations regarding Hebrews, James, Jude, and Revelation by placing them at the end and introducing them with prefaces highlighting their points of contrast with books like Romans, Galatians, 1 Peter, and the Gospel of John, which give unalloyed witness to the saving grace of Christ. Luther's practice was followed in William Tyndale's English New Testament of 1525, but was not taken up in other Protestant Bibles.

Luther criticized many practices of the medieval church, such as masses for the dead, invocation of the saints, monastic vows and clerical celibacy, branding them "human traditions" not grounded in Scripture. Protestants also applied the "Scripture principle" to exclude the sacraments other than Baptism and the Lord's Supper.

The Council of Trent's Fourth Session, following the lines of apologists like Johann Eck, Johann Dietenberger and St. John Fisher, accepted as binding those traditions of doctrine and practice that come down from the Apostles, linking these with the Scriptures, not as "sources" of revelation, but as essential mediations of the saving truth and rule of the gospel of Christ for all later ages. The Council also declared once more the normativity of the fuller canon of the Old Testament, including the deutero-canonical books, as long accepted in the Western Church.

In a second decree the Council declared "authentic" the Latin Vulgate, in reference to its reliability for liturgical and theological use. Here "authenticity" does not involve issues of the authorship of biblical books nor does it exclude a revision of the Vulgate, as many Tridentine theologians and bishops had desired and the post-Tridentine popes carried out.

The second decree includes as well a point of fundamental difference with the Protestant Reformation, in Trent's declaration that the Fathers of the Church constitute a negative norm of biblical interpretation and that the Church's tradition, that is, her creeds, dogma, and liturgy, embodies the global meaning of Scripture in a manner that makes her able to pass judgment on interpretations of the Bible's meaning for faith and life.

DECREE OF RECEPTION OF THE SACRED BOOKS AND APOSTOLIC TRADITIONS

(Written books and unwritten traditions)

210 The holy ecumenical and general Council of Trent[...]
1501 has always this purpose in mind that in the Church errors
be removed and the purity of the Gospel be preserved.
This Gospel was promised of old through the prophets in the
Sacred Scriptures; Our Lord Jesus Christ, Son of God, first
promulgated it from his own lips; he in turn ordered that it be
preached through the apostles to all creatures as the source of
all saving truth and norms of conduct. The Council clearly
perceives that this truth and rule are contained in the written
books and unwritten traditions which have come down to us,
having been received by the apostles from the mouth of Christ
himself or from the apostles by the dictation of the Holy Spirit,
and have been transmitted as it were from hand to hand.
Following, then, the example of the orthodox Fathers, it receives
and venerates with the same sense of loyalty and reverence all
the books of the Old and New Testament—for the one God is
the author of both—together with all the traditions concerning
faith and practice, as coming from the mouth of Christ or being
inspired by the Holy Spirit and preserved in continuous
succession in the Catholic Church.

(The Canon of Scripture)

211 The Council has thought it proper to insert in this decree
1502 a list of the sacred books, so that no doubt may remain
as to which books are recognised by the Council.

They are the following:

Old Testament: The five books of Moses, i..e., Genesis,
Exodus, Leviticus, Numbers. Deuteronomy; Joshua, Judges, Ruth,
four books of Kings, two of Chronicles, the first book of Ezra,
the second book of Ezra called the book of Nehemiah, Tobit,
Judith, Esther, Job, the Psalter of David containing 150 psalms,
Proverbs, Ecclesiastes, the Song of Songs, Wisdom, Ecclesiasticus,
Isaiah, Jeremiah with Baruch, Ezechiel, Daniel, the twelve minor
prophets, i.e., Hosea, Joel, Amos, Obadiah, Jonah, Micah, Nahum,
Habakkuk, Zephaniah, Haggai, Zachariah and Malachi; two
books of Maccabees, i.e.., the first and the second.

212 New Testament: The four Gospels according to Matthew,
1503 Mark, Luke and John; the Acts of the Apostles written
by Luke the Evangelist; fourteen epistles of the apostle
Paul, i.e., to the Romans, two to the Corinthians, to the Galatians,
Ephesians, Philippians, Colossians, two to the Thessalonians, two
to Timothy, to Titus, Philemon, and the Hebrews; two epistles of
the apostle Peter, three of the apostle John, one of the apostle
James, one of the apostle Jude, and the revelation of the apostle
John.

213 If anyone does not accept all these books in their entirety,
1504 with all their parts, as they are being read in the Catholic
Church and are contained in the ancient Latin Vulgate
editions, as sacred and canonical, and knowingly and deliberately
rejects the aforesaid traditions, *anathema sit*.

DECREE ON THE VULGATE
AND ON HOW SCRIPTURE IS TO BE INTERPRETED

(The Vulgate as the standard version)

214 Moreover, because the same holy Council thought it very
1506 useful to the Church if it were known which of all the
Latin editions of the sacred books now in circulation is
to be regarded as the authentic version, it declares and decrees:
This same ancient Vulgate version which has been preserved by
the Church for so many centuries is to be regarded as the
authentic translation in public readings, disputations, sermons
and expositions, and let no one dare or presume to reject it on
any grounds.

(The Church as interpreter of Holy Scripture)

215 Furthermore, to restrain irresponsible minds, it decrees
1507 that no one, relying on his own prudence, twist Holy
Scripture in matters of faith and practice that pertain to
the building up of Christian doctrine, according to his own mind,
contrary to the meaning that holy mother the Church has held
and holds—since it belongs to her to judge the true meaning
and interpretation of Holy Scripture—and that no one dare to
interpret the Scripture in a way contrary to the unanimous
consensus of the Fathers, even though such interpretations not
be intended for publication.

THE FIRST VATICAN GENERAL COUNCIL
THIRD SESSION
DOGMATIC CONSTITUTION *DEI FILIUS* ON THE CATHOLIC FAITH (1870)

In conjunction with the doctrine of revelation, Vatican I had to deal also with the question of the transmission of revelation. It reiterated the doctrine of Trent concerning Tradition and Scripture and interpreted it in view of contemporary opinons. It described inspiration against the doctrines of D. Haneberg who saw in it only a subsequent approbation by the Church and of J. Jahn who considered it as an external and negative assistance which wards off any and all errors.

Chapter II: On Revelation

(Scripture and Tradition as sources from which we know revelation)

216   Further, this supernatural revelation, according to the
3006   universal belief of the Church, declared by the sacred
           Synod of Trent, "is contained in the written books and
unwritten traditions which have come down to us, having been
received by the apostles themselves by the dictation of the Holy
Spirit, and have been transmitted as it were from hand to hand"
[cf. n.210]. These books of the Old and New Testaments are to
be received as sacred and canonical in their integrity, with all
their parts, as they are enumerated in the decree of the same
Council and are contained in the ancient Latin edition of the
Vulgate. These the Church holds to be sacred and canonical, not
because, having been carefully composed by mere human
industry, they were afterwards approved by her authority, nor
merely because they contain revelation with no admixture of
error, but because, having been written by the inspiration of the
Holy Spirit, they have God for their author and have been
delivered as such to the Church herself.

(Interpretation of Holy Scripture)

217   However, what the holy Council of Trent has laid down
3007   concerning the interpretation of the divine Scripture for
           the good purpose of restraining indisciplined minds, has
been explained by certain people in a distorted manner. Hence
we renew the same decree and declare this to be its sense. In
matters of faith and morals, affecting the building up of Christian

doctrine, that is to be held as the true sense of Holy Scripture which Holy Mother the Church has held and holds, to whom it belongs to judge the true sense and interpretation of Holy Scriptures. Therefore no one is allowed to interpret the same Sacred Scripture contrary to this sense, or contrary to the unanimous consent of the Fathers.

Canon 4 to Chapter II

218
3029
If anyone does not receive as sacred and canonical the books of Holy Scripture, entire and with all their parts, as the sacred Synod of Trent has enumerated them, or denies that they have been divinely inspired, *anathema sit.*

Chapter III: On Faith
(Scripture and Tradition contain the divine revelation)

219
3011
[...]All those things are to be believed with divine and Catholic faith which are contained in the word of God, written or handed down, and which by the Church, either in solemn judgment or through her ordinary and universal magisterium, are proposed for belief as having been divinely revealed.

LEO XIII

ENCYCLICAL LETTTER *PROVIDENTISSIMUS DEUS* (1893)

This encyclical on the study of Holy Scripture represents the magisterium's first treatment of the questions raised by modern Bible criticism. Leo XIII unhesitatingly recognises the services rendered by scientific methods of biblical research and wishes them to be used for a deeper understanding of the sacred books. But the Bible is inspired in all its parts (n.227) and is therefore inerrant. Scientific research can never ignore this fact. Therefore, no interpretation can neglect the criteria of faith and tradition.

The encyclical is based on the firm conviction that there can be no contradiction between the word of God and the findings of sciences, provided that on both sides researchers honestly seek the truth and are aware of their own limitations. God who created nature and is the author of Scripture cannot contradict himself.

(Catholic doctrine as norm for the interpretation of Scripture)

220
Where the sense of biblical texts has been authoritatively declared, either by the sacred authors themselves under

the inspiration of the Holy Spirit, as in many passages of the New Testament, or by the Church assisted by the same Holy Spirit, whether by means of a solemn judgement or by her ordinary and universal magisterium [cf. n. 219], it should be the religious concern of the Catholic interpreter to explain them in the same way and to prove by the help which science supplies that it is the only interpretation which can rightly be approved according to the laws of sound exegesis.

221 In other points the analogy of faith must be followed,
3283 and Catholic doctrine as it has been received from the authority of the Church must be considered as the supreme criterion. For, since it is the same God who is author of the sacred books and of the doctrine handed down by the Church, it is surely impossible to extract from the former a legitimate interpretation which in any way conflicts with the latter.

(The Catholic interpretation draws from the wealth of Tradition, mainly the Fathers of the Church)

222 The authority of the holy Fathers is very great whenever
3284 they explain unanimously in one and the same manner a biblical testimony as belonging to the doctrine of faith and morals, as "after the apostles they were the ones to plant and water, build, shepherd, and rear the Holy Church in her growth".[1] For, through their consensus, it becomes evident that such an explanation has been handed down from the apostles in accordance with the Catholic faith.

(Higher Criticism, and the limits for 'inner criteria')

223 Without foundation and to the detriment of religion a
3286 method has been introduced which parades under the name of higher criticism, according to which the origin, integrity, and authority of any book can be judged by what are called internal criteria. On the contrary, it is evident that in historical questions, such as the origin and preservation of books, historical testimonies are of greater value than others and should be sought out and weighed with greatest care. On the other hand, internal criteria are generally not important enough to be admitted except as a sort of confirmatory evidence.

---

1. St. Augustine, *Contra Iulianum Pelagianum*, II, 10, 37.

(The Bible and natural sciences)

224 No real disagreement can exist between the theologian
3287 and the scientist provided each keeps within his own
limits.[...]

3288 If nevertheless there is disagreement, [...] it should be
remembered that the sacred writers, or more truly "the
Spirit of God who spoke through them, did not wish to teach us
such truths (as the inner structure of visible objects) which are
of no help to salvation";[1] and that, for this reason, rather than
trying to provide a scientific exposition of nature, they sometimes
describe and treat these matters either in figurative language or
as the common manner of speech in those times required, and
indeed still requires nowadays in everyday life, even among
learned people.

(Historicity)

225 The same principles can also be transferred to related
3290 branches of knowledge, especially to history.

(Divine origin and inerrancy of Sacred Scripture)

226 It would be utterly impious to limit inspiration to
3291 some portions only of Sacred Scripture or to admit
that the sacred author himself has erred. Nor can one
tolerate the method of those who extricate themselves from
difficulties by allowing without hesitation that divine inspiration
extends to matters of faith and morals and to nothing
more.[...]

3292 For all the books in their entirety, which the Church
receives as sacred and canonical, with all their parts, have
been written under the dictation of the Holy Spirit. Now it is
utterly impossible that divine inspiration could give rise to any
error; it not only by its very nature excludes all error, but excludes
and rejects it with the same necessity by which it is impossible
that God, the highest Truth, be the author of any error
whatsoever.

3293 This is the ancient and constant faith of the Church.

---

1. St. Augustine, *De Genesi ad litt.*, II, 9, 20.

(References are given to the Councils of Florence, Trent, Vatican I).

227   It is futile to argue that the Holy Spirit took human
3293   beings as his instruments in writing, implying that some
          error could slip in, not indeed from the principal author,
but from the inspired writers. For by his supernatural power he
so stimulated and moved them to write, and so assisted them
while they were writing, that they properly conceived in their
mind, wished to write down faithfully, and expressed aptly with
infallible truth all those things, and only those things, which he
himself ordered; otherwise he could not himself be the author of
the whole of Sacred Scripture.

PIUS X

DECREE *LAMENTABILI* OF THE HOLY OFFICE (1907) ARTICLES OF MODERNISM CONDEMNED

Modernism (cf. n. 143i) subscribed to liberal scriptural sciences in matters of biblical criticism and exegesis. The articles condemned concern the relation of the Church's magisterium to Scripture (1-4), the modernist view on divine inspiration (9-12), and some specific questions (13-24).

[228/1]   The ecclesiastical law which requires that books
3401   treating of Holy Scripture be submitted to previous
          censorship does not apply to workers in the field
of criticism or of scientific exegesis of the Old and New
Testaments.

[228/4]   The Church's teaching office cannot, even by dogmatic
3404   definition, declare the genuine meaning of Sacred
          Scripture.

[228/9]   Those who believe that God is really the author of
3409   Holy Scripture show too much simplicity or ignorance.

[228/11]   Divine inspiration does not extend to the whole of
3411   Scripture in such a way that each and every part of it
          is kept free from error.

[228/14]   In many of their accounts the Evangelists narrated not
3414   so much the truth as what they thought would—
          even though it be false—be more helpful to their
          readers.

[228/15] Until the canon was defined and established, the
3415   gospels were constantly enlarged and amended:
           therefore in them no more than a slight and uncertain
trace of Christ's teaching has remained.

[228/16] John's narrations are not really historical but a mystical
3416   contemplation of the Gospel. The discourses in his
           gospel are theological meditations about the mystery
of salvation, devoid of historical truth.

[228/23] There can and in fact there does exist conflict
3423   between the facts related by Holy Scripture and the
           Church's dogma based upon them. The critic can
thus reject as false things which the Church believes as most
certain.

[228/24] An exegete is not to be censured when he sets up
3424   premises from which it follows that dogmas are
           historically false or doubtful, provided that he does
not directly deny the dogmas themselves.

BENEDICT XV

ENCYCLICAL LETTER *SPIRITUS PARACLITUS* (1920)

*The occasion for the encyclical was the fifteen-hundredth anniversary of
the death of St. Jerome, the great translator and interpreter of Sacred Scripture.
The doctrine developed is essentially that expressed by Leo XIII, but Benedict
XV's main task was to deal with the misinterpretation of the passage in which
his predecessor dealt with the historicity of the inspired books.*

(Divine inspiration of the Bible)

229   [St. Jerome consistently teaches the Catholic doctrine]
3650   that the sacred books were written under the inspiration
         of the Holy Spirit, have God for their author, and were
as such entrusted to the Church *[cf. n. 216]*. Indeed he asserts
that the books of Holy Scripture were written under the
inspiration of the Holy Spirit, by his instruction, stimulus, and
even dictation, and were indeed written and produced by him.
Besides he has no doubts that the individual writers freely placed
themselves at the service of God's inspiration according to each
one's nature and gifts. For he not only consistently asserts the
common features of all sacred writers, viz., that in writing they
followed the Spirit of God, so that God must be considered the

primary cause of every expression and affirmation of Scripture, but he also accurately distinguishes the special characteristics of each writer.

(Inspiration extends to both religious and profane matters)

230   Some recent writers distinguish between a primary or
3652   religious and a secondary or profane element in
        Scripture; while admitting that divine inspiration applies to every affirmation, even to every word of Holy Scripture, they restrict and narrow down its effects, especially its absolute truth and inerrancy, to the primary or religious element. They believe that only what deals with religion is intended and taught by God in the Scriptures. Everything else that belongs to profane subjects and serves the revealed doctrine, as it were as an outer garment of divine truth, was merely permitted and was left subject to the shortcomings of the writer. No wonder therefore that there are many things in Scripture concerning natural sciences, history, and the like, which cannot be reconciled with modern scientific progress[...]

But it is apparent from the very words of the Pope (Leo XIII) how rash and wrong such contentions are. [...] He rejected any distinction between primary and secondary elements, as they are called, removed all ambiguity, and clearly showed that the opinion of those who believe that concerning the truth of statements one does not need to ask what God said so much as why he said it, is very far from the truth. He likewise taught that the divine inspiration extends to all parts of Scripture without distinction, and that no error could occur in the inspired text. "It would be utterly impious to limit inspiration to some portions only of Sacred Scripture or to admit that the sacred author himself has erred" *[cf. n. 226]*

(Historical truth)

231   And those depart no less from the teaching of the Church
3653   [...] who hold the view that the historical parts of Holy
        Scripture are not based on the absolute truth of facts, but upon what they call relative truths, and upon the views of ordinary people. They are even bold enough to argue from the very words of Pope Leo, for he said that the principles of natural science could be transferred to historical disciplines *[cf. n. 225]*. Thus they maintain that, as the sacred writers wrote about the

physical order according to its outward appearance, so too, they reported events without accurate knowledge as they appeared in the eyes of ordinary people or from the false testimony of others, without indicating the source of their information or making the accounts of others their own.

Why should we refute with many words this entirely misleading and false assumption, unjust as it is to our predecessor? The physical order has to do with the appearances. But the principal law of history is that accounts of facts must agree with the facts as they actually occurred. If the false opinion just mentioned were once accepted, how would the truth of the sacred narration still be free from all error, as our predecessor in the whole context of his letter declared that we must believe?

PIUS XII

ENCYCLICAL LETTER *DIVINO AFFLANTE SPIRITU* (1943)

On the fiftieth anniversary of Leo XIII's Providentissimus Deus, Pius XII published the landmark document for modern Catholic biblical studies. The proximate occasion was a booklet circulated in 1941 by an Italian priest among the cardinals and Italian bishops. The booklet decried the grave danger for souls represented by the scholarly study of Scripture in the original languages. In place of philology and critical history, the author urged a meditative and spiritual interpretation based on the Latin Vulgate.

Pius XII responded with a strong recommendation of scholarly biblical studies: the knowledge and mastery of biblical and Oriental languages is fostered; the position of the Church with regard to the Latin Vulgate is clarified; Catholic exegetes are encouraged to make proper use of textual criticism and literary analysis of the sacred books, according to literary genres and form criticism; they must attach great importance to the literal meaning without neglecting the 'spiritual' or theological sense of the sacred texts.

(Original texts and the Latin Vulgate version)

232 One must explain the text in the original language which, since it was written by the sacred author himself, has greater weight and authority than even the best translation, either ancient or modern. Exegetes will be able to accomplish their task more easily and in a more effective way if to the knowledge of biblical languages they add a sound skill in textual criticism.

233
3825 As for the decree of the Council of Trent requiring that the Vulgate be used by all as the authentic Latin version [cf. n.214], it is common knowledge that this

concerns only the Latin Church and her public use of Scriptures, and obviously in no way detracts from the authority and value of the original texts. [...] This special authority or, as it is called, 'authenticity' which the Council attributes to the Vulgate was not given on account of special critical reasons but rather because of the lawful use the Vulgate had enjoyed in the Church for so many centuries. This long use proves that the Vulgate as the Church has understood and now understands, is free from all error in matters of faith and morals so that, as the Church herself testifies and confirms, it can be safely quoted, without the least fear of erring, in disputations, public readings, and sermons. Its authenticity is therefore more properly called 'juridical' than 'critical'.

Therefore this authority of the Vulgate in matters of doctrine by no means prevents—but instead today practically demands—both the verification and confirmation of this doctrine from the original texts, as well as constant recourse to these texts, by which the correct meaning of Holy Scripture is everywhere and each day being made more clear and evident. Neither does the Tridentine decree forbid translations into modern languages, also from the original texts themselves, for the use and benefit of the faithful and the easier understanding of the divine word, as, we know, has already been done in many places laudably and with the approval of the authority of the Church.

(Literal and spiritual meaning)

234   Equipped with knowledge of languages and skill in the
3826   tools of the critical method, Catholic exegetes should
          undertake as their most important task to ascertain and to explain the true meaning of the sacred books. In carrying out this task the exegetes should keep in mind that their chief task must be to discern and determine what is known as the literal sense of the words of the Bible. [...] Commentators must first and foremost show what is the theological doctrine concerning faith and practice of each book and text.[...]

3827   By giving an interpretation [...] that is primarily
          theological, they will effectively silence those who assert that in biblical commentaries they find hardly anything to raise their minds to God, nourish their souls and foster their interior life, and therefore maintain that we must have recourse to a spiritual and so-called mystical interpretation.[...]

235 It is true that not every spiritual sense is excluded
3828 from Sacred Scripture; what was said and done in the
Old Testament was wisely ordained and disposed by God
so that the past would spiritually foreshadow what was to
happen in the new covenant of grace. It is therefore the duty of
the exegete to discover and explain not only the literal meaning
of the words, i.e., that which the sacred writers intended and
expressed, but also their spiritual significance, provided that it
be established that such meaning has been given to them by
God himself. For God alone was able to know this spiritual
significance and to reveal it to us. In the gospels our divine
Saviour himself points out and teaches this kind of meaning;
the apostles, following the example of the Master, make use of it
in their preaching and writings; the traditional teaching of the
Church continuously gives proof of it; finally the ancient practice
of the liturgy bears out this meaning, wherever the well-known
saying can be applied in truth: the norm of prayer is the norm
of belief [*cf. n. 1913*]. Catholic exegetes should bring this divinely
intended spiritual meaning to light and propound it with the
carefulness that the dignity of the divine word demands. They
should be scrupulously careful not to propose other figurative
senses as though they were the original meaning of Holy
Scripture.

(Literary genres)

236 It is absolutely necessary for the interpreter to go back
3830 in spirit to those remote centuries of the East, and to
make proper use of the help given by history,
archaeology, ethnology and other sciences, in order to discover
what literary forms the writers of those early ages intended to
use and did in fact use. For, to express what they had in mind,
the ancients of the East did not always avail themselves of the
same forms and expression as we do today, they used those that
were current among people of their own time and place. The
exegete cannot determine what these were by an *a priori*
judgement but must first make a careful study of ancient
literature. [...] The sacred writers, like the other ancients, use
certain arts of exposition and narration, certain idioms known
as 'approximations' which are typical of Semitic languages,
certain hyperbolic ways of speaking, and certain paradoxes
intended for emphasis—all of which will cause no surprise to

those who understand biblical inspiration correctly. The sacred books need not exclude any of the forms of expression that were commonly used in human speech among the ancient peoples, especially of the East, so long as they are not incompatible with God's sanctity and veracity.[...]

In many cases in which the authors are accused of some historical inaccuracy or some inexact recording of certain events, there is in fact nothing else to be found than those customary and characteristic forms of expression or style of narration which were current among people of that time, and were in fact quite legitimately and commonly used. Just impartiality demands that when these are found in the word of God [...] they should no more be considered as error than when similar expressions are used in everyday speech.

LETTER OF THE BIBLICAL COMMISSION TO CARDINAL SUHARD, ARCHBISHOP OF PARIS (1948)

This letter, written by the Secretary, J.M. Vosté, has in fact the authority of a decree of the Biblical Commission; it contains an important application of the above principles (cf. n. 236) to the literary genre of Genesis, chapters 1-11, and stresses the caution needed to decide their historicity. It also somewhat rectifies previous decrees regarding the Mosaic origin of the Pentateuch and accepts "written documents or oral traditions and post-Mosaic modifications and additions".

237   The question of the literary forms of the first eleven
3864   chapters of Genesis is much more complicated and
        obscure. These literary forms do not correspond to any of our classic categories and cannot be judged in the light of Greco-Latin or modern literary genres. Their historicity can be neither affirmed nor denied *en bloc* without unjustifiably applying to them the rules of a literary genre in which they cannot be classified.[...] To declare *a priori* that the accounts found in them do not contain history in the modern sense of the word would easily lead to the misunderstanding that they contain no history in any sense of the word, while they do actually relate in simple and figurative language, adapted to the intelligence of less educated people, the fundamental truths underlying the divine plan of salvation. They are a popular description of the origins of the human race and of the chosen people.

ENCYCLICAL LETTER *HUMANI GENERIS* (1950)

From this document (cf. n. 144i) two texts referring to Scripture are quoted here:

The first text rejects once more the theory of the double meaning of Scripture, one human and one divine, the former fallible, the latter inerrant.

The second clarifies the letter to Cardinal Suhard (cf. n. 237) concerning the historical value of the first eleven chapters of Genesis.

(Interpretation of Scriptural inerrancy)

238   There are some who clearly distort the sense of the
3887   definition laid down by the first Vatican Council as to
the divine authorship of the Bible.[...] They even use misguided language about the human meaning of the sacred books, under which a divine meaning is said to be concealed, and claim that only this divine meaning is infallible. In their interpretation of Scripture they will not take into consideration the analogy of faith, nor pay attention to the tradition of the Church.

(Comment on the letter to Cardinal Suhard)

239   It was clearly laid down in that letter that the first eleven
3898   chapters of Genesis [...] do in some true sense come
under the heading of history; in what exact sense, it is for the further study of exegetes to determine. These chapters have a naive, symbolic way of speaking, well suited to the understanding of primitive people. But they do disclose important truths, upon which the attainment of our eternal salvation depends, and they do also give a popular description of the origin of the human race and of the chosen people. It may be true that the ancient authors of sacred history drew some of their material from current popular stories. So much may be granted. But it must be remembered that they did so under the impulse of divine inspiration which preserved them from all error in selecting and assessing the documents they used.

These excerpts from popular stories, which are taken over in the sacred books, must not be put on a level with mere myths, or with legend in general.[...] In the Old Testament a love of truth and a cult of simplicity shine out in such a way as to put these writers on a distinctly different level from their profane contemporaries.

INSTRUCTION OF THE BIBLICAL COMMISSION
SANCTA MATER ECCLESIA (1964)
ON THE HISTORICAL TRUTH OF THE GOSPELS

In this Instruction, concerned mainly with the genesis of the gospels, biblical scholars are encouraged and protected against unfair criticism. The most modern and scientific methods of research are approved, including a sane and balanced Form Criticism (5).

The three stages in which the Gospel message has come down to us are described at length: from Christ's own words and actions to the apostolic preaching, and from the Sitz im Leben of the apostolic Church to the writers of the gospels (6-10).

Besides, the Instruction points out the complexity of many problems of exegesis and insists on the ultimate pastoral purpose of biblical studies: to nourish the spiritual life and to bring people to salvation. The text is found in AAS (1964) 712 ff.., and in Enchiridion Biblicum (1993) nn. 644-659.

(Form Criticism)

240　5. In appropriate cases the interpreter is free to seek out
3999a　what sound elements there are in the method of form-criticism; one can freely make use of these to gain a fuller understanding of the gospels.

(The three stages in the formation of the Gospels)

241　6. In order to determine correctly the trustworthiness of
3999b　what is transmitted in the gospels, the interpreter must take careful note of the three stages of tradition by which the teaching and the life of Jesus came down to us.

242　7. (1) Christ our Lord attached to himself certain chosen disciples who had followed him from the beginning, had seen his works and heard his words, and thus were qualified to become witnesses of his life and teaching. Our Lord, when expounding his teaching by word of mouth, used the ways of reasoning and of expression which were in common use at that time.[...] He accommodated himself to the mentality of his hearers, and ensured that his teaching would be deeply impressed on their mind and would easily be remembered by the disciples.

243　8, (2) The apostles, bearing witness to Jesus, proclaimed
3999c　first and foremost the death and resurrection of the Lord.

They faithfully recounted his life and words and, as regards the manner of their preaching, took into account the circumstances of their hearers. After Jesus had risen from the dead and his divinity was clearly perceived, the faith of the disciples, far from blotting out the remembrance of the events that had happened, rather consolidated it since their faith was based on what Jesus had done and taught.[...] Yet, it need not be denied that the apostles, when handing on to their hearers the things which in actual fact the Lord had said and done, did so in the light of that fuller understanding which they enjoyed as the result of being instructed by the glorious events accomplished in Christ, and illumined by the Spirit of Truth.[...] They made use of such various forms of speech as were adapted to their own purpose and to the mentality of their hearers.

244   9. (3) The sacred authors took this earliest body of
3999d   instruction, which had been handed down orally at first
          and then in writing [...], and set it down for the benefit of the churches in the four gospels. In doing so, each of them followed a method suitable to the special purpose which he had in view. They selected certain things out of the many traditions; some they synthesised, some they elaborated in view of the situation of the churches, painstakingly using every means of bringing home to their readers the firm truth in which they had been instructed [cf. Lk 1:4]. For, out of the material which they had received, the sacred authors selected especially those items which were adapted to the various circumstances of the faithful as well as to the end which they themselves had in view; these items they recounted in a manner fitting those circumstances and that end. [...] In handing on the words and deeds of our Saviour, they explained them [...], one Evangelist setting them in one context, another in another. [...] The truth of the narrative is not affected in the least by the fact that the Evangelists report the sayings or doings of our Lord in a different order or that they use different words to express what he said, not keeping to the letter but nevertheless preserving the sense.

245   10. The result of recent studies has made it clear that
          the teaching and the life of Jesus were not simply recounted for the purpose of being kept in remembrance, but were 'preached' in such a way as to provide the Church with the foundation on which to build faith and practice.

THE SECOND VATICAN GENERAL COUNCIL
DOGMATIC CONSTITUTION *DEI VERBUM* (1965)

Chapter II: The Transmission of Divine Revelation

This Chapter unfolds the Council's teaching on the nature of revelation (nn. 149-153) by showing how Tradition, Scripture and the ecclesial magisterium work together to bring to every age a testimony of God's saving word, by which he continues to speak to believers and lead them into fuller communion of life with himself (cf. n. 149).

God's consummate revelation of himself in Christ (cf. n.151) was proclaimed in the apostolic gospel, which is the source of saving truth and rule of life (cf. n. 201, incorporated in DV 7). The gospel is further communicated through the Tradition of the church and the inspired books of the New Testament. Tradition is the global apostolic patrimony that the church hands on by prolonging her own life as a community of faith, worship and witness. Tradition develops and provides the ambience in which Scripture becomes God's loving discourse with believers and a vital evangelical message for the world (DV 8).

Scripture and Tradition differ, since the former is a fixed text and the latter includes a vital process of transmitting faith and a style of life, but they are intrinsically connected (DV 9). They are a single treasure entrusted to the whole church, within which the episcopal and papal magisterium has an interpretive and protective function that serves the integrity and vitality of the revealed message (DV 10)

(Sacred Tradition)

246   8. [...] The Tradition handed on by the apostles includes everything which contributes to the living of a holy life by the people of God and the increase of their faith; thus the Church, in her teaching, life and worship, perpetuates and hands on to all generations all that she herself is, all that she believes.

This Tradition, derived from the apostles, progresses in the Church with the help of the Holy Spirit *[cf. n. 136]*, for there is growth in the understanding both of the realities and of the words handed down. This happens through study and contemplation on the part of the believers who ponder them in their hearts *[cf. Lk 2:19, 51]*, through their interior understanding of the spiritual realities of their own experience, and through the preaching of those who have received a sure charism of truth together with episcopal succession. Thus the Church tends continually through the centuries towards the fulness of divine truth.[...]

The words of the holy Fathers bear witness to the life-giving presence of this Tradition, the riches of which are poured out in the practice and life of the Church that believes and prays. By the same tradition the entire canon of Sacred Scripture becomes known to the Church, and these Scriptures are more deeply understood and constantly actualized in the Church. In this way God, who spoke of old, still holds unbroken converse with the spouse of his beloved Son; and the Holy Spirit, through whom the living voice of the Gospel resounds in the Church, and through her in the world, introduces believers into all truth, and makes the word of Christ dwell abundantly in them [cf Col 3:16].

(Relation between Tradition and Scripture)

247   9. Hence there exists a close connection and commonality between Sacred Tradition and Sacred Scripture. For both of them, flowing from the same divine well-spring, in a certain way merge into unity, and tend toward the same end. For Sacred Scripture is the word of God in as much as it is consigned to writing under the inspiration of the Holy Spirit, while Sacred Tradition takes the word of God entrusted by Christ the Lord and the Holy Spirit to the apostles, and hands it on to their successors in its integrity, so that, led by the light of the Spirit of truth, they may, in their preaching of this word, preserve it faithfully, explain it and cause it to spread. Consequently, it is not from Sacred Scripture alone that the Church derives her certainty about the whole content of revelation. And so, both Sacred Scripture and Sacred Tradition are to be accepted and venerated with the same sense of loyalty and reverence [cf. n. 210].

(Scripture and Tradition in relation to the Church's magisterium)

248   10. [...] The office of authentically interpreting the word of God, whether written or handed down, has been entrusted to the living teaching office of the Church alone [cf. n. 859], whose authority is exercised in the name of Jesus Christ. This teaching office, however, is not above the word of God, but ministers to it, teaching only what has been handed on, listening to this word devoutly, guarding it religiously and expounding it faithfully, by divine commission and with the help of the Holy Spirit; it draws from the one deposit of faith everything which it proposes for belief as divinely revealed.

It is clear therefore, that, by God's most wise design, Sacred Tradition, Sacred Scripture and the Church's teaching authority are so linked and so associated together that one cannot stand without the others, and that all together and each in its own way contribute effectively to the salvation of souls under the action of the one Holy Spirit.

Chapter III: The Divine Inspiration of Sacred Scripture and its Interpretation

The Council affirms the inspiration of Scripture as a tenet of apostolic faith, adding a simple statement that God acted in and through the chosen human authors, leaving aside the often cited account given by Leo XIII of how the Spirit worked in their faculties (cf. n.227). Instead of "inerrancy", as in the biblical encyclicals, the Council affirms the saving truth of Scripture, as attested in 2 Tim 3:16-17 on the many-sided pastoral efficacy of the Bible.

The norms of correct interpretation begin with a concise recapitulation of Divino afflante (nn. 234, 236), but Vatican II then insists on reading Scripture "in the Spirit" with attention to factors that carry the interpreter beyond historical and literary considerations.

Finally, God's words to us in Scripture are marvelously tempered to our limitations, in analogy with his coming to us in the weakness of flesh in the incarnation of the eternal Word.

(Inspiration and truth of Holy Scripture)

249   11. [...] For the composing of these sacred books God chose human beings, and while he employed them, they made use of their own powers and abilities, so that with God acting in them and through them, they—as true authors— committed to writing all those things and only those that he wanted [cf. n.227].

Since therefore everything asserted by the inspired authors or sacred writers must be held to be asserted by the Holy Spirit, it must be acknowledged that the books of Scripture teach firmly, faithfully and without error the truth which God, for the sake of our salvation, wanted to be set down in the sacred writings.

(Interpretation)

250   12. [...] Sacred Scripture must be read and interpreted in the same Spirit in which it was written. In order therefore to discover the correct meaning of the sacred texts, no less serious attention must be paid to the content and unity of the whole of Scripture in the light of the living Tradition of the whole Church and of the analogy of faith.

(God's condescension)

251 13. [...] The words of God, expressed in human language, resemble human speech, just as once the Word of the eternal Father, taking to himself the weak flesh of humanity, became similar to human beings.

Chapters IV and V: The Old and the New Testaments

After a brief description of salvation history (14), the Constitution shows the importance of the Old Testament and its relation to the New Testament. According to the saying of St. Augustine, "The New Testament lies hidden in the Old and the Old is made manifest in the New"[1]

The New Testament has an excellence of its own (17), especially the gospels which are of apostolic origin and have a historical character; number 19 is a summary of the instruction of the Biblical Commission 'Sancta Mater Ecclesia' (cf. nn. 240-245). The chapter concludes with an extremely brief account of all the other New Testament writings (20).

(Importance of the Old Testament for Christians)

252 15. [...] Though these books contain also certain things which are imperfect and merely temporary, they still exhibit a true divine pedagogy.[...] They give expression to a lively sense of God, contain a storehouse of sublime teachings about God, of saving wisdom about human life, and a wonderful treasury of prayers; in sum, the mystery of our salvation is present in them in a hidden way.

(The unity of the two Testaments)

253 16. [...] The books of the Old Testament in their entirety have been assumed into the proclamation of Gospel, and it is in the New Testament that they acquire and manifest their full significance *[cf. Mt 5:17; Lk 24:27; Rom 16:25-26; 2 Cor 3:14-16]*. In their turn the Old Testament books shed light on the New Testament and explain it.

---

1. St. Augustine, *Quaest. in Hept.*, 2, 73.

(The apostolic origin of the gospels)

254   18. [...] What the apostles preached by the command of
            Christ, afterwards they and others of the apostolic
circle under the inspiration of the divine Spirit handed on to
us in writings which are the foundation of our faith, namely,
the fourfold Gospel, according to Matthew, Mark, Luke and
John.

Chapter VI: Sacred Scripture in the Life of the Church

All preaching must be nourished and governed by Sacred Scripture.
Suitable translations from the original text must be made available in the
language of the people; when possible, these may be made in collaboration
with other Christians (22).
   Exegetes and theologians are encouraged in the apostolic use of the Bible
(23). Theology must become more and more biblical. Finally, the Council
recommends guided reading of Holy Scripture as a stimulus to the life in the
Spirit (25).

(The importance of Holy Scripture for the Church)

255   21. [...] In the sacred books it is the heavenly Father
            himself who meets his children with tender love and
enters into conversation with them. Now there is such force and
efficacy in the word of God that it constitutes strength and
support for the Church, and for her children it provides strength
of faith, the food of the soul and a pure unfailing source of the
spiritual life.

(The importance of Scripture for theology)

256   24. [...] Let the study of the sacred page be as it were
            the soul of sacred theology. Through the same word of
Scripture the ministry of the word, which includes pastoral
preaching, catechesis, and all Christian instruction, where the
liturgical homily ought to have a privileged place, also must find
healthy nourishment and holy growth.

(The reading of Holy Scripture is recommended)

257   26. [...] Just as the life of the Church is strengthened
            through the persistent frequenting of the eucharistic
mystery, so also we may hope for a new stimulus for the life of
the Spirit from a growing devotion to the word of God which
lasts for ever *[Is 40:8; cf. 1 Pet 1:23-25].*

PAUL VI

S. CONGREGATION FOR CATHOLIC EDUCATION
THE THEOLOGICAL FORMATION OF FUTURE PRIESTS
(22 February 1976)

This lengthy document, issued by the Sacred Congregation for Catholic Education, was sent to all bishops and Directors of Seminaries. In an important section it outlines the principles to be observed in the teaching of Sacred Scripture, the relation of Scripture to Tradition and its place as the basis of all theological disciplines. The text is found in The Pope Speaks, *Vol. 21 (1976), pp. 265-366.*

(The place of Scripture in theology)

258   79. The basic fact which theological teaching must take into account is that Sacred Scripture is the starting point, the permanent foundation, and the life-giving and animating principle of all theology [*cf. DV 24; n. 256*]. The professor of biblical sciences must therefore carry out his mission with the competence and thorough scientific preparation that the importance of his discipline requires. To be faithful to his mission, he must deal, at different levels, with the text, with the event to which the text relates, and with the tradition which communicates and interprets the text. But, while he applies textual, literary and historical analysis, he must also keep alive in the minds of his students an awareness of the unity of the mystery and plan of God. Since Scripture is passed on to us by the Church and in part came into existence within the Church, it should be read and understood in the light of ecclesiastical tradition.[1]

80. The primordial role of Sacred Scripture determines the nature of its relation to theology and its various disciplines. We must recall here that Sacred Scripture cannot be taken into account in function solely of these disciplines (as though it were but a source of probative texts); on the contrary, theology in its entirety is called upon to help to a better and increasingly profound understanding of the sacred texts, that is, of the dogmatic and moral truths they contain. Consequently, after the introductory questions have been handled, the teaching of Sacred Scripture must culminate in a biblical theology which gives a unified vision of the Christian mystery.

---

1. Cf. Instruction *Sancta Mater Ecclesia*, 21 April 1964, *AAS* 56 (1964) 713f.

JOHN PAUL II

APOSTOLIC EXHORTATION *CATECHESI TRADENDAE*
(16 October 1979)

The Apostolic Exhortation takes up the theme of the 1977 Synod of Bishops in Rome on Catechesis in Our Day. See n. 163i. In the fourth chapter, "The Whole of the Good News Drawn from its Source", a passage shows the link between Scripture and tradition as source of catechesis. The text is found in AAS 71 (1979) 1277-1340.

(Tradition and Scripture as source of catechesis)

259 27. To speak of Tradition and Scripture as the source of catechesis is to draw attention to the fact that catechesis must be impregnated and penetrated by the thought, the spirit and the outlook of the Bible and the Gospels through assiduous contact with the texts themselves; but it is also a reminder that catechesis will be all the richer and more effective for reading the texts with the intelligence and the heart of the Church and for drawing inspiration from the two thousand years of the Church's reflection and life.

The Church's teaching, liturgy and life spring from this source and lead back to it, under the guidance of the pastors and, in particular, of the doctrinal Magisterium entrusted to them by the Lord.

CONGREGATION FOR THE DOCTRINE OF THE FAITH

LETTER TO THE BISHOPS OF THE CATHOLIC CHURCH ON CERTAIN QUESTIONS CONCERNING THE MINISTER OF THE EUCHARIST
(6 August 1983)

Although this document deals with questions concerning the minister of the Eucharist (cf. n 1756i), there is a relevant passage on the erroneous use of Scripture texts. The text of the letter is found in AAS 75 (1983) 1001-1009.

(Interpretation of Scripture and living Tradition)

260 This apostolic succession which constitutes the entire Church as apostolic is part of the living tradition which has been for the Church from the beginning, and continues to be, her particular form of life. And so, those who cite isolated texts of Scripture in opposition to this living tradition, trying thereby to justify different structures, stray from the truth.

CONGREGATON FOR THE DOCTRINE OF THE FAITH

INSTRUCTION *LIBERTATIS NUNTIUS* ON CERTAIN
ASPECTS OF THE THEOLOGY OF LIBERATION
(6 August 1984)

This Instruction purposes to give guidelines on the "theologies of liberation". It is not intended as a treatise on the theme of "Christian Freedom and Liberation"(as a subsequent Instruction, dated 22 March, 1986, will be), but only draws attention to the deviations and risks of deviation on the part of certain forms of liberation theology which use in an insufficiently critical manner concepts borrowed from various currents of Marxist thought. A passage from the fourth section, "Biblical Foundations", on the interpretation of the Exodus event, and another from the tenth section denounce a new, 'reductionist' hermeneutics. The text is found in AAS 76 (1984) 876-909.

(Against a reductionist interpretation of Exodus)

261   IV,3. The "theologies of liberation" make wide use of readings from the book of Exodus. The exodus, in fact, is the fundamental event in the formation of the chosen people. It represents freedom from foreign domination and from slavery. One will note that the specific significance of the event comes from its purpose, for this liberation is ordered to the foundation of the people of God and the Covenant cult celebrated on Mount Sinai *[cf. Ex 24]*. That is why the liberation of the Exodus cannot be reduced to a liberation which is principally or exclusively political in nature. Moreover, it is significant that the term *freedom* is often replaced in Scripture by the very closely related term, *redemption*.

(New hermeneutic: reductionist reading of the Bible)

262   X,5. The new hermeneutic inherent in the "theologies of liberation" leads to an essentially political re-reading of the Scriptures. Thus, a major importance is given to the Exodus event in as much as it is a liberation from political servitude. Likewise, a political reading of the *Magnificat* is proposed. The mistake here is not in bringing attention to a political dimension of the reading of Scripture, but in making of this one dimension the principal or exclusive component. This leads to a reductionist reading of the Bible.[...]

X,7. In giving such priority to the political dimension, one is lead to deny the radical newness of the New Testament and above all to misunderstand the person of Our Lord Jesus Christ, true God and true man, and thus the specific character of the salvation he gave us, that is above all liberation from sin, which is the source of all evils.

PONTIFICAL COMMISSION FOR RELIGIOUS RELATIONS WITH THE JEWS
NOTES ON THE PROPER WAY TO PRESENT THE JEWISH FAITH IN ROMAN CATHOLIC PREACHING AND TEACHING
(24 June 1985)

The Secretariat for Christian Unity previously published Guidelines and Suggestions for the implementation of the Declaration Nostra Aetate *(n.4) in relation to the Jews (1974). In this subsequent document, the Commission for Religious Relations with the Jews of the Secretariat not only urges the faithful to avoid any anti-semitism, but also to learn to appreciate and love Jews and Judaism. The "Notes" recall the organic unity and explain the relationship between the "Old" (in the sense of 'first', not of 'out-of-date') and the New Testaments. In this connection the document explains the use of typology and the right method of typological interpretation. The text is found in* Osservatore Romano, *24-25 June, 1985, pp. 6-7.*

(Relation between the two Testaments and typology)

263   II,3. From the unity of the divine plan derives the problem of the relation between the Old and New Testaments. The Church already from apostolic times *[cf. 1 Cor 10:11; Heb 10:1]* and then constantly in tradition resolved this problem by means of typology, which emphasises the primordial value that the Old Testament must have in the Christian view. Typology, however, makes many people uneasy and is, perhaps, the sign of a problem unresolved.

4. Hence in using typology [...] we should be careful to avoid any transition from the Old to the New Testament which might seem merely a rupture.[...]

(Typological interpretation and Christian reading)

264   II,5. It should[...] be emphasised that typological interpretation consists in reading the Old Testament as preparation and, in certain aspects, outline and foreshadowing of the New *[cf. e.g. Heb 5:5-10, etc]*. Christ is henceforth the key and point of reference to the Scriptures: "The rock was Christ" *[1 Cor 10:4]*.

6. It is true then and should be stressed that Christians read the Old Testament in the light of the event of the dead and risen Christ and that on these grounds there is a Christian reading of the Old Testament which does not necessarily coincide with the Jewish reading.[...] But this detracts nothing from the value of the Old Testament in the Church and does nothing to hinder Christians from profiting discerningly from the traditions of Jewish reading.

7. Typological reading only manifests the unfathomable riches of the Old Testament, its inexhaustible content and the mystery of which it is full, and should not lead us to forget that it retains its own value as revelation which the New Testament often does no more than reiterate [cf. Mk 12:29-31]. Moreover, the New Testament itself demands to be read in the light of the Old. Primitive catechesis constantly had recourse to this [cf. e.g. 1 Cor 5:6-8; 10:1-11].

JOHN PAUL II

LETTER REGARDING ARCHBISHOP LEFEBVRE
(8 April 1988)

In 1976 Pope Paul VI suspended Archbishop Marcel Lefebvre from his priestly functions after the Archbishop had ordained members of the traditionalist Fraternity of Pius X. In 1988, Pope John Paul II wrote to Cardinal Joseph Ratzinger, Prefect of the Congregation for the Doctrine of the Faith, to encourage him in his efforts to achieve reconciliation with Archbishop Lefebvre.

The letter was the occasion for the Pope to speak of two extreme tendencies in the church after Vatican II and to clarify the nature of tradition and its relation to church teaching authority (cf. n. 246-248).

Unfortunately, negotiations with Archbishop Lefebvre broke down and on June 30, 1988, he proceeded to ordain four members of the Fraternity to the episcopate. On July 2, he was declared excommunicated in the decree "Ecclesiam Dei" (AAS 80 [1988] 1495-98). The following text on progressivist and integrist reactions to Vatican II, found in the letter to Cardinal Ratzinger, is taken from Origins *17 (1987-88), pp. 803-804.*

(Progressivism heedless of fidelity to tradition)

265a In the period since the council [...] there have appeared tendencies which create a certain difficulty in putting the council into practice. One of the tendencies is characterized by a desire for changes which are not always in harmony with the teaching and spirit of Vatican II, even though they seek to appeal to the council. These changes claim to express progress, and this tendency is given the name progressivism. In this case, progress consists in an aspiration toward the future which breaks with the past, without taking into consideration the function of tradition, which is fundamental to the church's mission in order that she may continue in the truth which was transmitted to her by Christ the Lord and by the apostles, and which is diligently safeguarded by the magisterium.

(Integrism heedless of the dynamic character of tradition)

265b The opposite tendency, which is usually called traditionalism or integrism, stops at the past itself, without taking into account the correct aspiration toward the future which manifested itself precisely in the work of Vatican II. While the former tendency seems to recognize the correctness of what is new, the latter sees correctness only in what is ancient, considering it synonymous with tradition.

But it is not what is ancient as such, or what is new per se, which corresponds to the correct idea of tradition in the life of the church. Rather that idea means the church's remaining faithful to the truth received from God, throughout the changing circumstances of history. The church, like that householder in the Gospel, wisely brings "from the storeroom both the new and the old" [*Mt 13:52*], while remaining absolutely obedient to the Spirit of truth whom Christ has given to the church as her divine guide. And the church performs the delicate task of discernment through her authentic magisterium [*cf. LG 25*].

CONGREGATION FOR CATHOLIC EDUCATION

INSTRUCTION ON THE STUDY OF THE FATHERS OF THE CHURCH IN THE FORMATION OF PRIESTS
(10 November 1989)

In early 1990 the Vatican Congregation for Catholic Education released an instruction on the contribution of patristic studies to the programmes of seminaries and theological faculties. Recalling the place of the fathers in the genetic study of doctrine, as prescribed by Vatican II in Optatam totius, *n. 16, the Congregation noted that some currents of theology were attempting to relate biblical texts directly to today's questions without attending to the early tradition in which the church fathers set the direction for doctrinal development. Study of the fathers should be cultivated because of their essential role as witnesses of tradition and practitioners of sound theological method.*

The Latin original of the instruction is given in AAS 82 (1990), pp. 607-636. An English translation, based on an Italian version, is found in Origins 19 (1989-90), pp. 549-561.

(The fathers and the "constitutive" tradition of Christianity)

266a In the flow of living tradition that continues from the beginning of Christianity through the centuries to our present time, [the fathers] occupy a quite special place, which distinguishes them from other figures in the history of the church. They laid down the first basic structures of the church, together with doctrinal and pastoral traditions that remain valid for all times. [...] Some of them are witnesses to the apostolic tradition, the source from which subsequent tradition is drawn. The fathers of the first centuries especially can be considered the founders and teachers of a "constitutive" tradition, which has been preserved and continuously elucidated in subsequent ages.

It is from them that "the full canon of the sacred books" is known [*DV 8; n. 246*]; they composed the basic professions of faith, which are in fact the *regulae fidei* that defined the deposit of faith in response to heresies and contemporary culture, thus giving rise to theology. Furthermore, they laid the foundations of canonical discipline [...] and created the first forms of liturgy that remaind an obligatory reference point for all subsequent liturgical reforms. In this way the fathers gave the first conscious and reflective response to Sacred Scripture, formulating this, not as an abstract theory, but as daily pastoral practice and teaching in the heart of the liturgical assemblies gathered together to profess the faith and celebrate the worship of the risen Lord. They were in this way the authors of the first great Christian catechesis.

(The dynamism of tradition)

266b The tradition to which the fathers are witnesses is a living tradition that manifests unity amid variety and continuity in progress. This is seen in the great number of liturgical families and in the spiritual, disciplinary and exegetical-theological traditions that existed in the first centuries. [...] These were diverse traditions, which though were connected by being rooted in the firm and unchanging common foundations of the faith.

Tradition, therefore, as it was known and lived by the fathers, is not like a monolithic, immovable and obsolete block, but a pluriform organism pulsating with life. It is a way of life and teaching that on the one hand experienced uncertainty and controversy, while searching tentatively for answers, but on the other hand also reached timely decisions of notable creativity and decisive importance for the future. Following the living tradition of the fathers does not mean orienting oneself to the past as such, but adhering to the rule of faith in a spirit of assurance and interior freedom, with continuing attention to the foundations of everything, to that which is essential, enduring and unchanging. An absolute fidelity is at stake here, which is often tested *usque ad sanguinis effusionem*, for the sake of dogma and those moral and disciplinary principles that manifest their fecundity precisely at those times that open the way to innovations.

(The patristic approach to Scripture)

267a   The fathers are primarily and principally expositors of Sacred Scripture. [...] In this task, from our present-day point of view, their interpretative method is marked by certain undeniable limitations. [...] Nonetheless, their contribution toward a better understanding of the sacred books is of enormous value. They are still truly our teachers and are superior in many ways to the exegetes of the Middle Ages and the modern era due to "a sort of sweet intuition about heavenly things through an admirable penetration of spirit, whereby they go farther into the depths of the divine word".[1]

The example of the fathers can indeed teach modern exegetes a truly religious approach to Scripture as well as an interpretation that constantly adheres to the criterion of communion with the experience of the church proceeding through history under the guidance of the Holy Spirit. When these two interpretative principles, namely the religious and the specifically Catholic, are neglected or forgotten, modern exegetical studies often turn out to be impoverished and distorted.

For the fathers, Sacred Scripture was the object of supreme veneration, the foundation of the faith, the constant content of preaching, nourishment of devotion, the soul of theology. They

---

1. Pope Pius XII, *Divino afflante Spiritu*, AAS 35 (1943), 312.

always maintained its divine origin, lack of error, normativity and inexhaustible wealth and power for sprituality and doctrine.

(Characteristics of patristic interpretation of Scripture)

267b Theology was born out of the exegetical activity of the fathers *in medio ecclesiae* and especially in the liturgical assemblies where they responded to the spiritual needs of the people of God. Their exegesis, with its blend of the spiritual life and rational theological reflection, always aims at the essential point while being faithful to the entire sacred deposit of the faith. It is centred on the mystery of Christ, the point of reference and compendious expression of all particular truths. Rather than pursuing numerous marginal problems, the fathers seek to embrace the fullness of the Christian mystery and follow the basic movement of revelation and of the economy of salvation that goes from God through Christ to the church, sacrament of communion with God and dispenser of divine grace, in order to return to God. This insight gives rise to the fathers' lively sense of ecclesial communion. Their proximity to Christian origins and familiarity with Scripture make them see all things in reference to the centre and sense how this is present in each of its parts, so that secondary questions are answered in terms of the centre. Following the theological path of the fathers means, therefore, grasping more easily the essential nucleus of our faith and the *specificum* of our Christian identity.

(The faith initiated the inculturation of the Gospel)

268 Another important and very relevant characteristic of the fathers' theological method is that it sheds light on understanding "by what means the faith can be explained in terms of the philosophy and wisdom of the peoples" *[AG 22; n. 1144]*. They have in fact drawn from Scripture and tradition a clear awareness of Christian originality, that is, the firm conviction that Christian teaching contains an essential nucleus of revealed truths that then are normative in judging human wisdom and distinguishing truth from error. [...] Being anchored in the norm of faith, the fathers accepted many contributions from Greco-Roman philosophy, but they also rejected its grave errors and especially avoided the danger or syncretism which was then so widespread in the prevailing Hellenistic culture.[...]

Thanks to this careful discernment of the values and the limitations hidden in the various forms of ancient culture, new paths were opened up toward the truth and new possibilities realized for announcing the Gospel. Taught by the Greek, Latin and Syriac fathers, the church "learned early in its history to express the Christian message in the concepts and language of different peoples and tried to clarify it in the light of the wisdom of their philosophers. It was an attempt to adapt the Gospel to the understanding of all people and the requirements of the learned" [GS 44; n. 1145]. In other words, the fathers, being aware of the universal value of revelation, began the great task of Christian inculturation. [...] They become the example of a fruitful encounter between faith and culture, [...] which continues to be a guide for the church of all ages that is committed to preaching the Gospel to people of such different cultures and working in their midst.

(Theology both rational and religious)

269   Within the church, the encounter of reason with faith has given rise to many and long controversies regarding the major themes of trinitarian, christological, ecclesiological, anthropological and eschatological dogma. On such occasions, in defending the truths that touch on the very essence of faith, the fathers originated a notable advance in the understanding of dogmatic content and rendered a valuable service to the progress of theology. [...]

The fathers became the initiators of rational procedures suitable for the content of revelation and astute promoters of that *intellectus fidei* that belongs to the essence of every authentic theology. It was their providential task not only to defend Christianity, but also to rethink it in the Greco-Roman cultural environment; to find new formulas for expressing an ancient doctrine and non-biblical forms for a biblical doctrine; to present, in a word, the faith in the forms of human discourse that is fully Catholic and capable of expressing the divine content of revelation while always safeguarding its identity and transcendence. [...]

As theologians they did not use only the resources of reason, but much more the religious resources gained through their affective existential knowledge, rooted in intimate union with

Christ, nourished by prayer and sustained by grace and the gifts of the Holy Spirit. In their activities as theologians and pastors they showed to a marked degree a deep sense of mystery and experience of the things of God. This protected them against the recurring temptations both of exaggerated rationalism or of a flat and resigned fideism.

The first thing that strikes us in patristic theology is the vivid sense of the transcendence of divine truth contained in revelation.[...] Given this lively spiritual sense, the image of themselves that the fathers offer is that of men who are not only learning but even more are experiencing divine things.[...] Mostly they are specialists in the supernatural life who communicate what they have seen and experienced in their contemplation of divine things and what they have known through the path of love, *"per quandam connaturalitatem,"* as St. Thomas Aquinas said.[1] In their way of speaking and explaining, the delightful tones of the mystics are often perceptible, revealing an intense familiarity with God, a lived experience of the mystery of Christ and the church, and constant contact with the genuine sources of a theological existence that the Fathers see as fundamental to Christian life.

CATECHISM OF THE CATHOLIC CHURCH
(7 December 1992)

The Catechism of the Catholic Church *(cf. introduction to n. 185) devoted articles to the ecclesial transmission of revelation and to Scripture's witness to revelation (CCC 74-141).*

After explaining tradition in terms of DV 7-9, the Catechism set forth the distinction between Apostolic Tradition, given once for all, and the ecclesial traditions that form a variable complex of teachings and practices.

On Scripture, the Catechism goes beyond Vatican II by explaining more fully what DV 12 stated, after its recommendation of historical and literary study of authorial intention, about reading and interpreting Scripture "in the Spirit in which it was written" (cf. n. 250).

(Apostolic Tradition and ecclesial tradition)

270   83. The Tradition here in question *[CCC 75-82]* comes from the apostles and hands on what they received from

---

1. *S.T.,* II-II, 45, 2.

Jesus' teaching and example and what they learned from the Holy Spirit. The first generation of Christians did not yet have a written New Testament, and the New Testament itself demonstrates the process of living Tradition.

Tradition is to be distinguished from the various theological, disciplinary, liturgical or devotional traditions, born in the local churches over time. These are the particular forms, adapted to different places and times, in which the great Tradition is expressed. In the light of Tradition, these traditions can be retained, modified or even abandoned under the guidance of the Church's Magisterium. [...]

(Interpreting Scripture "in the Spirit")

271   111. But since Sacred Scripture is inspired, there is another and no less important principle of correct interpretation, without which Scripture would remain a dead letter. [...]

The Second Vatican Council indicates three criteria for interpreting Scripture in accordance with the Spirit who inspired it *[cf. n. 250].*

112. *Be especially attentive "to the content and unity of the whole Scripture".* Different as the books which compose it may be, Scripture is a unity by reason of the unity of God's plan, of which Christ is the centre and heart, open since his Passover *[cf. Lk 24:25-27; 44-46].* [...]

113. *Read the Scripture within "the living Tradition of the whole Church".* According to a saying of the Fathers, Sacred Scripture is written principally in the Church's heart rather than in documents and records, for the Church carries in her Tradition the living memorial of God's Word, and it is the Holy Spirit who gives her the spiritual interpretation of the Scripture ("[...] according to the Spiritual meaning which the Spirit grants to the Church").[1]

114. *Be attentive to the analogy of faith [cf. Rom 12:6].* By "analogy of faith" we mean the coherence of the truths of faith among themselves and with the whole plan of Revelation.

---

1. ORIGEN, *Homily on Leviticus,* 5, 5; *PG* 112, 454D.

PONTIFICAL BIBLICAL COMMISSION

THE INTERPRETATION OF THE BIBLE IN THE CHURCH
(1993)

In 1993, the Pontifical Biblical Commission completed a study of current methods and approaches in biblical interpretation. On April 23, Pope John Paul II accepted the Commission's document at a special audience held to commemorate the centenary of the first biblical encyclical, Providentissimus Deus, *by Leo XIII (nn. 220-227), and the fiftieth anniversary of Pius XII's* Divino afflante Spiritu *(nn. 232-236).*

The Pope underscored the importance of the new document in view of recent discoveries like the Dead Sea Scrolls and recent innovations in exegetical method, such as sociological and rhetorical analysis. He praised the breadth of vision of the new study along with its balance in evaluating current approaches to interpretation. It avoids a fundamentalist reduction of the true humanity of Scripture while recognizing that Catholic exegesis must serve the actualization of Scripture for the good of the whole world.

We give below sections of the document that clarify the interpretative task beyond what has gone before (cf. nn. 234-236, 250, 261-264, 271). The Commission clarifies the importance of the literal sense of the biblical text, while relating this to the "spiritual sense" which is given clear contours by relation to Christ's paschal mystery and our new life in the Spirit.

An English translation of the Pope's address and of the Commission document came out as a booklet published by the Liberia Editrice Vaticana, while the document is found in Origins *23 (1993-94), pp. 497-524.*

(Historical shifts regarding textual meaning)

272　　　The contribution made by modern philosophical hermeneutics and the recent developments of literary theory allows biblical exegesis to deepen its understanding of the task before it, the complexity of which has become ever more evident.

Ancient exegesis [...] attributed to every text of Scripture several levels of meaning. The most prevalent distinction was that between the literal sense and the spiritual sense. Medieval exegesis distinguished within the spiritual sense three different senses, relating, respectively, to the truth revealed, to the way of life commended and to the final goal to be achieved. [...]

In reaction to this multiplicity of senses, historical-critical exegesis adopted, more or less overtly, the thesis of the one single meaning. A text cannot have at the same time more than one meaning. All the effort goes into defining the precise sense of this or that biblical text seen within the circumstances in which it was produced.

But now this has run aground on the conclusions of theories of language and of philosophical hermeneutics, both of which affirm that written texts are open to a plurality of meaning.[...]

(The literal sense of Scripture)

273   It is not only legitimate, it is also absolutely necessary to seek to define the precise meaning of texts as produced by their authors—what is called the "literal" meaning. St. Thomas Aquinas had already affirmed the fundamental importance of this sense.[1][...]

The literal sense of Scripture is that which has been expressed directly by the inspired human authors. Since it is the fruit of inspiration, this sense is also intended by God, as the principal author. One arrives at this sense by means of a careful analysis of the text, within its literary and historical context.[...] To this end, the study of ancient literary genres is particularly necessary *[cf. n. 236].*

(The literal sense can develop in new directions)

274   One should be especially attentive to the dynamic aspect of many texts. [...] Historical-critical exegesis has too often tended to limit the meaning of texts by tying them too rigidly to precise historical circumstances. It should seek rather to determine the direction of thought expressed by the text; this direction, far from working toward a limitation of meaning, will on the contrary dispose the exegete to perceive extensions of it that are more or less foreseeable in advance.

One branch of modern hermeneutics has stressed that human speech gains an altogether fresh status when put in writing. A written text has the capacity to be placed in new circumstances, which will illuminate it in different ways, adding new meanings to the original sense. This capacity of written texts is especially operative in the case of the biblical writings, recognized as the word of God. Indeed, what encouraged the believing community to preserve these texts was the conviction that they would continue to be bearers of light and life for generations of believers to come. The literal sense is, from the start, open to further

---

1. *S.T.,* I, 10 ad 3.

developments, which are produced through the re-reading of texts in new contexts.

It does not follow from this that we can attribute to the biblical text whatever meaning we like, interpreting it in a wholly subjective way. On the contrary, one must reject as unauthentic every interpretation alien to the meaning expressed by the human authors in their written text. To admit the possibility of such alien meanings would be equivalent to cutting off the biblical message from its root, which is the word of God in its historical communication; it would also mean opening the door to interpretations of a wildly subjective nature.

(The spiritual sense of biblical texts)

275   There are reasons, however, for not taking *alien* in so strict a sense as to exclude all possibility of higher fulfilment. The paschal event, the death and resurrection of Jesus, has established a radically new historical context, which sheds fresh light upon the ancient texts and causes them to undergo a change in meaning. In particular, certain texts which in ancient times had to be thought of as hyperbole (e.g. the oracle where God speaking of a son of David, promised to establish his throne "forever": *2 Sam 7:12-13;1 Chron 17:11-14*), must now be taken literally, because "Christ, having been raised from the dead, dies no more " *[Rom 6:9]*.

In such cases one speaks of the "spiritual sense." As a general rule we can define the spiritual sense, as understood by Christian faith, as the meaning expressed by the biblical texts when read, under the influence of the Holy Spirit, in the context of the paschal mystery of Christ and of the new life which flows from it. This context really exists. In it the New Testament recognizes the fulfillment of the Scriptures. It is therefore quite acceptable to re-read the Scriptures in the light of this new context, which is that of life in the Spirit.

(The interrelation of literal and spiritual senses)

276   The above definition allows us to draw some useful conclusions of a more precise nature concerning the relationship between the spiritual and literal senses.

Contrary to a current view, there is not necessarily a distinction between the two senses. When a biblical text relates directly to the paschal mystery of Christ or to the new life that results from it, its literal sense is already a spiritual sense. Such is regularly the case in the New Testament. It follows that it is most often in dealing with the Old Testament that Christian exegesis speaks of the spiritual sense. But already in the Old Testament there are many instances where texts have a religious or spiritual sense as their literal sense. Christian faith recognizes in such cases an anticipatory relationship to the new life brought by Christ.

While there is a distinction between the two senses, the spiritual sense can never be stripped of its connection with the literal sense. The latter remains the indispensable foundation. Otherwise one could not speak of the "fulfillment" of Scripture. Indeed, in order that there be fulfillment, a relationship of continuity is essential. But it is also necessary that there be transition to a higher order of reality.

The spiritual sense is not to be confused with subjective interpretations stemming from the imagination or intellectual speculation. The spiritual sense results from setting the text in relation to real facts which are not foreign to it: the paschal event, in all its inexhaustible richness, which constitutes the summit of the divine intervention in the history of Israel, to the benefit of all humankind.

Spiritual interpretation, whether in community or in private, will discover the authentic spiritual sense only to the extent that it is kept within these perspectives. One then holds together three levels or reality: the biblical text, the paschal mystery and the present circumstances of life in the Spirit. [...]

One of the possible aspects of the spiritual sense is the typological. This is usually said to belong not to Scripture itself but to the realities expressed by Scripture: Adam as the figure of Christ [cf. Rom 5:14], and the flood as the figure of baptism [1 Pt 3:20-21], etc. Actually, the connection involved in typology is ordinarily based on the way in which Scripture describes the ancient reality (cf. the voice of Abel: Gen 4:10; Heb 11:4; 12:24) and not simply on the reality itself. Consequently, in such a case one can speak of a meaning that is truly scriptural.

CHAPTER III

THE TRIUNE GOD

"This is eternal life that they know thee, the only true God, and Jesus Christ whom thou hast sent" (Jn 17:3). This is how the substance of the Christian life is expressed in Jesus' words according to John's gospel. The core of the Christian message consists in the Mystery of Jesus Christ, but Jesus himself understood his coming as the manifestation of the Father. Through him all are made to share in the life and light of God. Hence the Christian doctrine about God is the foundation of the Church's faith.

Two series of problems concerning God figure in the documents of the Church from the outset. First among these is the right conception of God as compared to the distorted ideas found in the world surrounding the Christian fold. The Christian conception of God goes back to the Old Testament, is deepened in the revelation of Jesus Christ, and pervades all Christian life, worship and thought. God is one, the only source of all being, the material world included. He comprises all perfection. He is the living God, not an impersonal ground of the world's being, but the free and sovereign source of all salvation. This had to be maintained as an integral part of the Christian faith against the mythological, pantheistic and dualistic conceptions to which the Christians were constantly exposed. This Christian idea of God is expressed primarily in the liturgy and in the ordinary teaching of the Church; it is also contained in Creeds and doctrinal documents, mostly in brief formulas.

The second series of problems concerns the Holy Trinity. This occupies much more space in the doctrinal texts. The Christian concept of God unfolds itself in the mission and revelation of the Son and the Spirit. Since together with the Father they are truly divine, the unity in God and the mutual relations between the divine persons need to be clarified. This mystery became from the beginning the object of theological reflection.

From early times Trinitarian theology developed two different approaches. In the patristic theology of the East the idea prevailed that the one God is God the Father, and that the Son and the Spirit share with him his divine life. This conception had the merit of being based on Scripture, but it could lend itself to misinterpretations. It could lead to subordinationist ideas which, in fact, did spring up in the East and came to a climax with the heresy of Arius. The other conception, prominent in the West, conceived God as the one divine substance, comprising Father, Son and Spirit. In this view, the unity of God and the equality of Father, Son and Spirit were easily safeguarded; but, the basic truth of the oneness of the divine nature could be misunderstood in such a way as to lead to the denial of the real distinction between the three persons. Modalism in its various forms did, in fact, deny this distinction.

The documents of the Church reject the various misguided conceptions of the Trinity in order to preserve the revealed mystery in its integrity. This indeed is the significance of the Trinitarian Creeds and of the doctrinal precisions added to them by the Councils. They insist, on the one hand, on the oneness of God and on the divinity and full equality of the divine persons, and, on the other hand, on their origin and their mutual distinction from one another. In a later period, when the origin of the Holy Spirit from Father and Son became a major issue between the Eastern and Western Churches, this controversy took an important place in the documents of the Church.

The theological concepts and the terminology used in these documents became more and more technical and at times somewhat involved. This could hardly be avoided in view of the depth of the mystery which they had to convey. It should, however, be borne in mind that the subtlety in reasoning was never meant to rationalise the divine mystery but to preserve its integrity against all rationalistic simplifications. All Trinitarian heresies are such simplifications which, if they were allowed to prevail, would ultimately nullify the mystery.

* * *

The doctrinal points dealt with in this chapter are the following:

The Christian concept of God

There is one personal God: 5-14, 19, 39/1, 306/20, 327-329.
He transcends the world: 327, 330f;
and is of infinite perfections: 19, 39/2, 327.

One God, three persons

In God there are three persons, Father, Son, and Holy Spirit: 1-19,
39/2, 301, 303, 306/21.24, 308, 325.
The three are one undivided Godhead: 16, 19, 22, 39/3, 301, 303,
306/20.24, 308, 311-313, 315, 317-320, 325, 620/1, 627/1.
Each person is fully God: 16, 19, 22, 24, 306/3f.10.24, 312;
the Father: 308;
the Son: 6-14, 23, 206/3.12.13, 302f, 309;
the Holy Spirit: 12, 14, 16, 24, 39/6, 305, 306/1.3.16-18.22f, 310.
The divine persons are distinct from one another: 14, 16, 301, 306/2,
313f, 333;
they are distinct through mutual relationship: 39/2, 313, 325.

The origin of the divine persons

The Father is absolute origin, from himself; 16,19, 308, 325f, 339.
The Son is born from the Father, from eternity: 6-19, 23, 39/3-4,
302f, 306/11, 309, 318, 325.
The Holy Spirit proceeds from Father and Son: 14, 16, 19, 23, 39/3,
310, 319, 321-325, 339.
The Holy Spirit is uncreated Love-Gift: 337.
The divine persons are united through mutual indwelling: 316, 326.
The divine actions in the world are common to the three persons: 306/
19, 315, 326.
*The Trinitarian mystery is revealed in the mission of Son and Spirit
for the salvation of human beings:* (332);
in God's self-communication (337i).

DIONYSIUS

LETTER TO DIONYSIUS OF ALEXANDRIA (262)

The Trinitarian doctrine develops in the dialectic between the oneness of God and the distinction of the divine persons. The insistence on the oneness, predominant in the West, finds its extreme form in Sabellianism (Modalism) which denies the real distinction of the divine persons. The insistence on the distinction, prevalent in the East with Origen as primary representative, is in danger of placing the Word on the level of creatures.

Dionysius, bishop of Alexandria about the middle of the 3rd century, was concerned with combating the false doctrine of Sabellius; in the process he put too much emphasis on the real distinction of the divine persons with the result that his opponents accused him of tritheism. This discussion became the occasion for a first important statement on the Trinity by Pope Dionysius, striking the correct balance between the distinction of the divine persons and their unity and equality. This document anticipates to some extent the Arian controversy and difficulties over hupostasis *(understood in the West as "substance" and in the East as "person").*

(Unity and Trinity in God)

301 Next I should rightly speak against those who divide,
112 dismember, and so destroy the divine oneness
(*monarchia*), this most august teaching of the Church of God, into three powers and separate beings (*hupostaseis*) and into three Godheads. For I have heard that among you some preachers and teachers of the divine word hold this opinion which is, so to speak, diametrically opposed to the teaching of Sabellius. It is his [Sabellius'] blasphemy that the Son is the Father and vice versa, whereas they somehow preach three gods as they divide the sacred unity into three different beings (*hupostaseis*), entirely separate from each other. The Word of God must necessarily be united with the God of all, and the Holy Spirit must abide and dwell in God; it is also necessary that the divine Trinity be recapitulated and led back to One, as to a supreme point, that is to the almighty God of all things. For the doctrine of the misguided Marcion who cuts and divides the divine Oneness (*monarchia*) into three principles is truly diabolic and does not belong to the true disciples of Christ and to those who accept the discipline of the Saviour. For these know well that, while the Trinity is preached in the divine Scripture, neither in the Old nor in the New Testament are three gods taught.

(The divinity of the Son)

302   Equally guilty are those who believe that the Son is a
113   creature and that the Lord was made in the same way
         as one of the things that were really made, for the divine
Word testifies that he is born as it is proper and fitting for him
and not created or made. It is indeed not a small but an enormous
blasphemy to say that the Lord is in some way made by hand.
For if the Son was made there was a time when he was not. But
he was always since he is in the Father, as he himself declares
[cf. Jn 14:10f], and since Christ is Word, Wisdom and Power—
and, as you know, the divine Scriptures teach that Christ is all
that *[cf. Jn 1:14; 1 Cor 1:24]*—all of which are truly God's powers.
Hence, if the Son was made, there was a time when these were
not, which would mean that there was a time when God was
without them, which is truly absurd.[...]

(Conclusion)

303   Therefore, neither is the admirable and divine unity to
115   be separated into three Godheads, nor is the excellence
         and supreme greatness of the Lord to be diminished by
using the word 'made' *(poiêsis)*; but one must believe in God,
the almighty Father, in Christ Jesus his Son, and in the Holy
Spirit in such a way that the Word is united with the God of all,
for he says: "I and the Father are one " *[Jn 10:30]* and "I am in
the Father and the Father in me " *[Jn 14:11]*. In this way the
divine Trinity and the holy doctrine of the Oneness *(monarchia)*
will be preserved in their integrity.

THE FIRST GENERAL COUNCIL OF NICAEA

SYMBOL OF NICAEA (325)

(304)   *The Council of Nicaea condemned the heresy of Arius who
taught that the second person of the Godhead is not equal to the
Father but is created in time. Arius'doctrine is the extreme form of the trend
of subordinationism which is not absent among the early Fathers. It connects
the Son, through whom all things were made, with the created world in such
a way that he is no longer truly God but belongs already on the side of
creation.*

*The Council is a landmark in Trinitarian doctrine as it firmly places the
Son of God on the side of God. This is the meaning of the key word of the
Council, 'homoousios', "one in being" with the Father. The question, however,*

of the positive relation between Father and Son remains open and is not yet ripe for definition. Hence the struggle regarding the positive meaning of the 'homoousios' will arise only after the Council. See introduction and text, n.7.

THE FIRST GENERAL COUNCIL OF CONSTANTINOPLE
SYMBOL OF CONSTANTINOPLE (381)

The second ecumenical Council, the first of Constantinople, deals with the divinity of the Holy Spirit. All Arians had necessarily denied his divinity as a consequence of their denying the divinity of the Son. Some continued to do so even after the Arian heresy was rejected at Nicaea. It is only after Nicaea that the question of the Holy Spirit came up for serious theological reflection. The Creed is still today the common formula of faith between East and West.

The text of the Creed is found under n. 12. Here only the passage concerning the Holy Spirit is quoted. It expresses his divinity by his functions, mainly by his function of giving the divine life to us. The original text speaks only of the origin of the Holy Spirit from the Father. In the third Council of Toledo (589) the 'Filioque' was added so that the Creed asserts the origin of the Holy Spirit "from the Father and the Son". The addition became the object of the great controversy between the Eastern and Western Churches from the 8th century onwards (cf. n. 12, note 1).

305   [We believe] in the Holy Spirit, the Lord and Giver of
150   life, who proceeds from the Father (and the Son), who
        together with the Father and the Son is worshipped and
glorified, who has spoken through the prophets.

THE COUNCIL OF ROME
"TOME OF DAMASUS" (382)

Shortly after the General Council of Constantinople, Pope Damasus (366-384) called a Council at Rome to renew the condemnation of the errors of the time. Some of these refer to Christology (cf. nn. 603/6ff). Those regarding the Trinity are mainly concerned with the divinity of the Son and of the Holy Spirit.

306/1   We anathematise those who do not with full freedom
153   proclaim that he [the Holy Spirit] is of one power and
        substance with the Father and the Son.

306/2   We likewise anathematise those who follow the error
154   of Sabellius in saying that the Father and the Son are
        one and the same.

306/3   We anathematise Arius and Eunomius who, with equal
155   impiety though in different words, assert that the Son
and the Holy Spirit are creatures.

306/10 Anyone who denies that the Father is always, the Son
162   is always, and the Holy Spirit is always, is a heretic.

306/11 Anyone who denies that the Son is born of the Father,
163   that is of his divine substance, is a heretic.

306/12 Anyone who denies that the Son of God is true God,
164   as the Father is true God, that he can do all things, knows
all things, and is equal to the Father, is a heretic.

306/13 Anyone who says that the Son, while incarnate on earth,
165   was not in heaven with the Father, is a heretic.

306/16 Anyone who denies that the Holy Spirit, like the Son,
168   is really and truly from the Father, of the divine
substance, and true God, is a heretic.

306/17 Anyone who denies that the Holy Spirit can do all
169   things, knows all things and is everywhere present, just
as the Father and the Son, is a heretic.

306/18 Anyone who says that the Holy Spirit is a creature, or
170   made by the Son, is a heretic.

306/19 Anyone who denies that the Father made all things,
171   that is things visible and invisible, through the Son and
the Holy Spirit, is a heretic.

306/20 Anyone who denies that the Father, the Son and the
172   Holy Spirit have one Godhead, one might, one majesty,
one power, one glory, one Lordship, one kingdom, one
will and truth, is a heretic.

306/21 Anyone who denies that there are three true persons,
173   the Father, the Son and the Holy Spirit, equal, living
eternally, containing all things visible and invisible,
all powerful, judging, creating and saving all things, is a
heretic.

306/22 Anyone who denies that the Holy Spirit is to be adored
174   by all creatures just as the Son and the Father, is a heretic.

306/23 Anyone who has a correct idea about Father and Son,
175   but not about the Holy Spirit is a heretic, because all
heretics who do not think correctly about the Son and
the Spirit share in the unbelief of the Jews and pagans.

306/24 If anyone, while saying that the Father is God, that his
176   Son is God and that the Holy Spirit is God, divides them
and means [several] gods, and does not say that they
are God on account of the one Godhead and might which we
believe and know to belong to the Father and the Son and the
Holy Spirit; and if he excludes the Son and the Holy Spirit and
believes that only the Father is God and this is what he means
when he believes in one God, he is a heretic on all these points
and indeed a Jew. For, the name of gods has been appointed
and given by God to the angels and all the saints; but for the
Father, the Son and the Holy Spirit, because of their one and
equal divinity it is not the name of gods but of God which we
are shown and taught to believe; for we are baptised solely in
the Father, Son, and Holy Spirit, and not in the names of
archangels or angels, like the heretics, the Jews or even the
pagans in their folly.

177   This then is the salvation of Christians, that, believing
in the Trinity, that is in Father, Son and Holy Spirit, [and]
baptised in it, we must believe without doubt that to it belongs
the one and only true Godhead and might, majesty and
substance.

THE PSEUDO-ATHANASIAN SYMBOL *QUICUMQUE*

(307)   *The classical formula of the Trinitarian faith in the West is the so-
called "Athanasian Creed", which belongs to the end of the 5th
century, See introduction and text in nn. 16-17.*

THE ELEVENTH COUNCIL OF TOLEDO
SYMBOL OF FAITH (675)

*This small local Council, attended by only 17 bishops, has little
significance today except for the beautiful confession of faith which was recited
at its opening. The official value of this document consists in the fact that in
subsequent centuries it was very highly regarded and considered a genuine
expression of the Trinitarian faith; it is one of the important formulas of
doctrine. In fact, hardly anywhere is the reflection of the early Church on the
Trinitarian mystery and on Christ expressed with such precision and acumen*

*as in this Creed which sums up the tradition of the earlier Councils and
patristic theology of the West.*

(The divine Trinity)

308   We confess and believe that the holy and ineffable
525   Trinity, Father, Son and Holy Spirit, is one God by nature,
of one substance, of one nature as also of one majesty and power.

(The Father)

And we profess that the Father is not begotten, not created,
but unbegotten. For he himself, from whom the Son has received
his birth and the Holy Spirit his procession, has his origin from
no one. He is therefore the source and origin of the whole
Godhead. He himself of his own essence is the Father, who in
an ineffable way has begotten the Son from his ineffable
substance. Yet he did not beget something different *(aliud)* from
what he himself is: God has begotten God, light has begotten
light. From him, therefore, is "all fatherhood in heaven and on
earth" [*cf. Eph 3:15 Vulg.*].

(The Son)

309   We also confess that the Son was born, but not made,
526   from the substance of the Father, without beginning,
before all ages, for at no time did the Father exist without
the Son, nor the Son without the Father. Yet the Father is
not from the Son, as the Son is from the Father, because the
Father was not generated by the Son but the Son by the Father.
The Son, therefore, is God from the Father, and the Father
is God, but not from the Son. He is indeed the Father of the
Son, not God from the Son; but the latter is the Son of the
Father and God from the Father. Yet in all things the Son is
equal to God the Father, for he has never begun nor ceased
to be born. We also believe that he is of one substance with
the Father; wherefore he is called *homoousios* with the Father,
that is of the same being as the Father, for *homos* in Greek
means 'one' and *ousia* means 'being', and joined together they
mean 'one in being'. We must believe that the Son is begotten or
born, not from nothing or from any other substance, but
from the womb of the Father, that is from his substance. Therefore
the Father is eternal, and the Son is also eternal. If he was
always Father, he always had a Son, whose Father he was, and

therefore we confess that the Son was born from the Father without beginning. We do not call the same Son of God a part of a divided nature,[1] because he was generated from the Father, but we assert that the perfect Father has begotten the perfect Son, without diminution or division, for it pertains to the Godhead alone not to have an unequal Son. This Son of God is also Son by nature, not by adoption; of him we must also believe that God the Father begot him neither by an act of will nor out of necessity, for in God there is no necessity nor does will precede wisdom.

(The Holy Spirit)

310   We also believe that the Holy Spirit, the third person in
527   the Trinity, is God, one and equal with God the Father
and the Son, of one substance and of one nature, not, however, begotten nor created but proceeding from both, and that he is the Spirit of both. Of this Holy Spirit, we also believe that he is neither unbegotten nor begotten, for if we called him unbegotten we would assert two Fathers, or if begotten, we would appear to preach two Sons. Yet he is called the Spirit not of the Father alone, nor of the Son alone, but of both Father and Son. For he does not proceed from the Father to the Son, nor from the Son to sanctify creatures, but he is shown to have proceeded from both at once, because he is known as the love or the sanctity of both. Hence we believe that the Holy Spirit is sent by both, as the Son is sent by the Father. But he is not less than the Father and the Son, in the way in which the Son, on account of the body which he has assumed, testifies that he is less than the Father and the Holy Spirit.

(The oneness in the Trinity)

311   This is the way of speaking about the Holy Trinity as it
528   has been handed down: one must not call it or believe it
to be threefold, but Trinity. Nor can it properly be said that in the one God there is the Trinity, but the one God is the Trinity. In the relative names of the persons the Father is related

---

1. Cf. VIGILIUS OF THAPSUS, *Contra Arianos, Sabellianos et Photinianos dialogus*, II, 13.

to the Son, the Son to the Father, and the Holy Spirit to both. While they are called three persons in view of their relations, we believe in one nature or substance. Although we profess three persons, we do not profess three substances, but one substance and three persons. For the Father is Father not with respect to himself but to the Son, and the Son is Son not to himself but in relation to the Father; and likewise the Holy Spirit is not referred to himself but is related to the Father and the Son, in as much as he is called the Spirit of the Father and the Son. So when we say 'God', this does not express a relationship to another, as of the Father to the Son or of the Son to the Father or of the Holy Spirit to the Father and the Son, but 'God' refers to himself only.

312 For, if we are asked about the single persons, we must
529 confess that each is God. Therefore, we say that the
Father is God, the Son is God, the Holy Spirit is God, each one distinctly; yet there are not three gods, but one God. Similarly, we say that the Father is almighty, the Son is almighty, the Holy Spirit is almighty, each one distinctly; yet there are not three almighty ones, but one Almighty, as we profess one light and one principle. Hence we confess and believe that each person distinctly is fully God, and the three persons together are one God. Theirs is an undivided and equal Godhead, majesty and power, which is neither diminished in the single persons nor increased in the three. For it is not less when each person is called God separately, nor is it greater when all three persons are called one God.

313 This Holy Trinity, which is the one true God, is not
530 without number; yet it is not comprised by number,
because in the relationships of the persons there appears number, but in the substance of the Godhead nothing is comprised that could be counted. Therefore they imply number only in so far as they are mutually related, but they lack number in so far as they are by themselves (*ad se*). For one name referring to its nature so fits this Holy Trinity that it cannot be used in the plural with relation to the three persons. This then is, in our faith, the meaning of the saying in Holy Scripture: "Great is our Lord, abundant in power, and of his wisdom there is no number" [Ps 147 (146) 5 *Vulg.*].

(The Trinity in the oneness)

314   However, though we have said that these three persons
530   are one God, we are not allowed to say that the same
          one is the Father who is the Son, or that he is the Son
who is the Father, or that he who is the Holy Spirit is either the
Father or the Son. For he is not the Father who is the Son, nor is
the Son he who is the Father, nor is the Holy Spirit he who is
the Father or the Son, even though the Father is that which the
Son is, the Son that which the Father is, the Father and the Son
that which the Holy Spirit is, that is one God by nature. For,
when we say: he who is the Father is not the Son, we refer to
the distinction of persons; but when we say: the Father is that
which the Son is, the Son that which the Father is, and the Holy
Spirit that which the Father is and the Son is, this clearly refers
to the nature or substance whereby God exists, since in substance
they are one; for we distinguish the persons, but we do not divide
the Godhead.

531   Hence, we recognise the Trinity in the distinction of
          persons and we profess the unity on account of the
nature or substance. Thus the three are one by nature, not as
person.

(The undivided Trinity)

315   Nevertheless these three persons are not to be considered
531   separable since, according to our belief, none of them
          ever existed or acted before another, after another,
without another. For they are inseparable both in what they are
and in what they do, because, according to our faith, between
the Father who generates and the Son who is generated or the
Holy Spirit who proceeds, there has not been an interval of time
in which the one who generates would precede the one who is
generated, or there would be no begotten one for him who begets,
or the Holy Spirit in his proceeding would appear later than
Father or Son. For this reason we profess and believe that this
Trinity is inseparable and distinct *(inconfusa)*. We say, therefore,
of these three persons, as our forefathers defined it, that they
should be acknowledged, not separated. For if we listen to what
Holy Scripture says about Wisdom: "She is a reflection of eternal
light" *[Wis 7:26]*, we see that, as the reflection belongs inseparably
to the light, so too, according to our confession, the Son cannot

be separated from the Father. Therefore, neither do we confuse these three persons whose nature is one and inseparable, nor do we preach that they are in any way separable.

316
532
The Holy Trinity itself has indeed deigned clearly to reveal it to us: in these names by which he wanted the single persons to be known, it is impossible to understand one person without the other; one cannot conceive of the Father without the Son, nor can the Son be found without the Father. Indeed, the very relationship expressed in the personal names forbids us to separate the persons, for, though the personal names do not name them together, they imply them. No one can hear any one of these names without necessarily understanding also the other.

While then these Three are One and this One Three, each of the persons retains his own characteristics: The Father has eternity without birth; the Son has eternity with birth; the Holy Spirit has procession with eternity but without birth.

THE FOURTH LATERAN GENERAL COUNCIL (1215)

More than four hundred bishops answered Pope Innocent III's call to the Twelfth General Council held at the Lateran in Rome. Two documents of this Council are significant for the interpretation of the Trinitarian faith. The first is the solemn Creed composed for the occasion, directed against the heretical trends of the time, mainly against the Albigensian revolt. It contains the basic truths about the Holy Trinity (cf. n. 19).

The second document is a special statement against Abbot Joachim de Fiore (d. 1202). There had been two main approaches to the understanding of the Trinitarian mystery. According to the one coming mainly from the Eastern Fathers and which is centred on God the Father, God means the Father; the Son and Holy Spirit are conceived as participating in his divinity. The second, developed mainly in the West, especially by St. Augustine, was centred on the one divine nature which subsists as Father, Son and Holy Spirit. Peter the Lombard had systematised this approach, making the divine essence the centre of his speculation. Joachim de Fiore took up the Eastern trend, and attacked Peter. In doing so he exaggerated the distinction of the divine persons. The Council defends Peter against this false accusation and sanctions the doctrine which became the basis of the Trinitarian speculation of most scholastics.

Chapter II: The Error of Abbot Joachim

317
803
We condemn and reject the booklet or tract written by Abbot Joachim against Master Peter, the Lombard on the unity and essence of the Trinity, calling him heretical and

insane, because in his *Sententiae* he says: "There is no supreme
reality, the Father, the Son and the Holy Spirit, which is neither
generating, nor born, nor proceeding." Thus, Joachim asserts that
he [Peter] does not teach a Trinity but a quaternity of God, viz.,
three persons and that common essence as a fourth. Joachim
clearly professes that there is no such reality which is Father,
Son and Holy Spirit; there is no essence or substance or nature,
though he agrees that Father, Son and Holy Spirit are one essence,
one substance and one nature. But this unity he conceives not as
true and proper, but, so to say, as collective and by similitude,
just as many people are called one nation, and many faithful
one Church, as in the texts: "The multitude of believers had but
one heart and one soul" [*Acts 4:32 Vulg.*], and "he who is united
to the Lord becomes one Spirit with him" [*1 Cor. 6:17*]; and again:
"He who plants and he who waters are one" [*1 Cor 3:8*], and
"we all are one body in Christ" [*Rom. 12:5*]; and in the book of
Kings: "My people and your people are one" [*cf. Ruth 1:16*]. To
support his doctrine he relies mainly on the word which Christ
spoke in the Gospel about the faithful: "I will, Father, that they
be one in us as we are one, that they may be perfectly one" [*Jn
17:22f*]. This is how he argues: Christ's faithful are one not as
one reality which is common to all, but they are one in this way,
namely, one Church on account of the unity of the faith, and
finally one kingdom on account of the bond of indissoluble
charity. So we read in the canonical epistle of the apostle John
(as it is found in some codices): "There are three who give
testimony in heaven, the Father, the Son and the Holy Spirit,
and the three are one" [*1 Jn 5:7 Vulg.*], and immediately it is
added: "And there are three that give testimony on earth, the
Spirit, the water and the blood, and these three are one" [*1 Jn
5:8 Vulg.*].

318   We therefore, with the approval of the Sacred Council,
804   believe and confess with Peter the Lombard that there is
         one highest, incomprehensible and ineffable reality,
which is truly Father, Son, and Holy Spirit; the three persons
together, and each person distinctly; therefore in God there is
only Trinity, not a quaternity, because each of the persons is that
reality, viz., that divine substance, essence or nature which alone
is the beginning of all things, apart from which nothing else can
be found. This reality is neither generating nor generated, nor

proceeding, but it is the Father who generates, the Son who is generated and the Holy Spirit who proceeds, so that there be distinctions between the persons but unity in nature.

319 Hence, though "the Father is one person *(alius)*, the Son
805 another person, and the Holy Spirit another person, yet there is not another reality *(aliud)*",[1] but what the Father is, this very same reality is also the Son, this the Holy Spirit, so that in orthodox Catholic faith we believe them to be of one substance. For the Father gives his substance to the Son, generating him from eternity, as he himself testifies: "That which my Father has given me is greater than all" *[Jn 10:29 Vulg.]*. One cannot say that he gave him a part of his substance and retained a part for himself, since the substance of the Father is indivisible, being entirely simple. Nor can one say that in generating, the Father transferred his substance to the Son, as though he gave it to the Son in such a way as not to retain it for himself, for so he would have ceased to be substance. It is therefore clear that the Son, being born, received the substance of the Father without any diminution, and thus Father and Son have the same substance. Thus, the Father and the Son and the Holy Spirit who proceeds from both are the same reality.

320 When then he who is the Truth prays to the Father for
806 his faithful "that they may be one in us as we also are one" *[Jn 17:22]*, the word 'one' as applied to the disciples is to be taken in the sense of a union of charity in grace, but in the case of the divine persons in the sense of a unity of identity in nature. In the same way, in another occasion the Truth says: "you must be perfect as your heavenly Father is perfect" *[Mt 5:48]*, as though he were saying more explicitly; "you must be perfect" in the perfection of grace "as your heavenly Father is perfect" in the perfection of nature, i.e., each in his own way. For between Creator and creature no similitude can be expressed without implying a greater dissimilitude. Anyone therefore who presumes to defend or approve the opinion or doctrine of the above-mentioned Joachim in this matter should be rejected by all as a heretic.

---

1. Cf. Gregory of Nazianzus, *Epistola ad Cledonium*.

THE SECOND GENERAL COUNCIL OF LYONS
CONSTITUTION ON THE BLESSED TRINITY AND ON
THE CATHOLIC FAITH (1274)

The Council has significance as the first large-scale attempt to bring about the re-union of the Eastern and Western Churches (cf. n. 22i).

For the Trinitarian doctrine, two documents are important: 1) the so-called "Profession of Faith of Michael Palaeologus", a large part of which deals with the Trinitarian mystery (cf. nn. 22-25); 2) the 'Constitution on the Holy Trinity and the Catholic Faith", containing the explanation of the Latin doctrine on the origin of the Holy Spirit. Against Eastern misunderstandings it is stated that the origin of the Holy Spirit from Father and Son does not imply a double principle in God. This passage of the Constitution is quoted here.

(On the procession of the Holy Spirit)

321 We confess faithfully and devoutly that the Holy Spirit
850 proceeds eternally from Father and Son, not as from two principles but from one, not by two spirations but by one only. This the holy Roman Church, the mother and teacher of all the faithful, has so far professed, preached and taught; this she continues to hold, to preach, to profess and to teach. This is the unchangeable and true doctrine of the orthodox Fathers and Doctors, both Latin and Greek. However, some have fallen into various errors out of ignorance of the above indisputable truth. Therefore in order to forestall such errors, with the approval of the holy Council, we condemn and disapprove those who presume to deny that the Holy Spirit proceeds eternally from Father and Son, or who rashly dare to assert that the Holy Spirit proceeds from Father and Son as from two principles, not from one.

THE GENERAL COUNCIL OF FLORENCE

The 17th General Council, held at Florence, marks the second large-scale attempt to bring about union between the Eastern and the Western Churches. It was more successful than Lyons II; yet, again, it had no lasting effect. The Council treated the controversial questions between East and West.

For the Trinitarian doctrine two documents are important:

1. The Decree for the Greeks (1439): it explains the procession of the Holy Spirit from Father and Son, allowing, however, also the dynamic formula, more in keeping with Eastern thinking, according to which the Spirit proceeds from the Father through the Son. It also defends as legitimate the insertion of the 'Filioque' in the Creed.

2. *The Decree for the Copts (1442)*: it is addressed to Syrian Christians and contains an elaborate formulation of the Trinitarian faith, with special emphasis on the procession of the Holy Spirit. It also contains the classical formula, borrowed from St. Anselm, that in God everything is one except for the relative opposition of the persons, e.g., between Father and Son. It culminates in the doctrine of the mutual indwelling of the divine persons.

DECREE FOR THE GREEKS (1439)

(On the procession of the Holy Spirit)

322   In the name of the Holy Trinity, Father, Son and Holy
1300   Spirit, with the approval of this sacred universal Council
       of Florence, we define that this truth of faith must be believed and received by all and that all must profess: the Holy Spirit is eternally from Father and Son; he has his nature and subsistence at once *(simul)* from Father and Son; he proceeds eternally from both as from one principle and through one spiration *[cf. n. 321]*.

323   We declare: When the holy Doctors and Fathers say that
1301   the Holy Spirit proceeds from the Father through the
       Son, this must be understood in the sense that, as the Father, so also the Son is what the Greeks call 'cause' and the Latins 'principle' of the subsistence of the Holy Spirit. And, since the Father has through generation given to the only-begotten Son everything that belongs to the Father, except being Father, the Son has also eternally from the Father, from whom he is eternally born, that the Holy Spirit proceeds from the Son.

324   Moreover, we define that the explanatory words *'Filioque'*
1302   have been added in the Symbol legitimately and with
       good reason for the sake of clarifying the truth and under the impact of a real need at that time.

DECREE FOR THE COPTS (1442)

325   The holy Roman Church, founded on the word of our
1330   Lord and Saviour, firmly believes, professes and preaches
       the one true almighty, unchangeable and eternal God, Father, Son and Holy Spirit, one in essence, triune in persons: the Father not begotten, the Son begotten from the Father, and the Holy Spirit proceeding from Father and Son. The Father is

not the Son or the Holy Spirit; the Son is not the Father or the
Holy Spirit; the Holy Spirit is not the Father or the Son. But the
Father is only the Father, the Son only the Son, the Holy Spirit
only the Holy Spirit. The Father alone begot the Son out of his
substance; the Son alone was begotten from the Father alone;
the Holy Spirit alone proceeds from both Father and Son. These
three persons are one God and not three gods, for the three are
one substance, one essence, one nature, one Godhead, one infinity,
one eternity, and everything [in them] is one where there is no
opposition of relationship.[1]

326   "On account of this unity the Father is wholly in the
1331   Son and wholly in the Holy Spirit; the Son wholly in the
           Father and wholly in the Holy Spirit; the Holy Spirit
wholly in the Father and wholly in the Son. None precedes the
other in eternity, none exceeds the other in greatness, nor excels
the other in eternity, none exceeds the other in greatness, nor
excels the other in power. For it is from eternity and without
beginning that the Son has taken his origin from the Father, and
from eternity and without beginning that the Holy Spirit proceeds
from the Father and the Son."[2]

All that the Father is or has, he has not from another but
from himself; he is the origin without origin. All that the Son is
or has, he has from the Father; he is origin from origin. All that
the Holy Spirit is or has, he has at once (simul) from the Father
and the Son. But the Father and the Son are not two origins of
the Holy Spirit but one origin, just as Father, Son and Holy Spirit
are not three origins of creation but one origin.

THE FIRST VATICAN GENERAL COUNCIL
THIRD SESSION
DOGMATIC CONSTITUTION DEI FILIUS ON
THE CATHOLIC FAITH (1870)

*In its confrontation with the current errors (cf. n. 113i), the 20th General
Council, the first held at the Vatican, had to re-assert the genuine Christian
concept of God against materialistic and pantheistic trends. The following
text is found at the beginning of the Constitution Dei Filius.*

---

1. This fundamental principle of Trinitarian theology seems to have been
first enunciated by St. Anselm, De processione Spiritus Sancti, 1
2. Cf. Fulgentius of Ruspe, De fide liber ad Petrum, 1. 4.

Chapter I: God Creator of All Things

327 The holy, Catholic Roman Church believes and
3001 confesses: there is one God, true and living, Creator and
Lord of heaven and earth, almighty, eternal, immense,
incomprehensible, infinite in his intellect and will and in all
perfection. As he is one unique and spiritual substance, entirely
simple and unchangeable, we must proclaim him distinct from
the world in existence and essence, blissful in himself and from
himself, ineffably exalted above all things that exist or can be
conceived besides him.

Canons on God Creator of all Things

328 1. If anyone denies the one true God, Creator and Lord
3021 of things visible and invisible, *anathema sit*.

329 2. If anyone is not ashamed to assert that nothing exists
3022 besides matter, *anathema sit*.

330 3. If anyone says that the substance and essence of God
3023 and all things is one and the same, *anathema sit*.

331 4. If anyone says that finite beings, the corporeal as
3024 well as the spiritual, or at least the spiritual ones, have
emanated from the divine substance; or that the divine
essence becomes all things by self-manifestation or self-evolution;
or lastly that God is the universal or indefinite being which, by
self-determination, constitutes the universality of beings,
differentiated in genera, species and individuals, *anathema sit*.

THE SECOND VATICAN GENERAL COUNCIL

(332) *Vatican II did not treat systematically the theme of God and the
Trinity. Yet the deeper reflection on the human situation, needs and
aspirations in our time, demanded the re-thinking of our relation to God.
Besides, the new perspectives on the mystery of salvation, of revelation and of
the Church, implied a more elaborate presentation of the Trinitarian mystery
and of the missions of the Son and the Holy Spirit.*

*The Trinitarian structure of the entire work of salvation is unfolded in
LG 2-4, with the conclusion, borrowed from St. Cyprian, that "the Church is
clearly a people whose unity derives from that of the Father, the Son, and the
Holy Spirit." The same perspective is found in AG 2-4, with a special emphasis
on the mission of the Church. Moreover, the Trinitarian life is presented as
the model and source of the inter-personal relations in human society (GS
24).*

PAUL VI

DECLARATION *MYSTERIUM FILII DEI* OF THE
S. CONGREGATION FOR THE DOCTRINE OF THE FAITH

(21 February 1972)

This declaration is primarily concerned with a certain danger, to which recent theological re-thinking has given rise, of presenting Christological formulations which would reduce the mystery of Christ's person. The mystery of Christ is so intimately connected with the mystery of the Trinity that failures to enunciate one adequately often entail parallel failures as regards the other. This document recalls that, notwithstanding the fact that the mystery of the Trinity has been revealed to us in the history of salvation, God is in himself triune independently of, and prior to his self-manifestation in history. The eternity of the three persons, and in particular of the Holy Spirit, must be preserved. The pronouncements of the Councils of the Church are quoted to this effect; the document re-affirms that the doctrine "concerning the eternal person of the Holy Spirit belongs to the immutable truth of the Catholic faith" (cf. n. 671). The text is found in AAS 64 (1972) 237 ff.

(Recent errors concerning the most Holy Trinity and especially the Holy Spirit)

333   The opinion that Revelation has left us uncertain about the eternity of the Trinity, and in particular about the eternal existence of the Holy Spirit as a person in God distinct from the Father and the Son, is, therefore, contrary to the faith. It is true that the mystery of the Most Holy Trinity was revealed to us in the economy of salvation, and most of all in Christ himself who was sent into the world by the Father and together with the Father sends to the People of God the life-giving Spirit, But by this revelation there is also given to those who believe some knowledge of Gods's intimate life, in which "the Father who begets, the Son who is born, and the Holy Spirit who proceeds" are "of the same substance and fully equal, equally almighty and equally eternal" *[cf. n. 19].*

JOHN PAUL II

LETTER TO COMMEMORATE THE COUNCILS
OF CONSTANTINOPLE I AND OF EPHESUS

(25 March 1981)

To celebrate the 16th centenary of the First Council of Canstantinople (381) and the 1550th anniversary of the Council of Ephesus (431), Pope

John Paul II addressed to all the bishops of the Catholic Church a letter in which he highlights the significance of the two conciliar events for the life of the Church today, "as we look towards the coming of the third millennium of her life" (1). Of the Credo of Constantinople the Pope remarks that it is still "the expression of the common faith of the Church and of the whole of Christianity" (1). The specific contribution of Constantinople consisted in explicitly stating the Christian doctrine of the Holy Spirit, the "Hypostatic Gift", and its significance for the life of the Church and of the Christian. With this doctrine—complementing that of Nicaea—"the inscrutable mystery of God in his absolute Transcendence, Father, Son and Holy Spirit", has been "correctly" proclaimed. The Council of Ephesus is closely connected with the Creed of Constantinople which professed the doctrine of the incarnation of the "only-begotten Son of God". The value of Ephesus is "above all Christological, for it defined the two natures in Jesus Christ, the divine and the human, in order to state exactly the authentic doctrine of the Church already expressed in the Council of Nicaea in 325" (3). But it has also a "soteriological significance", for it illustrates the fact that "what is not assumed is not saved". Closely linked with those dogmatic truths was also that concerning the Blessed Virgin, "called to the unique and unrepeatable dignity of being the Mother of God, the Theotokos" (3). The Pope expresses the hope that the commemoration of the two Councils, whose faith we profess together with the other Churches of East and West, may hasten the journey towards unity. The text is found in AAS 73 (1981) 513-527.

(The doctrine of the Holy Spirit in Constantinople I)

334   2. In the present year we ought to give thanks to the Holy Spirit in a special way because, in the midst of the many fluctuations of human thought, he has enabled the Church to express her faith—in the manner of expression peculiar to that age—in complete harmony with 'all the truth'.

"I believe in the Holy Spirit, the Lord, the Giver of life, who proceeds from the Father. With the Father and the Son he is worshipped and glorified; he has spoken through the prophets": these are the words of the Creed of the First Council of Constantinople in 381, that elucidated the mystery of the Holy Spirit and his origin from the Father, thus affirming the unity and equality in divinity of the Holy Spirit with the Father and the Son.

(Ephesus on the redemptive incarnation and the divine motherhood)

335   3. It was a whole hymn raised by those ancient Fathers to the incarnation of the only-begotten Son of God, in the full truth of the two natures in the one person; it was a hymn to the work of salvation, accomplished in the world through the working of the Holy Spirit, and all of this could not fail to rebound to the honour of the Mother of God, the first cooperator with the power of the Almighty, which overshadowed her at the moment of the Annunciation in the luminous coming of the Holy Spirit.[...]

It therefore seems to be very opportune that this ancient Council too, the third in the history of the Church, should be remembered by us in its rich theological and ecclesiological context. The Most Blessed Virgin is she who, by the overshadowing of the power of the Trinity, was the creature most closely associated with the work of salvation. The incarnation of the Word took place beneath her heart, by the power of the Holy Spirit. In her there dawned the new humanity which with Christ was brought forth in the world in order to bring to completion the original plan of the Covenant with God, broken by the disobedience of the first man.

(Ecumenical significance of the commemoration of the Councils)

336   5. I also venture to hope that the commemoration of the Councils of Constantinople and Ephesus, which were expressions of the faith taught and professed by the undivided Church, will make us grow in mutual understanding with our beloved Brothers in the East and in the West, with whom we are still not united by full ecclesial communion but together with whom we seek in prayer, with humility and with trust, the paths to unity in truth.[...]

ENCYCLICAL LETTER *DOMINUM ET VIVIFICANTEM*
(18 May 1986)

The first part of this encyclical letter is entitled "The Spirit of the Father and of the Son, Given to the Church". It recalls that the Holy Spirit unceasingly continues, in the mystery and action of the Church, the historical presence on earth of Christ the Redeemer and his saving work (7). It goes on to explain the identity of the Holy Spirit within the mystery of God's intimate life, and his role in the economy of creation and salvation—repeating a notion popularized by Karl Rahner and others, God's "self-communication" (nn. 13, 14, 23, 50, 51, 58). The text is found in AAS 76 (1986) 809-900.

(The Holy Spirit within the divine life)

337   10. In his intimate life, "God is love" [1 Jn 4:8.16], the essential love shared by the three divine persons:

personal love is the Holy Spirit of the Father and of the Son. Therefore he "searches even the depths of God" *[1 Cor 2:10]*, as uncreated *Love-Gift*. It can be said that in the Holy Spirit the intimate life of the Triune God becomes totally gift, an exchange of mutual love between the divine persons, and that through the Holy Spirit God exists in the mode of gift. It is the Holy Spirit who is *the personal expression* of this self-giving, of this being-love.[1] He is Person-Love. He is Person-Gift. Here we have an inexhaustible treasure of the reality and an inexpressible deepening of the concept of *person* in God, which only divine revelation makes known to us.

(The Holy Spirit in the economy of salvation)

338   10. At the same time, the Holy Spirit, being consubstantial with the Father and the Son in divinity, is love and uncreated gift from which derives as from its source (*fons vivus*) *all giving of gifts* vis-à-vis creatures (created gift): the gift of existence to all things through creation; the gift of grace to human beings through the whole economy of salvation. As the Apostle Paul writes: "God's love has been poured into our hearts through the Holy Spirit which has been given to us" *[Rom 5:5]*.

PONTIFICAL COUNCIL FOR PROMOTING CHRISTIAN UNITY

CLARIFICATION ON THE GREEK AND LATIN TRADITIONS REGARDING THE PROCESSION OF THE HOLY SPIRIT

(13 September 1995)

Pope John Paul II, in a homily given in St Peter's Basilica on 29 June 1995, in the presence of the Ecumenical Patriarch Bartholomew I, asked that "the traditional doctrine of the Filioque, *present in the liturgical version of the Latin Credo [be clarified] in order to highlight its full harmony with what the Ecumenical Council of Constantinople of 381 confesses in its creed: the Father as the source of the whole Trinity, the one origin both of the Son and of the Holy Spirit". The Pontifical Council for Promoting Christian Unity prepared and published three months later such a clarification. The text is found in the* Osservatore Romano *for 13 September 1995.*

---

1. Cf. St. Thomas Aquinas. *Summa Theol.* Ia, qq. 37-38

339   The Father alone is the principle without principle of the two other persons of the Trinity, the sole source *(pègè)* of the Son and of the Holy Spirit. The Holy Spirit therefore takes his origin from the Father alone[...] in a principal, proper and immediate manner.[...] The doctrine of the *Filioque* must be understood and presented by the Catholic Church in such a way that it cannot appear to contradict the Monarchy of the Father nor the fact that he is the sole origin *(archè, aitia)* of the *ekporeusis* of the Spirit.

CHAPTER IV

HUMANKIND AND THE WORLD

Israel expressed its belief that the God of Abraham, Isaac and Jacob—the Saviour who had freed his chosen people from slavery—manifests his mercy and love through the vicissitudes of time, as the sole origin of all that there is. This God, whom they learned to identify by his mighty actions, is also the one who communicates himself in "deeds and words" (DV 2; cf. Gen 1) from the very origin of humankind and the beginning of time.

The Church, the new Israel, reinterprets this creation theology in the light of God's only begotten Son, made man. "As he chose us in" Jesus Christ "before the foundation of the world", God "has made known to us in all wisdom and insight the mystery of his will", "a plan for the fulness of time, to unite all things in him, things in heaven and things on earth" (Eph 1:4.9-10). Proclaiming the Father "Creator of heaven and earth", the early creeds attribute to him the work of creation. This same creation is also preordained towards "the first-born of all creation.[...] All things were created through him and for him" (Col 1:15f). The Father, therefore, brings about all things through, and in view of, his only-begotten Word; in the Spirit, he guides and spurs them on towards completion.

Acknowledging God as their creator, believers not only discern how he is at work in their very midst; they become aware of their own call to enter into communion with God as his unique representatives and direct collaborators on earth. Responsible stewards, they invest their energies and talents to manage their environment, that it may truly be according to God's own plan in Christ and, through the Spirit, to the glory of the Father.

In the course of history, many inevitably had to make the best of their own understanding of the universe—their cosmology—when they expressed their faith in God as the source and goal of all being. The Middle Ages reinterpreted the colourful, vivacious imagery of the Bible as an anthropocentric account of the universe itself. Since the 16th century, after new discoveries called into question that same imagery, *the Christian understanding of creation has to measure itself with many new and challenging insights about the macro- and the micro-cosmos.*

John Paul II calls on Christians to emulate what Israel did, at the time of the composition of the Genesis accounts: they must try to reformulate and reassert their faith in creation in contemporary culture, while taking into account and respecting scientific data. He looks at these countless new insights as opportunities to discern and encounter God's loving mercy in action.

At first sight, this might imply that the Church is reacting in a different way from when, during the first millennium of Christianity, it upheld the theology of creation against the dualism of the Manichaeans or the Cathars. These held some spiritual being other than God to be the creator; thus, they could sound an apocalyptic call against the forces of evil that they considered as obstacles to the creature's approach to God. Today, dualism is still to be reckoned with. Many continue to disjoin and separate material and spiritual processes, to uphold a form of scientific materialism or find refuge in forms of popular piety that tend to be poor imitations of Eastern religious traditions.

The Church has always avowed God's transcendence. Upholding creation 'out of nothing', it proclaims that God creates solely out of love and enjoys complete freedom of action. The universe cannot be some part of the divine (pantheism); nor can it ever bring itself into existence (emanation). Defining God as Creator, and nature as creation, the believer articulates the continual relationship between God and creature; God brings it into existence and sustains it all along. The Church's tradition refers to this foundational correlation as God's providence.

Though faith in creation centres on God's transcendence, it manifests also the sanctity and spiritual significance of God's work. From the 17th and 18th centuries, the Church continually insists on the sacredness of life as God's own gift and, since Vatican II, emphasizes the dignity of the human person as the source of inviolable rights and inalienable duties.

Tradition emphasizes the unity of the human being (body and soul) and the direct creation of each soul by God. The Church today proclaims "the noble destiny of man", champions "the godlike seed which has been sown in him" and fosters "that brotherhood of all human beings which corresponds to this dignity of theirs" (GS 3). From the very beginning, God wills every human to relate directly (immediately) to God and bring that relationship to completion in communion and solidarity. The Church today, more than ever, takes a stand against all kinds of theories that separate body and soul, and usher in division within individuals, and between nations and races.

The Second Vatican Council has restored to its rightful place the theology of humankind created in the "image of God". While Eastern Christianity has consistently interpreted the life of the faithful as a process of divinisation and sanctification, the West is rediscovering this long-lost patristic heritage and becoming more aware of its implications. The Church upholds also the specific autonomy of created realities as well as the exercise of personal responsibility towards society, the world at large, and the environment.

Ultimately, the first article of the creed calls for a theology of nature and work, culture and science, history and society. It constitutes the foundation of the very faith that credal formulations continue summing up in the articles that follow.

*   *   *

These are then the main doctrinal points contained in the following documents.

God

God created the whole world, spiritual and material: 5, 7, 12, 19 22, 39/1, 328, 331, 403f, 408f, 411/2, 412, 414f, 418, 440, 442, 627/1.

God created the world 'out of nothing': 19, 412, 440, 442;
   freely, and not from eternity: 19, 401/8, 406, 412, 418, 442;
   to manifest his goodness: 412, 440;
   for his glory: 418, 440, 441;
   to divinise creation: 440.

God guides the world through his providence: 402/9, 403, 411/2, 413, 627/1.

Creation

The world is distinct from God: 402/5, 406/27, 411/1, 416f.
It is a 'cosmos', not 'chaos': 434b, 442.
God reveals himself through creation (the 'book of nature'): 434c, 441.
All created things are good: 19, 402/7.11.13, (404), 408.
The created world has its own 'autonomy': 423.
The theories of evolution provide a new opportunity to rethink our faith: 419-420, 436-438, 516.

Science, philosophy and creation theology should stimulate and enrich each other: 176a-c, 184c, 430b, 434b, 437-439, 440-441.

In the dialogue between theology and science, one should avoid any form of unilateralism: 430b, 438.

Contemporary science calls us to emulate the sacred author's approach to understand God's word on all that exists: 176c.

The Human Person

The human being is created by God, in body and soul, as the crown of creation: 19, 39/1, 402/11-13, (404), 412, 421, 429, 435, 443;
  as God's image: 176c, 425, 431;
  with a unique dignity: (421i), 421, 425, 426, 431, 439;
  inviolable rights and inalienable duties: 426.

The human being is created free: 430.
  to enter into communion with God: 443;
  and live in solidarity with others: 438, 443.

The human soul is 'directly' created by God: 39/1, 402/5f, 406/27, 419.
  It does not pre-exist before conception: 401/1, 402/6.
  It is not begotten by the parents: 405, 407.
  It is individual and immortal: 410, 421.
  It is the 'form' of the body: 405, 410.

There is one human race: 420, 424.

Human beings are persons in society: 428, 435.

Equality of man and woman as persons: 431-432.

Woman's dignity essentially connected with love: 433.

Each human person is related to Christ and the Church: 427.

The human being is destined to rule over creation, in justice and holiness: 422;
  and collaborate with God through his work: 422, 423.

All racial ideologies contradict the biblical revelation: 434.

THE COUNCIL OF CONSTANTINOPLE

ANATHEMAS AGAINST THE ORIGENISTS (543)

Under patriarch Menas this provincial Council of Constantinople edited a series of canons against the Origenists which were later confirmed by Pope Vigilius. The doctrine condemned is not directly that of Origen, but of a group of monks of Jerusalem who exaggerated and proposed as firm doctrine what Origen had advanced as a hypothesis for theological thinking. Their doctrine is influenced by Platonist philosophy. Two canons refer to the doctrine of creation. Firstly, the theory according to which preexisting souls are inserted into bodies as a punishment for sin is condemned. As proposed by the Origenists the theory made use of a peculiar etymology of the word psuchè. This doctrine conceived the body as a degrading place of exile; besides, the idea of a sin committed before the union with the body dissolved the unity of the body and soul as constituents of one person. Here lies the main anthropological argument against the concept of the transmigration of souls. Secondly, the Origenists conceived the origin of the world as necessary; thus, they excluded the freedom of God's creative act. This opinion too is condemned.

401/1   If anyone says or thinks that human souls had a
403   previous existence viz., that first they were spirits or
blessed powers which, having become tired of the contemplation of God and turned to evil, grew cold *(apopsugeisas)* in the love of God, and for this reason came to be called souls *(psuchai)* and so were in punishment sent down into bodies, *anathema sit.*

401/8   If anyone says or holds that God's power is finite or
410   that he has created all that he could comprehend and
think, or that creatures are co-eternal with God, *anathema sit.*

THE COUNCIL OF BRAGA

ANATHEMAS AGAINST THE PRISCILLIANISTS (561)

Priscillian (d. 385) was the founder of a Manichaean sect in Spain. He taught that the devil was the evil principle and the creator of matter and of the human body, whereas the soul is divine by nature and tied to the body in punishment for previous sins. This teaching is borrowed from the Origenists. The canons of the Council of Braga, in Portugal, reject the radical dualism of matter and spirit and the contempt of the human body which it implies. All that exists is good because it is made by God.

402/5 If anyone believes that the human souls or the angels
455 come from the substance of God as Manes and Priscillian
have said, *anathema sit.*

402/6 If anyone says that the human souls first committed sin
456 in the heavenly abode and for this reason were thrown
down on earth into human bodies, as Priscillian has said,
anathema sit.

402/7 If anyone says that the devil was not first a good angel
458 created by God, or that his nature was not the work of
God, but that he emerged from darkness, and had no
creator but is himself the principle and substance of evil, as
Manes and Priscillian have said, *anathema sit.*

402/8 If anyone says that the devil made some of the creatures
458 in the world, and that he is by his own power the author
of thunder and lightning and storms and droughts, as
Priscillian has said, *anathema sit.*

402/9 If anyone believes that the human souls and bodies are
459 by their fate bound to the stars, as pagans and Priscillian
have said, *anathema sit.*

402/11 If anyone condemns human marriage and despises
461 (*perhorrescit*) the procreation of children, as Manes and
Priscillian have said, *anathema sit.*

402/12 If anyone says that the formation of the human body is
462 the work of the devil and that the conception of children
in their mothers' womb is brought about through the
activity of the devil, and for this reason does not believe in the
resurrection of the body, as Manes and Priscillian have said,
anathema sit.

402/13 If anyone says that the creation of all flesh is not the
463 work of God but of bad angels, as Manes and Priscillian
have said, *anathema sit.*

INNOCENT III

PROFESSION OF FAITH PRESCRIBED TO THE
WALDENSIANS (1208)

*The medieval followers of Manichaeism were known in France, from 1180
onwards, under the name of Albigensians. They taught that matter was evil,*

that the Old Testament came under the influence not of God but, of a demiurge or evil spirit. As to the dispensation of the New Testament, they denied the human body of Jesus Christ and rejected the sacraments as means of sanctification, while ascetical abstention from meat was considered by them as of high moral value. A similar teaching was held by the Waldensians in France, and the Lombards in Italy. These movements had a strong anti-clerical character and were directed against the display of worldliness and power in the Church.

The Creed prescribed by Innocent III for those returning from these movements to the doctrine of the Church contains the rejection of dualism in its various aspects: it insists on the creation of all things by God, who is the author of the Old Testament as well as of the New.

403
790
We believe with our heart and confess with our tongue that Father, Son, and Holy Spirit are one God.[...] creator, maker, ruler and provider of all things, corporeal and spiritual, visible and invisible. We believe that one and the same God is author of the Old and the New Testaments.

THE FOURTH LATERAN GENERAL COUNCIL
SYMBOL OF LATERAN (1215)

(404)   *This General Council held at the Lateran spoke the Church's final word against the Albigensian and Waldensian errors. Its teaching on creation was later adopted by the first Vatican Council (cf. nn. 412ff). The text is found in n. 19.*

THE GENERAL COUNCIL OF VIENNE (1311-1312)

This Council condemned the doctrine of John Olieu, O.F.M., who taught that the spiritual soul is not by itself the "form of the human body", i.e., the principle of organic life. Historically, this condemnation of Olieu, who in 1298 had died in peace with the Church, was an attempt to bring discredit on the so-called "Spirituals", namely on the radical Franciscans who had had Olieu as their leader. There is, however, a deeper meaning in the doctrine of the Council: the spiritualistic movements tended to separate the spirit from the realities of nature and history and so to split human nature into two heterogeneous spheres. The Council's doctrine affirming that the spiritual soul is by itself also the principle of organic life is a strong assertion of the unity of the person. It is in this sense that Olieu's teaching, which seems to be of merely philosophical interest, is said to go against the Catholic truth.

(The spiritual soul is the form of the body)

405
902
With the approval of the holy Council we reject as erroneous and contrary to the truth of the Catholic faith any doctrine or opinion which rashly asserts that

the substance of the rational and intellectual soul is not truly and of itself *(per se)* the form of the human body, or which calls this into doubt. In order that the truth of the pure faith may be known to all, and the path to error barred, we define that from now on whoever presumes to assert, defend, or obstinately hold that the rational and intellectual soul is not of itself and essentially the form of the human body, is to be censured as heretic.

JOHN XXII

ERRORS OF ECKHART ON THE RELATION BETWEEN GOD AND WORLD AND THE HUMAN BEING (1329)

Twenty-eight articles from Eckhart's sermons and writings were condemned after his death (1327). It is not clear whether he held these articles in the sense in which they are condemned by the Church. The condemnation, however, has doctrinal significance in so far as it brings out God's freedom in the work of creation.

The articles mentioned here, except 406/26, are condemned as "containing error or the blot of heresy, taken as they sound and according to the meaning of their words"; but article 406/26 is only condemned as "very offensive and rash and as suspect of heresy, even though with many supplementary explanations it can acquire or have a Catholic sense" (cf. DS 979).

[406/1]
951
Asked why God did not create the world sooner, he replied that God could not create the world sooner because nothing can act before it exists; therefore God created the world as soon as he existed.

[406/2]
952
Again, it can be granted that the world is from eternity.

[406/3]
953
Again, when God existed, and when he begot his Son, God co-eternal with himself and co-equal in all things, then at the same time and at once *(simul et semel)* he also created the world.

[406/26]
976
All creatures are one pure nothingness. I do not say that they are little or that they are anything, but that they are pure nothingness.

Objection was also raised against Eckhart that he preached two other articles with these words:

[406/27]   There is something in the soul that is uncreated and
977   cannot be created; this is the intellect. If the entire soul
               were such, it would be uncreated and could not be
created.

[406/28]   God is not good, nor better, nor best; whenever I call
978   God Good, I am equally wrong as if I were to call
               white black.

BENEDICT XII
LIBELLUS *CUM DUDUM* (1341)

Traducianism is the doctrine which teaches that not only the body but
also the soul is generated by the parents. It affords an easy explanation for the
inheritance of psychic qualities and defects, and, in theology, for the
transmission of original sin, one which is not, however, in keeping with the
Christian faith. Traducianism is unacceptable as it seems to exclude the
spirituality of the human soul. It was condemned by Pope Anastasius II (498)
(cf. DS 360). It is rejected again among various errors of the Armenians
condemned by Pope Benedict XII.

(Condemnation of Traducianism)

407   A teacher among the Armenians [...] again introduced
1007   the teaching that the human soul of a son is progagated
         from the soul of his father, as the body is from the body,
and that angels are also propagated one from another. He gave
as reason that, since the rational human soul and the intellectual
nature of angels are like spiritual lights, they propagate from
themselves other spiritual lights.

THE GENERAL COUNCIL OF FLORENCE
DECREE FOR THE COPTS (1442)

This decree (cf n. 322i) includes a statement on the Church's teaching on
creation, and a condemnation of Manichaean dualism.

408   [The Holy Roman Church] most firmly believes, professes
1333   and proclaims that the one true God, Father, Son, and
         Holy Spirit, is the creator of all things, visible and invisible,
who when he so willed, out of his bounty made all creatures,
spiritual as well as corporeal. They are good since they were made
by him who is the highest good, but they are mutable because they
were made out of nothing. She asserts that there is no such thing
as a nature of evil, because all nature, as nature, is good.

409   Furthermore, the Church condemns the error of the
1336   Manichaeans who asserted two first principles, one of
visible, the other of invisible things, and who said that
the God of the New Testament is different from the God of the
Old Testament.

THE FIFTH LATERAN GENERAL COUNCIL
BULL *APOSTOLICI REGIMINIS* (1513)

*Once more the oneness and individuality of the human person had to be
defended against Pietro Pomponazzi, Professor in Padua (1464-1525).
Influenced by Aristotelian philosophy, he taught that because of its ability to
grasp universal ideas, the spiritual soul of the human person is not an
individual entity but is common to all; in death it loses its individual identity
and merges with the universal spirit. The principle of organic life, on the
other hand, was understood by him to be bound up with matter and to perish
in death. The Council proclaims the unity, individuality and immortality of
the human soul, and thus re-asserts the oneness of the human nature,
comprising the intellectual and organic life.*

(The individuality and immortality of the soul)

410   The sower of cockle, the ancient enemy of the human
1440   race [...], has dared to sow and make grow in the Lord's
field some pernicious errors which at all times were
rejected by the faithful concerning in particular the nature of the
rational soul: viz., that it is mortal and one and the same in all
human beings. Some people, rash in their philosophising, assert
that this is true at least philosophically speaking. We therefore
wish to use the appropriate remedy against this error; and with
the approval of the Council we condemn and reprove all those
who assert that the intellectual soul is mortal or that it is one
and the same in all human persons, or who raise doubts in this
matter. The intellectual soul is not only truly, of itself and
essentially, the form of the human body, as it is stated in the
canon of Clement V, our pedecessor of blessed memory, issued
by the Council of Vienne *[cf. n. 405]*, but it is also immortal and,
according to the number of bodies in which it is infused, it can
be, has been and will be multiplied in individuals.

PIUS IX
SYLLABUS OF CONDEMNED ERRORS (1864)

On this syllabus, cf. n. 101i.

(Errors of Pantheism and Deism)

[411/1] There does not exist any supreme, all-wise, all-
2901   provident divine being *(numen)* distinct from this
universe of things; God is identical with the nature of
things, and therefore subject to change; God actually becomes
himself in the human being and in the world; all things are God
and have the very substance of God; God is one and the same
reality with the world, and so is spirit with matter, necessity
with liberty, truth with falsehood, good with evil and justice with
injustice.

[411/2] Any action of God on the human being and the world
2902   must be denied.

THE FIRST VATICAN GENERAL COUNCIL
THIRD SESSION

DOGMATIC CONSTITUTION *DEI FILIUS* ON THE
CATHOLIC FAITH (1870)

*The first Vatican Council expressed the Church's stand against the errors
of the 19th century. Among these figured in particular materialism according
to which only matter exists, and various forms of pantheism identifying in
one way or another the world with God. The Council states the doctrine of
creation and brings out its meaning. The first chapter on "God creator of all
things" is largely based on the text of the Fourth Lateran General Council (cf.
n. 19).*

Chapter I: God Creator of All Things

(Creation)

412 This one and only true God, of his own goodness and
3002   almighty power, not for the increase of his own
happiness, nor for the acquirement of his perfection, but
in order to manifest his perfection through the benefits which
he bestows on creatures, with absolute freedom of counsel, "from
the beginning of time made at once *(simul)* out of nothing both
orders of creatures, the spiritual and the corporeal, that is, the
angelic and the earthly, and then *(deinde)* the human creature,
who as it were shares in both orders, being composed of spirit
and body" [cf. n. 19].

(Providence)

413   By his providence God protects and governs all things
3003   which he has made, "reaching mightily from one end of
            the earth to the other, and ordering all things well" *[Wis
8:1]*. For "all are open and laid bare to his eyes" *[cf. Heb 4:13]*,
also those things which are yet to come to existence through the
free action of creatures.

Canons on Chapter I

414   1. If anyone denies the one true God Creator and Lord
3021   of things visible and invisible, *anathema sit.*

415   2. If anyone is not ashamed to assert that nothing exists
3022   besides matter, *anathema sit.*

416   3. If anyone says that the substance and essence of God
3023   and of all things is one and the same, *anathema sit.*

417   4. If anyone says that finite beings, the corporeal as well
3024   as the spiritual, or at least the spiritual ones, have
            emanated from the divine substance; or that the divine
essence becomes all things by self-manifestation or self-evolution;
or lastly that God is the universal or indefinite being which,
by self-determination, constitutes the universality of beings
differentiated into genera, species and individuals, *anathema sit.*

418   5. If anyone refuses to confess that the world and all
3025   things contained in it, the spiritual as well as the material,
            were in their whole substance produced by God out of
nothing; or says that God created not by an act of will free from
all necessity, but with the same necessity by which he necessarily
loves himself; or denies that the world was made for the glory
of God, *anathema sit.*

PIUS XII

ENCYCLICAL LETTER *HUMANI GENERIS* (1950)

*In the context of other errors, Pius XII treats two questions regarding
the origin of the human person. Firstly, the human being's origin through
evolution from other living beings: while formerly evolution was rejected
as irreconcilable with the biblical account of creation (which was interpreted
in too literal a sense), and as implying a materialistic conception of the
human being, the question is now left open to scholarly investigation,*

provided that the creation of the soul by God is maintained. Secondly, monogenism or polygenism, i.e., the question whethere the human race must be conceived as descending from a single couple or can be considered to originate from several couples: polygenism is rejected because "it does not appear" to be reconcilable with the doctrine of original sin inherited by all from Adam. Recent theology, however, is seeking explanations of original sin under the supposition of polygenism, and so tries to remove the reason for its rejection.

(The origin of man through evolution)

419   The teaching of the Church does not forbid that the
3896   doctrine of evolutionism, in so far as it inquires into the
          origin of the human body from already existing and
living matter, be, according to the present state of human disciplines and sacred theology, treated in research and discussion by experts on both sides; as to the souls, the Catholic faith requires us to hold that they are immediately created by God [...].

(Polygenism)

420   As regards the other conjecture, viz., what is called
3897   Polygenism, the sons of the Church do not at all have
          the same freedom. For the faithful cannot lend support
to a theory which involves either the existence on this earth, after Adam, of true human beings who would not originate from him, as the ancestor of all, by natural generation, or that 'Adam' stands for a plurality of ancestors. For, it is not at all apparent how such a view can be reconciled with the data which the sources of revealed truth and the documents of the Church propose concerning original sin, namely, that it originates from a sin truly committed by one Adam, is transmitted to all through generation and is in each, proper to each *[cf. Rom 5:12-19; nn. 508-511].*

THE SECOND VATICAN GENERAL COUNCIL

The Council took place at a time when in the world "according to the almost unanimous opinion of believers and unbelievers alike all things should be related to human beings as their centre and crown" (GS 12). Among the Council documents the Pastoral Constitution Gaudium et Spes on the Church in the modern world is the one most deeply centred on the question: "What is the human being?" (ibid), but the other documents are also strongly influenced by the concern for the human person.

In this broad anthropological outlook, the traditional doctrines about creation and human nature are taken for granted and re-asserted only in passing. The real concern of the Council is deeper. It consists in the Christian understanding of human existence, of the destiny and task of the human person in the world and beyond it.

The moral implications of the Conciliar doctrine are treated here in chapters XX and XXII. In this chapter doctrinal principles are enumerated.

Human beings, made of body and soul, are the crown of creation (GS 10,14). They are created in God's likeness (NA 5; AG 7; GS 12, 17, 29, 34), and, therefore, have a unique dignity (GS 12, 27, 40, 46, 63, 91; DH 1). This dignity is "known through the revealed word of God and by reason itself" (DH 2, 9). It is characteristic of modern persons to be deeply conscious of the human dignity (DH 1; GS 9, 27, 73).

All human beings are equal (GS 29; NA 5); man and woman are of equal dignity (GS 49). By nature the human being is social (GS 23, 24, 32); the human race has a common origin and shares in a common destiny (NA 1; AG 3).

Through work human persons extend their mastery over nature and better their life-conditions (GS 33-35)

Personal and social life unfolds in the life of the family (GS47-52), in culture (GS 53-62), in the socio-economic life (GS 25, 63-72), in the political life (GS 73-76), in the family of nations (GS 77-90).

PASTORAL CONSTITUTION *GAUDIUM ET SPES* (1965)

(The human being's nature, body and soul)

421 14. Though made up of body and soul, human beings are one. Through their bodily condition they gather into themselves the elements of the material world: through them these reach their crown and raise their voice freely to praise the Creator. Human beings, therefore, may not despise their bodily life; rather, they are bound to regard their very body, which was created by God and is to be raised again on the last day, as good and honourable [...].

Human beings are not mistaken when they regard themselves as superior to material things, and not a mere particle of nature or an anonymous element in human society. By their capacity for interior life, they outstrip the whole universe of things.[...] So, when they acknowledge in themselves a spiritual and immortal soul, they are not the plaything of a deceptive fantasy resulting only from their physical and social conditions; rather they are getting at the very depth of reality.

(The value of human activity)

422 34. Considered in itself, human activity, individual and collective—all that tremendous effort which people have made throughout the centuries to better their living conditions—is in keeping with God's design. Human beings, created in God's image, were given the mandate to subject the earth and all it contains, and to rule the world in justice and holiness; acknowledging God as the creator of all things, they were to refer to him their own person and all creation; and thus, by the subjection of all things to them, the name of God would be wonderful in all the earth.

(The rightful autonomy of the temporal order)

423 36. [...] If by the autonomy of earthly realities we understand that created things and societies have their own laws and values which the human person must gradually come to know, use and organise, then it is not only requested by people of our day but is also in concordance with the will of the Creator. It is by virtue of their very creation that all things are provided with a stability, truth and goodness of their own, with their own laws and order. People must respect all this, while acknowledging the methods proper to each science or art. Consequently, if methodical research in any branch of learning is carried out in a truly scientific manner, and in keeping with the norms of morality, it will never really conflict with the faith, because both secular things and the realities of faith derive from the same God [...].

But if by the phrase 'autonomy of temporal affairs' one means to say that created things do not depend on God, and that the human person can make use of them without any reference to the Creator, then anyone who believes in the existence of God will sense the falsehood of such opinions. For a creature without a creator vanishes into nothingness.[...] Indeed, forgetfulness of God makes the creature itself unintelligible.

DECLARATION *NOSTRA AETATE* (1965)

(The unity of the human race)

424 1. All peoples form a single community; their origin is one, for God made the whole human race to dwell over the entire face of the earth [cf. Acts 17:26]. One also is their final goal, God. His providence, the manifestations of his goodness, his plan of salvation extend to all human beings [cf. Wis 8:1; Acts 14:17; Rom 2:6f; 1 Tim 2:4], until the moment when the elect will be gathered in the Holy City whose light shall be the glory of God, when the nations will walk in his light [cf. Rev 21: 23f].

JOHN PAUL II

ADDRESS TO THE THIRD GENERAL ASSEMBLY OF

LATIN AMERICAN BISHOPS

(Puebla, 28 January 1979)

Inaugurating the Third General Assembly of the Latin American Bishops on the theme "The Present and the Future of Evangelisation in Latin America", Pope John Paul II reminded the bishops of their pastoral mission. In this context he exposed the "truth concerning the human person". The text of the address is found in AAS 71(1979) 187-205.

(The human person in God's image)

425   1. (9) Thanks to the Gospel, the Church has the truth about the human person. This truth is found in an anthropology that the Church never ceases to fathom more thoroughly and to communicate to others. The primordial affirmation of this anthropology is that the human person is God's image and cannot be reduced to a mere portion of nature or a nameless element in the human city [cf. n. 421 and GS 12]. This is the meaning of what St. Irenaeus wrote: "The human person's glory is God, but the recipient of God's every action, of his wisdom and of his power is the human person.[...]."[1]

(Basic rights)

426   3. (1) This dignity [of the human being] is infringed on the individual level when due regard is not had for values such as freedom, the right to profess one's religion, physical and mental integrity, the right to essential goods, to life.[...] It is infringed on the social and political level when one cannot exercise one's right of participation, or when one is subjected to

---

1. *Adv. Haer.*, III. 20.203

unjust and unlawful coercion, or submitted to physical or mental torture, etc.[...]

3: (5) In the face of what has been said hitherto, the Church sees with deep sorrow "the sometimes massive increase of human rights violations in many parts of the world.[...] Who can deny that today individual persons and civil powers violate basic rights of the human person with impunity: rights such as the right to be born, the right to life, the right to responsible procreation, to work, to peace, to freedom and social justice, the right to participate in the decisions that affect people and nations? And what can be said when we face the various forms of collective violence like discrimination against individuals and groups, the use of physical and psychological torture perpetrated against prisoners or political dissenters? The list grows when we turn to the instances of the abduction of persons for political reasons and look at the acts of kidnapping for material gain which attack so dramatically family life and the social fabric."[1] We cry once more: Respect the human persons! They are the image of God! Evangelise, so that this may become a reality, so that the Lord may transform hearts and humanise the political and economic systems with the human person's responsible commitment as the starting point.

ENCYCLICAL LETTER *REDEMPTOR HOMINIS* (1979)

The whole Encyclical Letter can be considered as a meditation on the Biblical understanding of the human person as the object of God's love and redemption in Jesus Christ, in the context of the present day world. The text is found in AAS 71 (1979) 257ff.

(Each concrete person is related to Christ and the Church)

427 13. What is in question here is the human person in all its truth and full stature. We are not dealing with an abstract human being, but the real, concrete, historical person. We are dealing with each one, for each one is included in the mystery of the Redemption and with each one Christ has united himself forever through this mystery. Every person comes into the world through being conceived in a mother's womb and being born of

---

1. Message of JOHN PAUL II to the Secretary General of the United Nations Organization on 2 December 1978 (*AAS* 71 (1979) 122).

a mother, and precisely on account of the mystery of the Redemption is entrusted to the solicitude of the Church. Her solicitude is about the whole person and is focussed on the person in an altogether special manner.

The object of her care is the human being in its unique, unrepeatable, real existence, which keeps intact the image and likeness of God himself [cf. Gen 1:26]. The Council points out this fact when, speaking of that likeness, it recalls that "the human being is the only creature on earth that God willed for itself" [GS 24]. Human being as "willed" by God, as "chosen" by him from eternity and called, destined for grace and glory— this is each person, the most *concrete* human being, the most *real*; this is, in all the fulness of the mystery in which one has become a sharer in Jesus Christ, the mystery in which each one of the four thousand million human beings living on our planet has become a sharer from the moment of one's conception beneath the heart of one's mother.

(Personal and social aspects of the human person)

428 14. The Church cannot abandon human beings, for their "destiny", that is to say, their election, calling, birth and death, salvation or perdition, is so closely and unbreakably linked with Christ. We are speaking precisely of each person on this planet, this earth that the Creator gave to the first parents, saying to man and woman: "Subdue it and have dominion" [Gen 1:28]; of each person in all the unrepeatable reality of what one is and one does, of intellect and will, conscience and heart. Human beings in their singular reality, because they are "persons", have a history of their life that is their own, and, most important, a history of their soul. In keeping with the openness of their spirit and also with the many diverse needs of their body and their existence in time, they write this personal history of theirs through numerous bonds, contacts, situations, and social structures that link them with others, beginning to do so from the first moment of their existence on earth, from the moment of conception and birth. Each one in the full truth of existence, of one's personal being, one's community and social being—in the sphere of one's own family, in the sphere of society and very diverse contexts, in the sphere of one's own nation or people (perhaps still only that of one's clan or tribe), and in the sphere of whole humankind—this person is the primary route that the Church must travel in fulfilling her mission: the person is the primary and fundamental way for the Church, the way traced out by Christ himself, the way that leads invariably through the mystery of the Incarnation and the Redemption.

It was precisely this person in the full truth of one's life, with one's conscience, one's continual inclination to sin and at the same time continual aspiration to truth, goodness, beauty, justice and love, that the Second Vatican Council had before its eyes, when, in outlining our situation in the modern world, it drew from the external elements and causes of this situation the immanent truth of humanity [cf. GS 10].

(People superior to their possessions)

429 16. The essential meaning of this "kingship" and "dominion" of people over the visible world, which the Creator himself gave them for their task, consists in the priority of ethics over technology, in the primacy of the person over things, and in the superiority of spirit over matter. This is why all phases of present day progress must be watched attentively. Each stage of that progress must, so to speak, be x-rayed from this point of view. What is in question is the advancement of persons, not just the multiplying of things that people can use. It is a matter—as a contemporary philosopher has said and as the Council has stated—not so much of "having more" as of "being more"[cf. nn. 2059, 2145].[...] Human beings cannot relinquish themselves or the place in the visible world that belongs to them; they cannot become the slaves of things, the slaves of economic systems, the slaves of their own products.

(Freedom)

430 21. Mature humanity means full use of the gift of freedom received from the Creator when he called to existence the human person made "in his image, after his likeness".[...] Nowadays it is sometimes held, though wrongly, that freedom is an end in itself, that each human being is free when one makes use of freedom as one wishes, and that this must be our aim in the lives of individuals and societies. In reality, freedom is a great gift only when we know how to use it consciously for everything that is our true good. Christ teaches us that the best use of freedom is charity, which takes concrete form in self-giving and in service. For this "freedom Christ has set us free" [Gal 5:1; cf. 5:13] and ever continues to set us free. The Church draws from this source the unceasing inspiration, the call and the drive for her mission and her service among all humankind. The full truth about human freedom is indelibly inscribed on the mystery of the Redemption.

LETTER TO THE DIRECTOR
OF THE VATICAN OBSERVATORY
(1 June 1988)

In his letter on the relationship between the natural sciences, philosophy and theology (cf. n. 176i), the Pope specifies the relationship between the sciences and the theology of creation. The text that follows continues on n. 176 above. John Paul clearly enumerates both the dangers to be avoided and the objects such a dialogue should aim at: mutual enrichment and the service of concrete humanity ("who we are and who we are becoming"). These indications prove to be good guidelines for any anthropological reflection. See nn. 176a-c.

(Dialogue between the Church and the scientific communities)

430b   What is important, as we have already stressed, is that the dialogue [between the church and the scientific communities] should continue and grow in depth and scope. In the process we must overcome every regressive tendency to a unilateral reductionism, to fear, and to self-imposed isolation. What is critically important is that each discipline should continue to enrich, nourish and challenge the other to be more fully what it can be and to contribute to our vision of who we are and who we are becoming.

APOSTOLIC LETTER *MULIERIS DIGNITATEM*
(15 August 1988)

This apostolic letter, written on the occasion of the Marian Year is devoted to the Dignity and Vocation of Woman. The "essential horizon", says the Pope, for a "reflection on the dignity and vocation of woman", is the mystery of the "woman-Mother of God" (5) (cf. n.723). Christian anthropology is based on the biblical doctrine of man's and woman's creation in the image and likeness of God (6). A part of the letter is devoted to the theme of the "great mystery" of the union of Christ with the Church. It goes on to explain the close bond between the dignity of woman and the order of love. The text is found in AAS 80 (1988) 1653-1729.

(Man and woman created in God's image and likeness)

431   6. [...] The revealed truth concerning the human person as "the image and likeness" of God constitutes the immutable basis of all Christian anthropology. "God created humanity in his own image, in the image of God he created it; male and female he created them" *[Gen 1:27]*. This concise passage contains the fundamental anthropological truths: The human being is the highpoint of the whole order of creation in the visible world; the human race, which takes its origin from the calling into existence of man and woman, crowns the whole work of creation; both man and woman are human beings to an equal degree, both are created in God's image. This image and likeness of God, which is essential for the human being, is passed on by the man and woman, as spouses and parents, to their descendants: "Be fruitful and multiply, and fill the earth and subdue it" *[Gen 1:28]*. The creator entrusts dominion over the earth to the human race, to all persons, to all men and women, who derive their dignity and vocation from their common "beginning".

(Equality of man and woman as persons)

432 6. The biblical text provides sufficient bases for recognizing the essential equality of man and woman from the point of view of their humanity. From the very beginning, both are persons, unlike the other living beings in the world about them. The woman is another "I" in a common humanity. From the very beginning they appear as a "unity of the two", and this signifies that the original solitude is overcome, the solitude in which man does not find "a helper fit for him" *[Gen 2:20]*. Is it only a question here of a "helper" in activity, in "subduing the earth" *[cf. Gen 1:28]*? Certainly it is a matter of life's companion with whom, as a wife, the man can unite himself, becoming with her "one flesh" and for this reason leaving "his father and his mother" *[cf. Gen 2:24]*. Thus in the same context as the creation of man and woman, the biblical account speaks of God instituting marriage as an indispensable condition for the transmission of life to new generations, the transmission of life to which marriage and conjugal love are by their nature ordered: "Be fruitful and multiply, and fill the earth and subdue it" *[Gen 1:18]*.

(Woman's dignity intimately connected with love]

433 30. A woman's dignity is closely connected with the love which she receives by the very reason of her feminity; it is likewise connected with the love which she gives in return. The truth about the person and about love is thus confirmed. With regard to the truth about the person, we must turn again to the Second Vatican Council: "The human person, who is the only creature on earth that God willed for its own sake, cannot fully find itself except through a sincere gift of self" [GS 24]. This applies to every human being as a person created in God's image, whether man or woman. This ontological affirmation also indicates the ethical dimension of a person's vocation. Woman can only find herself by giving love to others.

PONTIFICAL COMMISSION *JUSTITIA ET PAX*
THE CHURCH AND RACISM: TOWARDS A MORE
FRATERNAL SOCIETY (3 November 1988)

This is the first Vatican document dealing solely with racism. It condemns the various forms which racism has taken in the past or are current even today. It suggests the application of the "principle of the equal dignity of persons" to overcome racism. In Christian doctrine, this equal dignity is based on the revealed message of the creation of all human persons in God's image and likeness, with the same nature and origin, the same calling and destiny in Jesus Christ. This doctrine, often affirmed by the Magisterium (cf. v.g. GS 29), is here developed with vigour. The text is found in Origins 23 February, 1989, pp. 613-626.

(All racist ideologies contradict the biblical revelation)

434   19. According to biblical revelation, God created the human being—man and woman—in his image and likeness [cf. Gen 1:26-27; 5:1-2;,9:6]. This bond between the human person and the Creator provides the basis of his or her dignity and fundamental inalienable rights of which God is the guarantor. To these personal rights obviously correspond duties towards others. Neither the individual nor society, the state or any human institution can reduce a person or a group of persons to the status of an object.

The belief that God is at the origin of humankind transcends, unifies and gives meaning to all the partial observations that science can amass about the process of evolution and the development of societies. It is the most radical affirmation of the equal dignity of all persons in God. With this concept, a person eludes all those manipulations of human powers and of ideological propaganda which seek to justify the servitude of the weakest. Faith in the one God, creator and redeemer of all humankind, made in his image and likeness, constitutes the absolute and inescapable negation of any racist ideologies. It is still necessary to draw out all the consequences of this: "We cannot truly pray to God the Father of all if we treat any people in other than brotherly/sisterly fashion, for all human persons are created in God's image"[NA 5].

ADDRESS TO THE PONTIFICAL ACADEMY OF SCIENCES
(31 October 1992)

The covering note to n. 184a explains the context of the present document. From his previous analysis of the relationship between faith and science (cf. nn. 184 a-c), John Paul II draws the conclusions necessary to an understanding of humanity's development that leads to one's full realization "as a spiritual being and as homo sapiens". *At the same time, he invites one and all to look at nature in the light of God's own Logos ("Thought") and see that it truly becomes what God wants: a well-ordered* cosmos. *The complete text is in* Origins 22 *(1992-93), pp. 369-375.*

(Science and faith: two modes of development and growth)

434b 14. Humanity has before it two modes of development.
The first involves culture, scientific research and technology, that is to say whatever falls within the horizontal aspect of the human being and creation which is growing at an impressive rate. In order that this progress should not remain completely external to the human person, it presupposes a simultaneous raising of conscience, as well as its actuation. The second mode of development involves what is deepest in the human being, when transcending the world and transcending self, the human person turns to the One who is the Creator of all. It is only this vertical direction which can give full meaning to people's being and action, because it situates them in relation to their origin and end. In this twofold direction, horizontal and vertical, the human person realizes oneself fully as a spiritual being and as *homo sapiens*. But we see that development is not uniform and linear, and that progress is not always well ordered. This reveals the disorder which affects the human condition. The scientist who is conscious of this twofold development and takes it into account contributes to the restoration of harmony.

Those who engage in scientific and technological research admit as the premise of its progress, that the world is not a chaos but a "cosmos"—that is to say, that there exist order and natural laws which can be grasped and examined, and which, for this reason, have a certain affinity with the spirit. Einstein used to say: "What is eternally incomprehensible in the world is that it is comprehensible" [*The Journal of the Franklin Institute*, vol. 221, n. 3, March 1936]. This intelligibility, attested to by the marvellous discoveries of science and technology, leads us, in the last analysis, to that transcendent and primordial Thought imprinted on all things.

CATECHISM OF THE CATHOLIC CHURCH
(7 December 1992)

The Catechism of the Catholic Church *dedicates a long section to the themes of the present chapter (cf. CCC, 279-384). The Catechism's introduction to the human being as 'person' and to the world as God's own 'creation' can convey an adequate overview of the main themes that are developed more extensively in the paragraphs mentioned above. The fundamental dependence of the world, God's creation, and of humanity itself on the Creator indicates the immediacy of access in both directions: God needs no mediation whatsoever to reach out to his creatures, while the latter continue to depend on him, even when they decide they can do without him. God is the sole guarantor of the creature's meaning and claim on beauty and goodness, truth and love (the ways towards authentic transcendence and ultimate purpose).*

(Ways of coming to know God)

434c   31. Created in God's image and called to know and love him, the person who seeks God discovers certain ways of coming to know him. These are also called proofs for the existence of God, not in the sense of proofs in the natural sciences, but rather in the sense of "converging and convincing arguments", which allow us to attain certainty about the truth.

These "ways" of approaching God from creation have a twofold point of departure: the physical world, and the human person.

32. The *world*: starting from movement, becoming, contingency, and the world's order and beauty, one can come to a knowledge of God as the origin and the end of the universe.

As St. Paul says of the Gentiles: "For what can be known about God is plain to them, because God has shown it to them. Ever since the creation of the world his invisible nature, namely, his eternal power and deity, has been clearly perceived in the things that have been made" [*Rom* 1:19-20].

And St. Augustine issues this challenge: "Question the beauty of the earth, question the beauty of the sea, question the beauty of the air distending and diffusing itself, question the beauty of the sky, ... question all these realities. All respond: See, we are beautiful. Their beauty is a profession *[confessio]*. These beauties are subject to change. Who made them if not the Beautiful One *[Pulcher]* who is not subject to change?" [Augustine, *Sermones*, 241, 2: *PL* 38, 1134].

33. The *human person*: with one's openness to truth and beauty, one's sense of moral goodness, one's freedom and the voice of one's conscience, with one's longings for the infinite and for happiness, the individual questions oneself about God's existence. In all this the person discerns signs of one's own spiritual soul. The soul, the "seed of eternity we bear in ourselves, irreducible to the merely material" *[GS 18; cf. 14]*, can have its origin only in God.

34. The world, and humankind, attest that they contain within themselves neither their first principle nor their final end, but rather that they participate in Being itself, which alone is without origin or end. Thus, in different ways, the person can come to know that there exists a reality which is the first cause and final end of all things, a reality "that everyone calls God" [Thomas Aquinas, *Summa Theologiae* I, 2, 3].

JOHN PAUL II
ENCYCLICAL LETTER *VERITATIS SPLENDOR*
(6 August 1993)

The main concern of the Encyclical is the Church's moral teaching. However, some passages dealing with Christian anthropology further develop ideas previously proposed by the teaching authority. The text quoted here deepens the meaning and dignity of the human being as person. The text is found in AAS 85 (1993) 1133-1228.

(Dignity of the human person)

435 48. The spiritual and immortal soul is the principle of unity of the human being, whereby the human being exists as a whole [...], as a person. Such definitions not only point out that the body, which has been promised the resurrection, will also share in glory. They also remind us that reason and free will are linked with all the bodily and sense faculties. The person, including the body, is completely entrusted to oneself, and it is in the unity of body and soul that the person is the subject of one's own moral acts [...]. And since the human person cannot be reduced to a freedom which is self-designing, but entails a particular spiritual and bodily structure, that primordial moral requirement of loving and respecting the human person which is always an end and never a mere means also implies, by its very nature, respect for certain fundamental goods, without which one would fall into relativism and arbitrariness.

ADDRESS TO THE PONTIFICAL ACADEMY OF SCIENCES
(22 October 1996)

In 1936, Pius XI reconstituted the Pontifical Academy of Sciences as a "senatus scientificus at the service of truth". On the 60th anniversary of the Academy, John Paul II addresses the relationship between creation and science, evolution and faith. He recalls the theologian's vocation to delve deeper into his understanding of the faith and summarises the Church's stand on evolution. Reappraising Pius XII's contribution on the subject (cf. n. 419), he states that we need to look positively at the "several theories of evolution" while resisting any attempt to reduce the human individual to "a pure means or a pure instrument", a "mere epiphenomenon" subject to the species or to society. Quoting Thomas Aquinas, Pius XII and Vatican II, the Pope declares that the human's dignity as 'person' places him or her in a direct, immediate relationship with God. Everything else achieves its completion within the mystery of Christ, in and through which the person understands and implements the splendour of God's call to communion with him.

L' Osservatore Romano amended the official English translation it first published; the text that follows is taken from the second version and can be found in full in Origins 26 *(1996), pp. 414-416.*

(No opposition between evolution and faith)

436   3. In his encyclical *Humani Generis* (1950), my predecessor Pius XII had already stated that there was no opposition between evolution and the doctrine of the faith about man and his vocation, on condition that one did not lose sight of several indisputable points [cf. *AAS* 42 (1950), pp. 575-576].

For my part, when I received those taking part in your academy's plenary assembly on 31 October 1992, I had the opportunity, with regard to Galileo, to draw attention to the need of a rigorous hermeneutic for the correct interpretation of the inspired word. It is necessary to determine the proper sense of Scripture while avoiding any unwarranted interpretations that make it say what it does not intend to say. In order to delineate the field of their own study, the exegete and the theologian must keep informed about the results achieved by the natural sciences [cf. *AAS* 85 (1993), pp. 764-772: address to the Pontifical Biblical Commission, 23 April 1993, announcing the document on *The Interpretation of the Bible in the Church: AAS* 86 (1994), pp. 232-243].

(Several theories of evolution and their implications)

437   4. Taking into account the state of scientific research at the time as well as of the requirements of theology, the encyclical *Humani Generis* considered the doctrine of 'evolutionism' a serious hypothesis, worthy of investigation and in-depth study equal to that of the opposite hypothesis. Pius XII added two methodological conditions: that this opinion should not be adopted as though it were a certain, proven doctrine as though one could totally prescind from revelation with regard to the questions it raises. He also spelled out the condition on which this opinion would be compatible with the Christian faith, a point to which I will return.

Today, nearly half a century after the appearance of that encyclical, new knowledge leads us to the recognition of the theory of evolution as more than a hypothesis. It is indeed remarkable that this theory has been progressively accepted by researchers, following a series of discoveries in various fields of knowledge. The convergence, neither sought nor provoked, of the results of work that was conducted independently is in itself a significant argument in favour of this theory.

What is the significance of such a theory? To address this question is to enter the field of epistemology. A theory is a metascientific elaboration, distinct from the results of observation but consistent with them. By means of it a series of independent data and facts can be related and interpreted in a unified explanation. A theory's validity depends on whether or not it can be verified; it is constantly tested against the facts; whenever it can no longer explain the latter, it shows its limitations and unsuitability. It must then be rethought.

Furthermore, while the formulation of a theory like that of evolution complies with the need for consistency with the observed data, it borrows certain notions from natural philosophy.

And to tell the truth, rather than *the* theory of evolution, we should speak of *several* theories of evolution. On the one hand, this plurality has to do with the different explanations advanced for the mechanism of evolution, and on the other, with the various philosophies on which it is based. Hence the existence of materialist, reductionist, and spiritualist interpretations. What is to be decided here is the true role of philosophy and, beyond it, of theology.

(The Magisterium and evolution)

438   5. The church's magisterium is directly concerned with the question of evolution, for it involves the conception of the human person: Revelation teaches us that each person was created in the image and likeness of God *[cf. Gen 1:27-29]*. The conciliar constitution *Gaudium et Spes* has magnificently explained this doctrine, which is pivotal to Christian thought. It recalled that the human person is 'the only creature on earth that God wanted for its own sake' *[GS 24]*.

In other terms, the human individual cannot be subordinated as a pure means or a pure instrument, either to the species or to society; one has value per se. One is a person. With one's intellect and one's will, one is capable of forming a relationship of communion, solidarity, and self-giving with one's peers.

St. Thomas observes that the individual's likeness to God resides especially in one's speculative intellect; for the person's relationship with the object of one's knowledge resembles God's relationship with what he has created [*Summa Theologiae*, I-II, q. 3, a. 5, ad 1]. But even more, the person is called to enter into a relationship of knowledge and love with God himself, a relationship which will find its complete fulfilment beyond time, in eternity.

All the depth and grandeur of this vocation are revealed to us in the mystery of the risen Christ *[cf. GS 22]*. It is by virtue of one's spiritual soul that the whole person possesses such a dignity even in one's body. Pius XII stressed this essential point: If the human body takes its origin from pre-existent living matter, the spiritual soul is immediately created by God ['*animas enim a Deo immediate creari catholica fides nos retinere iubet*': encyclical *Humani Generis, AAS* 42 (1950), p. 575].

Consequently, theories of evolution which, in accordance with the philosophies inspiring them, consider the spirit as emerging from the forces of living matter or as a mere epiphenomenon of this matter are incompatible with the truth about the human individual. Nor are they able to ground the dignity of the person.

(Humankind and nature: an ontological difference)

439 6. With the human individual, then, we find ourselves in the presence of an ontological difference, an ontological leap, one could say. However, does not the posing of such ontological discontinuity run counter to that physical continuity which seems to be the main thread of research into evolution in the field of physics and chemistry? Consideration of the method used in the various branches of knowledge makes it possible to reconcile two points of view which would seem irreconcilable.

The sciences of observation describe and measure the multiple manifestations of life with increasing precision and correlate them with the time line. The moment of transition to the spiritual cannot be the object of this kind of observation, which nevertheless can discover at the experimental level a series of very valuable signs indicating what is specific to the human being. But the experience of metaphysical knowledge, of self-awareness and self-reflection, of moral conscience, freedom, or again, of aesthetic and religious experience, falls within the competence of philosophical analysis and reflection, while theology brings out its ultimate meaning according to the Creator's plans.

APOSTOLIC LETTER *DIES DOMINI*
(31 May 1998)

The need to revitalise the meaning of Sunday practice and the approaching millennium that would demand a restating of what the day of the Lord really stands for provide the occasion for the publication of this Apostolic Letter. The theology of the Sunday observance provides a mini-compendium of many theological themes that converge into the Church's understanding of its weekly encounter with the risen Lord. Sunday, the first day of the week, recalls the first day when God created all that there is. The Pope revisits the Genesis account to clarify the basic datum that life is fundamentally good and exists as a response to God's creative will. Life, therefore, should comprehend itself as a continuous thanksgiving and glorify its Creator. The text is in Origins *28 (1998), pp. 133-151.*

(Genesis, a story of intense religious significance)

440   9. The poetic style of the Genesis story conveys well the awe which people feel before the immensity of creation and the resulting sense of adoration of the One who brought all things into being from nothing. It is a story of intense religious significance, a hymn to the Creator of the universe, pointing to him as the only Lord in the face of recurring temptations to divinize the world itself. At the same time, it is a hymn to the goodness of creation, all fashioned by the mighty and merciful hand of God.[...]

ENCYCLICAL LETTER *FIDES ET RATIO* (1998)
(14 September 1998)

In what can surely be considered one of his major encyclicals (dated September 14, 1998), John Paul II tries to address the issue of the contemplation of the truth humankind receives from God who places in each heart a yearning and calls each person to its attainment. "Faith and reason are", in the Pope's words, "like two wings on which the human spirit rises to the contemplation of truth" that allow the latter to achieve the full truth about one's own self (Introduction). The contemplation of nature as creation becomes the first, fundamental instance of revelation: the foremost encounter between God and humankind. In line with Paul's speech to the Athenians ("In him we live and move and have our being": cf. Acts 17:24-28) and the tradition of the Church (cf. nn. 7, 39/1-2, 113, 131, 132), the Pope reclaims the so-called "books of nature" as a sure way to God and a "first stage" of revelation. The full text of the encyclical is in Origins *28 (1998), pp. 317-347.*

(The 'Book of Nature')

441   19. The Book of Wisdom contains several important texts which cast further light on this theme. There the sacred author speaks of God who reveals himself in nature. For the ancients, the study of the natural sciences coincided in large part with philosophical learning. Having affirmed that with their intelligence human beings can "know the structure of the world and the activity of the elements[...] the cycles of the year and the constellations of the stars, the natures of animals and the tempers of wild beasts" [*Wis* 7:17.19-20]—in a word, that he can philosophize—the sacred text takes a significant step forward. Making his own the thought of Greek philosophy, to which he seems to refer in the context, the author affirms that, in reasoning about nature, the human being can rise to God:

"From the greatness and beauty of created things comes a corresponding perception of their Creator" [*Wis 13:5*]. This is to recognize as a first stage of divine Revelation the marvellous "book of nature", which, when read with the proper tools of human reason, can lead to knowledge of the Creator. If human beings with their intelligence fail to recognize God as Creator of all, it is not because they lack the means to do so, but because their free will and their sinfulness place an impediment in the way.

ADDRESS TO THE PONTIFICAL ACADEMY OF SCIENCES
(27 October 1998)

At its annual meeting, the Pontifical Academy of Sciences took up the modern concepts of nature. In his address, the Pope returned to one of the major themes of his pontificate: the unique status and dignity of human nature within the order created by God. The believer, in line with the Church's tradition, looks at creation as God's work, at the course of time that recognizes in God its source and goal, and at his or her own self called to live as God's image and attain perfection in Christ. The text is in Osservatore Romano *(English Edition), 4 November 1998, p. 2.*

(Nature as God's 'creation')

442 4. In Catholic philosophy and theology and in the Magisterium, the concept of nature has an importance which it would be good to point out. First of all, it calls to mind the reality of God in his very essence, thus expressing the divine unity of "the holy and ineffable Trinity, Father, Son and Holy Spirit, [who] is one God by nature, of one substance, of one nature, and of one majesty and power" [*11th Council of Toledo, n. 308*]. The same term also explains creation, the visible world which owes its existence to God and is rooted in the creative act by which "the world began when God's word drew it out of nothingness" [*CCC, n. 338*]. According to the divine plan, creation finds its purpose in the glorification of its maker [*cf. LG 36*]. Thus we see that this concept also expresses the meaning of history, which comes from God and advances towards its end, the return of all created things to God; therefore history cannot be understood as cyclical, for the Creator is also the God of salvation history. "It is the one and the same God who establishes and guarantees the intelligibility and reasonableness of the natural order of things upon which scientists confidently depend,

and who reveals himself as the Father of our Lord Jesus Christ"
[*FR 34*].

Through reason and the various intellectual operations
belonging to the nature of the individual as such [cf. Thomas
Aquinas, *Summa Theologiae*, I-II, q. 71, a. 2], everyone "by [one's]
nature can discover the Creator" [*FR 8*] from contemplating the
work of creation, for the Creator makes himself known through
the greatness of his work. Its beauty and the interdependence of
created realities spur scientists to admire and respect creation's
own principles. 'Nature, philosophy's proper concern, can
contribute to the understanding of divine Revelation' [*FR 43*].
This rational knowledge does not, however, exclude another form
of knowledge, that of faith, based on revealed truth and on the
fact that the Lord communicates himself to humanity.

(The human person, the summit of creation)

443   5. The concept of nature acquires a particular meaning
when applied to the person, the summit of creation. The
only being on earth that God willed for one's own sake has a
dignity stemming from one's spiritual nature which bears the
mark of the Creator, for each person was created in his image
and likeness [*cf. Gen 1:26*] and endowed with the highest faculties
a creature can possess: reason and will. These make one capable
of free self-determination and enable one to communicate with
God, to answer his call and to fulfil oneself in accordance with
one's own nature. In fact, because one has a spiritual nature,
one can receive supernatural realities and attain the eternal
happiness freely offered by God. This communication is made
possible because God and the human person are both spiritual
beings. This is what Gregory of Nazianzus meant when he spoke
of the Lord having assumed our human nature: "Christ heals
like by like" [*Oratio 28, 13*]. In the view of this Cappadocian
Father, the metaphysical and ontological approach enables us to
learn the mystery of the Incarnation and Redemption, by which
Jesus, true God and true man, took on human nature [cf. *GS 22*].
Speaking of human nature also reminds us that there is a unity
and solidarity belonging to the whole human race. For this
reason, the individual is to be considered "in the full truth of
one's existence, of one's personal being and also of one's
community and social being" [*RH 14*].

CHAPTER V

ORIGINAL JUSTICE AND FALL

"Why evil? And where does it come from?" The ominous presence of evil has always troubled consciences and questioned the very meaning of existence. At times, the existence of a merciful God is put in doubt, together with the goodness of creation, and the capacity of a human being to decide and shape one's own being. Divine providence and love seems to be a sheer travesty of itself: cynical aloofness or radical impotence on God's part.

The whole biblical tradition presents God as abhorring evil and going out of his way to rescue humanity from its tentacles. The first account of creation presents God as the saviour of all that exists from amorphous darkness. Genesis shows how the Creator presents humanity with a well-ordered environment and demands that everyone give his or her contribution to the well-being of the whole. The Bible thus extricates 'evil' from the sphere of being and situates it squarely in the sphere of doing. According to Revelation, humanity responds to God's original gifts of holiness and justice by choosing to disobey him (cf. n. 508).

While the doctrine of creation illustrates what life within this world should be according to God's plan, the biblical account of the fall constitutes the interpretative key of evil, *"the mystery of lawlessness... at work"* (2 Thess 2:7) in our world. It consists in the creature's decision to account for one's own self, without any reference to the Creator. Revelation disdains any understanding of evil as a constitutive element of existence: it is the fruit of disobedience, an ethical choice that stems from the creature's own freedom.

While many cultures preserve some form of perception of a 'lost paradise', the Church looks on the succession of falls in Gen 3-11 not so much as an account of bygone days: it is a sapiential description and a theological exposition that illustrates the present human condition. The world is not what God wants it to be. According to the same chapters, sin spreads throughout history and augments its hold on humankind, because of the many individual decisions that redirect creation away from God and constitute what the Church refers to as "social sin". By means of the typical imagery of the time, these chapters illustrate the concrete situation in which the humanity we know struggles to achieve its living, combats against suffering, and yearns after a life that knows no end.

Humanity finds it hard to agree to the fact that only God gives life. In different ways, it attempts to master life, independently of the Creator. According to the doctrine of original sin, life exclusively comes from the Father, but is not always ready to acknowledge him as the source of all there is. Whenever one tries to redeem one's own self, one only distances oneself further from God and takes a deeper plunge into the abyss of meaninglessness and irrationality.

The Church recognised this danger already in the 4th century. According to Pelagius, the life of grace depends on humanity's moralistic effort; the individual has to decide whether he wants to be one with God, or not. Besides, the individual's freedom is now somewhat weakened, owing to sin that encompasses it from all sides. The magisterium emphasized the reality of original sin, to stress one simple fact: communion with God does not depend solely on the human person's decision; it is God's gift of himself. No human being can ever lay claim on God's gift of grace; one can receive it only as a "second gift", that of redemption.

At the end of the Middle Ages, life in general turned out to be insecure and unstable. That could not but raise the question of the certainty of salvation. Luther's experience of humanity's sinful state, and its irresistible inclination to evil, led him to overstate the effects of the fall and insist on the radical sinfulness of our present human condition. After the human will egotistically and freely chose to turn away from God, humankind can only await the Son of God made man to receive forgiveness on all counts. The unique, God-given remedy of forgiveness manifests itself in a person's conversion and renewal: two major gifts that stand out among the many we receive from the Father in Christ.

Trent could not but respond to the need of reformulating the theology of original sin and refocus it on the centrality of the Paschal mystery. Every single individual, including the children of the baptised, needs to embrace Christ and respond positively to him. In Christ, one truly dies to sin and rises to new life, though concupiscence lingers on as the after-effect of sin's presence in the world.

In spite of all the terminological difficulties, Trent opted to continue speaking of original sin in ethical terms, knowing too well that it was an act of active disobedience against God only in the case of our first parents. For all others, it can only be "a sin" by analogy, as it does not imply an exercise of one's will. (According to the IVth Lateran, in analogy "no similitude can be expressed without implying a greater dissimilitude": cf. n. 320). The Council tried to resist any approach that can turn evil into a constitutive element of our human condition.

On account of 20th century biblical research (cf. nn. 237ff) and contemporary scientific research, the theology of original sin must be restated. The Second Vatican Council explains original sin as "man[...] split within himself" and life as "a dramatic struggle between good and evil, light and darkness". "The Lord himself came to free and strengthen man" [GS 13]. Paul VI summarised the Church's teaching on original sin in three points: the privation of original holiness and justice as part and parcel of our present human condition, its universal character, and the "death of the soul" as its consequence.

The unequivocal importance of our rebirth in Christ is the object of the theology of original sin. This teaching of the Church looks at sin as a reality, limited within history: it is preceded and overwhelmed by God's mercy. The Church's teaching on original justice and original sin stresses, therefore, God's unwavering love, humankind's need of salvation, and the uniqueness of Christ's saving mission that reunites humanity with God, its origin and goal.

*   *   *

The documents on original justice and sin contain the following doctrinal points:

Our first parents were endowed with the life of 'holiness and justice': 503, 508f, (515).
God created them in communion with him: 518-519, 520a, 522b-c, 524, 525;
    free from death and concupiscence: 501, 508, 512.
These gifts were not due to our first parents: 501, 514/26, 1984, 1998.

Original Sin

Original sin is the 'reverse side' of the Good News: 521.
Humanity lost the God-given gift of grace through sin: 39/9, 503f, 508, 516, 518, 521 a-b.
Sin and its consequences form part of our human condition, transmitted to our offspring: 39/9, 420, 503, 505, 509-511, (515), 518, 520a-b, 522a-e, 523c, 523f, 524, 646, 1927.

Original sin differs from actual sin by the absence of personal consent:
506, 514, 523d;
 and, in today's humanity, begs for God's mercy without incurring his judgment: 523d.

It consists of the loss of 'holiness and justice': 503, 508f, 1925.

It brings in the 'death of the soul': 501, 508f, 516, 523a.

It alienates one from oneself; it brings about death and fratricide, and the earth's 'rebellion' against humanity: 518, 519, 523f.

It is the source of concupiscence which weakens the human will: 512, 523d, 527, 1921, 1925, 1987, 1989, 2007c.

It does not destroy freedom: 512, 1923/36, 1925, 1955f, 1987, 1989f, 1992.

Baptism

Baptism wipes out original sin and restores us to communion with God: 12, (502), 503, 506, 510-512, 524, 525, 1411, 1412, 1415, 1923-1927, 1932, 2006a, 2007a-c.

It conforms us to the image of the Son: 510, 524.

Even the children of the baptised need to be reborn in Christ: 511, 523b.

Thanks to the redemptive mediation of her Son, Mary has been preserved from original sin: 709, 716a, 718b.

THE SIXTEENTH COUNCIL OF CARTHAGE (418)

The first doctrinal decrees on original justice and sin were occasioned by Pelagianism. In the context of the appeal which he made for moral renewal, Pelagius denied the necessity of grace (cf.n. 1901) and the reality of original sin. In 416 he was censured in a synod of Carthage for the following heresies: Adam was created mortal; his sin harmed himself only, not his offspring: newborn children are in the same condition as Adam before his fall; Christ's death and resurrection are not the cause for human persons rising from death, since even before Christ's coming there were people without sin.

A number of decisions were made by the Church's teaching office in answer to these articles. First among these is the doctrine of the important provincial Council of Carthage attended by 200 bishops in 418; it is followed by the Indiculus *and the Council of Orange.*

501
222
1. This has been decided by all the bishops [...] gathered together in the holy Synod of Carthage: Whoever says that Adam, the first man, was made mortal in the sense that he was to die a bodily death whether he sinned or not, which means that to quit the body would not be a punishment for sin but a necessity of nature, *anathema sit.*

(502)
223
2. *(The second canon was later adopted with some minute additions by the Council of Trent: cf. n. 511)*

THE *INDICULUS* (between 435 and 442)

On this document, see n. 1907i.

503
239
1. In Adam's sin all human beings lost their natural power for good and their innocence. No one can of one's own free will rise out of the depth of this fall if one is not lifted up by the grace of the merciful God. This is the pronouncement of Pope Innocent of blessed memory in his letter to the Council of Carthage: "He [Adam] acted of his own free will when he used his gifts thoughtlessly; he fell into the abyss of sin and sank and found no means to rise again. Betrayed by his freedom for ever, he would have remained weighed down by his fall had not later the advent of Christ raised him up by his grace when through the cleansing of a new regeneration he washed away all previous guilt in the bath of his baptism."[1]

---

1. *Epistola "In requirendis", 7.*

THE SECOND COUNCIL OF ORANGE (529)

On this document, see n. 1915i.

504 1. If anyone says that through the offence of Adam's
371   sin the whole person, body and soul, was not changed
         for the worse, but believes that only the body was
subjected to corruption while the freedom of the soul remained
unharmed, such a one is misled by the error of Pelagius and
goes against Scripture which says: "the soul that sins shall die"
[Ez 18:20], and: "do you not know that if you yield yourselves
to anyone as obedient slaves you are slaves of the one whom
you obey?" *[Rom 6.16]*; and again:"whatever overcomes one, to
that one is enslaved" *[2 Pet 2:19]*.

505 2. If anyone maintains that the fall harmed Adam alone
372   and not his descendants, or declares that only bodily
         death which is the punishment of sin, but not sin itself
which is the death of the soul was passed on to the whole human
race by one man, he ascribes injustice to God and contradicts
the words of the apostle: "Sin came into the world through one
man, and death through sin, and so [death] spread to all as all
sinned in him" *[Rom 5:12 Vulg.]*.

INNOCENT III

LETTER TO HUMBERT, ARCHBISHOP OF ARLES (1201)

*Pope Innocent defends infant baptism by which sin is forgiven without
personal conversion. This is explained by the different nature of personal and
original sin. Original sin is inherent in the human being by birth without
implying a personal offence against God; it consists in the condition of non-
salvation in which one needs God's saving grace; it can be cleansed through
baptism without a personal act of repentance. The punishment also differs:
original sin excludes from the beatific vision but does not lead to a positive
punishment. See also n. 1409.*

(Original sin and actual sin)

506 We say that two kinds of sin must be distinguished,
780   original and actual: original which is contracted without
         consent and actual which is committed with consent.
Thus original sin, which is contracted without consent is remitted
without consent by the power of the sacrament [of baptism]; but
actual sin, which is committed with consent, is by no means
remitted without consent. [...]

Further, the punishment of original sin is the loss of the beatific vision, but the punishment of actual sin is the torture of eternal hell.

THE GENERAL COUNCIL OF TRENT
FIFTH SESSION
DECREE ON ORIGINAL SIN (1546)

Luther had taught that original sin consists in concupiscence which remains in the person after baptism. Thus a baptised person remains a sinner but concupiscence is no longer laid to one's charge because Christ's justice is imputed to the sinner.

The Council did not confine itself to the refutation of Luther's teaching but expounded the whole of Catholic teaching on the matter. The Pelagian errors were again refuted as well as those of the Manichaeans and Priscillianists who denied the existence of original sin in children born from a Christian marriage.

The doctrine is proposed in five canons:1) Adam's sin and its effect on Adam himself; 2) the transmission of Adam's sin to his descendants: Rom 5:12 is quoted against Erasmus who denied that it dealt with original sin; 3) the remission of original sin through the passion and death of Christ whose merits are applied to human persons in baptism; 4) the necessity of infant baptism: the Council quotes here, with slight modifications, canon 2 of the Council of Carthage (cf. n 502); the nature of original sin in opposition to the opinion of the Reformers. Two points of doctrine are here defined: original sin is wiped out by baptism; concupiscence remains after baptism, but is not sin.

The note on the Virgin Mary, as the only exception to the universality of original sin, is added to indicate the Council's intention not to cause prejudice to the doctrine of the Immaculate Conception.

507 Our Catholic faith "without which it is impossible to
1510 please God" [cf. Heb 11:6] must be kept free from errors, pure and unstained; Christian people should not be "carried about with every wind of doctrine" [Eph 4:14] while the ancient serpent, the perpetual enemy of humankind, has stirred up among the many evils that beset the Church of God in this time of ours both new and old controversies about original sin and its remedy. For these reasons the holy ecumenical and general Council of Trent, duly assembled in the Holy Spirit, in order to call back the erring and to strengthen the wavering, following the witness of Holy Scripture, of the holy Fathers and of the approved Councils, and the judgment and consensus of the Church herself, states, professes and declares the following concerning original sin:

508 1. If anyone does not profess that Adam, the first man,
1511 by transgressing God's commandment in paradise, at
once lost the holiness and justice in which he had been
constituted; and that, offending God by his sin, he drew upon
himself the wrath and indignation of God and consequently death
with which God had threatened him, and together with death
captivity in the power of him who henceforth "has the power of
death" [Heb 2:14], i.e., the devil; and that "the whole Adam, body
and soul, was changed for the worse through the offence of his
sin" [cf. n. 504], anathema sit.

509 2. If anyone asserts that Adam's sin harmed only him
1512 and not his descendants and that the holiness and justice
received from God which he lost was lost only for him and
not for us also; or that, stained by the sin of disobedience, he
transmitted to all humankind only death and the sufferings of the
body but not sin as well which is the death of the soul, anathema
sit. For, he contradicts the words of the apostle: "Sin came into
the world through one man, and death through sin, and so [death]
spread to all as all sinned in him" [Rom 5:12 Vulg.; cf. n. 505].

510 3. If anyone asserts that this sin of Adam, which is one
1513 in origin and is transmitted by propagation, not by
imitation, and which is in all human beings, proper to
each, can be taken away by the powers of human nature or by
any remedy other than the merits of the one mediator our Lord
Jesus Christ who reconciled us with God by his blood, being
"made our righteousness and sanctification and redemption"
[1 Cor 1:30]; or if anyone denies that the same merit of Christ
Jesus is applied to adults and children alike through the
sacrament of baptism duly administered in the form given by
the Church, anathema sit. "For there is no other name under
heaven given among humans by which we must be saved"
[Acts 4:12]. Hence the words "Behold the lamb of God who takes
away the sins of the world" [cf. Jn 1:29]; and "as many of you
as were baptised in Christ have put on Christ" [Gal 3:27].

511 4. If anyone denies that infants newly born from their
1514 mother's womb are to be baptised, even when born from
baptised parents; or says that, though they are baptised
for the remission of sins, yet they do not contract from Adam any
trace of original sin which must be expiated by the bath of

regeneration that leads to eternal life, so that in their case the formula of baptism 'for the forgiveness of sins' would no longer be true but would be false, *anathema sit*. For, what the apostle says: "Sin came into the world through one man, and death through sin, and so [death] spread to all as all sinned in him" [*Rom. 5:12 Vulg.*], should not be understood in another sense than that in which the Catholic Church spread over the whole world has understood it at all times. For, because of this rule of faith, in accordance with apostolic tradition, even children who of themselves cannot have yet committed any sin are truly baptised for the remission of sins, so that by regeneration they may be cleansed from what they contracted through generation. For "unless one is born of water and the Spirit, one cannot enter the Kingdom of God" [*Jn 3:5*].

512   5. If anyone denies that the guilt of original sin is
1515   remitted by the grace of our Lord Jesus Christ given in
baptism, or asserts that all that is sin in the true and proper sense is not taken away but only brushed over or not imputed, *anathema sit*. For, in those who are reborn God hates nothing, because there is no condemnation for those who were buried with Christ through baptism into death [*cf. Rom 8:1 and 6:4*], "who do not walk according to the flesh" [*Rom 8:4*] but who, putting off the old person and putting on the new, created after the likeness of God [*cf. Eph 4:22f; Col 3:9f*], innocent, unstained, pure and guiltless, have become the beloved children of God, "heirs of God and fellow heirs with Christ" [*Rom 8:17*], so that nothing henceforth holds them back from entering into heaven.

The holy Council, however, professes and thinks that concupiscence or the inclination to sin remains in the baptised. Since it is left for us to wrestle with, it cannot harm those who do not consent but vigorously resist it by the grace of Jesus Christ. Rather, "one who strives lawfully will be crowned" [*cf. 2 Tim 2:5*]. Of this concupiscence which the apostle occasionally calls "sin" [*cf. Rom 6 12ff; 7:7, 14-20*] the holy Council declares: The Catholic Church has never understood that it is called sin because it would be sin in the true and proper sense in those who have been reborn, but because it comes from sin and inclines to sin. If anyone thinks the contrary, *anathema sit*.

513   This same holy Synod declares that it is not its intention
1516   to include in this decree dealing with original sin the
Blessed and Immaculate Virgin Mary, Mother of God,

but that the Constitutions of Pope Sixtus IV of blesed memory are to be observed under the penalties contained in those Constitutions, which it renews [cf . n. 704]

PIUS V

BULL *EX OMNIBUS AFFLICTIONIBUS* (1567)
CONDEMNED PROPOSITIONS OF MICHAEL DE BAY

In his conception of grace, original justice and sin, M. de Bay was greatly influenced by the Reformers. He considered grace, immortality and freedom from concupiscence as due to the human being and given in creation; they were not gifts freely bestowed by God. Hence their loss through original sin was not merely the loss of a gratuitous privilege, but a wound of human nature itself. See on this document, n.1984i. See also the other propositions of M. de Bay under n. 1984, the condemnation of Quesnel (DS 2384-2387) and of the Synod of Pistoia (DS 2616).

[514/26]   The integrity at the beginning of creation was not a
1926   gratuitous exaltation of human nature but its natural
            condition.

[514/46]   Wilfulness does not belong to the essence and
1946   definition of sin; hence the question whether every
            sin must be voluntary does not concern the definition
of sin, but its cause and origin.

[514/47]   Therefore original sin has truly the nature of sin,
1947   irrespective and independently of the will from which
            it took its origin.

[514/48]   Original sin is wilful through the habitual will of a
1948   child. It habitually dominates the child because the
            child does not make any contrary decision of will.

[514/49]   And through this habitually dominating will it
1949   happens that a child dying without the sacrament of
            regeneration, when [after death] it reaches the use of
reason, actually hates God, blasphemes him and resists the law
of God.

THE SECOND VATICAN GENERAL COUNCIL

(515)   *Vatican II does not deal ex-professo with the doctrine of original justice and sin. However, in the context of the history of salvation and of the actual condition and task of human beings in the world, these doctrines are mentioned. They appear in their relevance for people today.*

The Constitution on the Church describes in a comprehensive vision the divine plan of our salvation: the human person's original dignity, the fall, and God's continued care (LG 2).

The Constitution on the Church in the modern world unfolds our actual condition today: the evils of our world point to a deeper root, the sinfulness of the human heart (GS 10) by which human persons are alienated from their original destiny (GS 13).

PAUL VI

ADDRESS TO THEOLOGIANS AT THE SYMPOSIUM ON ORIGINAL SIN (1966)

Paul VI had organised this symposium in order to take stock of the present state of exegetical studies and of the natural sciences, as anthropology and paleontology, with regard to the original condition of the human being. He demands an honest investigation of the existing problems, while at the same time stating the limits of this search. The text is found in AAS 58 (1966) 654.

516   It is evident that you will not consider as reconcilable with the authentic Catholic doctrine those explanations of original sin, given by some modern authors, which start from the presupposition of polygenism which is not proved, and deny more or less clearly that the sin which has been such an abundant source of evils for humankind has consisted above all in the disobedience which Adam, the first man and the figure of the future Adam, committed at the beginning of history. Consequently, these explanations do not agree either with the teachings of Holy Scripture, sacred Tradition and the Church's magisterium, which says that the sin of the first man is transmitted to all his descendants by way of propagation, not of imitation, that it is "proper to each", and is "the death of the soul", i.e., the privation and not merely the absence of holiness and justice, even in new-born infants [*cf. nn. 509, 510*].

As to the theory of evolutionism, you will not consider it acceptable if it is not clearly in agreement with the immediate creation of human souls by God and does not regard the disobedience of Adam, the first universal parent, as of decisive importance for the destiny of humankind [*cf. n. 509*]. This disobedience should not be understood as though it had not caused in Adam the loss of the holiness and justice in which he was constituted [*cf. n. 508*].

JOHN PAUL II
ENCYCLICAL LETTER *REDEMPTOR HOMINIS* (1979)

In chapter II of the Encyclical, entitled "The Mystery of the Redemption",
the Pope, alluding to the present state of the world, applies to it the Biblical
doctrine of the fall: the present threat to ecology from industry and to the
survival of humankind from the arms race witnesses today to the fall of the
human person and to the world still in need of being saved in Jesus Christ.
The text is found in AAS 71 (1979) 270-271.

(The present world in need of being recreated)

517 8. In Jesus Christ the visible world which God created
for the human being *[cf. Gen 1:26-30]*—the world that, when
sin entered, "was subjected to futility" *[Rom 8:20; cf. 8:19-22; GS 2,*
13]—recovers again its original link with the divine source of
Wisdom and Love. Indeed, "God so loved the world that he gave
his only Son" *[Jn 3:16]*. As this link was broken in the man Adam,
so in the Man Christ it was reforged *[cf. Rom 5:11-21]*. Are we of the
twentieth century not convinced of the overpoweringly eloquent
words of the Apostle of the Gentiles concerning the "creation [that]
has been groaning in travail together until now" *[Rom 8:22]* and
"waits with eager longing for the revelation of the children of God"
[Rom 8:19], the creation that "was subjected to futility"? Does not
the previously unknown immense progress—which has taken place
especially in the course of this century—in the field of the human
being's dominion over the world itself reveal to a previously
unknown degree that subjection "to futility"? It is enough to recall
certain phenomena, such as the threat of pollution of the natural
environment in areas of rapid industrialisation, or the armed
conflicts continually breaking out with growing intensity, or the
power, already present, of self-destruction through the use of
atomic, hydrogen, neutron and similar weapons, or the lack of the
respect for the life of the unborn. The world of the new age, the
world of space flights, the world of the previously unattained
conquests of science and technology—is it not also the creation,
"groaning in travail", that "awaits with eager longing for the
revelation of the children of God"?

MESSAGE FOR THE XXIII WORLD DAY FOR PEACE
(1 January 1990)

The message John Paul II wrote for the XXIII World Day for Peace—
entitled "Peace with God the Creator, Peace with All of Creation" — has

become the magisterium's Magna Charta *on the ecological crisis. Addressing the issue of common responsibility, the Pope starts with a clear reference to original sin and its after-effects. In a brief, terse statement, the Pope identifies the many ways in which believers can see sin at work, one of which is the destruction of the one world in which humanity can live. Ecological disasters are the effect of widespread sinfulness that one can hardly attribute to any single individual. In Christ, creation yearns to be freed from its bondage of sin and decay (cf. Rom 8:21) as believers wait for "new heavens and a new earth in which righteousness dwells" (2 Pt 3:13). The Pope concludes: "If man is not at peace with God, then earth itself cannot be at peace" (5). The text is found in* Origins *(1989), pp. 465-8.*

(Alienation and loss of harmony)

518 3.[...] Adam and Eve's call to share in the unfolding of God's plan of creation brought into play those abilities and gifts which distinguish the human being from all other creatures. At the same time, their call established a fixed relationship between humankind and the rest of creation. Made in the image and likeness of God, Adam and Eve were to have exercised their dominion over the earth *[Gen 1:28]* with wisdom and love. Instead, they destroyed the existing harmony *by deliberately going against the creator's plan,* that is, by choosing to sin. This resulted not only in humanity's alienation from itself, in death and fratricide, but also in the earth's "rebellion" against humankind *[cf. Gen 3:17-19; 4:12].* All of creation became subject to futility, waiting in a mysterious way to be set free and to obtain a glorious liberty together with all the children of God *[cf. Rom 8:20-21].*

(Creation and Original Sin)

519 5. These biblical considerations help us to understand better the relationship between human activity and the whole of creation. When a person turns his back on the Creator's plan, that individual provokes a disorder which has inevitable repercussions on the rest of the created order. If humanity is not at peace with God, then earth itself cannot be at peace: "Therefore the land mourns and all who dwell in it languish, and also the beasts of the field and the birds of the air and even the fish of the sea are taken away" *[Hos 4:3].* [...]

CATECHISM OF THE CATHOLIC CHURCH
(7 December 1992)

In the following paragraphs, the Catechism reformulates Trent's Decree on *Origina Sin* (*cf. nn. 507-513*), *especially in the light of 20th century biblical research. After the Second Vatican Council refrained from preparing a document on the subject (cf. n. 515), the magisterium challenges theologians and believers alike. The Catechism insists (a) on the positive dimension of the theology of original sin as "the 'reverse side' of the Good News" (cf. n. 521), (b) on the broken harmony with creation, and (c) on "the sin of the world" (Jn 1:29). In the brief historical note, it underlines the controversial dimension of this teaching. We have retained the subtitles carried in the Catechism itself.*

(*The reality of sin*)

520a   386. Sin is present in human history; any attempt to ignore it or to give this dark reality other names would be futile. To try to understand what sin is, one must first recognize the profound relation of every individual to God, for only in this relationship is the evil of sin unmasked in its true identity as humanity's rejection of God and opposition to him, even as it continues to weigh heavy on human life and history.

520b   387. Only the light of divine Revelation clarifies the reality of sin and particularly of the sin committed at humankind's origins. Without the knowledge Revelation gives of God we cannot recognize sin clearly and are tempted to explain it as merely a developmental flaw, a psychological weakness, a mistake, or the necessary consequence of an inadequate social structure, etc. Only in the knowledge of God's plan for humankind can we grasp that sin is an abuse of the freedom that God gives to created persons so that they are capable of loving him and loving one another.

(*Original sin - an essential truth of the faith*)

521   389. The doctrine of original sin is, so to speak, the "reverse side" of the Good News that Jesus is the Saviour of all, that all need salvation and that salvation is offered to all through Christ. The Church, which has the mind of Christ [*cf. 1 Cor 2:16*], knows very well that we cannot tamper with the revelation of original sin without undermining the mystery of Christ.

(*Humanity's first sin*)

522a   397. Man, tempted by the devil, let his trust in his Creator die in his heart and, abusing his freedom, disobeyed God's command. This is what man's first sin consisted of [*cf.*

Gen 3:1-11; Rom 5:19]. All subsequent sin would be disobedience toward God and lack of trust in his goodness.

522b 398. In that sin man preferred himself to God and by that very act scorned him. He chose himself over and against God, against the requirements of his creaturely status and therefore against his own good. Created in a state of holiness, man was destined to be fully "divinized" by God in glory. Seduced by the devil, he wanted to "be like God", but "without God, before God, and not in accordance with God" [St. Maximus the Confessor, *Ambigua: PG 91, 1156C; cf. Gen 3:5]*.

522c 399. Scripture portrays the tragic consequences of this first disobedience. Adam and Eve immediately lose the grace of original holiness *[cf. Rom 3:23]*. They become afraid of the God of whom they have conceived a distorted image—that of a God jealous of his prerogatives *[cf. Gen 3:5-10]*.

522d 400. The harmony in which they had found themselves, thanks to original justice, is now destroyed: the control of the soul's spiritual faculties over the body is shattered; the union of man and woman becomes subject to tensions, their relations henceforth marked by lust and domination *[cf. Gen 3:7-16]*.

Harmony with creation is broken: visible creation has become alien and hostile to humankind *[cf. Gen 3:17.19]*. Because of humanity, creation is now subject "to its bondage to decay" *[Rom 8:21]*. Finally, the consequence explicitly foretold for this disobedience will come true: all will "return to the ground" *[Gen 3:19; cf. 2:17]*, for out of it they were taken. Death makes its entrance into human history *[cf. Rom 5:12]*.

522e 401. After that first sin, the world is virtually inundated by sin. There is Cain's murder of his brother Abel and the universal corruption which follows in the wake of sin. Likewise, sin frequently manifests itself in the history of Israel, especially as infidelity to the God of the Covenant and as transgression of the Law of Moses. And even after Christ's atonement, sin raises its head in countless ways among Christians *[cf. Gen 4:3-15; 6:5, 12; Rom 1:18-32; 1 Cor 1-6; Rev 2-3]*. Scripture and the Church's Tradition continually recall the presence and universality of sin in human history.

What revelation makes known to us is confirmed by our own experience. For when we look into our own heart we find that we are drawn towards what is wrong and sunk in many evils which cannot come from our good creator. Often refusing to acknowledge God as one's source, the individual has also upset the relationship which should link all to their last end, and at the same time has broken the right order that should reign within oneself as well as between oneself and others and all creatures *[GS 13/1]*.

(The consequences of Adam's sin for humanity)

523a   402. All are implicated in Adam's sin, as St. Paul affirms: "By one man's disobedience many (that is, all) were made sinners": "sin came into the world through one man and death through sin, and so death spread to all men because all men sinned" *[Rom 5:12, 19]*. The Apostle contrasts the universality of sin and death with the universality of salvation in Christ. "Then as one man's trespass led to condemnation for all men, so one man's act of righteousness leads to acquittal and life for all men" *[Rom 5:18]*.

523b   403. Following St. Paul, the Church has always taught that the overwhelming misery which oppresses all and their inclination towards evil and death cannot be understood apart from their connection with Adam's sin and the fact that he has transmitted to us a sin with which we are all born afflicted, a sin which is the "death of the soul" *[cf. n. 509]*. Because of this certainty of faith, the Church baptizes for the remission of sins even tiny infants who have not committed personal sin *[cf. n. 511]*.

523c   404. How did the sin of Adam become the sin of all his descendants? The whole human race is in Adam "as one body of one man" [St. Thomas Aquinas, *De malo* 4,I]. By this "unity of the human race" all are implicated in Adam's sin, as all are implicated in Christ's justice. Still, the transmission of original sin is a mystery that we cannot fully understand. But we do know by Revelation that Adam had received original holiness and justice not for himself alone, but for all human nature. By yielding to the tempter, Adam and Eve committed a personal sin, but this sin affected the human nature that they would then transmit in a fallen state *[cf. nn. 508-509]*. It is a sin which will be transmitted by propagation to all humankind, that is, by the transmission of a human nature deprived of original holiness and justice. And that is why original sin is called "sin" only in an analogical sense: it is a sin "contracted" and not "committed"—a state and not an act.

523d 405. Although it is proper to each individual [cf. n. 510], original sin does not have the character of a personal fault in any of Adam's descendants. It is a deprivation of original holiness and justice, but human nature has not been totally corrupted: it is wounded in the natural powers proper to it, subject to ignorance, to suffering and the dominion of death, and inclined to sin—an inclination to evil that is called "concupiscence". Baptism, by imparting the life of Christ's grace, erases original sin and turns the individual back towards God, but the consequences for nature, weakened and inclined to evil, persist in all and summon them to spiritual battle.

523e 406. The Church's teaching on the transmission of original sin was articulated more precisely in the fifth century, especially under the impulse of St. Augustine's reflections against Pelagianism, and in the sixteenth century, in opposition to the Protestant Reformation. Pelagius held that one could, by the natural power of free will and without the necessary help of God's grace, lead a morally good life; he thus reduced the influence of Adam's fault to bad example. The first Protestant reformers, on the contrary, taught that original sin has radically perverted humankind and destroyed its freedom; they identified the sin inherited by each individual with the tendency to evil (*concupiscentia*), which would be insurmountable. The Church pronounced on the meaning of the data of Revelation on original sin especially at the second Council of Orange (529) [cf. nn. 504-505] and at the Council of Trent (1546) [cf. nn. 507-513].

523f 408. The consequences of original sin and of the personal sins of all put the world as a whole in the sinful condition aptly described in St. John's expression, "the sin of the world" [Jn 1:29]. This expression can also refer to the negative influence exerted on people by communal situations and social structures that are the fruit of people's sins [cf. nn. 2067 b-c].

JOHN PAUL II
ENCYCLICAL LETTER *EVANGELIUM VITAE*
(25 March 1995)

In paragraph 34 and 35 of his encyclical, dedicated to the value and

inviolability of human life, John Paul II returns to one of his favourite themes:
"Man, although formed from the dust of the earth (cf. Gen 2:7, 3:19; Job 34:15;
Ps 103(102)14; 104(103):29, is a manifestation of God in the world, a sign of
his presence, a trace of his glory (cf. Gen 1:26-27; Ps 8:6). This is what Saint
Irenaeus of Lyons wanted to emphasize in his celebrated expression: 'Man, living
man, is the glory of God' ("Gloria Dei vivens homo": Adversus Haereses, IV,
20, 7: SCh 100/2, 648-649)". In the Pope's words, life is "the seed of an existence
which transcends the very limits of time" (cf. Wis 2:23). Within this context of
a theology of glory, fulfilment and completion as the goal of human life, John Paul
gives us the following reappraisal of the theology of original sin. He focusses on
a christological understanding of original sin and its aftermath: new life in Christ's
image. The full text of the encyclical is in Origins 24 (1995), pp. 689-727.

("Called... to be conformed to the image of his Son"—Rom 8:28-29:
God's glory shines on the face of each person)

524   36. Unfortunately, God's marvellous plan was marred
by the appearance of sin in history. Through sin, the
individual rebels against one's Creator and ends up by *worshipping*
creatures: "They exchanged the truth about God for a lie and
worshipped and served the creature rather than the Creator" *[Rom*
1:25]. As a result one not only deforms the image of God in one's
own person, but is tempted to offences against it in others as well,
replacing relationships of communion by attitudes of distrust,
indifference, hostility and even murderous hatred. When *God* is
not acknowledged *as God,* the profound meaning of the human
being is betrayed and communion between people is compromised.

In the life of each person God's image shines forth anew
and is again revealed in all its fullness at the coming of the Son
of God in human flesh. "Christ is the image of the invisible God"
[Col 1:15], he "reflects the glory of God and bears the very stamp
of his nature" *[Heb 1:3].* He is the perfect image of the Father.

The plan of life given to the first Adam finds at last its
fulfilment in Christ. Whereas the disobedience of Adam had
ruined and marred God's plan for human life and introduced
death into the world, the redemptive obedience of Christ is the
source of grace poured out upon the human race, opening wide
to everyone the gates of the kingdom of life *[cf. Rom 5:12-21].* As
the Apostle Paul states: "The first man Adam became a living
being; the last Adam became a life-giving spirit" *[1 Cor 15:45].*
All who commit themselves to following Christ are given the
fulness of life: the divine image is restored, renewed and brought
to perfection in them. God's plan for human beings is this, that

they should "be conformed to the image of his Son" [Rom 8:29]. Only thus, in the splendour of this image, can the person be freed from the slavery of idolatry, rebuild lost fellowship and rediscover one's true identity.

APOSTOLIC LETTER *DIES DOMINI*
(31 May 1998)

If the Lord's day is the memorial of the first day of creation, it reminds the believer that humanity's contribution to God's work has not been what God desired it to be. Ever since the stance of the first humanity redirected the course of history, the Creator lovingly responds to the need that everything receive new life. If Sunday—the first day of the week—recalls the work of creation, it also reminds us of the first day of the new creation that dawned with the resurrection of our Lord, the "first-born from the dead" (Col 1:18). Though humanity is God's prime interlocutor, the rest of creation is assumed into the vicissitudes of its relationship with God. The text is in Origins 28 (1998), pp. 133-151.

525 9.[...] "God saw that it was good" [Gn 1:10,12, etc.]. Punctuating the story as it does, this refrain *sheds a positive light upon every element of the universe* and reveals the secret for a proper understanding of it and for its eventual regeneration: the world is good insofar as it remains tied to its origin and, after being disfigured by sin, it is again made good when, with the help of grace, it returns to the One who made it. It is clear that this process directly concerns not inanimate objects and animals but human beings, who have been endowed with the incomparable gift and risk of freedom. Immediately after the creation stories, the Bible highlights the dramatic contrast between the grandeur of the human persons, created in the image and likeness of God, and their fall, which unleashes on the world the darkness of sin and death [cf. Gn 3].

CONGREGATION FOR THE DOCTRINE OF THE FAITH
COMMENTARY ON *AD TUENDAM FIDEM*
(30 June 1998)

On May 28, 1998, John Paul II signed the Apostolic Letter "Motu Proprio" Ad Tuendam Fidem ("To Defend the Faith") to insert certain norms into the Code of Canon Law and into the Code of Canons of the Eastern Churches, "to protect the Catholic faith against errors arising on the part of some of the Christian faithful, in particular among those who studiously dedicate themselves to the discipline of sacred theology". The text is in Origins 28 (1998), pp. 113-116 (cf. n. 1891i).

On June 30th, 1998, the Letter was made public together with an explanatory note from the Congregation for the Doctrine of the Faith. Bearing the signatures of Cardinal Joseph Ratzinger and Archbishop Tarcisio Bertone, respectively prefect and secretary of the congregation, the note distinguishes between "the truths set forth by the church as divinely revealed (those of the first paragraph)" and truths of Catholic doctrine "to be held definitively (those of the second paragraph)" (8). It adds: "the magisterium of the Church [...] teaches a doctrine to be believed as divinely revealed (first paragraph) or to be held definitively (second paragraph) with an act which is either defining or nondefining" (9).

Original sin belongs to the first category. The Congregation refers to the Decree of the Council of Trent as the point of reference for this doctrine (cf. nn. 507-513). This brief text shows that one should interpret Carthage (nn. 501-2) in the light of Trent. The text is in Origins 28 (1998), pp. 116-119.

(Original sin is 'divinely revealed')

526   11.[...] To the truths of the first paragraph belong the articles of faith of the Creed, the various Christological dogmas and Marian dogmas; [...] the doctrine on the existence of original sin *[cf. nn. 507-513]*; the doctrine on the immortality of the spiritual soul and on the immediate recompense after death *[cf. nn. 2305-2307]* [...].

THE LUTHERAN WORLD FEDERATION AND THE CATHOLIC CHURCH
JOINT DECLARATION ON THE DOCTRINE OF JUSTIFICATION
(31 October 1999)

The Joint Declaration on Justification gives a succinct definition of concupiscence. This will be reported again within the fuller context of justification in Chapter XIX: cf. n 2000 k-s. The text of the document is carried in Origins 28 (1998), pp. 120-127.

(The Catholic understanding of concupiscence)

527   30.[...] There does, however, remain in the person an inclination (concupiscence) which comes from sin and presses toward sin. Since, according to Catholic conviction, human sins always involve a personal element and since this element is lacking in this inclination, Catholics do not see this inclination as sin in an authentic sense. They do not thereby deny that this inclination does not correspond to God's original design for humanity and that it is objectively in contradiction to God and remains one's enemy in a lifelong struggle. [...]

CHAPTER VI

JESUS CHRIST THE SAVIOUR

The eternal Son of God, "one of the Trinity", became man in order to save all men and women. Recapitulating all things in himself, he re-united the whole human race with God through the mystery of his death and resurrection, and reconciled all things among themselves. The mystery of the redemptive incarnation, together with that of the Trinity from which it is inseparable, constitutes the substance of the Christian message; it is at the centre of the Christian understanding of history and reveals to human beings their true vocation as sons and daughters of God in God's own Son.

The mysteries of Christ's person and of his work are also inseparable. If the man Jesus contains the fullness of God's revelation to the world, if his human actions have saving power for the entire human race, the reason is that in the Son incarnate God and man have been united in the unity of one person: the God-man is the mediator between God and human beings; his action flows from his being. This is why, in order to uphold and to proclaim the message of universal salvation in Christ, the Christian Tradition has had to preserve intact and to progressively explicitate the mystery of his person.

The mystery of the Word incarnate could be, and has in fact been approached since the earliest Christian Tradition, from two opposite directions with the humanity of Christ and the divinity of the Son of God, respectively, as their starting points. These two avenues gave rise to two schools, equally legitimate though faced with opposite problems, the Antiochian and the Alexandrian. Both had the burden of showing that Christ is truly God and truly man and that he is one. They could and did in fact lead to opposite errors: Nestorianism denied the unity of person, Monophysitism the duality of his natures after union. Against every threat either to the divinity or to the humanity of Christ, the leaders of the Church had to affirm clearly the integrity of his two natures; the great Christological Councils of the fifth century were faced with the task of expressing in unequivocal terms the mysterious union of the two natures in one person.

Later, it also became necessary to explicitate the same mystery on the level of Christ's actions: against the Monothelitist tendency the Church's teaching authority explained that the two wills and actions, the divine and the human, remain distinct in the one person of the God-man. Except for a document against the Agnoetes who attributed ignorance to Christ, the Church's teaching on the mysterious union of the divine and the human knowledge was reserved for a much later period. Thus the mystery of Christ, a mystery of unity in duality, has been through the centuries the object of deep reflection; in recent years this reflection has taken on new dimensions with the problem of the psychological unity of the God-man.

As compared with the mystery of Christ's person, that of his work has for many centuries been treated only cursorily in Church documents. The Church has always believed in the salvific significance of the totality of the Christ-event. The early Creeds enumerated its various phases from the incarnation down to the Paschal mystery, including in this the death on the cross, the resurrection and the ascension. In the early Tradition, different schools, the Greek and the Latin, laid greater emphasis on the incarnation and on the Paschal mystery, respectively. These various traditions were not, however, mutually exclusive: rather they complemented each other. It is only after the objective efficacy of Christ's redeeming death had been questioned in the Middle Ages that the doctrine of the merit and satisfaction of his expiatory sacrifice began to be explicitly stated. This doctrine needs even today to be harmoniously combined with the salvific meaning of the incarnation of the Word of God on the one hand and the saving power of his resurrection on the other. Nor must Christ's work be reduced to his redeeming function. Retrieving the earliest Christian Tradition, the Second Vatican Council explained Christ's revelatory function more clearly than previous Church documents: the Word incarnate is through his deeds and words the fulness of God's revelation to the world. The same Council also expressed better than previous official documents the central role of Christ in history and the significance of Christ for the Christian understanding of the human mystery.

*   *   *

The main points of doctrine considered in this chapter fall under the following headings:

Christ is truly God, eternally begotten from the Father: 1-12, 14, 17,

20, 23, 39/4, (601), 606/1, 606/5, 612, 617, 620/2, 627/4, 631, 632, 648, 650/27-30.

Christ is truly man, born in time from the Virgin Mary: 2-5, 7, 12, 15, 17, 20, 23, 39/4, (601), (602), 603/7, 610, 612, 617, 620/2, 620/6, 627/4, 628, 631, 632, 645, 648.

The two natures, divine and human, are united in the person of the Son of God: 17, 20, 23, 604, 606/2-4, 606/6-7, 607-608, 612, 613-616, 619/1-3, 620/4-5, 620/7-8, 621-623, 627/6-9, 629, 640, (641), (642), 644, 663, 670.

Christ has a double will and action, divine and human, both united in one person: 627/10-16, 635-637.

In his human will he is impeccable: 603/7, 614, 621, 627/5, 628, 634, 635.

Christ's human knowledge excludes ignorance and error: 619/4, 624-626, 650/32-34, 651/1-3, 661.

The divine Sonship of Christ excludes his being an adopted son of God: 23, 603/6, 619/5, 638, 639, (642).

The Word incarnate must be adored by one worship which extends to his humanity: 606/8, 619/5, 620/9, 649.

Divine cult must be rendered to his Sacred Heart: 664-667.

Christ brings the fulness of God's revelation: 149, 151, 679.

Mediator between God and human beings, he has saved everyone through the sacrifice of his cross: 6, 7, 10, 12, 15, 17, 20, 23, 39/5.10, 606/10, 606/12, 609, 611, 620/10, 627/2, 634, 645-646, 648, 650/38, 654-655, 712, 1546, 1989/5.

Christ saves and liberates: 672-673, 677-678.

He has satisfied and merited for all: 510, 643, 647, 712, 1631, 1926-1931, 1960.

By his resurrection he has become for all the source of a new life: 606/11, 650/36-37, 660.

Thus he has universal Lordship and Kingship: 9, 10, 12, 39/5, 652-653.

The Paschal Mystery is the supreme revelation of God's love: 680.

Christ is priest, prophet and king: 668, 848.

Christ is the goal of history: 669b.

As the new and perfect Adam, he manifests the true vocation for all human beings and associates them with his Easter mystery: 669a.

He exercises his priesthood for all: 668.

The truth about Jesus Christ may not be distorted: 670-671, 674-676.

Ecumenical christological declarations: 671a, 683, 684.

THE FIRST GENERAL COUNCIL OF NICAEA
SYMBOL OF NICAEA (325)

(601)   *Arius considered the "Word of God" as created by God in time and having in the fulness of time manifested himself in human flesh for our salvation. According to Arius, Christ was not God, for he did not share the divine nature; he was not man, for he did not have a complete human nature, made up of soul and body, but only human flesh. Thus Christ was a composite intermediary being— the Word made flesh—neither true God nor true man. He was not the mediator who unites God and us in his own person. Against Arius, the Symbol of faith of the Council of Nicaea affirms the strict divinity of the Son of God, "one in being with the Father"; against the gnostic and docetist currents which undermined the realism of Christ's humanity and Arius who reduced it to human flesh, the Council stresses the reality and completeness of Christ's humanity: He "became flesh, was made man." The mystery of Christ's full humanity united with his true divinity will later raise many problems and call for more precise answers. But the foundation for this fundamental affirmation of faith is already found in Nicaea. Cf. introduction and text, n. 7.*

THE FIRST GENERAL COUNCIL OF CONSTANTINOPLE
SYMBOL OF CONSTANTINOPLE (381)

(602)   *Unlike Arius, Apollinaris of Laodicaea (310-390) strongly professed the divinity of the Son of God, "one in being" with the Father, as stated by the Council of Nicaea. In the process of trying to express how the eternal Word of God became man, he nevertheless unduly reduced the humanity of Christ as Arius had done before him. Apollinaris followed the Greek anthropology according to which we are made up of body and soul, the soul itself being composed of a lower and a higher part, the principles of life and of spiritual activity respectively. Apollinaris understood the mystery of the incarnation in the sense that the eternal Word of God substituted for and replaced the highest part of the human composite. Christ, the Son incarnate, was the eternal Word to whom were united the lower part of the human soul and a human body, but he had no spiritual human soul. To Apollinaris this seemed necessary to ensure the unity of Christ and his absolute freedom from sin. Pope Damasus I rejected this doctrine in several documents. Making use of the soteriological argument according to which it was necessary that Christ, in order to redeem human beings,* *should have a complete human nature, the Pope explained that Christ's humanity is made up of a body and a soul with its lower and higher faculties; a full humanity is united to the eternal Son of God. See the fragment of a letter written c. 374 (DS 146), and the letter* Per Filium Meum *(375) (DS 148). In another letter (c. 378) the same Pope condemned the doctrine of Apollinarism: cf. DS 149. In this context, it is clear that the double affirmation of the Council of Constantinople, "He became flesh [...] and was made man" intends, more directly than did the profession of faith of Nicaea, to affirm the integrity of Christ's humanity. A letter sent after the Council to Pope Damasus clearly states the full and "perfect" humanity of Christ. The Council itself condemned Apollinarians along with other heretics (DS 151). Cf. introduction and text, n. 12.*

THE COUNCIL OF ROME. "TOME OF DAMASUS" (382)

Shortly after the General Council of Constantinople, Pope Damasus I (366-384) called a Council at Rome to renew the condemnation of various errors. Some of the canons of the "Tome of Damasus" condemn Trinitarian errors (cf. nn. 306/1ff); others Christological errors. Among these, the idea of a double sonship of Christ, one eternal, the other temporal (canon 6), was attributed to Diodorus of Tarsus (d. 394); the error of Apollinaris is once again condemned (canon 7); so too is the error of "Patripassianism" according to which the Father himself, not the Son incarnate, underwent the sufferings of the cross (canon 14).

603/6　We condemn those who affirm two sons, one who is
158　　before the ages, the other after the assumption of the
　　　　flesh from the Virgin.

603/7　We condemn those who say that the Word of God
159　　dwelling in human flesh took the place of the rational
　　　　and spiritual soul, since the Son and the Word of God
did not replace the rational and spiritual soul in his body but
rather assumed our soul (i.e., a rational and spiritual one) without
sin and saved it.

603/14　If anyone says that in the passion of the cross it is God
166　　himself who felt the pain and not the flesh and the soul
　　　　which Christ, the Son of God, had taken to himself—the
form of servant which he had accepted as Scripture says [cf. Phil
2:7]—he is mistaken.

THE GENERAL COUNCIL OF EPHESUS (431)

Christ is God and man. The extremist representatives of the Antiochian school conceived the distinction between the two natures in Christ as one between two persons. Nestorius (d.c. 450) belonged to this school. A priest in Antioch, he became patriarch of Constantinople in 428. There his doctrine met with strong opposition. A crisis broke out when Anastasius, a priest, publicly denied to Mary the title "Mother of God" (theotokos); according to him she was not the mother of God but only the mother of Christ (khristotokos) to whom the person of the Word of God had united himself. This amounted to affirming in Christ two persons, one divine and one human.

Nestorianism is based on the idea that a complete human nature, as faith affirms in Christ, necessarily implies a human person. Christ, therefore, was a human person to whom the divine person of the Word of God was united. Though this union was sublime and unique in the order of grace to the extent of constituting between the two a unique "figure" (prosôpon)—the Word of God dwelling in Christ "as in a temple"—it was nevertheless only an accidental union between persons. The divine and the human attributes which Scripture predicates of Christ belonged to either person respectively; accordingly Christ, not the Word of God, died on the cross.

Nestorius' most ardent opponent was Cyril, bishop of Alexandria (c.380-444). The final decision on the conflict which set Cyril against Nestorius fell to the General Council of Ephesus convened by emperor Theodosius II.

During the Council's first session (June 22), opened by Cyril before the arrival of the legates of Pope Celestine I, the second of three letters addressed by Cyril to Nestorius was read. This letter, dated Jan.-Feb. 430, was officially approved by the Fathers as being in conformity with the Church's orthodox faith in the incarnation of the Word and consequently in Mary's divine motherhood (cf. nn. 604-605); this letter represents the official faith of the Council of Ephesus. Cyril's third letter to Nestorius, dated Nov. 430, to which were added the "twelve anathemas" was also read before the Council Fathers but does not seem to have been officially approved by them; some of its formulations contain expressions which, though correctly meant by St. Cyril, could and in fact would be misinterpreted later. The "Twelve Anathemas" (cf.nn. 606/1-12) cannot be considered as definitions of faith. The first session ended with the formal condemnation and deposition of Nestorius. The Roman legates, soon after their arrival, gave their approval in the name of the Pope to the proceedings of the session. The second letter of St.Cyril must be understood in its historical context; the terminology had not yet acquired the precision which it would have later. For a recent reconciliation between the Catholic Church and the followers of Nestorius, cf. n. 683.

Cf. P.T. CAMELOT, *Ephèse et Chalcédoine* (Paris 1961) 13-75.

SECOND LETTER OF CYRIL OF ALEXANDRIA
TO NESTORIUS

604 For we do not say that the nature of the Word became
250 flesh by undergoing a change, nor that it was
transformed into a complete man, made up of soul and body. Rather, we affirm that the Word, having united to himself according to the hypostasis *(kath' hupostasin)* the flesh animated by a rational soul, became man in an ineffable and incomprehensible manner and was called Son of man. This union is not merely according to will or to good pleasure; nor does it consist in the assumption of a *prosôpon* ("personality") only. And though the natures which are brought together into a true unity are distinct, from both there results one Christ and one Son; not as though the distinction of natures were suppressed by their union, but rather because the divinity and the humanity by their mysterious and ineffable coming together into unity have constituted for us the one Lord, Christ and Son [...].

605 It was not that an ordinary man was born first of the
251 holy Virgin, on whom afterwards the Word descended;
what we say is that, being united with the flesh from the womb, [the Word] has undergone birth in the flesh, making the birth in the flesh his own.[...] Thus [the holy Fathers] have unhesitatingly called the holy Virgin "Mother of God" *(theotokos)*. This does not mean that the nature of the Word or his divinity received the beginning of its existence from the holy Virgin, but that, since the holy body, animated by a rational soul, which the Word united to himself, according to the hypostasis *(kath' hupostasin)*, was born from her, the Word was born according to the flesh.

THE TWELVE ANATHEMAS OF CYRIL

606/1 If any one does not confess that the Emmanuel is truly

252   God and, therefore, that the holy Virgin is the Mother of
             God *(theotokos)* (since she begot according to the flesh
the Word of God made flesh), *anathema sit.*

606/2   If anyone does not confess that the Word who is from
253   God the Father has been united to the flesh according to
             the hypostasis *(kath'hupostasin)* and that Christ is one with
his own flesh, that is to say that the same is at once God and
man, *anathema sit.*

606/3   If in Christ who is one anyone divides the hypostases
254   after union, connecting them by a mere association in
             dignity or authority or power, and not rather by a coming
together into "physical" *(phusikê)* union,[1] *anathema sit.*

606/4   If anyone ascribes separately to two persons *(prosôpa)*
255   or hypostases the words which in the gospel and
             apostolic writings are either spoken of Christ by the
saints or used by Christ about himself, and applies some to a
man considered by himself, apart from the Word, and others,
because they befit God, solely to the Word who is from God the
Father, *anathema sit.*

606/5   If anyone dares to say that Christ is a man "bearing
256   God" *(theophoros)* and does not say that he is truly
             God, the one Son by nature, since the Word became flesh
and shares as we do in blood and flesh, *anathema sit.*

606/6   If anyone says that the Word who is from God the
257   Father is the God or Lord of Christ and does not rather
             confess that the same is at once God and man
since, according to the Scriptures, the Word became flesh,
anathema sit.

606/7   If anyone says that Jesus is like a man acted upon by
258   the Word of God and that the glory of the Only-
             begotten has been added to him as belonging to
another distinct from him, *anathema sit.*

---

1. This expession which in the still fluid terminology of St. Cyril conveyed
the realism of the ineffable union of divinity and humanity was liable to be
misinterpreted. At a later period it would in fact be used, against St. Cyril's
intention, in a Monophysite sense.

606/8   If anyone dares to say that the man assumed ought
259   to be worshipped with God the Word and glorified
               with him, and that he is to be called God conjointly
with him as one person with another (for the continual addition
of "with" [sun] compels us to think in this way); and does
not rather venerate the Emmanuel with one worship and glorify
him with one praise because the Word became flesh, *anathema
sit.*

606/9   If anyone says that the one Lord Jesus Christ was
260   glorified by the Spirit, implying that through him he
               had access to a power that was not his own, and that
he received from the Spirit the power to overcome unclean spirits
and to work divine signs among us, and does not rather say
that he performed divine signs by virtue of the Spirit which was
his own, *anathema sit.*

606/10   Christ, divine Scripture says, has become "the High
261   Priest and Apostle of our confession" [Heb 3:1], and
               he offered himself for us a fragrant sacrifice [cf. Eph
5:2] to God the Father. If anyone, therefore, says that it is not the
Word of God himself who, when he became flesh and man like
us, became High Priest and our Apostle, but another, distinct
from him, who properly speaking is a man born of a woman, or
if anyone says that he offered by sacrifice for himself and not
for us only—for he who knew no sin had no need of sacrifice—
anathema sit.

606/11   If anyone does not confess that the flesh of the Lord
262   is life-giving and that it is the flesh of the Word of
               God himself who is from the Father, but [regards it]
as the flesh of another than him, united with him in dignity or
possessing only divine indwelling, and if he does not confess
that it is life-giving, as we have said, because it has become the
flesh of the Word himself who has the power to enliven all things,
anathema sit.

606/12   If anyone does not confess that the Word and God
263   suffered in the flesh and was crucified in the flesh,
               and that he tasted death in the flesh and became the
first born from the dead, being Life and giver of life as God,
anathema sit.

THE FORMULA OF UNION BETWEEN CYRIL OF ALEXANDRIA AND THE BISHOPS OF ANTIOCH (433)

The Council of Ephesus had not succeeded in dispelling all misunderstandings between Cyril of Alexandria, on the one hand, and the Orientals, mostly represented by the Antiochene bishops, on the other. These refused to adhere to some of the formulations used by St. Cyril, notably in his Twelve Anathemas against Nestorius. On the invitation of Emperor Theodosius II, John of Antioch wrote a profession of faith to which Cyril was able to subscribe. It expressed better than Cyril had done the reality of Christ's distinct human nature, and the distinction between the two natures united in one person. Pope Sixtus III congratulated both parties on their mutual agreement, thus implicitly approving the formula which consecrated their union. It is chiefly through this formula that the Antiochian school made its contribution to the subsequent development of the Christological dogma at Chalcedon (cf. nn. 613-616).

607 We confess therefore our Lord Jesus Christ, the only-
272 begotten Son of God, perfect God and perfect man
composed of rational soul and body, begotten before all
ages from the Father as to his divinity, and the same in the latter
days born of the Virgin Mary as to his humanity for us and for
our salvation. The same is one in being with the Father as to the
divinity and one in being with us as to the humanity, for a union
of two natures has taken place. Hence we confess one Christ,
one Son, one Lord. In accordance with this union without
confusion, we profess the holy Virgin to be Mother of God
(*theotokos*), for God the Word became flesh and was made man
and from the moment of conception united to himself the temple
he had taken from her.

608 As for the words of the gospels and of the apostles
273 concerning the Lord, we know that theologians have
considered some as common because they are said of
the one person (*prosôpon*), while they have distinguished others
as applying to the two natures (*phuseis*), reserving those which
befit God to Christ in his divinity while assigning those which
are lowly to Christ in his humanity.

LEO I

LETTER TO FLAVIAN OF CONSTANTINOPLE
(13 June 449)

Despite the formula of union, Dioscorus (d. 454), St. Cyril's successor in

Alexandria, remained too literally dependent on some ambiguous formulations from Cyril. In his zeal against Nestorianism, he tended to conceive the union of divinity and humanity in Christ as realised not in the person but at the level of nature: distinct before their union, divinity and humanity merged on being united into one theandric nature. In Constantinople, the monk Eutyches (378-d. after 454) carried this tendency to an extreme: according to him, on being united to the divine nature, the human nature became absorbed into it; there remained only one nature with the result that Christ's humanity was not consubstantial with ours. Condemned at a synod held in Constantinople in 448, Eutyches appealed to other synods in favour of his view. Dioscorus of Alexandria rehabilitated him in his communion.

But Leo the Great to whom Eutyches had also appealed took a definite stand against the new heresy of Monophysitism in a dogmatic letter addressed to Flavian, patriarch of Constantinople. The "Tome of Leo" contained the clearest expression to date of the doctrine of the incarnation. While distinguishing Christ's two natures clearly by use of antithetic expressions, it also upheld the unity of his person. The Tome of Leo I was immediately and universally accepted as a rule of faith. It remained famous because of the influence it exercised on the Council of Chalcedon (cf. nn. 613-616).

Cf. P.T. CAMELOT, *Ephèse et Chalcédoine* (Paris 1962) 79-114.

609 This eternal only-begotten Son of the eternal Father
291 "was born of the Holy Spirit and the Virgin Mary."
This temporal birth took nothing away from, and added nothing to, his divine and eternal birth. He spent himself entirely to repair man who had been deceived, to conquer death and to destroy by his power the devil who held sway over death. For we could not overcome the author of sin and death unless he, whom sin could not defile nor death hold in bondage, took on our nature and made it his own.

He was conceived by the Holy Spirit in the womb of the Virgin Mother, who gave him birth without losing her virginity just as she conceived him without losing her virginity.[...]

610 But this unique and wonderful generation must not be
292 understood as if the newness of this creation had
voided the condition proper to our race. It is the Holy Spirit who made the Virgin fruitful, but a true body has been taken from her body. "Wisdom has built herself a house" [Prov 9:1] and "the Word became flesh and dwelt among us" [Jn 1:14], that is, in the flesh which he took from a human being and which was animated by the breath of rational life.

611   The character proper to each of the two natures which
293   come together in one person being therefore preserved,
lowliness was taken on by majesty, weakness by strength,
mortality by eternity. And, in order to pay the debt of our condition,
the inviolable nature was united to a nature open to suffering so
that, as was fitting to heal our wounds, one and the same "mediator
between God and humankind, the man Christ Jesus" *[1 Tim 2:5]*
could die in one nature and not in the other. The true God, therefore,
was born with the complete and perfect nature of a true man; he
is complete in his own properties and complete in ours.[...]

612   And so, the Son of God, descending from his heavenly
294   throne, yet not leaving the glory of the Father, enters
into this lowly world. [He comes] in a new order,
generated by a new birth. In a new order, because, invisible in his
nature, he became visible in ours; surpassing comprehension, he
has wished to be comprehended; remaining prior to time, he
began to exist in time. The Lord of all things hid his immeasurable
majesty to take on the form of a servant. The impassible God has
not disdained to be a man subject to suffering nor the Immortal
to submit to the law of death. He is generated by a new birth,
because an inviolate virginity, untouched by concupiscence, has
provided the flesh of his body. From his mother, the Lord has
assumed the nature of man, not the guilt. Yet, the miraculous
manner of the birth of the Lord Jesus Christ, born from the womb
of a virgin, does not make his nature different from ours. For he
who is truly God is the same who is also truly man and there is
no deception in this unity in which human lowliness and the
divine majesty coincide. God suffers no change because of his
condescension, nor is man consumed by such dignity. For each of
the two natures performs the functions proper to it in communion
with the other: the Word does what pertains to the Word and the
flesh what pertains to the flesh. The one shines forth in miracles,
the other is subjected to insults. And as the Word does not lose
the glory which is his in equality with the Father, so the flesh
does not abandon the nature of our race.[...]

THE GENERAL COUNCIL OF CHALCEDON
SYMBOL OF CHALCEDON (451)

Despite the strong rebuff given by Pope Leo I to the Monophysite heresy,
Eutyches and Dioscorus, by using their influence at the imperial court,

succeeded in having a synod convened at Ephesus in August 449. The pressure exercised on the bishops at that synod prevented any freedom of voting; as a result Eutyches was rehabilitated and his doctrine approved, while his main opponents, notably Theodoret of Cyrus (d. 466) and Ibas of Edessa (d. 457), were deposed from their sees. Pope Leo called this Synod of Ephesus a "robbery" (latrocinium) and it is known as the Latrocinium of Ephesus even today. Its proceedings were condemned by a synod of Rome on September 29, 449. This synod requested Emperor Theodosius II to convoke a general Council in Italy. The emperor refused to comply with the Roman request; it was only under his successor Marcian that the fourth general Council was convened in Chalcedon. It defined solemnly the doctrine of the two natures of Christ united in the second person of the Trinity.

The Tome of Leo served as a preparation for the Council. When it was read in assembly, the Council Fathers exclaimed: "Peter has spoken through the mouth of Leo." The Symbol promulgated by the Council on Oct. 22 borrows from Leo's firm terminology to repudiate the Nestorian heresy on the one hand and the Eutychian on the other. It forms a synthesis of the Antiochian and the Alexandrian schools as regards the mystery of the Word Incarnate. For a 1973 reconciliation between the Coptic Church of Egypt and the Catholic Church, cf. n. 671a.

613
300
[The Council] opposes those who attempt to divide the mystery of the incarnation into two sons. It excludes from the sacred assembly those who dare to declare subject to suffering the divinity of the Only-begotten. It withstands those who imagine a mixture or confusion of Christ's two natures (*phusis*). It rejects those who fancy that the form of servant assumed by him among us is of a heavenly nature and foreign to ours in essence (*ousia*). It condemns those who invent the myth of two natures of the Lord before the union and of one nature after the union.

(Definition)

614
301
Following therefore the holy Fathers, we unanimously teach to confess one and the same Son, our Lord Jesus Christ, the same perfect in divinity and perfect in humanity, the same truly God and truly man composed of rational soul and body, the same one in being (*homoousios*) with the Father as to the divinity and one in being with us as to the humanity, like unto us in all things but sin [*cf. Heb 4:15*]. The same was begotten from the Father before the ages as to the divinity and in the latter days for us and our salvation was born as to his humanity from Mary the Virgin Mother of God.

615 We confess that one and the same Lord Jesus Christ, the
302 only-begotten Son, must be acknowledged in two
natures, without confusion or change, without division
or separation. The distinction between the natures was never
abolished by their union but rather the character proper to each
of the two natures was preserved as they came together in one
person *(prosôpon)* and one hypostasis. He is not split or divided
into two persons, but he is one and the same Only-begotten,
God the Word, the Lord Jesus Christ, as formerly the prophets
and later Jesus Christ himself have taught us about him and as
has been handed down to us by the Symbol of the Fathers.

(Sanction)

616 As these points have been determined by us with all
303 possible precision and care, the holy ecumenical Council
has ordained that no one may propose, put into writing,
devise, hold or teach to others any other faith than this.

JOHN II
LETTER TO THE SENATE OF CONSTANTINOPLE (534)

*Even after the important definitions on the person of Christ, the
implications of the mystery of the incarnation remained obscure to many. Some
bishops of Palestine and Egypt inclined to Monophysitism and thought that
the doctrine of Chalcedon had contradicted that of Ephesus. In 519 some
Scythian monks, also Monophysites, sought from Pope Hormisdas approbation
of the formula: "One of the three has suffered in the flesh"; they considered it
to reflect the 12th anathema of St. Cyril (n. 606/12) but interpreted it in a
Monophysite way. They did not obtain satisfaction. Wanting to rally all
Monophysite tendencies to the common faith, Emperor Justinian later enquired
from Pope John II whether the formula, with its implications for God's
passibility and Mary's divine motherhood, was acceptable. While answering
positively, the Pope explained that "one" refers to "one person" of the Trinity
who has suffered in the flesh, and drew the consequences as regards the "true
and proper" divine motherhood of Mary.*

617 [Emperor Justinian] has pointed out, as you have learned
401 from the contents of his letter, that disputes have arisen
over the following three questions: Can one say that
Christ our God is "one of the Trinity", that is one holy person
among the three persons of the Holy Trinity? Did Christ our
God who in his divinity is impassible suffer in the flesh? Must
Mary, the ever Virgin Mother of our Lord and God Jesus Christ,

be called truly and properly Mother of God and Mother of God the Word incarnate from her?[...]

Christ is one of the Holy Trinity, that is one holy person or subsistence *(subsistentia)*—one hypostasis as the Greeks say— among the three persons of the Holy Trinity.

(There follow among other quotations: Gen 3:22; 1 Cor 8:6; the Nicene Symbol).

The fact that God did truly suffer in the flesh we confirm likewise by the following witnesses *[Deut 28:66; Jn 14:6; Mal 3:8; Acts 3:15; 20:28; 1 Cor 2:8; Cyril of Alexandria, Anathema 12; Leo I, Tome to Flavian, etc.].*

We teach that it is right for Catholics to confess that the glorious and holy Mary, ever Virgin, is truly and properly the Mother of God and Mother of God the Word incarnate from her. For it is he himself who truly and properly became incarnate in these latter days and deigned to be born of the holy and glorious Virgin Mother. Hence, since the Son of God became incarnate and was born from her truly and properly, we confess her to be truly and properly the Mother of God incarnate and born from her. In proper terms lest one should believe that the Lord Jesus Christ received the name of God as a title of honour or as a favour as Nestorius foolishly taught; truly, lest one should believe that from the Virgin he took on a mere appearance of flesh or in some other way a flesh which was not real, as Eutyches irreverently declared.

SYNOD OF CONSTANTINOPLE
ANATHEMAS AGAINST THE ORIGENISTS (543)

Among the errors attributed to the disciples of Origen as regards the relation between soul and body (cf. n. 401i, 402), some touched on the doctrine of the incarnation of the Word.

618/2 If anyone says or holds that the soul of the Lord has
404   existed first and has been united to God the Word before the incarnation and the birth from the Virgin, *anathema sit.*

618/3 If anyone says or holds that the body of our Lord Jesus
405   Christ was first formed in the womb of the holy Virgin and that God the Word and the soul already in existence were later united with it, *anathema sit.*

VIGILIUS

CONSTITUTUM I (14 May 553)

The Monophysite danger persisted long after Chalcedon. In particular, there arose a "Neo-Chalcedonian" current which advocated a compromise between the Chalcedonian formula and Monophysitism. Its protagonists demanded the condemnation of the first opponents of Monophysitism, Theodoret of Cyrus (d. 466) and Ibas of Edessa (d. 457) as well as of Theodore of Mopsuestia (d. 428), the teacher of Nestorius, all of whom they accused of Nestorian tendencies. Attention was thus concentrated on the "three chapters", the term under which the three authors were grouped.

Emperor Justinian, anxious to re-unite the separated Churches, promulgated in 543 an edict favouring this condemnation. Pope Vigilius opposed it, the reason being the fact that the three authors had been recognised as orthodox by the Council of Chalcedon. Later, however, the Pope yielded to pressure and, having been transferred by force to Constantinople, assented in 548 to the condemnation of the three chapters (in the falsified form in which their works were then known). This capitulation caused much unrest in the West and led the Pope to suggest to the emperor the convocation of a general Council which would settle the conflict. As relations between Vigilius and Justinian deteriorated to the point of rupture, Pope Vigilius wrote a profession of faith (552) against the Monophysite tendencies of the emperor (cf. DS 412-415); in rebellion against the Pope the "Second Council of Constantinople" opened on May 5, 553.

The condemnations pronounced during the Council's first sessions led the Pope to dissociate himself from the assembly by publishing his first Constitutum. In this document he condemns some propositions attributed to Theodore of Mopsuestia but upholds the orthodoxy of the "three chapters". The document ends with five anathemas directed against the Nestorian heresy and uses the formulations of Ephesus and Chalcedon to affirm the union of both natures in the one person of Christ.

619/1 If anyone, in maintaining the immutability of the
416   divine nature, does not confess that the Word became
       flesh and from the very conception in the womb of the
Virgin united to himself according to the hypostasis the human
nature in its origin, but says that God the Word came to be with
a man who had already been in existence with the result that
the holy Virgin is not believed to be truly the Mother of God
but is so called in words only, *anathema sit.*

619/2 If anyone denies that the unity of natures was effected
417   in Christ according to the hypostasis, but says that God
       the Word dwelt in a man having a separate existence as
one among the just, and so does not confess the union of the

natures according to the hypostasis which means that God the Word remained and still remains one hypostasis or person with the flesh which he assumed, *anathema sit.*

619/3 If anyone so divides in the one Christ the words of the
418 Gospels and of the apostles that he also introduces a division between the natures which are united in him, *anathema sit.*

619/4 If anyone says that the one Jesus Christ who is both true
419 Son of God and true Son of man did not know the future or the day of the Last Judgment and that he could know only as much as the divinity, dwelling in him as in another, revealed to him, *anathema sit.*

619/5 If anyone, referring to the passage of the apostle in the
420 epistle to the Hebrews *[Heb 5:8,7]* where it is said that Christ learned through experience what it means to obey and that with loud cries and tears he offered up prayers and supplications to him who was able to save him from the dead, applies the passage to Christ divested of his divinity and reaching perfection through his virtuous efforts, with the result that he seems to introduce two Christs or two Sons and does not believe that we must confess and worship one and the same Christ, Son of God and son of man, of two natures and in two natures which are inseparable and undivided, *anathema sit.*

THE SECOND GENERAL COUNCIL OF CONSTANTINOPLE
ANATHEMAS AGAINST THE THREE CHAPTERS (553)

In the conflict which opposed Emperor Justinian to Pope Vigilius the Council sided with the emperor. It pursued its work, disregarding the first Constitutum of Vigilius (nn. 619/1-5). In its last session it formulated 14 anathemas. Among these the first ten (nn. 620/1-10) re-assert the mystery of the incarnation mostly as expressed by St. Cyril against Nestorius to whom they assimilate Theodore of Mopsuestia. Canon 8 (n. 620/8) defends the orthodoxy of an expression used correctly by St. Cyril but which could and had been misused by the Monophysites. Canon 11 is directed against various heresies (DS 433); the last three Canons, against the "three chapters" and the writings of Theodore of Mopsuestia (n. 621), Theodoret of Cyrus (n.622), and Ibas of Edessa (n. 623), respectively.

In his second Constitutum of February 554, Pope Vigilius explicitly approved the Council's condemnation of the "three chapters", thus conferring post factum the value of a general Council on part of the work of Constantinople

II. This approval does not, however, seem to extend to all the canons but only to the last three, directly concerned with the "three chapters". The Pope's approval of these canons implies the condemnation of the propositions attributed in them to the "three chapters", without passing judgment on the authors and their actual writings. The significance of the second general Council of Constantinople consists in a reiterated condemnation of the Nestorian heresy.

620/1 If anyone does not confess that Father, Son and Holy
421 Spirit, are one nature *(phusis)* or essence *(ousia)*, one might and power, a Trinity one in being *(homoousios)*, one Godhead to be worshipped in three hypostases or persons *(prosôpon), anathema sit.* For one is the God and Father from whom all things are, one is the Lord Jesus Christ through whom all things are and one the Holy Spirit in whom all things are.

620/2 If anyone does not confess the two births of the Word of
422 God, one from the Father before the ages which is timeless and incorporeal, the other [which took place] in the latter days when the same [Word], descending from heaven was made flesh from Mary, the holy and glorious Mother of God ever Virgin, and was born of her, *anathema sit.*

620/3 If anyone says that the Word of God who performed
423 miracles was someone other than the Christ who suffered, or that God the Word was with the Christ born of a woman *[cf. Gal 4:4]* or was in him as one in another, but [does] not [confess] one and the same our Lord Jesus Christ the Word of God incarnate and made man, to whom belong the miracles and the sufferings which he has voluntarily endured in the flesh, *anathema sit .*

620/4 If anyone says that the union of God the Word with
424 the man was no more than a union by grace or by operation *(energeia)*, or by equality of honour, or by authority or relation, affection or power; or if he says that it took place because of good-will, the Word of God being well pleased with the man for whom he had high esteem, as Theodore foolishly asserts; or if he speaks of a union by homonymy as the Nestorians who, by giving to God the Word the name of Jesus and of Christ and by calling the man separately considered Christ and Son, evidently speak of two persons while they pretend to speak of one person and one Christ because of the common

appellation, honour, dignity and adoration; but does not confess that the union of God the Word with the flesh animated by a rational and intellectual soul took place by way of synthesis, that is according to the hypostasis, as the holy Fathers have taught, and consequently denies that he has only one hypostasis who is our Lord Jesus Christ, one of the Holy Trinity, *anathema sit*.

425   For, since union can be understood in various ways, some following the impiety of Apollinaris and Eutyches and upholding the obliteration of the elements which come together, maintain a union by confusion. Others who think with Theodore and Nestorius, favouring division, introduce an accidental union. The Holy Church of God, rejecting these two impious heresies, confesses the union of God the Word with the flesh as being by synthesis, that is according to the hypostasis. For, in the mystery of Christ union by synthesis not only preserves from confusion what has come together but also tolerates no division.

620/5 If anyone understands the one hypostasis of our Lord
426   Jesus Christ as admitting the meaning of several hypostases, and so tries to introduce into the mystery of Christ two hypostases or two persons, and after having introduced two persons, speaks of one person as regards dignity, honour and adoration, as Theodore and Nestorius have written senselessly; and if he makes the slanderous assertion that the holy Council of Chalcedon has used the term "one hypostasis" in this impious way and does not confess that the Word of God has been united to the flesh according to the hypostasis and that, therefore, there is but one hypostasis or person, and that this is the sense in which the holy Council of Chalcedon confessed one hypostasis of our Lord Jesus Christ, *anathema sit*. For the Holy Trinity has had no person or hypostasis added to it, even by the incarnation of God the Word, one of the Holy Trinity.

620/6 If anyone says that the glorious holy Mary, ever virgin,
427   is not Mother of God in the true sense but only by an abuse of language, or that she is so by relation, meaning that a mere man was born from her and not God the Word made flesh in her, though, according to those who hold this, the birth of this man can be attributed to God the Word in so far as he

was with the man at his birth; and if he makes the slanderous assertion that it was in this blasphemous sense thought out by Theodore that the Holy Council of Chalcedon called the virgin "Mother of God"; or if anyone calls her mother of the man or mother of Christ as though Christ were not God, but does not confess that she is Mother of God in the true and proper sense since God the Word, begotten from the Father before the ages, became incarnate from her in the latter days, and this is the pious sense in which the holy Council of Chalcedon confessed her to be the Mother of God, *anathema sit.*

620/7 If anyone, while using the phrase "in two natures"
428 does not confess that the one Jesus Christ our Lord is acknowledged in divinity and humanity, signifying thereby the distinction of the natures of which the ineffable union was made without any confusion, without either the Word being transformed into the nature of the flesh or the flesh being translated into the nature of the Word—for each of the two remains what it is by nature, even after the union according to the hypostasis has taken place—, but if he applies the phrase to the mystery of Christ as meaning a division into parts, or if, while confessing the plurality of natures in one and the same Jesus, our Lord, the Word of God made flesh, he does not only accept in "theory" the distinction between the principles of which he [Christ] is constituted, a distinction which is not suppressed by their union — for one is from both and both are by one —, but uses the number with the intention of separating the natures and of attributing to each its own hypostasis, *anathema sit.*

620/8 If anyone, while confessing that the union was made
429 out of two natures, the divinity and the humanity, or while speaking of "one incarnate nature *(phusis)* of God the Word",[1] does not understand these expressions according to the teaching of the holy Fathers, that is as meaning that from the divine and the human natures, when the union according to the hypostasis was realised, there resulted one Christ; but if by

---

1. This expression was first used by Apollinaris who denied the completeness of Christ's humanity. It was later attributed to St. Athanasius and used by St. Cyril who understood it correctly though its terminology remanis deficient. Cf. also the third anathema of Cyril (n. 606/3 and note).

these expressions he attempts to introduce one nature or essence (*ousia*) of the divinity and of the flesh of Christ, *anathema sit*.

430 For when we say that the only-begotten Word was united according to the hypostasis, we do not say that there took place any confusion between natures; rather, we think that God the Word was united to the flesh, each of the two natures remaining what it is. This is why Christ is one, God and man; the same, one in being (*homoousios*) with the Father as to the divinity and one in being with us as to the humanity. For the Church of God repudiates and condemns equally those who introduce a separation or division and those who introduce a confusion into the mystery of the divine incarnation.

620/9 If anyone says that Christ is worshipped in two natures,
431 whereby he introduces two acts of worship, one proper to God the Word and the other proper to the man, or if anyone, in order to suppress the flesh or to fuse the divinity and the humanity, speaks falsely of one nature (*phusis*) or essence (*ousia*) of the elements which have been united and worships Christ in this sense but does not venerate by one act of worship God the Word made flesh together with his own flesh, according to the Tradition received in the Church of God from the beginning, *anathema sit*.

620/10 If anyone does not confess that he who was crucified in
432 the flesh, our Lord Jesus Christ, is true God, Lord of glory and one of the Holy Trinity, *anathema sit*.

621 12. If anyone defends the impious Theodore of
434 Mopsuestia who said that God the Word is one while Christ is another who, disturbed by the passions of the soul and the desires of the flesh, freed himself gradually from inferior inclinations and, having improved through the progress of his works and having become irreproachable in his conduct, was baptised as a mere man in the name of the Father and of the Son and of the Holy Spirit; who received through baptism the grace of the Holy Spirit and was deemed worthy of [divine] adoption; who, much like an image of the emperor, is worshipped in the person of God the Word; who after the resurrection became perfectly steadfast in his thoughts and wholly impeccable.

Furthermore, the same impious Theodore has said that the union of God the Word with Christ is similar to that of man and wife, of which the apostle says: "the two shall be in one flesh" [Eph 5:31]. And, in addition to his other countless blasphemies, he dared to say that, when after the resurrection the Lord breathed on the disciples and said, "Receive the Holy Spirit" [Jn 20:22], he did not give them the Holy Spirit but only breathed on them figuratively. He also said, as regards the confession of Thomas after the resurrection, when having touched the hands and the side of Christ he said, "My Lord and my God" [Jn 20:28], that it was not addressed to Christ by Thomas, but that, struck by the miracle of the resurrection, Thomas praised God who had raised Christ.

435   Worse still, in the commentary which he wrote on the Acts of the apostles, the same Theodore compares Christ with Plato, Manes, Epicurus and Marcion. As each one of these, he says, having devised his own doctrine, caused his disciples to be called Platonists, Manichaeans, Epicureans or Marcionites, similarly, Christ having devised a doctrine, it is after him that Christians were named.

If anyone, therefore, defends the afore-mentioned most impious Theodore and his impious writings in which he spreads the blasphemies mentioned and countless others against our great God and Saviour Jesus Christ, and if he does not condemn him and his impious writings and those as well who accept him either by justifying him or by saying that his positions are orthodox, and those who have written in his favour and in favour of his impious writings, and those who hold similar opinions or once held them and remained to the end in such heresy, *anathema sit*.

622   13. If anyone defends the impious works of Theodoret
436   against the orthodox faith, against the first holy Council of Ephesus and against St. Cyril and his twelve anathemas, and if he defends all that he has written in favour of the impious Theodore and Nestorius[...], and, because of this, brands as impious those teachers of the Church who confess the union of God the Word according to the hypostasis and does not condemn the above-mentioned impious writings and those who have held and hold like opinions together with all who have written against the orthodox faith and against St. Cyril and

his twelve anathemas and have died in such impiety, *anathema sit.*

623 14. If anyone defends the letter said to have been written
437 by Ibas to Maris the Persian, which denies that God the
Word, made flesh from Mary the holy Mother of God
ever virgin, became man; but asserts [instead] that a mere man
whom it terms Temple was born of her, as though God the Word
was one and the man another; in which also St. Cyril the herald
of the orthodox faith of Christians is accused of being a heretic
and of having written in the same vein as the impious
Apollinaris; in which furthermore the first holy Council of
Ephesus is blamed for having condemned Nestorius without
investigation; the same impious letter moreover qualifies as
impious and contrary to the orthodox faith the twelve anathemas
of St. Cyril and justifies Theodore and Nestorius together with
their impious doctrines and writings. If, therefore, anyone defends
the above-mentioned letter and does not condemn it and its
defenders who say that it is orthodox or that part of it is
orthodox, together with those who have written or are writing
in its favour or in favour of its impious contents, and those who
dare to justify it and its impious contents in the name of the
holy Fathers or of the holy Council of Chalcedon, and remain to
the end in these errors, *anathema sit.*

GREGORY THE GREAT
LETTER TO EULOGIUS, PATRIARCH OF ALEXANDRIA
(600)

*In the sixth century a sect originated from Monophysitism and held what
may be called an inverted monophysitism: the divine nature was reduced to
the human rather than the human absorbed into the divine. Thus, as regards
Christ's knowledge, this sect's adherents, basing themselves on a passage of
Mark's gospel, admitted lack of knowledge concerning the day of judgement.
Against these "Agnoetes", Eulogius, Patriarch of Alexandria (d.607) wrote
an important treatise. Pope Gregory the Great approved it as conformable to
the ideas of St. Augustine. This document is not, however, a document of
faith.*

(On the knowledge of Christ against the Agnoetes)

624 Concerning the passage of Scripture according to which
474 "neither the Son nor the angels know the day and the
hour" [*cf. Mk 13:32*], your Holiness is entirely correct in

judging that it is certainly not to be referred to the Son considered
as the Head, but considered as the Body which we are. In a
number of passages [...] Augustine understands it in this sense.
He also says that it can be understood as referring to the Son
himself, because almighty God sometimes speaks in human
fashion, as for instance when he says to Abraham: "Now I know
that you fear God" [cf. Gen 22:12], which does not mean that
God came then to know that he was feared but that he then
made Abraham recognise that he feared God. Just as we speak
of a joyful day not because the day is joyful but because it makes
us joyful, so the almighty Son says that he does not know the
day which he causes not to be known, not because he himself
does not know but because he does not in any way allow it to
be known.

625   Thus, it is also said that only the Father knows, because
475   the Son who is one in being with him (consubstantialis)
            has, from the nature which he receives from him and
which is superior to that of the angels, a knowledge which angels
do not have. This can also, therefore, be understood in a
more subtle way by saying that the only-begotten Son incarnate,
made perfect man for us, knew the day and the hour of judgment
in his human nature but did not know it *from* his human nature.
What he knew therefore *in* his humanity he did not *know from* it,
because it is by the power of his divinity that God-made-man
knew the day and the hour of judgment [...]. Thus it is that he
denied having the knowledge which he did not have from the
human nature by which he was a creature as the angels are, as
he also denied it to the angels because they are creatures. The
God-man knows therefore the day and the hour of judgment,
but precisely because God is man.

626   It is perfectly clear that whoever is not a Nestorian
476   cannot in any way be an Agnoete. For, how can one who
            professes that the Wisdom of God himself became
incarnate ever maintain that there is anything which the Wisdom
of God does not know? It is written: "In the beginning was the
Word and the Word was with God and the Word was God.[...]
All things were made through him" [Jn 1:1, 3]. If all things, then
undoubtedly the day and the hour also. Who would then be so
foolish as to say that the Word of the Father made something he
did not know? Scripture again says: "Jesus knowing that the

Father had given all things into his hands[...]" *[Jn 13:3]*. If all things, then certainly the day and the hour also. Who then is so foolish as to say that the Son received in his hands what he was ignorant of?[...]

THE LATERAN COUNCIL (649)

The first attempt to end the Monophysite schism by condemning the "three chapters" had not succeeded. Sergius, patriarch of Constantinople from 610 till 638, made a new effort to re-unite the separated Churches; he was sustained in this effort by Emperor Heraclius who wanted to strengthen his empire. The attempt of Sergius was not, however, without danger to the true faith. While acknowledging two natures in Christ after union, he transposed the Monophysite tendency to the level of Christ's actions and will, recognizing but one action (mono-energism) and one will (monothelitism).

Sergius first had recourse to Pope Honorius, suggesting that for the sake of maintaining peace among the Churches, the expression "two actions" which divided them be avoided; though holding the true faith, the Pope in a letter to Sergius (634) (DS 487-488) had for the sake of peace consented to the use of the expression "one will" and suggested that all controversial expressions be avoided. Emboldened by the Pope's failure to uphold the necessity of professing two wills and actions, Sergius developed Monothelitism more definitely in his Ecthesis, promulgated by Emperor Heraclius (638) after the death of Sergius and of Pope Honorius. This amounted to reviving Monophysitism by drawing the consequences naturally implied in it: if there is in Christ but one will and one action, the reason must be that there is only one nature, for action is derived from nature.

This is why Mono-energism and Monothelitism had to be condemned, notwithstanding the attempt made by Emperor Constans II in his Typos (648) to end the controversy. These errors were condemned more than once, notably and with great solemnity by the Lateran Council (649), convened by Pope Martin I, which gathered 105 bishops from Italy and Africa. This was not an ecumenical council but the authority of its canons grew with their recognition by the Pope as a rule of faith. The Greek text, more precise than the Latin, is followed here. Canons 5 (627/5) and 15 (627/15) give the official interpretation of expressions used by St. Cyril (cf.n. 620/8, note) and Pseudo-Dionysius respectively. The final condemnation of Monothelitism will come later in the Third General Council of Constantinople (680-681)(cf. nn. 635-637).

627/1 If anyone does not, according to the holy Fathers,
501 confess truly and properly the Father and the Son and the Holy Spirit, Trinity in unity and unity in Trinity, that is, one God in three consubstantial hypostases equal in glory; and for the three one and the same Godhead, nature, essence *(ousia)*, power, Lordship, kingship, authority, will, action *(energeia)*

and sovereignty; uncreated, without beginning, infinite, immutable, creator of all beings and holding them together in his providence, let him be condemned.

627/2 If anyone does not, according to the holy Fathers, 502   confess truly and properly that God the Word, one of the Holy, consubstantial and adorable Trinity, descended from heaven, became incarnate from the Holy Spirit and from the most holy Mary, ever virgin, and was made man; that he was crucified and of his own free will suffered in the flesh for us and our salvation and was buried, that he rose again on the third day and ascended into heaven, that he is seated at the right hand of the Father and will come again with the glory of the Father, with the flesh assumed by him and animated by an intellectual soul, to judge the living and the dead, let him be condemned.

(627/3) *(See text in n. 703)*

627/4 If anyone does not, according to the holy Fathers, 504   confess truly and properly two births of the one our Lord Jesus Christ himself, one incorporeal and eternal from God the Father before all ages, the other, corporeal and in the last age, from holy Mary, ever virgin, Mother of God; and one and the same Jesus Christ our Lord and God, one in being with the Father as to his divinity, one in being with us and with his mother as to his humanity, subject to suffering in his flesh while he is impassible in his divinity, limited in his flesh while he is illimited in his spirit, at once created and uncreated, earthly and heavenly, perceptible by sense and by intellect, bound by space and beyond space, in order that the whole human reality which had fallen a prey to sin be restored by one who is fully man and God at the same time, let him be condemned.

627/5 If anyone does not, according to the holy Fathers, 505   confess truly and properly "one incarnate nature of God the Word", by which is meant that our substance is incarnate perfectly and without restriction in Christ who is God, sin only being excepted, let him be condemned.

627/6 If anyone does not, according to the holy Fathers, 506   confess truly and properly that one and the same Lord and God, Jesus Christ, is out of two natures, the divinity and the humanity, and in two natures, the divinity and the humanity united according to the hypostasis without confusion or division, let him be condemned.

627/7
507
If anyone does not, according to the holy Fathers, confess truly and properly that, after their ineffable union by which the one and only Christ exists, the essential distinction of the natures is safeguarded in him without confusion or division, let him be condemned.

627/8
508
If anyone does not, according to the holy Fathers, confess truly and properly that the union of the natures by synthesis, that is according to the hypostasis, by which the one and only Christ exists, is verified in him without confusion or division, let him be condemned.

627/9
509
If anyone does not, according to the holy Fathers, confess truly and properly that the natural properties of the divinity of Christ and of his humanity are fully preserved in him, complete and undiminished, by which is truly confirmed the fact that the same is perfect God and perfect man by nature, let him be condemned.

627/10
510
If anyone does not, according to the holy Fathers, confess truly and properly two wills, the divine and the human, intimately united in one and the same Christ God, since it is one and the same who by each of his two natures has willed our salvation, let him be condemned.

627/11
511
If anyone does not, according to the holy Fathers, confess truly and properly two actions (*energeia*), the divine and the human, intimately united in one and the same Christ God, since it is one and the same who by each of his two natures has worked our salvation, let him be condemned.

627/12
512
If anyone, following the infamous heretics, confesses only one nature or one will or one action of divinity and humanity in the Christ God, destroying thereby what the holy Fathers confess and denying the mystery of the incarnation of our Saviour, let him be condemned.

627/13
513
If, in the Christ God in whom, as has been taught by our holy Fathers, the two wills and the two actions, the divine and the human, are essentially preserved

in their unity, anyone, following the infamous heretics, confesses against the doctrine of the holy Fathers one will only and only one action, let him be condemned.

627/14 If anyone, following the infamous heretics, confesses
514 their impious doctrine of one will and one action in the Christ God, and denies and rejects the two wills and two actions, the divine and the human, "physically" (*phusikôs*) preserved in their unity in the Christ God, as is professed about him by the holy Fathers according to orthodox doctrine, let him be condemned.

627/15 If anyone, following the infamous heretics, foolishly
515 admits the divine-human action which the Greeks call theandric (*theandrikên*) as being one action, but does not profess according to the holy Fathers that it is two-fold, that is divine and human, or if he professes that the new appellation "theandric" which has been introduced designates one action only and does not rather manifest the wonderful and glorious union of the two actions, let him be condemned.

627/16 If, while in the Christ God, as piously taught by the
516 holy Fathers, the essential union of the two wills and of the two actions, the divine and the human, is preserved, anyone, following the infamous heretics who seek to destroy, foolishly introduces oppositions and divisions in the mystery of his (incarnation) and for this reason does not refer the evangelical and apostolic sayings concerning the Saviour to the same Jesus Christ our Lord and God according to the illustrious Cyril in order to confirm the fact that one and the same is by nature truly God and truly man, let him be condemned.

THE ELEVENTH COUNCIL OF TOLEDO
SYMBOL OF FAITH (675)

For this Symbol of faith, see n. 308i. This Symbol of faith borrows from dogmatic statements already formulated in the professions of faith promulgated by previous synods held in the same city, especially the fourth Council of Toledo (633) (DS 485) and the sixth Council of Toledo (638) (DS 490-493). It also incorporates data from the Pseudo-Athanasian Symbol Quicumque (nn. 16-17) and from the great Latin doctors, especially St. Augustine. It reflects the Latin approach to the basic mysteries of the faith and contains its deepest insights and clearest formulations of the doctrine of the Trinity and of the incarnation. Here the doctrine of the incarnation and the redemption is quoted. For the doctrine on the Trinity, cf. nn 308-316; for the doctrine on the last things, cf. n. 2302.

(The Incarnation)

628
533
Of these three persons we believe that only the person of the Son has assumed a true human nature, without sin, from the holy and immaculate Virgin Mary, for the liberation of the human race. He was begotten from her in a new order and by a new birth: in a new order, because, invisible in his divinity, he is shown visible in the flesh; by a new birth, because an inviolate virginity, without knowing the contact of man, supplied the matter of his body, being made fruitful by the Holy Spirit. This virgin-birth is neither grasped by reason nor illustrated by example. Were it grasped by reason, it would not be wonderful; were it illustrated by example, it would not be unique. Yet we must not believe that the Holy Spirit is the Father of the Son because Mary conceived by the overshadowing of the same Holy Spirit, lest we should seem to affirm that the Son has two fathers—which it is certainly impious to say.

(One person and two natures)

629
534
In this wonderful conception, by which Wisdom built herself a house, "the Word became flesh and dwelt among us" *[Jn 1:14]*. The Word himself, however, was neither transformed nor changed in the flesh in such a way that he who willed to be man would have ceased to be God; but the Word became flesh in such a way that in him there is not only the Word of God and the flesh of man, but also a rational human soul, and that this whole is called God on account of God and man on account of man. In this Son of God we believe that there are two natures, one divine, the other human, which the one person of Christ has so united in himself that the divinity can never be separated from the humanity nor the humanity from the divinity. Christ, therefore, is perfect God and perfect man in the unity of one person. By asserting that there are two natures in the Son, we do not, however, set up two persons in him, lest—which God forbid—the Trinity should seem to become a quaternity. For God the Word did not take the person of man but his nature; he took the temporal substance of the flesh into the eternal person of the divinity.

(Only the Son is incarnate)

630   Likewise, we believe that the Father and the Son and
535   the Holy Spirit are one substance; we do not, however,
    say that the Virgin Mary gave birth to the unity of this
Trinity, but only to the Son who alone assumed our nature in
the unity of his person. We must also believe that the entire
Trinity brought about the incarnation of the Son of God, because
the works of the Trinity are inseparable. However, only the Son
took the form of a servant [cf. Phil 2:7] in the singleness of person,
not in the unity of the divine nature; he took it into what is
proper to the Son, not into what is common to the Trinity. This
form has been joined to him in the unity of person, so that the
Son of God and the Son of man are one Christ. Thus, the same
Christ in his two natures is made of three substances: that of the
Word which must be referred to the essence of God alone, that
of the body and of the soul which belong to the true man.

(Two births of the Son of God)

631   He has therefore in himself the double substance of his
536   divinity and of our humanity. By the fact that he has
    come forth from the Father without a beginning, he is
said only to be born, not to be made or predestined; but by the
fact that he was born from the Virgin Mary, we must believe
that he was born and made and predestined. Yet, in him both
births are wonderful, because he was begotten from the Father
without a mother before all ages, and in the end of the ages he
was generated from a mother without a father. He who in as
much as he is God created Mary, in as much as he is man was
created from Mary. He is at once the Father and the Son of his
Mother Mary. Similarly, by the fact that he is God, he is equal to
the Father; by the fact that he is man, he is less than the Father.
Likewise, we must believe that he is both greater and less than
himself: for in the form of God the Son himself is greater than
himself because of the humanity which he has assumed and
to which the divinity is superior; but in the form of the
servant he is less than himself, that is, in his humanity which
is recognised as inferior to the divinity. For, while by the
flesh which he has assumed he is recognised not only as less
than the Father but also as less than himself, according to the
divinity he is co-equal with the Father; both he and the Father

are greater than the man whom he person of the Son alone assumed.

(God and man)

632 Likewise, to the question whether the Son might be
537 equal to, and less than the Holy Spirit, as we believe
him to be now equal to, now less than the Father, we answer: according to the form of God he is equal to the Father and to the Holy Spirit; according to the form of the servant, he is less than both the Father and the Holy Spirit. For neither the Holy Spirit nor the Father but only the person of the Son has assumed the flesh by virtue of which he is believed to be less than those two persons. Similarly, we believe that this Son is distinct though inseparable from God the Father and the Holy Spirit as a person, and distinct by nature from the humanity *(ab homine)* which he has assumed. Again, with his human nature *(cum homine)* he is one person; but with the Father and the Holy Spirit he is one in the nature or substance of the Godhead.

(Trinity and Incarnation)

633 Yet we must believe that the Son was sent not only by
538 the Father but also by the Holy Spirit, for he himself
says through the prophet: "And now the Lord God and his Spirit has sent me" *[Is 48:16]*. He is also understood to be sent by himself, because not only the will but also the action of the whole Trinity is believed to be inseparable. For he who before all ages was called the only-begotten became the first-born in time: he is the only-begotten on account of the substance of the Godhead, the first-born on account of the nature of flesh which he has assumed.

(The redemption)

634 In the form of man which he assumed, we believe,
539 according to the truth of the Gospel, that he was
conceived without sin, he who alone "was made sin" *[cf. 2 Cor 5:21]* for our sake, that is who became sacrifice for our sins. And yet he endured his passion for our offences without losing his divinity. Condemned to death, he has experienced on the cross a real death in the flesh and on the third day, restored to life by his own power, he rose from the grave.

THE THIRD GENERAL COUNCIL OF CONSTANTINOPLE DEFINITION OF THE TWO WILLS AND ACTIONS IN CHRIST (681)

Monothelitism and Mono-energism had been condemned by the Counil of Lateran (nn. 627/10-14). The Third Council of Constantinople (680-681) gave to this condemnation the authority of an ecumencial Council. It was convoked by Emperor Constantine IV with the full consent of Pope Agatho. In March 680 the Pope had written a letter to the Emperor in which he explained the true doctrine as regards the two wills and actions in Christ and their union (cf. DS 544-545). This and a similar letter presented by a Synod of Rome (DS 547-548) were acclaimed by the Council in its fourth session in November 680. The Council meant to settle the matter definitively and to extirpate the Monothelistic tendency then mostly represented by Macarius, patriarch of Constantinople, who was condemned during the Council's 9th session. Pope Honorius too was taken to task in the 13th session for having failed to uphold the true doctrine against Sergius (DS 552) (cf. n. 627i). During its 18th and last session (16 Sept. 681), the Council approved a profession of faith, interspersed with anathemas directed against the Monothelitists. It explicitates what was already implicitly contained in the doctrine of Leo the Great (n. 612) and in the dogma of Chalcedon (cf. nn. 614ff). One year later, Pope Leo II, successor of Agatho, approved the proceedings of the Council.

635 We likewise proclaim in him, according to the teaching
556 of the holy Fathers, two natural volitions or wills and
two natural actions, without division, without change, without separation, without confusion. The two natural wills are not—by no means—opposed to each other as the impious heretics assert; but his human will is compliant, it does not resist or oppose but rather submits to his divine and almighty will. For, as the wise Athanasius says, it was necessary that the will of the flesh move itself *(kinêthênai)*, but also that it be submitted to the divine will;[1] because, just as his flesh is said to be and is the flesh of God the Word, so too the natural will of his flesh is said to be and is God the Word's very own, as he himself declares: "I have come down from heaven, not to do my own will but the will of him who sent me "*[Jn 6:38]*. He calls the will of his flesh his own will, because the flesh also has become his own. For just as his most holy and immaculate flesh, animated by his soul,

---

1. ATHANASIUS OF ALEXANDRIA, *Tractatus in illud "Nunc anima mea turbata est"* *(Jn 12:27)* (this treatise has not been preserved).

has not been destroyed by being divinised but remained in its own state and kind, so also his human will has not been destroyed by being divinised. It has rather been preserved, according to the words of Gregory the theologian: "For his will —referring to that of the Saviour—, being fully divinised, is not opposed to God."[1]

636   In the same our Lord Jesus Christ, our true God, we
557   glory in proclaiming two natural actions, without
        division, without change, without separation, without confusion, namely a divine action and a human action, as Leo, the master in matters related to God, asserts with utmost clarity: "For each of the two natures performs the function proper to it in communion with the other: the Word does what pertains to the Word and the flesh what pertains to the flesh" [cf. n. 612]. For we do not in any way admit one natural action of God and the creature, so as neither to raise to the divine essence what is created nor lower the sublime divine nature to the level proper to creatures. For we know that both the miracles and the sufferings belong to one and the same, according to the different natures of (ex) which he consists and in which he has his being, the admirable Cyril has said.[2]

637   Therefore, preserving entirely what is neither fused nor
558   divided, we proclaim the entire matter in this concise
        utterance: believing that one of the Holy Trinity, who after the incarnation is our Lord Jesus Christ, is our true God, we say that his two natures shine forth in his one hypostasis. In it, throughout his entire human existence in the flesh, he made manifest his miracles and his sufferings, not in mere apperance but in reality. The difference of natures in that same and unique hypostasis is recognised by the fact that each of the two natures wills and performs what is proper to it in communion with the other, Thus, we glory in proclaiming two natural wills and actions concurring together for the salvation of the human race.

---

1. Gregory of Nazianzus, *Oratio* 30, 12
2. These words are not found *ad litteram* in any of the extant works of Cyril of Alexandria. They seem to sum up freely the doctrine exposed for instance in the *Epistolae Synodales ad Nestorium*; see also the anathemas 4 and 9 of St. Cyril (*cf. nn. 603/4.9*) and the Second Council of Constantinople (*cf. n 620/3*).

HADRIAN I

LETTER *SI TAMEN LICET* ADDRESSED TO THE SPANISH BISHOPS (793)

Monothelitism represented an attempt to compromise with Monophysitism; it led back to it. In the opposite direction, a new Adoptionism arose in the eighth century which led back to Nestorianism by seeking a compromise with it. The movement originated in Spain where it was headed by Elipandus, archbishop of Toledo. Wishing to stress the perfect consubstantiality of Christ with the rest of humankind, the Spanish Adoptionists came to affirm in him a double sonship: his eternal, natural sonship due to his eternal generation from the Father and an adoptive sonship of God derived from his human birth from the Virgin Mary. This teaching overlooked the fact that the affirmation of a double sonship ultimately implied the affirmation of two persons and consequently was a return to Nestorianism. It met with opposition from Rome. Pope Hadrian I rejected it in a first letter to the Spanish bishops (cf. DS 595). The same Pope reiterated its condemnation in another letter, Si tamen licet, addressed to the same bishops in 793. The condemnation of the new Adoptionism would soon be taken up by local councils (cf. n. 693). It led to a further clarification of the mystery of the incarnation.

(Christ is not the Son of God by adoptive sonship but only by natural sonship)

638   The adoption of Jesus Christ the Son of God according
610   to the flesh [...] the Catholic Church has never believed, never taught, never accepted when it was asserted by a wrong belief. [...] But with one voice with Peter she proclaims that Christ is the Son of God, because there is one Christ, Son of God and of man, not by grace of adoption but by the dignity of natural sonship.[...]

THE COUNCIL OF FRIULI
PROFESSION OF FAITH (796 or 797)

The new Adoptionism had spread to Gaul. Several councils condemned it, among them the Council of Frankfurt (794) (DS 615) in which the Italian and French bishops played the leading role. Later, Paulinus, patriarch of Aquileia, who had drawn up the document submitted by the Italian bishops at Frankfurt, held his own Synod at Friuli. New precisions were added to the Symbol of Constantinople (cf. n. 12). Some of these are concerned with Trinitarian doctrine (cf. DS 616-618); others with the sonship of Christ: his unique natural, divine sonship excludes all adoptive sonship, without preventing him from being truly man by virtue of his human birth. The unity of person must be preserved. This is the clearest condemnation of the new

Adoptionism which affirmed a double sonship in Christ. The same precisions will later be reflected in the profession of faith of Pope Leo IX (1053) (DS 681).

639   The human and temporal birth did not interfere with
619   the divine timeless birth, but in the one person of Jesus Christ are the true Son of God and the true son of man. There is not one who is son of man and another who is Son of God, but one and the same Son of God and son of man, in two natures, the divine and the human, true God and true man. He is not the putative Son of God, but the true Son; not the adoptive Son but the real Son, for he was never estranged from the Father because of the man (human nature) which he assumed. [...] And, therefore, we confess him to be in each of the two natures the real, not the adoptive, Son of God, because, having assumed the human nature *(assumpto homine)*, one and the same is Son of God and son of man without confusion and without separation. He is naturally Son of the Father as to his divinity, naturally son of his Mother as to his humanity, but he is properly Son of the Father in both [natures].

INNOCENT III

PROFESSION OF FAITH PRESCRIBED TO THE
WALDENSIANS (1208)

The Waldensians held a sort of cosmological dualism, inherited from the Manichaeans, according to which matter is evil. This led them to several errors as regards creation (cf. n. 403). Applying the same principle to the mystery of Christ, they professed his human body to be but an appearance, not a real body. Thus, they returned to the early Christological heresy of Docetism. The profession of faith prescribed to them by Pope Innocent III lays stress on the reality of the human flesh of Christ from the incarnation down to his glorified state after the resurrection and to his return in glory. It also brings out the fact, already affirmed by the Council of Reims (DS 745i), that, since the three divine persons are one Godhead, in Christ the Godhead itself has become man, but only as subsisting in the person of the Son.

640   We heartily believe and we proclaim that the incarnation
791   of the Godhead has taken place, not in the Father or the Holy Spirit, but only in the Son; so that he who in his divinity was the Son of God the Father, true God from the Father, became in his humanity son of man, true man from a mother, with a true flesh taken from the womb of his mother and a rational human soul. [Subsisting] at once in two natures, as God

and as man, he is one person, one Son, one Christ; one God
with the Father and the Holy Spirit and with them creator and
ruler of all, he was born of the Virgin Mary by a true birth in
the flesh. He ate and drank, slept and rested when he was tired
from walking. He suffered a true passion in the flesh, died his
own true bodily death, rose again by a true resurrection of his
flesh and the true resumption of his body by his soul. He ate
and drank in his risen flesh, and then ascended to heaven and is
seated at the right hand of the Father. In the same flesh he will
come to judge the living and the dead.

THE FOURTH LATERAN GENERAL COUNCIL
SYMBOL OF LATERAN (1215)

(641)   *This important profession of faith (cf. n. 19i) explicitates the
       traditional doctrine of faith in the mystery of the incarnation. It is
fundamentally based on the doctrine of the Council of Ephesus (cf. nn. 604f)
and of Chalcedon (cf. nn 613ff), but also includes further developments. It
points out that the incarnation of the Son is the common work of the whole
Trinity. See text in n. 20.*

THE SECOND GENERAL COUNCIL OF LYONS
"PROFESSION OF FAITH OF MICHAEL PALAEOLOGUS"
(1274)

(642)   *The "Profession of Faith of Michael Palaeologus" (cf. n. 22i) is, in
       its Christological article, basically inspired by the doctrine of the
Council of Chalcedon (cf. nn. 613ff), to which are added further well-established
developments, as for instance the exclusion of an adoptive sonship of Christ
(cf. n. 639), and the reality of his human flesh (cf. n. 640). Its brief formulation
proposes the orthodox doctrine about Christ in a way which excludes all the
major Christological errors. See text in n.23*

CLEMENT VI
JUBILEE BULL *UNIGENITUS DEI FILIUS* (1343)

*The early documents of the Church were mostly concerned with the
mystery of the person of Christ and of the incarnation; in comparison with
this the doctrine of the redemption remained undeveloped. Christ's death on
the cross for our salvation had been mentioned in the early Symbols of the
faith (cf. nn. 2ff) and again in later Symbols. But the elaboration of the doctrine
of the expiatory sacrifice and atoning death came only later. Previous to the
document under review may be mentioned the following documents from the
Middle Ages: the condemnation by the Council of Sens (1141) of Abelard who
tended to reduce the efficacy of Christ's death to a purely subjective one (DS*

723); the affirmation made by the Council of Vienne (1312), against an opinion attributed to Peter John Olivi, that Christ truly died on the cross for our salvation (DS 901)...

While proclaiming the Jubilee indulgences in 1343, Pope Clement VI showed their foundation to lie in the sacrificial shedding of Christ's blood on the cross. Union with the Word of God gave infinite value to the merits of the Saviour's humanity; they are the main source of the treasure on which the Church's indulgences are based. The doctrine of Christ's merit and satisfaction will later be explicitated by the Council of Trent (cf. n. 647).

(The infinite merits of Christ)

643
1025 The only-begotten Son of God[...], "whom God made our wisdom, our righteousness, and sanctification and redemption" [cf. 1 Cor 1:30], "entered once for all into the Holy Place, taking not the blood of goats and calves but his own blood, thus securing an eternal redemption" [Heb 9:12]. For "it is not with perishable things such as silver or gold, but with his own precious blood that he who is the Lamb without blemish or spot redeemed us" [cf. 1 Pet 1:18f]. Immolated on the altar of the cross though he was innocent, he did not merely shed a drop of his blood—although this would have sufficed for the redemption of the whole human race because of the union with the Word—but a copious flood.[...]

1027 To this mass of treasure the merits of the Blessed Mother of God and of all the elect, from the first just man to the last, also contribute, as we know; nor is it at all to be feared that it could be exhausted or diminished, first on account of the infinite merits of Christ, as already mentioned, and further because the more people are drawn to righteousness by having this treasure applied to them, so much the more does the store of those merits increase.

THE GENERAL COUNCIL OF FLORENCE
DECREE FOR THE COPTS (1442)

In its Bull Cantate Domino, *the Council of Florence (cf. n. 322i), after exposing the doctrine of the Trinity (cf. nn. 325f), treats of the mystery of Christ. A first section deals with the mystery of the incarnation and of the person of Christ in terms mostly borrowed from previous documents. A second section recalls the mystery of the redemption as contained in the early professions of faith, and, after condemning the main Christological heresies (cf. DS 1339-1346), goes on to explain that Christ's redemptive work is the source of salvation for all people.*

644 The Church firmly believes, professes and preaches that
1337 one person of the Trinity, true God, Son of God begotten
from the Father, one in being with the Father and equally
eternal with him, has, in the fulness of time designed by the
divine counsel in its inscrutable majesty, assumed from the
immaculate womb of the Virgin Mary for the salvation of the
human race a true and complete human nature and united it to
himself in the unity of person *(in unitatem personae)*. This unity
is so intimate that neither is anything which in him belongs to
God separated from the man, nor is anything belonging to the
man divided from the divinity; one and the same is undivided,
each of the two natures perduring with its own properties. He is
God and man, Son of God and son of man, equal to the Father
as to the divinity, inferior to the Father as to the humanity;
immortal and eternal by his divine nature, subject to suffering
and to time by the human condition which he has assumed.

645 She firmly believes, professes and preaches that the Son
1338 of God was truly born of the Virgin in the humanity
which he assumed, that he truly suffered, truly died and
was buried, truly rose from the dead, ascended to heaven and is
seated at the right hand of the Father, and that he will come at
the end of times to judge the living and the dead.

646 She firmly believes, professes and preaches that no one
1347 ever conceived from man and woman has been freed
from the dominion of the devil, except through faith in
Jesus Christ our Lord, the mediator between God and human
beings, who, conceived without sin, having been born and having
died, alone crushed the enemy of the human race by his death
which destroyed our sins, and secured again entry into the
kingdom of heaven which the first man had lost by his sin and
all his descendants with him.[...]

THE GENERAL COUNCIL OF TRENT
SIXTH SESSION
DECREE ON JUSTIFICATION (1547)

*The Council of Trent was concerned with the doctrine of the redemption
only indirectly, in connection with the doctrine of justification which was the
fundamental issue raised by the Reformation. Nevertheless, the Decree on
Justification (cf. n. 1924i), when explaining the various causes of human
justification, clearly states the traditional doctrine of the Middle Ages on*

Christ's merit and satisfaction for all people. See the rest of the Decree on Justification, especially nn. 1926-1932, and Canon 10 (n. 1960); see also the Decree on Original Sin (n. 510).

(Christ is the meritorious cause of human justification)

647 The meritorious cause [of justification] is the beloved
1529 only-begotten Son of God, our Lord Jesus Christ who, "while we were sinners" *[Rom 5:10]*, "out of the great love with which he loved us" *[Eph 2:4]*, merited for us justification by his most holy passion on the wood of the cross *[cf. n. 1960]* and made satisfaction for us to God the Father.

PAUL IV

CONSTITUTION *CUM QUORUMDAM HOMINUM* (1555)

Soon after the Reformation emerged, rationalism, which set reason above Revelation, made its appearance and various sects issued from it. These denied the fundamental mysteries of the Trinity, of the incarnation and redemption. They were condemned by Pope Paul IV in virtue of his "apostolic authority". The same Constitution also condemns errors concerning Marian doctrine (cf. n. 707). It may be regarded as the first condemnation of rationalism. The section concerned with the mystery of Christ and his work is given here.

648 In the name of almighty God, Father, Son and Holy
1880 Spirit, in virtue of our apostolic authority we desire to admonish all those who up to this time have asserted, taught and believed [...] that our Lord is not true God, of the same substance in all things with the Father and the Holy Spirit, or that according to the flesh he was not conceived in the womb of the Blessed Mary ever Virgin from the Holy Spirit, but, as other humans, from the seed of Joseph; or that the same Jesus Christ our Lord and God did not undergo the very violent death of the cross to redeem us from sins and from eternal death and to reconcile us with the Father unto life eternal.

PIUS VI

CONSTITUTION *AUCTOREM FIDEI* (1794)

This Constitution condemns several sets of propositions from a synod which met at Pistoia in Tuscany (1786) under the leadership of Scipio Ricci; many of its propositions reflect the basic tenets of Jansenism. One set deals with the divine worship due to the humanity of Christ. To deny, as the Synod of Pistoia did, that Christ must be adored in his humanity, while professing the divine worship due to his divinity, amounted to denying the unity of person and, therefore, was a subtle return to Nestorianism. The text of the condemned propositions, given below, indicates that, because of the assumption of Christ's humanity to union in the person of the Son of God, the divine worship due to him extends to his humanity. Two other condemned propositions apply the same doctrine to the worship of the Sacred Heart: the cult of latria is due to it on account of the union of Christ's humanity with the person of the Word of God (cf. DS 2662-2663).

(On the adoration of the humanity of Christ)

649
2661
The proposition which affirms that "to adore directly the humanity of Christ and all the more any part of his humanity is always to render divine honour to a creature", where the use of the term "directly" is intended to bring condemnation on the cult of adoration which the faithful address to the humanity of Christ, as if such an adoration—by which the humanity and the living flesh of Christ is adored, not indeed for its own sake and merely as flesh *(tamquam nuda caro)* but as united to the divinity—were divine honour paid to a creature, and not rather one and the same adoration by which the Word incarnate together with his own flesh is adored, is false[...] and detracts from the pious and fitting cult rendered and rightly rendered by the faithful to the humanity of Christ.[...]

PIUS X

DECREE *LAMENTABILI* OF THE HOLY OFFICE (1907)
ARTICLES OF MODERNISM CONDEMNED

Despite some genuine insights, the Modernist current of the early twentieth century threatened the foundations of the faith (cf. n.143i). The Modernists reduced the message of Christ to the proclamation of the eschatological Kingdom which Christ, they maintained, believed to be imminent. This led them to affirm in Christ not only ignorance but also error as regards the day of judgment, and to question his divinity and even his messianic character. In addition, they so stressed the role played by the early Christian community in the formation of the Gospels as to contrast sharply the Christ of faith and the Jesus of history. Despite the dangers which it offered for the faith and which needed to be clearly pointed out, the Modernist current has had beneficial effects. It has prompted modern biblical scholarship to show the continuity between the Jesus of history and the Christ of faith, notwithstanding the fact that the New Testament writings contain primarily the proclamation of the faith of the early Christian community. The Decree Lamentabili *enumerates the Christological errors of the Modernists. In his Encyclical* Pascendi *of the same year, Pope Pius X mostly expatiates on the alleged opposition between the Jesus of history and the Christ of faith (cf. DS 3479, 3485).*

(Modernist errors about Christ condemned)

[650/27]   The divinity of Jesus Christ is not proved from the
3427   Gospels, but is a dogma which the Christian
          consciousness has deduced from the notion of the
Messiah.

[650/28]   When Jesus exercised his ministry, neither did he
3428   speak with the intention of teaching that he was the
          Messiah nor were his miracles meant to prove it.

[650/29]   It may be granted that the Christ shown by history
3429   is much inferior to the Christ who is the object of faith.

[650/30]   In all the Gospel texts the term 'Son of God' merely
3430   means the same as Messiah and does not at all mean
          that Christ is the true and natural Son of God.

[650/31]   The doctrine which Paul, John and the Councils of
3431   Nicaea, Ephesus and Chalcedon teach about Christ,
          is not what Jesus taught but what the Christian
consciousness conceived about Jesus.

[650/32]   The natural meaning of the Gospel texts cannot be
3432   reconciled with what our theologians teach about the
          consciousness and the infallible knowledge of Jesus
Christ.

[650/33]   It is evident to anyone with no preconceived opinions
3433   that either Jesus' teaching as regards the proximity of
          the Messianic advent was erroneous or else the greater
part of his teaching contained in the Synoptic Gospels is
inauthentic.

[650/34]   A critic cannot assert that Christ's knowledge was
3434   unlimited, unless by making the hypothesis, which is
          historically inconceivable and morally repugnant,
that Christ as man had God's knowledge and yet was unwilling
to communicate so much knowledge to his disciples and
posterity.

[650/35]   Christ did not always have the consciousness of his
3435   messianic dignity.

[650/36] The resurrection of the Saviour is not properly a fact
3436 of the historical order but a fact of the purely supernatural order, which is not and cannot be demonstrated, a fact which the Christian consciousness derived gradually from other sources.

[650/37] Faith in the resurrection of Christ has been from the
3437 beginning not so much faith in the fact of his resurrection as in the immortal life of Christ with God.

[650/38] The teaching about the expiatory death of Christ is
3438 not evangelical but Pauline only.

BENEDICT XV
DECREE OF THE HOLY OFFICE (1918)

The great conciliar definition had clearly exposed the main outlines of doctrine with regard to the person of Christ. They had opened the way for an attempt to penetrate more deeply into the mystery of the human psychology of the Son Incarnate. It is certain that by assuming human nature the Word took with him not only the strengths but also the weaknesses of the human soul, having become similar to us in all things but sin. But it is no less certain that the hypostatic union postulated in his human soul unique privileges and that other privileges were required for the exercise of his revelatory and redemptive functions. As regards Christ's knowledge, tradition had taught the absence of ignorance in him [cf.nn.624-626), but without always distinguishing clearly between the divine and the human knowledge. To penetrate more deeply into the mystery of the human knowledge of Christ was reserved to recent times; the questions raised by the Modernists invited such a study. Speculative attempts followed, some of which were not satisfactory in so far as they unduly undermined the privileges in the human soul of Christ. Having been consulted on definite questions by the Congregation for Seminaries and Universities, the Holy Office gave the following answers which were confirmed by Pope Benedict XV. The text must be carefully interpreted in its historical context; in particular, Christ's "beatific vision" remains open to different interpretations. As such it does not appear among the Christological doctrines taught by the 1992 Catechism of the Catholic Church.

Question: Can the following propositions be taught safely:

651/1 It is not certain that the soul of Christ during his life
3645 among us had the knowldege which the blessed, that is those who have achieved their goal (*comprehensores*), have.

651/2 The opinion cannot be declared certain, which holds
3646 that the soul of Christ was ignorant of nothing but from the beginning knew in the Word everything, past, present

and future, that is to say everything which God knows with the "knowledge of vision".

651/3   The recent opinion of some about the limited knowledge
3647   of the soul of Christ is not to be less favoured in Catholic
       schools than the ancient opinion about his universal
knowledge.

Answer: No

PIUS XI

ENCYCLICAL LETTER *QUAS PRIMAS* (1925)

In his encyclical letter on the Kingship of Christ, Pope Pius XI explains the double foundation of Christ's dominion over all things: it belongs to him as the God-man and as Redeemer. The Pope goes on to explain the various powers which Christ's Kingship comprises, and that, though his Kingship is primarily spiritual, it also extends in a certain sense to civil matters (cf.DS 3677-3679). It must be noted that Kingship is not attributed to Christ and the earthly Kings univocally. In our times, when earthly kings have lost much of their power and appeal little to the masses, the biblical roots and meaning of Christ's Lordship and Kingship need to be stressed.

(The Kingship of Christ as man)

652   If we ponder this matter more deeply, we cannot but
3675   see that the title and the power of King belong to Christ
      as man in the strict and proper sense also. For it is only as man that he may be said to have received from the Father "dominion and glory and Kingdom" [cf. Dan 7:13-14], since the Word of God, as consubstantial with the Father, has all things in common with him, and therefore has necessarily supreme and absolute dominion over all things created.

(The twofold foundation of Christ's Kingship)

653   The foundation of this power and dignity of our Lord is
3676   rightly indicated by Cyril of Alexandria. He says:
      "Christ has dominion over all creatures, a dominion not seized by violence nor usurped, but his by essence and by nature".[1] His Kingship is founded upon the ineffable hypostatic union. From this it follows not only that Christ is to be adored

---

1. CYRIL OF ALEXANDRIA, *Comment. in Joan.*, 12, 18.

by angels and humans, but that to him as man angels and humans are subject, and must recognise his empire: by reason of the hypostatic union Christ has power over all creatures. But a thought that must give us even greater joy and consolation is this, that Christ is our King by acquired as well as by natural right, for he is our Redeemer.[...]

ENCYCLICAL LETTER *MISERENTISSIMUS REDEMPTOR* (1928)

In his encyclical on the reparation due to the Sacred Heart of Jesus the same Pope explains that by the incarnation and redemption Christ has entered into an intimate communion with humanity: head and members constitute one Body. Though Christ's redemptive work has been historically accomplished once for all, the application of its effect to all generations is a work which continues through the centuries and in which Christians must join. Thus humankind is drawn into the ever operative mysteries of the incarnation and the redemption. By reason of the mysterious bond between the Head and the members, Christians must carry on in their own life Christ's redemptive passion.

(Christ's redemptive sacrifice)

654   The plentiful redemption of Christ brought us abundant forgiveness of all our sins *[cf. Col 2:13]*. Nevertheless, owing to the wonderful arrangement of divine Wisdom by which what is lacking in the sufferings of Christ is to be completed in our flesh for his Body which is the Church *[cf.Col 1:24]*, we are able and, in fact, we ought to join our own acts of praise and satisfaction to those which Christ has presented to God in the name of sinners.

655   However, we must always remember that the entire expiatory value [of our acts] depends on the one bloody sacrifice of Christ, which is uninterruptedly renewed on our altars in an unbloody manner; for "the victim is one and the same: the same now offers through the ministry of priests, who then offered himself on the cross; only the manner of offering is different" *[cf n.1548]*.

(Community of atonement with Christ)

656   Therefore, an act of immolation on the part of both priests and the rest of the faithful must be joined with this most august eucharistic sacrifice so that they too may offer themselves as living victims, holy and pleasing to God [cf.Rom 12:1]. Indeed, St. Cyprian unhesitatingly asserts that "the celebration of the Lord's sacrifice does not effect our proper sanctification, unless our sacrificial offering is in accord with his passion."[1] Accordingly, the apostle warns us that, "carrying in our body the death of Jesus" [2 Cor 4:10] and being buried with Christ and united with him in the likeness of his death [cf. Rom 6:4f], we ought to crucify our flesh with its vices and lusts [cf.Gal 5:24], "escaping from the corruption that is in the world because of passion" [2 Pet 1:4]; he exhorts us that "the life of Jesus may be manifested in our bodies" [2 Cor 4:10] and that, as sharers in his eternal priesthood, we may offer "gifts and sacrifices for sins" [Heb 5:1].

(The universal priesthood exercised in satisfaction and in the eucharistic sacrifice)

657 For participation in the mysterious priesthood and in the duty of offering satisfaction and sacrifice is not limited to those whom our High Priest Jesus Christ uses as his ministers to offer the clean oblation to the divine Majesty in every place from the rising of the sun to its setting [cf. Mal 1:11]; no, it is the duty of the entire Christian family, which the prince of the apostles rightly calls "a chosen race, a kingdom of priests" [1 Pet 2:9], to offer expiatory sacrifice [cf.Heb 5:3] not only for itself but also for the whole human race, in much the same way as every priest and "every high priest chosen from among men is appointed to act on their behalf in relation to God" [Heb 5:1].

658 We shall reap a more abundant harvest of mercy and forgiveness for ourselves and for others to the extent that our own offering and sacrifice correspond more perfectly to the sacrifice of our Lord; in other words, to the extent that we immolate our self-love and our passions and crucify our flesh with that mystical crucifixion of which the apostle speaks. For there is a wonderfully close relationship between Christ and all the faithful—a relationship like that of the head of a body to the rest of its members. Moreover, by the mysterious communion of saints, which we acknowledge by our Catholic faith, all human

---

1. St. CYPRIAN, *Epistola 63 ad Caecilium, 9.*

beings, as individuals and as nations, are joined not only in association with one another but also to him "who is the Head, Christ, from whom the whole Body, joined and knit together by every joint with which it is supplied, when each part is working properly makes bodily growth and upbuilds itself in love" [Eph 4:15]. This indeed is what the Mediator between God and human beings, Christ Jesus, prayed for to his Father when he was approaching death: "I in them and you in me, that they may become perfectly one" [Jn 17:23].

659   A further consideration is the truth that Christ's expiatory suffering is renewed and in a way continued and completed in his mystical Body, which is the Church. For, to use St. Augustine's words again: "Christ suffered all that he should have suffered; there is now nothing lacking in the measure of his sufferings. His sufferings as Head, then, were completed; yet, for Christ in his body sufferings still remained."[1] The Lord Jesus himself mercifully made this truth known when, speaking to Saul who was still breathing threats of slaughter against the disciples [cf. Acts 9:1], he said: "I am Jesus whom you are persecuting" [Acts 9:5]. Obviously he means that, when persecutions are directed against the Church, it is the divine Head of the Church himself who is attacked and afflicted. It is entirely proper, then, that Christ who is still suffering in his mystical Body should want to have us as his companions in the work of expiation. This is required of us also by our close union with him, since we are "the Body of Christ and individually members of it" [1 Cor 12:27], and all the members ought to suffer with the Head anything that the Head suffers [cf. 1 Cor 12:26].

PIUS XII

ENCYCLICAL LETTER *MYSTICI CORPORIS* (1943)

Pope Pius XII's Encyclical Letter on the mystery of the Church, the mystical Body of Christ (cf. n. 847i), had naturally to be based on Christological doctrine. In particular, the Pope points out that Christ is the Head of his Body the Church; he affirms the fulness of grace of his humanity from which all people receive; touching on the question of the human knowledge of Christ, he reaffirms that Christ's human intellect possessed the "beatific vision" and explains that his human knowledge extended to all people.

---

1. St.Augustine, *Enarrationes in Psalmos : in Ps*, 86.5.

(Christ, the Head of his mystical Body, has the fulness of grace)

660 A further reason why Christ is to be regarded as the Head of the Church lies in the surpassing plenitude and perfection of his supernatural gifts, in consequence of which his mystical Body draws upon that fulness. Many of the Fathers remark that just as the head of our mortal body is endowed with all the senses while the remainder has only the sense of touch, so all the virtues, gifts, and miraculous powers which are found in the Christian community exist in Christ its Head with the full perfection of their splendour. "For in him all the fulness of God was pleased to dwell" *[Col 1:19]*. He is adorned with all those supernatural gifts which accompany the hypostatic union; for in him the Holy Spirit dwells with a fulness of grace than which no greater can be conceived. To him has been given "power over all flesh" *[cf. Jn 17:2]* and "all the treasures of wisdom and knowledge" *[Col 2:3]* abound in him. He also enjoys the beatific vision in a degree, both as regards extent and clarity, surpassing that of all the saints in heaven. Indeed, so full of grace and truth is he that of his inexhaustible fulness we all receive *[cf. Jn 1:14-16]*.

(Christ's human knowledge)

661
3812 But the loving knowledge with which the divine Redeemer has pursued us from the first moment of his incarnation is such as completely to surpass all the searchings of the human mind; for by means of the beatific vision, which he enjoyed from the time when he was received into the womb of the Mother of God, he has for ever and continuously had present to him all the members of his mystical Body, and embraced them with his saving love. [...]

ENCYCLICAL LETTER *SEMPITERNUS REX* (1951)

This Encyclical celebrates the 15th centenary of the Council of Chalcedon. In the name of the Conciliar doctrine, the Pope rejects two errors. The first is that of the "kenotic theories" which were prominent in non-Catholic theology, especially in Germany and England, during the 19th century. These theories held that the Word of God, by becoming incarnate, had really given up all or some of his divine attributes. The other error is found among some Catholic theologians who, inspired by a Christology of the "assumptus homo", so conceived the autonomy of Christ's humanity as to practically contradict its hypostatic union with the Word of God. But the Pope leaves open the question of a human psychological personality in Christ. Theologians can speak of a human 'ego' or psychological personality in Christ, provided the unique ontological personhood of the Son Incarnate is safeguarded. Theology remains engaged in the study of the mysterious psychological unity of the God-man.

(Condemnation of the kenotic theory)

662 Likewise entirely opposed to Chalcedon's profession of faith is the erroneous opinion, rather widespread among non-Catholics, which imagines that in Christ the divinity of the Word is lost. Called the "kenotic theory", it finds a specious foundation in a rash misinterpretation of a text of the letter of the apostle Paul to the Philippians *[cf. Phil 2:7]*. It is truly a blasphemous theory, and, like the doctrine of Docetism directly opposed to it, it makes the whole mystery of the incarnation and the redemption a lifeless and meaningless illusion. "The true God[...] was born with the complete and perfect nature of a true man; he is complete in his nature and complete in ours": this is the exalted doctrine of Leo the Great *[cf.n. 611]*.

(Christ's human nature is not an independent subject)

663
3905 Though it is legitimate to study the humanity of Christ from the psychological view-point, yet in this difficult matter there are some who too rashly set up novel constructions which they wrongly place under the patronage of the Council of Chalcedon. These theologians describe the state and condition of Christ's human nature in such terms that it seems to be taken for an independent subject *(subiectum sui iuris)*, as though it did not subsist in the person of the Word. Yet, the Council of Chalcedon, in complete agreement with that of Ephesus, clearly asserts that the two natures of our Redeemer were united in one person, and it does not allow us to put in Christ two individuals, so that some *homo assumptus*, endowed with complete autonomy, is placed by the side of the Word *(penes Verbum collocetur)*.

ENCYCLICAL LETTER *HAURIETIS AQUAS* (1956)

This Encyclical Letter on the cult of the Sacred Heart broadens the perspectives opened by previous papal encyclicals on the same subject. A certain disaffection towards the cult of the Sacred Heart was due to a lack of perception of its true nature. It was necessary to give it a solid theological foundation and to show its intimate relationship with the mystery of Christ. The Pope

shows that the cult of the Sacred Heart has deep roots in the Scriptures
themselves. As for its theological foundation, it is to be found in the mystery
of the incarnation and of the hypostatic union. Because the Incarnate Word
has united to himself a complete human nature (cf. DS 3923), his human
heart can rightly be recognised as the symbol and the manifestation of his love
for the Father and for human beings. It is therefore the symbol of what is at
the centre of the mystery of Christ. Theological reflection serves here to show
that the cult of the Sacred Heart deserves a central place in the Christian life,
and is not just an ordinary devotion among others.

(The twofold reason for the cult of the Sacred Heart)

664　In order that all may more exactly grasp the import for
3922　this cult of the outstanding passages of the Old and of
　　　the New Testaments which contain a reference to it, we
must keep quite clearly in mind why the Church offers the
worship of *latria* to the divine Heart of the Redeemer.[...] This
reason is twofold. The first, which is applicable also to the other
members of the Body of Jesus Christ, rests on the principle
according to which we acknowledge that his Heart, the noblest
part of human nature, is hypostatically joined to the person of
the divine Word; and therefore it must be given the same worship
of adoration as that with which the Church honours the person
of the Incarnate Son of God himself.[...] The other reason, which
is proper to the Heart of the divine Redeemer, and hence calls
in a special way for the worship of *latria* to be offered to it, is
the fact that his Heart, more than all the other members of his
Body, is the natural sign and symbol of his boundless charity for
the human race.[...]

(The Heart of the Incarnate Word is the symbol of a threefold love)

665　The Heart of the Incarnate Word is quite rightly
3924　considered the chief sign and symbol of the threefold
　　　love with which the divine Redeemer continually loves
the eternal Father and all human beings. It is a symbol first of
that divine love which he has in common with the Father and
the Holy Spirit, but which only in him, as the Word Incarnate, is
manifested to us through a weak and frail human body.[...] It is
a symbol secondly of that burning charity which, infused into
his soul, enriches the human will of Christ; the exercise of this
charity is illumined and guided by a twofold perfect knowledge,
namely, beatific knowledge and infused knowledge. And finally,

in a more direct and natural way, it is a symbol also of emotional affection, since the body of Jesus Christ, formed by the action of the Holy Spirit in the womb of the Virgin Mary, enjoys the most perfect powers of feeling and perception, to a greater degree in fact than the bodies of all other human beings.

(In Christ three loves are united)

666
3925
This is why from the bodily organ of the Heart of Jesus Christ and from its natural meaning, we can and must, with the help of Christian faith, ascend not only to the contemplation of his sensitive love, but, higher still, to the consideration and the adoration of his infused spiritual love; and finally to the mediation and adoration of the divine love of the incarnate Word.[...] This is legitimate since the faith according to which the two natures, the human and the divine, are united in the person of Christ, allows us to conceive the close relationships which exist between the sensitive love of the physical Heart of Jesus and his double spiritual love, the human and the divine. For these [three] loves not only exist simultaneously in the adorable person of the divine Redeemer, but also are united between themselves by a natural bond, since the human and sensitive love is subordinate to the divine love and analogically reflects its image.[...]

(The natural symbolism of the physical Heart of Jesus is based on the hypostatic union)

667
3925
It is therefore necessary[...] that all hold ever in their mind that the natural symbolism by which the physical Heart of Jesus is related to the person of the Word rests completely on the primary truth of the hypostatic union. Those who deny this renew errors which have already often been condemned by the Church, because they deny the unity of person in Christ in the distinction and integrity of the two natures.

THE SECOND VATICAN GENERAL COUNCIL

"The Council did not expressly deal with dogmas related to Christ as did the Councils of Nicaea, Ephesus and Chalcedon. Its central theme was the Church. But just because it endeavoured to understand the Church in her inmost reality, in the source of her vitality rather than [merely] in her historical and juridical aspects, the Council was happily obliged to refer everything to Christ Our Lord, not only as to the founder, but as to the Head, the principle

of action and life of his Body which is the Church.[...] If then we wish to understand the central doctrine of the Council, we must understand the Church; but to understand the Church, we must refer everything to Christ[...]."[1]

These words of Pope Paul VI indicate the place which the mystery of Christ occupies in the Second Vatican Council. While no Council document is explicitly devoted to the mystery of Christ, not even a chapter—as is the case for the mystery of the Virgin Mary in LG—the mystery of Christ is everywhere present as the standard of the Church's teaching and the practical rule of her concrete attitudes. The "Council of the Church" may be described as that of Christ's presence to the Church. Its Christ-centredness seems to have grown as the Council progressed; it found its clearest expression in GS 22 and 45.

In this perspective, what retained primarily the attention of the Council Fathers is the meaning of Christ in the divine plan and his place in the history of salvation. Without getting embarrassed with scholastic disputes, the Council explains that the human race finds in Christ its centre, the whole cosmos its Head and history its goal (GS 45;cf.LG 13,17,48,etc.). The Church of Vatican II "believes that the key, centre and purpose of human history is to be found in her Lord and Master" (GS 10).

The Council does not fail to contemplate the sublime union of the divine and the human natures implied in Christological doctrine; witness to this is the parallel which it draws—"in virtue of an anology which is not farfetched"—between Christ's two natures and the Church's twofold element, the divine and the human (LG 8). Beyond the ontological reality of the mysterious union of the two natures, it prefers, however, to dwell on the economy of the saving incarnation (LG 3,AG 3), on the mysterious human condition of the Word incarnate, on Christ's kenôsis and glorification, on the depth of his identification with our human race in its concrete situation: "The Word Incarnate wished to enter fully into human fellowship" (GS 32; cf.22). Christ's kenôsis serves the pilgrim Church as a deep source of inspiration for her renewal and as guiding principle for her apostolic activity (LG 8; cf.AG 5). The same principle commands the Council's theology of the redemption. It is precisely in so far as by his incarnation the Son of God has united himself in some way to every person that "as an innocent Lamb, freely shedding his blood, he merited life for us" (GS 22).

A special feature of the Council's Christology must be pointed out, for it will provide a frame for much of its Ecclesiology: the Council teaches insistently the existence in Christ of a threefold function: prophetic, sanctifying and pastoral (LG 21; cf.13; OT 4). The same is found in the Church (LG 10-13), precisely in so far as she has been established by the risen Christ as the "universal sacrament of salvation" (LG 48). Christ's revelatory function is described in terms, inspired from Scripture, which had never before found in official documents the same deep echo: Christ is the mediator of God's revelation

---

1. PAUL VI, Public audience, Nov. 23, 1966

to the world; his person and his work contain the fulness of that revelation (DV 2,4;cf.nn.149, 151; SC 33). His saving action culminates in his Paschal Mystery (SC 5). Through the Church's liturgy the risen Christ remains present and active (cf. n. 1334); he also exercises his priestly office (cf. n. 1231) for the whole human race (SC 83). He is also the good Shepherd who gathers together the scattered people of God.

Thus, for Vatican II, the mystery of Christ is at every level the foundation of the mystery of the Church, whose task it is "faithfully (to) reveal in the world his mystery" (LG 8; cf. 15; GS 43) and so "to bring together all humankind with all its treasures under Christ the Head in the unity of the Holy Spirit" (LG 13). Christ is not merely the founder of the Church but the continuous source of her life (LG 8); her mission is the prolongation of his (LG 17); her action is destined to make his own action visibly present in the world (SC 7). Whether in doctrine or in action the Church lives by him. The mystery of Christ is the vivifying centre of the Christian message and consequently of priestly formation (OT 14)

It is so because Christ is the new Adam, who recapitulates all things in himself (GS 22,45), on whom the solidarity of all people is based (GS 32) and who leads them all to their eschatological fulfilment (GS 38). The problems that besiege modern people must find a solution in "the light and the principles that stem from Christ" (GS 46); above all, the human mystery is fully intelligible only in the light of the mystery of Christ (GS 22).

Thus, to put Christ at the centre of all things, both in practice and in doctrine, is one of the great concerns of Vatican II. The "Council of the Church" turns out to be a providential and inspired plea for her de-centring, so that she may appear to be what she is in reality, the sign of Christ raised among the nations.

CONSTITUTION *SACROSANCTUM CONCILIUM* (1963)

(Christ the High Priest for all)

668   83. Jesus Christ, the High Priest of the New and eternal Covenant, by assuming human nature, has introduced into this earthly exile that hymn which is sung throughout all ages in the halls of heaven. He unites to himself the entire human community and has them join him singing this divine song of praise.

PASTORAL CONSTITUTION *GAUDIUM ET SPES* (1965)

(Christ the new Adam, present to all)

669a   22. In actual fact, it is only in the mystery of the Word incarnate that the human mystery becomes clear. Adam the first human being was a figure of him who was to come, namely Christ the Lord. Christ, the new Adam, fully reveals human beings to themselves in the very revelation of the Father and his love, and discloses to them their sublime calling.[...]

He who is "the image of the invisible God" [Col 1:15] is himself the perfect human being, who has restored to the children of Adam the divine likeness deformed by the first sin. Since in him human nature was assumed, not absorbed, it was, by that very fact, raised to a sublime dignity in us also. For by his incarnation the Son of God has united himself in some way to every person. He worked with human hands, thought with a human mind, acted with a human will, and loved with a human heart. Born of the Virgin Mary, he truly became one of us, like unto us in all things except sin.

As an innocent Lamb, freely shedding his blood, he merited life for us. In him God has reconciled us with himself and among ourselves and delivered us from the bondage of the devil and of sin, so that now each one of us can say with the apostle: the Son of God "loved me and gave himself for me" [Gal 2:20]. By suffering for us he not only set an example for us to follow in his footsteps, but he also opened up a new path. If we follow it, life and death are made holy and take on a new meaning.[...]

The Christian is certainly bound both by need and by duty to struggle with evil through many afflictions and to suffer death; but, as one brought into association with the paschal mystery, and as one configured to the death of Christ, the Christian will go forward, strengthened by hope, to the resurrection [cf. Phil 3:10; Rom 8:17].

All this holds true not only for Christians but also for all individuals of good will in whose hearts grace is active invisibly [cf. n. 1018]. For since Christ died for all [cf. Rom 8:32], and since all human beings are in fact called to one and the same destiny, which is divine, we must hold that the Holy Spirit offers to all the possibility of being associated, in a way known to God, with the paschal mystery.

Such is the nature and the greatness of the mystery of our humanity as enlightened for the faithful by Christian revelation. It is therefore through Christ, and in Christ, that light is thrown on the riddle of suffering and death which, apart from his Gospel, overwhelms us. Christ has risen, destroying death by his death, and given life abundantly to us [cf. the Byzantine Easter Liturgy], so that becoming sons and daughters in the Son, we may cry out in the Spirit: Abba, Father! [cf. Rom 8:15 and Gal 4:6; also Jn 1:12 and 3:1-2].

(Christ Alpha and Omega)

669b   45. For the Word of God, through whom all things were
made, was himself made flesh so that, as the perfect
human being, he might save all people and recapitulate all things
in himself. The Lord is the goal of human history, the focal point
to which converge the longings of history and civilisation, the
centre of the humn race, the joy of all hearts and the fulfilment
of their aspirations. He it is whom the Father has raised from
the dead, exalted and placed at his right hand, establishing him
as judge of the living and the dead. And we, quickened and
united in his Spirit, we are on our pilgrimage towards the
fulfilment of human history which perfectly coincides with the
design of his love: "to unite all things in him, things in heaven
and things on earth" *[Eph 1:10]*.

It is the Lord himself who says: "Behold, I am coming soon,
bringing my recompense, to repay everyone for what he has
done. I am the Alpha and the Omega, the first and the last, the
beginning and the end" *[Rev 12:21f]*.

PAUL VI

DECLARATION *MYSTERIUM FILII DEI* OF THE
S. CONGREGATION FOR THE DOCTRINE OF THE FAITH
(21 February 1972)

*In the Church's documents the mystery of Christ, the God-man, has
traditionally been formulated with the terms: one person, two natures. These
concepts, however, are for various reasons gradually becoming more difficult
to understand. This is why several attempts have been made in recent years
to re-formulate the mystery of Christ in more intelligible terms. These attempts
have not been altogether successful. It is not enough to believe that Christ is
a man in whom God is fully present; the faith as formulated in the great
Christological Councils implies that he is God's eternal Son who in time became
man to reveal the Father fully. He is not a human person receiving the divine
presence, but a divine person accepting human becoming. While encouraging
theologians to expound the mystery of Christ in up-to-date terminology, the
S. Congregation for the Doctrine of the Faith draws attention to the
fundamental truth which must be preserved and to errors which would fall
short of it. The text is found in AAS 64 (1972) 237ff.*

(Recent errors with regard to the faith in the Son of God)

670   3. The opinions according to which it has not been
revealed and made known to us that the Son of God
subsists from all eternity in the mystery of the Godhead, distinct

from the Father and the Holy Spirit, are in open conflict with this belief [of the Councils]; likewise the opinions according to which we should abandon the notion of the one person of Jesus Christ, begotten in his divinity of the Father before all ages and, in time, begotten in his humanity of the Virgin Mary; and lastly the assertion that the humanity of Christ existed not as assumed into the eternal person of the Son of God, but in itself as human person, and therefore, that the mystery of Jesus Christ consists only in the fact that God, in revealing himself, was present in the highest degree in the human person of Jesus.

Those who think in this way are far removed from the true faith in Christ, even when they maintain that the special presence of God in Jesus results in his being the supreme and final expression of divine Revelation. Nor do they come back to the true belief in the divinity of Christ by adding that Jesus can be called God by reason of the fact that God is fully present in what they call his human person.

(The mysteries of the Incarnation and of the Trinity are to be faithfully preserved and expounded)

671　6.What is expressed in the documents of the Councils referred to above concerning the one and the same Christ, the Son of God, begotten before the ages in his divine nature and in time in his human nature, and also concerning the eternal person of the Holy Spirit [*cf. n.333*], belongs to the immutable truth of the Catholic faith.

This does not mean that the Church should not consider it her duty—taking also into account the progress of human thought—never to stop in her effort to reach a better understanding of these mysteries through contemplation and theological research, and to have them more fully expounded in up-to-date terminology. But, while this necessary task is being pursued, care must be taken that these profound mysteries be not interpreted in a meaning different from that in which the Church has understood and understands them.[...]

JOINT DECLARATION BY PAUL VI AND THE COPTIC POPE SHENOUDA III OF EGYPT

(19 May 1973)

This joint confession of Christological faith follows the definition of

Chalcedon, in particular that Council's use of four adverbs (which now become six phrases—"without mingling" etc.) and emphasis on the preservation of all the human and divine properties in Christ. At the same time, the confession respects Coptic sensibilities by not insisting on the Chalcedonian language of "one person in two natures". Cf. nn. 613-615. The text is found in Origins *3 (1973) 30.*

(Reconciliation over the language of Chalcedon)

671a　We confess that our Lord and God and Saviour and King of us all, Jesus Christ, is perfect God with respect to his divinity, perfect man with respect to his humanity. In him his divinity is united with his humanity in a real, perfect union without mingling, without commixtion, without confusion, without alteration, without division, without separation.[...] In him are preserved all the properties of the divinity and all the properties of the humanity together in a real, perfect, indivisible and inseparable union.

APOSTOLIC EXHORTATION *EVANGELII NUNTIANDI*
(8 December 1975)

This Apostolic Exhortation was published by Pope Paul VI after the Synod of Bishops in Rome on Evangelisation (1974) and in continuation of its work. Chapter I describes Jesus as the first evangeliser who preaches the Kingdom of God. It goes on to explain the content of Jesus' Good News as liberation-salvation. This Good News is now entrusted to the Church to be proclaimed by her. Hence in Chapter III on the Content of Evangelisation the Pope stresses that salvation in Jesus Christ is at the centre of the Church's message. He defines this salvation as not merely immanent and confined to temporal existence, but also transcendent and eschatological. The text is found in AAS 68 (1976) 5ff.

(Jesus proclaims liberating salvation)

672　9. At the kernel and centre of his Good News, Christ proclaims salvation, this great gift of God which is liberation from everything that oppresses human beings but which is above all liberation from sin and the Evil One, in the joy of knowing God and being known by him, of seeing him, and of being given over to him. All of this is begun during the life of Christ and definitively accomplished by his death and resurrection. But it must be patiently carried on during the course of history, in order to be realised fully on the day of the final coming of Christ, whose date is known to no one except the Father *[cf. Mt 24:36; Acts 1:7; 1 Thess 5:1-2].*

(Salvation in Jesus Christ at the centre of the Church's message)

673 27. Evangelisation will always contain—as the foundation, centre and at the same time summit of its dynamism—a clear proclamation that, in Jesus Christ, the Son of God made man, who died and rose from the dead, salvation is offered to all human beings as a gift of God's grace and mercy *[cf.Eph 2:8; Rom 1:16]*. And not an immanent salvation, meeting material or even spiritual needs, restricted to the framework of temporal existence and completely identified with temporal desires, hopes, affairs and struggles, but a salvation which exceeds all these limits in order to reach fulfilment in a communion with the one and only divine Absolute: a transcendent and eschatological salvation, which indeed has its beginning in this life but which is fulfilled in eternity.

JOHN PAUL II
ADDRESS TO THE THIRD GENERAL ASSEMBLY OF LATIN AMERICAN BISHOPS
(Puebla, 28 January 1979)

The Third General Assembly of Latin American Bishops, held at Puebla, Mexico, from January 27 to February 13, 1979, had for its theme "The Present and the Future of Evangelisation in Latin America". In his inaugural address Pope John Paul II warned against distortions of the revealed truth about Jesus Christ, the Church, and human beings (cf. nn. 425-426). In particular, he cautioned against "re-readings of the Gospel" which distort the person of Jesus and are at variance with the Church's faith in him as the Son of God. The text is found in AAS 72 (1979) 187-205.

(Truth concerning Jesus Christ)

674 1.(2). From you, pastors, the faithful of your countries expect and demand above all a careful and zealous transmission of the truth concerning Jesus Christ. This truth is at the centre of evangelisation and constitutes its essential content: "There is no true evangelisation if the name, the teaching, the life, the promises, the kingdom and the mystery of Jesus of Nazareth, the Son of God, are not proclaimed" *[EN 22]*.

On the living knowledge of this truth will depend the vigour of the faith of millions of people. On it will also depend the strength of their support of the Church and of their active presence as Christians in the world. From this knowledge there will derive choices, values, attitudes and modes of behaviour capable of orienting and defining our Christian life and of creating new people and hence a new humanity for the conversion of the individual and social conscience [EN 18].

It is from a solid Christology that there must come light on so many doctrinal and pastoral themes and questions that you intend to study in these coming days.

1.(3). And then we have to confess Christ before history and the world with a conviction that is profound, deeply felt and lived, just as Peter confessed him: "You are the Christ, the Son of the Living God" [Mt 16:16].

This is the Good News, in a certain sense unique: the Church lives by it and for it, just as she draws from it everything that she has to offer to people, without any distinction of nation, culture, race, time, age or condition. For this reason "from that confession of faith [Peter's] the sacred history of salvation and of the People of God could not fail to take on a new dimension".[1]

This is the one Gospel, and "even if we, or an angel from heaven, should preach to you a gospel contrary to that which we preached to you, let him be accursed" [Gal 1:8], as the apostle wrote in very clear terms.

(Re-readings of the Gospel)

675　1.(4)In fact, today there occur in many places—the phenomenon is not a new one—"re-readings" of the Gospel, the result of theoretical speculations rather than authentic meditation on the word of God and a true commitment to the Gospel. They cause confusion by diverging from the central criteria of the faith of the Church, and some people have the temerity to pass them on, under the guise of catechesis, to the Christian communities.

In some cases either Christ's divinity is passed over in silence or some people in fact fall into forms of interpretation at variance with the Church's faith. Christ is said to be merely a "prophet", one who proclaimed God's kingdom and love, but not the true Son of God, and therefore not the centre and object of the very gospel message.

---

1. Homily of Pope JOHN PAUL II at the Solemn inauguration of his pontificate, 22 October 1978.

In other cases people claim to show Jesus as politically committed, as one who fought against Roman oppression and the authorities, and also as one involved in the class struggle. This idea of Christ as a political figure, a revolutionary, as the subversive man from Nazareth, does not tally with the Church's catechesis. By confusing the insidious pretexts of Jesus'accusers with the—very different—attitude of Jesus himself, some people adduce as the cause of his death the outcome of a political conflict, and nothing is said of the Lord's will to deliver himself and of his consciousness of this redemptive mission. The Gospels clearly show that for Jesus anything that would alter his mission as the servant of Yahweh was a temptation *(Mt 4:8; Lk 4:5)*. He does not accept the position of those who mixed the things of God with merely political attitudes *(Mt 22:21; Mk 12:17; Jn 18:36)*. He unequivocally rejects recourse to violence. He opens his message of conversion to everybody, without excluding the very publicans. The perspective of his mission is much deeper. It consists in complete salvation through a transforming, peace-making, pardoning and reconciling love. There is no doubt, moreover, that all this is very demanding for the attitude of the Christian who wishes truly to serve his least brethren, the poor, the needy, the marginalised, in a word, all those who in their lives reflect the sorrowing face of the Lord *(LG 8)*.

(Affirmation of the Church's faith)

676 1.(5)Against such "re-readings", therefore, and against the perhaps brilliant but fragile and inconsistent hypotheses flowing from them, "evangelisation in the present and future of Latin America" cannot cease to affirm the Church's faith: Jesus Christ the Word and the Son of God, become man in order to come close to human beings and to offer them, through the power of his mystery, salvation, the great gift of God *(EN 19 and 27)*

ENCYCLICAL LETTER *REDEMPTOR HOMINIS* (1979)

The first Encyclical Letter of Pope John Paul II published on 4 March,1979, is devoted to "Jesus Christ, the Redeemer of Man."In Chapter II on the "Mystery of the Redemption", the Pope explains that redemption in Jesus Christ is a new creation brought about by God in his Son. He goes on to expand the "divine" and the "human dimension of the mystery of the redemption". Quoting the Pastoral Constitution Gaudium et Spes, 22 (cf. n.

669a), the Pope concludes that in Jesus Christ not only is God fully revealed to human beings but also their dignity is fully manifested.The text is found in AAS 71(1979)257ff.

(The divine dimension of the mystery of redemption)

677   9. Jesus Christ, the Son of the living God, became our reconciliation with the Father *[Rom 5:11; Col 1:20]*. He it was, and he alone,who satisfied the Father's eternal love,that fatherhood that from the beginning found expression in creating the world, giving human beings all the riches of creation, and making them "little less than God"*[Ps 8:6]*, in that they were created "in the image and after the likeness of God" *[cf. Gen 1:26]*. He and he alone also satisfied that fatherhood of God and that love which human beings in a way rejected by breaking the first Covenant *[cf. Gen 3:6-13]* and the later Covenants that God "again and again offered to them" *(cf. Eucharistic Prayer IV)*. The redemption of the world—this tremendous mystery of love in which creation is renewed *[GS 37]*—is, at its deepest root, the fulness of justice in a human Heart—the Heart of the first-born Son—in order that it may become justice in the hearts of many human beings, predestined from eternity in the first-born Son to be childern of God *[cf. Rom 8:29-30; Eph 1:8]* and called to grace, called to love. The Cross on Calvary, through which Jesus Christ—a Man, the Son of the Virgin Mary, thought to be the son of Joseph of Nazareth—"leaves" this world, is also a fresh manifestation of the eternal fatherhood of God, who in him draws near again to humanity, to each human being, giving him the thrice holy "Spirit of truth" *[cf.Jn. 16:13]*.

(The human dimension of the mystery of redemption)

678   10. Human beings cannot live without love. They remain beings that are incomprehensible for themselves, their life is senseless, if love is not revealed to them, if they do not encounter love, if they do not experience it and make it their own, if they do not participate intimately in it. This [...] is why Christ the Redeemer fully reveals them to themselves. If we may use the expression, this is the human dimension of the mystery of the Redemption. In this dimension human beings find again the greatness, dignity and value that belong to their humanity. In the mystery of the Redemption they become newly "expressed" and in a way, are newly created.[...] Those who wish to understand themselves throughly—and not just in accordance with immediate, partial, often superficial, and even illusory standards and measures of their being—must with their unrest, uncertainty and even their weakness and sinfulness, with their life and death, draw near to Christ. They must, so to speak, enter into him with all their self, they must "appropriate" and assimilate the whole of the reality of the Incarnation and Redemption in order to find themselves.

(Christ fully reveals God to humanity and humanity to itself)

679 11. The opening made by the Second Vatican Council has enabled the Church and all Christians to reach a more complete awareness of the mystery of Christ, "the mystery hidden for ages" *[Col 1:26]* in God, to be revealed in time in the Man Jesus Christ, and to be revealed continually in every time. In Christ and through Christ God has revealed himself fully to humankind and has definitively drawn close to it; at the same time, in Christ and through Christ human beings have acquired full awareness of their dignity, of the heights to which they are raised, of the surpassing worth of their own humanity, and of the meaning of their existence.

ENCYCLICAL LETTER *DIVES IN MISERICORDIA*
(30 November 1980)

This encyclical letter, devoted to the mercy of God, shows that already in the Old Testament God's justice is subordinate to his mercy. This revelation culminates in the Paschal Mystery of Christ's death and resurrection. The text is found in AAS 72 (1980) 1177-1232.

(God's love and mercy supremely revealed in the Paschal Mystery)

680 8. The Paschal Mystery is at the summit of the revelation of the inscrutable mystery of God. It is precisely then that the words pronounced in the Upper Room are completely fulfilled: "He who has seen me has seen the Father" *[Jn 14:9]*. In fact, Christ, whom the Father "did not spare" *[Rom 8:32]* for our sake and who in his Passion and in the torment of the Cross did not obtain human mercy, has revealed in his Resurrection the fulness of the love that the Father has for him and, in him, for all people. "He is not God of the dead, but of the living" *[Mk 12:27]*. In his Resurrection Christ has revealed the God of merciful love precisely because he accepted the Cross as the way to the resurrection. And it is for this reason that, when we recall the Cross of Christ, his Passion and death, our faith and hope are centred on the Risen One.[...]

Here is the Son of God, who in his Resurrection experienced in a radical way mercy shown to himself, that is to say the love of the Father which is more powerful than death. And it is also the same Christ, the Son of God, who at the end of his messianic mission—and, in a certain sense, even beyond the end—reveals himself as the inexhaustible source of mercy, of the same love that, in a subsequent perspective of the history of salvation in the Church, is to be everlastingly confirmed as more powerful than sin. The paschal Christ is the definitive incarnation of mercy, its living sign: in salvation history and in eschatology [...].

LETTER TO COMMEMORATE THE COUNCILS OF CONSTANTINOPLE I AND OF EPHESUS
(25 March 1981)

The letter celebrates conjointly the 16th centenary of the First Council of Constantinople (381) and the 1550th anniversary of the Council of Ephesus (431). The Pope highlights the Christological and soteriological significance of Ephesus. Cf. n. 334i. The text is found in AAS 73 (1981) 513-527.

(Ephesus on the redemptive incarnation and the divine motherhood)

(681)   See text in n.335.

ENCYCLICAL LETTER *REDEMPTORIS MISSIO*
(7 December 1990)

This encyclical on the permanent validity of the Church's missionary mandate dedicates Chapter I to Christ as the only Saviour and Chapter II to the kingdom of God in its relation to Christ and the Church. The text is found in Origins 20 (1991) 541-567.

(Jesus reveals the Kingdom)

682   13. The Kingdom which Jesus inaugurates is the Kingdom of God. Jesus himself reveals who this God is, the One whom he addresses by the intimate term "Abba", Father [cf. Mk 14:36]. God, as revealed above all in the parables [cf. Lk 15:3-32; Mt 20:1-16] is sensitive to the needs and sufferings of every human being.

14. Jesus gradually reveals the characteristics and demands of the Kingdom through his words, his actions and his

own person. The Kingdom of God is meant for all humankind, and all people are called to become members of it.

COMMON CHRISTOLOGICAL DECLARATION BETWEEN THE CATHOLIC CHURCH AND THE ASSYRIAN CHURCH OF THE EAST
(11 November 1994)

This joint declaration, signed by John Paul II and Mar Dinkha IV, Patriarch of the Assyrian Church of the East, echoes the language of Chalcedon (e.g. the one "person" and two "natures", as well as the famous four adverbs, here translated as "without confusion or change, without division or separation"). It respects the sensibilities of the followers of Nestorius by not insisting on the Mariological title "Mother of God" as being absolutely necessary. Cf. nn. 604-605. The text is found in the Osservatore Romano *(12 November 1994) 1.*

683 Therefore our Lord Jesus Christ is true God and true man, perfect in his divinity and perfect in his humanity, consubstantial with the Father and consubstantial with us in all things but sin. His divinity and his humanity are united in one person, without confusion or change, without division or separation. In him has been preserved the difference of the natures of divinity and humanity, with all their properties, faculties and operation. But far from constituting "one and another", the divinity and humanity are united in the person of the same and unique Son of God and Lord Jesus Christ, who is the object of a single adoration.

Christ therefore is not an "ordinary man" whom God adopted in order to reside in him and inspire him, as in the righteous ones and the prophets. But the same God the Word, begotten of his Father before all worlds without beginning according to his divinity, was born of a mother without a father in the last times according to his humanity . The humanity to which the Blessed Virgin Mary gave birth always was that of the Son of God himself. That is the reason why the Assyrian Church of the East is praying [to] the Virgin Mary as "the Mother of Christ our God and Saviour". In the light of this same faith the Catholic tradition addresses the Virgin Mary as "the Mother of God" and also as "the Mother of Christ". We both recognize the legitimacy and rightness of these expressions of the same faith and we both respect the preference of each Church in her liturgical life and piety.

COMMON DECLARATION BY POPE JOHN PAUL II AND CATHOLICOS KAREKIN I
(13 December 1996)

This joint declaration, signed by John Paul II and Catholicos Karekin I, the Supreme Patriarch and Catholicos of all Armenians, repeats the famous four adverbs from the Council of Chalcedon, here translated as "without confusion, without alteration, without division, without any form of separation". When confessing the unity of perfect divinity and perfect humanity in the one Person of the Son of God, the declaration does not use the terminology of "consubstantial" or "natures". The text is found in AAS 89 (3 February 1997) 90-92.

684 Pope John Paul II and Catholicos Karekin I [...] particularly welcome the great advance that their Churches have registered in their common search for unity in Christ, the Word of God made flesh, perfect God as to his divinity, perfect man as to his humanity. His divinity is united to his humanity in the person of the Only-begotten Son of God, in a union which is real, perfect, without confusion, without alteration, without division, without any form of separation.

CHAPTER VII

THE MOTHER OF THE SAVIOUR

The significance of the Mother of God in the divine plan of salvation and in the order of grace cannot be brought out adequately in a collection of doctrinal documents directly concerned with her. Comparatively few official pronouncements deal exclusively with Mary. The doctrine on Mary is so closely linked with that about Jesus Christ and his work that the most fundamental affirmations regarding her are found in the Church's Christological documents.

There is, nevertheless, need for a special chapter on Mary, which is, as it were, a complement to Christology. It contains those documents on Mary which have not been mentioned in the Christological context. To gather these documents together in a separate chapter could create the impression that Mariology is dealt with as a special branch of theology. Indeed, the objection raised against Mariology in the past decades has been that it tended to remain isolated from the broader context of Christian doctrine, and was at times developed beyond proportion. Similar objections have been raised against the onesidedness and exaggerations of certain forms of Marian devotion. It surely is the merit of the Second Vatican Council to have re-integrated the doctrine on Mary into the comprehensive view of divine revelation and salvation. This integration is clearly manifested by the fact that the Marian doctrine of the Council forms part of the Constitution on the Church.

The documents mentioned here witness to three stages through which the mystery of Mary has been progressively unfolded in the consciousness of the Church. There are first the documents in which Mary's divine motherhood is taught: she is not merely the mother of the man Jesus, of a man united to the Son of God, but the Mother of God himself; God truly became man through her. The doctrine of the 'theotokos' is central for the correct understanding of the person of Jesus Christ himself.

The unique privilege of Mary's divine motherhood having been clearly stated, the way was open for a growing understanding of its implications for Mary herself. In the course of the centuries the doctrine on Mary's sinlessness, on her Immaculate Conception and on her bodily Assumption into heaven have been gradually expounded; this process has led to the two definitions of the Immaculate Conception and the Assumption.

Mariology would not, however, be complete were it to stop at the contemplation of Mary's personal vocation. Mary must be understood in the context of her role within the entire mystery of salvation; her place is in the midst of the people of God. This last phase in the unfolding of Marian doctrine has its root in early patristic theology, but it has been developed extensively by modern Mariology. It is contained in recent papal documents, mainly since Leo XIII; it has been brought to a climax by the Second Vatican Council.

* * *

The main points of doctrine mentioned in this chapter may be grouped under the following headings:

Mary is Mother of God: 5, 10, 605, 606/1, 607, 614, 617, 620/6, (701), (702), 703;
through the overshadowing of the Holy Spirit: 3, 4, 5, 10, 12, 15, 23, 39/4, 609, 703, 707;
without loss of her virginity: 5, 10, 39/7, 609, 612, 620/2, 628, 703, 704, 707, 709.
Motherhood and virginity united: 724.
Mary is free from original sin: 39/7, 704, 705, 708, 709;
and sinless: 706, 716, 1973.
Mary's faith: 721a, 721b.
Mary was assumed into heaven: 39/8, 713-715.
She played an active role in Christ's redemptive work: 710, 712, 716a, 716d.
Her shared mediation is motherly: 716a, 716c, 721-722.
She intercedes for all: 39/8, 704, 710, 712, 717.
She is the type of the Church: 718.
She is the mother of Christians and of the Church: 716a, 718b, 718c.
Mary, the model of womanhood: 719, 723.
Mary, sign of hope for modern people: 720.

THE GENERAL COUNCIL OF EPHESUS (431)

(701) *The basic Mariological dogma of the true divine motherhood of Mary is in fact a Christological dogma asserted in the general Council of Ephesus (431) against Nestorius. It is contained in the second letter of Cyril of Alexandria to Nestorius which was solemnly approved by the Council Fathers as representing the Catholic faith; it is also explicitly affirmed in the first of the twelve anathemas of St. Cyril against Nestorius. See the texts under nn. 605, 606/1.*

JOHN II
LETTER TO THE SENATE OF CONSTANTINOPLE (534)

(702) *The Christological dogma was formulated more precisely in the Council of Chalcedon (451) than it had been at Ephesus; along with it the doctrine of the divine motherhood of Mary was also repeated. Later still, the import of the title'Mother of God' (theotokos) was officially declared by John II in a letter to the Senate of Constantinople. Among other points under discussion, the Pope explains that this title must be strictly understood against both the Nestorian and the Monophysite interpretations. See text under n.617.*

THE LATERAN COUNCIL (649)

Martin I gathered a Council in the Lateran against the heresy of Monothelitism (cf.n.627i) In the context of the Christological doctrine this Council also teaches in peremptory terms the perpetual virginity of Mary.

(Mary, Mother of God and Virgin)

703
503

3. If anyone does not, according to the holy Fathers, confess truly and properly that holy Mary, ever virgin and immaculate, is Mother of God, since in this latter age she conceived in true reality without human seed from the Holy Spirit, God the Word himself, who before the ages was born of God the Father, and gave birth to him without corruption, her virginity remaining equally inviolate after the birth, let him be condemned.

SIXTUS IV
CONSTITUTION *CUM PRAEEXCELSA* (1477)

Once Mary's divine motherhood and the unique place which it confers upon her in God's plan of salvation had been clearly stated and understood, the reflection of the Church turned to the implications of her role for Mary herself. If she was to be at the service of God in the act by which God brought about the salvation of humankind and the conquest of sin, she could not be herself subject to sin. Thus the doctrine of Mary's Immaculate Conception, i.e., her freedom from sin from the very beginning of her existence, became more and more firmly established.

In fact already the Council of Basel had decreed in its thirty-sixth session (1439): "The doctrine which asserts that the glorious Virgin Mary, Mother of God, through the working of a singular prevenient grace of the divine power was never subject to original sin and was always immune from original and actual sin, holy and immaculate, is a pious doctrine which accords with the liturgy of the Church, with Catholic faith, with sound reasoning and Holy Scripture; we define that it is to be approved by all Catholics and that from now on no one should be allowed to preach or teach the contrary".[1]

This session of the Council of Basel, however, took place at a time when the Council was no longer in communion with the Pope and, therefore, its decrees were not held as binding. The controversy to which the doctrine of the Immaculate Conception had already previously been subjected went on. The Dominican school opposed it because it seemed to contradict the dogma of the universality of original sin; the Franciscans on the contrary defended it.

Pope Sixtus IV, himself a Franciscan, approved the feast of the Immaculate Conception in this Constitution; later, in Grave Nimis *(1483) he forbade anyone to censure those who celebrated the feast and held the Immaculate Conception as doctrine of faith (cf. DS 1425-1426).*

(On the Immaculate Conception)

704
1400   [...] In His divine providence the almighty God looked from eternity on this humble virgin. Having prepared her by the Holy Spirit, he made her the dwelling place of his only-begotten in order to reconcile to its author the human nature that had been subject to eternal death through the fall of the first parent. From her he was to receive the flesh of our mortality for the redemption of his people, while she would remain an immaculate virgin also after his birth. All the faithful of Christ should give thanks and praise to almighty God for the wonderful conception of the immaculate virgin and should celebrate the Mass and the other divine offices instituted to this end in the Church of God and attend them. With indulgences for the forgiveness of sins we invite them to do so in order that through the merits and the intercession of the same virgin they may become more capable of receiving divine grace.

---

1.   Cf. Mansi, 29, 183 BC

THE GENERAL COUNCIL OF TRENT

The council of Trent was concerned with re-asserting the Catholic faith against the challenge of the Reformers. It speaks of Mary only incidentally, with regard to the unique place which she holds in God's plan of salvation. The first reference is found in the Decree on Original Sin (1546). The Council states that it is not its intention to include Mary in the general condition of sinfulness of our race. The second reference is contained in the Decree on Justification (1547): while human beings in general are subject to sin in their daily life, Mary is free from it through a special grace.

FIFTH SESSION

DECREE ON ORIGINAL SIN (1546)

705 This same holy Synod declares that it is not its intention
1516 to include in this decree dealing with original sin the
Blessed and Immaculate Virgin Mary, Mother of God,
but that the Constitutions of Pope Sixtus IV of blessed memory
are to be observed under the penalties contained in those
Constitutions, which it renews *[cf.n.704]*.

SIXTH SESSION

DECREE ON JUSTIFICATION (1547)

706 Canon 23: If anyone says[...] that a person once justified
1573 can avoid all sins, even venial ones, throughout one's
entire life, unless it be by a special privilege of God as
the Church holds of the Blessed Virgin, *anathema sit.*

PAUL IV

CONSTITUTION *CUM QUORUMDAM HOMINUM* (1555)

Soon after the emergence of the Reformation rationalist theology, which set reason above revelation, made its appearance within Protestantism. It denied all supernatural elements in revelation and attacked the doctrine of the Trinity, the incarnation and the redemption (cf. n. 648). The Constitution of Paul IV reflects the attacks of rationalism. The texts referring to Mary are quoted here.

(Mary's Virginity)

707 [...] We question and admonish all those who [...] have
1880 asserted, taught and believed [...] that our Lord [...] was
not conceived from the Holy Spirit according to the flesh
in the womb of the Blessed Mary ever Virgin but, as other human

beings, from the seed of Joseph; [...] or that the same Blessed
Virgin Mary is not truly the mother of God and did not retain
her virginity intact before the birth, in the birth, and perpetually
after the birth.

PIUS V

BULL *EX OMNIBUS AFFLICTIONIBUS* (1567)
CONDEMNED PROPOSITIONS OF MICHAEL DE BAY

*The teaching of de Bay and the Jansenists about Mary forms part of their
rigorist views about the fundamental sinfulness of the human will (cf. n. 1984i),
to which they did not admit any exception. See a similar Jansenist error about
Mary in DS 2324.*

[708]   73. Nobody but Christ is free from original sin; hence
1973   the Blessed Virgin died on account of the sin inherited
        from Adam, and all her afflictions in this life were, like
those of the rest of the just, punishment for actual or original
sin.

PIUS IX

BULL *INEFFABILIS DEUS* (8 Dec. 1854)

*The doctrine of the Immaculate Conception had developed through many
centuries (cf. n. 708). After the position taken by Trent (cf. nn. 705-706) and
the condemnation of de Bay (cf. n. 708), Alexander VII in 1661 explained
and defended the doctrine (cf. DS 2015-2017) in terms similar to those used
in the definition of Pius IX. This Pope thus raised to a dogma of faith a
doctrine which had behind it a long tradition.*

709   To the glory of the holy and undivided Trinity, to the
2803   honour and renown of the Virgin Mother of God, the
        exaltation of the Catholic faith and the increase of
Christian religion; by the authority of our Lord Jesus Christ, of
the blessed apostles Peter and Paul, and our own authority, we
declare, pronounce and define: the doctrine which holds that the
most Blessed Virgin Mary was, from the first moment of her
conception, by a singular grace and privilege of almighty God
and in view of the merits of Christ Jesus the Saviour of the
human race, preserved immune from all stain of original sin, is
revealed by God and, therefore, firmly and constantly to be
believed by all the faithful.

2804   If, therefore, any person shall dare to think—which God
         forbid—otherwise than has been defined by us, let them
clearly know that they stand condemned by their own judgment,
that they have made shipwreck of their faith and fallen from
the unity of the Church. Furthermore, they subject themselves
ipso facto to the penalties provided by law if by speech or writing
or in any other exterior way they shall dare to express their
views.

LEO XIII

ENCYCLICAL LETTER *OCTOBRI MENSE* (1891)

*Modern Mariology is centred round the problem of Mary's place in God's
plan of salvation. Though a purely gratuitous and free gift on the part of
God, salvation depends on one's free response to and acceptance of God's gift.
Mary was the first to respond to the divine invitation made by God to human
beings in Jesus Christ; this is why she plays a unique role in the work of
salvation. She plays this role in two ways; first, through her share in the
mystery of salvation itself, in her "fiat" to God at Nazareth which came to its
full expression as she stood at the foot of the cross; secondly, in her heavenly
role of intercession for all the faithful.*

*Until the Second Vatican Council this double role of Mary has been
much debated. At times it has been exaggerated, as though her place were
somewhat similar to that of her Son; at times, on the contrary, it has been
unduly played down out of fear of obscuring the unique mediation of Christ.
Since Vatican II strikes the correct balance most felicitously, only a few
characteristic texts need to be quoted from among the many Mariological
declarations of the last Popes before the Council. In this encyclical the Pope
stresses the significance of Mary's consent to her divine motherhood.*

(Mary's role in our salvation)

710   When the eternal Son of God willed to take the human
3274   nature for the redemption and honour of human beings,
         and so wanted in a certain sense to enter into a mystical
marriage with the whole of the human race, he did not do so
before his chosen mother had given her totally free consent. She
impersonated in some way the human race, as Thomas Aquinas
says beautifully and in full truth: "In the Annunciation the
consent of the Virgin was awaited in place of that of the whole
human nature."[1] Therefore, one may in truth and aptly say

---

1. *Summa Theologica*, III, 30, I

that nothing of the vast treasure of all grace which the Lord has brought—since "grace and truth came through Jesus Christ" [*Jn 1:17*]—is, according to God's will, given to us without Mary.

PIUS X

ENCYCLICAL LETTER *AD DIEM ILLUM* (1904)

This encyclical marks the fiftieth anniversary of the proclamation of the dogma of the Immaculate Conception. It develops mainly the theological foundations for Mary's mediation of grace.

(*The union of Mary with the sacrifice of her Son*)

712
3370
From the community of will and suffering between Christ and Mary she merited to become the restorer (*reparatrix*) of the world that was lost, and the dispenser (*dispensatrix*) of all the benefits which Jesus won for us by his death and at the price of his blood. We do not deny indeed that the distribution of these gifts belongs personally to Christ by a unique right. For they were won through his death alone and he alone has the power to be mediator between God and human beings. Nevertheless, on account of the union of sorrow and pain between mother and Son, of which we have spoken, it has been given to the august Virgin to be the most powerful mediator (*mediatrix*) and advocate (*conciliatrix*) for the whole world with her only-begotten Son [....]. Since she stands above all others in sanctity and in union with Christ, and was drawn by Christ into the work of our salvation, she merits for us by equity (*de congruo*), as it is said, what Christ merited by right (*de condigno*), and she is the primary minister in the distribution of the divine graces.

PIUS XII

APOSTOLIC CONSTITUTION *MUNIFICENTISSIMUS DEUS* (1950)

On November 1, 1950, Pius XII solemnly defined the Assumption of Mary to the glory of heaven. The Constitution offers a survey of the belief in Mary's Assumption, expressed in doctrine, popular piety and liturgy through the ages. The final theological synthesis given by the Constitution, and the definition itself are quoted here.

(Mary's Assumption into heaven)

713 From all eternity and by one and the same decree of
3902 predestination the august Mother of God is united in a
sublime way with Jesus Christ; immaculate in her
conception, a spotless virgin in her divine motherhood, the noble
companion of the divine Redeemer who won a complete triumph
over sin and its consequences, she finally obtained as the
crowning glory of her privileges to be preserved from the
corruption of the tomb and like her Son before her, to conquer
death and to be raised body and soul to the glory of heaven, to
shine refulgent as Queen at the right hand of her Son, the
immortal King of ages [cf. 1 Tim 1:17].

714 The universal Church, in which the Spirit of truth
actively dwells, and which is infallibly guided by him to
an ever more perfect knowledge of revealed truths, has down the
centuries manifested her belief in many ways; the bishops from
all over the world ask almost unanimously that the truth of the
bodily Assumption of the Blessed Virgin Mary into heaven be
defined as a dogma of divine and catholic faith; this truth is based
on Sacred Scripture and deeply embedded in the minds of the
faithful; it has received the approval of liturgical worship from the
earliest times; it is perfectly in keeping with the rest of revealed
truth, and has been lucidly developed and explained by the
studies, the knowledge and wisdom of theologians. Considering
all these reasons we deem that the moment pre-ordained in the
plan of divine providence has now arrived for us to proclaim
solemnly this extraordinary privilege of the Virgin Mary.[...]

715 Therefore, having directed humble and repeated prayers
3903 to God, and having invoked the light of the Spirit of
Truth; to the glory of almighty God who has bestowed
his special bounty on the Virgin Mary, for the honour of his Son
the immortal King of ages and victor over sin and death, for the
greater glory of his august mother, and for the joy and exultation
of the whole Church; by the authority of our Lord Jesus Christ,
of the blessed apostles Peter and Paul, and by our own authority,
we proclaim, declare and define as a dogma revealed by God:
the Immaculate Mother of God, Mary ever Virgin, when the
course of her earthly life was ended, was taken up body and
soul into the glory of heaven.

Wherefore, if anyone—which God forbid—should wilfully dare to deny or call in doubt what has been defined by us, let him know that he certainly has abandoned the divine and Catholic faith.

THE SECOND VATICAN GENERAL COUNCIL

The references of the Council texts to the Blessed Virgin are many. She has her place in the documents concerning liturgy, the ministry and life of priests, religious and lay-people, the formation of seminarians; she is mentioned in the description of the Eastern Churches (UR 15 and OE 30) and also in the outline of the faith of Muslims (NA 3)

However, the Council could not limit itself to such occasional references. It had to fulfil a difficult and urgent task with regard to the doctrine on the Blessed Virgin and her place in the life of the Church. Different, even contrasting tendencies existed within the Church, often described as maximalist and minimalist trends (however inadequate such terms may be). The impression was created that there existed two different Mariologies which tended to drift apart. It was a matter of grave concern for the Council to propose a coherent synthesis of the Catholic teaching about Mary which would meet with the approval of the various tendencies. It had to fulfil the following demands: 1) not to formulate a new dogma (some were apprehensive that Mary's mediation of all graces might be defined); 2) to dispel the impression that Mariology is a separate and isolated domain of theological research and reflection, by integrating it into a comprehensive view of the mystery of salvation; 3) to show in particular its connection with, and relevance for, the life of the Church, and the Christian life in general; 4) to avoid unnecessary tensions on the ecumenical plane, and present the Catholic position in a way which could be intelligible for Protestants.

Thus the document of the Council on Mary became a comprehensive and constructive document, reconciling different tendencies through "studied ambiguities", yet sufficiently articulated and founded on Scripture, Tradition and modern theological reflection. To emphasise its intimate connection with the whole mystery of salvation, the Council Fathers, after a heated discussion and a close vote, decided to join this document to the Constitution Lumen Gentium *on the Church, of which it constitutes the eighth and last chapter.*

DOGMATIC CONSTITUTION *LUMEN GENTIUM* (1964)

The introduction to chapter eight outlines the intention of the Council to describe Mary's place in the mystery of salvation: on the one hand, she plays a unique role; on the other hand, she fully belongs to our race, being "redeemed in an eminent manner" (52-54).

Part I describes Mary's role in the work of salvation: it is foreshadowed in the Old Testament (55); she enters into her role through the free assent to her vocation to be mother of the Saviour; thus she is not a passive instrument of God's design, but through her obedience plays an irreplaceable part in the salvation of humankind. Her response, asked for by God and freely offered by her, is the core of the Marian mystery, and the starting point of Mariology (56). Her role is unfolded in the mysteries of the infancy of Jesus (57) and in his public life (58). It is fulfilled in her presence in the midst of the Church on Pentecost, and finally in the Assumption (59).

Part II unfolds the continuation of Mary's role in the life of the Church. First, the exclusive role of Jesus Christ as the only mediator between God and human beings is stressed; Mary's role does not rival that of her Son but rather enhances it (60). It flows from her co-operation in our salvation (61), and consists in her maternal solicitude and intercession for all, until the end of time (62). Her virginal motherhood is the 'type'(63) which is fulfilled in the Church (64); while she has already reached the final glory, the Church is still on her pilgrimage, following her (65).

Part III treats of the veneration of Mary. From the beginning Mary held a unique place in the cult of the Church (66). Her cult must be fostered, though in the right direction and measure; it must also be conceived in an ecumenical spirit (67).

The conclusion considers Mary in her glory as a sign of hope for all the faithful (68). All Christians should join in venerating her and imploring her intercession (69).

The following few texts are characteristics of this Mariological document, the most important to date.

(Mary, Mother of the members of Christ)

716a   53. [...] Redeemed, in a more exalted fashion, by reason of the merits of her Son and united to him by a close and indissoluble tie, she is endowed with the high office and dignity of the Mother of the Son of God, and therefore she is also the beloved daughter of the Father and the temple of the Holy Spirit. Because of this gift of sublime grace she far surpasses all creatures, both in heaven and on earth. But, being of the race of Adam, she is at the same time also united to all those who are to be saved; indeed, "she is clearly the mother of the members of Christ [...] since she has by her charity joined in bringing about the birth of believers in the Church, who are members of its head."[1] Wherefore she is hailed as pre-eminent

---

1. Cf. St. AUGUSTINE, *De S. Virginitate*, 6.

and as a wholly unique member of the Church, and as its type and outstanding model in faith and charity. The Catholic Church taught by the Holy Spirit, honours her with filial affection and devotion as a most beloved mother.

(Mary's free consent to the divine motherhood)

716b 56. [...] Adorned from the first moment of her conception with the radiance of a unique holiness, the virgin of Nazareth is greeted, in the name of God, by an angel as "full of grace" *[cf. Lk 1:28]*; and she replies to the heavenly messenger: "Behold I am the handmaid of the Lord; let it be to me according to your word" *[Lk 1:38]*. Thus it came to pass that Mary, a daughter of Adam, became mother of Jesus through her consent to the divine word. With her whole heart, unhindered by sin, she embraced the salvific will of God and consecrated herself totally as handmaid of the Lord to the person and work of her Son, under whom and with whom, by the grace of the Almighty, she served in the mystery of the redemption. Justly, therefore, do the holy Fathers consider Mary not merely as a passive instrument in the hands of God, but as freely co-operating in the salvation of humankind by her faith and obedience. As St. Irenaeus says: "Through her obedience she became cause of salvation both for herself and for the whole human race."[1]

(Unique mediation of Christ and maternal role of Mary)

716c 60. In the words of the apostle there is but one mediator; "for there is one God, and there is one mediator between God and humankind, the man Jesus Christ, who gave himself as a ransom for all" *[1 Tim 2:5-6]*. But Mary's function as mother of human beings in no way obscures or diminishes this unique mediation of Christ, but rather shows its power. But the blessed Virgin's salutary influence on human persons originates not in any inner necessity but in the disposition of God. It flows forth from the superabundance of the merits of Christ, rests on his mediation, depends entirely on it and draws all its power from it. It does not hinder in any way the immediate union of the faithful with Christ but on the contrary fosters it.

---

1. St. Irenaeus, *Adversus Haereses*, III, 22, 4.

(Mary associated with Christ in the work of redemption)

716d 61. The predestination of the Blessed Virgin Mary as Mother of God was associated with the incarnation of the divine Word: in the designs of the divine Providence she was the gracious mother of the divine Redeemer here on earth, and above all others and in a singular way the generous associate and humble handmaid of the Lord. She conceived, brought forth, and nourished Christ, she presented him to the Father in the temple, shared her son's sufferings as he died on the cross. Thus in a wholly singular way she cooperated by her obedience, faith, hope and burning charity in the work of the Saviour in restoring supernatural life to souls. For this reason she is a mother to us in the order of grace.

(Mary's intercession)

717 62. Mary's motherhood in the economy of grace continues without interruption, from the moment of her consent—which she gave at the annunciation and maintained unwaveringly under the cross—until the eternal fulfilment of all the elect. Her assumption into heaven does not mean that she has laid aside her salvific role; she continues to obtain by her constant intercession the graces we need for eternal salvation. In her maternal love, she takes care of her Son's brothers and sisters, still journeying on earth surrounded by dangers and difficulties, until they reach their blissful home. That is why the Blessed Virgin is invoked in the Church under the titles of Advocate, Auxiliatrix, Helper, Mediatrix. All of which, however, have to be so understood that they in no way diminish or add to the dignity and efficacy of Christ the one Mediator.

(Mary, type of the Church)

718a 63. [...] The Blessed Virgin is also intimately united with the Church. Already St. Ambrose called her the type of the Church, or exemplar, in the order of faith, charity and perfect union with Christ.[1] Indeed, in the mystery of the Church, who herself is rightly called mother and virgin, the Blessed Virgin

---

1. St. Ambrose, *Expos. Lc.*, II, 7.

Mary came first, standing out as an eminent and unequalled exemplar of both motherhood and virginity. For, by her faith and obedience she brought forth on earth the Father's own Son, without loss of her virginity but overshadowed by the Holy Spirit, not listening to the serpent as Eve of old, but as the new Eve believing God's messenger with unhesitating faith.[...]

PAUL VI

ALLOCUTION TO THE COUNCIL FATHERS
(21 November 1964)

In this allocution to the Conciliar Fathers held on the day of the Presentation of Our Lady, Pope Paul VI proclaimed her "Mother of the Church". The text is found in AAS 56 (1964) 1007-1018.

(Mary, Mother of the Church)

718b   [...] We declare the most holy Mary Mother of the Church, that is, of the entire Christian people, faithful and pastors alike, who call her most loving mother; and we decree that henceforth the whole Christian people give to the divine mother ever greater honour by invoking her and having recourse to her with that sublime name.

[...] This name belongs indeed to genuine Marian piety, since it is firmly rooted in the dignity with which Mary is endowed as Mother of God's Incarnate Word.

Divine Motherhood is the reason why Mary is related to Christ in a unique way and is present in the work performed by Jesus Christ for human salvation. Similarly, her divine motherhood is also the main source of the relations between Mary and the Church. Indeed, Mary is the Mother of Christ who, while assuming human nature in her virginal womb, united to himself as Head his Mystical Body which is the Church. Hence, as Mother of Christ she must also be considered mother of all the faithful and pastors, that is, Mother of the Church.

APOSTOLIC EXHORTATION *SIGNUM MAGNUM*
(13 May 1967)

This apostolic exhortation confirms and completes the allocution to the Council Fathers mentioned above (n. 718b). The text is found in AAS 59 (1967) 465-475.

(Mary's continued motherhood of the redeemed)

718c There is first the following truth: Mary is Mother of the Church, not only because she is mother of Jesus Christ and his closest associate in the new plan of salvation "when the Son of God took human nature from her, that he might in the mysteries of his flesh free human beings from sin" *[LG 55]*, but also because she "shines forth to the whole community of the elect as the model of virtues" *[LG 65]*. Just as no human mother may limit her role strictly to the procreation of a new human person but must continue it by nourishing and educating her offspring, so does also the Virgin Mary. After sharing in the Sacrifice of her Son, cause of our Redemption, so closely as to deserve to be called by him mother not only of John the disciple but also—it may be said—of the whole human race represented by the disciple, she continues now in heaven to fulfil her motherly role by contributing to bring forth and increase the divine life in the souls of all the redeemed.

APOSTOLIC EXHORTATION *MARIALIS CULTUS* (1974)

This lengthy document bears the date of 2 February, 1974, but was published on 21 March. Its intention is to give guidelines for the "right ordering and development of the devotion to the Blessed Virgin Mary". It shows the place of the Marian devotion in the context of the liturgical reform of Vatican II and indicates its theological and pastoral significance for our time. Its theology is widely based on Chapter VIII of Lumen Gentium. *The document also shows the significance of Marian devotion in the context of modern movements for the liberation of women. Thus it describes Mary as presenting an ideal of womanhood widely different from that of traditional Marian piety. The Gospel shows Mary in the essential situations of womanhood, responding to God's will; it is for each generation to articulate this ideal within the context of its own culture. In the last section the document points to Mary's significance in the crisis of the modern world. The text is found in AAS 66 (1974) 113ff.*

(Mary, the model of womanhood)

719 34. The picture of the Blessed Virgin presented in a certain type of devotional literature cannot easily be reconciled with today's life-style, especially the way women live today.

(Women strive for co-responsibility in the home and for their legitimate role in the social, political, cultural spheres of society).

In consequence of these phenomena some people are becoming estranged from devotion to the Blessed Virgin and find it difficult to take as an example Mary of Nazareth because the horizons of her life, so they say, seem rather restricted in comparison with the vast spheres of activity open to humankind today[...]

35. First, the Virgin Mary has always been proposed to the faithful by the Church as an example to be imitated, not precisely in the type of life she led, and much less for the socio-cultural back-ground in which she lived and which today scarcely exists anywhere. She is held as an example to the faithful rather for the way in which, in her own particular life, she fully and responsibly accepted the will of God [cf. Lk 1:38]; because she received the word of God and acted on it; because charity and a spirit of service were the driving force of her actions; because she was the first and the most perfect of Christ's disciples. All of this has a permanent and universal exemplary value.

36. Secondly [...] the difficulties alluded to above are not connected with the true Gospel image of Mary nor with the doctrinal data [...]. It is not surprising that Christians who lived in different social and cultural conditions [...] saw in Jesus' mother the outstanding type of womanhood and the prominent example of a life lived according to the Gospel, and expressed their sentiments with the mentality and images corresponding to their age. They looked at Mary and her mission as the New Woman and the perfect Christian who united in herself the characteristic situations of a woman's life as Virgin, Spouse and Mother. When the Church considers the long history of Marian devotion she rejoices at the continuity of her veneration, but she does not bind herself to any particular expression of an individual cultural epoch or to the particular anthropological ideas underlying such expressions.

(Mary in the crisis of the modern world)

720   57. Mary, the New Woman, stands at the side of Christ, the New Man, within whose mystery the mystery of the human being alone finds true light [cf. n. 668]; she is given to us as a pledge and guarantee that God's plan in Christ for the salvation of the whole human person has already achieved realisation in a creature: in her. Contemplated in the vicissitudes of her earthly life and in the heavenly bliss which she already possesses in the City of God, the Blessed Virgin Mary offers a calm vision and a reassuring word to modern people, torn as they often are between anguish and hope, defeated by the sense of their own limitations and assailed by limitless aspirations, troubled in their mind and divided in their heart, uncertain before the riddle of death, oppressed by loneliness while yearning for fellowship, a prey to boredom and disgust. She shows forth the victory of hope over anguish, of fellowship over solitude, of peace over anxiety, of joy and beauty over boredom and disgust, of eternal visions over earthly ones, of life over death.

JOHN PAUL II

ENCYCLICAL LETTER *REDEMPTORIS MATER*
(25th March 1987)

In the first part of this Marian encyclical Pope John Paul II shows the place of Mary in the Mystery of Christ, stressing especially the "obedience of faith" by which she is perfectly united with her son. The second part is entitled " The Mother of God at the Centre of the Pilgrim Church": She who first believed accompanies the Church's pilgrimage of faith. The third part is devoted to Mary's "motherly mediation". The text is found in AAS 79 (1987) 361-433.

(The faith of Mary)

721a   19. In the expression "Blessed is she who believed", we can [...] rightly find a kind of "key" which unlocks for us the innermost reality of Mary, whom the angel hailed as "full of grace". If as "full of grace" she has been eternally present in the mystery of Christ, through faith she became a sharer in that mystery in every extension of her earthly journey.

(The extension of Mary's faith)

721b   26. From [the moment of Pentecost] there [...] begins that journey of faith, the Church's pilgrimage through the history of individuals and peoples. We know that at the beginning of this journey Mary is present. We see her in the midst of the apostles in the Upper Room, "prayerfully imploring the gift of the Spirit" [LG 59].

In a sense her journey of faith is longer. The Holy Spirit had already come down upon her, and she became his faithful spouse at the annunciation, welcoming the Word of the true God, offering "the full submission of intellect and will [...] and freely assenting to the truth revealed by him", indeed abandoning herself totally to God through the "obedience of faith" [DV 5].

(Mary's shared mediation bound to her motherhood)

721c 38. In effect, Mary's mediation is intimately linked with her motherhood. It possesses a specifically maternal character, which distinguishes it from the mediation of the other creatures who in various and always subordinate ways share in the one mediation of Christ, although her own mediation is also a shared mediation. In fact, while it is true that "no creature could ever be classed with the Incarnate Word and Redeemer", at the same time "the unique mediation of the Redeemer does not exclude but rather gives rise among creatures to a manifold cooperation which is but a sharing in this unique source". And thus "the one goodness of God is in reality communicated diversely to his creatures" [LG 62].

(Motherly mediation)

722 39. Mary' motherhood, completely pervaded by her spousal attitude as the "handmaid of the Lord", constitutes the first and fundamental dimension of that mediation which the Church confesses and proclaims in her regard [LG 62] and continually "commends to the hearts of the faithful", since the Church has great trust in her. For it must be recognized that before anyone else it was God himself, the eternal Father, who entrusted himself to the Virgin of Nazareth, giving her his own Son in the mystery of the Incarnation. Her election to the supreme office and dignity of mother of the Son of God refers, on the ontological level, to the very reality of the union of the two natures in the person of the Word (hypostatic union). This basic fact of being the mother of the Son of God is from the very beginning a complete openness to the person of Christ, to his whole work, to his whole mission. The words "Behold, I am the handmaid of the Lord" testify to Mary's openness of spirit: She perfectly unites in herself the love proper to virginity and the love characteristic of motherhood, which are joined and as it were fused together.

APOSTOLIC LETTER *MULIERIS DIGNITATEM*
(15 August 1988)

Written on the occasion of the Marian year, the Apostolic Letter shows that the "essential horizon" for a "reflection on the dignity and vocation of women" is the mystery of the "woman-mother of God". Cf. n. 431i. Motherhood and virginity are "two particular dimensions" of woman's personality, both of which are realized conjointly in Mary in an outstanding manner. Thus Mary stands out as the perfect model for woman in both motherhood and virginity. The text is found in AAS 80 (1988) 1653-1719.

(The mystery of the Mother of God and the dignity of woman)

723   5. [The] reality [woman-mother of God] [...] determines the essential horizon of reflection on the dignity and the vocation of women. In anything we think, say or do concerning the dignity and the vocation of women, our thoughts, hearts and actions must not become detached from this horizon. The dignity of every human being and the vocation corresponding to that dignity find their definitive measure in union with God. Mary, the woman of the Bible, is the most complete expression of this dignity and vocation. For no human being, male or female, created in the image and likeness of God, can in any way attain fulfilment apart from this image and likeness.

(Motherhood and virginity united in Mary)

724   17. [...] Virginity and motherhood [are] two particular dimensions of the fulfilment of woman's personality. In the light of the Gospel, they acquire their full meaning and value in Mary, who as a virgin became the mother of the Son of God. These two dimensions of woman's vocation were united in her in an exceptional manner, in such a way that one did not exclude the other but wonderfully complemented it.[...] Virginity and motherhood coexist in her: They do not mutually exclude each other. Indeed, the person of the mother of God helps everyone— especially women—to see how these two dimensions, these two paths in the vocation of women as persons, explain and complete each other.

ENCYCLICAL LETTER *REDEMPTORIS MISSIO*
(7 December 1990)

For an introduction to the encyclical see n.1166i. The passage quoted here is from the conclusion. The text is found in AAS 83 (1991) 249-340.

(Mary, model of the Church's maternal love)

725   92. On the eve of the third millennium, the whole Church is invited to live more intensely the mystery of Christ by gratefully cooperating in the work of salvation. The Church does this together with Mary and following the example of Mary, the Church's mother and model: Mary is the model of the maternal love which should inspire all who cooperate in the Church's apostolic mission for the rebirth of humanity.

ENCYCLICAL LETTER *VERITATIS SPLENDOR*
(6 August 1993)

For an introduction to the encyclical see n. 2072i. The passage quoted here is from the conclusion. The text is found in AAS 85 (1993) 1134-1228.

(Mary mother of mercy)

726   118. Mary is mother of mercy because her Son, Jesus Christ, was sent by the Father as the revelation of God's mercy *[cf. Jn 3:16-18]*.[...]

120. Mary is also mother of mercy because it is to her that Jesus entrusts his Church and all humanity. [...] Thus Mary becomes mother of each and everyone of us, the mother who obtains for us divine mercy.

CHAPTER VIII

THE CHURCH

Salvation in Christ is offered to all men and women. However, as the Second Vatican Council teaches, " it has pleased God to call human beings to share his life not merely as individuals without relation to each other"—irrespective of their social nature and the continuity of human history—"but to make of them a people in which his children who were scattered far and wide may be brought together into one" (AG 2). Thus the word of God and the saving grace of Jesus Christ are enshrined in the Church.

The Church is not primarily an object of theology, but its subject. The revealed word of God is entrusted to her; she must teach it, interpret it and defend it. The Church has exercised her function long before she enunciated it explicitly. This is why her reflection on her own nature belongs to a late period. In fact, this reflection has developed in relation to the situations and problems with which the Church found herself confronted in the fulfillment of her mission.

In the early Church two questions required explicit consideration. First was the unity of the Church, expressed in the hierarchical authority with its centre in the bishop of Rome, successor of the apostle Peter. In the second place came a question more directly related to the Church's inner life: the necessity of belonging to the Church in order to find salvation. These questions remained alive throughout the centuries and are of central importance in modern ecclesiology.

In the Middle Ages new factors influenced the reflection on the Church. The rivalry between the secular and the ecclesiastical powers led to acute canonical controversies about the nature of Church authority. The defence of the rights of the hierarchy, and mainly of the papacy, often resulted in presenting a one-sided view of the Church, mostly garbed in juridical language. The great Schism gave rise to an acute crisis of ecclesiastical authority, viz., the idea of conciliarism, or the theory of the superiority of the Council over the Pope. This could be resolved only in the General Council of Constance. The increasing worldliness of the hierarchy and the frequent misuse of ecclesiastical power for political and other earthly interests disfigured the Church and made it difficult to recognise in her the mystery of Jesus Christ. To this current must be traced the attacks launched against, and the rejection of, the ecclesiastical authority by the various anticlerical movements of the Middle Ages. The crisis came to a climax with the Reformation. The historical context thus explains why ecclesiastical documents up to recent times are mostly concerned with the rejection of errors and the answer to problems related to authority.

The first large scale attempt to frame an official document on the nature of the Church was made in preparation for the first Vatican General Council. Political circumstances, however, prevented this Council from completing its work. The comprehensive schema had to be abandoned and only papal primacy and infallibility were in fact defined. This unhappy situation contributed to the one-sided stress laid on central authority in the Church and to a defensive attitude against disruptive forces. This attitude is reflected even in relatively recent documents, as in the rejection of Modernism and in the encyclical Humani Generis *of Pope Pius XII.*

These facts notwithstanding, it is also certain that a new understanding of the inner reality of the Church has developed during the last decades. It found expression in the great encyclical letter Mystici Corporis *of Pope Pius XII. It is fully expounded by the doctrine of the Second Vatican Council. Among the conciliar documents two have a special significance for the Council's ecclesiology: the dogmatic Constitution* Lumen Gentiun *unfolds the various aspects of the Church's life; the pastoral Constitution* Gaudium et Spes *on the Church in the modern world explains her place and mission in human society. In these documents two extremes are avoided: a one-sided juridical conception of the Church, on the one hand, and, on the other, an unearthly spiritualisation which would separate the mystery of Christ from society and history. The Church is presented as the universal sign and sacrament of salvation, for she is at once a "visible assembly and a spiritual community,[...] one complex reality composed of a divine and a human element" (LG 8).*

* * *

Thus the documents mentioned here contain the following points:

Jesus Christ founded one Church: 21, 25, 39/12, 143/3, 804, 818, 846/52, 848, 854, (860), (866f), (869), (871), 900Ed.
The Church is a visible community (802), 808, (812), 847, (860), (866-869).

The Church is inseparable from Christ: 884, 890, 899a, 899c.

She is Christ's Mystical Body: 847-849, 852, (862);

animated by his Spirit: 3, 851, (860), (867), (881).

The Church continues Christ's saving mission : 818, (860), (862), (864f), (867-870).

The Church is communion; 891, 900Ba-c, 900Da. 900Eh, 900Ej, 932c-e.

The Church as sacrament: 887-888, 889.

The charismatic and the hierarchical aspects of the Church must not be separated: 848, 853, (860), (869), 1710, 1719.

The Church is a pilgrim community with an eschatological destiny: (861), (862), (865), (868), (882).

The Church, universal and particular: 885, 892, 900Ba-c, 900Eb, 900Ed, 900Eh, 900F.

The word of revelation is entrusted to the Church who interprets the Scriptures authoritatively: 31, 39/13, 121, 123, 134, 139f, 143/3.9.11, 208, 210, 215, 217, 220, 221, 228/1.4, 238, 248, 836f, 858f, (863), (877), 898b-d.

The Church is infallible in her teaching; in particular the Roman Pontiff is infallible when speaking 'ex cathedra': 831-840, 841, (862f), 883, 900Ef.

The Church exercises a legitimate authority to which submission is due: 805, 807f, (811f), 815, 818, 846, 848, 858f, (863), (876f), (879), 898d, 900Eg.

The college of the bishops, united with the Pope, and the general Councils constitute the highest authority in the Church: 806, (863), (875), 900Db-c, 900Eb-c.

Peter and his successors, the Roman Pontiffs, are given authority over the whole Church: 29, 36, 143/3, 801, 803-805, 807-809, (811f), 815f, 818-830, 841, 846/55f, (860), (863), 900Bc, 900Ea-j.

Different realizations of collegiality: 893.

Episcopal Conferences: 900Dd-h.

Continental synods of bishops: 900F.

Bishops have ordinary jurisdiction over the particular Churches of their dioceses: 827, 841, 850, (863), (874), (876), (878f), 1711, 1720f, 900De, 900Dg.

Lay faithful in the Church : 880, 894-895.

Ministries, offices and roles of lay faithful: 896.

The members of the Church are those who, being baptized, confess their faith and acknowledge her authority: 847, 849, 854, (862), (864), (871), 1412, 1427, 1439-1440, 1441.

The Church is necessary for salvation : 21, 38, 39/16, (802), 804, 810, 813f, 849, 854f, (862), (871), 899a.

At least the implicit desire of the Church, accompanied with faith and charity, is required for salvation: 813f, 847, 855-857, (862), (871-873).

The Church is for human beings: 886, 900Ab.

The missionary nature of the Church: (862), 884, 886, 888, 889, 896, 899b, 899c, 899d, 900Aa, 900Ab, 900Ef, 900F.

The catholicty of the Church includes diversity and pluriformity: 852, 885, 891, 892, 895, 897, 930a, 932b, 932e, 932g, 900F.

Basic Ecclesial Communities and the criteria of ecclesiality of groups in the Church: 896a, 899e.

The object about which the magisterium is competent to teach, which includes moral and social doctrine: 121, 217, 248, 836, 839, (877), 883, 898c, 900Aa, 900Ca, 900Cb.

Various levels of magisterial teaching and corresponding levels of response : (877), 898d, 900Df, 900Dh.

The sensus fidei and the indefectibility of the whole People of God: (862), (870), 900Cc.

The role of theology in the Church: 858, 859, 898a.

INNOCENT I

LETTER *IN REQUIRENDIS* TO THE AFRICAN BISHOPS
(417)

In the fifth and sixth centuries, the doctrine of the primacy of authority of the See of Rome was very much developed and affirmed by the reigning Pontiffs. Two important documents from this period were later embodied in the decree of the First Vatican Council. They are: 1) the declaration made by the Papal Legate to the Council of Ephesus (431) about the primacy of the Bishop of Rome (cf. n. 822); 2) the "Formula of Pope Hormisdas" whose signature by some two hundred and fifty Oriental bishops put an end to the Acacian Schism (484-519) and which was later adopted by the fourth general Council of Constantinople (869) (cf. n. 832). In these texts the authority of the Roman Pontiffs is based on the authority given by Christ to Peter (Mt 16:18-19) who lives on in his successor. In the following letter praising the bishops of Africa for their condemnation of the Pelagians, Innocent I takes up the idea, first found in Africa and adopted by St. Cyprian, that the episcopate had its birth or origin in Peter. The Pope closely associated the See of Rome and the apostle Peter. And where Cyprian thought of the unity of the episcopate manifested in the oneness of its origin, Innocent proposes the Roman See as the source and norm of the life and teaching of the Church. This position was very much developed in later centuries.

801
217

In your pursuit of the things of God, [...] following the examples of ancient tradition, [...] you have made manifest by your proper course of action the vitality of our religion [...] when you agreed to have recourse to our judgment, knowing what is due to the apostolic See, since all of us placed in this position wish to follow the apostle [Peter], from whom have come this episcopate and all the authority belonging to this dignity. By following him we know how to condemn what is wrong, and approve what is praiseworthy. Moreover, in safeguarding the ordinances of the Fathers with your priestly zeal, you certainly believe that they must not be trodden underfoot. They decreed, not with human but with divine judgment, that no decision (even though it concerned the most remote provinces) was to be considered final unless this See were to hear of it, so that all the authority of this See might confirm whatever just decision was reached. From this See the other Churches receive the confirmation of what they ought to ordain, just as all waters proceed from their source and through diverse regions of the world remain pure liquids of an uncorrupted source.

THE FOURTH LATERAN GENERAL COUNCIL
SYMBOL OF LATERAN (1215)

(802)   *The spiritualist and anti-ecclesial movements of the 12th
            century were in great part a protest against a worldly Church whose
ecclesiology (following on the Gregorian Reform) was often dominated by the
category of power and favoured a clerical, sacerdotal, and even curialist
conception of the Church. They advocated a lay fraternity with emphasis on
personal evangelism. Their critique contained a part of truth and was nourished
by profound religious perceptions, but in conceiving of the Church uniquely
as the "congregatio fidelium" they denied its incarnational and mediatory
nature, and consequently its visible sacramental structure. Thus in the
definition against the Albigensians and Cathars the Fourth Council of the
Lateran included a profession of faith in the visible sacramental and eucharistic
community, "outside which no one at all is saved." See text in n. 21.*

THE SECOND GENERAL COUNCIL OF LYONS
"PROFESSION OF FAITH OF MICHAEL PALAEOLOGUS"
(1274)

(803)   *The formula on the role and authority of the Roman Pontiff, proposed
            by Clement IV in 1267 to the emperor in the East, Michael VIII
Palaeologus, was finally accepted by him through his ambassadors at the Second
Council of Lyons, which sought to bring about reunion with the Greek Church.
This formula (the first enuntiated on the level of the solemn magisterium, and
explicitly quoted by the First Vatican Council: cf. DS 3066) sums up the
entire development, theological and canonical, that had taken place during the
13th century: the universal pre-eminence of the Roman Church in the sense
of an ecclesial monarchy: the function of the supreme magisterium; the supreme
and universal judging function of Rome in matters of faith; the "fulness of
power" understood in the sense that Rome is the source of power for the other
Churches, including the patriarchal 'privileges'. The document lacked
appreciation for, and openness to a tradition other than that of the Latin Church,
and was severely criticised in the East. The reunion itself was short-lived. See
text in n. 29.*

BONIFACE VIII
BULL *UNAM SANCTAM* (1302)

*During the reign of Boniface VIII and the Avignon Popes, the question
of the two powers, spiritual and temporal, and of their inter-relationship
dominated ecclesiastical thought. This Bull, which issued from the acrimonious
dispute between Boniface and Philip the Fair of France over the rights of the
King in temporal matters, admits that there are two swords (the temporal
and the spiritual powers), but, dominated as it is by the idea and ideal of
unity, affirms that the temporal is under the control of the spiritual; concretely*

of the Pope. Boniface, therefore, seems to propose the hierocratic theory in an extreme form. In any case, it is necessary to distinguish the conclusion of the Bull, which is a doctrinal declaration (submission to the Roman Pontiff is necessary for salvation), and the body of the document which develops an ideology bound to the concepts of the time. Positively, the Bull affirms clearly the unity of the Church, its necessity for salvation, its divine origin, and the foundation of the authority of the Roman Pontiff. But Boniface goes on to assert that Christ and the Pope form one head; the Pope is therefore head of the mystical Body, which in the process is identified with the juridical reality, the body of people submitting themselves to the jurisdiction of the Pope.

(The one Church, necessary for salvation)

804
870
That there is only one, holy, catholic and apostolic Church we are compelled by faith to believe and hold, and we firmly believe in her and sincerely confess her, outside of whom there is neither salvation nor remission of sins[...] She represents one mystical Body; the head of this body is Christ, but the head of Christ is God. In her there is "one Lord, one faith, one baptism" *[Eph 4:5]*.[...]

872
This one and unique Church, therefore, has not two heads, like a monster, but one body and one head, viz., Christ and his vicar, Peter's successor, for the Lord said to Peter personally: "Feed my sheep" *[Jn 21:17]*. 'My' he said in general, not individually, meaning these or those; whereby it is understood that he confided all his sheep to him. If therefore Greeks or others say that they were not confided to Peter and his successors, they must necessarily confess that they are not among Christ's sheep, for the Lord said in John: "there shall be one fold and one shepherd"*[Jn 10:16]*.

875
Furthermore we declare, state and define that it is absolutely necessary for the salvation of all human beings that they submit to the Roman Pontiff.

JOHN XXII

CONDEMNATION OR ERRORS OF MARSILIUS OF PADUA ON THE CONSTITUTION OF THE CHURCH (1327)

The book Defensor Pacis *written by Marsilius of Padua (1280-1343) (it is not certain whether his pupil, John of Jandun collaborated in writing it) was one of the most famous of the 14th century, and influenced conciliarist thought and the theologians of the Reformation, especially Luther. Marsilius attributed a normative value to Scripture alone, and rigorously applied the political philosophy of Aristotle to the Church. Pope John XXII in the Bull* Licet Juxta Doctrinam *condemned especially the following points: denial of the divine institution of the hierarchy, of the papal primacy, of all ecclesial coercive power; and the subordination of the Pope to the emperor.*

[805/2] That the apostle St. Peter had no more authority than
942   the other apostles had; [...] similarly, that Christ did
         not provide any head for his Church, nor appoint
anyone his vicar.

[805/3] That it is the emperor's duty to correct the Pope, to
943   appoint and depose him, and to punish him.

[805/4] That according to the institution of Christ, every priest,
944   whether he be Pope, archbishop or simple priest, has
         equal authority and jurisdiction.

THE GENERAL COUNCIL OF CONSTANCE
DECREE *HAEC SANCTA* (1415)

The Council of Constance is of crucial importance in the history of the Church, for it succeeded in bringing to an end the 40 years old "Western Schism" when the allegiance of the Church was divided between 2 (later 3) rival popes. Gregory XII of the Roman obedience resigned spontaneously (July 4, 1415); Benedict XIII of the Avignon obedience and John XXIII of the Pisan obedience were deposed (May 29, 1415, and July 26, 1417). In their place Martin V was elected on November 11, 1417. Besides the condemnation of the errors of Wyclif and Hus, the Council is important for ecclesiology because of its famous decree Haec Sancta *adopted at the fifth session of the Council, April 6, 1415. While many historians today would agree that* Haec Sancta *has to be counted as a valid decree of an ecumenical Council, disagreement remains with regard to the interpretation of its content.* Haec Sancta *affirms two things: 1) the general Council receives its power not from the Pope but immediately from Christ: 2) every Catholic, including the Pope, owes obedience to the Council in matters of faith, for the extinction of actual heresy and for the reform of the Church in its head and members. The wording is ambivalent, and was later interpreted in a conciliarist sense (permanent superiority of a Council over the Pope); yet it seems to be in keeping with the traditional heresy clause of the canonists, who, to the principle of the immunity of the "first See" (Prima sedes a nemine indicatur), added the words; "unless he is found to deviate from the faith" (nisi deprehendatur a fide devius). The text is found in COD, p. 408.*

806 This holy Synod of Constance holding a general Council
     in order to uproot the present schism, and to unite and
reform the Church in its head and members,[...] orders, defines,

fixes, decrees and declares the following in order to achieve more easily, securely, fully and freely the union and reform of the Church of God.

And first of all it declares that, having assembled legitimately in the Holy Spirit, and being a general Council and representing the Catholic Church militant, it has its power immediately from Christ, which every state and dignity, even if it be the papal dignity, must obey in what concerns faith, the eradication of the mentioned schism and the reformation of the said Church in head and members.

CONDEMNATION OF THE ERRORS OF WYCLIF AND HUS
(1415)

John Wyclif (1324-1384) was the forerunner of the Reformation in England. A reformer, his main attack was directed against the riches and temporal pretensions of the clergy. He refused to define the Church by profession of the true faith or as a sacramental institution, because he desired a spiritual Church, defined by a purely divine element. This element for him was predestination: that which constitutes the Church and its unity is the predestining love of Christ. The Church, therefore, is the congregation of all the predestined; the reprobate (the "foreknown") are not members of it and cannot hold office in it. John Hus (1369-1415), patriot and reformer in Bohemia, was Wyclif's spiritual heir. In his De Ecclesia *(1412-1413) he reproduced entire passages from Wyclif's writings. Summoned to the Council of Constance, he was tried and condemned, and then turned over to the secular authorities to be burnt at the stake (July 6, 1415). The errors of Wyclif and Hus were collated and condemned by the Council.*

(Wyclif's errors condemned)

[807/8]   If the Pope be a reprobate and an evil man and,
1158   consequently, a member of the devil, he has no power
         over the faithful given him by anyone, except perhaps
by the state.

[807/37]   The Roman Church is the synagogue of Satan, and
1187   the Pope is not the proximate and immediate vicar of
         Christ and of the apostles.

(Hus' errors condemned)

808/1]   The only and holy universal Church is the aggregate
1201   of the predestined. And it follows: the holy universal
         Church is one only, just as the number of all the
predestined is one.

[808/3]   The reprobates are not parts of the Church, since no
1203   part of the Church will ultimately fall away from it
              for the charity of predestination, which keeps it
together, will not fail.

[808/5]   Even if sometimes a reprobate in grace according to
1205   his actual state of justice, he is, nevertheless, never a
              part of the holy Church, and a predestined always
remains a member of the Church, even though sometimes he may
fall from temporary grace, but not from the grace of predestination.

[808/6]   The Church is an article of faith only if by the Church
1206   is meant the gathering of the predestined, whether
              they are in grace according to their actual state of
justice or not.

[808/10]   It would be unreasonable for anyone without a
1210   revelation to make the claim for himself or for anyone
              that he is the head of a particular Church; and not even
the Roman Pontiff is the head of the particular Roman Church.

[808/13]   The Pope is not the true and manifest successor of
1213   Peter, the first of the apostles, if he lives in a manner
              contrary to Peter; and if he be avaricious, then he is
the vicar of Judas Iscariot.[...]

[808/15]   Ecclesiastical obedience is obedience according to the
1215   invention of the priests of the Church without the
              express authority of the scriptures.

THE GENERAL COUNCIL OF FLORENCE

*Florence, under the leadership of Pope Eugene IV, was yet another attempt
to bring about reunion between the Eastern churches and Rome. This sinuous
and eventful "Council of union" held its sessions from 1431 till 1445. It
started its career at Basel, was transferred to Ferrara in 1438 and to Florence
the following year where the decrees of union with the Armenian, Greek and
Coptic ("Jacobite") Churches were approved. In 1443 it was finally transferred
to Rome where other decrees of union with the Syrians of Mesopotamia, with
the Chaldeans and with the Maronites of Cyprus were passed. The decrees of
Ferrara, Florence and Rome are in the form of Bulls, as these sessions were
presided over by the Roman Pontiff himself. The Council endorsed the Roman
texts presented to it for approval.*

*The Decree for the "Jacobites" or Copts from Egypt was partly inspired
by the* Treatise on Faith *of Fulgentius of Ruspe (647-533), an African bishop,*

disciple of St. Augustine. This decree deals less with specific points of dissent than does the one for the Greeks; it rather offers a summary of the Christian belief.

The question at issue with the Greeks was that of the Papal primacy. The act of union with the Greeks uncompromisingly delineates the dogma of the privileges of the apostolic See and the Roman Pontiff while at the same time recognising the traditional privileges of the ancient patriarchates.

In the Decree for the Copts, the necessity of the Church for salvation is expressed in a rigid formula taken verbatim from Fulgentius. It exposes the order of salvation as follows: Jesus Christ is the final revelation of God; his mission is entrusted to the Church; thus, separation from this Church means separation from Christ and hence loss of salvation. This is the first official church document in which mention is made of the "pagans" in connection with the axiom Extra Ecclesiam nulla salus. *Previous documents had made use of the axiom in relation to Christian schism and heresy (cf. nn. 802i,804; cf. also DS 792, 1051). In view of the historical context, this remains even in this Decree the first intention of the Council. See also n. 1003i.*

DECREE FOR THE GREEKS (1439)

(The Primacy of the Roman Pontiff)

809
1307

Likewise, we define that the holy apostolic See and the Roman Pontiff have the primacy over the whole world, and that the same Roman Pontiff is the successor of St. Peter, the prince of the apostles, and the true vicar of Christ, the head of the whole Church, the father and teacher of all Christians; and that to him, in the person of St. Peter, was given by our Lord Jesus Christ the full power of feeding, ruling, and governing the whole Church as is also contained in the acts of the ecumenical Councils and in the sacred canons.

(The order of patriarchates)

1308

Besides, we declare anew the order of the other venerable patriarchates, as transmitted in the canons: the patriarch of Constantinople is second after the most holy Roman Pontiff; third is that of Alexandria, fourth that of Antioch, fifth that of Jerusalem; all of whose privileges and rights evidently remain intact.

DECREE FOR THE COPTS (1422)

(The unity of the Catholic Church and its necessity for salvation)

810
1351

The holy Roman Church] [...] firmly believes, professes and preaches that "no one remaining outside the Catholic Church, not only pagans", but also Jews, heretics or schismatics, can become partakers of eternal life; but they will go to the "eternal fire prepared for the devil and his angels' [*Mt 25:41*], unless before the end of their life they are joined to (*aggregati*) it. For union with the body of the Church is of so great importance that the sacraments of the Church are helpful to salvation only for those remaining in it; and fasts, almsgiving, other works of piety, and the exercises of a militant Christian life bear eternal rewards for them alone. "And no one can be saved, no matter how much alms one has given, even if shedding one's blood for the name of Christ, unless one remains in the bosom and unity of the Catholic Church."[1]

LEO X

BULL *EXSURGE DOMINE* (1520)
ERRORS OF LUTHER CONDEMNED

(811) *The protest against the misuse of ecclesiastical authority and the worldly patterns of the hierarchical regime came to a climax with the Reformation. Luther and the other Reformers took up the ideas of Wyclif and Hus, based on the conceptions of Marsilius of Padua (cf. n. 805). Among the propositions of Luther condemned by Pope Leo X there is the denial of papal authority and of ecclesiastical authority in general (cf. DS 1475-1479). Since they contain no new elements, they need not be quoted here. Many of the ecclesiological problems raised by the Reformers were in fact treated by the Council of Trent in the context of the sacraments, especially of the sacrament of Order (cf. nn 1706ff). It was, however, only at Vatican I and mainly Vatican II that the most basic ecclesiological issues raised by the Reformation were explicitly dealt with.*

PIUS VI

CONSTITUTION *AUCTOREM FIDEI* (1794)

(812) *The two most powerful movements that affected the life of the Church in the post-Reformation period were Jansenism (cf. n. 1989i) and Febronianism with its tendency to subordinate the life of the Church to political interests, and therefore to play down the ecclesiastical authority. These trends found expression in the synod of the Italian province of Tuscany in Pistoia (1786). A series of 85 propositions taken from the Acts of this synod were condemned by Pius VI in the Constitution* Auctorem Fidei *(1794). Among the propositions condemned, 1-15 belong to the doctrine on the Church (DS 2601-2615). They concern the origin of ecclesiastical authority, and mainly of the authority of the Pope, which is attributed to the Christian*

---

1. FULGENTIUS OF RUSPE, *De fide liber ad Petrum*, 38, 79 and 39, 80.

community, not to an institution by Christ (2,3); the denial of the Church's disciplinary authority over the faithful (4,5); the independence of bishops from the papal authority (6-8); the democratic conception of ecclesiastical authority according to which the entire Christian people is established as judge of the faith (9-11); the Jansenistic conception of a Church constituted only by saints (15). All these issues, however, are dealt with more explicitly in the documents of the 19th and 20th centuries.

PIUS IX

ALLOCUTION *SINGULARI QUADAM* (1854)

Denial of supernatural revelation entails denying the Church as the unique God-given community necessary for salvation. Rationalism and indifferentism (according equal value to all forms of religion) are closely connected. Again and again they were condemned alongside one another in Church documents of the nineteenth century. The present document is of importance because it makes a clear distinction between the objective necessity of the Church for salvation as willed by God, and the subjective guilt or innocence of people outside the Church.

(Salvation in the Church)

813   It must, of course, be held as a matter of faith that outside
2865i   the apostolic Roman Church no one can be saved, that
          the Church is the only ark of salvation, and that whoever does not enter it will perish in the flood. On the other hand, it must likewise be held as certain that those who live in ignorance of the true religion, if such ignorance be invincible, are not subject to any guilt in this matter before the eyes of the Lord. But then, who would dare to set limits to this ignorance, taking into consideration the natural differences of people, lands, native talents, and so many other factors?

ENCYCLICAL LETTER *QUANTO CONFICIAMUR MOERORE* (1863)

This encyclical addressed to the bishops of Italy warns again against a liberal indifferentism that would deny the necessity of the Church for salvation, but also states in a more positive way the possibility of salvation for those living in ignorance of the Christian revelation.

(Salvation in the Church)

814   And here, beloved Sons and venerable Brethren, it is
2865   necessary once more to mention and censure the serious
          error into which some Catholics have unfortunately fallen. For they are of the opinion that those who live in errors,

estranged from the true faith and Catholic unity, can attain eternal life. This is in direct opposition to Catholic teaching.

2866   We all know that those who suffer from invincible ignorance with regard to our holy religion, if they carefully keep the precepts of the natural law which have been written by God in the hearts of all persons, if they are prepared to obey God, and if they lead a virtuous and dutiful life, can, by the power of divine light and grace, attain eternal life. For God, who knows completely the minds and souls, the thoughts and habits of all persons, will not permit, in accord with his infinite goodness and mercy, anyone who is not guilty of a voluntary fault to suffer eternal punishment.

2867   However, also well known is the Catholic dogma that no one can be saved outside the Catholic Church, and that those who obstinately oppose the authority of the definitions of the Church, and who stubbornly remain separated from the unity of the Church and from the successor of Peter, the Roman Pontiff, to whom the Saviour had entrusted the care of his vineyard, cannot obtain salvation.

ENCYCLICAL LETTER *QUANTA CURA* (1864)

In this doctrinal letter, issued on the same day as the Syllabus *of condemned errors,* Pius IX *reviews some of the errors of his time on the relationship between Church and State. He stresses the Church's full independence from temporal power and the divine origin of its authority. See also the* Syllabus: *DS 2919 - 2938.*

(Eccesiastical authority)

815   Others have revived the evil and often condemned errors
2893   of the Reformers. Acting with extraordinary boldness they dare to submit to the judgment of civil authority the supreme authority of the Church and of this apostolic See— an authority which was received from Chirst our Lord. And they deny the Church and this See any rights in matters belonging to the external order.

816   They do not hesitate to profess openly and publicly an
2895   heretical principle that has led to very many perverse opinions and errors. For they say : "It is not of divine law that the power of the Church be distinct and independent from the civil power. Indeed it is impossible to keep such

independence and distinction without having the Church infringe upon and usurp essential rights of the civil power." Nor can we be silent about the arrogant claim of those who [.....] maintain: "It is possible, without sinning and without at all departing from the profession of the Catholic faith, to refuse assent and obedience to those decisions and decress of the apostolic See whose declared object is the general good of the Church and its rights and discipline, provided only that such decisions do not touch upon dogmas of faith or morals." No one can fail to see that this doctrine directly opposes Catholic dogma according to which Christ our Lord with his divine authority gave to the Roman Pontiff the supreme power of shepherding, ruling, and governing the Church.

THE FIRST VATICAN GENERAL COUNCIL
THIRD SESSION
DOGMATIC CONSTITUTION *DEI FILIUS* ON THE CATHOLIC FAITH (1870)

(817) *In its Dogmatic Constitution on the Catholic Faith (nn. 113ff), Vatican I dealt with the role of the Church as guardian and teacher of the revealed word. This Constitution contains important affirmations about the ordinary universal magisterium and the "irreformability" of dogmas, as well as the affirmation that the Church as a sign raised among the nations manifests in its life and structures the victorious grace of Christ, and so is in itself a perpetual motive of credibility of its divine mission. See text in nn. 121, 122, 123, 136, 139.*

FOURTH SESSION
DOGMATIC CONSTITUTION *PASTOR AETERNUS* ON THE CHURCH OF CHRIST (1870)

Vatican I's solemn definition of the primacy of jurisdiction of the Roman Pontiff and his infallible teaching function was the culmination of a long development in the ecclesiology of the Western Church that had in great part been centred on the theme of the unity of the universal Church and on the role of the Petrine office as the centre and support of that unity. Against all attempts to limit juridically the scope and extent of the primatial authority, it affirms in precise juridical terminology the universal authority of the Roman Pontiff as the centre and guardian of the Church's unity in faith and communion. The Council's definition of the universal and infallible (under precise conditions) teaching office of the Popes flows from its teaching regarding the nature and role of the primatial See in the Church. The Council had prepared and intended to debate and promulgate a Constitution on the Church as a whole. Unfortunately, the untimely termination of the Council prevented it from carrying out this project. As a result the definitions regarding the primacy tend to give a one-sided view of the Church's life and structure. The Second Vatican Council in its Constitution on the Church, while re-affirming the teaching of Vatican I, will seek to integrate that teaching in a much more complete exposition of the mystery of the Church and its hierarchical structure.

Introduction: The Institution and Foundation of the Church

818   The eternal Shepherd and Guardian of our souls
3050   *[cf. 1 Pet 2:25]*, in order to continue for all time the saving
work of redemption, determined to build his holy Church
so that in it, as in the house of the living God, all who believe
might be united together in the bond of one faith and one love.
For this reason, before he was glorified, he prayed to the Father
not for the apostles only but for those also who would believe
in him on their testimony, that all might be one as he, the Son,
and the Father are one *[cf. Jn 17:20ff]*. Therefore, just as he sent
the apostles, whom he had chosen for himself out of the world,
as he himself was sent by the Father *[cf. Jn 20:21]*, so also he
wished shepherds and teachers to be in his Church until the
consummation of the world *[cf. Mt 28:20]*.

3051   In order that the episcopate itself might be one and
undivided, and that the whole multitude of believers
might be preserved in unity of faith and communion by means
of a closely united priesthood, he placed St. Peter at the head of
the other apostles, and established in him a perpetual principle
and visible foundation of this twofold unity, in order that on his
strength an everlasting temple might be erected and on the
firmness of his faith a Church might arise whose pinnacle was
to reach into heaven.

3052   But the gates of hell, with a hatred that grows greater
every day, are rising up everywhere against the Church's
divinely established foundation with the intention of
overthrowing the Church, if this were possible. We, therefore,
with the approval of the sacred Council, judge it necessary, for
the protection, the safety and the increase of the Catholic flock,
to propose to all the faithful what is to be believed and held,
according to the ancient and constant belief of the universal
Church, with regard to the establishment, the perpetuity and the

nature of his sacred apostolic primacy, in which is found the strength and solidity of the entire church. Likewise we judge it necessary to proscribe with sentence of condemnation the contrary erroneous opinions so detrimental to the Lord's flock.

Chapter I: The Establishment of the Apostolic Primacy in St. Peter

819
3053

We, therefore, teach and declare, according to the testimony of the Gospel, that the primacy of jurisdiction over the whole Church was immediately and directly promised to and conferred upon the blessed apostle Peter by Christ the Lord. To Simon alone he had first said: "You shall be called Cephas" [Jn 1:42]; to him alone, after he had acknowledged Christ with the confession: "You are the Christ, the Son of the living God" [Mt 16:16], these solemn words were also spoken: "Blessed are you, simon Bar-Jona! For flesh and blood have not revealed this to you, but my Father who is in heaven. And I tell you: you are Peter, and on this rock I will build my Church, and the powers of death shall not prevail against it. I will give you the keys of the Kingdom of heaven, and whatever you bind on earth shall be bound in heaven, and whatever you loose on earth shall be loosed in heaven" [Mt 16:17-19]. And after his resurrection, Jesus conferred upon Simon Peter alone the jurisdiction of supreme shepherd and ruler over his whole flock with the words: "Feed my lambs.[...] Feed my sheep" [Jn 21:15, 17].

820
3054

In clear opposition to this very clear teaching of the Holy Scripture, as it has always been understood by the Catholic Church, are the perverse opinions of those who wrongly explain the form of government established by Christ in his Church; either by denying that Peter alone in preference to the other apostles, either singly or as a group, was endowed by Christ with the true and proper primacy of jurisdiction; or by claiming that this primacy was not given immediately and directly to blessed Peter, but to the Church and through the Church to Peter as a Minister of the Church.

Canon

821
3055

Therefore, if anyone says that the blessed apostle Peter was not constituted by Christ the Lord as the Prince of all the apostles and the visible head of the whole Church militant, or that he received immediately and directly from Jesus Christ our Lord only primacy of honour and not a true and proper primacy of jurisdiction, *anathema sit.*

Chapter II: The Perpetuity of
St. Peter's Primacy in the Roman Pontiffs

822 Now, what Christ, the Lord, the Prince of Shepherds and
3056 the great Shepherd of the flock, established in the person of
the blessed apostle Peter for the perpetual safety and everlasting good of the Church must, by the will of the same, endure without interruption in the Church, which was founded on the rock and which will remain firm until the end of the world. Indeed, "no one doubts, in fact it is obvious to all ages, that the holy and most blessed Peter, Prince and head of all the apostles, the pillar of faith and the foundation of the Catholic Church, received the keys of the Kingdom from our Lord Jesus Christ, the saviour and redeemer of the human race; and even to this time and forever he lives", and governs, "and exercises judgment in his successors", the bishops of the holy Roman See, which he established and consecrated with his blood.[1]

823 Therefore, whoever succeeds Peter in this Chair,
3057 according to the institution of Christ himself, holds
Peter's primacy over the whole Church. "Therefore, the dispositions made by truth perdure, and St. Peter still has the rock-like strength that has been given to him, and he has not surrendered the helm of the Church with which he has been entrusted."[2] For this reason, "because of its more powerful principality", it was always "necessary for every Church, that is, the faithful who are everywhere, to be in agreement" with the Roman Church;[3] thus in that See from which "the bonds of sacred communion"[4] are imparted to all, the members will be joined as members under one head and coalesce into one compact body.

Canon

824 Therefore , if anyone says that it is not according to the

---

1. PHILIP, legate of the Pope, *Oratio* at the Council of Ephesus (11 July, 431).
2. LEO THE GREAT, *Sermo 3 de natali ipsius*, 3.
3. IRENAEUS, *Adversus Haereses*, III, 3,2.
4. AMBROSE, *Epistola* 11,4.

3058   institution of Christ our Lord himself, that is, by divine
           law, that St. Peter should have perpetual successors in
the primacy over the whole Church; or if anyone says that the
Roman Pontiff is not the successor of St. Peter in the same
primacy, *anathema sit.*

Chapter III : The Power and Nature of the
Primacy of the Roman Pontiff

(Declaration of the Primacy)

825   Wherefore, relying on the clear testimony of the
3059   Holy Scriptures and following the express and definite
           decrees of our predecessors, the Roman Pontiffs, and
of the general Councils, We reaffirm the definition of the
ecumenical Council of Florence. According to this definition all
the faithful must believe "that the holy apostolic See and the
Roman Pontiff have the primacy over the whole world; the Prince
of the apostles, and the true vicar of Christ, the head of the whole
Church, the father and teacher of all Christians; and that to him,
in the person of St. Peter, was given by our Lord Jesus Christ
the full power of feeding, ruling and governing the whole
Church, as is also contained in the proceedings of the ecumencial
Council and in the sacred canons" *[cf. DS 1307].*

(Consequences that the Reformers denied)

826   And so We teach and declare that, in the disposition of
3060   God, the Roman Church holds the pre-eminence of
           ordinary power over all the other Churches, and that
this power of jurisdiction of the Roman Pontiff, which is truly
episcopal, is immediate. Regarding this jurisdiction, the shepherds
of whatever rite or jurisdiction and the faithful, individually and
collectively, are bound by a duty of hierarchical subjection and
of sincere obedience; and this not only in matters that pertain
to faith and morals, but also in matters that pertain to the
discipline and government of the Church throughout the whole
world. The result is that, when this bond of unity, both of
communion and of profession of the same faith, is guarded, then
the Church of Christ is one flock under one supreme shepherd.
This is the doctrine of Catholic truth; and no one can deviate
from it without loss of faith and salvation.

(The jurisdiction of the Roman Pontiff and the Bishops)

827   This power of the Supreme Pontiff is far from standing
3061   in the way of the power of ordinary and immediate
            episcopal jurisdiction by which the bishops who, under
appointment of the Holy Spirit *[cf. Acts 20:28]*, succeeded in the
place of the apostles, feed and rule individually, as true
shepherds, the particular flock assigned to them. Rather this latter
power is asserted, confirmed and vindicated by this same
supreme and universal shepherd, as in the words of St. Gregory
the Great: " My honour is the honour of the whole church. My
honour is the firm strength of my brothers. I am truly honoured
when due honour is paid to each and every one".[1]

(The right to deal freely with all the faithful)

828   Furthermore, from his supreme power of governing the
3062   whole Church, the Roman Pontiff has the right of freely
            communicating with the shepherds and flocks of the
whole Church in the exercise of his office so that they can be
instructed and guided by him in the way of salvation. Hence,
we condemn and reject the opinions of those who say that it can
be licit to hinder the communication of the supreme head
with the shepherds and the flocks; or those who make this
communication subject to the secular power in such a way that
they claim that whatever is decreed for the government of the
Church by the apostolic See or by its authority has no binding
force unless it is confirmed by the *placet* of the secular power.

(The right of recourse to the Roman Pontiff as supreme judge)

829   And because, by the divine right of apostolic primacy,
3063   the Roman Pontiff is at the head of the whole Church,
            we also teach and declare that he is the supreme judge
of the faithful; and that one can have recourse to his judgement
in all cases pertaining to ecclesiastical jurisdiction. We declare
that the judgment of the apostolic See, whose authority is
unsurpassed, is not subject to review by anyone; nor is anyone
allowed to pass judgment on its decision. Therefore, those
who say that it is permitted to appeal to an ecumenical Council
from the decisions of the Roman Pontiff, as to an authority

---

1. GREGORY THE GREAT, *Epistola and Eulogium Alexandrinum.*

superior to the Roman Pontiff, are far from the straight path of truth.

Canon

830 And, so, if anyone says that the Roman Pontiff has only
3064 the office of inspection and direction, but not the full
and supreme power of jurisdiction over the whole
Church, not only in matters that pertain to faith and morals but
also in matters that pertain to the discipline and government of
the Church throughout the whole world; or if anyone says that
he has only a more important part and not the complete fulness
of this supreme power; or if anyone says that this power is not
ordinary and immediate either over each and every Church or
over each and every shepherd and faithful, *anathema sit*.

Chapter IV : The Infallible Magisterium of the Roman Pontiff

(Arguments based on doctrinal documents)

831 Moreover, this holy See has always held, the perpetual
3065 practice of the Church confirms, and the ecumenical
Councils, especially those in which the Western and
Eastern Churches were united in faith and love, have declared
that the supreme power of teaching is also included in this
apostolic primacy which the Roman Pontiff, as the successor of
St. Peter, the Prince of the apostles, holds over the whole
Church.

832 For the Fathers of the Fourth Council of Constantinople,
3066 following closely in the footsteps of their predecessors,
made this solemn profession: "The first condition of
salvation is to keep the norm of the true faith.[...] And because
it is impossible that those words of our Lord Jesus Christ: "You
are Peter and upon this rock I will build my Church" *[Mt 16:18]*,
should not be verified, their truth has been proved by the course
of history, for in the apostolic See the Catholic religion has always
been kept unsullied, and its teaching kept holy. Desiring in no
way to be separated from this faith and doctrine[...], we hope
that we may deserve to be associated with you in the one
communion which the apostolic See proclaims, in which the
whole truth and perfect security of the Christian religion resides"
[cf. DS 363f].

833 Furthermore, with the approval of the Second Council
3067 of Lyons, the Greeks professed that "the holy Roman
Church possesses the supreme and full primacy and
authority over the universal Catholic Church, which she
recognises in truth and humility to have received with fulness
of power from the Lord himself in the person of Blessed Peter,
the Prince or head of the apostles, of whom the Roman Pontiff
is the successor. And, as she is bound above all to defend the
truth of faith, so too, if any questions should arise regarding the
faith, they must be decided by her judgment" [cf. n. 29].

834 Finally, the Council of Florence defined "that the Roman
3068 Pontiff is the true vicar of Christ, the head of the whole
Church, the father and teacher of all Christians; and that
to him, in the person of St. Peter, was given by our Lord Jesus
Christ the full power of feeding, ruling, and governing the whole
Church" [cf. n. 809].

(Argument based on the agreement of the Church)

835 To satisfy this pastoral care, our predecessors have
3069 always expended untiring effort to propagate Christ's
doctrine of salvation among all the peoples of the world,
and with similar care they were watchful that the doctrine might
be preserved genuine and pure wherever it was received.
Therefore, the bishops of the whole world, sometimes singly,
sometimes assembled in Councils, following the long-standing
custom of the Churches and the form of the ancient rule, reported
to this apostolic See those dangers especially which arose in
matters of faith, so that here where the faith can suffer no
diminution, the harm suffered by the faith might be repaired.
For their part, the Roman Pontiffs, according as the conditions
of the times and the circumstances dictated, sometimes by calling
together ecumenical Councils or sounding out the mind of the
Church throughout the world, sometimes through regional
Councils, or sometimes by using other helps which divine
Providence supplied, have defined as having to be held those
matters which, with the help of God, they had found consonant
with the Holy Scripture and with the apostolic Tradition.

836 For the Holy Spirit was not promised to the successors
3070 of Peter that they might disclose a new doctrine by his
revelation, but rather, that, with his assistance, they might

jealously guard and faithfully explain the revelation or deposit of faith that was handed down through the apostles. Indeed it was this apostolic doctrine that all the Fathers held, and the holy orthodox Doctors reverenced and followed, fully realising that this See of Saint Peter always remains untainted by any error, according to the divine promise of our Lord and Saviour made to the Prince of his disciples: "But I have prayed for you that your faith may not fail; and when you have turned again, strengthen your brethren" [Lk 22:23].

837   Now this charism of truth and of never-failing faith
3071   was conferred upon Peter and his successors in this
           Chair, in order that they might perform their supreme office for the salvation of all; that by them the whole flock of Christ might be kept away from the poison of error and be nourished by the food of heavenly doctrine; that, the occasion of schism being removed, the whole Church might be preserved as one, and, resting on its foundation, might stand firm against the gates of hell.

(The definition of infallibility)

838   But since in this present age, which especially requires
3072   the salutary efficacy of the apostolic office, not a few are
           found who minimise its authority, We think it extremely necessary to assert solemnly the prerogative which the only-begotten Son of God deigned to join to the highest pastoral office.

839   And so, faithfully keeping to the tradition received from
3073   the beginning of the Christian faith, for the glory of God
           our Saviour, for the exaltation of the Catholic religion, and for the salvation of Christian peoples, We, with the approval of the sacred Council, teach and define:

3074   It is a divinely revealed dogma that the Roman Pontiff,
           when he speaks *ex cathedra*, that is, when, acting in the office of shepherd and teacher of all Christians, he defines, by virtue of his supreme apostolic authority, a doctrine concerning faith or morals to be held by the universal Church, possesses through the divine assistance promised to him in the person of Blessed Peter, the infallibility with which the divine Redeemer willed his church to be endowed in defining the doctrine concerning faith or morals; and that such definitions of the

Roman Pontiff are therefore irreformable of themselves, not because of the consent of the Church *(ex sese, non autem ex consensu ecclesiae).*

Canon

840
3075
But if anyone presumes to contradict this our definition, which God forbid, *anathema sit.*

COLLECTIVE DECLARATION BY THE GERMAN HIERARCHY (1875)

On May 14, 1872, Bismark, the German Chancellor, issued a circular in which he maintained that the teaching of Vatican I about the direct and universal jurisdiction of the Pope made bishops into mere executive organs of the Pope, and that they were thus degraded to the status of mere officials. Against this view the collective declaration of the German hierarchy was issued (January-February 1875). In an apostolic brief of March 6, 1875, Pius IX gave approval to this declaration in an unusually solemn form. He wrote: "Your declaration gives the genuine Catholic doctrine, which is also that of the holy Council and of this holy See; it defends it with illuminating and irrefutable reasoning, and sets it out so clearly that it is plain to any honest person that there is no innovation in the definitions attacked..." (cf. DS 3117). The document is important because of the clarification which it gives regarding the relationship between the papal and episcopal authority as understood in the era immediately following upon the definition of papal primacy at Vatican I. This is brought out clearly in the passage given below.

841
3115
It is in virtue of the same divine institution upon which the papacy rests that the episcopate also exists. It, too, has its rights and duties, because of the ordinance of God himself, and the Pope has neither the right nor the power to change them. Thus it is a complete misunderstanding of the Vatican decrees to believe that because of them "episcopal jurisdiction has been absorbed into the papal", that the Pope has "in principle taken the place of each individual bishop", that the bishops are now "no more than tools of the Pope, his officials, without responsibility of their own." According to the constant teaching of the Catholic Church, expressly declared at the Vatican Council itself, the bishops are not mere tools of the Pope, nor papal officials without responsibility of their own, but, "under appointment of the Holy Spirit, they succeeded in the place of the apostles, and feed and rule individually, as true shepherds, the particular flock assigned to them" *[cf. n. 827].*

PIUS X

DECREE *LAMENTABILI* OF THE HOLY OFFICE (1907)
ARTICLES OF MODERNISM CONDEMNED

In the decree Lamentabili, *published by the Holy Office, several errors connected with the doctrine of the Church which were bound up with the Modernist position (cf. n. 143i) were explicitly condemned. They flow from the Modernist ideas either with regard to the understanding of revelation and dogma, or with regard to exegetical and historical conclusions about the founding of the Church by Christ and its essential structures.*

[846/6] The learning Church and the teaching Church so
3406   work together in defining truths, that the only function
        of the teaching Church is to ratify the generally held
opinions of the learning Church.

[846/7] In proscribing errors the Church cannot exact from
3407   the faithful any internal assent by which the judgments
        that it has decreed are accepted.

[846/52] It was far from the mind of Christ to establish the
3452   Church as a society that would last on earth for a long
         succession of centuries; in fact, in the mind of Christ
the kingdom of heaven together with the end of the world was
imminent.

[846/53] The organic constitution of the Church is not
3453   unchangeable; rather, the Christian society is just
         as subject to perpetual evolution as human society
is.

[846/54] Dogmas, sacraments, hierarchy—both in their notion
3454   and their reality—are nothing but evolutions and
         interpretations of Christian thought which caused the
tiny seed, hidden in the Gospel, to grow through external
accretions and to be brought to fruition.

[846/55] Simon Peter never even suspected that the primacy in
3455   the Church was entrusted to him by Christ.

[846/56] The Roman Church became the head of all Churches
3456   not because of any determination on the part of divine
         providence but because of political conditions.

PIUS XII
ENCYCLICAL LETTER *MYSTICI CORPORIS* (1943)

Between the two world wars there was a renewed interest in and development of the theology of the Church as the mystical Body of Christ (cf. especially the works of Emile Mersch and Sebastian Tromp). Along with the positive developments, there also appeared a trend toward a sort of pan-Christianism. In his great encyclical, Pius XII, while warning against such excesses, gave official recognition and expression to the riches of this theology. While taking as his point of departure the Counter-Reformation theology of the Church as a visible hierarchical society, which he identified with the mystical Body of Christ, the Pope sought to incorporate into this theology the stress laid by patristic and scholastic thought on the interior reality of grace and the role of the Holy Spirit. According to the teaching of the encyclical the Church is a body because it is one visible, hierarchically structured, society. It is the Body of Christ, because he is its founder, head, sustainer and saviour. It is called mystical Body in order to distinguish it clearly both from the physical body of Christ as well as from any other body, whether physical or moral. The passages given here bring out the most important teachings of the encyclical: the identification of the Roman Catholic Church with the mystical Body of Christ (reaffirmed in the encyclical Humani Generis*); the requirements for membership (distinguishing between those who are 'really' members, and those who are members only 'in voto'); the demonstration that without prejudice to the Church's juridical structure and official 'offices', the charismatic element also pertains to the Church; the unity of the Church of law and the Church of love in the true Church of Christ; the nature and significance of the episcopal office (with the statement that the bishops' power of ordinary jurisdiction is received directly from the Pope); the theology of the Holy Spirit as the 'soul' of the Church, a doctrine which is important in combating a naturalistic conception of the Church with undue emphasis on its sociological and juridical aspects. The text is found in AAS (1943) 193-248.*

(The Catholic Church is the Mystical Body)

847   If we would define and describe this true Church of Jesus Christ—which is the holy, catholic, apostolic, Roman Church—we shall find no expression more noble, more sublime or more divine than the phrase which calls it "the mystical Body of Jesus Christ". This title is derived from and is, as it were, the fair flower of the repeated teaching of Sacred Scripture and the holy Fathers.

That the Church is a body is frequently asserted in Sacred Scripture. "Christ", says the apostle,"is the head of his body, the Church" [Col 1:18]. If the Church is a body, it must be an unbroken unity according to those words of Paul: "So we, though many, are one body in Christ" *[Rom 12:5]*. But it is not enough that the Body of Christ be an unbroken unity: it must be also something definite and perceptible to the senses, as our predecessor of happy memory, Leo XIII, in his encyclical *Satis Cognitum* asserts: "The Church is visible because she is a body". It is an error in the matter of divine truth to imagine that the Church is invisible, intangible, something merely spiritual *(pneumaticum)*, as they say, by which many Christian communities, though they differ from each other in their profession of faith, are united by a bond that is invisible to the senses.

(Church, hierarchical and charismatic)

848   One must not think, however, that this ordered or
3801   'organic' structure of the body of the Church contains
        only hierarchical elements and with them is complete; or, as an opposite opinion holds, that it is composed only of those who enjoy charismatic gifts—though members gifted with miraculous powers will never be lacking in the Church. It is certainly true that those who hold sacred power in this body are its first and chief members. It is through them, in accordance with the plan of the divine Redeemer himself, that Christ's functions as Teacher, King and Priest endure forever. However, when the Fathers of the Church mention the ministries of this body, its grades, professions, states, orders and offices, they rightly have in mind not only persons in sacred orders, but also all those who have embraced the evangelical counsels and lead either an active life among men and women or a hidden life in cloister, or else contrive to combine the two, according to the institution to which they belong; those also who, though living in the world, actively devote themselves to spiritual or corporal works of mercy; and also those who are joined in chaste wedlock.

(Members of the Mystical Body)

849   Only those are to be accounted as members of the
3802   Church in reality *(reapse)* who have been baptised and
        profess the true faith and who have not had the misfortune of withdrawing from the Body or for grave faults been cut off by legitimate authority. For, as the apostle says: "For by one Spirit we were all baptised into one body—*Jews or Greeks, slaves or free*" *[1 Cor 12:13]*. As, therefore, in the true Christian

community there is only one Body, one Spirit, one Lord, one baptism, so there can be only one faith [cf. Eph 4:5]. And so, whoever refuses to listen to the Church should be considered, so the Lord commands, as a heathen and publican [cf. Mt 18:17]. It follows that those who are divided in faith and government cannot be living in one body such as this, and cannot be living the life of its one divine Spirit.

(Bishops in the Church)

850
3804
What we have thus far said of the universal Church must be understood also of the individual Christian communities, whether Eastern or Latin, which go to make up the one Catholic Church. For they, too, are ruled by Christ Jesus through the authoritative voice of their own respective bishops. Bishops, then, must be considered as the nobler members of the universal Church, for they are linked in an altogether special way to the divine Head of the whole Body and so are rightly called "first among the members of the Lord";[1] what is more, as far as each one's own diocese is concerned, they each and all as true shepherds feed the flocks entrusted to them and rule them in the name of Christ. Yet in exercising this office they are not altogether independent, but are duly subordinate to the authority of the Roman Pontiff; and although their jurisdiction is inherent in their office, yet they receive it directly from the same supreme Pontiff. Hence, they should be revered by the faithful as divinely appointed successors of the apostles.[...]

(The Holy Spirit in the Church)

851
3807
If we examine closely this divine principle of life and power given by Christ, in so far as it constitutes the very source of every gift and created grace, we easily see that it is nothing else than the Holy Spirit, the Paraclete who proceeds from the Father and the Son, and who is called in a special way the "Spirit of Christ" or the "Spirit of the Son" [cf. Rom 8:9; 2 Cor 3:17; Gal 4:6]. For it was by his breath of grace and truth that the Son of God adorned his own soul in the immaculate womb of the Blessed Virgin; this Spirit delights to dwell in the dear soul of our Redeemer as in his most cherished shrine; this Spirit Christ merited for us on the cross by shedding

---

1. Gregory the Great, *Moralia, XIV*, 35, 43.

his own blood; this Spirit he bestowed on the Church for the remission of sins, when he breathed on the apostles [cf.Jn 20:22]; and while Christ alone received this Spirit without measure [cf.Jn 3:34], to the members of the mystical Body he is imparted only according to the measure of the giving of Christ, from Christ's own fulness [cf. Eph 1:8; 4:7]. But after Christ's glorification on the cross, his Spirit is communicated to the Church in an abundant outpouring, so that the Church and each of its members may become daily more and more like to our Saviour. It is the Spirit of Christ that has made us adopted children of God [cf. Gal 4:6-7; Rom 8:14-17] in order that one day all of us with faces unveiled, reflecting as in a mirror the glory of the Lord, may be transformed into his very image from glory to glory [cf.2 Cor 3:18].

852 To this Spirit of Christ, too, as an invisible principle, is
3808 to be ascribed the fact that all the parts of the Body are joined one with the other and with their exalted Head; for the whole Spirit of Christ is in the Head, the whole Spirit is in the Body, and the whole Spirit is in each of the members. He is present in the members and assists them in proportion to their various tasks and offices and to the degree of spiritual health which they enjoy. It is he who through his heavenly grace is the principle of every truly supernatural act in all parts of the Body. It is he who, while he is personally present and divinely active in all the members, also acts in the inferior members through the ministry of the higher members. Finally, while with his grace he provides for the constant growth of the Church, he yet refuses to dwell with sanctifying grace in members that are wholly severed from the Body. This presence and activity of the Spirit of Jesus Christ are tersely and vigorously described by our predecessor of immortal memory Leo XIII in his Encyclical Letter *Divinum Illud* in these words: "Let it suffice to say that, as Christ is the head of the Church, so is the Holy Spirit its Soul."[1]

(The juridical Church and the Church of love)

853 We, therefore, deplore and condemn the pernicious error of those who conjure up from their fancies an imaginary Church, a kind of Society that finds its origin and growth in charity, to which they somewhat contemptuously oppose another

---

1. *ASS* 29 (1896-97) 650.

which they call juridical. To draw such a distinction is utterly futile. For they fail to understand that the divine Redeemer had one single purpose in view when he wanted the community of men and women of which he was the founder to be established as a society perfect in its own order and possessing all juridical and social elements—the purpose, namely, of perpetuating the salutary work of the redemption here on earth. And it was for the very same purpose that he wanted that society to be enriched with the heavenly gifts of the consoling Spirit. The eternal Father, indeed, wished it to be the "Kingdom of his beloved Son" [Col 1:13], but it was to be a real kingdom, in which all believers would make the obeisance of their intellect and will, and humbly and obediently model themselves on him, who for our sake "became obedient unto death" [Phil 2:8]. There can, then, be no real opposition or conflict between the invisible mission of the Holy Spirit and the juridical commission of ruler and teacher received from Christ. Like body and soul in us, they complement and perfect one another, and have their source in our one Redeemer, who not only said, as he breathed on the apostles: "Receive the Holy Spirit" [Jn 20:22], but also clearly commanded: "As the Father has sent me, even so I send you" [Jn 20:21], and again: "He who hears you, hears me" [Lk 10:16].

LETTER OF THE HOLY OFFICE TO THE ARCHBISHOP OF BOSTON (1949)

An unfortunate controversy in the United States (the Leonard Feeney case) over the meaning of the axiom Extra Ecclesiam nulla salus *was the occasion of the following letter, dated August 8, 1949. It is important because, while emphasising once more the ancient doctrine of the necessity of the Church for salvation, it clarifies what this must mean for each and every individual. All, in order to be saved, must be in some way related to the Church, but actual membership is not absolutely required. Provided that one is related to the Church in desire or longing, even implicitly, and this desire is informed by supernatural faith and love, he or she can be saved.*

854
3866
The infallible dictum which teaches us that outside the Church there is no salvation, is among the truths that the Church has always taught and will always teach. But this dogma is to be understood as the Church itself understands it. For the Saviour did not leave it to private judgment to explain what is contained in the deposit of faith, but to the doctrinal authority of the Church.

3867   The Church teaches, first of all, that there is question
          here of a very strict command of Jesus Christ. In
unmistakable words he gave his apostles the command to teach
all nations to keep whatever he had commanded [cf. Mt 28:19f].
Not least among Christ's commands is the one which orders us
to be incorporated by baptism into the mystical Body of Christ,
which is the Church, and to be united to Christ and to his vicar,
through whom he himself governs the Church on earth in a
visible way. Therefore, no one who knows that the Church has
been divinely established by Christ and nevertheless, refuses to
be a subject of the Church or refuses to obey the Roman Pontiff,
the vicar of Christ on earth, will be saved.

3868   The Saviour did not make it merely a necessity of
          precept for all nations to enter the Church. He also
established the Church as a means of salvation without which
no one can enter the kingdom of heavenly glory.

855   As regards the helps to salvation which are ordered to
3869   the last end only by divine decree, not by intrinsic
          necessity, God, in his infinite mercy, willed that their
effects which are necessary to salvation can, in certain
circumstances, be obtained when the helps are used only in desire
or longing. We see this clearly stated in the Council of Trent
about the sacrament of regeneration and about the sacrament of
penance [cf. nn.1928, 1944].

3870   The same, in due proportion, should be said of the
          Church in so far as it is a general help to salvation. To
gain eternal salvation it is not always required that a person be
incorporated in reality (*reapse*) as a member of the Church, but it
is required that one belong to it at least in desire and longing
(*voto et desiderio*). It is not always necessary that this desire be
explicit, as it is with catechumens. When one is invincibly
ignorant, God also accepts an implicit desire, so called because
it is contained in the good disposition of soul by which a person
wants his or her will to be conformed to God's will.

856   This is clearly taught by the Sovereign Pontiff Pope Pius
3871   XII in his doctrinal letter on the mystical Body of
          Christ.[...] In this letter the Sovereign Pontiff clearly
distinguishes between those who are actually (*re*) incorporated
into the Church as members and those who belong to the Church

only in desire *(voto tantummodo)*. In treating of members who make up the mystical Body on earth, the Sovereign Pontiff says: "Only those are to be accounted as members of the Church in reality *(reapse)* who have been baptised and profess the true faith and who have not had the misfortune of withdrawing from the Body or for grave faults been cut off by legitimate authority" *[cf.n.849]*. Towards the end of the same encyclical, when with all his heart he invites to union those who do not pertain to the body of the Catholic Church, the Pope mentions those "who are ordained to the mystical Body of the Redeemer by some kind of unconscious desire or longing". He by no means excludes these persons from eternal salvation; but, on the other hand, he does point out that they are in a condition "in which they cannot be secure about their salvation.[...] since they lack many great gifts and helps from God which they can enjoy only in the Catholic Church" *(cf. DS 3821)*.

3872	With these prudent words the Pope censures those who exclude from eternal salvation all those who adhere to the Church only with an implicit desire, and he also censures those who falsely maintain that people can be saved equally well in any religion.

857	It must not be imagined that any desire whatsoever of entering the Church is sufficient for a person to be saved. It is necessary that the desire by which one is related to the Church be informed with perfect charity. And an implicit desire cannot have its effect unless one has supernatural faith. "Without faith it is impossible to please him. For whoever would draw near to God must believe that he exists and that he rewards those who seek him" *[Heb 11:6]*. And the Council of Trent says: "Faith is the beginning of human salvation, the foundation and source of all justification, without which it is impossible to please God and to come into the fellowship of his children" *[cf. n. 1935]*.

ENCYCLICAL LETTER *HUMANI GENERIS* (1950)

The following extract from the encyclical Humani Generis *(cf. n. 144i) is an important statement about the relationship between theologians and the official teaching authority in the Church. It brings out the fact that the theologian, as a member of the believing community, cannot pursue his scientific investigations independently of the magisterium, to whose teaching, even when not definitive, should be given due submission. Though the Pope stresses the role of the theologian to illuminate and defend the Church's official teaching by recourse to Scripture and Tradition, he also recognises that the theologian must not stop there, but probe ever deeper into the inexhaustible riches of the divine revelation.*

(The ordinary teaching authority)

858   It is not to be supposed that a position advanced in an
3885   encyclical does not, *ipso facto*, claim assent. In writing them, it is true, the Popes do not exercise their teaching authority to the full. But such statements come under the day-to-day teaching of the Church, which is covered by the promise: "He that hears you hears me" *[Lk 10:16]*. For the most part the positions advanced and the duties inculcated by these encyclical letters are already bound up, under some other title, with the general body of Catholic teaching. And when the Roman Pontiffs carefully pronounce on some subject which has hitherto been controverted, it must be clear to everybody that, in the mind and intention of the Pontiffs concerned, this subject can no longer be regarded as matter of free debate among theologians.

859   It is true, again, that a theologian must constantly have
3886   recourse to the fountains of divine revelation. It is for him to show how the doctrine of the teaching authority of the Church is contained in Scripture and in the sacred Tradition, whether explicitly or implicitly. This twofold spring of doctrine divinely made known to us contains, in any case, treasures so varied and so rich that it must ever prove inexhaustible. That is why the study of these hallowed sources, gives the sacred sciences a kind of perpetual youth, while, on the contrary, if the labour of probing deeper and deeper into the sacred deposit is neglected, speculation—as experience shows—grows barren. Theology, however, even what is called positive theology, cannot for that reason be put on a level with the merely historical sciences. For, side by side with these hallowed sources God has given his Church a living teaching authority to make clear for us and to unravel what in the deposit of faith is contained only in an obscure manner and implicitly. The task of interpreting the deposit authentically was entrusted by our divine Redeemer not to the individual Christian, nor even to the theologians, but only to the Church's teaching authority.

THE SECOND VATICAN GENERAL COUNCIL

The teaching of the Second Vatican Council on the Church is found primarily in the Dogmatic Constitution Lumen Gentium. *This Constitution must, however, be studied along with the other conciliar documents, for it can be said that the Church, in all the manifold aspects of its mystery and structure, of its life and mission, constitutes the central and unifying object of the Council's teaching.*

Since it is impossible, within the limits of this chapter, to do justice to the richness of the entire Council doctrine, some introductory guide-lines to the Constitution on the Church only are given here; a reading list is added which refers to some of the most significant passages of the Constitution.

DOGMATIC CONSTITUTION *LUMEN GENTIUM*
(21 November 1964)

(The nature and mission of the Church)

(860)   *The nature and mission of the Church are first situated in the only context in which they can be adequately understood, that of the mystery of salvation: God's gracious will and purpose, hidden from all eternity, but now revealed and realised in Christ through the Church, to share with human beings the riches of his own divine life in an ineffable communion of love through Christ in the sanctification of the Holy Spirit (2-4). This is the mystery of the Kingdom of God which Christ proclaimed and manifested in his person and work; it will be fully realised only at the end of time when Christ comes in his glory, but the Church on earth both announces this mystery of God's saving love revealed in Christ, and already experiences it as a present reality (5). This inner nature of the Church is made known to us in the Scriptures by various images, above all by the Pauline doctrine of the Body of Christ (6-7). As both the manifestation and the present realisation of the mystery of our salvation through Christ in the Spirit, it is at once and inseparably a visible hierarchically structured community and the spiritual communion of those who have been incorporated into Christ through the Spirit: "one complex reality composed of a divine and of a human element" (8). This one Church of Christ, "constituted and organised in this world as a society, subsists in the Catholic Church, which is governed by the successor of Peter and the bishops in communion with him, although many elements of sanctification and truth can be found outside of her visible structure" (8). This important affirmation, more nuanced than that of Pope Pius XII in his encyclical* Mystici Corporis *(cf. n. 847), both re-affirms the traditional teaching about the unique ecclesial status of the Catholic communion, and opens the way for a positive evaluation of the ecclesial reality of the other Christian communions (15) (cf. nn.909, 913).*

(The pilgrim Church)

(861)   *The first chapter concludes with some important reflections on the present status of the Church on earth, situated as she is between* *the definitive revelation of God's saving will in Christ and the final and perfect restoration of all things at the time of his second coming. She must follow Christ's path toward glory in poverty, humility and suffering; she is upheld by the victorious grace of Christ and hence is essentially indefectible in her faith and structures, but at the same time is always called to renewal and repentance. This pilgrim situation of the Church in the context of her eschatological nature and goal, and the consequences that flow from this for our understanding of her structures, life and mission, are emphasized throughout the Constitution: see mostly 48; but also 9, 12, 13, 17, 39, etc.*

(The People of God)

(862)   *Reflection on the pilgrim status of the Church leads naturally to the theme of the Church as the people of God of the new and eternal Covenant, which is developed in chapter II. The mystery of the Church finds its concrete expression and realisation in an historical people (9), the sacramentally structured community of believers in Jesus Christ, which he uses as his instrument for the redemption of humankind (10-11). Throughout this chapter the emphasis is on the common dignity and vocation of all the members of the Church, and it is significant that it has been deliberately placed before the consideration of the Church's hierarchical structure in chapter III. Of special doctrinal importance is the teaching about the 'sensus fidei' and the specifically charismatic element as a perduring reality in the life of the church (12).*

Chapter II, 13-17, forms a whole. In the context of the Church's true catholicity, which is both an essential property and a dynamic exigency of the Church's life (13), the Constitution exposes the different ways by which men and women belong or are related to the Catholic unity of the people of God: Catholics (14), other Christians (15), non-Christians (16); and this exposition leads naturally to the essentially missionary nature of the Church (17). In its teaching (14-16), the Constitution avoids the terminology of membership, because of the continuing theological debate about its precise meaning. While not conflicting with the teaching of Pope Pius XII in Mystici Corporis *(cf. n. 849), the council's doctrine is more descriptive and flexible and takes more adequately into account the ecclesial status of non-Catholic Christians. Number 15 should be studied in the context of the Decree* Unitatis Redintegratio *on Ecumenism (cf. n.909i); number 16 in that of the Declaration* Nostra Aetate *on non-Christian religions (cf. n.1019i); number 17 in that of the Decree* Ad Gentes *on the Church's missionary activity (cf.n. 1136i).*

(The hierarchical structure of the Church)

(863)   *The teaching of chapter III on the hierarchical structure of the Church and in particular the episcopate both complements and qualifies the teaching of Vatican I on the primatial office of the bishop of Rome (cf.nn. 818ff). The teachings on the sacramentality of the episcopate (21), and on the nature, meaning and implications of the collegiality of the bishops (22-*

23) are doctrinally the most important of this chapter, and perhaps of the entire Constitution. This teaching may be briefly summarised. The bishops, who succeed to the apostles as shepherds of the flock (19-20), form a college or stable group (22), which, united with its head is also the subject of full and supreme authority over the universal Church (23). As members of the episcopal college, the bishops must live in communion with one another, be solicitous for the unity in faith and love of the entire Church (23), and promote the preaching of the Gospel, a task which pertains to all of them in common (23) One is constituted a member of the college by the sacramental consecration and hierarchical communion with the head and the other members of the college (22). Episcopal consecration confers the fulness of the sacrament of Order; it confers, together with the function of sanctifying, the function also of teaching and governing, though these latter of their nature can only be exercised in hierarchical communion with the head and other members of the college (21). This teaching should be read in conjunction with the Nota Explicativa, which though not an integral part of the Constitution, is an authoritative declaration of its meaning and import.

Chapter III contains a number of other points that are doctrinally important for understanding the nature and exercise of the episcopal office in the Church. A few are noted here: 1) all ecclesiastical authority is seen as essentially a service or diakonia within the context of the Spirit-filled community and ordained toward the building up of the Body in truth and love (18, 24, 27); 2) number 27 further clarifies the teaching of Vatican I (cf. n. 827) on the ordinary pastoral function of each bishop in his own diocese, and its relationship with the ordinary and universal authority of the Pope; 3) number 25 on the magisterial authority of the hierarchy explains more adequately the 'ex sese, non autem ex consensu Ecclesiae' of Vatican I (cf. n. 839); cf. also its nuanced statement on the object of the infallible magisterium.

This chapter also contains important statements on the collegial nature of the Church herself, which, though one and universal, is made present and realised in each fully constituted local community. Hence the Church is seen as a communion of local Churches united in the bonds of faith, love and mutual service (especially 26 and 23; cf. also 13).

(The laity)

(864)   *Chapter IV on the laity summarises recent developments in the theology of the laity. In this descriptive definition of the laity, special emphasis is placed on their secular character (31). While making special reference to the laity as distinguished from the hierarchy, this chapter further develops the teaching of chapter II on the common dignity of all the members of the Church (32): all share in her mission (33), and in her priestly (34), prophetic (35) and kingly (36) nature and function, each according to his or her specific state in the Church and his or her own gifts. Number 37 states the general principle that should govern the relationship between the laity and the hierarchy.*

(Universal call to holiness and religious life; eschatological nature of the Church)

(865)   *Chapter V and VI on the universal call to holiness and the religious life respectively express, as it were, the end of all the Church's activity, viz., the building up of the Body of Christ in holiness. With regard to chapter VII, reference has already been made to the important number 48 on the eschatological character of the pilgrim Church (cf. n. 2311). As is clear from the Constitution as a whole, this eschatological perspective is vital for our understanding of the entire structure and life of the Church. The rest of chapter VII contains important teaching on the communion of the Church on earth with the glorified Church of heaven, and on the meaning and veneration of the saints (cf.nn. 2312-2314; 1258i). For chapter VIII on the Blessed Virgin Mary in the mystery of Christ and the Church, cf. n. 716i.*

READING LIST OF IMPORTANT TEXTS

(866)   1.   *(The sacramentality of the Church)*
(867)   2-4. *(The Church in the divine plan of salvation)*
(868)   5.   *(The Church and the Kingdom of God)*
(869)   8.   *(The Church: one complex reality, divine and human; the Church subsists in the Catholic Church; the Church in constant need of reform)*
(870)   12. *(The prophetic office of the faithful; sense of faith and charisms)*
(871)   14. *(The necessity of the Church)*
(872)   15. *(Ties between the Catholic Church and other Christians)*
(873)   16. *(The members of other religions and the People of God)*
(874)   21. *(The episcopate as sacrament)*
(875)   22. *(The college of bishops and its head)*
(876)   23. *(Relations of bishops in the college; the Church as communion of Churches)*
(877)   25. *(The magisterium of the Church)*
(878)   26. *(The function of bishops as sanctifiers and the local Churches)*
(879)   27. *(The pastoral function of bishops)*
(880)   31. *(The identity of the laity)*
(881)   39. *(The indefectible holiness of the Church)*
(882)   48. *(The eschatological nature of the Church)*

PAUL VI

DECLARATION *MYSTERIUM ECCLESIAE* OF THE
S. CONGREGATION FOR THE DOCTRINE OF THE FAITH
(11 May 1973)

The mystery of the Church has been the object of much theological rethinking in recent years. Among the attempts made at presenting the mystery in more understandable language, not all have been equally successful.

This Declaration issued by the S. Congregation for the Doctrine of the Faith, "intends to gather together and explain a number of truths concerning the mystery of the Church which at the present time are being either denied or endangered". It is mostly concerned with the question of infallibility, intended by God in order that "what he has revealed for the salvation of all nations would abide perpetually in its full integrity" (DV 7). The Declaration first speaks of the charism of "shared infallibility" granted by God to the whole Church: "The Body of the faithful as a whole[...] cannot err in matters of belief". However, "the Holy Spirit enlightens and assists the people of God in as much as it is the Body of Christ united in a hierarchical community." Thus there must be recognized a special charism of infallibility of the Church's teaching authority, for "by divine institution it is the exclusive task of the pastors, the successors of Peter and the other apostles, to teach the faithful authentically, that is with the authority of Christ shared in different ways". The infallibility of the Magisterium has its source in Christ. Explaining its object, the Document repeats the doctrine of the First and Second Vatican Councils: it "extends not only to the deposit of faith but also to those matters without which that deposit cannot be rightly preserved and expounded"; but, while its application to the deposit of faith itself is a matter of revealed truth, the extension to its secondary object merely belongs to "Catholic doctrine" (cf. LG 25). Thus, "the matter of Catholic faith" is limited to things "to be believed as having been divinely revealed" (cf.n. 121). The Declaration proceeds to reject three ways in which the Church's gift of infallibility would be unduly diminished. The text is found in AAS 65 (1973) 396-408.

(The Church's gift of infallibility is not to be diminished)

883   From what has been said about the extent of the conditions governing the infallibility of the people of God and of the Church's Magisterium, it follows that the faithful are in no way permitted to see in the Church merely a fundamental permanence in truth which, as some assert, could be reconciled with errors contained here and there in the propositions that the Church's Magisterium teaches to be held irrevocably, as also in the unhesitating assent of the People of God concerning matters of faith and morals.

It is of course true that through the faith that leads to salvation men and women are converted to God, who reveals himself in his Son Jesus Christ; but it would be wrong to deduce from this that the Church's dogmas can be belittled or even denied. Indeed, the conversion to God which we should undergo through faith is a form of obedience [cf. Rom 16:26], which should correspond to the nature of divine Revelation and its demands. Now this Revelation, in the whole plan of salvation, reveals the mystery of God who sent his Son into the world [cf.1 Jn 4:14] and teaches its application to Christian conduct. Moreover it demands that, in full obedience of the intellect and will to God who reveals, we accept the proclamation of the good news of salvation as it is infallibly taught by the pastors of the Church. The faithful, therefore, through faith are converted as they should to God, who reveals himself in Christ, when they adhere to him in the integral doctrine of the Catholic faith.

It is true that there exists an order and as it were a hierarchy of the Church's dogmas, as a result of their varying relationship to the foundation of the faith [cf. n. 912]. This hierarchy means that some dogmas are founded on other dogmas which are the principal ones, and are illuminated by these latter. But all dogmas, since they are revealed, must be believed with the same divine faith.

APOSTOLIC EXHORTATION *EVANGELII NUNTIANDI*
(8 December 1975)

As a result of the Synod of bishops on Evangelisation in 1974, on the 10th anniversary of the conclusion of the Council, Paul VI published this Apostolic Exhortation which is an important document on the Church's mission (cf. Chapter XI). Two paragraphs are of special significance for the understanding of the mystery of the Church: the Pope explains the inseparable link between Christ and the Church, and the relation of the particular Church to the universal Church. The text is found in AAS 68 (1979) 5-76.

(The Church is inseparable from Christ)

884 16. There is a profound link between Christ, the Church and evangelisation. In this era of the Church, the mandate to evangelise is entrusted to her. It is not right to carry out this mandate without her, much less against her. It is certainly fitting to recall this fact at the present moment when, not without sorrow, we can hear people—whom we wish to believe are well intentioned, but who are certainly misguided from the right path—continually claiming that they want to love Christ but not the Church. The absurdity of this dichotomy is clearly evident from this phrase of the Gospel: "he who rejects you rejects me" [Lk 10:16]. And how can we wish to love Christ without loving the Church, if the finest witness to Christ is that of Saint Paul: "Christ loved the Church and gave himself up for her" [Eph 5:25]?

(The universal and the particular Church)

885   62. The universal Church is in reality incarnate in the particular Churches that are made of this or that part of humanity, use such or such a language, are heirs of a cultural patrimony, of a vision of the world, of an historical past, of a particular human substratum, and remain closely linked to it. Receptivity to the wealth of the particular Church corresponds to a special sensitivity of modern men and women.

Let us, however, be very careful not to conceive of the universal Church as the sum or, if one can say so, the more or less heterogeneous federation of essentially different particular Churches. In the mind of the Lord the Church is universal by vocation and mission, but when she puts down her roots in a variety of cultural, social and human, terrains, she takes on different external expressions and appearances in each part of the world.

Thus each particular Church that would voluntarily cut itself off from the universal Church would lose its relationship to God's plan and would be impoverished in its ecclesial dimension. But at the same time a Church which is spread all over the world would become an abstraction if she did not take body and life precisely through the particular Churches. Only continuous attention to these two poles of the Church will enable us to perceive the richness of this relationship between the universal Church and the particular Churches.

JOHN PAUL II

ENCYCLICAL LETTER *REDEMPTOR HOMINIS*
(4 March 1979)

In his first encyclical John Paul II sees his ministry for the Church linked with the incarnation in which God's concern and love for humankind find their full expression. God's saving presence to human beings must be embodied in his Church. Thus the Pope sees the very essence of the Church in her service to men and women to help them realise and fulfil their full human destiny in Christ. This vision contains the guidelines for his pontificate. The text is found in AAS 71 (1979) 257-324.

(The Church is for men and women)

886   18. If Christ united himself with each human being *[cf. n. 668]*, the Church lives more profoundly her own nature and mission by penetrating into the depth of this mystery and into its rich universal meaning. It was not without reason that the Apostle spoke about Christ's Body, the Church. If this Mystical Body of Christ is God's People, [...] this means that each man or woman who belongs to it is filled with that breath of life that comes from Christ. This means that the Church herself, who is a body, an organism, a social unit, when she turns to human beings with their real problems, their hopes and sufferings, their achievements and falls, receives the same divine influences, the light and strength of the Spirit that comes from the crucified and risen Christ. It is for this very reason that she lives her life. The Church has no other life but that which is given her by her Spouse and Lord. Indeed, precisely because Christ united her to himself in the mystery of Redemption, the Church must be firmly united with each human being.

APOSTOLIC EXHORTATION *RECONCILIATIO ET PAENITENTIA*
(2 December 1984)

One year after the Sixth General Assembly of the Synod of Bishops on Reconciliation and Penance in the Mission of the Church (1983), the Pope issued an Apostolic Exhortation integrating many of the insights that emerged in the discussion of the bishops. He speaks of the Church herself being a reconciled community, with ecumenical openness, and applies to the mission of reconciliation the theme of Vatican II on the Church as sacrament of salvation. The text is found in AAS 77 (1985) 185-275.

(The reconciled Church)

887   9. My Venerable Predecessor Paul VI commendably highlighted the fact that the Church, in order to evangelise, must begin by showing that she herself has been evangelised, that is to say that she is open to the full and complete proclamation of the Good News of Jesus Christ in order to listen to it and put it into practice *[EN 13]*. I too, by bringing together in one document the reflections of the Fourth General Assembly of the Synod, have spoken of a Church that is catechised to the extent that she carries out catechesis *[Catechesi Tradendae 24]*.

I now do not hesitate to resume the comparison, in so far as it applies to the theme I am dealing with, in order to assert that the Church, if she is to be reconciling, must begin by being a reconciled Church. Beneath this simple and indicative expression lies the conviction that the Church, in order ever more effectively to proclaim and propose reconciliation to the world, must become ever more genuinely a community of disciples of Christ[...], united in the commitment to be continually converted to the Lord and to live as new people in the spirit and practice of reconciliation.

(The Church, the great sacrament of reconciliation)

888　11. The Church has the mission of proclaiming this reconciliation and as it were of being its sacrament in the world. The Church is the sacrament, that is to say the sign and means of reconciliation in different ways, which differ in value but which all come together to obtain what the divine initiative of mercy desires to grant to humanity.

She is a sacrament in the first place by her very existence as a reconciled community which witnesses to and represents in the world the work of Christ.

She is also a sacrament through her service as the custodian and interpreter of Sacred Scripture, which is the Good News of reconciliation in as much as it tells each succeeding generation about God's loving plan and shows to each generation the paths to universal reconciliation in Christ.

Finally she is a sacrament by reason of the seven Sacraments which, each in its own way, "make the Church".[1] For since they commemorate and renew Christ's Paschal Mystery, all the Sacraments are a source of life for the Church, and in the Church's hands they are means of conversion to God and of reconciliation among people.

SECOND EXTRAORDINARY SYNOD OF BISHOPS
RELATIO FINALIS
(9 December 1985)

To celebrate the twentieth anniversary of the close of the Second Vatican Council Pope John Paul II called the Second Extraordinary Synod of Bishops in Rome in November-December, 1985. The "Relatio Finalis" of the Synod, entitled "The Church, in the Word of God, Celebrates the Mysteries of Christ for the Salvation of the World", has been published with the approval of the

---

1. St. Augustine, *De Civitate Dei*, XXII, 17: *CCL* 48, 835s; St. Thomas Aquinas, *Summa Theologiae*, pars q. 64, a.2 ad tertium.

Pope. The main part of the document is centred on the ecclesiology of the Church as communion. The principle of communion is highlighted and applications are made, among others, to the Church universal and particular, and to the collegiality of bishops. The text is found in Origins 15 (1985) 444-450.

(The mystery of God through Jesus Christ in the Holy Spirit)

889   II.A.2. The primary mission of the Church, under the impulse of the Holy Spirit, is to preach and to witness to the good and joyful news of the election, the mercy and the charity of God which manifest themselves in salvation history, which through Jesus Christ reach their culmination in the fulness of time, and which communicate and offer salvation to human beings by virtue of the Holy Spirit. Christ is the light of humanity! The Church, proclaiming the Gospel, must see to it that this light clearly shines out from her countenance *[cf. LG]*. The Church makes herself more credible if she speaks less of herself and ever more preaches Christ crucified *[cf. 1 Cor 2:2]* and witnesses with her own life. In this way the Church is sacrament, that is, sign and instrument of communion with God and also of communion and reconciliation of human beings with one another. The message of the Church, as described in the Second Vatican Council, is Trinitarian and Christocentric.

(The mystery of the Church)

890   II.A.3. The whole importance of the Church derives from her connection with Christ. The Council has described the Church in diverse ways: as the People of God, the Body of Christ, the bride of Christ, the temple of the Holy Spirit, the family of God. These descriptions of the Church complete one another and must be understood in the light of the mystery of Christ or of the Church in Christ. We cannot replace a false unilateral vision of the Church as purely hierarchical with a new sociological conception which is also unilateral. Jesus Christ is ever present in his Church and lives in her as risen. From the Church's connection with Christ we clearly understand the eschatological character of the Church herself *[cf. LG 7]*. In this way the pilgrim Church on earth is the messianic people *[cf. LG 9]* that already anticipates in itself its future reality as a new creation. Yet she remains a holy Church that has sinners in her midst, that must ever be purified, and that moves, amidst the persecutions of this world and the consolations of God, towards the future Kingdom [cf. LG 8]. In this sense the mystery of the Cross, and the mystery of the Resurrection are always present in the Church.

(The meaning of Communion)

891   II.C.1. The ecclesiology of communion is the central and fundamental idea of the Council's documents. *Koinônia* (communion), founded on the Sacred Scripture, has been held in great honour in the early Church and in the Oriental Churches to this day. Thus, much was done by the Second Vatican Council so that the Church as communion might be more clearly understood and concretely incorporated into life. What does the complex word "communion" mean? Fundamentally, it is a matter of communion with God through Jesus Christ, in the Holy Spirit. This communion is had in the Word of God and in the sacraments. Baptism is the door and the foundation of communion in the Church. The Eucharist is the source and the culmination of the whole Christian life [cf. LG 11]. The communion of the eucharistic Body of Christ signifies and produces, that is, builds up, the intimate communion of all the faithful in the Body of Christ which is the Church [1 Cor. 10:16].

For this reason the ecclesiology of communion cannot be reduced to purely organizational questions or to problems which simply relate to powers. Still, the ecclesiology of communion is also the foundation for order in the Church, and especially for a correct relationship between unity and pluriformity in the Church.

(Unity and pluriformity in the Church)

892   IIC.2. Just as we believe in one God alone and one mediator, Jesus Christ, in one Spirit, so we have but one baptism and one Eucharist with which the unity and the uniqueness of the Church are signified and built up. This is of great importance especially today, because the Church, in as much as she is one and unique, is as a sacrament, a sign and instrument of unity and reconciliation, of peace among individuals, nations, classes and peoples. In the unity of the faith and the sacraments and in the hierarchical unity, especially with the centre of unity given to us by Christ in the service of Peter, the Church is that messianic people of which the Constitution *Lumen Gentium* (9) speaks. In this way, ecclesial communion with

Peter and his successors is not an obstacle but the anticipation and prophetic sign of a fuller unity. On the other hand, the one and unique Spirit works with many and varied spiritual gifts and charisms [1 Cor 12:4ff], the one Eucharist is celebrated in various places. For this reason the unique and universal Church is truly present in all the particular Churches [CD 11], and these are formed in the image of the universal Church in such a way that the one and unique Catholic Church exists in and through the particular Churches [LG 23]. Here we have the truly theological principle of variety and pluriformity in unity, but it is necessary to distinguish pluriformity from pure pluralism. When pluriformity is true richness and carries with it fulness, this is true catholicity. The pluralism of fundamentally opposed positions instead leads to dissolution, destruction and the loss of identity.

(Collegiality)

893 II.C.3. The ecclesiology of comunion provides the sacramental foundation of collegiality. Therefore the theology of collegiality is much more extensive than its mere juridical aspect. The collegial spirit is broader than effective collegiality understood in an exclusively juridical way. The collegial spirit is the soul of the collaboration between the bishops at the regional, national and international levels. Collegial action in the strict sense implies the activity of the whole college, together with its head, over the entire Church. Its maximum expression is found in an ecumenical council. In the whole theological question regarding the relationship between primacy and the college of bishops a distinction cannot be made between the Roman Pontiff and the bishops considered collectively, but between the Roman Pontiff alone and the Roman Pontiff together with the bishops [LG expl. note 3], because the college exists with its "head" and never without him, the subject of supreme and full power in the whole Church [LG 22].

From this first collegiality understood in the strict sense one must distinguish the diverse partial realizations, which are authentically sign and instrument of the collegial spirit: the Synod of Bishops, the Episcopal Conferences, the Roman Curia, the "ad limina" visits, etc. All of these actualizations cannot be directly deduced from the theological principle of collegiality; but they are regulated by ecclesial law. Nonetheless, all of these other forms, like the pastoral journeys of the Supreme Pontiff, are a service of great importance for the whole college of bishops together with the Pope, and also for the individual bishops whom the Holy Spirit has made guardians in the Church of God [*Acts 20:28*].

APOSTOLIC EXHORTATION *CHRISTIFIDELES LAICI*
(30 Dcember 1988)

In this Apostolic Exhortation Pope John Paul II resumes the work of the 1987 Synod of Bishops in Rome on the "Vocation and Mission of Lay People in the Church and in the World Twenty Years after the Second Vatican Council". Characteristically, the Pope's document is interspersed with many quotations from the "propositions" handed over to him by the Synod. The exhortation proposes a "positive description" of lay people in the Church. Returning to the central reality of the Church-communion, the Pope shows it to be an "organic communion" to which lay people contribute according to their proper vocation and mission. He goes on to explain which ministries are open to lay people according to the present discipline. The text is found in AAS 81 (1989) 393-521.

(Who are the lay faithful?)

894   9. In giving a response to the question, who are the lay faithful?, the Council went beyond previous interpretations, which were predominantly negative. Instead it opened itself to a decidedly positive vision and displayed a basic intention of asserting the full belonging of the lay faithful to the Church and to its mystery. At the same time it insisted on the unique character of their vocation, which is in a special way to "seek the Kingdom of God by engaging in temporal affairs and ordering them according to the plan of God" [*LG 31*]. "The term lay faithful"—we read in the Constitution on the Church, *Lumen Gentium*—"is here understood to mean all the faithful except those in holy orders and those who belong to a religious state sanctioned by the Church. Through baptism the lay faithful are made one body with Christ and are established among the People of God. They are in their own way made sharers in the priestly, prophetic and kingly office of Christ. They carry on their own part in the mission of the whole Christian people with respect to the Church and to the world" [*LG 31*].

Pius XII once stated: "The faithful, more precisely the lay faithful, find themselves on the front lines of the Church's life; for them the Church is the animating principle for human society. Therefore, they in particular ought to have an ever clearer consciousness not only of belonging to the Church, but of being the Church, that is to say, the community of the faithful on earth under the leadership of the Pope, the head of all, and of the bishops, in communion with him. These are the Church".[1]

(An organic communion: diversity and complementarity)

895   20. Ecclesial communion is more precisely likened to an "organic" communion, analogous to that of a living and functioning body. In fact, at one and the same time it is characterised by a diversity and complementarity of vocations and states in life, of ministries, of charisms and responsibilities. Because of this diversity and complementarity, every member of the lay faithful is seen in relation to the whole body and offers a totally unique contribution on behalf of the whole body.

(The ministries, offices and roles of the lay faithful)

896   23. The Church's mission of salvation in the world is realized not only by the ministers in virtue of the sacrament of orders, but also by all the lay faithful; indeed, because of their baptismal state and their specific vocation, in the measure proper to each person the lay faithful participate in the priestly, prophetic and kingly mission of Christ.

The pastors, therefore, ought to acknowledge and foster the ministries, the offices and roles of the lay faithful that find their foundation in the sacraments of baptism and confirmation, indeed, for a good many of them, in the sacrament of matrimony.

When necessity and expediency in the Church require it, the pastors, according to established norms from universal law, can entrust to the lay faithful certain offices and roles that are connected to their pastoral ministry but do not require the character of orders [...] *[cf. canon 230, 3]*. However, the exercise of such tasks does not make pastors of the lay faithful: in fact, a person is not a minister simply in performing a task, but through sacramental ordination. Only the sacrament of orders gives the ordained minister a particular participation in the office of Christ, the shepherd and head, and in his eternal priesthood *[cf. PO 2 and 5]*. The task exercised in virtue of supply takes its legitimacy

---

1. Pius XII, Discourse to the New Cardinals, 20 February, 1946: *AAS* 38 (1946) 149.

formally and immediately from the official deputation given by the pastors as well as from its concrete exercise under the guidance of ecclesiastical authority [cf. AA 24].

("Criteria of Ecclesiality" for Lay Groups)

896a 30. It is always from the perspective of the Church's communion and mission, and not in opposition to the freedom to associate, that one understands the necessity of having *clear and definite criteria for discerning and recognizing* such lay groups, also called "Criteria of Ecclesiality". The following basic criteria might be helpful in evaluating an association of the lay faithful in the Church:

–*The primacy given to the call of every Christian to holiness,* as it is manifested "in the fruits of grace which the Spirit produces in the faithful" [LG 39] and in a growth towards the fulness of charity [cf. LG 40].[...]

–*The responsibility of professing the Catholic faith,* embracing and proclaiming the truth about Christ, the Church and humanity, in obedience to the Church's Magisterium, as the Church interprets it.[...]

–*The witness to a strong and authentic communion* in filial relationship to the Pope, in total adherence to the belief that he is the perpetual and visible centre of unity of the universal Church [cf. LG 23], and with the local Bishop, "the visible principle and foundation of unity" *(ibid.)* in the particular Church, and in "mutual esteem for all forms of the church's apostolate" [AA 23].[...]

–*Conformity to and participation in the Church's apostolic goals,* that is, "the evangelization and sanctification of humanity and the Christian formation of people's conscience, so as to enable them to infuse the spirit of the gospel into the various communities and spheres of life" [AA 20].[...]

–*A commitment to a presence in human society,* which in light of the Church's social doctrine, places it at the service of the total dignity of the person.[...]

PONTIFICAL BIBLICAL COMMISSION
UNITY AND DIVERSITY IN THE CHURCH
(11-15 April 1988)

In light of the potentially fruitful tension between the desire of local churches to express their distinctive characteristics and the need to maintain the catholic unity of the whole Church, the Pontifical Biblical Commission was asked to examine the teaching of Holy Scripture on the relationship between local Churches, or between particular groups, and the universality of the one People of God. The text was published in pamphlet form by the Vatican Polyglot Press in 1991.

(Synthesis of the biblical evidence explaining communion in diversity in the Church)

897 B.2.2. [...]There are diversities of ministry: apostles and prophets, *episkopoi* and presbyters, deacons, teachers, shepherds and so on. The nomenclature varies from place to place, and some of these ministries may be entrusted to persons of either sex. As a result of this diversity one single faith receives doctrinal and theological expressions, cultural and social realizations, in which the diversity of thought and tradition of the entire human race is enabled both to flourish and to refine itself, and in which the inventiveness of *agapê* may exercise itself.

It is by reason of this love which is poured into our hearts by the Spirit [Rom 5:5], and through the breaking of the bread [1 Cor 10:16-17], and as a consequence of the testimony of the Twelve, of whom Peter, "the first" [Mt 10:2] was charged by Jesus to feed his sheep [Jn 21:16-17], and through the preaching of Paul, continued by his collaborators, by Titus and Timothy, and by the message of the four gospels, that the unity of the Church of Christ is achieved and maintained amid all diversity. For the Church as the Body of Christ is the reconciliation of those who are divided by hatred [Eph 2:14-16]. By the mercy of God, by the action of the risen Christ and by the power of the Spirit, the unity of the Church can overcome divisions which are apparently insurmountable. In her, all legitimate diversity discovers a wonderful fruitfulness.

CONGREGATION FOR THE DOCTRINE OF THE FAITH INSTRUCTION ON THE ECCLESIAL VOCATION OF THE THEOLOGIAN *DONUM VERITATIS*
(24 May 1990)

This Instruction places the vocation of the theologian within the context of the Church as a communion in the truth which is given to it by God. Within this ecclesial context, the Instruction also describes the aim and form of the exercise of official teaching by the Church's pastors as well as the relationship which should obtain between the magisterium and theologians. Carefully distinguishing "dissent" from legitimate tensions which, instead of diminishing the credibility of official teaching authority, can lead to clearer and more convincing teaching and, moreover, defining dissent as "public opposition to the magisterium of the Church," which gives rise to a "parallel magisterium" of theologians, the congregation examines and argues against the reasons sometimes given to establish the legitimacy of dissent. The text can be found in AAS 82 (1990) 1550-1570.

(The necessity and role of theology)

898a 7. Theology, which seeks the "reasons of faith" and offers these reasons as a response to those seeking them, thus constitutes an integral part of obedience to the command of Christ, for men and women cannot become disciples if the truth found in the word of faith is not presented to them [cf. Rom. 10:14f].

(The necessity and role of the magisterium)

898b 14. The function of the magisterium is not, then, something extrinsic to Christian truth nor is it set above the faith. It arises directly from the economy of the faith itself, in as much as the magisterium in its service to the word of God is an institution positively willed by Christ as a constitutive element of his Church.

(The competence of the magisterium in the areas of morality and natural law)

898c 16. By its nature, the task of religiously guarding and loyally expounding the deposit of divine revelation (in all its integrity and purity), implies that the magisterium can make a pronouncement "in a definitive way" [cf. n. 41] on propositions which, even if not contained among the truths of faith, are nonetheless intimately connected with them in such a way that the definitive character of such affirmations derives in the final analysis from revelation itself [cf. LG 25; Mysterium Ecclesiae 3-5; n. 41]. What concerns morality can also be the object of authentic magisterium because the Gospel, being the word of life, inspires and guides the whole sphere of human behaviour. The magisterium, therefore, has the task of discerning by means of judgments normative for the consciences of believers those acts which in themselves conform to the demands of faith and foster their expression in life and those which, on the contrary, because intrinsically evil, are incompatible with such demands. By reason of the connection between the orders of creation and redemption, and by reason of the necessity, in view of salvation, of knowing and observing the whole moral law, the competence of the magisterium also extends to that which concerns the natural law.[1]

(Levels of teaching and corresponding levels of response)

898d 23. When the magisterium of the church makes an infallible pronouncement and solemnly declares that a teaching is found in revelation, the assent called for is that of theological faith. This kind of adherence is to be given even to the teaching of the ordinary and universal magisterium when it proposes for belief a teaching of faith as divinely revealed.

When the magisterium proposes "in a definitive way" truths concerning faith and morals, which even if not divinely revealed are nevertheless strictly and intimately connected with revelation, these must be firmly accepted and held.[2]

When the magisterium, not intending to act "definitively", teaches a doctrine to aid a better understanding of revelation and make explicit its contents, or to recall how some teaching is in conformity with the truths of faith or finally to guard against ideas that are incompatible with these truths, the response called for is that of religious submission of will and intellect [*cf. LG 25; CIC 752*]. This kind of response cannot be simply exterior or disciplinary, but must be understood within the logic of faith and under the impulse of obedience to the faith.

24. Finally, in order to serve the people of God as well as possible, in particular by warning them of dangerous opinions which could lead to error, the magisterium can intervene in questions under discussion which involve, in addition to solid principles, certain contingent and conjectural elements. It often becomes possible with the passage of time to distinguish between what is necessary and what is contingent.

The willingness to submit loyally to the teaching of the magisterium on matters per se not irreformable must be the rule. It can happen, however, that a theologian may, according to the case, raise questions regarding the timeliness, the form or even the contents of magisterial interventions.

---

1. Cf. PAUL VI, Encyclical Letter *Humanae Vitae*, 4.
2. Cf. New Formula for the Profession of Faith (*cf. n 41*). "Firmly accepted and held" is suggested by the Latin: *"Firmiter etiam amplector et retineo"*.

ENCYCLICAL LETTER *REDEMPTORIS MISSIO*
(7 December 1990)

The encyclical is devoted to the "permanent validity of the Christian mission." Chapter I places this mission within the context of the fact that Jesus Christ is the sole saviour of human beings and Chapter II relates the Church to the Kingdom of God which Christ proclaimed. Chapter V includes a description of an important phenomenon in the period after Vatican II: the basic ecclesial community. The text is found in AAS 83 (1991) 249-340.

(God's universal salvific will does not render the Church unnecessary)

899a 9. It is necessary to keep these two truths together, namely, the real possibility of salvation in Christ for all humankind and the necessity of the Church for salvation. Both these truths help us to understand the one mystery of salvation, so that we can come to know God's mercy and our own responsibility. Salvation, which always remains a gift of the Spirit, requires one's cooperation, both to save oneself and to save others. This is God's will, and this is why he established the Church and made her a part of his plan of salvation.

(The motivation of the Church's mission)

899b 11. To the question, Why mission?, We reply with the Church's faith and experience that true liberation consists in opening oneself to the love of Christ. In him, and only in him, are we set free from all alienation and doubt, from slavery to the power of sin and death. Christ is truly "our peace" [Eph. 2:14]; "the love of Christ impels us" [2 Cor 5:14], giving meaning and joy to our life. Mission is an issue of faith, an accurate indicator of our faith in Christ and his love for us.

(The Church is not identified with but is intimately related to Christ and the Kingdom)

899c 18. [...] If the kingdom is separated from Jesus, it is no longer the kingdom of God which he revealed. [...] Likewise one may not separate the kingdom from the Church. It is true that the church is not an end unto herself, since she is ordered toward the kingdom of God of which she is the seed, sign and instrument. Yet, while remaining distinct from Christ and from the kingdom, the Church is indissolubly united to both. Christ endowed the church, his body, with the fulness of the benefits and means of salvation. The Holy Spirit dwells in her, enlivens her with his gifts and charisms, sanctifies, guides and constantly renews her. The result is a unique and special relationship which, while not excluding the action of Christ and the Spirit outside the Church's visible boundaries, confers upon her a specific and necessary role; hence the Church's special connection with the kingdom of God and of Christ, which she has "the mission of announcing and inaugurating among all peoples" [LG 5].

(Values of the Kingdom outside the visible confines of the Church)

899d   20. The Church serves the kingdom by spreading throughout the world the "Gospel values" which are an expression of the kingdom and which help people to accept God's plan. It is true that the inchoate reality of the kingdom can also be found among peoples everywhere to the extent that they live "Gospel values" and are open to the working of the Spirit, who breathes when and where he wills [cf. Jn. 3:8]. But it must immediately be added that this temporal dimension of the kingdom remains incomplete unless it is related to the kingdom of Christ present in the Church and straining toward eschatological fulness [cf. EN 34].

(Basic Ecclesial Communities)

899e   51. A rapidly growing phenomenon in the young churches—one sometimes fostered by the bishops and their conferences as a pastoral priority—is that of "ecclesial basic communities" (also known by other names), which are proving to be good centres for Christian formation and missionary outreach. These are groups of Christians who, at the level of the family or in a similarly restricted setting, come together for prayer, Scripture reading, catechesis and discussion on human and ecclesial problems with a view to a common commitment. These communities are a sign of vitality within the Church, an instrument of formation and evangelization and a solid starting point for a new society based on a "civilization of love."

ENCYCLICAL LETTER *CENTESIMUS ANNUS*
(1 May 1991)

The encyclical celebrates the hundredth anniversary of Leo XIII's Rerum Novarum by pointing out the abiding principles of the Church's social doctrine and applying them to the new conditions of the present time. In doing so, the

Pope relates the social doctrine of the Church, which is built upon the fundamental principle of the dignity of every human person, to the very nature of the Church. The text can be found in AAS 83 (1991) 793-867.

(Social doctrine is an essential part of the Christian message and, hence, essential to the Church's evangelizing mission)

900Aa 5. In effect, to teach, and to spread her social doctrine pertains to the Church's evangelizing mission and is an essential part of the Christian message, since this doctrine points out the direct consequences of that message in the life of society and situates daily work and struggles for justice in the context of bearing witness to Christ the saviour.

(Human beings are the "way of the Church")

900Ab 53. During the last hundred years the Church has repeatedly expressed her thinking, while closely following the continuing development of the social question. She has certainly not done this in order to recover former privileges or to impose her own vision. Her sole purpose has been care and responsibility for the human person, who has been entrusted to her by Christ himself: for this person, who, as the Second Vatican Council recalls, is the only creature on earth which God willed for its own sake, and for which God has his plan, that is a share in eternal salvation. We are not dealing here with human beings in the "abstract," but with the real, "concrete," "historical" person. We are dealing with each individual, since each one is included in the mystery of redemption and through this mystery Christ has united himself with each one forever *[RH 13]*. It follows that the Church cannnot abandon the human person and that "this person is the primary route that the Church must travel in fulfilling her mission[...], the way traced out by Christ himself, the way that leads invariably through the mystery of the incarnation and the redemption" *(RH 14)*.

CONGREGATION OF THE DOCTRINE OF THE FAITH

LETTER TO THE BISHOPS OF THE CATHOLIC CHURCH ON SOME ASPECTS OF THE CHURCH UNDERSTOOD AS COMMUNION (28 May 1992)

This letter reaffirms the suitability and value of the concept of communion for expressing the mystery of the Church. At the same time the congregation warns that the notion of communion must not be isolated from other important concepts such as People of God, Body of Christ and sacrament, which tend to underscore the catholic unity of the church as a whole. The five chapters of the letter speak of the Church as a mystery of communion, of the interrelation between the universal and the particular church, of the importance of the eucharist and the episcopacy in an ecclesiology of communion, of unity and diversity in ecclesial communion and of ecumenism. The text can be found in AAS 85(1993) 838-850.

(The particular church is not complete in itself; the universal church is not the result of reciprocal recognition of particular churches)

900Ba 8. The universal church is therefore the body of the churches *[LG 23, 2]*.[1] Hence it is possible to apply the concept of communion in analogous fashion to the union existing among particular churches and to see the universal church as a communion of churches. Sometimes, however, the idea of a "communion of particular churches" is presented in such a way as to weaken the concept of the unity of the Church at the visible and institutional level. Thus it is asserted that every particular church is a subject complete in itself, and that the universal church is the result of a reciprocal recognition on the part of the particular churches. This ecclesiological unilateralism, which impoverishes not only the concept of the universal church but also that of the particular church, betrays an insufficient understanding of the concept of communion.

(The mutual interiority between the particular churches and the Church as a whole; the ontological and temporal priority of the universal Church)

900Bb 9. In order to grasp the true meaning of the analogical application of the term communion to the particular churches taken as a whole, one must bear in mind above all that particular churches, insofar as they are "part of the one Church of Christ" *[CD 6, 3]*, have a special relationship of "mutual interiority"[2] with the whole, that is with the universal church,

---

1. Cf. St. HILARY OF POITIERS, *In Psalm* 14, 3: *PL* 9, 301; St. GREGORY THE GREAT, *Moralia,* IV, 7, 12: *PL* 75, 643.

2. JOHN PAUL II, *Address to the Roman Curia,* in December 1990, no 9. *AAS* 83 (1991) 745-747.

because in every particular church "the one, holy, catholic and apostolic Church of Christ is truly present and active" [CD 11,1]. For this reason, "the universal church cannot be conceived as the sum of the particular churches or as a federation of particular churches".[1] It is not the result of the communion of the churches, but in its essential mystery it is a reality ontologically and temporally prior to every individual particular church.

(The relation of primacy to the particular church)

900Bc 13. But for each particular church to be fully church, that is, the particular presence of the universal church with all its essential elements, and hence constituted after the model of the universal church, there must be present in it, as a proper element, the supreme authority of the church: the episcopal college "together with their head, the supreme pontiff, and never apart from him" [LG 22, 2; cf. also 19]. The primacy of the bishop of Rome and the episcopal college are proper elements of the universal church that are "not derived from the particularity of the churches"[2] but are nevertheless interior to each particular church. Consequently "we must see the ministry of the successor of Peter not only as a 'global' service, reaching each particular church from 'outside', as it were, but as belonging already to the essence of each particular church from 'within'."[3] Indeed, the ministry of the primacy involves, in essence, a truly episcopal power which is not only supreme, full and universal but also immediate, over all, whether pastors or other faithful[cf. Pastor Aeternus, Ch. 3:n. 830; LG 22, 2]. The ministry of the successor of Peter as something interior to each particular church is a necessary expression of that fundamental mutual interiority between universal church and particular church.[4]

---

1. JOHN PAUL II, *Address to the Bishops of the United States*, 16 September 1987, no. 3, in *Insegnamenti di Giovanni Paolo II*, X, 555.

2. JOHN PAUL II, *Address to be Roman Curia*, no. 9.

3. JOHN PAUL II, *Address to the Bishops of the United States*, no. 4.

4. JOHN PAUL II, *Address to the Bishops of the United States*, no. 9

JOHN PAUL II

ENCYCLICAL LETTER *VERITATIS SPLENDOR*
(6 August 1993)

"This is the first time, in fact," states VS 115, "that the Magisterium of the Church has set forth in detail the fundamental elements of [Christian moral] teaching, and presented the principles for the pastoral discernment necessary in practical and cultural situations which are complex and even crucial." Within this context, the encyclical also points out the deep connection between moral life and doctrine, on the one hand, and the unity of the Church on the other. The text can be found in AAS 85 (1993) 1133-1228.

(The essential unity of the church in moral life and doctrine)

900Ca 26. [...]No damage must be done to the harmony between faith and life: the unity of the Church is damaged not only by Christians who reject or distort the truths of faith but also by those who disregard the moral obligations to which they are called by the Gospel [cf. 1 Cor 5:9-13]. The Apostles decisively rejected any separation between the commitment of the heart and the actions which express or prove it [cf. 1 Jn 2:3-6]. And ever since Apostolic times the Church's pastors have unambiguously condemned the behaviour of those who fostered divisions by their teaching or by their actions.

(The competence of pastors in teaching moral doctrine)

900Cb 27. Within the unity of the Church, promoting and preserving the faith and the moral life is the task entrusted by Jesus to the Apostles [cf. Mt. 28:19-20], a task which continues in the ministry of their successors. This is apparent from the living Tradition, whereby—as the Second Vatican Council teaches—"the Church, in her teaching, life and worship, perpetuates and hands on to every generation all that she is and all that she believes" [DV 8]. [...]

In particular, as the Council affirms, "the task of authentically interpreting the word of God, whether in its written form or in that of the Tradition, has been entrusted only to those charged with the Church's living Magisterium, whose authority is exercised in the name of Jesus Christ" (DV 10). The Church, in her life and teaching is thus revealed as "the pillar and bulwark of the truth" [1 Tim 3:15], including the truth regarding moral action.

(In virtue of the supernatural sense of the faith [sensus fidei], the whole body of the faithful cannot be mistaken in belief)

900Cc 109.[...] Thanks to the permanent presence of the Spirit of truth in the Church *[cf. Jn. 14:16-17]*, "the universal body of the faithful who have received the anointing of the holy one *[cf. 1 Jn 2:20, 27]* cannot be mistaken in belief. It displays this particular quality through a supernatural sense of the faith in the whole people when, 'from the Bishops to the last of the lay faithful', it expresses the consensus of all in matters of faith and morals" *[LG 12]*.

MOTU PROPRIO *APOSTOLOS SUOS*
(21 May 1998)

Vatican II's decree on bishops, Christus Dominus, 37, *stated that "it would be in the highest degree helpful if in all parts of the world the bishops of each country or region would meet regularly, so that by sharing their wisdom and experience and exchanging views they may jointly formulate a program for the common good of the church." In 1966, with the* motu proprio *"Ecclesiae Sanctae," Paul VI called for episcopal conferences to be established wherever they did not yet exist. The Extraordinary Synod of Bishops of 1985, celebrating the twentieth anniversary of the close of the council, called for a fuller and more profound study of the theological and juridical status of episcopal conferences. The present document is a fruit of that study, its aim being "to set out the basic principles [...] indispensable for helping to establish a theologically well-grounded and juridically sound praxis for the conferences" (paragraph 7). The text can be found in* AAS 90, 1998, 641-658.

(The collegial union of bishops and the unity of the church)

900Da 8.[...] The unity of the episcopacy is one of the constitutive elements of the unity of the church. In fact, through the body of bishops "the apostolic tradition is manifested and preserved throughout the world" *[Lumen Gentium 20]*, and the essential components of ecclesial communion are the sharing of the same faith, the deposit of which is entrusted to their care, the taking part in the same sacraments, "the regular and fruitful distribution of which they direct by their authority" *[Lumen Gentium 26]*, and the loyalty and obedience shown to them as pastors of the church. This communion, precisely because it extends throughout the whole church, forms the structure also of the college of bishops, and is "an organic reality which demands a juridical form, and is at the same time animated by charity" *[Lumen Gentium, Nota Explicativa Praevia 2]*.

(The collegial exercise of supreme power in the church; the bishops are not vicars or delegates of the pope)

900Db 9.[...] The supreme power which the body of bishops possesses over the whole church cannot be exercised by them except collegially, either in a solemn way when they gather together in ecumenical council or spread throughout the world, provided that the Roman pontiff calls them to act collegially or at least freely accepts their joint action. In such collegial acts the bishops exercise a power which is proper to them for the good of their faithful and of the whole church, and although conscientiously respecting the primacy and pre-eminence of the Roman pontiff, head of the college of bishops, they are not acting as his vicars or delegates. There it is clear that they are acting as bishops of the Catholic Church, for the benefit of the whole church, and as such they are recognized and respected by the faithful.

(The power of the college of bishops and the "affectus collegialis")

900Dc 12. When the bishops of a territory jointly exercise certain pastoral functions for the good of their faithful, such joint exercise of the episcopal ministry is a concrete application of collegial spirit *(affectus collegialis)*, which "is the soul of the collaboration between the bishops at the regional, national and international levels" *[Synod of 1985, Relazione finale, II, C, 4].* Nonetheless, this territorially based exercise of the episcopal ministry never takes on the collegial nature proper to the actions of the order of bishops as such, which alone holds the supreme power over the whole church. In fact, the relationship between the individual bishops and the college of bishops is quite different from their relationship to the bodies set up for the above-mentioned joint exercise of certain pastoral tasks.

[...] Likewise the college of bishops is not to be understood as the aggregate of the bishops who govern the particular churches nor as the result of their communion; rather, as an essential element of the universal church it is a reality which precedes the office of being the head of a particular church. In fact, the power of the college of bishops over the whole church is not the result of the sum of the powers of the individual bishops over their particular churches; it is a pre-existing reality in which individual bishops participate. They have no competence to act over the whole church except collegially. Only the Roman pontiff, head of the college, can individually exercise supreme power over the church. In other words, "episcopal collegiality in the strict and proper sense belongs only to the entire college of bishops, which as a theological subject is indivisible" [John Paul II, *Discourse to the Roman Curia*, Dec. 20, 1990, n. 6]. And this is the express will of the Lord [cf. *Lumen Gentium* 22]. This power, however, should not be understood as dominion; rather, essential to it is the notion of service, because it is derived from Christ, the Good Shepherd who lays down his life for the sheep.

(Description and competence of episcopal conferences)

900Dd 14. Episcopal conferences constitute a concrete application of the collegial spirit. Basing itself on the prescriptions of the Second Vatican Council, the Code of Canon Law gives a precise description: "The conference of bishops, a permanent institution, is a grouping of bishops of a given country or territory whereby, according to the norm of law, they jointly exercise certain pastoral functions on behalf of the Christian faithful of their territory in view of promoting that great good which the church offers humankind, especially through forms and programs of the apostolate which are fittingly adapted to the circumstances of the time and place" *[canon 447]*.

15.[...] It escapes no one that issues which currently call for the joint action of bishops include the promotion and safeguarding of faith and morals, the translation of liturgical books, the promotion and formation of priestly vocations, the preparation of catechetical aids, the promotion and safeguarding of Catholic universities and other educational centers, the ecumenical task, relations with civil authorities, the defense of human life, of peace and of human rights, also in order to ensure their protection in civil legislation, the promotion of social justice, the use of the means of social communication, etc.

(Relation of the episcopal conference to the individual bishop)

900De 19. The authority of the episcopal conference and its field of action are in strict relation to the authority and action of the diocesan bishop and the bishops equivalent to them in law. Bishops "preside in the place of God over the flock whose shepherds they are as teachers of doctrine, priests of sacred worship and ministers of government. [...] By divine institution, bishops have succeeded to the apostles as shepherds of the church" [*Lumen Gentium 20*], and they "govern the particular churches entrusted to them as the vicars and ambassadors of Christ by their counsel, exhortations and example, but also by their authority and sacred power.[...] This power, which they personally exercise in Christ's name, is proper, ordinary and immediate" [*Lumen Gentium 27*]. Its exercise is regulated by the supreme authority of the church, and this is the necessary consequence of the relation between the universal church and the particular church, since the latter exists only as a portion of the people of God "in which the one catholic church is truly present and operative" [*Christus Dominus 11*].[...]

20. In the episcopal conference the bishops jointly exercise the episcopal ministry for the good of the faithful of the territory of the conference, but for the exercise to be legitimate and binding on the individual bishops there is needed the intervention of the supreme authority of the church which, through universal law or particular mandates, entrusts determined questions to the deliberation of the episcopal conference.

(The episcopal conference in relation to the teaching office of bishops)

900Df 21.[...] The concerted voice of the bishops of a determined territory, when in communion with the Roman pontiff they jointly proclaim the catholic truth in matters of faith and morals, can reach their people more effectively and can make it easier for their faithful to adhere to the magisterium with a sense of religious respect. In faithfully exercising their teaching office, the bishops serve the word of God, to which their teaching is subject, they listen to it devoutly, guard it scrupulously and explain it faithfully in such a way that the faithful can receive it in the best manner possible.

22. In dealing with new questions and in acting so that the message of Christ enlightens and guides people's consciences in resolving new problems arising from changes in society, the bishops assembled in the episcopal conference and jointly exercising their teaching office are well aware of the limits of their pronouncements. While being official and authentic and in communion with the Apostolic See, these pronouncements do not have the characteristics of a universal magisterium.[...]

Taking into account that the authentic magisterium of the bishops, namely what they teach insofar as they are invested with the authority of Christ, must always be in communion with the head of the college and its members, when the doctrinal declarations of episcopal conferences are approved unanimously they may certainly be issued in the name of the conferences themselves, and the faithful are obliged to adhere with a sense of religious respect to that authentic magisterium of their own bishops. However, if this unanimity is lacking, a majority alone of the bishops of a conference cannot issue a declaration as authentic teaching of the conference to which all the faithful of the territory would have to adhere, unless it obtains the *recognitio* of the Apostolic See, which will not give it if the majority requesting it is not substantial.

(The episcopal conference as an aid and not an obstacle to the effective ministry of the individual bishop)

900Dg 24. At present, episcopal conferences fulfill many tasks for the good of the church. They are called to support in a growing service "the inalienable responsibility of each bishop in relation to the universal church and to his particular church" [*Synod of 1985, Relazione finale*, II, C, 5] and naturally not to hinder it by substituting themselves inappropriately for him where the canonical legislation does not provide for a limitation of his episcopal power in favour of the episcopal conference or by acting as a filter or obstacle as far as direct contact between the individual bishops and the Apostolic See is concerned.

(Complementary norms regarding the conferences of bishops)

900Dh Article 1- In order that the doctrinal declarations of the conference of bishops referred to in No. 22 of the present letter may constitute authentic magisterium and be published in the name of the conference itself, they must be unanimously approved by the bishops who are members or receive the *recognitio* of the Apostolic See if approved in plenary assembly by at least two-thirds of the bishops belonging to the conference and having a deliberative vote.

Article 2- No body of the episcopal conference outside of the plenary assembly has the power to carry out acts of authentic magisterium. The episcopal conference cannot grant such power to its commissions or other bodies set up by it.

Article 3- For statements of a different kind, different from those mentioned in Article 2, the doctrinal commission of the conference of bishops must be authorized explicitly by the permanent council of the conference.

Article 4- The episcopal conferences are to review their statutes in order that they may be consistent with the clarifications and norms of the present document as well as the Code of Canon Law[...].

CONGREGATION FOR THE DOCTRINE OF THE FAITH
REFLECTIONS ON THE PRIMACY OF PETER

(30 October 1998)

In his 1995 encyclical on ecumenism, Ut unum sint, *Pope John Paul II invited the leaders of other Christian communities, along with their theologians, to dialogue with him about how the ministry of primacy might be exercised in a way which, "while in no way renouncing what is essential to its mission, is nonetheless open to a new situation" (see, below, n. 937c). As part of its contribution to such a dialogue, the Congregation for the Doctrine of the Faith organized a symposium concerning "The Primacy of the Successor of Peter in the Mystery of the Church" in December of 1996. The following reflections by the Congregation were appended to the Acts of this symposium, published in 1998, and "are meant only to recall the essential points of Catholic doctrine on the primacy." The text can be found in* Origins 28, *1998-1999, 560-563.*

(Origin, purpose and development of Petrine ministry)

900Ea 3.[...] In Peter's person, mission and ministry, in his presence and death in Rome—attested to by the most ancient literary and archeological tradition—the church sees a deeper reality essentially related to her own mystery of communion and salvation: *"Ubi Petrus, ibi ergo Ecclesia"* [St. Ambrose of Milan, *Enarr. in Ps., 40, 30*]. From the beginning and with increasing clarity, the church has understood that just as there is a succession of the apostles in the ministry of bishops, so too the ministry of unity entrusted to Peter belongs to the permanent structure of Christ's church and that this succession is established in the see of his martyrdom.

4. On the basis of the New Testament witness, the Catholic Church teaches as doctrine of faith that the bishop of Rome is the successor of Peter in his primatial service in the universal church; this succession explains the pre-eminence of the church of Rome, enriched also by the preaching and martyrdom of St. Paul.

In the divine plan for the primacy as "the office that was given individually by the Lord to Peter, the first of the apostles, and to be handed on to his successors" [*Lumen gentium 20*], we already see the purpose of the Petrine charism, i.e., "the unity of faith and communion" [*Pastor aeternus,* Prologue] of all believers. The Roman Pontiff, as the successor of Peter, is "the perpetual and visible principle and foundation of unity both of the bishops and of the multitude of the faithful" [*Lumen gentium 23*], and therefore he has a specific ministerial grace for serving that unity of faith and communion which is necessary for the church to fulfill her saving mission [cf. *Jn* 17:21-23].

(Harmony between primatial and episcopal ministry)

900Eb 5. The constitution *Pastor Aeternus* of the First Vatican Council indicated the purpose of the primacy in its prologue and then dedicated the body of the text to explaining the content or scope of its power. The Second Vatican Council, in turn, reaffirmed and completed the teaching of Vatican I, addressing primarily the theme of its purpose, with particular attention to the mystery of the church as *corpus ecclesiarum*. This consideration allowed for a clearer exposition of how the primatial office of the bishop of Rome and the office of the other bishops are not in opposition, but in fundamental harmony.

Therefore, "when the Catholic Church affirms that the office of the bishop of Rome corresponds to the will of Christ, she does not separate this office from the mission entrusted to the whole body of bishops, who are also 'vicars and ambassadors of Christ' (*Lumen Gentium* 27). The bishop of Rome is a member of the 'college,' and the bishops are his brothers in the ministry" [*Ut Unum Sint 95*]. It should also be said, reciprocally, that episcopal collegiality does not stand in opposition to the personal exercise of the primacy nor should it relativize it.

(The pastoral care of the whole church)

900 Ec 6. All the bishops are subjects of the *sollicitudo omnium ecclesiarum* [*2 Cor. 11:28*] as members of the episcopal college which has succeeded to the college of the apostles, to which the extraordinary figure of St. Paul also belonged. This universal dimension of their *episkopê* (overseeing) cannot be separated from the particular dimension of the offices entrusted to them. In the case of the bishop of Rome—Vicar of Christ in the way proper to Peter as head of the college of bishop—the *sollicitudo omnium ecclesiarum* acquires particular force because it is combined with the full and supreme power in the church: a truly episcopal power, not only supreme, full and universal, but also immediate, over all pastors and other faithful. The ministry of Peter's successor, therefore is not a service that reaches each church from outside, but is inscribed in the heart of each particular church, in which "the church of Christ is truly present and active" [*Christus Dominus 11*], and for this reason it includes openness to the ministry of unity. This interiority of the bishop of Rome's ministry to each particular church is also an expression of the mutual interiority between universal church and particular church.

(Divine institution of the primatial-episcopal structure of the Church; providential origin of the patriarchates)

900Ed 6.[...] The episcopacy and the primacy, reciprocally related and inseparable, are of divine institution. Historically there arose forms of ecclesiastical organization instituted by the church in which a primatial principle was also practiced. In particular, the Catholic Church is well aware of the role of the apostolic sees in the early church, especially those considered Petrine—Antioch and Alexandria—as reference points of the apostolic tradition, and around which the patriarchal system developed; this system is one of the ways God's providence guides the church, and from the beginning it has included a relation to the Petrine tradition.

(Limits to the exercise of primatial authority)

900Ee 7.[...] The primacy differs in its essence and in its exercise from the offices of governance found in human societies: it is not an office of coordination or management, nor can it be reduced to a primacy of honour or be conceived as a political monarchy.

The Roman pontiff—like all the faithful—is subject to the word of God, to the Catholic faith and is the guarantor of the church's obedience; in this sense he is *servus servorum Dei*. He does not make arbitrary decisions, but is spokesman for the will of the Lord, who speaks to man in the Scriptures lived and interpreted by tradition; in other words, the *episkopê* of the primacy has limits set by divine law and by the church's divine, inviolable constitution found in revelation. The successor of Peter is the rock which guarantees a rigorous fidelity to the word of God against arbitrariness and conformism: hence the martyrological nature of his primacy.

(The teaching office of the successor of Peter)

900Ef   9. Given its episcopal nature, the primacy of the bishop of Rome is first of all expressed in transmitting the word of God; thus it includes a specific, particular responsibility for the mission of evangelization, since ecclesial communion is something essentially meant to be expanded: "Evangelization is the grace and vocation proper to the church, her deepest identity" [*Evangelii Nuntiandi 14*].

The Roman pontiff's episcopal responsibility for transmission of the word of God also extends within the whole church. As such, it is a supreme and universal magisterial office; it is an office that involves a charism: the Holy Spirit's special assistance to the successor of Peter, which also involves, in certain cases, the prerogative of infallibility.

(The governing office of the successor of Peter)

900Eg   10. Together with the magisterial role of the primacy, the mission of Peter's successor for the whole church entails the right to perform acts of ecclesiastical governance necessary or suited to promoting and defending the unity of faith and communion[...] Since the power of the primacy is supreme, there is no other authority to which the Roman pontiff must juridically answer for his exercise of the gift he has received: *"Prima sedes a nemine iudicatur"* [*Canon* 1404; *Eastern Canon* 1058]. This does not mean, however, that the pope has absolute power. Listening to what the churches are saying is, in fact, an earmark of the ministry of unity, a consequence also of the unity of the episcopal body and of the *sensus fidei* of the entire people of God; and this bond seems to enjoy considerably greater power and certainty than the juridical authorities—an inadmissible hypothesis, moreover, because it is groundless—to which the Roman pontiff would supposedly have to answer. The ultimate and absolute responsibility of the pope is best guaranteed, on the one hand, by its relationship to tradition and fraternal communion, and, on the other, by trust in the assistance of the Holy Spirit, who governs the church.

(The relation of primacy of the church's life of worship)

900Eh 11. The unity of the church, which the ministry of Peter's successor serves in a unique way, reaches its highest expression in the eucharistic sacrifice, which is the centre and root of ecclesial communion; this communion is also necessarily based on the unity of the episcopate. Therefore, "every celebration of the eucharist is performed in union not only with the proper bishop, but also with the pope, with the episcopal order, with all the clergy, and with the entire people. Every valid celebration of the eucharist expresses this universal communion with Peter and with the whole church, or objectively calls for it" *[Congregation for the Doctrine of the Faith, Aspects of the Church as Communion, 14]*, as in the case of churches which are not in full communion with the Apostolic See.

(Discerning the ways of exercising the Petrine ministry)

900Ei 12.[...] The concrete contents of its exercise distinguish the Petrine ministry insofar as they faithfully express the application of its ultimate purpose (the unity of the church) to the circumstances of time and place. The greater or lesser extent of these concrete contents will depend in every age on the *necessitas ecclesiae*. The Holy Spirit helps the church to recognize this necessity, and the Roman pontiff, by listening to the Spirit's voice in the churches, looks for the answer and offers it when and how he considers it appropriate.

13. In any case, it is essential to state that discerning whether the possible ways of exercising the Petrine ministry correspond to its nature is a discernment to be made *in ecclesia*, i.e., with the assistance of the Holy Spirit and in fraternal dialogue between the Roman pontiff and the other bishops, according to the church's concrete needs. But at the same time it is clear that only the pope (or the pope with an ecumenical council) has, as the successor of Peter, the authority and the competence to say the last word on the ways to exercise his pastoral ministry in the church.

(Primatial ministry and the reestablishment of full communion)

900Ej 15. The full communion which the Lord desires among those who profess themselves his disciples calls for the common recognition of a universal ecclesial ministry "in which all the bishops recognize that they are united in Christ and all the faithful find confirmation for their faith" [*Ut Unum Sint* 97]. The Catholic Church professes that this ministry is the primatial ministry of the Roman pontiff, successor of Peter, and maintains humbly and firmly "that the communion of the particular churches with the church of Rome, and of their bishops with the bishop of Rome, is—in God's plan—an essential requisite of full and visible communion" [*ibid.*]. Human errors and even serious failings can be found in the history of the papacy; Peter himself acknowledged he was a sinner [*Lk 5:8*]. Peter, a weak man, was chosen as the rock precisely so that everyone could see that victory belongs to Christ alone and is not the result of human efforts. Down the ages the Lord has wished to put his treasure in fragile vessels [*cf. 2 Cor 4:7*]: Human frailty has thus become a sign of the truth of God's promises.

JOHN PAUL II
APOSTOLIC EXHORTATION *ECCLESIA IN ASIA*
(6 November 1999)

As part of the preparation for the celebration of the two thousandth anniversary of the birth of Christ, Pope John Paul II adopted the suggestion of various cardinals and bishops that regional synods be held to address the evangelical task of the Church in the various continents at the dawn of the new millennium (cf. Tertio Millennio adveniente, *38). This appeal was made shortly after the close of the Special Assembly of Synod of Bishops for Africa (April 10 - May 8, 1994), whose theme was: "The Church in Africa and its Mission of Evangelization Towards the Year 2000; 'You Shall Be My Witnesses' (Acts 1:8)." Other continental synods followed: the Special Assembly for America (November 16 - December 12, 1997), with the theme "Encounter with the Living Jesus Christ: The Way to Conversion, Communion and Solidarity"; the Special Assembly for Asia (April 18 - May 14, 1998), whose theme was "Jesus Christ the Saviour and His Mission of Love and Service in Asia:'... that they may have life, and have it abundantly' (Jn 10:10)"; the Special Assembly for Oceania (November 22 - December 12, 1998), with the theme "Jesus Christ and the Peoples of Oceania: Walking His Way, Telling His Truth, Living His Life"; and the second Special Assembly for Europe (October 1_23, 1999), whose theme was "Jesus Christ Alive in His Church, Source of Hope for Europe."*

The documentation for each of these synods includes not only the post-synodal apostolic exhortation by the Holy Father, who has chosen to entitle them with the similar opening phrase "Ecclesia in Africa, ...America, ...Asia, ...Oceania, ...Europa." Also important are the series of texts which belong to the synodal process as a whole, principally the Lineamenta, *the* Instrumentum laboris, *and the various texts which emerge during the synod itself, such as the addresses of the individual bishops and observers, the message and the propositions. The value of this material lies in its exploration of ways of more effective evangelization in light of the particular situation of the Catholic Church in the various continents. Such continental synods represent a rather unique post-Vatican II exercise of episcopal ministry in which the primatial service to the unity of the universal church collaborates in a special way with the bishops of a particular region as they address the particular challenges for evangelization in their local churches. The pope refers to those synods in his post-synodal exhortation for Asia. The text is found in AAS 92 (2000) 449-528.*

(On continental synods of bishops)

900F   2. In my apostolic letter *Tertio Millennio Adveniente*, I set out a programme for the Church to welcome the Third Millennium of Christianity, a programme centred on the challenge of the new evangelization. An important feature of that plan was the holding of *continental synods* so that the bishops could address the question of evangelization according to the particular situation and needs of each continent. This series of synods, linked by the common theme of the new evangelization, has proved an important part of the Church's preparation for the Great Jubilee of the Year 2000.

CHAPTER IX

THE CHURCH AND THE CHURCHES

In view of the perfect Kingdom of the future, the Church is sent into the world to be the efficacious sign and instrument of the reconciling grace of Christ, drawing men and women into a unity of faith, hope and love, across all the barriers of sin and human division. It is, therefore, and is called to be the sacrament of unity (cf. LG 1), a unity that is at once visible and invisible, human and divine. Yet from the very beginning of the life and mission of the Church there were rifts, and in the course of the centuries large bodies of Christians were separated from one another, and continue to this day to live in isolation and opposition. This is the scandal of Christian disunity, and the problem and challenge of ecumensim, which seeks the restoration of unity among Christians in one visible communion, in the one Church of Christ.

In the first millennium of the Church's history movements toward disunity were blunted and checked by the great Councils of the times, especially the first four. Arianism, Donatism, Novatianism, Priscillianism, Montanism and Nestorianism—all movements that could have torn the Church apart—were rejected by the Councils and gradually disappeared, not without the help of the secular power. Yet the efforts to preserve the unity of the Church were not completely successful: the Monophysite Churches, which rejected the Council of Chalcedon (431), still exist today, mainly in Egypt and Ethiopia.

The first great and lasting division between Christians was that between the Churches of the East and the Church of the West. The gradual estrangement between West and East took a decisive turning point in 1054 with the severing of relations between the patriarch of Constantinople and the pope. Even then the break was not complete, and two attempts were made on the conciliar level to heal the wounds of disunity. The first was that of the Council of Lyons (1274), when the emperor Michael Palaeologus accepted the Roman terms of reunion. Politically motivated, and manifesting little understanding of the theological and ecclesial position of the East, the settlement was doomed to failure from the beginning. The second was that of the

Council of Florence (1439 - 1445), in which East and West took part as equal partners, and real agreement was reached in the disputed question of the Filioque. *However, agreement was only apparent with regard to the understanding of the primacy of the Pope, especially in its relationship to the rights and privileges of the patriarchs of the East. Officially rejected in 1483, the union actually came to an end as early as 1453 when Constantinople was captured by the Turks. Both before and after these attempts to reunite East and West, individual Eastern Churches or sections of these Churches again entered into communion with Rome, e.g., the Maronites already in the 13th century, the Byzantine Ukranians at the union of Brest-Litovsk in 1595, the Malankara Catholics in India in the 20th century. Despite considerable degree of latinisation, these "Uniate Churches" have preserved their own spirituality, liturgy, and, to a lesser extent, their own ecclesiastical structures within Catholic communion.*

As a result of the upheaval of the Protestant Reformation in the 16th century, the Church in the West was split into numerous Churches and Ecclesial Communities. In the early part of the 16th century, before positions hardened, attempts were made to stem the tide of division. But the leaders of the Catholic Church did not at first realise the seriousness of the situation; the Protestants too were unwilling to compromise and, in drawing up their own confessional statements, they settled down into their own separate communities. Desire for reconciliation gave way to polemics and mutual antagonism, and from the 17th century to almost the present day little serious effort was made to bring about union with the Protestants. In fact the ecclesiology of the counter-Reformation with its understanding of the Church as one visible hierarchical society left little or no room for dialogue with the Protestant communities as such. It is against the historical background and in relation to the ecclesiology of the times that the documents issued by the Magisterium in the 19th century and at the beginning of the 20th century must be read and understood.

The renewed ecclesiology which found its official expression in the Second Vatican Council offers possibilities to approach the ecumenical problems in a new light. Its vision is no longer limited to the firmly established Catholic Church to which all must return; it starts from the divine plan for the human race and the common Christian calling. It is God's will that the Christian life be lived in a visible community which is one and comprehensive; a community which prefigures the final communion to which all nations are called at the end of time. This mystery of unity is sacramentally present in the Catholic Church, but is also expressed, in various degrees, in other Christian communities; they too may contain ecclesial elements by virtue of which they may be called Churches. Vatican II no longer views these communities in their deficiencies only; it sees the positive values of their life and traditions. Thus the solution to the problem of Christian unity is no longer sought by merely inviting other Christians to join the Catholic Church, but by integrating into the one Church willed by Christ whatever Christian values are found also in non-Catholic Christian communities. The aim must be the fulness of the Christian life, comprising all traditions, for "whatever is truly Christian is never opposed to the genuine values of the faith; indeed it can always help to a better realisation of the mystery of Christ and the Church" (UR 4).

All the documents given here belong to the 19th and 20th centuries; they are a rapid survey of the evolution in the attitude of the Catholic Church towards the ecumenical movement characteristic of modern times. Earlier pertinent documents are found in other chapters, especially in the chapter on the Church. Besides, the doctrinal differences that separate Christians cover almost the entire spectrum of christian doctrine; these are dealt with directly under their specific headings.

* * *

The main points of doctrine covered in this chapter may be grouped under the following headings:

The Church is the sacrament of unity: (866), 888, 889.
The sole Church of Christ subsists in the Catholic Church in which is found the fulness of the means of salvation: (869), 909, 932f;
but it is also present, though imperfectly and in various degrees, in Churches and ecclesial communities which do not have full communion with Rome: 39/15, (872) 909.
In particular, the Eastern Churches separated from Rome share with it the same faith and sacramental life: 904, 914, 930a, 938.
The Church's reform is an essential requirement for Church unity: 910, 911, 933a, 933c, 936a.
The status and privileges of the Eastern patriarchates must be respected: 809, 900Ed, 906.
*On proselytism, especially regarding the Eastern Churches :*930b.
The ancient traditions and customs of these Churches must also be preserved: 914, 1206, 1207, 1235-1236.
All Christians must strive after Christian unity: 39/15, 902, 903, 905, 907, 908, 914, 933b.

The hierarchy of truths must be kept in mind: 913.

Principles for common worship: 912.

Principles for admission of other Christians to the Eucharist: 915.

Dialogue with the Orthodox Churches : 916-921.

Dialogue with the Communities of the Reformation: 922-927, 940.

Importance of historical truth in ecumenism: 928, 933a, 938, 939, 940.

The nature of the ecumenical movement: 908, 909i, 922, 929, 932a, 932g, 933c, 939.

The relation of ecumenism to the ecclesiology of communion: 914, 915, 918, 921, 932b, 932c, 932d, 932e, 939.

Unity in faith: 816, 826, 835, 849, 900Ca, 904, 907a, 913, 915, 917, 920, 992, 924, 925, 929, 931, 932c, 932h, 935b, 938. 940.

Unity includes diversity: 852, 885, 891, 895, 897, 914, 930a, 932b, 932c, 932g, 934a-b, 935c-d, 940.

Church unity in relation to the Successor to Peter: 804, 809, 818, 826, 900Ej, 909, 917, 932b, 932f, 937a-c.

PIUS IX

LETTER *IAM VOS OMNES* TO PROTESTANTS AND OTHER NON-CATHOLICS
(13 September 1868)

After announcing to them his intention to convoke a general Council, the Pope invites Christians who are not Catholics to examine whether or not they are walking in the way of salvation, and to seize upon the occasion of the Council to return to the unity of the Catholic Church. The text is from ASS 4 (1868) 131-135.

(Religious societies separated from Rome do not constitute the true Church)

901
2998
Now anyone who wishes to examine with care and to meditate on the condition of the different religious societies divided among themselves and separated from the Catholic Church, who, since the time of our Lord Jesus Christ and his apostles has always exercised by her legitimate pastors and still exercises today the divine power which was given to her by the same Lord, will easily be convinced that no one of these societies nor all of them together in any way constitute or are that one Catholic Church which our Lord founded and established and which he willed to create. Nor is it possible, either, to say that these societies are either a number or a part of this same Church, since they are visibly separated from Catholic unity. [...]

(Exhortation to return to the Catholic Church)

902
2999
Let all those, therefore, who do not possess the unity and truth of the Catholic Church seize upon this occasion of the Council, where the Catholic Church to which their ancestors belonged is going to give again a striking proof of her unity and her invincible life-force, to strive conformably to the needs of their hearts to disengage themselves from a state where they cannot be assured of their own salvation. And let them not cease to offer the most fervent prayers to the God of mercies so that he will break down the wall of division, dissipate the clouds of error, and bring them back to holy Mother Church, in the bosom of which their fathers found the saving food of life, in which alone is kept and transmitted in its entirety the doctrine of Jesus Christ, and where alone are dispensed the mysteries of heavenly grace.[...]

ENCYCLICAL LETTER *QUARTUS SUPRA* TO THE ARMENIANS (6 January 1873)

This Encyclical Letter was addressed by Pope Pius IX to the Armenians in the context of a recent schism among them. The Pope strongly urges the indispensable need of recognition of and communion with the apostolic See of Rome in order for a local Church to be truly part of the Church of Christ. The text is found in ASS 7 (1873) 225-253.

903   If, therefore, the sovereign Pontiff is called a stranger by any one of the Churches, that Church will be, in consequence, a stranger to the apostolic See, that is, to the Catholic Church which is one, and which alone was founded on Peter by the Lord's word. Whoever separates the Church from this foundation no longer preserves the divine and Catholic Church, but is striving to make a human church. Now a church like that, united solely by human bonds, bonds that are called national, would not be united by the bond of priests firmly attached to the Chair of Peter; it would not be made firm by the solidity of that same Chair, and would not belong to the universal and perfect unity of the Catholic Church.

LEO XIII

ENCYCLICAL LETTER *PRAECLARA GRATULATIONIS* (20 June 1894)

Written on the occasion of the fiftieth anniversary of his episcopal consecration, this letter by Pope Leo XIII expresses a sincere and ardent desire for Christian unity. In its appeal to first the Eastern Churches, and then the Protestant 'nations', it brings out clearly the consistent recognition by the Roman Pontiffs of the ecclesial status of the Eastern Churches separated from Rome. They are always referred to as 'Churches'; the appeal made to them is for the re-establishment of full communion with the See of Rome. The often repeated assurance is given that in any reunion with Rome, the special status and privileges of the Patriarchates (cf. n 809), as well as the ancient traditions and customs of these Churches (cf. n. 1206) will be fully respected and safeguarded. Though in practice some latinisation of the oriental Catholic Churches did occur—as was, perhaps, inevitable in the ecclesial situation of the time—the affirmation of the principle of legitimate diversity was in itself significant. It is all the more important today in the context of a broader ecclesiology. The text is found in ASS 16 (1894) 705-717.

904   First of all, then, we cast an affectionate look upon the East, from where in the beginning came forth salvation to the whole world. Yes, and the yearning desire of our heart bids us to conceive the hope that the day is not far distant when the Eastern Churches, so illustrious in their ancient faith and glorious past, will return to the fold they have abandoned. We hope it, all the more, because that which divides them from us is not so great: nay, with few exceptions, we agree so entirely on other topics that, in defence of the Catholic faith, we often have recourse to arguments and testimonies borrowed from the teaching, the rites, and customs of the East. [...]

905   Weigh carefully in your minds and before God the nature of our request. It is not for any human motive, but impelled by divine charity and a desire for the salvation of all, that we urge your reconciliation and union with the Church of Rome; and we mean a perfect and complete union, such as could not subsist in any way if nothing else were brought about but a certain degree of agreement in the tenets of belief and an exchange of fraternal love. The true union between Christians, and that which Jesus Christ, the Author of the Church, instituted and desired, consists in oneness of faith and of government.

906   Nor is there any reason for you to fear that we or any of our successors will ever diminish your rights, the privileges of the patriarchs, or the established rite of any one of your Churches. It has been and always will be the intent and discipline of the apostolic See, to allow a just and good place to the primitive traditions and special customs of every nation. Indeed, if you return to communion with us, you will see how much, by God's bounty, the glory and dignity of your Churches will be increased.[...]

PIUS XI

ENCYCLICAL LETTER *MORTALIUM ANIMOS*
(6 January 1928)

This letter, which was occasioned by the Faith and Order Conference held at Lausanne in 1927, took a very negative attitude towards the modern ecumenical movement. The Pope condemned wholesale the various conferences, Congresses and assemblies of the time, which sought to bring about unity among Christians. The reasons for this stern attitude was the persuasion that the movement among "pan-Christians", as he called them, was based on a false religious indifferentism which "holds any religion whatever to be more or less good and praiseworthy, although not all in the same way, because they all reveal and explain the significance of the native, inborn instinct which turns us towards God and makes us acknowledge his sovereignty". While forbidding Catholics to have anything to do with this movement, the Pope laid down the principles which should guide Catholics at all times. There can be no true religion other than that revealed by God. That revelation, which reached its perfection in Jesus Christ, has been entrusted by him to the one and only Church which he founded on Peter. This Church, which is a perfect society, remains always indentical to itself and visibly one. It is the guardian of the immutable deposit of revelation, and, within it, it belongs to the Roman Pontiff and the Bishops in communion with him to teach authoritatively and infallibly the deposit of faith. This document, which must be read in the context of the narrow ecclesiology of its time, concludes as follows. The text of the encyclical is found in ASS 20 (1928) 5-16.

907   It is clear, therefore, Venerable Brothers, why this apostolic See has never permitted its subjects to take part in the Congresses of non-Catholics. The union of Christians cannot be fostered otherwise than by promoting the return of the dissidents to the one true Church of Christ, which in the past they so unfortunately abandoned; return, we say, to the one true Church of Christ which is plainly visible to all and which by the will of her Founder forever remains what he himself destined her to be for the common salvation of human beings. For the mystical Spouse of Christ has never been contaminated in the course of centuries, nor will she ever be contaminated. [...] No one is in the Church of Christ, and no one remains in it, unless he acknowledges and accepts with obedience the authority and power of Peter and his legitimate successors.[...] Therefore to this apostolic See, founded in the City which Peter and Paul, the princes of the apostles, consecrated with their blood, to this See which is the 'root and matrix of the Catholic Church,' may our dissident children return; let them do so, not with the thought and hope that the Church of the living God, the pillar and ground of the truth, will sacrifice the integrity of the faith, but on the contrary, with the intention of submitting to her authority and government.[...]

(Because faith responds to the authority of God who reveals, one cannot consider some doctrines as non-fundamental and, therefore, optional)

907a   Besides, as to those things which must be believed, it is in no way allowed to use that distinction which some have thought fit to introduce between articles of faith which are called fundamental and those called non-fundamental, as if some must be accepted by all and others may be left to the free assent of the faithful. For the supernatural virtue of faith has as its formal object the authority of the revealing God, an authority which does not allow for a distinction of this sort. Wherefore, all who are truly disciples of Christ adhere, for example, to the Immaculate Conception with the same faith as that in which they hold the mystery of the august Trinity and, similarly, faith in the incarnation of the Lord is not other than that in the infallible teaching office of the Roman pontiff, in the sense that it has been defined in the ecumenical Vatican synod. For while the Church sanctioned and defined various truths at various times, some even quite recently, are these not all equally certain and equally to be believed? Has not God revealed them all?

PIUS XII

INSTRUCTION *ECCLESIA CATHOLICA* OF THE HOLY OFFICE (20 December 1949)

This instruction is important because it marks a turning point in the official approach of the Catholic Church to the modern ecumenical movement. Within clearly defined limits, it encourages the ecumenical dialogue between Catholics and other Christians, though stopping short of any official Catholic participation in ecumenical conferences. More significantly, it takes a cautiously positive approach toward the ecumenical movement, and in this contrasts sharply with Pius XI's encyclical Mortalium animos. *Due to more recent developments in doctrine and in attitudes, the practical directives of the instruction have since been superseded. The text is found in AAS 42 (1950) 142-147.*

908　　The Catholic Church takes no part in 'Ecumenical' conferences or meetings. But, as may be seen from many papal documents, she has never ceased, nor ever will, from following with deepest interest and furthering with fervent prayer every attempt to attain that end which Christ our Lord had so much at heart, namely, that all who believe in him "may become perfectly one" *[Jn 17:23]*.[...] The present time has witnessed in different parts of the world a growing desire amongst many persons outside the Church for the reunion of all who believe in Christ. This may be attributed, under the inspiration fo the Holy Spirit, to external factors and the changing attitude of peoples' minds, but above all to the united prayers of the faithful. To all children of the true Church this is a cause for holy joy in the Lord; it urges them to extend a helping hand to all those sincerely seeking after truth by praying fervently that God may enlighten them and give them strength.[...]

THE SECOND VATICAN GENERAL COUNCIL

It was Pope John XXIII's explicit intention that the Second Vatican Council should have an ecumenical orientation. The creation of the Secretariat for Promoting Christian Unity in 1960 and the presence at the Council of observers from the other Churches helped to ensure this. The Council made its own the new perspectives in Catholic ecclesiology which had developed in the years preceding it, and whose renewed outlook also commanded new attitudes.

Symptomatic of the ecumenical apprach of the Council is the fact that references to ecumenism, in its theory and practice, pervade the various conciliar documents. The theological foundation for the new Catholic ecumenism is explained in the Dogmatic Constitution Lumen Gentium *(15): this fundamental text enumerates the ties that bind the Catholic Church in various ways to the members of other Churches or ecclesial communities (cf. n. 872). The Decree* Ad Gentes *on the Church's missionary activity recommends the right ecumenical orientation in newly founded Churches; it does not merely advocate practical collaboration between Christian communities, but also calls for a common witness of faith as far as the already existing unity in faith permits (15; cf. 12, 41). Ecumenical formation and orientation is expected to be given in seminaries (OT 16), especially in mission countries (AG 16), and among religious (PC 2). Special attention is given by the Council to the Oriental Churches. The Decree* Orientalium Ecclesiarum, *after paying due respect to the rich patrimony of the Oriental tradition and to the Oriental patriarchates, explains at length the Catholic Church's present attitude towards the Eastern Churches separated from it (24-30).*

DECREE *UNITATIS REDINTEGRATIO*
(21 November 1964)

Passing references to ecumenism could not, however, suffice. It was necessary that a special Decree be devoted to ecumenism, in which the fundamental principles and basic attitudes would be explicitly stated. The Decree Unitatis Redintegratio *was promulgated in November 1964 after prolonged debate. The openness of this decree and its positive evaluation of the other Christian Churches have no real precedent in official Church teaching. It proposes a clear and coherent theological foundation for the full and unequivocal participation of the Catholic Church in the modern ecumenical movement.*

The document is devided into an introduction and three Chapters. The introduction states the purpose of the decree, namely, to set before all Catholics the ways and means by which they can respond to the grace and divine call so obviously present in the concerted efforts of Christians everywhere to overcome the scandal of Christian disunity.

Chapter I is doctrinally the most important, for it lays down the Catholic principles of ecumenism: It exposes the mystery of the Church's unity as that of a dynamic communion in faith and sacramental life, at once visible and invisible, and it affirms that this communion is realised, acording to the will of Christ, in the Catholic Church governed by the Pope and the bishops in communion with him. The ecclesial reality and the salvific efficaciousness of the other Christian Communities, however, are also affirmed. They are said to be in real, though imperfect, communion with the Catholic Church, and the establishment of full and perfect communion which is hoped for is seen as enriching and perfecting not only the other communities, but also the Catholic Church itself.

Chapter II is concerned with the practice of ecumenism. Of special significance is the affirmation of the need for inner renewal and reform in the Church and for a conversion of heart, without which the Church cannot contribute to Christian unity. Also of ecumenical importance is the statement regarding the manner of exposing the faith: although the doctrine of the Church should be clearly presented in its entirety, it must be remembered that there is a "hierarchy" of truths, since not all the truths of Catholic doctrine are equally connected with the foundation of Christian faith (n. 912).

Chapter III turns the attention to a concrete exposition of the Churches and Ecclesial Communities separated from the See of Rome. The special position of the Eastern Churches is clearly underlined: their origin; their situation as fully constituted Churches; their rich heritage of spirituality and liturgy, of law and theology, which belong to the full catholic and apostolic character of the Church, and which must be fully respected in any reunion. The Decree is more guarded in its exposition of the ecclesial reality, faith and structures of the separated Churches and Ecclesial Communities in the West, which have arisen as a result of the Reformation in the 16th century. Yet here also the exposition is positive. Emphasis is placed upon their essential faith in Christ and the Trinity, their zeal for and devotion to the word of God in Scripture, their sacramental life founded on Baptism, and the richness of their Christian life.

The Decree must be read and studied in its entirety, together with the Council's Dogmatic Constitution on the Church. Here only those passages are quoted which are of special doctrinal importance.

(The ecclesial reality of the other Christian Communities and their relationship to the Catholic Church)

909   3. Moreover, from among the elements and endowments which together go to build up and give life to the Church itself, some and indeed very many and significant ones can exist outside the visible boundaries of the Catholic Church: the written word of God, the life of grace, faith, hope and charity with the other interior gifts of the Holy Spirit, and visible elements too. All of these, which come from Christ and lead back to Christ, belong by right to the one Church of Christ.

The brethren divided from us also use many liturgical actions of the Christian religion. These most certainly can truly engender a life of grace in ways that vary according to the condition of each Church or Community; they must be regarded as capable of giving access to the community of salvation.

It follows that the separated Churches and Communities as such, though we believe them to be deficient in some respects, are by no means deprived of significance and importance in the mystery of salvation. For the Spirit does not decline to use them as means of salvation—means which derive their efficacy from the very fulness of grace and truth entrusted to the Catholic Church.

Nevertheless, our separated brethren, whether considered as individuals or as Communities and Churches, are not blessed with that unity which Jesus Christ wished to bestow on all those who through him were born again into one body and with him quickened to newness of life—that unity which the Holy Scriptures and the ancient Tradition of the Church proclaim. For it is only through Christ's Catholic Church, which is the all-embracing means of salvation, that the fulness of the means of salvation can be enjoyed. We believe that our Lord entrusted all the treasures of the new Covenant to the apostolic college alone, of which Peter is the head, in order to build up the one Body of Christ on earth into which all should be fully incorporated who already belong in any way to the People of God.[...]

(Renewal of the Church)

910   6. Since every renewal of the Church essentially consists in a greater fidelity to her vocation, this unquestionably is also the basis of the movement towards unity. The pilgrim Church is summoned by Christ to continual reformation—of which, as an institution made up of men and women here on earth, she stands ever in need. If then, in various times and circumstances, there have been deficiencies in moral conduct or in Church discipline, or even in the formulation of Church teaching—to be clearly distinguished from the deposit of faith itself—these should be set right at the opportune moment.

(Conversion of heart)

911   7. There can be no ecumenism worthy of the name without a change of heart. For it is from renewal of our minds, from self-denial and generous love that desires of unity arise and come to maturity.[...] The words of St. John hold good also about faults against unity:"If we say we have not sinned, we make him a liar, and his word is not in us" *[1 Jn 1:10]*. So we humbly beg pardon of God and of our separated brothers and sisters, just as we forgive them that trespass against us.

(Communicatio in sacris)

912   8. Worship in common may not be considered as a means to be used indiscriminately for the restoration of Christian unity. There are two main principles governing the practice of such common worship: first the bearing witness to the unity of the Church, and second, the sharing in the means of grace. Witness to the unity of the Church generally forbids common worship; the grace to be obtained from it sometimes commends it.

(The manner of exposing the faith)

913   11. In ecumenical dialogue, when Catholic theologians, while standing fast by the teaching of the Church, join with separated brothers and sisters in common study of the divine mysteries, they should pursue the work with love for the truth, with charity and with humility. When comparing doctrines with one another, they should remember that among the truths of Catholic doctrine there exists an order or 'hierarchy', since not all these truths are equally connected with the foundation of the Christian faith. Thus, by this kind of 'fraternal rivalry' all will be spurred on to a deeper knowledge and a clearer expression of the unfathomable riches of Christ.

(Special position of the Eastern Churches)

914   14. For many centuries the Church of the East and that of the West each followed its own ways, though linked in a sisterly union of faith and sacramental life; the Roman See by common consent acted as guide when disagreements arose between them over matters of faith or discipline. Among other matters of moment, it is a pleasure for this Council to remind everyone that there exist in the East many particular or local Churches, among which the patriarchal Churches hold first place, many of which trace their origins back to the apostles themselves. Hence a matter of primary concern and care among the Easterners has been, and still is, to preserve the bonds of common faith and charity which ought to exist between local Churches as between sisters.

It must not be forgotten that from the beginning the Churches of the East have had a treasury from which the Western Church has drawn extensively—in liturgical practice, spiritual tradition and law. Nor must we undervalue the fact that it was the ecumenical Councils held in the East that defined the basic dogmas of the Christian faith, on the Trinity and the Word of God who took flesh of the Virgin Mary. To preserve this faith these Churches have suffered and still suffer much.

However, the inheritance handed down by the apostles was received with differences of form and manner, so that from the earliest times of the Church it was explained variously in different places, owing to diversities of genius and conditions of life. All this, besides external causes, and combined with a lack of charity and mutual understanding, prepared the way for divisions.

For this reason the Council urges all, but especially those who intend to devote themselves to the restoration of the desired full communion between the Churches of the East and the Catholic Church, to give due consideration to this special feature of the origin and growth of the Eastern Churches, and to the character of the relations which obtained between them and the Roman See before separation. A right appreciation of these elements will greatly contribute to the dialogue in view.

POST-CONCILIAR DOCUMENTS ON ECUMENISM

The Vatican II Council Decree on Ecumenism laid down the goal and principles of ecumenism and gave general norms for its practice. These new attitudes and the practical ways of proceeding had to be spelled out in subsequent documents. As these are easily accessible in A. FLANNERY (ed.), Vatican Council II, The Conciliar and Post-Conciliar Documents,

Dominican Publications, Dublin 1975, and Vatican Council II. More Postconciliar Documents, Dominican Publications, Dublin 1982, and other sources, only their nature is indicated here.

There are first the joint declarations of the Popes, with heads of other ecclesial communities:

—The common Declaration of Paul VI and Patriarch Athenagoras I at the conclusion of the Council, 7 December, 1965, withdrawing the mutual excommunication of the Churches of Rome and Constantinople in a spirit of forgiveness, and pledging mutual trust and dialogue towards complete communion. Text in AAS 58 (1966) 20-21.

—The Joint Declaration of Paul VI and Archbishop Ramsey of Canterbury on cooperation and dialogue (24 March 1966). Text in AAS 58 1996) 286-288.

—The Joint Declaration of Paul VI and Vasken I, Catholicos, Supreme Patriarch of the Armenians pledging to work for more profound unity on the basis of reciprocal acknowledgment of the common Christian faith and sacramental life (12 May 1970). Text in AAS 62 (1970) 416-417.

—The Joint Declaration of Paul VI and Ignatius Jacob III, Patriarch of Antioch of the Syrians on common profession of Christological faith (27 October 1971). Text in AAS 63 (1971) 814.

—The Joint Profession of Faith of Paul VI and Shenouda III, Patriarch of Alexandria, Egypt (10 May 1973). Text in AAS 65 (1973) 299-301 (See above,n.671a).

—The Joint Declaration of Paul VI and Archbishop Coggan of Canterbury, encouraging continued dialogue (29 April 1977). Text in AAS (1977) 286-289.

—The Joint Declaration of John Paul II and Patriarch Dimitrios I pledging to work towards full communion (30 November 1979). Text in AAS 71 (1979) 1603ff.

—The Joint Declaration of John Paul II and Archbishop Runcie of Canterbury, pledging to pursue the theological dialogue in view of the restoration of full communion (29 May 1982). Text in AAS 74 (1982) 924-926.

—The Joint Declaration of John Paul II and Ignatius Zakka I Iwas, Syrian Orthodox Patriarch of Antioch, with the common profession of Christological faith (23 June 1984). Text in Documentation Catholique, 2 September 1984, pp. 824-826 and, later, in AAS 85 (1993) 238-241.

—The Joint Declaration of John Paul II and Dimitrios I, Patriarch of Constantinople, expressing their hope for future unity between the Roman

Catholic and Orthodox Churches (7 December 1987). Text in AAS *80 (1988) 252-255.*

—*The Joint Declaration of John Paul II and Archbishop Runcie of Canterbury (2 October 1989). Text in* AAS *82 (1990) 323-326.*

—*The Joint Declaration of John Paul II and Patriarch Mar Dinkha IV, "Common Christological Declaration between the Catholic Church and the Assyrian Church of the East" (11 November 1994). Text in* Osservatore Romano, *12 November 1994 (See above n. 683).*

—*The Joint Declaration of Pope John Paul II and Catholicos Karekin I on christological faith (13 December 1996). Text in* AAS *89 (1997) 90-92.*

There are, besides, various documents regarding ecumenism which apply to the whole Catholic Church:

—*Congregation for the Doctrine of the Faith, Instruction on Mixed Marriages,* Matrimonii Sacramentum *(18 March 1966). Text in* AAS *58 (1966)235-239.*

—*Congregation for Oriental Churches, On Marriages between Roman Catholics and Orthodox* Crescens Matrimoniorum *(22 February 1967). Text in* AAS *59 (1967) 165-166.*

—*Secretariat for Promoting Christian Unity [SPCU], Directory concerning Ecumenical Matters, published in two parts: Part I,* Ad Totam Ecclesiam *(14 May 1967), text in* AAS *59 (1967) 574-592; and Part II,* Spiritus Domini, *on ecumenism in higher education (16 April 1970), in* AAS *62 (1970) 705-724.*

—*Paul VI, Apostolic Letter Motu Proprio* Matrimonia Mixta, *which finalises earlier norms concerning marriages of Catholics and non-Catholics, whether Christian or non-Christain. Text in* AAS *62 (1970) 257-263.*

—*SPCU, Declaration on the Common Eucharistic Celebration by Christians of Different Confessions, "Dans ces derniers temps" (7 January 1970). Text in* AAS *62 (1970) 184-187.*

—*SPCU, Reflections and Suggestions Concerning Ecumenical Dialogue (15 August 1970) (a semi-official document for practical guidance). Text in* SPCU, *Information Service 12 (1970) 5-11.*

—*SPCU, On admitting other Christians to Eucharistic Communion in the Catholic Church,* In Quibus Rerum Circumstantiis *(1 June 1972). Text in* AAS *64 (1972) 518-525.*

—*SPCU, Note interpreting the preceding instruction (17 October 1973). Text in* AAS *65 (1973) 616-619.*

—*SPCU, Ecumenical Collaboration at the Regional, National and Local Levels (22 February 1975). Text in* SPCU, *Information Service 29 (1975) 8-31*

PAUL VI

SECRETARIAT FOR PROMOTING CHRISTIAN UNITY
IN QUIBUS RERUM CIRCUMSTANTIIS
(1 June 1972)

Two problems of ecumenism have special theological relevance: the question of baptism and its validity, and, if necessary, of re-baptising in the Catholic Church (cf. Chapter XIV); and the question of admitting Christians of other Churches to the Eucharist in the Catholic Church. In this matter the Directory had already restated the guidelines of the Council Decree (n.912) and given detailed norms with regard to admission of Christians of Eastern Churches and of members of other Christian communities to the Eucharist. In the statement of 1 June, 1972, the Secretariat explains the theological rationale which underlies these norms. The text is found in AAS 64 (1972) 518-525.

(Norms for admission of other Christians to Catholic eucharistic communion)

915 The ecumenical directory has already shown how we must safeguard simultaneously the integrity of ecclesial communion and the good of souls. Behind the directory lie two main governing ideas:

1. The strict relationship between the mystery of the Church and the mystery of the Eucharist can never be altered, whatever pastoral measures we may be led to take in given cases. Of its very nature, the celebration of the Eucharist signifies the fulness of profession of faith and the fulness of ecclesial communion. This principle must not be obscured and must remain our guide in this field.

2. The principle will not be obscured if admission to Catholic eucharistic communion is confined to particular cases of those Christians who have a faith in the sacrament in conformity with that of the Church, who experience a serious spiritual need for the eucharistic sustenance, who for a prolonged period are unable to have recourse to a minister of their own community, and who ask for the sacrament of their own accord; all this provided that they have proper dispositions and lead lives worthy of a Christian. This spiritual need should be understood in the sense defined above: a need for the increase in spiritual life and a need for a deeper involvement in the mystery of the Church and of its unity.

(Disturbance of Catholics should be avoided; the assessment of the actual situation belonging to the bishop, and, in cases of similar conditions in a wider region, to episcopal conferences).

JOHN PAUL II

DISCOURSE AT THE LITURGY IN ST GEORGE'S AT PHANAR (30 November 1979)

Following the example of John XXIII and Paul VI in their cordial relations with Patriarch Athenagoras, John Paul II visited Patriarch Dimitrios I in Istanbul for the celebration of the feast of St. Andrew in November 1979. On this occasion the Pope and the Patriarch signed a Joint Declaration in which they announced the inauguration of the theological dialogue between the Catholic and the Orthodox Churches. This theological dialogue aims "not only at progressing towards the re-establishment of full communion between the Catholic and Orthodox Sister-Churches, but also at contributing to the multiple dialogues that are developing in the Christian world in search of its unity" (Osservatore Romano, English Edition, 10 December 1979, p.4). The Pope also attended the Byzantine Liturgy celebrated by Patriarch Dimitrios in the Greek Orthodox Cathedral of St. George at the Phanar, and at the end of the Liturgy delivered a discourse which gives fresh impetus to the re-union movement between the two Churches. In particular, the Pope placed the emphasis on the communion of the Churches; he presented the Petrine office as one in the service of unity, without mentioning papal jurisdiction. The text of this address, from which the quotations below are taken, is found in AAS 71 (1979) 1599-1603.

(Rome and Constantinople are Sister-Churches)

916   The Apostle Andrew, patron saint of the illustrious Church of Constantinople, is Peter's brother.[...] Today's celebration reminds us that special bonds of sisterhood and intimacy exist between the Church of Rome and the Church of Constantinople, and that a closer collaboration is natural between these two Churches.

(Peter's ministry of unity)

917   Peter, Andrew's brother, is the leader *(choryphée)* of the Apostles. Thanks to the inspiration given him by the Father, he fully recognized in Jesus Christ the Son of the living God *[cf. Mt 16:16]*. For this act of faith he received the name 'Peter' in order that the Church might be founded on this rock. He was commissioned with the task of ensuring unity in the apostolic preaching. As a brother among brothers he received the mission of strengthening them in faith [cf. Lk 22:32]; he is the first to have the responsibility of watching over the union of all, of ensuring the symphony of the holy Churches of God, in faithfulness to "the faith which was once for all delivered to the saints" [Jude 3]. It is in this spirit, animated by these sentiments, that the successor of Peter has wished on this day to visit the Church whose patron is St. Andrew.[..]

(Union with the Orthodox Churches is basic for ecumenism)

918   The visit to the primatial See of the Orthodox Church shows clearly the will of the entire Catholic Church to go forward in the march towards the unity of all, and also its conviction that the restoration of full communion with the Orthodox Church is a fundamental stage of the decisive progress of the entire ecumenical movement. Our division may not, perhaps, have been without an influence on the other divisions that followed it.

(Revising canonical rules)

919   We must not be afraid to reconsider, on both sides, and in consultation with one another, canonical rules established at a time when awareness of our communion—now close even if still incomplete—was still obscured. These rules are perhaps no longer consistent with the results achieved in our dialogue of love and with the possibilities opened up for us by these results.

(The theological dialogue)

920   The theological dialogue which is about to begin will have the task of overcoming the misunderstandings and disagreements which still exist between us, if not at the level of faith, at least at the level of theological formulation. It should be carried on not only in the atmosphere already created by the dialogue of love, which must be developed and intensified, but also in an atmosphere of worship and availability.

(Duty to be united)

921   It is only in worship, with a keen sense of the transcendence of the ineffable mystery "which surpasses knowledge" [Eph 3:19] that we will be able to situate our differences and "lay on[...]no greater burden than the things necessary" [*Acts* 15:28] to re-establish communion. It seems to me, in fact, that the question we must ask ourselves is not so much whether we can re-establish full communion, as whether we still have the right to remain separated. We must ask ourselves this question in the very name of our faithfulness to Christ's will for his Church.[...]

HOMILY TO THE DIASPORA-CATHOLICS AT OSNABRÜCK (16 November 1980)

The visit of the Pope to Germany in November 1980 had great ecumenical significance. Germany had been the cradle of the Reformation and continues to be a center of Protestant life and theology. 1980 was the 450th anniversary of the Confessio Augustana, *compiled by Melanchton, with Luther's approval, in an attempt to demonstrate the doctrinal orthodoxy of the Protestant movement before the Emperor and the diet of the empire. It was later accepted as an official document of the evangelical Churches. It contains the common basis of faith of Catholics and Protestants but remains ambiguous mostly in the understanding of the Church, grace and the sacraments. The possibility of accepting it as a basis for reunion was discussed again in the last years.*

At various occasions during his visit to Germany the Pope spoke about different aspects of ecumenism. In the homily he pronounced during the eucharistic celebration at Osnabrück, he insisted on what Catholics and evangelical Christians already have in common and hoped that this unity may grow. The text is found in AAS 73 (1981) 64-71.

(The growing union with other ecclesial communities)

922   5. The ecumenical movement in the last few decades has clearly shown you how much evangelical Christians are united with you in their concerns and joys, and how much you have in common with them when you live your faith in Our Lord Jesus Christ together, sincerely and consistently. So let us thank God from the bottom of our hearts that the various ecclesial communities in your regions are no longer divided by misunderstanding or even barricaded against one another in fear. You rather have already had the happy experience that mutual understanding and acceptance were particularly easy when both sides knew their own faith well, professed it joyfully, and encouraged concrete communion with their own brothers and sisters in faith. I would like to encourage you to continue along this way.

Live your faith as Catholics with gratitude to God and to

your ecclesial community. Bear a credible witness, in all humility and without any complacency, to the deep values of your faith, and encourage, discreetly and amiably, also your evangelical fellow Christians to strengthen and deepen in Christ their own convictions and forms of religious life. If all Churches and communities really grow in the fulness of the Lord, his Spirit will certainly indicate to us the way to reach the full internal and external unity of the Church.

ADDRESS TO THE EVANGELICAL LUTHERAN CHURCH COUNCIL OF GERMANY
(Mainz, 17 November 1980)

On the third day of his visit to Germany (cf. n. 922i), Pope John Paul II addressed the Council of the German Evangelical (Lutheran) Church in Mainz. He stressed the urgency for a common confession of faith and the need of conversion on the part of all in order that full unity may be obtained. Remarkable here is the positive way in which the Pope referred to Luther. The text is found in AAS 73 (1981) 71-75.

(The need of conversion of all)

923   There is no Christian life without repentance. There can be no ecumenism worthy of the name without a change of heart "[n. 911]. Let us no more pass judgment on one another" [Rom 14:13]. Let us rather recognise our guilt. "All have sinned" [Rom 3:23], applies also with regard to the grace of unity.

(The urgency of common confession of faith)

924   All the gratitude for what remains common to us and unites us [the common faith in Jesus Christ] cannot make us blind to what still divides us. We must examine it together as far as possible, not to widen the gaps, but to bridge them. We cannot stop at the acknowledgment : "we are and remain divided for ever and against each other". We are called to strive together, in a dialogue of truth and love, towards full unity in faith. Only full unity gives us the possibility of gathering with the same sentiments and the same faith at the Lord's one table.

(We are divided through the doctrine of the Church)

925   [In] the lectures given by Luther on the Letter to the Romans in the year 1516-1517, [...] he teaches that "faith in Christ through which we are justified, is not just belief in

Christ , or more exactly in the person of Christ, but belief in what is Christ's". [...] "We must believe in him and what is his". For the question: "What is this then?", Luther refers to the Church and to her authentic teaching. If the difficulties that exist between us were only a question of "ecclesiastical structures set up by human beings",[1] we could and should eliminate them immediately. According to the conviction of Catholics, disagreement revolves around "what is Christ's", around "what is his": his Church and her mission, her message, her sacraments, and the ministries placed in the service of the Word and the Sacrament. The dialogue established since the Council has brought us a good way further in this respect.

(The efforts for unity must continue)

926 We must remain in dialogue and in contact [...] I hope that we will find together the way to continue our dialogue. [...] We must leave no stone unturned. We must do what unites. We owe it to God and to the world. "Let us then pursue what makes for peace and for mutual upbuilding" *[Rom 14:19]*.[...] Christ's message requires us to bear witness together. Allow me to repeat what I said on 25 June of this year on the occasion of the jubilee of the *Confessio Augustana:* "The will of Christ and the signs of the times urge us to common witness in growing fulness of truth and love".

ADDRESS TO THE GERMAN EPISCOPAL CONFERENCE
(Fulda, 18 November 1980)

Also during his visit to Germany (cf. n. 922i), Pope John Paul II addressed the German Episcopal Conference in Fulda. He again returned to the theme of ecumenism, this time stressing that the way to unity must pass through the Cross. The text is found in AAS 73 (1981) 82-92.

(Unity in truth through the cross)

927 We often hear it said today that the ecumenical movement of the Churches is at a standstill.[...] I cannot agree with this judgment. Unity, which comes from God, is given to us at the Cross. We must not want to avoid the Cross, passing to rapid attempts at harmonising differences, excluding the

---

1. Cf. *Confessio Augustana,* VIII.

question of truth. But neither must we abandon one another, and go on our separate ways, because drawing closer calls for the patient and suffering love of Christ crucified. Let us not be diverted from the laborious way in order to remain where we are or to choose ways that are apparently shorter and lead astray.

LETTER TO CARDINAL WILLEBRANDS
(31 October 1983)

To mark the 500th anniversary of Luther's birth Pope John Paul II addressed an important letter to Cardinal Willebrands, President of the Secretariat for Promoting Christian Unity. A remarkable passage of this letter on the importance of historical truth is included here. The full text of the letter was published in Osservatore Romano, *English edition, 14 November 1983, p.9.*

(Importance of historical truth)

928   A twofold effort is necessary, both in regard to Martin Luther and also for the re-establishment of unity. In the first place it is necessary to continue an accurate historical work. By means of an investigation without preconceived ideas, motivated only by a search for the truth, one must arrive at a true image of the reformer, of the whole period of the Reformation, and of the persons involved in it. Fault, where it exists, must be recognized, wherever it may lie. Where controversy has beclouded one's view, that view must be corrected independently of either party. Besides, we must not allow ourselves to be guided by the intention of setting ourselves up as judges of history, but solely by the motive of understanding better what happened and of becoming messengers of truth.

SECRETARIAT FOR PROMOTING CHRISTIAN UNITY
CATHOLIC RESPONSE TO BEM
(August 1987)

The Faith and Order document, "Baptism, Eucharist and Ministry" (BEM), fruit of a long inter-church consultation and study, was approved at a January 1982 meeting of more than 100 theologians in Lima, Peru. The Faith and Order Commission that produced the document is made up of Anglicans, Orthodox and Protestants, with 12 Catholic members officially designated by the Vatican. Churches have been invited to respond to the text "at the highest appropriate level of authority". After consulting the episcopal conferences, theological faculties and others throughout the world, the

Secretariat for Promoting Christian Unity finalized the official Catholic Response to BEM in conjunction with the Congregation for the Doctrine of the Faith. The Response—the first of its kind in the recent ecumenical dialogue—observes that the document, while claiming to have achieved a "remarkable degree of agreement" and "major areas of theological convergence" between the communities participating in Faith and Order dialogue, recognized nevertheless that full consensus has not been reached. The Catholic Response acknowledges that there is much in the BEM document which the Catholic Church can affirm. At the same time it identifies the main issues on which the document does not accord with full Catholic teaching. The Response goes on to suggest that in order to achieve further progress the work of the Faith and Order Commission should focus more directly on ecclesiology; meanwhile only an incomplete response can be given to BEM, which does not directly refer to the Catholic ecclesiological self-understanding developed by the Second Vatican Council. Only a short passage can be quoted here in which the Response looks upon BEM as an important step, yet only one stage on the way to unity. The text is found in Origins *17 (1987-1988) 401-416.*

(Status of the document)

929   Even though we think that the text falls short at certain points, we believe that if it were accepted by the various Churches and ecclesial communities, it would bring the Churches to an important step forward in the ecumenical movement, although still only one stage along the way in the ecumenical process of working towards visible unity of divided Christians. If through this process of response and reception of BEM now being undertaken, many of the convergences, even agreements reported by BEM were affirmed by the Churches and ecclesial communities, we believe that this would be an advance in the ecumenical movement.

BEM is also a *stage along the way*, one of the "various stages" the Churches will have to pass through on "their way towards their goal of visible unity" (preface). Its claims therefore are limited: "We have not yet fully reached 'consensus'.[...] Full consensus can only be proclaimed after the Churches reach the point of living and acting together in unity." The text does not offer a full systematic treatment of baptism, eucharist or ministry, but focuses rather on those aspects which have been related to the problems of mutual recognition leading to unity. It is also formulated with the help of a new theological vocabulary which necessarily includes a new horizon of thought.

At important junctions of the document, contrasting

statements and language open the way to a variety of interpretations. The commentaries related to the text identify disputed issues still in need of further research and reconciliation. And there are occasional passages which suggest options in theology and practice not consistent, for example, with the Catholic faith.

JOHN PAUL II

LETTER TO BISHOPS OF EUROPE ON RELATIONS BETWEEN CATHOLICS AND ORTHODOX IN THE NEW SITUATION OF CENTRAL AND EASTERN EUROPE
(31 May 1991)

Tensions between Catholic churches of oriental rite and Orthodox churches arose during the period after the collapse of communist governments in Central and Eastern Europe and the subsequent religious liberty, which allowed for the reestablishment of ecclesiastical structures in service to those Christians in full communion with the Bishop of Rome. In this letter in preparation for the Special Assembly for Europe of the Synod of Bishops (November 28-December 14, 1991), Pope John Paul II expresses the Catholic church's approach to unity with the Orthodox church and draws several pastoral consequences regarding the tensions between the communities. The text is from The Pontifical Council for Promoting Christian Unity, Information Service, N. 81, 1992 (III-IV), 101-103.

(The nature of the unity sought between the Catholic and Orthodox churches).

930a 4.Hence with these Churches (Orthodox) relations are to be fostered as between sister Churches, to use the expression of Pope Paul VI in his Brief to the Patriarch of Constantinople Anthengaoras I.[1]

The unity with these Churches which is sought—and must be sought—is full communion in one faith, in the sacraments and in ecclesial government [cf.LG 14], with full respect for legitimate liturgical, disciplinary and theological diversity, as I explained in my apostolic Epistle *Euntes in Mundum Universum*, on the occasion of the Millennium of the Baptism of Kievan Rus'.[2]

---

1. *Anno Ineunte,* 25 July 1967: *AAS* 59 (1967) 852-854.
2. 25 January 1988, no. 10: *AAS* (1988) 949-950.

(Pastoral consequence of this ecumenical vision)

930b From this there follow immediate and practical consequences. The first of these was stated by Pope Paul VI in the Address which he gave in the Cathedral of the Ecumenical Patriarchate on the occasion of his visit and it retains all of its validity today: "We see more clearly thus that it belongs to the leaders of the Churches, to their hierarchy, to guide the Churches on the path which leads to recovering full communion. They must do so recognizing each other and respecting each other as shepherds of that part of the flock of Christ which has been entrusted to them, caring for the cohesion and faith of the people of God and avoiding all that could divide it or bring confusion into its ranks."[1]

A second consequence is the rejection of all undue forms of proselytism, with the avoidance in the most absolute way in pastoral action of any temptation to violence and any form of pressure. At the same time, pastoral action will not fail to respect the freedom of conscience and the right which each individual has to join, if he wishes, the Catholic Church. In brief, it is a matter of respecting the action of the Holy Spirit, who is the Spirit of truth [cf. Jn. 16:13]. The Council's Decree on Ecumenism stated this and gave the reason thus: "it is evident that the work of preparing and reconciling those individuals who wish for full Catholic communion is of its nature distinct from ecumenical action, but there is no opposition between the two, since both proceed from the wondrous providence of God" [UR 4].

The third consequence is that it is obviously not enough just to avoid mistakes: it is also necessary to promote positively coexistence with mutual and harmonious respect. This attitude has certainly been proposed and re-affirmed as the rule of conduct in relations between Catholics and Orthodox, as was stated by the Pope Paul VI and the Patriarch Athenagoras I in their joint declaration: "The dialogue of charity among their Churches must bear fruits of disinterested collaboration on the common plan of action at the pastoral, social and intellectual level, in mutual respect for the faithfulness that both must have

---

1. 25 July 1967: *AAS* 59 (1967) 841.

for their own Churches."[1] As I had occasion to state in my
Encyclical *Slavorum Apostoli*, all this will help the mutual
enrichment of the two great traditions, the Eastern and the
Western, and the path towards full unity.

CATHOLIC RESPONSE TO THE FINAL REPORT OF
ARCIC-I
(1991)

*Produced by the Congregation for the Doctrine of the Faith in consultation
with the Pontifical Council for Promoting Christian Unity, this response was
made to the final report of the first Anglican-Roman Catholic International
Commission (ARCIC-I), whose work spanned the years from 1967-1982,
resulting in documents on the themes of the eucharist, ordained ministry and
authority. The response welcomes "the achievement of points of convergence
and even of agreement which many would not have thought possible before
the Commission began its work," noting, however, that "substantial agreement"
has not yet been achieved "on all the questions studied by the Commission."
At times the response evaluates the text in light of expressions drawn from
official formulations of Catholic doctrine, such as "propitiatory sacrifice" with
regard to the Eucharist or "priestly character" with regard to ordained ministry.
Some commentators question whether such an evaluation adequately reflects
the approach recommended by the popes since Vatican II, who encouraged
dialogue partners to go beyond patterns of thought or expression which were
nourished in controversy and to formulate the great common heritage in a
language which is both traditional and expressive of an ecumenical spirit. The
text is from The Pontifical Council for Promoting Christian Unity, Information
Service, N. 82, 1993 (I), 47-51, whose source is the Osservatore Romano of
December 6, 1991.*

(Ecumenical method and nature of the Vatican response to ARCIC I)

931   Conclusion.[...] The objection may be made that this reply
          does not sufficiently follow the ecumenical method, by
which agreement is sought step by step, rather than in full
agreement at the first attempt. It must, however, be remembered
that the Roman Catholic Church was asked to give a clear answer
to the question: are the agreements contained in this Report
consonant with the faith of the Catholic Church? What was asked
for was not a simple evaluation of an ecumenical study, but an
official response as to the identity of the various statements with
the faith of the Church.

---

1. 28 October 1967: *AAS* 59 (1967) 1055.

PONTIFICAL COUNCIL FOR PROMOTING CHRISTIAN UNITY
DIRECTORY FOR THE APPLICATION OF PRINCIPLES AND NORMS ON ECUMENISM

(25 March 1993)

This Directory is a revision of the original Ecumenical Directory (Ad Totam Ecclesiam), published in two parts in 1967 and 1970, which attempted to apply the general principles of Vatican II concerning Catholic participation in the ecumenical movement to such areas as the establishment of Church structures to promote unity and ecumenical sharing in prayer, education and witness. This new directory brings its predecessor up to date in light of important documents bearing on ecumenism which subsequently had been published (such as the codes of canon law for the Latin and the Eastern Churches and the new catechism) and in light of the ecumenical experience of the Church after the Second Vatican Council. It also improves the earlier directory by adding an opening chapter explaining the search for Christian unity in terms of an ecclesiology of communion and by including directives concerning mixed marriages (cf.n. 1852). The text can be found in AAS 85 (1993) 1039-1119.

(The ecumenical movement in light of the Trinity, the mystery of the Church and the theological virtues)

932a   9. The ecumenical movement seeks to be a response to the gift of God's grace which calls all Christians to faith in the mystery of the Church according to the design of God who wishes to bring humanity to salvation and unity in Christ through the Holy Spirit. This movement calls them to the hope that the prayer of Jesus "that they all may be one" will be fully realized. It calls them to that charity which is the new commandment of Christ and the gift by which the Holy Spirit unites all believers.

(The Church and its unity in the plan of God)

932b   11. The Council situates the mystery of the Church within the mystery of God's wisdom and goodness which draws the whole human family and indeed the whole of creation into unity with himself [cf. LG 1-4 and UR 2]. To this end, God sent into the world his only Son, who was raised up on the cross, entered into glory and poured out the Holy Spirit through whom he calls and draws into unity of faith, hope and charity the people of the new Covenant which is the Church. In order to establish this holy Church in every place until the end of the ages, Christ entrusted to the college of the Twelve to which he chose Peter as head, the office of teaching, ruling and sanctifying. It is the will of Jesus Christ, that through the faithful preaching of the Gospel, the administration of the sacraments, and through government in love exercised by the apostles and their successors under the action of the Holy Spirit, this people should grow and its communion be made ever more perfect. The Council presents the Church as the new People of God, uniting within itself, in all the richness of their diversity, men and women from all nations, all cultures, endowed with manifold gifts of nature and grace, ministering to one another and recognizing that they are sent into the world for its salvation [LG 2 and 5].

(The threefold bond of communion)

932c 12. The People of God in its common life of faith and sacraments is served by ordained ministers: bishops, priests and deacons [LG, Chapter III]. Thus united in the threefold bond of faith, sacramental life and hierarchical ministry, the whole People of God comes to be what the tradition of faith from the New Testament [Acts 2:42] onwards has called *koinônia/* communion.

(The Church as communion)

932d 13. The communion in which Christians believe and for which they hope, is in its deepest reality, their unity with the Father through Christ in the Spirit. Since Pentecost, it has been given and received in the Church, the communion of saints. It is accomplished fully in the glory of heaven, but it is already realized in the Church on the earth as it journeys towards that fullness. Those who live united in faith, hope and love, in mutual service, in common teaching and sacraments, under the guidance of their pastors [cf. LG 14] are part of that communion which constitutes the Church of God. This communion is realized concretely in the particular Churches, each of which is gathered together around its Bishop. In each of these "the one, holy, catholic and apostolic Church of Christ is truly present and alive" [CD 11]. This communion is, by its very nature, universal.

(Communion as a gift and a task; the catholic diversity which communion includes)

932e 16. Communion within the particular Churches and between them is a gift of God. It must be received with joyful thanks and cultivated with care. It is fostered in a special way by those who are called to minister in the Church as pastors. The unity of the Church is realized in the midst of a rich diversity. This diversity in the Church is a dimension of its catholicity. At times the very richness of this diversity can engender tensions within the communion. Yet, despite such tensions, the Spirit continues to work in the Church calling Christians in their diversity to ever deeper unity.

(The Church of Christ subsists in the Catholic Church)

932f 17. Catholics hold the firm conviction that the one Church of Christ subsists in the Catholic Church "which is governed by the successor of Peter and by the Bishops in communion with him" *[LG 8]*. They confess that the entirety of revealed truth, of sacraments, and of ministry that Christ gave for the building up of his Church and carrying out of its mission is found within the Catholic communion of the Church. Certainly Catholics know that personally they have not made full use of and do not make full use of the means of grace with which the Church is endowed. For all that, Catholics never lose confidence in the Church. Their faith assures them that it remains "the worthy bride of the Lord, ceaselessly renewing herself through the action of the Holy Spirit until, through the cross, we may attain to that light which knows no setting" *[LG 9]*. Therefore, when Catholics use the words "Churches," "other Churches," "other Churches and ecclesial Communities", etc., to refer to those who are not in full communion with the Catholic Church, this firm conviction and confession of faith must always be kept in mind.

(The goal of the ecumenical movement)

932g 20. [...]This unity which of its very nature requires full visible communion of all Christians is the ultimate goal of the ecumenical movement. The Council affirms that this unity by no means requires the sacrifice of the rich diversity of spirituality, discipline, liturgical rites and elaborations of revealed truth that has grown up among Christians in the measure that this diversity remains faithful to the apostolic Tradition [cf. UR 4 and 15-16]

CATHOLIC ACCEPTANCE OF CLARIFICATIONS ON EUCHARIST AND MINISTRY IN ARCIC I

(11 March 1994)

The official Roman Catholic response to the Final Report of the Anglican-Roman Catholic International Commission (ARCIC I; see the introduction to number 931 above) had called for clarifications concerning several points touching upon the Eucharist and Ordained Ministry. In working out its reply, ARCIC-II listed the issues concerning Eucharistic doctrine as follows: "a) the essential link of the eucharistic Memorial with the once-for-all sacrifice of Calvary which it makes sacramentally present; b) 'the propitiatory nature of the eucharistic sacrifice, which can be applied also to the deceased'; [...] c) certitude that Christ is present sacramentally and substantially when 'under the species of bread and wine these earthly realities are changed into the reality of his Body and Blood, Soul and Divinity'; and d) the adoration of Christ in the reserved sacrament." Concerning the Ordained Ministry, the following affirmations were asked to be made clearer: "a) only a validly ordained priest, acting 'in the person of Christ', can be the minister offering sacramentally the redemptive sacrifice of Christ in the Eucharist; b) the institution of the sacrament of orders which confers the priesthood of the New Covenant, comes from Christ; c) the 'character of priestly ordination implies a configuration to the priesthood of Christ'; and d) the apostolic succession in which the unbroken lines of episcopal succession and apostolic teaching stand in causal relation to each other." Cardinal Cassidy's letter is addressed to the co-chairmen of ARCIC II, Bishop Mark Santer (Anglican) and Bishop Cormac Murphy-O'Connor (Roman Catholic). The text can be found in The Pontifical Council for Promoting Christian Unity, Information Service, N. 87, 1994 (IV), 237.

932h   On September 4th last, you sent me a document containing *"Clarifications of Certain Aspects of the Agreed Statements on Eucharist and Ministry"* which had been submitted to and approved by the ARCIC-II meeting taking place in Venice at that time.

This document has been examined by the appropriate dicasteries of the Holy See and I am now in a position to assure you that the said clarifications have indeed thrown new light on the questions concerning Eucharist and Ministry in the Final Report of ARCIC-I for which further study had been requested.

The Pontifical Council for Promoting Christian Unity is therefore most grateful to the members of ARCIC-II, and to those from ARCIC-I who prepared these clarifications. The agreement reached on Eucharist and Ministry by ARCIC-I is thus greatly strengthened and no further study would seem to be required at this stage.

APOSTOLIC LETTER *TERTIO MILLENNIO ADVENIENTE*
(10 November 1994)

This epistle explains the rationale and sets in motion various stages in preparation for the celebration of the beginning of the Third Millennium after the birth of Jesus Christ. Within the context of commenting on various failures for which the Church needs to repent as she looks back over the past, the pope makes several points about ecumenism. He places Christian divisions within historical perspective and underscores the urgency of and the commitment needed for seeking full Christian unity. The text can be found in AAS 87 (1995) 5-41.

(Historical perspective for considering Christian divisions)

933a   34. Among the sins which require a greater commitment to repentance and conversion should certainly be counted those which have been detrimental to the unity willed by God for his people. In the course of the 1,000 years now drawing to a close, even more than in the first millennium, ecclesial communion has been painfully wounded, a fact "for which, at times, people of both sides were to blame" *[UR 3]*. Such wounds openly contradict the will of Christ and are a cause of scandal to the world *[UR 1]*.

(Urgency of the ecumenical task and commitment of the Catholic Church)

933b   34. [...] In these last years of the millennium, the Church should invoke the Holy Spirit with ever greater insistence, imploring from him the grace of Christian unity. This is a crucial matter for our testimony to the Gospel before the world. Especially since the Second Vatican Council many ecumenical initiatives have been undertaken with generosity and commitment: It can be said that the whole activity of the local churches and of the Apostolic See has taken on an ecumenical dimension in recent years.

(Aspects and dimensions of the ecumenical task)

933c   34. [...] The approaching end of the second millennium demands of everyone an examination of conscience and the promotion of fitting ecumenical initiatives so that we can celebrate the Great Jubilee, if not completely united, at least much closer to overcoming the divisions of the second millennium. As everyone recognizes, an enormous effort is needed in this regard. It is essential not only to continue along the path of dialogue on doctrinal matters, but above all to be more committed to prayer for Christian unity. Such prayer has become much more intense after the council, but it must increase still more, involving an ever greater number of Christians, in unison with the great petition of Christ before his passion: "Father, [...] that they also may all be one in us" *[Jn. 17:21]*.

APOSTOLIC LETTER *ORIENTALE LUMEN*

(2 May 1995)

This letter, published on the feast of St. Athanasius, celebrates the one hundredth anniversary of Leo XIII's Apostolic Letter Orientalium Dignitas. *It reaffirms the legitimate diversity "of methods and approaches in understanding and confessing divine things" (5) and that the uses and customs of each Church must not be considered "as absolutely unchangeable, lest the Tradition lose its quality of being a living reality: (8). The pope expresses deep appreciation for many aspects of the Orthodox expression of Christianity, singling out eastern monasticism for special praise (9-16).*

(Role of the pope in promoting unity)

934a 20.[...] I would like to reassert that this commitment [on the part of the pope to Christian unity] is rooted in the conviction that Peter *[cf. Mt 19:17-19]* intends to place himself at the service of a Church united in charity. "Peter's task is to search constantly for ways that will help preserve unity. Therefore he must not create obstacles but must open up paths. Nor is this in any way at odds with the duty entrusted to him by Christ: 'Strengthen your brothers in the faith' *[cf. Lk 22:32]*. It is significant that Christ said these words precisely at the moment when Peter was about to deny him. It was as if the Master himself wanted to tell Peter: 'Remember that you are weak, that you too, need endless conversion. *You are able to strengthen others only insofar as you are aware of your own weakness.* I entrust to you as your responsibility the truth, the great truth of God, meant for human salvation, but this truth cannot be preached or put into practice except by loving'. *Veritatem facere in caritate* [to live the truth in love; *cf. Eph 4:15*]: this is what is always necessary."[1]

(Unity of East and West; Respect of traditions and autonomy of each)

934b 20. Today we know that unity can be achieved through the love of God only if the Churches want it together, in full respect for the traditions of each and for necessary autonomy. We know that this can take place only on the basis of the love of Churches which feel increasingly called to manifest the one Church of Christ, born from one Baptism and from one Eucharist, and which want to be sisters [*cf. UR 14*]. As I had occasion to say: "The Church of Christ is one. If divisions exist, that is one thing; they must be overcome, but the Church is one, the Church of Christ between East and West can only be one, one and united."[2]

Of course, in today's outlook it appears that true union is possible only in total respect for the other's dignity, without claiming that the whole array of uses and customs in the Latin Church is more complete or better suited to showing the fulness of correct doctrine; and again, that this union must be preceded by an awareness of communion that permeates the whole Church and is not limited to an agreement among leaders. Today we are conscious—and this has frequently been reasserted—that unity will be achieved as and when the Lord desires, and that it will require the contribution of love's sensitivity and creativity, perhaps even going beyond the forms already tried in history [*cf. OE 30*].

ENCYCLICAL LETTER *UT UNUM SINT*

(25 May 1995)

This encyclical letter, written at "the threshold of the Third Millennium," is the first in the period after Vatican I to be specifically and primarily concerned with the ecumenical movement. Toward the end of the letter, Pope John Paul II explains his intention in writing it: "Given the importance which the Council attributed to the work of rebuilding Christian unity, and in this

---

1. JOHN PAUL II, *Crossing the Threshold of Hope*, New York 1994, pp. 154-155.
2. JOHN PAUL II, Greetings to the Faculty of the Pontifical Oriental Institute (12 December 1993), *Osservatore Romano*, 13-14 December 1993, p. 4.

our age of grace for ecumenism, I thought it necessary to reaffirm the fundamental convictions which the Council impressed upon the consciousness of the Catholic Church, recalling them in the light of the progress subsequently made towards the full communion of all the baptized" (100). In an optimistic and encouraging tone, its three chapters address 1) the Catholic Church's commitment to ecumenism, 2) the fruits already achieved by dialogue and 3)the path that yet lies ahead.

The encyclical reaffirms Vatican II's fundamental convictions about ecumenism, especially as expressed in Unitatis redintegratio, *underscoring the ecclesiology of communion with its affirmation that Christ's Church subsists in the Catholic Church and, at the same time, its recognition of the ecclesiality of Churches and Ecclesial Communities not in full communion with the Catholic Church (7-14). "Ecumenism is directed precisely to making the partial communion existing between Christians grow towards full communion in truth and love" (14). The encyclical's catalogue of progress made since the Council includes steps such as ecumenical dialogues (28-39, 50-51, 59, 64, 77-79), Christological agreements (62-63), papal writings (53-54), pilgrimages and visits by Church leaders (52,72) and cooperation on behalf of justice, peace and the integrity of creation (40, 43, 74-76). Special emphasis is placed upon the primacy and necessity of "ecumenical prayer" as a valuable means for healing divisions (22, 26, 70, 102). The encyclical embraces Paul VI's affirmation that the Churches of the East and West are "Sister Churches" (55-58) and proposes such a framework as the context for addressing the special problems between the Orthodox and Catholics which arise in connection with the Eastern Catholic Churches (60). Finally, the role of the bishop of Rome in promoting and serving the unity of the Church is made the object of special reflection (4, 88-97).*

(Unity as an essential characteristic of the Church)

935a 9. Jesus himself, at the hour of his Passion, prayed "that they may all be one" *[Jn 17:21]*. This unity, which the Lord has bestowed on his Church and in which he wishes to embrace all people, is not something added on, but stands at the very heart of Christ's mission. Nor is it some secondary attribute of the community of his disciples. Rather, it belongs to the very essence of this community. God wills the Church, because he wills unity, and unity is an expression of the whole depth of his *agapê*. In effect, this unity bestowed by the Holy Spirit does not merely consist in the gathering of people as a collection of individuals. It is a unity constituted by the bonds of the profession of faith, the sacraments and hierarchical communion *[LG 14]*. [...] To believe in Christ means to desire unity; to desire unity means to desire the Church; to desire the

Church means to desire the communion of grace which corresponds to the Father's plan from all eternity. Such is the meaning of Christ's prayer: *"Ut unum sint."*

(Unity in faith as adherance to the whole of revelation)

935b 18. The unity willed by God can be attained only by the adherence of all to the content of revealed faith in its entirety. In matters of faith, compromise is in contradiction with God who is Truth. In the Body of Christ, "the way, and the truth, and the life" *[Jn 14:6]*, who could consider legitimate a reconciliation brought about at the expense of truth? The Council's Declaration of Religious Freedom, *Dignitatis Humanae*, attributes to human diginity the quest for truth, "especially in what concerns God and his Church" *[DH 1]*, and adherence to truth's demands. A "being together" which betrayed the truth would thus be opposed both to the nature of God who offers his communion and to the need for truth found in the depths of every human heart.

36. Love for the truth is the deepest dimension of any authentic quest for full communion between Christians. [...] There must be charity towards one's partner in dialogue, and humility with regard to the truth which comes to light and which might require a review of assertions and attitudes. [...] Full communion of course will have to come about through the acceptance of the whole truth into which the Holy Spirit guides Christ's disciples. Hence all forms of reductionism or facile "agreement" must be absolutely avoided. Serious questions must be resolved, for if not, they will reappear at another time, either in the same terms or in a different guise.

79. To uphold a vision of unity which takes account of all the demands of revealed truth does not mean to put a break on the ecumenical movement.[1] On the contrary, it means preventing it from settling for apparent solutions which would lead to no firm and solid results.[2]

---

1. Cf. Address to Cardinals and the Roman Curia (28 June 1985), 6:*AAS* 77 (1985) 1153.
2. *ibid.*

(Differing forms of truth's expression)

935c   19. Because by its nature the content of faith is meant
for all humanity, it must be translated into all cultures.
Indeed, the element which determines communion in truth is
the meaning of truth. The expression of truth can take different
forms. The renewal of these forms of expression becomes
necessary for the sake of transmitting to the people of today the
Gospel message in its unchanging meaning.[1]

(Complementary, not incompatible, doctrinal formulations)

935d   39. [...] Ecumenical dialogue, which prompts the parties
involved to question each other, to understand each other
and to explain their positions to each other, makes surprising
discoveries possible. Intolerant polemics and controversies have
made incompatible assertions out of what was really the result
of two different ways of looking at the same reality. Nowadays
we need to find the formula which, by capturing the reality in
its entirety, will enable us to move beyond partial readings and
eliminate false interpretations. One of the advantages of
ecumenism is that it helps Christian Communities to discover
the unfathomable riches of the truth. Here too, everything that
the Spirit brings about in "others" can serve for the building up
of all Communities *[UR 4]* and in a certain sense instruct them
in the mystery of Christ. Authentic ecumenism is a gift at the
service of truth.

(Sharing in sacramental life)

935e   46.[...] It is a source of joy to note that Catholic ministers
are able, in certain particular cases, to administer the
Sacraments of the Eucharist, Penance and Anointing of the Sick
to Christians who are not in full communion with the Catholic
Church but who greatly desire to receive these sacraments, freely
request them and manifest the faith which the Catholic Church
professes with regard to these sacraments. Conversely, in specific
cases and in particular circumstances, Catholics too can request
these same sacraments from ministers of Churches in which these
sacraments are valid. The conditions for such reciprocal reception

---

1. Cf. Saint Vincent of Lerins, *Commonitorium primum*, 23: PL 50, 667-668.

have been laid down in specific norms; for the sake of furthering ecumenism these norms must be respected.[1]

(The importance of constant reform for ecumenism)

936a 82. Only the act of placing ourselves before God can offer a solid basis for that conversion of individual Christians and for that constant reform of the Church, insofar as she is also a human and earthly institution *[UR 6]*, which represent the preconditions for all ecumenical commitment. One of the first steps in ecumenical dialogue is the effort to draw the Christian Communities into this completely interior spiritual space in which Christ, by the power of the Spirit, leads them all, without exception, to examine themselves before the Father and to ask themselves whether they have been faithful to his plan for the Church.

(Christian Communities are already united in their martyrs and saints)

936b 84. In a theocentric vision, we Christians already have a common *Martyrology*. This also includes the martyrs of our own century, more numerous than one might think, and it shows how, at a profound level, God preserves communion among the baptized in the supreme demand of faith, manifested in the sacrifice of life itself.[2] The fact that one can die for the faith shows that other demands of the faith can also be met. I have already remarked, and with deep joy, how an imperfect but real communion is preserved and is growing at many levels of ecclesial life. I now add that this communion is already perfect in what we all consider the highest point of the life of grace, *martyria* unto death, the truest communion possible with Christ who shed his Blood, and by that sacrifice brings near those who once were far off *[Cf. Eph 2:13]*.

While for all Christian communities the martyrs are the proof of the power of grace, they are not the only ones to bear witness to that power. Albeit in an invisible way, the communion between our Communities, even if still incomplete, is truly and solidly

---

1. Cf. *UR* 8 and 15, *CIC* c. 844; *CCEC* c. 671; PCPCU, *Directory for the Application of Principles and Norms on Ecumenism* (25 March 1993), 122--125, 129-131, 123 and 132; AAS 85 (1993), 1086, 1087, 1088-1089, 1087 and 1089.

2. Cf. JOHN PAUL, II, Apostolic Letter *Tertio Millennio Adveniente* (10 November 1994), 37: *AAS* 87 (1995), 29-30.

grounded in the full communion of the Saints—those who, at the end of a life faithful to grace, are in communion with Christ in glory. These *Saints* come from all the Churches and Ecclesial Communities which gave them entrance into the communion of salvation.

When we speak of a common heritage, we must acknowledge as a part of it not only the institutions, rites, means of salvation and the traditions which all the communities have preserved and by which they have been shaped, but first and foremost this reality of holiness.[1]

(Positive outcome of divisions)

936c   85. Since God in his infinite mercy can always bring good even out of situations which are an offense to his plan, we can discover that the Spirit has allowed conflicts to serve in some circumstances to make explicit certain aspects of the Christian vocation, as happens in the lives of the Saints. In spite of fragmentation, which is an evil from which we need to be healed, there has resulted a kind of rich bestowal of grace which is meant to embellish the *koinônia*. God's grace will be with all those who, following the example of the Saints, commit themselves to meeting its demands.

(Papal primacy and its power as service; a request for forgiveness)

937a   88. In the beautiful expression of Pope Saint Gregory the Great, my ministry is that of *servus servorum Dei*. This designation is the best possible safeguard against the risk of separating power (and in particular the primacy) from ministry. Such a separation would contradict the very meaning of power according to the Gospel: "I am among you as one who serves" *[Lk 22:27]*, says our Lord Jesus Christ, the Head of the Church. On the other hand, as I acknowledged on the important occasion of a visit to the World Council of Churches in Geneva on 12 June 1984, the Catholic Church's conviction that in the ministry of the Bishop of Rome she has preserved, in fidelity to the Apostolic Tradition and the faith of the Fathers, the visible sign and guarantor of unity, constitutes a difficulty for most other Christians, whose memory is marked by certain painful

---

1. Cf. Paul VI, Address at the Shrine in Namugongo, Uganda (2 August 1969): *AAS* 61 (1960) *590-591*.

recollections. To the extent that we are responsible for these, I join my Predecessor Paul VI in asking forgiveness.[1]

(Papal primacy as a service to unity , in communion with other bishops and with the whole Church)

937b 94. This service of unity, rooted in the action of divine mercy is entrusted within the College of Bishops to one among those who have received from the Spirit the task, not of exercising power over the people—as the rulers of the Gentiles and their great men do [cf. Mt 20:25; Mk 10:42]—but of leading them towards peaceful pastures. [...]The mission of the Bishop of Rome within the College of all the Pastors consists precisely in "keeping watch" *(episkopein)*, like a sentinel, so that, through the efforts of the Pastors, the true voice of Christ the Shepherd may be heard in all the particular Churches. [...] With the power and the authority without which such an office would be illusory, the Bishop of Rome must ensure the communion of all the Churches. For this reason, he is the first servant of unity. This primacy is exercised on various levels, including vigilance over the handing down of the Word, the celebration of the Liturgy and the Sacraments, the Church's mission, discipline and the Christian life. It is the responsibility of the Successor of Peter to recall the requirements of the common good of the Church, should anyone be tempted to overlook it in the pursuit of personal interests. He has the duty to admonish, to caution and to declare at times that this or that opinion being circulated is irreconcilable with the unity of faith. When circumstances require it, he speaks in the name of all the pastors in communion with him. He can also—under very special conditions clearly laid down by the First Vatican Council—declare *ex cathedra* that a certain doctrine belongs to the deposit of faith [n. 839].

95. All this however must always be done in communion. When the Catholic Church affirms that the office of the Bishop of Rome corresponds to the will of Christ, she does not separate this office from the mission entrusted to the whole body of Bishops, who are also "vicars and ambassadors of Christ" [LG 27]. The Bishop of Rome is a member of the "College", and the Bishops are his brothers in the ministry.

---

1. Cf. Discourse at the Headquarters of the World Council of Churches, Geneva (12 June 1984), 2: *Insegnamenti* VII/1 (1984), 1686.

(Discerning the forms which Petrine ministry may take)

937c   95.[...] Christ ardently desires the full and visible communion of all those Communities in which, by virtue of God's faithfulness, his Spirit dwells. I am convinced that I have a particular responsibility in this regard, above all in acknowledging the ecumenical aspirations of the majority of the Christian Communities and in heeding the request made of me to find a way of exercising the primacy which, while in no way renouncing what is essential to its mission, is nonetheless open to a new situation. For a whole millennium Christians were united in "a brotherly/sisterly communion of faith and sacramental life. [...] If disagreements in belief and discipline arose among them, the Roman See acted by common consent as moderator"*[UR 14]*. In this way the primacy exercised its office of unity. When addressing the Ecumenical Patriarch His Holiness Dimitrios I, I acknowledged my awareness that "for a great variety of reasons, and against the will of all concerned, what should have been a service sometimes manifested itself in a very different light. But [...] it is out of a desire to obey the will of Christ truly that I recognize that as Bishop of Rome I am called to exercise that ministry. [...] I insistently pray the Holy Spirit to shine his light upon us, enlightening all the pastors and theologians of our Churches, that we may seek—together, of course—the forms in which this ministry may accomplish a service of love recognized by all concerned."[1]

96. This is an immense task, which we cannot refuse and which I cannot carry out by myself. Could not the real but imperfect communion existing between us persuade Church leaders and their theologians to engage with me in a patient and fraternal dialogue on this subject, a dialogue in which, leaving useless controversies behind, we could listen to one another, keeping before us only the will of Christ for his Church and allowing ourselves to be deeply moved by his plea "that they may all be one [...] so that the world may believe that you have sent me" *[Jn 17:21]*.

---

1. Cf. Homily in the Vatican Basilica in the presence of Dimitrios I, Archbishop of Constantinople and Ecumenical Patriarch (6 December 1987), 3: *AAS* 80 (1988), 714.

PONTIFICAL COUNCIL FOR PROMOTING CHRISTIAN UNITY

CLARIFICATION ON THE GREEK AND LATIN TRADITIONS REGARDING THE PROCESSION OF THE HOLY SPIRIT

(13 Sptember 1995)

Pope John Paul II, in a homily delivered in the presence of the Ecumenical Patriarch Bartholomew I, on June 29, 1995, expressed the desire that "the traditional doctrine of the Filioque, present in the liturgical version of the Latin Credo," be clarified "in order to highlight its full harmony with what the Ecumenical Council of Constantinople of 381 confesses in its creed: the Father as the source of the whole Trinity, the one origin both of the Son and of the Holy Spirit." In September of the same year, the Pontifical Council for the Promotion of Christian Unity published such a clarification, carefully reviewing the terminology used by various Fathers, both from the East and the West. Partly because of the way Greek New Testament texts were translated into Latin and partly because of the differences in the shades of meaning inherent in the Greek and Latin terms used by theologians to express the Trinitarian faith of the Church, "a false equivalence was involuntarily created with regard to the eternal origin of the Spirit between the Oriental theology of the ekporeusis and the Latin theology of the processio. Since the latter term was used to describe the eternal origin both of the Son and of the Holy Spirit, the "Filioque" was added by various Latin Fathers, to more adequately distinguish the Son from the Holy Spirit. The Pontifical Council argues that such differences of expression were not intended to and should not be interpreted as denying the doctrine that the Father is the one origin and source of the whole Trinity (cf. n. 339). From an ecclesiological point of view, the importance of the text lies in its forceful reaffirmation that the Catholic Church considers herself fully committed to and bound by the doctrine established in the ecumenical councils of the fourth century. The text can be found in The Pontifical Council for Promoting Christian Unity, Information Service, N. 89, 1995 (II-III), 88-92.

938 The Catholic Church acknowledges the conciliar, ecumenical, normative and irrevocable values, as expression of the one common faith of the Church of all Christians, of the Symbol professed in Greek at Constantinople in 381 by the Second Ecumenical Council. No profession of faith peculiar to a particular liturgical tradition can contradict this expression of the faith taught and professed by the undivided Church.[...]

Being aware of this, the Catholic Church has refused the addition of *kai tou Uiou* to the formula *ek tou Patros ekporeuomenon* of the Symbol of Nicaea-Constantinople in the Churches, even of Latin rite, which use it in Greek. The liturgical use of this original text remains always legitimate in the Catholic Church.

COMMON DECLARATION BY POPE JOHN PAUL II AND CATHOLICOS KAREKIN I

(13 December 1996)

This declaration intends principally to affirm the unity of faith between the Roman Catholic Church and the Armenian Apostolic Church concerning the manner of the union of the incarnate Word, without using the phrase "two natures" of the Council of Chalcedon (451). Thus Jesus Christ is confessed to be "Perfect God as to his divinity, perfect man as to his humanity, His divinity is united to his humanity in the Person of the Only-begotten Son of God, in a union which is real, perfect, without confusion, without alteration, without division, without any form of separation (cf. n. 684)." In addition to this Christological confession, the declaration also contains several sentences which express the vision which these churches share regarding their growth toward full communion. The text can be found in AAS 89, 1997, 90-92.

939 Pope John Paul II and Catholicos Karekin I recognize the deep spiritual communion which already unites them and the bishops, clergy and lay faithful of their Churches. It is a communion which finds its roots in the common faith in the Holy and life-giving Trinity proclaimed by the Apostles and transmitted down the centuries by the many Fathers and Doctors of the Church and the bishops, priests, and martyrs who have followed them. They rejoice in the fact that recent developments of ecumenical relations and theological discussions carried out in the spirit of Christian love and fellowship have dispelled many misunderstandings inherited from the controversies and dissensions of the past. Such dialogues and encounters have prepared a healthy situation of mutual understanding and recovery of the deeper spiritual communion based on the common faith in the Holy Trinity that they have been given through the Gospel of Christ and in the Holy Tradition of the Church.

[...] The reality of this common faith in Jesus Christ and in the same succession of apostolic ministry has at times been obscured or ignored. Linguistic, cultural and political factors have immensely contributed towards the theological divergences that have found expression in their terminology of formulating their doctrines. His Holiness John Paul II and His Holiness Karekin I have expressed their determined conviction that because of the fundamental common faith in God and in Jesus Christ, the controversies and unhappy divisions which sometimes have followed upon the divergent ways in expressing it, as a result of the present declaration, should not continue to influence the life and witness of the Church today.

OFFICIAL COMMON STATEMENT CONCERNING THE LUTHERAN-ROMAN CATHOLIC JOINT DECLARATION ON JUSTIFICATION
(31 October 1999)

On June 25, 1998, the Pontifical Council for Promoting Christian Unity announced that the Vatican had approved the Lutheran-Catholic "Joint Declaration on the Doctrine of Justification," which had just been unanimously accepted by the council of the Lutheran World Federation on June 16. This declaration was built upon the results of the dialogue about the doctrine of justification which had taken place between Lutherans and Catholics at the international and regional levels over the previous thirty years. Its forty-four numbered paragraphs explore the biblical and ecumenical contexts for the doctrine, culminating in a statement of the common understanding of justification, which is further explained in seven specific points. After an initial period of misunderstanding in which the recognition by the Catholic Church was further clarified, Cardinal Edward Idris Cassidy, president of the Pontifical Council for the Promotion of Christian Unity, and Rev. Dr. Ishmael Noko, general secretary of the Lutheran Word Federation, signed a common statement accepting the Joint Declaration on behalf of their respective communities. The signing occurred on reformation day, October 31, 1999, in the city of Augsburg, where, in 1530, the famous Confessio augustana *was proposed as the first summary of Lutheran doctrine, during the earliest years of the protestant reformation. While the Catholic Church has issued "joint declarations" about doctrinal questions with other Christian communions in the recent past, especially the Christological declarations issued by Pope John Paul II and the leaders of various non-Chalcedonian churches, this is the first joint declaration on a specific doctrinal issue between the Catholic Church and one of the churches of the Reformation. Moreover, it addresses the central issue of contention at the time. The content of the agreement about justification is more properly included in Chapter XIX of the present collection, where one finds the condemnations of Luther and the decree on justification of the Council of Trent. Of precisely ecumenical interest is the text signed by Cardinal Cassidy and Rev. Dr. Noko, which follows. The complete text of the Joint Declaration can be found in The Pontifical Council for Promoting Christian Unity,* Information Service, *N. 98, 1998 (III), 81-93. The "Official Common Statement" signed at Augsburg can be found in* Origins *29, 1999-2000, 85-88. For the Joint Declaration, cf. nn. 2000k-s.*

940 1. On the basis of the agreements reached in the Joint Declaration on the Doctrine of Justification, the Lutheran World Federation and the Catholic Church declare together: "The understanding of the doctrine of justification set forth in this declaration shows that a consensus in basic truths of the doctrine of justification exists between Lutherans and Catholics" (*Joint Declaration, 40*). On the basis of this consensus the Lutheran World Federation and the Catholic Church declare together: "The teaching of the Lutheran churches presented in this declaration does not fall under the condemnations from the Council of Trent. The condemnations in the Lutheran Confessions do not apply to the teaching of the Roman Catholic Church presented in this declaration" (*JD 41*).

2. With reference to the resolution on the joint declaration by the council of the Lutheran World Federation of June 16, 1998, and to the response to the joint declaration by the Catholic Church of June 25, 1998, and to the questions raised by both of them, the annexed statement (called Annex) further substantiates the consensus reached in the joint declaration; thus it becomes clear that the earlier mutual doctrinal condemnations do not apply to the teaching of the dialogue partners as presented in the joint declaration.

3. The two partners in dialogue are committed to continued and deepened study of the biblical foundations of the doctrine of justification. They will also seek further common understanding of the doctrine of justification beyond what is dealt with in the joint declaration and the annexed substantiating statement. Based on the consensus reached, continued dialogue is required specifically on the issues mentioned especially in the joint declaration itself (*JD 43*) as requiring further clarification, in order to reach full church communion, a unity in diversity, in which remaining differences would be "reconciled" and no longer have a divisive force. Lutherans and Catholics will continue their efforts ecumenically in their common witness to interpret the message of justification in language relevant for human beings today, and with reference both to individual and social concerns of our times.

By this act of signing, the Catholic Church and the Lutheran World Federation confirm the Joint Declaration on the Doctrine of Justification in its entirety.

CHAPTER X

THE CHURCH AND THE WORLD RELIGIONS

The problem of the significance of the many religions of humankind in God's plan of salvation has struck modern Christians with full force especially after World War II. The collapse of the colonial system, the revolution in world communications, the emergence of a truly pluralistic international society, have forced them to consider more seriously, indeed often with anguish, the meaning of the religions which they encounter constantly and come to know better and better. Moreover, the new discoveries in the human sciences and a better knowledge of population statistics make them realise that in the enormous span of human history the Judaeo-Christian event fills only a tiny fraction, and that those who profess Jesus as the Lord are a diminishing minority of the world population. This naturally leads to a more intense theological reflection on the "other" religions. This is why, "in our time" especially, the Church "examines with great attention what is her relation to non-Christian religions" (NA 1).

In her proclamation of the Gospel of Christ she had, of course, always encountered people professing various forms of religious beliefs, more or less at variance with the contents of her own preaching; but in the earliest centuries the teaching Church did not find it necessary to make any statement about these religions. The Christian attitude towards them was in fact for the main part a negative one; it was taken for granted that the other religions cannot lead to salvation. This, however, was a negative way of expressing an important aspect of the Christian faith, viz., the uniqueness of Jesus Christ as the only Mediator between God and human beings (cf. 1 Tim. 2:5). Little positive thinking was done about the possible role of those religions in God's plan.

The first official pronouncements bearing on other religions appeared in the social and political context of the Middle Ages, and were occasioned by the continued presence of distinct Jewish communities in the Western world and by the Muslim threat. The sociological background of these conciliar or papal statements is that of a Christian commonwealth threatened by the economic power of the Jews and the military advances of Islam. In this context sociological discrimination based on religious principles was often practised. This negative attitude notwithstanding, the need was also recognised of sending to various peoples preachers full of sympathy and understanding (see chapter XI). And, though pressure could be exerted on the Jews to listen to the Gospel message, nobody was to be forced to conversion. Of this early period only three documents are given here which keep some relevance today.

A second group of documents deals mostly with the danger of indifferentism which contact with non-Christian religions can bring about. These documents are written against the background of nineteenth century liberalism. They contain harsh statements, much influenced by the current theology; at the same time they keep an element of permanent value. For, they witness to the Church's awareness of an objective order of salvation to which the human being is called to submit, and to a consciousness of the fact that the salvific grace of God comes to all people through Christ. Therefore, the Church, because of her unique relation to Christ, cannot be reduced to the level of other religious communities; her function is unique. This does not prevent the fact, already acknowledged in the documents of this period, that the grace of Christ reaches beyond the visible boundaries of the Catholic Church. The Jansenist proposition, "no grace is granted outside the Church", had already been condemned by Clement XI in 1713 (cf. DS 2429). As regards the danger of indifferentism, the documents quoted here show that the Church's stern attitude has gradually softened down. More and more recognition is given to the principle of religious liberty; the previous attitude will be completely superseded by the new theological climate of Vatican II.

The third group of documents concerning the religions of the world reflects mostly the new and much more open theological outlook characteristic of the Second Vatican Council. The Council recognises the moral and spiritual values of these religions and urges the Church not only to enter into friendly dialogue with their adherents but also to learn from contact with their traditions. After the Council Church documents have further developed this open attitude.

*   *   *

The Church's doctrine on the religions of the world covers the following points:

Religions in relation to the Gospel

Though abrogated by the Gospel, practices of Judaism were allowable in early Christianity: 1003, 1004.

Religions are related to the Christian economy of salvation: 39/16,
    1003, 1018, 1034.
Outside this relationship they have no salvific power: 810, 1003, 1005,
    1008, 1009, 1013/16f, 1168.
Yet their votaries can find salvation: 39/16, 814, 854-857, 1010, 1018.
They are not on an equal footing with the Christian faith; hence
    indifferentism is condemned: 1006f, 1008, 1013/15, 1013/21.77.
    78.79, 1016, 1036, 1053, 1060, 1066.
Yet they play a role in the salvation of their members: 1059-1060.
The Gospel must be announced to them: 1036, 1039.

Religions considered in themselves

They contain many spiritual, moral and human values, though often
    mixed with error, and hence need to be purified: 1017, 1018, 1025,
    1026, 1030, 1035.
They even contain elements of the supreme Truth, seeds of the Word;
    divine grace is at work in them: 1021, 1023, 1025, 1036, 1037,
    1038, 1040, 1046.
The Holy Spirit is at work in their members: 1044, 1048, 1172, 1176.
They deal with the one God and with the ultimate questions of
    humankind: 1002, 1019f, 1031, 1033, 1038.

The Christian attitude to world religions

There must be true religious freedom, tolerance and respect: 1001, 1014f,
    1027, 2048-2050.
There should reign an attitude of acceptance, collaboration and dialogue:
    1022, 1024, 1027, 1028, 1029, 1032, 1037, 1039, 1040.
The place of dialogue within the mission: 1041, 1054, 1058, 1164.
Foundation of inter-religious dialogue: 1042-1044, 1049-1052, 1056.
Fruits of inter-religious dialogue: 1047, 1057, 1061, 1063.
The Christian attitude is charity towards all: 1011, 1012.
Christians should learn from the values of other religious traditions:
    1025, 1037.
The Church together with others advances towards the fulness of the
    Kingdom: 1045.
The Kingdom of God is already universally present: 1062, 1171.
Dialogue and proclamation, two distinct activities of the Church: 1055,
    1064.
Dialogue open to proclamation: 1065.
Anti-Semitism and Anti-Judaism condemned: 1067-1070.

THE SECOND GENERAL COUNCIL OF NICAEA (787)

The Council was convoked in the midst of the iconoclast controversy by Irene and her son Emperor Constantine IV, at the request of Paul IV, patriarch of Constantinople, and Tarasius, his successor. The Council was presided over, at least nominally, by the legate of Pope Hadrian I. Besides settling the doctrinal matters on the veneration of images (cf. nn. 1251f), it passed several disciplinary canons, among which is found the following one. The canon states the obligation laid on all those who claim to be Christians of professing the Christian faith without ambiguity. An open allegiance to Judaism is preferable to a Christian profession which is not sincere. The text is found in COD, pp 145-146.

(Jews must not be received, unless sincerely converted)

1001   *Canon 8:* Since those who live in the error of the Hebrew religion seem to make a mockery of Christ, our God, pretending to be Christians while in fact they deny him and secretly keep the Sabbath and other customs of the Jews, we determine that such people must not be received into the communion, nor in prayer, nor in the Church; but let them be Hebrews openly according to their own religion. Nor should their children be baptised or their slaves bought or acquired. But if any among them should with a sincere heart and true faith be converted and profess [the faith] with their whole heart, showing that they have triumphed over their customs and practices by striving that others be convinced and corrected, those should be received and baptised, and their children too. And we determine that it must be made sure that they have turned away from the Jewish practices; and if this is not the case, they should by no means be received.

GREGORY VII

LETTER TO ANZIR, KING OF MAURITANIA (1076)

In a letter to the Muslim King of Mauritania, referred to in the Council Vatican II (NA 3), the Pope thanks Anzir for gifts he has received from him as well as for freeing some prisoners and for his promise to free others. He also sends him a delegation as a token of Christian friendship and love and as a proof of his desire to be of service to him "in all things agreeable to our Fathers". The most significant part of the letter is the following extract in which the Pope explains that Christians and Muslims worship the same God. See Epistola 21. PL 48, 450-452.

(Christians and Muslims adore the same God)

1002 God, the Creator of all, without whom we cannot do or even think anything that is good, has inspired to your heart this act of kindness. He who enlightens all people coming into this world *[Jn 1:9]* has enlightened your mind for this purpose. Almighty God, who desires all people to be saved *[1 Tim 2:4]* and none to perish, is well pleased to approve in us most of all that besides loving God human beings love others, and do not do to others anything they do not want to be done unto themselves *[cf. Mt 7:14]*. We and you must show in a special way to the other nations an example of this charity, for we believe and confess one God, although in different ways, and praise and worship him daily as the creator of all ages and the ruler of this world. For as the apostle says: "He is our peace who has made us both one" *[Eph 2:14]*. Many among the Roman nobility, informed by us of this grace granted to you by God, greatly admire and praise your goodness and virtues.[...] God knows that we love you purely for his honour and that we desire your salvation and glory, both in the present and the future life. And we pray in our heart and with our lips that God may lead you to the abode of happiness, to the bosom of the holy patriarch Abraham, after long years of life here on earth.

THE GENERAL COUNCIL OF FLORENCE
DECREE FOR THE COPTS (1442)

On this document, see n. 809i. This is the first official document in which reference is explicitly made to the "pagans" in connection with the axiom Extra Ecclesiam nulla salus; *previous official pronouncements had applied the principle to situations of schisms and heresy within the Christian fold. The formulation of the axiom is borrowed from Fulgentius of Ruspe (467-533). As it stands, the document takes a negative attitude as regards the role of "pagan" religions in the objective economy of salvation. It does not, however, deny what it was beyond its scope to consider, viz., the presence of grace beyond the boundaries of the Church and the limitations of subjective human knowledge and responsibility. As regards the place of the Jewish religion in the Christian economy of salvation, the attitude is also rather negative: though tolerated at the beginning of the Church's existence, it must eventually disappear. As far as Christians are concerned, it states clearly that, though Jewish religious practices could licitly be kept by them in the earliest period of the Church's existence, this is no longer true in the present. At the same time, it insists that Christian freedom makes all human customs lawful, provided that the faith is intact and edification ensured.*

(Jewish religious practices are abrogated with the promulgation of the Gospel)

1003   [The Holy Roman Church] firmly believes, professes and
1348   teaches that the legal [statutes] of the Old Testament or
         Mosaic Law, divided into ceremonies, holy sacrifices and
sacraments, were instituted to signify something to come, and
therefore, although in that age they were fitting for divine worship,
they have ceased with the advent of our Lord Jesus Christ, whom
they signified. [With him] the sacraments of the New Testament
have begun. Whoever puts his hope in these legal [statutes] even
after the passion [of Christ] and submits oneself to them as though
faith in Christ was unable to save without them, sins mortally. Yet
[the Church] does not deny that between the passion of Christ and
the promulgation of the Gospel they could be observed, provided
one in no way believed that they were necessary for salvation. But
she asserts that after the promulgation of the Gospel *(post
promulgatum evangelium)* they cannot be observed without the loss
of eternal salvation. Therefore, she denounces as foreign to the
faith of Christ all those who after that time observe circumcision,
the Sabbath and other laws, and she asserts that they can in no
way be sharers of eternal salvation, unless they sometime turn
away from their errors. She therefore commands to all who glory
themselves in the Christian name that they must, sometime or
other, give up circumcision fully, either before or after baptism,
because, whether one puts one's hope in it or not, it cannot in any
way be observed without the loss of eternal salvation.

(All things are lawful but not all things are helpful)

1004   [The Holy Roman Church] firmly believes, professes and
1350   preaches that "everything created by God is good and
         nothing is to be rejected if it is received with thanksgiving"
[1 Tim 4:4]; because, according to the word of the Lord, it is "not
what goes into the mouth that defiles a man" [Mt 15:11]. She
asserts that the distinction of clean and unclean food in the Mosaic
Law belongs to the religious observances which have passed away
with the rise of the Gospel and have ceased to be efficacious. It
also asserts that the command of the apostles to "abstain from
what has been sacrificed to idols and from blood and from what
is strangled" [Acts 15:29] was fitting in those times when the one
Church was emerging from the Jews and the Gentiles, who

previously had observed different religious customs and moral habits. For, in this way the Gentiles would share some observances in common with the Jews, and, the causes of dissent being removed, it would be possible to come to a common worship and profession of faith. For, to the Jews, because of their ancient traditions, blood and what is strangled is abhorrent; thus, if they saw the Gentiles eat what was sacrificed to idols, they could suspect them of returning to idolatry. But, once the Christian religion has been so well spread that no Jew according to the flesh is found in it but all who enter the Church agree on the same rites of the Gospel and modes of worship, believing that "to the pure all things are pure" [Tit 1:15], the reason for the apostolic prohibition has ceased to exist and, therefore, the prohibition itself has also ceased. The Church declares, therefore, that none among the kinds of food which human civilisation admits must be condemned; and that no distinction must be made between animals, whoever be the person, man or woman by whom they are killed, and whatever be the way in which they are killed. However, for the sake of bodily health, for the exercise of virtue, for the observance of monastic and ecclesiastical discipline, a person may and must refrain from many things which are not condemned. For, as the apostle says: "All things are lawful but not all things are helpful" [1 Cor 6:12; 10:22].

(The necessity of the Church for salvation)

1005 [The Holy Roman Church][...] firmly believes, professes
1351 and preaches that "no one remaining outside the Catholic Church, not only pagans", but also Jews, heretics or schismatics, can become partakers of eternal life; but they will go to the "eternal fire prepared for the devil and his angels" [Mt. 25:41], unless before the end of their life they are joined [aggregati] to it. For union with the body of the Church is of so great importance that the sacraments of the Church are helpful to salvation only for those remaining in it; and fasts, almsgiving, other works of piety, and the exercises of a militant Christian life bear eternal rewards for them alone. "And no one can be saved, no matter how much alms one has given, even if shedding one's blood for the name of Christ, unless one remains in the bosom and unity of the catholic Church."[1]

---

1. Cf. FULGENTIUS OF RUSPE, *De fide liber and Petrum*, 38, 79 and 39, 80.

LEO XII

ENCYCLICAL LETTER *UBI PRIMUM* (1824)

The intellectual climate of Europe in the nineteenth century was largely derived from Descartes. It was a strange combination of rationalism and fideism. The rationalistic tenets led to the doctrine of religious indifferentism which ascribed equal value to all religions. The philosophical roots of this movement were clearly incompatible with the Christian faith; they tended to deny all divine revelation or at least to refuse any finality to God's revelation in Christ. No word of God was recognised as demanding a religious assent. The doctrine was vigorously opposed by the official teaching of the Church, especially by Pope Pius IX. Pope Leo XII, in his first Encyclical Letter, Ubi Primum, defined what the Church understood by indifferentism.

(Condemnation of religious indifferentism)

1006   [A certain sect], putting on airs of piety and liberality,
2720   professes what they call 'tolerantism' or indifferentism,
and extols it not only in matters of politics, about which
we are not speaking, but also in matters of religion. It teaches
that God has given to every one a great freedom, so that one can
embrace and adopt without any danger to salvation any sect that
attracts one according to one's own private judgment and opinion.

(Against this, Rom 16:17f is quoted.)

GREGORY XVI

ENCYCLICAL LETTER *MIRARI NOS ARBITRAMUR* (1832)

In this letter the Pope condemns the liberal doctrines spread by the French writer, F. de Lamennais (1782-1854), who after having first submitted, later reiterated the same teaching. He was again condemned by the same Pope in the Encyclical Singulari Nos *(1834) (D 1617).*

(Condemnation of religious indifferentism)

1007   We now come to another important cause of the evils
2730   with which we regret to see the Church afflicted, namely
indifferentism, or that wrong opinion according to which
[...] one can attain the eternal salvation of one's soul by any
profession of faith, provided one's moral conduct conforms to
the norms of right and good [...] From this foulest source of
indifferentism there flows the absurd and wrong view, or rather
insanity, according to which freedom of conscience must be
asserted and vindicated for everybody.

PIUS IX

ENCYCLICAL LETTER *QUI PLURIBUS* (1846)

In this first encyclical Pius IX already condemns the doctrine of indifferentism, which he was to reject repeatedly later: in the allocution Singulari Quaedam (1854), in the encyclical Quanto Conficiamur Moerore (1863) (cf. DS 2865-2867), and again in the Syllabus of Condemned Errors (1864). His teaching, which today sounds very harsh, must, in order to be correctly interpreted, be placed in its historical context. The presupposition of indifferentism was the negation of revelation upon which there followed the equality of all religions. This context did not favour the recognition of what is good in religions outside Christianity. What remains valid in this teaching found a more careful theological expression in the Dogmatic Constitution on the Catholic Faith of the First Vatican Council (cf. nn. 113ff).

(Condemnation of religious indifferentism)

1008 [Among errors against the Catholic Faith] must be
2785 included the horrible system, repugnant even to the
natural light of reason, according to which there is no
difference between religions [indifferentism]. These crafty people
doing away with all distinction between virtue and vice, truth
and error, honesty and dishonesty, feign that people can attain
to eternal salvation by the practice of any religion whatever.

ALLOCUTION *SINGULARI QUADAM* (1854)

In this allocution, delivered one day after the definition of the dogma of the Immaculate Conception, the Pope exposed to the Cardinals the dangers that beset the right doctrine of the Church, i.e., rationalism and indifferentism. For the first time an official document on the necessity of the Church for salvation speaks of the "invincible ignorance" by which people are subjectively excused from embracing Christianity. This admission, completing the previous doctrine (cf. n. 1003i), considerably tempers its harshness. The same doctrine was repeated nine years later in the encyclical Quanto Conficiamur Moerore (cf. DS 2865-2867).

(There is no salvation outside the Church)

1009 We have learnt not without sorrow that another error,
no less destructive than the previous one, has invaded
some parts of the Catholic world and affects the minds of many
Catholics. They think that there is good hope for the eternal
salvation of all those who do not in any way belong to the
Church of Christ. Therefore they are in the habit of frequently

inquiring about the future lot and condition after death of those who in no way have given their adherence to the Catholic faith. Advancing the flimsiest arguments, they expect a reply that will support their erroneous opinion. Far from us, Venerable brethren, be the idea of daring to set limits to the divine mercy, which is infinite; far also from us to want to penetrate the secret plans and judgments of God which are "like the great deep" [cf. Ps 36 (35) 6], impenetrable to human thought. But, in accordance with our apostolic office, we want you to be on the alert, with episcopal care and vigilance, so as to keep away from people's minds, by all possible efforts, that opinion which is as unholy as it is deadly, namely that the way of eternal salvation can be found in any religion whatever. With all the learning and ingenuity that is yours, teach the people entrusted to your care that the dogmas of the Catholic faith are not in the slightest manner opposed to the divine mercy and justice.

(Invincible ignorance excuses from belonging to the Church)

1010   It must, of course, be held as of faith that no one can be saved outside the apostolic Roman Church, that the Church is the only ark of salvation, and that whoever does not enter it will perish in the flood. Yet, on the other hand, it must likewise be held as certain that those who are in ignorance of the true religion, if this ignorance is invincible, are not subject to any guilt in this matter before the eyes of the Lord. Now, who could presume for oneself the ability to set the boundaries of such ignorance, taking into consideration the natural differences of peoples, lands, talents and so many other factors? Only when we have been released from the bonds of this body and "shall see God as he is" [1 Jn 3:2], shall we understand how closely and wonderfully the divine mercy and justice are linked. But, as long as we dwell on earth, encumbered by this mortal body that dulls our soul, let us tenaciously hold the Catholic doctrine that there is "one God, one faith, one baptism" [cf. Eph 4:5]. To push our inquiry further is not right.

(Condemnation of religious indifferentism)

1011   For the rest, as charity demands, let us pray continually for the conversion to Christ of all nations everywhere. Let us devote ourselves to the salvation of all as far as we can, for "the Lord's hand is not shortened" [Is. 59:1]. The gifts of heavenly grace will assuredly not be denied to those who sincerely wish and pray to be renewed by the divine light. These truths need to be deeply fixed in the minds of the faithful, so that they may not be infected with doctrines tending to foster the religious indifferentism which we see spreading widely, with growing strength, and with destructive effect upon souls.

ENCYCLICAL LETTER *QUANTO CONFICIAMUR MOERORE* (1863)

In this letter addressed to the Bishops of Italy, Pius IX repeats the teaching he had given nine years earlier (cf. nn. 1009-1011), but he further stresses the duty of brotherly relations with people of all religions.

1012   But let it never happen that the children of the Catholic Church be in any way at enmity with those who are not joined to them by the bonds of the same faith and love. On the contrary, if they are poor or sick or afflicted by any other evils, let the children of the Church endeavour to succour and help them with all the services of Christian love. First and foremost, let them try to lead them from the shadows of error in which they lie to the Catholic truth and to the most loving mother the Church. She never ceases to extend lovingly her maternal arms towards them and to call them to her bosom, so that, grounded in faith, hope and love, and "bearing fruit in every good work" [Col. 1:10], they may find eternal salvation.

SYLLABUS OF CONDEMNED ERRORS (1864)

The full title of this document is: "A Syllabus containing the most important errors of our time which have been condemned by our holy Father Pius IX in allocutions, at consistories, in encyclicals and other apostolic letters." It is the final outcome of the Pope's protracted effort to comply with the request made to him by the Council of Spoleto in 1851 that he should list and condemn the principal errors of the times. The final list of 80 errors, divided into ten sections, draws from previous statements of the Pope, and, although not signed by him, was sent together with his Encyclical **Quanta Cura**, *accompanied by a letter of the Cardinal Secretary of State. The Syllabus is very harsh in some respects, but its propositions must be interpreted in the light of the original documents to which they refer. These documents generally belonged to European ideological movements which were much more in conflict with Christian revelation than the ambiguous and vague wording used in the Syllabus would suggest. The errors listed here are taken from the third section of the Syllabus dealing with indifferentism (15-17), from the fourth section on various errors*

(21), and from the last or tenth section on modern liberalism (77-79). Cf. also other propositions in n. 112.

(Errors of indifferentism condemned)

[1013/15]
2915
Every one is free to embrace and profess the religion which by the light of reason one judges to be true.

[1013/16]
2916
Human beings can find the way of eternal salvation and attain eternal salvation by the practice of any religion whatever.

[1013/17]
2917
We should at least have good hopes for the eternal salvation of all those who are in no way in the true Church of Christ.

(Errors against the Church condemned)

[1013/21]
2921
The Church has no power to define dogmatically that the religion of the Catholic Church is the only true religion.

(Errors of liberalism condemned)

[1013/77]
2977
In our age it is no longer advisable that the Catholic religion be the only State religion, excluding all the other cults.

[1013/78]
2978
Therefore it is praiseworthy that in some Catholic regions the law has allowed people immigrating there to exercise publicly their own cult.

[1013/79]
2979
It is false to assert that civil freedom of cult and the full right granted to all to express openly and publicly any opinions and views lead to an easier corruption of morality and of the minds of people and help to propagate the pest of indifferentism.

LEO XIII

ENCYCLICAL LETTER *IMMORTALE DEI* (1885)

From their opposition to indifferentism earlier Popes had drawn the conclusion that the secularism of the State was also wrong, since it seemed to be intimately linked with religious indifferentism. Thus Pius IX had condemned it in the Encyclical Quanta Cura *(1864) (cf. DS 2890). Leo XIII softens this unnecessary conclusion. The condemnation of the secularism of the State will be completely superseded by the doctrine of the Second Vatican Council in its declaration* Dignitatis Humanae *on religious freedom (cf. nn. 2048-2050).*

(On the secularism of the State)

1014 Although the Church does not consider it licit that
3176 various forms of worship of God should have the same
rights as the true religion, yet she does not thereby
condemn the authorities of the nations who, for the sake of
attaining a great good or of avoiding to cause evil, tolerate in
practice and by custom that they all have the same place in the
city.

(There must be no forced conversion)

1015 The Church is also always very careful that no one be
3177 forced to join the Catholic faith against one's will, for,
as Augustine wisely admonishes: "only one who wills
so can believe."[1]

THE FIRST PLENARY COUNCIL OF INDIA (1950)

This Council, demanded by the bishops of India and convoked in Bangalore by the papal legate Cardinal Gilroy, is the only fully official statement of doctrine and practice made by the Magisterium of the Church in India. Its decrees, approved by Pope Pius XII in 1951, contain a doctrinal part and a much larger disciplinary and pastoral part. While it rejects the indifferentist attitude, the Council is the first official Church document offering a clearly positive approach to the spiritual values of the world religions. It represents a first step in the Church's new understanding of these religions, which will find its full expression in the Second Vatican Council. The texts quoted here belong to the doctrinal section, dealing with the true religion. See Acta et Decreta primi Concilii plenarii Indiae, *2nd ed. (Ranchi 1959), pp. 24, 25.*

(Against indifferentism and syncretism)

1016 11. We therefore reject the view so widely spread in our
regions which holds that all religions are equal among
themselves, and that, provided they are adhered to with sincerity,
all are various ways to one and the same end, namely God and
eternal salvation. We equally reject the syncretism according to
which the ideal religion or the religion of the future is conceived
as a sort of synthesis to be worked out by humanity from various
religions that exist.

---

1. *In evang. Ioan. tract.,* 26, 2.

(Positive values and limitations of world religions)

1017   We acknowledge indeed that there is truth and goodness outside the Christian religion, for God has not left the nations without a witness to himself, and the human soul is naturally drawn towards the one true God. But with the passage of the centuries serious errors have almost everywhere been mixed with these truths, and this is why the various religions contradict each other even on essential points. But the inadequacy of all non-Christian religions is principally derived from this, that, Christ being constituted the one Mediator between God and human beings, there is no salvation by any other name.

THE SECOND VATICAN GENERAL COUNCIL

While maintaining unshaken the belief in the uniqueness of Christ and of his revelation, the Second Vatican Council took a clearly positive approach to the religions of the world. It devoted a special declaration, Nostra Aetate, to the relation of the Church to these religions. This is the first Conciliar document to deal with this important subject. Besides the Declaration, other documents of Vatican II, especially LG and AG, also contain important references to the place of these religions in God's plan of salvation.

The Council does not intend to provide on this point an elaborate theology; but it clearly adopts a new attitude by stressing what Christians share with other people, and thereby fosters unity (NA 1). It mentions with respect the great world religions (AG 10); more specifically, it refers to the traditional religions (NA 2), Hinduism (ibid.), Buddhism (ibid.), Islam (NA 3 and LG 16) and Judaism (NA 4; LG 16 and passim). It recognises in them not only human answers to the fundamental problems of life (NA 2), but also precious religious values (GS 12). They represent a wealth of goodness embedded in the hearts of people, which finds expression in rites and symbols, and is a true preparation for the Gospel (LG 16; AG 9). They contain treasures of ascetical and contemplative life whose seeds have been planted in human beings by God before the preaching of the Gospel (AG 15, 18); hence in them are found "Seeds of the Word" (AG 11, 15).

The Council thus acknowledges in the faith of the adherents of these religions a response to the voice and self-manifestation of God (GS 16 and 22). It mentions that the Holy Spirit was already at work in the world before Christ was glorified (AG 4), referring to St. Leo who said: "When on Pentecost day the Holy Spirit filled the disciples of the Lord, he did not bring his first gift, but came with new graces; for the patriarchs and prophets and priests and all the saints of former times were enlivened and sanctified by the same Spirit[...], though they did not receive the same measure of his gifts."[1] Hence

---

1. Leo the Great, *Sermo* 76.

the Council recognises that the religious traditions have their place in God's universal design of salvation (AG 3), although it does not explain theologically the exact nature of the role they play in it. The Church of Vatican II looks at the religious traditions of humankind not as rivals, nor as historical movements wholly foreign to her, but as values intimately related to the divine mystery of which she is the repositary (LG 16; NA 2).

It is not surprising therefore that the Council makes a strong appeal to Christians for a new attitude towards the religions of the world (cf. especially NA 1-5). The Church rejects nothing of the truth and holiness found in them (NA 2); it considers with respect even those doctrines of theirs which differ from her teaching but often contain a ray of the eternal Truth (NA 2; GS 57). Hence Christians must not only discover what is true and good in other religions (OT 16) and feel at home in the national and religious traditions of various peoples (AG 11); they must also learn to acknowledge, preserve and foster their spiritual, moral and socio-cultural values (NA 2). Thus they will appreciate the riches of the gifts which God in his generosity has dispensed to the peoples of the world (AG 11, 18).

Moreover, in Vatican II the Church asserts vigorously the right to religious freedom (cf. nn. 2048ff). Christians must oppose every form of discrimination among people, based on status, race or creed (NA 5). They must be open to all forms of dialogue, imbued with the spirit of justice and love (GS 92; AG 11, 16, 34; NA 2,3). Dialogue must be practised not only at the level of co-operation in humanitarian tasks (AA 27; AG 12; GS 92); it is also a common search for socio-cultural, moral and spiritual enrichment (NA 5; AG 18). This requires discernment, for sin and evil have not been absent in human, even religious, endeavours (LG 16, 17; AG 9); but it is part of the Church's task and can be done without detriment to her duty of witnessing to the fulness of revelation addressed by God to all people in Jesus Christ (NA 2, 5; GS 28, etc).

DOGMATIC CONSTITUTION *LUMEN GENTIUM* (1964)

(The members of other religions and the People of God)

1018   16. There are finally those who have not yet received the Gospel; they too are ordained *(ordinantur)* in various ways to the People of God. In the first place there stands that people to which the covenants and promises were given and from which Christ was born according to the flesh *[cf. Rom 9:4-5]*, a people of election most dear to God because of their Fathers; for the gifts and the call of God are irrevocable *[cf. Rom 11:28-29]*. The plan of salvation includes those also who acknowledge the Creator; foremost among these are the Muslims: they profess fidelity to the faith of Abraham and, with us, adore the one and merciful God who will judge humankind on the last day. Nor is God far from those who in shadows and images seek the unknown God; for he gives to all life and breath and all things [cf. Acts 17:25-28], and as Saviour desires all to be saved [cf. 1 Tim 2:4]. For those also can attain eternal salvation who without fault on their part do not know the Gospel of Christ and his Church, but seek God with a sincere heart, and under the influence of grace endeavour to do his will as recognised through the promptings of their conscience [cf. nn. 855-857]. Nor does divine Providence deny the help necessary for salvation to those who, without fault on their part, have not yet reached an explicit knowledge of God, and yet endeavour, not without divine grace, to live a good life, for whatever goodness or truth is found among them is considered by the Church as a preparation for the Gospel[1], a gift from him who enlightens all human beings that they may finally have life. But, often enough, deceived by the evil one, human beings have become futile in their thinking and have exchanged the truth about God for a lie, serving a creature rather than the Creator [cf. Rom 1:21, 25]; there are some who, living and dying without God in this world, are a prey to utter despair. That is why the Church, in order to promote God's glory and the salvation of all these human beings, fosters the missions with great solicitude, mindful as she is of the Lord's command: "Preach the Gospel to the whole creation" [Mk 16:15].

DECLARATION *NOSTRA AETATE* (1965)

This is the first conciliar document dealing directly and explicitly with other religions. Its title, "Declaration on the relationship (habitudo) *of the Church to the non-Christian religions", is already in itself a theological statement. The history of this document is long and complex. It began with the wish expressed by Pope John XXIII that the Council should issue a statement on the Jews, to clarify the Church's stand with regard to them. Various drafts for such a statement met with difficulties, caused by political (anti-Zionism of the Arabs) and theological (Jews and Christ's death) tensions. After an abortive attempt to push the declaration on to other documents, its scope was finally enlarged so as to include the attitude of the Church not only to Judaism, but also to Islam and other religions; the final draft was approved and voted on October 28, 1965. The whole document breathes an atmosphere of respect and sympathy for the religions of the world, whose authentic values it expounds while at the same time showing the finality of Christ's revelation which the Church is commissioned to proclaim.*

---

1. Cf. Eusebius of Caesarea, *Praeparatio Evangelica*, 1,1.

Number 1 places the meeting of the Church with the world religions in the broad context of the common origin and destiny of all peoples and their search for an answer to the ultimate questions that beset them. Number 2 gives a positive description of the so-called "traditional religions", of Hinduism and of Buddhism; it explains the Church's attitude to these religions as one not merely of acceptance, but of respect and appreciation; it calls for dialogue and collaboration, whereby, while proclaiming Christ, Christians will share in the authentic values possessed by others. Number 3 describes appreciatively the Muslim beliefs; referring to the historical frictions between Christians and Muslims, it exhorts all to mutual understanding and to collaboration in common tasks. Number 4 deals with the mystery of Judaism and the Church's close relationship to it; it calls for mutual support, especially in biblical studies, and condemns all forms of anti-Semitism. Number 5 condemns in general all forms of discrimination between people.

(The unity of the human race)

1019   1. For all peoples form a single community; their origin is one for God made the whole human race to dwell over the entire face of the earth *[cf. Acts 17:26]*. One also is their final goal, God. His Providence, the manifestations of his goodness, his plan of salvation extend to all people *[cf. Wis 8:1; Acts, 14:17; Rom 2:6f: 1 Tim 2:4]*, until the moment when the elect will be gathered in the Holy City whose light shall be the glory of God, when the nations will walk in his light *[cf.Rev 2:23f]*.

(The place of religion in people's life)

1020   Human beings expect from the various religions answers to those unsolved riddles of the human condition—riddles which today as in olden times deeply stir the hearts of people: What is the human person? What is the meaning and the goal of our life? What is moral good and what is sin? What is the origin of suffering and what purpose does it serve? What is the way to true happiness? What are death, judgment, retribution after death? What, finally, is that ultimate and ineffable mystery which enfolds our existence, from which we come and to which we are going?

(The Church's stand towards other religions)

1012   2. The Catholic Church rejects nothing of what is true and holy in these religions. With sincere respect she looks on those ways of conduct and life, those precepts and teachings which, though differing on many points from what she herself holds and teaches, yet not rarely reflect a ray of that Truth which enlightens all human beings. But she proclaims and must ever proclaim Christ, "the way, the truth and the life" [*Jn* 14:6], in whom human beings find the fulness of religious life, and in whom God has reconciled all things to himself [*cf. 2 Cor* 5:18].

(The Church's concrete attitude)

1022 And so the Church has this exhortation for her children: prudently and lovingly, through dialogue and collaboration with the followers of other religions, and in witness to the Christian faith and life, acknowledge, preserve and promote the spiritual and moral good, as well as the socio-cultural values found among them.

DECREE *AD GENTES* (1965)

(Religions are a preparation for the Gospel)

1023 3. This universal design of God to save the human race is not achieved only in secret, as it were, in the hearts of people; nor merely through the undertakings *(incepta)*, including religious ones, by which they seek God in many ways, in the hope that they may feel after him and find him, though indeed he is not far from each one of us [*cf. Acts* 17:27]. For these undertakings need to be enlightened and healed, even though, in the merciful design of the provident God, they may sometimes be taken as leading the way *(paedagogia)* to the true God and as a preparation for the Gospel [*cf. n. 1018*].

(Christ heals and perfects all religious values)

1024 9. But whatever truth and grace is already found among the nations as a sort of secret presence of God [the missionary activity] frees from evil influences and restores to Christ, their author, who overthrows the reign of the devil and wards off the manifold malice of sin. So whatever good is found sown in the hearts and minds of human beings, or in the rites and cultures proper to various peoples, is not only saved from destruction but is also healed, ennobled and brought to perfection, for the glory of God, the confusion of the devil and the happiness of the human person [*cf. n. 1136*]. Thus missionary activity tends towards the eschatological fulfilment. For through it the People of God grows to the measure and time which the Father has fixed by his own authority [*cf. Acts 1:7*].

(The seeds of the Word must be illumined by the Gospel)

1025   11. In order to be able to witness to Christ fruitfully, Christians must be united to those [other] people in esteem and love. They must regard themselves as real members of the groups in which they live. They must take part in the cultural and social life through the various dealings and occupations of human life. They must be familiar with their national and religious traditions; with joy and reverence they must discover the seeds of the Word hidden in these traditions.[...] Just as Christ searched the hearts of people and led them to the divine by truly human contacts, so his disciples, deeply imbued with the Spirit of Christ, should know the human persons among whom they live and associate with them. In this way, through sincere and patient dialogue they will learn what treasures the bountiful God has distributed among the nations. At the same time they should strive to illumine those riches with the light of the Gospel, to liberate them and bring them under the dominion of God the Saviour.

(The Christian religious life must assume the religious traditions of the nations)

1026   18. The religious institutes which are working for the planting of the Church and are deeply imbued with the treasures of mysticism for which the religious tradition of the Church is so remarkable, should strive to express and hand on these treasures in a way suitable to the natural gifts and character of each people. There are ascetical and contemplative traditions in some ancient cultures the seeds of which were implanted by God before the Gospel was ever preached there. The religious institutes should carefully study how best these ascetical and contemplative traditions may be assimilated into Christian religious life.

PASTORAL CONSTITUTION *GAUDIUM ET SPES* (1965)

The Pastoral Constitution on the Church in the Modern World complements the Dogmatic Constitution on the Church (LG) and the Decree on the Church's Missionary Activity (AG). It presents a Church open and in dialogue with the world and all its values, including religious ones.

After a preliminary description of the cultural and spiritual situation of the world today the Constitution in its first part speaks of the Church in relation to the vocation of the human being. Chapter I of this first part, dealing with the mystery of the human person, recognises that the grace of the risen Lord acts invisibly in the heart of all people of good will (22). Chapter II on human society stresses the need for love, mutual understanding and dialogue, whereby, while error is rejected, persons will always find acceptance (28). Chapter III is dedicated to human activity and Chapter IV to the Church's role in the modern world. This world is ever stirred by the Holy Spirit (41); this is why for the unique contribution which she must make the Church receives help from all forms of human culture which open new ways towards truth (44) (cf. n. 1145).

This point is taken up especially in the second part which deals with particular problems, especially in the important Chapter II on promoting cultural values, a task which above all requires openness (57). The conclusion of the Constitution finds the roots for the Christian attitude of dialogue with all people, specifically of inter-religious dialogue, in the missionary call of the Church (92).

(The Holy Spirit offers to all the possibility of salvation)

1027a 22. All this holds true not only for Christians but also for all individuals of good will in whose hearts grace is active invisibly [cf. n. 1018]. For since Christ died for all [cf. Rom 8:32], and since all human beings are in fact called to one and the same destiny, which is divine, we must hold that the Holy Spirit offers to all the possibility of being associated, in a way known to God, with the paschal mystery.

(Respect and love of adversaries)

1027b 28. Respect and love ought to be extended also to those who think and act differently from us in social, political and even religious matters. In fact, the more deeply we come to understand their ways of thinking through sympathy and love, the more easily shall we be able to enter into dialogue with them.

Of course, this love and kindness must never make us in any way indifferent to what is true and good. Rather, love itself impels the disciples of Christ to announce the saving truth to all people. But we must distinguish between the error, which is always to be repudiated, and the human person in error who always keeps the dignity of being a person, even when flawed by false or less accurate religious ideas [cf. n. 2140]. God alone is the judge and searcher of hearts; hence he forbids us to make judgment about the interior guilt of any one [cf. Lk 6:37f; Mt 7:1f; Rom 2:1-11; 14:10-12].

(Dialogue among all people)

1028   92. By virtue of her mission to shed on the whole world the light of the Gospel message and to gather together in the one Spirit all people of every nation, race and culture, the Church stands forth as a sign of that kinship which makes possible, indeed stimulates, a sincere dialogue.

But this requires that first of all within the Church itself we foster esteem, respect and concord, with full recognition of legitimate differences. [...]

We also turn our thoughts to all those who acknowledge God and preserve in their traditions precious elements of religion and humanity. We wish that a frank dialogue may lead us all to welcome faithfully the impulses of the Spirit and to carry them out courageously.

For our part, the desire for such dialogue—which should be guided by the sole love of truth though with due prudence— does not exclude any one: neither those who cultivate noble human values without as yet recognising their Author, nor those who oppose the Church and persecute her in various ways. Since God the Father is the beginning and the end of all human beings, we are all called to be brothers and sisters. And thus, sharing the same vocation, both human and divine, we can and must work together, without violence or deceit, to build up the world in true peace.

PAUL VI

ENCYCLICAL LETTER *ECCLESIAM SUAM* (1964)

While presenting the programme of his pontificate in his first Encyclical Letter, Pope VI spoke of the attitudes which the Church must develop in our times. He stressed the need for friendly dialogue with all people. This fundamental openness to others gives to the Letter a tone which is in sharp contrast with the polemic attitude of many earlier documents. Dialogue is not merely a matter of policy; it is based on God's free initiative in revealing himself to humanity from which he expects a free response. God's revelation discloses nis own intimate life. The same notion of dialogue is found in the later documents of Vatican II (cf. especially NA 2-3; AG 16, 34, 41; cf. also n. 1027). In the encyclical the Pope distinguishes by way of concentric circles four classes of people with whom the Church must be in dialogue. The first and the widest circle comprises all human beings, for there is scope for dialogue with all on the fundamental problems of human life (cf. nn 155-159). In the second circle, the Church reaches out to all believers, in the third to all Christians; the fourth or inner circle concerns dialogue within the Church. The extract quoted here belongs to the second circle, that of dialogue with all believers. The text is found in AAS 56 (1964) 654-655. The Pope came back on the same topic in his Djakarta address (December 3, 1970) (cf. AAS 63 [1971] 74).

(Dialogue with all believers)

1029   Then we see another circle around us. This too is vast in extent; yet it is not so far away from us. It is made first and foremost of those people who adore the one, supreme God, whom we also worship. We refer here to the children of the Hebrew race, worthy of our respect and love. They are faithful to the tradition proper to what we call the Old Testament. We refer also to those who adore God according to the conception of monotheism, especially that of the Muslims, whom we rightly admire for the truth and goodness found in their religion. Finally we refer to the followers of the great religions of Africa and Asia. It is obvious that we cannot agree with various aspects of these religions, and that we cannot overlook differences or be unconcerned with them, as if all religions had, each in its own way, the same value, which would dispense those who follow them from the need of inquiring whether God has revealed a way free from all error and certain, by which he desires to make himself known, loved and served. Indeed, honesty compels us to declare openly what we believe, namely that there is one true religion, the Christian religion, and that we hope that all who seek God and adore him, will come to acknowledge this.

1030   Yet we do, nevertheless, acknowledge with respect the spiritual and moral values of various non-Christian religions, for we desire to join them in promoting and defending common ideals in the spheres of religious liberty, human kinship, teaching and education, social welfare and civil order. On these great ideals that we share with them we can have dialogue, and we shall not fail to offer opportunities for it whenever, in genuine mutual respect, our offer would be received with good will.

ADDRESS TO REPRESENTATIVES OF VARIOUS RELIGIONS (1964)

During the 38th International Eucharistic congress held in Bombay, the Pope, in an address to representatives of various religions, stressed the need of mutual respect and acceptance. In this and in other Bombay speeches he quoted approvingly from the sacred books of Hinduism. The text quoted below is found in AAS 57(1965) 132-33.

(The Indian religious heritage)

1031 This visit to India is the fulfilment of a long cherished desire. Yours is a land of ancient culture, the cradle of great religions, the home of a nation that has sought God with a relentless desire, in deep meditation and silence, and in hymns of fervent prayer. Rarely has this longing for God been expressed with words so full of the spirit of Advent as in the words written in your sacred books many centuries before Christ: "From the unreal lead me to the real; from darkness lead me to light; from death lead me to immortality."[1] This is a prayer which belongs also to our time. Today more than ever it should rise from every human heart.

(Towards a universal communion based on love)

1032 Therefore we must come closer together, not only through the modern means of communication, through press and radio, through steamships and jet planes; we must come together with our hearts, in mutual understanding, esteem and love. We must meet not merely as tourists, but as pilgrims who set out to find God, not in buildings of stone but in human hearts. Person must meet person, nation meet nation, as brothers and sisters, as children of God. In this mutual understanding and friendship, in this sacred communion, we must also begin to work together to build the common future of the human race. We must find the concrete and practical way of organisation and cooperation, so that all resources be pooled and all efforts united towards achieving a true communion among all nations. Such a union cannot be built on universal terror or the fear of mutual destruction; it must be built on a common love that embraces all and has its roots in God who is Love.

---

1. *Bṛhādaraṇyaka Upaniṣad*, 1, 3, 28.

LETTER *AFRICARUM TERRARUM* TO THE HIERARCHY AND THE PEOPLES OF AFRICA (1967)

In this important letter the Pope dwells at length on the basic religious experience of persons belonging to the traditional religions. A similar but less elaborate description is found in Vatican II (NA 2), where it is followed by the religious experience proper to Hinduism and Buddhism. The Pope shows the value of this fundamental religious experience. The text is found in AAS 59 (1967) 1077-1078, 1080.

(Basic religious experience)

1033   7.[...]We think it opportune to dwell on some general concepts, characteristic of the ancient cultures of Africa, as their moral and religious value demands, we think, a careful consideration.

8. As firm foundation there is in all the traditions of Africa a sense of the spiritual realities. This sense must not be understood merely as what scholars of the history of religion at the end of the last century used to call animism. It is something different, something deeper, vaster and more universal. It is the realisation that all created realities, and in particular visible nature itself, is united with the world of invisible and spiritual realities. As for human beings, they are not considered as mere matter or limited to their earthly life, but are recognised as having a spiritual active element, so that their mortal life is seen as connected at every moment with life after death.

A very important and common factor of this sense of spiritual realities is the notion of God as the first and ultimate cause of things. Such a notion is more experienced than described, more realised in life than apprehended by thought. It is expressed in many different ways according to the variety of cultural forms. In reality, a living sense of God as the supreme, personal and mystical Being, pervades the whole of African culture.

People have recourse to God in all the more important moments of life, when recourse to another intercessor is thought to be useless. Generally he is invoked as father, without any fear of the divine power. The prayers addressed to him either individually or collectively are very genuine and often touch deeply the hearts of those who hear them. Among the ritual actions performed by people one of the purest and most significant is the sacrifice of the first fruits.[...]

(Christianity assumes all that is good)

1034   14. The Catholic Church holds in great regard the moral and religious values proper to the African traditions, not only because of their own significance but also because she sees them as a providential and most fruitful foundation on which the preaching of the Gospel can be based and a new society centred on Christ can be built.[...]

In fact the doctrine and redemption of Christ fulfils, renews and perfects whatever good is found in all human traditions. Therefore, the African who is consecrated as a Christian is not forced to renounce one's own self, but assumes the ancient values of one's people "in spirit and in truth" *[Jn 6:24]*.

RADIO-MESSAGE TO THE GOVERNMENTS AND PEOPLES OF ASIA (1970)

This message was transmitted from Manila over Radio Veritas during the visit of the Pope to East Asia and Oceania, on November 1, 1970. In it the Pope salutes an immense land, "the source of great civilisations, the birthplace of world religions, the treasure-house of ancient wisdom." The whole speech is imbued with the concern to show how the values of material progress can be combined with those of the spirit. The text is found in AAS 63(1971) 37-38.

(Spiritual values and human progress)

1035   In fact, brethren, while we contemplate the past history of your nations, we are impressed most of all by the sense of spiritual values dominating the thoughts of your sages and the lives of your vast multitudes. The discipline of your ascetics, the deep religious spirit of your peoples, your filial piety and attachment to the family, your veneration of ancestors:—all point to the primacy of the spirit; all reveal your unceasing quest for God, your hunger for the supernatural.

These characteristics are not only of value for your spiritual life. For, taken together, they not only constitute no obstacle for the attainment of the technical, economic and social progress to which your immense peoples rightly aspire; but, indeed, they offer a foundation of immeasurable might for full development which does not sacrifice the deepest and most precious values, those namely which make of the human being a being directed by spiritual influences, the master, at least potentially, of the cosmos and of its forces, and likewise master of oneself.

APOSTOLIC EXHORTATION *EVANGELII NUNTIANDI*
(8 December 1975)

In his Apostolic Exhortation on Evangelization in which he resumes the work of the Synod of Bishops in Rome on the same topic (1974), Pope Paul VI speaks of the religions of the world in the context of the Church's evangelizing mission. While recognising after Vatican II that authentic values are found in those religions, he notes that their relationship to Christianity raises many questions which need to be further studied, and stresses what distinguishes the religion of Jesus which the Church proclaims through evangelization. The text is found in AAS 68(1976) 41-42.

(World religions and the Church's evangelizing mission)

1036   53. This first proclamation [of the Gospel] is also addressed to the immense sections of humankind that practice non-Christian religions. The Church respects and esteems highly these non-Christian religions, the living expression of the soul of vast groups of people. They carry within them the echo of thousands of years of searching for God, a quest incomplete indeed but often made with great sincerity and righteousness of heart. They possess an impressive heritage of deeply religious texts and have taught generations of people how to pray. They are impregnated with innumerable "Seeds of the Word" and therefore constitute an authentic "preparation for the Gospel", to quote felicitous expressions used by the Second Vatican Council [nn. 1025, 1136; 1018] and borrowed from Eusebius of Caesarea.

As we reflect on this there certainly arise many complex questions that require a great deal of prudence. These questions, which are neither light nor easy, have still to be studied by theologians, with due regard for the Christian tradition and the Church's teaching authority so as to open to missionaries of today and of tomorrow new ways in their contacts with non-Christian religions.

But neither respect and high esteem for these religions nor the complexity of the theological questions raised is an invitation to the Church to withhold from these non-Christians the proclamation of Jesus Christ. On the contrary, the Church holds that these multitudes have the right to know the riches of the mystery of Christ [cf. Eph 3:8]— riches in which, we believe, the whole humanity can find in unsuspected fulness everything that it is gropingly searching for concerning God, human beings and their destiny, life and death, and truth.

Therefore, even in the face of the highest forms of natural religions, the Church thinks that she has a unique function: the religion of Jesus which she proclaims through evangelization truly puts human beings in contact with the plan of God, with his living presence and his action. It thus enables them to meet the mystery of the Fatherhood of God that bends over towards humanity. In other words, through our religion an authentic and living relationship with God is truly established, such as other religions cannot bring about even though they have, as it were, their arms stretched out towards heaven.

JOHN PAUL II

ENCYCLICAL LETTER *REDEMPTOR HOMINIS* (1979)

At the beginning of his first Encyclical Letter on "Jesus Christ Redeemer of the human being" Pope John Paul II expresses appreciation for the progress of inter-religious dialogue between Christians and others, showing what benefit Christians can derive from such dialogue. In chapter II, entitled "The Mystery of Redemption," he describes the values contained in other religions and exhorts Christians of various denominations to share in the same mission towards them in an open spirit. The text is found in AAS 71 (1979) 257ff.

(Fostering inter-religious dialogue)

1037   6. It is obvious that this new stage in the Church's life demands of us a faith that is particularly enlightened, profound and responsible. True ecumenical activity means openness, drawing closer, availability for dialogue, and a shared investigation of the truth in the full Gospel and Christian sense; but in no way does it or can it mean giving up or in anyway underestimating the treasures of divine truth that the Church has constantly confessed and taught.[...]

What we have just said[about ecumenical action]must also be applied—although in another way and with due differences— to activity for coming closer together with representatives of the non-Christian religions, an activity expressed through dialogue, contacts, prayer in common, investigation of the treasures of human spirituality, in which, as we well know, the members of these religions are indeed not lacking. Does it not sometimes happen that the firm belief of the followers of the non-Christian religions—a belief that is also an effect of the Spirit of truth operating outside the visible confines of the Mystical Body—can make Christians ashamed at often being themselves so disposed to doubt concerning the truths revealed by God and proclaimed by the Church and so prone to relax moral principles and open the way to ethical permissiveness?It is a noble thing to have a predisposition for understanding every person, analysing every system and recognizing what is right; this does not at all mean losing certitude about one's faith [cf. n 130] or weakening the principles of morality.[...]

(Union with God and full humanity, goal of all religions)

1038   11. The Council document on non-Christian religions[...]
is filled with deep esteem for the great spiritual values, indeed for the primacy of the spiritual, which in the life of humankind finds expression in religion and then in morality, with direct effects on the whole of culture. The Fathers of the Church rightly saw in the various religions as it were so many reflections of the one truth, "seeds of the Word" [cf. nn. 1025, 1136], attesting that, though the routes taken may be different, there is but one single goal to which is directed the deepest aspiration of the human spirit as expressed in its quest for God, and also in its quest, through its tending towards God, for the full dimension of its humanity, or, in other words, for the full meaning of human life.

(Missionary attitude towards members of other religions)

1039   12. Thanks to this unity [of all Christians in mission]
we can together come close to the magnificent heritage of the human spirit that has been manifested in all religions, as the Second Vatican Council's Declaration *Nostra Aetate* says [cf. nn. 1019-1022]. It also enables us to approach all cultures, all ideological concepts, all people of good will. We come to them with the esteem, respect and discernment that since the time of the apostles has marked the missionary policy and the attitude of the missionary. Suffice it to mention St. Paul and, for instance, his address in the Areopagus at Athens[Acts 17:22-31]. The missionary attitude always begins with a feeling of deep esteem for "what is in the human being" [Jn 2:26], for what one has worked out in the depths of one's spirit concerning the most profound and important problems. It is a question of respecting

everything that has been brought about in one by the Spirit, which "blows where it wills" *[Jn 3:8]*. The mission is never destruction, but instead is a taking up and fresh building, even if in practice there has not always been full correspondence with this high ideal. And we know well that the conversion that is begun by the mission is a work of grace, in which human beings must fully find themselves again.

MESSAGE TO THE PEOPLE OF ASIA
(Manila, 21 February, 1981)

During his journey to several Asian Churches in 1981 Pope John Paul II delivered a message to the people of Asia from the Auditorium of Radio Veritas in Manila. After summarising the teaching of the Declaration Nostra Aetate *of Vatican II (cf. nn. 1019-1023), the Pope expressed the desire that inter-religious dialogue may grow, especially in Asia which is the cradle of ancient religions, in common concern for spiritual values and for the dignity of the human person. The text is found in AAS 73 (1981) 391-398.*

(Fostering inter-religious dialogue)

1040 4. In this age the Church of Jesus Christ experiences a profound need to enter into contact and dialogue with all these religions. She pays homage to the many moral values contained in these religions, as well as to the potential for spiritual living which so deeply marks the traditions and the cultures of whole societies. What seems to bring together and unite, in a particular way, Christians and believers of other religions is an acknowledgement of the need for prayer as an expression of human spirituality directed towards the Absolute. Even when, for some, he is the Great Unknown, he nevertheless remains always in reality the same living God. We trust that wherever the human spirit opens itself in prayer to this Unknown God, an echo will be heard of the same Spirit who, knowing the limits and weakness of the human person, himself prays in us and on our behalf, "expressing our plea in a way that could never be put into words" *[Rom 8:26]*. The intercession of the Spirit of God who prays in us and for us is the fruit of the mystery of the Redemption of Christ, in which the all-embracing love of the Father has been shown to the world.

5. All Christians must therefore be committed to dialogue with the believers of all religions, so that mutual understanding and collaboration may grow; so that moral values may be

strengthened; so that God may be praised in all creation. Ways must be developed to make this dialogue become a reality everywhere, but especially in Asia, the continent that is the cradle of ancient cultures and religions.[...] Christians will, moreover, join hands with all men and women of good will who share a belief in the inestimable dignity of each human person. They will work together in order to bring about a more just and peaceful society in which the poor will be the first to be served. Asia is the continent where the spiritual is held in high esteem and where the religious sense is deep and innate: the preservation of this precious heritage must be the common task of all.

SECRETARIAT FOR NON-CHRISTIANS
DIALOGUE AND MISSION (1984)

On Pentecost, 1984, the Secretariat for non-Christians published a document entitled "The Attitude of the Church toward the Followers of Other Religions: Reflections and Orientations on Dialogue and Mission." The document aims at situating inter-religious dialogue within the evangelising mission of the Church. The mission is a single but complex and articulated reality"; inter -religious dialogue is among its "principal elements" (13) (cf. n. 1164). Addressing the Plenaria of the Secretariat on the occasion of its 1984 session, Pope John Paul II remarked that "dialogue is fundamental to the Church" (2). He added: "Dialogue finds its place within the Church's salvific mission: for this reason it is dialogue of salvation" (5); nor is any local Church "exempt from this duty which is made urgent by continuous changes" (5) (AAS 76 (1984) 709-712). The document of the Secretariat gives a broad definition of inter-religious dialogue: "It means not only discussion, but also includes all positive and constructive inter-religious relations with individuals and communities of other faiths which are directed at mutual understanding and enrichment" (3). Dialogue takes on different forms: dialogue of life, of deeds, of specialists, of religious experience (28-35). The document stresses the importance of inter-religious dialogue among the "different aspects and manners of mission" (12), and expands on its theological foundation. The text is found in Bulletin. Secretariatus pro non christianis *19 (1984) 126-141.*

(The importance of dialogue within the mission)

1041   19. Respect for every person ought to characterize the missionary activity of the Church today *[cf. ES 77; EN 79-80; RH 12]*. "The human being is the first path which the Church ought to traverse in carrying out its mission" *[RH 14]*. These values, which the Church continues to learn from Christ its teacher, should lead the Christians to love and respect all that is good in the culture and the religious commitment of the other. "It concerns respect for everything which the Spirit, who blows where he wills, has produced in the human being" *[RH 12; cf. EN 79]*. The fact that Christian mission can never be separated from love and respect for others is proof for Christians of the place of dialogue within that mission.

(Dialogue is rooted in faith in God the Father...)

1042 22. The Church [...] feels itself called to dialogue principally because of its faith. In the Trinitarian mystery, Christian revelation allows us to glimpse in God a life of communion and interchange.[...]

The Church has the duty of discovering and bringing to light and fulness all the richness which the Father has hidden in creation and history, not only to celebrate the glory of God in its liturgy but also to promote among all humankind the circulation of the gifts of the Father.

(...in the Son who is united with every person)

1043 23. In God the Son we are given the Word and Wisdom in whom everything was already contained and subsisting even from the beginning of time. Christ is the Word who enlightens every person because in him is manifested at the same time the mystery of God and the mystery of humankind *[cf. RH 8, 10, 13; n. 679]*. He is the redeemer present with grace in every human encounter, to liberate us from our selfishness and to make us love one another as he has loved us.

(... in the Spirit who is at work)

1044 24. In God the Holy Spirit, our faith allows us to perceive the force of life and movement and continuous regeneration *[cf. LG 4]* which acts in the depth of people's consciences and accompanies them on the sacred path of hearts towards the truth *[cf. GS 22]*. The Spirit also works "outside the visible confines of the Mystical Body" *[RH 6; cf. LG 16; GS 22; AG 15]*. The Spirit both anticipates and accompanies the path of the Church which, nevertheless, feels itself impelled to discern the signs of his presence, to follow him wherever he leads and to serve him as a humble and discreet collaborator.

(The Church advances towards the fulness of the Kingdom, along with the rest of humankind)

1045 25. The reign of God is the final end of all persons, the Church, which is to be "its seed and beginning" *[LG. 5, 9]*, is called from the first to start out on the path towards the kingdom and, along with the rest of humanity, to advance towards that goal.

[...]The Church is thus oriented towards God's reign until its fulfilment in the perfect communion of all humankind as brothers and sisters in God.

Christ is the guarantee for the Church and the world that the "last days" have already begun, that the final age of history is already fixed *[LG 48]*, and that, therefore, the Church is equipped and commissioned to work so that there come about the progressive fulfilment of all things in Christ.

(Values preserved in the religious traditions, an invitation to dialogue)

1046 26. This vision induced the Fathers of the Second Vatican Council to affirm that in the religious traditions of non-Christians there exist "elements which are true and good" *[LG 16]*, "precious things, both religious and human" *[GS 92]*, "seeds of contemplation" *[AG 18]*, "elements of truth and grace" *[AG 9]*, "seeds of the Word" *[AG 11,15]*, and "rays of that Truth which illumines all human kind" *[NA 2]*. According to explicit conciliar indications, these values are found preserved in the great religious traditions of humanity. Therefore, they merit the attention and the esteem of Christians, and their spiritual heritage is a genuine invitation to dialogue *[cf. NA 2,3; AG 11]*, not only in those things which unite us, but also in our differences.

ADDRESS TO THE LEADERS OF OTHER RELIGIONS
(5 February, 1986)

Addressing the leaders of other religions in Madras, during the visit to India, Pope John Paul II expressed his appreciation for the spiritual values enshrined in the Indian religious traditions. He again stressed the importance of inter-religious dialogue and described its fruits both on the spiritual and the human plane. The text is found in AAS 78 (1986) 766-771.

(The fruits of inter-religious dialogue)

1047 4. Dialogue between members of different religions increases and deepens mutual respect and paves the way for relationships that are crucial in solving the problems of human suffering. Dialogue that is respectful and open to the opinions of others can promote union and a commitment to this noble cause. Besides, the experience of dialogue gives a sense of solidarity and courage for overcoming barriers and difficulties in the task of nation-building. For without dialogue the barriers of prejudice, suspicion and misunderstanding cannot be effectively removed. With dialogue, each partner makes an honest attempt to deal with the common problems of life and receives courage to accept the challenge of pursuing truth and achieving good. The experience of suffering, disappointment, disillusionment and conflict are changed from signs of failure and doom to occasions for progress in friendship and trust.

Again, dialogue is a means of seeking after truth and of sharing it with others. For truth is light, newness and strength. The Catholic Church holds that "the search for truth, however, must be carried out in a manner that is appropriate to the dignity of the human person and its social nature, namely by free enquiry with the help of teaching or instruction, communication and dialogue. It is by these means that people share with each other the truths they have discovered, or are convinced they have discovered, in such a way that they help one another in the search for truth" [DH 3]. The modern human being seeks dialogue as an apt means of establishing and developing mutual understanding, esteem and love, whether between individuals or groups. In this spirit of understanding, the Second Vatican Council urges Christians to acknowledge, preserve and promote the spiritual and moral values found among non-Christians, as well as their social and cultural values [n. 1022].

The fruit of dialogue is union between people and union of people with God, who is the source and revealer of all truth and whose Spirit guides them in freedom only when they meet one another in all honesty and love. By dialogue we let God be present in our midst; for as we open ourselves in dialogue to one another, we also open ourselves to God. We should use the legitimate means of human friendliness, mutual understanding and interior persuasion. We should respect the personal and civic rights of the individual. As followers of different religions we should join together in promoting and defending common ideals in the spheres of religious liberty, human kinship, education, culture, social welfare and civic order. Dialogue and collaboration are possible in all these great projects.

ENCYCLICAL LETTER *DOMINUM ET VIVIFICANTEM* (18 May, 1986)

Already in the Encyclical letter Redemptor Hominis *(1979), Pope John Paul II had stressed the operative presence of the Holy Spirit in the religious life of the people belonging to other religious traditions (6) (n. 1037). In this new encyclical he broadens the perspective, affirming the universal action of the Holy Spirit in the world before the Christian dispensation, to which this action was ordained, and referring to the universal action of the same Spirit today, outside the confines of the visible body of the Church. The text is found in AAS 78 (1986) 809-900.*

(The universal presence of the Holy Spirit)

1048   53.[...]We cannot limit ourselves to the two thousand years which have passed since the birth of Christ. We need to go further back, to embrace the whole of the action of the Holy Spirit even before Christ—from the beginning, throughout the world, and especially in the economy of the Old Covenant. For this action has been exercised, in every place and at every time, indeed in every individual, according to the eternal plan of salvation, whereby this action was to be closely linked with the mystery of the incarnation and redemption, which in its turn exercised its influence on those who believed in the future coming of Christ. [...] Grace, therefore, bears within itself both a Christological aspect and a pneumatological one, which becomes evident above all in those who expressly accept Christ.[...]

But [...] we need to look further and go further afield, knowing that "the wind blows where it will" [...] [*cf. Jn 3:8*]. The Second Vatican Council, centred primarily on the theme of the Church, reminds us of the Holy Spirit's activity also "outside the visible body of the Church". The Council speaks precisely of "all people of good will in whose hearts grace works in an unseen manner [*cf. n. 1018*]. For, since Christ died for all [*cf. Rom 8:32*], and since the ultimate vocation of the human person is in fact one, and divine, we must hold that the Holy Spirit, in a manner known to God, offers to all the possibility of being associated with the Paschal Mystery" [*GS 22; n. 1027a*].

ADDRESS TO THE ROMAN CURIA
(22 December, 1986)

In the address which he delivered to the Roman Curia after the World Day of Prayer for Peace in Assisi with leaders of different religious traditions (27 October 1986), Pope John Paul II insisted once more on the universal presence of the Holy Spirit in all people, stating that "every authentic prayer is called forth by the Holy Spirit, who is mysteriously present in the heart of every person" (11). Going beyond the individual perspective, he articulated the main elements which together can be seen as constituting the theological basis for a positive appraisal of other religious traditions and the practice of inter-religious dialogue. There is first the fact that the whole of humankind forms one family due to the common origin of all, created by God in his own image. Correspondingly, there is the common destiny of all, as all are called to the fulness of life in God. There is, moreover, God's unique plan of salvation, with its centre in Jesus Christ, who in his incarnation "has united himself in some manner to every person" [RH 13; n. 668]. There is finally the active presence of the Holy Spirit in the religious life of the members of the other religious traditions. From all this the Pope concludes to a "mystery of unity", which was manifested clearly at Assisi, "inspite of the differences between the religious professions" (8). The Pope sees in the day of Assisi a practical expression, in a new form of ministry, of the insights of Vatican II regarding the Church and its relations to other religions. The text is found in ASS 79 (1987) 1082-1090.

(Unity in creation)

1049 3. More than once, the Council established a relationship between the very identity and the mission of the Church on the one hand, and the unity of the human race, on the other, especially when it chose to define the Church as "a sacrament, ie. a sign and instrument of intimate unity with God and of the unity of the whole human race" [LG 9; cf. GS 42].

The radical unity, which belongs to the very identity of the human being, is based on the mystery of the divine creation. The one God in whom we believe, Father, Son and Holy Spirit, the Most Holy Trinity, created man and woman with a particular attention, according to the narrative of Genesis [cf. Gen 1:26ff; 2:7, 18-24]. This affirmation contains and communicates a profound truth: the unity of the divine origin of all the human family, of every man and woman, reflected in the unity of the divine image which each bears in oneself [cf. Gen 1:26] and itself gives the orientation to a common goal [cf. n. 1019]. "You have made us for yourself, O Lord", exclaims St. Augustine, in the fulness of his maturity as a thinker, "and our heart has no rest, until it rests in you."[1] The Dogmatic Constitution *Dei Verbum* declares that "God, who creates and conserves all things by his Word, provides people with constant evidence of himself[...] and he never ceases to take care of the human race, for he wishes to give eternal life to all who seek salvation through perseverance in doing good" [DV 3].

Accordingly, there is only one divine plan for every human being who comes into this world [cf. Jn 1:9], one single origin and goal, whatever may be the colour of the skin, the historical and geographical framework within which one happens to live and act, or the culture in which one grows up and expresses oneself. The differences are a less important element, when confronted with the unity which is radical, fundamental and decisive.

(Mystery of unity)

1050   5. In the light of this mystery, it becomes clear that the differences of every type, and first of all the religious differences, belong to another order, to the extent that they reduce the design of God. If it is the order of unity that goes back to creation and redemption and is therefore, in this sense, "divine", such differences—and even religious divergences—go back rather to a "human fact", and must be overcome in progress towards the realization of the mighty plan of unity which dominates the creation. There are undeniably differences that reflect the genius and the spiritual "riches" which God has given to the peoples [cf. AG 11]. I am not referring to these divergences: I intend here to speak of the differences in which are revealed the limitation, the evolutions and the falls of the human spirit which is undermined by the spirit of evil in history [LG 16].

It may be the case that persons are often unaware of this radical unity of their origin and destiny, and their place in one and the same divine plan; and when they profess religions which are diverse and mutually incompatible, they can also feel that their divisions are insuperable. Yet despite these divisions, they are included in the great and unique design of God, in Jesus

---

1. *Confessions*, 1

Christ, who "has united himself in some manner to every person" [GS 22], even if the person in question is not aware of this.

(The Church, sacrament of unity)

1051 6. In this great design of God for humanity, the Church finds her identity and her task as "universal sacrament of salvation" precisely in being "a sign and instrument of intimate union with God and of the unity of the whole human race" [LG 1]; this means that the Church is called to work with all her energies (evangelization, prayer, dialogue) so that the wounds and divisions— which separate people from their Origin and Goal, and make them hostile to one another—may be healed; it means also that the entire human race, in the infinite complexity of its history, with its different cultures, is "called to form the new People of God" [LG 13] in which the blessed union of God with people and the unity of the human family are healed, consolidated and raised up: "All persons, accordingly, are called to this *catholic unity* of the People of God, which prefigures and promotes universal peace, and to which, in various ways, belong or are oriented both the Catholic faithful and the others who believe in Christ, and finally all who have been called to salvation by the grace of God" [ibid.].

(The day of Assisi)

1052 9. The day of Assisi, showing the Catholic Church holding the hands of fellow Christians, and all these joining hands with the brothers and sisters of other religions, was a visible expression of the statements of the Second Vatican Council. With this day, and by means of it, we have succeeded, by the grace of God, in realizing this conviction of ours, inculcated by the Council, about the unity of the origin and goal of the human family, and about the meaning and the values of the non-Christian religions—without the least shadow of confusion or syncretism.

Has not the day taught us to read afresh, in our turn, with eyes more open and penetrating, the rich teaching of the Council about the salvific plan of God, about the centrality in this plan of Jesus Christ, and about the profound unity which is the starting-point and the goal of this plan, by means of the ministry of the Church? The Catholic Church revealed herself to her children and to the world in the exercise of her function of "promoting unity and charity among human persons, indeed, among the peoples" [NA 1].

In this sense, one must say also that the very identity of the Catholic Church and her self-awareness have been reinforced at Assisi. For the Church—that is, we ourselves—has understood better, in the light of this event, what is the true sense of the mystery of unity and reconciliation which the Lord has entrusted to us, and which he himself carried out first, when he offered his life" not for the nation only, but to gather into one the children of God who are scattered abroad" [Jn 11:52].

LETTER TO THE BISHOPS OF ASIA
(23 January, 1990)

The fifth Plenary Assembly of the Federation of Asian Bishops' Conferences took place in Bandung, Indonesia, 17-27 July, 1990. On this occasion Pope John Paul II addressed a letter to the Asian bishops in which he wrote that the possibility of salvation in Christ outside the Church does not lessen the Church's duty to proclaim Jesus Christ. The text is found in GIOVANNI PAOLO II, *Insegnamenti, 1990, XIII/1, pp. 1653-1654.*

(Salvation in other Religions and the Proclamation of Jesus Christ)

1053   4. Although the Church gladly acknowledges whatever is true and holy in the religious traditions of Buddhism, Hinduism and Islam as a reflection of that Truth which enlightens all people, this does not lessen her duty and resolve to proclaim without fail Jesus Christ who is "the way, the truth and the life [Jn 14:6].[...] The fact that the followers of other religions can receive God's grace and be saved by Christ apart from the ordinary means which he has established does not thereby cancel the call to faith and baptism which God wills for all people [cf. AG 7]. It is a contradiction of the Gospel and of the Church's very nature to assert, as some do, that the Church is only one way of salvation among many, and that her mission towards the followers of other religions should be nothing more than to help them to be better followers of those religions.

5. The mission of God's people[...] is twofold: to bear witness to Christ and "the things that are above, where Christ is, seated at the right hand of God" [Col 3:1], and to be a leaven of love and goodness in the affairs of this world until Christ returns in glory.

ENCYCLICAL LETTER *REDEMPTORIS MISSIO*
(7 December, 1990)

The encyclical is devoted to the "permanent validity of the Christian mission". Chapter V explains the "various paths of mission" in the following order: witness, first proclamation, conversion and baptism, forming local Churches, ecclesial basic communities, inculturation; and, finally, dialogue and the promotion of human development. The text is found in AAS 83 (1991) 249-340.

(Interreligious dialogue, part of the evangelising mission)

1054 55. Interreligious dialogue is a part of the Church's evangelising mission. Understood as a method and means of mutual knowledge and enrichment, dialogue is not in opposition to the mission *ad gentes;* indeed, it has special links with the mission and is one of its expressions. This mission, in fact, is addressed to those who do not know Christ and his Gospel, and who belong for the most part to other religions. In Christ, God calls all people to himself and he wishes to share with them the fulness of his revelation and love. He does not fail to make himself present in many ways, not only to individuals but also to entire peoples through their spiritual riches, of which their religions are the main and essential expression, even when they contain "gaps, insufficiencies and errors" *[cf. nn. 1021-1022; 1018; 1024: 1036].*

(Interreligious dialogue in the Church's mission)

1055 55. In the light of the economy of salvation, the Church sees no conflict between proclaiming Christ and engaging in interreligious dialogue. Instead, she feels the need to link the two in the context of her mission *ad gentes.* These two elements must maintain both their intimate connection and their distinctiveness; therefore they should not be confused, manipulated or regarded identical, as though they were interchangeable.

(Guiding principles of dialogue)

1056 56. Dialogue does not originate from tactical concerns or self-interest, but is an activity with its own guiding principles, requirements and dignity. It is demanded by deep respect for everything that has been brought about in human beings by the Spirit who blows where he wills *[cf. n. 1039].*

Through dialogue the Church seeks to uncover the "seeds of the Word" [cf. n. 1025], a "ray of that Truth which enlightens all people" [cf. n 1021]; these are found in individuals and in the religious traditions of humankind. Dialogue is based on hope and love, and will bear fruit in the Spirit.

(Spirit and fruits of dialogue)

1057   56. Those engaged in this dialogue must be consistent with their own religious traditions and convictions, and be open to understanding those of the other party without pretence or close-mindedness, but with truth, humility and frankness, knowing that dialogue can enrich each side. There must be no abandonment of principles or false irenicism, but instead a witness given and received for mutual advancement on the road of religious inquiry and experience, and at the same time for the elimination of prejudice, intolerance and misunderstandings. Dialogue leads to inner purification and conversion which, if pursued with docility to the Holy Spirit, will be spiritually fruitful.

(Dialogue may be the only way to witness to Christ)

1058   57.[...]Many missionaries and Christian communities find in the difficult and often misunderstood path of dialogue their only way of bearing witness to Christ and offering generous service to others.[...] Dialogue is a path towards the Kingdom and will certainly bear fruit, even if the times and seasons are known only to the Father [cf. Acts 1:7].

PONTIFICAL COUNCIL FOR INTERRELIGIOUS DIALOGUE CONGREGATION FOR THE EVANGELISATION OF PEOPLES

DIALOGUE AND PROCLAMATION (19 May, 1991)

In 1984 the Secretariat for non-Christians had published "Dialogue and Mission" (cf. nn. 1041-1046; 1164) in which it explained that dialogue is part of the Church's evangelising mission. This, however, raised the further question of the relationship between interreligious dialogue and the proclamation of Jesus Christ. This question is studied in the present document, conjointly published by the Pontifical Council for Interreligious Dialogue and the Congregation for the Evangelisation of Peoples. It is entitled "Dialogue and Proclamation. Reflections and Orientations on Interreligious Dialogue and the Proclamation of the Gospel of Jesus Christ". The document is made up of three parts: 1. Dialogue; 2. Proclamation; 3. Dialogue and Proclamation. Extracts dealing with dialogue and its relationship to proclamation are given here; others directly dealing with proclamation are found in Chapter XI (nn. 1176-1179). The first part of the document begins with "A Christian approach to Religious Traditions";' it then reaffirms the place of interreligious dialogue in the mission of the Church. The relationship between dialogue and proclamation is found in the third part. The text is found in Bulletin n. 77;26 (1991/2) 210-250.

(Positive role of the religious traditions)

1059   29. From this mystery of unity *[cf. n. 1049i]* it follows that all men and women who are saved, share, though differently, in the same mystery of salvation in Jesus Christ through his Spirit. Christians know this through their faith, while others remain unaware that Jesus Christ is the source of their salvation. The mystery of salvation reaches out to them, in a way known to God, through the invisible action of the Spirit of Christ. Concretely, it will be in the sincere practice of what is good in their own religious traditions and by following the dictates of their conscience that the members of other religions respond positively to God's invitation and receive salvation in Jesus Christ, even while they do not recognise or acknowledge him as their Saviour *[cf. nn. 1023-1025].*

(Discernment is required to identify elements of grace in the religious traditions)

1060   30. To identify in other religious traditions elements of grace capable of sustaining the positive response of their members to God's invitation[...] requires a discernment for which criteria have to be established. Sincere individuals marked by the Spirit of God have certainly put their imprint on the elaboration and the development of their respective religious traditions. It does not follow, however, that everything in them is good.

31. To say that other religious traditions include elements of grace does not imply that everything in them is the result of grace. For sin has been at work in the world, and so religious traditions, notwithstanding their positive values, reflect the limitations of the human spirit, sometimes inclined to choose evil. An open and positive approach to other religious traditions cannot overlook the contradictions which may exist between them and Christian revelation. It must, where necessary, recognise

that there is incompatibility between some fundamental elements of the Christian religion and some aspects of such traditions.

(Mutual challenge)

1061 32.[...]While entering with an open mind into dialogue with the followers of other religious traditions, Christians may have also to challenge them in a peaceful spirit with regard to the content of their belief. But Christians too must allow themselves to be questioned. Notwithstanding the fulness of God's revelation in Jesus Christ, the way Christians sometimes understand their religion and practice it may be in need of purification.

(Universality of the Reign of God present in history)

1062 35. To the Church, as the sacrament in which the Kingdom of God is present "in mystery", are related or oriented *(ordinantur) [cf. n 1018]* the members of other religious traditions who, in as much as they respond to God's calling as perceived by their conscience, are saved in Jesus Christ and thus already share in some way in the reality which is signified by the Kingdom. The Church's mission is to foster "the Kingdom of our Lord and his Christ" *[Rev 11:15]*, at whose service she is placed. Part of her role consists in recognising that the inchoate reality of this Kingdom can be found also beyond the confines of the Church, for example in the hearts of the followers of other religious traditions, insofar as they live evangelical values and are open to the action of the Spirit. It must be remembered, however, that this is indeed an inchoate reality, which needs to find completion through being related to the Kingdom of Christ already present in the Church yet realized fully only in the world to come.

(Aim of interreligious dialogue)

1063 40. In dialogue Christians and others are invited to deepen their religious commitment, to respond with increasing sincerity to God's personal call and gracious self gift which, as our faith tells us, always passes through the mediation of Jesus Christ and the work of his Spirit.

41. Given this aim, a deeper conversion of all towards God, interreligious dialogue possesses its own validity.[...] Sincere dialogue implies, on the one hand, mutual acceptance of

differences, or even of contradictions, and on the other, respect for the free decision of persons taken according to the dictates of their conscience [cf. nn 1021-1022].

(Dialogue and proclamation, interrelated yet not interchangeable)

1064 77. Interreligious dialogue and proclamation, though not on the same level, are both authentic elements of the Church's evangelising mission. Both are legitimate and necessary. They are intimately related, but not interchangeable: true interreligious dialogue on the part of the Christian supposes the desire to make Jesus Christ better known, recognised and loved; proclaiming Jesus Christ is to be carried out in the Gospel spirit of dialogue. The two activities remain distinct but, as experience shows, one and the same person, can be diversely engaged in both.

(Dialogue remains open to proclamation)

1065 82. [...]Dialogue[...] does not constitute the whole mission of the Church[...]; it cannot simply replace proclamation, but remains oriented towards proclamation in so far as the dynamic process of the Church's evangelising mission reaches in it its climax and its fulness. As they engage in interreligious dialogue they will discover the "seeds of the Word" sown in people's hearts and in the religious traditions to which they belong. In deepening their appreciation of the mystery of Christ they will be able to discern the positive values in the human search for the unknown or incompletely known God.[...] Christians in dialogue have the duty of responding to their partners' expectations regarding the contents of the Christian faith, of bearing witness to this faith when this is called for, of giving an account of the hope that is within them [cf. 1 Pet 3:15].

APOSTOLIC LETTER *TERTIO MILLENNIO ADVENIENTE*
(10 November 1994)

In spite of his repeated insistence on the universal presence of the Holy Spirit not only in all people but also in their religious traditions, in this apostolic letter on the forthcoming third millennium (cf. n. 933i) John Paul II explains the relationship between Christianity and the other religions in a way which is reminiscent of Paul VI's assessment in the apostolic exhortation Evangelii Nuntiandi *(cf. n. 1036), echoing the "fulfilment theory" of religions. The text is found in* AAS 87 (1995) 8-9.

(Christianity and World Religions)

1066   6. Jesus does not [...] merely speak "in the name of God" like the prophets, but he is God himself speaking in his eternal Word made flesh. Here we touch upon the essential point by which Christianity differs from all the other religions, by which the human search for God has been expressed from earliest times. Christianity has its starting-point in the incarnation of the Word. Here, it is not simply a case of the human search for God, but of God who comes in person to speak to human beings of himself and to show them the path by which he may be reached [...]. The incarnated Word is thus the fulfilment of the yearning present in all the religions of humankind: this fulfilment is brought about by God himself and transcends all human expectations. It is the mystery of grace.

In Christ, religion is no longer a "blind search for God" [*cf. Acts 17:27*] but the response of faith to God who reveals himself[...]. Christ is thus the fulfilment of the yearning of all the world's religions and, as such, he is their sole and definitive completion.

COMMISSION FOR RELIGIOUS RELATIONS WITH THE JEWS

WE REMEMBER: A REFLECTION ON THE "SHOAH"

(16 March 1998)

Since the Second Vatican Council (cf. Lumen Gentium 16, here n. 1018; Nostra Aetate 4), efforts have been made to develop renewed relations between Judaism and Christianity. The visit of pope John Paul II to the synagogue in Rome (1986) and his recent visit to Israel (20-26 March 2000) are important landmarks in these renewed relations. So are many recent pronouncements by the pope himself and by episcopal conferences. In the document that follows below the Vatican Commission for Religious Relations with the Jews writes: "The spoiled seeds of anti-Judaism and anti-Semitism must never again be allowed to take root in any human heart". In an accompanying letter addressed to Cardinal Edward Cassidy, president of the commission, pope John Paul II said he hoped that the document would "enable memory to play its necessary part in the process of shaping a future in which the unspeakable iniquity of the "Shoah" will never again be possible". The document refers to the "Shoah" as "the work of a thoroughly modern neopagan regime" whose "anti-Semitism had its roots outside of Christianity". But, the document says, "it may be asked whether the Nazi persecution of the Jews was not made easier by the anti-Jewish prejudices imbedded in some Christian minds and hearts". Document in English in Origins, n. 40; 27 (1998) 670-675.

(What we must remember)

1067   While bearing their unique witness to the Holy One of Israel and to the Torah, the Jewish people have suffered much at different times and in many places. But the Shoah was certainly the worst suffering of all. The inhumanity with which the Jews were persecuted and massacred during this century is beyond the capacity of words to convey. All this was done to them for the sole reason that they were Jews.

(Nazi Anti-Semitism and the Shoah)

1068   We cannot ignore the difference which exists between *anti-Semitism*, based on theories contrary to the consistent teaching of the Church on the unity of the human race and on the equal dignity of all races and people, and the long-standing sentiments of mistrust and hostility that we call *anti-Judaism*, of which, unfortunately, Christians also have been guilty [...].

[...] The *Shoah* was the work of a thoroughly modern neopagan regime. Its anti-Semitism had its roots outside of Christianity, and in pursuing its aims, it did not hesitate to oppose the Church and persecute her members also.

But it may be asked whether the Nazi persecution of the Jews was not made easier by the anti-Jewish prejudices imbedded in some Christian minds and hearts. Did anti-Jewish sentiment among Christians make them less sensitive or even indifferent to the persecutions launched against the Jews by National Socialism when it reached power?

(A matter of deep regret)

1069   We deeply regret the errors and failures of those sons and daughters of the church. We make our own what is said in the Second Vatican Council's declaration *Nostra Aetate*, which unequivocally affirms: "The church [...], mindful of her common patrimony with the Jews and motivated by the Gospel's spiritual love and by non political considerations, deplores the hatred, persecutions and displays of anti-Semitism directed against the Jews at any time and from any source" [NA 4].

(Looking together to a common future)

1070   Looking to the future of relations between Jews and Christians, in the first place we appeal to our Catholic

brothers and sisters to renew the awareness of the Hebrew roots
of their faith. We ask them to keep in mind that Jesus was a
descendant of David; that the Virgin Mary and the apostles
belonged to the Jewish people; that the Church draws sustenance
from the root of that good olive tree onto which have been
grafted the wild olive branches of the gentiles [cf. Rm 11:17-24];
that the Jews are our dearly beloved brothers, indeed in a certain
sense they are "our elder brothers"[1].[...]

We pray that our sorrow for the tragedy which the Jewish
people have suffered in our century will lead to a new
relationship with the Jewish people. We wish to turn awareness
of past sins into a firm resolve to build a new future in which
there will be no more anti-Judaism among Christians or anti-
Christian sentiment among Jews, but rather a shared mutual
respect as befits those who adore the one Creator and Lord and
have a common father in faith, Abraham.

---

1. JOHN PAUL's speech at the Rome synagogue (April 13, 1986) 4: AAS 78
(1986) 1120.

CHAPTER XI

THE CHURCH AND THE MISSIONS

"Go and make disciples of all nations" (Mt 28:19): *such was the command of the risen Christ to his apostles; "and they went forth and preached everywhere"* (Mk 16:20). *The Acts of the Apostles testify to the missionary activity of the apostolic Church. Ever since, the Church obeying Christ's mandate, has continued to proclaim his message to new peoples. This effort sustained through the centuries witnesses to the Church's sure instinct as regards her missionary vocation.*

To be missionary is not for the Church a merely accidental function; it belongs to her very nature. The reason is that in God's plan of salvation for the world her mission prolongs the mission of the Incarnate Son. What God has once for all accomplished in Jesus Christ for the salvation of people is, as it were, actuated in space and time through the Church: his saving word remains audible in her proclamation of the Gospel; his redeeming work becomes tangible in her actions. Established by Christ as the "universal sacrament of salvation" (AG 1), the Church must fulfill her function at all times and in every place. Through her God's design must be realised that all may come to the full knowledge of the Truth. Hence the Church's urge to communicate the Good News to all people.

In the early centuries few official documents spoke of the Church's missionary activity. Here as in other areas of the Church's life, practice has preceded theory; the conversion of the ancient Christian world witnesses, however, to the vitality of the Church's mission during that period. The conditions created by the Middle Ages, while offering to the Church new opportunities to meet the outside world, did not favour a profound reflection on the mission. A few texts belonging to this period are mentioned here; they witness to the positive and negative elements in the Church's discharge of her mandate. The modern times have brought with them a great missionary movement. It is a well known fact that the vast extension of the boundaries of the Church to remote lands during this period has sometimes been unduly linked to worldly interests and has suffered from this association. Yet, not to mention the boundless zeal of missionaries, this period is also marked with deep missionary insights and with a great foresight on the part of the Church in the exercise of her missionary action. Texts testify to both. The elaboration of an explicit theology of the missions remains, nevertheless, a later development, characteristic of this century. Its progress can be followed through the missionary encyclicals of the Popes. The fundamental principles of missionary theology emerge more and more definitely in these documents. An adequate definition of the purpose of missionary activity evolves gradually; the role of the local clergy and hierarchy stands out more and more clearly; progressive recognition is given to the principle of missionary adaptation.

This impressive elaboration notwithstanding, the missions have in recent years met with new questioning. A first reason for this is the Church's renewed awareness of the fact that God can save people by ways known to him; prolonged and sincere contact with other religions and their adherents has, moreover, convinced the Church that they too already live by God's grace which reaches them in the concrete circumstances of their religious life. Another reason is that to the outsider the Christian mission appears as imposing a narrow institutional set-up with its inherent limitations and its own cultural heritage; the Church herself has become more conscious of the constant danger that threatens her of sacrificing the mystery to the institution. All this has led to a new reflection on the true nature of the Church and of her missionary activity which it is the merit of the Second Vatican Council to have brought to fruition. The Council has shown that the institution of the Church is rooted in the mystery of Christ. She is not an end in herself, but has for her only purpose to make Christ and his work visibly present in the world. This renewed understanding of the Church, implying a radical de-centring, brings with it a new theological perception of her missionary activity and a new approach to her missionary practice. Based essentially on presence and witnessing, it overcomes all the antinomies and embraces all the various forms of Christian action. It is shared responsibility of the whole Church, especially of all the members of the local Churches where Christ remains unknown to many. It is in order to be as perfect a sign of Christ as possible that the local Churches must be endowed with all the elements that constitute the mystery of the Church. The evangelising mission of the Church is a complex reality, including various aspects among which is involvement for human liberation. It needs to be deeply inserted into the culture of different peoples through inculturation.

*   *   *

The doctrinal points dealt with in this chapter may be grouped under the following headings:

The Church is essentially missionary: (1136i), 1136, 1137, 1141.

Her missionary activity takes a special form in the missions: 1136, 1138, 1143

The purposes of the missions is to evangelise and to establish the Church: 1116, 1123, 1126, 1138, 1149.

Missionary motivation is to bring others to Christ and the Church: 1115, 1139, 1140.

The local Churches must develop to maturity: 1142, 1143.

They must make their contribution to the universality of the Church: 1119, 1120, 1124, 1125, 1131, 1144, 1145.

They must have their local hierarchy: 1107, 1112, 1116, 1142;

their local priests : 1107, 1112, 1116, 1142;

their local religious and an active laity: 1117, 1128, 1133, 1135, 1142.

All share in the missionary activity of the local Church: 1118, (1136i).

Priests of local Churches must be well trained : 1112, 1132,(1136i).

The laity must be well trained: 1101, 1133, 1134, (1136i).

The local Church must be rooted in the culture of the land and assume all its values: 1102, 1109, 1120, 1121, 1122, 1125, 1129, 1136, 1144.

Adaptation to local customs is the law of the mission: 1102, 1108, 1109, 1120, 1121, 1129, 1144, 1145, 1233.

Theological reflection must seek ways of presenting the message adapted to the country: 1132, 1144, 1145, 1175, 1182, 1183.

The inculturation of the message must preserve its content intact: 1158-1160, 1161, 1165, 1174, 1180-1181, 1184.

The law of adaptation applies especially to foreign missionaries: 1104, 1105, 1106, 1109, 1113, 1114, 1122.

They are destined to become auxiliaries to the local clergy: 1127.

Evangelisation means the renewal of humanity and of culture: 1150-1152.

Witnessing, dialogue and proclamation, all belong to missionary activity: 1111, (1136i), 1164.

Proclamation has the permanent priority: 1173.

Divine pedagogy of proclamation: 1176-1179.

Evangelisation and development complement each other: 1146-1148, (1155).

Evangelisation includes liberation: (1153)-(1154).

Two dimensions of liberation proclaimed by the Church : (1156), 1162.

Evangelisation includes the promotion of justice: 1163, 1164, 2159.

The Reign of God, universally present, is related to Christ and the Church : 1169, 1170, 1171.

THE FIRST GENERAL COUNCIL OF NICAEA (325)

Besides its Symbol of faith (cf. n. 7), the first Council of Nicaea promulgated a series of canons. Among these one recommends a long catechesis for new converts to the faith and forbids that neophytes be promoted to the episcopate or presbyterate without adequate probation. The text is found in COD, p.6.

(On neophytes)

1101   Canon 2: Many things have been done against the ecclesiastical rule, either out of necessity or under pressure from human beings.Thus people acceding to the faith from the life of the gentiles are soon led to the spiritual cleansing, and at once after baptism are promoted to the episcopate or the presbyterate. It has seemed best that nothing of the sort be done hereafter. For catechesis requires time and after baptism a long probation is needed. The text of the apostle is indeed clear where it says: "he must not be a recent convert, or he may be puffed up with conceit and fall into condemnation and the snare of the devil" *[cf. 1 Tim 3:6-7]* [...]

GREGORY THE GREAT (590-604)
LETTER TO ABBOT MELLITUS

This letter was addressed by Pope Gregory the Great to Mellitus, abbot in France, who was about to join St. Augustine of Canterbury as a fellow missionary. The Pope instructs his correspondent to show his letter to Augustine, as it is concerned with the missionary methods to be used for an easier conversion of England. This instruction is a practical combination of sound psychology, tolerance and firmness. Rather than destroy the temples of the people they evangelise, missionaries should aim at converting them into churches. Thus there will be continuity and newness between the peoples' ancient religion and their new faith; being allowed to retain their places of worship, they will more readily accept the mystery of Christ celebrated in them. Nor is it to be expected that new Christians will grasp at once the full meaning of the Christian faith; this requires time. If allowed to continue some of their time-honoured customs, they will gradually discover the new meaning they take on in Christianity. See Epistola 76, PL 77, 1215-1216.

(The temples must not be destroyed but converted into Christian Churches)

1102   Tell Augustine that he should by no means destroy the temples of the gods but rather the idols within those temples. Let him, after he has purified them with holy water, place altars and relics of the saints in them. For, if those temples are well built, they should be converted from the worship of demons to the service of the true God. Thus, seeing that their places of worship are not destroyed, the people will banish error from their hearts and come to places familiar and dear to them in acknowledgment and worship of the true God.

Further, since it has been their custom to slaughter oxen in sacrifice to the demons, they should receive some solemnity in exchange. Let them, therefore, on the day of the dedication of their churches, or on the feast of the martyrs whose relics are preserved in them, build themselves huts around their one-time temples and celebrate the occasion with religious feasting. They will sacrifice and eat the animals not any more as an offering to the devil, but for the glory of God to whom, as to the giver of all things, they will give thanks for having been satiated. Thus, it they are not deprived of all the exterior joys, they will more easily taste the interior ones. For surely it is impossible to efface all at once everything from their strong minds, just as, when one wishes to reach the top of a mountain one must climb by stages and step by step, not by leaps and bounds [......]

Mention this then to our brother the bishop, that he may dispose of the matter as he sees fit according to the conditions of time and place [.....]

THE FOURTH LATERAN GENERAL COUNCIL (1215)

Besides its doctrinal pronouncements on the Catholic faith (cf. nn. 19-21) and on the mystery of the Trinity (cf. nn. 317-320), the Council also promulgated other "Constitutions" mostly concerned with practical matters, for instance liturgical (cf. nn. 1201-1202). Among these is found a chapter forbidding converts from Judaism to retain their Jewish practices. The text must be understood in the historical context of the times when the Church was engaged in her effort to free the Holy Land from the Saracens. This context was not conducive to a friendly attitude towards Judaism. Christianity appeared as a complete break with Judaism and little attention was given to the religious heritage which it inherited from the Jewish tradition. In fact, as the Council testifies (68, 69), social discrimination against the Jews, including distinction in dress and exclusion from public offices, was part of the policy enforced by the Church. Neither were converts from Judaism allowed to identify themselves with their people of origin; sincere conversion seemed to demand a complete break. The text is found in COD, p. 267.

Chapter LXX: Jewish Converts to the Faith May not Retain their
Ancient Practices.

1103   There are some, as has been reported to us, who after
having freely approached the sacred bath of baptism do
not put off the old person fully in order the better to put on the
new one [cf. Col. 3:9]; they retain elements of their former rites
and thus by a sort of mixture introduce confusion in the
splendour of the Christian religion. Since it is written: Woe to
the one who walks along two ways [cf. Sir 2:14; 3:28], and that
one must not wear mingled dress, wool and linen together [cf.
Deut 22:11], we decide that such converts must be forced by those
who preside over the Churches to abandon altogether the
observance of their ancient rites so that, after having given to
the Christian religion the assent of their free will, they may be
preserved in its observance by the pressure of salutary
compulsion. For it is a lesser evil not to recognise the way of the
Lord than to step back after having recognised it.

THE GENERAL COUNCIL OF VIENNE (1131-1312)

This Council also met in the context of the long drawn-out crusade for
the liberation of the Holy Land from the Saracens. Besides its doctrinal decrees
(cf. n. 405), it contains others on practical matters. One of these (25) legislates
that the cult rendered to Muhammad by the Saracens must be forbidden in
Christian lands. This stricture notwithstanding, the Council recognises the
demands which the work of evangelisation makes on the preachers of the Gospel
in foreign lands: they must be thoroughly conversant with the languages
required for convincingly presenting the message of Christ. In the historical
context mention is made of the languages needed for the evangelisation of the
Muslims. The text of this decree 24 is found in COD, pp. 379.

(On the knowledge of languages required for the work of evangelisation)

1104   24.[...]Therefore, unworthy as we are of the commission
which Christ has entrusted to us in this world, following
his own example when he wished that the apostles who were to
go to evangelise the whole world should be well versed in all
languages [cf. Acts 2:4; 1 Cor 12:30], we desire that the holy
Church should have an abundant number of Catholics well
versed in the languages, especially in those of the infidels, so as
to be able to instruct them in the sacred doctrine and to join
them to the Christian community by the acceptance of the
Christian faith and the reception of holy baptism.[...] Once they

have learned and are sufficiently proficient in those languages (Hebrew, Arabic, Chaldaean), they will be able by God's grace to bear the fruit which is hoped for and to present the faith adequately to the infidel peoples.[...]

THE GENERAL COUNCIL OF BASEL
DECREE ON JEWS AND NEOPHYTES (1434)

This decree belongs to the Basel period of the 17th general Council celebrated from 1431 to 1445, which held its sessions at Basel, Ferrara, Florence and Rome, successively. The decrees of sessions I to XXI of Basel though passed almost in their entirety while the Council was under censure from Pope Eugene IV, were subsequently approved by him and form an integral part of the work of the general Council. The decree quoted here (session XIX) again witnesses to the Church's stern attitude towards the Jews during this entire period; various strictures were imposed on them, including the prohibition of mixed marriage. At the same time it was recognised that missionaries ought to be not only learned but also full of sympathy in order to bring the Jews to the faith and though pressure could be exercised on them to hear the Christian message, yet conversions had to be free and sincere. The text of the decree is found in COD, pp 483-484.

A similar decree of the same session, "on those who wish to be converted to the faith" (ibid., 484-485), strongly forbids Jews who have become Christians to return to Jewish practices; but it also expects all Christians to show the greatest charity towards those who have been converted to the faith and to help them materially when in need. Nor should pastors be satisfied with exhorting their flock in this respect; they themselves should set an example for them to emulate.

(The qualities required from missionaries to the Jews)

1105   [...] Following in the steps of Jesus Christ our Saviour [cf. 1 Pet 2:21], this holy Synod desires with the most intense love that all may come to recognise the truth of the Gospel and, after they have accepted it, that they may persevere in it faithfully. It wishes, therefore, to take salutary measures in order that the Jews and other infidels may be converted to the orthodox faith and that converts may persevere in it steadfastly. First of all it decrees that all bishops must sometimes each year send some men well grounded in the divine word to those parts where Jews and other infidels live, to preach and explain the truth of the Catholic faith in such a way that the infidels who hear them may come to recognise their errors. Let them compel them to hear their preaching[...]; but let also the bishops and preachers show themselves so full of sympathy and charity towards their hearers as to win them to Christ not only by declaring the truth to them but also through other human good offices.[...]

ALEXANDER VII

S. CONGREGATION *DE PROPAGANDA FIDE* INSTRUCTION TO THE VICARS APOSTOLIC OF TONKIN AND COCHINCHINA (1659)

In May 1658 the S. Congregation de Propaganda Fide *presented to Pope Alexander VII the first two candidates for the episcopate in Indochina. Bishop Francis Pallu was appointed Vicar apostolic of Tonkin and put in charge of all missions in Western China, while Bishop Lambert de la Motte was appointed Vicar apostolic of Cochinchina, responsible for all the missions in Southern China. Before their departure for the missions the new Vicars apostolic received specific instructions from the S.Congregation. Conditions were not favourable to Catholic missionaries in those countries at that particular time and Propaganda wished to ensure in missionaries the necessary qualities. More important, however, was the need to promote a local clergy. It was recognised as imperative to establish the local Church with its own clergy and, eventually, its own hierarchy. The S. Congregation was also anxious to respect the traditions and customs of those countries, thus carrying on the early tradition of the Church to assume into Christianity whatever was good in the ways of the people and gradually to eradicate what was not compatible with it. The text is found in* Collectanea Sacrae Congregationis de Propaganda Fide *(Rome, 1907) 1, 42-43.*

(Qualities required of missionaries)

1106   Your first care must be to seek out and select with great diligence, from among many, people whose age and health will enable them to cope with sustained work, and—what is more important—who are distinguished for their charity and prudence. These qualities must be ascertained, not through the opinion or conjectures of others, but through the candidates' sustained behaviour and successful accomplishment of diverse responsible tasks. They must be persons who can keep secrets and guard them tenaciously; who, by the integrity of their conduct, by their courtesy, meekness, patience, humility and the example of all their virtues, bear witness in their lives to the Christian faith which their lips profess. Finally, by conforming to the norms of evangelical charity, they must be ready to adapt themselves to the mentality and customs of others so as not to be a burden to the companions with whom they live, nor earn the disfavour or even the dislike of outsiders but rather become, like the apostle, all things to all.

(On preparing a local clergy)

1107   The chief reason which has induced the S. Congregation to send you as bishops to these regions is that, by every means and method possible, you so take in hand the education of young people that they may become capable of attaining to the priesthood. You will then ordain them and assign them in those vast territories, each to his own region, with the mission to serve Christianity there with the utmost diligence, under your direction. Therefore, you must always have this end in view; to lead to holy orders as many and as suitable candidates as possible, to form them and to promote them in due time.

If, among those whom you have promoted, there are some worthy of the episocpate,[...] inform the S. Congregation of their names, age, qualities and whatever else it may be useful to know about them such as where they could be consecrated, in charge of which dioceses they could be appointed.[...]

(The directives of Propaganda must not be imposed forcibly)

1108   If, in carrying out the order of the S. Congregation, you meet or foresee difficulties to the extent that these orders will not be accepted without revolt, avoid at all cost imposing them on the persons concerned against their will. Do not urge them by force or the fear of censures and avoid sowing the seed of division which would result from the disobedience of some, for you would thus alienate them and arouse strong passions. On the contrary, it will be better to take into account the recent conversion and consequent weakness of the neophytes and therefore not to apply the decree immediately. Take time to write and explain fully and sincerely the whole question to the S. Congregation and await its instructions on what you must do.

(Western customs must not be introduced but local ones adopted)

1109   Do not in any way attempt, and do not on any pretext persuade these people to change their rites, habits and customs, unless they are openly opposed to religion and good morals. For what could be more absurd than to bring France, Spain, Italy or any other European country over to China? It is not your country but the faith you must bring, that faith which does not reject or belittle the rites or customs of any nation as long as these rites are not evil, but rather desires that they be preserved in their integrity and fostered. It is, as it were, written in the nature of all human beings that the customs of their country and especially their country itself should be esteemed, loved and respected above anything else in the world. There is no greater cause of alienation and hatred than to change the customs of a nation, especially when they go back as far as the memory of ancestors can reach. What then if, having abrogated them, you attempt to replace them with the customs of your country imported from abroad? Never make comparisons between the customs of these peoples and those of Europe; on the contrary show your anxiety to become used to them. Admire and praise whatever merits praise. As regards what is not praiseworthy, while it must not be extolled as is done by flatterers, you will be prudent enough not to pass judgment on it, or, in any case, not to condemn it rashly or exaggeratedly. As for what is evil, it should be dismissed by a nod of the head or by silence rather that by words, without losing the occasions, when souls have become disposed to receive the truth, to uproot it imperceptibly.

(The witness of evangelical poverty)

1110   You would not wish to incur hatred as a result of material interests. Remember the poverty of the apostles who earned with their own hands what was needed for themselves and their companions. All the more reason why you who emulate and imitate them, being content with your food and clothing, should abstain from any base profit. Do not beg alms or collect money, gifts or riches. If some of the faithful force you to accept offerings inspite of your protests, distribute them to the poor under their own eyes, knowing well that nothing is more astounding to people and nothing attracts their attention more than to witness contempt for temporal goods. This is the Gospel poverty which prepares for itself a treasure in heaven by raising itself above all things human and earthly.

BENEDICT XV

APOSTOLIC LETTER *MAXIMUM ILLUD* (1919)

This Apostolic Letter by Pope Benedict XV, the first in a series of great encyclicals explicitly concerned with the full organisation of mission work in this century, represents an important break-through for the modern concept of the Church's missionary activity. Written at a time when the mission lands had been considerably depleted of foreign personnel as a consequence of the first world war, it does not only plead for the recruitment of more foreign missionaries and for help in alms and prayers from Catholics in Christian countries; it exposes in a forceful manner some of the basic principles which must guide the authentic growth of the Church in mission lands. Insistence is laid on the Church's responsibility to all the inhabitants of mission countries; on the primary importance of training a local clergy which will be able to take into their hands the destiny of the Church in their country, on the disinterestedness required from foreign missionaries and their full adaptation to the country of their adoption. The text is found in AAS 11 (1919) 440ff.

(Missionary zeal must extend to all the inhabitants of the land)

1111 The superior of a mission should make it one of his primary concerns to expand and fully develop his mission. The entire region within the boundaries of his mission has been committed to his care. Consequently, he must work for the eternal salvation of all its inhabitants. If, out of an immense population, he has converted a few thousand people he has no reason to fall into complacency. He must become a guide and a protector for these children he has brought forth in Jesus Christ; he must see to their spiritual nourishment and he must not let a single one of them slip away and perish. But he must do more than this. He must not consider that he is properly discharging the duties of his office unless he is working constantly and with all the vigour he can muster to bring the other, far more numerous, inhabitants of the area to partake of the Christian truth and the Christian life.

(The primary concern is the formation of the local clergy)

1112 Anyone who has charge of a mission must make it his special concern to secure and train local candidates for the sacred ministry. In this policy lies the greatest hope of the new Churches. For the local priest, one with his people by birth, by nature, by his sympathies and his aspirations, is remarkably effective in appealing to their mentality and thus attracting them to the faith. Far better than anyone else he knows the kind of argument they will listen to, and, as a result, he often has easy access to places where a foreign priest would not be tolerated.

If, however, the local clergy is to achieve the results we hope for, it is absolutely necessary that they be well trained and well prepared. We do not mean a rudimentary preparation, the bare minimum for ordination. No, their education should be complete and finished, excellent in all its phases.[...] For the local clergy is not to be trained merely to perform the humbler duties of the ministry, acting as the assistants of foreign priests. On the contrary, they must take up God's work as equals, so that some day they will be able to enter upon the spiritual leadership of their people. The Church of God is Catholic, and cannot be a stranger to any nation nor alien to any people. It is only right, then, that she chooses in every nation ministers of the Lord to instruct their country people in the faith and to lead them on the way to salvation. Wherever the local clergy exist in sufficient numbers and are suitably trained and worthy of their holy vocation, there you can justly assume that the work of the missionaries has been successful and that the Church has laid her foundations well.[...]

(Foreign missionaries must forget their country of origin)

1113   [...]Remember that your duty is not the extension of a human realm, but of Christ's and remember too that your goal is the acquisition of citizens for a heavenly homeland and not for an earthly one. It would be tragic indeed if any of our missionaries forgot the dignity of their office so completely as to busy themselves with the interests of their terrestrial homeland instead of with those of their homeland in heaven. It would be a tragedy indeed if an apostolic person were to spend oneself in attempts to increase and exalt the prestige of the native land one once left behind. Such behaviour would infect their apostolate like a plague. It would destroy in them, the representatives of the Gospel, the sinews of their love for souls and it would destroy their reputation with the people.[...] For they will subject them in their own way to a very searching investigation, and if one has any object in view other than their spiritual good, they will find out about it. If it becomes clear that one is involved in worldly schemes of some kind, and that, instead of devoting oneself exclusively to the work of the apostolate, one is serving the interests of one's homeland as well, the people will immediately suspect everything one does. And, in addition, such a situation could easily give rise to the conviction that the Christian religion is the national religion of some foreign people and that anyone converted to it is abandoning one's loyalty to one's people and submitting to the pretensions and domination of a foreign power.

(The command of the local language is needed)

1114   Among the attainments necessary for the life of missionaries, a place of paramount importance must obviously be given to the language of the people to whose salvation they will devote themselves. They should not be content with a smattering of the language, but should be able to speak it readily and competently. For in this respect they are under an obligation to all those they deal with, the learned and the ignorant alike, and they will soon realise the advantage a command of their language gives them in the task of winning the confidence and sympathy of the people.[...] There will be occasions when, in their position as representatives and interpreters of our holy faith, they will have to associate with the dignitaries of the place, or they may be invited to appear at scholarly gatherings. How will they maintain their dignity under these circumstances if they cannot make themselves understood because they do not know the language?

PIUS XI
ENCYCLICAL LETTER *RERUM ECCLESIAE* (1926)

Following in the footsteps of his predecessor Benedict XV, Pope Pius XI made it one of the main preoccupations of his pontificate to foster the growth of the Church in mission countries. In his encyclical the "Pope of the missions" wrote: "As long as divine Providence shall grant us life, we shall ardently busy ourselves with this duty of our apostolic office." The Pope appeals to all the bishops, who share in his own solicitude, for more missionaries. He defines the purpose of the missions, stresses the role of the local clergy and the need to prepare them adequately for their task; he insists on the creation in mission lands of new religious congregations better adapted than foreign ones to local conditions; he recommends the creation of the religious contemplative life in the missions and the cooperation of all, diocesan clergy and religious institutes, at the service of the local Church. The text on this encyclical is found in AAS 18 (1926) 65ff.

(Missionary motivation)

1115   [...]. Our obligation of charity towards God demands that we labour to the utmost not only to increase the number of those who know and adore him "in spirit and in truth" *[Jn 4:24]*, but also to bring as many as possible under our Saviour's sweet yoke. Thus will "the profit in his blood" [cf. Ps. 30(29) 10 Vulg.] become daily more fruitful. Thus also will we ourselves become more acceptable to him to whom, indeed, there is nothing more agreeable than that people be saved and come to the knowledge of the truth [cf. 1 Tim. 2:4]. Since Christ himself proclaimed as characteristic of his disciples their sincere love for one another [cf. Jn 13:35; 15:12], can we possibly render our neighbours a greater or more signal charity than by trying to lead them out of the darkness of fear and to communicate to them the true faith in Christ?

(The purpose of the missions and the role of the local clergy)

1116   [...]Unless you provide to the very best of your ability for priests from the land, your apostolate will remain crippled and the establishment of a fully organised Church in your territories will encounter still further delay.[...]

What, we may ask, is the purpose of the missions, if not that the Church of Christ be established and solidly rooted in those immense regions? And how will this be realised today among the nations, if not through all the forces which brought it about among us in olden times, namely the faithful, the clergy, the religious men and women of each nation?

[...]You must supply your territories with enough local priests to extend the frontiers of Christianity and to govern the faithful by themselves alone, without the help of any outside clergy.[...]

(The role of local religious congregations and the contemplative life)

1117   Since you should make use of all the means offered by divine Providence for the organisation of Christ's Church in your territory, you ought to consider as one of the principal duties of your office the establishment of indigenous religious communities both of men and women. For if these new followers of Christ feel called by God to a more perfect life, what is to prevent their pronouncing the vows of religion?[...] However, you should seriously and impartially consider whether it might not be more useful to establish new congregations more in keeping with the local character and temperament, and therefore better suited to the particular needs of your region.[...]

[...] We have earnestly exhorted the superiors of[...] contemplative orders to establish monasteries in missionary regions, so that their austere mode of life may there flourish and grow more widespread. You should second our efforts [...]by extending to them repeated invitations, for these solitary monks will win for you and your labours an abundance of heavenly graces. One cannot doubt, moreover, that these foundations will find in your missions a very favourable soil, for their people— especially in some countries where precisely the non-Christians are a vast majority—have a natural bent for solitude and contemplative prayer.

(Collaboration of all)

1118   [...]Since the territories which the Holy See has entrusted to your devoted labour in order that you may win them to Christ Our Lord are in most instances very extensive, it may easily happen that your own particular institute is unable to supply as many missionaries as are needed. In such cases, even in well established dioceses, it is customary for religious congregations of men and women, both clerical and lay, to assist the bishop in his work. Therefore, do not hesitate to seek help from other institutes in order to promote the Christian faith Welcome these missionaries to your territory, to help you in preaching the faith, teaching the youth, and directing other useful projects. The various religious orders and congregations can justly be proud of their conquests for Christ among the people entrusted to their care, but they should remember that they possess no exclusive or permanent title to their mission areas.[...]

PIUS XII

ENCYCLICAL LETTER *SUMMI PONTIFICATUS* (1939)

In his first Encyclical Letter Pope Pius XII outlines the programme of his pontificate. A section is devoted to the missions; it states clearly the principle of adaption which must pervade the entire activity of the Church in mission countries. The doctrine is based on the unity of the human race and the equality of all people. Hence the right for all nations to preserve and develop their cultural heritage, and the duty for the Church to assume it into the life of the new Churches. So will the Church show her true catholicity; her ideal is not exterior uniformity, but a healthy pluralism in the unity of faith. The Pope sees this spirit exemplified in the recent decrees of Propaganda promulgated by his predecessor and by himself (1935 to 1939), which recognise the liceity in China and Japan of certain rites and ceremonies connected with the veneration of Confucius and of ancestors and with patriotic festivities. These decrees abrogate the censures imposed by Benedict XIV in the apostolic

Constitutions Ex quo Singulari *(1742)* and Omnium Sollicitudinem *(1744),
thus bringing to an end the long drawn-out controversy on the Chinese rites.
The Pope also declares his intention of fostering the formation of the local
clergy in mission lands and of "gradually increasing the number of native
bishops". The text of the encyclical is found in* AAS 31(1939) 413 ff.

(The unity of the human race and diversity of nations)

1119   The nations, despite a difference of development due to
diverse conditions of life and culture, are not destined
to break the unity of the human race but rather to enrich and
embellish it by the sharing of their own peculiar gifts and by
that reciprocal interchange of goods which can be possible and
efficacious only when a mutual love and a lively sense of charity
unite all the sons of the same Father and all those redeemed by
the same divine blood.

(The aim of the Church is supernatural unity in the diversity of gifts)

1120   The Church of Christ, the faithful depositary of the
teaching of divine Wisdom, cannot and does not think
of depreciating or disdaining the peculiar characteristics which
each people, with jealous and understandable pride, cherishes
and retains as a precious heritage. Her aim is supernatural union
in all-embracing love, deeply felt and practised, and not a
uniformity which can only be external and superficial and by
that very fact weak. The Church hails with joy and follows with
her maternal blessing every method of guidance and care which
aims at a wise and orderly evolution of peculiar forces and
tendencies having their origin in the individual character of each
race, provided that they are not opposed to the duties incumbent
on people from their unity of origin and common destiny.

*(The spiritual values of the nations must be assumed into the Church's
mission)*

1121   She has repeatedly shown in her missionary enterprises
that such a principle of action is the guiding star of her
universal apostolate. Pioneer research and investigation, involving
sacrifice, devotedness and love on the part of her missionaries
of every age, have been undertaken in order to gain a deeper
appreciative insight into the civilisation and customs of diverse
people so as to put their intellectual and spiritual endowments
to account for a living and vital preaching of the Gospel of Christ.

All that in such usages and customs is not inseparably bound up with religious errors will always be the object of sympathetic consideration and, whenever possible, will be preserved and developed.[...] Those who enter the Church, whatever be their origin or their speech, must know that they have equal rights as children in the house of the Lord, where the law of Christ and the peace of Christ prevail.

ADDRESS TO THE DIRECTORS OF PONTIFICAL MISSION WORKS (1944)

In this address the Pope spoke of the future of the Church in mission countries. Having taken stock of the fact that the modern view of the mission leans more and more towards the principle of adaptation, he re-expresses his faith in this principle which in Summi Pontificatus *he had already considered as the "guiding star" of the Church's apostolate (cf. n. 1121). Referring to the universality of the Church "which is above all national frontiers", he defines the aim of the missions as the exercise of the catholicity of the Church. The text is found in* AAS 36(1944) 210.

(The principle of missionary adaptation)

1122 [...]The specific character, the traditions, the customs of each nation must be preserved intact, so long as they are not in contradiction with the divine law. Missionaries are apostles of Jesus Christ. Their task is not to propagate European civilisation in mission lands, like a tree which is transposed to foreign soil. Rather it is their function so to train and guide other peoples, some of whom glory in their ancient and refined civilisation, as to prepare and dispose them for the willing and hearty acceptance of the principles of Christian life and behaviour. These principles, moreover, are compatible with any wholesome and healthy civilisation whatever and can imbue it with a keener zest for the protection of human dignity and the attainment of happiness. Granted that Catholic inhabitants of a country are primarily members of God's noble family and citizens of his Kingdom, they do not on that account cease to be citizens of their earthly homeland also.

(The purpose of missionary activity)

1123 [...] It is this universality [of the Church] which spurs you on towards the goal you want to reach, namely, to make the frontiers of the Kingdom of God coincide with those of the world.[...] It is the great aim of the missions to establish the Church in new regions and to make her take root there, so that one day she may be able to live and develop without the assistance of Mission Works. The Mission Work is not an end in itself; it ardently tends to the realisation of that lofty goal, but retires when it has reached its aim.

CHRISTMAS MESSAGE (1945)

In this allocution the Pope insists on the Catholic and supra-national character of the Church which is the foundation of its missionary activity; he explains that this universal character does not make the Church less sensitive to human realities for it is founded on the mystery of the incarnation. The text is found in AAS 38(1946) 18, 20.

(The supra-national character of the Church)

1124 The Catholic Church of which Rome is the centre is supranational by her very nature.[...] The Church is a Mother, *Sancta Mater Ecclesia,* a true mother, mother of all nations and all peoples no less than of all persons individually. And because she is a Mother, she does not and cannot belong exclusively to this or that people, not more to one than to others, but must belong equally to all. Since she is a Mother, she is not and cannot be a stranger anywhere; she dwells, or at least should, because of her nature, dwell among all peoples. Nay more, while a mother with her spouse and children forms one family, the Church in virtue of a union incomparatively more intimate, constitutes more and better than a family, the mystical Body of Christ. The Church is thus supra-national because she is an indivisible and universal whole.

(The Church's catholicity is based on the mystery of the incarnation)

1125 The Church is not, because of her supra-natural character, a remote reality, as though suspended in an inaccessible and intangible isolation above the nations.[...] As the Son of God assumed a real human nature, so too the Church takes to herself the fulness of all that is genuinely human wherever and under whichever form she finds it, and transforms it into a source of supernatural energy. She lives and develops her life in all the countries of the world, and all the countries of the world contribute to her life and development.

ENCYCLICAL LETTER *EVANGELII PRAECONES* (1951)

Pope Pius XII wrote this encyclical at the occasion of the 25th anniversary of Rerum Ecclesiae *of Pius XI. The great themes of the previous encyclicals are taken up anew, but the Pope also turns his attention to other problems as, for instance, the Church's responsibility for promoting social justice in mission lands. Especially noteworthy are the purpose assigned to the Church's missionary activity and the insistence on the role to be played by the laity in the work of evangelisation. In view of the recent growth of the local clergy, the Pope explains how to conceive the function which foreign missionaries still retain. He recommends that they should "look upon the country where they come to shed the Gospel light as a second homeland and love it with due charity". Again he stresses the need of preserving and promoting the local culture and explains the principle of Christian adaptation. The text of this encyclical is found in AAS 43(1951) 497ff.*

(The purpose of the missions)

1126 The primary object of the missions, as everyone knows, is to bring the shining light of Christian truth to new peoples and to form new Christians. But, in view of this, the ultimate goal to which they must tend—and which one must always keep before his eyes—is that the Church be established on firm and definitive foundations among new peoples and that it be endowed with its own hierarchy, chosen from among the people of the place.

(The subordinate role of foreign missionaries)

1127 It is not expected that a religious society whose members have laboured to plough a field for the Lord should forsake it entirely when the vineyard, now prospering and filled with ripe fruit, is handed over to other husbandmen.[...] Such a society will perform a useful and gratifying service if it offers to assist the new bishop born in the land. Just as religious usually tender their help to local ordinaries in all the rest of the Catholic dioceses in the world, so too, in missionary regions they, though of a different country of origin, will not cease to fight the holy fight as auxiliary troops.[...]

(The role of the laity)

1128 It is altogether imperative[...] that magnanimous lay people should contribute their diligent and self-sacrificing cooperation to the hierarchical apostolate of the clergy. This they can do by forming solid ranks of Catholic Action[...]. Although [...] Catholic Action should employ its energies specifically to further the activities of the Christian apostolate, nothing prevents its members from joining associations intended to bring social and political affairs into conformity with the principles and methods of the Church. This is a right which they enjoy not only as citizens but also as Catholics. It is, moreover, a duty to which they are obligated.

(The local culture must be preserved and fostered)

1129　When the Gospel is accepted by diverse nations, it does not crush or repress anything good and honourable and beautiful which they have achieved by their inborn genius and natural endowments. When the Church calls and guides a people to a higher refinement and a better way of life under the inspiration of the Christian religion, she does not act like a woods-person who recklessly cuts down and devastates a luxuriant forest. Rather she acts like an orchardist who grafts an excellent scion upon the wild stock so that later on fruits of a more tasty and richer quality may issue forth and mature.

Although human nature by Adam's unhappy sin has been tainted with an hereditary blemish, it still keeps in itself something that is 'naturally Christian'. If this is illumined by divine light and nurtured by God's grace, it can in time rise to genuine virtue and supernatural life.

Accordingly, the Catholic Church has neither scorned nor rejected the learning of the nations, but rather has freed it from all error and alloy, and then sealed and perfected it by Christian wisdom. The same holds true for the fine arts and culture, which in some countries have reached a high degree of perfection. The Church received them in sympathy, encouraged them assiduously, and lifted them up to a peak of beauty never, perhaps, previously excelled. So too, with regard to particular customs and traditional institutions of peoples. The Church did not simply suppress them but in some way sanctified them. Even in the matter of local feasts, she merely altered their meaning by transforming them into commemorations of the martyrs or into occasions for celebrating the mysteries of the faith

ENCYCLICAL LETTER *FIDEI DONUM* (1957)

From this other letter of Pope Pius XII, dedicated to the development of missionary activity especially in Africa, only two passages are quoted here, in which the Pope stresses the Church's mission in the social field and explains the Catholic spirit which must inspire its whole action. The text is found in AAS 49 (1957) 231, 237.

(The Church's social responsibility in mission lands)

1130 At a moment when new structures are being sought, [...] it is the Church's sacred duty to make all people share as fully as possible in the outstanding advantages of her way of life and culture, so that a new social order may arise, based on Christian principles.

(The missionary spirit is based on the catholicity of the Church)

1131 The missionary spirit and the Catholic spirit[...] are one and the same thing. To be Catholic is the Church's principal distinguishing mark. Hence the individual can scarcely be called a Christian and a member of the Church if he/she is not at the same time a devoted fellow-member of the whole body of the faithful, desiring the Church to strike her roots and flourish everywhere on earth.

JOHN XXIII
ENCYCLICAL LETTER *PRINCEPS PASTORUM* (1959)

This encyclical Letter on the missions was written by Pope John XXIII at the occasion of the 40th anniversary of Maximum Illud. It prolongs the thought of Pope Benedict XV and his successors and applies it to new circumstances obtaining in mission lands. There is a new insistence on the thorough training of the local clergy. A special characteristic of this letter is the stress it lays on the cooperation of the laity in the Church's mission, to which Pope Pius XII had already given impetus. The laity, as the clergy themselves, must be adequately prepared to assume fully their responsibility, especially in the field of public life. The organisation of lay missionary activity must be adapted to local circumstances. The text of the encyclical is found in AAS 51 (1951) 833ff.

(The study of missiology in seminaries)

1132 Local seminaries in mission lands will not fail to provide study courses in the various branches of missiology and in such special skills and techniques as are likely to be of particular value to the clergy of those regions in their future ministry. [...] This instruction[...] should[...] be aimed at sharpening the students' minds, so as to enable them to form a true estimate of the cultural traditions of their own homelands, especially in matters of philosophy and theology, and to discern the special points of contact which exist between these systems and the Christian religion.

(The responsibility of the laity and its training)

1133   There is need for organising the Church in all those lands where she has led her armies of peace, and this organic structure of hers consists not merely in the hierarchy and its various orders, but in the laity as well. In pursuing her work of salvation the Church must act through the medium of the clergy and the laity alike.

[...]It is necessary[...] to give the people a Christian education suited to their age and environment, an education which will fit them to make their own contribution to the present and future welfare of the Church and to its spread throughout the world.[...] The profession of the Christian faith is no mere question of statistics. It is the creation of a new person. It is a supernatural vitality that takes possession of the whole person, inspiring, directing, and governing all one's actions.[...] It is a primary and fundamental duty of every Christian to witness to the truth he/she believes in, and to the grace that has transformed him/her.[...]

(The lay apostolate must be adapted to local conditions)

1134   We must insist[...]upon the need to adapt this form of the apostolate to local needs and conditions. What has proved successful in one country cannot without more ado be transferred to another[...] What may appear suitable in one area may be less advantageous in another where needs and circumstances differ materially.

(The responsibility of the laity in public life)

1135   It is in the sphere of public life that the laity of mission lands have their most direct and influential part to play. It is, therefore, a matter of utmost urgency that the Christian communities be able to offer people to take up public life in their own homelands for the common good; people who will be a credit to their various professions and the public offices they hold, and will also, by reason of their truly Christian lives, reflect honour on the Church that has regenerated them through grace.[...]

THE SECOND VATICAN GENERAL COUNCIL

The Dogmatic Constitution Lumen Gentium *had stressed the full Catholicity of the Church in which "each individual part contributes by its special gifts to the gifts of the other parts and of the whole Church:" (13). It had devoted its number 17 to the missionary character of the Church, conceived as derived from the Son's own mission, and prompting her to send heralds of the Gospel to foreign lands "until the young Churches are fully established and are able themselves to carry on the task of evangelising." It was, however, necessary to issue a special conciliar document on the missions.*

The Decree Ad Gentes *on the Church's Missionary Activity reflects the Church's new understanding of her mystery, her new openness to all that is good and her new attitude towards the religions of the world. It provides a deep theological concept of the missions which, while owing much to the teaching of the great missionary encyclicals of this century, also completes them and leads to a further stage of development.*

The Decree is divided into six chapters, dealing respectively with the doctrinal principles, missionary work, particular Churches, missionaries, the organisation of missionary activity, and cooperation.

Chapter I on doctrinal principles (2-9) offers a synthesis of missiological doctrine in line with the Council's ecclesiology. "The pilgrim Church is missionary by her very nature, since she draws her origin from the mission of the Son and the mission of the Holy Spirit according to the design of the Father" (2). A Trinitarian preamble traces the origin of her missionary activity to the Father's calling of all people (2) through the Son incarnate (3) in the Holy Spirit (4). The Church, born of the Spirit at Pentecost to continue Christ's mission, is essentially missionary (5). Her role as "universal sacrament of salvation" (1) is to unfold in the course of history the mission of Christ himself (5). Her function is fundamentally the same in all parts of the world and is realised by her presence and action (5); but the exercise of the mission takes different forms according to circumstances (6). One special form is found in those countries where the Church still remains to be fully planted; these are the 'missions' commonly so-called (6.)

The necessity of the missions flows from Christ's explicit command (5) as well as from the Church's intimate nature (6). She must become present to all nations in order to make Christ known to them and to gather them into one people of God according to the divine plan of salvation and for God's glory (7). Thus she must be missionary, irrespective of what God can do and does for the salvation of those whom the Gospel does not reach (7). To make Christ known to them is to bring them to the full knowledge of their dignity and vocation, for Christ is the principle of a new humanity(8). Missionary activity, which is the manifestation of God's plan of salvation, extends from the first

coming of the Lord to the second and tends to its eschatological fulfilment
when the Church will be gathered into the Kingdom of God(9).

The purpose of the missions finds here a theological structure, and
missionary motivation a theological foundation, which integrate the recent
theology on salvation 'outside the Church' and on the significance of the
religions of the world in God's plan, as well as the new awareness regarding
the meaning and implications of the Church's catholicity.

Chapter II deals with missionary work (10-18). It proposes to combine
Christian witness through dialogue (11) and the presence of charity (12), on
the one hand, and, on the other hand, evangelisation which gathers the people
of God through the preaching of the Gospel (13-14). The first, which is already
missionary activity, will normally lead to the second. Christians, by the witness
of their lives and by promoting spiritual and moral values, already contribute
to the salvation of other people and "gradually open the way to a fuller access
to God" (12); but, when the way is open for the Gospel, the full mystery of
Christ must be announced (13). Conversion is a personal and free response to
God's calling "to enter into a personal relationship with him in Christ" (13)
For the building up of a Christian community a solid training of its members
(15), and especially of its local clergy (16), is necessary, as well as the training
of catechists to whose role the Council gives full recognition (17), and the
advancement of the religious life, particularly in forms deeply rooted in the
religious tradition of the nation (18).

Chapter III on particular Churches (19-22) is symptomatic of the renewed
awareness regarding the significance of the local Church in the Church
universal. The local Church must grow to full maturity (19); to the end of
representing the mystery of the Church as perfectly as possible in a particular
place, it must be endowed with all its constitutive elements (20), which include
a mature Christian laity (21), fully equipped to co-operate with the local
hierarchy in the Church's mission (22); following the economy of the
incarnation, it must also be fully at home in the traditions of the land in view
of which a clear plan of adaptation is necessary (22).

Chapter IV is concerned with missionaries (23-27). It draws considerably
from the missionary encyclicals of recent Popes as regards the formation,
spiritual, doctrinal and apostolic, of missionaries, whether local or from abroad
(24-26); it stresses the special role to be played by missionary institutes (27).
Chapter V is devoted to the organisation of missionary activity (28-34). Coordination is needed at all levels; between the local Church and the centre in
Rome (29), and in the field between bishops and missionaries (30) as well as
among bishops (31) and missionary institutes (32). Chapter VI on co-operation
explains that the entire People of God must co-operate in the Church's
missionary activity (36). It analyses the missionary duty of Christian
communities (37), of bishops (38), priests (39), religious (40), and laity (41).

Thus the Decree offers a synthetic structure of the Church's missionary
activity which is remarkably coherent and new. That activity is the immediate
task of all those who in a given territory constitute the Church's presence.

The whole local Church and each one of her groups and members are missionary; in communion with one another and with the Church universal, they are in a particular country the sign of Christ's salvation for all people.

DOGMATIC CONSTITUTION *LUMEN GENTIUM* (1964)

(The Church's missionary character)

1136 17. [...] It is the Holy Spirit who impels the Church to do her part in bringing about the full realisation of the plan of God who has established Christ as the source of salvation for the whole world. By proclaiming the Gospel she moves her hearers to receive and to profess the faith, she prepares them for baptism, she sets them free from the slavery of error and incorporates them into Christ, so that they may grow up through charity into full maturity in Christ. By her activity whatever good is found sown in the hearts and minds of human beings or in the rites and cultures proper to various people, is not only saved from destruction, but is also healed, ennobled and brought to perfection, for the glory of God, the confusion of the devil and the happiness of human persons.[...]

DECREE *AD GENTES* (1965)

(The Church's mission)

1137 5. [...]The Church fulfills her mission by that activity by which, in obedience to the command of Christ and under the impulse of the grace and love of the Holy Spirit, she becomes fully and actively present among all people or nations so as to lead them, by living example, by preaching, by the sacraments and other channels of grace, to the faith, the liberty and the peace of Christ. Thus a free and safe path is opened for people to fully participate in the mystery of Christ.

(Missionary activity)

1138 6. This duty must be fulfilled by the order of bishops with the successor of Peter as their head and with the prayers and co-operation of the whole Church. It remains one and the same everywhere and in every situation, even though it is not exercised in the same way in all circumstances. It follows that the differences which must be recognised in the activity of the Church do not derive from the intimate nature of the mission itself but from the conditions in which the mission is carried out.

[...]The special undertakings by which the heralds of the Gospel, sent by the Church into the whole world, discharge their task of preaching the Gospel and planting the Church among the peoples and groups which do not as yet believe in Christ, are commonly called "missions". These are carried out by missionary activity and are usually exercised in certain territories recognised by the Holy See. The specific aim of this missionary activity is evangelisation and the planting of the Church among the peoples and groups in which she has not yet taken root. Thus from the seed of the word of God there should increase everywhere enough autochtonous local Churches, endowed with their own resources and maturity. These must have their own hierarchy united with the faithful, and be provided with sufficient and apt means to live a fully Christian life, and so to contribute their share to the good of the whole Church. The chief means for this planting of the Church is the preaching of the Gospel of Jesus Christ. It was to announce the Gospel that the Lord sent his disciples into the whole world, so that people, reborn by the word of God [cf. 1 Pet 1:23], might by baptism be joined to the Church which, as the Body of the Word Incarnate, is nourished and lives by the word of God and the eucharistic bread [cf. Acts 2:43].

(Motives for and necessity of missionary activity)

1139   7. Though God can, by ways known to himself, lead people who through no fault of their own are ignorant of the Gospel, to the faith without which it is impossible to please him [cf. Heb 11:6], yet there is incumbent upon the Church both the necessity [cf. 1Cor 9:16] and the sacred right to evangelise; consequently, the missionary activity retains its full force and necessity today as ever.

[...]Through it God's design is fulfilled[...] that the entire human race should form one People of God, should coalesce into one Body of Christ, should be built together into one temple of the Holy Spirit.[...]

(Missionary activity in the life and history of people)

1140   8.[...]By the very fact of manifesting Christ, the Church reveals to people the real truth about their condition and their complete vocation. For Christ is the principle and exemplar of that new humanity, animated by brotherly and sisterly love, sincerity and a spirit of peace, which all persons long for. Christ, and the Church which by the preaching of the Gospel bears testimony to him, transcend all peculiarity of race and nation; therefore, they cannot be considered foreign anywhere or to anybody. Christ himself is the truth and the way which the preaching of the Gospel lays open to all people.[...] All are in need of Christ as their exemplar, their master, their liberator, their Saviour and life-giver.[...]

(Eschatological aspect of missionary action)

1141   9.[...]Missionary activity is nothing else and nothing less than the manifestation or the epiphany of God's plan and its fulfilment in the world and its history, in which God through the mission visibly accomplishes the history of salvation. By the preaching of the word and the celebration of the sacraments whose centre and culminating point is the Holy Eucharist, it makes present Christ, the author of salvation.[...] Thus missionary activity tends towards the eschatological fulfilment.[...]

(The growth of the particular Church)

1142   19.The work of planting the Church in a particularly human community reaches a definite turning point when the community of the faithful, firmly established in the social life and to some extent adapted to the culture of the place, possesses a certain stability and firmness; equipped with its own supply, insufficient though it be, of local priests, religious and laity, it is endowed with those ministries and institutions which are necessary for leading the life of the People of God and expanding it, under the direction of its own bishop.

(Missionary activity in particular Churches)

1143   20. Since the particular Church must represent the universal Church as perfectly as possible, it must realise that it is sent also to those in the same territory who do not believe in Christ, in order that, by the witness of the life of each individual faithful and of the whole community, it may be a sign showing Christ to them.

(Diversity in unity)

1144   22.[...]Following the economy of the incarnation, the new Churches, rooted in Christ and built upon the foundation of the apostles, take to themselves in a wonderful intercourse all the riches of the nations which have been given to Christ as his inheritance *[cf. Ps 2:8]*. They borrow from the customs, traditions, wisdom, learning, arts and sciences of their own people everything which can serve to confess the glory of the Creator, to illustrate the grace of the Saviour and rightly order the Christian life *[cf. LG 13]*.

To achieve this purpose, it is necessary that theological reflection should be stimulated in every large socio-cultural area. The deeds and words revealed by God, as contained in Holy Scripture and explained by the Fathers and magisterium of the Church, should be subjected to a new investigation in the light of the Tradition of the universal Church. Thus it will become clearer in what ways the faith can seek understanding by taking into account the philosophy and wisdom of the peoples concerned; how the customs, outlook on life and social order may be harmonised with the norms indicated in divine revelation. This will open the way for a more profound adaptation covering the whole compass of the Christian life. By proceeding in this way every appearance of syncretism and false particularism will be avoided; the Christian life will be accommodated to the mentality and characteristics of each culture, and particular traditions together with the endowments of each family of peoples will be illuminated by the light of the Gospel and taken up into Catholic unity. The new local Churches, adorned with their own traditions, will take their place in the ecclesial communion, without prejudice to the primacy of Peter's chair, which presides over the universal assembly of charity *[cf. LG 13]*.[...]

PASTORAL CONSTITUTION *GAUDIUM ET SPES* (1965)

(Adaptation of the message is the law of evangelisation)

1145 44. [...]The experience of the past centuries, the progress of sciences, the treasures hidden in the various forms of human culture which manifest more fully human nature itself and lay open new ways towards the truth—all these profit also the Church. For from the beginning of her history, she has endeavoured to express the message of Christ by means of the concepts and the languages of various peoples, and has, besides, tried to clarify it with the help of the wisdom of the philosophers. She has done so for the purpose of adapting the Gospel, as far as is proper, to both the understanding of all and the demands of the learned. Indeed, this adaptation of the preaching of the revealed word must remain the law of all evangelisation. For thus every nation develops the ability to express the message of Christ in its own way, and at the same time a living exchange is fostered between the Church and the diverse cultures of peoples [cf. LG 13].

PAUL VI
MISSION SUNDAY MESSAGE (1970)

In this message, Pope Paul VI notes that in the last years "a new era has dawned for the missions". This is due partly to the fast developing means of communication among people, in the growth of which he recognises a 'sign of the times'. "This means[...] that a new approach is needed in the underlying principles, in publicity, recruitment, training[...]." The Pope examines especially the relationship between evangelisation and human development. After defining clearly the two concepts, he goes on to show that, though distinct, the two realities complement each other. There is between them no dilemma. If in the order of ends and intentions priority must be given to evangelisation, pastoral priority may be given to development according to circumstances. The mission of the Church must be seen in its totality. The text is found in AAS 62 (1970) 534ff.

(Definition of evangelisation and development)

1146 In the rethinking of the Church's missionary vocation there is one question that stands out in particular, opposing two concepts of what the general direction of missionary activity should be—concepts which may be summed up in two words: evangelisation and development. By evangelisation is meant the strictly religious activity, aimed at the preaching of God's Kingdom, of the Gospel as a revelation of the plan of salvation in Christ, through the action of the Holy Spirit. This activity has the ministry of the Church as its instrument, the building up of the Church itself as its aim, and God's glory as its final end. This is the traditional doctrine and to it the Council has given its authoritative support. By development is meant the human, civil, temporal promotion of those peoples who, by contact with modern civilisation and with the help that it provides, are becoming more conscious of themselves and are stepping out on the road to higher levels of culture and prosperity. Missionaries cannot excuse themselves from taking an interest in this promotion [cf. AG 11].

(Evangelisation and development complement each other)

1147 The confrontation between these two concepts is a serious one and entails two dangers: that we may consider them as mutually exclusive, and that we may fail to establish a correct relationship between them. We hope that the confrontation will not be looked upon as a dilemma that precludes a synthesis between evangelisation and development in which the one complements the other. For us believers it would be unthinkable that missionary activity should make of earthly realities its only or principal end and lose sight of its essential end, namely, to bring all people to the light of faith, to give them a new birth in baptism, to incorporate them into the mystical Body of Christ that is the Church, to teach them what is the life beyond. It is equally inadmissible that the Church's missionary activity should be indifferent to the needs and aspirations of developing countries and, because of its religious orientation, neglect the basic duties of human charity.[...] We ourselves, in our encyclical *Populorum Progressio*, have stressed the duty of resolutely and intelligently fostering the growth of economic, cultural, social and spiritual well-being among peoples, especially those of the so-called Third World where missionary activity finds its main scope for the carrying out of its programme *[cf AG 12]*.

There should be no dilemma. It is a question of priority of ends, of intentions, of duties; and there is no doubt that missionary activity is concerned primarily with evangelisation and that it must maintain this priority both in the concept that inspires it and in the way in which it is organised and exercised. Missionary activity would be failing in its *raison d'être* if it turned aside from its religious axis: the Kingdom of God before everything else; the Kingdom of God understood in its vertical, theological, religious sense, freeing people from sin and presenting them with the love of God as their ultimate destiny; that is to say, the *"kerygma"*, the word of Christ, the Gospel, faith, grace, prayer, the Cross, Christian living.[...]

(A question of method)

1148 The debate between evangelisation and development is rather, then, a question of method: must evangelisation precede or come after development? The answer cannot be the same for all cases, but must depend on particular circumstances.[...] We could distinguish three phases: before, during and after evangelisation— evangelisation always retaining its essential and intentional priority, while development, with its use of temporal means, may be given pastoral priority. There is first what some refer to as pre-evangelisation, that is, making contact with future Christians by living among them, helping them and giving the example of a good Christian life. Then there is service, when the Gospel comes to a place, charity comes with it, bearing witness to the human validity of Christ's message, and taking the form of schools, hospitals, social assistance and technical training. In the third phase, there comes the result of this activity, in a new way of life.

APOSTOLIC EXHORTATION *EVANGELII NUNTIANDI* (1975)

In his Apostolic Exhortation on Evangelisation which resumes and prolongs the work of the 1974 Synod of Bishops in Rome devoted to the same topic, Pope Paul VI dwells on the Church's mission in the world and clarifies theologically the nature of her evangelising activity. Showing the link between Jesus the evangeliser [cf n. 672] and the Church, the Pope affirms that evangelisation is the Church's essential mission. But evangelisation is a complex activity. The Pope develops a comprehensive view of evangelisation, centred on the renewal of humanity and the transformation of culture. He further shows that human liberation—not only development— is part of the Church's evangelizing mission. After having explained the relationship between the universal and the particular Church (62)(cf.n 885), the Pope also takes up the subject of the adaptation of the Christian life and message to the local culture of particular Churches. This process extends to the fields of liturgical expression, of theological formulation, and of secondary ecclesial structures and ministries. It involves a "transposition" into a new language, new signs and symbols, which, however, must be done in full fidelity to the deposit of faith, which is unchangeable. The text is found in AAS 68 (1976)5ff.

(Evangelisation, vocation proper to the Church)

1149   14. The Church[...] has a vivid awareness of the fact that the Saviour's words, "I must proclaim the Good News of the Kingdom of God" *[Lk 4:43]*, apply in all truth to herself. She willingly adds with Saint Paul: "Not that I boast of preaching the Gospel, since it is a duty that has been laid on me; I should be punished if I did not preach it!" *[1 Cor 9:16]*. It is with joy and consolation that at the end of the great Assembly of 1974 we heard these illuminating words: "We wish to confirm once more that the task of evangelizing all people constitutes the essential mission of the Church."[1] It is a task and mission which the vast and profound changes of present day society make all the more urgent. Evangelizing is in fact the grace and vocation proper to the Church, her deepest identity. She exists in order to evangelize, that is to say in order to preach and teach, to be the channel of the gift of grace, to reconcile sinners with God, and to perpetuate Christ's sacrifice in the Mass, which is the memorial of his death and glorious Resurrection.

(Evangelization means the renewal of humanity...)

1150　18. For the Church, evangelizing means bringing the Good News into all the strata of humanity, and through its influence transforming humanity from within and making it new: "Now I am making the whole of creation new" *[Rev 21:5; cf. 2 Cor 5:17; Gal 6:15].* But there is no new humanity if there are not first of all new persons renewed by baptism *[cf. Rom 6:4]* and by lives lived according to the Gospel *[cf. Eph 4:23-24; Col 3:9-10].* The purpose of evangelization is therefore precisely this interior change, and, if it had to be expressed in one sentence, the best way of stating it would be to say that the Church evangelizes when she seeks to convert *[cf. Rom 1:16; 1 Cor 1:18, 2:4],* solely through the divine power of the message she proclaims, both the personal and collective consciences of people, the activities in which they engage, and the lives and concrete milieux which are theirs.

(... and of the strata of humanity)

1151　19. We spoke of the strata of humanity which are transformed: indeed, for the Church it is a question not only of preaching the Gospel in ever wider geographic areas or to ever greater numbers of people, but also of affecting and as it were upsetting, through the power of the Gospel, humankind's criteria of judgment, scales of values, points of interest, ways of thinking, sources of inspiration and models of life, which are in conflict with the Word of God and the plan of salvation.

---

1. Declaration of the Synod Fathers, 4. *See Ossevatore Romano,* English Edition, 27 October 1974, p.6.

(Evangelization of cultures)

1152   20. All this could be expressed in the following words:
What matters is to evangelize people's culture   and cultures (not in a purely decorative way as it were by applying a thin veneer, but in a vital way, in depth and right to their very roots), in the wide and rich sense which these terms have in *Gaudium et Spes* (53), always taking the person as one's starting-point and always coming back to the relationships of people among themselves and with God.

The Gospel, and therefore evangelization, are certainly not identical with culture, and they are independent in regard to all cultures. Nevertheless, the Kingdom which the Gospel proclaims is lived by people who are profoundly linked to a culture, and the building up of the Kingdom cannot avoid borrowing the elements of human culture or cultures. Though independent of cultures, the Gospel and evangelization are not necessarily incompatible with them; rather they are capable of permeating them all without becoming subject to any one of them.

The split between the Gospel and culture is without a doubt the drama of our time just as it was of other times. Therefore every effort must be made to ensure a full evangelization of culture, or, more correctly, of cultures. They have to be regenerated by an encounter with the Gospel. But this encounter will not take place if the Gospel is not proclaimed.

(Evangelization includes liberation)

(1153) See text in n. 2167.

(The Church's task in people's liberation)

(1154) See text in n. 2168.

(Evangelization necessarily linked with human promotion)

(1155) See text in n. 2169.

(The Church's mission not to be reduced to a temporal project)

(1156) See text in n. 2170.

(True liberation involves a necessary conversion)

(1157) See text in n. 2171.

(Adaptation and fidelity in expression)

1158 63. The particular Churches, intimately composed not only of people but also of aspirations, of riches and limitations, of ways of praying, of loving, of looking at life and the world which distinguish this or that human gathering, have the task of assimilating the essence of the Gospel message and of transposing it, without the slightest betrayal of its essential truth, into the language that these particular people understand, then of proclaiming it in this language.

The transposition has to be done with the discernment, seriousness, respect and competence which the matter calls for in the field of liturgical expression [cf. SC 37-40], and in the areas of catechesis, theological formulation, secondary ecclesial structures, and ministries. And the word "language" should be understood here less in the semantic or literary sense than in the sense which one may call anthropological and cultural.

The question is undoubtedly a delicate one. Evangelization loses much of its force and effectiveness if it does not take into consideration the actual people to whom it is addressed, if it does not use their language, their signs and symbols, if it does not answer the questions they ask, and if it does not have an impact on their concrete life. But on the other hand evangelization risks losing its power and disappearing altogether if one empties or adulterates its content under the pretext of translating it; if, in other words, one sacrifices this reality and destroys the unity without which there is no universality, out of a wish to adapt a universal reality to a local situation.[...]

(Openness to the universal Church)

1159 64. The more a particular Church is attached to the universal Church by solid bonds of communion, in charity and loyalty, in receptiveness to the magisterium of Peter, in the unity of the *lex orandi* which is also the *lex credendi*, in the desire for unity with all the other Churches which make up the whole—the more such a Church will be capable of translating the treasure of faith into the legitimate variety of expressions of the profession of faith, of prayer and worship, of Christian life and conduct and of the spiritual influence of the people among which it dwells.

(The unchangeable deposit of faith)

1160 65.[...]While being translated into all expressions, [the]content [of the Catholic faith which the Lord entrusted to the apostles] must be neither impaired nor mutilated. While being clothed with the outward forms proper to each people, and made explicit by theological expression which takes account of differing cultural, social and even racial milieux, it must remain the content of the Catholic faith just exactly as the ecclesial magisterium has received it and transmits it.

JOHN PAUL II

APOSTOLIC EXHORTATION *CATECHESI TRADENDAE*
(16 October 1979)

The Message of the Synod of Bishops on Catechesis (1977) is the first official Church document, in which the term "inculturation" is used. It said: "The Christian message must strike roots in human cultures and must also assume and transform these cultures. In this sense we can say that catechesis is an instrument of inculturation.[...] Christian faith must become incarnate in the cultures [...]" (5). In the Apostolic Exhortation which follows up the work of the Synod, Pope John Paul II takes up the question of "inculturation", specially in relation to catechesis. The inculturation of the message is based on the principle of incarnation. It will enable cultures to "bring forth from their own living tradition original expressions of Christian life, celebration and thought." Inculturation, however, requires discernment; the Gospel does not change, while it transforms cultures by its power. The text is found in AAS 71(1979) 1277-1340.

(The message embodied in cultures)

1161 53. As I said recently to the members of the Biblical Commission: "The term 'acculturation', or 'inculturation' may be a neologism, but it expresses very well one factor of the great mystery of the Incarnation."[1] We can say of catechesis, as well as of evangelization in general, that it is called to bring the power of the Gospel into the very heart of culture and cultures. For this purpose, catechesis will seek to know these cultures and their essential components; it will learn their most significant expression; it will respect their particular values and riches. In

---

1.   *AAS* 71 (1979) 607

this manner it will be able to offer these cultures the knowledge of the hidden mystery [cf. Rom 16:25; Eph 3:5] and help them to bring forth from their own living tradition original expressions of Christian life, celebration and thought. Two things must, however, be kept in mind.

On the one hand the Gospel message cannot be purely and simply isolated from the culture in which it was first inserted (the biblical world or, more concretely, the cultural milieu in which Jesus of Nazareth lived), nor, without serious loss, from the cultures in which it has already been expressed down the centuries; it does not spring spontaneously from any cultural soil; it has always been transmitted by means of an apostolic dialogue which inevitably becomes part of a certain dialogue of cultures.

On the other hand, the power of the Gospel everywhere transforms and regenerates. When that power enters into a culture, it is no surprise that it rectifies many of its elements. There would be no catechesis if it were the Gospel that had to change when it came into contact with the cultures.

To forget this would simply amount to what Saint Paul very forcefully calls "emptying the cross of Christ of its power" [1 Cor 1:17].

It is a different matter to take, with wise discernment, certain elements, religious or otherwise, that form part of the cultural heritage of a human group and use them to help its members to understand better the whole of the Christian mystery.

ADDRESS TO WORKMEN IN SÃO-PAULO
(4 July, 1980)

During his journey to Brazil, Pope John Paul II addressed a large gathering of workers at São-Paulo. The Pope affirmed that the world willed by God is a just world. He went on to show that the promotion of justice is part of the Church's evangelizing mission, whose message of salvation has both a historical and an eschatological dimension. The text is found in AAS 72(1980) 887-896.

(The Church's message of salvation has two dimensions)

1162   3. It is Christ who sends his Church to all people and to all societies with a message of salvation. This mission of the Church is carried out in two perspectives at the same time: the eschatological perspective which considers the human being as a being whose definitive destiny is God; and the historical perspective which regards this same person in its concrete situation, incarnate in the world of today.

(The promotion of justice is part of the Church's mission)

1163   This message of salvation which the Church, by virtue of her mission, brings to every person and also to the family, to the different social environments, to the nations and to the whole of humankind, is a message of love and kinship, a message of justice and solidarity, in the first place for the neediest. In a word, it is a message of peace and of a just social order.

[...]The world willed by God is a world of justice. The order that must govern relations between people is based on justice. This order must be continually realized in this world, and it must even always be realized anew, as situations and social systems grow and develop, in proportion to new conditions and economic possibilities, new possibilities of technology and production, and at the same time new possibilities and necessities of distributing goods.

The Church, when she proclaims the Gospel, also tries to ensure, without, however, forgetting her specific task of evangelisation, that all aspects of social life in which injustice is manifested undergo a change towards justice.

SECRETARIAT FOR NON-CHRISTIANS
DIALOGUE AND MISSION (1984)

The Apostolic Exhortation Evangelii Nuntiandi *(1975) of Pope Paul VI had set forth a broad notion of evangelisation. Evangelisation which is the mission of the Church and her very* raison d'être *(14), involves the entire person of the evangelizer: words, deeds, and the witness of life (21-22); as for its object, it extends to all that is human, aiming as it does at the renewal of humanity and the transformation by the power of the Gospel of human culture and cultures (18-20) (cf. n. 1150-1152). In a document entitled " The Attitude of the Church towards the Followers of Other Religions: Reflections and Orientations on Dialogue and Mission", published on Pentecost 1984, the Secretariat for non-Christians views the Church's mission as "a single but complex and articulated reality" of which, without pretending to be exhaustive, it enumerates the principal elements. The text is found in* Bulletin. Secretariatus pro non Christianis *19(1984) 126-141.*

(The Church's evangelizing mission expresses itself in many ways)

1164   13. Mission is [...] presented in the consciousness of the Church as a single but complex and articulated reality. Its principal elements can be mentioned.

Mission is already constituted by the simple presence and living witness of the Christian life *[cf. EN 21]*, although it must be recognised that "we bear this treasure in earthen vessels" *[2 Cor 4:7]*. Thus the difference between the way the Christian appears existentially and that which he professes to be is never fully overcome.

There is also the concrete commitment to the service of humankind and all forms of activity for social promotion and for the struggle against poverty and the structures which produce it.

Also, there is liturgical life and that of prayer and contemplation, eloquent testimonies to a living and liberating relationship with the active and true God who calls us to his Kingdom and to his glory*[cf. Acts 2:42]*.

There is, as well, the dialogue in which Christians meet the followers of other religious traditions in order to walk together towards truth and to work together in projects of common concerns.

Finally, there is proclamation and catechesis in which the good news of the Gospel is proclaimed and its consequences for life and culture analysed.

The totality of Christian mission embraces all these elements.

JOHN PAUL II

ENCYCLICAL LETTER *SLAVORUM APOSTOLI*
(2 June 1985)

This Encyclical Letter was written on the occasion of the eleventh centenary of the death of St. Methodius in Velerhad (Tchekoslovakia) (885). It commemorates Saints Cyril and Methodius, the Greek brothers who in the ninth century brought the Gospel to the Slav peoples of Eastern Europe. Reflecting on the "vision of the catholicity of the Church" which inspired the apostles of the Slavs, the Pope notes: "Men of Hellenistic culture and Byzantine training", they were "connecting links or spiritual bridges between the Eastern and the Western traditions, which both come together in the one Tradition of the universal Church." He sees in the two saints an "up-to-date version of the catholicity of the Church", because they recognized that the Gospel could be expressed in any language or culture. They are models of inculturation of the Gospel: "The work of evangelisation which they carried out[...] contains both a model of what today is called 'inculturation' — the incarnation of the Gospel in native cultures—and also the introduction of those cultures into the life of the Church" (21). The text is found in AAS 77 (1985) 779-813.

(The catholicity of the Church)

1165   18. The Church is catholic also because she is able to present in every human context the revealed truth preserved by her intact in its divine content, in such a way as to bring it into contact with the lofty thoughts and just expectations of every individual and every people. Moreover, the entire heritage of good which every generation transmits to posterity, together with the priceless gift of life, forms as it were an immense and many-coloured collection of tesserae that together make up the living mosaic of the *Pantocrator,* who will manifest himself in his total splendour only at the moment of the parousia.

The Gospel does not lead to the impoverishment or extinction of those things which every individual, people and nation and every culture throughout history recognizes and brings into being as goodness, truth and beauty. On the contrary, it strives to assimilate and to develop all these values: to live them with magnanimity and joy and to perfect them by the mysterious and ennobling light of revelation.

The concrete dimension of catholicity, inscribed by Christ the Lord in the very make-up of the Church, is not something static, outside history and flatly uniform. In a certain sense it wells up and develops every day as something new from the unanimous faith of all those who believe in God, One and Three, revealed by Jesus Christ and preached by the Church through the power of the Holy Spirit. This dimension issues quite spontaneously from mutual respect—proper to brotherly and sisterly love—for every person and every nation, great or small, and from the honest acknowledgment of the qualities and rights of brothers and sisters in the faith.

ENCYCLICAL LETTER *REDEMPTORIS MISSIO*
(7 December 1990)

After an introduction in which the Pope stresses the permanent validity and the urgency of the mission ad gentes, chapters I to V develop the theology of mission. Chapter I is entitled: "Jesus Christ, the Only Saviour"; chapter II: "The Kingdom of God"; chapter III: "The Holy Spirit, the Principal Agent of Mission"; chapter IV "The paths of Mission". The remaining part of the encyclical

is devoted to leaders and workers in mission, to cooperation and spirituality.
Cf. also nn. 1054-1059. The text is found in AAS 83 (1991) 249-340.

(Jesus Christ's unique mediation does not exclude participated mediations)

1166   5. Christ is the only mediator between God and humankind: "For there is one God, and there is one mediator between God and human beings, the man Christ Jesus,who gave himself as a ransom for all..." *[1 Tim 2:5-7; cf. Heb 4:14-16]*. No one, therefore, can enter into communion with God except through Christ, by the working of the Holy Spirit. Christ's one, universal mediation, far from being an obstacle in the journey towards God, is the way established by God himself.[...] Although participated forms of mediation of different kinds and degrees are not excluded, they acquire meaning and value only from Christ's own mediation, and they cannot be understood as parallel or complementary to his.

(The Church sign and instrument of salvation)

1167   9. It is necessary to keep these two truths together, namely, the real possibility of salvation in Christ for all humankind and the necessity of the Church for salvation. Both these truths help us to understand the one mystery of salvation, so that we can come to know God's mercy and our own responsibility. Salvation, which always remains a gift of the Spirit, requires the person's cooperation, both to save oneself and to save others. This is God's will and this is why he established the Church and made her a part of his plan of salvation. Referring to "this messianic people", the Council says: "It has been set up by Christ as a communion of life, love and truth; by him too it is taken up as the instrument of salvation for all, and sent on a mission to the whole world as the light of the world and the salt of the earth" *[LG 9]*.

(Salvation without membership of the Church implies a mysterious relationship with her)

1168   10. The universality of salvation means that it is granted not only to those who explicitly believe in Christ and have entered the Church. Since salvation is offered to all, it must be made concretely available to all.[...]

For[...]people [outside the Church] salvation in Christ is available in virtue of a grace which, while having a mysterious relationship to the Church, does not make them formally part of the Church but enlightens them in a way which is accommodated to their spiritual and material situation. This grace comes from Christ; it is the result of his Sacrifice and is communicated by the Holy Spirit. It enables each person to attain salvation through his or her free cooperation.

(Universality of the Reign of God)

1169 15. The Kingdom is the concern of everyone: individuals, society, and the world. Working for the Kingdom means acknowledging and promoting God's activity, which is present in human history and transforms it. Building the Kingdom means working for liberation from evil in all its forms. In a word, the Kingdom of God is the manifestation and the realization of God's plan of salvation in all its fullness.

(A Kingdom-centred perspective may not overlook the role of Christ and the Church)

1170 17. There are [...] conceptions which deliberately emphasise the Kingdom and which describe themselves as "Kingdom-centred". They stress the image of a Church which is not concerned about herself, but which is totally concerned with bearing witness to and serving the Kingdom. It is a "Church for others" just as Christ is the "man for others". The Church's task is described as though it had to proceed in two directions: on the one hand, promoting such "values of the Kingdom" as peace, justice, freedom, brotherhood, etc.; on the other hand, fostering dialogue between peoples, cultures and religions, so that through a mutual enrichment they might help the world to be renewed and to journey ever closer towards the Kingdom.

Together with positive aspects these conceptions often reveal negative aspects as well. First, they are silent about Christ: the Kingdom of which they speak is "theocentrically" based, since, according to them, Christ cannot be understood by those who lack Christian faith, whereas different peoples, cultures and religions are capable of finding common ground in the divine reality, by whatever name it is called.[...] Furthermore, the Kingdom, as they understand it, ends up either leaving very little room for the Church or undervaluing the Church in reaction to a presumed "ecclesiocentrism" of the past, and because they

consider the Church herself only a sign, for that matter a sign
not without ambiguity.

This is not the Kingdom of God as we know it from
revelation. The Kingdom cannot be detached either from Christ
or from the Church.

[...]The Kingdom of God is not a concept, a doctrine, or a
programme subject to free interpretation, but is before all else a
person with the face and name of Jesus of Nazareth, the image
of the invisible God [*cf. n. 668*]. If the Kingdom is separated
from Jesus, it is no longer the Kingdom of God which he
revealed. The result is a distortion of the meaning of the
Kingdom, which runs the risk of being transformed into a purely
human or ideological goal, and a distortion of the identity of
Christ, who no longer appears as the Lord to whom everything
must one day be subjected [*cf. 1 Cor 15:27*].

Likewise, one may not separate the Kingdom from the
Church. It is true that the Church is not an end unto herself,
since she is ordered towards the Kingdom of God of which she
is the seed, sign and instrument. Yet, while remaining distinct
from Christ and the Kingdom, the Church is indissolubly united
to both. Christ endowed the Church, his Body, with the fulness
of the benefits and means of salvation. The Holy Spirit dwells in
her, enlivens her with his gifts and charisms, sanctifies, guides
and constantly renews her [*cf. LG 4*]. The result is a unique and
special relationship which, while not excluding the action of
Christ and the Spirit outside the Church's visible boundaries,
confers upon her a specific and necessary role; hence the Church's
special connection with the Kingdom of God and of Christ, which
she has "the mission of announcing and inaugurating among all
peoples"[*cf. LG 5*].

(The Reign of God is present outside the boundaries of the Church)

1171   20.[...]The Church serves the Kingdom by spreading
              throughout the world the "Gospel values" which are an
expression of the Kingdom and which help people to accept
God's plan. It is true that the inchoate reality of the Kingdom can
also be found beyond the confines of the Church among peoples
everywhere, to the extent that they live "Gospel values" and are
open to the working of the Spirit who breathes when and
wherever he wills [*cf. Jn 3:8*]. But it must immediately be added
that this temporal dimension of the Kingdom remains incomplete

unless it is related to the Kingdom of Christ present in the Church and straining towards eschatological fulness [cf. EN 34].

(Universal presence of the Spirit)

1172   28. The Spirit manifests himself in a special way in the Church and in her members. Nevertheless, his presence and activity are universal, limited neither by space nor time.[...]

The Spirit's presence and activity affect not only individuals but also society and history, people, cultures and religions. Indeed, the Spirit is at the origin of the noble ideals and undertakings which benefit humanity on its journey through history. [...] [cf. GS 26, 38]. Again, it is the Spirit who sows the "seeds of the Word" present in the various customs and cultures, preparing them for full maturity in Christ [cf. n. 1136].

(Among the forms of mission   permanent priority belongs to proclamation)

1173   44. Proclamation is the permanent priority of mission.
The Church cannot elude Christ's explicit mandate, nor deprive men and women of the "Good News" about their being loved and saved by God.[...] All forms of missionary activity are directed to this proclamation, which reveals and gives access to the mystery hidden for ages and made known in Christ [cf. Eph 3:3-9; Col 1:25-29], the mystery which lies at the heart of the Church's mission and life, as the hinge on which evangelisation turns.

In the complex reality of mission, initial proclamation has a central and irreplaceable role, since it introduces people "into the mystery of the love of God, who invites them to enter into a personal relationship with himself in Christ" [cf. AG 13] and opens the way to conversion .[...] Just as the whole economy of salvation has its centre in Christ, so too all missionary activity is directed to the proclamation of his mystery.

(Inculturation of the Gospel)

1174   52. Through inculturation the Church makes the Gospel incarnate in different cultures and at the same time introduces people, together with their cultures, into her own community. She transmits to them her own values, at the same time taking the good elements that already exist in them and renewing them from within [cf. n. 1161]. Through inculturation the Church, for her part, becomes a more intelligible sign of what she is, and a more effective instrument of mission.

Thanks to this action within the local Churches, the universal Church herself is enriched with forms of expression and values in the various sectors of Christian life, such as evangelisation, worship, theology and charitable works. She comes to know and to express better the mystery of Christ, all the while being motivated to continual renewal.

(Legitimate variety of expressions of faith)

1175 53. Developing ecclesial communities, inspired by the Gospel, will gradually be able to express their Christian experience in original ways and forms that are consonant with their own cultural traditions, provided that those traditions are in harmony with the objective requirements of the faith itself. To this end, especially in the more delicate areas of inculturation, particular Churches of the same region should work in communion with each other *[cf. n. 1144]* and with the whole Church, convinced that only through attention both to the universal Church and to the particular Churches will they be capable of translating the treasure of faith into a legitimate variety of expressions *[cf. n. 1159]*. Groups which have been evangelised will thus provide the elements for a "translation" of the Gospel message *[cf. n. 1158]*, keeping in mind the positive elements acquired down the centuries from Christianity's contact with different cultures and not forgetting the dangers of alterations which have sometimes occurred.

PONTIFICAL COUNCIL FOR INTERRELIGIOUS DIALOGUE
CONGREGATION FOR THE EVANGELISATION OF PEOPLES
DIALOGUE AND PROCLAMATION
(19 May 1991)

The second part of the joint document is concerned with proclamation; the third with the relationship between dialogue and proclamation (cf. n. 1059i; cf. also nn. 1059, 1064). The text is found in Bulletin *n. 77; 26 (1991/2) 210-250.*

(The action of the Spirit precedes the Church's proclamation)

1176 68. While proclaiming the message of God in Jesus Christ, the evangelising Church must always remember that her task is not exercised in a complete void. For the Holy Spirit, the Spirit of Christ, is present and active among the hearers of the Good News even before the Church's missionary action comes into operation [cf. n. 1039; DV 53]. They may in many cases have already responded implicitly to God's offer of salvation in Jesus Christ, a sign of this being the sincere practice of their own religious traditions, in so far as these contain authentic religious values. They may have already been touched by the Spirit and in some way associated unknowingly to the paschal mystery of Jesus Christ [cf. GS 22].

(Divine pedagogy of proclamation)

1177 69. Mindful of what God has already accomplished in those addressed, the Church seeks to discover the right way to announce the Good News. She takes her lead from divine pedagogy. This means learning from Jesus himself, and observing the times and seasons as prompted by the Spirit. Jesus only progressively revealed to his hearers the meaning of the Kingdom, God's plan of salvation realized in his own mystery. Only gradually, and with infinite care, did he unveil for them the implications of his message, his identity as the Son of God, the scandal of Cross. Even his closest disciples, as the Gospels testify, reached full faith in their Master only through their Easter experience and the gift of the Spirit. Those who wish to become disciples of Jesus today will pass through the same process of discovery and commitment. Accordingly, the Church's proclamation must both be progressive and patient, keeping pace with those who hear the message, respecting their freedom and even their "slowness to believe" [EN 79].

(Aim and progressive way of proclamation)

1178 81. Proclamation.[...] aims at guiding people to explicit knowledge of what God has done for all men and women in Jesus Christ, and at inviting them to become disciples of Jesus through becoming members of the Church. When in obedience to the command of the Risen Lord and the Spirit's promptings, the Church fulfills this task of proclamation, this will often need to be done in a progressive manner. A discernment is to be made concerning how God is present in each one's personal history. The followers of other religions may discover, as may Christians also, that they already share many values. This can lead to a challenge in the form of a witness of the Christian community or a personal profession of faith, in which the full identity of Jesus is humbly confessed. Then, when the time is ripe, Jesus' decisive question can be put: "Who do you say that I am?" The true answer to this question can come only through faith. The preaching and the confession, under the movement of grace, that Jesus of Nazareth is the Son of God the Father, the Risen Lord and Saviour, constitutes the final stage of proclamation. One who freely professes this faith is invited to become a disciple of Jesus in his Church and to take a responsible part in her mission.

(Proclamation, a mystery of love)

1179   83. In [a] dialogue approach, how could [Christians] not hope and desire to share with others their joy in knowing and following Jesus Christ, Lord and Saviour? We are here at the heart of the mystery of love. Insofar as the Church and the Christians have a deep love for the Lord Jesus, the desire to share him with others is motivated not merely by obedience to the Lord's command, but by this love itself. It should not be surprising, but quite normal, that the followers of other religions should also desire sincerely to share their faith. All dialogue implies reciprocity and aims at banishing fear and aggressiveness.

JOHN PAUL II

OPENING ADDRESS TO THE FOURTH GENERAL CONFERENCE OF LATIN AMERICAN BISHOPS
(Santo Domingo, 12 October 1992)

"New Evangelisation" was the central theme to be addressed by the Santo Domingo Assembly of Latin American Bishops. The Pope had already previously explained what is meant by "new evangelisation", as "a fresh forward impulse, capable of creating, with a Church still more rooted in the undying power and strength of Pentecost, a new period of evangelisation." In his opening address to the Santo Domingo conference he further stresses the content of new evangelisation. The text is found in AAS 85 (1993) 808-832.

(The mystery of Jesus Christ is the content of new evangelisation)

1180   6. The new evangelisation does not consist in a "new gospel", which would always arise from ourselves, our culture, our analysis of human need. Hence, it would not be

"Gospel" but mere human invention, and there would be no salvation in it. Nor does it consist of trimming away from the Gospel everything that seems difficult for the contemporary mind-set to accept. Culture is not the measure of the Gospel; rather, Jesus Christ is the measure of all culture and all human endeavour. No, the new evangelization does not arise from the desire "to curry favour with human beings" or to "please people" [Gal 1:10], but from responsibility for the gift that God has made to us in Christ, in which we accede to the truth about God and about the human being, and to the possibility of true life. The starting point for the new evangelisation is the certainty that in Christ are "inscrutable riches" [Eph 3:8] that are not exhausted by any culture or any age and that we human beings can always approach in order to be enriched. That wealth is first and foremost Christ himself, his person, for he himself is our salvation. By approaching him through faith and being incorporated in his body, which is the Church, we human beings of any period and any culture can find the answer to those ever old and ever new questions with which we face the mystery of our existence and which we bear indelibly engraved in our hearts from creation and from the wound of sin.

(The unchangeable Gospel is to be preached in complete faithfulness)

1181 7. Newness does not touch the content of the Gospel message, which is unchangeable, for Christ is the same "yesterday, today and forever" [Heb 13:8]. Hence, the Gospel is to be preached with complete faithfulness and purity as it has been guarded and transmitted by the tradition of the Church. To evangelise is to announce a person; who is Christ. Indeed, "there is no true evangelisation if the name, the teaching, the life, the promises, the kingdom and the mystery of Jesus of Nazareth, Son of God, are not proclaimed" [EN 22]. Hence, reductive Christologies, whose errors I have pointed out on several occasions [cf. nn. 674-676], cannot be accepted as instruments for the new evangelisation. When evangelisation takes place, the unity of the Church's faith must shine forth not only in the authentic magisterium of the bishops but also in the service to truth by pastors of souls, theologians, catechists and all those who are committed to proclaiming and preaching the faith.

ENCYCLICAL LETTER *FIDES ET RATIO*
(14 September 1998)

For an introduction to the document, cf. n. 190a. In this chapter two texts of the encyclical are being mentioned, which deal with the need of cultural pluralism in the proclamation of the Gospel, especially in the Indian context. The text of the encyclical is found in AAS 91 (1999) 5ff.

(Cultural pluralism in the proclamation of the Gospel)

1182   71. While it demands of all who hear it the adhesion of faith, the proclamation of the Gospel in different cultures allows people to preserve their own cultural identity. This in no way creates division, because the community of the baptized is marked by a universality which can embrace every culture and help to foster whatever is implicit in them to the point where it will be fully explicit in the light of truth.

This means that no one culture can ever become the criterion of judgment, much less the ultimate criterion of truth with regard to God's revelation. The Gospel is not opposed to any culture, as if in engaging a culture the Gospel would seek to strip it of its native riches and force it to adopt forms which are alien to it. On the contrary, the message which believers bring to the world and to cultures is a genuine liberation from all the disorders caused by sin and is, at the same time, a call to the fulness of truth. Cultures are not only not diminished by this encouter; rather, they are prompted to open themselves to the newness of the Gospel's truth and to be stirred by this truth to develop in new ways.

(On tasks of inculturation, especially in India)

1183   72. In preaching the Gospel, Christianity first encountered Greek philosophy; but this does not mean at all that other approaches are precluded. Today, as the Gospel gradually comes into contact with cultural worlds which once lay beyond Christian influence, there are new tasks of inculturation, which means that our generation faces problems not unlike those faced by the Church in the first centuries.

My thoughts turn immediately to the lands of the East, so rich in religious and philosophical traditions of great antiquity. Among these lands, India has a special place. A great spiritual impulse leads Indian thought to seek an experience which would liberate the spirit from the shackles of time and space and would therefore acquire absolute value. The dynamic of this quest for liberation provides the context for great metaphysical systems.

In India particularly, it is the duty of Christians to draw from this rich heritage the elements compatible with their faith, in order to enrich Christian thought. In this work of discernment, which finds its inspiration in the Council's Declaration *Nostra Aetate*, certain criteria will have to be kept in mind. The first of these is the universality of the human spirit, whose basic needs are the same in the most disparate cultures. The second, which derives from the first, is this: in engaging great cultures for the first time, the Church cannot abandon what she has gained from her incluturation in the world of Greco-Latin thought. To reject this heritage would be to deny the providential plan of God who guides his Church down the paths of time and history. This criterion is valid for the Church in every age, even for the Church of the future, who will judge herself enriched by all that comes from today's engagement with Eastern cultures and will find in this inheritance fresh cues for fruitful dialogue with the cultures which will emerge as humanity moves into the future. Thirdly, care will need to be taken lest, contrary to the very nature of the human spirit, the legitimate defense of the uniqueness and originality of Indian thought be confused with the idea that a particular cultural tradition should remain closed in its difference and affirm itself by opposing other traditions.

What has been said here of India is no less true for the heritage of the great cultures of China, Japan and the other countries of Asia, as also for the riches of the traditional cultures of Africa, which are for the most part orally transmitted.

APOSTOLIC EXHORTATION *ECCLESIA IN ASIA*
(6 November 1999)

In the apostolic letter Tertio Millennio Adveniente *(10 November 1994), Pope John Paul II announced, in preparation for the third millennium of Christianity, different synods of bishops in Rome "of a continental character". The Synod for Asia took place in Rome from 20 April 1998 till 14 May. In the apostolic exhortation which followed, the pope resumed and commented on the findings of the Asian Synod. One extract of the apostolic exhortation is mentioned here. It deals with the need in Asia for an inculturated theology and sets the necessary criteria in order that such inculturation may proceed correctly. The text is found in AAS 92 (2000) 449-528.*

(On inculturated theology)

1184 22. The Synod expressed encouragement to theologians in their delicate work of developing an inculturated theology, especially in the area of Christology *(Proposition 43)*. They noted that "This theologising is to be carried out with courage, in faithfulness to the Scriptures and to the Church's Tradition, in sincere adherence to the Magisterium and with an awareness of pastoral realities" *(Proposition 7)*. I too urge theologians to work in a spirit of union with the Pastors and the people, who—in union with one another and never separated from one another—"reflect the authentic *sensus fidei* which must never be lost sight of" [cf. *RM 54*]. Theological work must always be guided by respect for the sensibilities of Christians, so that by a gradual growth into inculturated forms of expressing the faith people are neither confused nor scandalized. In every case inculturation must be guided by compatibility with the Gospel and communion with the faith of the universal Church, in full compliance with the Church's Tradition and with a view to strenghtening people's faith *[RM 54]*. The test of true inculturation is whether people become more committed to their Christian faith because they perceive it more clearly with the eyes of their own culture.

CHAPTER XII

CHRISTIAN WORSHIP OR LITURGY

Liturgy or worship is at the centre of the Church's life. Founded by Christ as the sign of the salvation which he gained for all people, enlivened by the Spirit of Christ to signify this mystery effectively, the Church finds the deepest raison d'être *of her entire activity in her union with Christ. But nowhere does the Church signify the mystery of Christ and the Church as deeply as in her liturgical life. In her liturgy the Church is mysteriously united with her Head, the Lord of glory, from whose glorified humanity there proceed at once the sanctification of human beings and the perfect worship of God. This is why, in different ways and at different levels, the Church in her various liturgical actions prolongs on earth the communication of God's grace to men and women and renders to God fitting worship in spirit and truth. The liturgy, then, is the exercise of Christ's mediatory and priestly function through his Body, the Church. It is Jesus Christ calling all people to salvation through the signs of the Church and calling them through the same signs to true worship in spirit and in truth. In the liturgy, heaven and earth are united; in it Christians discover their true vocation to serve God and humanity; from it we draw the Christian spirit at its deepest source.*

From the apostolic age down through the centuries the Church has always lived her liturgical life. She did so with great spontaneity and creativeness during the first centuries. At various intervals of her history the Church has also experienced the need for liturgical reform; for, in an institution which is at once divine and human, the human forms must constantly evolve in order adequately to convey the mystery which they contain. But never before had the Church experienced such a deep current of liturgical renewal as she has known this century; this renewal has been officially sanctioned by the Second Vatican Council. The Council of Trent had previously initiated a liturgical reform which was set in motion by Pope Pius V. At that time it was found necessary, in the context of a universal reform of Church traditions, to unify the existing liturgical trends. Later unification and stabilisation, however, resulted in uniformity and formalism. The progressive clericalisation of the liturgy and an individualistic approach obscured the traditional doctrine that conscious and active participation by the people of God is required if they are to derive profit from the Church's liturgical life. The rediscovery of this basic principle was bound to lead and has in fact led in recent years to far-reaching changes. For participation requires a certain intelligibility, meaningfulness and adaptation in order to enter into the mystery being celebrated.

The documents mentioned in this chapter outline the new awareness which has developed in this century as regards the nature and laws of the Church's liturgy and the constant need of renewal it imposes on the Church in order that through it the people may be able to enter more deeply, as persons and as members of a community, into the mystery of Christ.

*   *   *

The main points of doctrine considered in this chapter fall under the following headings:

The liturgy is an exercise of Christ's priestly function through the Church: 1218.

It is the work of the entire Body of Christ, Head and Members: 1216, 1228, 1229, 1231.

Christ is present in the Church's liturgy: (1217), 1331, 1334.

His mysteries are present in the Church's liturgical cycle: (1226), 1234, 1333.

Liturgical prayer can be addressed to Christ: 1215.

The liturgy of the Word must be fostered: 1202, 1203-1205, 1242, 1243.

Lex orandi, lex credendi: 1211, 1212, 1223.

There are various degrees of efficacy in the Church's liturgical actions: 1221.

Active participation is required on the part of the people: 1208, 1219-1220, 1230.

Subjective dispositions are needed to derive profit from the liturgy: 1209/1-4, 1232.

Liturgy implies interior and exterior worship: 1219-1220, 1230.

Liturgical and personal piety are related to each other: 1214, 1222.

The liturgy must be adapted to the people, especially in mission countries: 1129, 1213, 1214, 1224, 1227, 1233, 1237-1239, 1241, 1245-1249.

The different liturgical rites of the Church must be fostered: 39/14,
    1201, 1206, 1207, 1210, 1235-1236.
Guidelines for liturgical renewal: 1240-1241.
Ecumenical guidelines for liturgico-sacramental life: (1244).
Notion of "celebration" of Christian liturgy/sacraments: 1241b.
The meaning of Sunday : 1250a-d

THE FOURTH LATERAN GENERAL COUNCIL (1215)

The fourth Lateran Council, convened by Pope Innocent III, is one of the greatest Western Councils. Its profession of faith (cf. nn. 19-20) and its Trinitarian doctrine (cf. nn. 317-320) are important documents. But the Council also dealt with practical matters which had a bearing on Church union. It required from the Greeks re-uniting with the Church that they show respect for Roman liturgical customs as Rome respected their own rites (cf. DS 810). Basing its legislation on the equality of all liturgical traditions in the unity of faith, it prescribed that worship according to their own traditions be made available to the people in all ecclesiastical provinces where the case arose. Regarding Church reform, the Council gave much importance to the preaching of the word of God and called on bishops unable to perform this duty by themselves to see to it that it be adequately fulfilled by others. The text is found in COD, p. 239.

Chapter IX: On the Diversity of Rites in the Unity of Faith

1201   Because in many regions people of different languages live in the same city or diocese, keeping different rites and customs in the unity of faith, we clearly prescribe that the bishops of such cities or dioceses must provide men capable of celebrating for them the divine liturgy and of administering to them the sacraments of the Church as the variety of rites and languages will require, and who will instruct them by word and example. But we altogether forbid one and the same city or diocese to have several bishops, like one body having several heads, which is a monstrous thing. If for the reasons mentioned above, it is found urgent and necessary, let the bishop of the place after due consideration appoint a Catholic prelate *(praesul)* from those nations to be his vicar in these matters; he will be subject and obedient to the bishop in all things.[...]

Chapter X: On Providing Preachers

1202   Among other things pertaining to the salvation of the Christian people, it is known that the food of the word of God is of the utmost necessity, since, as the body is nourished by material food, so the soul is by spiritual food, for "one does not live by bread alone, but by every word that comes from the mouth of God" *[Mt 4:4]*. Hence, since it often happens that bishops because of many occupations or ill-health or hostilities or other reasons[...]cannot by themselves suffice to administer the word of God to their people, especially in vastly spread-out dioceses, in order that the sacred duty of preaching be duly fulfilled, we ordain by this general Constitution that bishops must enrol for it capable men, mighty in deed and in word [cf. Lk 24:19]. When the bishops are not able to do so themselves, these men will visit the people entrusted to the bishops, in their name and with due solicitude, and will edify them by word and example. When the preachers are in need, the bishops will provide them with what is reasonable and necessary, lest because of want they be compelled to give up the ministry they have undertaken.[...]

THE GENERAL COUNCIL OF TRENT
FIFTH SESSION
DECREE ON TEACHING AND PREACHING THE WORD OF GOD (1546)

In its 7th session the Council of Trent stressed the efficacy of the sacraments against the denial of the Reformers (cf. nn. 1310ff); in its 22nd session, however, while exposing the doctrine of the sacrifice of the Mass, it ordered that, during the celebration of the Mass, pastors frequently explain to the people some of its readings (cf. n. 1554). Previous to this, the primary obligation to preach had been the object of detailed legislation in a Decree of Reformation promulgated by the Council's 5th session. This decree shows the importance which the Council attributed to the ministry of teaching and preaching the word of God. The Council refers to the legislation previously made by the fourth Lateran Council (cf. n. 1202). The full text is found in COD, pp. 667-670; only three paragraphs of the Decree's second chapter, dealing with preaching, are quoted here (COD, p. 669).

(On preaching the word)

1203 In view of the fact that the preaching of the Gospel meets as important a need of the Christian people as does lecturing about it—and indeed preaching is the main *(praecipuum)* office of the bishops—the Holy Synod has ordained and decreed that all bishops, archbishops, primates and all other prelates of the Church are bound to preach the Holy Gospel of Jesus Christ by themselves, unless a legitimate reason prevents them.

1204 If it should happen that bishops or the other persons mentioned here above are prevented by a legitimate reason, they are bound to follow the decision taken by the

General Council *[cf. n. 1202]* to enrol capable men who will duly fulfil this duty of preaching.[...]

1205   Let archbishops, parish-priests, priests in rural areas *(plebani)* and whoever has the care of souls in any Church, either by themselves or, if they are prevented by a legitimate reason, through other capable persons, provide the people entrusted to their care, at least on Sundays and feast-days, with salutary preaching, according to their own ability and in keeping with the level of their people.[...]

PIUS IX
ENCYCLICAL LETTER *AMANTISSIMUS* (1862)

In this Encyclical Letter, Pius IX, after explaining that the Holy See is the foundation of unity and faith in the Church, remarks that the plurality of liturgical rites in no way obscures but rather enhances this unity. The pluralism of liturgical forms is legitimate and must be preserved. The text is found in Acta, Vol. 3, 424.

(Unity of the Church and diversity of rites)

1206   The rich variety of legitimate rites is not in any way opposed to the unity of the Catholic Church; rather, it is most conducive to the Church's dignity, majesty, ornament and splendour.[...] Our predecessors[...] have repeatedly affirmed their express will that the rites of the Oriental Churches, provided they contain no error on the Catholic faith[...], be preserved intact.[...]

LEO XIII
CONSTITUTION *ORIENTALIUM DIGNITAS* (1894)

In this Constitution, the Pope shows, better than previous documents had done, the rich contribution which the Oriental rites make to the catholicity of the Church. The text is found in ASS 1894, pp. 257ff.

(On preserving the Oriental rites)

1207   The most important thing, it seems to us, is to give our attention and care to the preservation of the particular discipline of the East; and this we have always done.[...]

The noble and glorious antiquity of those various rites is the ornament of the whole Church; it enhances the divine unity of the Catholic faith. [Those rites] clearly manifest to the main

Eastern Churches their apostolic origin, while illustrating at the same time their intimate union with the Roman Church from the origin of Christianity. For nothing, perhaps, manifests better the catholicity of the Church of God than does the singular homage of ceremonies of various forms, celebrated in languages of venerable antiquity, and ennobled even more by the use which the apostles and the Fathers made of them. It imitates as it were the exquisite worship which Christ, the divine founder of the Church, received at his birth when the Magi came from various regions of the East.

Here it is worth noting that, though holy ceremonies have not been directly instituted to prove the truth of Catholic doctrine, they nevertheless show forth its vitality in a wonderful manner. Thus, while the Church of Christ jealously preserves in their integrity the dogmas she has received, which their divine character makes immutable, she allows and makes provision for some innovations in exterior forms, mostly when they are in conformity with the ancient past. Thus is made manifest the vigour of the Church's eternal youth, and she shines with ever renewed brightness. This is the Church of which the Fathers found a type in the words of David: "The princess is decked in her chamber with gold-woven robes[...] in many-coloured robes" [cf. Ps 45 (44):13-14].

PIUS X

MOTU PROPRIO *TRA LE SOLLECITUDINI* (1903)

In this Motu Proprio Pope Pius X gives directives to be followed in order that sacred music be truly worthy of the liturgical worship of God. The introduction contains a passage, often quoted later, in which the Pope considers active participation in the Church's liturgy as the principal source of renewal for the Christian life. The text is found in ASS 1903, pp. 329ff.

(Active participation in the liturgy is the primary source of true Christian life)

1208 [...] Since we have very much at heart that the true Christian spirit be revived in all possible ways and that it be maintained among all the faithful, it is above all necessary to provide for the holiness and dignity of the sacred places where precisely the faithful gather to draw this spirit at its primary and indispensable source, that is, active participation in the sacred mysteries and in the public and solemn prayer of the Church.[...]

DECREE *SACRA TRIDENTINA* (1905)

By this Decree Pope Pius X allowed the practice of daily communion which he considered to be "the desire of Christ and of the Church". After a brief survey of the history of frequent communion and of the discussions regarding the necessary dispositions, the Pope gives definite rules on the observance of which the fruit of the practice depends. Though partly conditioned by the theology of the time, this is a clear statement of the personal appropriation required from the recipient of the sacrament for its fruitful reception. The first four rules, theologically more important, are quoted here.

(Decree on daily communion)

1209/1 Frequent and daily communion, because ardently
3379   desired by Christ and the Church, must be open to all
        the faithful of whatever class or condition, so that none
who is in the state of grace and approaches the holy table with
a right intention may be turned away from it.

1209/2 The right intention consists in this, that a person
3380   approach the holy table, not from routine, vanity or
        human motives, but because he wishes to please God,
to be more closely united with him in charity, and to overcome
his infirmities and defects by means of this divine remedy.

1209/3 Though it is extremely desirable that those who practice
3381   frequent and daily communion be free from venial sins,
        or at least from fully deliberate ones, and from all
attachment to them, yet it is enough that they be free from mortal
sins and resolved never to sin again; with this sincere proposal,
it is impossible that they should not gradually correct themselves
from venial sin and from attachment to it.

1209/4 Though the sacraments of the New Law obtain their
3382   effect *ex opere operato*, yet their fruit increases with
        the dispositions of the recipient; hence care must be
taken that holy communion be preceded by a solid preparation
and followed by a proper thanksgiving, according to each one's
strength, condition and duties.

APOSTOLIC CONSTITUTION *TRADITA AB ANTIQUIS*
(1912)

As a result of the practice of daily Communion, the desire was expressed in regions with Catholics belonging to different rites, that the faithful be allowed to receive the sacrament in any rite in which it was available to them. In this Apostolic Constitution Tradita ab antiquis, *Pope Pius X recalls that in the ancient tradition the faithful, when travelling, were allowed to participate in the celebration of the mysteries in the local rite. The Schism and the controversy on the validity of consecration with unleavened bread interrupted this practice. But the Council of Florence recognised the validity of the discipline of both the Roman and the Oriental rites as regards the matter of the Eucharist (cf. n. 1508), and allowed the faithful to partake of it in either form. If the practice of inter-ritualism was short-lived after the Council of Florence, the reason is that the union attempted by the Council was itself short-lived. Later, the Holy See again permitted the practice in various circumstances. The Pope recalls that, in his Constitution* Orientalium Dignitas, *his predecessor Leo XIII gave permissions in that direction, while for the sake of respecting the equal rights of the Oriental rites (cf. n. 1207), he also recommended that Oriental priests be provided in order that the Orientals living in Rome be able to partake of the Eucharist in their own rite. Now, in view of the fact that such priests are not always easily available, and considering especially the new needs that have arisen from the practice of daily Communion, the Pope grants without any restriction to all Catholics the permission to share in the Eucharist celebrated in any Catholic rite. The text is found in AAS 4 (1912) 609ff.*

(All restriction about rites is abrogated with regard to the reception of the Eucharist)

1210   Therefore, considering the unanimity of the Catholic faith as regards the validity of consecration done with either unleavened or leavened bread; convinced, moreover, that for many Latins as well as Orientals the prohibition to share in each other's rite is a source of annoyance and a matter of scandal; having consulted the S. Congregation of Propaganda for the affairs of the Oriental rites, and having closely examined the question, we have deemed it opportune to abrogate all the decrees forbidding or restricting the mutual sharing of rites in the reception of the Holy Eucharist, and to allow all, Latins and Orientals, to be fed with the august sacrament of the Body of the Lord consecrated by Catholic priests either with unleavened or leavened bread, in Catholic churches of either rite according to the ancient custom of the Church, in order that "all Christians may be joined together and united in this symbol of unity and charity" [cf. n. 1512].

PIUS XI
ENCYCLICAL LETTER *QUAS PRIMAS* (1925)

In this Encyclical Letter, Pope Pius XI, after explaining the theology of the kingship of Christ (cf. nn. 652-653), prescribes the celebration of the feast of Christ the King for the universal Church. On this occasion, he explains the educative value of the liturgy in the life of Christians. The text is found in AAS 17 (1925) 593ff.

(On the didactic role of the liturgy)

1211 That these blessings may be abundant and lasting in Christian society, it is necessary that the kingship of our Saviour should be as widely as possible recognised and understood, and to this end nothing would serve better than the institution of a special feast in honour of the kingship of Christ. For people are instructed in the truths of the faith and brought to appreciate the inner joys of religion far more effectively by the annual celebration of our sacred mysteries than by any pronouncement, however weighty, made by the teaching of the Church. Such pronouncements usually reach only a few and the more learned among the faithful; feasts reach them all. The former speak but once; the latter speak every year—in fact, for ever. The Church's teaching affects primarily the mind; her feasts affect both mind and heart, and have a salutary effect upon the whole of human nature. Human beings are composed of body and soul, and they need these external festivities so that the sacred rites, in all their beauty and variety, may stimulate them to drink more deeply of the fountain of God's teaching, to make it a part of themselves and to use it with profit for their spiritual life.

APOSTOLIC CONSTITUTION *DIVINI CULTUS* (1928)

In this Apostolic Constitution, Pope Pius XI recalls the Motu proprio of Pius X on sacred music (1903) and gives further directives on the same subject. The document shows the important place which music occupies in the sacred action of the liturgy. It situates the liturgy in the life of the Church by showing, according to the ancient axiom Lex orandi, lex credendi, that it is a privileged expression of the Church's faith and therefore a source of theological knowledge. The text is found in AAS 21 (1929) 33ff.

(Lex orandi, lex credendi)

1212 The liturgy is indeed sacred. Through it we lift ourselves to God and we are united with him, we profess our faith and fulfil our grave duty of giving thanks to God for the benefits and the help which he bestows on us and which we constantly need. There exists, therefore, a close relationship between dogma and the sacred liturgy, as also between the Christian cult and the sanctification of the people. This is why Pope Celestine I thought that the rule of faith is expressed in the ancient liturgical formulations; he said that "the norm of prayer establishes the norm of belief." "For, when the leaders of the holy assemblies exercise the office entrusted to them, they plead the cause of the human race before the divine mercy and they offer prayers and supplications while the whole Church joins in their entreaty" *[cf. n. 1913].*

LETTER *MISSIONALIUM RERUM* (1937)

In a letter addressed to Cardinal Fumasoni-Biondi on the occasion of an exhibition devoted to sacred art in mission lands, the Pope explains the function of sacred art in the liturgy and states the principle of missionary adaptation in its application to sacred art. The text is found in AAS 29 (1937) 413ff.

(On sacred art in the missions)

1213 Art ranks among the highest manifestations of the genius and culture of all peoples; it also offers to the Church the most worthy and the most important elements which the exterior celebration of the divine cult must assume.[...] The exhibition will show the truly Catholic spirit and action of the Church of Christ, for the holy Church respects the artistic and cultural patrimony, the laws and customs of each people, provided that they are not contrary to the holy law of God. Since its origin the Church repeats with St. Paul that it seeks souls only *[cf. 2 Cor 12:14-15]* and that it wishes to be all things to all people *[cf. 1 Cor 9:22].* The exhibition will also show to all the inexhaustible fecundity of Christian doctrine even in the field of art; it will show that, overcoming many painful divisions, Christian doctrine is capable of gathering in the house of the common Father under the same wonderful spiritual unity the artistic productions by which various people seek to glorify God through the homage of beauty.

PIUS XII

ENCYCLICAL LETTER *MYSTICI CORPORIS* (1943)

In his great Encyclical Letter on the mystery of the Church, Pius XII shows the place which the sacraments occupy in the Church's life (cf. nn. 1328-1330); the doctrine of the Eucharist, the visible sign of the Church's unity, receives special treatment (cf. nn. 1564-1565). Broadening the perspective, the encyclical touches on several themes pertaining to the liturgy in general. The Pope considers how liturgical and private prayer must be combined in the life of Christians. He also explains why liturgical prayer can be addressed to Christ himself and need not always be directed to God through him: Christ is not only mediator between God and humankind, but God himself. The early centuries had made it a rule to address liturgical prayer to the Father, as the Council of Hippo (393) for instance testifies: "At the altar, let prayer always be addressed to the Father" (cf. Mansi, 3. 922). This rule is not, however, exclusive as more recent liturgical developments show. The text is found in AAS 35 (1943) 193ff.

(Liturgical and private prayer)

1214   There are some[...]who deny to our prayers of petition
3819   any real efficacy, or who suggest that private prayers to
         God are to be accounted of little value, inasmuch as it is
rather the public prayers offered in the name of the Church which
have real worth, since they proceed from the mystical Body of
Jesus Christ. This suggestion is quite untrue. For the divine
Redeemer holds in close union with himself not only his Church,
as his beloved Bride, but in her also the souls of each one of the
faithful, with whom he ardently desires to have intimate
converse, especially after they have received holy communion.
And although public prayer, as proceeding from Mother Church
herself, excels beyond any other by reason of the dignity of the
Bride of Christ, nevertheless all prayers, even those said most
privately, have their dignity and their efficacy, and are also of
great benefit to the whole mystical Body, for in that Body there
can be no good and virtuous deed performed by individual
members which does not, through the communion of saints,
redound also to the welfare of all.[...]

(Liturgical prayer can be addressed to Christ)

1215   Finally, there are those who say that our prayers ought
3820   not to be addressed to the person of Jesus Christ himself,
         but rather to God, or through Christ to the eternal Father,

on the ground that our Saviour in his capacity as Head of his mystical Body is to be regarded only as the "mediator between God and humankind" [cf. 1 Tim 2:5]. But this is not only contrary to the mind of the Church and to Christian practice; it is also untrue. For Christ, strictly speaking, is Head of the whole Church according to both natures together; moreover he himself has solemnly declared: "whatever you ask in my name, I will do it" [Jn 14:14]. Thus, although it is true that prayers are usually addressed to the eternal Father through his only begotten Son, especially in the eucharistic sacrifice where Christ being both Priest and Victim, discharges in a special manner his office of Mediator, nevertheless, on not a few occasions, even during the holy Sacrifice, prayers are directed also to the divine Redeemer; because it is necessary for all Christians to know and to understand clearly that the man Christ Jesus is truly the Son of God, and himself truly God.[...]

ENCYCLICAL LETTER *MEDIATOR DEI* (1947)

This encyclical is the first "magna charta" of the liturgical renewal of this century. It is the result of several decades of scientific research directed to giving new vigour to the Church's liturgy; it marks also a new point of departure for a more pastorally oriented liturgical life. It is divided into four parts: 1) the nature, origin and development of the liturgy; 2) eucharistic worship; 3) the divine office and the liturgical year; 4) pastoral instruction. Here are mentioned mostly passages dealing with the general principles of the liturgy, exposed in the first part of the encyclical. For the doctrine of the Eucharist, cf. nn. 1566-1570 and nn. 1735-1736; for the sacraments in general, cf. nn. 1331-1333. Are found there the passages of the encyclical dealing with the various modalities of Christ's presence and action in the Church's liturgy and the presence in it of his mysteries; this doctrine extends beyond the Church's sacramental actions to other liturgical celebrations and applies to the entire liturgical cycle. The text is found in AAS 39 (1947) 521ff.

(Christ's priestly function is continued in the Church's liturgy)

1216 [...] The Church at the bidding of her founder continues the priestly office of Jesus Christ, especially in the liturgy. This she does first and chiefly at the altar, where the sacrifice of the cross is perpetually represented [cf. n. 1546] and, with a difference only in the manner of offering, for ever renewed [cf. n. 1548]. She does it secondly by means of the sacraments, those special means for communicating supernatural life to people. She does it thirdly by the tribute of praise which is daily offered to almighty God.[...]

(The presence of Christ in the Church's liturgy)

(1217)   *(See text in n. 1331)*

(Definition of the sacred liturgy)

1218   The sacred liturgy, then, is the public worship which
3841   our Redeemer, the Head of the Church, offers to the
heavenly Father, and which the community of Christ's
faithful pays to its Founder, and through him to the eternal
Father; briefly, it is the whole public worship of the mystical
Body of Jesus Christ, Head and members.

(External and internal worship: the external element is necessary)

1219   The whole of the Church's divine worship must be both
3842   external and internal. It must be external; for this is
required by the nature of the human being, composed
of soul and body, and it is also required by the divine plan
according to which, "while recognising God in visible form, we
may through him be rapt to the love of things invisible."[1]
Moreover, it is natural that the outpourings of the soul should
be expressed by the senses. Furthermore, divine worship is a
duty for human society as such and not only for individuals;
and how can religion be social unless it too has its external bonds
and signs? Finally, the external element in divine worship is an
important manifestation of the unity of the mystical Body; it also
fosters its holy endeavours, invigorates its powers and intensifies
its activity.[...]

(External and internal worship: internal worship is the chief element)

1220   But most important in divine worship is the internal
3842   element. If it is with Christ and through him that
due glory is to be given to our heavenly Father, then we
must always live in Christ and devote ourselves entirely to him.
The sacred liturgy itself requires these two elements to be closely
combined and repeatedly insists on this whenever it enjoins some

---

1. Cf. *Roman Missal*, Preface for Christmas

external act of divine worship—as when it exhorts us that our acts of fasting "may inwardly effect what they outwardly proclaim."[1] Otherwise, religion becomes nothing but an empty ceremony and pure formalism.[...] Consequently, it is a total misunderstanding of the true meaning of the liturgy to regard it as the merely external and visible element in divine worship, or as the outward splendour of ceremonial; it is equally wrong to see in it a mere catalogue of rules and regulations issued by the hierarchy of the Church for the conduct of the sacred rites.

(Efficacy ex opere operato and ex opere operantis Ecclesiae)

1221   [...] God cannot be worthily honoured unless the mind
3844   and will are intent upon spiritual perfection; and for
      the achievement of holiness the worship which the Church, united with her divine Head, offers to God is the most efficacious possible means.

This efficacy, so far as the eucharistic sacrifice and the sacraments are concerned, is primarily *ex opere operato*. In the case of the prayers and sacred ceremonies which Christ's immaculate Bride the Church uses to adorn the sacrifice and the sacraments, and also in the case of the sacramentals and other rites instituted by the hierarchy of the Church, the efficacy is rather *ex opere operantis Ecclesiae*, inasmuch as the Church is holy and acts in the closest union with her Head.

(Complementarity of various elements)

1222   [...] In the spiritual life there can be no discrepancy
3846   between the divine action which, perpetuating the work
      of our redemption, pours out grace into our souls, and the active human co-operation which must ensure that the gift of God is not in vain; no opposition between the *ex opere operato* efficacy of the external sacrament and the meritorious or *ex opere operantis* action of its minister or recipient; no opposition between public and private prayer, between the active and the contemplative life, between the ascetical life and liturgical piety.[...]

---

1. Cf. *Roman Missal*, Prayer over the gifts for Thursday after the second Sunday of Lent

(Lex orandi, lex credendi: a shift from the more traditional meaning of this well known adage; a double interaction)

1223   [...] In the liturgy we make explicit profession of our Catholic faith; not only by celebrating the various mysteries, not only by offering the sacrifice and administering the sacraments, but also by reciting or singing the Creed (the Christian watchword), by reading other documents as well as the divinely inspired Scriptures. Thus the whole liturgy contains the Catholic faith, inasmuch as it is a public profession of the faith of the Church.[...] This is the origin of the well-known and time-honoured principle: "the norm of prayer establishes the norm of belief" *[cf. n. 1913].*

Thus the sacred liturgy does not absolutely or of itself designate or constitute the Catholic faith. The fact is that the liturgy, besides being divine worship, is also a profession of heavenly truth subject to the Church's supreme teaching authority, and therefore it can provide important indications to decide some particular point of Catholic doctrine. Indeed, if we wanted to state quite clearly and absolutely the relation existing between the faith and the sacred liturgy, we could rightly say that "the norm of our faith must establish the norm of our prayer".[...]

(Divine and human elements in the liturgy)

1224   [...] In the liturgy there are human elements as well as divine ones. The latter, obviously, having been established by the divine Redeemer, cannot under any circumstances be changed by human beings; but the human elements may be modified in various ways approved by the hierarchy under the guidance of the Holy Spirit, according as time, circumstances, and the needs of the souls may demand. This explains the admirable variety of rites in East and West; it explains the progressive development whereby particular religious customs and pious practices gradually come into existence though earlier times show very little trace of them, while others which in course of time had fallen into disuse are revived. It is a proof that the immaculate Bride of Jesus Christ is vigorously alive, that in the course of ages there has been development in the language which she uses to express to her divine Bridegroom her own faith and inexhaustible love and that of her people. It is a proof of her skill as a teacher, always inculcating and increasing in the faithful the 'sense of Christ'.

(The divine office is the prayer of the mystical Body of Christ)

1225 The divine Office is the prayer of the mystical Body of Jesus Christ, offered to God in the name of all Christians and for their benefit, since it is recited by priests, by other ministers of the Church and by religious, who are officially appointed by the Church to that function.[...]

The Word of God, when he assumed a human nature, introduced into this land of exile the hymn that in heaven is sung throughout all ages. He unites the whole community of humankind with himself and associates it with him in singing this divine canticle of praise.[...]

(The presence of the mysteries of Christ in the Church's liturgical cycle)

(1226) *(See text in n. 1333)*

ENCYCLICAL LETTER *MUSICAE SACRAE DISCIPLINA* (1955)

In his Encyclical Letter on Sacred Music, Pope Pius XII stresses the need to create in mission countries a genuine sacred music by which the people will be able to celebrate the mysteries of the faith in a manner congenial to their culture. The text is found in AAS 48 (1956) 5ff.

(On sacred music in mission lands)

1227 It is remarkable how, among the peoples entrusted to the ministry of missionaries, many delight in musical chants and adorn the ceremonies dedicated to the worship of images with sacred singing. The heralds of Christ the true God cannot afford to overlook or to neglect this effective help of apostolate. Therefore, in the discharge of their apostolic duty, let the messengers of Christ in mission lands gladly promote the love for religious music characteristic of the peoples entrusted to their care. Thus, beside the religious songs of those peoples which often arouse the admiration of the most cultured nations there will flourish a Christian sacred music, similar to it, by means of which the truths of the faith, the life of Christ the Lord and of the Blessed Virgin Mary and the praise of the saints will be celebrated in the language and with melodies congenial to those peoples.

DISCOURSE AT THE INTERNATIONAL CONGRESS ON PASTORAL LITURGY (Assisi 1956)

In his address at the International Congress on Pastoral Liturgy held at Assisi in 1956, Pope Pius XII recalled the teaching of the encyclical Mediator Dei, according to which the liturgy is the work of the whole Church (cf. n. 1218). He showed, even better than in the encyclical, that in the liturgy the ordained ministers and the faithful are united in a common action, though exercising distinct functions. The text is found in AAS 48 (1956) 711ff.

(The liturgy is the work of the whole Church)

1228   The contributions which the hierarchy and the faithful make to the liturgy are not added to each other as separate entities; they rather represent the co-operation of members of one and the same organism acting as one living being. Pastors and flock, the teaching Church and the Church which is taught, constitute only one Body of Christ.[...] Thus, it is in this unity that the Church prays, offers, is sanctified; and it can truly be said that the liturgy is the work of the whole Church.

INSTRUCTION OF THE S. CONGREGATION OF RITES ON SACRED MUSIC AND THE SACRED LITURGY (1958)

This instruction prolongs Pope Pius XII's two encyclicals on the liturgy (Mediator Dei) and sacred music (Musicae Sacrae Disciplina); it gives practical norms for the application of their doctrine. It contains a clear definition of the liturgical action which it distinguishes from exercises of piety. In connection with the liturgy of the Mass it explains what is meant by interior and exterior participation and what is the relationship between both. The text is found in AAS 50(1958) 630-663.

(Definition of liturgical action)

1229   Liturgical actions are those sacred actions which are instituted by Jesus Christ or the Church and are performed in their name by legitimately deputed persons, in accordance with the prescriptions of the liturgical books approved by the Holy See, in order to render to God, the saints and the blessed the cult due to them. The other sacred actions, performed either in Church or outside, even if presided over or conducted by the priest, are called 'pious exercises'.

(Active participation, interior and exterior)

1230 The Mass by its very nature requires that all present participate in it according to the mode proper to them. This participation must first of all be interior; this consists in the pious attention of the mind and intimate sentiments of the heart. By this participation the faithful "are intimately united with the sovereign Priest[...] and, together with him and through him, offer the sacrifice and dedicate themselves with him" [cf. n. 1734].

The participation of those present becomes more effective if to interior participation is joined exterior participation, that, namely, which is expressed in external actions like postures[...], gestures, and especially responses to prayers and singing.

THE SECOND VATICAN GENERAL COUNCIL
CONSTITUTION *SACROSANCTUM CONCILIUM* (1963)

The Council of Trent had been concerned with liturgical reform, but in the historical context of the times its scope for liturgical renewal remained very limited: besides stressing the priest's duty to preach (cf. n. 1203ff) it mostly decreed a reform of liturgical books, which did not, however, animate the liturgy with a new spirit and a new life. The context of Vatican II is entirely different. The deep renewal to which it was to give official sanction had been prepared by the liturgical movement of the last half century, marked, as the years went by, with a more and more definite pastoral orientation. The Council itself, being essentially pastoral in purpose, turned to the liturgy as one of the important areas in which renewal would contribute to the aim it had in view (SC 1). In fact, Vatican II is the first general Council to have set in motion a liturgical renewal of such large proportions, based, moreover, on a thorough statement of doctrine on the liturgy: the Constitution Sacrosanctum Concilium *has no precedent in the history of the Councils.*

This Constitution represents the first fruits of the Council, and in a true sense made a break-through for the entire conciliar work. In particular, much of the doctrinal statements made by the Constitution Lumen Gentium *on the mystery of the Church is already implied and virtually contained in the theological concept of the liturgy proposed here. Thus, for instance, the idea of the liturgical action as the action of the whole Church in which all play their respective part led to that of the Church as the People of God with distinct and complementary functions. The mystery of the Church as a structured communion finds a privileged field of application in the liturgy, which is "the summit towards which the activity of the Church is directed and at the same time the fount from which all her power flows" (SC 10).*

The Constitution is divided into seven chapters. The first is devoted to general principles for the restoration and promotion of the sacred liturgy; the second treats of the Eucharist, the centre of the Church's liturgical life; the third deals with the other sacraments and with sacramentals. One chapter lays down the principles for a reform of the liturgy of the hours. There follow three chapters on the liturgical year, sacred music and sacred art, respectively.

The first chapter on general principles is the most elaborate and important; the following chapters represent various applications of those principles. To explain the nature of the sacred liturgy and its place in the Church's life, the Constitution goes back to Christ himself in whom "our perfect reconciliation (with God) has been achieved and the fulness of divine worship has been inserted among us" (SC 5). The Church continues on earth the priestly mediation of Christ, especially in the liturgy; Christ associates her with himself and is present in her action (SC 7); hence, the twofold end of the Church's liturgical action "wherein God is perfectly glorified and human beings are sanctified" (SC 7). Hence also, the liturgy is an exercise of the priestly office of Jesus Christ by his entire Body, Head and members (SC 7). Though it does not exhaust the Church's entire activity, it represents nevertheless its summit (SC 9-10).

In order that the liturgy may attain its twofold end, it is necessary that the members of the Church take part in it "fully aware of what they are doing, actively engaged in the rite and enriched by it" (SC 11). A constant preoccupation to promote in all the conscious and active participation "which is demanded by the very nature of the liturgy" (SC 14) underlies all the guide-lines laid down by the Constitution in view of the liturgical reform (SC 14) This participation supposes that all are effectively involved in the liturgical actions (SC 20) and that each person does all that belongs to one's role and only that (SC 28); it requires that the rites be meaningful (SC 21), which in turn implies intelligibility and a noble simplicity (SC 34). All the rest flows naturally from these premises, from the adoption of the local language (SC 36) down to the principle of liturgical adaptation, especially in mission countries. This principle often stated by papal documents as regards the Church's missionary activity in general (cf. chapter XI), had never before been as directly applied as it is here to all that belongs to the liturgical life of the Church (SC 37-40); particular applications are also made to sacred art (123) and music (119). In order that the aim which the Council has in view be attained, it is not enough that liturgical books be revised and, where the need arises, adapted; a whole programme for promoting the liturgical life of dioceses and parishes (SC 41f) and for pastoral liturgical action (SC 43ff) is necessary.

Among the most significant reforms made by the Constitution the new emphasis given to the liturgy of the word deserves special mention (SC 35). The Council strikes a new balance between Word and Sacrament, as appears most clearly in its doctrine on the eucharistic celebration: the liturgy of the word and the eucharistic liturgy proper "form but one single act of worship" (SC 56). In order to restore the liturgy of the word to its due place in the eucharistic celebration, the Council directs that "the treasures of the Bible are to be opened up more lavishly, so that a richer fare may be provided for the faithful at the table of God's word" (SC 51).

The Constitution Sacrosanctum Concilium *provides a plan of action for a far-reaching liturgical renewal, which has not finished to produce its fruits. Symptomatic of the potential for change contained in the spirit of the Constitution is the fact that, when in post-conciliar years the Church entered on the way opened by the Council, some of the norms explicitly set by it soon appeared too restrictive and needed to be broadened. Examples of this are: the use of the local language (SC 36) and the practice of concelebration (SC 57).*

(The liturgy is the work of the whole Church, Head and members)

1231   7. Christ indeed always associates the Church with himself in this great work wherein God is perfectly glorified and men and women are sanctified. The Church is his beloved Bride who calls to her Lord, and through him offers worship to the eternal Father.

Rightly, then, the liturgy is considered as an exercise of the priestly office of Jesus Christ. In the liturgy the sanctification of humankind is signified by signs perceptile to the senses and is effected in a way which corresponds with each of these signs; in the liturgy the whole public worship is performed by the mystical Body of Jesus Christ, that is, by the Head and his members.

From this it follows that every liturgical celebration, because it is an action of Christ the priest and of his Body which is the Church, is a sacred action surpassing all others: no other action of the Church can equal its efficacy by the same title and to the same degree.

(Place of the liturgy in the life of the Church: the two ends of the liturgical action)

1232   10. [...] The liturgy is the summit towards which the activity of the Church is directed; at the same time it is the fount from which all her power flows. For the aim of apostolic endeavour is that all, after being made children of God by faith and baptism, should come together to praise God in the midst of his Church, to take part in the sacrifice, and to eat the Lord's Supper.

The liturgy in its turn moves the faithful, filled with "the paschal sacraments", to be "one in holiness";[1] it prays that "they

---

1. Cf. *Roman Missal*, Prayer after communion in the Mass of Easter Vigil and Easter Sunday.

may hold fast in their lives to what they have grasped by their faith"[1], the renewal in the Eucharist of the Covenant between the Lord and humankind draws the faithful and sets them aflame with Christ's insistent love. From the liturgy, therefore, and especially from the Eucharist, as from a fountain, grace is poured forth upon us; and the sanctification of men and women in Christ and the glorification of God, to which all other activities of the Church are directed as towards their end, are achieved with maximum effectiveness.

(On liturgical adaptation, especially in mission lands)

1233   37. Even in the liturgy, the Church has no wish to impose a rigid uniformity in matters which do not involve the faith or the good of the whole community; rather does she respect and foster the genius and talents of the various races and nations. Anything in these people's way of life which is not indissolubly bound up with superstition and error she studies with sympathy and, if possible, preserves intact. Sometimes she even admits such things into the liturgy itself, provided they harmonise with its true and authentic spirit.

38. Provision shall also be made, when revising the liturgical books, for legitimate variations and adaptations to different groups, regions and peoples especially in mission countries, provided that the substantial unity of the Roman rite is preserved.[...]

(The mystery and the mysteries of Christ in the liturgical year)

1234   102. Holy Mother Church believes that it is for her to celebrate the saving work of her divine Spouse in a sacred commemoration on certain days throughout the course of the year. Once each week, on the day which she has called the Lord's Day, she keeps the memory of the Lord's resurrection. She also celebrates it once every year, together with his blessed passion, at Easter, that most solemn of all feasts.

In the course of the year, moreover, she unfolds the whole mystery of Christ from the incarnation and nativity to the ascension, to Pentecost and the expectation of the blessed hope of the coming of the Lord.

---

1. Cf. *Roman Missal*, Prayer of the Mass of Tuesday in the octave of Easter.

Thus recalling the mysteries of the redemption, she opens up to the faithful the riches of her Lord's powers and merits, so that these are in some way made present for all time; the faithful lay hold of them and are filled with saving grace.

(The Divine Office—the Liturgy of the Hours: prayer of the whole Church; source of personal prayer)

1234a 83. Jesus Christ, High Priest of the New and Eternal Covenant, taking human nature, introduced into this earthly exile that hymn which is sung throughtout all ages in the halls of heaven. He attaches to himself the entire community of humankind and has them join him in singing his divine song of praise.

90. The divine office, because it is the public prayer of the Church, is a source of piety and a nourishment for personal prayer.

99. [...] The divine office is the voice of the Church, that is, of the whole mystical body publicly praising God[...].[1]

DECREE *ORIENTALIUM ECCLESIARUM* (1964)

This Decree on the Oriental Catholic Churches states in all clarity the equal rights of the various traditions, liturgical and spiritual, proper to the Eastern and Western Churches. All must be fostered and allowed to develop their own genius, for all contribute to the catholicity of the Church universal. The doctrine is based on a clear theology of the mystery of the Church as a communion of particular Churches in the bond of unity which is effectively symbolised by the Roman See.

(The particular Churches or Rites)

1235 2. The holy Catholic Church, which is the mystical Body of Christ, consists of believers who are organically united in the Holy Spirit by the same faith, the same sacraments and the same government. Grouped in different communities around their hierarchies, the faithful constitute particular Churches or Rites. Between these Churches there exists a wonderful communion, so that diversity, far from harming the Church's

---

1. The *General Instruction on the Liturgy of the Hours (Feb. 2, 1971)* expresses more forcibly that the "divine office" or Liturgy of the Hours is the prayer of all the Christian community and can be celebrated, at least in part and in an adapted form, by different groups within the whole Church (20-27, 270)

unity, rather manifests it. The Catholic Church, indeed, means to keep intact the traditions of each particular Church or Rite and she wants to adapt her mode of life to the various needs of times and places.

1236 3. These particular Churches of both East and West, though partially differing from one another by their 'rites'—i.e., their liturgy, ecclesiastical discipline and spiritual patrimony—are all equally entrusted to the pastoral direction of the Roman Pontiff, who by divine institution succeeds St. Peter in the primacy over the universal Church. All have the same dignity, none is higher than the others by reason of its rite; all have the same rights and the same obligations, also as regards the preaching of the Gospel in the whole world [cf. Mk 16:15], under the guidance of the Roman Pontiff.

POST-CONCILIAR DOCUMENTS ON SACRED WORSHIP

The Constitution Sacrosanctum Concilium *of the Second Vatican Council had laid down the principles of liturgical renewal. After the Council several Roman documents applied those principles to various aspects of the Church's liturgical life. New rites were promulgated for the celebration of the sacraments; the documents promulgating these new rites are mentioned here in the various chapters on the sacraments. Other documents applied the principles of the Council to the Church's liturgy in general. Among these may be mentioned:*

—*The Motu Proprio of Pope Paul VI on the Sacred Liturgy,* Sacram Liturgiam *(25 January 1964);*

—*The First Instruction on the Proper Implementation of the Constitution on the Sacred Liturgy by the Sacred Congregation of Rites,* Inter Oecumenici *(26 September 1964);*

— *The Instruction on Music in the Liturgy by the Sacred Congregation of Rites,* Musicam Sacram *(5 March 1967);*

—*The Second Instruction on the Proper Implementation of the Constitution on the Sacred Liturgy by the Sacred Congregation of Rites,* Tres Abhinc Annos *(4 May 1967);*

—*The Third Instruction on the Correct Implementation of the Constitution on the Sacred Liturgy by the Sacred Congregation for Divine Worship,* Liturgiae Instaurationes *(5 September 1970).*

—*Directory on Children's masses, Sacred Congregation for Divine Worship*, Pueros baptizatos *(1 November 1973).*

As these documents are easily accessible in A.Flannery *(ed.)*, Vatican Council II, The Conciliar and Post-Conciliar Documents, *Costello Publishing Co. N.Y., 1988, revised edition, they are not included here.*

N.B. *The general introduction (the* praenotanda*) in each of the new liturgical books published after Vatican II, contains valuable doctrinal elements for the contemporary understanding of the liturgico-sacramental celebrations. Besides the "seven" sacraments, these new rituals include the* Liturgy of the Hours, *the* Rite of Funerals, *the* Rite of Dedication of a Church and Altar, *the* Book of Blessings, *the* Ceremonial of Bishops, *etc.*

JOHN PAUL II
ADDRESS TO THE BISHOPS OF ZAÏRE
(3 May, 1980)

The Constitution Sacrosanctum Concilium *of the Second Vatican Council foresaw the need for a profound adaptation of the liturgy to different regions and peoples, especially in mission lands (cf. n. 1233). After the Council, efforts began to be made to adapt the Roman liturgy, especially the celebration of the sacraments, to the culture of the people in mission lands. This process of inculturation of the liturgy has unhappily been to a large extent hindered by a cumbersome procedure and the continued dependence on the central authority for liturgical adaptations. During his visit to Africa in 1980, Pope John Paul II, addressing the bishops of Zaïre, clearly stated the principle of inculturation of the Gospel. He went on to stress the responsibility of the local bishops in this matter, and applied the principle of inculturation to various fields, in particular to theology and to liturgy. The text is found in* Osservatore Romano *(English Edition), 12 May 1980, pp. 6-7.*

(The inculturation of the Gospel)

1237   4. One of the aspects of evangelisation is the inculturation of the Gospel, the *Africanisation* of the Church.[...] That is part of the indispensable efforts to incarnate the message of Christ. The Gospel, certainly, is not identified with cultures, and transcends them all. But the Kingdom that the Gospel proclaims is lived by people deeply tied to a culture; the building up of the Kingdom cannot dispense with borrowing elements of human culture [*cf. n. 1152*]. Indeed, evangelisation must help the latter to bring forth out of their own tradition original expressions of Christian faith, celebration and thought[1].

(The responsibility of the local hierarchy)

1238 It is up to you, bishops, to promote and harmonize the advance in this field, after mature reflection, in concerted action among yourselves, in union also with the universal Church and with the Holy See. Inculturation, for the people as a whole, cannot be, moreover, but the fruit of gradual maturity in faith. For you are convinced as I am that this work [...] requires a great deal of theological lucidity, spiritual discernment, wisdom and prudence, and also time.

(Liturgical inculturation)

1239 5. In the field of sacred action and the liturgy, a whole enrichment is possible *[cf. n. 1233]*, provided the meaning of the Christian rite is always preserved and the universal, Catholic element of the Church is clearly seen ("the substantial unity of the Roman rite"), in union with other local Churches and in agreement with the Holy See.

MORE POST-CONCILIAR DOCUMENTS

—*On January 16, 1988 a Circular Letter was issued by the Congregation for Divine Worship and Sacraments,* Preparing and Celebrating the Paschal Feasts. *This letter has a special focus on the importance of the celebration of the Easter Vigil (while noting certain abuses in the manner of observing it), but it also treats the season of Lent, penitential celebrations during Lent, Holy Week, each day of the Triduum and the Paschal season. It stresses the need of catechesis and a deeper knowledge of the rites and texts, especially of the Easter Vigil, so that the Christian community will experience more deeply the paschal mystery. (English text in* Origins, *March 17, 1998, vol. 17: no. 40, pp. 677-687).*

—*John Paul II,* Christifideles Laici: Apostolic Exhortation on the Vocation and Mission of the Lay Faithful in the Church and in the World. *This document, issued on Jan. 30, 1988, though not directly on the liturgy, has implications for the full participation of all the baptized in diverse ministries of liturgical celebrations. (Cf. SC 14: full, conscious and active participation—a right and duty by virtue of baptism). The English text is found in* Origins, *Feb 9, 1989, vol. 18: no. 35, pp. 561-595 (cf. nn. 894-896, 1758).*

---

1. Apostolic Exhoration *Catechesi Tradendae,* 53.

—*On May 21, 1988, the Congregation for Divine Worship issued the* Directory for Sunday Celebrations in the Absence of a Priest. *The intent of this document is to guide and prescribe what needs to be done when real circumstances require such Sunday celebrations. The Directory discusses the meaning of Sunday (the Day of the Lord), the conditions for these kinds of liturgical celebrations and the order of celebration. It contains helpful guidelines for the different ministries in the liturgical celebration. (Translation by the ICEL in* Origins, *Oct, 20, 1988, vol. 18: no 19, pp 301-307).*

APOSTOLIC LETTER *VICESIMUS QUINTUS ANNUS*
(4 December, 1988)

On the occasion of the twenty-fifth anniversary of the Vatican II Constitution Sacrosanctum Concilium, *the Pope reviews the growth and difficulties of the liturgical movement in the post-conciliar era. He recalls the guiding principles of the Constitution : a) on the liturgy as the re-enactment of the Paschal Mystery, b) the liturgy as the self-manifestation of the Church, and c) on the liturgy of the word of God. The Pope offers some guidelines for the ongoing task of fostering a robust liturgical life. He also reflects on the practical application of liturgical renewal in the past years and on the tasks ahead for further renewal. The text is found in* Osservatore Romano *(English Edition), 22 May, 1989, pp. 7-10.*

(Guidelines for liturgical renewal)

1240   10. From these principles are derived certain norms and guidelines which must govern the renewal of liturgical life. While the reform of the liturgy desired by the Second Vatican Council can be considered already accomplished, the pastoral promotion of the liturgy constitutes a permanent commitment to draw ever more abundantly from the riches of liturgy that vital force which spreads from Christ to the members of his Body which is the Church.

Since the liturgy is the exercise of the priesthood of Christ, it is necessary to keep ever alive the affirmation of the disciples faced with the mysterious presence of Christ: "It is the Lord!" [Jn 21:7]. Nothing of what we do in the liturgy can appear more important than what in an unseen but real manner Christ accomplishes by the power of his Spirit. A faith alive in charity, adoration, praise of the Father and silent contemplation will always be the prime objective of liturgical and sacramental pastoral care.

Since the liturgy is totally permeated by the word of God, any other word must be in harmony with it, above all in the homily, but also in the various interventions of the minister and in the hymns which are sung. No other reading may supplant the biblical word, and human words must be at the service of the word of God without obscuring it.

Since liturgical celebrations are not private acts but "celebrations of the Church, the 'sacrament of unity' "[SC 26]. their regulation is dependent solely upon the hierarchical authority of the Church [SC 22,26]. The liturgy belongs to the whole body of the Church [SC 26]. It is for this reason that it is not permitted to anyone, even the priest, or any group, to add, subtract or change anything whatsoever on their own initiative [SC 22]. Fidelity to the rites and to the authentic texts of the liturgy is a requirement of the lex orandi, which must always be in conformity with the lex credendi. A lack of fidelity on this point may even affect the very validity of the sacraments.[...]

Since the liturgy has great pastoral value, the liturgical books have provided for a certain degree of adaptation to the assembly and to individuals, with the possibility of openness to the traditions and culture of different people [SC 37-40]. The revision of the rites has sought a noble simplicity [SC 34], and signs that are easily understood, but the desired simplicity must not degenerate into an impoverishment of the signs. On the contrary, the signs, above all the sacramental signs, must carry the greatest possible expressiveness. Bread and wine, water and oil, and also incense, ashes, fire and flowers, and indeed almost all the elements of creation have their place in the liturgy as gifts to the Creator and as a contribution to the dignity and beauty of the celebration.

(Adaptation)

1241   16. Another important task for the future is that of the adaptation of the liturgy to different cultures. The Constitution set forth the principles, indicating the procedure to be followed by the episcopal conferences [SC 39]. The adaptation to languages has been rapidly accomplished, even if on occasions with some difficulties. It has been followed by the adaptation of rites, which is a more delicate matter but equally necessary. There remains the considerable task of continuing to implant the liturgy in diverse cultures, welcoming from them those expressions which are compatible with aspects of *the true and authentic spirit* *of the liturgy,* in respect for the *substantial unity of the Roman Rite* as expressed in the liturgical books *[SC 37-40].* The adaptation must take account of the fact that in the liturgy, and notably that of the sacraments, there is *a part which is unchangeable,* because it is of divine institution, and of which the Church is the guardian. There are also *parts open to change,* which the Church has the power and on occasion also the duty to adapt to the cultures of recently evangelised people *[SC 21].* This is not a new problem for the Church. Liturgical diversity can be a source of enrichment, but it can also provoke tensions, mutual misunderstandings and even divisions. In this field it is clear that diversity must not damage unity. It can only gain expression in fidelity to the common faith, to the sacramental signs that the Church has received from Christ and to hierarchical communion. Cultural adaptation also requires a conversion of heart and even, where necessary, a breaking with ancestral customs incompatible with the Catholic faith. This demands a serious formation in theology, history and culture, as well as sound judgment in discerning what is necessary or useful and what is not useful or even dangerous to faith. "A satisfactory development in this area cannot but be the fruit of a progressive maturing in faith, one which encompasses spiritual discernment, theological lucidity, and a sense of the universal Church, acting in broad harmony."[1]

THE CATECHISM OF THE CATHOLIC CHURCH
(7 December, 1992)

(Notion of the celebration of liturgy)

1241a 1135. The catechesis of the liturgy entails first of all an understanding of the sacramental economy[...]. In this light, the innovation of its *celebration* is revealed. This chapter [II]will therefore treat of the celebration of the sacraments of the Church. It will consider that which, through the diversity of liturgical traditions, is common to the celebration of the seven sacraments.[...]This fundamental catechesis on the sacramental celebrations responds to the first questions posed by the faithful

---

1. Address to a group of bishops of the episcopal conference of Zaïre (12 April, 1983), (5), *AAS* 75 (1983) 620.

regarding this subject: Who celebrates the liturgy? How is the liturgy celebrated ? When is the liturgy celebrated? Where is the liturgy celebrated ?

PONTIFICAL BIBLICAL COMMISSION
THE INTERPRETATION OF THE BIBLE IN THE CHURCH
(15 April, 1993)

This important document on the value of the Bible and its function in the Christian community contains a section (IV), re-affirming Vatican II's statements of the role of the Bible "in the liturgy" [cf. SC 35, 51-52). The proclamation of the Word and the homily in the sacramental liturgies (cf. nn. 255-257, 1202, 1203-1205), especially the Eucharist; the use of the Psalms, especially in the Liturgy of the Hours; the hymns and prayers of sacramental celebrations—all are inspired by the language of the Bible, all are forms of "actualisation" and "inculturation" of the Bible as Word of God for the believing communities of today. The document affirms that this process has been part of the living tradition of the Church since the beginning. English text: Pontifical Biblical Commission, The Interpretation of the Bible in the Church, *Libreria Editrice Vaticana, Roma 1993, pp. 119-124. (Cf. nn. 1202, 1203-1205; 246-257).*

(Bible and liturgy)

1242   [...]Today, too, it is above all through the liturgy that Christians come into contact with Scripture, particularly during the Sunday celebration of the Eucharist.

In principle, the liturgy, and especially the sacramental liturgy, the high point of which is the Eucharistic celebration, brings about the most perfect actualisation of the biblical texts, for the liturgy places the proclamation in the midst of the community of believers, gathered around Christ so as to draw near to God. Christ is then "present in his word, because it is he himself who speaks when Sacred Scripture is read in the Church" *[SC 7]*. Written text thus becomes living word.

[...]The liturgy of the Word is a crucial element in the celebration of each of the sacraments of the Church[...]. It ought to involve[...] periods of silence and of prayer[...]. In particular, the Liturgy of the Hours makes selections from the body of Psalms to help the Christian community pray. Hymns and prayers are all filled with the language of the Bible and the symbolism it contains.[...]

If in the readings "God addresses the word to his people" *[Roman Missal, n. 33]*; the liturgy of the Word requires that great care be taken both in the proclamation of the readings and in their interpretation[...], that the formation of those who are to preside at the assembly and of those who serve with them take full account of what is required for a liturgy of the Word of God that is fully renewed.[...]

1243 Analogous remarks [to those for catechesis] apply to the ministry of *preaching*[...]. Today, this ministry is exercised especially[...] through the *homily* which follows the proclamation of the Word of God.

The explanation of the biblical texts given in the course of the homily cannot enter into great detail. It is, accordingly, fitting to explain the central contribution of texts, that which is most enlightening for faith and most stimulating for the progress of the Christian life, both on the community and individual level. Presenting this central contribution means striving to achieve its actualisation and inculturation [...]. Want of preparation in this area leads to the temptation[...] to being content simply to moralize or to speak of contemporary issues in a way that fails to shed upon them the light of God's Word.

[...]The biblical message must preserve its principal characteristic of being the good news of salvation freely offered by God[...] to "know the gift of God" *[Jn 4:10]*; [...]they will then understand in a positive light the obligations that flow from it.

PONTIFICAL COUNCIL FOR PROMOTING CHRISTIAN UNITY DIRECTORY FOR THE APPLICATION OF PRINCIPLES AND NORMS ON ECUMENISM (1993)

(1244) *This new text contains three sections which give helpful and positive guidelines apropos the liturgico-sacramental life of the Church in its ongoing ecumenical dialogue: Sharing in non-sacramental liturgical worship (116-121); Sharing in sacramental life, especially the Eucharist (122-136); and Mixed marriages (143-160). On this document, cf. also nn. 932a-f.*

CONGREGATION FOR WORSHIP AND SACRAMENTS
THE ROMAN LITURGY AND INCULTURATION:
FOURTH INSTRUCTION FOR THE RIGHT APPLICATION OF THE CONCILIAR CONSTITUTION ON THE LITURGY
(29 March, 1994)

This document is a further theological reflection and pastoral application of Vatican II's statements of ongoing cultural adaptation of the Roman rite

(SC 37-40). The experience of the Church's life and the reform of the liturgy during the last 30 years in the diverse cultures of the human family call for a more serious application of the principles of Vatican II's Constitution on the Liturgy on liturgical renewal. This text uses the word "inculturation", a term which defines more precisely the incarnation of the Gospel in the cultures of the world. After an introduction indicating the theological meaning of "inculturation" and the various situations envisaged by this Instruction (1-8), Chapter I outlines the process of inculturation throughout the history of salvation (9-20); Chapter II notes the requirements and preliminary conditions for liturgical inculturation (21-32); Chapter III assigns the principles and practical norms for incultration of the Roman rite (33-51); in the final chapter (IV) it indicates the areas of adaptation in the Roman rite (52-70). While this document seems highly concerned with maintaining "the substantial unity of the Roman rite", it does open up new possibilities of liturgical expression in language, singing and music, gesture and posture, movement and dance, art forms, etc., among the various cultures where the Gospel is proclaimed and lived. The text is found in Origins, *April 14, 1994, Vol 23: No. 43, pp 745-756.*

(Inculturation and the Liturgy)

1245 4. The term inculturation is a better expression to designate a double movement [...]. On the one hand the penetration of the gospel into a given sociocultural milieu "gives inner fruitfulness to the spiritual qualities and gifts proper to each people[...], strengthens these qualities, perfects them and restores them in Christ" *[GS 58]*.

On the other hand, the Church assimilates these values when they are compatible with the Gospel, "to deepen understanding of Christ's message and give it more effective expression in the liturgy and in the many different aspects of the life of the community of believers" *(ibid)*.

5.[...]The inculturation of the Christian life and of liturgical celebrations must be the fruit of a progressive maturity in the faith of the people.[1]

(General principles)

1246 34. In the planning and execution of the inculturation of the Roman rite, the following points should be kept in

---

1. Cf. JOHN PAUL II, Discourse to the Bishops of Zaïre (12 April 1983), no. 5, *AAS* 75(1983) 617-622.

mind: 1) the goal of inculturation; 2) the substantial unity of the Roman rite; 3) the competent authority.

(Adaptations which can be made)

1247 39. Language, which is a means of communication between people [...] must express, along with the truths of the faith, the grandeur and holiness of the mysteries which are being celebrated.[...]

40. Music and singing, which expresses the soul of people, have pride of place in the liturgy. [...] Due importance is to be attached to their music and a suitable place given to it[...].

41. The liturgy is an action, and so gesture and posture are especially important.[...] Each culture will choose those gestures and bodily postures which express the attitude of humanity before God, giving them a Christian significance[...].

42. Among some people, singing is instinctively accompanied by handclapping, rhythmic swaying and dance movements on the part of the participants. Such forms of external expression can have a place in the liturgical action of these people.[...]

43. The liturgical celebration is enriched by the presence of art, which helps the faithful to celebrate, meet God and pray [...]. Preference should be given to materials, forms and colours which are in use in the country.

(Necessary prudence)

1248 47. The liturgy is the expression of faith and Christian life, and so it is necessary to ensure that liturgical inculturation is not marked, even in appearance, by religious syncretism.

(Adaptation envisaged by No. 40 of the Conciliar Constitution on the Liturgy)

1249 64.[...]The Congregation for Divine Worship and the Discipline of the Sacraments is ready to receive the proposals of episcopal conferences and examine them, keeping in mind the good of the local Churches concerned and the common good of the universal Church, and to assist the process of inculturation where it is desirable or necessary. It will do this in accordance with the principles laid down in this instruction *[cf. Nos. 33-51]*, and in a spirit of confident collaboration and shared responsibility.

JOHN PAUL II

APOSTOLIC LETTER *DIES DOMINI*
(31 May 1998)

The Apostolic Letter shows the foundation of the Sunday precept in the Christian mystery and in Christian life. The pope writes: "More than a precept, the observance [of Sunday] should be seen as a need arising from the depths of Christian life". The pope shows the deep meaning of the Sunday eucharistic celebration. The exhortation is divided into five main parts: 1. The Day of the Lord; 2. The Day of Christ; 3. The Day of the Church; 4. The Day of Man; 5. The Day of Days. The extracts below belong to the second and third parts. The text is found in Origins *28 (1998-1999) 133-154.*

(Sunday, the Day of the Risen Lord)

1250a   19. "We celebrate Sunday because of the venerable resurrection of our Lord Jesus Christ, and we do so not only at Easter but also at each turning of the week": so wrote Pope Innocent I at the beginning of the fifth century [*Ep. ad Decentium XXV, 4, 7: PL 20, 555*], testifying to an already well-established practice which had evolved from the early years after the Lord's resurrection [...]. The intimate bond between Sunday and the resurrection of the Lord is strongly emphasized by all the churches of East and West. In the tradition of the Eastern churches in particular, every Sunday is the *anastasimos hemera*, and this is why it stands at the heart of all worship.

In the light of this constant and universal tradition, it is clear that, although the Lord's Day is rooted in the very work of creation and even more in the mystery of the biblical "rest" of God, it is nonetheless to the resurrection of Christ that we must look in order to understand fully the Lord's Day. This is what the Christian Sunday does, leading the faithful each week to ponder and live the event of Easter, true source of the world's salvation.

(Sunday, the Day of the Church)

1250b   31. As the day of resurrection, Sunday is not only the remembrance of a past event: It is a celebration of the living presence of the risen Lord in the midst of his own people. For the presence to be properly proclaimed and lived, it is not enough that the disciples of Christ pray individually and commemorate the death and resurrection of Christ inwardly, in the secrecy of their hearts. Those who have received the grace of baptism are not saved as individuals alone, but as members of the mystical Body, having become part of the people of God [LG 9]. It is important, therefore, that they come together to express fully the very identity of the Church, the *ekklesia*, the assembly called together by the risen Lord, who offered his life "to reunite the scattered children of God" [Jn 11:52]. They have become "one" in Christ [cf. Gal 3:28] through the gift of the Spirit.

(The eucharistic assembly)

1250c 32. The eucharist is not only a particularly intense expression of the reality of the church's life, but also in a sense its "fountainhead" [Dominum et Vivificantem 62-64]. The eucharist feeds and forms the church: "Because there is one bread, we who are many are one body, for we all partake of the one bread" [1 Cor 10:17]. Because of this vital link with the sacrament of the body and blood of the Lord, the mystery of the Church is savoured, proclaimed and lived supremely in the eucharist.[...]

35-36. Therefore, the *dies Domini* is also the *dies ecclesiae*.[...] The Sunday assembly is the privileged place of unity: It is the setting of the celebration of the *sacramentum unitatis*, which profoundly marks the church as a people gathered "by" and "in" the unity of the Father, of the Son and of the Holy Spirit [LG 4; SC 26].

(A pilgrim people)

1250d 37. As the church journeys through time, the reference to Christ's resurrection and the weekly reference of this solemn memorial help to remind us of the pilgrim and eschatological character of the people of God. Sunday after Sunday the church moves toward the final "Lord's Day", that Sunday which knows no end. The expectation of Christ's coming is inscribed in the very mystery of the church [LG 48-51] and is evidenced in every eucharistic celebration. But with its specific remembrance of the glory of the risen Christ, the Lord's Day recalls with greater intensity the future glory of his "return". This makes Sunday the day on which the church, showing forth more clearly her identity as "bride", anticipates in some sense the eschatological reality of the heavenly Jerusalem.[...]

(The Sunday obligation)

1250e 81. It is crucially important that all the faithful should be convinced that they cannot live their faith and share fully in the life of the christian community unless they take part regularly in the Sunday eucharistic assembly.

APPENDIX
ON THE CULT OF SAINTS AND SACRED IMAGES

In appendix to this chapter are mentioned the Church's most important documents on the cult of saints, of relics and of sacred images. Though she submits it to some laws, the Church has always defended as legitimate the veneration of sacred images; the reason is that their veneration goes to the person whom they represent. As for the veneration of saints, it arises naturally from the lively awareness of the deep communion which binds together in Christ all those redeemed by him. While venerating the saints, the Church celebrates in them the triumph of the mystery of Christ; she draws inspiration from their example and pleads for God's favour through their intercession. It is an historical fact that protests against the veneration of saints have always resulted from a loss of ecclesial consciousness, prompted by a tendency towards a purely interior and individualistic religion. While speaking out against abuses, the Church has upheld such veneration as being based on the mystery of the communion of saints.

*   *   *

The Church recommends the cult of saints: 35, 39/22-23, 1255, 1258, 2311f, (2313f).

It also recommends the cult of relics and sacred images: 35, 1251-1252, 1253, 1254, 1256, 1257, 1260.

It also recommends popular piety, provided this is purified of possible distortions: 1259.

Christian art must express the faith of the Church: 1261.

THE SECOND GENERAL COUNCIL OF NICAEA
DEFINITION ON SACRED IMAGES (787)

The 8th century of Christianity has known the outburst of a heated controversy over sacred images; opposition to the veneration of sacred images representing Christ can be considered as remotely inspired by a Monophysite tendency. It is true that the cult of images in the East sometimes led to reprehensible abuses; some Fathers of the Church, rigorist in tendency, even feared the danger of idolatry. Iconoclasm first made its appearance in Constantinople under Manichaean influence. The crisis broke out when in 730 Emperor Leo III ordered the destruction of icons, a special object of piety in the Byzantine tradition. This action met with much opposition and was condemned by Rome. But it is only after the accession to the throne of Empress Irene, who favoured the cult of images, that the case could be submitted to the judgment of a general Council which met at Nicaea.

In its 7th session the Second Council of Nicaea solemnly defined that the cult of images is legitimate and explained that the veneration of images is addressed to the persons whom they represent. In order to distinguish the adoration due to God alone from the veneration which is given to the cross and to images of Christ and the saints, the Council reserved the Augustinian term latria (latreia) *to the cult or worship addressed to God himself while it applies the ancient term of adoration* (proskunêsis) *to the veneration of sacred images. This verbal distinction will not, however, impose itself later. Nor did the Council distinguish, as later tradition will, the relative cult of divine worship due to the images of Christ from the veneration addressed to those of the saints.*

1251   We define that [...]the representations of the precious and
600   life-giving cross, and the venerable and holy images as
           well[...], must be kept in the holy Church of God[...], in
houses and on the roads, whether they be images of God our
Lord and Saviour Jesus Christ or of our immaculate Lady the
Mother of God, or of the holy angels and of all the saints and
just.

1252   For, the more frequently one contemplates these pictorial
601   representations, the more gladly will one be led to
           remember the original subject whom they represent, the
more too will one be drawn to it and inclined to give it[...] a
respectful veneration *(proskunêsis, adoratio)*, which, however, is
not the true adoration *(latria, latreia)* which, according to our faith,
is due to God alone. But, as is done for the image of the revered
and life-giving cross and the holy Gospels and other sacred

objects and monuments, let an oblation of incense and light be made to give honour to those images according to the pious custom of the ancients. For "the honour given to an image goes to the original model"[1], and one who venerates an image, venerates in it the person represented by it.

THE FOURTH GENERAL COUNCIL OF CONSTANTINOPLE
(869-870)

The iconoclast crisis which seemed to have been settled by the Second Council of Nicaea was revived two decades after the Council. Three Asiatic emperors convened iconoclast Councils and persecuted the patriarchs and monks who favoured the veneration of images. The persecution was once again brought to an end by an Empress, Theodora by name, who had come to power in 842. The conflict nevertheless went on and had to be dealt with by the Fourth Council of Constantinople. The Council treated the question of images in its 10th session held in 870. Canon 3 develops the definition of the Second Council of Nicaea and explains that colours play in images the role which words play in writing. Thus images constitute a language accessible to the illiterate.

(On the veneration of sacred images.)

1253 Canon 3: We decree that the sacred image of our Lord
653 Jesus Christ, the liberator and Saviour of all people, must be venerated with the same honour as is given to the book of holy Gospels.

654 For, as through the language of the words contained in this book all can reach salvation, so, due to the action which these images exercise by their colours, all, wise and simple alike, can derive profit from them. For, what speech conveys in words, pictures announce and bring out in colours. It is fitting, in accordance with sane reason and with the most ancient tradition, since the honour is referred to the principal subject, that the images derived from it be honoured and venerated, as is done for the sacred book of the holy Gospels and for the image of the precious cross.[...]

---

1. St. Basil, *De Spiritu Sancto*, 18, 45.

MARTIN V
BULL *INTER CUNCTAS* (1418)

The list of questions proposed to the followers of Wyclif and Hus which are contained in this Bull mostly pertains to the doctrine of the sacraments (cf. n. 1304; nn. 1507/16-17; 1611/20ff). One deals with the cult of saints. Some exaggerations and deviations of medieval piety had provoked legitimate reactions. But, with the forerunners of the Reformation, Wyclif and Hus and their followers, the reaction against abuses took the form of a contestation of the cult itself.

(Question proposed to the followers of Wyclif and Hus)

1254 Does he believe and does he affirm that it is legitimate
1269 for the faithful of Christ to venerate relics and images of
saints?

THE GENERAL COUNCIL OF TRENT
TWENTY-FIFTH SESSION
DECREE ON THE INVOCATION, THE VENERATION AND THE RELICS OF SAINTS AND ON SACRED IMAGES (1563)

After Wyclif and Hus, the Reformers took an even more hostile attitude towards the cult of saints which they soon came to view as opposed to the spirit of Christianity. Luther, while admitting the legitimacy of the veneration and the imitation of saints, rejected their invocation and denied their intercession. Zwingli advocated suppressing all cult of saints because God alone must be invoked; Calvin considered the cult of saints as the devil's invention and the veneration of images as idolatry.

The Council of Trent meant to condemn the new iconoclasm of the Reformation, while at the same time suppressing the abuses to which an ill-inspired piety had often given rise on the Catholic side (cf. DS 1825). This Decree, promulgated during the Council's 25th session, provides a clearer statement on the subject of the veneration of saints and of sacred images than was found in previous documents.

(Veneration of saints)

1255 The holy Council, in accordance with the practice of the
1821 Catholic and apostolic Church from the early years of
the Christian religion, and in accordance with the
common teaching of the holy Fathers and the decrees of the
sacred Councils, orders all bishops and others who have the
official charge of teaching to instruct the faithful diligently, in
particular as regards the intercession and the invocation of the
saints, the honour due to their relics, and the lawful use of

images. Let them teach the faithful that the saints, reigning together with Christ, pray to God for men and women; that it is good and useful to invoke them humbly and to have recourse to their prayers, to their help and assistance, in order to obtain favours from God through his Son, our Lord Jesus Christ, who alone is our Redeemer and Saviour. Those who deny that the saints enjoying eternal happiness in heaven are to be invoked, or who claim that saints do not pray for human beings or that calling upon them to pray for each of us is idolatry or is opposed to the word of God and is prejudicial to the honour of Jesus Christ, the one Mediator between God and humankind [cf. 1 Tim 2:5]; or who say that it is foolish to make supplication orally or mentally to those who are reigning in heaven; all those entertain impious thoughts.

(Veneration of relics)

1256   The sacred bodies of the holy martyrs and of the other
1822   saints living with Christ, which have been living
members of Christ and the temple of the Holy Spirit [cf. 1 Cor 3:16; 6:19; 2 Cor 6:16], and which are destined to be raised and glorified by him unto life eternal, should also be venerated by the faithful. Through them many benefits are granted to human beings by God. For this reason, those who say that veneration and honour is not due to the relics of the saints, or that these relics and other sacred memorials are honoured in vain by the faithful, and that it is futile to visit the places where the martyrs have died to implore their assistance, are to be condemned absolutely, just as the Church has already condemned them and even now condemns them.

(Veneration of images)

1257   Further, the images of Christ, of the Virgin Mother of
1823   God and of other saints are to be kept and preserved, in
places of worship especially; and to them due honour and veneration is to be given, not because it is believed that there is in them anything divine or any power for which they are revered, nor in the sense that something is sought from them or that a blind trust is put in images as once was done by the gentiles who placed their hope in idols [cf. Ps 135 (134):15ff]; but because the honour which is shown to them is referred to the original subjects which they represent. Thus, through these

images which we kiss and before which we kneel and uncover our heads, we are adoring Christ and venerating the saints whose likeness these images bear. That is what was defined by the decrees of the Councils, especially the Second Council of Nicaea, against the opponents of images [cf. nn 1251f].

THE SECOND VATICAN GENERAL COUNCIL

The Council of Trent had stated clearly that the veneration of saints is legitimate and in accordance with the Church's Tradition. Reigning with Christ, they intercede for us and can be invoked for help. The Second Vatican Council has further deepened the theological foundation for the cult of saints. It is treated in the Constitution Lumen Gentium *in the context of the eschatological nature of the pilgrim Church and her union with the Church of heaven (49-50). The Constitution explains the full significance of the mystery of the communion of saints. If the saints intercede for us, it is in virtue of the mysterious communion between the pilgrim Church and the Church triumphant. Nor does the intercession of saints exhaust the meaning of the cult rendered to them by the Church. The saints are for the pilgrim Church on earth striking examples of conformity to the mystery of Christ and a powerful incentive to holiness. What the Church primarily celebrates in their cult is the triumph of the mystery of Christ in their lives. See nn. 2311-(2314). Here is mentioned a short passage of the Constitution* Sacrosantum Concilium *to which the Constitution* Lumen Gentium *gave a more ample development (51)*

CONSTITUTION *SACROSANCTUM CONCILIUM* (1963)

(The memory of saints in the liturgical cycle)

1258   104. The Church has also included in the annual cycle days devoted to the memory of the martyrs and of the other saints. Raised up to perfection be the manifold grace of God, and already in possession of eternal salvation, they sing God's perfect praise in heaven and offer prayers for us. By celebrating the passage of these saints from earth to heaven the Church proclaims the paschal mystery achieved in the saints who have suffered and been glorified with Christ; she proposes them to the faithful as examples drawing all to the Father through Christ, and through their merits she pleads for God's favours.

PAUL VI
APOSTOLIC EXHORTATION *EVANGELII NUNTIANDI* (1975)

During the 1974 Synod of Bishops in Rome on Evangelization, Bishops, especially from Latin America stressed the value of popular religiosity for evangelization. Though popular piety needs to be purified of possible distortions, if well oriented it can bring people to a true encounter with God in Jesus Christ. The Apostolic Exhortation published by Pope Paul VI after the Synod echoes the bishops' positive appraisal of popular piety. The text is found in AAS 68 (1976) 37-38.

(Popular piety)

1259 48. One finds among the people particular expressions of the search for God and for faith, both in the regions where the Church has been established for centuries and where she is in the course of becoming established. These expressions were for a long time regarded as less pure and were sometimes despised, but today they are almost everywhere being rediscovered. During the last Synod the Bishops studied their significance with remarkable pastoral realism and zeal.

Popular religiosity, of course, certainly has its limits. It is often subject to many distortions of religion and even superstitions. It frequently remains at the level of forms of worship not involving a true acceptance by faith. It can even lead to the creation of sects and endanger the true ecclesial community.

But if it is well oriented, above all by a pedagogy of evangelization, it is rich in values. it manifests a thirst for God which only the simple and poor can know. It makes people capable of generosity and sacrifice even to the point of heroism, when it is a question of manifesting belief. It involves an acute awareness of profound attributes of God: his fatherhood, providence, his loving and constant presence. It engenders interior attitudes rarely observed to the same degree elsewhere: patience, the sense of the cross in daily life, detachment, openness to others, devotion. By reason of these aspects, we readily call it "popular piety", that is, religion of the people, rather than religiosity.

Pastoral charity must dictate to all those whom the Lord has placed as leaders of the ecclesial communities the proper attitude in regard to this reality, which is at the same time so rich and so vulnerable. Above all one must be sensitive to it, know how to perceive its interior dimensions and undeniable values, be ready to help it overcome its risks of deviation. When it is well oriented, this popular religiosity can be more and more for multitudes of our people a true encounter with God in Jesus Christ.

JOHN PAUL II
APOSTOLIC LETTER *DUODECIMUM SAECULUM*
(4 December 1987)

On the occasion of the twelfth centenary of the Second Council of Nicaea the Pope published an Apostolic Letter in which he recalls the main issues which were clarified in the seventh Ecumenical Council, the last to have been fully recognised by the Catholic and the Orthodox Churches. To the Council's doctrine on Tradition and the veneration of images (cf. nn. 1251-1252), the Pope adds some reflections on the meaning of images and of Christian art. The text is found in AAS 80 (1988) 241-252.

(The meaning of images in the economy of incarnation)

1260 9. The dilemma posed by the iconoclasts involved much more than the question of the possibility of Christian art: it called into question the whole Christian perception of the truth of the Incarnation and therefore the relationships of God and the world, grace and nature; in short, the specific character of the "new covenant" that God made with humanity in Jesus Christ. The defenders of images saw it well: according to the Patriarch of Constantinople, Saint Germain, an illustrious victim of the iconoclast heresy, it is "the divine economy according to the flesh" that was being questioned. For, to see the human face of the Son of God, "image of the invisible God" [Col 1:15], is to see the Word made flesh [cf. Jn 1:14], the Lamb of God who takes away the sin of the world [cf. Jn 1:29]. Therefore art can represent the very form, the effigy of God's human face and lead the one who contemplates it to the ineffable mystery of God made flesh for our salvation. Thus Pope Hadrian could write: "Sacred images are honoured by the faithful so that by means of a visible face, our spirit may be carried in a spiritual attraction towards the invisible majesty of the divinity, through the contemplation of the image where the flesh that the Son of God deigned to take for our salvation is represented. May we thus adore and praise him together while glorifying in spirit this same Redeemer for, as it is written, 'God is spirit', and that is why we spiritually adore his divinity."[2]

---

1. Cf. THEOPHANE, *Chronographia ad annum*, 6221, ed. C. de Boor, I, Leipzig, 1883, p. 404 or PG 108, 821C.

2. Letter of HADRIAN I to the Emperors, in: Mansi XII, 1061C-D.

Hence, Nicaea II solemnly reaffirmed the traditional distinction between "the true adoration" *(latreia)* which "according to our faith is rendered to the unique divine nature" and "the prostration of honour" *(timêtikê proskunêsis)* which is attributed to icons, for "he who prostrates before the icon does so before the person *(hupostasis)* who is represented."[2]

Therefore the iconography of Christ involves the whole faith in the reality of the incarnation and its inexhaustible meaning for the Church and the world. If the Church practices it, it is because she is convinced that the God revealed in Jesus Christ has truly redeemed and sanctified the flesh and the whole sensible world, that is human beings with their five senses, to allow them "to be renewed in knowledge after the image of [their] creator" *[cf. Col 3:10].*

(Christian art must express the faith of the Church)

1261   11. Over the past several decades we have observed a resurgence of interest in the theology and spirituality of Oriental icons, a sign of the growing need for a spiritual language of authentically Christian art. In this regard, with the Council I can only invite my brothers in the episcopate to "maintain firmly the practice of proposing to the faithful the veneration of sacred images in the Churches" *[SC 125]* and to do everything so that more works of art of truly ecclesial quality may be produced. Believers of today, like those of yesterday, must be helped in their prayer and spiritual life by contemplating works of art which seek to express the mystery, not to hide it. That is why today as ever before faith is the necessary inspiration of Church art.

Art for art's sake, which only refers to the author, without establishing a relationship with the divine world, does not have its place in the Christian concept of the icon. No matter what style is adopted, all sacred art must express the faith and hope of the Church. The tradition of the icon shows that the artist must be conscious of fulfilling a mission of service to the Church.

Authentic Christian art is that which, through sensible perception, gives the intuition that the Lord is present in his Church, that the events of salvation history give meaning and

---

2. *Horos*, in: Mansi XIII, 378E.

orientation to our life, that the glory that is promised to us already transforms our existence. Sacred art must tend to offer us a visual synthesis of all the dimensions of our faith. Church art must aim at speaking the language of the Incarnation and, with the elements of matter, express the One who "deigned to dwell in matter and bring about our salvation through matter", according to Saint John Damascene's beautiful expression.[1]

The rediscovery of the Christian icon will also help in raising the awareness of the urgency of reacting against the depersonalization and at times degrading effects of the many images that condition our lives in advertisements and the media. For it is an image that turns towards us the look of Another who is invisible and gives us access to the reality of the spiritual and eschatological world.

1. *Discourse on images*, 1, 6,. in: *PG* 94, 1246A.

CHAPTER XIII

THE SACRAMENTS OF THE CHURCH

This chapter on the Sacraments of the Church is inseparable from that of Christian worship or liturgy, since all sacraments are forms of Christian worship; that is, they celebrate the saving mystery of God in Christ. Through signs they effect the grace proper to each sacrament in the persons who celebrate these sacraments.[1]

Salvation history is the history of God's personal dealings with men and women and the unfolding in history of his saving design. This personal encounter of God with human beings, the initiative for which comes from God and can only come from him, has been accomplished once for all in Jesus Christ: in the one Mediator the infinite distance which separates human beings from God has been bridged; through Christ's Paschal Mystery all humankind has been saved and united with God. Yet, the mystery accomplished once for all must remain present and operative at all times and in all places, and its saving effects must be applied to all people. The celebration of the sacraments are privileged means instituted by Christ and entrusted by him to the Church, by which the mystery of salvation becomes, for every age till the end of the world, a living and tangible reality. Through them the mystery of Christ is ever actual and effective. Christ who has died and is risen is present in them and exercises through them his saving power. In them men and women come in personal contact with the risen Lord and his saving action. Humble human signs which of themselves could never have any supernatural efficacy have become the channels of God's grace because Christ has made their dispensation by the Church the visible expression of his sanctifying will.

Thus, two fundamental affirmations belong to the Church's teaching on the sacraments. First, the Church is the depository of the signs instituted by Christ, which he entrusted to her to be faithfully preserved

---

1. On June 28, 1988, Pope JOHN PAUL II announced that the two former Congregations for Divine Worship and for the Sacraments would henceforth be one Congregation for Divine Worship and Sacraments.

and celebrated. Second, these signs, because they are the signs of the action of the glorified Christ, are efficacious signs of grace. Designed by him to communicate his salvation and assumed by him as his own actions, they are not hindered in their validity by the human deficiencies of those who administer them, so long as they mean to communicate what Christ has entrusted to the Church. The fruitful reception of them does depend on the disposition of those celebrating them.

Through the centuries the Church has progressed in the explicit awareness of her sacramental life. Her sacramental doctrine has grown out of the exercise of her sacramental life; in particular, the doctrine on the number of seven sacraments has been explicitly stated at a relatively late period. After having long been tranquilly possessed, the Church's sacramental doctrine was seriously challenged for the first time by the Reformation. The Church defended her sacred deposit and affirmed clearly the objective efficacy attached to the sacraments by Christ's institution. But, in the process of stressing the ex opere operato efficacy of the sacramental signs, post-Tridentine theology has, to an extent, lost sight of their personal aspect. This has once again been stressed in recent years: the sacraments are personal encounters of Christ with human beings in the signs of the Church. Their significance in the life of the Church has also received new emphasis: as the visible expression and continued actuality of the mystery of Christ, they are also a manifestation or epiphany of the mystery of the Church.

*   *   *

The main points of doctrine found in the official documents can be summarised as follows:

The sacraments are instituted by Christ: 32, 1311, 1326/39-40, 1327.
Their celebration is entrusted by Christ to the Church: 32, 1323, 1324.
There are seven sacraments: 28, 32, (1302), 1305, 1311, 1328.
They differ from the sacraments of the Old Law: 1003, 1305, 1312.
The sacraments confer the grace which they signify: 1305, 1309, 1316, 1317, 1318, 1327, 1335.
They sanctify human beings and give worship to God: 1334, 1335.
They are the actions of Christ: 1329, 1330, 1334.
Christ is present and active in them: 1331, 1332, 1334.
Christ's mysteries are present in the sacraments: 1333, 1334.
Three sacraments imprint an indelible character: 1308, 1319, 1710.

The sacraments are necessary, but not all equally, for salvation: 32, 810, 1313, 1314.

The sacraments are validly administered by carrying out the sign with the proper intention: 1304, 1307, 1321, 1325.

The validity of the sacraments is independent of the worthiness of the minister: 1301, 1303, 1304, 1322, 1504, 1627, 1650.

Not all are equally qualified to administer all the sacraments: 1320, 1627.

The fruitful reception of the sacraments depends on the disposition of the recipient: 1209/1-4, 1309, 1316, 1332, 1335.

Word, faith and sacrament are linked together: 1336.

INNOCENT III

PROFESSION OF FAITH PRESCRIBED TO THE WALDENSIANS (1208)

The thirteenth century was marked by a spirit of reform which found its expression in the orders founded by St. Francis of Assisi and St. Dominic. No less zealous for reform were the followers of Peter Waldo. Nevertheless, they inherited some of the errors of the Albigensians (cf. n. 403i). In their zeal to counteract the worldliness and unworthiness of the clergy which they held responsible for the decay of the religious life, they regarded only those who embraced religious poverty in its most extreme form as worthy ministers of the sacraments. Accordingly, the hierarchy of orders was to yield to a hierarchy of saints. In the process they made the validity of the sacraments dependent on the worthiness of the minister, thus failing to distinguish between the person and the office. The profession of faith prescribed by Innocent III shows that the validity of a sacrament does not depend on the worthiness of the minister.

1301 Furthermore, we do not reject the sacraments which
793 are conferred in the Church, in co-operation with the
inestimable and invisible power of the Holy Spirit, even
though these sacraments be administered by a sinful priest, as
long as he is recognised by the Church. And we do not disparage
ecclesiastical duties and blessings performed by such a one; but
we accept them with benevolence, as we would those performed
by the most just man. For the evil life of a bishop or a priest has
no harmful effect on either the baptism of an infant or the
consecration of the Eucharist or other ecclesiastical duties
performed for the faithful.

THE SECOND GENERAL COUNCIL OF LYONS
"PROFESSION OF FAITH OF MICHAEL PALAEOLOGUS"
(1274)

(1302) *Despite divergences of opinions among theologians as regards their
significance and divine efficacy, the number of seven major rites or
sacraments in the strict sense came to be explicitly recognised in the West
towards the middle of the twelfth century. Though less precise, the faith of the
Eastern Church was fundamentally the same. The profession of faith of Michael
Palaeologus (cf. n. 22i) affirms that there are seven sacraments and enumerates
them. Previous to this document the catalogue of seven sacraments is found
with less clarity in the profession of faith prescribed to the Waldensians (cf.
DS 794). See text in n. 28.*

THE GENERAL COUNCIL OF CONSTANCE
CONDEMNATION OF ERRORS OF WYCLIF AND HUS
(1415)

Wyclif's errors on the sacraments were not without relation to his ideas about the Church to which only the predestined belonged (cf. n. 807/8i). The same ideas were taken over by John Hus and spread by him in Bohemia. After healing the schism, Church reform and the campaign against the errors of Wyclif and Hus were for the Council of Constance the most urgent tasks. It condemned those errors in its 8th session (May 4, 1415). According to Wyclif, a sinful person loses all power in both the civil and the religious spheres. Sacraments administered by a sinner, priest or bishop, are not true sacraments.

(Error of Wyclif condemned)

[1303] If a bishop or priest is in mortal sin, he does not
1154   ordain, he does not consecrate, he does not perform [the
        Eucharist], he does not baptise.

MARTIN V
BULL *INTER CUNCTAS* (1418)

Soon after his election as Pope, Martin V meant to sanction the decisions taken by the Council of Constance. In this Bull he comes back to the errors of Wyclif and Hus already condemned by the Council; he adds a series of 39 questions addressed to their followers. One of these is again concerned with the problem of the validity of a sacrament administered by an unworthy minister.

(Question proposed to the followers of Wyclif and Hus)

1304 Likewise, whether he believes that a bad priest who uses
1262   the correct matter and form and has the intention of
        doing what the Church does, truly performs [the
Eucharist], truly absolves, truly baptises, truly confers the other
sacraments.

THE GENERAL COUNCIL OF FLORENCE
DECREE FOR THE ARMENIANS (1439)

Soon after the Bull Laetentur Coeli *destined to bring about the union of the Greeks which in fact did not materialise (cf. n. 322i), the Council issued a decree for the union of the Armenians; this document too was published as a Bull of Pope Eugene IV, entitled* Exsultate Domino. *The Decree for the Armenians was accepted by the delegates of their Church. The Bull mentions the doctrine of the early Councils on the Trinity (including the Filioque in the profession of faith of the Council of Constantinople: cf. n. 12), and on the two natures and two wills of Christ; it insists on the authority of Chalcedon and of St. Leo. It then comes to its main purpose, the sacraments.*

It recalls that there are seven sacraments and determines their effects; it explains that the sacraments are made up of matter and form, and the minister, all three elements constituting together the sacramental action; it further declares that baptism, confirmation and Order confer an "indelible character". A development on each of the sacraments follows, in which their constitutive elements are respectively determined (cf. nn. 1412-1418, 1509-1511, 1612-1613, 1705, 1803). This entire sacramental doctrine follows very closely St. Thomas Aquinas' short treatise "On the articles of faith and the sacraments of the Church". The document is neither an infallible definition, nor a document of faith. It is a clear exposition of the sacramental theology commonly held at that time in the Latin Church. The limits of its authority must be borne in mind, especially with regard to the question of the essential rite of the sacrament of Order (cf. n. 1705).

The Bull ends by repeating the Pseudo-Athanasian Symbol of faith (cf. nn. 16-17), by recalling the Council's Decree for the Greeks, and by making prescriptions regarding dates for the celebration of feasts by the Armenians.

1305 [...]We here set out the true doctrine of the sacraments
1310 of the Church in a brief formula which will facilitate the
instruction of the Armenians, both now and in the future.
There are seven sacraments of the New Law, namely, baptism,
confirmation, the Eucharist, penance, extreme unction, Order and
matrimony; and they differ greatly from the sacraments of the
Old Law. For these did not cause grace but were only a figure
of the grace that was to be given through the passion of Christ;
but our sacraments both contain grace and confer it on those
who receive them worthily.

1306 The first five of these are ordained to the interior
1311 spiritual perfection of the person; the last two are
ordained to the government and the increase of the
whole Church. For by baptism we are spiritually reborn and by
confirmation we grow in grace and are strengthened in the faith;
being reborn and strengthened, we are nourished with the divine
food of the Eucharist. If by sin we become sick in soul, we are
healed spiritually by penance; we are also healed in spirit, and
in body in so far as it is good for the soul, by extreme unction.
Through Order the Church is governed and receives spiritual
growth; through matrimony she receives bodily growth.

1307 All these sacraments are constituted by three elements:
1312 by things as the matter, by words as the form, and by
the person of the minister conferring the sacrament with

the intention of doing what the Church does. And if any one of these three is lacking, the sacrament is not effected.

1308 Among these sacraments there are three, baptism,
1313 confirmation and Order, which imprint on the soul an indelible character, that is a certain spiritual sign distinguishing [the recipient] from others. Hence, these are not repeated for the same person. The other four, however, do not imprint a character and may be repeated.

LEO X
BULL *EXSURGE DOMINE* (1520)

The Bull Exsurge Domine *condemns 41 propositions extracted from Luther's writings. Based on his doctrine of salvation through faith alone, they mostly refer to his teaching on the Church (cf. n. 811), on grace (cf. n. 1923/ 2i), on the sacrament of penance (cf. n. 1614/5i), on indulgences (cf. n. 1685/ 17i) and on purgatory. One proposition denied the efficacy of the sacraments; it is quoted here. The condemnation by Leo X did not stop Luther from spreading his ideas; it rather prompted him to write the major works which will give to the Reformation its definitive orientation.*

(Error of Luther condemned)

[1309] It is a heretical, though widespread, opinion that the
1451 sacraments of the New Law give justifying grace to those who do not place an obstacle in the way.

THE GENERAL COUNCIL OF TRENT
SEVENTH SESSION
DECREE ON THE SACRAMENTS (1547)

Aftert having exposed the doctrine on justification in its 6th session (cf. nn. 1924ff), the Council of Trent devoted its 7th session to the doctrine of the sacraments, and in particular to baptism and confirmation (cf. nn. 1420ff). The Decree on the Sacraments comprises no chapters but only canons preceded by a brief foreword. The canons are mostly directed against the errors of Luther, of the Augsburg confession (1530) and of Melanchton. Canon 1 maintains that there are seven sacraments, against Luther who reduced their number to three and later to two (baptism and Eucharist). It affirms that the seven sacraments are instituted by Christ, but without excluding the possibility of the "mediate institution" of some as held then by some Catholic theologians. Canon 4 is directed against Luther's opinion according to which, salvation being through faith alone, the sacraments are superfluous; canon 5 against an article of the Augsburg confession which reduced their efficacy to the arousing of faith. Canons 6-8 determine the efficacy of grace proper to the sacraments and its necessary conditions. Canon 9 affirms the existence in three sacraments of a sacramental character, which it describes in terms of the theology of St. Thomas Aquinas (cf. n. 1308). Canons 10 to 12 are directed against Luther who taught that, since the sacraments are effective only through the faith of the recipient, their efficacy in no way depends on the person and intention of the minister.

Foreword

1310   In order to bring to completion the salutary doctrine of
1600   justification promulgated with the unanimous consent
of the Fathers in the session immediately preceding, it seemed fitting to deal with the holy sacraments of the Church. For all true justification either begins through the sacraments, or, once begun, increases through them, or when lost is regained through them. Therefore, in order to do away with errors and to root out heresies which in this our age are directed against the holy sacraments—partly inspired by heresies already condemned in the past by our Fathers and partly newly devised—and which are doing great harm to the purity of the Catholic Church and to the salvation of souls, the most holy, ecumenical and general Council of Trent, lawfully assembled in the Holy Spirit under the presidency of the same legates of the apostolic See, adhering to the teaching of the Holy Scriptures, to the apostolic traditions and to the consensus of the Fathers and of the other Councils, has thought that the present canons should be drawn up and decreed. The canons which remain for the completion of the work begun, the Council will, with the help of the Holy Spirit, publish hereafter.

Canons on the Sacraments in General

1311   1. If anyone says that the sacraments of the New Law
1601   were not all instituted by Jesus Christ our Lord; or that
there are more or fewer than seven that is: baptism, confirmation, the Eucharist, penance, extreme unction, Order and matrimony; or that any one of these is not truly and properly a sacrament, *anathema sit.*

1312   2. If anyone says that these same sacraments of the
1602   New Law do not differ from the sacraments of the Old
Law, except that the ceremonies and external rites are different, *anathema sit.*

1313   3. If anyone says that these sacraments are so equal to
1603   one another that one is not in any way of greater worth
than another, *anathema sit.*

1314 4. If anyone says that the sacraments of the New Law
1604 are not necessary for salvation, but that they are superfluous; and that without the sacraments or the desire of
them human beings obtain from God the grace of justification
through faith alone, although it is true that not all the sacraments
are necessary for each person, *anathema sit*.

1315 5. If anyone says that these sacraments are instituted
1605 only for the sake of nourishing the faith, *anathema sit*.

1316 6. If anyone says that the sacraments of the New Law
1606 do not contain the grace which they signify or that they
do not confer that grace on those who do not place
an obstacle in the way, as if they were only external signs of
the grace or justice received through faith and a kind of
mark of the Christian profession by which among human beings
the faithful are distinguished from the unbelievers, *anathema
sit*.

1317 7. If anyone says that, as far as God's part is concerned,
1607 grace is not given through these sacraments always and
to all, even if they receive them rightly, but only
sometimes and to some, *anathema sit*.

1318 8. If anyone says that through the sacraments of the
1608 New Law grace is not conferred by the performance of
the rite itself *(ex opere operato)* but that faith alone in the
divine promise is sufficient to obtain grace, *anathema sit*.

1319 9. If anyone says that in three sacraments, namely,
1609 baptism, confirmation and Order, a character is not
imprinted on the soul, that is, a kind of indelible spiritual
sign by reason of which these sacraments cannot be repeated,
anathema sit.

1320 10. If anyone says that all Christians have the power
1610 [to preach] the word and to administer all the
sacraments, *anathema sit*.

1321 11. If anyone says that the intention, at least of doing
1611 what the Church does, is not required in the ministers
when they are performing and conferring the sacraments,
anathema sit.

1322 12. If anyone says that a minister in the state of mortal
1612 sin, though he observes all the essentials that belong to
the performing and conferring of the sacrament, does
not perform or confer the sacrament, *anathema sit.*

1323 13. If anyone says that the accepted and approved rites
1613 of the Catholic Church which are customarily used in
the solemn administration of the sacraments may be
despised or omitted without sin by the ministers as they please,
or that they may be changed to other new rites by any pastor in
the Church, *anathema sit.*

TWENTY-FIRST SESSION

DOCTRINE ON COMMUNION UNDER BOTH SPECIES AND ON COMMUNION OF LITTLE CHILDREN (1562)

In its 21st session the Council of Trent dealt with the much disputed question of the admission of lay people to communion with the chalice (cf. nn. 1537ff). The legitimacy of communion under one kind only which had become the received practice is based on the principle that, the substance of the sacraments instituted by Christ being preserved, the Church has power to determine the modality of their dispensation. Much later (1947), Pope Pius XII will refer to the same principle in order to determine the essential rite of the sacrament of Order (cf. n. 1737i). He will further define the "substance" of the sacraments over which the Church has no power, as consisting of "those things which, on the testimony of the sources of divine revelation, Christ the Lord himself has determined as having to be preserved in the sacramental sign" (DS 3857).

Chapter II: The Power of the Church concerning the Dispensation of the Eucharist

1324 [The Holy Council] furthermore declares that in the
1728 dispensation of the sacraments, provided their substance
is preserved, the Church has always had the power to
determine or change, according to circumstances, times and
places, what she judges more expedient for the benefit of those
receiving them or for the veneration of the sacraments. It seems
that the apostle referred to this power rather clearly when he
said: "This is how one should regard us, as servants of Christ
and stewards of the mysteries of God" *[1 Cor 4:1].* It is sufficiently
clear that he himself used this power not only in many other
instances but also with regard to this very sacrament, when he

laid down certain regulations for its use and said: "About the other things I will give directions when I come" *[1 Cor 11:34]*. Therefore,[...] holy Mother Church, conscious of her authority in the administration of the sacraments[...].

(There follows the approval of Communion under one kind.)

ALEXANDER VIII

DECREE OF THE HOLY OFFICE (1690)

The Council of Trent had purposely left indeterminate the "intention of doing what the Church does" which is required in the celebration of the sacraments. Among the errors of the Jansenists condemned by this decree of the Holy Office is found a proposition attributed to Farvacques according to which a sacrament is validly conferred by a minister who duly performs the rite even though he interiorly resolves not to do what the Church does. From this condemnation (which is not a document of faith), it results that the so-called "external intention" (shown in the performance of the rite itself) is not sufficient, but that a certain "interior intention" is required on the part of the minister for a valid celebration of the sacraments.

(Jansenist error condemned)

[1325] Baptism is valid, when conferred by a minister who
2328 observes all the external rites and the form of baptising,
      but interiorly within his heart resolves: I do not intend what the Church does.

PIUS X

DECREE *LAMENTABILI* OF THE HOLY OFFICE (1907)
ARTICLES OF MODERNISM CONDEMNED

The Church's doctrine on the institution of the sacraments by Christ and their efficacy ex opere operato were regarded by the Modernists, in accordance with their basic tenets (cf. n. 143i), as typical examples of the way in which religious forms established in the first centuries of Christianity were progressively fixed and presented in the Church's teaching as immutable dogmas. According to them, the sacraments are an interpretation, in no way absolute, of the mind of Christ by early Christianity. The Decree Lamentabili condemns three fundamental errors of the Modernists on the sacraments in general (cf. also nn. 1437/42ff; 1660/46ff; 1729//49).

[1326/39] The opinions on the origin of the sacraments with
3439   which the Tridentine Fathers were imbued and
         which undoubtedly influenced their dogmatic canons

are far removed from those which are now rightly held by research historians of Christianity.

[1326/40] The sacraments owe their origin to the fact that the
3440   apostles and their successors interpreted some idea
     and intention of Christ under the influence and
pressure of circumstances and events.

[1326/41] The purpose of the sacraments is only to recall to
3441   the human mind the ever beneficent presence of the
     Creator.

ENCYCLICAL LETTER *PASCENDI* (1907)

Completing the Decree Lamentabili, *the encyclical* Pascendi *of Pius X exposes at length and attempts to synthetise in their diversity the ideas of the Modernists (cf. n. 143i). One passage refers to the Modernist opinion according to which the sacraments, as all that belongs to the cult, have no sanctifying action as proposed by the Council of Trent.*

1327   On the question of worship, little would have to be said
3489   were it not for the fact that the sacraments come under
     this heading; and here the Modernists fall into the gravest errors. They attempt to show that worship results from a twofold impulse or necessity; for, as we have seen, everything in their system is explained by inner impulses or necessities. The first impulse is to attribute some sensible element to religion; the second impulse is to make it known, and this could not be done without some sensible form and sanctifying actions which we call sacraments. For the Modernists, the sacraments are mere symbols or signs, though not altogether without power. To explain the nature of this power, they compare it to the power of certain phrases which in common parlance "have caught on", inasmuch as they have acquired the power of propagating mighty ideas capable of deeply striking people's minds. What these phrases are to ideas, the sacraments are to the religious sense— that, and nothing more. Now, surely, the Modernists would speak more plainly, were they to affirm that the sacraments were instituted solely to foster faith. But this the Council of Trent has condemned: "If anyone says that these sacraments were instituted only for the sake of nourishing the faith, *anathema sit*" [*cf. n. 1315*].

PIUS XII

ENCYCLICAL LETTER *MYSTICI CORPORIS* (1943)

In his great Encyclical Letter on the mystery of the Church (cf. nn. 847ff),
Pope Pius XII shows the meaning of the various sacraments for the spiritual
life of individual Christians and in relation to the mystery of the Church.
Linking up with the persuasion of the early tradition, he re-states the theological
principle that the sacraments are the actions of Christ through the Church.

(The Church, Mystical Body of Christ, and the sacraments)

1328   The human body[...] has its own means for fostering the life,
health and growth of itself and each of its members. And
the Saviour of the human race in his infinite goodness has in like
manner admirably equipped his mystical Body by endowing it with
the sacraments, making available for its members a progressive
series of graces to sustain them from the cradle to their last breath,
and abundantly providing also for the social needs of the whole
Body. By baptism those who have been born to this mortal life are
regenerated from the death of sin and made members of the Church,
and also invested with a spiritual character which makes them able
and fit to receive the other sacraments. The chrism of confirmation
gives believers new strength so that they may strenuously guard
and defend Mother Church and the faith which they have received
from her. The sacrament of penance offers a saving remedy to
members of the Church who have fallen into sin, and this not only
for the sake of their own salvation but also in order that their fellow-
members may be saved from the danger of contagion, and receive
instead an example and incentive to virtue. Nor is this all: in the
Holy Eucharist the faithful are nourished and fortified at a common
banquet, and by an ineffable and divine bond united with one
another and with the divine Head of the whole Body. And when
at last they are mortally ill, loving Mother Church is at their side
with the sacrament of extreme unction, and although, God so
willing, she may not always thereby restore health of the body, she
nevertheless applies a supernatural balm to the wounded soul, thus
providing new citizens for heaven and new heavenly intercessors
for herself, who will enjoy the divine goodness for all eternity.

For the social needs of the Church Christ has also provided
in a particular way by two other sacraments which he instituted.
The sacrament of matrimony, in which the partners become the
ministers of grace to each other, ensures the regular numerical

increase of the Christian community, and, what is more important, the proper and religious education of the offspring, the lack of which would constitute a grave menace to the mystical Body. And holy Order, finally, consecrates to the perpetual service of God those who are destined to offer the eucharistic victim, to nourish the flock of the faithful with the bread of angels and with the food of doctrine, to guide them by the divine commandments and counsels, and to fortify them by their other supernatural functions.

(The sacraments are the actions of Christ through the Church)

1329   Christ is the author and efficient cause of holiness; for there can be no salutary act which does not proceed from him as from its supernatural source: "Apart from me you can do nothing", he said *[Jn 15:5]*.[...] His inexhaustible fulness is the fount of grace and glory.[...] And when the Church administers the sacraments with external rites, it is he who produces their effect in the soul. He it is, too, who feeds the redeemed with his own flesh and blood.[...]

1330   [...]In the first place, in virtue of the juridical mission by which the divine Redeemer sent forth his apostles into the world as he himself had been sent by the Father *[cf. Jn 17:18; 20:21]*, it is indeed he who baptises through the Church, he who teaches, governs, absolves, binds, offers and makes sacrifice.

ENCYCLICAL LETTER *MEDIATOR DEI* (1947)

This Encyclical Letter prolongs Mystici Corporis and further develops its doctrine with regard to the Church's liturgical life. Regarding the sacraments, it lays stress on Christ's presence and action; it explains that Christ's action does not dispense the recipient from personally appropriating to oneself the gift of grace. It also touches on the difficult question of the presence of the historical mysteries of Christ in the sacraments and in the entire liturgical life of the Church. The theological discussion on this point had received impetus mostly from the works of Dom Odo Casel (1886-1948), a Benedictine monk of Maria Laach, and the theory of the "mysteric presence" proposed by him. The encyclical does not favour explanations which would seem too obscure, but neither does it propose one which would answer all the questions. It leaves open a discussion in which theologians are engaged even today.

(Christ's presence in the sacraments)

1331   [...] In the whole conduct of the liturgy the Church has
3840   her divine founder present with her. Christ is present in the august sacrifice of the altar, both in the person of his

minister and especially under the eucharistic species; he is present in the sacraments by his power which he infuses into them as instruments of sanctification; he is present, finally, in the prayer and praise which are offered to God, in accordance with his promise: "Where two or three are gathered in my name, there am I in the midst of them" [Mt 18:20].

(Christ's action must be personally appropriated)

1332 It is certainly true that the sacraments and the Mass possess an intrinsic efficacy, because they are actions of Christ himself transmitting and distributing the grace of the divine Head to the members of the mystical Body. But to have their proper effect they require our souls also to be in the right dispositions. This is why St. Paul warns us in regard to the Eucharist: "Examine yourselves, and only then eat of the bread and drink of the cup" [1 Cor 11:28].[...] For it must be borne in mind that the members of this body are living members, endowed with intellect and will; therefore they must deliberately set their lips to this source of grace, absorb and assimilate this food of life, and uproot from themselves anything that may obscure its efficacy. So the work of our redemption, though in itself something independent of our will, really calls for an interior effort from our souls if we are to attain eternal salvation.

(The presence of the mysteries of Christ)

1333
3855 [...]The liturgical year, animated throughout by the devotion of the Church, is no cold and lifeless representation of past events, no mere historical record. It is Christ himself, living on in his Church, and still pursuing that path of boundless mercy which, going about doing good [cf. Acts 10:38], he began to tread during his life on earth. This he did in order that the souls of human beings might come into contact with his mysteries and, so to speak, live by them. And these mysteries are still now constantly present and active, not in the vague and nebulous way which recent authors describe, but as Catholic doctrine teaches us. The Doctors of the Church tell us that the mysteries of Christ's life are at the same time most excellent models of virtue for us to imitate and also sources of divine grace for us by reason of the merits and intercession of the Redeemer. They live on in their effect in us, since each of them is, according to its nature and in its own way, the cause of our salvation.

THE SECOND VATICAN GENERAL COUNCIL

Though the Council of Trent in its Decree on Justification referred to Christ's continuous vital action on his members (cf. n. 1947), its canons on the sacraments made no reference to Christ beyond stating that they have been instituted by him. Partly prepared by the encyclicals Mystici Corporis *and* Mediator Dei, *the sacramental doctrine of Vatican II is more comprehensive than that of the Council of Trent. It is deeply Christocentric, while at the same time stressing the ecclesial dimension of the sacraments. It combines harmoniously two complementary aspects of the sacraments, at once efficacious signs of Christ's sanctifying power and concrete expressions of the faith of the Church; for God's gratuitous initiative does not dispense human beings from responding to it in faith. Again, without toning down the idea of efficacy, the Council makes a strong plea for the meaningfulness of the signs (SC 59). Its doctrine is found in the two Constitutions on the Sacred Liturgy(SC) and on the Church (LG).*

The perfect achievement of our reconciliation and the fulness of divine worship are found in Christ the Word Incarnate (SC 5); his earthly work consisted in "redeeming humankind and giving perfect glory to God" (SC 5). The Church as "universal sacrament of salvation" (LG 48; cf. 1, 9: SC 5, 26; GS 45...) prolongs Christ's action; for Christ associates her with himself in the work by which God is perfectly glorified and men and women sanctified (SC 7). This is true especially of the liturgy (SC 10); hence the twofold end which the Council assigns to it (SC 10) (cf. n. 1232). In the liturgical life of the Church, however, the sacraments have a privileged place: "around the sacrifice and the sacraments the entire liturgical life revolves" (SC 6; cf. 2, 7, etc.). The sacraments draw their power from the Paschal Mystery (SC 61). Like the Paschal Mystery itself, they are directed to a double end, the sanctification of men and women and the praise of God (SC 61); thus, they build up the Body of Christ (SC 59).

While referring to the mystery of salvation contained in the sacraments, the Council purposely avoids the controversial phrase ex opere operato. *It is replaced by the concept of Christ's presence and action. Christ's presence in the Church's sacraments is stressed in SC 7. This text, partly prepared by* Mediator Dei *(cf. n. 1731), is among the most profound and far-reaching theological statements of Vatican II. By affirming Christ's presence in the liturgy of the word (not mentioned in* Mediator Dei*), it opens the way for a theology which will combine harmoniously the efficacy of the word of God and of the sacraments. Not only is Christ present in the sacramental actions of the Church, but his mysteries too are present there in a mysterious manner: by baptism men and women are inserted into the Paschal mystery of Christ (SC 6; cf. 61); this indicates that Christ's Paschal Mystery is present and operative in the sacraments. SC 102 extends the presence of the mysteries of Christ to the Church's liturgical year (cf. n. 1234).*

The sacraments are also a mystery of divine worship on the part of the Church: they not only presuppose faith, but also nourish, strengthen and

express it; this is why they are called "sacraments of faith" (SC 59). Thus,
correlative to the stress put on Christ's presence and action in the sacraments,
Vatican II insists on the role of faith. It rejuvenates the phrase of an old
tradition: the sacraments are sacramenta fidei. *On the part of the Church,*
they are communal acts of worship, in so far as here, even more than in other
liturgical actions, Christ associates her with himself in the work of God's
glorification (SC 7). As to the recipients of the sacrament, what the Council
says explicitly of the faithful participating in the liturgy applies to them in a
special manner: "It is necessary that the faithful come to it with proper
dispositions, that their minds should be attuned to their voices, and that they
should co-operate with divine grace lest they receive it in vain" (SC 11).

CONSTITUTION *SACROSANCTUM CONCILIUM* (1963)

(Christ's manifold presence and action in the Church's liturgy)

1334   7. To accomplish so great a work, Christ is always present
to his Church, especially in her liturgical celebrations.
He is present in the sacrifice of the Mass, not only in the person
of his minister, "the same now offering through the ministry of
priests, who then offered himself on the cross" *[cf. n. 1548]*, but
especially under the eucharistic species. By his power he is
present in the sacraments, so that when someone baptises it is
really Christ himself who baptises. He is present in his word,
since it is he himself who speaks when the Holy Scriptures are
read in the Church. He is present, lastly, when the Church prays
and sings, for he promised: "Where two or three are gathered in
my name, I am there among them" *[Mt 18:20]*.

Christ indeed always associates the Church with himself in
this great work wherein God is perfectly glorified and human
beings are sanctified. The Church is his beloved Bride who calls
to her Lord and through him offers worship to the eternal Father.

Rightly, then, the liturgy is considered as an exercise of the
priestly office of Jesus Christ. In the liturgy the sanctification of
humanity is signified by signs perceptible to the senses, and is
effected in a way which corresponds with each of these signs; in
the liturgy the whole public worship is performed by the mystical
Body of Jesus Christ, that is, by the Head and his members.[...]

(Sanctification of men and women and worship of God in the
sacraments)

1335   59. The purpose of the sacraments is to sanctify human
beings, to build up the Body of Christ, and finally, to

give worship to God; because they are signs, they also instruct. They not only presuppose faith, but by words and objects they also nourish, strengthen and express it; that is why they are called "sacraments of faith". They do indeed impart grace, but, in addition, the very act of celebrating them most effectively disposes the faithful to receive this grace in a fruitful manner, to worship God duly, and to practice charity.

It is therefore of the highest importance that the faithful should easily understand the sacramental signs, and should frequent with great eagerness those sacraments which were instituted to nourish the Christian life.

PAUL VI

APOSTOLIC EXHORTATION *EVANGELII NUNTIANDI* (1975)

Chapter III of the Apostolic Exhortation on Evangelization of Pope Paul VI is devoted to the "Methods of Evangelization". It affirms the need for preaching and verbal proclamation and in this context stresses the role of the liturgy of the word. It goes on to show the link between word, faith and sacrament and concludes that sacramentalization cannot be opposed to evangelization. The text is found in AAS 68 (1976) 36-37.

(Word, faith and sacrament)

1336   47. Evangelization exercises its full capacity when it achieves the most intimate relationship, or better still a permanent and unbroken inter-communication, between the Word and the sacraments. In a certain sense it is a mistake to build a contrast between evangelization and sacramentalization, as is sometimes done. It is indeed true that a certain way of celebrating the sacraments, without the solid support of catechesis regarding these same sacraments and a global catechesis, could end up by depriving them of their effectiveness to a great extent. The role of evangelization is precisely to educate people in the faith in such a way as to lead each individual Christian to live the sacraments as true sacraments of faith—and not to receive them passively or to undergo them.

CHAPTER XIV

BAPTISM AND CONFIRMATION

To be a Christian is to be conformed to the mystery of Christ's death and resurrection in order to live a new life in Christ and to continue his mission in the world as a member of his Church. Baptism, confirmation and the Eucharist are the three sacraments that initiate the members of the Church into this new life; but, while the Eucharist is meant to strengthen day by day the Christian life, baptism and confirmation mark a person once for all as a member of Christ in his Church. This is why these two sacraments are closely connected; together they confer full Church membership.

Through baptism "as through a door" (cf.AG 7) human beings enter the Church. Plunged into the mystery of Christ's death and resurrection, they are once for all sacramentally conformed to this mystery, become members of Christ's mystical Body and receive a spiritual rebirth. But, though already destined through baptism to share in the life of the Church and its mission, they are even more directly ordained to witness to Christ in word and deed through confirmation.

The sacrament of baptism has from the earliest tradition been present to the explicit consciousness of the Church. In it all who bear the name Christian are united; no heresy claiming that name ever could or did question it seriously. Doubts were raised only as regards the manner of conferring it, its effects and its mode of efficacy. The Church clarified these issues as they arose. For the most part, official documents answer concrete questions and refute errors; they do not exhaust the riches of the 'sacrament of faith' upon which the patristic catechesis had dwelt with predilection.

The church has grown through the centuries in its explicit awareness of confirmation as a distinct sacrament. Its intrinsic connection with baptism and the early practice of conferring the Christian initiation in one liturgical celebration caused this distinction to remain latent. Yet, the early documents witness to the fact that the Christian initiation conferred by the priest is completed by the bishop. This element has played a decisive role in the explicitation of the faith *about confirmation. As sacramental doctrine developed in the 12th century, confirmation found its proper place in the sacramental system. Its specific significance, however, was not always equally well understood; linking with Scripture and a strong current of tradition, the recent documents show more and more clearly that confirmation strengthens Christians with the gift of the Spirit to enable them to bear witness to Christ.*

Summing up the data of the Christian Tradition, the Second Vatican Council has brought out the distinction and complementarity of the two sacraments that make the Christian. Both together constitute the foundation of the common priesthood of the People of God and are the basis for the lay aspotolate. Baptised in Christ and confirmed with the Spirit, all Christians are called upon to take an active part in the Church's life and mission.

The documents of the Second Vatican Council also indicate more explicitly the practical and social effects which the grace of baptism and that of confirmation should encourage Christians to manifest in the life and mission of the Church. Since Jesus was baptised in the Jordan so as "to fulfill all justice"(Mt 3:15), and since he was anointed at the start of his ministry so that "justice would be brought to victory and people would hope in his name" (Mt 12:20-21), the sanctifying grace conferred by baptism leads Christians to be just human beings in their society, and that conferred by confirmation urges them to be hopeful people who set up in history concrete signs of the inauguration of the Kingdom. The many references in the conciliar documents to the obligation of the faithful to create a more just social order (cf.AG 8) and to give witness to the renewing force of the paschal mystery in human endeavours (cf.GS 22) can rightly be considered the consequences of being justified through baptism and anointed through confirmation.

*   *   *

The main points of doctrine contained in this chapter may be summed up under the following headings:

Baptism

Baptism is a true sacrament instituted by Christ: 25, 28, 32, 39/11, 1305f, 1311, 1412, 1420.
It introduces into the Church and incorporates into Christ: 849, 1412, 1439, 1440, 1441, 1447,1618.

It confers a sacramental character by which Christians share in the priesthood of Christ: 32,1308,1319, 1410, 1439, 1441, 1710.

It confers all the rights and enjoins all the duties of the Christian life: 1425-1429, 1433.

It cannot be repeated: 32, 1401, 1404, 1430, 1432, 1440a-1440b.

It remits sins, original and personal, and confers the life of grace: 9, 10, 12, 39/11,503, 510-512, 1306, (1407) 1409, 1411, 1412, 1415, 1439, 1441, 1615, 1619, 1923/2, 1932, 1944, 2302.

It is administered with water and the Trinitarian formula: 21,1413,1421.

Baptism at least of desire is necessary for salvation: 510, 1405, 1408,1419, 1424, 1437/42,1928.

Infants can and should be baptised: 21,39/11,511,1405,(1407),1409, 1411, 1419, 1431f, 1437/43, 1443-1446.

Adults must be free in receiving baptism: 1410.

Every human being can baptise validly: 1401, 1402, 1403, 1404, 1414,1423.

Catechumenate as formation in the communal and apostolic life of the Church: 1439d.

Baptism as the beginning of acquiring fullness of life in Christ:1439d.

The baptised are to manifest their paschal existence by resisting evil and acting justly: 1439b, 1439c, 1448.

The faithful are to view the search for social justice as prior to the practice of charity: 1440

Confirmation

Confirmation is a true sacrament, instituted by Christ: 28, 32, 1305, 1311, 1416, 1434, 1435.

It completes baptism but is distinct from it: 1402, 1404, 1437/44, 1439, 1440, 1441.

It confers a sacramental character which binds Christians more deeply to the Church: 32, 1319, 1439, 1440, 1441, 1710.

It confers the gift of the Spirit for strength in Christian witness: 1306, 1404, 1406, 1416, 1418, 1439, 1440, 1441.

It is administered by an anointing with chrism accompanied with the words: 28, 1308, 1404, 1406, 1416, 1442.

The chrism must be blessed by the bishop: 1417

The bishop is the ordinary minister of confirmation, the priest the extraordinary minister: 28, 1404, 1406, 1417, 1436, (1438).

The confirmed are to manifest their anointing with the Holy Spirit by living according to Christian hope: 1439b.

The missionary task of the confirmed consists in giving witness to the power of the Holy Spirit in their lives: 1439c.

Baptism and Confirmation

Baptism and confirmation form the foundation of the common priesthood of all Christians and of the lay apostolate: 1439,1440,1441.

Baptism and confirmation are aimed at Christian maturity by serving others through charity: 1439e, 1440.

Baptism and confirmation urge Christians to give witness to the new liberty of the paschal mystery by practicing justice and love: 1439c, 1439e, 1440, 1446a, 1448.

Baptism and confirmation lead Christians to discover the seeds of the Word and the actions of the Spirit in non-Christians: 1439c.

Eucharistic ministry and the non-ordained: 1449-1450.

STEPHEN I

LETTER TO CYPRIAN, BISHOP OF CARTHAGE (256)

In Rome as in Alexandria and Palestine, the custom when receiving heretics who had been baptised was to lay hands on them as a sign of reconciliation. In Carthage the persuasion was that persons baptised in heresy had to be re-baptised. Pope Stephen I who had received notification of this practice objects to it and claims his right to impose the Roman practice. The same doctrine on the validity of baptism received in heresy will later be repeated by Pope Innocent I (cf.DS 211) and Pope Gregory II (cf DS 580).

(On baptism of heretics)

1401 If therefore some come to you from any heresy
110 whatsoever let no innovation be made except according
to what has been handed down, namely let an imposition
of hands be made on them by way of penance; for the heretics
themselves are right in not baptising other heretics who come
over to them but simply receiving them into their communion.

THE COUNCIL OF ELVIRA (c.300-303)

This local Council held in Spain shows the distinction in and connection between baptism and its "perfection" through an imposition of hand by the bishop. See also canon 77 of the same Council (DS 121)

(On baptism and its completion by the bishop)

1402 Canon 38: [...]A faithful who has been fully baptised and
120 is not bigamous may in case of need arising from sickness
baptise a catechumen, so that, if he survives, he will bring
him to the bishop that he may be perfected by the imposition of
hand.

THE FIRST GENERAL COUNCIL OF NICAEA (325)

The decision of Pope Stephen notwithstanding (cf. n. 1401), conditions could arise in which heretics had to be re-baptised. Such was the case with the Paulianists (followers of Paul of Samosata, bishop of Antioch, c. 260) who denied the divinity of the Son and therefore were not baptised in the name of the Blessed Trinity. The Council of Nicaea orders that they be re-baptised. See similar decisions by the Council of Arles (314) (DS 123) and later by Pope Innocent I (DS 214) and Pope Gregory I (DS 478).

(Some baptisms of heretics are not valid)

1403   Canon 19: As for the Paulianists who seek refuge in the
128   Catholic Church, the decision has been taken that they
be re-baptised by all means.

SIRICIUS

LETTER TO HIMERIUS, BISHOP OF TARRAGONA (385)

In this letter the Pope distinguishes baptism from the gift of the Spirit through the bishop's imposition of hand; the first is not repeated in the case of heretics, while the other is conferred on them (see also Leo I: DS 320). After having insisted on the observance of the liturgical time (Easter and Pentecost) for the conferring of baptism, he goes on to explain the necessity of baptism for salvation (see also Innocent I: DS 219) which may require that other provisions be made.

(Baptism and its completion by the bishop)

1404   These (Arians) as well as the Novatians and other
183   heretics we join to the Catholic assembly merely by the
invocation of the septiform Spirit through the bishop's
imposition of hand, as has been decided by the Synod. The same
is observed everywhere in East and West.[...]

(Necessity of baptism for salvation)

1405   As we maintain that the observance of the holy Paschal
184   time should in no way be relaxed, in the same way we
desire that infants who, on account of their age, cannot
yet speak, or those who, in any necessity, are in want of the
water of holy baptism, be succoured with all possible speed, for
fear that if those who leave this world should be deprived of
the life of the Kingdom for having been refused the source of
salvation which they desired, this may lead to the ruin of our
souls. If those threatened with shipwreck, or the attack of
enemies, or the uncertainties of a siege, or those put in a hopeless
condition due to some bodily sickness, ask for what in their faith
is their only help, let them receive at the very moment of their
request the reward of the regeneration they beg for. Enough of
the past mistakes! From now on, let all the priests observe the
aforesaid rule if they do not want to be separated from the
solid apostolic rock on which Christ has built his universal
Church.

INNOCENT I

LETTER TO DECENTIUS, BISHOP OF GUBBIO (416)

In this letter the Pope distiguishes clearly basptism (comprising an anointing with chrism) which is conferred by the presbyter from the signing (consignatio) with chrism reserved to the bishop.

(Signing with chrism is reserved to the bishop)

1406 As for the signing of infants [with chrism] *(de*
215 *consignandis infantibus)* it is clear that it may only be
done by the bishop. For, though the presbyters are priests of the second order, yet they do not have the fulness of the pontificate. That this pontifical authority of confirming *(ut consignent)* or of conferring the Spirit the Paraclete is proper only to the bishop is clearly shown not only by the Church's custom but by that passage of the Acts of the Apostles which affirms that Peter and John were directed to confer the Holy Spirit to those who were already baptised *[cf. Acts 8:14-17]*. For it is allowed to presbyters when they baptise either in the absence of the bishop or in his presence to anoint with chrism those who are being baptised, though only with chrism consecrated by the bishop; but not to sign their forehead with the same oil, which is reserved to the bishops when they confer the Spirit the Paraclete.[...]

THE SIXTEENTH COUNCIL OF CARTHAGE (1418)

(1407) *In its Canon 2 on original sin this local Council clearly states that*
223 *baptism truly remits original sin in infants and that, therefore, baptism for the remission of sins is properly verified in them. For the historical context of this document, see n. 501i. The text of the Council of Carthage was adopted with minute additions by the Council of Trent in its Decree on Original Sin; the text of Trent is quoted in n. 511.*

INNOCENT II (1130-1143)

LETTER TO THE BISHOP OF CREMONIA (time unknown)

In this letter Pope Innocent II explains that "baptism of desire" can remit original sin and lead to salvation. The same doctrine is taught by Pope Innocent III in a letter to Bertolius, bishop of Metz (1206) (cf. DS 788).

(On baptism of desire)

1408 We affirm without hesitation that the old man who,

741   according to the information received from you, died
           without having received the baptism of water has been
relieved of original sin and granted the joy of the heavenly home,
because he has persevered in the faith of holy Mother the Church
and in the confession of Christ's name. Read on this the eighth
book of Augutine's *"The City of God"*[1] where among other things
we read the following; "Baptism is invisibly administered which
has been impeded, not by contempt for religion but by
unavoidable death". And read over again the book of St. Ambrose
"On the Death of Valentianus"[2] which affirms the same doctrine.[...]

INNOCENT III

LETTER TO HUMBERT, ARCHBISHOP OF ARLES (1201)

*Some heretics, perhaps the Waldensians, considered infant baptism
profitless. In this letter, the Pope explains the effect of baptism of children and
compares it with the effect of circumcision: circumcision made men belong to
the chosen people, remission of original sin included, but only baptism opens
the Kingdom of heaven. Thus it is eminently fruitful. A second passage of the
same letter (quoted under n. 506) explains why original sin can in baptism be
remitted without consent; this is due to the nature of original sin as distinct
from personal sin (cf. n. 506i). A third passage, while treating of the freedom
required for the baptism of adults, alludes to the character produced by the
sacrament.*

(The effect of baptism)

1409   Even though original sin was remitted by the mystery
780   of circumcision and the danger of damnation avoided,
            human beings could not reach the Kingdom of heaven,
which remained closed for all till the death of Christ. But through
the sacrament of baptism[...] the guilt is remitted and one also
reaches the Kingdom of heaven, whose gate the blood of Christ
mercifully opened to his faithful. Far from us the thought that
all the small children, of whom such a great multitude dies every
day, should perish without the merciful God, who wishes no
one to perish, having provided for them also some means of
salvation.[...]

---

1. The correct reference is to St Augustine's *De baptismo contra Donatistas*,
IV, 22, 29.
2. St. Ambrose, *De obitu Valentiani*, 51.

(Freedom required for baptism; its character)

1410 It is contrary to the Christian religion to force others
781 into accepting and practicing Christianity if they are
always unwilling and totally opposed. Wherefore, some,
not without reason, distinguish between unwilling and unwilling,
forced and forced. For whoever are violently drawn by fear of
punishments and receive the sacrament of baptism to avoid harm
to themselves, such persons just like those who come to baptism
in bad faith, receive the imprint of the Christian character; and,
since they gave their consent conditionally though not absolutely,
they are to be held to the observance of the Christian faith.[...]
But one who never consents and is absolutely unwilling receives
neither the reality nor the character of the sacrament because
express dissent is something more than the absence of any
consent.[...]

PROFESSION OF FAITH PRESCRIBED TO THE
WALDENSIANS (1208)

*For this document, see n. 403i. One article treats baptism and explains
the effect of baptism in general.*

1411 We therefore approve the baptism of infants. We profess
794 and believe that they are saved if they die after baptism
before having committed any sins. And we believe that
all sins are remitted in baptism, the original sin which has been
contracted as well as those committed voluntarily.

THE GENERAL COUNCIL OF FLORENCE
DECREE FOR THE ARMENIANS(1439)

*For the doctrinal value of this document see n. 1306i.After treating the
sacraments in general, the Decree turns to each in particular, explaining its
matter, form, minister and effect, successively. It begins with baptism and
confirmation. For confirmation see, previous to this document, the question
which, in 1351,Pope Clement VI put to Catholicos Mekhitar to ascertain the
correct faith of the Armenians at a time (1198 to 1375) when they were united
with Rome (DS 1068-1071); the various elements mentioned there are included
in this Decree. As regards the matter of confirmation, the Decree merely says
that it is the chrism with which the candidate is signed. It does not mention
that this signing with chrism implies in itself an imposition of hand, as had been
explained by some earlier documents. Thus, for instance, in 1204 Innocent III had
written:"By the chrismation of the forehead is signified the imposition of hand
which is also called confirmation[...]"(DS 785; see also Innocent IV(DS 831).*

1412   Among all the sacraments holy baptism holds the first
1314   place because it is the gateway to the spiritual life; by it
        we are made members of Christ and belong to his body,
the Church. And since through the first man death has entered
into all [cf Rom 5:12], unless we are born again of water and the
Spirit we cannot, as the Truth said, enter into the Kingdom of
heaven [cf. Jn 3:5].

1413   The matter of this sacrament is true natural water; it
1314   does not matter whether it is cold or warm. The form is:
        "I baptise you in the name of the Father and of the Son
and of the Holy Spirit." We do not deny, however, that true
baptism is also effected by these words: "May the servant of
Christ, N., be baptised in the name of the Father and of the Son
and of the Holy Spirit", or: "By my hands N. is baptised in the
name of the Father and of the Son and of the Holy Spirit." For
as the principal cause from which baptism derives its virtue is
the Holy Trinity, while the instrumental cause is the minister
who confers the sacrament externally, the sacrament is performed
whenever the act carried out by the minister is expressed along
with the invocation of the Holy Trinity.

1414   The minister of this sacrament is the priest, to whom by
1315   reason of his office it belongs to baptise. But in case of
        necessity not only priests or deacons, but also laymen
or laywomen, or even pagans and heretics may baptise, provided
they observe the Church's form and intend to do what the
Church does.

1415   The effect of this sacrament is the remission of all guilt,
1316   original and actual, and also of all punishment due to
        the guilt itself. For this reason, no satisfaction is to be
enjoined on the baptised for their past sins; and if they die before
committing any fault, they immediately gain access to the
Kingdom of heaven and the beatific vision.

1416   The second sacrament is confirmation. Its matter is
1317   chrism made from oil, signifying the purity of
        conscience, and balsam, signifying the fragrance of a
good reputation; it is blessed by the bishop. The form is: "I sign
you with the sign of the cross and I confirm you with the chirsm
of salvation, in the name of the Father and of the Son and of the
Holy Spirit."

1417 The ordinary minister is the bishop. Whereas other
1318 anointings may be performed by a simple priest, this
one must only be conferred by the bishop. For we read
that only the apostles, whose place the bishops hold, imparted
the Holy Spirit by the laying on of hand. Reading the Acts of
the Apostles makes this clear, for it is said: "Now when the
apostles at Jersualem heard that Samaria had received the word
of God, they sent to them Peter and John, who came down and
prayed for them that they might receive the Holy Spirit; for it
had not yet fallen on any of them, but they had only been
baptised in the name of the Lord Jesus. Then they laid their hands
on them and they received the Holy Spirit" [Acts 8:14-17].
Confirmation given by the Church takes the place of that
imposition of hand. Nevertheless, we read that sometimes
through a dispensation of the apsotolic See for a reasonable and
very urgent cause a simple priest has administered the sacrament
of confirmation with chrism prepared by the bishop.

1418 The effect of this sacrament is that in it the Holy Spirit
1319 is given for strength, as he was given to the apostles on
the day of Pentecost, in order that Christians may
courageously confess the name of Christ. And, therefore, those
to be confirmed are anointed on the forehead which is the seat
of shame, so that they may not be ashamed to confess the name
of Christ, and chiefly his cross, which, according to the apostle,
is a stumbling block for the Jews and foolishness for the Gentiles
[cf. 1 Cor 1:23]. This is why they are signed with the sign of the
cross.

DECREE FOR THE COPTS (1442)

*For this document see nn. 809i and 1003i. The scope of the Decree is
limited. It states the objective order of salvation through the Church without
considering how those outside can subjectively be saved. A fortiori where infants
are concerned, it does not consider any other means of salvation than the
objective means of sacramental baptism. Only later theology will consider the
possibility of a baptism of desire in infants. For adults this possibility had
already been recognised in documents previous to this (cf n.1408); its
application to children who have not reached the age of reason is a more recent
development and remains even today the object of theological reflection.*

(The necessity of baptism of children)

1419 With regard to children, on account of the danger of

1349   death which can often occur, since no other remedy
         can help them than the sacrament of baptism by which
they are snatched away from the devil's dominion and made the
adopted children of God, [the Church] warns that holy baptism
should not be delayed for forty or eighty days or for some other
length of time according to the custom observed by some; but it
must be conferred as soon as can suitably be done, with the
provision that if the peril of death is imminent, the children be
baptised at once without any delay even if no priest is available,
by a layman or a laywoman, in the form of the Church as is more
fully explained in the decree for the Armenians [cf. n. 1414].

THE GENERAL COUNCIL OF TRENT
SEVENTH SESSION
CANONS ON THE SACRAMENT OF BAPTISM (1547)

*Trent contains no doctrinal chapter on the sacrament of baptism, as it
merely intended to condemn the heresies that had become widespread.
Nevertheless, these canons are of decisive importance for the Catholic doctrine
of baptism.*

*Canon 1 affirms the difference between the baptism of John and that of
Christ against an error of Melanchton. Canon 2 deals with the matter of
baptism. Canon 3 affirms the truth of the Catholic doctrine of baptism against
the Anabaptists and Luther. Canon 4 on the minister and form of baptism
contains the final definition of a doctrine which had been firmly held for
centuries. The validity of baptism conferred by heretics had been affirmed from
the earliest times (cf.n.1401); it was considered as proving that the efficacy of
the sacrament does not depend on the faith or worthiness of the minister but
on the proper carrying out of Christ's command. Canon 5 affirms the necessity
of baptism against the Manichaens and Messalians. Canons 6 to 10 reject
conclusions wrongly derived by the Reformers from the doctrine of baptism,
which had been partly dealt with in the decree and canons on justification (cf
nn. 1934, 1968-1970). Canon 6 is directed against Luther's opinion that the
only sin whereby a human being loses justification is unbelief (cf nn.1945,
1977). Canons 11 to 13 are directed against the Anabaptists. Canon 14 opposes
the "liberal" opinions of Erasmus and Bucer.*

1420   1. If anyone says that the baptism of John had the same
1614   force as the baptism of Christ, *anathema sit.*

1421   2. If anyone says that true and natural water is not
1615   necessary for baptism and therefore reduces to some sort
            of metaphor the words of our Lord Jesus Christ: "Unless
one is born of water and the Spirit" [Jn 3:5], *anathema sit.*

1422   3. If anyone says that the Roman Church (the mother
1616   and teacher of all Churches) does not have the true
      doctrine concerning the sacrament of baptism, *anathema*
sit.

1423   4. If anyone says that baptism, even that given by
1617   heretics in the name of the Father and of the Son and of
      the Holy Spirit, with the intention of doing what the
Church does, is not true baptism, *anathema sit.*

1424   5. If anyone says that baptism is optional, that is, not
1618   necessary for salvation, *anathema sit [cf. n. 1928].*

1425   6. If anyone says that the baptised cannot lose grace,
1619   even if they wish to, no matter how much they sin, unless
      they are unwilling to believe, *anathema sit [cf. n. 1945].*

1426   7. If anyone says that those baptised are by the fact
1620   of their baptism obliged merely to faith alone. but
      not to the observance of the whole law of Christ,
      anathema sit.

1427   8. If anyone says that those baptised are free from all
1621   the precepts of holy Church, whether written or handed
      down, so that they are not bound to observe them unless,
of their own accord, they wish to submit to them, *anathema sit.*

1428   9. If anyone says that the remembrance of the baptism
1622   which they have received ought to be so impressed on
      human beings that they be brought to understand that all
vows taken after baptism are void in virtue of the promise
already made in baptism itself, as if those vows detracted from
the faith which they have professed and from baptism itself,
anathema sit.

1429   10. If anyone says that all sins committed after baptism
1623   are either remitted or made venial by the mere
      remembrance of, and faith in, the baptism once received,
anathema sit.

1430   11. If anyone says that for those who have denied the
1624   faith of Christ before infidels, baptism truly and rightly
      conferred must be repeated when they are converted to
repentance, *anathema sit.*

1431   12 If anyone says that no one is to be baptised except
1625   at the age at which Christ was baptised, or on the point
of death, *anathema sit.*

1432   13. If anyone says that because little children do not
1626   have actual faith, they are not to be numbered among
the faithful after receiving baptism, and that, for
this reason, they are to be re-baptised when they have reached
the age of discretion; or that it is better to omit their baptism
rather than to baptise them solely in the faith of the Church
while they do not believe by an act of their own, *anathema sit.*

1433   14. If anyone says that when the little children thus
1627   baptised have grown up, they are to be asked whether
they wish to ratify what their sponsors promised in their
name when they were baptised; and if they answer that they are
unwilling, they are to be left to their own judgment; and if one
says that they are not meanwhile to be forced to a Christian life
by any penalty other than the exclusion from receiving the
Eucharist and the other sacraments until they repent, *anathema
sit.*

CANONS ON THE SACRAMENT OF CONFIRMATION
(1547)

*The specific teaching of the Council of Trent on the sacrament of
confirmation is limited to the following three canons which, mainly in
opposition to Luther, Melanchton and Calvin, affirm that confirmation is a
true sacrament. Its institution by Christ and the sacramental character it
confers had already been taught in the general doctrine on the sacraments
(cf.nn.1311,1319). The Augsburg Confession considered confirmation as
instituted by the apostles. As regards its meaning, Melanchton in particular
reduced it to a solemn confession of belief; Canon 1 is directed against this
opinion. Canon 3 lays down that the ordinary minister of confirmation is the
bishop, but does not disavow the practice of the Greeks among whom the
sacrament is usually administered by priests.*

1434   1. If anyone says that the confirmation of those baptised
1628   is a useless ceremony and not a true and proper
sacrament; or that of old it was nothing more than a
sort of catechesis in which those nearing adolescence gave an
account of their faith before the Church, *anathema sit.*

1435   2. If anyone says that those who ascribe any power to

1629   the sacred chrism of confirmation are offending the Holy
          Spirit, *anathema sit.*

1436   3. If anyone says that the ordinary minister of holy
1630   confirmation is not the bishop but any simple priest,
           anathema sit.

PIUS X

DECREE *LAMENTABILI* OF THE HOLY OFFICE (1907)
ARTICLES OF MODERNISM CONDEMNED

*On this document see n. 143i. The articles of Modernism mentioned here
were part of their attempt to explain the contents of the Catholic faith and, in
particular, the origin and development of the doctrine of the sacraments (cf. n.
1327) as a natural development of the religious life of the Christian community.
To this evolution were assigned the idea of the necessity of baptism, the
distinction between baptism and penance on the one hand, and baptism and
confirmation on the other,*

[1437/42]   The Christian community introduced the necessity
3442   of baptism by adopting it as a necessary rite and
                attaching to it the obligation of Christian profession.

[1437/43]   The custom of conferring baptism on infants was a
3443   disciplinary evolution which was one of the reasons
                why the sacrament became divided into two,
baptism and penance.

(1437/44)   There is no proof that the rite of the sacrament of
3444   confirmation was used by the apostles; the formal
                distinction of the two sacraments, baptism and
confirmation, has nothing to do with the history of primitive
Christianity.

PIUS XII

DECREE *SPIRITUS SANCTI MUNERA* ON THE MINISTER
OF CONFIRMATION (1946)

(1438)   *By this decree, dated 14 September, 1946, the Pope grants to some
             categories of priests a general indult empowering them to confer as
extraordinary ministers the sacrament of confirmation to the faithful in their
territories who, due to serious illness, are in danger of death, provided that no
bishop is available. The list of priests to whom the indult is given includes
parish priests to whom is entrusted the stable care of souls in territories not yet*

erected as parishes. The text is found in AAS 38 (1946) (349-358). This is the first step, followed by others, in the extension of the faculty to confirm to priests of the Latin Church. The latest legislation on the subject is found in the Apostolic Constitution Divinae Consortium Naturae *of Pope Paul VI, dated August 15, 1971 (cf. AAS 63 (1971) 657ff). While the bishop remains the ordinary minister* (minister originarius)*, priests who in virtue of their office (parish priests,...) baptise adults or children of "catechetical age" or receive baptised persons into the Church, may confirm them; thus the connection between baptism and confirmation becomes more apparent. In case of danger of death any priest may confirm if neither bishop nor priest in charge is available.*

THE SECOND VATICAN GENERAL COUNCIL

The Council mentions several times the intrinsic connection between baptism, confirmation and the Eucharist, as constituting together the full initiation into the Christian life (cf.LG 11; AA 3) which is a share in the Paschal mystery (AG 14). The renewal of the baptismal promises just before confirmation and the celebration of confirmation within the Mass, are destined to make this connection apparent (cf. SC 71). The link between baptism and confirmation is particulary evident from the fact that both assign the Christian to the apostolate (LG 33; AA 3; cf AG 11): yet, the two sacraments remain distinct.

Through baptism, human beings enter the Church (LG 14), Christ's mystical Body (SC 6; AA 3); being plunged into Christ's Paschal mystery (SC 6; AG 14) which makes them children of God (LG 40; SC 6, 10) and of the Church (LG 64). Freed from the power of darkness (AG 14; SC 6), they are reborn to a new life (LG 64; UR 22; AG 15, 21); consecrated as members of the kingdom of priests (cf. 1 Pet 2:9), they are enabled by their baptismal character (LG 11) to offer spiritual sacrifices (AA 3) and to participate in the Church's liturgical life (SC 14; cf. LG 10,11). Finally their being members of the People of God through baptism already requires from them that they bear witness to their faith and participate in the Church's salvific mission (LG 33; AA3; cf AG, 11, 36). As to the profession of the evangelical counsels in the religious life, it is deeply rooted in baptism; its special consecration expresses the baptismal consecration in its fulness (PC 5; cf. LG 44).

The Council rejoices at the "sacramental bond of unity" which baptism establishes among all Christians (UR 22), even though communion with the Catholic Church remains imperfect for those belonging to other Churches (UR 3). Through baptism as through a door human beings enter the Church (AG 7) which, as the "universal sacrament of salvation" (LG 48) making Christ present to them, is necessary for salvation (LG 14;) this is why missionary activity seeks to incorporate into Christ through baptism those who have come to recognise him as their Saviour (AG 7).

The Council's description of the effect of confirmation lays stress on a special gift of the Holy Spirit ordained to the Christian witness in word and deed (AA 3; LG 10, 11). The participation of the laity in the Church's mission *was one of the Council's important themes (cf. LG 30ff; AA). It is based on the two sacraments of baptism and confirmation which together constitute the foundation of the common priesthood of the people of God (LG 11).*

The Council reaffirms that the bishop is the ordinary minister of confirmation (LG 26). But it also decrees that in Catholic Eastern Churches the discipline allowing priests to confer the sacrament with holy chrism blessed by the patriarch or bishop will be fully restored (OE 13).

DOGMATIC CONSTITUTION *LUMEN GENTIUM* (1964)

(The common priesthood founded on baptism and confirmation)

1439 11. The sacred and organic nature of the priestly community enters into operation through the sacraments and the practice of virtues. Through baptism, the faithful are incorporated into the Church and receive a character that destines them to the worship of the Christian religion; they are reborn as children of God and, as such, they are in duty bound to profess before others the faith they have received from God through the Church. Through the sacrament of confirmation, they are bound more perfectly to the Church; they are endowed with special strength of the Holy Spirit, and are thus more strictly obliged, as true witnesses of Christ, to spread and defend the faith by word and by deed.[...]

DECREE *UNITATIS REDINTEGRATIO* (1964)

(Baptism as the beginning of acquiring fulness of life in Christ)

1439a 22. Baptism constitutes the sacramental bond of unity existing among all who through it are reborn. But baptism, of itself, is only a beginning, a point of departure, for it is wholly directed toward the acquiring of fulness of life in Chirst. Baptism is thus ordained toward a complete profession of faith, a complete incorporation into the system of salvation such as Christ himself willed it to be, and finally, toward a complete integration into eucharistic communion.

PASTORAL CONSTITUTION *GAUDIUM ET SPES* (1965)

(The baptised and confirmed are to live by the paschal mystery through resisting evil and being strengthened by hope)

1439b 22. Christians are certainly bound both by need and duty to struggle with evil through many afflictions and to suffer death; but as those who have been made partners in the paschal mystery, and have been configured to the death of Christ, they will go forward strengthened by hope, to the resurrection [cf. Phil 3:10; Rom 8:17].

DECREE *AD GENTES* (1965)

(The obligation of the baptised to manifest their new existence, and of the confirmed to give witness to the power of the Spirit)

1439c   11. The Church must be present to these [non-Christian] groups through those of its members who live among them or have been sent to them. All Christians by the example of their lives and the witness of the word, wherever they live, have an obligation to manifest the new existence *(novum hominem)* which they put on in baptism, and to reveal the power of the Holy Spirit by whom they were strengthened at confirmation, so that others, seeing their good works, might glorify the Father [cf. Mt 5:16] and more perfectly perceive the true meaning of human life and the universal solidarity of humankind.[...] They should be familiar with their national and religious traditions and uncover with gladness and respect those seeds of the Word which lie hidden among them.

(The catechumenate as formation in the communal and apostolic life of the Church)

1439d   14. Those who have received from God the gift of faith in Christ, through the Church [LG 17], should be admitted with liturgical rites to the catechumenate which is not a mere exposition of dogmatic truths and norms of morality, but a period of formation in the whole Christian life, and apprenticeship of sufficient duration, during which the disciples will be joined to Christ their teacher. The catechumens should be properly initiated into the mystery of salvation and the practice of the evangelical virtues, and they should be introduced into the life of faith, liturgy and charity of the People of God by successive sacred rites [SC 64-65].

[...] This Christian initiation, which takes place during the catechumenate, should not be left entirely to the priests and catechists, but should be the concern of the whole Christian community, especially of the sponsors, so that from the beginning the catechumens will feel that they belong to the People of God. Since the life of the Church is apostolic, the catechumens must learn to cooperate actively in the building up of the Church and in its work of evangelization, both by the example of their lives and the profession of their faith.

DECREE *PRESBYTERORUM ORDINIS* (1965)

(The baptised and the confirmed are to attain Christian maturity by serving others through charity)

1439e 6. It is the priests' part as instructors of the people in the faith to see to it either personally or through others that all the faithful shall be led in the Holy Spirit to the full development of their own vocation in accordance with the Gospel teaching, and to sincere and active charity and the liberty with which Christ has set us free *[cf. Gal 4:3; 5:1, 13]*. Very little good will be achieved by ceremonies however beautiful, or societies however flourishing, if they are not directed towards educating people to reach Christian maturity.[...] Christians must also be trained so as not to live only for themselves. Rather, according to the demands of the new law of charity, all as they have received grace ought to minister to the others *[cf.1 Pet 4;10ff]*, and in this way all should carry out their duties in a Christian way in the community of other human beings.

DECREE *APOSTOLICAM ACTUOSITATEM* (1965)

(Foundations of the apostolate of the laity)

1439f 3. The laity derive the duty and the right to the apostolate from their very union with Christ the Head. Incorporated into the mystical Body of Christ by baptism, and strengthened by the power of the Holy Spirit in confirmation, they are assigned to the apostolate by the Lord himself. They are consecrated to form a kingdom of priests and a holy people *[cf. 1Pet 2:4-10]*, so that by all their actions they may offer spiritual sacrifices and bear witness to Christ throughout the world.[...]

(The faithful are to view the search for social justice as prior to the practice of charity)

1440 8. If the exercise of charity is to be above all criticism, and seen to be so, all should see in their neighbours the image of God to which they have been created, and Christ the Lord to whom is really offered all that is given to the needy.The liberty and dignity of the persons helped must be respected with the greatest sensitivity. Purity of intention should not be stained by any self-seeking or desire to dominate. The demands of justice must first of all be satisfied; that which is already due in justice is not to be offered as a gift of charity. The cause of evils, and not merely their effect ought to disappear. The aid contributed should be organized in such a way that beneficiaries are gradually freed from their dependence on others and become self-supporting.

PAUL VI

DIRECTORY CONCERNING ECUMENICAL MATTERS, PART I, *AD TOTAM ECCLESIAM* (14 May, 1967)

The Secretariat for Promoting Christian Unity, created by John XXIII in 1960, issued a set of norms for the implementation of the Vatican II decision regarding ecumenism. The document was published with the approval and authority of Paul VI (cf. AAS 59 (1967) 574 -592 and 62 (1970) (705-724). The following doctrinal and pastoral teachings regarding the sacrament of baptism are found in the first part of the document.

(Validity of all Christians' baptism)

1440a 11. Baptism is[...]the sacramental bond of unity, indeed the foundation of communion among all Christians. Hence its dignity and the manner of administering it are matters of great importance to all Christ's disciples. Yet a just evaluation of the sacrament and the mutual recognition of each other's baptism by different communities is sometimes hindered because of a reasonable doubt about the baptism conferred in some particular case. To avoid difficulties which may arise when some Christians separated from us, led by the grace of the Holy Spirit and by their conscience, seek full communion with the Catholic Church, the following guiding principles are put forward.

12. There can be no doubt cast upon the validity of baptism as conferred among separated Eastern Christians. It is enough therefore to establish the fact that baptism was administered.[...]

13. In respect of other Christians a doubt can sometimes arise:

(a) Concerning *matter and form*. Baptism by immersion, pouring or sprinkling, together with the Trinitarian formula, is of itself valid. Therefore if the rituals and liturgical books or established customs of a Church or Community prescribe one of these ways of baptising, doubt can only arise if it happens that the minister does not observe the regulations of his own Community or Church. What is necessary and sufficient, therefore, is evidence that the ministers of baptism were faithful to the norms of their own Community or Church. For this purpose generally one should obtain a written baptismal certificate with the name of the minister. It will normally be possible to request the other community to cooperate in establishing whether or not in general or in a particular case, a minister is to be considered as having baptised according to the approved ritual.

(b) Concerning *faith and intention.* Because some consider that insufficiency of faith or intention in a minister can create a doubt about baptism, these points should be noted:

— The minister's insufficient faith never of itself makes baptism invalid.

— Sufficient intention in baptising ministers is to be presumed unless there is serious ground for doubting that they intend to do what Christians do.

(c) Concerning the *application of matter.* Where doubt arises about the application of matter, both reverence for the sacrament and respect for the ecclesial nature of the other communities demand that a serious investigation of the Community's practice and of the circumstances of the particular baptism be made before any judgment is passed on the validity of a baptism by reason of its manner of administration.

(Baptism is not to be repeated)

1440b 14. Indiscriminate conditional baptism of all who desire full communion with the Catholic Church cannot be approved. The sacrament of baptism cannot be repeated, and therefore to baptize again conditionally is not allowed unless there is prudent doubt of the fact, or of the validity, of a baptism already administered [*cf. n. 1423*].

CONGREGATION FOR DIVINE WORSHIP

ORDO BAPTISMI PARVULORUM

(15 May 1969/1973 *(editio typica altera)*)

(1440c) *Following the directives of Vatican II's* Sacrosanctum Concilium—Constitution on the Liturgy, *art. 67-69, to revise the*

rite of baptism for children, this new liturgical book (1973 second edition),
Rite of Baptism for Children, *includes the general doctrinal introduction to
Christian initiation, the introduction for baptism of children, as well as the
various forms of the baptismal rites for diverse situations.*

APOSTOLIC CONSTITUTION *DIVINAE CONSORTIUM NATURAE* (1971)

*In this Apostolic Constitution the Pope determines the essential rite of
the sacrament of confirmation and approves the revised rite of confirmation,
Ordo Confirmationis (22 August, 1971) prepared by the S. Congregation
for Divine Worship. The sacrament is conferred by the anointing with chrism
(which implies a laying on of hand) and the accompanying words.
The traditional 'form' is replaced by the Byzantine formula, more expressive of
the meaning of the sacrament. More important than the determination of the
rite is the statement of the meaning of the sacrament which no previous
document had ever expressed with the same clarity. Christ himself in his
baptism at the Jordan was anointed with the Holy Spirit for the exercise of his
public ministry (cf. Mk 1:10); this was a prophetic anointing (cf. Lk 4:17-21).
Similarly, Christ promised to the apostles that the Spirit would come upon
them in order that they might be his witnesses (cf. Jn 15:26-27; Acts 1:8).
This promise was realised at Pentecost (Acts 2). The Pentecostal gift of
the Spirit is ordained to the mission, common to all Christians, to be witnesses
to Christ. As in the apostolic Church the gift of the Spirit was communicated
to the neophytes by a laying on of hand, so it is now through the sacrament
of confirmation "which in a certain way perpetuates in the Church the
grace of Pentecost". On these premises the Pope explains what he calls "the
specific significance of confirmation." The text is found in AAS 63 (1971)
657ff.*

(The specific significance of confirmation)

1441   [...]In baptism, neophytes receive forgiveness of sins and
adoption as children of God as well as the character of
Christ whereby they are made members of the Church and given
first sharing in the priesthood of their Saviour *[cf. 1 Pet 2:2-9].*
Through the sacrament of confirmation, those who have been
born anew in baptism receive the ineffable gift, the Holy Spirit
himself, by which "they are endowed with special strength" and
by the character of this sacrament "are bound more perfectly to
the church" *[cf. n. 1439],* and "are more strictly obliged, as true
witnesses of Christ, to spread and defend the faith by word and
by deed" *[cf. n 1439].[...]*

(The essential rite)

1442   The sacrament of confirmation is conferred through the anointing with chrism on the forehead, which is done by the laying on of hand, and through the words: "Receive the seal of the gift of the Holy Spirit" *(Accipe signaculum doni Spiritus Sancti)*.

CONGREGATION FOR DIVINE WORSHIP

ORDO INITIATIONIS CHRISTIANAE ADULTORUM
(6 January, 1972/1974 (editio emendata))

(1442a)   *According to arts. 64-66 of the Constitution on the Liturgy, a new* Rite of Christian Initiation of Adults *was promulgated. This new ritual contains a doctrinal introduction as well as the rites for the various stages of adult Christian initiation.*

JOHN PAUL II

INSTRUCTION ON INFANT BAPTISM *PASTORALIS ACTIO* OF THE S. CONGREGATION FOR THE DOCTRINE OF THE FAITH (20 October, 1980)

With the approval of Pope John Paul II, the S. Congregation for the Doctrine of the Faith issued an instruction on infant Baptism. The practice of infant baptism appears more problematic in the present pluralistic society. The Instruction first reviews the practice of baptising infants in the data of early tradition, stating that "both in the East and in the West the practice of baptising infants is considered a rule of immemorial tradition" (4). It goes on to reaffirm the validity and normativeness of the traditional practice, bringing out its theological meaning. But it also gives important pastoral guidelines to protect the practice from possible abuses. The text is found in AAS 72 (1980) 1137-1156.

(Theological meaning of infant baptism)

1443   9. Baptism is a manifestation of the Father's prevenient love, a sharing in the Son's paschal Mystery, and a communication of new life in the Spirit; it brings people into the inheritance of God and joins them to the Body of Christ, the Church.

10. In view of this, Christ's warning in St. John's Gospel, "Unless one is born of water and the Spirit, one cannot enter the kingdom of God" *[Jn 3:5]*, must be taken as an invitation of universal and limitless love, the words of a Father calling all his children and wishing them to have the greatest of blessings. This

pressing and irrevocable call cannot leave us indifferent or neutral, since its acceptance is a condition for achieving our destiny.[...]

12. This is how the Church has understood its mission from the beginning, and not only with regard to adults. It has always understood the words of Jesus to Nicodemus to mean that children should not be deprived of baptism. Jesus' words are so universal and absolute in form that the fathers employed them to establish the necessity of baptism, and the magisterium applied them expressly to infants: the sacrament is for them too the entry into the People of God and the gateway to personal salvation.

(Infants baptised in the faith of the Church)

1444 14. The fact that infants cannot yet profess personal faith does not prevent the Church from conferring this sacrament on them, since in reality it is in its own faith that it baptises them. This point of doctrine was clearly defined by St. Augustine: "When children are presented to be given spiritual grace", he wrote, "it is not so much those holding them in their arms who present them—although, if they are good Christians they also present the children—as the whole company of saints and faithful Christians.[...] It is done by the whole of Mother Church which is in the saints, since it is as a whole that she gives birth to each and every one of them."[1] This teaching is repeated by Saint Thomas Aquinas and all subsequent theologians: the children who are baptised believe not on their own account, by a personal act, but through others, "through the Church's faith communicated to them".[2] This same teaching is also expressed in the new Rite of Baptism, when the celebrant asks the parents and godparents to profess the faith of the Church, the faith in which the children are baptised.[3]

(Limits to infant baptism)

1445 15. Although the Church is truly aware of the efficacy of its faith operating in the baptism of children, and aware of the validity of the sacrament that it confers on them, it recognises limits to its practice, since, apart from cases of danger

---

1. *Epist.* 98, 5: *PL* 33, 362; cf. *Sermo* 176, 2, 2: *PL* 38, 950.
2. *Summa Theologiae,* III, q. 69, a.6, ad 3; cf. q. 68, a. 9, ad 3.
3. *Ordo baptismi parvulorum,* Praenotanda, 2; cf. 56.

of death, it does not admit children to baptism without their parents' consent and serious assurance that after baptism they will be given a Catholic upbringing. This is because it is concerned both for the natural rights of the parents and for the requirements of the development of faith in the children.

(Practical guidelines for infant baptism)

1446   28. It is important to recall that the baptism of infants must be considered a serious duty. The questions which it poses to pastors can be settled only by faithful attention to the teaching and the constant practice of the Church. Concretely, pastoral practice regarding infant baptism must be governed by two great principles, the second of which is subordinate to the first:

1) Baptism, which is necessary for salvation, is the sign and the means of God's prevenient love, which frees us from original sin and communicates to us a share in divine life. Considered in itself, the gift of these blessings to infants must not be delayed.

2) Assurances must be given that the gift thus granted can grow by an authentic education in the faith and Christian life, in order to fulfil the true meaning of the sacrament. As a rule, these assurances are to be given by the parents or close relatives, although various substitutions are possible within the Christian community. But if these assurances are not really serious there can be grounds for delaying the sacrament; and if they are certainly non-existent the sacrament should be refused.

ENCYCLICAL LETTER *SOLLICITUDO REI SOCIALIS*
(30 December 1987)

At the conclusion of this encyclical on the social concern of the Church, explicit reference is made to the sacrament of baptism and to the commitment, which is inherent in baptismal grace, to carry out the messianic programme initiated by Jesus among oppressed people. The following text manifests the truly noteworthy convergence, gradually promoted by the Magisterium in the twentieth century, between the dogmatic affirmations and the social teaching of the Church. As witnesses and agents of peace and justice in their culture, the baptised manifest the power of sanctifying grace to illumine the mind and to strengthen the will regarding the obligation to denounce social evil and to foster human progress. The text is found in Origins 17 (1987-1988) 658.

(Christians as witnesses and agents of peace and justice)

1446a 47. In this commitment [solidarity with and love of the poor], the sons and daughters of the Church must serve as examples and guides, for they are called upon, in conformity with the program announed by Jesus himself in the synagogue at Nazareth, to "preach good news to the poor[...], to proclaim release to the captives and recovery of sight to the blind, to set at liberty those who are oppressed, to proclaim the acceptable year of the Lord" *[Lk 4:18-19]*. It is appropriate to emphasize the preeminent role that belongs to the laity, both men and women, to animate temporal realities with Christian commitment, by which they show that they are witnesses and agents of peace and justice.

APOSTOLIC LETTER *EUNTES IN MUNDUM UNIVERSUM* ON THE OCCASION OF THE MILLENNIUM OF THE BAPTISM OF KIEVAN RUS' (25 January, 1988)

The Pope wishes to associate himself with the Russian Orthodox Church in the celebration of its millennium. In his Apostolic Letter he offers a reflection on the meaning of baptism based on Scripture and the Eastern liturgy. Later in the letter he explains the relation between the baptism of Kievan Rus' and the emergence of the Byzantine-Slav form of Christianity and culture. The text is found in AAS 80 (1988) 935-956.

(The meaning of baptism)

1447 1.[...] We wish first of all to concentrate our attention upon the saving mystery of baptism itself. This is—as Christ the Lord teaches—the sacrament of rebirth "of water and the Spirit" *[Jn 3:5]*, which introduces the candidates, made adopted children of God, into the eternal Kingdom. Saint Paul speaks of baptism "into the death" of the Redeemer in order to "rise again" together with him to a new life in God *[cf. Rom 6:4]*. Thus the Eastern Slav people who lived in the great principality of Kievan Rus' extending up to Novgorod descended into the water of holy baptism and entrusted themselves—when the fulness of time came for them *[cf. Gal 4:4]*— to the saving plan of God. The news of the "great works of God" reached them, therefore, and, just as once at Jerusalem, Pentecost shone for them too *[cf. Acts 2:37-39]*. Immersing themselves in the water of baptism, they experienced "the bath of rebirth".

How eloquent, in the Byzantine Rite, is the ancient prayer for the blessing of the baptismal water, which Oriental theology likes to identify with the waters of the Jordan, in which the Redeemer of humanity entered, in order to receive the baptism of repentance, in the same way as the people of Judea and Jerusalem [cf. Mk 1:5]: "Grant to it[...] the blessing of the Jordan; make it a spring of incorruptibility, the gift of holiness, absolution of sins.[...] You, Lord of all things, show it to be the water of redemption, the water of sanctification, expiation of the body and of the spirit, liberation from bonds, remission of faults, enlightenment of souls, the washing of regeneration, renewal in the Spirit, the grace of adoption, the garment of incorruptibility, and fount of life.[...] Show yourself, O Lord, also in this water and transform those who are to be baptized in it, that they may put aside the old nature[...] and put on the new humanity, renewed according to the image of him who created it; so that, made completely one with him through baptism in the likeness of his death, they may become sharers in his resurrection; and having preserved the gift of your Holy Spirit[...], they may be enabled to receive the reward of the heavenly calling and may be included among the first-born who are recorded in heaven."[1]

Those who were far away have found themselves immersed, through baptism, into that cycle of life, in which the most Holy Trinity—Father, Son and Holy Spirit—gives itself to us and creates in us a new heart, freed from sin and capable of filial obedience to the eternal design of love. At the same time those people and their individual members entered into the great family of the Church, in which they can celebrate the Holy Eucharist, listen to the word of God and bear witness to it, live in Christian love and share in the mutual exchange of spiritual goods. This was symbolically expressed by the ancient rites of holy baptism when the newly baptised, clad in white robes, went in procession from the baptistry to the assembly of the faithful gathered in the cathedral. This procession was at once a liturgical entrance and the symbol of the Body of Christ.

---

1. Prayer for the blessing of baptismal water, the most ancient testimony of which is found in the Codex Vaticanus Barberino Graeco 336, p. 201.

APOSTOLIC EXHORTATION *CHRISTIFIDELES LAICI*
(30 January, 1989)

*This exhortation resumes the interventions made by the participants at
the 1987 Synod of Bishops on the Laity. The following text focuses on the
eschatological dimension of the pastoral activities to be undertaken by the
baptised and confirmed. Through the practice of justice and charity, the faithful
are constantly to show forth how the sacraments of Christian initiation urge
them to order creation according to the contours of the coming Kingdom. The
graces conferred by these sacraments enable Christians to share in the universal
mission of the risen Christ who leads all things to the Father. The text is
found in* Origins *18 (1988-1989) 567.*

*(The pastoral function of the baptised and confirmed as manifesting
the justice and charity of the Kingdom of God)*

1448   14. Because the lay faithful belong to Christ, Lord and
King of the universe, they share in his pastoral mission
and are called by him to spread the Kingdom in history. They
exercise this pastoral role as Christians, above all in the spiritual
combat in which they seek to overcome in themselves the
kingdom of sin *[cf. Rom 6:12]*, and thus to make a gift of
themselves so as to serve, in justice and charity, Jesus who is
himself present in all his brothers and sisters, above all in the
very least *[cf. Mt 25:40]*. But in particular, the lay faithful are
called to restore to creation all its original value. In ordering
creation to the authentic well-being of humanity in an activity
governed by the life of grace, they share in the exercise of the
power with which the risen Christ draws all things to himself
and subjects them along with himself to the Father, so that God
might be everything to everyone *[cf. 1 Cor 15:28; Jn 12:32]*. The
participation of the lay faithful in the threefold mission of Christ
as priest, prophet and pastor finds its source in the anointing of
baptism, its further development in confirmation, and its
realisation and dynamic sustenance in the holy Eucharist.

CONGREGATION FOR THE CLERGY AND SEVEN OTHER
VATICAN OFFICES
INSTRUCTION *ECCLESIAE EX MYSTERIO*
(15 August, 1997)

*While admitting that, through the sacraments of baptism and confirmation,
Christ himself grants all the faithful a proper share in the prophetic, sanctifying
and pastoral aspects of his priesthood, this instruction attests to the special*

ministry restricted to the clergy who have received the sacrament of orders. Collaboration with them, on the part both of the lay faithful and of lay members of institutes of consecrated life and societies of apostolic life, does not mean substitution for their unique ministry. The instruction consists in thirteen practical provisions (for example, regarding preaching, administering baptism, distributing communion, assisting at marriages, giving pastoral care to the sick, and leading funeral rites) which are based on the following theological principles: (1) the essential difference between the common priesthood of the faithful and the ministerial priesthood; (2) the unity and diversity of ministerial functions; and (3) the necessary collaboration of the nonordained faithful in pastoral ministry. The texts cited below are found in Origins 27 (1997-1998) 404; 405.

(On the homily at the eucharistic liturgy as reserved to the ordained)

1449 Article 3.1. The homily during the celebration of the holy eucharist must be reserved to the sacred minister, priest or deacon to the exclusion of the nonordained faithful, even if these should have responsibilities as "pastoral assistants" or catechists in whatever type of community or group. This exclusion is not based on the preaching ability of sacred ministers nor their theological preparation, but on that function which is reserved to them in virtue of having received the sacrament of holy orders. For the same reason, the diocesan bishop cannot validly dispense from the canonical norm since this is not merely a disciplinary law, but one which touches upon the closely connected functions of teaching and sanctifying. Similarly, the practice on some occasions of entrusting the preaching of the homily to seminarians or theology students who are not clerics is not permitted. Indeed, the homily should not be regarded as a training for some future ministry. All previous norms which may have admitted the nonordained faithful to preaching the homily during the holy eucharist are to be considered abrogated by Canon 767.1.

(Practical provisions regarding Sunday celebration in the absence of a priest)

1450 Article 7.1. In some places in the absence of priests or deacons, nonordained members of the faithful lead Sunday celebrations. In many instances, much good derives for the local community from this useful and delicate service when it is discharged in accordance with the spirit and the specific norms issued by the competent ecclesiastical authority. A special mandate of the bishop is necessary for the nonordained members of the faithful to lead such celebrations. This mandate should contain specific instructions with regard to the term of applicability, the place and conditions in which it is operative, as well as indicate the priest responsible for overseeing these celebrations.

Article 7.2. It must be clearly understood that such celebrations are temporary solutions, and the text used at them must be approved by the competent ecclesiastical authority. The practice of inserting into such celebrations elements proper to the holy Mass is prohibited. So as to avoid causing error in the minds of the faithful, the use of the eucharistic prayers even in a narrative form at such celebrations is forbidden. For the same reasons, it should be emphasised for the benefit of those participating that such celebrations cannot substitute for the eucharistic sacrifice and that the obligation to attend Mass on Sunday and holy days of obligation is satisfied only by attendance at holy Mass. In cases where distance or physical conditions are not an obstacle, every effort should be made to encourage and assist the faithful to fulfil this precept.

CHAPTER XV

THE EUCHARIST

The new Covenant between God and human beings has been sealed by the mystery of Christ's death and glorification. Summing up in himself the entire human race, Christ has once for all offered to the Father the sacrifice of atonement; in him humankind has been reunited to God. Accomplished once for all in time, the Paschal mystery remains sacramentally present to every successive generation of humankind in the mystery of the Eucharist. For, at the last Supper, Christ instituted the memorial of his death and resurrection and gave it to the Church to celebrate. The Eucharist is the Church's greatest treasure. It is the summit of its liturgy, the centre of its life, the source of its power, the visible sign on which its unity is built.

The Eucharist is at once sacrifice and meal: it perpetuates the sacrifice of Christ in the Church and makes its members share in the sacred banquet of his body and blood. For it contains Christ himself, who in it is present to the Church not merely by the power of his grace but in the reality of his glorified humanity. In this it surpasses all the other sacraments given by Christ to the Church.

Sacrifice, presence, meal: all three aspects of the eucharistic mystery are united by an indissoluble bond. But the truth of the sacrifice and of the banquet stands or falls with the reality of the presence; this is why the Church has always maintained its realism. During the first millennium of Christianity this faith remained tranquilly possessed. It is not suprising, however, that this aspect of the mystery, which the human mind can hardly conceive and words hardly express, gave rise to questions. Doubts called for a clear affirmation of the Church's faith by official documents. Besides the eucharistic presence, the Reformers also challenged the sacrificial value of the Eucharist, which they feared would detract from the uniqueness of Christ's sacrifice. The Church explained that the eucharistic sacrifice takes nothing away from the sacrifice accomplished once for all in history, for the one is entirely related to the other. The sacrifice of the Mass rather enhances the uniqueness of Christ's sacrifice than it detracts from it, for it perpetuates its memory and applies its power.

The eucharistic mystery is so rich in meaning as to defy comprehension. Historically conditioned as they often were, the Church's documents have at different times emphasised different aspects: these, however, must always be perceived within the totality of the mystery. In particular, the stress often laid on the eucharistic presence must not be allowed to obscure in the Christian consciousness its essential relation to that totality; there is no eucharistic presence which is not ordained to the eucharistic meal: "Take, eat; this is my body" (Mt 26:26). Similarly, the eucharistic meal is prepared only by the eucharistic sacrifice: "This is my body which is given up for you; do this as a memorial of me" (Lk 22:19).

In our own day the Church is seeking through its renewed eucharistic life to establish the balance between the various facets of the mystery. The Second Vatican Council has contributed to such a balance. Better than previous documents it has also shown the intrinsic relationship which exists between the mystery of the eucharist and the mystery of the Church. Furthermore, this eucharistic ecclesiology is viewed as the basis of a eucharistic style of life, by which Christians engage in sharing themselves, their talents and their resources with the most needy in society. Such self-giving love corresponds to the specific quality of eucharistic grace as a participation in the kenotic thoughts, feelings and actions of Jesus in the Cenacle and on Calvary. The union of Christians with the sacrifice of Jesus is thus not so much an interior attitude as a public stance, whereby Christians adhere to the words of Jesus concerning the hungry: "They need not go away; you give them something to eat" (Mt 14: 16; cf. Mt 25:35, 42). The social dimension of eucharistic grace is a pronounced theme in recent papal encyclicals, since the authenticity of Christians and their credibility at the present time are judged by their actions more than their words. The practico-social development of dogma regarding eucharistic grace corresponds quite well to the poignant comment of Jesus after having washed the feet of his disciples: "If you know these things, blessed are you if you do them" (Jn 13:17).

* * *

The main points of doctrine on the Eucharist can be grouped under the following headings:

The eucharistic mystery is the completion of the catechumenate and the centre of the Church's life: (1574i), 1574, 1576, 1576b, 1582.

Various aspects of the eucharistic celebration: 1575, 1576a, 1581, 1588-1589.

All, priests and laity together, play an active, though distinct, part in the whole celebration: 1576, 1583.

Eucharistic Sacrifice

The Mass is a true sacrifice instituted by Christ at the Last Supper: 34, 1546, 1555, 1592.

It perpetuates the memory of the sacrifice of the cross: 39/17, 655, 1546, 1558, 1566, (1574i), 1575, 1581, 1588.

Christ is the priest and the victim of the sacrifice: 21, 1546, 1548.

He offers himself in an unbloody manner through the priest acting in his name: 39/17, 655, 1546, 1548, 1556, 1566, (1567), 1570, 1572, 1734, 1740.

The faithful offer the sacrifice through the priest and with him: 1564, (1568), 1572, (1574i), 1576, 1735-1736, 1738, 1740.

The sacrifice of the Mass is offered to God in praise and thanksgiving, petition and propitiation: 34, 1546, 1548, 1549, 1555, 1557.

It is offered for the living and the dead: 34, 1548, 1557.

Every Mass, even celebrated privately, is the Mass of the Church: 1569.

Concelebration is the eminent manner of celebrating the Eucharist: 1584.

It requires that concelebrants say the words of consecration: 1573.

The determination of the rites of the Mass belongs to the Church's authority: 1550, (1551), (1553), 1554, 1560, 1561, (1574i).

Eucharistic Presence

Among the various modes of Christ's presence it is his presence par excellence: (1574i), 1578, 1585, 1588.

Christ himself, whole and entire, is substantially present under each species: 21, 34, 39/17, 1501, 1502, 1504, (1505), 1506, 1507/16f, 1510, 1513, 1516-1518, 1526, 1528, 1579.

This presence is realised by a complete change of the substance of bread and wine into the body and blood of Christ: 21, 28, 34, 39/17-18, 1501, (1505), 1510, 1519, 1527, 1571, 1577, 1580.

This change is aptly called transubstantiation: 21, 28, 34, 39/18, 1502, (1505), 1519, 1527, 1571, 1577, 1580.

Of bread and wine only the appearances remain: 39/19, 1502.

Christ is present under the species even outside communion: 39/19, 1516, 1529.

Hence the sacred species deserve honour and adoration: 39/19, 1520, 1521, 1531, 1532.

The consecration is done by the ministerial priest: 21, 1504, (1505), 1510, 1546, 1556, 1572, 1703, 1707, 1714.

Eucharistic Meal

The Eucharist is a true sacrament instituted by Christ at the Last Supper: 28, 32, 1305, 1311, 1514, 1515.
Christ is received in the eucharistic banquet: 1533, 1575, 1576a, 1581.
The whole Christ is received under one species: 34, 1506, (1537-1539), 1541-1543.
Communion under both kinds shows forth better the sacramental sign: (1574i) 1581i.
Only the communion of the priest is required: 1552, 1563
Communion perfects the participation of the faithful in the Mass: 1552, 1570, (1574i), 1576, 1583.
The sacred banquet must be received worthily, which supposes the state of grace: 1209/1-3, 1511, 1522, 1523, 1536.
Little children are not bound to communion: (1540), 1544.

Eucharistic Worship

The worship due to the eucharist: 1520, 1524, 1531.
The reservation of the Blessed Sacrament: 1521, 1532.
Prayer before the Blessed Sacrament: 1586.
Eucharistic devotions: 1587.

Eucharistic Grace

The Eucharist is the sacrament of unity and love: 21, 1511, 1515, 1524, 1565, (1574i), 1575, 1576, 1576a.
It is also the sacrament of life, by which the life of grace is nourished: 1306, 1511, 1515, 1524, 1530.
The sacrament contains the whole spiritual good of the Church and is the source and summit of all evangelization: 1576b, 1593.
Eucharist and the coming of the Lord: 1595.
On Sunday precept: 1594
Social implications of participating in the broken bread and the poured out wine: 1576a, 1576c, 1580a, 1587a, 1590, 1591, 1592.
The perfect and mystical analogy between the presence of Christ in the Eucharist and in the poor: 1587a.
The pneumatological and eschatological dimensions of eucharistic grace: 1576a, 1592.

THE COUNCIL OF ROME
OATH OF BERENGAR OF TOURS (1079)

In the 11th century the "ontological symbolism" by which some of the Church Fathers had expressed their faith in the reality of the sacramental presence of Christ's body and blood in the Eucharist was no longer understood. The Church had recourse to other categories to express the same reality. Berengar (1005-1088), head of the school of St. Martin at Tours, was the first to deny the change of substance; he seemed to reduce the eucharistic presence to a dynamic presence of Christ, sign of our spiritual union with him. Repeatedly condemned, he also retracted more than once. A Council of Rome (1059) prescribed to him a profession of faith some formulations of which St. Thomas Aquinas himself (cf. S.T. III, 71, 7 ad 3m) will later consider as ultra-realistic (cf. DS 690). Another Council of Rome (1079), more sober in its wording, asked Berengar to subscribe to the following oath. The oath states that the eucharistic signs are no mere signs but Christ is present by a change of substance.

(On the eucharistic presence of Christ)

1501
700

I, Berengar, believe in my heart and confess with my lips that the bread and wine which are placed on the altar are, by the mystery of the sacred prayer and the words of the Redeemer, substantially changed into the true and proper and life-giving body and blood of Jesus Christ our Lord; and that, after consecration, they are Christ's true body, which was born of the virgin and hung on the cross, being offered for the salvation of the world, and which sits at the right hand of the Father; and Christ's true blood, which was poured forth from his side; not only by way of sign and by the power of the sacrament, but in their true nature and in the reality of their substance *(in proprietate naturae et veritate substantiae)*.[...]

INNOCENT III
LETTER *CUM MARTHAE CIRCA* TO JOHN,
FORMER ARCHBISHOP OF LYONS (1202)

Pope Innocent III had been consulted on the words of Christ at the Last Supper, and especially on the meaning and origin of the words "Mystery of faith" (mysterium fidei) which are found inserted in the institution narrative for the first time in the Gelasian sacramentary. Some had recourse to these words to support the interpretation according to which the eucharistic presence is a purely figurative one. The Pope, answering as a private theologian, seems wrongly to attribute these words to Christ himself. He nevertheless distinguishes well the faith of the Church in the change of substance from minimalist spiritualistic interpretations of Christ's presence in the Eucharist. The letter also reflects the clear terminology and the elaborate distinctions which contemporary scholasticism used in its theology of the eucharistic presence.

(On the sacramental form of the Eucharist)

1502   You have asked who has added to the words of the
782   formula used by Christ himself when he
           transubstantiated *(transubstantiavit)* the bread and wine
into his body and blood, the words which are found in the Canon
of the Mass generally used by the Church, but which none of
the evangelists has recorded. [...] Namely, in the Canon of the
Mass, we find the words "Mystery of faith" inserted into the
words of Christ.[...] Surely there are many words and deeds of
the Lord which have been omitted in the gospels; of these we
read that the apostles have supplemented them by their words
and expressed them in their actions.[...] But, in the words which
are the object of our inquiry, Brother, namely the words "Mystery
of faith", some have thought to find support for their error; they
say that in the sacrament of the altar it is not the reality of the
body and blood of Christ which is [there] but only an image, an
appearance, a symbol *(figura)*, since Scripture sometimes mentions
that what is received at the altar is sacrament, mystery, figure
(exemplum). These people fall into such error because they neither
understand correctly the testimony of the Scriptures nor receive
respectfully the divine sacraments, ignorant of both the Scriptures
and the power of God *[cf. Mt 22:29].*[...] Yet, the expression
"Mystery of faith" is used, because here what is believed differs
from what is seen, and what is seen differs from what is believed.
For what is seen is the appearance of bread and wine and what
is believed is the reality of the flesh and blood of Christ and the
power of unity and love.[...]

(On the elements of the Eucharist)

1503   We must, however, distinguish accurately between three
783   [elements] which in this sacrament are distinct; namely:
           the visible form, the reality of the body, and the spiritual
power. The form is of bread and wine; the reality is the flesh and
blood; the power is for unity and charity. The first is 'sacrament
and not reality'; the second is 'sacrament and reality'; the third is
'reality and not sacrament'. But, the first is the sacrament of a
twofold reality; the second is the sacrament of one [element] and

the reality of the other; the third is the reality of a twofold sacrament. Therefore, we believe that the apostles have received from Christ the words of the formula found in the Canon, and their successors have received them from the apostles.[...]

PROFESSION OF FAITH PRESCRIBED TO THE WALDENSIANS (1208)

After affirming in general the validity of sacraments administered by unworthy ministers (cf. n. 1301), the profession of faith prescribed by Pope Innocent III to the Waldensians treats the various sacraments successively. The sacraments of the Eucharist and of Order are considered together. The Waldensians are urged to profess the reality of the presence of Christ's body and blood in the Eucharist which only the ordained priest can consecrate.

(The Eucharist contains the true body and blood of Christ)

1504   [...]With sincere hearts, we firmly and unhesitatingly
794   believe and loyally affirm that after consecration the
             Sacrifice, that is, the bread and the wine are the true body and the true blood of our Lord Jesus Christ. And we believe that in the Sacrifice a good priest effects nothing more than a bad priest; because it is not by the merit of the one consecrating that the sacrifice is accomplished, but by the word of the Creator and by the power of the Holy Spirit.

(There follows the text mentioned under n. 1703)

THE FOURTH LATERAN GENERAL COUNCIL SYMBOL OF LATERAN (1215)

(1505) *In its ecclesiology which is centred on the sacraments of the Church the Fourth Lateran Council mentions in the first place the Eucharist, considered as effecting the mystery of unity between God and human beings. This document also reflects a long theological elaboration. The term 'transubstantiation', previously used by Pope Innocent III (cf. n. 1502), is found here for the first time in an official document. The term will be used again soon after by the Second General Council of Lyons (1274) (cf. n. 28). The text of this profession of faith is found under n. 21.*

THE GENERAL COUNCIL OF CONSTANCE DECREE ON COMMUNION UNDER THE SPECIES OF BREAD ALONE (1415)

First to claim communion from the chalice for the laity were the disciples of John Hus in Bohemia. Their claim was based on the precept given by the

Lord at the Last Supper and the practice of the early centuries. For reasons of expediency the Council thought it appropriate to maintain the practice of communion under one kind. What remains of value in this document is the doctrinal reason advanced to justify, against those who denied it, the validity of the practice: both the body and blood of Christ are present under each kind. The Council of Trent will further explain the same doctrine (cf. nn. 1537ff).

1506 The present custom has been introduced for good reasons
1199 to avoid some dangers and scandals and thus it has been legitimate to maintain and observe it for similar or even greater reasons. It is true that in the early Church this sacrament was received by the faithful under both kinds, but later it came to be received under both kinds by those who consecrate it and under the species of bread alone by the laity. [This custom is legitimate] for it must be firmly believed and can in no way be doubted that the body and the blood of Christ are truly and integrally contained under the species of bread as well as under that of wine.

MARTIN V
BULL *INTER CUNCTAS* (1418)

Among the errors of the followers of Wyclif and Hus condemned by Martin V several are related to the Eucharist. First the opinion is condemned according to which the reality of bread and wine continue to exist after consecration. The second error is more directly concerned with the modality of the presence of Christ's body and blood. This is a delicate point of doctrine which requires a well-balanced exposition: while the realism of the eucharistic presence must be maintained, its sacramental modality must also be kept in mind. Too materialistic a concept of the presence of Christ's body and blood and a purely symbolical conception of the same are equally erroneous. The Church rejected the ultra-realism stigmatised as Capharnaitic eating which led to false problems (cf. DS 1101-1103). In this text, the Pope upholds the realism of the eucharistic presence against the tendency of the followers of Wyclif and Hus to reduce it to a mere symbol. The errors of Wyclif on this point had already been condemned by the Council of Constance (DS 1151-1153), of which the Bull of Martin V is a confirmation.

(Questions proposed to the followers of Wyclif and Hus)

1507/16 Likewise, whether they believe that in the sacrament
1256 of the altar, after the consecration by the priest, there is under the veil of bread and wine no material bread and wine, but the very same Christ who suffered on the cross and sits at the right hand of the Father.

1507/17 Likewise, whether they believe and affirm that after
1257 the priest has consecrated, the true flesh and blood of
Christ, his soul and divinity, the whole Christ, are
present under the species of bread alone, even apart of the species
of wine, and that the same body is present absolutely and under
each of these species taken separately.

THE GENERAL COUNCIL OF FLORENCE
DECREE FOR THE GREEKS (1439)

*The Decree of the Council of Florence for the Greeks, which attempted to
bring about their union with Rome, recognised that the Eucharist can be
consecrated with either unleavened or leavened bread according to the different
practice of the Western and the Eastern traditions.*

1508 Likewise, we define that the body of Christ is truly
1303 effected with either unleavened or leavened wheaten
bread; and that priests must consecrate the body of the
Lord in one way or the other, namely each following the custom
of their Church, either the Western or the Oriental Church.

DECREE FOR THE ARMENIANS (1439)

*For the Eucharist as for the other sacraments (cf. n. 1305i), the Decree
for the Armenians was an elaborate exposition of then current Latin theology
which followed very closely St. Thomas Aquinas; it cannot be considered as a
document of faith but rather as a clear statement, for the benefit of the
Armenians, of what was then the sacramental theology commonly received in
the Western Church. The sacramental form of the Eucharist is said to consist
in the words of institution; no mention is made of the epiclesis to which the
Eastern tradition attributed sacramental value. Following the decree, later
documents will go on exposing the Latin view without consideration for the
Eastern one. Examples of this are a brief of Pope Pius VII (1822) (cf. DS
2718) and a letter of Pius X (1910) (cf. DS 3556). It is important to note that
none of these documents is a document of faith. In recent years, a broader
approach to sacramental efficacy has sought to reconcile the Western and the
Eastern traditions by attributing complementary sacramental value to the words
of institution and to the epiclesis.*

(The matter of the Eucharist)

1509 The third sacrament is the Eucharist. The matter of this
1320 sacrament is wheat-bread and grape-wine with a small
amount of water to be mixed in before the consecration.
Water is mixed in because, according to the testimony of the holy

Fathers and Doctors of the Church mentioned in the preceding discussions, it is believed that our Lord himself instituted this sacrament with wine mixed with water. Furthermore this is a fitting representation of our Lord's passion. For, as Blessed Alexander, the fifth Pope after St. Peter, says: "In the oblation of the mysteries which are offered to the Lord during the solemnities of the Mass, let only bread and wine mixed with water be offered in sacrifice. Not wine only nor water only should be offered in the chalice of the Lord, but a mixture of both. For we read that both, that is, blood and water, flowed from the side of Christ"*[cf. Jn 19:34]*.[1] Finally, this is a fitting way to signify the effect of this sacrament, that is, the union of the Christian people with Christ. For, water represents the people as the Apocalypse says: "many waters[...] many peoples" *[cf. Rev 17:15]*. And Julius, the second Pope after Blessed Sylvester, says: "According to the prescription of the canons, the Lord's chalice should be offered with wine mixed with water. For we see that the water represents the people and the wine manifests the blood of Christ. Thus, when wine and water are mixed in the chalice, the people are united with Christ, and the faithful people are closely joined to him in whom they believe."[2] Therefore, since the holy Roman Church which was instructed by the Blessed apostles Peter and Paul, and all the other Churches of Latins and Greeks, in which have shone luminaries of sanctity and learning, have followed this custom from the beginning of the early Church and still follow it, it seems entirely improper for any region whatsoever not to follow this reasonable and universal practice. We therefore decree that the Armenians must conform to the whole Christian world and that their priests must mix a small amount of water with the wine, as has been said, in the offering of the chalice.

(The form of the Eucharist)

1510   The form of this sacrament is the words of the Saviour
1321   with which he effected this sacrament; for the priest
         effects the sacrament by speaking in the person of Christ.
It is by the power of these words that the substance of bread is changed into the body of Christ, and the substance of wine into his blood; in such a way, however, that the whole Christ is

---

1. PSEUDO-ALEXANDER I, *Epistola ad omnes orthodoxos*, 9.
2. PSEUDO-IULIUS I, *Epistola ad episcopos Aegypti*.

contained under the species of bread and the whole Christ under the species of wine. Further, the whole Christ is present under any part of the consecrated host or the consecrated wine when separated from the rest.

(The effect of the Eucharist)

1511 The effect which this sacrament produces in the souls of
1322 persons who receive it worthily, is to unite them with Christ. For, since it is by grace that persons are incorporated into Christ and united to his members, it follows that those who receive this sacrament worthily receive an increase of grace. And all the effects which material food and drink have on the life of the body—maintaining and increasing life, restoring health and giving joy—all these effects this sacrament produces for the spiritual life. As Pope Urban says [*cf. DS 846*], in this sacrament we celebrate in thanksgiving the memory of our Saviour, we are drawn away from evil, we are strengthened in what is good, and we advance and increase in virtue and in grace.

THE GENERAL COUNCIL OF TRENT
THIRTEENTH SESSION
DECREE ON THE MOST HOLY EUCHARIST (1551)

The doctrine of the Eucharist is among those on which the Council of Trent had to pronounce clearly in the face of the violent attacks it met with on the part of the Reformers. For this as for other matters the Council did not mean to propose a complete doctrine but to affirm clearly the important points which were being denied. In the historical circumstances, the Council found it necessary first to state the doctrine related to the presence of Christ's body and blood in the Eucharist; this would be complemented by another decree on the sacrifice of the Mass, which, because of the unfortunate interruption of the Council, was promulgated only eleven years later.

The discussion on the Eucharist began as early as 1547, though the decree on the eucharistic presence could be published only by the Council's 13th session in 1551. The decree contains eight chapters and eleven canons. It deals with the following points.

1) The fact and the meaning of the presence of Christ's body and blood in the Eucharist, based on scriptural evidence. This is not directed against Luther who never denied the "real presence", but against Zwingli (1484-1531) who opposed Luther on this point; according to Zwingli, Christ is present in the Eucharist "in sign" only. Also opposed to the Church's doctrine was the theory of Christ's dynamic presence "by his power" as proposed by Calvin (nn. 1513-1515, 1526).

2) The presence of Christ is complete under each species. This point already affirmed in previous documents against the fore-runners of the Reformation (cf. nn. 1506, 1507/17) is further elaborated because of the new denials (n. 1516).

3) Though it is ordained to sacramental communion, the eucharistic presence exists prior to it and continues in the sacred species which have not been consumed. Luther himself was hesitant on this point; Melanchton clearly denied it (nn. 1516, 1529).

4) The eucharistic presence is effected by transubstantiation. Following Wyclif (cf. n. 1507/16), Luther thought that bread and wine subsist together with Christ's body and blood. Against this, the Council affirms a complete change of substance with the result that of the bread and wine only the outward appearances remain; it declares appropriate the term "transubstantiation" which since the fourth Lateran Council (cf. n. 1505) was officially used to express this change of substance (nn. 1519, 1527).

5) From this exposition of doctrine, the Council derives concrete conclusions as regards mostly the reception and use of the sacrament (nn. 1521-1524, 1532-1536) and the cult of the Eucharist (nn. 1520, 1531).

This decree requires careful interpretation. In particular, the doctrine of faith proposed by the Council must be distinguished from the theological concept of "transubstantiation" which is recognised only as an appropriate enunciation of its content.

For a detailed analysis of the text, cf. K. RAHNER, Theological Investigations, vol. 4, pp. 291 ff.

Foreword

1512   The holy, ecumenical and general Council of Trent,
1635   lawfully assembled in the Holy Spirit, and presided over
         by the aforementioned legates and nuncios of the holy,
apostolic See, under the special guidance and direction of the
Holy Spirit, has assembled to set forth the true and ancient
doctrine on the faith and on the sacraments and to supply a
remedy for all the heresies and the other serious evils which
now deeply trouble God's Church and divide it into so many
different parts. But, from the beginning it has always been the
Council's special desire to uproot completely the cockle of the
damnable errors and schisms which in these fateful times of ours
the enemy has sown [cf. Mt 13:25] in the doctrine of faith, and
in the use and worship of the most holy Eucharist; that very
Eucharist which our Saviour has left in his Church precisely as
a symbol of the unity and charity with which he desired all

Christians to be joined together and united. And so this holy
Council teaches the true and genuine doctrine about this
venerable and divine sacrament of the Eucharist—the doctrine
which the Catholic Church has always held and which it will
hold until the end of the world, as it learned it from Jesus Christ
our Lord himself, from his apostles, and from the Holy Spirit,
who continually reminds it of all truth [cf. Jn 14:26]. The Council
forbids all the faithful of Christ henceforth to believe, teach, or
preach anything about the most holy Eucharist that is different
from what is explained and defined in this present decree.

*Chapter I: The real presence of our Lord Jesus Christ in the most
holy sacrament of the Eucharist*

1513   To begin with, the holy Council teaches and openly and
1636   straightforwardly professes that in the blessed sacrament
        of the holy Eucharist, after the consecration of the bread
and wine, our Lord Jesus Christ, true God and man, is truly,
really and substantially contained under the appearances of those
perceptible realities [cf. n. 1526]. For, there is no contradiction in
the fact that our Saviour always sits at the right hand of the
Father in heaven according to his natural way of existing and
that, nevertheless, in his substance he is sacramentally present
to us in many other places. We can hardly find words to express
this way of existing; but our reason, enlightened through faith,
can nevertheless recognise it as possible for God, and we must
always believe it unhesitatingly.

1514   For all our predecessors in the true Church of Christ
1637   who treated of this most holy sacrament very clearly
        professed that our Redeemer instituted this wonderful
sacrament at the Last Supper, when, after he had blessed bread
and wine, he declared in plain, unmistakable words, that he was
giving to them his own body and his own blood. These words,
recorded by the evangelists [cf. Mt 26:26ff; Mk 14:22ff; Lk 22:19f]
and afterwards repeated by St. Paul [1 Cor 11:23ff], have this
proper and obvious meaning and were so understood by the
Fathers. Consequently, it is indeed the greatest infamy that some
contentious, evil persons, distort these words into fanciful,
imaginary figures of speech where the truth about the body and
blood of Christ is denied, contrary to the universal undestanding
of the Church. The Church, which is "the pillar and bulwark of

the truth" [cf. 1 Tim 3:15], has detested as satanical these interpretations invented by impious persons, and it acknowledges in a spirit of unfailing gratitude this most precious gift of Christ.

Chapter II: The reason for the institution of this most holy sacrament

1515 Our Saviour, therefore, instituted this sacrament before
1638 leaving this world to go to the Father. He poured out, as it were, in this sacrament the riches of his divine love for human beings, "causing his wonderful works to be remembered" [cf. Ps. 111(110)4], and he wanted us when receiving it to celebrate his memory [cf. 1 Cor 11:24] and to proclaim his death until he comes to judge the world [cf. 1 Cor 11:26]. His will was that this sacrament be received as the soul's spiritual food [cf. Mt 26:26] which would nourish and strengthen [cf. n. 1530] those who live by the life of him who said: "He who eats me will live because of me" [Jn 6:57]; and that it be also a remedy to free us from our daily faults and to preserve us from mortal sin. Christ willed, moreover, that this sacrament be a pledge of our future glory and our everlasting happiness and, likewise, a symbol of that one "Body" of which he himself is "the Head" [cf. 1 Cor 11:3; Eph 5:23], and to which he willed that we, as members, should be linked by the closest bonds of faith, hope and love, so that we might all say the same thing, and that there might be no dissensions among us [cf. 1 Cor 1:10].

Chapter III: The pre-eminence of the most holy Eucharist over the other sacraments

1516 In common with the other sacraments, the most holy
1639 Eucharist is "a symbol of a sacred thing and a visible form of invisible grace".[1] But the Eucharist also has this unique mark of distinction that, whereas the other sacraments have the power of sanctifying only when someone makes use of them, in the Eucharist the Author of Sanctity himself is present before the sacrament is used [cf. n. 1529].

1517 For the apostles had not yet received the Eucharist from
1640 the hands of the Lord [cf. Mt 26:26; Mk 14:22] when he himself told them that it was truly his body that he was

---

1. Cf. St. Augustine, *Quaestionum in Heptateuchum*, 3, 84.

giving them. This has always been the belief of the Church of God that immediately after the consecration the true body and blood of our Lord, together with his soul and divinity, exist under the species of bread and wine. The body exists under the species of bread and the blood under the species of wine by virtue of the words. But the body too exists under the species of wine, the blood under the species of bread, and the soul under both species in virtue of the natural connection and concomitance by which the parts of Christ the Lord, who has already risen from the dead to die no more [cf. Rom 6:9], are united together. Moreover, the divinity is present because of its admirable hypostatic union with the body and the soul [cf. nn. 1526, 1528].

1518 It is, therefore, perfectly true that just as much is present
1641 under either of the two species as is present under both.

For Christ, whole and entire, exists under the species of bread and under any part of that species, and similarly the whole Christ exists under the species of wine and under its parts [cf. n. 1528].

Chapter IV : Transubstantiation

1519 Because Christ our Redeemer said that it was truly his
1642 body that he was offering under the species of bread
[cf. Mt 26:26ff; Mk 14:22ff; Lk. 22:29f; 1 Cor 11:24ff], it has always been the conviction of the Church of God, and this holy Council now again declares that, by the consecration of the bread and wine there takes place a change of the whole substance of bread into the substance of the body of Christ our Lord and of the whole substance of wine into the substance of his blood. This change the holy Catholic Church has fittingly and properly named transubstantiation [cf. n. 1527].

Chapter V: The worship and veneration to be shown to this most holy sacrament

1520 There remains, therefore, no room for doubting that all
1643 the faithful of Christ, in accordance with the perpetual
custom of the Catholic Church, must venerate this most holy sacrament with the worship of *latria* which is due to the true God [cf. n. 1531]. Nor is it to be less adored because it was instituted by Christ the Lord to be received (*ut sumatur*) [cf. Mt 26:26ff]. For in it we believe that the same God is present

whom the eternal Father brought into the world, saying: "Let all God's angels worship him" [Heb 1:6; cf. Ps 97:(96)7], whom the Magi fell down to worship [cf. Mt 2:11] and whom, finally, the apostles adored in Galilee as Scripture testifies [cf. Mt 28:17].[...]

Chapter VI: The reservation of the sacrament of the holy Eucharist and taking it to the sick

1521 The custom of reserving the holy Eucharist in a sacred
1645 place is so ancient that it was recognised already in the
century of the Council of Nicaea. That the holy Eucharist should be taken to the sick and that it should be carefully kept in the churches for this purpose is right and very reasonable. Moreover, this is prescribed by many Councils and goes back to the most ancient custom in the Catholic Church. Consequently, this holy Council has decreed that this most salutary and necessary custom be retained [cf. n. 1532].

Chapter VII: The preparation to be made to receive the holy Eucharist worthily

1522 It is not right that anyone should participate in any
1646 sacred functions except in a holy manner. Certainly, then,
the more Christians are aware of the holiness and the divinity of this heavenly sacrament, the more careful they should be not to receive it without great reverence and sanctity [cf. n. 1536], especially since we read in the apostle the fearful words: "Those who eat and drink unworthily, without discerning the body of the Lord, eat and drink judgment upon themselves" [1 Cor 11:29 Vulg.]. Therefore, whoever desires to communicate must be reminded of the precept: "Let them examine themselves" [1 Cor 11:28].[...]

Chapter VIII: The use of this wonderful sacrament

1523 As regards the use, our Fathers have correctly and
1648 appropriately distinguished three ways of receiving this
holy sacrament. They teach that some receive it only sacramentally because they are sinners. Others receive it only spiritually; they are the ones who, receiving in desire the heavenly bread put before them, with a living faith "working through love" [cf. Gal 5:6], experience its fruit and benefit from it. The third

group receive it both sacramentally and spiritually [cf. n. 1533]; they are the ones who examine and prepare themselves beforehand to approach this divine table, clothed in the wedding garment [cf. Mt 22:1ff].[...]

1524 Finally, with fatherly affection the holy Council warns, *1649* exhorts, asks and pleads, "through the tender mercy of our God" [Lk 1:78], that each and all who bear the name of Christians meet at last in this "sign of unity", in this "bond of charity",[1] in this symbol of concord, to be finally of one heart. Keeping in mind the great majesty and the most excellent love of our Lord Jesus Christ, who laid down his precious life as the price of our salvation, and who gave us his flesh to eat [cf. Jn 6:48ff], may all Christians have so firm and strong a faith in the sacred mystery of his body and blood, may they worship it with such devotion and pious veneration, that they will be able to receive frequently their "super-substantial bread" [cf. Mt 6:11 Vulg.]. May it truly be the life of their souls and continual health for their minds; strengthened by its power [cf. 1 Kings 19:8], may they, after journeying through this sorrowful pilgrimage, reach their home in heaven, where they will eat without any veil the same "bread of angels" [cf. Ps 78(77) 25] which they eat now under sacred veils.

1525 But, since it is not enough to state the truth without *1650* pointing out and refuting errors, it has pleased the holy Council to add the following canons so that all, already knowing the Catholic doctrine, may also realise what are the heresies that they must beware of and avoid.

Canons on the most holy sacrament of the Eucharist

1526 1. If anyone denies that in the sacrament of the most *1651* holy Eucharist the body and blood, together with the soul and divinity, of our Lord Jesus Christ and, therefore, the whole Christ is truly, really and substantially contained, but says that he is in it only as in a sign or figure or by his power, *anathema sit* [cf. nn. 1513, 1517].

1527 2. If anyone says that in the holy sacrament of the

---

1. Cf. St. Augustine, *In evang. Iohan. tract.*, 26, 13.

1652 Eucharist the substance of bread and wine remains together with the body and blood of our Lord Jesus Christ, and denies that wonderful and unique change of the whole substance of the bread into his body and of the whole substance of the wine into his blood while only the species of bread and wine remain, a change which the Catholic Church very fittingly calls transubstantiation, *anathema sit [cf. n. 1519].*

1528 3. If anyone denies that in the venerable sacrament of *1653* the Eucharist the whole Christ is contained under each species and under each part of either species when separated, *anathema sit [cf. n. 1518].*

1529 4. If anyone says that after the consecration the body *1654* and blood of our Lord Jesus Christ are not in the marvellous sacrament of the Eucharist but that they are there only in the use of the sacrament *(in usu)*, while it is being received, and not before or after, and that in the consecrated hosts or particles which are preserved or are left over after communion the true body of the Lord does not remain, *anathema sit [cf. n. 1516f].*

1530 5. If anyone says that the principal fruit of the most holy *1655* Eucharist is the forgiveness of sins, or that no other effects come from it, *anathema sit [cf. n. 1515].*

1531 6. If anyone says that Christ, the only-begotten Son of *1656* God, is not to be adored in the holy sacrament of the Eucharist with the worship of *latria*, including external worship, and that the sacrament therefore is not to be honoured with special festive celebrations nor solemnly carried in processions according to the praise-worthy universal rite and custom of the holy Church; or that it is not to be publicly exposed for the people's adoration, and that those who adore it are idolaters, *anathema sit [cf. n. 1520].*

1532 7. If anyone says that it is not lawful to keep the sacred *1657* Eucharist in a sacred place, but that it must necessarily be distributed immediately after the consecration to those who are present; or that it is not lawful to carry it with honour to the sick, *anathema sit [cf. n. 1521].*

1533 8. If anyone says that Christ presented in the Eucharist *1658* is only spiritually eaten and not sacramentally and really as well, *anathema sit [cf. n. 1523].*

1534 9. If anyone denies that each and all of Christ's faithful
1659 of both sexes are bound, when they reach the age of
reason, to receive communion every year, at least during
the Paschal season, according to the precept of Holy Mother
Church, *anathema sit [cf. DS 812].*

1535 10. If anyone says that it is not lawful for the
1660 celebrating priest to communicate himself, *anathema sit
[cf. DS 1648].*

1536 11. If anyone says that faith alone is a sufficient
1661 preparation for receiving the sacrament of the most holy
Eucharist, *anathema sit.* And, lest so great a sacrament be
received unworthily and hence unto death and condemnation,
this holy Council determines and decrees that those whose
conscience is burdened with mortal sin, no matter how contrite
they may think they are, first must necessarily make a
sacramental confession if a confessor is availble. If anyone
presumes to teach, or preach, or obstinately maintain, or defend
in public disputation the opposite of this, he shall by the very
fact be excommunicated *[cf. DS 1647].*

TWENTY-FIRST SESSION

DOCTRINE ON COMMUNION UNDER BOTH SPECIES AND ON COMMUNION OF LITTLE CHILDREN (1562)

*After having been interrupted since 1552, the Council resumed its
deliberations in 1562 under Pope Pius IV. In its 21st session it turned to the
controversial questions of communion from the chalice for the laity and
communion of little children. Adopting the position of Hus and his followers
(cf. n. 1506i), the Reformers were also claiming the chalice for the laity. In
this decree, made up of four chapters and four canons, the Council affirms the
following:*

*1) No divine precept requires the faithful to communicate under both kinds
(cf. nn. 1537, 1541).*
*2) Consequently, the Church has the power to determine the modality of the
administration of the sacrament (cf. nn. 1538, 1542).*
*3) Communion under one kind only causes no substantial spiritual loss (cf.
nn. 1539, 1543). The Council, however, deliberately left undecided the question
whether or not communion under both kinds gives grace more abundantly;
the reason is that different schools held different opinions on this point.*
*4) As for little children, there is no need to admit them to communion (cf. nn.
1540, 1544).*

While maintaining the principles laid down by the Council of Trent, and in no way contradicting its doctrine, the Second Vatican Council in its Constitution on the Sacred Liturgy will decree that "communion under both kinds may be granted when the bishops think fit, not only to clerics and religious, but also to the laity [...]" (SC 55). This new attitude does not necessarily imply the persuasion that grace is more abundantly given when communion is received under both kinds; it is inspired by a new appreciation of the sign-value of the Church's sacramental actions, especially in the Eucharist.

Chapter I: Lay people and clerics who do not celebrate are not bound by divine law to communion under both kinds

(1537) *(The reception of the one specis of bread is sufficient for salvation.*
1726 *Those who advocate the chalice for the laity cannot claim it to be a*
1727 *binding precept of the Lord, for Christ himself in St. John's Gospel sometimes speaks of his body and blood (cf. Jn 6:54, 55, 57), and sometimes mentions only his body (cf. Jn 6:52, 59).)*

Chapter II: The power of the Church concerning the dispensation of the sacrament of the Eucharist

(1538) *(The substance of the sacraments being preserved, the Church has*
1728 *the power to determine the modality of their dispensation. St. Paul taught this and took steps in this direction. It is by making use of this power that the Church has for serious reasons decreed communion under one kind).*

(The principle laid down here is an important principle of sacramental theology; the text is found under n. 1324).

Chapter III: The whole and entire Christ and the true sacrament are received under either species

(1539) *(Those who receive the sacrament under one species only are not*
1729 *deprived of any grace necessary for salvation, for the whole Christ is received under one species.)*

Chapter IV: Little children are not obliged to receive sacramental communion

(1540) *(They are incorporated into Christ by baptism and cannot at their*
1730 *age lose grace. Nevertheless, the practice of the early centuries when small children occasionally received communion is not to be condemned. But communion is not necessary for salvation before the age of reason.)*

Canons on communion under both species and on communion of little children

1541 1. If anyone says that each and all of Christ's faithful
1731 ought to receive both species of the most holy sacrament of the Eucharist, because of a command from God or because it is necessary for salvation, *anathema sit [cf. n. 1537].*

1542 2. If anyone says that the holy Catholic Church was not
1732 led by lawful and good reasons to have the laity and the clerics who are not celebrating communicate under the species of bread alone, or that the Church erred in so doing, *anathema sit [cf. n. 1538].*

1543 3. If anyone denies that the whole and entire Christ, the
1733 source and author of all graces, is received under the species of bread alone, because, as some falsely affirm, he is not received under both species in accordance with the institution of Christ himself, *anathema sit [cf. n. 1737].*

1544 4. If anyone says that eucharistic communion is necessary
1734 for little children before they reach the age of reason, *anathema sit [cf. n. 1540].*

TWENTY-SECOND SESSION
DOCTRINE ON THE MOST HOLY SACRIFICE
OF THE MASS (1562)

In its 13th session the Council had re-affirmed the Church's faith in the reality of the presence of Christ's body and blood in the Eucharist. There remained to state, against the denial of the Reformers, the sacrificial value of the Mass. This decree brings the eucharistic doctrine of the Council to completion. Its first chapters contain a remarkable synthesis, deeply rooted in Scripture, on the Mass as sacrifice and its relationship to the sacrifice of the cross. The Council does not, however, decide what is the essence of sacrifice, a point on which various opinions were held by theologians. The document is made up of nine chapters and nine canons, of vastly different doctrinal import:

1) The salvation of humankind has been effected by the sacrifice of the cross. Holy Mass is not a sacrifice independent of the cross. It is the sacrifice of the cross now offered by the Church, whenever, following Christ's command, it celebrates the ritual of the Last Supper in which Christ offered himself. This doctrine is directed against Luther, Melanchton, Calvin, who, restricting Christ's sacrifice to the cross and denying all relationship of the Last Supper to his sacrificial death, reduced the Lord's Supper celebrated by the Church to a sacred meal without sacrificial value (cf. nn. 1546, 1556).

2) The sacrifice of the Mass is a true propitiatory sacrifice as was the sacrifice of the cross. Its propitiatory value takes nothing away from the uniqueness of the sacrifice of the cross, since it is essentially related to it. All share in the fruits of the sacrifice of the Mass (cf. nn. 1548, 1557-1558).

3) Against the objections advanced by the Reformers, the Council explains in what sense Masses are legitimately offered in honour of the saints (cf. nn. 1549, 1559).

4) Explanations are given regarding some special rites in the celebration of the Mass. The chapters and canons dealing with these are of secondary importance and must be read in the historical context. Some of their disciplinary prescriptions have, for liturgical and pastoral reasons, been changed by and after the Second Vatican Council (cf. nn. 1550-1554, 1560-1563).

Primarily intent on defending the Church's doctrine on the sacrificial aspect of the Mass which was denied by the Reformers, the Council did not attempt a complete exposition of doctrine on the significance of the Eucharist. The historical circumstances explain why the meal-aspect receives less emphasis than the sacrificial aspect; it had been partly dealt with in the Decree on the most holy Eucharist. In a climate with no controversial issues involved, the Second Vatican Council established the balance between the two inseparable aspects of the Eucharist, sacrifice and meal.

Foreword

1545 In order to retain in the holy Catholic Church and to
1738   preserve in its purity the ancient, absolute and
       completely perfect faith and doctrine about the great
mystery of the Eucharist and to avert heresies and errors, the
holy, ecumenical and general Council of Trent, lawfully
assembled in the Holy Spirit, presided over by the same apostolic
legates, teaches and lays down, under the guidance and light of
the Holy Spirit, the following doctrine about the Eucharist as
true and unique sacrifice and declares that this doctrine is to be
preached to the faithful.

Chapter I: The institution of the most holy sacrifice of the Mass

1546 As the Apostle testifies, there was no perfection under
1739   the former Covenant because of the insufficiency of the
       levitical priesthood. It was, therefore, necessary
(according to the merciful ordination of God the Father) that
another priest arise after the order of Melchizedek [cf. Gen 14:18; Ps 110 (109): 4; Heb 7:11], our Lord Jesus Christ who could make perfect all who were to be sanctified [cf. Heb 10:14] and bring them to fulfilment.

1740   He, then our Lord and God, was once and for all to offer himself to God the Father by his death on the altar of the cross, to accomplish for them an everlasting redemption. But, because his priesthood was not to end with his death [cf. Heb 7:24, 27], at the Last Supper, "on the night when he was betrayed" [1 Cor 11:23], in order to leave to his beloved Spouse the Church a visible sacrifice (as human nature demands) [cf. n. 1555]—by which the bloody sacrifice which he was once for all to accomplish on the cross would be present, its memory perpetuated until the end of the world and its salutary power applied for the forgiveness of the sins which we daily commit—; declaring himself constituted "a priest for ever after the order of Melchizedek" [Ps 110 (109):4], he offered his body and blood under the species of bread and wine to God the Father, and, under the same signs (sub earundem rerum symbolis) gave them to partake of to the disciples (whom he then established as priests of the New Convenant), and ordered them and their successors in the priesthood to offer, saying: "Do this as a memorial of me", etc. [Lk 22:19; 1 Cor 11:24], as the Catholic Church has always understood and taught [cf. n. 1556].

1741   For, after he celebrated the old Pasch, which the multitude of the children of Israel offered (immolabat) to celebrate the memory of the departure from Egypt [cf. Ex 12:1ff], Christ instituted a new Pasch, namely himself to be offered by the Church through her priests under visible signs in order to celebrate the memory of his passage from this world to the Father when by the shedding of his blood he redeemed us, "delivered us from the dominion of darkness and transferred us to his Kingdom" [cf. Col 1:13].

1547   This is the clean oblation which cannot be defiled by
1742   any unworthiness or malice on the part of those who offer it, and which the Lord foretold through Malachi would be offered in all places as a clean oblation to his name [cf. Mal 1:11]. The apostle Paul also refers clearly to it when, writing to the Corinthians, he says that those who have been defiled by partaking of the table of devils cannot be partakers of the table of the Lord. By 'table' he understands 'altar' in both cases [cf. 1 cor 10:21]. Finally, this is the oblation which was prefigured by various types of sacrifices under the regime of nature and of the law [cf. Gen 4:4; 8:20; 12:8; 22; Ex, passim]. For

it includes all the good that was signified by those former sacrifices; it is their fulfilment and perfection.[...]

Chapter II: The visible sacrifice is propitiatory for the living and the dead

1548 In this divine sacrifice which is celebrated in the Mass,
1743 the same Christ who offered himself once in a bloody manner [cf. Heb 9:14, 27] on the altar of the cross is contained and is offered in an unbloody manner. Therefore, the holy Council teaches that this sacrifice is truly propitiatory [cf. n. 1557], so that, if we draw near to God with an upright heart and true faith, with fear and reverence, with sorrow and repentance, through it "we may receive mercy and find grace to help in time of need" [cf. Heb 4:16]. For the Lord, appeased by this oblation, grants grace and the gift of repentance, and he pardons wrong-doings and sins, even grave ones. For, the victim is one and the same: the same now offers through the ministry of priests, who then offered himself on the cross; only the manner of offering is different. The fruits of this oblation (the bloody one, that is) are received in abundance through this unbloody oblation. By no means, then, does the latter detract from the former [cf. n. 1558]. Therefore, it is rightly offered according to apostolic tradition, not only for the sins, punishments, satisfaction and other necessities of the faithful who are alive, but also for those who have died in Christ but are not yet wholly purified [cf. n. 1557].

Chapter III: Masses in honour of the saints

1549 And, although it is the custom of the Church occasionally
1744 to celebrate some Masses in honour and in remembrance of the saints, the Church teaches that sacrifice is offered not to the saints, but to God alone who has given them their crown [cf. n. 1559]. Therefore, "the priest does not say: 'I offer the sacrifice to you, Peter and Paul'",.[1] but giving thanks to God for the victory of the saints, he implores their protection "in order that those whose remembrance we celebrate on earth may intercede for us in heaven."[2]

---

1. Cf. St. Augustine, *Contra Faustum Manichaeum, XX*, 21.
2. *Roman Missal*, Order of the Mass.

Chapter IV: The canon of the Mass

1550 Holy things must be treated in a holy way and this
1745   sacrifice is the most holy of all things. And so, that this
            sacrifice might be worthily and reverently offered and
received, the Catholic Church many centuries ago instituted the
sacred Canon. It is so free from all errors [cf. n. 1560] that it
contains nothing which does not savour strongly of holiness and
piety and nothing which does not raise to God the minds of those
who offer. For it is made up of the words of our Lord himself, of
apostolic traditions, and of devout instructions of the holy pontiffs.

Chapter V: The solemn ceremonies of the sacrifice of the Mass

(1551) (The Council upholds the legitimacy of some prescriptions made by
1746   the Church for the celebration of the Mass (cf. n. 1563) and of some
            ceremonies to be observed (cf. n. 1561)).

Chapter VI: The Mass in which the priest alone communicates

1552 The holy Council would wish that in every Mass the
1747   faithful who are present communicate not only in desire,
            but by a sacramental reception of the Eucharist, so that
they may derive more abundant fruits from this most holy
sacrifice. Nevertheless, if such is not always the case, the Council
does not on that account condemn the Masses in which the priest
alone communicates sacramentally as private and illicit [cf. n.
1562]. Rather, it approves them and endorses them since such
Masses too are to be considered as truly public, partly because the
people communicate at them spiritually and partly because they
are celebrated by a public minister of the Church, not for himself
alone, but for all the faithful who belong to the Body of Christ.

Chapter VII: Water must be mixed with the wine to be offered in the chalice

(1553) (The Council reminds priests of the precept of the Church. It
1748   attributes to the rite the same symbolism as was already proposed by
            the Council of Florence in the decree for the Armenians (cf. n. 1509).
See also n. 1563.)

Chapter VIII: Mass should not be celebrated in the vernacular indiscriminately; the mysteries of the Mass are to be explaiend to the people

1554 Although the Mass contains much instruction for the

1749   faithful, the Fathers did not think that it should be celebrated in the vernacular indiscriminately *[cf. n. 1563]*. Therefore, the ancient rite of each Church, approved by the holy Roman Church, the mother and teacher of all the Churches, being everywhere maintained, the holy Council, in order that the sheep of Christ may not go unfed, lest "the children beg for food but no one gives to them" *[Lam 4:4]*, orders that pastors and all who have the care of souls must frequently, either by themselves or through others, explain during the celebration of Masses some of the readings of the Mass, and among other things give some instruction about the mystery of this most holy sacrifice, especially on Sundays and feastdays.

Canons on the most holy sacrifice of the Mass

1555   1. If anyone says that in the Mass a true and proper
1751   sacrifice is not offered to God or that the offering consists merely in the fact that Christ is given to us to eat, *anathema sit.*

1556   2. If anyone says that by the words "Do this as a
1752   memorial of me" *[Lk 22:19; 1 Cor 11:24]* Christ did not establish the apostles as priests or that he did not order that they and other priests should offers his body and blood, *anathema sit [cf. n. 1546]*.

1557   3. If anyone says that the sacrifice of the Mass is merely
1753   an offering of praise and thanksgiving, or that it is a simple commemoration of the sacrifice accomplished on the cross, but not a propitiatory sacrifice, or that it benefits only those who communicate; and that it should not be offered for the living and the dead, for sins, punishments, satisfaction and other necessities, *anathema sit [cf. n. 1548]*.

1558   4. If anyone says that the sacrifice of the Mass constitutes
1754   a blasphemy against the most holy sacrifice which Christ accomplished on the cross, or that it detracts from that sacrifice, *anathema sit [cf. n. 1548]*.

1559   5. If anyone says that it is an imposture to celebrate
1755   Masses in honour of the saints and in order to obtain their intercession with God as the Church intends, *anathema sit [cf. n. 1549]*.

1560 6. If anyone says that the Canon of the Mass contains
1756 errors and therefore should be abolished, *anathema sit*
[*cf. n. 1550*].

1561 7. If anyone says that the ceremonies, vestments and
1757 external signs which the Catholic Church uses in the
celebration of Masses are incentives to impiety rather
than works of piety, *anathema sit [cf. n. 1551].*

1562 8. If anyone says that Masses in which the priest alone
1758 communicates sacramentally, are illicit and therefore
should be abolished, *anathema sit [cf. n. 1552].*

1563 9. If anyone says that the rite of the Roman Church
1759 prescribing that part of the Canon and the words of
consecration be recited in a low voice, must be
condemned; or that Mass should be celebrated only in the
vernacular; or that water should not be mixed with the wine to
be offered in the chalice because this would be contrary to
Christ's institution, *anathema sit [cf. nn. 1551, 1553].*

PIUS XII

ENCYCLICAL LETTER *MYSTICI CORPORIS* (1943)

The more recent documents of the Church have brought to light, in accordance with the tradition of the early centuries, the close relationship between the mystery of the Eucharist and the mystery of the Church. Previous to this document may be mentioned the Encyclical Letter **Mirae Caritatis** *(1902) of Pope Leo XIII (cf. DS 3360-3364) in which the Eucharist is said to be "as it were the soul of the Church" (DS 3364). The great Encyclical Letter of Pope Pius XII rightly considers (after a previous encyclical of Leo XIII) the Holy Spirit to be the soul of the Church (cf. n. 852); the Eucharist has, nevertheless, a unique significance for the mystery of the Church, for it is the visible sign of the mysterious union which binds together the members of Christ's mystical Body with their Head and among themselves. In the Eucharist Christ unites the Church to his sacrifice: the priests, representing at once Christ and his mystical Body, offer the sacrificial victim while the faithful offer through the priests; in the sacramental banquet of Christ's body and blood, all receive the life of Christ which binds together the members of his Body. The text is found in AAS 35 (1943) 193ff.*

(The eucharistic sacrifice and the Church)

1564 [...] Christ our Lord willed that in the eucharistic sacrifice
this wonderful and inestimable union, binding us with

one another and with our divine Head, should find a special manifestation before the eyes of the faithful. Herein the sacred ministers represent not only our Saviour but also the whole mystical Body and each one of its members; in that sacrifice the faithful are associated in the common prayer and supplication and, through the hands of the priest, whose voice alone renders the immaculate Lamb present on the altar, they themselves offer to the eternal Father this most pleasing Victim of praise and propitiation for the needs of the whole Church. And as the divine Redeemer, when he was dying on the cross, offered himself as the Head of the whole human race to the eternal Father, so in this "clean oblation" [cf. Mal 1:11] he offers to the heavenly Father not only himself as the Head of the Church, but in himself also his mystical members, for he embraces them all, even the weak and the frail among them, most lovingly in his heart.

(The sacrament of the Eucharist and the Church)

1565 Moreover, the sacrament of the Eucharist, while also presenting a vivid and marvellous picture of the unity of the Church—since the bread to be consecrated results from the kneading together of many grains of wheat[1]—gives to us the very author of supernatural grace, from whom we are enabled to draw that Spirit of charity which bids us live not our own life, but the life of Christ, and whereby we love the Redeemer himself in all the members of his social Body.

ENCYCLICAL LETTER *MEDIATOR DEI* (1947)

Pope Pius XII's great encyclical on the liturgy continues Mystici Corporis, *but contains a much more elaborate treatment of the Eucharist. The Pope shows the central place which the Eucharist occupies in the Church's liturgical life; the Eucharist is "the summit of the Christian religion". The doctrine is to a great extent based on the Council of Trent but it also reflects recent theological advances. It explains that Christ is offered in the state of victim in which he is made present on the altar and which is symbolised by the double consecration (cf. n. 1566). It goes beyond* Mystici Corporis, *when it states that the faithful, though exercising no ministerial priestly power as does the priest representing Christ at the altar (cf. n. 1567), nevertheless do*

---

1. Cf. *Didachê* IX, 4.

not merely offer through the priest (cf. n. 1564), but also together with him (n. 1568). It shows that every Mass, even celebrated privately, has a public and social character and is the Mass of the Church (n. 1569). In line with, but more precise than the Council of Trent (cf. n 1562), it explains that communion, though a participation in the sacrifice, belongs to its integrity, not to its essence; this is why only the communion of the priest is required though the communion of the faithful is highly recommended (n. 1570). The text is found in AAS 39 (1947) 521ff.

(Christ is offered in the Mass under signs symbolic of his death)

1566 [...] On the cross Christ offered to God the whole of
3848 himself and his sufferings, and the victim was immolated
by a bloody death voluntarily accepted. But on the altar, by reason of the glorious condition of his humanity "death no longer has dominion over him" *[Rom 6:9]*, and therefore the shedding of his blood is not possible. Nevertheless, the divine wisdom has devised a way in which our Redeemer's sacrifice is marvellously shown forth by external signs symbolic of death. By the transubstantiation of bread into the body of Christ and of wine into his blood both his body and blood are rendered really present; but the eucharistic species under which he is present symbolise the violent separation of his body and blood, and so a commemorative showing forth of the death which took place in reality on Calvary is repeated in each Mass, because by distinct representations Christ Jesus is signified and shown forth in the state of victim.

(At the altar the priest represents Christ)

(1567) *(See text under n. 1734)*

(The faithful offer through the priest and with him)

(1568) *(See text under nn. 1735-1736)*

(Every Mass, even celebrated privately, is the Mass of the whole Church)

1569 [...]Every time the priest re-enacts what the divine
3853 Redeemer did at the Last Supper, the sacrifice is really
accomplished; and this sacrifice, always and everywhere, necessarily and of its nature, has a public and social character. For he who offers it acts in the name both of Christ and of the faithful, of whom the divine Redeemer is the Head, and he offers it to God for the holy Catholic Church, and for the living and

the dead. And this happens whether the faithful are present—and we would indeed have them assisting in great numbers and with great devotion—or whether they are absent, because it is in no way necessary that the people should ratify what has been done by the sacred minister.[...]

(Communion belongs to the integrity, not to the essence of the Mass)

1570 [...]The eucharistic sacrifice is essentially the unbloody
3854 immolation of the divine Victim, an immolation
mystically manifested in the separation of the sacred species and the offering made of them to the eternal Father. The communion belongs to the integrity of the sacrifice; it is a participation of the sacrifice by the reception of the blessed sacrament. And, while it is quite necessary for the sacrificing minister, to the faithful it is only to be highly recommended.

ENCYCLICAL LETTER *HUMANI GENERIS* (1950)

Modern scientific research, probing the secret of the composition of matter, has led to a physical concept of substance which is considerably new, and consequently to a re-consideration of the meaning of transubstantiation. Some assumed that the doctrine of transubstantiation is based on the philosophical concept of substance which is no longer tenable; on the other hand, they perceived the difficulty of applying to the eucharistic presence of Christ's body and blood the new physical concept of substance. Hence they could be tempted to reduce that presence to a symbolic one. Pope Pius XII rejects a solution which would tend to destroy the Church's doctrine.

1571 There are some who pretend that the doctrine of
3891 transubstantiation, based, as they say, on a philosophical
notion of substance which is now out of date, must be corrected in such a way that the presence of Christ in the most holy Eucharist is reduced to some sort of symbolism; the consecrated species would be merely efficacious signs of Christ's spiritual presence and of his intimate union with his faithful members in the mystical Body.

DISCOURSE AT THE INTERNATIONAL CONGRESS ON PASTORAL LITURGY (Assisi 1956)

Recent years have witnessed a growing awareness of the communitarian meaning of the Eucharist; consequently, the desire has also been felt that this aspect be expressed in the way in which the Eucharist is celebrated. The ancient practice of sacramental concelebration which, though always retained in the Oriental Churches, had almost entirely disappeared in the West, brought out this aspect in striking manner. At a time when it could not be foreseen that the practice of concelebration would soon be re-introduced in the Latin rite by the Second Vatican Council, some theologians advocated the attendance by priests and people at a Mass celebrated by one priest. Pope Pius XII draws the attention to the action which only the celebrating priet performs, as acting in the person of Christ. Not only the personal fruit derived from the Mass but also the nature of the action must be linked to the participation by priests in the celebration of the Eucharist. The Discourse delivered at the Assisi congress repeats this point and further elaborates a previous allocution (2 Nov. 1954), the text of which is found in AAS 46 (1954) pp. 668-670. The Pope also states that for sacramental concelebration it is required that concelebrants recite the words of institution together with the main celebrant; he does not, however, attribute this requirement to the "institution of Christ" as does a decree of the Holy Office issued the following year (1957) (cf. DS 3928). The text is found in AAS 48 (1956) 711ff.

(Only the celebrating priest performs the act of Christ offering himself, as representing his person)

1572 The priest-celebrant, putting on the person of Christ, alone offers sacrifice, and not the people, nor the clerics, nor even the priests who reverently assist. All, however, can and should take an active part in the sacrifice.[...] With regard to the offering of the eucharistic sacrifice, the actions of Christ, the High Priest, are as many as are the priests celebrating, not as many as are the priests reverently hearing the Mass of a bishop or a priest; for those present at the Mass in no sense sustain, or act in, the person of Christ sacrificing, but are to be compared to the faithful lay people who are present at the Mass.[...] The central element of the eucharitic sacrifice is that in which Christ intervenes as "offering himself"—to adopt the words of the Council of Trent *[cf. n. 1548]*. That happens at the consecration when, in the very act of transubstantiation worked by the Lord, the priest-celebrant is "acting in the person of Christ" (*personam Christi gerens*).[...] After the consecration is performed, the "offering of the victim placed on the altar" (*oblatio hostiae super altare positae*) can be accomplished and is accomplished by the priest-celebrant, by the Church, by the other priests, by each of the faithful. But this action is not the action of Christ himself through the priest representing him (*actio ipsius Christi per sacerdotem ipsius personam sustinentem et gerentem*).

(Sacramental concelebration requires that the concelebrants say the words of consecration)

1573 In reality, the action of the consecrating priest is the very action of Christ who acts through his minister. In the case of a concelebration in the proper sense of the word, Christ, instead of acting through one minister, acts through several. On the other hand, in a merely ceremonial concelebration, which could also be the act of a lay person, there is no question of simultaneous consecration, and this fact raises the important question: What intention and what exterior action are required to have a true concelebration and simultaneous consecration?[...] It is not sufficient to have and to indicate the will to make one's own the words and the actions of the celebrant. The concelebrants must, themselves, say over the bread and the wine: "This is my body", "This is my blood". Otherwise, their concelebration is purely ceremonial.

THE SECOND VATICAN GENERAL COUNCIL

The Council of Trent devoted separate sessions to the "sacrament of the Eucharist" (cf. nn. 1512ff) and the "sacrifice of the Mass" (cf. nn. 1545ff). The doctrine of the sacrifice of the Mass is among the most beautiful documents issued by it. Yet, the twofold division between sacrament and sacrifice, imposed by the context of the Reformation as well as the lapse of eleven years that— due to historical circumstances—separated the two sessions, was not conducive to a fully integrated doctrine. Vatican II is less doctrinal in purpose than Trent had been; its oulook is primarily pastoral. Nevertheless, its eucharistic doctrine, if less technically elaborated, is more complete and provides a more balanced view of the mystery than that of the Tridentine Council. The main documents are the constitutions on the Sacred Liturgy (SC) and on the Church (LG), as well as the decrees on ecumenism (UR) and on the priestly ministry (PO).

Three main features characterise the eucharistic doctrine of Vatican II: its comprehensiveness; the stress it lays on the intrinsic relationship between the eucharistic mystery and the mystery of the Church; its keen sense of the value of signs in the eucharistic celebration.

SC 47 enumerates the various aspects of the eucharistic mystery; it perpetuates the sacrifice of the cross through the centuries; it is a Paschal banquet in which Christ is eaten; it is the memorial of Christ's death and resurrection, the sacrament of love, sign of unity and bond of charity. In the Mass, therefore, the sacrifice and sacred meal belong to the same mystery (cf. LG 11). Sacrifice and meal, the eucharistic mystery is the sacramental celebration of Christ's Paschal mystery (SC 6); this is why it is especially from it "as from a fount" that are derived "the sanctification of human beings in Christ and the glorification of God" (SC 10; cf. LG 3).

As a sacrifice, the eucharistic mystery makes Christ's sacrifice present to the Church. Christ instituted it in order to perpetuate the sacrifice of the cross through the centuries and to entrust to the Church a memorial of his death and resurrection (SC 47; cf. LG 3, 7, 26, 28; SC 2, 6, 7; PO 2, 5, 13; CD 15 etc.). Thus, in the Mass the sacrifice which Christ made of himself once for all is represented and the offerings of the faithful are joined to the sacrifice of their Head (LG 28). The faithful do not merely offer through the priest; for even though the priest alone, acting in the name of Christ the Head, consecrates and makes the sacrifice of Christ present on the altar, they too offer "not only through the hands of the priest, but also together with him" (SC 48 after Mediator Dei; cf. n. 1568). This is why every Mass, even celebrated privately, is "an act of Christ and of the Church" (PO 13; cf. LG 26; SC 26). As to the assembled congregation, it is urged to enter into the Mass effectively through active participation (SC 48).

The eucharistic presence of Christ is viewed in its relationship to the mysteric action by which the Paschal mystery is represented. SC 7 distinguishes various modalities of Christ's presence in the liturgical celebration. The liturgy of the word and the eucharistic liturgy proper constitute one single act of worship (SC 56). However, Christ is present "especially" under the eucharistic species (SC 7).

The eucharistic mystery is also the sacred banquet in which the sacrificial victim is shared. Through sacramental communion the faithful achieve a more perfect participation in the Mass (SC 55). This is why communion is strongly recommended to them. Pronounced emphasis is laid on the Eucharist as the sacrament of unity: the unity of God's people is "aptly signified and admirably realised by this most august sacrament" (LG 11; cf. LG 26; UR 2). In fact, "no Christian community can be built up unless it be rooted and centred in the celebration of the Holy Eucharist: all education in community spirit must start there" (PO 6). The unity signified and effected by the eucharistic banquet has a double aspect, ecclesial and Christological: the Eucharist unites the members among themselves and through Christ with God. "By really partaking of the Lord's body in the breaking of the eucharistic bread, we are taken up into communion with him and with one another" (LG 7); we are day by day drawn "into ever more perfect a union with God and with each other" (SC 48). Through the eucharistic celebration, the Covenant of God with human beings, ratified once for all in the blood of Christ, is renewed (SC 10). While looking back to the Christ-event, the eucharistic reality also looks towards eschatological salvation: it is a pledge of resurrection. Hence, the threefold dimension of the eucharistic banquet: it is at once a memorial of the Paschal mystery, an event of grace, and a pledge of future glory (SC 47).

The 'Council of the Church' was bound to throw new light on the theme: Eucharist and Church. In fact, the emphasis laid on the close relationship between the two mysteries is one of the remarkable achievements of Vatican II.

From the outset, SC notes that the Eucharist, which occupies the central place among the Church's sacraments (PO 5) and in its entire liturgical life (SC 10), is quite particularly "the outstanding means whereby the faithful can express in their lives and manifest to others the mystery of Christ and the real nature of the true Church" (SC 2). The sacramental representation of the mystery of Christ is also the celebration of the mystery of the Church. The social character of the Eucharist is inscribed in its very nature: as sacrifice it is the one sacrifice of Christ represented in the Church (LG 28); as meal, it is "a meal of fraternal communion" (GS 38). However, the Church is a hierarchical communion; hence the hierarchical character of the eucharistic assembly. From the bishop, the high priest of his flock, "the life of Christ in his faithful is in some way derived and dependent" (SC 41). The bishop exercises his function as steward of grace mostly in the Eucharist (LG 26). Thus, the Eucharist at which he presides, surrounded by his college of priests, is the eucharistic celebration par excellence (SC 41; cf. LG 26). Every other celebration is related to him (SC 42). At the same time, each eucharistic assembly is a sign of the unity of the mystical body (SC 26; LG 26). On the relationship between Church and Eucharist, cf. also LG 3, 7, 11, 15, 26, 28, 50; UR 2, 3, 15; PO 5, 7, etc.

A last important feature of the eucharistic doctrine of Vatican II is its sense of the value of sacramental symbolism. The reforms introduced by the Constitution SC for the celebration of the Eucharist as for other liturgical actions are directed to a greater intelligibility of the sacramental signs (cf. SC 59, 33). This is the reason for the restoration of the communion under both kinds (SC 55). Of sacramental concelebration SC 57 affirms that by it "the unity of the priesthood is appropriately manifested".

CONSTITUTION *SACROSANCTUM CONCILIUM* (1963)

(The Liturgy, especially the Eucharist, in the life of the Church)

1574   2. The liturgy, "through which the work of our redemption is accomplished", most of all in the divine sacrifice of the Eucharist, is the outstanding means whereby the faithful can express in their lives and manifest to others, the mystery of Christ and the real nature of the true Church. It is of the essence of the Church that it be both human and divine, visible and yet invisibly endowed, eager to act and yet intent on contemplation, present in this world and yet a pilgrim; and it is all these things in such a wise that in it the human is directed and subordinated to the divine, the visible likewise to the invisible, action to contemplation, and this present world to that city yet to come, which we seek [cf. Heb 13:14]. Hence, while the liturgy daily builds up those who are within into a holy temple in the Lord, into a dwelling place for God in the Spirit [cf. Heb 2:21-22] to the mature measure of the fulness of Christ [cf. Eph 4:13], at the same time it marvellously strengthens their power to preach Christ, and thus shows forth the Church to those who are outside as a sign lifted up among the nations [cf. Is. 11:12] under which the scattered children of God may be gathered together [cf. Jn 11:52] until there is one sheepfold and one shepherd [cf. Jn 10:16].

(The various aspects of the Eucharist)

1575 47. At the Last Supper, on the night when he was betrayed, our Saviour instituted the eucharistic sacrifice of his body and blood. He did this in order to perpetuate the sacrifice of the cross throughout the centuries until he should come again, and so to entrust to his beloved Spouse, the Church, a memorial of his death and resurrection: a sacrament of love, a sign of unity, a bond of charity, a paschal banquet "in which Christ is eaten, the mind is filled with grace, and a pledge of future glory is given to us."[1]

DOGMATIC CONSTITUTION *LUMEN GENTIUM* (1964)

(Participation by all)

1576 11. Whenever they take part in the eucharistic sacrifice, fount and summit of the entire Christian life, [the faithful] offer to God the divine victim and themselves along with it; and thus, both for the offering and in holy communion, all act their own part in the liturgical action, not indeed indiscriminately but in various ways. Strengthened at the holy table by the body of Christ, they manifest in a concrete manner the unity of God's people, aptly signified and admirably realised by this most august sacrament.

PASTORAL CONSTITUTION *GAUDIUM ET SPES* (1965)

(The Eucharist in connection with the Spirit, human freedom and ethical responsibility for the future of created reality)

1576a 38. But of all Christians the Spirit makes free human beings, who are ready to put aside love of self and

---

1. *Roman Breviary*, Feast of Corpus Christi.

integrate earthly resources into human life, in order to reach out to that future day when humankind itself will become an offering accepted by God [Rom 15:16]. Christ left to his followers a pledge of this hope and food for the journey in the sacrament of faith, in which natural elements, the fruits of human cultivation, are changed into his glorified body and blood, as a supper of brotherly fellowship and a foretaste of the heavenly banquet.

DECREE *PRESBYTERORUM ORDINIS* (1965)

(The Spirit-filled flesh and blood of Christ as source and summit of all evangelization, and as completion of the catechumenate)

1576b 5. The other sacraments, and indeed all ecclesiastical ministries and works of the apostolate, are bound up with the Holy Eucharist and are directed towards it. For in the most blessed Eucharist is contained the whole spiritual good of the Church, namely Christ himself our Pasch and the living bread which gives life to humankind through his flesh—that flesh which is given life and gives life through the Holy Spirit. Thus all are invited and led to offer themselves, their works and all creation with Christ. For this reason the Eucharist appears as the source and the summit of all preaching of the Gospel: catechumens are gradually led up to participation in the Eucharist, while the faithful who have already been consecrated in baptism and confirmation are fully incorporated in the body of Christ by the reception of the Eucharist.

(The full and sincere celebration of the Eucharist leads to the practice of mutual help, missionary activity and public witness)

1576c 6. No Christian community is built up which does not grow from and hinge on the celebration of the most holy Eucharist.[1] From this all education for community spirit must begin. This eucharistic celebration, to be full and sincere, ought to lead on the one hand to the various works of charity and mutual help, and on the other hand to missionary activity and the various forms of Christian witness.

---

1. Cf. *Didascalia* II, 59, 1-3.

PAUL VI

ENCYCLICAL LETTER *MYSTERIUM FIDEI* (1965)

The Constitution of the Second Vatican Council on the Sacred Liturgy had shown the various modalities of the presence of Christ in the liturgy (cf. n. 1334). The encyclical Mysterium Fidei states that all these different modalities of Christ's presence must be called "real". Yet, the presence of Christ under the eucharistic species surpasses them all and is "presence in the fullest sense". Alluding to attempts made by recent theologians to express the eucharistic presence in terms of 'transignification' and 'transfinalisation', the Pope remarks that these terms do convey a real aspect of the mystery; they do not, however, by themselves suffice to express it adequately. The term of transubstantiation must continue to be used, for it is the change of substance which gives to the eucharistic species their new meaning and their new finality. The text is found in AAS 57 (1965) 753 ff.

(The change of substance must be preserved)

1577 It is not allowable [...] to exaggerate the element of sacramental sign as if the symbolism, which all certainly admit in the Eucharist, expressed fully and exhausted the mode of Christ's presence in this sacrament. Nor is it allowable to discuss the mystery of transubstantiation without mentioning what the Council of Trent stated about the marvellous change of the whole substance of bread into the body and of the whole substance of wine into the blood of Christ [*cf. n. 1519*], speaking rather only of what is called "transignification" and "transfinalisation".[...]

(The presence of Christ under the eucharistic species is his presence in the fullest sense)

1578 But there is yet another manner in which Christ is present to his Church, a manner which surpasses all the others; it is his presence in the sacrament of the Eucharist, which is for this reason "a more consoling source of devotion, a more lively object of contemplation, a more effective means of sanctification than all the other sacraments."[1] The reason is clear: it contains Christ himself.[...]

This presence is called "real" not in an exclusive sense, as if the other kinds of presence were not real, but 'par excellence', because

---

1. St. Thomas Aquinas, *S.T.*, III, 73, 3c.

it is a substantial presence by which Christ, the Godman, whole and entire, becomes present *[cf. nn. 1516ff].* It would therefore be wrong to explain this presence by imagining a "spiritual" nature, as it is called, of the glorified body of Christ, which would be present everywhere, or by reducing it to a kind of symbolism, as if this most august sacrament consisted of nothing else than an efficacious sign "of Christ's spiritual presence and of his intimate union with his faithful members in the mystical Body" *[cf. n. 1571].*

(Eucharistic symbolism is no adequate expression of this presence)

1579   While the eucharistic symbolism brings us to an understanding of the effect proper to this sacrament which is the unity of the mystical Body, it does not indicate or explain the nature of this sacrament which makes it different from all others. The constant teaching which the Catholic Church passes on to its catechumens, the understanding of the Christian people, the doctrine defined by the Council of Trent, the very words used by Christ when he instituted the most holy Eucharist, compel us to acknowledge that "the Eucharist is the flesh of our Saviour Jesus Christ which suffered for our sins and which the Father in his loving kindness raised again."[1]

(The change of substance gives to the eucharistic species their new signification and finality)

1580   The way Christ is made present in this sacrament is none other than by the change of the whole substance of the bread into his body and of the whole substance of the wine into his blood, and this unique and truly wonderful change the Catholic Church rightly and properly calls transubstantiation *[cf. nn. 1519, 1527].* As a result of transubstantiation, the species of bread and wine undoubtedly take on a new meaning and a new finality, for they no longer remain ordinary bread and ordinary wine, but become the sign of something sacred, the sign of a spiritual food. However, the reason why they take on this new significance and this new finality is because they contain a new "reality" which we may justly term ontological. For there no longer lies under those species what was there before, but something quite different; and that, not only because of the faith

---

1. St. Ignatius of Antioch, *Epistola ad Smyrnas*, 7, 1.

of the Church, but in objective reality, since after the change of the substance or nature of the bread and wine into the body and blood of Christ, nothing remains of the bread and wine but the appearances, under which Christ, whole and entire, in his physical "reality" is bodily present, although not in the same way as bodies are present in a given place.

(The presence of the eucharistic Christ is a strong stimulus to the practice of Christian love in society)

1580a You know very well, my dear Christians, that the Eucharist is conserved in the churches and oratories as the spiritual centre of the religious and parochial community, and indeed of the universal Church and of all humanity because, under the veil of the sacred species, it contains Christ the invisible Head of the Church and Redeemer of humankind, the centre of all hearts, "for whom all things exist and we for him" *[1 Cor 8:6]*. It follows that eucharistic worship forcefully moves the soul to cultivate "social" love *(ad amorem "socialem" excolendum)* which places the common good before the private good; let us make our own the cause of the community, of the parish, of the universal Church; and let us extend charity to the entire world, so that people everywhere might know that we are the living members of Christ.

INSTRUCTION *EUCHARISTICUM MYSTERIUM* OF THE S. CONGREGATION OF RITES (1967)

This instruction, published by the Sacred Congregation of Rites to put into effect the renewal desired by the Second Vatican Council in the celebration of the eucharistic mystery, is essentially practical and pastoral in scope. Nevertheless, it is based on doctrine and on more than one point expresses the doctrine of Vatican II even better than the conciliar documents. It enumerates the various aspects of the eucharistic mystery and stresses the close bond which exists between sacrifice and meal (cf. n. 1581). It shows the relationship between the Eucharist and the mystery of the Church (cf. n. 1582). It brings out the full import of the people's active participation in the eucharistic celebration (cf. n. 1583). It shows how in the unfolding of the eucharistic celebration the various modes of Christ's presence in the liturgical assembly are progressively revealed (cf. n. 1585). It insists that the social aspect inscribed in the very nature of the Eucharist be brought out in the manner of celebration; in this regard it points to concelebration as the "eminent manner" of celebrating, and brings out its full significance not merely in the order of signification but also of efficacy.

A remarkable feature of this document is its insistence on the full orchestration of sacramental symbolism in the celebration of the Eucharist. On the foundation of what the Second Vatican Council has stated concerning the need for intelligibility of the sacramental signs (cf. SC 59, 33), the instruction concludes that "the more intelligible the signs by which [the Eucharist] is celebrated and worshipped, the more firmly and effectively will it enter into the lives and minds of the faithful" (4). All the norms and directives given in view of a renewal of the Church's eucharistic life are based on this fundamental principle (20). Hence the expression "ratione signi" recurs everywhere in the instruction: "even through signs" communion ought to be perceived as a participation in the sacrifice (31); the sign of the eucharistic banquet is more complete in communion under both kinds (32); "by reason of the sign" it is fitting that priests participate in the common Eucharist by actually exercising their priestly order (43). Similarly, all eucharistic devotions must by signs be perceived as essentially related to the celebration of the mystery (cf. nn. 60, 55, etc.). The text is found in AAS 59 (1967) 539ff.

(The various aspects of the eucharistic celebration)

1581   3. The Mass, the Lord's Supper, is at the same time and inseparably: a sacrifice in which the sacrifice of the cross is perpetuated; a memorial of the death and resurrection of the Lord, who said: "Do this as a memorial of me" [Lk 22:19]; a sacred banquet in which, through the communion of the body and blood of the Lord, the people of God share the benefits of the Paschal sacrifice, renew the new Covenant which God has made with human beings once for all through the blood of Christ, and in faith and hope foreshadow and anticipate the eschatological banquet in the Kingdom of the Father, proclaiming the Lord's death "until he comes" [1 Cor 11:26].

In the Mass, therefore, the sacrifice and sacred meal belong to the same mystery—so much so that they are linked by the closest bond.

(The Eucharist is the centre of the Church's life)

1582   6. The catechesis of the eucharistic mystery should aim to help the faithful to realise that the celebration of the Eucharist is the true centre of the whole Christian life both for the universal Church and for the local congregations of that Church. For "the other sacraments as well as every ecclesiastical ministry or work of the apostolate are connected with the Holy Eucharist and directed towards it. For the Holy Eucharist contains the whole of the Church's spiritual treasure, namely Christ himself, our Pasch and the living bread who gives life to humankind by his flesh made living and vivifying by the Holy Spirit. Thus, all are invited and led to offer themselves and their labours and all things created together with Christ" [PO 5].

(The fulness of the people's active participation in the eucharistic celebration)

1583 12. It should be made clear that all who gather together for the Eucharist constitute the holy people which, together with the minister, plays its part in the sacred action. It is indeed the priest alone, who, acting in the person of Christ, consecrates the bread and wine, but the role of the faithful in the Eucharist is to recall the passion, resurrection and glorification of the Lord, to give thanks to God, and to offer the immaculate victim not only through the hands of the priest, but also together with him, and finally, by receiving the body of the Lord, to perfect their communion with God and among themselves which should be the effect of participation in the sacrifice of the Mass. For the faithful achieve a more perfect participation in the Mass, when, with proper dispositions, they receive the body of the Lord sacramentally in the Mass itself, in obedience to his words: "Take and eat."

(The meaning of concelebration)

1584 47. Concelebration in the Eucharist aptly demonstrates the unity of the sacrifice and of the priesthood. Moreover, whenever the faithful take an active part, the unity of the people of God is strikingly manifested, particularly if the bishop presides.

Again, concelebration both symbolises and strengthens the brotherly bond between priests, because "by virtue of the sacred ordination and mission which they have in common, all priests are bound together in an intimate brotherhood" [cf. LG 28].

Therefore, unless it conflicts with the needs of the faithful, which must always be attended to with the deepest pastoral concern, and although every priest retains the right to celebrate alone, it is desirable that priests should celebrate in this eminent manner.[...]

(The various modes of Christ's presence are progressively revealed in the eucharistic celebration)

1585 55. In the celebration of the Mass, the principal modes of Christ's presence to his Church are gradually revealed.

First of all, Christ is seen to be present in the assembly of the faithful gathered in his name; then in his word, as the scriptures are read and explained; in the person of the minister; finally and in a unique way *(modo singulari)* under the species of the Eucharist.[...]

(Prayer before the Blessed Sacrament)

1586 50. When the faithful adore Christ present in the sacrament, they should remember that this presence derives from the sacrifice and is directed towards both sacramental and spiritual communion.

In consequence, the devotion which leads the faithful to visit the Blessed Sacrament draws them into an ever deeper participation in the Paschal Mystery. It leads them to respond gratefully to the gift of him who through his humanity constantly pours divine life into the members of his Body *[PO 5]*. Dwelling with Christ our Lord, they enjoy his personal friendship and pour out their hearts before him for themselves and their dear ones, and pray for the peace and salvation of the world. They offer their entire lives with Christ to the Father in the Holy Spirit, and receive in this wonderful exchange an increase of faith, hope and charity. Thus they nourish those right dispositions which enable them with all devotion to celebrate the memorial of the Lord and receive frequently the bread given us by the Father.

The faithful should therefore strive to worship Christ our Lord in the Blessed Sacrament, in harmony with their way of life.

(Eucharistic devotion)

1587 58. Devotion, both private and public, towards the sacrament of the altar even outside Mass, provided it observes the norms laid down by the legitimate authority and those of the present instruction, is highly recommended by the Church, since the eucharistic sacrifice is the source and summit of the whole Christian life *[n. 1576]*.

In determining the form of such devotions, account should be taken of the regulation of the Second Vatican Council concerning the relationship to be maintained between the liturgy and other non-liturgical celebrations. Especially important is the rule which states: "the liturgical seasons must be taken into account, and those devotions must harmonize with the liturgy, be in some way derived from it and lead the people towards the liturgy as to something which, of its nature, is far superior to these devotions" *[SC 13]*.

ADDRESS TO PEASANT WORKERS AT THE INTERNATIONAL EUCHARISTIC CONGRESS IN BOGOTA, COLUMBIA

(23 August 1968)

In this address, the Pope not only exemplifies the "social" love which he had claimed is fostered by eucharistic grace (cf. n. 1580a), but also refers to the peasant workers themselves as "a sacrament", or as "a mystery of the presence of Christ", thus pointing out an analogical correspondence between the real presence in the eucharistic species and the real presence in the poor and oppressed. Furthermore, the care shown to such human signs and images of the presence of Christ is said to be based on the powerful "sociology of the Gospel" which should be adhered to by those who have received holy communion. The text is found in Insegnamenti di Paolo VI, *Vol. 6, Tipografia Poliglotta Vaticana, 1968, p. 377.*

(Poor people as the sacrament of Christ in a perfect, analogical and mystical correspondence to the eucharistic presence)

1587a We have come to Bogota to honour Jesus in his eucharistic mystery, and we are full of joy that he has given us the opportunity to do so by coming into your midst to celebrate the presence of the Lord among us, in the midst of his Church and of the world, and in your very selves. You are a sign, you are in image, you are a mystery of the presence of Christ. The sacrament of the Eucharist offers us his living and real presence in a hidden way; but you also are a sacrament, that is, a sacred image of the Lord among us, as a representative reflection, but one which is not hidden, of his human and divine face. We recall that which at one time the reknown and wise bishop Bossuet said concerning "the eminent dignity of the poor". And the entire tradition of the Church recognizes in the poor the sacrament of Christ, certainly not identical to the reality of the Eucharist, but in a perfect, analogical and mystical correspondence to it. Moreover, Jesus himself has said this to us on a solemn page of his Gospel, where he proclaims that every human being who suffers, who is hungry or sick, distressed or in need of compassion and help, is he himself, as if he were that unfortunate person, according to the mysterious and powerful sociology of the Gospel [cf. Mt 25:35ff], according to the humanism of Christ.

GENERAL INSTRUCTION ON THE ROMAN MISSAL OF THE SACRED CONGREGATION FOR DIVINE WORSHIP
(26 March 1970)

On 3 April, 1969, Pope Paul VI, by the Apostolic Constitution Missale Romanum, *approved the new Roman Missal prepared by the Sacred Congregation for Divine Worship in accordance with the Constitution on Liturgy of the Second Vatican Council. On 26 March, 1970, the Sacred Congregation, at the mandate of the Pope, promulgated and published the new edition of the Roman Missal. The new Missal is preceded by a General Instruction. The passages quoted here explain the nature of the eucharistic celebration and its basic structure.*

(Nature of the eucharistic celebration)

1588 7. The Lord's Supper or Mass gathers together the people of God, with a priest presiding in the person of Christ, to celebrate the memorial of the Lord or eucharistic sacrifice [cf. PO 5; SC 33]. For this reason the promise of Christ is particularly true of such a local congregation of the Church: "Where two or three are gathered in my name, there am I in their midst" [Mat 18:20]. In the celebration of Mass, which perpetuates the sacrifice of the cross [n. 1740], Christ is really present in the assembly itself, which is gathered in his name, in the person of the minister, in his word, and indeed substantially and unceasingly under the eucharistic species [SC 7].

(General structure of the Mass)

1589 8. Although the Mass is made up of the liturgy of the word and the liturgy of the eucharist, the two parts are so closely connected as to form one act of worship [SC 56]. The table of God's word and of Christ's body is prepared and from it the faithful are instructed and nourished [SC 48, 51]. In addition, the Mass has introductory and concluding rites.

JOHN PAUL II
LETTER TO THE BISHOPS OF THE CHURCH,
DOMINICAE CENAE
(24 February 1980)

On the occasion of Maundy Thursday, 1980, Pope John Paul II addressed to all the Bishops of the Church, and through them to all priests, a letter on the mystery and the cult of the Eucharist. One section of the letter develops the traditional doctrine on the Eucharist as sacrament of unity and love. The Pope prolongs this traditional doctrine by showing the social implications of the sacrament. The text is found in AAS 72 (1980) 123-124.

(Eucharist and neighbour)

1590   6. The authentic sense of the Eucharist becomes of itself the school of active love for neighbour. We know that this is the true and full order of love that the Lord has taught us: "By this all will know that you are my disciples, if you have love for one another" *[Jn 13:35]*. The Eucharist educates us to this love in a deeper way, it shows us, in fact, what value each person, our brother or sister, has in God's eyes, if Christ offers himself equally to each one, under the species of bread and wine. If our eucharistic worship is authentic, it must make us grow in awareness of the dignity of each person. The awareness of that dignity becomes the deepest motive of our relationship with our neighbour.

We must also become particularly sensitive to all human suffering and misery, to all injustice and wrong, and seek the way to redress them effectively. Let us learn to discover with respect the truth about the inner self that becomes the dwelling-place of God present in the Eucharist. Christ comes into the hearts of our brothers and sisters and visits their consciences. How the image of each and every one changes, when we become aware of this reality, when we make it the subject of our reflections! The sense of the Eucharistic Mystery leads us to love for our neighbour, to love for every human being.

HOMILY AT THE INAUGURAL MASS OF THE NATIONAL EUCHARISTIC CONGRESS AT FORTALEZA
(8 July 1980)

During his visit to Brazil, Pope John Paul II inaugurated the X National Eucharistic Congress at Fortaleza. During the inaugural Mass he delivered a homily in which he stressed the social implications of the Eucharist. One passage of the homily is quoted here. The text is found in Osservatore Romano *(English Edition), 11 August 1980, p. 7.*

(Social implications of the Eucharist)

1591   4. Eucharistic communion is the sign of the meeting of all the faithful. A truly inspiring sign, because at the holy table all the differences of race or social class disappear, leaving only the participation of all in the same holy food. This participation, identical in all, signifies and realizes the suppression of all that divides people, and brings about the meeting of all at a higher level, when all opposition is eliminated. Thus the Eucharist becomes the great instrument of bringing people closer to one another. Whenever the faithful take part in it with a sincere heart, they receive a new impetus to establish a better relationship among themselves, leading to recognition of one another's rights and corresponding duties as well. In this way the satisfaction of the requirements of justice is facilitated, precisely because of the particular climate of interpersonal relations that Christian charity creates within the same community.

ENCYCLICAL LETTER *SOLLICITUDO REI SOCIALIS*
(30 December 1987)

The acute perception, which has developed in various sectors of the Christian world since Vatican II, regarding the inextricable relationship between orthodoxy, or proper faith, and orthopraxy, or proper action, is clearly expressed in the following eucharistic passage found in conclusion of an encyclical on the social concerns of the Church. This passage is noteworthy not only because of its context, but also because of its content. Eucharistic grace is described as a union with Christ which in turn becomes a mission in his name. This eucharistic mission is eschatological, since it both gives witness to the definitive love of Jesus in society through faith and works, and anticipates the definitive goal of such witness in the kingdom.

(The Eucharist as the profound meaning of Christian efforts on behalf of development and peace in anticipation of the Kingdom)

1592 48. Thus the Lord unites us with himself through the Eucharist—sacrament and sacrifice—and he unites us with himself and with one another by a bond stronger than any natural union; and thus united, he sends us into the whole world to bear witness through faith and works to divine love, preparing the coming of his kingdom and anticipating it, though in the obscurity of the present time. All of us who take part in the Eucharist are called to discover, through this sacrament, the profound meaning of our actions in the world in favour of development and peace; and to receive from it the strength to commit ourselves ever more generously, following

the example of Christ, who in this sacrament lays down his life
for his friends [cf. Jn 15:3]. Our personal commitment, like that
of Christ, and in union with it, will not be in vain but certainly
fruitful.

APOSTOLIC LETTER *DIES DOMINI*
(31 May, 1998)

*In the face of lessening church attendance on Sundays and holy days of
obligation, the faithful are invited to rediscover the Lord's day despite growing
secularisation, and are reminded of their serious obligation to participate in
the Mass. Besides appealing to the scripture, the tradition, and the post-conciliar
canon law and catechism, the Pope offers an extensive theological argument
which, from five diverse yet related perspectives, views Sunday as: (1) The
Day of the Lord; (2) The Day of Christ; (3) The Day of the Church; (4) The
Day of Man; and (5) The Day of Days. For these reasons, it is most appropriate
to receive the Eucharist especially on the Lord's day, so that the force of this
sacrament may have its effect on all the dimensions of Christian life. The
entire text is found in* Origins *28 (1998-1999) 133-151.*

(From the Mass, Christians are sent on their evangelical mission)

1593 45. Receiving the Bread of Life, the disciples of Christ
ready themselves to undertake with the strength of the
risen Lord and his Spirit the tasks which await them in their
ordinary life. For the faithful who have understood the meaning
of what they have done, the eucharistic celebration does not stop
at the church door. Like the first witnesses of the resurrection,
Christians who gather each Sunday to experience and proclaim
the presence of the risen Lord are called to evangelise and bear
witness in their daily lives. Given this, the prayer after communion
and the concluding rite—the final blessing and the dismissal—
need to be better valued and appreciated, so that all who have
shared in the eucharist may come to a deeper sense of the
responsibility which is entrusted to them. Once the assembly
disperses, Christ's disciples return to their everyday surroundings
with the commitment to make their whole life a gift, a spiritual
sacrifice pleasing to God [cf. Rom 12:1]. They feel indebted to their
brothers and sisters because of what they have received in the
celebration, not unlike the disciples of Emmaus who, once they had
recognised the risen Christ "in the breaking of the bread" [cf. Lk
24: 30-32], felt the need to return immediately to share with their
brothers and sisters the joy of meeting the Lord [cf. Lk 24:33-35].

(On the grave obligation to observe the Sunday precept)

1594 47. The Code of Canon Law of 1917 for the first time gathered this tradition into a universal law *[canon 1248]*. The present code reiterates this, saying that "on Sundays and other holy days of obligation the faithful are bound to attend Mass" *[canon 1247]*. This legislation has normally been understood as entailing a grave obligation. This is the teaching of the *Catechism of the Catholic Church [2118]*, and it is easy to understand why if we keep in mind how vital Sunday is for the Christian life.

(Sunday as the invitation to look ahead to the day of the coming of the Lord)

1595 84. Sustaining Christian life as it does, Sunday has the additional value of being a testimony and a proclamation. As a day of prayer, communion and joy, Sunday resounds throughout society, emanating vital energies and reasons for hope. Sunday is the proclamation that time, in which he who is the risen Lord of history makes his home, is not the grave of our illusions but the cradle of an ever new future, an opportunity given to us to turn the fleeting moments of this life into seeds of eternity. Sunday is an invitation to look ahead; it is the day on which the Christian community cries out to Christ, *"Marána tha: Come, O Lord!" [1 Cor 16:22]*. With this cry of hope and expectation, the church is the companion and support of human hope. From Sunday to Sunday, enlightened by Christ, it goes forward toward the unending Sunday of the heavenly Jerusalem, which "has no need of the sun or moon to shine upon it, for the glory of God is its light and its lamp is the Lamb" *[Rv 21:23]*

CHAPTER XVI

RECONCILIATION AND THE ANOINTING OF THE SICK

The beginning of the Christian vocation is marked by a call to repentance, to metanoia, linked with the promise of forgiveness, and leading to God's kingdom. Thus, repentance has its first place in the initiation to the Christian life; but it is not limited to it. It is called for even after baptism and it always includes the assurance of God's mercy.

There is, however, a difference between the first turning to God and the reconciliation of those who have fallen into sin after baptism. The first forgiveness is given in the birth to a new existence; it coincides with a person's entrance into the Church, the communion of those who believe and have life in Jesus Christ through the Holy Spirit. The Christian's new situation after baptism gives to sin and repentance a new dimension: both affect a human being's relation not only to God but also to the Church. Sin remains, no doubt, an offence against the Creator and Saviour; but it also implies an inner dissociation from the spiritual communion with God's people. Similarly, repentance requires, together with a return to God, the desire to share once again in the life of the community. Forgiveness comes from God's mercy but includes the re-admission into the Church's life. From the earliest times this has been concretely apparent in the fact that a grave offence was sanctioned by the exclusion from the Eucharist, and forgiveness signified by the re-admission to the sacrificial banquet.

Hence the doctrine of sacramental penance must take into account two distinct yet closely interwoven realities: firstly, the inner renewal of the sinner whose relation to God, severed by sin, is restored in conversion and repentance; secondly, the ecclesial discipline by which the reconciliation of the sinner takes place within the Christian community.

No other sphere of the Church's life has, perhaps, undergone through the centuries such radical changes as has the penitential discipline. The patristic period was characterised by the practice of public penance. Having been excluded from the community, the sinner was reconciled after a period of penance; the reconciliation was granted only once in a life-time and therefore was frequently postponed to the time of death. Some rigoristic groups, however, denied altogether the power of the Church to remit sins; others made the demands for reconciliation too exacting. Hence the early ecclesiastical documents had to be concerned with the Church's right to forgive; they stressed the obligation to grant forgiveness at least at the time of death.

The documents of the early Middle Ages reflect the transition to a new penitential system, which gradually led to the present practice. With the fourth Lateran Council the general framework of the penitential discipline, including confession at least once a year, was settled.

Most documents reflect the theology of sacramental penance progressively developed by scholastic theology. It took its specific orientation at the time of the pre-Reformation period. Thus, in the Council of Trent, emphasis was laid on the acts of the penitent and on the Church's sacramental action; but the relation of sin and forgiveness to the community of the faithful was not stressed. In recent years, however, the renewed ecclesiology which the Second Vatican Council made its own once again brought to the fore the relation of sin and reconciliation to the life of the Christian community.

The introduction to the **Ordo Paenitentiae** *(1973) and the Post-Synodal Apostolic Exhortation (1984) elaborate on the themes of sin, reconciliation and the forms of celebrating sacramental reconciliation. For sin, see chapter XX.*

The anointing of the sick is closely related to penance. Classical theology conceived it as the Christian's final preparation and purification for the heavenly glory, according to the prevalent interpretation given to this sacrament during the middle Ages. The biblical text on which it is based (James 5.14f), however, already testified to the fact that it is ordained to the healing of both soul and body. A certain ambiguity has long prevailed in the ecclesiastical documents concerning this sacrament. Early texts witness to its practice in the early Church as an anointing of the sick; the documents of the Middle Ages and the Council of Trent conceive it more as "extreme unction", i.e., as the sacrament of the dying, though it is also called "sacred anointing of the sick". Once again it is the merit of the Second Vatican Council to have restored the more ancient tradition of this sacrament of the sick. The general introduction to the **Ordo unctionis infirmorum** *(1972) gives a more balanced understanding and practice of this sacrament.*

* * *

Thus the main points of doctrine in the Church documents on sacramental reconciliation and anointing of the sick are the following:

Reconciliation

The Church must herself be reconciled through dialogue, catechesis and the celebration of the sacraments: 1673, 1674, 1675, 1676b.

The Church has the power to forgive sins: 21, 25, 1601, 1615, 1616, 1617, 1643, 1660/46.47, 1943, 1979.

Penance is a sacrament instituted by Jesus Christ: 28, 32, 1305, 1311, 1612, 1615, 1617, 1641, 1943.

It is distinct from baptism as a judicial act: 1618, 1619, 1642, 1944.

Sacramental penance is necessary: 1429, 1610, 1611/20, 1623, 1626, 1646, 1944, 1979.

The Church must offer reconciliation at least at the time of death: 1602, 1604.

On the part of the penitent are required contrition, confession and satisfaction: 1612, 1614/5.14, 1620, 1644, 1944.

Contrition, its nature and necessity: 1612, 1614/6.7.11.12.14, 1622, 1645, 1944.

Through perfect contrition sins are forgiven: 1623.

Imperfect contrition, i.e., attrition, is a sufficient disposition for confession and is salutary: 1614/6.7, 1624, 1645.

Confession of all mortal sins committed after baptism is required: 1610, 1611/20, 1612, 1614/8.9, 1625, 1626, 1646-1648, 1670, 1676c, 1944.

It must be practised at least once a year: 1608, 1670.

Confession should be private: 1606, 1608, 1609, 1672.

Satisfaction, its need and meaning: 1611/21, 1612, 1630-1634, 1652-1655, 1944.

On the part of the Church sacramental absolution is required: 1612, 1614/10, 1620.

It is a judicial act: 1628, 1649, 1676d.

The confessor must have the requisite qualities: 1676b.

Formula of absolution: 1671.

Cases can be reserved: 1611/25, 1614/13, 1629, 1651.

The minister of the sacrament of penance is the priest, authorised by the bishop: 1605, 1611/20.21, 1612, 1614/12.13, 1627, 1629, 1650, 1707, 1714, 1740.

Role of penitent: 1669b.

Norms of general absolution are to be followed: 1670, 1676e.

The fruit of sacramental penance is the reconciliation with God: 1306, 1612, 1614/10, 1621, 1943f, 1980;
and with the Church: 1662, 1667, 1669a.
Not all temporal punishment is remitted: 1630, 1652, 1944, 1980.
Various forms of doing penance: 1669.
The Church asks pardon for the sins of the past: 1677a-e, 1678, 1679, 1680b.
Penance and conversion: 1680a.

Anointing of the Sick

It is a true sacrament: 28, 32, 1305, 1311, 1635, 1636, 1656, 1660/ 48;
instituted by Christ: 1311, 1636, 1637, 1656; 1668a.
The death and resurrection of Christ are the source of the sacrament's power: 1668b.
It is promulgated by St. James: 1636, 1656.
It is administered by an anointing with oil accompanied by a prayer: 1603, 1613, 1636, 1658, 1668.
The minister of the sacrament is the priest: 1603, 1613, 1659.
It is to be received by the faithful who are seriously ill: 1603, 1613, 1635, 1638, 1661, 1664.
The fruit of the sacrament is the strength of the soul: 1306, 1613, 1637, 1657;
and, at times, health of the body: 1306, 1613, 1637, 1664, 1665, 1667.
It can also remit sins: 1637, 1657.
The role of community and minister: 1668c, 1668d.

THE FIRST GENERAL COUNCIL OF NICAEA (325)

Many local Councils of the early centuries dealt with the reconciliation of sinners, e.g., Carthage (251 and 252) at the time of the Decian persecution, Elvira in Spain (c. 300-303) during the persecution of Diocletian, the general Council of the Western Church in Arles (314), the Synod of Ancyra (314). Great differences as regards practical norms of the reconciliation of apostates and other public sinners are found in these Councils. Yet in the general Council of Nicaea a consensus on the basic attitudes was reached. This gathering of 318 bishops took a definite stand against Novatianism, which denied the power of the Church to forgive sins; against rigoristic practices it also decided that reconciliation must not be denied at the time of death, though with the proviso that in case of recovery such persons would be ranked among the penitents.

(The reconciliation of Novatians)

1601   Canon 8: As to those who call themselves Cathars, i.e.,
127   the "pure" [the Novatians], if they come to the Catholic and apostolic Church, this holy and great Synod has decided that after receiving the imposition of hands they remain in the ranks of the clergy. They must, however, above all promise in writing to accept and follow the doctrines of the Catholic and apostolic Church, to have communion with 'digamists' [people living in a second marriage] and with those who have lapsed in persecution, for whose reconciliation provision has been made and a time has been fixed.

(Reconciliation of the dying and viaticum)

1602   Canon 13: As to those who are departing from this life,
129   the old canonical law is now to be kept: anyone about to die should not be deprived of the ultimate and most necessary viaticum. If, after having been reconciled and received again into the fellowship, one should recover one's health, such a one should be placed in the ranks of those who share only in the communion of prayer. In general, to anyone who is departing from this life and asks to partake of the Eucharist the bishop after investigation should grant it.

INNOCENT I

LETTER TO DECENTIUS, BISHOP OF GUBBIO (416)

This letter intends merely to clarify practical points regarding the administration of the anointing of the sick, viz., who is to administer it; but in reality it sums up the contemporary teaching. It links the anointing with the text of James; the oil is blessed by the bishop; it is used, apart from the sacramental rite, also for other purposes; the anointing is done by bishops or priests; it is called a 'sacrament' which, however, must not be understood in the later technical sense as one of the seven sacraments. Still, the fact that those who undergo penance and hence are excluded from the Eucharist cannot receive it, indicates that it is considered as something more than a pious custom.

(On the anointing of the sick)

1603 [Your next question] concerns the text from the epistle
216 of the blessed apostle James: "Are any among you sick?
They should call for the elders of the Church and have them pray over them, anointing them with oil in the name of the Lord. The prayer of faith will save the sick, and the Lord will raise them up; and anyone who has committed sins will be forgiven" [*James 5:14f*]. This must undoubtedly be accepted and understood as referring to the oil of Chrism, prepared by the bishop, which can be used for anointing not only by priests but also by all Christians whenever they themselves or their people are in need of it. The question whether the bishop can do what undoubtedly can be done by priests seems superfluous, for priests are mentioned simply because bishops are prevented by other occupations and cannot visit all the sick. But if a bishop is in a position to do so and thinks it proper, he, to whom it belongs to prepare the Chrism, can himself without hesitation visit the sick to bless them and anoint them with Chrism. But it may not be used on those undergoing penance for it is of the nature of a sacrament. How could one think that one kind of sacrament should be allowed to those to whom the rest is denied?

CELESTINE I

LETTER TO THE BISHOPS OF VIENNE AND NARBONNE (428)

Reconciliation at the time of death remained controversial on various grounds: 1) suspicions concerning the sincerity of those in danger of death, as they seemed to seek absolution only out of fear; 2) the need for works of satisfaction which seemed indispensable for reconciliation. In this official letter Pope Celestine insists on offering reconciliation to the dying who ask for it. His letter reflects a great pastoral concern for the faithful in the decisive hour of their death, and an absolute trust in God's mercy.

(Reconciliation at the time of death)

1604   It came to our notice that penance is denied to the dying,
236   and the desire of those who in the hour of death wish to
           be helped by this remedy for their souls is not fulfilled.
We confess to be horrified that anyone should be so impious as
to despair of God's mercy, as if he could not succour one who
takes refuge in him at any time and liberate him or her who is
oppressed by the weight of sins, from the burden of which one
wishes to be freed. What else is this but to inflict death on the
dying, and by one's cruelty to kill his/her soul that it may not
be absolved? Because God is most ready with his assistance, he
adds this promise to the invitation to penance: "On whatever
day sinners will turn to me, their sins will not be remembered
against them" *[cf. Ez 33:12 and 16 Vulg].*[...] Since God is the
knower of the heart, at no time must penance be denied to one
who asks for it.

LEO I

LETTER TO THEODORE, BISHOP OF FREJUS (452)

*This great Pope also takes up the doctrinal and pastoral problems of the
penitential discipline, mainly the need to offer reconciliation to the dying. In
this letter, he explains the role of the priest in reconciliation. His role is
indispensable. It is described by Leo as 'supplication', which reflects the
consciousness of the early Church that in forgiving sins the priest does not
act in his own right but carries out the mediating mission of Christ. Yet this
supplication is not merely a personal prayer of the priest, but the official
intercession of the Church who has the mandate to lead sinners through penance
to reconciliation with God.*

(The priest's role in reconciliation)

1605   God's manifold mercy comes to the aid of human beings
308   who have fallen so that the hope of eternal life may be
           restored not only through the grace of baptism but also
through the remedy of penance. Thus, those who have violated
the gifts of their new birth can come to the forgiveness of their
crimes by a judgment in which they condemn themselves. These
remedies of the divine goodness have been so ordained that
God's forgiveness cannot be obtained except through the
supplication of the priests. For "the one mediator between God
and humankind, the man Jesus Christ" *[1 Tim 2:5]* gave to

those who hold authority in the Church the power to grant the discipline of penance to those who confess and, after they have been purified through salutary satisfaction, to admit them to the communion of the sacraments through the door of reconciliation.

LETTER TO THE BISHOPS OF ROMAN RURAL DISTRICTS (459)

In this letter, the same Pope deals with the secrecy required in confession to safeguard the reputation of the penitent; the practice is presented as apostolic tradition.

(Confession in secret)

1606   I order that all measures be taken to eradicate the
323   presumptuous deviation from the apostolic rule through
           an illicit abuse of which I have learned of late. In the procedure of penance, for which the faithful ask, there should be no public confession of sins in kind and number read from a written list, since it is enough that the guilt of conscience be revealed to the priests alone in secret confession. Though such fulness of faith seems praiseworthy which out of the fear of God is not afraid of shame before human beings, yet not all sins are such that those who ask for penance would not fear them to become publicly known. Hence this objectionable practice must be removed lest many be kept away from the remedies of penance, either out of shame or for fear that their enemies may come to know of facts which could bring harm to them through legal procedures. For that confession is sufficient which is first offered to God, then also to the priest whose role is that of an intercessor for the sins of the penitents. Finally a greater number will be induced to penance only if the conscience of the penitent is not made public for all to hear.

THE THIRD COUNCIL OF TOLEDO (589)

The 11th canon of this regional Council is of particular interest as it belongs to a period of transition. It sternly reasserts the old penitential order with its basic structure of exclusion from the community, satisfaction through a protracted period of time, and finally reconciliation. Ever since Hermas, this way of penance was granted only once in a life-time. The Council reflects the new practice of granting reconciliation to penitents as often as they ask for it, according to a new code of canons. The new practice had come from Ireland and England to France, and from there had spread also to Spain. The text is found in Mansi, IX, 995.

(The old penitential system against the new procedure)

1607 It came to our knowledge that in some Churches in Spain people go through the discipline of penance for their sins, not according to the canons but in a most shameful manner, viz., as often as they happen to fall into sin they ask for reconciliation from the priest. To eradicate this execrable presumption this holy Council commands that penance be granted according to the old canons, which means that [the priest] first suspends from the communion the person who repents of one's deed, that he lets the person come frequently to the imposition of hands along with the other penitents, that after he or she has completed the time of satisfaction with the approval of the priest, the priest restores the person to communion. But those who fall back into their former vices, either during the time of penance or after reconciliation, should be condemned in accordance with the severity of the earlier canons.

THE FOURTH LATERAN GENERAL COUNCIL (1215)

This Council is a landmark in the history of ecclesial penance. In its Symbol it re-asserts the power of the Church to forgive sins, against the anti-clerical sects of the Albigensians and the Waldensians (cf. n. 21). Concerning the discipline of penance it prescribes as a minimum the annual reception of the Eucharist. Such a legislation was called for, once the possibility of repeated absolution was generally accepted (cf. n. 1607i). The rule of annual confession puts an end to the many fluctuations of the previous centuries. The Council also exhorts the priests to fulfil their spiritual and pastoral office in the administration of sacramental penance (cf. DS 813); finally it puts strict sanctions on the breach of the seal of sacramental confession.

(The rule of annual confession)

1608 Every faithful of either sex who has reached the age of
812   discretion should at least once a year faithfully confess all one's sins in secret to one's own priest. They should strive as far as possible to fulfil the penance imposed on them, and with reverence receive at least during Easter time the sacrament of the Eucharist.[...] But if anyone wishes for good reasons to confess one's sins to another priest, one must first ask and obtain permission from one's own priest because otherwise that priest has no power to bind or loose him or her.

(The seal of confession)

1609 Let [the confessor] take absolute care not to betray the
814   sinner through word or sign, or in any other way
     whatsoever. In case he needs expert advice he may seek
it without, however, in any way indicating the person. For we
decree that he who presumes to reveal a sin which has been
manifested to him in the tribunal of penance is not only to be
deposed from the priestly office, but also to be consigned to a
closed monastery for perpetual penance.

THE GENERAL COUNCIL OF CONSTANCE
CONDEMNATION OF ERRORS OF
WYCLIF AND HUS (1415)

*Wyclif in England (d. 1384) and Hus in Bohemia (d. 1415, burned at
the stake) were the forerunners of the Reformation. In accordance with their
doctrine of the Church (cf. n. 807/8i) and the sacraments (cf. n. 1303i), they
maintained that the forgiveness of sins is obtained not through the ecclesiastical
authority but simply by the contrition of the heart.*

(Error of Wyclif condemned)

[1610] 7. If a person is duly contrite, any exterior confession
1157   is superfluous and useless

MARTIN V
BULL *INTER CUNCTAS* (1418)

On this document, see n. 1304i.

(Questions proposed to the followers of Wyclif and Hus)

1611/20 Whether he believes that, apart from heartfelt
1260   contrition, if a qualified priest is available, a Christian
     is bound by a necessity of salvation to confess only to
him, and not to one or more laypersons, however good and
devout they may be.

1611/21 Whether he believes that a priest, in the cases
1261   permitted to him, can absolve from sin a sinner who
     has confessed and is contrite, and impose a penance
on him or her.

1611/25 Whether he believes that the jurisdictional authority

1265   of the Pope, of an archbishop and bishop, in loosing
and binding is greater than the authority of a simple
priest, even if he has the care of souls.

THE GENERAL COUNCIL OF FLORENCE
DECREE FOR THE ARMENIANS (1439)

On this document see n. 1305i. The decree proposes an interpretation of sacramental penance along the lines of Thomas Aquinas' theology. Thus, it keeps the balance between the pre-Thomist conception which placed the essence of sacramental penance on the side of the penitent, one's works of satisfaction, confession and contrition, and the later Scotist view for which the essence of the sacrament consists only in the absolution, while the acts of the penitent are considered merely as preparatory disposition. With St. Thomas the Decree considers the acts of the penitent as the 'quasi-matter', therefore as a constitutive element of the sacrament, and the absolution as the 'form'.

The text on "extreme unction" is also based on St. Thomas. It includes the positive aspect of healing for mind and body; thus the sacrament is presented not as that of the dying only, but of the sick.

(The Sacrament of Penance)

1612   The fourth sacrament is penance. Its quasi-matter consists
1323   in the actions of the penitent which are divided into three
parts. The first of these is contrition of the heart, which
requires that one be sorry for the sin committed with the resolve
not to sin in the future. The second is oral confession which
requires that the sinner confess to one's priest in their integrity
all the sins he or she remembers. The third is satisfaction for the
sins according to the judgment of the priest, which is mainly
achieved by prayer, fasting and almsgiving. The form of this
sacrament is the words of absolution spoken by the priest who
has authority to absolve, either ordinary or by commission from
his superior. The effect of this sacrament is absolution from sins.

(The sacrament of "extreme unction")

1613   The fifth sacrament is extreme unction. Its matter is olive
1324   oil blessed by the bishop. This sacrament may not be
given except to a sick person whose life is feared for. He
is to be anointed on these parts: on the eyes on account of sight,
on the ears on account of hearing, on the nostrils on account of
smelling, on the mouth on account of taste and speech, on the
hands on account of touch, on the feet on account of movement,
on the loins on account of the lust seated there.

1325   The minister of this sacrament is the priest. The effect
         is the healing of the mind and, as far as it is good for
the soul, of the body as well. Of this sacrament blessed James
the apostle says: "Is anyone among you sick?[...]" *[James 5:14f]*.

LEO X

BULL *EXSURGE DOMINE* (1520)

*Luther's theology of penance is part and parcel of his doctrine on
justification: grace is exclusively God's gift; it is ours not on account of any
work or merit on our part, but only through faith. As regards penance, Luther
considered it a sacrament, and he encouraged confession as a means of
awakening faith in God's forgiveness; but confession had to be entirely free
from any coercion. In the words of absolution the sinner found the assurance
of God's promise. Luther polemised against the practice of the Church in which,
he thought, the works of the penitent were considered more important than
the faith in God's mercy, so that human beings relied on themselves more
than on God. He further objected to the reservation of the power of forgiveness
to priests because of which, in his view, the sacrament of penance became a
means of clerical domination.*

The Bull Exsurge Domine *is the first official rejection of Luther's
doctrine. The propositions which are condemned are selected from his works,
mostly in his own words. To understand Luther's position and the significance
of the conflict, the propositions must, however, be read in the wider context of
his theology.*

(Errors of Luther condemned)

[1614/5]   That there are three parts of penance: contrition,
1455   confession and satisfaction, is not founded on Holy
               Scripture nor on the holy ancient Christian Doctors.

[1614/6]   Contrition   which   arises   from   examination,
1456   consideration and detestation of sins, whereby one
               recounts one's years in the bitterness of one's soul,
pondering over the grievousness, number and ugliness of one's
sins, over the loss of eternal happiness and the fall into eternal
damnation, such a contrition makes one a hypocrite and a greater
sinner than before.

[1614/7]   Very true, and better than all the previous teaching
1457   on the kinds of contrition is the maxim: not to do it
               again is the height of penance; the best penance is a
new life.

[1614/8] Do not on any account presume to confess venial sins,
1458   nor even all mortal sins, for it is impossible for you
            to recall all mortal sins. This is why only public mortal
sins were confessed in the early Church.

[1614/9] If we wish to confess everything clearly, we desire in
1459   reality to leave nothing to the mercy of God to forgive.

[1614/10] Sins are not remitted to anyone unless, when the priest
1460   remits them, one believes that they are remitted; rather
            the sin would remain if one did not believe that it is
remitted. For, the remission of sin and the giving of grace are
not sufficient; it is also necessary to believe that sin is remitted.

[1614/11] Do not believe that you are absolved on account of
1461   your contrition, but on account of Christ's word:
            "Whatever you loose...", etc. [Mt 16:19]. Hence I say:
If you have received the absolution of a priest, have confidence
and firmly believe that you are absolved; and absolved you will
truly be, whatever your contrition.

[1614/12] In the impossible supposition that one who confesses
1462   would not be sorry, or that the priest would give
            absolution not seriously but in jest, yet, if one believes
that one is absolved, the penitent is in very truth absolved.

[1614/13] In the sacrament of penance and the remission of guilt,
1463   the Pope or the bishop does no more than the lowliest
            priest; in fact, where there is no priest, any Christian
can do as much, even a woman or a child.

[1614/14] No one needs to answer a priest that one is sorry;
1464   nor should the priest inquire.

THE GENERAL COUNCIL OF TRENT

FOURTEENTH SESSION

DOCTRINE ON THE SACRAMENT OF PENANCE (1551)

*The Council of Trent not only answers the attacks of the Reformers against
sacramental penance, but at the same time gives a coherent exposition of the
nature and structure of this sacrament as understood then. It insists primarily
on the fact that penance is a sacrament instituted by Christ (Chapter 1),
distinct from baptism since it consists, on the part of the minister, in a judicial
act exercised on the members of the Christian community (Chapter 2). Thus*

the basis of the Catholic doctrine is proposed against the Protestant position. In the following chapter the parts of sacramental penance are described in general terms: the three acts of the penitent are contrition, confession and satisfaction (Chapter 3). Then these parts are described in detail: first contrition, with special reference to imperfect contrition, i.e., attrition, which is vindicated against Luther's attacks (Chapter 4); then confession of all mortal sins (Chapter 5); the absolution by the minister, who is the priest only (Chapter 6); the need for the priest to have jurisdiction, and the possibility of reserving cases to the bishops (Chapter 7); finally the need of imposing a penance, along with the meaning of satisfaction (Chapters 8 and 9).

Chapter I: The necessity and the institution of the sacrament of penance

1615
1668
If in all those who are regenerated there were such gratitude towards God that through his kindness and grace they constantly preserved the justice which they have received in baptism, there would have been no need to institute another sacrament for the forgiveness of sins besides baptism itself. But since God, who is "rich in mercy" [*Eph 2:4*], "knows how we are made" [*Ps 103 (102):14*], he has given a remedy of life also to those who after baptism have delivered themselves up to the bondage of sin and the devil's power, namely the sacrament of penance whereby the benefit of Christ's death is applied to those who have fallen after baptism.

1616
1669
Penance was indeed at all times necessary for all who had stained themselves by any mortal sin in order to obtain grace and justice—not excepting those who desired to be cleansed by the sacrament of baptism—so that they might turn from their perversion, make amendment, and detest so great an offence of God with hatred of sin and a sincere and heartfelt sorrow. Therefore the Prophet says: "Repent and turn from all your iniquities, otherwise iniquity shall be your ruin" [*Ez 18:30 Vulg.*]. The Lord also said: "Unless you repent, you will all perish" just as they did [*Lk 13:5*]. And Peter, prince of the apostles, recommended penance to sinners who were about to receive baptism with the words: "Repent and be baptised everyone of you" [*Acts 2:38*].

1617
1670
Yet before the coming of Christ penance was not a sacrament; nor is it one after his coming for anyone who has not been baptised. But the Lord instituted the

sacrament of penance, principally when after his resurrection he breathed upon his disciples and said: "Receive the Holy Spirit. If you forgive the sins of any, they are forgiven them; if you retain the sins of any, they are retained" [Jn 20:22]. The universal consensus of the Fathers has always acknowledged that by so sublime an action and such clear words the power of forgiving and retaining sins was given to the apostles and their lawful successors for reconciling the faithful who have fallen after baptism; and with good reason the Catholic Church denounced and condemned as heretics the Novatians who in the past stubbornly denied the power of forgiveness. Therefore this holy Council approves and accepts the words of the Lord in their full and true meaning and condemns the fictitious interpretations of those who, in contradiction with the institution of this sacrament, distort these words to make them refer to the power of preaching the word of God and of proclaiming the Gospel of Christ.

Chapters II: The difference between the sacraments of penance and baptism

1618
1671 Besides, it is clear that this sacrament differs in many ways from baptism. Apart from the fact that it differs very widely in matter and form, which constitute the essence of a sacrament, it is beyond question that the minister of baptism need not be a judge since the Church does not exercise judgment on anyone who has not first entered it through the gate of baptism. "For what have I to do", the apostle asks, "with judging those outside?" [1 Cor 5:12]. It is otherwise with those who are of the household of the faith, whom Christ the Lord has once made members of his Body by the bath of baptism [1 Cor 12:12]. For, it was his will that, if afterwards they should defile themselves by some crime, they would not be cleansed by receiving baptism again—this is not allowed under any condition in the Catholic Church—but that they would present themselves before this tribunal in order that they might be set free through the sentence of the priest; and this not once only, but as often as, repentant of the sins committed, they turn to that tribunal.

1619
1672 Moreover, the effect of baptism is different from that of penance. For by baptism we "put on Christ" [Gal 3:27] and are made an entirely new creature in him, receiving full and integral remission of all sins. To this newness and

integrity, however, we are by no means able to arrive by the sacrament of penance without many tears and labours on our part, as divine justice demands. Hence penance has rightly been called by the holy Fathers "a laborious kind of baptism".[1] This sacrament of penance is necessary for salvation for those who have fallen after baptism, just as baptism itself is for those who have not yet been regenerated.

Chapter III: The parts of penance and its effect

1620　The holy Council teaches moreover that the form of the
1673　　sacrament of penance, in which its power principally resides, consists in these words of the minister: I absolve you, etc. In accordance with a custom of the holy Church certain prayers are laudably added to these words; they do not, however, in any way belong to the essence of the form, nor are they necessary for the administration of the sacrament. The "quasi-matter" (*quasi materia*) of this sacrament is the acts of the penitent oneself, viz., contrition, confession and satisfaction. In as much as these acts are by divine institution required in the penitent for the integrity of the sacrament and for the full and complete forgiveness of sins, they are called parts of penance.

1621　As to the reality (*res*) and the effect of this sacrament, so
1674　　far as concerns its power and efficacy, it consists in reconciliation with God. In persons who are pious and receive this sacrament with devotion, it is likely to be followed at times by peace and serenity of conscience with an overwhelming consolation of spirit.

1675　　In declaring this doctrine on the parts and the effect of this sacrament, the holy Council at the same time condemns the view of those who maintain that the parts of penance consist in the terrors of a striken conscience and in faith.

Chapter IV: Contrition

1622　Contrition holds the first place among the acts of the
1676　　penitent mentioned above. It consists in the sorrow of the soul and the detestation of the sin committed, together with the resolve not to sin any more. This disposition

---

1. Cf. v.g. GREGORY OF NAZIANZUS, *Oratio* 39, 17.

(motus) of contrition was necessary at all times for the attainment of the remission of sins. In a person who has fallen after baptism it prepares for the forgiveness of sins if it is joined with trust in the divine mercy and the intention to fulfil whatever else is required for the right reception of this sacrament. Therefore the holy Council declares that this contrition implies not only cessation from sin and the resolve and beginning of a new life, but also the hatred of the old according to the word: "Cast away from you all the transgressions that you have committed against me, and get yourselves a new heart and a new spirit" *[Ez. 18:31].*[...]

1623   Moreover, the Council teaches that, although it sometimes
1677   happens that this contrition is perfect through charity
and reconciles humanity to God before this sacrament is actually received, this reconciliation, nevertheless, is not to be ascribed to contrition itself without the desire of the sacrament, a desire which is included in it.

1624   As to imperfect contrition, which is called attrition, since
1678   it commonly arises either from the consideration of the
heinousness of sin or from the fear of hell and of punishment, the Council declares: If it excludes the will to sin and implies the hope for pardon, it not only does not make one a hypocrite and a greater sinner, but is a gift of God and a prompting of the Holy Spirit, not indeed as already dwelling in the penitent but only moving one—an impulse by which the penitent is helped to prepare for oneself a way unto justice. Though without the sacrament of penance it cannot of itself lead the sinner to justification, it nevertheless disposes one to obtain the grace of God in the sacrament of penance. For, it is thanks to this salutary fear that the Ninivites, after the terrifying preaching of Jonas, did penance and obtained mercy from the Lord *[cf. Jonah 3].* Falsely, therefore, do some accuse Catholic writers as if they maintained that the sacrament of penance confers grace without any good disposition *(motu)* on the part of those receiving it; this is something which the Church of God never taught or accepted. Falsely also do they assert that contrition is extorted or forced, not free and voluntary.

Chapter V: Confession

1625   From the institution of the sacrament of penance as

1679   already explained the whole Church has always understood that the complete confession of sins was also instituted by the Lord [cf. James 5:16; 1 Jn 1:9], and is by divine Law necessary for all who have fallen after baptism. For, when he was about to ascend from earth to heaven, our Lord Jesus Christ left priests to represent him [cf. Mt 16:19; 18:18; Jn 20:23] as presiding judges to whom all mortal sins into which the faithful of Christ would have fallen should be brought that they, in virtue of the power of the keys, might pronounce the sentence of remission or retention of sins. For it is clear that without knowledge of the case priests could not exercise this judgment, nor could they observe equity in the imposition of penances if the penitents declared their sins only in general and not specifically and in particular.

1626   Thus it follows that all mortal sins of which penitents
1680   after a diligent self-examination are conscious must be recounted by them in confession, though they may be most secret and may have been committed only against the last two precepts of the decalogue [cf. Ex 20:17; Mt 5:28]; for these sins sometimes wound the souls more grievously and are more dangerous than those which are committed openly. As regards venial sins by which we are not excluded from the grace of God and into which we fall more frequently, it is right and profitable, and implies no presumption whatever, to declare them in confession, as can be seen from the practice of devout people; yet, they may be omitted without guilt and can be expiated by many other remedies. But since all mortal sins, also those of thought, make of human beings "children of wrath" [Eph 2:3] and enemies of God, there is need to seek God's pardon equally for them all through an open and humble confession. Hence when Christ's faithful strive to confess all sins that occur to their memory, they undoubtedly place all of them before the divine mercy for pardon. But those who fail to do so and knowingly withhold some, place nothing before the divine goodness for remission, "for if the sick is ashamed to lay open one's wound before the physician, the medicine does not heal what it does not know."[1]

---

1. St. Jerome, *Comment. in Ecclesiasten*, 10, 11.

(Also those circumstances which change the species of the sin must be confessed (DS 1681). Confession is not a torture since only confession of those sins is required which after diligent examination come to mind; sins which are not remembered are included in the confession and forgiven (DS 1682). The practice of secret confession is based on old traditions; public confession is never obligatory. The obligation to confess was not introduced by the fourth Lateran Council; this Council only determined that the existing precept of confession should be fulfilled at least once a year (DS 1682).)

Chapter VI: The minister of the sacrament and absolution

1627 With regard to the minister of this sacrament the holy
1684 Council declares: False and totally foreign to the truth
of the Gospel are all doctrines which in a very destructive manner extend the ministry of the keys to all other persons besides bishops and priests. They do so in the belief that the words of the Lord: "Whatever you bind on earth shall be bound in heaven, and whatever you loose on earth shall be loosed in heaven" [Mt 18:18] and: "If you forgive the sins of any, they are forgiven; if you retain the sins of any, they are retained" [Jn 20:23], were, in contradiction with the institution of this sacrament, addressed to all the faithful of Christ without difference or distinction, with the result that everyone has the power to forgive sins, public ones by public correction, if the sinner complies, and secret ones by spontaneous confession to anyone. The Council likewise teaches that even priests who are in mortal sin exercise the office of forgiving sins as ministers of Christ through the power of the Holy Spirit conferred in ordination, and that the opinion of those who maintain that bad priests do not possess this power is wrong.

1628 It is true that priestly absolution is the dispensation of
1685 another's kindness; yet, it does not consist in the mere
ministry of proclaiming the Gospel or of declaring that the sins have been forgiven, but it has the pattern of a judicial act in which the priest pronounces sentence as judge. Hence the penitent should not be so complacent about one's faith as to consider oneself truly absolved before God on account of his or her faith alone, even if one has no contrition, or if the priest has no mind to act seriously and to absolve truly. For faith without penance would effect no remission of sins, and one would be most negligent about one's salvation if, knowing that a priest absolved one jokingly, one would not diligently seek another who would act seriously.

Chapter VII: Jurisdiction and reservation of cases

1629 It is in the nature and meaning of a judgment that the
1686 sentence be pronounced only over one's subjects. Hence
the Church of God has always been convinced, and this
Synod confirms as fully true, that absolution is of no value if it
is pronounced by a priest on one over whom he has neither
ordinary nor delegated jurisdiction.

*(For pastoral reasons the absolution of special sins may be reserved to the
bishop; but on the point of death all reservations are cancelled (DS 1687f).)*

Chapter VIII: The necessity and fruit of satisfaction

1630 Finally, as regards satisfaction: it is among the parts of
1689 penance the one which, though at all times recommended
to the Christian people by our Fathers, yet in our age
has become the main target of attack under the pretext of piety
by those "holding to the outward form of godliness but denying
its power" *[2 Tim 3:5]*. The holy Synod declares: It is utterly false
and contrary to the word of God that the guilt is never remitted
by the Lord, without the entire punishment also being condoned.
For, apart from the divine Tradition, clear and striking examples
are found in Holy Scripture by which this error is refuted in the
plainest possible manner *[cf. Gen 3:16ff; Num 12:14f; 20:11f; 2 Sam
12:13f, etc.]*.

1631 Indeed, the nature of divine justice seems to demand
1690 that those who have sinned through ignorance before
baptism be received in grace in one manner, and in
another manner those who have already once been liberated from
the slavery of sin and the devil, who have received the gift of
the Holy Spirit, and yet have not feared knowingly to "violate
the temple of God" *[1 Cor 3:17]* and to grieve the Holy Spirit
[Eph 4:30]. It is also in keeping with the divine clemency that
sins should not be pardoned to us without any satisfaction, with
the consequence that we would consider sin as trivial and, when
the occasion arises, would fall into more grievous sins, insulting
as it were and outraging the Holy Spirit *[cf. Heb 10:29]*, storing
up wrath for ourselves on the day of wrath *[cf. Rom 2:5; James
5:3]*. For without doubt these satisfactory penances greatly detach
penitents from sin; they act like a bridle to keep them in check,
and make them more cautious and vigilant in the future. They

also heal the after-effects of sin and destroy evil habits, acquired through a bad life, by acts of virtues opposed to them. And no way of averting the punishments which threaten us from the Lord was ever held in the Church of God more secure than the practice of the works of penance done with a sorrowful heart [Mt 3:2, 8; 4:17; 11:21, etc.]. Besides, when we suffer in satisfaction for our sins we conform ourselves to Christ Jesus who made satisfaction for our sins [cf. Rom 5:10; 1 Jn 2:1f], from whom comes all our sufficiency [cf. 2 Cor 3:5]; this gives us the surest pledge that, while suffering with him, we shall also be glorified with him [cf. Rom 8:17].

1632 However, this satisfaction which we made for our sins
1691 is not ours in such a way that it be not through Christ Jesus. For, while we can do nothing of ourselves as of ourselves, we can do everything with the cooperation of him who strengthens us [cf. Phil 4:13]. Thus humankind has nothing wherein to glory, but all our glorying is in Christ [cf. 1 Cor 1:31; 2 Cor 10:17; Gal 6:14], in whom we live [cf. Acts 17:28], in whom we merit, in whom we make satisfaction, bringing forth worthy fruits of penance [cf. Lk 3:8]; these fruits have their efficacy from him, by him they are offered to the Father, and through him they are accepted by the Father.

1633 Hence the priests of the Lord have the duty to impose
1692 salutary and proportionate satisfactions as suggested by spiritual prudence, in accordance with the nature of the crime and the ability of the penitents, lest they become partakers of the sins of others [cf. 1 Tim 5:22] if they connive at their sins and deal too leniently with them by imposing only some sort of slight penance for very grave faults. Let them keep in mind that the satisfaction imposed by them is meant not merely as a safeguard for the new life and as a remedy to weakness, but also as a vindicatory punishment for former sins. For the early Fathers also believe and teach that the keys of the priests are given not only to loose but also to bind [cf. Mt 16:19; 18:18; Jn 20:23]. They did not for that reason consider the sacrament of penance as a tribunal of wrath and punishment; similarly no Catholic ever thought that through these satisfactions of ours the value of the merit and satisfaction of our Lord Jesus Christ is obscured or to some extent diminished. This is the interpretation of the innovators when they teach that a new life

is the best penance, with the result that they do away with all efficacy and practice of penance.

Chapter IX: The works of satisfaction

1634 Moreover, [this Council] teaches that the generosity of
1693 the divine goodness is so great that we are able to make satisfaction before God the Father through Christ Jesus, not only by the penances which we voluntarily undertake for the expiation of sin, or which are imposed on us by the priest's judgment according to the measure of the sin, but also—and this is the most forceful proof of love—by the temporal affliction imposed on us by God, if we bear them with patience.

DOCTRINE ON THE SACRAMENT OF EXTREME UNCTION (1551)

The Council of Trent enunciated the doctrine on the anointing of the sick in the same session as, and in continuation with, the doctrine on the sacrament of penance, to which it is related. The document offers a suitable treatment of the subject.

The introduction places the sacrament in the context of the Christian life. Chapter 1 deals with the controversial question of its institution. Some theologians had taught that it was instituted by St. James. Luther had vigorously denied that an apostle could institute a sacrament. The Council teaches the institution of the sacrament by Christ, and its promulgation by the apostle James. Chapter 2 treats the effect of the sacrament; chapter 3 its minister and recipient. Luther had objected to the practice of anointing only the dying, a restriction not found in James' text. The Council still partly continues the Scholastic tradition which had considered this anointing the "extreme" unction, but uses as well the more ancient term of this sacrament— "the anointing of the sick". It also extends the sacrament to those seriously ill and includes among its effects psychological comfort and the restoration of bodily health.

Foreword

1635 It seemed good to the holy Council to add to the
1694 preceding doctrine on penance the following concerning the sacrament of extreme unction, which was considered by the Fathers as the complement not only of penance but also of the whole Christian life, which ought to be a continual penance. First, therefore, with regard to its institution, it declares and teaches the following: our most merciful Redeemer wished his servants to be provided at all times with salutary remedies

against all weapons of all enemies; as in the other sacraments he prepared the greatest aids for Christians to keep themselves, during their lifetime, free from every grave spiritual evil, so did he protect the end of life with the sacrament of extreme unction as with a very strong safeguard. For, though throughout our whole life, our adversary seeks and seizes upon occasions to devour our souls in any possible way [cf 1 Pet 5:8], yet there is no time when he strains more vehemently all the powers of his cunning to ruin us utterly, and, if possible, to make us lose even faith in the divine mercy, than when he perceives that the end of our life is near.

Chapter I: The institution of the sacrament of extreme unction

1636 This sacred anointing of the sick was instituted by Christ
1695 our Lord as a true and proper sacrament of the New Testament. It is alluded to indeed by Mark [6:13], but is recommended to the faithful and promulgated by James the apostle and brother of the Lord: "Are any among you sick?", he says, "they should call for the elders of the Church, and have them pray over them, anointing them with oil in the name of the Lord. The prayer of faith will save the sick, and the Lord will raise them up; and anyone who has committed sins will be forgiven" [James 5:14f]. By these words, as the Church has learned from the apostolic Tradition handed down and received by her, he teaches the matter, the form, the proper minister and the effect of this salutary sacrament. For the Church has understood that the matter is oil blessed by the bishop, because the anointing very aptly represents the grace of the Holy Spirit with which the soul of the sick is invisibly anointed. And the form consists of these words: "By this unction", etc.

Chapter II: The effect of this sacrament

1637 Further, the reality (res) and effect of this sacrament are
1696 explained in the words: "and the prayer of faith will save the sick, and the Lord will raise them up; and anyone who has committed sins will be forgiven" [James 5:15]. For the reality is the grace of the Holy Spirit, whose anointing takes away the sins if there be any still to be expiated, and also the remains of sin; it comforts and strengthens the soul of the sick person by awakening in him or her great confidence in the

divine mercy; supported by this, the sick person bears more lightly the inconveniences and trials of one's illness and resists more easily the temptations of the devil who lies in wait for one's heel [cf. Gen 3:15]; at times it also restores bodily health when it is expedient for the salvation of the soul.

Chapter III: The minister of this sacrament, and the time of its administration

1638 The directives as to who must receive and administer
1697   this sacrament are also clearly transmitted in the words
already quoted. They indicate that the proper ministers of this sacrament are the presbyters of the Church. In this text this word does not refer to those who are senior in age or more influential among the people, but either to bishops or to priests duly ordained by them through the laying on of hands of the presbyterium [cf. 1 Tim 4:14].

1698   It is also declared that this anointing is to be administered
to the sick, especially to those who are so seriously ill that they seem near to death; hence it is also called the sacrament of the dying. If, however, the sick recover after receiving this anointing, they can again receive the help and assistance of this sacrament if they fall into another similar critical condition.

1639 On no account, then, should any attention be paid to
1699   those who, contradicting this plain and lucid doctrine of
the apostle James, teach that this anointing is a human invention or a rite received from the Fathers, which has no mandate from God and no promise of grace; nor to those who assert that this anointing has already ceased, as if it referred only to the gift of healing in the primitive Church; nor to those who maintain that the rite and usage observed in the holy Roman Church in the administration of this sacrament is contrary to the doctrine of the apostle James and, therefore, must be changed; nor finally to those who say that this extreme unction can, without sin, be held in contempt by the faithful. For all this is very plainly contrary to the clear words of this great apostle. Indeed, in the administration of this anointing, as far as what constitutes the substance of this sacrament is concerned, the Roman Church, the mother and teacher of all other Churches, observes nothing different from what blessed James has

prescribed. No contempt of so great a sacrament is then possible without a great sin and without offence to the Holy Spirit himself.

1640
1700   These are the points concerning the sacraments of penance and extreme unction which this holy, ecumenical Synod professes and teaches, and proposes to all the faithful to be believed and held. Besides, it submits the following canons to be observed without violation; those who affirm the contrary it condemns and anathematises for ever.

Canons on the sacrament of penance

1641
1701   1. If anyone says that in the Catholic Church penance is not truly and properly a sacrament, instituted by Christ our Lord to reconcile the faithful with God himself as they fall into sin after baptism, *anathema sit* [cf. nn. 1615ff].

1642
1702   2. If anyone confuses the sacraments and says that baptism itself is the sacrament of penance, as though these two sacraments were not distinct, and that, therefore, penance is not correctly called "the second plank after shipwreck", *anathema sit* [cf. nn. 1618f, 1943].

1643
1703   3. If anyone says that these words of the Lord Saviour: "Receive the Holy Spirit. If you forgive the sins of any, they are forgiven; if you retain the sins of any, they are retained" [Jn 20:22f], are not to be understood as referring to the power of forgiving and retaining sins in the sacrament of penance, as the Catholic Church has always understood them from the beginning; but if one distorts them, in contradiction with the institution of this sacrament, to make them refer to the authority of preaching the Gospel, *anathema sit* [cf. n. 1617].

1644
1704   4. If anyone denies that for the full and perfect remission of sins three acts are required of the penitent, constituting as it were the matter of the sacrament of penance, namely, contrition, confession and satisfaction, which are called the three parts of penance; or says that there are only two parts of penance, namely, the terrors of a conscience stricken by the realisation of sin, and the faith derived from the Gospel or from absolution, by which one believes that one's sins are forgiven through Christ, *anathema sit* [cf. nn. 1620, 1621].

1645   5. If anyone says that the contrition which is evoked by

1705   examination, consideration and hatred of sins, whereby
        one recounts one's years in the bitterness of one's soul
[cf. Is 38:15], reflecting on the grievousness, the multitude and
baseness of one's sins, the loss of eternal happiness and the
incurring of eternal damnation, along with the resolve of
amendment, is not a true and beneficial sorrow and does not
prepare for grace, but makes one a hypocrite and a greater sinner;
or finally that this sorrow is forced and not free and voluntary,
anathema sit [cf. 1622, 1614/6].

1646   6. If anyone denies that sacramental confession was
1706   instituted, and is necessary for salvation, by divine Law;
        or says that the manner of confessing secretly to a priest
alone, which the Catholic Church has always observed from the
beginning and still observes, is at variance with the institution
and command of Christ and is a human invention, *anathema sit*
[cf. nn. 1625ff].

1647   7. If anyone says that for the remission of sins in the
1707   sacrament of penance it is not necessary by divine Law
        to confess each and all mortal sins which one remembers
after a due and diligent examination, also secret ones, and those
against the last two precepts of the decalogue, as also the
circumstances that change the species of a sin; but says that such
a confession is useful only to instruct and console the penitent,
and that in olden times it was observed only in order to impose
a canonical penance; or says that those who endeavour to confess
all sins want to leave nothing to the divine mercy to pardon; or
finally that it is not allowed to confess venial sins, *anathema sit*
[cf. nn. 1625ff].

1648   8. If anyone says that confession of all sins as it is
1708   observed in the Church is impossible and is a human
        tradition which pious people must abolish; or that it
is not binding on each and all of the faithful of Christ of either
sex once a year in accordance with the Constitution of the
great Lateran Council, and that for this reason the faithful of
Christ are to be persuaded not to confess during Lent, *anathema
sit*.

1649   9, If anyone says that the sacramental absolution of the
1709   priest is not a judicial act but a mere ministry of
        pronouncing and declaring to one who confesses that

one's sins are forgiven, provided only one believes oneself absolved, even if the priest does not absolve seriously but in jest; or says that the confession of the penitent is not required in order that the priest be able to absolve one, *anathema sit [cf. nn. 1628, 1614/12]*.

1650   10. If anyone says that priests who are in mortal sin do
1710   not have the power of binding and loosing, or that priests
are not the only ministers of absolution, but that to each and all of the faithful it was said: "Whatever you bind on earth shall be bound in heaven, and whatever you loose on earth shall be loosed in heaven" *[Mt. 18:18]*, and "If you forgive the sins of any, they are forgiven; if you retain the sins of any, they are retained" *[Jn 20:23]*, so that by virtue of these words everyone could absolve from sins, from public ones merely by correction, if the sinner complies, and from secret ones by voluntary confession, *anathema sit [cf. n. 1627]*.

1651   11. If anyone says that bishops do not have the right to
1711   reserve cases to themselves, except such as pertain to
external government, and that, therefore, the reservation of cases does not prevent a priest from truly absolving from such reserved sins, *anathema sit*.

1652   12. If anyone says that the whole punishment is always
1712   remitted by God together with the guilt and that the
satisfaction of penitents is nothing else but the faith by which they realise that Christ has satisfied for them, *anathema sit [cf. n. 1630]*.

1653   13. If anyone says, concerning temporal punishments,
1713   that no satisfaction is made to God through the merits
of Christ by means of the punishments inflicted by him and patiently borne, or of those imposed by the priest, or finally of those voluntarily undertaken, as fasts, prayers, alms-giving or other works of piety; and that, therefore, the best penance is merely a new life, *anathema sit [cf. nn. 1631ff]*.

1654   14. If anyone says that the satisfactions by which
1714   penitents atone for their sins through Christ Jesus are
not worship of God but human traditions which obscure the doctrine of grace, the true worship of God and the benefit of Christ's death itself, *anathema sit [cf. n. 1633]*.

1655 15. If anyone says that the keys have been given to the
1715 Church only to loose and not also to bind and that,
therefore, the priests, when imposing penances on those
who confess, act contrary to the purpose of the keys, and to the
institution of Christ; and that it is a fiction that, after the eternal
punishment has been removed by virtue of the keys, there often
remains a temporal punishment to be expiated, *anathema sit [cf.
n. 1633].*

Canons concerning extreme unction

*Canon 1 teaches, against Luther, Calvin and Melanchton, that the
anointing of the sick is a true sacrament. Canon 2 teaches its spiritual effect.
The text of James is not to be interpreted, as Calvin did, as referring merely to
the charism of healing. Canon 4 affirms that the priest is the only minister of
the sacrament, and rejects the interpretation given by the Reformers to the
text of James, namely that 'presbyters' has a purely secular meaning, referring
to seniority or social influence on the community.*

1656 1. If anyone says that extreme unction is not truly and
1716 properly a sacrament instituted by Christ our Lord *[cf.
Mt 6:13]* and promulgated by the blessed apostle James
[James 5:14], but only a rite received from the Fathers or a human
invention, *anathema sit [cf. nn. 1636, 1639].*

1657 2. If anyone says that the sacred anointing of the sick
1717 neither confers grace, nor remits sins, nor comforts the
sick; but that it does no longer exist as if it consisted
only in the grace of healing of olden days, *anathema sit [cf. nn.
1639, 1637].*

1658 3. If anyone says that the rite and usage of extreme
1718 unction which the holy Roman Church observes is
contrary to the doctrine of the blessed apostle James and,
therefore, must be changed; and that it can without sin be held
in contempt by Christians, *anathema sit [cf. n. 1639].*

1659 4. If anyone says that the presbyters of the Church who,
1719 as blessed James exhorts, should be brought to anoint
the sick are not priests ordained by a bishop but the
senior members of each community, and that, for this reason,
the proper minister of extreme unction is not only the priest,
anathema sit [cf. n. 1638].

PIUS X
DECREE *LAMENTABILI* OF THE HOLY OFFICE (1907)
ARTICLES OF MODERNISM CONDEMNED

Though the practice of penance and reconciliation underwent profound changes in the Church, its substance as an authoritative action of the Church, expressed already in the biblical texts, always remained intact. But the way in which Modernists used biblical criticism and historical research, led them to unduly undermine the foundation of the doctrinal tenets on sacramental penance. Hence some of the Modernist articles condemned by Pius X refer to penance. As regards the anointing of the sick, the Modernists understood the text of James as alluding merely to a pious custom. The text affirms more, though obviously it does not imply a definition of sacrament which came much later in history. For this document, cf. n. 143i.

(Modernist errors about penance and anointing condemned)

[1660/46] In the primitive Church the concept of a Christian
3446   sinner reconciled through the authority of the Church
          did not exist; only very slowly did the Church become
accustomed to such an idea. Furthermore, even after penance
was acknowledged as an institution of the Church it was not
called a sacrament, because it would have been taken for a
shameful sacrament.

[1660/47] The words of the Lord: "Receive the Holy Spirit. If
3447   you forgive the sins of any, they are forgiven; if you
          retain the sins of any, they are retained" *[Jn 20:22f]*,
refer in no way to the sacrament of penance, inspite of what the
Fathers of Trent were pleased to affirm.

1660/48] In his epistle *[5:14f]* James does not intend to
3448   promulgate a sacrament of Christ, but he recommends
          some pious custom; if perhaps he sees in this custom
a certain means of grace, he does not accept it in the rigorous
sense in which it is understood by theologians who determined
the notion and the number of sacraments.

BENEDICT XV
APOSTOLIC LETTER *SODALITATEM NOSTRAE DOMINAE* (1921)

Canon Law (1917) followed the scholastic tradition which required that those receiving the anointing of the sick be "in danger of death on account of illness or old age" (canon 940). However, in a letter addressed to the sodality of 'Bona Mors', dedicated to the care of the dying, the Pope interpreted the law in a liberal sense. Shortly later Pius XI took the same attitude (cf. AAS 15 (1923) 105). The text of this letter is found in AAS 13 (1921) 345.

(The time for the anointing of the sick)

1661   The members join this sodality in order to exercise the apostolate of 'good health' according to the rules of the sodality. They should make every effort in order that those who are in their last crisis may not delay the reception of the viaticum and the extreme unction till they are about to lose their consciousness. On the contrary, according to the teaching and the precepts of the Church, they should be strengthened by these sacraments as soon as their condition worsens and one may prudently judge that there is danger of death.

PIUS XII
ENCYCLICAL LETTER *MYSTICI CORPORIS* (1943)

In keeping with its general theme, this encyclical views sin and reconciliation in their ecclesial context. The sinner is not separated from the Church, but he or she defiles Christ's Body; one must be restored to full life with the help of the Body. Text in AAS 35 (1943) 203. The same encyclical contains an exhortation to frequent devotional confession (ibid., 235).

1662   The fact that the Body of the Church bears the august name of Christ must not lead anyone to suppose that, also during this time of its earthly pilgrimage, its membership is restricted to those who are eminent in sanctity, or that it is composed only of those whom God has predestined to eternal beatitude. For it is in keeping with the infinite mercy of our Saviour that he does not here refuse a place in his mystical Body to those whom he formerly admitted to his table [cf. Mt 9:11; Mk 2:16 Lk 15:2]. Schism, heresy, or apostasy are such of their very nature that they sever a person from the Body of the Church; but not every sin, even the most grievous, is of such a kind. Nor does all life depart from those, who, though by sin they have lost charity and divine grace and are consequently no longer capable of a supernatural reward, nevertheless retain Christian faith and hope, and illuminated by heavenly light, are moved by the inner promptings and stirrings of the Holy Spirit to conceive a salutary fear and divinely urged to prayer and repentance of their sin.

Let all, therefore, abhor sin, which defiles the mystical members of the Redeemer; but should anyone have unhappily fallen, if one has not by his obstinacy rendered oneself unworthy of the fellowship of the faithful, then let him or her be welcomed most lovingly, and let a practical charity see in him or her a frail member of Jesus Christ. For it is better, as St. Augustine says, "to be healed within the organism of the Church than to be cut off from its body as an incurable member."[1] "So long as a member still adheres to the body its cure is not beyond all hope; but if it has been cut off it cannot be cured or made whole."[2]

THE SECOND VATICAN GENERAL COUNCIL

With regard to sacramental penance, the Council continues the general pastoral tradition of the Church; priests must be aware of the importance of the sacrament; they must instruct the faithful, and be available for hearing confessions (CD 30; PO 5, 13). They too should frequently avail themselves of this sacrament (PO 18).

Two texts, however, open new perspectives: the very brief description of sacramental penance in the Constitution on the Church presents the sacrament in its ecclesiological context; the Constitution on the liturgy decrees that a new rite, more expressive of the meaning of the sacrament, must be prepared to overcome the dangers of routine and individualism inherent in the present practice.

The constitution on the Church gives to the anointing of the sick a rich meaning in the life of the Church. It clearly repudiates the trend which connected this sacrament too exclusively with the time of death. While accepting the scholastic conception according to which the sacrament is the ultimate purification and the preparation for final glory, it connects it with the other tradition which included healing among its effects. Most of all, it integrates the sufferings of the sick into the mystery of Christ's saving passion and death; conformation to the mystery of Christ makes human sufferings fruitful for the entire people of God.

The change in outlook had been prepared by the Constitution on the liturgy where the more ancient term 'anointing of the sick' is used in preference to the more popular term 'extreme unction'. The Constitution states that the sacrament should be administered early, when illness becomes serious. It further requests that the ritual be revised; a continuous ceremony must be prepared, which will integrate the various rites for the sick in a new sequence: confession,

---

1. Cf. St. Augustine, *Epistola* 157, 3, 22.
2. Cf. St. Augustine, *Sermo* 137, 1.

anointing and viaticum, as against the former sequence of confession, viaticum and anointing.

CONSTITUTION *SACROSANCTUM CONCILIUM* (1963)

(The Sacrament of penance)

1663 72. The rite and formulas for the sacrament of penance are to be revised so that they more clearly express both the nature and the effect of the sacrament.

(The anointing of the sick)

1664 73. "Extreme unction", which may also and more fittingly be called "Anointing of the sick", is not a sacrament for those only who are at the point of death. Hence, as soon as one of the faithful begins to be in danger of death from sickness or old age, the fitting time for him or her to receive this sacrament has certainly already arrived.

1665 74. In addition to the separate rites for anointing of the sick and for viaticum, a continuous rite shall be prepared according to which the sick person is anointed after one has made one's confession and before one receives viaticum.

1666 75. The number of anointings is to be adapted to the occasion, and the prayers which belong to the rite of anointing are to be revised so as to correspond with the varying conditions of the sick who receive the sacrament.

DOGMATIC CONSTITUTION *LUMEN GENTIUM* (1964)

(On penance and the anointing of the sick)

1667 11.[...] Those who approach the sacrament of Penance obtain pardon from God's mercy for the offence committed against him, and are, at the same time, reconciled with the Church which they have wounded by their sins and which by charity, by example and by prayer labours for their conversion. By the sacred anointing of the sick and the prayer of the presbyters the whole Church commends those who are ill to the suffering and glorified Lord that he may raise them up and save them [cf. James 5:14-16]. And indeed she exhorts them to contribute to the good of the People of God by freely uniting themselves to the passion and death of Christ [cf. Rom 8:17, Col 1:24; 2 Tim 2:11-21; 1 Pet 4:13].

PAUL VI

APOSTOLIC CONSTITUTION *SACRAM UNCTIONEM INFIRMORUM* (30 November 1972)

By this Apostolic Constitution, Pope Paul VI promulgates the new rite for the sacrament of the anointing of the sick, prepared by the S. Congregation for Divine Worship in 1971. The rite is called "Rite of Anointing and Pastoral Care of the Sick". In promulgating it, the Pope uses his apostolic authority, as the sacramental rite itself has been modified "in such a way that, in view of the words of St. James, the effects of the sacrament might be better expressed". The Pope quotes the doctrine of the Second Vatican Council with regard to the serious illness required for receiving the sacrament (cf. n. 1664); he adds that the sacrament "can be repeated if the sick person, having once received the anointing, recovers and then again falls ill, or if, in the course of the same illness, the danger becomes more serious". The text is found in AAS 65 (1973) 5ff.

(The rite of the anointing of the sick)

1668   Since this revision in certain points touches upon the sacramental rite itself, by our apostolic authority we lay down that the following is to be observed for the future in the Latin Rite:

The sacrament of the anointing of the sick is administered to those who are seriously ill, by anointing them on the forehead and hands with properly blessed olive oil, or, according to circumstances, with another blessed plant oil, and saying once only the following words: *Per istam sanctam unctionem et suam piissimam misericordiam adiuvet te Dominus gratia Spiritus Sancti, ut a peccatis liberatum te salvet atque propitius allevet* (Through this holy anointing may the Lord in his love and mercy help you with the grace of the Holy Spirit. May the Lord who frees you from sin save you and raise you up).

THE NEW *ORDO UNCTIONIS INFIRMORUM* (7 December, 1972)

The general introduction to the new Rite of Anointing and the Pastoral Care of the Sick is both theologically and pastorally constructive in its tone and content. The first section sets the context: the meaning of human sickness in the mystery of salvation (nos. 1-4). The second part deals with the meaning of the celebration of the sacraments of the sick: A. Anointing, including those who are to be anointed, the minister of anointing and the requirements for a proper celebration (nos. 5-25); B. Viaticum (nos. 16-29); C. A Continuous

Rite—penance, anointing, and eucharist as viaticum—(nos. 30-31). The third, fourth and fifth sections treat: III. the offices and ministries for the sick; IV. the adaptations possible by the conferences of bishops; and V. the adaptations by the minister of the sacraments (nos. 32-41).

The new ritual includes a rich variety of rites and texts (Scripture and prayers) for a diversity of situations: visit to the sick, communion of the sick, anointing of the sick (outside or within the Eucharistic celebration), as well as pastoral care of the dying: Viaticum, commendation of the dying, rites for exceptional circumstances, etc.

1668a 1. Suffering and illness have always been among the greatest problems that trouble the human spirit. Christians feel and experience pain as do all other people; yet their faith helps them to grasp more deeply the mystery of suffering and to bear their pain with greater courage. From Christ's words they know that sickness has meaning and value for their own salvation and for the salvation of the world. They also know that Christ, who during his life often visited and healed the sick, loves them in their illness.

1668b 7. In the anointing of the sick, which includes the prayer of faith [*cf. James* 5:15], faith itself is manifested. Above all this faith must be made actual both in the minister of the sacrament and, even more importantly, in the recipient. The sick person will be saved by personal faith and the faith of the Church, which looks back to the death and resurrection of Christ, the source of the sacrament's power [*cf. James* 5:15][1] and looks ahead to the future kingdom that is pledged in the sacraments.

1668c 33. It is thus especially fitting that all baptised Christians share in this ministry of mutual charity within the Body of Christ by doing all they can to help the sick return to health, by showing love for the sick, and by celebrating the sacraments with them. Like the other sacraments, these too have a community aspect, which should be brought out as much as possible when they are celebrated.

1668d 40. The minister should take into account the particular circumstances, needs, and desires of the sick and of other members of the faithful and should willingly use the various opportunities that the rites provide.

---

1. St. Thomas, *In 4 Sententiarum*, d. 1, q. 1, a. 4, quaestioncula 3.

THE NEW *ORDO PAENITENTIAE*
(2 December, 1973)

The Decree Reconciliationem inter Deum et homines *of the S. Congregation for Divine Worship, dated December 2, 1973, promulgates with the approval of Pope Paul VI the new order for the celebration of the sacrament of penance. The Second Vatican Council had requested that the rite for this sacrament be revised (cf. n. 1663). The old ritual was found too jejune: no place was given in it to the word of God, nor did it express the ecclesial dimension of sin and reconciliation. The deficiencies often led to a routine performance of the rite. The text of the Decree of promulgation of the new rite is found in AAS 66 (1974) 172-173.*

The new Ordo Paenitentiae, *published shortly after, begins with an extensive doctrinal exposition of the sacrament of penance. It then outlines the various forms in which the sacrament can be celebrated: reconciliation of individual penitents; of several penitents with individual confession and absolution; and communal reconciliation without individual confession, with general absolution. Non-sacramental penitential services are also foreseen. Norms are given for the adaptation of the new rites to varying circumstances; the rites are marked by considerable flexibility. Insistence is laid on the use of the Bible for the preparation of the penitent and on a greater personal commitment on the part of both priest and penitent.*

The first part of the general introduction places the sacrament of reconciliation in the context of God's saving action through Jesus Christ in the Church. Thus its doctrinal presentation becomes more biblical, spiritual and pastoral than has been customary in former documents. The nature of the sacrament is described as reconciliation with God (in a Trinitarian perspective), as reconciliation among human beings and as the expression of a common striving for peace and justice in the world. Thus the ecclesial dimension of the sacrament is made to stand out clearly.

The norms for reconciliation of several penitents without individual confession are repeated in a condensed form. These norms had been given earlier in the Normae Pastorales of June 16, 1972; cf. AAS 64 (1972) 510-514. The obligation of confessing mortal sins individually, affirmed by the Council of Trent, is maintained; it cannot be replaced by general confession and absolution. Where grievous sins are absolved in a general absolution, they must be confessed individually afterwards. These norms, repeated in both documents, while meeting urgent pastoral needs, reflect an anxiety lest the practice of individual confession be undermined.

(Penance in the Life and Liturgy of the Church)

1669   4. The people of God do penance continually in many and various ways. Sharing in the sufferings of Christ by their own suffering, performing works of mercy and charity, undergoing a constant conversion to the Gospel of Christ, they become to the world a symbol of conversion to God. This the Church expresses in its life and celebrates in its liturgy, when the faithful profess themselves sinners and ask pardon of God and their brothers and sisters—as happens in penitential services, in the proclamation of the word of God, in prayer, in the penitential elements of the Mass.

And in the sacrament of Penance, the faithful "obtain pardon from God's mercy for the offence committed against him, and are, at the same time, reconciled with the Church which they have wounded by their sins and which by charity, by example and by prayer labours for their conversion" [cf. n. 1667].

1669a   5. Since sin is an offence against God and breaks our friendship with him, penance "has for its ultimate objective that we should love God and commit ourselves wholly to him."[1] When the sinner, therefore, by God's mercy takes the road of penance, he or she returns to the Father who "first loved us" [1 Jn 4:19], to Christ who gave himself up for us [cf. Gal 2:20; Eph 5:25], and to the Holy Spirit who is poured out on us abundantly [cf. Tit 3:6].

But, "because of a secret and loving mystery of dispensation, human beings are joined together by a supernatural bond in such wise that the sin of one injures the others, and the holiness of one benefits the others."[2] In the same way, penance always brings with it reconciliation with the brothers and sisters whom sin likewise injures.

Further human beings often act together in perpetrating injustice. In the same way they help one another when doing penance so that, freed from sin by the grace of Christ, they might, with all people of good will, make peace and achieve justice in the world.

(Both penitent and priest celebrate the sacrament)

1669b   11. The role of the penitent is of the greatest importance in this sacrament.

---

1. PAUL VI, Apostolic Constitution *Paenitemini* (17 February 1966); *AAS* 58 (1966) 179.
2. PAUL VI, Apostolic Constitution *Indulgentiarum Doctrina* (1 January 1967); *AAS* 59 (1967) 9.

When, properly disposed, one approaches this saving remedy which Christ instituted, and confesses one's sin, one's actions form part of the sacrament itself. The words of absolution, pronounced by the minister in the name of Christ, complete the sacrament.

Thus the penitent, while experiencing the mercy of God in one's life and proclaiming it, joins the priest in celebrating the liturgy of a Church engaged in the holy task of self-renewal.

(Norms for general absolution)

1670   31. It can happen that, because of a particular combination of circumstances, absolution may be, or even ought to be, given to a number of people together, without individual confession of sins.

Aside from danger of death, it is permissible, in a case of grave necessity, to absolve a number of people together, even though they have confessed only in general terms, if they are truly repentant. This can happen when the number of penitents is too great for the number of confessors present to hear their confessions properly, individually, in the time available, with the result that the penitents through no fault of their own would be compelled to remain without sacramental grace or holy communion for a long time. This can happen on the missions especially, but also in other places, in any gathering where the need arises.

If enough confessors are available, the mere presence of a large crowd of penitents—as on a great festival or at a pilgrimage—does not justify communal confession and absolution.

32. It is for the bishop of the diocese to judge whether the conditions are such as to justify communal sacramental absolution, after he has taken counsel with the other members of the episcopal conference.

Apart from the instances laid down by the bishop of the diocese, if on other occasions there should arise grave need for communal sacramental absolution, the priest should, for legality, apply to the local ordinary beforehand, if this is possible. But if it is not possible to approach the bishop beforehand, he should at the earliest opportunity inform him of the necessity which arose and that he had administered communal absolution.

(No. 33 stresses the need of proper disposition on the part of the penitents in case of general absolution. No. 34 demands that those who have received absolution from a grave sin in general absolution, confess this sin within one year; besides, the obligation to confess all grave sins at least once a year remains in force).

(The formula of absolution)

1671 46. The priest with his hands extended over the penitent's head (or at least with his right hand extended), says: *Deus, Pater misericordiarum, qui per mortem et resurrectionem Filii sui mundum sibi reconciliavit et Spiritum Sanctum effudit in remissionem peccatorum, per ministerium Ecclesiae indulgentiam tibi tribuat et pacem. Et ego te absolvo a peccatis tuis in nomine Patris, et Filii, + et Spiritus Sancti.* (God, the Father of mercy, reconciled the world to himself through the death and resurrection of his Son and poured out the Holy Spirit for the forgiveness of sins. May he grant you pardon and peace through the ministry of the Church. And I absolve you from your sins in the name of the Father, and of the Son, + and of the Holy Spirit).

JOHN PAUL II
ENCYCLICAL LETTER *REDEMPTOR HOMINIS* (1979)

In the concluding section of the encyclical the Pope speaks about the Church's role in realising the redemptive mission of Jesus Christ. In particular, a fuller realisation of the central place of the Eucharist is needed and a deeper understanding of sacramental penance. He develops the reasons why individual confession remains important in the Christian life. The text is found in AAS 71 (1979) 314-315.

(The significance of individual celebration of the sacrament of penance)

1672 20. In the last years much has been done to highlight in the Church's practice—in conformity with the most ancient tradition of the Church—the community aspect of penance and especially of the sacrament of penance itself. Such efforts are certainly very useful and are bound to contribute much to the enrichment of the penitential practice in the Church today. However, we cannot forget that conversion is a particularly profound inward act in which the individual cannot be replaced by others, where the community cannot become a substitute in place of the single members. Although participation by the brotherly and sisterly community of the faithful in a common penitential celebration is a great help for the act of personal conversion, nevertheless, in the final analysis, it is necessary that in this act there should be a pronouncement of the individual oneself from the depth of one's conscience with one's full sense of guilt and of trust in God, placing oneself like the Psalmist before him to confess: "Against you, you alone have I sinned" *[Ps 51 (50):4]*. Thus, in faithfully observing the century old practice of the sacrament of Penance—i.e., the practice of individual confession with a personal act of sorrow and the intention to amend and make satisfaction—the Church defends the human soul's individual right to a more personal encounter of each one with the crucified forgiving Christ, with Christ who says through the minister of the sacrament of Reconciliation: "Your sins are forgiven" *[Mk 2:5]*, "go your way, and from now on do not sin again" *[Jn 8:11]*. As is evident, this is also a right on Christ's part with regard to every human being redeemed by him: his right to meet each one of us in that key moment in the soul's life, in the moment of conversion and forgiveness. By guarding the sacrament of Penance, the Church expressly affirms her faith in the mystery of the Redemption as a living and life-giving reality that fits in with our human inward truth, with human guilt and also with the desires of the human conscience.

APOSTOLIC EXHORTATION *RECONCILIATIO ET PAENITENTIA*

(2 December 1984)

In a shattered world there is a great longing for reconciliation. The Apostolic Exhortation, using the "Propositions" prepared by the Synod of 1983 on Reconciliation and Penance in the Mission of the Church speaks about the role of the Church in carrying out her mission of reconciliation. It indicates the radical cause of the wounds and divisions between different people, and between people and God. Finally, it indicates the means that enable the Church to promote reconciliation. The reconciling Church is herself called to reconciliation which is a gift of God (cf. also n. 887). The loving kindness of God calls for a response of the Christian to live a reconciled life. The pastoral activity of presence and reconciliation is to be carried out by dialogue, catechesis, and the sacraments, especially that of reconciliation. John Paul II puts an added restriction, not found in the liturgical books, of the use of the first and third forms of reconciliation. The text is found in AAS 77 (1985) 185-275.

(The reconciling Church must herself be reconciled)

1673   9.[...]The Church, if she is to be *reconciling*, must begin by being a *reconciled Church*. Beneath this simple and indicative expression lies the conviction that the Church, in order ever more effectively to proclaim and propose reconciliation to the world, must become ever more genuinely a community of disciples of Christ[...], united in the commitment to be continually converted to the Lord and to live as new people in the spirit and practice of reconciliation.

To the people of our time, so sensitive to the proof of concrete living witness, the Church is called upon to give an example of reconciliation especially within herself. And for this purpose we must all work to bring peace to people's minds, to reduce tensions, to overcome divisions and to heal wounds that may have been inflicted by one person on another when the contrast of choices in the field of what is optional becomes acute; and on the contrary we must try to be united in what is essential for Christian faith and life, in accordance with the ancient maxim: In what is doubtful, freedom; in what is necessary, unity; in all things, charity.

(Method of dialogue)

1674   24. The Church in fact uses the method of dialogue in order the better to lead people—both those who through baptism and the profession of faith acknowledge their membership of the Christian community and also those who are outside—to conversion and repentance, along the path of a profound renewal of their own consciences and lives, in the light of the mystery of the redemption and salvation accomplished by Christ and entrusted to the ministry of the Church. Authentic dialogue is above all, therefore, aimed at the rebirth of individuals, through interior conversion and repentance, but always with profound respect for consciences and with patience and at the step-by-step pace indispensable for modern conditions.

(Catechesis on reconciliation and penance)

1675   26. From the pastors of the Church one expects, first of all, a *catechesis on reconciliation*. This must be founded on the teaching of the Bible, especially the New Testament, on the need to rebuild the Covenant with God in Christ the Redeemer and Reconciler. And, in the light of this new commission and friendship, and as an extension of it, it must be founded on the teaching concerning the need to be reconciled with one's brothers and sisters, even if this means interrupting the offering of the sacrifice [cf. Mt 5:23ff]. Jesus strongly insists on this theme of fraternal reconciliation: for example, when he invites us to turn the other cheek to the one who strikes us, and to give our cloak too to the one who has taken our coat [cf. Mt 5:38-40], or when he instils the law of forgiveness which each one receives to the measure that he or she forgives [cf. Mt 6:12[, forgiveness to be offered even to enemies [cf. Mt 5:43ff], forgiveness to be granted seventy times seven times [cf. Mt 18:2ff], which means in practice without any limit.[...]

The pastors of the Church are also expected to provide *catechesis on penance* Here too the richness of the biblical message must be its source. With regard to penance this message emphasises particularly its value for *conversion*, which is the term that attempts to translate the word in the Greek text, *metanoia*, which literally means to allow the spirit to be *overturned* in order to make *it turn towards* God.

(Renewal of the sacrament of reconciliation)

1676a   28. It is good to *renew and reaffirm this faith* at a moment when it might be weakening, losing something of its completeness or entering into an area of shadow and silence, threatened as it is by the negative elements of the above mentioned crisis. For the sacrament of confession is indeed being undermined, on the one hand by the obscuring of the moral and religious conscience, the lessening of a sense of sin, the distortion of the concept of repentance, and the lack of effort to live an authentically Christian life. And on the other hand it is being undermined by the sometimes widespread idea that one can obtain forgiveness directly from God, even in an habitual way, without approaching the sacrament of reconciliation. A further negative influence is the routine of a sacramental practice sometimes lacking in fervour and real spontaneity, deriving perhaps from a mistaken and distorted idea of the effects of the sacrament.

(Ministry of this sacrament)

1676b   29. For the effective performance of this ministry, the confessor must necessarily have *human qualities* of prudence, discretion, discernment and a firmness tempered by gentleness and kindness. He must likewise have a serious and careful preparation, not fragmentary but complete and harmonious, in the different branches of theology, pedagogy and psychology, in the methodology of dialogue, and above all in a living and communicable knowledge of the word of God. But it is even more necessary that he should live an intense and genuine spiritual life. In order to lead others along the path of Christian perfection the minister of penance himself must *first* travel this path. More by action than by long speeches he must give proof of real experience of lived prayer, the practice of the theological and moral virtues of the Gospel, faithful obedience to the will of God, love of the Church and docility to the Magisterium.

(Importance and function of the sacrament)

1676c 31.1 The first conviction is that, for a Christian, *the sacrament of penance is the ordinary way* of obtaining forgiveness and the remission of serious sins committed after baptism. Certainly, the Saviour and his salvific action are not so bound to a sacramental sign as to be unable in any period or area of the history of salvation to work outside and above the sacraments. But in the school of faith we learn that the same Saviour desired and provided that the simple and precious sacraments of faith would ordinarily be the effective means through which his redemptive power passes and operates. It would therefore be foolish, as well as presumptuous, to wish arbitrarily to disregard the means of grace and salvation which the Lord has provided.

1676d 31.2 The second conviction concerns *the function of the sacrament of penance* for those who have recourse to it. According to the most ancient traditional idea, the sacrament is a kind of *judicial action*; but this takes place before a tribunal of mercy rather than of strict and rigorous justice, which is comparable to human tribunals only by analogy, namely in so far as sinners reveal their sins and their condition as creatures subject to sin, commit themselves to renouncing and combatting sin, accept the punishment (*sacramental penance*) which the confessor imposes on them and receive absolution from him.

(Forms of celebration)

1676e   32. The first form—*reconciliation of individual penitents*—
is the only normal and ordinary way of celebrating the
sacrament, and it cannot and must not be allowed to fall into
disuse or to be neglected. The second form—*reconciliation of a
number of penitents with individual confession and absolution*—even
though in the preparatory acts it helps to give greater emphasis
to the community aspects of the sacrament, is the same as the
first form in the culminating sacramental act, namely individual
confession and individual absolution of sins. It can thus be
regarded as equal to the first form as regards the normality of
the rite. The third form however—*reconciliation of a number of
penitents with general confession and absolution*—is exceptional in
character. It is therefore not left to free choice but is regulated
by a special discipline.

JOHN PAUL II

APOSTOLIC LETTER *TERTIO MILLENNIO ADVENIENTE*

(10 November 1994)

*Since the very first Jubilee celebration in 1300, conversion has consistently
been one of the major objectives in every jubilee. On the verge of the third
millennium of Christianity, John Paul II invites the whole Church to do an
examination of conscience that it might respond better to Christ's call to make
disciples of all nations (Mt 28:19). That meant taking into account the very
ways that the Church itself has hindered the access of many to her and their
Lord. The Pope goes into details and invites believers to avoid past mistakes
and respond with their whole self to the Lord. The text can be found in AAS
87 (1994), pp. 5-41; Origins 24 (1994), pp. 401-416.*

(The Joy of Conversion)

1677a   32. [...] Nevertheless, the joy of every Jubilee is above all
a *joy based upon the forgiveness of sins, the joy of conversion.*
It therefore seems appropriate to emphasize once more the theme
of the *Synod of Bishops in 1984: penance and reconciliation* [*cf.
Apostolic Exhortation* Reconciliatio et Paenitentia]. That Synod was
an event of extraordinary significance in the life of the post-
conciliar Church. It took up the ever topical question of
conversion [*"metanoia"*], which is the pre-condition for
reconciliation with God on the part of both individuals and
communities.

(Forms of Counterwitness and Scandal)

1677b 33. Hence it is appropriate that, as the Second Millennium of Christianity draws to a close, the Church should become more fully conscious of the sinfulness of her children, recalling all those times in history when they departed from the spirit of Christ and his Gospel and, instead of offering to the world the witness of a life inspired by the values of faith, indulged in ways of thinking and acting which were truly forms of counter-witness and scandal.

Although she is holy because of her incorporation into Christ, the Church does not tire of doing penance: before God and humankind she always acknowledges as her own her sinful sons and daughters. As *Lumen Gentium* affirms: "The Church, embracing sinners to her bosom, is at the same time holy and always in need of being purified, and incessantly pursues the path of penance and renewal" [*LG* 8].

The Holy Door of the Jubilee of the Year 2000 should be symbolically wider than those of previous Jubilees, because humanity, upon reaching this goal, will leave behind not just a century but a millennium. It is fitting that the Church should make this passage with a clear awareness of what has happened to her during the last ten centuries. She cannot cross the threshold of the new millennium without encouraging her children to purify themselves, through repentance, of past errors and instances of infidelity, inconsistency, and slowness to act. Acknowledging the weaknesses of the past is an act of honesty and courage which helps us to strengthen our faith, which alerts us to face today's temptations and challenges and prepares us to meet them.

1677c 34. Among the sins which require a greater comitment to repentance and conversion should certainly be counted those which *have been detrimental to the unity willed by God for his People*. In the course of the thousand years now drawing to a close, even more than in the first millennium, ecclesial communion has been painfully wounded, a fact "for which, at times, people of both sides were to blame" [*UR* 3]. Such wounds openly contradict the will of Christ and are a cause of scandal to the world [*UR* 1]. These sins of the past unfortunately still burden us and remain ever present temptations. It is necessary to make amends for them, and earnestly to beseech Christ's forgiveness. [...]

1677d   35. Another painful chapter of history to which the sons and daughters of the Church must return with a spirit of repentance is that of the acquiescence given, especially in certain centuries, to *intolerance and even the use of violence* in the service of truth.

It is true that an accurate historical judgment cannot prescind from careful study of the cultural conditioning of the times, as a result of which many people may have held in good faith that an authentic witness to the truth could include suppressing the opinions of others or at least paying no attention to them. Many factors frequently converged to create assumptions which justified intolerance and fostered an emotional climate from which only great spirits, truly free and filled with God, were in some way able to break free. Yet the consideration of mitigating factors does not exonerate the Church from the obligation to express profound regret for the weaknesses of so many of her sons and daughters who sullied her face, preventing her from fully mirroring the image of her crucified Lord, the supreme witness of patient love and of humble meekness. From these painful moments of the past a lesson can be drawn for the future, leading all Christians to adhere fully to the sublime principle stated by the Council: "The truth cannot impose itself except by virtue of its own truth, as it wins over the mind with both gentleness and power" [*DH* 1].

1677e   36. Many Cardinals and Bishops expressed the desire for a serious examination of conscience above all on the part of *the Church of today*. On the threshold of the new Millennium Christians need to place themselves humbly before the Lord and examine themselves on *the responsibility which they too have for the evils of our day*. The present age in fact, together with much light, also presents not a few shadows.

How can we remain silent, for example, about the *religious indifference* which causes many people today to live as if God did not exist, or to be content with a vague religiosity, incapable of coming to grips with the question of truth and the requirement of consistency? To this must also be added the widespread loss of the transcendent sense of human life, and confusion in the ethical sphere, even about the fundamental values of respect for life and the family. The sons and daughters of the Church too need to examine themselves in this regard. To what extent have they been shaped by the climate of secularism and ethical relativism? And what responsibility do they bear, in view of the increasing lack of religion, for not having shown the true face of God, by having "failed in their religious, moral, or social life"? [GS 19].

It cannot be denied that, for many Christians, the spiritual life is passing through *a time of uncertainty* which affects not only their moral life but also their life of prayer and the *theological correctness of their faith*. Faith, already put to the test by the challenges of our times, is sometimes disoriented by erroneous theological views, the spread of which is abetted by the crisis of obedience vis-à-vis the Church's Magisterium.

And with respect to the Church of our time, how can we not lament *the lack of discernment*, which at times became even acquiescence, shown by many Christians concerning the violation of fundamental human rights by totalitarian regimes? And should we not also regret, among the shadows of our own day, the responsibility shared by so many Christians *for grave forms of injustice and exclusion?* It must be asked how many Christians really know and put into practice the principles of the Church's social doctrine.

An examination of conscience must also consider the *reception given to the Council*, this great gift of the Spirit to the Church at the end of the second millennium. To what extent has the word of God become more fully the soul of theology and the inspiration of the whole of Christian living, as *Dei Verbum* sought? Is the liturgy lived as the "origin and summit" of ecclesial life, in accordance with the teaching of *Sacrosanctum Concilium?* In the universal Church and in the particular Churches, is the ecclesiology of communion described in *Lumen Gentium* being strengthened? Does it leave room for charisms, ministries, and different forms of participation by the People of God, without adopting notions borrowed from democracy and sociology which do not reflect the Catholic vision of the Church and the authentic spirit of Vatican II? Another serious question is raised by the nature of relations between the Church and the world. The Council's guidelines—set forth in *Gaudium et Spes* and other documents—of open, respectful and cordial dialogue, yet accompanied by careful discernment and courageous witness to the truth, remain valid and call us to a greater commitment.

APOSTOLIC LETTER *ORIENTALE LUMEN*
(2 May 1995)

This Apostolic Letter comes a hundred years after Leo XIII published his Orientalium Dignitas *(cf.* Leonis XIII Acta, 14 *[1894], 358-370). Leo recalled the esteem and the concrete help which the Holy See gives the Eastern Churches, and its willingness to safeguard their specific qualities. John Paul II, in the wake of his* Tertio Millennio Adveniente, *mentions the division in the Church as an urgent call to conversion. Paragraph 17 starts off with a long quotation from* Tertio Millennio Adveniente, 34 *(n. 1677c). The text is in* Origins 25 *(1995-1996) 1-13.*

(The Sin of Division among Christians)

1678   17.[...] The sin of our separation is very serious: I feel the need to increase our common openness to the Spirit who calls us to conversion, to accept and recognize others with fraternal respect, to make fresh, courageous gestures, able to dispel any temptation to turn back. We feel the need to go beyond the degree of communion we have reached.

PONTIFICAL COUNCIL FOR JUSTICE AND PEACE
TOWARDS A BETTER DISTRIBUTION OF LAND: THE CHALLENGE OF AGRARIAN REFORM
(23 November 1997)

This document, the full title of which is Towards a Better Distribution of Land: the Challenge of Agrarian Reform *is quite unprecedented; but the situation of our world is reaching dramatic proportions. Humanity urgently needs to increase and quicken its awareness of the human, social and ethical problems caused by the phenomenon of the concentration and misappropriation of land. Such problems affect millions of persons and deprive many peoples of the possibility of true peace. This "scandalous situation of property and land use, present on almost all continents"—as the Council refers to it in its presentation—demands that there is not even a moment to lose. Drawing on John Paul II's* Tertio Millennio Adveniente, *it renews the Pope's challenging call to conversion in the social and political fields, to re-establish the right of the poor and marginalized. Only thus can they enjoy the use of the land and its goods that the Lord has given to all and to each one of his sons and daughters. The text is in* Origins 27 *(1997), pp. 129ff.*

(Equitable redistribution of land)

1679   60.[...] This exceptional ecclesial event [the Great Jubilee of the Year 2000] should prompt all Christians to make a serious examination of conscience on their witness in the present and also to a fuller awareness of the sins of the past, "recalling those times in history when [Christians][...] indulged in ways of thinking and acting which were truly forms of counterwitness and scandal" [John Paul II, *Tertio Millennio Adveniente*, 33: n. 1677b].

In treating the subject of an equitable redistribution of land, central to the jubilee tradition in the Bible, the Pontifical Council for Justice and Peace wants to focus the attention of all on one of the most squalid and painful spectacles—that of the shared responsibility, including that of many Christians, for grave forms of injustice and exclusion, and the acquiescence of too many of them in the violation of fundamental human rights [cf. 36: n. 1677e].

61. In many contexts, acquiescence in evil, which is a troubling sign of spiritual and moral degeneration not for Christians alone, is producing a disturbing cultural and political void which makes people incapable of change and renewal. While social relations are not changing, and justice and solidarity remain absent and invisible, the doors of the future are closing, and the destiny of many peoples remains locked into an increasingly uncertain and precarious present.

The spirit of the Jubilee urges us to cry "Enough!" to the many individual and collective sins that bring about intolerable situations of dire poverty and injustice. By calling attention to the special and essential significance of justice in the biblical message—that of protection of the weak and of their right, as children of God, to the wealth of creation—we strongly hope that, as in the biblical experience, the jubilee year will help us today to restore social justice through a distribution of land ownership carried out in a spirit of solidarity in social relations.

BULL OF INDICTION *INCARNATIONIS MYSTERIUM*
(29 November 1998)

The Bull of Indiction of the Jubilee could not but draw on the above documents (nn. 1677-1679) and specify what the believer's understanding of true conversion should be. John Paul II insists on the profound and intrinsic unity of "sacramental action" and "existential act". As a direct and immediate consequence, he invites all Christians (a) to purify their desires and intentions, and (b) to render pleasing to God their historical and economic heritage. The text is in Origins 28 (1998), 445-452.

(Penance, Conversion and Indulgence)

1680a   9. [...] The Sacrament of Penance offers the sinners "a new possibility to convert and to recover the grace of justification" [CCC, *n. 1446*] won by the sacrifice of Christ. The sinner thus enters the life of God anew and shares fully in the life of the Church. Confessing his own sins, the believer truly receives pardon and can once more take part in the Eucharist as the sign that he has again found communion with the Father and with his Church. From the first centuries, however, the Church has always been profoundly convinced that pardon, freely granted by God, implies in consequence a real change of life, the gradual elimination of evil within, a renewal in our way of living. The sacramental action had to be combined with an existential act, with a real cleansing from fault, precisely what is called penance. Pardon does not imply that this existential process becomes superfluous, but rather that it acquires a meaning, that it is accepted and welcomed.

Reconciliation with God does not mean that there are no enduring consequences of sin from which we must be purified. It is precisely in this context that the indulgence becomes important, since it is an expression of the "total gift of the mercy of God" [John Paul II, Bull *Aperite portas Redemptori* (6 January 1983), 8: *AAS* 75 (1983), 98]. With the indulgence, the repentant sinner receives a remission of the temporal punishment due for the sins already forgiven as regards the fault.

(The Purification of Mind and Heart)

1680b   11. These signs have long been part of the traditional celebration of Jubilees. Nor will the People of God fail to recognize other possible signs of the mercy of God at work in the Jubilee. In my Apostolic Letter *Tertio Millennio Adveniente*, I suggested some which may help people to live the exceptional grace of the Jubilee with greater fervour [cf. *33.37.51: AAS* 87 (1995), 25-26; 29-30; 36]. I recall them briefly here.

First of all, the sign of *the purification of memory;* this calls everyone to make an act of courage and humility in recognizing the wrong done by those who have borne or bear the name of Christian.

By its nature, the Holy Year is a time when we are called to conversion. This is the first word of the preaching of Jesus, which significantly enough is linked with readiness to believe: "Repent and believe the Good News" [Mk 1:15]. The imperative put by Christ flows from realization of the fact that "the time is fulfilled" [Mk 1:15]. The fulfilment of God's time becomes a summons to conversion, which is in the first place an effect of grace. It is the Spirit who impels each of us to "return into ourselves" and to see the need to go back to the Father's house [cf. Lk 15:17-20]. Examination of conscience is therefore one of the most decisive moments of life. It places each individual before the truth of one's own life. Thus one discovers the distance which separates one's deeds from the ideal which one had set oneself.

The history of the Church is a history of holiness. The New Testament strongly states this mark of the baptized: they are "saints" to the extent that, being separate from the world insofar as the latter is subject to the Evil One, they consecrate themselves to worshipping the one true God. In fact, this holiness is evident not only in the lives of the many Saints and Blessed recognized by the Church, but also in the lives of the immense host of unknown men and women whose number it is impossible to calculate [cf. Rev 7:9]. Their lives attest to the truth of the Gospel and offer the world a visible sign that perfection is possible. Yet it must be acknowledged that history also records events which constitute a counter-testimony to Christianity. Because of the bond which unites us to one another in the Mystical Body, all of us, though not personally responsible and without encroaching on the judgement of God who alone knows every heart, bear the burden of the errors and faults of those who have gone before us. Yet we too, sons and daughters of the Church, have sinned and have hindered the Bride of Christ from shining forth in all her beauty. Our sin has impeded the Spirit's working in the hearts of many people. Our meagre faith has meant that many have lapsed into apathy and been driven away from a true encounter with Christ.

As the Successor of Peter, I ask that in this year of mercy the Church, strong in the holiness which she receives from her Lord, should kneel before God and implore forgiveness for the past and present sins of her sons and daughters. All have sinned and none can claim righteousness before God [cf. 1 Kings 8:46]. Let it be said once more without fear: "We have sinned" [Jer 3:25], but let us keep alive the certainty that "where sin increased, grace abounded even more" [Rom 5:20].

The embrace which the Father reserves for repentant sinners who go to him will be our just reward for the humble recognition of our own faults and the faults of others, a recognition based upon awareness of the profound bond which unites all the members of the Mystical Body of Christ. Christians are invited to acknowledge, before God and before those offended by their actions, the faults which they have committed. Let them do so without seeking anything in return, but strengthened only by "the love of God which has been poured into our hearts" (*Rom* 5:5). At the same time, there will be no lack of fair-minded people able to recognize that past and present history also records incidents of exclusion, injustice and persecution directed against the sons and daughters of the Church. [...]

Let us therefore look to the future. The merciful Father takes no account of the sins for which we are truly sorry [*cf. Is 38:17*]. He is now doing something new, and in the love which forgives he anticipates the new heavens and the new earth. Therefore, so that there may be a renewed commitment to Chritian witness in the world of the next millennium, let faith be refreshed, let hope increase and let charity exert itself still more.

12. One sign of the mercy of God which is especially necessary today is the sign of *charity*, which opens our eyes to the needs of those who are poor and excluded.[...]

There is also a need to create a new culture of international solidarity and cooperation, where all—particularly the wealthy nations and the private sector—accept responsibility for an economic model which serves everyone.[...]

The Jubilee is a further summons to conversion of heart through a change of life. It is a reminder to all that they should give absolute importance neither to the goods of the earth, since these are not God, nor to man's dominations or claim to domination, since the earth belongs to God and to him alone: "the earth is mine and you are strangers and sojourners with me" [*Lev 25:23*]. May this year of grace touch the hearts of those who hold in their hands the fate of the world's people!.

APPENDIX
INDULGENCES

Not all the temporal punishment for sins is forgiven through sacramental absolution. The penances imposed on the penitent are meant to reduce this punishment. In the Middle Ages penances were protracted and burdensome. They could be reduced or remitted by the ecclesiastical authority on certain conditions; good works, prayers, and contributions to pious causes played an important role in this discipline. This remission of penances, and with them of the temporal punishment of sins, either partially or totally, is called indulgences. These are to be clearly distinguished from the forgiveness of the sins themselves which must first be obtained in the sacrament of penance. The foundation of the Church's power to remit temporal punishment is the treasury of the merits of Jesus Christ himself, and with him of all the saints, whose life is pleasing to God.

Indulgences have, in the course of history, given rise to many problems. During the Middle Ages there was, on the part of those who granted them, the danger of misusing their power for the sake of material gains; on the part of those who made use of them, there was the danger of a mechanical, superstitious conception of good works and supernatural merits. In fact, abuses in the practice of indulgences and misunderstandings as regards their meaning were among the primary causes that brought about the Reformation.

At a deeper level, indulgences raise important theological problems. What does the Church's power to grant the remission of temporal punishment consist in? What is meant by the "treasury" of the Church which can be applied to all the faithful, living and dead? This theology developed only gradually, and found its mature expression in the Apostolic Constitution of Pope Paul VI (1976).

Thus, the ecclesiastical documents concerned with indulgences treat mainly two aspects: the practical problems of abuses to be remedied; the progressive theological understanding of indulgences.

* * *

The main doctrinal points covered by these documents are the following:

Indulgences are granted from the "treasury" of the merits of Christ and the Saints: 1681, 1683, 1685/17, 1687, 1688. 1691.

The Church has the authority to grant the faithful the remission of temporal punishments: 35, 1682, 1684/26.27, 1685/17-19, 1686, 1690/1-5, 1692/5.

Indulgences may be applied to the dead: 1685/22, 1689, 1690/3.

The use of indulgences is salutary: 35, 1685/20-22, 1686.

Abuses must be avoided: 1686.

CLEMENT VI

JUBILEE BULL *UNIGENITUS DEI FILIUS* (1343)

The Bull of Clement VI is the most important document in the early history of indulgences. In 1300 Boniface VIII had proclaimed a Jubilee year which was to be celebrated every hundred years, with a plenary indulgence for all who made a pilgrimage to Rome and fulfilled certain conditions. In 1343 Clement VI decided that the Jubilee should be held every fiftieth year, beginning with 1350. He took this occasion to set out the doctrinal foundation of indulgences as it had been developed by scholastic theology. The doctrine comprises three points: Christ's merits are superabundant; to the treasure of Christ's merits, the merits of the Saints are added; this treasury is entrusted to the Church. A more complete understanding of this 'treasury' will only be worked out by later theology.

1681   The only-begotten Son of God[...] "whom God made our
1025   Wisdom, our righteousness, and sanctification and
         redemption" *[1 Cor 1:30]*, "entered once for all into the
Holy place, not with the blood of goats and calves but with his
own blood, thus obtaining eternal redemption" *[Heb 9:12]*. For
"you were ransomed not with perishable things like silver or
gold, but with the precious blood of Christ like that of a lamb
without defect or blemish" *[1 Pet 1:18f]*. Immolated on the altar
of the cross though he was innocent, he did not merely shed a
drop of his blood—although this would have sufficed for the
redemption of the whole human race because of the union with
the Word—but a copious flood, like a stream, so that "from the
sole of the foot even to the head there was no soundness in
him" *[cf. Is 1:6]*. What a great treasure, then, has the good Father
acquired for the Church militant, if the merciful shedding of
blood is not to be empty, meaningless and superfluous. He
wanted to lay it up for his children, so that there might be "an
unfailing treasure for human beings; those who draw from it
"obtain friendship with God" *[cf. Wis 7:14]*.

1682   This treasure[...][Christ] committed to the care of St. Peter,
1026   who holds the keys of heaven, and to his successors, his
         own vicars on earth, who are to distribute it to the
faithful for their salvation. And they are to apply it with
compassion, for pious and good reasons, in order that it may
benefit those who are truly contrite and who have confessed, at
times for the complete remission of the temporal punishment
due to sin, at times for the partial remission, either by general or
particular disposition, as before God they judge more expedient.

1683   To this mass of treasure the merits of the Blessed Mother
1027   of God and of all the elect, from the first just person to
             the last, also contribute, as we know; nor is it at all to
be feared that it could be exhausted or diminished, first on
account of the infinite merits of Christ, as already mentioned,
and further because the more men and women are drawn to
righteousness by having this treasure applied to them, so much
the more does the store of those merits increase.

MARTIN V
BULL *INTER CUNCTAS* (1418)

On this document, see n. 1304i.

(Questions proposed to the followers of Wyclif and Hus)

1684/26   Whether he believes that for a pious and just cause
1266   the Pope can grant indulgences for the remission of
              sins to all Christians who are truly contrite and have
confessed, especially to the pilgrims to the holy places and those
who offer them a helping hand.

1684/27   Whether he believes that through this grant those who
1267   visit the churches and those who offer them a helping
              hand can obtain such indulgences.

LEO X
BULL *EXSURGE DOMINE* (1520)

*The abuses in granting and popularising indulgences had already led to
the attacks made against the Church by Wyclif and Hus (cf. n. 1684). The
indulgence offered by Pope Julius II to all those who contributed in the
sumptuous restoration of the Basilica of St. Peter (1510), and its popular
promulgation through Tetzel in Germany became the occasion for Luther's
revolt against the Church. The condemnation of Luther by Leo X contains six
propositions concerning indulgences.*

(Errors of Luther condemned)

[1685/17]   The treasures of the Church from which the Pope gives
1467   indulgences are not the merits of Christ and of the
                Saints.

[1685/18]   Indulgences are a pious fraud on the faithful

1468   dispensing them from doing good works; they are
              among those things that are allowed, not among those
that are expedient.

[1685/19]   Indulgences, for those who really gain them, do not
1469   have the value of remitting the punishment incurred
              before the divine justice by actual sins.

[1685/20]   They are led astray who believe that indulgences are
1470   salutary and spiritually fruitful.

[1685/21]   Indulgences are necessary only for public crimes; they
1471   are rightly granted only to the hardened and
              impatient.

[1685/22]   There are six kinds of people for whom indulgences
1472   are neither necessary nor useful, viz., the dead or the
              dying, the infirm, those who are legitimately
prevented, those who have committed no crimes, those who have
committed crimes but not public ones, those who perform better
works.

THE GENERAL COUNCIL OF TRENT
TWENTY-FIFTH SESSION
DECREE ON INDULGENCES (1563)

*The council of Trent first took up the pending question of indulgences at
the disciplinary level. In its 21st Session (1562) it decided that no fees should
be collected on granting indulgences. In this way one of the rampant
malpractices was stopped. However, deep doctrinal problems had been raised
by the controversy with the Reformers. These questions were postponed to the
end of the Council which had to be precipitated, partly on account of the
illness of Pope Pius IV. Hence only a short decree was issued in the 25th
Session (1563). In this Decree the deeper theological issues about the meaning
of temporal punishment, the Church's authority to remit them, and the concept
of the treasury of the Church were bypassed; only the basic truths about
indulgences were re-stated: the Church's power to grant them and the need of
discernment in the use of this power.*

1686   Since the power of granting indulgences was conferred
1835   on the Church by Christ, and as she made use of this
              power divinely given to her [cf. Mt. 16:19; 18:18] even in
the early times, the holy Council teaches and commands that
the use of indulgences, most salutary to the Christian people
and approved by the authority of the holy Councils, is to be

retained in the Church; and it condemns with anathema those who assert that they are useless or who deny that the Church has the power to grant them.

In granting them, however, it desires that moderation be observed in accordance with the ancient custom approved in the Church, lest too much relaxation should weaken the ecclesiastical discipline.[...]

(Abuses must be suppressed and all evil traffic in indulgences, which is a source of scandal, must be abolished. The people must get proper instruction so that superstition, ignorance and irreverence be avoided. Synods should study the problems that arise and report their findings to the Holy See).

PAUL VI

APOSTOLIC CONSTITUTION *INDULGENTIARUM DOCTRINA* (1967)

During the Second Vatican Council the Bishops' Conferences were asked to submit their opinion on a reform of the system of indulgences. Though the question referred only to the canonical and pastoral aspects of indulgences, the doctrinal problems, shelved ever since the Council of Trent, could not be ignored. The Apostolic Constitution of Jan. 1, 1967, provides an answer to these problems.

Most important in this document is the explanation of the 'treasury' of the Church, which is presented not in terms of a quantitative storing up of treasures, but in a personalistic way as being identical with Jesus Christ himself. Also significant is the new definition of indulgences and the way in which the role of the Church in granting them is conceived. New norms are then laid down for gaining plenary and partial indulgences. The text is found in AAS 59 (1967) 5-24.

1687 Christ who committed no sin, suffered for us *[cf.1 Pet 2:21f]*; he was wounded for our transgressions, crushed for our iniquities, and by his bruises we are healed *[cf. Is 53:4f]*.

Following in Christ's footsteps, the faithful have always endeavoured to help one another on their pilgrimage to the heavenly Father by prayer, the performance of good works and by penitential expiation. The more fervently they were inspired by charity, the more closely they followed the suffering Christ carrying each one's own cross in expiation of their sins and of the sins of others, convinced that they could assist their brothers and sisters to obtain salvation from God the Father of mercy. This is the ancient dogma of the communion of saints, according to which the life of each of the children of God is joined, in

Christ and through Christ, to the lives of all one's fellow Christians by a wonderful link in the supernatural oneness of the mystical Body of Christ, in one mystical person as it were.

1688   It is thus that one should understand the term 'treasury of the Church'. It is not to be regarded as something akin to a hoard of material wealth accumulated over the centuries. Rather it is the infinite and inexhaustible value which the expiation and merits of Christ have in the sight of God, offered to the end that the whole of humanity might be freed from sin and arrive at fellowship with the Father. It is Christ the Redeemer himself in whom the satisfaction and merits of his redemption still exist and retain their efficacy. Further, this treasury also includes the truly immense value, immeasurable and constantly renewed, which the prayers and good works of the Blessed Virgin Mary and all the saints possess in the sight of God; they followed in the footsteps of Christ the Lord with the help of his grace, sanctified themselves and completed the work which the Father had given them to do, so that, effecting their own salvation, they also contributed to the salvation of their brothers and sisters in the unity of the mystical Body.

1689   "For all who belong to Christ and have his Spirit are brought together into one Church and cleave together in him [cf. Eph. 4:16]. Therefore the union of the wayfarers with the brethren who have gone to sleep in the peace of Christ is in no way interrupted; on the contrary, according to the perennial faith of the Church it is strengthened through the exchange of spiritual goods. For, because those in heaven are more closely united with Christ, they establish the whole Church more firmly in holiness[...] and in many ways contribute to its further upbuilding [cf. 1 Cor 12:12-27]. This is because, from the moment they have been received into the heavenly home and enjoy the presence of the Lord [cf. 2 Cor 5:8], through him and with him and in him they unceasingly intercede with the Father for us, laying before him the merits which through Christ Jesus, the one Mediator between God and humankind [cf. 1 Tim 2:5], they have won on earth while they were serving God in all things and completing in their flesh what is lacking in the sufferings of Christ on behalf of his Body, the Church [cf. Col 1:24]. In this way, their fraternal interest is of great help for our weakness" [LG 49].

Thus there is indeed a perennial bond of charity and an abundant exchange of all goods among the faithful, whether they have already taken possession of the heavenly home, or expiate their failings in purgatory, or are still on their pilgrimage on earth; thereby all the sins of the entire mystical Body are expiated and the divine justice is placated; and the divine mercy is moved to forgiveness so that the contrite sinners be brought sooner to the full fruition of the goods of God's family.

(Norms for indulgences)

1690/1 An indulgence is the remission in the sight of God of the temporal punishment due to sins which have already been blotted out as far as guilt is concerned; the Christian believer who is properly disposed gains it on certain conditions with the help of the Church which, as the minister of redemption, authoritatively dispenses and applies the treasury of the satisfactions of Christ and the saints.

1690/2 An indulgence is either plenary or partial, according to whether it involves total or partial remission of the temporal punishment due to sins.

1690/3 Indulgences, either plenary or partial, can always be applied to the dead by way of intercession (*suffragium*).

1690/4 Henceforth a partial indulgence will be described merely by the term 'partial indulgence', with no additional determination of days or years.

1690/5 The Christian faithful who is contrite at least interiorly and fulfils a work to which a partial indulgence is attached, obtains through the help of the Church a remission of temporal punishment equal to that which one has already obtained through one's own action.

CATECHISM OF THE CATHOLIC CHURCH
(7 December 1992)

Taking note of the fact that "the doctrine and practice of indulgences in the Church are closely linked to the effects of the sacrament of Penance" (§ 1471), the Catechism quotes the brief definition of Paul VI of what indulgences are (cf. n. 1690/1). It then insists on the positive dimension of indulgences and repeats the traditional teaching that they can be applied to the living and the dead.

(The practice of indulgences)

1691   1478. An indulgence is obtained through the Church who,
by virtue of the power of binding and loosing granted
her by Christ Jesus, intervenes in favour of individual Christians
and opens for them the treasury of the merits of Christ and the
saints to obtain from the Father of mercies the remission of the
temporal punishments due for their sins. Thus the Church does
not want simply to come to the aid of these Christians, but also
to spur them to works of devotion, penance, and charity [cf.
Paul VI, *Indulgentiarum Doctrina: n. 1689/5*].

1498. Through indulgences the faithful can obtain the
remission of temporal punishment resulting from sin for
themselves and also for the souls in Purgatory.

JOHN PAUL II

BULL OF INDICTION *INCARNATIONIS MYSTERIUM*
(29 November 1998)

The Apostolic Letter Tertio Millennio Adveniente *placed the years of
immediate preparation to the Jubilee year "under the sign of the Most Holy
Trinity: through Christ—in the Holy Spirit—to God the Father" (3). It
thus announced and paved the way to the celebration of the year 2000, but
only mentioned the practice of indulgences: "The tradition of jubilee years
involves the granting of indulgences on a larger scale than at other times"
(14).*

*The Bull of Indiction then applied the Apostolic Letter's intuitions to the
impending celebration of the Jubilee, the dates and modalities for its celebration,
and the granting of indulgences. Summing up the main lines of his Apostolic
Letter, John Paul II gives the pride of place—on the theological level—to the
"communion of saints". On the practical level, there are two major novelties:
the Church is invited to "kneel before God and implore forgiveness for the
past and present sins of her sons and daughters", while nations are called to
"create a new culture of international solidarity and cooperation".*

*The Bull was published together with a decree from the Sacred
Penitentiary, signed on 29 November 1998 and meant to define "the discipline
to be observed for gaining the Jubilee indulgence" (introduction to the Decree).
The text of both documents can be found in* Origins 28 *(1998), pp. 445-452
and 452-453 respectively.*

(Vigorous language of conversion and penance)

1692/1   2. [...] The period of the Jubilee introduces us to the
vigorous language which the divine pedagogy of

salvation uses to lead people to conversion and penance. These are the beginning and path of people's healing, and the necessary condition for them to recover what they could never attain by their own strength: God's friendship and grace, the supernatural life which alone can bring fulfilment to the deepest aspirations of the human heart.

(Pilgrimage as exercise of pious asceticism)

1692/2 7. In the course of its history, the institution of the Jubilee has been enriched by signs which attest to the faith and foster the devotion of the Christian people. Among these, the first is the notion of *pilgrimage*, which is linked to the situation of one who readily describes one's life as a journey. From birth to death, the condition of each individual is that of the *homo viator*. Sacred Scripture, for its part, often attests to the special significance of setting out to go to sacred places. [...]

Pilgrimages have always been a significant part of the life of the faithful, assuming different cultural forms in different ages. A pilgrimage evokes the believer's personal journey in the footsteps of the Redeemer: it is an exercise of practical asceticism, of repentance for human weaknesses, of constant vigilance over one's own frailty, of interior preparation for a change of heart. Through vigils, fasting and prayer, the pilgrim progresses along the path of Christian perfection, striving to attain, with the support of God's grace, "the state of the perfect man, to the measure of the full maturity of Christ" [*Eph 4:13*].

(Christ, the 'door')

1692/3 8. In addition to pilgrimage, there is the sign of the *holy door*, opened for the first time in the Basilica of the Most Holy Saviour at the Lateran during the Jubilee of 1423. It evokes the passage from sin to grace which every Christian is called to accomplish. Jesus said: "I am the door" [*Jn 10:7*], in order to make it clear that no one can come to the Father except through him. This designation which Jesus applies to himself testifies to the fact that he alone is the Saviour sent by the Father. There is only one way that opens wide the entrance into the life of communion with God: this is Jesus, the one and absolute way to salvation. To him alone can the words of the Psalmist be applied in full truth: "This is the door of the Lord where the just may enter" [*Ps 118:20*].

To focus upon the door is to recall the responsibility of every believer to cross its threshold. To pass through that door means to confess that Jesus Christ is Lord; it is to strengthen faith in him in order to live the new life which he has given us. It is a decision which presumes freedom to choose and also the courage to leave something behind, in the knowledge that what is gained is divine life [cf. Mt 13:44-46]. [...]

(The Sacrament of Reconciliation and Indulgences)

1692/4 9. Another distinctive sign, and one familiar to the faithful, is the indulgence, which is one of the constitutive elements of the Jubilee. The indulgence discloses the fulness of the Father's mercy, who offers everyone his love, expressed primarily in the forgiveness of sins. Normally, God the Father grants his pardon through the Sacrament of Penance and Reconciliation [cf. John Paul II, Post-Synodal Apostolic Exhortation *Reconciliatio et Paenitentia, 28-34: AAS* 77 (1985), 250-273; see nn. 1676a-e]. Free and conscious surrender to grave sin, in fact, separates the believer from the life of grace with God and therefore excludes the believer from the holiness to which he is called. Having received from Christ the power to forgive in his name [cf. *Mt* 16:19; *Jn* 20:23], the Church is in the world as the living presence of the love of God who leans down to every human weakness in order to gather it into the embrace of his mercy. It is precisely through the ministry of the Church that God diffuses his mercy in the world, by means of that precious gift which from very ancient times has been called "indulgence".

The Sacrament of Penance offers the sinner "a new possibility to convert and to recover the grace of justification" [*CCC, 1446*] won by the sacrifice of Christ. [...] The sacramental action had to be combined with an existential act, with a real cleansing from fault, precisely what is called penance. Pardon does not imply that this existential process becomes superfluous, but rather that it acquires a meaning, that it is accepted and welcomed.

Reconciliation with God does not mean that there are no enduring consequences of sin from which we must be purified. It is precisely in this context that the indulgence becomes important, since it is an expression of the "total gift of the mercy of God" [John Paul II, Bull *Aperite portas Redemptori* (6 January 1983), 8: *AAS* 75 (1983), 98] With the indulgence, the repentant sinner receives a remission of the temporal punishment due for the sins already forgiven as regards the fault.

(Vicariousness and Punishment)

1692/5 10. Because it offends the holiness and justice of God and scorns God's personal friendship with the human being, sin has a twofold consequence. In the first place, if it is grave, it involves deprivation of communion with God and, in consequence, exclusion from a share in eternal life. To the repentant sinner, however, God in his mercy grants pardon of grave sin and remission of the "eternal punishment" which it would bring.

In the second place, "every sin, even venial, entails an unhealthy attachment to creatures, which must be purified either here on earth, or after death in the state called purgatory. This purification frees one from what is called the "temporal punishment" of sin" [CCC, 1472], and this expiation removes whatever impedes full communion with God and with one's brothers and sisters.

Revelation also teaches that the Christian is not alone on the path of conversion. In Christ and through Christ, one's life is linked by a mysterious bond to the lives of all other Christians in the supernatural union of the Mystical Body. This establishes among the faithful a marvellous exchange of spiritual gifts, in virtue of which the holiness of one benefits others in a way far exceeding the harm which the sin of one has inflicted upon others. There are people who leave in their wake a surfeit of love, of suffering borne well, of purity and truth, which involves and sustains others. This is the reality of "vicariousness", upon which the entire mystery of Christ is founded. His superabundant love saves us all. Yet it is part of the grandeur of Christ's love not to leave us in the condition of passive recipients, but to draw us into his saving work and, in particular, into his Passion. This is said in the famous passage of the Letter to the Colossians: "In my flesh I complete what is lacking in Christ's afflictions for the sake of his Body, that is, the Church" [1:24]. [...]

Everything comes from Christ, but since we belong to him, whatever is ours also becomes his and acquires a healing power. This is what is meant by "the treasures of the Church", which are the good works of the saints. To pray in order to gain the indulgence means to enter into this spiritual communion and therefore to open oneself totally to others. In the spiritual realm, too, no one lives for himself alone. And salutary concern for the salvation of one's own soul is freed from fear and selfishness only when it becomes concern for the salvation of others as well. This is the reality of the communion of saints, the mystery of "vicarious life", of prayer as the means of union with Christ and his saints. He takes us with him in order that we may weave with him the white robe of the new humanity, the robe of bright linen which clothes the Bride of Christ.

This doctrine on indulgences therefore "teaches firstly how sad and bitter it is to have abandoned the Lord God [cf. Jer 2:19]. When they gain indulgences, the faithful understand that by their own strength they would not be able to make good the evil which by sinning they have done to themselves and to the entire community, and therefore they are stirred to saving deeds of humility" [Paul VI, Apostolic Constitution *Indulgentiarum doctrina* (1 January 1967), 9: *AAS 59 (1967), 18*]. Furthermore, the truth about the communion of saints which unites believers to Christ and to one another, reveals how much each of us can help others—living or dead—to become ever more intimately united with the Father in heaven.

CHAPTER XVII

ORDER

Christ, the Only mediator between God and humankind [cf. 1 Tim 2:5], possesses a unique and absolute priesthood which, while fulfilling the Old Testament priesthood, surpassed it and abolished it (cf. Heb.). He exercised his priesthood as Prophet by revealing the Father and as Shepherd by gathering God's scattered people; he crowned it in his Paschal Mystery by the offering of the sacrifice of the Cross. He communicated his priesthood to the Church in order that through the latter it might be present in the world for all ages; the Church is established by him as a "kingdom of priests" (1 Pet 2:9). Consecrated and sent on a mission through baptism and confirmation, all Christians are made to share in Christ's priesthood; as members of the priestly people they share in the Church's mission of representing Christ's unique mediatory function. The Church, however, as the Body of Christ, is a living organism with various functions exercised by various members. Christ entrusted a special function to the apostles whom he chose to be his authentic witnesses, the dispensers of his mysteries and the shepherds of his flock. They passed on their ministry to their successors, who in turn shared it with others in various degrees through the sacrament of Order. Through the ministerial priesthood Christ's function as Head is represented in the hierarchical communion which is the Church. The common priesthood of all Christians and the ministerial priesthood entrusted to the hierarchy are two inseparable and essentially related elements of its mystery.

For many centuries the Church lived in the quiet possession of this doctrine. The only serious crisis it encountered is that of the Reformation. Reacting excessively against a one-sided stress on the ministerial priesthood which did not do full justice to the common priesthood of all, the Reformers were led to deny the existence of a sacrament of Order instituted by Christ, and considered the ministry as a function delegated by the Christian community to some of its members. The denial of a sacramental ministry deprived the Church of one of the constitutive elements willed for it by Christ. This is why the Church upheld strongly against the Reformers the existence of the sacrament of Order. Due to the historical circumstances of the times, it did so with special stress on the ministerial power to offer the eucharistic sacrifice and to remit sins. This emphasis on the cultic aspect of the ministry led, in the post-Tridentine period to a certain impoverishment of its theology. Recent times, however, have been marked by a return to the biblical and patristic sources of the full dimension, as a service, at once prophetic, sanctifying and pastoral, to the community of the faithful. At the same time, the essential relatedness between the common priesthood and the ministerial priesthood in the mystery of the Church is once again brought to the fore. The Second Vatican Council has made this rich and well poised doctrine its own; by clearly declaring that the episcopate confers the fulness of the ministerial priesthood, it has further high-lighted the three sacramental degrees of the sacrament of Order.

* * *

The main points of doctrine on the sacrament of Order fall under the following headings:

Order is a true sacrament: 28, 32, 1305, 1311, 1709, 1714, 1716.

It is instituted by Christ: 32, 1305, 1311, 1707, 1716, 1731, 1749.

It is conferred through the imposition of hands and the key-phrases of the ordination preface: 1705, 1722-1726, 1737, (1744).

The minister of the sacrament of Order is the bishop: 1704, 1720, 1730.

The sacrament of Order confers the Holy Spirit: 1717, 1741c.

It imprints a sacramental character which conforms to Christ the Priest: 32, 1308, 1319, 1710, 1717, 1733, 1750.

The ordained ministers can never become lay persons again: 1710.

The sacrament also confers grace for the exercise of the ministry: 1709, 1733.

Ordination is not subject to civil authority: 1712, 1720.

Bishops are superior to priests: 1711, 1719, 1720.

The episcopate confers the fulness of the ministerial priesthood: 1739.

On episcopal conferences: (1763)

The presbyterate is required to preside over the Eucharist and to remit sins: 21, 39/17, 1546, 1556, 1627, 1650, 1703, 1707, 1714, 1729/1, 1734, 1738, 1740, 1756a-1757d.

The priesthood has a threefold function, prophetic, sanctifying and pastoral: 1740.

Only men can be ordained to the priestly ministry: 1752, 1758, 1760, 1761.

The law of priestly celibacy in the Latin Church: 1743, 1753.

The diaconate confers a ministry of service: 1741, 1741a, (1742), (1748), 1762

The ministerial priesthood differs in essence from the common priest-hood: 1710, 1732, 1734, 1735, 1738, 1746, 1751, 1754.

Some ministries can be conferred on lay people by 'installation': 1747, 1751, 1754;

Similarly some offices and tasks can be entrusted to them: 896.

These may not obscure the distinct role of ordained priests: 1754.

Some movements and associations are forbidden to the clergy: 1755a-1755e.

The eschatological dimension of ordained ministry: 1741b, 1741c.

The practico-social or messianic aspect of ordained ministry: 1741d.

The ordained refashion creation and restore it in God's image: 1759.

CLEMENT I
LETTER TO THE CORINTHIANS (c. 96)

Some seditious members of the Christian community of Corinth had unjustly taken upon themselves to depose several "episkopoi" from their office. The report had reached Rome and Pope Clement intervenes to restore order.

(The Church's hierarchy)

1701 40. Exploring the depths of the divine knowledge, we
101 must methodically carry out all that the Lord has commanded us to perform at stated times: namely, he has enjoined the offerings and the services to be performed, not at random or without order, but at fixed times and seasons. He himself, by his sovereign will, has determined where and by whom he wants them to be performed. Then, everything being religiously accomplished with his approval, will be acceptable to his will.[...] To the high priest special functions have been attributed; to the priest a special place has been assigned, and special services fall to the levite.The lay people are bound by the precept laid down for them.

42. The apostles received the Gospel for us from the Lord Jesus Christ; Jesus Christ was God's ambassador. Thus Christ [is sent] from God and the apostles from Christ; both these dispositions originated in an orderly way from God's will. Having thus received their mandate and fully convinced by the resurrection of [our] Lord Jesus Christ, and committed to the Word of God, they went forth with the full assurance of the Holy Spirit, announcing the good news that the Kingdom of God was close at hand. Preaching from country to country and from city to city, they established some of their first followers as *"episkopoi"* and *"diakonoi"* of the future believers, after having tested them by the Spirit.

44. Our apostles were also given to know by Jesus Christ our Lord that the name [office] *"episkopos"* would give rise to rivalries. This is why, endowed as they were with a perfect knowledge, they established the ministers mentioned above and for the future laid down the rule that, after their death, others who are approved should succeed them in their office. Therefore, those who are established by them or later by other eminent leaders with the consent of the whole Church, and have served Christ's flock faultlessly, humbly[...]we judge it an injustice to

deprive them of their office.[...] For it will be no small sin if we eject from the episcopacy those who have offered the gifts [sacrifice] piously and without reproach.

GREGORY I

LETTER TO THE BISHOPS OF GEORGIA (c. 601)

(Orders of heretics)

1702   Without any doubt let your Holiness receive them [the
478   converts from Nestorianism] into your assembly,
      preserving their own Orders, so that[...] you will snatch
them away from the mouth of the ancient enemy, while by your gentleness you do not raise any opposition or difficulty as regards their own Orders.

INNOCENT III

PROFESSION OF FAITH PRESCRIBED TO THE WALDENSIANS (1208)

On this profession of faith, cf. n. 1301i and n. 1504.

(Priestly ordination is necessary to celebrate Mass)

1703   [...]Hence we firmly believe and confess that no Christian,
794   however honest, religious, holy and prudent they may
      be, either can or should consecrate the Eucharist and
perform the Sacrifice of the altar, if they are not priests regularly ordained by a bishop, visible and tangible. According to our faith, three things are necessary for this office, namely: a definite person, i.e., a priest who, as we have said above, has been properly constituted in that office by a bishop; those solemn words which have been expressed in the canon by the holy fathers; the faithful intention of the one who pronounces them. And, therefore, we firmly believe and confess that any Christians who believe and contend that they can perform the Sacrifice of the Eucharist without having first been ordained by a bishop as mentioned above, are heretics.

BONIFACE IX

BULL *SACRAE RELIGIONIS* (1400)

The Bull Sacrae Religionis *concedes to the Abbot of St. Osith in Essex, who was not a bishop, and to his successors, the privilege of conferring minor and major Orders, including the priesthood, on the members of their community. This privilege was revoked three years later by the Bull Apostolicae Sedis of the same Pope (1403) (cf. DS 1146). The reason for the revocation was not doctrinal; it was meant, at the instance of the bishop of London himself, to safeguard the jurisdiction of the local bishop. By the Bull Gerentes ad vos (1427), Pope Martin V granted, for a period of five years, a similar privilege to the Abbot of the Cistercian Monastery of Altzelle in Saxony; it included the permission to confer on his monks "all, even the sacred Orders" (cf. DS 1290). Pope Innocent VIII's Bull (Exposcit tuae devotionis) (1489) granted to the Cistercian Abbots of the Monastery of Citeaux (France) and its four main sub-foundations, and to their successors, the privilege of conferring the Subdiaconate and the Diaconate on their own monks (cf. DS 1435). This privilege has been used by the Cistercians till the end of the 18th century.*

The authenticity of these three documents cannot reasonably be questioned. In view of the definition of Trent (cf. nn. 1711, 1720) regarding the bishop as minister of the sacrament of Order, they can be understood either as "untying" a radical power conferred by priestly ordination which needs to be untied for its valid exercise, or as an exceptional power granted to priests as extraordinary ministers of the sacrament, in virtue of the Pope's own "eminent power" (potestas excellentiae) over the sacramental rites and their ministers.

(Extraordinary minister of ordination)

1704   [...]In compliance with the request made by the abbot
1145   and community [of the monastery of St. Osith in the
           diocese of London], we concede to the same abbot, and
to his successors in perpetuity as abbots of the same monastery, the power to confer freely and licitly on each and all professed canons of the same monastery, now and in future, all the minor orders as well as the orders of the subdiaconate, diaconate and presbyterate at the time fixed by law; and we decree that the aforesaid canons who have thus been promoted by the aforementioned abbots may freely and licitly exercise their ministry in the Orders thus received, no apostolic constitution whatsoever withstanding.[...]

THE GENERAL COUNCIL OF FLORENCE
DECREE FOR THE ARMENIANS (1439)

For the doctrinal value of this document, cf. n. 1305i. As regards the matter and form of the sacrament of Order, the Decree follows the teaching of St. Thomas which departs from the earlier persuasion expressed for instance in the Ancient Statutes of the Church (DS 326-328) or by Pope Gregory IX (DS 826). St.Thomas' teaching on this point has later been almost universally abandoned, even before Pope Pius XII promulgated the Apostolic

Constitution Sacramentum Ordinis *on the matter and form of Order(cf. n. 1737).*

1705   The sixth sacrament is that of Order. Its matter is that
1326   by the handing over *(traditio)* of which the Order is
             conferred: thus the presbyterate is conferred by handing
over *(porrectio)* the chalice with wine and the paten with the
bread; the diaconate by giving the book of the gospels; the
subdiaconate by handing over the empty chalice covered with
an empty paten: and similarly the other Orders by assigning the
things pertaining to their office. The form of the presbyterate is
this: "Receive the power of offering the Sacrifice in the Church
for the living and the dead, in the name of the Father and of the
Son and of the Holy Spirit." And similarly for the forms of the
other Orders, as is contained in detail in the Roman Pontifical.The
ordinary minister of this sacrament is the bishop. The effect is
an increase of grace so that one may be a suitable minister of
Christ.

THE GENERAL COUNCIL OF TRENT
TWENTY-THIRD SESSION
DOCTRINE ON THE SACRAMENT OF ORDER (1563)

*According to the doctrine of the Reformers, there exists in the Church no
ministerial power received through the sacrament of Order. The unicity of the
priesthood of Christ, the only Mediator, and of his redemptive act leaves room
only for the universal priesthood of all Christians.To preside over the Christian
communities, ministers do not require any special sacramental power. This
doctrine is closely linked with the basic tenet of the Reformation, according to
which justification by faith, being a personal commitment to God in Christ,
allows no human mediation. Consequently, the Reformers considered the
ministry as a power delegated by the community and denied its sacramental
character. Faith was not communicated by a visible teaching body; grace was
not conferred through outward signs entrusted to a special sacramental
ministry; the Church was not governed by an authority instituted by Christ.
In particular, the denial of the sacrificial value of the Eucharist made the
ministerial power of Order superfluous.*

*The Council had rejected the foundation of the Reformers' doctrine in its
Decree on Justification (cf. nn. 1924ff). In subsequent sessions, it reaffirmed
against them the Church's doctrine of the sacraments. Thus it was led to
reassert the existence in the Church of a ministerial priesthood based on the
sacrament of Order. The XXIIIrd session devoted to this sacrament is that
which together with the session on justification required the most thorough
preparatory work.*

1706 This is the true and Catholic doctrine on the sacrament
1763 of Order. It is decreed and published by the holy
Tridentine Council in its seventh session [under Pius IV],
to condemn the errors of our time.

Chapter I: The institution of the priesthood of the new law

1707 Sacrifice and priesthood are by the ordinance of God so
1764 united that both have existed under every law. Since,
therefore, in the New Testament the Catholic Church has
received from the institution of Christ the holy, visible sacrifice
of the Eucharist, it must also be acknowledged that there exists
in the Church a new, visible and external priesthood [*cf. n 1714*]
into which the old one was changed [*cf. Heb 7:12ff*]. Moreover,
the Sacred Scriptures make it clear and the Tradition of the
Catholic Church has always taught that this priesthood was
instituted by the same Lord our Saviour [*cf. n. 1716*], and that
the power of consecrating, offering and administering his body
and blood, and likewise of remitting and retaining sins, was given
to the apostles and to their successors in the priesthood [*cf. n.
1714*].

Chapter II: The seven orders

1708 But since the ministry of so holy a priesthood is
1765 something divine, in order that it might be exercised in
a more worthy manner and with greater veneration, it
was fitting that in the perfectly ordered disposition of the Church
there should be several distinct Orders of ministers [*cf. Mt 16:19;
Lk 22:19; 20:22f*], serving in the priesthood by virtue of their office,
and that they be so distributed that those already having the
clerical tonsure should ascend through the minor to the major
Orders [*cf. n. 1715*]. For the Sacred Scriptures mention
unmistakably not only the priests but also the deacons [*Acts 6:5;
1 Tim 3:8ff; Phil 1:1*], and teach in the most authoritative words
what is chiefly to be observed in their ordination. And from the
very beginning of the Church the names of the following Orders
and the ministries proper to each one, namely, those of
subdeacon, acolyte, exorcist, lector and porter, are known to have
been in use, though they were not of equal rank. For the
subdiaconate is counted among the major orders by the Fathers

and the Holy Councils, in which very frequently we also read about the other, lower Orders.

Chapter III: Order is truly a sacrament

1709 Since from the testimony of Scripture, apostolic Tradition
1766 and the unanimous agreement of the Fathers it is clear
that grace is conferred by sacred Ordination, which is performed by words and outward signs, no one ought to doubt that Order is truly and properly one of the seven sacraments of Holy Church *[cf.n. 1716]*. For the Apostle says: "I remind you to rekindle the gift of God that is within you through the laying on of my hands: for God did not give us a spirit of timidity but a spirit of power and love and self-control" *[2 Tim 1:6f; cf 1 Tim 4:14]*.

Chapter IV: The ecclesiastical hierarchy and ordination

1710 But since in the sacrament of Order, as also in baptism
1767 and confirmation, a character is imprinted *[cf. n. 1717]*
which can neither be erased nor taken away, the Holy Council justly condemns the opinion of those who say that priests of the New Testament have only a temporary power, and that those who have once been rightly ordained can again become lay persons if they do not exercise the ministry of the word of God *[cf. n. 1714]*. And if Christians should assert that all Christians are without distinction priests of the New Testament, or that all are equally endowed with the same spiritual power, they seem to be doing nothing else than upset the Church's hierarchy which is "like an army with banners" *[cf. Song 6:3] [cf. n. 1719]*, as if, contrary to the teaching of St. Paul, all were apostles, all prophets, all evangelists, all pastors, all doctors *[cf. 1 Cor 12:39; Eph 4:11]*.

1711 Therefore the holy Council declares that, besides the
1768 other ecclesiastical grades, the bishops, who have
succeeded the apostles, principally belong to this hierarchical Order and have been, as the same apostle says, "established by the Holy Spirit to govern *(regere)* the Church of the Lord" *[cf. Acts 20:28 Vulg.]*; that they are superior to priests, confer the sacrament of confirmation, ordain ministers of the Church, and can perform most of the other functions over which those of a lower Order have no power *[cf. n. 1720]*.

1712 The holy Council teaches, furthermore, that in the
1769 ordination of bishops, of priests and of other grades, the
consent, call or mandate, neither of the people nor of
any civil power or authority, is necessary to the extent that
without it the ordination would be invalid. Rather it decrees
that all those who ascend to the exercise of these ministries being
called and installed only by the people or by the civil power or
authority, and those who in their rashness assume them on their
own, are not to be regarded as ministers of the Church [cf. n.
1721], but "as thieves and robbers, who have not entered by the
door" [cf. Jn 10:1].

1713 Such are the main points which the Council wanted to
1770 teach the faithful regarding the sacrament of Order. It
was decided to condemn the contrary propositions with
definite and special canons in the way that follows, so that all
those who with Christ's help observe the rule of faith may more
easily discern and hold the Catholic truth amid the darkness of
so many errors.

Canons on the sacrament of Order

1714 1. If anyone says that there is in the New Testament no
1771 visible and external priesthood, or that there is no power
of consecrating and offering the true body and blood of
the Lord and of remitting and retaining sins, but only the office
and bare ministry of preaching the Gospel; or that those who do
not preach are not priests at all, *anathema sit*[cf. nn. 1707, 1710].

1715 2. If anyone says that besides the priesthood there are
1772 in the Catholic Church no others Orders, major and
minor, by which, as by various steps, one advances
towards the priesthood, *anathema sit* [cf. n. 1708].

1716 3. If anyone says that Order or sacred ordination is not
1773 truly and properly a sacrament instituted by Christ the
Lord, or that it is a kind of human invention devised by
those inexperienced in ecclesiastical matters, or that it is only a
kind of rite by which are chosen the ministers of the word of
God and of the sacraments, *anathema sit* [cf.n. 1709]

1717 4. If anyone says that by sacred ordination the Holy
1774 Spirit is not given and that, therefore, the bishops say in
vain: "Receive the Holy Spirit"; or if anyone says that

no character is imprinted by ordination: or that they who have once been priests can again become lay persons, *anathema sit [cf. n. 1710]*.

1718 5. If anyone says that the sacred anointing which the
1775 Church uses at holy ordination not only is not required but is despicable and pernicious, and so are also the other ceremonies, *anathema sit*.

1719 6. If anyone says that in the Catholic Church there is no
1776 hierarchy instituted by divine ordinance, which consists of bishops, priests and ministers, *anathema sit [cf. n. 1711]*.

1720 7. If anyone says that bishops are not superior to priests;
1777 or that they do not have the power to confirm and ordain, or that the power they have is common both to them and to priests; or if anyone says that Orders conferred by them without the consent or call of the people or of the civil power are invalid; or that those who have neither been rightly ordained by ecclesiastical and canonical authority nor sent by it, but come from some other source, are lawful ministers of the word and of the sacraments, *anathema sit[cf. n. 1711f]*.

1721 8. If anyone says that bishops chosen by the authority
1778 of the Roman Pontiff are not true and legitimate bishops but a human invention, *anathema sit*.

LEO XIII
BULL *APOSTOLICAE CURAE* ON ANGLICAN ORDINATIONS (1896)

In the Edwardine Ordinal (1552) the rites of ordination of the Roman Pontifical were changed by Cranmer acting under the influence of Bucer. The Anglican ordinations performed with the new rite were already considered invalid from the Catholic stand-point by Pope Julius III in a letter to Card. Reginald Pole (1554) and by two letters of Pope Paul IV (Jan 20 and Oct. 30 1555).

The Bull Apostolicae Curae *of Pope Leo XIII declared them invalid because of a double defect of form and intention: the new rites did not mention adequately the offices of bishops and priests; the changes had been introduced with the explicit intention of excluding the idea of a sacrificial ministerial priesthood exercised in the Eucharist. More than a century later, the rites of ordination of bishops and priests were amended, but by then the Anglican hierarchy validly ordained according to the Roman Pontifical was already extinguished. In a letter to Cardinal Richard, Archbishop of Paris (1896),*

Pope Leo XIII stated that by issuing the Bull Apostolicae Curae *he intended to give "a final judgment and to completely settle the matter", his decision "being definitively fixed, valid and irrevocable". The Pope did not, however, intend to give to this decision the value of an infallible pronouncement.*

In the new ecumenical climate created in recent years, it is felt that the question of the value of orders derived from the Anglican hierarchy should once more be re-examined. Several Catholic bishops have expressed the desire that a mixed commission of Anglican and Catholic historians make an impartial examination of the facts with a view to clarifying the issue and dispelling misunderstandings. Independently of the historical facts, a further question has arisen of late, concerning the possibility of a Catholic recognition of the ministry of Christian Churches living outside the apostolic succession as traditionally understood, provided the integrity of the faith has been restored. This intricate question, which is at the centre of the ecumenical problem, is today the object of a new theological reflection.

(Defect of form)

1722   The words which, until quite recent times, have been
3316   generally held by Anglicans to be the proper form of
          priestly ordination: "Receive the Holy Spirit", certainly
do not signify definitely the Order of the priesthood or its grace
and power, which is pre-eminently the power "to consecrate and
offer the true body and blood of the Lord" *[cf. n. 1714]* in that
sacrifice which is no "mere commemoration of the sacrifice
accomplished on the Cross" *[cf. n. 1557]*.

It is true that this form was subsequently amplified by the
addition of the words, "for the office and work of a priest"; but
this proves, rather than anything else, that the Anglicans
themselves had recognised that the first form had been defective
and inadequate. Even if this addition could have lent the form a
legitimate signification, it was made too late, when a century
had already elapsed since the adoption of the Edwardine Ordinal
and when, consequently, with the hierarchy now extinct, the
power of ordaining no longer existed.

1723   Of late, some have sought an argument for their case in
          other prayers of the same Ordinal, but in vain. To say
nothing of other reasons which show such prayers to be
inadequate, when occurring in the Anglican rite, for the purpose
suggested, let this one argument serve for all: namely, these
prayers have been deliberately stripped of everything which in
the Catholic rite clearly sets forth the dignity and functions of
the priesthood. It is, then, impossible for a form to be suitable

and sufficient for a sacrament if it suppresses that which it ought distinctively to signify.

1724   The case is the same with episcopal consecration.[...] It
3317   follows that, since the sacrament of Order and the true
            priesthood of Christ has been totally expunged from the
Anglican rite, and since accordingly the priesthood is in no way conferred in the episcopal consecration of the same rite, it is equally impossible for the episcopate itself to be truly and properly conferred thereby; the more so because a chief function of the episcopate is that of ordaining ministers for the Holy Eucharist and for the sacrifice.[...]

1725   [...] Hence not only is there in the whole Ordinal no
3317a   clear mention of sacrifice, of consecration, of priesthood,
            of the power to consecrate and offer sacrifice, but, as we
have already indicated, every trace of these and similar things found in the prayers of the Catholic rite which were not completely rejected, was purposely removed and obliterated.

3317b   The original character and spirit of the Ordinal, as one
            might say, is thus objectively evident.[...]

(Even the amended form remains invalid)

1726   The efforts [made to vindicate the validity of the
3317b   amended form] have been, we say, and remain fruitless.
            And they are fruitless for this reason also, that, even
though some words of the Anglican Ordinal as it now stands may present the possibility of ambiguity, they cannot bear the same meaning as they have in the Catholic rite. For, as we have seen, when once a new rite has been introduced denying or falsifying the sacrament of Order and repudiating any notion whatsoever of consecration and sacrifice, then the formula: "Receive the Holy Spirit"—the Spirit, namely, who is infused into the soul with the grace of the sacrament—is deprived of its force; nor have the words "for the office and work of a priest" or "of a bishop" and similar expressions any longer their force, being now mere names, voided of the reality which Christ instituted.

The strength of this argument is felt by many Anglicans themselves who interpret the Ordinal more accurately than others; and they use it openly against those who are vainly attempting, by a new interpretation of the rite, to attach to the Orders conferred by this rite a value and efficacy which they do not possess.[...]

(Defect of intention)

1727 Then with this intrinsic defect of form has been combined
3318 a defect of intention—of that intention which is equally
necessary for the existence of the sacrament.[...] If the rite is changed with the manifest purpose of introducing another rite which is not accepted by the Church, and of repudiating what in fact the Church does and by Christ's institution belongs to the nature of the sacrament, then it is evident, not only that the intention necessary for a sacrament is lacking, but even that an intention is present which is adverse to, and incompatible with the sacrament.[...]

(The decision)

1728 Therefore, adhering entirely to the decrees of the Pontiffs
3319 our predecessors on this subject, and fully ratifying and
renewing them by our own authority, on our own initiative and with sure knowledge, we pronounce and declare that ordinations performed according to the Anglican rite have been and are absolutely null and utterly void.

PIUS X

DECREE *LAMENTABILI* OF THE HOLY OFFICE (1907) ARTICLES OF MODERNISM CONDEMNED

On this document, see n. 1326i.

(Modernist errors on the origin of priesthood condemned)

[1729/49] As the Christian Supper little by little took on
3449 the nature of a liturgical action, those who had been
usually presiding over it acquired the priestly character.

[1729/50] The elders, who discharged the function of
3450 overseers in the Christian communities, were
established by the apostles as presbyters and *episkopoi* in order to see to the good order made necessary by the growth of the communities; not properly in order to perpetuate the apostolic mission and power.

PIUS XII

APOSTOLIC CONSTITUTION
EPISCOPALIS CONSECRATIONIS (1944)

The Constitution authoritatively decrees that the two bishops who assist the main consecrator in an episcopal ordination are really co-consecrators and must act as such. The text is found in AAS 37 (1945)131ff.

(Ministers of the ordination of a bishop)

1730 With the fulness of the apostolic power we declare, decree and lay down the following. Though one bishop is necessary and sufficient for the validity of an episcopal consecration, since he performs the essential rites, nevertheless the two bishops who, according to the Roman Pontifical, assist at the consecration as stated by the ancient rule, must not only touch with both hands the head of the bishop elect together with the consecrator while saying: "Receive the Holy Spirit", but also recite the prayer: "Be propitious" with the entire Preface that follows, after having duly made their mental intention of conferring the episcopal consecration together with the consecrating bishop. For they are themselves consecrators and, therefore, they must henceforward be called co-consecrators.

ENCYCLICAL LETTER *MEDIATOR DEI* (1947)

Pope Pius XII's encyclical on the sacred liturgy (cf. nn. 1216ff) contains an extensive treatment on the priesthood. It shows that the foundation of the Church's priesthood lies in the priesthood of Christ himself. It distinguishes clearly the ministerial priesthood (based on the sacrament of Order) from the common priesthood of the faithful, and shows how both are differently exercised in the eucharistic sacrifice. The text is found in AAS 39 (1947) 521-595.

(Priesthood of Christ and priesthood of the Church)

1731 The divine Redeemer wished that the priestly life begun by him in his mortal body by his prayers and his sacrifice should continue unceasingly through the centuries in his mystical Body which is the Church: and therefore he instituted a visible priesthood to offer everywhere a "pure oblation"[cf. Mal 1:11], so that all people all over the world, being freed from sin, might serve God conscientiously and of their own free will.

(There follows the text quoted under n. 1216)

(The ministerial priesthood)

1732   The Church is a society, and, therefore, must have its
          own authority and hierarchy. Although it is true that all
members of the mystical Body share the same benefits and tend
to the same end, this does not mean that they all enjoy the same
powers or are competent to perform the same actions. The divine
Redeemer has established his Kingdom upon the stable
foundation of a sacred order; and that order is a kind of reflection
of the heavenly hierarchy.

Only the apostles and those who since have duly received
from them and their successors the imposition of hands possess
that priestly power in virtue of which they stand before their
people as Christ's representatives and similarly before God as
the representatives of the people. This priesthood is not
transmitted by heredity or blood relationship; nor does it
originate in the Christian community, nor is it derived by
delegation from the people. Before acting in God's sight on behalf
of the people, priests are the ambassadors of the divine
Redeemer; and because Jesus Christ is the Head of that Body of
which Christians are members, priests are God's representative
for the people entrusted to their care. The power committed to
them, therefore, has by nature nothing human; it is supernatural
and comes from God: "As the Father has sent me, even so I
send you" *[Jn 20:21].*[...]

Therefore, the visible and external priesthood of Jesus Christ
is not given in the Church universally, generally, or
indeterminately; it is imparted to chosen members and constitutes
a sort of spiritual birth which takes place in one of the seven
sacraments, holy Order.

(Effects of the sacrament of Order)

1733   This sacrament not only confers the grace proper to this
          particular function and state of life; it also confers an
indelible character which conforms the sacred ministers to Christ
the Priest, and enables them lawfully to perform the acts of
religion by which human beings are sanctified and God duly
glorified according to the divine ordinance.

*(The exercise of the ministerial priesthood and of the common priest-
hood in the eucharistic sacrifice)*

1734   It is therefore important, venerable brethern, for all the
3849   faithful to understand that it is their duty and highest
            privilege to take part in the eucharistic sacrifice [...] with
such active devotion as to be in the closest union with the High
Priest[...] and to offer it together with him, and with him to
surrender themselves.[...]

But the fact that the faithful take part in the eucharistic
sacrifice does not mean that they also possess the power of the
priesthood.[...]

3850   There are some who, holding a view not far removed
            from errors that have been already condemned (*cf. nn.*
1710ff), teach that the New Testament knows of no priesthood
other than that which is common to all the baptised; that the
command which Jesus Christ gave to his apostles at the Last
Supper, to do what he himself had done, was addressed directly
to the whole community of the faithful; and that thence and only
later the hierarchical priesthood took its rise. They therefore
maintain that the people possess the true priestly power, and
that priests act only in virtue of a function delegated to them by
the community.[...]

It is necessary to show how plainly these captious errors
contradict the truths we asserted above, in speaking of the special
position that priests hold in the mystical Body of Jesus Christ.
One thing we think it advisable to repeat: that priests act in the
name of the people precisely and only because they represent
the person of our Lord Jesus Christ, considered as Head of all
the members and offering himself for them; that priests, therefore,
approach the altar as Christ's ministers, lower than Christ, but
higher than the people; that the people, on the other hand,
because it in no way represents the person of the divine
Redeemer and is not mediator between itself and God, can in
no way possess the priestly right.

All this is certain with the certainty of faith. Yet, it must be
said that the faithful do also offer the divine victim, though in a
different way.

(The faithful offer through the priest and with him)

1735   "Not only do priests offer", wrote Pope Innocent III, "but
3851   all the faithful offer too; what is performed in a special
            way by the ministry of priests is done in a universal

manner by the votive offering of the faithful."[1][...] The rites and prayers of the Mass show no less clearly that the offering of the victim is made by the priests and the people together.[...]

And there is no wonder that the faithful are accorded that privilege; for, by reason of their baptism Christians become by a common title members of the Body of Christ the Priest; by the character that is as it were engraved upon their soul, they are appointed to the worship of God, and therefore according to their condition, they share in the priesthood of Christ himself.[...]

1736 To avoid any mistake in this very important matter
3852 we must clearly define the exact meaning of the word 'offer'. The unbloody immolation by which, after the words of consecration have been pronounced, Christ is rendered present on the altar in the state of victim, is performed by the priests alone, insofar as they act in the name of Christ, not insofar as they represent the faithful. But, precisely because the priests place the divine Victim on the altar they present it as an oblation to God the Father for the glory of the Blessed Trinity and for the benefit of the whole Church. Now, understood in this restricted sense, the oblation is in their own way shared by the faithful on a twofold ground; for they do not only offer the sacrifice through the hands of the priests, but also, in a certain sense, together with them. In virtue of this participation, the people's offering also pertains to liturgical worship.

That the faithful offer that sacrifice through the hands of the priests is clear from the fact that the ministers at the altar act in the person of Christ considered as Head, and as offering in the name of all the members; this is why it is true to say that the whole Church makes the offering of the Victim through Christ. But when the people are said to offer with the priests, this does not mean that all the members of the Church, like the priests themselves, perform the visible liturgical rite; this is done only by the ministers divinely appointed for the purpose. Rather they are said to offer with the priests inasmuch as they unite their votive offerings of praise, entreaty, expiation and thanksgiving with the votive offering or mental intentions of the priests, indeed with those of the High Priest himself, in order that they may be

---

1. INNOCENT III, *De Sacro Altaris Mysterio*, 3, 6.

presented to God the Father in the external rite itself performed
by the priests offering the victim. The external rite of sacrifice
must, indeed, of its very nature, be a sign of internal worship;
and what is signified by the sacrifice of the New Law is that
supreme homage by which Christ, the principal offerer, and with
him and through him all his mystical members, pay to God due
honour and veneration.[...]

APOSTOLIC CONSTITUTION *SACRAMENTUM ORDINIS*
(1947)

*By this constitution Pope Pius XII determined the matter and form of
the ordinations to the diaconate, the presbyterate and the episcopate. By
authoritatively restating the doctrine of the ancient tradition, he brought to a
conclusion the controversy of past centuries (cf. n. 1705i). Without pronouncing
on the historical question whether the rite did in fact undergo a substantial
change in the Western Church, the Pope, in virtue of his supreme apostolic
authority, makes a practical declaration and decision for the future: henceforth
for all three ordinations the matter is the imposition of hands alone, and the
form the words determining its meaning. This is first stated for all three
ordinations in general, and then for each in particular. The Pope's decision is
based on the Church's power to determine the sacramental rites, provided that
the "substance" of the sacrament—which is here very accurately defined (cf.
n. 1324i)—be preserved. Noteworthy is the fact that the Constitution considers
the three orders as sacramental; they produce a sacramental effect, which
includes the power of Order and the grace of the Holy Spirit.*

(Matter and form of diaconate, presbyterate and episcopate)

1737 3. [...]Even according to the mind of the Council of
3858   Florence itself [*cf. n. 1705*], the handing over of the
         instruments *(traditio instrumentorum)* was not required for
the substance and validity of this sacrament in virtue of the will
of our Lord Jesus Christ himself. If the same handing over of
the instruments has at some time been necessary, even for
validity, in virtue of the will and precept of the Church, all
know that the Church has the power to change and abrogate
what it has determined.

3859   4. By virtue of our supreme apostolic authority we
         declare with sure knowledge and, as far as it may be
necessary, we determine and ordain: the matter of the holy orders
of diaconate, presbyterate and episcopate is the laying on of
hands alone, and the sole form is the words determining the

application of the matter, words by which the effects of the sacrament—that is, the power of Order and the grace of the Holy Spirit—are unequivocally signified, and which for this reason are accepted and used by the Church. This leads us to declare, and, if other provisions have been legitimately made in the past at any time, we now determine that, at least in future, the handing over of the instruments is not necessary for the validity of the holy Orders of the diaconate, the presbyterate and the episcopate.

THE SECOND VATICAN GENERAL COUNCIL

The Council first dealt with the sacrament of Order when in the Constitution Lumen Gentium it spoke of the hierarchical structure of the Church (chapter 3). It devoted a decree to the pastoral office of bishops (CD) and another to the priestly ministry and life (PO).

The more characteristic points of doctrine in the conciliar documents are the following:

1. The ministerial priesthood in the context of the Church

LG speaks first of Christ's unique priesthood which is communicated by him to his Church and is shared by the entire people of God (LG 10-13) Its function is to make Christ's unique priesthood present in the world The basic priestly function is exercised differently by the Church's various members, laity and minister (LG 18) but, in the context of the Church's fundamental priestly reality, the ministerial priesthood which differs from the common priesthood "in essence and not only in degree" (LG 10) is essentially related to it; it is viewed as a service to the people of God, the powers which it confers being ordained to that service. It consists of three degrees: the episcopate conferred on the bishops as successors of the apostles (LG 20-27; cf. 18-19), the presbyterate (LG 28) and the diaconate (LG 29).

2. The three degrees of the ministerial priesthood

The episcopate

One of the most important doctrinal points made by the Council is its clear affirmation of the sacramentality of the episcopate. The episcopal consecration confers the fulness of the sacrament of Order (LG 21); this is why it is mainly through the bishops that Christ, the supreme High Priest, is present in the midst of his people (LG 21). The bishops are the successors of the apostles and continue Christ's work (CD 2); to them is entrusted the care of the portion of God's people which is the diocese, a charge which they must exercise in communion with the Supreme Pontiff who is the centre of unity of the whole Church (LG 21). United with their head, the supreme Pontiff, the bishops constitute an apostolic college (LG 22), and share in his solicitude for the whole Church (LG 23-24).

The presbyterate

The presbyterate confers a specific degree of participation in the ministerial priesthood possessed in its fulness by the episcopal college (LG 28). Thus the priests are united with the bishops in priestly dignity (LG 28). Their ordination enables them to act in the person of Christ (LG 28) and to represent him among their flock as Head of his Body, the Church (PO 2). They are established in the order of the presbyterate as collaborators of the bishop (LG 28; CD 29-30) and his necessary helpers and counsellors (PO 7). Together with him and around him they constitute "one college of priests" (unum presbyterium) (LG 28). The sacrament of Order creates a bond of union between bishop and priests as well as between the priests themselves as co-members of the priestly college (LG 28).

The diaconate

It is a sacramental degree of Order (LG 29) and makes the deacons participate in their own degree in the function of the hierarchy. The Council determines the ministerial functions exercised by the deacons in communion with the bishops and the priestly college (LG 29). It recommends the restoration of the permanent diaconate in the Western Church (LG 29).

3. The twofold perspective of consecration and mission

In its teaching the Council synthesises two aspects of the ministerial priesthood; consecration to God and mission to the Christian community and to the World. Both are inseparable and complementary; if priests are "set apart", they are so "within the fold of the people of God" (PO 3), not in order to be "separated from it or from any person", but to be fully engaged in the service of the community (PO 3). In order to exercise their ministerial function, priests must live in contact with others; they cannot remain strangers to their life (PO 3).

4. The threefold function of the ministerial priesthood

Christ's unique priesthood has a threefold function: He is at once Teacher, High Priest and Shepherd. These three functions of Christ's unique mediation are continued in the Church; hence the Church's threefold function, prophetic, sanctifying and pastoral. These three functions are shared by the entire people of God; the laity exercise them in their own way (LG 34-36). The same three functions are indissolubly linked in the ministerial priesthood and exercised in various degrees by bishops, presbyters and deacons. Going beyond the problematic of post-Tridentine theology, the Council links up here with the early Tradition to give to the priestly ministry its full significance. It cannot be reduced to the cultic function exercised mostly in the offering of the sacrifice of the Mass; its prophetic and pastoral aspects too are derived from the sacramental ordination. The bishops have the fulness of the threefold priestly function (LG 20). Their primary function is to preach the Gospel (LG 25), as authentic teachers of the faith (CD 2). The bishops are also the principal dispensers of the means of grace (LG 26) and the shepherds of their flock (LG 27; CD 16:19). Presbyters share in their own degree in the three functions attached to the priestly ministry (PO

2); *as helpers of the bishops their first duty is to preach the Gospel to all people and to be the educators of the faith (PO 4); their prophetic function is oriented to their sanctifying function (PO 5) which finds its climax in the eucharistic celebration (PO 5; LG 28), centre of the life of the Christian community; they shepherd the community entrusted to them and thus build up the Body of Christ which is the church (PO 6.) Deacons too, in union with bishops and priests, share in their own way in the threefold function of the ministry, in preaching, liturgy and the exercise of charity (LG 29).*

DOGMATIC CONSTITUTION *LUMEN GENTIUM* (1964)

(The common priesthood and the ministerial priesthood)

1738   10. The Lord Christ, High Priest taken from among people *[cf. Heb 5:1-5]*, made this new people into "a new Kingdom, priests to his God and Father" *[Rev 1;6; 5:9-10]*. For they who are regenerated by baptism and anointed by Holy Spirit, are consecrated to be a spiritual household and a holy priesthood, so that in all their actions as Christians they may offer spiritual oblations and proclaim the marvels of him who has called them out of darkness into his admirable light *[cf. 1 Pet 2:4-10]*. Therefore, all Christ's disciples must, in persevering prayer and praise of God *[cf. Acts 2:42-47]*, show themselves living victims, holy and pleasing to God *[cf. Rom 12:1]*; they must bear witness to Christ throughout the world and give an answer to those who seek an account of that hope of eternal life which is in them *[cf. 1 Pet 3:1]*.

Though the common priesthood of the faithful and the ministerial or hierarchical priesthood do, indeed, differ from one another in essence and not only in degree, they are nonetheless ordained to each other; for both, in their respective manner, share in the one priesthood of Christ. In virtue of the sacred power with which they are endowed, the ministerial priests instruct and rule the priestly people, perform in the person of Christ the eucharistic sacrifice and offer it to God in the name of all the people; while the faithful on their part, in virtue of their royal priesthood, join in the eucharistic offering, and exercise their priesthood in receiving the sacraments, in prayer and thanksgiving, in the witness of a holy life, in self-denial and active charity.

(The episcopate as a sacrament)

1739   21. Thus in the bishops, who are assisted by priests, the Lord Jesus Christ, the Supreme High Priest, is present in the midst of those who believe. For, while he is sitting at the right hand of God the Father, he is not absent from the community of his high priests; it is mainly through their signal service that he preaches the word of God to all nations and ceaselessly administers the sacraments of the faith to the believers; through their paternal action [cf. 1 Cor 4:15], he incorporates new members into his body by divine regeneration; through their wisdom and prudence, he directs and guides the People of the New Testament during their pilgrimage towards eternal happiness. These pastors, chosen to be shepherds of the Lord's flock, are servants of Christ and stewards of the mysteries of God [cf. 1 Cor 4:1]; to them has been entrusted the task of bearing witness to the good tidings of God's grace [cf. Rom 15:16; Acts 20:24], and the ministration of the Spirit and of justice in glory [cf. 2 Cor 3:8, 9].

In view of carrying out these lofty functions, the apostles were enriched by Christ with a special outpouring of the Holy Spirit [cf. Acts 1:8; 2:4; Jn 20:23]; this spiritual gift they passed on to their fellow-labourers by the imposition of hands [cf. 1 Tim 4:14; 2 Tim 1:6-7], and it has come down to us in the episcopal consecration. This holy Council teaches that, through the episcopal consecration, the fulness of the sacrament of Order is conferred, that fulness, namely, which both in the Church's liturgical practice and in the language of the early Fathers is truly called the high priesthood and the apex of the sacred ministry. The episcopal consecration bestows, together with the function of sanctifying, the functions also of teaching and governing, though these functions, of their very nature, can be exercised only in hierarchical communion with the Head and the members of the College. For, from Tradition, as expressed chiefly both in the East and in the West, it is clear that through the imposition of hands and the words of consecration the grace of the Holy Spirit is so conferred and the sacred character so impressed that the bishops continue in an eminent and visible way Christ's own roles of Teacher, Shepherd and High Priest and that they act in his person. It belongs to the bishops to admit new members into the episcopal body by means of the sacrament of Order.

(The Presbyterate)

1740 28. Christ, whom the Father sanctified and sent into the world [cf. Jn 10:36], made his apostles partakers of his consecration and mission, and through them their successors the bishops. The bishops, in turn, legitimately handed on to different members of the Church various degrees of participation in their ministry. Thus, the divinely established ecclesiastical ministry is exercised in different ranks by those who from early times have been called bishops, presbyters, deacons. Although the presbyters do not possess the highest degree of the priesthood and depend on the bishops in the exercise of their power, they are nevertheless united with the bishops in sacerdotal dignity. By the power of the sacrament of Order they are, after the image of Christ, the supreme and eternal Priest [cf. Heb 5:1-10; 7:24; 9:11-28], consecrated true priests of the New Testament, to preach the Gospel, to shepherd the faithful and to celebrate the divine worship. Sharing, according to their degree of the ministry, in the function of Christ, the sole Mediator [cf. 1 Tim 2:5], they announce the word of God to all. They exercise their sacred function especially in the eucharistic liturgy or synaxis. In the sacrifice of the Mass, acting in the person of Christ and proclaiming his mystery, they join the offerings of the faithful to the sacrifice of their Head and, until the coming of the Lord [cf. 1 Cor 11:26], represent and apply the one sacrifice of the New Testament, namely the sacrifice of Christ offering himself, once and for all, to the Father as a spotless victim [cf. Heb 9:14-28]. For the benefit of the sinners and the sick among the faithful, they exercise in a special manner the ministry of reconciliation and of alleviation. They lay before God the Father the needs and prayers of the faithful [cf. Heb 5:1-4]. By performing within the limits of their authority the function of Christ, Shepherd and Head, they gather together the family of God as a community that has but one heart and one soul, and lead them through Christ in the Spirit to God the Father.[...]

(The diaconate and its restoration)

1741 29. At a lower level of the hierarchy stand the deacons, upon whom hands are imposed "not unto the priesthood, but unto a ministry [of service]".[1] Indeed, strengthened with the sacramental grace, they serve the people of God in the service *(diakonia)* of the liturgy, of the word and of charity in communion with the bishop and his priestly college *(presbyterium)*.[...]

---

1. *Constitutiones Ecclesiae Aegyptiacae,* III, 2.

Since the present discipline of the Latin Church makes it difficult, in many regions, to fulfill these functions so necessary in the life of the Church, the diaconate can in the future be restored as a proper and permanent rank in the hierarchy. It is left to the various competent territorial bodies of bishops, with the approval of the Supreme Pontiff, to decide whether and where it is opportune to introduce permanent deacons for the care of souls.[...]

DECREE *AD GENTES* (1965)

(Restoration of the diaconate in mission countries)

1741a   16. Where the bishops' conferences deem it opportune, the order of diaconate should be restored as a permanent state of life, as laid down in the Constitution "On the Church" *[n. 1741]*. For it is beneficial that those who are really performing diaconal functions, whether preaching the word of God as catechists, or ruling remote Christian communities in the name of the parish priest or the bishop, or exercising charity in social and charitable works, should be strengthened and more closely joined to the altar by the imposition of hands, as handed down by the Apostles. They will more efficaciously fulfil their ministry through the sacramental grace of the diaconate.

DECREE *PRESBYTERORUM ORDINIS* (1965)

(The eschatological dimension of ordained ministry)

1741b   2. Thus, presbyters, whether they devote themselves to prayer and adoration, or preach the Word, or offer the eucharistic sacrifice and administer the other sacraments, or exercise other services for the benefit of the faithful, are contributing at once to the increase of God's glory and to the growth of human beings in the divine life. And all these activities, since they flow from the pasch of Christ, will find their consummation in the glorious coming of the same Lord, when he shall have delivered up the kingdom to God the Father.

(The ordained, ecclesial service leading people to God)

1741c   6. Presbyters exercise the function of Christ as Pastor and Head in proportion to their share of authority. In the name of the bishop they gather the family of God as a community endowed with the spirit of unity and lead it in Christ through the Spirit to God the Father. For the exercise of this ministry, as for the rest of the presbyters' functions, a spiritual power is given them, a power whose purpose is to build up. And in building up the Church, they ought to treat everybody with the greatest kindness after the model of our Lord. They should act towards people not according to what may please them, but according to the demands of Christian doctrine and life.

(The practico-social or messianic aspect of ordained ministry)

1741d 6. Although presbyters owe service to everybody, the poor and the weaker ones have been committed to their care in a special way. It was with these that the Lord himself associated, and the preaching of the Gospel to them is given as a sign of his messianic mission.[...] Presbyters ought to be especially devoted to the sick and the dying, visiting them and comforting them in the Lord.

PAUL VI
MOTU PROPRIO *SACRUM DIACONATUS ORDINEM*
(1967)

(1742) *The Second Vatican Council had made the restoration of the permanent diaconate in the Latin Church possible. In this* Motu Proprio *Paul VI promulgates the general rules that govern this restoration. He determines the procedure; the choice of candidates: either young men who will be bound to celibacy, or older men, either unmarried or married; their training; their upkeep; their functions and spiritual life; the special case of religious deacons; the rite of their ordination. The text is found in AAS 59 (1967) 697-704.*

ENCYCLICAL LETTER *SACERDOTALIS COELIBATUS* (1967)

Till the third century, bishops and priests were mostly married. As a result of the growing awareness of a close bond between priesthood and celibacy, by the fourth century the unmarried clergy became the majority; by then too, ordained ministers were forbidden to enter the married state. Celibacy, however, was not imposed as a rule, but continence in marriage was gradually required from the married clergy of the Western Church. The first document which witnesses to this is found in the Council of Elvira, Spain (c. 300-303) (cf. DS 119). In the sixth century continence became a clear obligation for the clergy of the Western Church. Recent popes have reaffirmed that, though there is no bond of necessity between ministry and celibacy, as is made clear by the practice of the Eastern Church, there exists nevertheless a clear harmony between the two which recommends that the long tradition of the Western Church be preserved. The Second Vatican Council spoke in the same line (PO 16). A major document on the subject is the Encyclical Letter of Pope Paul VI. Aware of the recent questioning to which the law of clerical celibacy has been subjected and of the difficulties met by priests in the modern world, the Pope considers that, nevertheless, the impressive testimony of the past and the present in favour of celibacy cannot be wiped out and that the law must be maintained. In a doctrinal part, the Pope states the reasons in favour of priestly celibacy: celibacy has a christological, an ecclesial and an eschatological meaning; he further shows the place of celibate ministry in the life of the Church and its relation to human values. The second part deals with practical questions such as the priestly life and training, priests abandoning the ministry, and the relations of priests with their bishops and the people (cf. AAS 59 (1967) 657-696).

1743 We consider then that the law of celibacy actually in force must still in our time, and firmly, be linked to the ecclesiastical ministry; it must sustain the ministers of the Church in their choice, exclusive, definitive and total, of the one and sovereign love of Christ, of dedication to the worship of God and the service of the Church; and it must be the mark of their state of life, both in the community of the faithful and in secular society.

APOSTOLIC CONSTITUTION *PONTIFICALIS ROMANI*
(1968)

(1744) *The Second Vatican Council had prescribed a revision of the rites of ordination (SC 76). In this Apostolic Constitution the Pope approves and promulgates the new rites of ordination to the diaconate, the presbyterate and the episcopate, prepared by the Consilium for the implementation of the Council's Constitution on the Sacred Liturgy (SC). The rites have been simplified, unified and given a richer doctrinal content. Since changes are introduced into the essential rites decreed by Pius XII (cf. n. 1738), the Pope uses his supreme authority to decree the new rites. For each order, the entire "consecratory prayer" which follows the laying on of hands is considered as the sacramental "form", but in each of the consecratory prayers one passage is singled out, which the Pope declares to be required for the validity of the ordination. In the ordination to the episcopate the consecratory prayer borrows from the* Apostolic Tradition *of Hippolytus; this is done in order that the meaning of the episcopal function, as "apex of the sacred ministry" (cf.n. 1739) in the apostolic succession, may be expressed more clearly than it was in the former Roman Pontifical. The new rite no longer limits the number of "consecrating bishops"; they not only lay on their hands on the bishops elect (cf. SC 76), but recite together with the "principal* *consecrator" the essential part of the consecratory prayer. The text is found in AAS 60 (1968) 369-373.*

On June 29, 1988, the Congregation for Divine Worship and the Discipline of the Sacraments promulgated the editio altera of De Ordinatione Episcopi, Presbyterorum et Diaconorum. The new edition of the ritual of Ordination includes the new doctrinal general introduction, and one for each order: bishop, presbyter and deacon.

THE THIRD SYNOD OF BISHOPS IN ROME

DE SACERDOTIO MINISTERIALI (1971)

The recent questioning on the ministerial priesthood, including the question of the specific character which distinguishes it from the common priesthood of the faithful, led to the topic of the priestly ministry being introduced for discussion at the Third Synod of bishops in Rome. The official Synodal document, submitted to the Pope for his consideration, has been published by him in Dec. 1971. The text is made up of two parts, one stating doctrinal principles, the other proposing guide-lines for the priestly life and ministry. The doctrinal part points to the newness of the priesthood which Christ has brought to the world and which remains present in the Church; it goes on to show, along the lines of the Second Vatican Council (cf. n. 738), the mutual link between flock and pastors which is inscribed in the very constitution of the Church. It is in this context that the specific function of the hierarchical ministry must be understood. The text is found in AAS 63(1971) 898ff.

(The priesthood of Christ)

1745 [...] Exercising a supreme and unique priesthood,[...] he [Christ] surpassed, by fulfilling them, all the ritual priesthoods and holocausts of the Old Testament and indeed of the nations.[...] When therefore we speak of the priesthood of Christ, we should have before our eyes a unique, incomparable reality, which includes the prophetic and royal office of the Incarnate Word of God.

(The origin and nature of the hierarchical ministry)

1746 The Church, which through the gift of the spirit is built up organically, participates in different ways in the functions of Christ as Priest, Prophet and King, in order to carry out its mission of salvation in his name and by his power, as a priestly people [cf. n. 1738].

It is clear from the New Testament writings that an apostle and a community of faithful united with one another by a mutual link under Christ as Head and the influence of his Spirit belong to the original inalienable structure of the Church.[...]

This essential structure of the Church—consisting of a flock and of pastors appointed for this purpose [cf. 1 Pet 5:1-4]—according to the tradition of the Church itself was always and remains the norm. Precisely as a result of this structure, the Church can never remain closed in on itself and is always subject to Christ as its origin and Head.

Among the various charisms and services, the priestly ministry of the New Testament, which continues Christ's function as mediator, and which differs from the common priesthood of all the faithful in essence and not only in degree [cf. n. 1738], alone perpetuates the essential work of the apostles: by effectively proclaiming the Gospel, by gathering together and leading the community, by remitting sins, and especially by celebrating the Eucharist, it makes Christ, the Head of the community, present in the exercise of his work of redeeming humankind and glorifying God perfectly.

APOSTOLIC LETTER *MINISTERIA QUAEDAM*
(15 August 1972)

By this Apostolic Letter, Pope Paul VI decrees the reform of the minor orders and of the subdiaconate in the Latin Church. The Council of Trent had considered those orders as "various steps" by which "one advances towards the priesthood" (n. 1715; cf. n. 1708). The reform suppresses the subdiaconate and restores lay ministries in the Latin Church. These are not called orders but "ministries"; they are not conferred through ordination but by "installation". Thus they are clearly distinguished from the sacramental orders of the diaconate, the presbyterate and the episcopate conferred through ordination. Belonging also to the laity, they do not introduce Christians into the clerical state; the tonsure being suppressed, it is henceforward the ordination to the diaconate that introduces into that state.

The Apostolic Letter establishes two lay ministries, those of lector and acolyte, by which the part in the service of the word and of the altar open to lay people is officially sanctioned in view of its stable exercise. It also foresees that, besides these two lay ministries which are of value for the universal Church, episcopal conferences may request the creation of others, among which the ministry of catechist is mentioned. Thus the possibility of a certain diversification of lay ministries and of their adaptation to circumstances of place and time is recognised. The official installation in the lay ministries of lector and acolyte is reserved to males. The text is found in AAS 64 (1972) 529ff.

1747   Among the special offices to be preserved and adapted to contemporary needs, there are those which are especially connected with the ministries of the word and of the altar and in the Latin Church are called the offices of lector and acolyte, and the subdiaconate. It is fitting to preserve and adapt these in such a way that, from this time on, there will be two offices: that of acolyte, which will include the functions of the subdiaconate.[...]

It is in accordance with the reality itself and with the contemporary outlook that the above mentioned ministries should no longer be called minor orders; their conferring should not be called 'ordination' but 'installation'; it is also proper that only those who have received the diaconate be considered as clerics. Thus there will better appear the distinction between clergy and laity, between what is proper and reserved to the clergy and what can be entrusted to the laity; thus there will appear more clearly their mutual relationship insofar as "the common priesthood of the faithful and the ministerial or hierarchical priesthood, though they differ in essence and not only in degree, are nonetheless ordained to each other; for both, in their respective manner, share in the one priesthood of Christ" [cf. n. 1738].

APOSTOLIC LETTER *AD PASCENDUM* (15 August, 1972)

(1748)   Issued on the same day as the previous document, this Motu Proprio fixes precise norms concerning the diaconate. These norms partly complete the general rules promulgated earlier by Pope VI for the restoration of the permanent diaconate (cf. n. 1742); their scope, however, is broader, for they also extend to the "transitional" diaconate of the candidates to the order of presbyters. Some of the new rules are suggested by the restoration of lay ministries. Aspirants to the permanent or transitional diaconate must during their formation, be officially received among the candidates for that order by a rite of admission which is the first public manifestation of their vocation and of its recognition by the bishop. They must be installed in the ministries of lector and acolyte and exercise them as a preparation for their ministry of the word and of the altar in the sacrament of Order. They are introduced into the clerical state by the ordination to the diaconate. In the case of candidates for the presbyterate and of unmarried candidates for the permanent diaconate the consecration to a celibate life and its obligation are linked with the ordination to the diaconate. The text is found in AAS 64(1972) 534ff.

DECLARATION *MYSTERIUM ECCLESIAE* OF THE
S. CONGREGATION FOR THE DOCTRINE OF THE FAITH
(11 May, 1973)

This Declaration on the mystery of the Church devotes a section to the priestly ministry, in which it intends to clarify the nature and especially the permanent character of the priestly ministry. Repeating the doctrine of the Second Vatican Council and of the Third Synod of Bishops in Rome (cf. nn. 1745-1746), the document begins by situating the Church's priesthood in relation to Christ's perfect priesthood. The Church's share in the priesthood of Christ "consists of the common priesthood of the faithful and the ministerial and hierarchical priesthood, both of which, though they differ from one another in essence and not only in degree, are nonetheless ordained to each other within the communion of the Church" (cf. nn. 1738, 1746). The document proceeds to show the origin in the Church of the priestly ministry derived from the apostolic succession. It shows how the permanent "character" of the ministry came progressively to be recognised in the Church. Though its nature is explained in different ways by theologians, the "permanent existence" or the "enduring nature of the priestly character through life" has traditionally been considered as "pertaining to the doctrine of faith" and must continue to be so considered. The text is found in AAS 65 (1973) 405-407.

(The origin of the priestly ministry in the Church)

1749 Christ, the Head of the Church which is his mystical Body, appointed as ministers of his priesthood, his apostles and through them their successors, that they might act in his person within the Church [*cf. n. 738; PO 2*] and also in turn legitimately hand on to priests in a subordinate degree the sacred ministry which they had received [*cf. n. 1740*]. Thus there arose in the Church the apostolic succession of the ministerial priesthood for the glory of God and for the service of his people and of the entire human family which must be converted to God.

(Ordination to the ministry confers a permanent character)

1750 The Church has ever more closely examined the nature of the ministerial priesthood, which can be shown to have been invariably conferred from apostolic times [*cf. 1 Tim 4:15; 2 Tim 1:6*]. By the assistance of the Holy Spirit, it recognised more clearly as time went on that God wished it to understand that this rite conferred upon priests not only an increase of grace for carrying out ecclesiastical duties in a holy way, but also a permanent designation by Christ, or character, by virtue of which they are equipped for their work and endowed with the necessary power that is derived from the supreme power of Christ.

APOSTOLIC EXHORTATION *EVANGELII NUNTIANDI* (1975)

By the Apostolic Letter Ministeria Quaedam *(1972) Pope Paul VI restored lay ministries in the Latin Church (cf. n. 1747). These have developed since and new lay ministries have been created, especially in some local churches, to the benefit of the mission of evangelisation. The 1974 Synod of Bishops on evangelisation encouraged the installation of lay people in ministries by which their participation in the Church's mission is officially recognised. The Apostolic Exhortation on evangelisation of Paul VI gives new impetus to lay ministries, while clearly distinguishing them from the ordained ministries. The Pope explains what is the specific role of all the laity in the Church's evangelising mission; in this context he shows the special contribution which lay ministries make to the ecclesial mission. The text is found in AAS 68 (1976) 61-63.*

(Lay ministries)

1751 73. The laity can also feel themselves called, or be called, to work with their pastors in the service of the ecclesial community, for its growth and life, by exercising a great variety of ministries according to the grace and charisms which the Lord is pleased to give them.

We cannot but experience a great inner joy when we see so many pastors, religious and lay people, fired with their mission to evangelize, seeking ever more suitable ways of proclaiming the Gospel effectively. We encourage the openness which the Church is showing today in this direction and with this solicitude. It is an openness to meditation first of all, and then to ecclesial ministries capable of renewing and strengthening the evangelizing vigour of the Church.

It is certain that, side-by-side with the ordained ministries, whereby certain people are appointed pastors and consecrate themselves in a special way to the service of the community, the Church recognises the place of non-ordained ministries which are able to offer a particular service to the Church.

A glance at the origins of the Church is very illuminating, and gives the benefit of an early experience in the matter of ministries. It was an experience which was all the more valuable in that it enabled the Church to consolidate itself and to grow and spread. Attention to the sources, however, has to be complemented by attention to the present needs of humankind and of the Church. To drink at these ever inspiring sources without sacrificing anything of their values, and at the same time to know how to adapt oneself to the demands and needs of today—these are the criteria which will make it possible to seek wisely and to discover the ministries which the Church needs and which many of its members will gladly embrace for the sake of ensuring greater vitality in the ecclesial community. These ministries will have a real pastoral value to the extent that they are established with absolute respect for unity and adhering to the directives of the pastors, who are the ones who are responsible for the Church's unity and the builders thereof.

These ministries, apparently new but closely tied up with the Church's living experience down the centuries—such as catechists, directors of prayer and chant, Christians devoted to the service of God's word or to assisting their brethren in need, the heads of small communities, or other persons charged with the responsibility of apostolic movements—these ministries are valuable for the establishment, life, and growth of the Church, and for its capacity to influence its surroundings and to reach those who are remote from it. We owe also our special esteem to all the lay-people who accept to consecrate a part of their time, their energies, and sometimes their entire lives, to the service of the missions.

DECLARATION OF THE SACRED CONGREGATION FOR THE DOCTRINE OF THE FAITH, *INTER INSIGNIORES*, ON THE QUESTION OF THE ADMISSION OF WOMEN TO THE MINISTERIAL PRIESTHOOD.
(15th October, 1976)

The question of the possibility of admitting women to the priestly ministry has been asked in recent years and has become a theological, pastoral and ecumenical problem. It led to this declaration by the Sacred Congregation for the Doctrine of the Faith which, though dated 15 October, 1976, was made public only on 27 January, 1977. In an introduction the document points to the increasing role played by women both in society and the Church's apostolate in modern times including, in some Christian Churches, the admission of "women to the pastoral office on a par with men". To the question whether the Catholic Church too could consider admitting women to the priestly ministry, the Document answers: "The Church, in fidelity to the example of the Lord, does not consider itself authorized to admit women to priestly ordination" (Introduction). The Document proceeds to justify its negative answer with dogmatic and theological reasons, not all of which have the same weight and value. Six considerations are made: 1) The Church's constant tradition has been to ordain only men to the priestly ministry; 2) Jesus did not call any women to be members of the Twelve: 3) the apostles did not include any women in the apostolic group: 4) the practice of Christ and the apostles in this regard is permanently normative: 5) the priest must have a "natural resemblance" to Christ, and the male sex is constitutive of this resemblance; 6) the issue of equality in the Church and of human rights is irrelevant to the question of priestly ministry for women. The most weighty among these arguments, and, in the mind of the S. Congregation, the decisive one, is the dogmatic value which it attributes to the Church's constant tradition, based on the practice of Jesus himself and of the apostles: the exclusion of women from priestly ordination is considered as belonging to the substance of the sacrament which the Church has no power to change (cf. nn. 1324; 1737i). The text is found in AAS 69 (1977) 98-116.

(The tradition of ordaining only men to the priestly ministry is normative)

1752 4. Could the Church today depart from the attitude of Jesus and the Apostles, which has been considered as normative by the whole of tradition up to our own day?[...]

[...]The priestly ministry is not just a pastoral service; it ensures the continuity of the functions entrusted by Christ to the Apostles and the continuity of the powers, related to those functions. Adaptation to civilisations and times therefore cannot abolish, on essential points, the sacramental reference to the constitutive events of Christianity and to Christ himself.

In the final analysis, it is the Church, through the voice of its magisterium, that, in these various domains decides what can change and what must remain immutable.When it judges that it cannot accept certain changes, it is because it knows that it is bound by Christ's manner of acting. Its attitude, despite appearances, is therefore not one of archaism but of fidelity; it can be truly understood only in this light. The Church makes pronouncements in virtue of the Lord's promise and the presence of the Holy Spirit, in order to proclaim better the mystery of Christ and to safeguard and manifest the whole of its rich content.

This practice of the Church therefore has a normative character: in the fact of confering priestly ordination only on men, it is a question of an unbroken tradition throughout the history of the Church, universal in the East and in the West, and alert to repress abuses immediately. This norm, based on Christ's example, has been and is still observed because it is considered to conform to God's plan for his Church.

JOHN PAUL II
LETTER TO ALL THE PRIESTS OF THE CHURCH ON THE OCCASION OF HOLY THURSDAY, 1979
(9 April, 1979)

The Pope's letter is directly concerned with strengthening priests in their priestly vocation; it has no intention to develop at length a theology of the priestly ministry. It is a direct and unambiguous appeal for "fidelity to Christ", including fidelity to the commitment to celibacy freely entered upon by ordination. Though priestly ministry and celibacy are distinct charisms, the Latin Church has a long tradition of linking the latter to the former. Like Pope Paul VI (cf. n. 1743), Pope John Paul II considers that this link must be preserved. The reason is that celibacy is not only an eschatological sign, but has also a social meaning in the present life as a sign of freedom for service of the people of God. Once freely assumed, it becomes a matter of fidelity to Christ and his Church. No allusion is made in the letter to the possibility, often advocated in recent years, of admitting married men to priestly ordination, where the pastoral care of Christian communities would seem to demand it. The text is found in Osservatore Romano *(English Edition), 17 April, 1979, pp. 6-9.*

(On priestly celibacy)

1753 8. The Latin Church has wished, and continues to wish, referring to the example of Christ the Lord himself, to the apostolic teaching and to the whole tradition that is proper to it, that all those who receive the sacrament of Orders should embrace this renunciation [of marriage] "for the sake of the kingdom of heaven". This tradition, however, is linked with respect for different traditions of other Churches. In fact, this tradition constitutes a characteristic, a peculiarity and a heritage of the Latin Catholic Church, a tradition to which it owes much and in which it is resolved to persevere, inspite of all the difficulties to which such fidelity could be exposed.

Why does the Latin Catholic Church link this gift [of celibacy] not only with the life of those who accept the strict programme of the evangelical counsels in religious institutes, but also with the vocation to the hierarchical and ministerial priesthood? The Church does it because celibacy "for the sake of the kingdom" is not only an eschatological sign; it also has a great social meaning, in the present life, for the service of the People of God. Through his celibacy, the priest becomes a "person for others". [...] Celibacy is a sign of a freedom that exists for the sake of service. According to this sign, the hierarchical or "ministerial" priesthood is, according to the tradition of our Church, more strictly "ordered" to the common priesthood of the faithful.

HOMILY AT THE CONCLUSION OF THE PARTICULAR SYNOD OF THE DUTCH BISHOPS IN ROME
(31 January, 1980)

A particular Synod of the Dutch Bishops with Pope John Paul II was held in Rome, January 14-31, 1980. It was convoked in order that, together with the Pope, the bishops might take collegial decisions on problems affecting the life and pastoral activity of the Church in Holland. One of the problems discussed at the Synod was that of the concrete forms of activity open to lay "pastoral workers" and the limits to be imposed on them. The distinction between the common priesthood and the ministerial priesthood may not be obscured as would be the case if a "parallel" ministry by lay people were to operate as an alternative for the ordained ministry of presbyter and deacon. In his homily on the last day of the Synod the Pope made special reference to this point. The text is found in Osservatore Romano *(English Edition), 11 February, 1980, p. 3.*

(Pastoral tasks of lay people may not obscure the priestly ministry)

1754　　4. Allow me to stress a special point which turned out to be at the centre of all the other questions raised and which will have a very great impact on the future of the Church. I am referring here to the true ministerial priesthood of priests, in its nature as well as in its relations with the bishops and in its relationship to the commitment of lay people in the mission of the Church.

The building up of the ecclesial community and the implementation of its mission are entrusted to the whole community, but, as the Dogmatic Constitution *Lumen Gentium* says [cf. LG 30-38], this responsibility is exercised in harmony with the charism and the place of each one in the Body of Christ. All vocations, all services, all charisms are ordained to manifesting in their variety the riches of the Church and to serving its unity. The church must be able to express the fulness of its life through the riches of vocations and charisms, in the ministerial priesthood as well as in the apostolate of the laity, and also in religious consecration according to the spirit and the specific purpose of every institute.

But each of these ministries and these services has its own specific character, and they all complete one another without merging[...]. It is important [...] to safeguard, in the attribution of tasks and in the delimitation of responsibilities, the distinction between the contribution of the laity and the tasks entrusted to priests and deacons.

S. CONGREGATION FOR THE CLERGY
DECLARATION ON SOME MOVEMENTS AND ASSOCIATIONS FORBIDDEN TO THE CLERGY

(8 March, 1982)

The question of priests unions and associations has been raised frequently in recent years. In this Declaration the S. Congregation for the clergy specifies which kind of unions are compatible with the priestly office and which are not. The text is found in AAS 74 (1982) 642-645.

(The right of clerics to associate)

1755a 1. From ancient times, many diocesan priests experienced the necessity and the profit of availing themselves of the personal advantages that are derived from uniting themselves in association with others in order to cultivate the spiritual life, to foster the education of the clergy, to exercise works of charity and holiness, and to pursue other goals which are in full conformity with their sacramental consecration and their divine mission. The Church hierarchy has very willingly recognised that clerics also have the right to associate among themselves either by establishing or by joining associations, always however for reasons that are in accord with the nature of the ministerial priesthood [PO 8].

(Limits of the right)

1755b 2. At the same time, however, the sacred hierarchy has never permitted, nor can it now permit, that the right of the clergy to associate, both in the realm of the ecclesial community and in the civil field, be exercised by joining associations or movements of any type which, by their nature, finality or modes of action, would be an impediment to the hierarchical communion of the Church and damage the priestly identity and the fulfillment of the duties which the priests themselves, "in the name of Christ", exercise in the service of God's People [cf LG 11: PO 2]. Both diocesan as well as religious priests, in fact, while striving to build up the Christian community, "are never to put themselves at the service of any ideology or human faction. Rather, as heralds of the Gospel and shepherds of the Church, they must devote themselves to the spiritual growth of the Body of Christ" [PO 6].

(Associations irreconcilable with the clerical state)

1755c   3. Those associations of clerics, even if they are only civilly established or constituted, whether they directly or indirectly, openly or secretly pursue goals that pertain to politics, without doubt, are irreconcilable with the clerical state, and, therefore, are forbidden to all members of the clergy, even if they may outwardly appear to promote humanitarian ideals, peace and social progress. Such associations or movements, in fact, cause division and discord in the heart of the People of God, both among the faithful and among the clergy in their relationships to one another and to their ordinaries, and undoubtedly cast a shadow over the priestly mission and shatter ecclesial communion: mission and communion, the realities which constitute an essential element in the life and ministry of priests.

(Trade unions irreconcilable with the clerical state)

1755d   4. In the same way, those associations which seek to unite deacons or priests in a type of "trade union" are also irreconcilable with the clerical state and, therefore, are forbidden to members of the clergy. Such associations actually reduce the sacred ministry of these deacons and priests to a *profession* or a *trade*, comparable to secular tasks. Such associations, in fact, envision the exercise of the functions of the ministerial priesthood like a job description, and thus can easily place the clergy in opposition to their sacred pastors, who would be considered merely as employers.

(Right and duty of the competent authority)

1755e   4. It is the right and duty of the competent ecclesiastical authority to see to it that clerics refrain from establishing or from belonging to associations or movements of any type which are not in harmony with the priesthood, a fact which is verified in the cases described above in nos. 3 and 4. Furthermore, whoever acts against the legitimate prohibition of the same competent authority can be punished with a just penalty or even censure, *servatis de iure servandis.*

It is the conviction of the Holy See that the prudent and firm application of these norms will allow the true charisms, which the Holy Spirit never ceases to pour out upon the Church, to bring forth abundant fruits to the benefit of the order of presbyters, the ministerial priesthood and the whole People of God. Through the watchful and solicitous action of the Church's sacred pastors [cf. LG 27; CD16], false charisms, which sometimes spread about and can lead some priests astray, will be exposed and completely rejected.

S. CONGREGATION FOR THE DOCTRINE OF THE FAITH LETTER TO THE BISHOPS OF THE CATHOLIC CHURCH ON CERTAIN QUESTIONS CONCERNING THE MINISTER OF THE EUCHARIST

(6 August, 1983)

From the various forms of Church organisation reflected in the New Testament writings some theologians concluded to the possibility for a Christian Community to celebrate the eucharist, at least in exceptional circumstances, with a president appointed from among its members, who has not been sacramentally ordained. The Letter of the S.Congregation for the Doctrine of the Faith, Sacerdotium Ministeriale, rejects this position as against the faith. The text is found in AAS 75 (1983) 1001-1009.

(Introduction)

1756a I,1. In teaching that the ministerial or hierarchical priesthood differs essentially and not only in degree from the common priesthood of the faithful, the Second Vatican Council expressed the certainty of faith that only the bishops and priests can confect the eucharistic mystery. Although all the faithful indeed share in the one and the same priesthood of Christ and are one in the offering of the eucharist, it is only the ministerial priest who, in virtue of the sacrament of Holy Orders has the power to confect the eucharistic sacrifice in the person of Christ and offer it in the name of all the Christian people [LG 10, 17, 26, 28; SC 7; CD 15; PO 2, 3].

1756b 2. In recent years, however, certain opinions have come to be propagated, and at times translated into practice, which deny the above teaching of the magisterium and consequently cause harm to the innermost life of the Church. Such opinions which are spread in various forms and with different lines of argument have begun to attract some of the faithful themselves, either because they claim to be based on a scholarly foundation, or because they are presented as responding to the needs of the pastoral care and sacramental life of Christian communities.

1756c   3. This is why this Sacred Congregation, prompted by a desire to offer its subsidiary services to the bishops in a true collegial spirit, wishes to restate here some of the essential points of the Church's doctrine on the minister of the eucharist, transmitted by its living tradition and expressed in previous documents of the magisterium [cf. nn. 1734, 1746, 1749-1750, 1752...] The Congregation takes for granted the integral vision of the priestly ministry as presented by the Second Vatican Council, but in the present situation it considers it a matter of urgency to bring to clearer light the special and essential role of priests.

(The doctrine of the Church)

1757a   III,1. Although they may be expressed in various ways with different nuances, all the above-mentioned opinions lead to the same conclusion: that the power to confect the sacrament of the eucharist is not necessarily connected with sacramental ordination. It is evident that such a conclusion is absolutely incompatible with the faith as it has been handed down, since not only does it deny the power conferred on priests but it distorts the entire apostolic structure of the Church and undermines the sacramental economy of salvation itself.

(Apostleship, apostolicity and apostolic succession)

1757b   2. According to the teaching of the Church, the word of the Lord and divine life which he has given to us have been destined from the very beginning to be lived and shared in a single body, which the Lord builds up for himself throughout the course of the ages. This body, which is the Church of Christ, is continually endowed with gifts of service *(ministratio)* by him "from whom the whole body, nourished and knit together through its joints and ligaments, grows with a growth that is from God" *[Col 2:19] [cf. LG 7, 18, 19, 20; CD 1, 3; PO 2]*. This structure of service finds clear expression in sacred tradition in the three powers entrusted to the Apostles and their successors: to sanctify, to teach and to govern in the name of Christ.

The apostolicity of the Church does not mean that all believers are Apostles *[cf. n. 1710]*, not even in a collective sense, and no community has the power to confer the apostolic ministry which is essentially bestowed by the Lord himself. Therefore, when the Church in its creeds calls itself apostolic, it expresses, beside the doctrinal identity of its teaching with that of the Apostles, the reality of the continuation of their work, by means of the structure of succession, in virtue of which the apostolic mission is to endure until the end of time *(LG 20)*.

This apostolic succession which constitutes the entire Church as apostolic is part of the living tradition which has been for the Church from the beginning, and continues to be, its particular form of life. And so, those who cite isolated texts of scripture in opposition to this living tradition, trying thereby to justify different structures, stray from the truth.

(Apostolic structure maintained)

1757c 3. The Catholic Church, which has developed through the ages and continues to grow by the life given to it by the Lord through the outpouring of the Holy Spirit, has always maintained its apostolic structure, faithful to the tradition of the Apostles which lives and endures in it. When it imposes hands on those to be ordained and invokes upon them the Holy Spirit, it is conscious of handing on the power of the Lord who makes the bishops, as successors of the Apostles, partakers in a special way of his threefold office, priestly, prophetic and royal. In turn, the bishops impart, in varying degrees, the office of their ministry to various persons in the Church *[LG 28]*.

And so, even though all the baptised enjoy the same dignity before God, in the Christian community, which was deliberately structured hierarchically by its divine founder, there have existed from its earliest days specific apostolic functions deriving from the sacrament of Holy Orders.

(Confecting the eucharist, a priestly power)

1757d 4. To be included among these functions which Christ entrusted exclusively to the apostles and their successors is the power of confecting the eucharist. To the bishops alone, and to the priests they have made sharers in their ministry which they themselves have received, is reserved the power of renewing in the mystery of the eucharist what Christ did at the last Supper [LG 21: PO 2].

In order that they may be able to carry out their functions, especially a work so important as confecting the eucharistic mystery, our Lord marks out in a spiritual manner those whom he calls to the episcopate and to the priesthood. He does this with a special seal through the sacrament of Orders, a seal also called a "character" in solemn documents of the Church's magisterium [LG 21:PO 2]. In this way he so configures them to himself that when they pronounce the words of consecration, they do not act on a mandate from the community but "in persona Christi, which means more than just 'in the name of Christ' or even 'in the place of Christ'[...], since the celebrant, by reason of this special sacrament, identifies himself with the eternal High Priest, who is both author and principal agent of his own sacrifice in which truly no one can take his place."[1] Since it is of the very nature of the Church that the power to consecrate the eucharist is imparted only to the bishops and priests who are constituted his ministers by the reception of Holy Orders, the Church holds that the eucharistic mystery can be celebrated in every community by no one except by an ordained priest, as expressly declared by the Fourth Lateran Council [cf. n. 21].

Individual faithful or communities who, because of persecution or lack of priests, are deprived of the holy eucharist for either a short or even a long period of time, do not thereby lack the grace of the Redeemer. If they are intimately animated by a desire for the sacrament and, united in prayer with the whole Church, call upon the Lord and raise their hearts to him, by virtue of the Holy Spirit they live in communion with the Church, the living body of Christ, and with the Lord himself. United, therefore, to the Church through their desire of the sacrament, no matter how physically distant they may seem to be, they intimately and really share in its life and therefore receive the fruits of the sacrament; whereas those who would illegally

---

1. John Paul II, Letter *Dominicae Cenae*, (8): *AAS* 72 (1980) 128-129.

take upon themselves the right to confect the eucharistic mystery end up by having their communion closed upon itself.[1]

None of this derogates from the serious obligation of bishops, priests, and all members of the Church to pray that "the Lord of the harvest" may send workers according to the needs of the times and of places [cf. Mt 9:39ff], and to work with all their energy to make the Lord's call to the ministerial priesthood heard and welcomed, with humble and generous heart.

JOHN PAUL II

APOSTOLIC EXHORTATION *CHRISTIFIDELES LAICI*
(30 December, 1988)

On this Apostolic Exhortation which resumed the theme of the 1987 Synod of bishops on the "Vocation and Mission of Lay People in the Church and in the World Twenty Years after the Second Vatican Council", cf. nn. 894i-896. After having shown which ministries are open to lay people, the Pope, while stressing the part which women can and must assume in the Church's mission, reaffirms that in fidelity to Christ's will the Church may not allow the promotion of women to the ordained ministry (cf. n. 1752). The text is found in AAS 81 (1989) 393-521.

(Women may not receive the sacrament of Orders)

1758   51. In speaking about participation in the apostolic mission of the Church, there is no doubt that in virtue of baptism and confirmation, a woman—as well as a man—is made a sharer in the threefold mission of Jesus Christ, priest, prophet and king, and is thereby charged and given the ability to fulfill the fundamental apostolate of the Church: evangelization. However, a woman is called to put to work in this apostolate the "gifts" which are properly hers: first of all, the gift that is her very dignity as a person exercised in word and testimony of life, gifts therefore, connected with her vocation as a woman.

In her participation in the life and mission of the Church a woman cannot receive the sacrament of Orders and therefore cannot fulfill the proper function of the ministerial priesthood. This is a practice that the Church has always found in the expressed will of Christ, totally free and sovereign, who called

---

1. JOHN PAUL II, Letter *Novo Incipiente Nostro*, (10): *AAS* 71 (1979) 411-415.

only men to be his Apostles [cf. n. 1752]; a practice that can be understood from the rapport between Christ, the spouse, and his bride, the Church.[1] Here we are in the area of function, not of dignity and holiness. In fact, it must be maintained: "Although the Church possesses a 'hierarchical' structure, nevertheless this structure is totally ordered to the holiness of Christ's members."[2]

CATECHISM OF THE CATHOLIC CHURCH
(7 December, 1992)

(The ordained refashion creation and restore it in God's image)

1759 1589. Before the grandeur of the priestly grace and office, the holy doctors felt an urgent call to conversion in order to conform their whole lives to him whose sacrament had made them ministers. Thus St. Gregory of Nazianzus, as a very young presbyter, exclaimed: "We must begin by purifying ourselves before purifying others; we must be instructed to be able to instruct, become light to illuminate, draw close to God to bring him close to others, be sanctified to sanctify, lead by the hand and counsel prudently. I know whose ministers we are, where we find ourselves and to where we strive. I know God's greatness and man's weakness, but also his potential. [Who then is the priest? He is] the defender of truth, who stands with angels, gives glory with archangels, causes sacrifices to rise to the altar on high, shares Christ's priesthood, refashions creation, restores it in God's image, recreates it for the world on high, and, even greater, is divinised and divinises."[3]

APOSTOLIC LETTER *ORDINATIO SACERDOTALIS*
(22 May, 1994)

(The definitive nature of the restriction of priestly ordination to males)

1760 4. Therefore, the teaching on priestly ordination as reserved only to men has been preserved by the constant and universal tradition of the Church, has been constantly and universally taught by the Church, and has been taught firmly

---

1. *Mulieris Dignitatem*, 26.
2. *Mulieris Dignitatem*, 27; cf. *Inter Insigniores*, 6.
3. St. Gregory of Nazianzus, *Oratio* 2, 71, 74, 73: *PG* 35, 480-481.

by the magisterium in its recent documents, even though in our time and in diverse places it is considered open to discussion, in the sense that there is to be attributed a merely disciplinary value to the decision of the Church not to admit women to such ordination. Thus, so as to remove every doubt regarding a question of such great importance, which entails the divine constitution of the Church, and in virtue of my ministry to confirm the brethern in the faith [cf. Lc 22:32], I declare that the Church does not possess in any way the faculty to confer priestly ordination on women, and that this statement ought to be considered as definitive by all the faithful of the Church.

CONGREGATION FOR THE DOCTRINE OF THE FAITH

REPLY TO THE *DUBIUM* CONCERNING THE TEACHING

CONTAINED IN THE APOSTOLIC LETTER *ORDINATIO SACERDOTALIS*

(28 October, 1995)

To a doubt expressed about the teaching of the Apostolic Letter (cf. n. 1760), the following reply was adopted by the congregation in question at an ordinary session, and was presented to John Paul II for approval. This was granted along with the order that it be published.

1761 *Dubium:* Whether the teaching that the church has no authority whatsoever to confer priestly ordination on women, which is presented in the apostolic letter *Ordinatio Sacerdotalis* to be held definitively, is to be understood as belonging to the deposit of the faith.

Responsum: In the affirmative.

This teaching requires definitive assent, since, founded on the written word of God and from the beginning constantly preserved and applied in the tradition of the church, it has been set forth infallibly by the ordinary and universal magisterium [cf. Second Vatican Council, Dogmatic Constitution on the Church *Lumen Gentium*, 25.2]. Thus, in the present circumstances, the Roman pontiff, exercising his proper office of confirming the brethren [cf. Lk 22: 32], has handed on this same teaching by a formal declaration, explicitly stating what is to be held always, everywhere and by all as belonging to the deposit of the faith.

CONGREGATION FOR CATHOLIC EDUCATION
"BASIC NORMS FOR THE FORMATION OF PERMANENT DEACONS"
CONGREGATION FOR THE CLERGY
"DIRECTORY FOR THE MINISTRY AND LIFE OF PERMANENT DEACONS"
(22 February 1998)

After world-wide consultation, these co-ordinated documents were drawn up separately by the two congregations in question, but were published together with a "joined declaration" and introduction. Their purpose is to clarify already existing universal and local legislation, to unify the formation programme and the style of ministry of permanent deacons throughout the Church, and to encourage those unmarried, married and widowed men who have the charism of ecclesial service to seek, prepare for and receive the sacrament of Order as permanent sacred ministers. The text of the documents is found in Origins *28 (1998-1999) 177-204.*

(*The sacramental grace of the diaconate as necessary to the Church's life*)

1762 Introduction, III, 3: The permanent diaconate is an important enrichment for the mission of the church. Since the *munera* proper to deacons are necessary to the church's life, it is both convenient and useful, especially in mission territories, that men who are called to a truly diaconal ministry in the church, whether liturgical or pastoral, charitable or social, "be strengthened by the imposition of hands, which has come down from the apostles, and more closely united to the altar so as to exercise their ministry more fruitfully through the sacramental grace of the diaconate" [AG 16].

MOTU PROPRIO *APOSTOLOS SUOS*
(21 May 1998)

(1763) *This document on the theological and canonical nature of the episcopal conferences is meant to meet a specific request, expressed at the Special Synod of 1985, that their relationship to the authority of the individual local bishops, to that of the college of bishops, and to that of the supreme authority of the Holy See be clarified. In order to achieve this goal, the document is divided into four parts: (1) an historical introduction, (II) reflections on the collegial union of the bishops, (III) comments on the episcopal conferences, and (IV) norms to be observed by them. See text in nn. 900 Da-h.*

CHAPTER XVIII

MATRIMONY

All peoples have recognised a sacred character in the marriage union. In the Old Testament the sanctity of marriage is clearly attributed to the will of the Creator; marriage becomes, moreover, a prophetic symbol of the union of God with his people. St. Paul shows how this union is fully realised in the mystical bond between Christ and the Church, of which Christian marriage is an image and reflection. Thus, Christian marriage is one of the means by which the mystery of the Church is actualised, for in the marriage covenant of her members she manifests herself as the mystery of the union of Christ with humanity. The Christian family is a fundamental expression of the mystery of the Church, the most incarnate form of her charity; hence it is rightly called the "Church in miniature".

It is only in this perspective that the Christian doctrine of marriage can be fully understood. Its direct object is not the fundamental properties of marriage, its unity and indissolubility, as already inscribed in nature; it is rather the new significance which the institution of marriage takes on in the context of the Christian mystery, in which it is raised by Christ to the dignity of a sacrament.

The Christian dignity of marriage explains why the Church's teaching authority has from the earliest times vindicated its goodness against dualistic and rigoristic errors; why she upheld its sacred character against all tendencies to reduce it to a merely profane reality; why again she has claimed for herself the right to legislate in matrimonial matters.

The Church, however, has grown in the explicit awareness of Christian marriage as an effective sharing in the mystery of Christ's union with her, and hence as an efficacious sign of grace. Implicitly contained in the early tradition and practice, this doctrine could only be clearly formulated when the Church came to a more explicit possession of her sacramental doctrine. It was then clearly recognised that if Christian marriage endows the natural bond of marriage with new compelling force and firmness, this is precisely due to the participation in the Christian mystery which the sacrament confers.

Moreover, the sacrament also gives the spouses the grace necessary to foster indefectible fidelity and to achieve the ends of mutual union and of fruitfulness which in the supernatural order results in the increase of the People of God. Traditionally, the stress has been laid on the end of procreation, consonant with the institutional aspect of marriage. The aspect of partnership, however, has recently found increasing recognition and is clearly brought out in the Pastoral Constitution Gaudium et Spes *of the Second Vatican Council.*

Long before the sacramental doctrine of marriage was explicitly formulated, the Church's teaching authority had already stated that the constitutive element of Christian marriage is the mutual consent of the partners. This forcibly brings out the fact that in Christian marriage it is the human reality of marriage itself which has been raised by Christ to the dignity of a sacrament: contract and sacrament are inseparable. This is also why the magisterium has claimed the right to determine the "canonical form" under which the contract must be made and to subject it to various conditions of validity.

Thus the Church documents uphold the dignity of the human reality of marriage and its place in her sacramental economy. At the same time, they show that the doctrine on marriage reflects in a particular manner the developments characteristic of the doctrine on the sacraments and on the Church herself. Against the denial of the Reformers the Council of Trent exposed clearly the sacramentality of Christian marriage and the consequences derived from it. Pope Leo XIII emphasised the intrinsic relation between the marriage contract and the sacrament. Pope Pius XI explained how Christian marriage and family life are a way to Christian perfection. Lately, the Second Vatican Council has stressed the central role which conjugal love plays in Christian marriage; it has shown how the covenant relationship between the spouses reflects the union of Christ with the Church.

Although the Church never grants dissolution of a sacramental consummated bond, she does grant annulment in the case of an invalid marriage. The tribunals are to proceed judiciously.

*   *   *

The moral aspects of conjugal life are dealt with in chapter XXII. The main doctrinal points treated in this chapter are the following:

Marriage is willed by God: 1824, 1835.

It has been raised by Christ to the dignity of a sacrament: 28, 32, 1305, 1311, 1803, 1806, 1807, 1808, 1820, 1822, 1823, 1824, 1830, 1834, 1836, 1843.

Marriage is good: 21, 402/11-12, 1802.

It may not be considered superior to the state of virginity: 1817.

Christian marriage is a sharing in the mystery of Christ and the Church: 1803, 1806, 1820, 1823, 1831, 1834, 1836, 1843.

Marriage as covenant: 1852 a-b.

Marriage as a communion of persons: 1852c.

Husband and wife, a uni-duality: 1854.

The essential rite of the sacrament is the mutual consent of the spouses: (1801), 1803, 1823, 1825, 1835.

Contract and sacrament are inseparable: 1822, 1823.

Marriage comes under the legal competence of the Church: 1821.

The Church's teaching authority can establish impediments: 1810, 1811, 1816

Vasectomy does not invalidate marriage: 1842.

The Church's magisterium may determine the rite to be observed: 1818.

Matrimonial cases are in the competence of ecclesiastical courts: 1819.

The essential laws of marriage are not subject to human will: 1824, 1825.

The marital bond is exclusive: 28, 1805, 1809.

It is indissoluble: 1802, 1803, 1804, 1805, 1813, 1831, 1835, 1836, 1844.

It cannot be dissolved because of adultery: 1814.

Its indissolubility is perfected by the sacrament: 1806, 1820, 1844.

Marriage which has not been consummated can be dissolved in certain circumstances: 1812.

Recent advances are to be used responsibly in annulment cases: 1845.

Marriage is a partnership of love in fidelity: 1803, 1804, 1828, 1830, 1835, 1837, 1839, 1841, 1852b.

This partnership is uniquely expressed through the conjugal act: 1837, 1838.

The conjugal act is by its nature ordained to procreation resulting in the increase of the People of God: 1306, 1803, 1826, 1827, 1834, 1841.

Union between the spouses is intimately linked with the end of procreation: 1840, 1841.

The sacrament sanctifies the spouses and gives them graces necessary for their state: 1806, 1807, 1808, 1820, 1823, 1832, 1833, 1836.

Christian marriage is a way to perfection: 1834, 1836.

The Christian family is the primary cell of the Church: 1834.

The equal personal dignity of man and woman in the unity of marriage: 1839.

Progress in Christian marriage: 1841a.

Human and ecclesial meaning (canonical aspect): (1846), (1847), (1848).

Adaptation and inculturation of sacramental rite: 1841b, (1849).

Participation in celebrations of marriages: 1850, 1851.

Mixed marriages: 1852.

Communion and divorced and remarried Catholics: 1853.

ALEXANDER III (1159-1181)
LETTER TO THE ARCHBISHOP OF SALERNO
(time unknown)

(1801)   *In answer to the inquiry made by the Emperor of the Bulgarians,*
755   *converted to Christianity, as regards the essence of Christian*
756   *marriage, Pope Nicholas I, in a letter to the Bulgarians (866) had*
          declared that the consent of the partners is as in the Roman law the
essential element of Christian marriage (cf.DS 643). But in the early Middle
Ages a controversy arose between those who, basing their doctrine on the
Germanic law, held that the conjugal act is necessary for the 'formation' of
marriage and those who with Peter Lombard held the traditional view that the
consent is sufficient. Alexander III settled the issue by declaring that mutual
consent makes the marriage, but the bond is perfected and becomes absolutely
indissoluble through consummation. Previous to consummation, marriage can
be dissolved by solemn religious profession.

INNOCENT III
PROFESSION OF FAITH PRESCRIBED TO THE
WALDENSIANS (1208)

In the early times the main controversy on marriage centred on its recognition
as a true human value. Dualistic tendencies, advocating two principles, one of
good and one of evil, attributed marriage to the principle of evil. The Manichaean
and Priscillianist denigration of marriage had been condemned by the first
Council of Toledo (400) (cf. DS 206) and by the Council of Braga (561) (cf.
nn.402/11-12). The goodness of marriage is again affirmed in the profession of
faith prescribed by Innocent III to the Waldensians who, like the Albigensians,
held Manichaean views (cf.n.403i), and forbade marriage to the 'perfect'.

1802   We do not deny that marriage can be contracted as the
794   apostle says *[cf. 1 Cor 7]*; but we strictly forbid that those
          rightly contracted be broken. We believe and confess that
a man can be saved even if he has a wife, and we do not
condemn a second marriage or even subsequent marriages.

THE GENERAL COUNCIL OF FLORENCE
DECREE FOR THE ARMENIANS (1439)

After affirming the sacramentality of marriage, the Decree for the
Armenians exposes the triple good of marriage according to the patristic
tradition. For the value of this document, see n. 1305i.

1803   The seventh is the sacrament of matrimony which is
1327   the sign of the union of Christ and the Church according
          to the saying of the apostle: "This is a great mystery,

and I am applying it to Christ and the Church" *[Eph 5:32]*. The efficient cause of matrimony is the mutual consent duly expressed in words relating to the present. A triple good is found in Matrimony. The first is the begetting of children and their education to the worship of God. The second is the faithfulness which each spouse owes to the other. Third is the indissolubility of marriage, inasmuch as it represents the indissoluble union of Christ and the Church. But, although it is permitted to separate on account of adultery, nevertheless it is not permitted to contract another marriage since the bond of a marriage legitimately contracted is perpetual.

THE GENERAL COUNCIL OF TRENT
TWENTY-FOURTH SESSION
DOCTRINE ON THE SACRAMENT OF MATRIMONY (1563)

The Reformers upheld the sacredness of marriage in the order of creation, but denied that it belongs to the order of grace as a Christian sacrament in the strict sense. Consequently, they rejected the Church's juridical function in matrimonial matters. They admitted the legitimacy of divorce because of adultery and other causes; some also held lenient opinions on bigamy. Besides, Luther's conception was not free from Augustinian pessimism. Hence the Council sought to defend the supernatural character of matrimony as a sacrament, giving new firmness to the bond of Christian marriage; it also defended the Church's teaching authority's claim to be competent in matrimonial matters. After a short exposition of the main doctrinal points concerning the sacrament, there follow the canons directed against the errors of the time.

In the second canon, the Council has specifically in mind the compliance of the Reformers in the case of Philip of Hesse's bigamous marriage. Canons 3 and 4 affirm the competence of the Church authority in matrimonial matters since the sacraments are entrusted to the Church's teaching authority. Canon 5 is categorical in rejecting the grounds for divorce, other than adultery, which were accepted by the Reformers, while Canon 6 defends the traditional view that marriage is dissolved by religious profession. Canon 7 deals with adultery as a ground for divorce. Tradition on this point was not absolutely clear and the Council did not wish to give offence to the Orientals among whom remarriage was allowed in such cases. The Canon is, therefore, carefully worded so as to demand acceptance of the Latin doctrine without expressly condemning the Oriental standpoint. Hence it does not seem to imply a dogmatic definition.[1] In the encyclical Casti Connubii *(1930), however, Pope Pius XI will take a*

---

1. Cf. P.F. FRANSEN, "Reflexions sur l'anathème du Concile de Trente", *Ephemerides Theologicae Lovanienses* 29 (1953) 657-672.

more definite standpoint: "The Church was not, and is not now, in error when she taught and still teaches this doctrine; consequently, it is certain that the marriage bond cannot be dissolved even on the grounds of adultery" (AAS 22 (1930) 574). *Canon 9 is so framed as not to include in the condemnation the Oriental custom of marriage before ordination to the priesthood. Canon 10 affirms the excellence of virginity as compared to marriage; this is stated against the Protestant depreciation of virginity. Canon 12 carefully asserts the competence of ecclesiastical tribunals in matrimonial cases, without entirely excluding that of the State regarding certain matters. Later Church law has interpreted this in such a way as to leave only the civil effects of marriage to the responsibility of the State.*

1804   The first father of the human race, inspired by the divine
1797   Spirit, proclaimed the perpetual and indissoluble bond
of matrimony when he explained: "This at last is bone of my bones and flesh of my flesh.[...] Therefore a man leaves his father and his mother and cleaves to his wife, and they become one flesh" [Gen 2:23f].

1805   But that only two are united and joined together by this
1798   bond, Christ the Lord taught more clearly when, referring
to these words as having been uttered by God, he said: "So they are no longer two but one flesh" [Mt 19:6], and immediately confirmed the stability of the bond which was proclaimed long ago by Adam in these words: "What therefore God has joined together, let no one separate" [Mt 19:6; Mk 10:9].

1806   Christ himself, who instituted the holy sacraments and
1799   brought them to perfection, merited for us by his passion
the grace which perfects that natural love, confirms the indissoluble union and sanctifies the spouses. St. Paul suggests this when he says: "Husbands, love your wives, just as Christ loved the Church and gave himself up for her" [Eph 5:25], adding immediately: "This is a great mystery, and I am applying it to Christ and the Church" [Eph 5:32].

1807   Since, because of the grace of Christ, matrimony under
1800   the Law of the Gospel is superior to the marriage unions
of the old Law, the holy Fathers, the Councils and the tradition of the universal Church have with good reason always taught that it is to be numbered among the sacraments of the New Law. Contrary to this teaching, ungodly and foolish people of this age, not only have entertained false ideas concerning this holy sacrament but, in their usual way, under the pretext of the

Gospel they have given freedom to the flesh, and, by word and writing, they have asserted—not without great harm to Christ's faithful—many things alien to the understanding of the Catholic Church and to customs approved since the apostolic times. Wishing to counteract their temerity, this holy ecumenical Council [...] declares as follows the condemnation of these heretics and of their errors.

Canons on the sacrament of matrimony

1808   1. If anyone says that matrimony is not truly and
1801   properly one of the seven sacraments of the Law of the Gospel, instituted by Christ the Lord, but that it was devised in the Church by human beings and does not confer grace, *anathema sit [cf. n. 1807]*.

1809   2. If anyone says that it is lawful for Christians to have
1802   several wives at the same time and that this is not forbidden by any divine law *[Mt 19:9ff]*, *anathema sit [cf.n. 1805]*.

1810   3. If anyone says that only those degrees of consan-
1803   guinity and affinity which are mentioned in *Leviticus [18:6ff]* can impede contracting marriage and invalidate the contract; and that the Church cannot dispense from some of them or declare other degrees impedient and diriment, *anathema sit*.

1811   4. If anyone says that the Church did not have the power
1804   to establish diriment impediments for marriage or that she has erred in establishing them, *anathema sit*.

1812   5. If anyone says that the marriage bond can be dissolved
1805   because of heresy, or irksome cohabitation, or because of the wilful desertion of one of the spouses, *anathema sit*.

1813   6. If anyone says that marriage contracted but not
1806   consummated is not dissolved by the solemn religious profession of one of the spouses, *anathema sit*.

1814   7. If anyone says that the Church is in error for having
1807   taught and for still teaching that in accordance with the evangelical and apostolic doctrine *[cf. Mk 10; 1 Cor 7]*, the marriage bond cannot be dissolved because of adultery on the part of one of the spouses, and that neither of the two, not

even the innocent one who has given no cause for infidelity, can contract another marriage during the lifetime of the other; and that the husband who dismisses an adulterous wife and marries again and the wife who dismisses an adulterous husband and marries again are both guilty of adultery, *anathema sit.*

1815 8. If anyone says that the Church errs when she de-
1808 clares that for many reasons separation may take place
between husband and wife with regard to bed and board or cohabitation for a definite period or even indefinitely, *anathema sit.*

1816 9. If anyone says that clerics in sacred orders or regulars
1809 who have made solemn profession of chastity can
contract marriage, and that one so contracted is valid despite the ecclesiastical law or the vow; and that the contrary opinion is nothing but a condemnation of marriage; and that all those who feel that they do not have the gift of chastity, even though they have vowed it, can contract marriage, *anathema sit.* For God does not refuse that gift to those who ask for it rightly, and "he will not let you be tested beyond your strength" [1 Cor 10:13].

1817 10. If anyone says that the married state surpasses that
1810 of virginity or celibacy, and that it is not better and
happier to remain in virginity or celibacy than to be united in matrimony [cf.Mt 19:11f;1 Cor 7:25f, 38, 40], *anathema sit.*

1818 11. If anyone says that the prohibition of the
1811 solemnisation of marriages at certain times of the year
is a tyrannical superstition derived from pagan superstition; or condemns the blessing and other ceremonies which the Church uses in solemn nuptials, *anathema sit.*

1819 12. If anyone says that matrimonial cases do not belong
1812 to ecclesiastical judges, *anathema sit.*

LEO XIII
ENCYCLICAL LETTER *ARCANUM DIVINAE SAPIENTIAE*
(1880)

After explaining the Tridentine doctrine on matrimony, Leo XIII strongly vindicates the Church's authority over the marriages of Christians, which he derives from the fact that the marriage contract and the sacrament are inseparable. The fact that with some previous Popes (cf.DS 2598,2990) he claims exclusive jurisdiction for the Church's teaching authority over the marriage contract, can in the historical context be understood as a reaction against various secularist tendencies which tried to deny the Church all right over it. Hence this teaching does not exclude the possibility of an amicable agreement between the Church and the civil power.

(Marriage is a sacrament)

1820 Christ the Lord raised matrimony to the dignity of a
3142 sacrament and at the same time provided that the spouses, sheltered and strengthened by the grace which his merits have won, should attain sanctification in marriage itself; and in it, marvellously modelled on the pattern of his mystical marriage with the Church, he has both perfected the love proper to human nature and by the bond of divine love strengthened the naturally indissoluble partnership of man and woman.

(The Church's authority over marriage)

1821 When Christ, therefore, renewed matrimony and raised
3144 it to such a great excellence, he gave and confided to the Church the entire legislation in the matter. And the Church has at all times and in all places exercised this power over the marriages of Christians in such a manner that it appeared clearly as something proper to her, not a concession sought from human beings but a right granted to her by the will of her divine Founder.

(The marriage contract and the sacrament are inseparable)

1822 Let no one be misled by the distinction which supporters
3145 of the civil power try to make, whereby they separate the marriage contract from the sacrament so that, leaving the sacramental aspects to the Church, the contractual element becomes subject to the power and judgment of the civil power. For there is no basis for such a distinction, or rather such a disruption, since it is clear that in Christian marriage the contract cannot be dissociated from the sacrament; thus there can be no true legitimate contract which is not also a sacrament. For Christ the Lord raised matrimony to the dignity of a sacrament, and matrimony is the contract itself provided it is legally made.

(Internal proof that the contract itself is the sacrament)

1823 Further, matrimony is a sacrament because it is a sacred
3146 and efficient sign of grace and the image of the mystical
marriage of Christ with the Church. This image and figure
are expressed by the bond of most intimate union by which man
and woman bind themselves together, which bond is nothing
other than matrimony itself. Hence it is clear that every valid
marriage between Christians is, in and of itself, the sacrament;
and nothing is further from the truth than to say that the sacrament
is a sort of ornament superadded, or an extrinsic property that
can be dissociated and separated from the contract by human will.

PIUS XI
ENCYCLICAL LETTER *CASTI CONNUBII* (1930)

This is a more developed exposition of the Catholic teaching on marriage.
It deals elaborately with the divine institution and sacramentality of marriage,
its laws and properties, the three "goods" of marriage, as exposed by the Fathers
of the Church, and the errors contrary to the Christian ideal of marriage.
Though the stress is somewhat on the institutional aspect, the encyclical also
brings out many personal elements. While, according to the prevailing view,
it calls the procreation and education of offspring the primary end of marriage,
it also refers to mutual union as "primary cause and reason" of marriage
looked at, not as an institution, but as a partnership, according to the Catechism
of the Council of Trent.

(Marriage as a divine institution)

1824 [...] Matrimony was not instituted or restored by human
3700 beings, but by God; not humankind, but God, the Author
of nature and Christ our Lord, the restorer of nature,
provided marriage with its laws, confirmed it and elevated it;
and consequently those laws can in no way be subject to human
wills or to any contrary pact made even by the contracting parties
themselves.

(Divine order and human freedom)

1825 But, although matrimony by nature is of divine
3701 institution, yet the human will has a part, and a very
important part, to play in it. Each marriage, in so far as
it is a conjugal union between a particular man and a particular
woman, arises solely out of a free consent of the two partners;
and this free act by which each yields and receives the specifically
marital right is so necessary for the constitution of marriage that

it cannot be supplied by any human power. But the only role of this human freedom is to decide that each of the partners in fact wishes to enter the state of matrimony, and to marry this particular person. The freedom of human beings has no power whatever over the nature of matrimony itself, and therefore, when once a person has contracted marriage, he or she becomes subject to its essential laws and properties[...].

(The goods of marriage: offspring)

1826 [...] The Creator of the human race himself, who in his
3704 goodness has willed to use human beings as his
ministers in the propagation of life, taught us this truth when instituting matrimony in the Garden of Eden he bade our first parents, and through them all married persons who should come after: "Be fruitful and multiply" *[Gen 1:28]*[...].

1827 Christian parents should, moreover, understand that their
3705 duty is not only to propagate and maintain the human
race on earth; it is not even merely to rear any sort of worshippers of the true God. They are called to provide children to the Church, to beget "fellow citizens with the saints and members of the household of God" *[Eph 2:19]*, in order that the people dedicated to the worship of our God and Saviour may increase from day to day.[...]

(The goods of marriage: conjugal fidelity)

1828 The second blessing of marriage [...] is fidelity, that is
3706 the mutual faithfulness of husband and wife in
observing the marital pledge. This implies that the right, which in virtue of his divinely ratified agreement belongs to each spouse, will neither be denied to the other nor be granted to any third party.[...]

1829 This mutual interior conformation of husband and wife,
3707 this persevering endeavour to bring each other to the
state of perfection, may in a true sense be called, as the Roman Catechism calls it,[1] the primary cause and reason of matrimony, so long as marriage is considered, not in its stricter sense as the institution destined for the procreation and education

---

1. Cf. *Roman Catechism,* 1566, 11, 8, 13.

of children, but in the wider sense as a complete and intimate life-partnership and association.

(The goods of marriage: the sacrament)

1830
3710
But the complement and crown of all is the blessing of Christian marriage which [...] we have called the sacrament. It denotes both the indissolubility of the matrimonial bond, and the consecration of this contract by Christ who elevated it to the rank of a sign which is a cause of grace.[...]

(The supernatural mystery of marriage)

1831
3712
If we seek with reverence to discover the intrinsic reason of this divine ordinance [the indissolubility of marriage][...], we shall easily find it in the mystical signification of Christian marriage, the full perfection of which is realised in consummated marriage between the faithful. The apostle in the epistle to the Ephesians[...] tells us that Christian marriage signifies that most perfect union which exists between Christ and the Church: "This is a great mystery, and I am applying it to Christ and Church" *[Eph 5:32]*; and this is a union which, certainly, as long as Christ lives and the Church lives by him, can never cease and be dissolved.[...]

(Graces of the sacrament)

1832
3714
[...] This sacrament, in those who do not, as is said, place an obstacle, not only increases in the soul sanctifying grace, the permanent principle of supernatural life; but also adds special gifts, good impulses and seeds of grace, amplifying and perfecting the power of nature and enabling the recipients, not only to understand with their minds, but also to relish immediately, grasp firmly, will effectively and fulfil in deed all that belongs to the conjugal state and its purpose and duties; it also gives them the right to obtain the help of actual grace whenever they need it for the discharge of their duties belonging to the married state.

(An abiding sacrament)

1833
Let them constantly be mindful that they have been consecrated and strengthened for the duties and the dignity of their state by a sacrament whose efficacy, though it does not confer a character, remains nonetheless permanently.

THE SECOND VATICAN GENERAL COUNCIL

In comparison with earlier documents, the Second Vatican Council adopts a striking personalistic standpoint. In the Dogmatic Constitution Lumen Gentium *(11), the ecclesial character of the sacrament of matrimony is explained, the family being called "the domestic church". It is meant to perpetuate the People of God.*

Marriage is a path to holiness (LG 11). It is the "primary form of interpersonal communion" (GS 12). It is of the highest importance for the well-being of the individual, and of the human and Christian society (GS 47). The pastoral Constitution Gaudium et Spes *vindicates the sanctity and indissolubility of marriage and insists on the personal nature of married love which pervades the whole of marital life and is uniquely expressed through the conjugal act (GS 48-49). Husband and wife are equal in personal dignity (GS 49). By cultivating constancy of love, they give witness to faithfulness, and thus help to bring about a renewal of marriage and the family (GS 49).*

The same Constitution Gaudium et Spes *has deliberately refrained from determining the 'hierarchy' of the ends of marriage; but it has clearly shown how the ends of mutual love and procreation are intimately linked together (GS 50). The importance of sexual intimacy for the total marital relationship is also pointed out (GS 49).*

DOGMATIC CONSTITUTION *LUMEN GENTIUM* (1964)

(Ecclesial character of marriage)

1834 [11] Finally, in virtue of the sacrament of matrimony by which they signify and share *[cf. Eph 5:32]* the mystery of the unity and faithful love between Christ and the Church, Christian married couples help one another to attain holiness in their married life and in the rearing of their children. Hence by reason of their state in life and of their position they have their own gifts in the People of God *[cf. 1 Cor 7:7]*. From the marriage of Christians there comes the family in which new citizens of human society are born and, by the grace of the Holy Spirit in Baptism, those are made children of God so that the People of God may be perpetuated throughout the centuries. In what might be regarded as the domestic Church, the parents, by word and example, are the first heralds of the faith with regard to their children.

PASTORAL CONSTITUTION *GAUDIUM ET SPES* (1965)

(Sacredness of marriage and the family)

1835 48. The intimate partnership of life and the love which constitutes the married state has been established by the creator and endowed by him with its own proper laws: it is rooted in the contract of its partners, that is, in their irrevocable personal consent. It is an institution confirmed by the divine law and receiving its stability, even in the eyes of society, from the human act by which the partners mutually surrender themselves to each other; for the good of the partners, of the children, and of society this sacred bond no longer depends on human decision alone. For God himself is the author of marriage and has endowed it with various benefits and with various ends in view: all of these have a very important bearing on the continuation of the human race, on the personal development and eternal destiny of every member of the family, on the dignity, stability, peace, and prosperity of the family and of the whole human race. By its very nature the institution of marriage and married love is ordered to the procreation and education of the offspring and it is in them that it finds its crowning glory. Thus the man and woman, who "are no longer two but one" [Mt 19:6], help and serve each other by their marriage partnership; they become conscious of their unity and experience it more deeply from day to day. The intimate union of marriage, as a mutual giving of two persons, and the good of the children demand total fidelity from the spouses and require an unbreakable unity between them.

1836 Christ our Lord has abundantly blessed this love, which is rich in its various features, coming as it does from the spring of divine love and modelled on Christ's own union with the Church. Just as of old God encountered his people with a covenant of love and fidelity, so our Saviour, the spouse of the Church now encounters Christian spouses through the sacrament of marriage. He abides with them in order that by their mutual self-giving spouses will love each other with enduring fidelity, as he loved the Church and delivered himself for it. Authentic married love is caught up into divine love and is directed and enriched by the redemptive power of Christ and the salvific action of the Church, with the result that the spouses are effectively led to God and are helped and strengthened in their lofty role as fathers and mothers. Spouses, therefore, are fortified and, as it were, consecrated for the duties and dignity of their state by a special sacrament; fulfilling their conjugal and family role by virtue of this sacrament, spouses are penetrated with the Spirit of Christ and their whole life is suffused by faith, hope, and charity; thus they increasingly further their own perfection and their mutual sanctification, and together they render glory to God.

(Marital love: undivided love, expressed in the conjugal act proper to marriage; the equality of man and woman in marriage)

1837   49. On several occasions the Word of God invites the betrothed to nourish and foster their betrothal with chaste love, and likewise spouses their marriage.[...] Married love is an eminently human love because it is an affection between two persons rooted in the will and it embraces the good of the whole person; it can enrich the sentiments of the spirit and their physical expression with a unique dignity and ennoble them as the special elements and signs of the friendship proper to marriage. The Lord, wishing to bestow special gifts of grace and divine love on it, has restored, perfected, and elevated it. A love like that, bringing together the human and the divine, leads the partners to a free and mutual giving of self, experienced in tenderness and action, and permeates their whole lives; besides, this love is actually developed and increased by the exercise of it. This is a far cry from mere erotic attraction, which is pursued in selfishness and soon fades away in wretchedness.

1838   Married love is uniquely expressed and perfected by the exercise of the acts proper to marriage. Hence the acts in marriage by which the intimate and chaste union of the spouses takes place are noble and honourable; the truly human performance of these acts fosters the self-giving they signify and enriches the spouses in joy and gratitude.[...]

1839   The unity of marriage, distinctly recognised by our Lord, is made clear in the equal personal dignity which must be accorded to man and wife in mutual and unreserved affection. Outstanding courage is required for the constant fulfilment of the duties of this Christian calling: spouses, therefore, will need grace for leading a holy life [...].

(Fruitfulness of marriage)

1840   50. Marriage and married love are by nature ordered to the procreation and education of children. Indeed children are the supreme gift of marriage and greatly contribute to the good of the parents themselves. God himself said: "It is not good that the man should be alone" *[Gen 2:18]*, and "from the beginning [he] made them male and female" *[Mt 19:4]*; wishing to associate them in a special way with his own creative work, God blessed man and woman with the words: "Be fruitful and multiply" *[Gen 1:28]*. Without intending to underestimate the other ends of marriage, it must be said that true married love and the whole structure of family life which results from it is directed to disposing the spouses to cooperate valiantly with the love of the Creator and Saviour, who through them will increase and enrich his family from day to day.

PAUL VI

ENCYCLICAL LETTER *HUMANAE VITAE* (1968)

The encyclical situates the problem of planned parenthood in the framework of a total vision of humankind and its vocation. The love of the spouses has its origin in God, who is Love. It must be fully human, faithful and exclusive, fruitful and raising up new human lives. Responsible parenthood is deeply related to the moral order established by God; it requires that the finality of the conjugal act ordained to the union of the spouses and to procreation be respected. The Pope shows the intimate union of these two aspects. See also n. 2220i. The text is found in AAS 60 (1968) 481ff.

1841   12. This doctrine, often set forth by the teaching authority, is founded upon the inseparable connection, willed by God and which human beings cannot break on their own initiative, between the two meanings of the conjugal act: union and procreation. For, by its intimate structure, the conjugal act, while most closely uniting the spouses, enables them to procreate new lives according to laws inscribed in the very being of man and woman. It is by safeguarding these two essential aspects, union and procreation, that the conjugal act preserves in its fulness the sense of true mutual love and its ordination towards humankind's most high calling to parenthood. We believe that the men and women of our day are particularly capable of understanding the deeply reasonable and human character of this fundamental principle.

S. CONGREGATION OF RITES

ORDO CELEBRANDI MATRIMONIUM
(19 March, 1969/1990)

The general introduction (the Praenotanda) *to this new ritual reaffirms in summary form the teaching of the Church for this sacrament. The "second typical edition" of 1990 expands the introduction and the possible choices of the forms of celebrating the sacrament. Part I (1-11) reiterates the importance and dignity of the sacrament of marriage; Part II (12-27) treats of the offices and ministries in preparation and celebration of the sacrament; Part III (28-38) describes the elements of the celebration of the sacrament itself; Part IV (39-44) deals with the right of the Conferences of Bishops to adapt this rite in various cultural situations. There follow the rites, the texts of prayers and Scripture readings for the various situations in celebrating the sacrament (within or outside the Eucharist, between a catholic and an unbaptised person etc.).*

(Marriage as sign of the mystery of Christ and Church is a "process")

1841a   11. For the God who calls husband and wife to marriage, calls them also to make progress in it. Those who marry are empowered to celebrate effectively with faith in God's word the mystery of Christ and Church, to live rightly, and to bear witness in the eyes of all.[...]

(Adaptation and inculturation of this sacrament)

1841b   42. In keeping with the provisions of the Constitution on the Liturgy [SC 63b], each conference of bishops may draw up its own marriage rite suited to the usages of the place and the people and approved by the Apostolic See. A necessary condition [...] is that in the rite the assisting minister must ask for and receive the consent of the contracting parties, and the nuptial blessing should always be given.[...]

43. As for the marriage customs of nations that are now receiving the Gospel for the first time, whatever is good and is not indissolubly bound up with superstition and error should be sympathetically considered and, if possible, preserved intact. Such things may in fact be taken over into the liturgy itself as long as they harmonise with its true and authentic spirit.

DECREE *CIRCA IMPOTENTIAM* OF THE S. CONGREGATION FOR THE DOCTRINE OF THE FAITH
(13 May, 1977)

In this decree, the S. Congregation settles a long-standing doubt regarding the requirement of male conjugal potency for valid marriage. The text is found in AAS 69(1977) 426.

1842   The S. Congregation for the Doctrine of the Faith has always held that persons who have undergone vasectomy and others in similar conditions are not to be prevented from marriage, inasmuch as their impotence is not certainly proved.

Now, however, after examining this practice and after renewed studies done by this S. Congregation and by the Commission for the Revision of the Code of Canon Law the Fathers [...] deemed that the following response should be given to questions proposed to them:

1. Whether impotence which invalidates marriage consists in the incapacity, antecedent and permanent, whether absolute or relative, of completing conjugal copulation.

2. If *affirmative*, whether ejaculation of semen elaborated in the testicles is necessarily required for conjugal copulation.

To the first, *affirmative*. To the second, *negative*.

JOHN PAUL II

APOSTOLIC EXHORTATION *FAMILIARIS CONSORTIO*
(22 November, 1981)

As a follow-up of the Synod of Bishops, 1980, on the Family, the Pope issued an elaborate exhortation regarding the Role of the Christian Family in the Modern World. He points out that an evangelical discernment on the subject is to be practised in relation to the sense of faith of all the faithful. Marriage like celibacy is a way of expressing and living the one mystery of the covenant of God with his people. It is a sacrament or symbol of the event of salvation in Christ, from which flow the unity and indissolubility of the marriage bond. The Pope strongly defends the sanctity and the indissolubility of Christian marriage. He reaffirms the teaching of the Church regarding responsible transmission of human life and asks that its practice be helped by proper sex education and research into human fertility (see n. 2236). The family as the first vital cell of society must be the prime concern of the whole of society. It has a share in the life and mission of the Church. It is a community in dialogue with God through worship and prayer. The Pope emphasises the need for pastoral care of the family. The text is found in AAS 74 (1982) 81-191.

(Sacramentality of Marriage)

1843   13. Like each of the seven sacraments, so also marriage is a real symbol of the event of salvation, but in its own way. The spouses participate in it as spouses, together, as a couple, so that the first and immediate effect *(res et sacramentum)* of marriage is not supernatural grace itself, but the Christian bond, a typically Christian communion of two persons which represents the mystery of Christ's incarnation and the mystery of his convenant. The participation in Christ's life which it confers is also specific: conjugal love involves a totality, in which all the elements of the persons enter—the appeal of the body and instinct, the power of feeling and affectivity, the aspiration of the spirit and the will. It aims at deeply personal unity, the unity that, beyond union in the flesh, leads to forming one heart and soul; it demands indissolubility and faithfulness in definitive mutual self-giving; and it opens to fertility.

(Indissolubility of marriage)

1844   20.It is a fundamental duty of the Church to reaffirm strongly, as the Synod Fathers did, the doctrine of the indissolubility of marriage. To all those who, in our times, consider it too difficult, or indeed impossible, to be bound to one person for the whole of life, and to those who are caught up in a culture that rejects the indissolubility of marriage and openly mocks the commitment of spouses to fidelity, it is necessary to reaffirm the good news of the definitive nature of that conjugal love that has its foundation and strength in Christ.

Being rooted in the personal and total self-giving of the couple, and being required by the good of the children, the indissolubility of marriage finds its ultimate truth in the plan that God has manifested in his revelation; he wills and he communicates the indissolubility of marriage as a fruit, a sign and a requirement of the absolutely faithful love that God has for humankind and that the Lord Jesus has for the Church.

DISCOURSE TO OFFICIALS OF THE ROMAN ROTA
(26 January, 1984)

The Pope asks for responsible use of recent advances in marriage in tribunal procedures. The text is found in AAS 76 (1984) 643-649.

(Tribunal procedure in marriage)

1845   But the concern to safeguard the dignity and indissolubility of marriage by opposing the abuses and irresponsibility which unfortunately must often be sadly noted in this matter, cannot prescind from the real and undeniable progress of the biological, psychological, psychiatric and social sciences; otherwise, one would contradict the very value which it is desired to safeguard, namely, a truly existing marriage, not one which has only the appearance of such, since it is null and void from the outset.

It is here that the impartiality and the wisdom of the ecclesiastical judges must shine: to know the law well, by penetrating its spirit in order to be able to apply it; to study the auxiliary sciences, which allow a more thorough knowledge of the facts and, above all, of persons; and, finally, to be able to find the balance between the inescapable duty to defend the indissolubility of marriage and the due attention to the complex human reality of the concrete case.

OTHER DISCOURSES TO THE ROMAN ROTA

(Human and ecclesial meaning of marriage)

(1846)   *(Discourse to the Roman Rota, January 30, 1986. The text is found in* Origins *15 (1986) 608-610)*

(An adequate anthropology for judging marriage cases)

(1847)   *(Discourse to the Roman Rota, February 5, 1987. Text in* AAS *79 (1987) 1453-1459)*

(Defender of the bond and psychic incapacity in marriage cases)

(1848)   *(Discourse to the Roman Rota, January 25, 1988. Text in* AAS *80 (1988) 1178-1185)*

(Marriage and culture)

(1849)   *(Discourse to the Roman Rota, January 28, 1991. Text in* AAS *83 (1991) 947-953)*

PONTIFICAL COUNCIL FOR PROMOTING CHRISTIAN UNITY

DIRECTORY FOR THE APPLICATION OF PRINCIPLES AND NORMS ON ECUMENISM (25 March, 1993)

This text contains new guidelines with regard to marriage within the ecumenical context; sharing in sacramental life, (nos. 127, 128, 136); and mixed marriages (143-160). The text is found in AAS *85 (1993) 1039-1119.*

(Participation in celebrations of marriage)

1850   127. A Catholic minister may be present and take part in the celebration of a marriage being properly celebrated between Eastern Christians or between a Catholic and an Eastern Christian in the Eastern Church if invited to do so by the Eastern

Church authority and if it is in accord with the norms given below concerning mixed marriages, where they apply.

128. A member of an Eatern Church may act as bridesmaid or best man at a wedding in a Catholic church; a Catholic also may be bridesmaid or best man at a marriage properly celebrated in an Eastern church.[...]

1851   136. Members of other churches or ecclesial communities may be witnesses at the celebration of marriage in a Catholic church. Catholics may also be witnesses at marriages which are celebrated in other churches or ecclesial communities.

(Mixed marriages)

1852   145. In view, however of the growing number of mixed marriages in many parts of the world, the Church includes within its urgent pastoral solicitude couples preparing to enter, or already having entered, such marriages. These marriages, even if they have their own particular difficulties, "contain numerous elements that could well be made good use of and developed both for their intrinsic value and for the contribution they can make to the ecumenical movement. This is particularly true when both parties are faithful to their religious duties. Their common baptism and the dynamism of grace provide the spouses in these marriages with the basis and motivation for expressing unity in the sphere of moral and spiritual values".[1]

JOHN PAUL II

LETTER TO FAMILIES
(2 February 1994)

Welcoming joyfully the decision of the United Nations Organization to declare 1994 the International Year of the Family, John Paul II indicted for the whole ecclesial community a Year of the Family "as one of the important steps along the path of preparation for the Great Jubilee of the Year 2000", to redirect thoughts and hearts towards the Holy Family of Nazareth (3). The Pope considers in depth all the major themes in the theology of marriage and basically provides us with a commentary to the Second Vatican Council on marriage (nn. 1834-1840). The text is in Origins *23 (1994), pp. 637-659.*

---

1. JOHN PAUL II, *Familiaris Consortio, 78*

(The marital covenant)

1852a 7. The family has always been considered as the first and basic expression of the human person's *social nature*. Even today this way of looking at things remains unchanged. Nowadays, however, emphasis tends to be laid on how much the family, as the smallest and most basic human community, owes to the personal contribution of a man and a woman. The family is in fact a community of persons whose proper way of existing and living together is communion: *communio personarum*. Here too, while always acknowledging the absolute transcendence of the Creator with regard to his creatures, we can see the family's ultimate relationship to the divine "We". *Only persons are capable of living "in communion"*. The family originates in a marital communion described by the Second Vatican Council as a "covenant", *in which man and woman "give themselves to each other and accept each other"*.

The Book of Genesis helps us to see this truth when it states, in reference to the establishment of the family through marriage, that "a man leaves his father and his mother and cleaves to his wife, and they become one flesh" *[Gen 2:24]*. In the Gospel, Christ disputing with the Pharisees, quotes these same words and then adds: "So they are no longer two but one flesh. What therefore God has joined together, let no one put asunder" *[Mt 19:6]*. In this way, he reveals anew the binding content of a fact which exists "from the beginning" *[Mt 19:8]* and which always preserves this content. If the Master confirms it "now", he does so in order to make clear and unmistakable to all, at the dawn of the New Covenant, the *indissoluble character* of marriage as the *basis of the common good of the family*.

When, in union with the Apostle, we bow our knees before the Father from whom all fatherhood and motherhood is named *[cf. Eph 3:14-15]*, we come to realize that parenthood is the event whereby the family, already constituted by the conjugal covenant of marriage, is brought about "in the full and specific sense". *Motherhood necessarily implies fatherhood*, and in turn, *fatherhood necessarily implies motherhood*. This is the result of the duality bestowed by the Creator upon human beings "from the beginning".

I have spoken of two closely related yet not identical concepts: the concept of "communion" and that of "community".

"*Communion*" has to do with the personal relationship between the "I" and the "thou". "*Community*" on the other hand transcends this framework and moves towards a "society", a "we". The family, as a community of persons, is thus the first human "society". It arises whenever there comes into being the conjugal covenant of marriage, which opens the spouses to a lasting communion of love and of life, and it is brought to completion in a full and specific way with the procreation of children: the "communion" of the spouses gives rise to the "community" of the family. The "community" of the family is completely pervaded by the very essence of "communion". On the human level, can there be any other "*communion*" comparable to that *between a mother and a child* whom she has carried in her womb and then brought to birth?

In the family thus constituted there appears a new unity, in which the relationship "of communion" between the parents attains complete fulfilment. Experience teaches that this fulfilment represents both a task and a challenge. The task involves the spouses in living out their original covenant. *The children* born to them—and here is the challenge—*should consolidate that covenant*, enriching and deepening the conjugal communion of the father and mother. When this does not occur, we need to ask if the selfishness which lurks even in the love of man and woman as a result of the human inclination to evil is not stronger than this love. Married couples need to be well aware of this. From the outset they need to have their hearts and thoughts turned towards the God "from whom every family is named", *so that their fatherhood and motherhood will draw from that source the power to be continually renewed in love.*

Fatherhood and motherhood are themselves a particular proof of love; they make it possible to discover love's extension and original depth. But this does not take place automatically. Rather, it is a task entrusted to both husband and wife. In the life of husband and wife together, fatherhood and motherhood represent such a sublime "novelty" and richness as can only be approached "on one's knees".[...]

(*The unity of the two*)

1852b   8. Only "persons" are [...] able to live "in communion" on the basis of a mutual choice which is, or ought to be, fully conscious and free. The Book of Genesis, in speaking of a man who leaves father and mother in order to cleave to his wife [cf. Gen 2:24], highlights the conscious and free choice which gives rise to marriage, making the son of a family a husband, and the daughter of a family a wife. How can we adequately understand this mutual choice, unless we take into consideration the full truth about the person, who is a rational and free being? The Second Vatican Council, in speaking of the likeness of God, uses extremely significant terms. It refers not only to the divine image and likeness which every human being as such already possesses, but also and primarily to "a certain similarity between the union of the divine persons and the union of God's children in truth and love".

This rich and meaningful formulation first of all confirms what is central to the identity of every man and every woman. This identity consists in the *capacity to live in truth and love;* even more, it consists in the need of truth and love as an essential dimension of the life of the person. The human person's need for truth and love opens him/her both to God and to creatures: it opens him/her to other people, to life "in communion", and in particular to marriage and to the family. In the words of the Council, the "communion" of persons is drawn in a certain sense from the mystery of the Trinitarian "We", and therefore "conjugal communion" also refers to this mystery. The family, which originates in the love of man and woman, ultimately derives from the mystery of God. This conforms to the innermost being of man and woman, to their innate and authentic dignity as persons.

In marriage man and woman are so firmly united as to become—to use the words of the Book of Genesis—"one flesh" [Gen 2:24]. Male and female in their physical constitution, the two human subjects, even though physically different, *share equally in the capacity to live "in truth and love".* This capacity, characteristic of the human being as a person, has at the same time both a spiritual and a bodily dimension. It is also through the body that man and woman are predisposed to form a "communion of persons" in marriage. When they are united by the conjugal covenant in such a way as to become *"one flesh"* [Gen 2:24], their *union* ought to take place *"in truth and love",* and thus express the maturity proper to persons created in the image and likeness of God.

The family which results from this union draws its inner solidity from the covenant between the spouses, which Christ raised to a Sacrament. The family draws its proper character as a community, its traits of "communion", from that fundamental communion of the spouses which is prolonged in their children.[...] Their unity, however, rather than closing them up in themselves, opens them towards a new life, towards a new person. As parents, they will be capable of giving life to a being like themselves, not only bone of their bones and flesh of their flesh [cf. Gen 2:23], but an image and likeness of God—a person.

When the Church asks "Are you willing?", she is reminding the bride and groom that they stand before the creative power of God. They are called to become parents, to cooperate with the Creator in giving life. Cooperating with God to call new human beings into existence means contributing to the transmission of that divine image and likeness of which everyone "born of a woman" is a bearer.

(The common good of marriage and the family)

1852c 10. Marital consent defines and consolidates the good common to marriage and to the family. [...] Marriage is a unique communion of persons, and it is on the basis of this communion that the family is called to become a community of persons. This is a commitment which the bride and groom undertake "before God and his Church", as the celebrant reminds them before they exchange their consent. Those who take part in the rite are witnesses of this commitment, for in a certain sense they represent the Church and society, the settings in which the new family will live and grow.

The words of consent define the common good of the *couple and of the family*. First, the common good of the spouses: love, fidelity, honour, the permanence of their union until death—"all the days of my life". The good of both, which is at the same time the good of each, must then become the good of the children. The common good, by its very nature, both unites individual persons and ensures the true good of each.[...]

The words of consent, then, express what is essential to the common good of the spouses, and *they indicate what ought to be the common good of the future family*. In order to bring this out, the Church asks the spouses if they are prepared to accept the children God grants them and to raise the children as Christians.[...] The question about children and their education is profoundly linked to marital consent, with its solemn promise of love, conjugal respect, and fidelity until death. The acceptance and education of children—two of the primary ends of the family—are conditioned by how that commitment will be fulfilled. Fatherhood and motherhood represent a responsibility which is not simply physical but spiritual in nature; indeed, through these realities there passes the genealogy of the person, which has its eternal beginning in God and which must lead back to him. [...]

CONGREGATION FOR THE DOCTRINE OF THE FAITH

LETTER ON THE RECEPTION OF COMMUNION BY DIVORCED AND REMARRIED CATHOLICS

(14 September, 1994)

The text of the Letters is found in Origins 24 *(1994) 337-340. To be noted is the Response to the Vatican Letter: Message to their People, by three German bishops (K. Lehmann, O. Saier, W. Kasper). Text in* Origins 24 *(1994) 341-344.)*

1853   3. Aware however that authentic understanding and genuine mercy are never separated from the truth, pastors have the duty to remind these faithful of the Church's doctrine concerning the celebration of the sacraments, in particular the reception of the Eucharist.[...]

6. [...] This does not mean that the Church does not take to heart the situation of the faithful, who moreover are not excluded from ecclesial communion. She is concerned to accompany them pastorally and invites them to share in the measure that is compatible with the disposition of divine law, from which the Church has no power to dispense. On the other hand, it is necessary to instruct these faithful so that they do not think their participation in the life of the Church is reduced exclusively to the question of the reception of the Eucharist.

LETTER TO WOMEN

(29 June 1995)

This is the first letter a successor of Peter has addressed "cordially" to "women throughout the world", "as a sign of solidarity and gratitude on the eve of the Fourth World Conference on Women" that the United Nations organised in Beijing in September 1995 (8). He rereads Gen 1:28 and marriage in the relational terms of a uni-duality and sees the creation of history as one of the main goals of marital life. The text is in Origins 24 91995), pp.

(Husband and wife: a uni-duality)

1854 8. After creating human beings male and female, God says to both: "Fill the earth and subdue it" *[Gen 1:28]*. Not only does he give them the power to procreate as a means of perpetuating the human species throughout time, *he also gives them the earth, charging them with the responsible use of its resources.* As rational and free beings, they are called to transform the face of the earth. In this task, which is essentially that of culture, *man and woman alike* share equal responsibility from the start. In their fruitful relationship as husband and wife, in their common task of exercising dominion over the earth, woman and man are marked neither by a static and undifferentiated equality nor by an irreconcilable and inexorably conflictual difference. Their most natural relationship, which corresponds to the plan of God, is the "unity of the two", a relational "uni-duality", which enables each to experience their interpersonal and reciprocal relationship as a gift which enriches and which confers responsibility.

To this "unity of the two" God has entrusted not only the work of procreation and family life, but the creation of history itself. *While the 1994 International Year of the Family* focused attention on *women as mothers*, the Beijing Conference, which has as its theme "Action for Equality, Development and Peace", provides an auspicious occasion for heightening awareness of *the many contributions made by women to the life of whole societies and nations.* This contribution is primarily spiritual and cultural in nature, but socio-political and economic as well. The various sectors of society, nations and states, and the progress of all humanity, are certainly deeply indebted to the contribution of women!

CHAPTER XIX

THE LIFE OF GRACE

Ever since the beginning of time, God calls humanity to full communion that entails concourse and collaboration with him. Though the history of sin radically changes the human condition, it does not modify God's original call. In "his goodness and love", the invisible God continues to "speak to men as friends, and lives among them so that he may invite and take them into fellowship with himself" (DV 2). "In many and various ways", the Father renews his call: in his Son made man, he raises us to new life and communicates his "innermost being" (DV 4).

The Church has always understood the Father's invitation to humankind as a call to adoptive sonship, a configuration to Christ, and an indwelling of the Spirit. Cherishing Christ's gift of himself in word and flesh, the Christian life enters into a direct and intimate relationship with all three divine Persons. The Church turns to biblical imagery, to fathom this intimacy with God, which it understands as (a) the gift of the Spirit, as (b) a grace that hallows and sanctifies, and as (c) new life that makes us all "partakers of the divine nature" (2 Pt 1:4).

Faith in God comes first, in humanity's response to God's call. But communion with God demands the love of God and neighbour, the yearning after the completion of God's plan, and the manifestation of creation's maturity in God (cf. Rom 8:19ff). Within the ecclesial milieu and through one's sacramental life, the believer can live more fully one's communion with God and with others, configure oneself further to Christ, and express creation's yearning after the fulness that only God can give.

The Fathers tried to explain the novelty of life in communion with the Father through Christ, in the Spirit in the context of baptismal catechesis. That provided the first occasion in which the magisterium clarified in depth what the creedal forms already stated. The teaching authority of the Church refrained from systematically developing a treatise on the life of grace. (Theology itself can never exhaust the treasures contained in revelation and tradition.) On the contrary, it tries to address issues that, from time to time, promote a partial, limited understanding of the life of grace, one that falls short of the gift God makes to humankind.

Pelagius and his followers insisted so much on human freedom—and the positive attitude all must assume in the life of grace—that they seemed to question the very nature of God's gift: the divinisation of humankind. The teaching Church reacted against this call, meant to overcome spiritual lethargy by resorting to self-reliance. God is the one who calls into communion every human person; he empowers the latter to live it to the full, to such an extent that sanctification becomes the goal of the believer's whole being.

During the Reformation crisis, the brevity and precariousness of life forced humanity to grope after security. While Catholics stressed the need of one's compliance with the grace of God, the Reformers accentuated God's role in forgiving humanity and promising final salvation. According to the latter, original sin renders the human will flawed to the extent that it becomes incapable of any good deed; the Council of Trent therefore had to address the issue. In line with tradition, Trent underlined both the reality of humanity's justification by God in Christ as well as humanity's need to respond to God's grace that continues to come first and precede every human act.

When the dialogue with other Christian confessions was interrupted in the period after Trent, the whole debate on grace centred on the definition of its 'nature' and the clarification of human freedom. In overstating the 'objective' dimension of grace and the importance of merit, the biblical understanding of grace as personal relationship and as communion with the Father, through Christ, in the Spirit, almost vanished into oblivion. The ecclesial dimension of the life of grace—of the fact that new life in the Spirit gives birth to the new people of God and brings about a renewed creation—gave way to an intimistic and ascetic understanding of the individual's response to God's gift of himself.

The biblical and patristic renewal of theology and the liturgical renaissance at the end of the 19th century and the beginning of the 20th led to a reappraisal of the life of grace. Pius XII's teaching, particularly his 'dogmatic' encyclicals, paved the way to Vatican II's ecclesial understanding of the life of grace as humankind's call to holiness and communion with God, and of divinisation as a process of collaboration with God that encompasses the being and activity of believers. It fully understands personal gifts and charisms as God's benefits to humanity and his response to creation's yearning after the fulfilment, that ultimately is God himself.

*   *   *

The Church's teaching on grace covers the following points:

God universal salvific will

God desires the salvation of all: 1922, 1989/5, 2000d/2, 2000g, 2000k, 2000q.

No one is predestined to evil: 1922, 1956, 1967.

No one can with absolute certainty affirm to be predestined to eternal life: 1941, 1965-67, 2000q.

The human person's new creation

Justification is the work of the triune God: 1916, 1997, 2000d, 2000d/4, 2000d/5, 2000g-h, 2000j, 2000k, 2000n, 2000q.

In Justification, Christ liberates us from sin: 1023, 1901, 1927, 1931f, 1934, 1943, 1961, 2000d/3, 2000d/5, 2000g, 2000j, 2000k.

Sins are forgiven and humanity is reconciled with God : 1023, 1927, 1931f, 1934, 1943, 1961, 2000d/5, 2000d/6, 2000 m.

The Holy Spirit dwells in the justified: 1624, 1932f, 1993-95, 1997, 1998, 2000d, 2000d/5, 2000d/6, 2000e, 2000g.

The justified become living members of Christ's body: 1618, 1934, 1995, 2000d/5, 2000j.

They become children of the Father: 1928, 1932, 1946, 1997, 2000c, 2000d/3, 2000g, 2000j.

Eternal life is bestowed on them: 1927f, 1932-1934, 1960f, 1985, 2000d/7, 2000j.

Aided by grace, they must prepare themselves for justification: 1914, 1929f, 1954-1959, 2000d/5, 20001.

Faith is necessary for justification: 118, 122, 1918, 1930, 1935, 2000d/1, 2000n, 2000p.

Faith alone without one's response as conversion to God, is not sufficient: 1935f, 1939, 1959, 1962-1964, 1969-1971, 2000g.

Grace is gratuitous and supernatural: 1925, 1929, 1935f, 1984, 1988, 1996, 2000d/3, 2000d/7, 20001, 2000o.

With justification, the virtues of faith, hope and charity are infused: 1933f, 1961, 2000d/4, 2000n.

The life of grace

The first impulse to justification comes from grace: 1911, 1913-1915, 1921, 1929, 1951-1953, 2000d/6, 2000d/7.

Humankind partakes of the divine nature, conforming itself to the image of the Son: 524 (2000i), 2000d/2, 2000d/6, 2000j.

The life of grace increases through the fulfilment of the commandments and good works: 1937, 1939f, 1969-1971, 1974f, 1981f, 2000j, 2000p, 2000r.

Already before justification one is able to perform good actions: 1923, 1940, 1957, 1986/20, 1988, 1990-1991, 2000d/6.

Only through grace do human actions receive supernatural value: 1908, 1910f, 1913f, 1917, 1921f, 1925, 1951-1953, 2000d/6, 2000o.

The merit of good works is the result of justification: 1946, 1982, 1985/13, 2000d/7, 2000r.

One must respond to grace actively and freely: 120, 1914, 1929, 1954f, 1987, 1989, 1992, 2000f, 2000l.

Everyone receives the grace necessary to keep the commandments: 1922, 1938, 1968, 1972f, 1986/54, 1989, 2000o;

but not to avoid all venial sins: 1904-1906, 1938, 1973.

Grace is necessary to persevere in avoiding grievous sin: 1901-1903, 1909, 1972, 2000o.

Perseverance to the end is a special grace: 1942, 1966, 1972, 2000n.

The justified merit eternal life through deeds done in grace: 1914, 1946-1948, 1976, 1981, 1985/13, 2000d/7, 2000j.

Grace and Sin

Grace is lost through every mortal sin: 1425, 1943, 1945, 1973, 1977;
but not through venial sin: 1905-1906, 1938, 1973.
Sin against the Holy Spirit: 2000b.

THE SIXTEENTH COUNCIL OF CARTHAGE (418)

Since Constantine had made Christianity the State religion, worldliness and laxity had crept into the Church. By the beginning of the fifth century the British monk Pelagius came to Rome where he expounded the strict demands of Christianity in the midst of general moral decay. Law, nature and especially the person's freedom and acquired virtue are the watchwords of Pelagius' austere moral preaching, later organised into a system by his disciple Celestius.

The Pelagian heresy is a mentality rather than a logically structured body of doctrine. Its kernel is the assumption of the complete freedom of the human person, who by choosing good can achieve salvation unaided by grace. Several errors followed from this assertion of the person's self-sufficiency; human liberty essentially consists in the absence of all compelling forces bending towards good or evil; original sin as a natural inclination towards evil must be denied; therefore Adam's sin is reduced to a bad example set by him to his descendants and freely followed by them in their own personal decisions; baptism of children is not necessary, since no original sinfulness needs to be remitted. Christ's redemption is confined to the forgiveness of personal sins; his grace, moreover, is not absolutely necessary to avoid them. The contrary would be derogatory to the intrinsic dignity of self-sufficient human nature. Impoverishing greatly the Christian message according to which our sufficiency comes from Christ alone, this system left no room for trust in God and personal commitment to his action.

The main condemnation of Pelagius is that of the Council of Carthage, a city where he had spent some time after Alaric's conquest of Rome. The sentence of the two hundred Bishops gathered at Carthage was soon confirmed by Pope Zosimus, at least in part. The Pope's Epistola tractoria *addressed to all the Churches, explicitly confirms canons 3-5, those namely which were also included later in the* Indiculus *(cf. n. 1912); no similar papal confirmation is however extant as regards the other canons, which, nevertheless, have always been held in great esteem by the later magisterium, as containing the doctrine of faith. For canons 1-2 on original sin, cf. nn. 501-502.*

1901 3. Likewise it has been decided: Whoever says that the
225   grace of God by which the human person is justified
       through Jesus Christ our Lord serves only for the
remission of sins already committed, and is not also a help not
to commit them, *anathema sit.*

1902 4. Again: Whoever says that this same grace of God
226   through our Lord Jesus Christ helps us not to sin solely
       because through it an understanding of the
commandments is revealed and opened to us that we may know
what we should seek and what we should avoid, but not because
through it is given to us the love and the strength to do what

we have recognised to be our duty, *anathema sit*. For, since the apostle says: "Knowledge puffs up, but love builds up" *[1 Cor 8:1]*, it would be very wrong to believe that we have the grace of Christ for knowledge which puffs up and not for love which builds up; for both are the gift of God: the knowledge of what we should do and the love to do it, so that built up by love we may not be puffed up by knowledge. Just as it is written of God: "He teaches human beings knowledge" *[Ps 94 (93)10]*, so too it is written: "love is of God" *[1 Jn 4:7]*.

1903 5. Likewise it has been decided: Whoever says that the
227 grace of justification is given to us so that we may do
more easily with grace what we are ordered to do by our free will, as if even without grace we were able, though without facility, to fulfil the divine commandments, *anathema sit*. For when the Lord spoke of the fruits of the commandments, he did not say that apart from him we could do things with greater difficulty, but rather: "Apart from me you can do nothing" *[Jn 15:5]*.

1904 6. Likewise it has been decided: When St. John the
228 apostle says: "If we say we have no sin we deceive
ourselves, and the truth is not in us" *[1 Jn 1:8]*, whoever takes this to mean that we must say we have sin out of humility, not because it is true, *anathema sit*. For the apostle continues: "If we confess our sins, he is faithful and just, and will forgive our sins and cleanse us from all unrighteousness" *[1 Jn 1:9]*. From this passage it is quite clear that that is not said only out of humility, but also in truth. For the apostle could have said: "If we say that we have no sin, we are boasting and humility is not in us." But since he says: "We deceive ourselves and the truth is not in us", he clearly shows that anyone who says he has no sin is not speaking truly but falsely.

1905 7. Likewise it has been decided: Whoever says that the
229 reason why the saints say in the Lord's prayer: "Forgive
us our debts" *[Mt 6:12]* is not that they are saying this for themselves—for such a petition is no longer necessary for them—but for others among their people who are sinners, and that this is why none of the saints says: "Forgive me my debts", but: "Forgive us our debts", so that the just person is understood to pray for others rather than for self, *anathema sit*. For the apostle

James was a holy and just man when he said: "We all offend in many things" [James 3:2 Vulg.]. Why was the word "all" added, if not to bring the expression into agreement with the Psalm where we read: "Enter not into judgment with thy servant, for none living is righteous before thee" [Ps 143(142):2]? And in the prayer of Solomon, the wise man [we read]: "There is no one who does not sin" [1 Kings 8:46]; and in the book of the holy man Job: "He seals up the hand of every one, that every one may know one's weakness" [cf. Job 37:7, old mistranslation]. Even the holy and just Daniel used the plural form in his prayer, when he said: "We have sinned, we have done wickedly" [Dan 9:5, 15], and other things which he there truly and humbly confesses. And lest anyone should think, as some do, that he was not speaking of his own sins, but of those of his people, he said further: "While I was [...] praying and confessing my sin and the sin of my people" [Dan 9:20] to the Lord my God. He would not say "our sins", but he spoke of the sins of his people and of his own sins for as a prophet he foresaw that in the future there would be some who would badly misunderstand him.

1906 8. Likewise it has been decided: Whoever holds that
230   the words of the Lord's prayer where we say: "Forgive us our debts" [Mt 6:12] are said by the saints out of humility but not truthfully, *anathema sit*. For who could tolerate that those who pray be lying not to human beings but to the Lord himself, by saying with their lips that they wish to be forgiven while in their heart they deny that they have any debts to be forgiven?

THE *INDICULUS* (between 435 and 442)

In his constant struggle with the Pelagians, particularly with Julian of Eklanus, Augustine focused his attention on the relationship between human freedom and divine grace, between God's universal saving will and the divine predestination of the elect. Fierce controversies followed. The strongest opposition came from Southern France, where a group of monks led by Cassian (d. 435) opposed certain aspects of the Augustinian teaching. According to these monks (later called Semi-Pelagians), all human beings, being equal before God, receive from him an equal measure of grace; any difference in the bestowal of grace comes solely from the difference in people's dispositions; the person needs grace to perform good works, but the beginning of conversion (or the 'beginning of faith', as it was technically called) is one's own doing for which grace is not required; after this foundation has been laid by one's own strength,

God will grant a further increase of faith. The conception of salvation by God as a transaction between equal partners at least in its initial stage implied a practical denial of the supremacy of grace.

It is in the midst of the semi-Pelagian controversy that the Indiculus *was composed. Redacted probably by Prosper of Aquitaine (c. 390-460), a disciple of St. Augustine and Cassian's strongest opponent, this document is a summary of the doctrine of grace, based on papal pronouncements, the decrees of African Councils which had subsequently received papal approval, and the Church's faith as expressed mainly in her liturgy. By the end of the fifth century it was already accepted as the standard exposition of the Church's doctrine of grace, and gradually acquired great authority, due mainly to its tacit approval by the universal Church. For chapter 1 on original sin, cf. n. 503.*

1907 Some people who pride themselves on the name of
238 Catholics, still remain, either through malice or through ignorance, under the sway of opinions condemned as heretical and have the presumption to contradict the most holy defenders [of the faith]. While these people do not hesitate to condemn Pelagius and Celestius, still they oppose our teachers as though they had gone beyond the necessary bounds. Since they profess to follow and approve only what the most Holy See of the blessed apostle Peter has sanctioned and taught through the ministry of its bishops against the enemies of the grace of God, it has been necessary to make a diligent investigation as to what judgment the rulers of the Roman Church passed on the heresy that arose during their time and what opinion they thought should be held about the grace of God against the dangerous upholders of free will. We are also adding sentences of the African Councils which the apostolic bishops certainly made their own when they approved them. In order therefore that those who are in doubt about some point may be more fully instructed, we are publishing in this short catalogue *(Indiculus)* the constitutions of the holy Fathers. Thus, if one is not too contentious, one will admit that the conclusion of all these discussions is contained in the brief statements of the authorities adduced, and that there is no ground left for asserting the contrary, if with Catholics one believes and professes the following:

(Papal condemnation of errors on grace)

1908 2. No one is good of oneself unless he who alone is
240 good makes him share in himself. This is what the same pontiff declares in the same letter where he says: "Can

we henceforth expect anything good from people who think they can attribute to themselves the fact that they are good without considering him whose grace they receive every day, and who trust that without him they are able to achieve so much?"[1]

1909 3. Nobody, not even one who has been renewed by the
241 grace of baptism, is capable of overcoming the snares of
the devil and of conquering the concupiscence of the flesh, unless one receives perseverance in good conduct through the daily help of God. This truth is confirmed by the doctrine of the same pontiff in the above quoted letter: "For although he redeemed human beings from their past sins, still, knowing that they could sin again, he kept many means whereby he could restore them and set them straight thereafter, offering them those daily remedies upon which we must always rely with confidence and trust; for by no other means shall we ever be able to overcome our human errors. For it is inevitable that, as with his help we conquer, without his help we are conquered."[2]

1910 5. All the efforts and all the works and merits of the
243 saints must be referred to the praise and glory of God,
for no one can please him except by what he himself has given.[...]

(Are quoted as authorities one passage of the Epistola tractoria of Pope Zosimus and its specific approval by the African bishops).

1911 6. God so works in the hearts of people and in the free
244 will itself that a holy thought, a good counsel and every
movement of a good will come from God, because it is through him that we can do any good, without whom we can do nothing [cf. Jn 15:5]. The same teacher Zosimus instructed us to profess this doctrine when, speaking to the bishops of the whole world about the assistance of divine grace, he said: "Is there ever a time when we do not need his help? Therefore in all our actions and affairs, in all our thoughts and inclinations, we must pray to him as to our helper and protector. For it is pride on the part of human nature to arrogate anything to itself, when the apostle

---

1. This refers to the Epistola in Requirendis, 3, addressed by Pope Innocent to the Council of Carthage, already mentioned in chapter 1 of the Indiculus (cf. n. 503).

2. Epistola in Requirendis, 7.

proclaims: "We are not contending against flesh and blood, but against the principalities, against the powers, against the world rulers of this present darkness, against the spiritual hosts of wickedness in the heavenly places" [Eph 6:12]. And as he says elsewhere: "Wretched man that I am! Who will deliver me from the body of death? The grace of God through our Lord Jesus Christ" [Rom 7:24 Vulg.]. And again: "By the grace of God I am what I am, and his grace towards me was not in vain. On the contrary, I worked harder than any of them, though it was not I but the grace of God which is in me" [1 Cor 15:10]."[1]

(Pontifical approval of the decrees of the Council of Carthage)

1912 7. We likewise uphold as the teaching proper to the Holy
245 See what was laid down in the decrees of the Council of
Carthage; namely, what was defined in the third chapter
[there follows the text quoted in n. 1901], and again in the fourth chapter *[n. 1902]*, and similarly in the fifth chapter *[n. 1903]*.

(The liturgy and the necessity of grace)

(1913) *(The necessity of grace is further established from the*
246 *liturgy, the many prayers offered for the conversion of people,*
so that "the norm of prayer may establish the norm of belief".)

1914 9.[...] Therefore, with the help of the Lord, we are so
248 strengthened by these Church norms and these
documents derived from divine authority that we
acknowledge God as the author of all good desires and deeds, of all efforts and virtues by which from the beginning of faith the human person tends towards God. And we do not doubt that all human merits are preceded by the grace of him through whom it is that we begin to will and to do any good work [cf. Phil 2:13]. By this help and gift of God, free will is assuredly not destroyed but liberated, so that from darkness it is brought to light, from evil to rectitude, from sickness to health, from imprudence to circumspection. For such is God's goodness towards all that he wants his own gifts to be our merits and that he will give us an eternal reward for what he has bestowed upon us. Indeed God so acts in us that we both will and do what he wills; he does not permit to lie idle in us what he has

---

1. *Epistola tractoria.*

given us to be employed, not neglected, so that we may be cooperators with the grace of God. And if we notice that something is slackening in us because of our negligence, we should earnestly have recourse to him, who heals all our diseases and redeems our life from destruction [cf. Ps 103(102): 3f)] and to whom we say daily: "Lead us not into temptation but deliver us from evil" [Mt 6:13].

249 [...]Whatever is contrary to the above statements we clearly consider as not being Catholic.

THE SECOND COUNCIL OF ORANGE (529)

The Semi-Pelagian conflict continued well into the sixth century, and was finally settled by the Council of Orange in 529, nearly a hundred years after St. Augustine's death. Caesarius of Arles, disciple of Augustine, sent to Pope Felix IV nineteen chapters on grace culled from Augustine's works. The Pope accepted eight and added others taken from a list drawn up by Prosper of Aquitaine. It is this complex document which was accepted by the local Council of Orange and later approved by Felix's successor, Boniface II. In general, therefore, it can be said that the Council reflects a moderate Augustinianism, without upholding each one of Augustine's propositions. As for its doctrinal authority, the precise nature and the extent of the Pope's approval remain doubtful; the decrees of the Council soon fell into oblivion, which lasted until the sixteenth century. However, the Council was later explicitly quoted by both Vatican I (cf. n. 120) and Vatican II (cf. n. 152).For the canons on original sin, cf. nn. 504-505.

Canons on grace

1915 3. If anyone says that the grace of God can be conferred
373   because of human prayer, and not rather that it is grace
     itself that prompts us to pray, one contradicts the prophet
Isaiah, or the apostle who says the same thing: "I have been found by those who did not seek me; I have shown myself to those who did not ask for me" [Rom 10:20; cf. Is 65:1].

1916 4. If anyone contends that God awaits our will before
374   cleansing us from sin, but does not confess that even
     the desire to be cleansed is aroused in us by the infusion and action of the Holy Spirit, he opposes the Holy Spirit himself speaking through Solomon: "The will is prepared by the Lord" [Prov. 8:35 Septuag.] and the apostle's salutary message: "God is at work in you, both to will and to work for his good pleasure" [Phil 2:13].

1917 5. If anyone says that the increase as well as the
375 beginning of faith and the very desire of faith—by which
we believe in him who justifies the sinner and by which
we come to the regeneration of holy baptism—proceeds from
our own nature and not from a gift of grace, namely from an
inspiration of the Holy Spirit changing our will from unbelief to
belief and from godlessness to piety, such a one reveals oneself
in contradiction with the apostolic doctrine, since Paul says: "I
am sure that he who began a good work in you will bring it to
completion at the day of Christ Jesus" [Phil 1:6]; and again: "It
has been granted to you that for the sake of Christ you should
not only believe in him but also suffer for his sake" [Phil 1:29];
and also: "By grace you have been saved, through faith; and
this is not your own doing, it is the gift of God" [Eph 2:8]. For
those who say that the faith by which we believe in God is
natural, declare that all those who are strangers to the Church
of Christ are, in some way, believers.

1918 6. If anyone says that mercy is divinely conferred upon
376 us when, without God's grace, we believe, will, desire,
strive, labour, pray, keep watch, endeavour, request, seek,
knock, but does not confess that it is through the infusion and
inspiration of the Holy Spirit that we believe, will or are able to
do all these things as is required; or if anyone subordinates the
help of grace to humility or human obedience, and does not
admit that it is the very gift of grace that makes us obedient and
humble, one contradicts the apostle who says: "What have you
that you did not receive?" [1 Cor 4:7]; and also: "By the grace of
God I am what I am" [1 Cor 15:10].

1919 7. If anyone asserts that to be able by one's natural
377 strength to think as is required or choose anything good
pertaining to one's eternal salvation, or to assent to the
saving message of the Gospel without the illumination and
inspiration of the Holy Spirit, who gives to all ease and joy in
assenting to the truth and believing it, one is deceived by the
heretical spirit and does not understand the word said by God
in the Gospel: "Apart from me you can do nothing" [Jn 15:5],
nor the word of the Apostle: "Not that we are sufficient of
ourselves to claim anything as coming from us; our sufficiency
is from God" [2 Cor 3:5].

1920 8. If anyone maintains that some are able to come to the
378 grace of baptism through [God's] mercy, but others
through their own free will—which, it is clear, is
wounded in all those who are born from the transgression of
the first parent—one shows that one has departed from the
orthodox faith. For one does not acknowledge that free will has
been weakened in all by the sin of the first parent, or at least
holds that free will has been wounded only in such a way that
some are still able to attain to the mystery of eternal salvation
by themselves without divine revelation. Yet that the opposite is
true is proved by the Lord himself, who does not testify that
some can come to him, but that nobody can, unless drawn by
the Father [cf. Jn 6:55], as he also says to Peter: "Blessed are you,
Simon Bar Jona! For flesh and blood has not revealed this to
you, but my Father who is in heaven" [Mt 16:17]. And the apostle
too says: "No one can say: 'Jesus is the Lord', except by the
Holy Spirit" [1 Cor 12:3].

Conclusion redacted by Caesarius of Arles

(The teaching of Tradition on grace)

1921 Thus, according to the texts of Holy Scripture and the
396 explanations of the early Fathers quoted above, we must
with God's help preach and believe the following: free
will has been so distorted and weakened by the sin of the first
parent, that thereafter no one could love God as was required,
or believe in God, or perform for the sake of God what is good,
unless first reached by the grace of the divine mercy. Therefore
we believe that excellent faith so highly proclaimed to their praise
by St. Paul [Heb 11] which was given to the just Abel, to Noah,
to Abraham, Isaac and Jacob, and to that vast multitude of saints
of old, was conferred through the grace of God, and not through
the natural goodness which had first been given to Adam. And
we know and believe that, even after the coming of the Lord,
for all those who desire to be baptised this grace [of faith] is not
found in their free will, but is conferred by the generosity of
Christ, according to what has been repeatedly said above and
which the apostle Paul preaches: "It has been granted to you
that for the sake of Christ you should not only believe in him
but also suffer for his sake" [Phil 1:29]; and also: "he who began
a good work in you will bring it to completion at the day of

Jesus Christ" *[Phil 1:6]*; and again: "By grace you have been saved through faith; and this is not your own doing, it is the gift of God" *[Eph 2:8]*. And of himself the apostle says: "I have obtained mercy that I might be faithful" *[1 Cor 7:25 Vulg.]*; where he does not say: "because I was faithful", but rather: "that I might be faithful." And again: "What have you that you did not receive?" *[1 Cor 4:7]*; and again: "Every good endowment and every perfect gift is from above, coming down from the Father of lights" *[James 1:17]*; and again: "No one can receive anything except what is given him from heaven" *[Jn 3:27]*. There are innumerable passages of Sacred Scripture that could be adduced as testimonies in favour of grace, but they have been omitted for the sake of brevity. For, indeed, more texts will not help anyone for whom a few do not suffice.

(The teaching of Tradition on predestination)

1922   According to the Catholic faith we also believe that after
397   grace has been received through baptism, all the
baptised, if they are willing to labour faithfully, can and
ought to accomplish with Christ's help and cooperation what
pertains to the salvation of their souls. Not only do we not believe
that some are predestined to evil by the divine power, but if there
are any who wish to believe such an enormity, we with great
abhorrence anathematise them. We also believe and profess for
our salvation that in every good work it is not we who begin and
afterwards are helped by God's mercy, but he himself who, without
any previous merits on our part, first instils in us faith in him and
love for him, so that we may faithfully seek the sacrament of
baptism and, after baptism, we may with his help accomplish
what is pleasing to him. Therefore we must clearly believe that
the wonderful faith of the thief whom the Lord called to his home
in paradise *[cf. Lk. 23:43]*, of Cornelius the centurion to whom an
angel of the Lord was sent *[cf. Acts 10:3]* and Zacchaeus who
merited to receive the Lord himself *[cf. Lk 19:6]* did not come from
nature but was a gift from the bounty of divine grace.

LEO X
BULL *EXSURGE DOMINE* (1520)

*The protracted controversies on grace which shook the Church from the
time of Augustine onwards had undoubtedly the salutary effect of focussing
the theological attention on, and throwing into bold relief, such important*

doctrines as the necessity of grace, the gratuitousness of faith as the initial step on the way to salvation, the right understanding of God's universal saving will, of divine predestination, original sin and the necessity of baptism. But there were liabilities as well, for there resulted a gradual departure from the biblical and patristic viewpoint. The theology of grace was no longer centred on the person of the Spirit dwelling in the justified but rather on the created reality of grace. An effort made by Peter Lombard to stress the role of the Holy Spirit proved unsuccessful in so far as he wrongly identified created grace with the divine person of the Spirit. Hence it happened that in their zeal to vindicate the reality of created grace as distinct from the indwelling Spirit, medieval theologians began so to stress sanctifying grace as to almost entirely overlook the place of the Spirit in the mystery of grace. The description of the reality of created grace and of its action in terms of Aristotelian categories further contributed to separate the theological language from the biblical sources.

The Reformers reacted sharply against too juridical and metaphysical a conception of grace. Their reaction, however, was marred by an extreme pessimism and an extrinsic conception of justification. Luther's teaching on grace can be summarised as follows: original sin has so deeply affected human nature that, steeped in sinfulness, one sins in every action one does. One finds salvation through total faith in Jesus Christ which gives the assurance that sins are forgiven. One is thus justified before God; yet, inwardly, remains a sinner because of concupiscence. Justification consists in the fact that God in his mercy no longer imputes sin. Thus, one is at once and simultaneously just on account of Christ's justice, and sinner by one's own ineradicable sinfulness. In spite of the ambiguity of some of his expressions, Luther holds the human beings to be radically transformed by a gratuitous justification which is deeply Christological. For according to him the righteousness of Christ is not merely attributed to the justified legally and externally, but is rather Christ's presence in the person through faith and the Holy Spirit. Thus justified, one is bound to perform good works, which are the external signs of justification; but these works cannot cause an increase in grace.

Among Luther's propositions condemned by Pope Leo X in the Bull Exsurge Domine (cf. n. 1309i), some pertaining to grace are quoted here.

(Errors of Luther condemned)

[1923/2] 1452	To deny that sin remains in a child after baptism is to disregard both Paul and Christ alike.
[1923/3] 1453	The seed of sin *(fomes peccati)* hinders a soul departing from the body from entering into heaven, even though there is no actual sin.
[1923/31] 1481	In every good work the just person sins.
[1923/32] 1482	A good work perfectly performed is a venial sin.

[1923/36]   After sin, free will is an empty concept; and when
1486   it does what is in its power, it sins mortally.

THE GENERAL COUNCIL OF TRENT
SIXTH SESSION
DECREE ON JUSTIFICATION (1547)

The preparatory work for this most important decree of the Council took seven months. Its purpose was not only to reject the objectionable teaching of the Reformers, but to give a coherent exposition of the Catholic doctrine on grace. The Decree steers a middle course between the two extremes of Pelagian self-sufficiency and of the Protestant diffidence regarding the capabilities of the human person's wounded nature. The Decree is not concerned with the justification of children, who receive the grace of justification by baptism without their personal cooperation, but exclusively with that of adults. The entire document is built on the conception of a triple justification: the moment when justification is first attained; the preservation and increase of this justification; and the recovery of justification after it has been lost through sin.

Chapter I-III offer on overall view of God's plan of salvation: people are unable to justify themselves (chapter I), but, thanks to the divine dispensation manifested in Christ (chapter II), they attain justification through him (chapter III). Chapters IV-IX deal with the first justification as the concrete realisation of the divine plan of salvation: a brief outline of this first justification (chapter IV) is followed by the conciliar exposition of the necessity of preparing for it (chapter V) and the manner of this preparation (chapter VI). The causes of justification are briefly stated within the framework of the categories of scholastic theology then prevalent (chapter VII). The two concluding chapters of this section explain the correct understanding of the Pauline formula stressed by Luther, according to which the sinner is justified through faith (chapter VIII), and the reasons for rejecting Luther's conception of the certainty of justification through faith (chapter IX). Chapters X-XIII deal with the second justification, the preservation and the increase of grace; one's justice can and ought to increase (chapter X) through the observance of the commandments, which bind also the justified (chapter XI). No one should rashly consider oneself among the predestined (chapter XII), for final perseverance remains a gratuitous gift of God (chapter XIII).

Finally, chapters XIV-XV treat the possibility of recovering justification (chapter XIV), if it has been lost through sin (chapter XV), while the last chapter is devoted to merit (chapter XVI) as the fruit of justification; this chapter, completely biblical in conception, is one of the most satisfactory of the entire decree. To the chapters are appended corresponding canons, where the same doctrine is found in the form of the condemnation of opposite errors.

Foreword

1924   Since at this time a certain erroneous doctrine about

1520   justification is being disseminated not without the loss
         of many souls and serious damage to Church unity, this
holy, ecumenical and general Council of Trent, lawfully
assembled in the Holy Spirit for the praise and glory of almighty
God, for the tranquillity of the Church and for the salvation of
souls[...], intends to set forth for all the faithful of Christ the
true and sound doctrine of justification which the "Sun of justice"
[Mal 4:2], Jesus Christ, "the pioneer and perfecter of our faith"
[Heb 12:2], has taught, which the apostles have handed down
and which the Catholic Church, under the inspiration of the Holy
Spirit, has always preserved. The Council strictly forbids that
henceforth anyone dare to believe, preach or teach anything
contrary to what is determined and declared in this Decree.

Chapter I: The inability of nature
and the law to justify human beings

1925   First the holy Council declares that for a correct and
1521   clear understanding of the doctrine of justification it is
         necessary that each one admits and confesses that all,
having lost innocence through the sin of Adam [cf. Rom 5:12; 1
Cor 15:22], "became unclean" [Is 64:6] and, according to the
apostle, were "by nature children of wrath" [Eph 2:3], as the
Council taught in its decree on original sin. So completely were
they the slaves of sin [cf. Rom 6:20] and under the power of the
devil and of death, that not only the gentiles by means of the
power of nature [cf. n. 1951] but even the Jews by means of the
letter of the Law of Moses were unable to liberate themselves
and to rise from that state, even though their free will, weakened
and distorted as it was, was in no way extinct [cf. n. 1955].

Chapter II: The divine dispensation
and the mystery of Christ's coming

1926   And so it came to pass that, when the blessed "fulness
1522   of time" [Eph 1:10; Gal 4:4] had come, the heavenly
         Father, "the Father of all mercies and God of all comfort"
[2 Cor 1:3] sent to human beings his own son Jesus Christ [cf. n.
1951], who had been announced and promised to many holy
fathers before the Law and during the time of the Law [cf. Gen
49:10, 18]. He was sent that the Jews, who were under the Law,
might be redeemed, and that the Gentiles "who were not

pursuing righteousness" *[Rom 9:30]* might attain it, and that all "might receive adoption as sons" *[Gal 4:5]*. God has "put him forward as an expiation by his blood, to be received by faith" *[Rom 3:25]*, for our sins and "not for our sins only, but also for the sins of the whole world" *[1 Jn 2:2]*.

Chapter III: On those who are justified through Christ

1927 But even though "Christ died for all" *[2 Cor 5:15]*,
1523 still not all receive the benefit of his death, but only
those to whom the merit of his passion is imparted. For, as truly as people would not be born unrighteous if they were not born children of Adam's seed, since it is because of their descent from him that in their conception they contract unrighteousness as their own, likewise they would never be justified if they were not reborn in Christ *[cf. nn. 1952, 1960]*, for it is this rebirth that bestows on them, through the merit of his passion, the grace by which they become just. It is for this favour that the apostle exhorts us always to give thanks to the Father, "who has qualified us to share in the inheritance of the saints in light" *[Col 1:12]* and "has delivered us from the dominion of darkness and transferred us to the Kingdom of his beloved Son in whom we have redemption, the forgiveness of sins" *[Col 1:13f]*.

Chapter IV: A brief description of the sinner's justification: its manner under the dispensation of grace

1928 In these words a description is outlined of the
1524 justification of the sinner as being a transition from the
state in which one is born a child of the first Adam, to the state of grace and adoption as children of God *[cf. Rom 8:15]* through the second Adam, Jesus Christ our Saviour. After the promulgation of the Gospel, this transition cannot take place without the bath of regeneration *[cf. n. 1424]* or the desire for it, as it is written: "Unless one is born of water and the Spirit, one cannot enter the kingdom of God" *[Jn 3:5]*.

Chapter V: The necessity for adults to prepare themselves for justification and the origin of this justification

1929 The Council moreover declares that in adults the
1525 beginning of justification must be attributed to God's
prevenient grace through Jesus Christ *[cf. n. 1953]*, that

is, to his call addressed to them without any previous merits of theirs. Thus, those who through their sins were turned away from God, awakened and assisted by his grace, are disposed to turn to their own justification by freely assenting to and cooperating with that grace [cf. nn. 1954-1955]. In this way, God touches the heart of the human being with the illumination of the Holy Spirit, but one is not inactive while receiving that inspiration, since one can reject it; and yet, without God's grace, one cannot by one's own free will take one step towards justice in God's sight [cf. n. 1953]. Hence, when it is said in sacred Scripture: "Return to me and I will return to you" [Zech 1:3], we are reminded of our freedom; but when we reply: "Restore us to thyself, O Lord, that we may be restored" [Lam 5:21], we acknowledge that God's grace precedes us.

Chapter VI: The manner of preparation

1930   Adults are disposed for that justice [cf. nn. 1957, 1959]
1526   when, awakened and assisted by divine grace,they
conceive faith from hearing [cf. Rom 10:17] and are freely led to God, believing to be true what has been divinely revealed and promised [cf. nn. 1962-1964], especially that the sinner is justified by God's grace "through the redemption which is in Christ Jesus" [Rom 3:24]; when, understanding that they are sinners and turning from the fear of divine justice—which gives them a salutary shock [cf. n. 1958]—to the consideration of God's mercy, they are aroused to the confident hope that God will be propitious to them because of Christ; when they begin to love God as the source of all justice and are thereby moved by a certain hatred and detestation for sin [cf. n. 1959], that is, by that repentance that must be practiced before baptism [cf. Acts 2:38]; when, finally, they determine to receive baptism, to begin a new life and to keep the divine commandments.

1931   Scripture says about this disposition: "Whoever would
1527   draw near to God must believe that he exists and that
he rewards those who seek him" [Heb 11:6] and: "The fear of the Lord drives out sin" [Sir 1:27 Vulg.]; and: "Repent and be baptised everyone of you in the name of Jesus Christ for the forgiveness of sins; and you shall receive the gift of the Holy Spirit" [Acts 2:38]; and: "Go therefore and make disciples of the nations, baptising them them in the name of the Father, and of

the Son and of the Holy Spirit, teaching them to observe all that I have commanded you" *[Mt 28:19]*; and finally: "Direct your heart to the Lord" *[1 Sam 7:3]*.

Chapter VII: The nature and the causes of the sinner's justification

1932 This disposition or preparation is followed by
1528   justification itself, which is not only the remission of
         sins *[cf. n. 1961]* but also the sanctification and renewal of the interior person through the voluntary reception of grace and of the gifts, whereby from unjust the person becomes just, and from enemy a friend, that one may be "an heir in hope of eternal life" *[Tit 3:7]*.

1529   The causes of this justification are the following: the final
         cause is the glory of God and of Christ, and life everlasting. The efficient cause is the merciful God who gratuitously washes and sanctifies *[cf. 1 Cor 6:11]*, sealing and anointing "with the promised Holy Spirit, who is the guarantee of our inheritance" *[Eph 1:13]*. The meritorious cause is the beloved only-begotten Son of God, our Lord Jesus Christ who, "while we were sinners" *[Rom 5:10]*, "out of the great love with which he loved us" *[Eph 2:4]* merited for us justification by his most holy passion on the wood of the Cross *[cf. n. 1960]* and made satisfaction for us to God the Father. The instrumental cause is the sacrament of baptism which is the 'sacrament of faith', without which [faith] no one has ever been justified. Finally, the single formal cause is "the justice of God, not that by which he himself is just, but that by which he makes us just"[1] *[cf. nn. 1960-1961]*, namely the justice which we have as a gift from him and by which we are spiritually renewed. Thus, not only are we considered just, but we are truly called just and we are just, each one receiving within oneself one's own justice, according to the measure which "the Holy Spirit apportions to each one individually as he wills" *[1 Cor 12:11]*, and according to each one's personal disposition and cooperation.

1933 For although no one can be just unless the merits of

---

1. Cf. St. Augustine, De *Trinitate*, XIV, 12, 15.

1530   the passion of our Lord Jesus Christ are imparted to
him/her, still this communication takes place in the
justification of the sinner, when by the merit of the same most
holy passion, "God's love is poured through the Holy Spirit into
the hearts" *[Rom 5:5]* of those who are being justified and inheres
in them *[cf. n. 1961]*. Hence, in the very act of justification,
together with the remission of sins, one receives through Jesus
Christ, into whom one is inserted, the gifts of faith, hope and
charity, all infused at the same time.

1934   For faith without hope and charity neither unites a
1531   person perfectly with Christ, nor makes one a living
member of his body. Therefore it is rightly said that "faith
by itself, if it has no works, is dead" *[James 2:17]* and unprofitable
[cf. n. 1969], and that "in Christ Jesus neither circumcision nor
uncircumcision is of any avail, but faith working through love"
[Gal 5:6; 6:15]. This is the faith which, in keeping with apostolic
tradition, the catechumens ask of the Church before the reception
of baptism when they ask for "the faith that gives eternal life",[1]
a life which faith without hope and charity cannot give. Hence
they immediately hear Christ's words: "If you would enter life,
keep the commandments: *[Mt 19:17; cf. nn. 1968-1970]*.
Accordingly, while they receive the true Christian justice, as soon
as they have been reborn, they are commanded to keep it
resplendent and spotless, like their "best robe" *[Lk 15:22]* given
to them through Jesus Christ in place of the one Adam lost for
himself and for us by his disobedience, so that they may wear it
before the tribunal of our Lord Jesus Christ and have eternal life.

*Chapter VIII: The correct understanding of the sinner's
gratuitous justification through faith*

1935   When the apostle says that the human person is justified
1532   "through faith" *[cf. n. 1959]* and "gratuitously" *[Rom
3:22, 24]*, those words are to be understood in the sense
in which the Catholic Church has held and declared them with
uninterrupted unanimity, namely, that we are said to be justified
through faith because "faith is the beginning of the human being's
salvation",[2] the foundation and root of all justification, "without

---

1. *Roman Ritual,* Order of Baptism, 1.
2. FULGENTIUS OF RUSPE, De *fide liber ad Petrum* prologue 1.

which it is impossible to please God" *[Heb 11:6]* and to come into the fellowship of his sons. And we are said to be justified gratuitously because nothing that precedes justification, neither faith nor works, merits the grace of justification; for "if it is by grace, it is no longer on the basis of works; otherwise (as the same apostle says) grace would no longer be grace" *[Rom 11:6].*

Chapter IX: Against the vain confidence of heretics

1936   It is necessary to believe that sins are not forgiven and
1533   have never been forgiven except gratuitously by the
divine mercy on account of Christ. And yet it must not be said that sins are forgiven or have been forgiven to anyone who boasts of one's confidence and certainty that one's sins are forgiven and who relies upon this confidence alone. This vain confidence which is foreign to all piety may exist and actully exists in our times among heretics and schismatics and is preached very vigorously against the Catholic Church *[cf. n. 1962].*

1534   Moreover it must not be asserted that those who are
truly justified should unhesitatingly determine within themselves that they are justified, and that no one is absolved from one's sins and justified unless one believes with certainty that one is absolved and justified, and that absolution and justification are brought about by this faith alone *[cf. n. 1964],* as if whoever lacks this faith were doubting God's promises and the efficacy of Christ's death and resurrection. For just as no devout human person should doubt God's mercy, Christ's merit and the power and efficacy of the sacraments; so also, whoever considers oneself, one's personal weakness and lack of disposition, may fear and tremble about one's own grace *[cf. n. 1963],* since no one can know with a certitude of faith which cannot be subject to error, that one has obtained God's grace.

Chapter X: The increase of justification in the justified

1937   In this way therefore the justified become both "friends
1535   of God" and "members of his household" *[Jn 15:15; Eph
2:19];* "they go from strength to strength" *[Ps 84(83)7],* "renewed (as the apostle says) every day" *[2 Cor 4:16],* that is "by putting to death the members of their flesh" *[Col 3:5 Vulg.]* and using them "as instruments of righteousness" *[Rom 6:13, 19]*

unto sanctification by observing the commandments of God and of the Church. When "faith is active along with works" *[James 2:22]*, they increase in the very justice they have received through the grace of Christ, and are further justified *[cf. nn. 1974, 1982]*, as it is written: "Let the holy still be holy" *[Rev 22:11]*; and again: "Fear not to be justified until you die" *[Sir 18:22] Vulg.]*; and again: "You see that one is justified by works and not by faith alone" *[James 2:24]*. It is this increase in faith that the holy Church asks for when she prays: "Give us, O Lord, an increase of faith, hope and charity."[1]

Chapter XI: The observance of the commandments; its necessity and possibility

1938 Nobody, however much justified, should consider oneself
1536 exempt from the observance of the commandments *[cf. n. 1970]*; and no one should say that the observance of God's commandments is impossible for the person justified—a rash statement censured by the Fathers with anathema *[cf. nn. 1968, 1972]*. "For God does not command the impossible, but when he commands he admonishes you to do what you can and to pray for what you cannot do",[2] and he helps you to be able to do it. "His commandments are not burdensome" *[1 Jn 5:3]*; his "yoke is easy and his burden light" *[Mt 11:30]*. For those who are children of God love Christ, and those who love him keep his words, as he himself testifies *[cf. Jn 14:23]*, and this they certainly can do with God's help.

1537 For although in this mortal life human beings, however just and holy they may be, fall, sometimes at least, into those slight and daily sins which are also called venial *[cf. n. 1973]*, they do not on that account cease to be just. For the petition of the just: "forgive us our debts" *[Mt 6:12]*, is both humble and true. Hence the just themselves should feel all the more obliged to walk in the way of justice because, having been "set free from sin and become the slaves of God" *[Rom 6:22]*, they can, by living "sober, upright and godly lives" *[Tit 2:12]*, progress through Jesus Christ, through whom "they have obtained access to this grace" *[Rom 5:2]*. For God "does not

---

1. *Roman Missal*, Thirteenth Sunday after Pentecost.
2. St. Augustine, *De natura et gratia*, 43, 50.

desert" those who have been once justified by his grace "unless they desert him first".[1]

1939   Therefore nobody should flatter oneself with faith
1538   alone [cf. nn. 1959, 1969, 1970], thinking that by faith
alone one is made an heir and will obtain the inheritance, even if one does not "suffer with Christ in order that one may also be glorified wth him "[Rom 8:17]. For even Christ himself, as the apostle says, "although he was a Son, learned obedience through what he suffered, and, being made perfect, he became the source of eternal salvation to all who obey him" [Heb 5:8]. That is why the apostle himself admonishes the justified, saying: "Do you not know that in a race all the runners compete, but only one receives the prize? So run that you may obtain it.[...] Well, I do not run aimlessly, I do not box as one beating the air; but I pommel my body and subdue it, lest after preaching to others I myself should be disqualified" [1 Cor 9:24-27]. Similarly Peter the prince of the apostles says: "Be the more zealous to confirm your call and election through good works; for if you do this you will never sin" [2 Pet 1:10] Vulg.].

1940   Hence it is clear that those are opposed to the orthodox
1539   doctrine of religion who maintain that the just sin at
least venially in every good work [cf. n. 1975], or (what is even more intolerable) that they merit eternal punishment. They too are opposed to it who assert that the just sin in all their works if in those works, while overcoming their sloth and encouraging themselves to run the race, they look for an eternal reward in addition to their primary intention of glorifying God [cf. nn. 1976, 1981]. For it is written: "I have disposed my heart to perform your statutes for the sake of the reward [Ps 119(118) 112 Vulg.]; and speaking of Moses the apostle says that "he looked to the reward" [Heb 11:26].

Chapter XII: Rash presumption of one's own predestination must be avoided

1941   Furthermore, no one, so long as one lives in this mortal
1540   condition, ought to be so presumptuous about the deep
mystery of divine predestination as to determine with

---

2. St. Augustine, *De natura et gratia*, 26, 29.

certainty that one is definitely among the number of the predestined [cf. n. 1965], as if it were true either that the one justified cannot sin anymore [cf. n. 1973] or that, if one sins, one should promise oneself an assured repentance. For without special revelation it is impossible to know whom God has chosen for himself [cf. n. 1966].

Chapter XIII: The gift of perseverance

1942 The same is to be said of the gift of perseverance [cf. n.
1541 1966], about which it is written: "The one who endures to the end will be saved" [Mt 10:22; 24:13]. This gift can be had only from him who has the power to uphold one who stands that one may stand with perseverance (cf. Rom 14:4) and who can lift one who falls. Let no one promise oneself any security about this gift with absolute certitude, although all should place their firmest hope in God's help. For, unless they themselves are unfaithful to his grace, God, who began the good work, will bring it to completion, effecting both the will and the execution [cf. Phil 2:13; n. 1972]. Yet "let anyone who thinks to be standing take heed not to fall" [1 Cor 10:12] and let one "work out one's salvation with fear and trembling" [Phil 2:12], in labours, in vigils, in almsgiving, in prayers and offerings, in fastings and chastity [cf. 2 Cor 6:3ff]. Knowing that they are reborn unto the hope of glory [cf. 1 Pet 1:3] and not yet unto glory, they should be in dread about the battle they still have to wage with the flesh, the world and the devil, in which they cannot be the winners unless with God's grace they obey the apostle who says: "We are debtors, not to the flesh to live according to the flesh, for if you live according to the flesh you will die, but if by the Spirit you put to death the deeds of the body, you will live" [Rom 8:12].

Chapter XIV: Those who sin after justification and their restoration to grace

1943 Those who through sin have forfeited the grace of
1542 justification they had received, can be justified again [cf. n. 1979] when, awakened by God, they make the effort to regain through the sacrament of penance and by the merits of Christ the grace they have lost. This manner of justification is the restoration of the sinner which the holy Fathers aptly called

"the second plank after the shipwreck of the loss of grace".[1] For Christ Jesus instituted the sacrament of penance for those who fall into sin after baptism, when he said: "Receive the Holy Spirit. If you forgive the sins of any, they are forgiven; if you retain the sins of any, they are retained" [Jn 20:22f].

1944 Hence it must be taught that the repentance of a
1543 Christian after sin differs vastly from repentance at the time of baptism. It includes not only giving up sins and detesting them, or "a broken and contrite heart" [Ps 51(50) 17], but also their sacramental confession or at least the desire to confess them when a suitable occasion will be found, and the absolution of a priest; it also includes satisfaction by fasts, almsgiving, prayer and other pious exercises of the spiritual life, not indeed for the eternal punishment which, together with the guilt, is remitted by the reception or the desire of the sacrament, but for the temporal punishment [cf. n. 1980] which, as sacred Scripture teaches, is not always entirely remitted, as is done in baptism, to those who, ungrateful to the grace of God they have received, have grieved the Holy Spirit [cf. Eph 4:30] and have not feared to violate the temple of God [cf. 1 Cor 3:17]. Of this form of repentance it is written: "Remember from what you have fallen, repent and do the works you did at first" [Rev. 2:5]; and again: "Godly grief produces a repentance that leads to salvation" [2 Cor 7:10]; and again: "Repent" [Mt 3:2; 4:17]; and: "Bear fruit that befits repentance" [Mt 3:8].

*Chapter XV: By every mortal sin grace is lost,
but not faith*

1945 It must also be asserted against the cunning wits of some
1544 who "by fair and flattering words deceive the hearts of the simple-minded" [Rom 16:18], that the grace of justification, once received, is lost not only by unbelief [cf. n. 1977] which causes the loss of faith itself, but also by any other mortal sin, even though faith is not lost [cf. n. 1978] Thus is defended the teaching of divine law that excludes from the Kingdom of God not only unbelievers, but also the faithful who are "immoral, adulterers, homosexuals, thieves, greedy,

---

1. See for instance, TERTULLIAN, *De paenitentia*, 4, 2; ST. JEROME, *Epistola 84 ad Pammachium et Oceanum*, 6; *Epistola 130 ad Demetriadem*, 9.

drunkards, revilers, robbers" *[1 Cor 6:9]*, and all others who commit mortal sins which they can avoid with the help of divine grace and which separate them from the grace of Christ *[cf. n. 1977]*.

Chapter XVI: The merit of good works as a result of justification and the nature of merit

1946 Therefore, it is with this in mind that the people justified,
1545 whether they have continuously kept the grace they have once received or have lost it and recovered it, should be asked to consider the words of the apostle: "Abound in the good work of the Lord, knowing that in the Lord your labour is not in vain" *[1 Cor 15:58]*; "God is not so unjust as to overlook your work and the love which you showed for his sake" [Heb 6:10]; and: "Do not throw away your confidence, which has a great reward" *[Heb 10:35]*. And eternal life should therefore be set before those who persevere in good works "to the end" *[Mt 10:22]* and who hope in God, both as a grace mercifully promised to the children of God through Jesus Christ, and "as a reward"[1] which, according to the promise of God himself, will faithfully be given them for their good works and merits *[cf. nn. 1976, 1982]*. For this is the crown of justice which the apostle says is laid up for him after the fight and the race; the crown that will be given him by the just Judge, and not to him alone but to all who love his coming *[cf. 2 Tim 4:7]*.

1947 For Jesus Christ himself continuously infuses strength
1546 into the justified, as the head into the members *[cf. Eph 4:15]* and the vine into the branches *[cf. Jn 15:5]*; this strength always precedes, accompanies and follows their good works which, without it, could in no way be pleasing to God and meritorious *[cf. n. 1952]*. Therefore, we must believe that nothing further is wanting to the justified for them to be regarded as having entirely fulfilled the divine law in their present condition by the works they have done in the sight of God; they can also be regarded as having truly merited eternal life, which they will obtain in due time, provided they die in the state of grace *[cf. Rev. 14:13; n. 1982]*, since Christ our Saviour says:

---

1. St. Augustine, *De gratia et libero arbitrio*, 8, 20.

"Whoever drinks of the water that I shall give will never thirst; the water that I shall give one will become in one a spring of water welling up to eternal life" *[Jn 4:14]*.

1547   Thus, neither is our justice considered as coming from us, nor is God's justice disregarded or denied *[cf.Rom 10:3]*; for the justice which is said to be ours because we become just by its inherence in us *[cf. nn.1960, 1961]* is that of God himself, since it is infused in us by God through the merit of Christ.

1948   Nor should this be overlooked: although in Holy
1548   Scripture such a high value is placed on good works that Christ promises that the person "who gives to one of his little ones even a cup of cold water shall not lose a reward" *[Mt 10:42]* and the apostle testifies that "this slight momentary affliction is preparing for us an eternal weight of glory beyond all comparison" *[2 Cor 4:17]*, nevertheless, a Christian should never rely on oneself or glory in oneself instead of in the Lord *[cf. 1 Cor 1:31; 2 Cor 10:17]*, whose goodness towards all is such that he wants his own gifts to be their merits *[cf. n. 1982]*.

1949   And since "we all offend in many things" *[James 3:2*
1549   *Vulg; cf. n. 1973]*, everyone ought to keep in mind not only God's mercy and goodness but also his severity and judgment. Neither should anyone pass judgment on oneself, even if one is conscious of no wrong, because the entire life of a person should be examined and judged, not by human judgment but by the judgment of God, "who will bring to light the things now hidden in darkness and will disclose the purposes of the heart. Then every one will receive commendation from God" *[1 Cor 4:5]* who, as it is written, "will render to everyone according to one's works" *[Rom 2:6]*.

1950   No one can be justified unless one faithfully and firmly
1550   accepts this Catholic doctrine on justification *[cf. n. 1983]*, to which the holy Council has decided to add the following canons, so that all may know, not only what they should hold and follow, but also what they should shun and avoid.

Canons on justification

1951   1. If anyone says that, without divine grace through
1551   Jesus Christ, one can be justified before God by one's own works, whether they be done by one's own

natural powers or through the teaching of the Law, *anathema sit* [*cf. n. 1925*].

1952 2. If anyone says that divine grace is given through Jesus
1552 Christ only in order that one may more easily live justly and merit eternal life, as if by one's free will without grace one could do both, although with great difficulty, *anathema sit* [*cf. nn. 1928f*].

1953 3. If anyone says that without the prevenient inspiration
1553 of the Holy Spirit and without his help one can believe, hope and love or be repentant, as is required, so that the grace of justification be bestowed upon one, *anathema sit* [*cf. n. 1929*].

1954 4. If anyone says that the free will of the human person,
1554 moved and awakened by God, in no way cooperates by an assent to God's awakening call, through which one disposes and prepares oneself to obtain the grace of justification; and that one cannot refuse assent if one wishes, but like a lifeless object does nothing at all and is merely passive, *anathema sit* [*cf. n. 1929*].

1955 5. If anyone says that after Adam's sin the free will of
1555 the human person is lost and extinct, or that it is an empty concept, a term without real foundation, indeed a fiction introduced by Satan into the Church, *anathema sit* [*cf. nn. 1925, 1929*].

1956 6. If anyone says that it is not in one's power to make
1556 one's ways evil, but that God performs the evil works just as he performs the good, not only by allowing them but properly and directly, so that Judas' betrayal no less than Paul's vocation was God's own work, *anathema sit*.

1957 7. If anyone says that all works performed before
1557 justification, no matter how they were performed, are truly sins or deserve God's hatred; or that the more earnestly one tries to dispose oneself for grace, the more grievously one sins, *anathema sit* [*cf. n. 1930*].

1958 8. If anyone says that the fear of hell, which makes us
1558 turn to the mercy of God in sorrow for our sins, or which makes us avoid sin, is a sin or that it makes sinners worse, *anathema sit* [*cf. n. 1930*].

1959 9. If anyone says that the sinner is justified by faith
1559 alone in the sense that nothing else is required by way
of cooperation in order to obtain the grace of justification,
and that it is not at all necessary that one should be prepared
and disposed by the movement of one's will, *anathema sit [cf. nn.
1935, 1939]*.

1960 10. If anyone says that human persons are justified
1560 without the justice of Christ, by which he merited for
us, or that they are formally just by his own justice,
anathema sit [cf. nn. 1927, 1932].

1961 11. If anyone says that people are justified either by the
1561 imputation of Christ's justice alone, or by the remission
of sins alone, excluding grace and charity which is
poured into their hearts by the Holy Spirit and inheres in them,
or also that the grace which justifies us is only the favour of
God, *anathema sit [cf. nn. 1932f, 1946ff]*.

1962 12. If anyone says that justifying faith is nothing else
1562 than confidence in the divine mercy that remits sins on
account of Christ, or that it is this confidence alone that
justifies us, *anathema sit [cf. n. 1936]*.

1963 13. If anyone says that, to attain the remission of sins,
1563 one must believe with certainty and without any
hesitation based on one's own weakness and lack of
disposition, that one's sins are forgiven, *anathema sit [cf. n. 1936]*.

1964 14. If anyone says that a person is absolved from sins
1564 and is justified because one believes with certainty to be
absolved and justified; or that no one is truly justified
except one who believes oneself to be justified, and that
absolution and justification are effected by this faith alone,
anathema sit [cf. n. 1936]

1965 15. If anyone says that one who has been reborn and
1565 justified is bound by faith to believe oneself to be
certainly among the number of the predestined, *anathema
sit (cf. n. 1941)*.

1966 16. If anyone claims with absolute and infallible
1566 certitude that one surely will have the gift of final
preseverance, unless one has learned this by a special
revelation, *anathema sit [cf. n. 1941f]*.

1967 17. If anyone says that the grace of justification is given
1567   only to those who are predestined to life, and that all
the others who are called, are called indeed, but do not
receive grace, as they are predestined to evil by the divine power,
anathema sit.

1968 18. If anyone says that the commandments of God are
1568   impossible to observe even for one who is justified and
established in grace, *anathema sit [cf. n. 1938].*

1969 19. If anyone says that nothing is commanded in the
1569   Gospels except faith, and that everthing else is
indifferent, neither prescribed nor prohibited, but free;
or that the ten commandments in no way concern Christians,
anathema sit [cf. n. 1938].

1970 20. If anyone says that a justified person, however
1570   perfect, is not bound to observe the commandments of
God and of the Church, but is bound only to believe, as
if the Gospel were merely an absolute promise of eternal life
without the condition that the commandments be observed,
anathema sit [cf. n. 1938].

1971 21. If anyone says that Jesus Christ was given by God
1571   to human beings as a redeemer in whom they are to
trust, but not also as a law-giver whom they are to obey,
anathema sit.

1972 22. If anyone says that without God's special help a
1572   justified person can persevere in the justice received, or
that with it one cannot persevere, *anathema sit [cf.n.1942].*

1973 23. If anyone says that a person once justified cannot
1573   sin again and cannot lose grace and that therefore the
one who falls and sins was never truly justified; or, on
the contrary, says that once justified one can avoid all sins, even
venial ones throughout one's entire life, unless it be by a special
privilege of God as the Church holds of the Blessed Virgin Mary,
anathema sit[cf. nn. 1938, 1949.]

1974 24. If anyone says that the justice received is not
1574   preserved and even increased before God through good
works, but that such works are merely the fruits, and
the signs of the justification obtained, and not also the cause of
its increase, *anathema sit [cf. n. 1937].*

1975 25. If anyone says that the just sins at least venially in
1575 every good work or (what is even more intolerable) sins
mortally, and therefore merits eternal punishment, and
that the only reason why such a one is not damned is that God
does not impute those works unto damnation, *anathema sit[cf. n.
1940]*.

1976 26. If anyone says that for the good works performed in
1576 God the just ought not to expect and hope for an eternal
reward from God through his mercy and the merits of
Jesus Christ, if they persevere to the end in doing good and in
keeping the divine commandments, *anathema sit [cf. nn. 1939f]*.

1977 27. If anyone says that there is no mortal sin except that
1577 of unbelief, or that grace, once received, cannot be lost
by any other sin, no matter how grievous and great,
except that of unbelief, *anathema sit [cf. n. 1945]*.

1978 28. If anyone says that with the loss of grace through
1578 sin faith is also always lost, or that the faith which
remains is not true faith, granted that it is not a living
faith; or that the person who has faith without charity is not a
Christian, *anathema sit [cf. n.1945]*.

1979 29. If anyone says that one who has fallen after baptism
1579 cannot rise again through God's grace, can indeed
recover the justice lost, but by faith alone without the
sacrament of penance, contrary to what the holy Roman and
universal Church, instructed by Christ the Lord and his apostles,
has always professed, observed and taught, *anathema sit [cf. nn.
1943f]*.

1980 30. If anyone says that after the grace of justification
1580 has been received the guilt is so remitted and the debt
of eternal punishment so blotted out for any repentant
sinner, that no debt of temporal punishment remains to be paid,
either in this world or in the other, in purgatory, before access can
be opened to the Kingdom of heaven, *anathema sit [cf. n. 1944]*.

1981 31. If anyone says that the justified sins when performing
1581 good works with a view to an eternal reward, *anathema
sit [cf. n. 1940]*.

1982 32. If anyone says that the good works of the justified

1582 person are the gifts of God in such a way that they are not also the good merits of the person justified; or that by the good works one performs through the grace of God and the merits of Jesus Christ (of whom one is a living member), the justified does not truly merit an increase of grace, eternal life and, provided one dies in the state of grace, the attainment of this eternal life, as well as an increase of glory, *anathema sit [cf. nn. 1948, 1946f].*

1983 33. If anyone says that this Catholic doctrine of
1583 justification, expounded by the holy Council in the present decree, is in any way derogatory to the glory of God or to the merit of Jesus Christ our Lord, and does not rather manifest the truth of our faith and ultimately the glory of God and of Jesus Christ, *anathema sit.*

PIUS V
BULL *EX OMNIBUS AFFLICTIONIBUS* (1567)
CONDEMNED PROPOSITIONS OF MICHAEL DE BAY

Even after the Reformation the relationship between nature and grace remained one of the principal concerns of the Church's teaching on grace. In 1551 Michael de Bay, professor of theology at Louvain began, under Protestant influence, to spread erroneous opinions which were subsequently condemned by three Popes: by Pius V in 1567, by Gregory XIII in 1579, and by Urban VIII in 1641.

According to de Bay grace, immortality and freedom from concupiscence were not gratuitous gifts of God to Adam; they were due to the human being and given in creation. Concupiscence, which is a wrong attitude of the will is a continual transgression of the law: "You shall not covet". Human freedom consists only in the absence of external coercion; it does not necessarily imply the possibility of choosing between good and evil. Grace is not a supernatural, gratuitous gift of God; it consists rather in the capability of fulfilling God's commandments. Justification is accompanied by pure love, the opposite of concupiscence, which alone can be the principle of morally good actions.

The condemnation by Pope Pius V extends to 79 propositions culled from de Bay's works and listed without systematic order. The most important ones concerning grace are given below; they are grouped after the main lines of his system. For the propositions on original sin, cf. nn. 514/26ff.

(On the original state of the human person)

[1984/21] The sublimation of human nature and its elevation
1921 to participation in the divine nature was due to the integrity of the human being in its first state, and is therefore to be called natural, not supernatural.

[1984/23]   It is absurd to hold that from the beginning the
1923   human being was raised above the natural human
                condition through a certain supernatural and
gratuitous gift so as to worship God supernaturally with faith,
hope and charity.

[1984/55]   God could not have created the human being from the
1955   beginning in the condition in which one is now born.

[1984/78]   The immortality of the first human being was not a
1978   gift of grace but a natural condition.

[1984/79]   The opinion of those doctors is wrong who hold
1979   that God could have created and constituted the
                human being without natural justice.

(On justification and merit)

[1985/13]   The good works performed by the children of
1913   adoption are meritorious, not because they are done
                through the Spirit of adoption dwelling in the hearts
of the children of God, but only because they conform to the law
and because through them the person shows obedience to the law.

[1985/42]   The justice by which the sinner is justified through
1942   faith consists formally in the observance of the
                commandments: it is the justice of works. It does
not consist in any sort of grace infused in the soul by which one
becomes God's adopted child, is internally renewed and is made
a sharer in the divine nature so that, renewed in this way through
the Holy Spirit, one may henceforward lead a good life and obey
the commandment of God.

[1985/63]   The distinction of a twofold justice must also be
1963   rejected: one which is effected through the
                indwelling of the Spirit of charity; the other which
consists in the inspiration of the Holy Spirit, who awakens the
heart to repentance but does not yet dwell in the heart nor diffuse
in it the charity by which the observance of the divine law can
be fulfilled.

(On sin and concupiscence)

[1986/20]   No sin is of its nature venial, but every sin deserves
1920   eternal punishment.

[1986/50] Evil desires to which reason does not consent and
1950 which one experiences against one's will, are
forbidden by the commandment: "You shall not
covet" [Ex 20:17].

[1986/54] The proposition that God has not commanded the
1954 human person to do the impossible is falsely
attributed to Augustine, since it belongs to Pelagius.

[1986/67] One sins and even merits damnation in that which
1967 one does of necessity.

[1986/74] In baptised persons who have fallen back into mortal
1974 sin and in whom concupiscence holds sway,
concupiscence, like the other evil habits, is sin.

(On the concept of freedom)

[1987/27] Without the help of God's grace free will can do
1927 nothing but sin.

[1987/28] It is a Pelagian error to say that free will is capable
1928 of avoiding any sin.

[1987/39] What is done voluntarily, even if done of necessity,
1939 is nevertheless a free action.

[1987/40] In all one's actions a sinner is the slave of a passion
1940 that overpowers one.

[1987/41] In the Scriptures the term 'freedom' does not mean
1941 freedom from necessity, but only freedom from sin.

[1987/66] The only thing opposed to the human being's natural
1966 freedom is violence.

(On love and the fulfilment of the Law)

[1988/16] Without charity, obedience to the Law is not true
1916 obedience.

[1988/34] The distinction of a twofold love of God, namely a
1934 natural love whose object is God as the author of
nature, and a gratuitous love whose object is God as
beatifying, is meaningless and imaginary; it has been devised as
a mockery of the sacred Scriptures and of the numerous
testimonies of ancient authors.

[1988/38] All love of a rational creature is either vicious
1938 cupidity by which the world is loved, which is
forbidden by John, or that praiseworthy charity
which, "poured into the hearts by the Holy Spirit" [cf. Rom 5:5],
makes them love God.

INNOCENT X

CONSTITUTION *CUM OCCASIONE* (1653)

ERRORS OF CORNELIUS JANSEN CONDEMNED

Jansenism is but a further development of Baianism. Cornelius Jansen,
bishop of Ypres, after an exhaustive study of St. Augustine's works, wrote his
famous Augustinus *with the purpose of restoring to its place of honour the*
African doctor's teaching on grace and free will. Jansen's work was published
posthumously, after its author had submitted in advance to the decision of the
Holy See. The work met with considerable success but was condemned by
Pope Urban VIII in 1642. Despite this papal condemnation, however, the work
of Jansen continued to spread until finally Innocent X condemned again five
propositions from Augustinus, *dealing with the possibility of keeping the divine*
commandments and of resisting grace, the concept of freedom and
predestination. The first four propositions are condemned as heretical, the fifth
one as false and scandalous, and if understood in the sense that Christ died
only for the predestined, heretical. The prolonged Jansenist controversies were
centred around these propositions.

[1989/1] Some of God's commandments cannot be observed
2001 by just persons with the strength they have in the
present state, even if they wish and strive to observe
them; nor do they have the grace that would make their
observance possible.

[1989/2] In the state of fallen nature interior grace in never
2002 resisted.

[1989/3] In order to merit or demerit in the state of fallen
2003 nature, it is not necessary for the human person to
have freedom from necessity, but freedom from
coercion suffices.

[1989/4] The Semi-Pelagians admitted the necessity of a
2004 prevenient interior grace for every act, even for the
beginning of faith; and their heresy consisted in
this, that they held this grace to be such that the human will
could either resist it or submit to it.

[1989/5] It is Semi-Pelagian to say that Christ died or shed
2005 his blood for all human beings without exception.

CLEMENT XI

CONSTITUTION *UNIGENITUS DEI FILIUS* (1713)

PROPOSITIONS OF PASQUIER QUESNEL CONDEMNED

In spite of repeated papal condemnations, Jansenism continued to spread. Quesnel (1634-1719), relying exclusively on the unchallenged authority of St. Augustine, brought out a new conception of grace as the principle of the human being's renewal. Without this grace the person was wholly corrupt, but grace itself was irresistible; it endowed one with pure charity, the only moral motive for action. In the dogmatic Constitution Unigenitus, *the last and most thorough rebuttal of Jansenism, Pope Clement XI condemned 101 propositions extracted from Quesnel's works.*

(Errors concerning the necessity of grace)

[1990/1] What else is left in the soul that has lost God and
2401 his grace except sin and its effects, proud poverty
and sluggish indigence, that is, general inability to
work, to pray and to do any good work?

[1990/38] Without the grace of the Redeemer the sinner is not
2438 free except for evil.

[1990/39] The will that is not preceded by grace has no light
2439 except to go astray, no eagerness except for self-
destruction, no strength except to wound itself; it is
capable of all evil and incapable of any good.

[1990/40] Without grace we cannot love anything except to
2440 our own condemnation.

[1990/41] Any knowledge of God, even natural, even among
2441 heathen philosophers, can only come from God; and
without grace it produces nothing but presumption,
vanity and opposition to God himself instead of a sense of
adoration, gratitude and love.

[1990/59] The prayer of sinners is a new sin and what God
2459 grants them is a new judgment against them.

(Propositions on the two loves)

[1991/44] There are only two loves that are the sources of all

2444   our volitions and actions: the love of God that does everything for the sake of God and which God rewards; and the love by which we love ourselves and the world, and which, because it does not refer to God what ought to be referred to him, becomes evil.

[1991/45]   When the love of God no longer reigns in the heart
2445   of sinners, it is inevitable that carnal desires reign in it and corrupt all its actions.

[1991/46]   It is covetousness or charity that makes the use of
2446   senses good or evil.

[1991/47]   Obedience to the Law ought to flow from a source,
2447   and this source is charity. When the love of God is the interior principle of this obedience and the glory of God its end, then its exterior manifestation is pure; otherwise it is nothing but hypocrisy or false righteousness.

(Propositions on the compelling force of divine grace)

[1992/10]   Grace is the working of the omnipotent hand of
2410   God which nothing can hinder or retard.

[1992/11]   Grace is nothing but the omnipotent will of God,
2411   commanding and doing what he commands.

[1992/23]   God himself has taught us the notion of the
2423   omnipotent working of his grace, signifying it by the operation which produces creatures out of nothing and restores life to the dead.

LEO XIII
ENCYCLICAL LETTER *DIVINUM ILLUD* (1897)

After the Council of Trent, due largely to the subsequent controversies De auxiliis *between the followers of Bañez and Molina, and to the diffusion and official condemnation of the systems of de Bay and Jansen, theological attention became narrowly focussed on the nature of actual grace. The doctrine of the indwelling of the Spirit in the justified, with which the Pauline epistles and the Greek tradition were deeply imbued, had receded to the background. Pope Leo XIII's encyclical* Divinum Illud *(1897) tries to restore this prominent biblical theme to the place of honour due to it. Although epoch-making because of the central role it attributes to the person of the Holy Spirit, the encyclical is influenced almost exclusively by the Western Fathers, while the rich theology of the Spirit, characteristic of the Eastern tradition, is hardly represented in it. With regard to the mode of presence of the Spirit in the justified, the Pope adopts the classical theory of appropriation, prevalent at that time.*

(The indwelling of the Holy Spirit)

1993 It is indeed certain that also in the just who lived before
3329 Christ the Holy Spirit resided by grace, as we read in the Scriptures concerning the prophets, Zachary, John the Baptist, Simeon and Anna. Thus, the self-communication of the Holy Spirit at Pentecost was not such that "then for the first time he would have begun to dwell in the saints, but that he was poured on them more abundantly; crowning, not beginning his gifts; not beginning a new work, but giving more abundantly.[...]"[1]

1994 The beginning of this regeneration and renovation of
3330 the human person takes place at baptism. In this sacrament[...] the Holy Spirit for the first time enters it [the soul] and makes it like to himself. "That which is born of the Spirit is spirit" *[Jn 3:6]*. The same Spirit gives himself more abundantly in holy confirmation for the steadfastness and the strength of the Christian life. [...] He not only brings to us divine gifts, but is the author of them and is himself the supreme gift, who, proceeding from the mutual love of the Father and the Son, is rightly considered and called "the gift of the most high". [...] Besides, by grace God abides in the just soul as in a temple, in a most intimate and singular manner. From this follows that bond of charity by which the soul adheres most closely to God, more than it could adhere to the most loving and beloved friend, and enjoys God in all fulness and sweetness.

3331 Now this wonderful union, which is properly called indwelling and differs only by reason of our condition or state from that in which God embraces and beatifies the citizens of heaven, is most certainly produced by the divine presence of the whole Trinity: "We will come to them and make our home with them" *[Jn 14:23]*; nevertheless it is attributed in a particular manner to the Holy Spirit. For, whilst traces of the

---

1. St. Leo the Great, *Sermo*, 77,1

divine power and wisdom appear even in a sinful person, only the just shares in charity, which is, as it were, the special mark of the Holy Spirit.

PIUS XII

ENCYCLICAL LETTER *MYSTICI CORPORIS* (1943)

This encyclical, devoted to the nature of the Church as the mystical Body of Christ (cf. n. 847i), contains some notable passages on the union of the justified with the risen Christ, and especially on the indwelling of the Holy Spirit. As the encyclical Divinum IIIud *of Leo XIII, it centres the mystery of the human being's transformation in justification on the person of the Holy Spirit, rather than on the created reality of sanctifying grace. But Pius XII goes beyond the doctrine of Leo XIII.* Mystici Corporis *is based not exclusively on the Western Fathers, but integrates to a large extent the views of the Eastern tradition. The mode of the divine indwelling is not reduced to mere appropriation, though its precise nature is ultimately left undecided. Clear norms are laid down for a balanced presentation of this doctrine that will avoid all danger of pantheistic interpretations.*

(*Union of the justified with Christ and the indwelling of the Holy Spirit*)

1995 Whereas in a physical body the principle of unity
3810 joins the parts together in such a way that each of them completely lacks a subsistence of its own, on the contrary in the mystical Body the cohesive force, intimate though it is, unites the members with one another in such a way that each of them wholly retains one's own personality.[...]

3811 Comparing now the mystical Body with a moral body, we must also notice between these a difference which is by no means slight but, on the contrary, of the very highest importance. For in a moral body the only principle of unity is a common end, and a common aspiration of all to that end by means of the social authority. But in the mystical Body, with which we are concerned, there is in addition to this common aspiration another internal principle, really existing and operative both in the whole structure and in each of its parts, and this principle is of such surpassing excellence that by itself it immeasurably transcends all the bonds of unity by which any physical or moral body is knit together. It is, as we have said above, something not of the natural, but of the supernatural order; indeed, in itself it is infinite and uncreated, namely the divine Spirit, who, in the words of the Angelic Doctor, "numerically one and the same, fills and unifies the whole Church".[1]

3813   Christ is in us through his Spirit, whom he imparts to us and through whom he so acts within us that any divine effect operated in our souls by the Holy Spirit must be said to be operated in us also by Christ.[2] "Anyone who does not have the Spirit of Christ", says the apostle, "does not belong to him. But if Christ is in you,[...] your spirits are alive because of righteousness" [Rom 8:9f]. It is due also to this communication of the Spirit of Christ that all the gifts, virtues and miraculous powers which are found eminently, most abundantly and fontally in the Head, stream into all the members of the Church and in them are perfected daily according to the place of each in the mystical Body of Jesus Christ.[...]

(Warning against misunderstandings)

1996   Under pain of departing from pure doctrine and from
3814   the true teaching of the Church, all must hold this as quite certain: that any explanation of this mystical union is to be rejected if it makes the faithful in any way pass beyond the order of created things, and so trespass upon the divine sphere that even one single attribute of the eternal God could be predicted of them in the proper sense. Moreover, this certain truth must be firmly borne in mind, that in these matters all things are to be held common to the Blessed Trinity, so far as the same relate to God as the supreme efficient cause. It must also be remembered that we are dealing with a hidden mystery which during our exile on earth can never be completely unveiled, never altogether understood, nor adequately expressed in human language.

(The indwelling of the divine Persons)

1997   The divine Persons are said to indwell inasmuch as,
3815   being present in a mysterious way to living intellectual creatures, they are attained by these through knowledge

---

1. St. Thomas Aqiunas, *De Veritate*, 29, 4c.
2. St. Thomas Aquinas, *Comment. in Eph.* c. 2, lect. 5.

and love, but in a manner which transcends all nature and is quite intimate and unique. If we would reach some little understanding of this, we shall do well to use the method recommended by the Vatican Council in such matters, the method by which light is successfully sought for some partial perception of God's hidden truths in a comparison of mysteries with one another and with the last end to which they are directed [*cf. n. 132*]. Thus, when our wise predecessor of happy memory, Leo XIII, was treating of this union of ours with Christ and the indwelling of the divine Paraclete within us, he appropriately turned his gaze to that beatific vision wherein one day in heaven this mystical union will find its perfect consummation. "This wonderful union", he wrote, "which is properly called indwelling[...] differs only by reason of our condition or state from that in which God embraces and beatifies the citizens of heaven" [*cf. n. 1994*]. In that vision it will be granted to the eyes of the mind, its powers augmented by supernatural light, to contemplate the Father, the Son and the Holy Spirit, for all eternity to witness closely the processions of the divine Persons, and to enjoy a beatitude very similar to that with which the most holy and undivided Trintiy is blessed.

THE SECOND VATICAN GENERAL COUNCIL

The doctrine of grace in Vatican II consists in passing references scattered in the Council's doctrinal documents. As compared with earlier declarations of the Church's teaching office, Vatican II lays greater emphasis on the ecclesial aspect of grace, which concerns not only the individual Christian, but affects the entire life of the Church. Along with this communitarian aspect of grace, the personal dimension comes strongly to the fore. During the Council sessions the Oriental bishops repeatedly voiced the complaint that full justice was not being done to the Eastern tradition with regard to the role of the Holy Spirit. In order to comply with their request, and also in keeping with modern theological trends in the West, greater stress is put on the action of the Spirit than in previous documents.

The sanctifying action of the Holy Spirit is described in two brief but dense passages in the frame-work of the Trinitarian structure of the Church and the Trinitarian origin of her mission (LG 2-4; AG 2-4). It is the Holy Spirit who guarantees the genuineness of the Church Tradition (DV 7-10, 19); he is the agent of biblical inspiration (DV 12,18,20). He is especially the principle of Christian unity (UR 2), whose influence extends outside the visible boundaries of the Catholic Church (UR 3-4; cf. LG 15); union can only be realised through the obedience of the Church to the promptings of the Spirit (UR 24).

Possibly one of the most important contributions made by the Council to the teaching on grace is the liberating paragraph on charisms (LG 12). According to St. Paul they are not peripheral to the life of the Church, but as essential an element of its structure as the institutional element. Two norms for the discernment of true charisms are mentioned: their orientation to the service of the Church, and the proper balance between their rich variety and necessary unity. The Holy Spirit distributes these gifts to the faithful of every rank; but charismatics are also subject to the Church authority (LG 7).

The Holy Spirit arouses in the Christian the faith in divine revelation (DV 5), which is the beginning of justification. He is the principle of life, dwelling in the Christian as in a temple, making one a child of God in worship and service. The sanctifying work of the Spirit renews the whole person, not only the soul (GS 22; cf, 41). The Council echoes the Eastern Fathers when it asserts that it is the Spirit himself who makes us partakers of the divine nature (UR 15).

DOGMATIC CONSTITUTION *LUMEN GENTIUM* (1964)

(The Sanctifying Spirit)

1998   4. When the Son had accomplished on earth the task entrusted to him by the Father, the Holy Spirit was sent on Pentecost day that he might for ever sanctify the Church. Thus, all who believe have access to the Father, through Christ, in one Spirit [*cf. Eph 2:18*]. He is the Spirit of life, the fountain of water springing up to life everlasting [*cf.Jn 4:14; 7:38f*]; it is through him that the Father gives life to human beings who were dead through sin; till at last, in Christ, he raises even their mortal bodies [*cf. Rom 8:10f*]. The Spirit dwells in the Church and in the hearts of the faithful as in a temple [*cf. 1 Cor 3:16; 6:19*]; he prays in them and bears witness to the fact that they are adopted children [*cf. Gal 4:6; Rom 8:15f, 26*]. He guides the Church into the fulness of truth [*cf. Jn 16:13*]; he unites her in mutual communion and in service; he teaches and directs her through his hierarchic and charismatic gifts, and adorns her with his fruits [*cf. Eph 4:11f; 1 Cor 12:4; Gal 5:22*]. By the power of the Gospel, he preserves the Church's youthfulness, renews her incessantly and leads her to perfect union with her spouse. Together, the Spirit and the Bride say to the Lord Jesus: "Come" [*Rev 22:17*]. Thus the universal Church is clearly a "people whose unity is derived from the unity of the Father, the Son and the Holy Spirit".[1]

---

1. St. Cyprian, *De Orat. Dom*, 23.

(The charisms of faith and of Christian life)

1999   12. God's holy people shares also in Christ's prophetic function when radiating his living testimony, mainly by a life of faith and charity, and offering to God a sacrifice of praise, the tribute of lips confessing his name [*cf. Heb 13:15*]. Because they are anointed by the Holy One [*cf. 1 Jn 2:20, 27*], the faithful as a body cannot err in their faith. They manifest this special prerogative of theirs by means of a supernatural sense of faith that belongs to the people as a whole, when "from the bishops down to the last lay believer",[2] they show universal agreement in matters of faith and morals. It is the Spirit of truth who awakens and sustains that sense of faith which enables the People of God, led by and obedient to the teaching authority of the Church, to accept not the word of human beings but the very word of God [*cf. 1 Thes. 2:13*], to cling unfailingly to the faith once communicated to the saints [*cf. Jude 3*], to penetrate more deeply into it and to live it more fully.

Further, the same Holy Spirit does not only sanctify the People of God, lead it and enrich it with virtues by means of the sacraments and the ministers of the Church, but he "apportions to each one individually as he wills" [*1 Cor 12:11*], he distributes among the faithful of every rank special graces that make them fit and ready to undertake various tasks and functions conducive to the renewal and further development of the Church; for, so writes the Apostle, "to each is given the manifestation of the Spirit for the common good" [*1 Cor 1:27*].[...]

JOHN PAUL II

ENCYCLICAL LETTER *DOMINUM ET VIVIFICANTEM*

(18 May, 1986)

In the general audience of 6 June, 1973, Pope Paul VI had stated: "The christology and ecclesiology of the Council [Vatican II] must be succeeded by a new study and devotion to the Holy Spirit, precisely as the indispensable complement to the teaching of the Council". This passage is quoted at the beginning of the encyclical, the first in nearly one century to be entirely devoted to the Holy Spirit. Unlike Divinum Illud of Leo XIII and Mystici Corporis

---

2. St. Augustine, *De Praed. Sanct.*, 14,27; PL 44, 980

*of Pius XII, which had shifted the focus from the reality of sanctifying grace
to the person of the Holy Spirit, this encyclical reverts on the whole to the
previous perspective. Thus the realities of divine filiation, partaking in the
divine nature and the indwelling itself of the Holy Spirit are said to be the
result of created sanctifying grace. Though a few Oriental Fathers are quoted,
the theology of the Holy Spirit present in the encyclical is rather Latin. The
text is found in AAS 78 (1986) 809-900.*

(The Spirit of love)

(2000a) *See text in nn. 337-338.*

(Sin against the Holy Spirit)

2000b   46. The blasphemy against the Holy Spirit consists
precisely in the radical refusal to accept [...] forgiveness,
of which he is the intimate giver and which presupposes
the genuine conversion which he brings about in the conscience.
If Jesus says that blasphemy against the Holy Spirit cannot be
forgiven either in this life or in the next, it is because this "non-
forgiveness" is linked, as to its cause, to "non-repentance", in
other words to the radical refusal to be converted. [...] One closes
oneself up in sin, thus making impossible one's conversion, and
consequently the remission of sins.[...]

(Supernatural filiation and partaking in the divine nature)

2000c   52. The birth, or rebirth, happens when the Father "sends
the Spirit of his Son into our hearts" [cf. Gal 4:6; Rom
5:5; 2 Cor 1:22]. Then "we receive a Spirit of adopted children
by which we cry 'Abba, Father' [cf. Rom 8:15]. Hence the divine
filiation planted in the human soul through sanctifying grace is
the work of the Holy Spirit. [...] And in the superabundance of
the uncreated gift there begins in the heart of all human beings
that particular created gift whereby they "become partakers of
the divine nature" [2 Pet 1:4].

(Indwelling of the three divine persons)

2000d   52. Through the gift of grace, which comes from the Holy
Spirit, the human being enters a "new life", is brought
into the supernatural reality of the divine life itself and becomes
a "dwelling place of the Holy Spirit", a living temple of God [cf.
Rom 8:9; 1 Cor 6:19]. For through the Holy Spirit, the Father and
the Son come to one and take their abode with one [cf. Jn 14:23].

CATECHISM OF THE CATHOLIC CHURCH
(7 December 1992)

This is but a selection of the many times the Catechism refers to the themes of grace, justification, sanctifying grace, and merit. It reiterates the traditional teaching of the magisterium on these subjects, emphasising the unity and uniqueness of the one mystery of Christ.

(The necessity of faith)

2000d/1   161. Believing in Jesus Christ and in the One who sent him for our salvation is necessary for obtaining that salvation [*cf. Mk 16:16; Jn 3:36; 6:40 et al*]. "Since 'without faith it is impossible to please [God]' and to attain to the fellowship of his children, therefore without faith no one has ever attained justification, nor will anyone obtain eternal life 'but those who endure to the end'" [*Dei Filius 3: n. 122; cf. Mt 10:22; 24:13 and Heb 11:6; Council of Trent: n. 1935*].

(Why did the Word become flesh?)

2000d/2   460. The Word became flesh to make us "partakers of the divine nature" [*2 Pt 1:4*]. "For this is why the Word became man, and the Son of God became the Son of man: so that man, by entering into communion with the Word and thus receiving divine sonship, might become a son of God" [St Irenaeus, *Adv. Haereses, 3, 19, 1*]. [...]

(The meaning and saving significance of the Resurrection)

2000d/3   654. The Paschal mystery has two aspects: by his death, Christ liberates us from sin; by his Resurrection, he opens for us the way to a new life. This new life is above all justification that reinstates us in God's grace, "so that as Christ was raised from the dead by the glory of the Father, we too might walk in newness of life" [*Rom 6:4; cf. 4:25*]. Justification consists in both victory over death caused by sin and a new participation in grace [*cf. Eph 2:4-5; 1 Pt 1:3*]. It brings about filial adoption so that we become Christ's brethren, as Jesus himself called his disciples after the Resurrection: "Go and tell my brethren" [*Mt 28:10; Jn 20:17*]. We are brethren not by nature, but by the gift of grace, because that adoptive filiation gains us a real share in the life of the only Son, which was fully revealed in his Resurrection.

("A new creature")

2000d/4 1265. The most Holy Trinity gives the baptized sanctifying grace, the grace of justification:
— enabling them to believe in God, to hope in him, and to love him through the theological virtues;
— giving them the power to live and act under the prompting of the Holy Spirit through the gifts of the Holy Spirit;
— allowing them to grow in goodness through the moral virtues.

This whole organism of the Christian's supernatural life has its roots in Baptism.

(Justification)

2000d/5 1989. The first work of the grace of the Holy Spirit is conversion, effecting justification in accordance with Jesus's proclamation at the beginning of the Gospel: "Repent, for the kingdom of heaven is at hand" *[Mt 4:17]*. Moved by grace, the person turns toward God and away from sin, thus accepting forgiveness and righteousness from on high. "Justification is not only the remission of sins, but also the sanctification and renewal of the interior person [*Council of Trent: n. 1932*].

1990. Justification detaches the person from sin which contradicts the love of God, and purifies one's heart of sin. Justification follows upon God's merciful initiative of offering forgiveness. It reconciles the person with God. It frees from the enslavement to sin, and it heals.

1991. Justification is at the same time the acceptance of God's righteousness through faith in Jesus Christ. Righteousness (or "Justice") here means the rectitude of divine love. With justification, faith, hope, and charity are poured into our hearts, and obedience to the divine will is granted us.

1993. Justification establishes cooperation between God's grace and the person's freedom. On the human person's part it is expressed by the assent of faith to the Word of God, which invites one to conversion, and in the cooperation of charity with the prompting of the Holy Spirit who precedes and preserves his assent.

When God touches one's heart through the illumination of the Holy Spirit, one is not inactive while receiving that inspiration, since one could reject it; and yet, without God's grace, one cannot by one's own free will move oneself toward justice in God's sight [*Council of Trent: n. 1929*].

(*Grace*)

2000d/6 2000. Sanctifying grace is an habitual gift, a stable and supernatural disposition that perfects the soul itself to enable it to live with God, to act by his love. Habitual grace, the permanent disposition to live and act in keeping with God's call, is distinguished from actual graces which refer to God's interventions, whether at the beginning of conversion or in the course of the work of sanctification.

2001. The preparation of the human person for the reception of grace is already a work of grace. This latter is needed to arouse and sustain our collaboration in justification through faith, and in sanctification through charity. God brings to completion in us what he has begun, "since he who completes his work by cooperating with our will began by working so that we might will it" [St. Augustine, *De gratia et libero arbitrio*, 17: PL 44, 901] [...].

2002. God's free initiative demands the person's free response, for God has created the person in his image by conferring on one, along with freedom, the power to know him and love him. The soul only enters freely into the communion of love. God immediately touches and directly moves the heart of the person. He has placed in one a longing for truth and goodness that only he can satisfy. The promises of "eternal life" respond, beyond all hope, to this desire[...].

2003. Grace is first and foremost the gift of the Spirit who justifies and sanctifies us. But grace also includes the gifts that the Spirit grants us to associate us with his work, to enable us to collaborate in the salvation of others and in the growth of the Body of Christ, the Church. There are sacramental graces, gifts proper to the different sacraments. There are furthermore special graces, also called charisms after the Greek term used by St. Paul and meaning "favour," "gratuitous gift", "benefit" [*cf. LG 12*]. Whatever their character—sometimes it is extraordinary, such as the gift of miracles or of tongues—charisms are oriented toward sanctifying grace and are intended for the common good of the Church. They are at the service of charity which builds up the Church [*cf. 1 Cor 12*].

(Merit)

2000d/7 2009. Filial adoption, in making us partakers by grace in the divine nature, can bestow true merit on us as a result of God's gratuitous justice. This is our right by grace, the full right of love, making us "co-heirs" with Christ and worthy of obtaining "the promised inheritance of eternal life." [*Council of Trent: n. 1947*]. The merits of our good works are gifts of the divine goodness [*cf. Council of Trent: n. 1948*]. "Grace has gone before us; now we are given what is due. [...] Our merits are God's gifts" [St Augustine, *Sermo* 298, 4-5: *PL* 38, 1367].

2010. Since the initiative belongs to God in the order of grace, no one can merit the initial grace of forgiveness and justification, at the beginning of conversion. Moved by the Holy Spirit and by charity, we can then merit for ourselves and for others the graces needed for our sanctification, for the increase of grace and charity, and for the attainment of eternal life. Even temporal goods like health and friendship can be merited in accordance with God's wisdom. These graces and goods are the object of Christian prayer. Prayer attends to the grace we need for meritorious actions.

JOHN PAUL II
ENCYCLICAL LETTER *VERITATIS SPLENDOR*
(6 August, 1993)

Only through the gift of God can the human person follow and imitate Christ. That gift which makes the following of Christ possible is the very person of the Holy Spirit. The Spirit does not substitute for our freedom but brings about and sustains our free response to the love of God.

(The Holy Spirit source of our love)

2000e 22. To imitate and live out the love of Christ is not possible for the human being by one's own strength alone. One becomes capable of this love only by virtue of a gift received. As the Lord receives the love of his Father, so he in turn freely communicates that love to his disciples: "As the Father has loved me, so have I loved you; abide in my love" [*Jn 15:9*]. Christ's gift is his Spirit, whose first "fruit" [*cf. Gal 5:22*] is charity: "God's love has been poured into our hearts through the Holy Spirit which has been given to us" [*Rom 5:5*].

2000f 24. Precisely the awareness of having received the gift, of possessing in Jesus Christ the love of God, generates and sustains the free response of a full love for God and our fellow Christians, as the apostle John insistently reminds us in his first Letter: "Beloved, let us love one another; for love is of God, and he who loves is born of God and knows God. He who does not love does not know God; for God is love. [...] Beloved, if God so loved us, we also ought to love one another.[...] We love, because he first loved us" *[1 Jn 4: 7-8, 11, 19]*.

APOSTOLIC LETTER *TERTIO MILLENNIO ADVENIENTE*
(10 November 1994)

The event of the Incarnation attests and justifies the need to celebrate a jubilee at the end of the second millennium of Christianity. John Paul II dwells on God's initiative as regards humanity's millennium of Christianity. John Paul II dwells on God's initiative as regards humanity's communion with him: it is God himself who "goes in search of humankind [...] because he loves them eternally in the Word" (n. 2000g). Whenever the person does respond, the immediate effects of God's action consist of abandoning and overcoming evil—redemption—and "dwelling in the immost life of God"—grace. The magisterium continues in its efforts (a) to refound its theology of sanctifying grace on revelation and reinterpret it in the light of the Christ event, (b) insist on its communitarian and personalistic dimensions, and (c) recuperate a dynamic understanding of grace as the process of divinisation. From patristic times, the Churches of the East consistently turn to the last point as the key to interpret and fathom the life of grace, while in Western Christianity, it needs to be sustained and developed further.

The text can be found in AAS 87 (1994), pp. 5-41; Origins 24 (1994), pp. 401ff.

(God in search of the human person)

2000g 7. *In Jesus Christ* God not only speaks to humankind but also *seeks it out*. The Incarnation of the Son of God attests that God goes in search of humankind. Jesus speaks of this search as the finding of a lost sheep [*cf. Lk 15:1-7*]. It is a search which *begins in the heart of God* and culminates in the Incarnation of the Word. If God goes in search of human beings, created in his own image and likeness, he does so because he loves them eternally in the Word, and wishes to raise them in Christ to the dignity of adoptive children. God therefore goes in search of one who is his special possession in a way unlike any other creature. The human being is God's possession by virtue of a choice made in love: God seeks one out, moved by his fatherly heart.

Why does God seek the human person out? Because one has turned away from him, hiding oneself as Adam did among the trees of the Garden of Eden [*cf. Gen 3:8-10*]. *He allowed himself to be led astray* by the enemy of God [*cf. Gen 3:13*]. Satan deceived him, persuading him that he too was a god, that he, like God, was capable of knowing good and evil, ruling the world according to his own will without having to take into account the divine will [*cf. Gen 3:5*]. Going in search of humankind through his Son, God wishes to persuade them to abandon the paths of evil which lead them farther and farther afield. "Making them abandon" those paths means making them understand that they are taking the wrong path; it means *overcoming the evil* which is everywhere found in human history. *Overcoming evil: this is the meaning of the Redemption.* This is brought about in the sacrifice of Christ, by which humankind redeems the debt of sin and is reconciled to God. The Son of God became man, taking a body and soul in the womb of the Virgin, precisely for this reason: to become the perfect redeeming sacrifice. The religion of the Incarnation is the *religion* of the world's *Redemption* through the sacrifice of Christ, wherein lies victory over evil, over sin and over death itself. Accepting death on the Cross, Christ at the same time reveals and gives life, because he rises again and death no longer has power over him.

(Dwelling in the heart of God)

2000h 8. The religion which originates in the mystery of the Redemptive Incarnation, is the religion of *"dwelling in the heart of God"*, of sharing in God's very life. Saint Paul speaks of this in the passage already quoted: "God has sent the Spirit of his Son into our hearts, crying, 'Abba! Father!'" [*Gal 4:6*]. Humankind cries out like Christ himself, who turned to God "with loud cries and tears" [*Heb 5:7*], especially in Gethsemane and on the Cross: it cries out to God just as Christ cried out to him, and thus it bears witness that it shares in Christ's sonship through the power of the Holy Spirit. The Holy Spirit, whom the Father has sent in the name of the Son, enables humankind to share in the inmost life of God. He also enables them *to be a son, in the likeness of Christ,* and an heir of all that belongs to the Son [*cf. Gal 4:7*]. In this consists the religion of "dwelling in the inmost life of God", which begins with the Incarnation of the Son of God. The Holy Spirit, who searches the depths of God

[cf. 1 Cor 2:10], leads us, all humankind, into these depths by
virtue of the sacrifice of Christ.

ENCYCLICAL LETTER *EVANGELIUM VITAE*
(25 March 1995)

"Life is always a good": *John Paul II restates the fundamental message of
his encyclical at the beginning of paragraph 34. He adds: "This is an instinctive
perception and a fact of experience, and human persons are called to grasp the
profound reason why this is so." To help the believer do that, he reflects on
the Genesis accounts of creation (34 and 35; cf. n. 524i) and then draws his
conclusions on our human condition: the multifaceted presence of sin and
new life in Christ (36). He then reflects on Christ's gift of life which consists
of "existence in time" and its "divine dimensions": "eternal life already springs
forth and begins to grow" in our existence on earth. Justification, therefore, is
to be understood in the light of God's twofold gift of life, as it projects the
former towards the latter, while enabling the latter—i.e. eternal life—to give
meaning to the former. The text of the encyclical is in* Origins 24 (1995), pp.
689-727.

*("Called ... to be conformed to the image of his Son"—Rom 8:28-29:
God's glory shines on the face of the human person)*

(2000i) *(See text under n. 524)*

*("Whoever lives and believes in me shall never die"—Jn 11:26: the gift
of eternal life)*

2000j   37. The life which the Son of God came to give to
human beings cannot be reduced to mere existence in
time. The life which was always "in him" and which is the "light
of men" *[Jn 1:4]* consists *in being begotten of God and sharing in the
fullness of his love:* "To all who received him, who believed in his
name, he gave power to become children of God; who were born,
not of blood nor of the will of the flesh nor of the will of man,
but of God" *[Jn 1:12-13]*.

Sometimes Jesus refers to this life which he came to give
simply as "life", and he presents being born of God as a necessary
condition if one is to attain the end for which God has created
them: "Unless one is born anew, he cannot see the kingdom of
God" *[Jn 3:3]*. To give this life is the real object of Jesus' mission:
he is the one who "comes down from heaven, and gives life to
the world" *[Jn 6:33]*. Thus can he truly say: "He who follows me
[...] will have the light of life" *[Jn 8:12]*.

At other times, Jesus speaks of "eternal life". Here the

adjective does more than merely evoke a perspective which is beyond time. The life which Jesus promises and gives is "eternal" because it is a full participation in the life of the "Eternal One". Whoever believes in Jesus and enters into communion with him has eternal life [cf. Jn 3:15; 6:40] because one hears from Jesus the only words which reveal and communicate to one's existence the fullness of life. These are the "words of eternal life" which Peter acknowledges in his confession of faith: "Lord, to whom shall we go? You have the words of eternal life; and we have believed, and have come to know, that you are the Holy One of God" [Jn 6:68-69]. Jesus himself, addressing the Father in the great priestly prayer, declares what eternal life consists in: "This is eternal life, that they may know you the only true God, and Jesus Christ whom you have sent" [Jn 17:3]. To know God and his Son is to accept the mystery of the loving communion of the Father, the Son and the Holy Spirit into one's own life, which *even now* is open to eternal life because it shares in the life of God.

38. Eternal life is therefore the life of God himself and at the same time the life of the children of God. As they ponder this unexpected and inexpressible truth which comes to us from God in Christ, believers cannot fail to be filled with ever new wonder and unbounded gratitude. They can say in the words of the Apostle John: "See what love the Father has given us, that we should be called children of God; and so we are. Beloved, we are God's children now; it does not yet appear what we shall be, but we know that when he appears we shall be like him, for we shall see him as he is" [1 Jn 3:1-2].

Here the Christian truth about life becomes most sublime. The dignity of this life is linked not only to its beginning, to the fact that it comes from God, but also to its final end, to its destiny of fellowship with God in knowledge and love of him. In the light of this truth Saint Irenaeus qualifies and completes his praise of man: "the glory of God" is indeed, "man, living man", but "the life of man consists in the vision of God" ["*Vita autem hominis visio Dei*": Adversus Haereses IV, 20, 7, SCh 100/2, 648-649].

Immediate consequences arise from this for human life in its *earthly state*, in which, for that matter, eternal life already springs forth and begins to grow. Although the human person instinctively loves life because it is a good, this love will find further inspiration and strength, and new breadth and depth, in the divine dimensions of this good. Similarly, the love which every human being has for life cannot be reduced simply to a desire to have sufficient space for self-expression and for entering into relationships with others; rather, it develops in a joyous awareness that life can become the "place" where God manifests himself, where we meet him and enter into communion with him. The life which Jesus gives in no way lessens the value of our existence in time; it takes it and directs it to its final destiny: "I am the resurrection and the life [...]; whoever lives and believes in me shall never die" [Jn 11:25-26].

THE LUTHERAN WORLD FEDERATION AND THE CATHOLIC CHURCH JOINT DECLARATION ON THE DOCTRINE OF JUSTIFICATION
(31 October 1999)

The Joint Declaration on Justification addresses one of the major theological issues in the crisis that led to the Lutheran Reformation and the Council of Trent, in the 16th century. Taking into account the Lutheran-Roman Catholic dialogue since the Second Vatican Council (Preamble: 1-7), the document reiterates the Biblical understanding of justification (Part 1: 8-12) and then, keeping in mind its ecumenical implications (Part 2:13), traces an outline of the doctrine that is common to both Catholics and Lutherans (Part 3: 14-18). It then enumerates the main topics involved and explicates the divergences that, in reality, account for the depth and the richness of the theme under discussion (Part IV: 19-39). The conclusion (Part V: 40-44) deals with the significance and the scope of the consensus attained through the Joint Declaration.

The document therefore proposes "a consensus in the basic truths" with which "the differing explications in particular statements are compatible" (14). The document constitutes a "decisive step forward on the way to overcoming the division of the church". The signatories beseech "the Holy Spirit to lead" them "further toward that visible unity which is Christ's will" (44). The text of the document is carried in Origins 28(1998), pp. 120-127. *A presentation of the document and the speeches accompanying its signing can be found in* Origins 29 (1999), pp. 341,343-349. *See also n. 940 for the Official Common Statement on the Joint Declaration.*

(The Common Understanding of Justification)

2000k 15. In faith we together hold the conviction that justification is the work of the triune God. The Father sent his Son into the world to save sinners. The foundation and presupposition of justification is the incarnation, death, and resurrection of Christ. Justification thus means that Christ himself is our righteousness, in which we share through the Holy Spirit in accord with the will of the Father. Together we confess: By grace alone, in faith in Christ's saving work and not because of any merit on our part, we are accepted by God and receive the Holy Spirit, who renews our hearts while equipping and calling us to good works ("All Under One Christ", para.14, in *Growth in Agreement*, 241-247).

16. All people are called by God to salvation in Christ. Through Christ alone are we justified, when we receive this salvation in faith. Faith is itself God's gift through the Holy Spirit who works through word and sacrament in the community of believers and who, at the same time, leads believers into that renewal of life which God will bring to completion in eternal life.

17. We also share the conviction that the message of justification directs us in a special way towards the heart of the New Testament witness to God's saving action in Christ: it tells us that as sinners our new life is solely due to the forgiving and renewing mercy that God imparts as a gift and we receive in faith, and never can merit in any way.

18. Therefore the doctrine of justification, which takes up this message and explicates it, is more than just one part of Christian doctrine. It stands in an essential relation to all truths of faith, which are to be seen as internally related to each other. It is an indispensable criterion which constantly serves to orient all the teaching and practice of our churches to Christ. When Lutherans emphasize the unique significance of this criterion, they do not deny the interrelation and significance of all truths of faith. When Catholics see themselves as bound by several criteria, they do not deny the special function of the message of justification. Lutherans and Catholics share the goal of confessing Christ in all things, who alone is to be trusted above all things as the one Mediator *(1 Tim 2:5f)* through whom God in the Holy Spirit gives himself and pours out his renewing gifts.

(Human Powerlessness and Sin in Relation to Justification)

2000l 19. We confess together that all persons depend completely on the saving grace of God for their salvation. The freedom they possess in relation to persons and the things of this world is no freedom in relation to salvation, for as sinners they stand under God's judgment and are incapable of turning by themselves to God to seek deliverance, of meriting their justification before God, or of attaining salvation by their own abilities. Justification takes place solely by God's grace. Because Catholics and Lutherans confess this together, it is true to say:

20. When Catholics say that persons "cooperate" in preparing for and accepting justification by consenting to God's justifying action, they see such personal consent as itself an effect of grace, not as an action arising from innate human abilities.

21. According to Lutheran teaching, human beings are incapable of cooperating in their salvation, because as sinners they actively oppose God and his saving action. Lutherans do not deny that a person can reject the working of grace. When they emphasize that a person can only receive (mere passive) justification, they mean thereby to exclude any possibility of contributing to one's own justification, but do not deny that believers are fully involved personally in their faith, which is effected by God's Word.

(Justification as Forgiveness of Sins and Making Righteous)

2000m 22. We confess together that God forgives sin by grace and at the same time frees human beings from sin's enslaving power and imparts the gift of new life in Christ. When persons come by faith to share in Christ, God no longer imputes to them their sin and through the Holy Spirit effects in them an active love. These two aspects of God's gracious action are not to be separated, for persons are by faith united with Christ, who in his person is our righteousness *(1 Cor 1:30)*: both the forgiveness of sin and the saving presence of God himself. Because Catholics and Lutherans confess this together, it is true to say that:

23. When Lutherans emphasize that the righteousness of Christ is our righteousness, their intention is above all to insist that the sinner is granted righteousness before God in Christ through the declaration of forgiveness and that only in union with Christ is one's life renewed. When they stress that God's grace is forgiving love ('the favour of God'), they do not thereby deny the renewal of the Christian's life. They intend rather to express that justification remains free from human cooperation and is not dependent on the life-renewing effects of grace in human beings.

24. When Catholics emphasize the renewal of the interior person through the reception of grace imparted as a gift to the believer *(cf. n. 1932)*, they wish to insist that God's forgiving grace always brings with it a gift of new life, which in the Holy Spirit becomes effective in active love. They do not thereby deny that God's gift of grace in justification remains independent of human cooperation.

(Justification by Faith and through Grace)

2000n 25, We confess together that sinners are justified by faith in the saving action of God in Christ. By the action of the Holy Spirit in baptism, they are granted the gift of salvation, which lays the basis for the whole Christian life. They place their trust in God's gracious promise by justifying faith, which includes hope in God and love for him. Such a faith is active in love and thus the Christian cannot and should not remain without works. But whatever in the justified precedes or follows the free gift of faith is neither the basis of justification nor merits it.

26. According to Lutheran understanding, God justifies sinners in faith alone *(sola fide)*. In faith they place their trust wholly in their Creator and redeemer and thus live in communion with him. God himself effects faith as he brings forth such trust by his creative word. God's act is a new creation, it affects all dimensions of the persons and leads to a life in hope and love. In the doctrine of "justification by faith alone", a distinction but not a separation is made between justification itself and the renewal of one's way of life that necessarily follows from justification and without which faith does not exist. Thereby the basis is indicated from which the renewal of life proceeds, for it comes forth from the love of God imparted to the person in justification. Justification and renewal are joined in Christ, who is present in faith.

27. The Catholic understanding also sees faith as fundamental in justification. For without faith, no justification can take place. Persons are justified through baptism as hearers of the word and believers in it. The justification of sinners is forgiveness of sins and being made righteous by justifying grace, which makes us children of God. In justification the righteous receive from Christ faith, hope, and love and are thereby taken into communion with him *(cf.n.1933)*. This new personal relation to God is grounded totally on God's graciousness and remains constantly dependent

on the salvific and creative working of this gracious God, who remains true to himself, so that one can rely upon him. Thus justifying grace never becomes a human possession to which one could appeal over against God. While Catholic teaching emphasizes the renewal of life by justifying grace, this renewal in faith, hope, and love is always dependent on God's unfathomable grace and contributes nothing to justification about which one could boast before God *(Rom 3:27)*.

(The Justified as Sinner)

2000o 28. We confess together that in baptism the Holy Spirit unites one with Christ, justifies, and truly renews the person. But the justified must all through life constantly look to God's unconditional justifying grace. They also are continuously exposed to the power of sin still pressing its attacks (cf. *Rom 6:12-14*) and are not exempt from a lifelong struggle against the contradiction to God within the selfish desires of the old Adam *(cf. Gal 5:16; Rom 7:7-10)*. The justified also must ask God daily for forgiveness as in the Lord's Prayer *(Mt 6:12; 1 Jn 1:91)*, are ever again called to conversion and penance, and are ever again granted forgiveness.

29. Lutherans understand this condition of the Christian as a being "at the same time righteous and sinner". Believers are totally righteous, in that God forgives their sins through Word and Sacrament and grants the righteousness of Christ which they appropriate in faith. In Christ, they are made just before God. Looking at themselves through the law, however, they recognize that they remain also totally sinners. Sin still lives in them *(1 Jn 1:8; Rom 7:17,20)*, for they repeatedly turn to false gods and do not love God with that undivided love which God requires as their Creator *(Deut 6:5; Mt 22:36-40 pr.)*. This contradiction to God is as such truly sin. Nevertheless, the enslaving power of sin is broken on the basis of the merit of Christ. It no longer is a sin that "rules" the Christian for it is itself "ruled" by Christ with whom the justified are bound in faith. In this life, then, Christians can in part lead a just life. Despite sin, the Christian is no longer separated from God, because in the daily return to baptism, the person who has been born anew by baptism and the Holy Spirit has this sin forgiven. Thus this sin no longer brings damnation and eternal death(*cf. Apology* II:38-45; *Book of Concord*, 105f). Thus, when Lutherans say that justified persons

are also sinners and that their opposition to God is truly sin, they do not deny that, despite this sin, they are not separated from God and that this sin is a "ruled" sin. In these affirmations, they are in agreement with Roman Catholics, despite the difference in understanding sin in the justified.

30. Catholics hold that the grace of Jesus Christ imparted in baptism takes away all that is sin "in the proper sense" and that is "worthy of damnation" *(Rom 8:1: cf.n. 512)*. There does, however, remain in the person an inclination (concupiscence) which comes from sin and presses toward sin. Since, according to Catholic conviction, human sins always involve a personal element and since this element is lacking in this inclination, Catholics do not see this inclination as sin in an authentic sense. They do not thereby deny that this inclination does not correspond to God's original design for humanity and that it is objectively in contradiction to God and remains one's enemy in lifelong struggle. Grateful for deliverance by Christ, they underscore that this inclination in contradiction to God does not merit the punishment of eternal death *(cf. n. 512)* and does not separate the justified person from God. But when individuals voluntarily separate themselves from God, it is not enough to return to observing the commandments, for they must receive pardon and peace in the Sacrament of Reconciliation through the word of forgiveness imparted to them in virtue of God's reconciling work in Christ.

(Law and Gospel)

2000p 31. We confess together that persons are justified by faith in the gospel "apart from works prescribed by the law" *(Rom 3:28)*. Christ has fulfilled the law and by his death and resurrection has overcome it as a way to salvation. We also confess that God's commandments retain their validity for the justified and that Christ has by his teaching and example expressed God's will which is a standard for the conduct of the justified also.

32. Lutherans state that the distinction and right ordering of law and gospel is essential for the understanding of justification. In its theological use, the law is demand and accusation. Throughout their lives, all persons, Christians also, in that they are sinners, stand under this accusation which uncovers their sin so that, in faith in the gospel, they will turn unreservedly to the mercy of God in Christ, which alone justifies them.

33. Because the law as a way to salvation has been fulfilled and overcome through the gospel, Catholics can say that Christ is not a lawgiver in the manner of Moses. When Catholics emphasize that the righteous are bound to observe God's commandments, they do not thereby deny that through Jesus Christ God has mercifully promised to his children the grace of eternal life (cf. n.1946).

(Assurance of Salvation)

2000q   34. We confess together that the faithful can rely on the mercy and promises of God. In spite of their own weakness and the manifold threats to their faith, on the strength of Christ's death and resurrection they can build on the effective promise of God's grace in Word and Sacrament and so be sure of this grace.

35. This was emphasized in a particular way by the Reformers: in the midst of temptation, believers should not look to themselves but look solely to Christ and trust only him. In trust in God's promise they are assured of their salvation, but are never secure looking at themselves.

36. Catholics can share the concern of the Reformers to ground faith in the objective reality of Christ's promise, to look away from one's own experience, and to trust in Christ's forgiving word alone (cf. Mt 16:19; 18:18). With the Second Vatican Council, Catholics state: to have faith is to entrust oneself totally to God (DV 5), who liberates us from the darkness of sin and death and awakens us to eternal life (DV 5). In this sense, one cannot believe in God and at the same time consider the divine promise untrustworthy. No one may doubt God's mercy and Christ's merit. Every person, however, may be concerned about one's salvation when one looks upon one's own weaknesses and shortcomings. Recognizing one's own failure, however, the believer may yet be certain that God intends one's salvation.

(The Good Works of the Justified)

2000r   37. We confess together that good works—a Christian life lived in faith, hope and love—follow justification and are its fruits. When the justified live in Christ and act in the grace they receive, they bring forth, in biblical terms, good fruit. Since Christians struggle against sin their entire lives, this consequence of justification is also for them an obligation they must fulfil. Thus both Jesus and the apostolic Scriptures admonish Christians to bring forth the works of love.

38. According to Catholic understanding, good works, made possible by grace and the working of the Holy Spirit, contribute to growth in grace, so that the righteousness that comes from God is preserved and communion with Christ is deepened. When Catholics affirm the "meritorious" character of good works, they wish to say that, according to the biblical witness, a reward in heaven is promised to these works. Their intention is to emphasize the responsibility of persons for their actions, not to contest the character of those works as gifts, or far less to deny that justification always remains the unmerited gift of grace.

39. The concept of preservation of grace and a growth in grace and faith is also held by Lutherans. They do emphasize that righteousness as acceptance by God and sharing in the righteousness of Christ is always complete. At the same time, they state that there can be growth in its effects in Christian living. When they view the good works of Christians as the fruits and signs of justification and not as one's own "merits", they nevertheless also understand eternal life in accord with the New Testament as unmerited "reward" in the sense of the fulfilment of God's promise to the believer.

(The Significance and Scope of the Consensus Reached)

2000s 40. The understanding of the doctrine of justification set forth in this Declaration shows that a consensus in basic truths of the doctrine of justification exists between Lutherans and Catholics. In light of this consensus the remaining differences of language, theological elaboration, and emphasis in the understanding of justification described in paras. 18 to 39 are acceptable. Therefore the Lutheran and the Catholic explications of justification are in their difference open to one another and do not destroy the consensus regarding the basic truths.

41. Thus the doctrinal condemnations of the 16th century, in so far as they relate to the doctrine of justification, appear in a new light: The teaching of the Lutheran churches presented in this Declaration does not fall under the condemnations from the Council of Trent. The condemnations in the Lutheran Confessions do not apply to the teaching of the Roman Catholic Church presented in this Declaration.

42. Nothing is thereby taken away from the seriousness of the condemnations related to the doctrine of justification. Some were not simply pointless. They remain for us "salutary warnings" to which we must attend in our teaching and practice (*Condemnations of the Reformation Era*, 27).

43. Our consensus in basic truths of the doctrine of justification must come to influence the life and teachings of our churches. Here it must prove itself. In this respect, there are still questions of varying importance which need further clarification. These include, among other topics, the relationship between the Word of God and church doctrine, as well as ecclesiology, ecclesial authority, church unity, ministry, the sacraments, and the relation between justification and social ethics. We are convinced that the consensus we have reached offers a solid basis for this clarification. The Lutheran churches and the Roman Catholic Church will continue to strive together to deepen this common understanding of justification and to make it bear fruit in the life and teaching of the churches.

CHAPTER XX

PRINCIPLES OF CHRISTIAN LIFE

In baptism the Christian has been sacramentally conformed to the mystery of Christ's death and resurrection and dedicated to God as a member of the Church. Christian living must carry out day by day this fundamental consecration. The Christian life consists essentially in the following of Christ through the perfection of charity. Each Christian lives this life not as an isolated individual person but as a member of the Christian community which constitutes the People of God willed by him and established by Christ to act in the human race as a leaven, to be the living sign of God's kindness towards men and women and to witness to their divine destiny. Hence, the Christian life is by nature a testimony; it implies for all Christians a call to perfection and holiness to which each must respond according to his or her own charism, in the state of life God has destined for each, either lay or religious. This is to say that in Christian morality there is no minimum standard laid down; rather, every Christian is summoned to grow daily in the love of God and in the love of people and to unify these two loves.

Though the Christian life is based on fundamental principles which go far beyond the natural demands of morality, it builds upon these demands which it brings to their perfection. This is why the Church has always been concerned with upholding the existence of a natural law, based on the dignity of the human person and inscribed in the heart by God, the Creator and last end. She has stressed human responsibility to obey this law in a free assent and according to the dictates of conscience; she has through the centuries explained the implications of this law in the various spheres of human life. In this process, the Church has often been led to react against two opposite extreme tendencies: on the one hand, a pessimistic and rigorist conception of human life, denying our ability to do good; on the other hand, liberalism and laxism, emancipating us from law and objective norms of moral conduct. Thus, the Church has greatly contributed to defending and preserving the most fundamental human values. If her official documents often have a negative form, the reason is that they are directly intended to meet concrete threats to the moral and spiritual order and to human dignity. It must, however, be admitted that the Church documents are not always free of a certain legalistic approach which has long characterised the elaboration of moral doctrine.

As to the specifically Christian principles of human conduct, they are poorly represented in some official documents which deal with Christian morality in a general way. Intimately connected as these principles are with life itself, they have often been taken for granted rather than explicitly stated by the Church's teaching office. Besides the life of the Church, the main source for her teaching on Christian living remains her doctrinal documents on the Christian faith itself, especially her doctrine on our salvation through Christ, on the life of grace and on the sacraments, the Eucharist in particular, which have been dealt with in previous chapters.

In recent decades, however, papal encyclicals have brought out more explicitly the implications of the faith for the Christian life. These documents witness to the fact that legalism in Christian morality has largely been overcome and that a return to the radical demands of the Gospel is felt as a pressing need. The doctrine of the Second Vatican Council reflects this new spirit, its moral teaching being characterised by a positive appeal to all Christians as members of the People of God to live up to their high calling in all the spheres of human life.

Pope John Paul II, while upholding a person-centred approach has thought fit to recall the traditional notions of moral absolutes and intrinsically evil actions. He has also pointed out that science and technology are to be at the service of the human person and that the magisterium has the role of expounding criteria for judgment regarding their application, especially in relation to human life and its beginnings. He has explained the different senses in which social sin could be rightly understood, insisting that sin is primarily personal.

On the occasion of the promulgation of the New Code of Canon Law (1983), the Pope explains the role of law in Christian life and outlines the principles of its interpretation.

*   *   *

The main points dealt with in this chapter are the following :

The human person has a unique dignity: 2011, 2027, 2051, 2056f.
This dignity brings with it rights and duties: 2028-2042.
Human persons are social by nature: 2054

This social character also entails rights and obligations: 2055, 2058.
Human dignity is shown mostly in the exercise of moral freedom: 2053
Though impaired by sin, human freedom is not destroyed: 1929, 1954-1957, 1987/27ff, 1989/1ff, (2002)
The human person as individual and in groups has a right to religious liberty: 2048-2050.
In the exercise of moral freedom persons must obey the dictates of conscience: 2052
Human conscience reveals the natural law, inscribed by God in nature, which we must obey: 2008/2, 2012, 2020, 2022-2025, 2026, 2059, 2080b.
Invincible error is possible: 2009/2;
without loss of dignity: 2080d.
It is licit to follow a probable opinion, though not a tenuous one: 2006/3, 2009/3.
Human laws made by a legitimate authority in conformity with the natural law must be obeyed: 2005, 2010/56.63, 2013.
Church law is to foster development of ecclesial society and the human person: 2066.
Its interpretation must take into account the mind of the legislator and the reason of the law: 2066.
Moral evil can be tolerated but not willed: 2014.
There are absolute norms and intrinsically evil acts: 2067, 2068-2069, 2082e.
All Christians, sharing the same dignity, are called to perfection: 2044, 2045
Charity is the essence of and the way to perfection: 2001, 2046, 2060
it includes the love of God and the love of others: 2021;
it goes beyond the demands of justice: 2019, 2161.
Active supernatural virtues must be practised: 2007/1ff, 2015-2018.
The laity must seek Christian perfection according to their specific vocation: 2043;
they are called to moral responsibility: 2061.
The religious profession is a specific vocation in the Church implying a special call to holiness: 2047.
A fundamental option defines a person's moral disposition: 2062 2081a.
Mortal sin is a serious violation of the order of love: 2063, 2067d.
Loss of the sense of sin is to be deplored: 2067e.
Social sin ultimately derives from personal sin: 2067b.
Science and technology are to be at the service of the human person: 2071.

The magisterium expands the criteria for their application: 2070.

Within the tradition, the interpretation of the moral law develops: 2072a.

There is a difference between the deposit of the truth of faith and the manner of its expression: 2072b.

The magisterium does not impose a particular system: 2072c.

Conscience applies universal knowledge to a particular situation: 2073, 2080b.

God's law does not reduce but promotes freedom: 2074.

An incorrect interpretation of autonomous reason is rejected: 2075a.

There is a rightful autonomy of the person: 2075b.

The new law is the interior law of the Spirit: 2076.

The unity of the human person: 2077.

It is an error to dissociate the moral act from its bodily dimensions: 2078.

The natural law refers to the nature of the person: 2079.

An incorrect and correct understanding of "creative conscience": 2080a.

The verdict of conscience is a pledge of mercy: 2080c.

Separating fundamental option from concrete behaviour and choice is against Catholic doctrine: 2081b, 2081c.

The theories of proportionalism and consequentialism are mistaken: 2082a, 2082b, 2082c, 2082d, 2082e.

The moral life sometimes calls for heroic commitment : 2083

Moral norms are not decided by empirical surveys or democratic processes: 2084a, 2084b.

Dissent, when organised and public, is against ecclesial communication: 2085.

The responsibilities of Bishops regarding Catholic institutions: 2086.

The place of philosophy in moral theology: 2087.

JOHN XXII
BULL *AD CONDITOREM* (1322)

In his Bull Ad Conditorem *to the Friars Minor on their poverty, Pope John XXII has this incidental sentence which seems to be the first expression, in an official document, of the essential role of charity in Christian perfection.*

(Charity is the essence of perfection)

2001 [...] The perfection of Christian life consists principally and essentially in charity, which is called by the apostle the bond of perfection [*cf. Col 3:14*] and somehow unites or joins the human being with its end.[...]

THE GENERAL COUNCIL OF TRENT
SIXTH SESSION
DECREE ON JUSTIFICATION (1547)

(2002) *In its decree on justification, the Council of Trent has defined the existence and reality of human liberty. In the process of justification the human person freely assents to, and cooperates with grace and thus disposes and prepares oneself to obtain justification. One can also dissent and refuse grace and is thus responsible for making one's ways evil (cf. text in nn. 1929, 1954, 1956). The person's free will was not destroyed by original sin (cf. text in nn. 1925, 1929, 1955); the moral acts that one performs before one's justification are not necessarily sinful (cf. text in n. 1957).*

ALEXANDER VII
ERRORS OF LAXIST MORALITY CONDEMNED BY THE HOLY OFFICE (1605)

Among other propositions condemned as at least causing scandal, one is concerned with obedience to civil law.

(Obedience to civil law)

[2005] People do not sin even if, without any reason, they
2048   do not accept the law promulgated by the ruler.

INNOCENT XI
ERRORS OF LAXIST MORALITY CONDEMNED BY THE HOLY OFFICE (1679)

The following proposition is condemned as at least causing scandal and harmful in practice.

(On probabilism)

[2006/3] Speaking in general, we are always acting prudently
2103   whenever we do something relying on an intrinsic
     or extrinsic probability, tenuous as this may be,
provided we do not go beyond the limits of what is probable.

CONSTITUTION *CAELESTIS PASTOR* (1687)

PROPOSITIONS OF MICHAEL MOLINOS CONDEMNED

     By this Constitution, Pope Innocent XI confirmed the condemnation of
68 propositions of M. Molinos, already condemned the same year by a decree
of the Holy Office. All the condemned propositions are related to Molinos'
false quietism which excluded from the spiritual life every moral effort. For
the propositions quoted below, the highest censures affixed by the theologians
of the Holy Office are as follows: 14 is condemned as heretical; 2, 4, 5 as
smacking of heresy.

(On quietism)

[2007/1] It is necessary that [one] reduce [one's] powers to
2201   nothingness and in this consists the interior way.

[2007/2] The will to work actively is an offence to God, who
2202   wishes to be himself the sole agent; and, therefore,
     one must totally abandon one's whole self in God
and thereafter remain like a lifeless body.

[2007/4] Natural activity is the enemy of grace and it hinders
2204   God's action and true perfection, because God
     wishes to act in us without us.

[2007/5] By doing nothing the soul annihilates itself and
2205   returns to its principle and to its origin, which is
     the essence of God, in which it remains transformed
and divinised, and God then remains in himself; because then
there are no longer two things which are united but only one,
and in this way, God lives and reigns in us and the soul
annihilates itself as far as its active being is concerned.

[207/14] For one who is resigned to the divine will it is not
2214   proper to ask anything from God; because asking
     is an imperfection, since it is an act of one's own
will and choice, and it is to wish that the divine will be
conformed to our own, and not our own to the divine will; and

the passage of the Gospel saying:"Ask and you will receive" *[Jn 16:24]* was not said by Christ for interior souls who refuse to have a will; moreover, these kinds of souls reach the point when they cannot ask anything from God.

ALEXANDER VIII
DECREE OF THE HOLY OFFICE (24 August, 1690)

Of the two propositions condemned in this decree, the following is considered as causing scandal and erroneous.

(On philosophical sin)

[2008/2]   A philosophical or moral sin is a human act which
2291   does not agree with rational nature and the right
           reason: a theological and mortal sin is the free
transgression of the divine law. A philosophical sin, however grievous it may be, if committed by one who either does not know God, or does not actually think of God, is a grievous sin but not an offence against God; nor is it a mortal sin which breaks off the friendship with God and deserves eternal punishment.

DECREE OF THE HOLY OFFICE (7 December, 1690)

This other decree of the Holy Office condemned, under the same Pope Alexander VIII, a number of Jansenist errors. The censure attached to those propositions, among which two are quoted here, varies from temerarious to heretical.

(On conscience in invincible ignorance about the natural law)

[2009/2]   Although there is such a thing as invincible
2302   ignorance about the natural law, this, in the state of
           fallen nature, does not excuse from formal sin anyone
acting out of ignorance.

(On probable opinion)

[2009/3]   It is not licit to follow a (probable) opinion, even
2303   the most probable among the probable ones.

PIUS IX
SYLLABUS OF CONDEMNED ERRORS (1864)

On this document, cf. n. 1013i. Among the errors condemned some are concerned with matters of morality, natural and Christian, notably the following three:

(On moral and human laws)

[2010/56]   The moral laws do not need a divine sanction, and
2956   it is not in the least required that human laws
             conform to the natural law, or receive from God their
binding force.

(On the nature of right)

[2010/59]   Right consists in a material fact; all the duties of
2959   human beings are an empty name, and all human
             deeds have the force of right.

(On submission to authority)

[2010/63]   It is licit to withhold obedience to, or even to rebel
2963   against, the legitimate rulers.

LEO XIII

ENCYCLICAL LETTER *LIBERTAS PRAESTANTISSIMUM*
(1888)

*In this encyclical, the Pope exposes the meaning of true freedom against
the doctrine of a certain liberalism according to which liberty consists in freedom
from law, with the result that every person has the right to believe and do
what pleases.*

(Dignity of the human person as free)

2011   Liberty, the highest of human endowments, being the
3245   portion only of intellectual or rational natures, confers
         on people their dignity; they are in the hand of their
counsel and have power over their actions.[...]

Such, then, being the condition of human liberty, it necessarily
stands in need of light and strength to direct its actions towards
good and to restrain them from evil. Without this the freedom
of our will would be our ruin. First of all there must be law;
that is, a fixed rule of teaching what must be done and what
must be avoided.[...] In one's free will, therefore, or in the moral
necessity for voluntary acts to be in accordance with reason lies
the very root of the necessity of law. Nothing more foolish can
be said or conceived than the idea that, because one is free by
nature, one is exempt from law. Were this the case, it would
follow that in order to be free we must be without reason;
whereas the truth is that we are bound to submit to law precisely

because we are free by our very nature. For law is the guide of the person's actions.[...]

(Nature of law)

2012 [...] First among all [laws] is the natural law, which is
3247 written and engraved in the mind of every human being
for it is the human reason itself, commanding to do right and forbidding sin. Nevertheless all prescriptions of human reason can have force of law only inasmuch as they are the voice and the interpreter of some higher power on which our reason and liberty necessarily depend. For, since the force of law consists in the imposing of obligations and the granting of rights, it is wholly founded on authority, that is, on a true power to fix duties and define rights, as also to assign the necessary sanctions of reward and punishment for each and all of its commands. But all this, clearly, cannot be found in human persons, as if, being their own supreme legislator, they themselves were laying down the norm for their actions. It follows, therefore, that the law of nature is the eternal law itself, implanted in rational creatures and inclining them to the right course of action and to their end; it is the eternal reason of God, the Creator and Ruler of the whole world.[...]

(Human law)

2013 What reason and natural law do for individuals, human
3248 law, promulgated for the common good of citizens, does
for persons in society. Among the laws established by human beings, some are concerned with what is good or bad by its very nature.[...] But such decrees by no means derive their origin from society; because just as society did not create human nature, so neither does it depend on society whether something is a good which befits human nature or an evil which is contrary to it. Rather, laws precede human society itself, and have their origin in the natural, and consequently in the eternal law.[...] There are other enactments of the civil authority, which do not follow immediately and directly, but somewhat remotely and indirectly, from the natural law; these determine many issues for which nature provides only in a general and indefinite way.[...] It is in the constitution of these particular rules of life, suggested by reason and prudence, and put forth by competent

authority, that human law, properly so called, consists, and in so far as human law is in conformity with the dictates of the natural law, it leads to what is good and deters from evil. From this it is manifest that the norm and rule of freedom lies entirely in the eternal law of God, not only for each individual but also for the community and human society.

(Tolerance)

2014 While the Church does not concede any right to
3251 anything save what is true and honest, she does not object to public authority tolerating what is at variance with truth and justice, for the sake of avoiding some greater evil or of obtaining or preserving some greater good. God himself, in his providence, though infinitely good and all-powerful, permits evil to exist in the world, partly in order that greater good may not be impeded, and partly that greater evil may not ensue. In the government of States it is sound to imitate the Ruler of the world; moreover, since human authority is powerless to prevent every evil, it has, as St. Augustine says, "to tolerate and leave unpunished many things which are rightly punished by divine Providence".[1] But if, under such circumstances, for the sake of the common good—and this is the ony legitimate reason— human law may or even must tolerate evil, it may not and must not approve or will evil in itself (*per se*), for evil, of itself, being the privation of good, is opposed to the common welfare which every legislator is bound to seek and defend to the best of one's ability. In this too, human law must endeavour to imitate God, who, in allowing evil to exist in the world, "neither wills evil to be done, nor wills evil not to be done, but wills to allow evil to be done, and this is good".[2] This sentence of the angelic Doctor contains in brief the doctrine concerning the permission of evil.

LETTER *TESTEM BENEVOLENTIAE* TO CARDINAL GIBBONS, ARCHBISHOP OF BALTIMORE (1899)

On the occasion of the publication of a life of Fr. I.T. Hecker by Fr. W. Elliot, in which ways of adapting Catholicism to modern conditions were proposed, a controversy arose, chiefly in Europe, about what was called "Americanism". It is to end this controversy that Pope Leo XIII wrote this

---

1. St. Augustine, *De libero arbitrio*, I, 41
2. St. Thomas Aquinas, *Summa theologica*, I, 19, 9, and 3.

letter to Cardinal Gibbons. It mostly condemns unsafe or false doctrinal trends bearing on Christian morality, without however disapproving either Fr. Hecker himself or his writings.

(On the contempt for supernatural and so-called "passive" virtues)

2015 It is chiefly in the practice of virtues that the help of the
3343 Holy Spirit is absolutely required. But those who are
enthusiastic about following the new trends exalt beyond measure the natural virtues as though these suited more aptly the manners and the needs of the present times, and as if it was preferable to possess them, because they render one more fit and more vigorous for action. It is hard to understand that those who are imbued with Christian wisdom could prefer natural virtues to supernatural ones and ascribe to them a greater efficacy and fruitfulness.[...]

2016 Intimately connected with this opinion about natural
3344 virtues is another one according to which the Christian
virtues as a whole are divided, as it were, into two classes: the passive ones, as they say, and the active ones; and they add that, while the former were more suited for the past ages, the latter agree better with the present times.[...] Now, that some Christian virtues are more appropriate to one time and some to another will only be held by one who does not remember the words of the apostle: "Those whom he foreknew he also predestined to be conformed to the image of his Son" [*Rom 8:29*]. The teacher and the model of all holiness is Christ; all those who wish to be admitted in the home of the blessed must be adapted to that rule. Now Christ does not change in the course of centuries, but he remains the same yesterday and today and for ever [*cf. Heb 13:8*]. Hence the saying applies to people of all ages: "Learn from me; for I am gentle and lowly in heart" [*Mt 11:29*]; and there is no period when Christ does not present himself to us made "obedient unto death" [*Phil 2:8*]; and this saying of the apostle is valid for all times: "Those who belong to Christ Jesus have crucified the flesh with its passions and desires" [*Gal 5:24*].

2017 From this kind of contempt for the evangelical virtues,
3345 wrongly called passive, it was likely to follow that a
disregard for the religious life would also gradually pervade the minds. and that this is commonly the case with the

champions of the new opinions, we gather from some of their sayings about the vows which are pronounced in religious orders. For they say that these vows are very remote from the spirit of our time inasmuch as they restrict the field of liberty; that they are suited to the weak souls rather than to the strong ones; and that they have absolutely no value to foster Christian perfection and the good of human society, but are rather an obstacle and a hindrance to both.[...]

2018   From what we have dealt with up to now, it is clear
3346   that those opinions which, taken as a whole, some
           designate as "Americanism", cannot have our approval.

PIUS XI
ENCYCLICAL LETTER *QUADRAGESIMO ANNO* (1931)

In this encyclical on the social order (cf. nn. 2106ff), Pope Pius XI shows, in connection with social justice, the relationship which exists between the virtues of justice and charity: charity supposes that the demands of justice be respected, but it goes beyond them; the observance of justice does not by itself fulfil the Christian ideal.

(Justice and charity)

2019   [...] Charity which is "the bond of perfection" [*cf. Col*
           3:14] must always play a leading part. How completely deceived are those rash reformers who, satisfied with enforcing commutative justice, proudly disdain the help of charity! Certainly the practice of charity cannot be considered as taking the place of justice unfairly withheld. But, even though a state of things be pictured in which every person receives at last all that is one's due, a wide field will always remain open for charity. For justice alone, however faithfully observed, though it can indeed remove the cause of social strife, can never by its own power bring about a union of hearts and minds. Yet this spiritual bond which unites the members together is the main principle of stability in all institutions, no matter how perfect they may seem, which aim at establishing social peace and promoting mutual help among people. In its absence, as repeated experience proves, the wisest regulations come to nothing. Then only will it be possible to unite all in harmonious striving for the common good, when all sections of society have the intimate conviction that they are members of one great family, and children of the

same heavenly Father, and further, that they are "one body in Christ, and individually members one of another" [Rom 12:5], so that, "if one member suffers, all suffer together" [1 Cor 12:26].

PIUS XII

ENCYCLICAL LETTER *SUMMI PONTIFICATUS* (1939)

In this first encyclical of his pontificate, Pope Pius XII deplores the evils that flow from the growth of secularism. He considers their root to be the rejection of the natural law, of which he re-states the doctrine.

(Natural law)

2020
3780 It is certain that the first and deeper source from which derive the evils which afflict today's society is the strong denial and rejection of a universal norm of morality in the private life of individuals, as well as in public life and in the mutual relationships between people and nations; namely, the natural law is being undermined through criticism and disregard.

3781 This natural law has as its foundation God, the almighty Creator and Father of all, the supreme and perfect lawgiver, the most wise and just judge of human actions. When the eternal will is rashly denied, the foundation of all moral honesty crumbles, the voice of nature becomes silent and grows faint, that voice which teaches even the unlearned or those to whom civilisation has not yet penetrated, what is right and what is wrong, what is allowed and what is forbidden, and gives them awareness that one day they will have to give to the supreme judge an account of their good and evil deeds.

ENCYCLICAL LETTER *MYSTICI CORPORIS* (1943)

In his great Encyclical Letter on the mystery of the Church as the mystical Body of Christ (cf. nn. 847ff), Pope Pius XII shows the supreme role of the virtue of charity which surpassses faith and hope in creating ties between the members of the Church. He also shows how the love of God and of neighbour are inseparable.

(Charity surpasses all other virtues)

2021 [...]Charity, more than any other virtue, unites us closely with Christ.[...]Therefore our divine Saviour earnestly exhorts us: "Abide in my love." And because charity is a poor thing unless it is shown and as it were put into practice by good works, he immediately adds: "If you keep my commandments, you will abide in my love, just as I have kept my Father's commandments and abide in his love" [Jn 15:9-10].

But our love of God, our love of Christ, must be accompanied by a corresponding charity towards our neighbour. How can we say that we love the divine Redeemer if we hate those he has redeemed with his precious blood to make them members of his mystical Body? [...] Indeed it must be said that our union with God, our union with Christ, will become proportionately closer as we become more and more members one of another [cf. Rom 12:5], more and more mutually careful one for another [cf. 1 Cor 12:25]; and, similarly, our union with each other by charity will become more intimate as we cleave more ardently to God and our divine Head.

INSTRUCTION OF THE HOLY OFFICE ON "SITUATION ETHICS" (1956)

As explained in this document and as the name suggests, "Situation Ethics" rejects the absolute value of objective norms and places the ultimate criterion of morality in each one's personal intuitive judgment exercised in the concrete situation. Fundamentally it is based on the tenets of some currents of existentialist philosophy. It represents a reaction against too legalistic an approach which has often prevailed in matters of morality. At present it must be understood in the light of the current discussion on Moral Absolutes.

2022   Contrary to the moral doctrine and its application which
3918   is traditional in the Catholic Church, there has begun to be spread abroad in many regions even among Catholics an ethical system which generally goes by the name of a certain "Situation Ethics". This ethics, they say, does not depend on the principles of objective ethics (which is ultimately based on ontological categories); nor it is merely put on the same plane as objective ethics, but it is ranked above it. The authors who follow this system hold that the decisive and ultimate norm of conduct is not the objective right order, determined by the law of nature and known with certainty from that law, but a certain intimate judgment and light of the mind of each individual, by means of which, in the concrete situation in which one is placed, one learns what one ought to do. And so, according to them, this ultimate decision a person makes is not, as the objective ethics handed

down by authors of great weight teaches, the application of the objective law to a particular case, which at the same time takes into account and weighs according to the rules of prudence the particular circmstances of the "situation", but that immediate, internal light and judgment. Ultimately, at least in many matters, this judgment is not measured, must not and cannot be measured, as regards its objective rectitude and truth, by any objective norm situated outside the human being and independent of subjective persuasion, but is entirely self-sufficient.

2023 According to these authors, the traditional concept of
3919 "human nature" does not suffice; but recourse must be had to the concept of "existent" human nature which in many respects does not have absolute objective value, but only a relative and, therefore, changeable value, except, perhaps, for those few factors and principles which pertain to metaphysical (absolute and unchangeable) human nature. Of the same merely relative value is the traditional concept of the "law of nature". Thus, many things which are commonly considered today as absolute postulates of the natural law, according to their opinion and doctrine rest upon[...]the aforesaid concept of existent nature, and are, therefore, but relative and changeable; they can always be adapted to every situation.

2024 Having accepted these principles and put them into
3920 practice, they assert and teach that individuals are preserved or easily liberated from many otherwise insoluble ethical conflicts when each one judges in one's own conscience, not primarily according to objective laws, but by means of that internal, individual light based on personal intuition, what one must do in a concrete situation.

2025 Many of the things set forth in this system of " Situation
3921 Ethics" contradict the truth of the matter and the dictates of sound reason, betray traces of relativism and modernism, and wander far from the Catholic doctrine handed down through the centuries. In not a few assertions they are akin to various systems of non-Catholic ethics.

Having considered all this, in order to avert the danger of the "New Morality" of which the Supreme Pontiff Pope Pius XII spoke in the Allocutions delivered on March 23 and April 18,

1952,[1] and in order to safeguard the purity and safety of Catholic doctrine, this supreme Congregation of the Holy Office forbids and prohibits this doctrine of "Situation Ethics" by whatever name it be designated, to be taught or approved in universities, academies, seminaries and houses of formation of religious, or to be propagated and defended in books, dissertations, assemblies or, as they are called, conferences, or in any other manner whatever.

JOHN XXIII
ENCYCLICAL LETTER *PACEM IN TERRIS* (1963)

In this encyclical, Pope John XXIII reminds all people of good will that peace in the world can be established only if the moral order laid down by God is respected. The encyclical comprises four parts : 1) the rights and duties of the human person; 2) the relations between persons and the State; 3) the relations between States; 4) the relations between States and the world community. The document belongs to the series of great social encyclicals. The first part, however, dealing with the fundamental rights and duties of the person, comes under the scope of general principles of morality; quotations from this part are given here. For the application of these fundamental principles to the social order, cf. nn. 2124ff.

(Order imposed by God on human beings)

2026 [....] The Creator of the world has imprinted in the heart
3956 of human beings an order which their conscience reveals
to them and strongly enjoins them to obey : " They show that what the law requires is written on their hearts, while their conscience also bears witness" [*Rom 2:15*]

(Dignity of the person)

2027 The foundation of a well ordered and prosperous society
3957 lies in the principle that every human being is a person
endowed by nature with intelligence and free will. Hence each one has rights and duties of one's own, flowing directly and simultaneously from one's very nature and, therefore, universal, inviolable and inalienable.

If we look upon the dignity of the human person in the light of the divinely revealed truth, we cannot help but esteem it far more highly. For human beings are redeemed by the blood of

---

1. Cf. AAS 44 (1952) 270ff, 413ff

Jesus Christ; they are by grace the children and friends of God and heirs of eternal glory.

(Human rights)

2028   [....] Everyone has the right to life, to bodily integrity
3958   and to the means necessary and suitable for a decent
way of life. These are primarily food and clothing, shelter, rest, medical care and finally the necessary services which the State must provide for all. Therefore each one also has the right to security in case of sickness or inability to work, of widowhood or old age, of unemployment, or in any other case in which one is deprived of the means of subsistence through no fault of one's own.

2029   By the natural law, every one has also the right to
3959   respect for one's person and to good reputation, to
freedom in seeking for truth, in the expression and communication of one's opinions and in the pursuit of art, within the limits of the moral order and the common good; the right also to truthful information about public events.

2030   Again, natural law gives each one the right to share in
3960   the benefits of culture and, hence, the right to a basic
education and technical and professional training in keeping with the stage of educational development of one's country. Efforts must be made to enable people, on the basis of their ability, to go on to higher studies, so that, as far as possible, they may occupy posts and assume responsibilities in human society in accordance with their natural gifts and the skills they have acquired.

2031   Among people's rights must also be counted that to
3961   honour God according to the norm of a right conscience
and to profess one's religion privately and publicly [.....]

2032   Moreover, people have the right to choose freely the state
3962   of life which they prefer, and, therefore, either to set up
a family with equal rights and duties for man and woman, or to follow a vocation to the priesthood or to the religious life.

The family, based on marriage freely contracted, monogamous and indissoluble, must be considered as the first and natural cell of human society. Hence the need to provide for it with the greatest care in the economic, social, cultural and moral fields, so as to strengthen its stability and facilitate the fulfilment of its specific mission. The right to see to the upkeep and the education of children belongs, however, primarily to the parents.

2033   [....] It is clear that persons have the natural right not
3693   only to get an opprotunity for work but also to choose
their work freely. Indissolubly linked with these is the right to demand working conditions in which physical health is not endangered, moral integrity is not threatened and the normal development of young people is not impaired. As for women, they have the right to work in such conditions as are in accordance with their needs and duties as wives and mothers.

2034   From the dignity of the human person there also arises
3964   the right to exercise economic activities duly and with
a proper sense of personal responsibility. Hence there is also — and this must not be overlooked — the right to a wage determined according to criteria of justice, and therefore sufficient, in proportion to the available resources, to give the worker and the family a standard of living in keeping with the dignity of the human person [...].

2035   From the nature of the human person derives also the
3965   right to private property, even of productive goods [...].
Finally—and this must be pointed out—the right of private property entails a social duty.

2036   From the fact that human persons are by nature social,
3966   they have the right of assembly and association, the
right to give their association the form they consider more conducive to the end they have in view, and to act in those societies on their own initiative and responsibility in order to achieve their desired objectives. [...] Such intermediate groups and societies [between State and family] must be considered as indispensable means of safeguarding the dignity and liberty of the human person, without interference with one's sense of responsibility.

2037   Every person has the right to freedom of movement
3967   and of residence within the boundaries of one's own
country, and, when there are just reasons for it, to emigrate to other countries and take up residence there. [...]

2038 The dignity of the human person involves further the
3968 right to take an active part in public affairs and to
contribute to the common good of the citizens [...].

2039 The human person is also entitled to a legal protection
3969 of one's rights, a protection that should be efficacious,
impartial and in conformity with the true norm of
justice. [...]

(Duties)

2040 The natural rights with which we have been dealing
3970 are, however, inseparably connected, in the person who
is their subject, with just as many respective duties, and
rights as well as duties find their source, their sustenance and
their inviolability in the natural law which grants or enjoins them.

For example, the right of life is correlative with the duty to
preserve it; the right to a decent standard of living with the duty
of living becomingly; the right to investigate the truth freely with
the duty of seeking it ever more deeply and completely.

[...] In human society, to each particular right of one person
there corresponds a duty in the other persons, the duty namely
of acknowledging and respecting that right. [...] Those, therefore,
who claim their own rights, yet altogether forget or neglect to
carry out their respective duties, are like people who build with
one hand and destroy with the other.

2041 [...] A well-ordered human society requires that persons
3971 recognise their mutual rights and discharge their mutual
duties. By so doing they also contribute generously
to the establishment of a civic order in which rights and duties
are progressively more diligently and more effectively
observed.

It is not enough, for example, to acknowledge the right of
all to the necessary means of subsistence: we must also seek
according to our means to provide them with adequate food and
nourishment.

Moreover, society must not only be organised, but must
also provide people with abundant resources. This [...] also
requires that all join for combined action in the many enterprises
which modern civilisation either allows, or encourages or
demands.

2042   The dignity of the human person also requires that every
3972   one enjoy the right to act freely and   responsibly.

THE SECOND VATICAN GENERAL COUNCIL

The Second Vatican Council has called for a renewal in the teaching of moral theology. "Its scientific exposition should lean more on the teaching of Sacred Scripture and set out the loftiness of the Christian vocation and the obligation of the faithful to bear fruit in charity for the life of the world" (OT 16). This teaching programme reflects the Council's conception of the Christian life which theology is meant to articulate, and sums up the fundamental principles which, according to the Council, constitute its foundation. Because of the Council's primarily pastoral orientation, all the conciliar documents are concerned with various aspects of the Christian life; its basic principles, however, are mostly expounded in the Dogmatic Constitution Lumen Gentium and in the Pastoral Constitution Gaudium et Spes.

The Council's approach to Christian living is essentially positive in character; going straight to the essentials, it proposes lofty Christian ideals beyond all juridical attitudes. It is also universal in so far as these ideals are proposed to all Christians without distinction. Thus, in the Constitution Lumen Gentium, the conception of the Christian life is essentially based on the theology of the Church as the People of God (LG 9ff); from this follows the common call to holiness addressed to all the members of the Church (LG 40). This fulness of the Christian life consists in the following of Christ (LG 41) which leads to the perfection of charity (LG 42)—a charity which does not separate the love of God from the love of people (GS 24). Applying this to the laity, the Constitution explains their specific vocation (LG 31), their dignity (LG 32) and their participation in the Church's mission (LG 33; AA; AG 21, 41). Against this background, it is clear that the profession of the evangelical counsels in the religious life does not give to the religious an exclusive claim to Christian perfection. The religious life entails nevertheless a special call to holiness (LG 42), which summons a Christian to follow Christ more closely and to live the baptismal consecration in a more radical manner (LG 44) by the practice of the evangelical counsels (LG 43; PC 1, 12-14). The Council shows the ecclesial significance of the religious life and its eschatological dimension as a sign of the Kingdom (LG 44). The Decree Perfectae Caritaris is chiefly concerned with its renewal and adaptation to the modern world. It states as the main principles of renovation a double faithfulness: to the sources, namely the Gospel and the inspiration of the founder, and to the demands of our time (PC 2).

Another general feature of the moral doctrine of the Council is its social character. Here too the Constitution Lumen Gentium sets the scene with its doctrine of the Church as the People of God, and the Body of Christ in which all members are mutually dependent. In a diversity of vocations and charisms, of functions and ministries, all share a common responsibility to build up the Church into God's holy people and the sign of the salvation he has wrought *for all in Jesus Christ. But to this common Christian calling, the Constitution* Gaudium et Spes *on the Church in the Modern World opens even broader perspectives. This vast document which embodies best the new spirit of the Church's openness to the world contains also its most far-reaching moral teaching. It gives to the Christian life its full dimension by bringing out its implications not only for the Christian community but for the world at large. It shows that Christian morality cannot remain centred on the individual, or even on the life of the Church; it must have in view the common good of the world community (GS 30).*

The first part of the Constitution Gaudium et Spes *deals with the Church and the human person's calling; four chapters treat of the dignity of human persons, the community of persons, their activity in the world, and the role of the Church in the modern world, respectively. This part lays down the basic principles of a broad-based Christian morality which the second part of the document applies to specific problems: marriage and the family, the development of culture, socio-economic life, the political community, peace and the building up of the community of nations.*

Among the fundamental principles the Constitution stresses first of all the dignity of the human person created in God's image (GS 12), the dignity and primacy of the moral conscience (GS 16), and the excellence of freedom (GS 17). This doctrine does not overlook the reality of sin (GS 13) and the consequent possibility of misusing one's freedom (GS 17); but the light of faith also allows it an optimistic view of the concrete human person: marred by sin, Christian activity has been redeemed by Christ (GS 37), who through his Paschal Mystery has opened the way to true freedom (GS 38).

Secondly the Constitution stresses the essentially social character of human persons and their destiny in the plan of God (GS 24). Emphasis is laid on the fact that person and society are interdependent: one realises one's personality through an interpersonal exchange with others; one fulfils one's destiny in the context of a human society (GS 26). Hence the need to promote the common good, which, however, is always ordained to the welfare of the persons (GS 26). Respect for the person and for all persons (GS 27), who all are equal (GS 29), is a supreme norm; it is in particular the norm on which social justice must be based (GS 29). Redeemed by Christ, human activity is at all levels a positive value (GS 34), willed by God for the full development of persons and the realisation of their divine destiny (GS 35). In this context the Constitution explains the rightful autonomy of secular realities (GS 36; cf. n. 423). Against this general background it goes on to expose the role of the Church in the world of today (GS 40ff). The laity are called upon to exercise moral responsibility (GS 43). The Constitution suggests a more personalistic understanding of the natural law (GS 51).

Insistence on the value of human freedom led the Council to make a special Declaration on religious liberty, the highest level at which persons are called to exercise their freedom. The Declaration Dignitatis Humanae *shows the foundation of religious liberty to lie in the dignity of the person itself (DH*

2). All must be able to search for truth according to the dictates of conscience (DH 3) and allowed to practice their religion, both interiorly and exteriorly, according to the same dictates (DH 3). Since in the practice of religion too the person is a social being, this liberty applies not only to individuals but to groups (DH 4), among which the Declaration singles out the family (DH 5). Religious liberty being the person's highest endowment, to protect it is the common responsibility of all and of society (DH 6); at the same time, it is each one's and each group's responsibility to exercise it rightly and in keeping with the common good (DH 7). Here most of all education in the correct use of freedom is required (DH 8). To this freedom the Church herself claims an inalienable right (DH 13) for the exercise of her divine mission (DH 14).

DOGMATIC CONSTITUTION *LUMEN GENTIUM* (1964)

(The vocation of the laity)

2043   31. [...] It is the special vocation of the laity to seek the Kingdom of God engaging in temporal affairs and ordering them according to the mind of God. They live in the world, that is, in the various secular professions and occupations and in the ordinary circumstances of family and social life, from which the web of their existence is woven. There they are called by God to work for the sanctification of the world like a leaven, from within, by exercising their proper function according to the spirit of the Gospel. Especially by the testimony of their lives, by the radiance of their faith, hope and charity, they are to manifest Christ to others. It is their specific task to shed light upon and to order all the temporal affairs with which they are closely connected, in such a way that these may constantly be carried on and develop in keeping with the spirit of Christ, to the praise of the Creator and the Redeemer.

(The Common dignity of all the members of the Church)

2044   32. [...]Thus, the chosen people of God is one: "one Lord, one faith, one baptism" [*Eph 4:5*]. As members, they share a common dignity from their rebirth in Christ; they have the same grace of God's children, the same call to perfection; they share in common one salvation, one hope and one undivided charity. In Christ, therefore, and in the Church there is no inequality on the basis of race or nationality, of social condition or sex, because "there is neither Jew nor Greek, there is neither slave nor free person; there is neither male nor female. For you are all 'one' in Christ Jesus" [*Gal 3:28; cf. Col 3:11*].[...]

(Universal call to holiness)

2045   40.[...] Thus it is evident that all the faithful, whatever their station or rank, are called to the fulness of Christian life and to the perfection of charity—a holiness which promotes even in the earthly society a more human manner of life.[...]

(Charity is the way to holiness)

2046   42. [...]Charity, as the bond of perfection and the fulness of the law [*cf. Col 3:14*], directs all the means that lead to holiness, animates them and makes them reach their end. Hence it is love for God and the neighbour that distinguishes the true disciple of Christ.[...]

(The religious: their triple function in the Church)

2047   44. [...]By their vows[...] Christians take upon themselves the obligation of observing the three above-mentioned evangelical counsels. Thereby they dedicate themselves totally to God, whom they love above all things, and thus are ordained to the service and honour of God under a new and special title. By baptism they have already died to sin and have been consecrated to God; but, in order to draw more abundant fruit from the baptismal grace, they seek by the profession of the evangelical counsels in the Church to free themselves from impediments that could withdraw them from the fervour of charity and from the perfection of divine worship; and so they are more intimately consecrated to the service of God.[...]

It is clear that the evangelical counsels, through the charity which they develop, unite their followers in a special way with the Church and her mystery; therefore, the spiritual life of religious should also be dedicated to the welfare of the whole Church. Hence their duty of labouring for the implantation and strengthening of Christ's Kingdom in souls and for its extension to all regions.[...]

The profession of the evangelical counsels, then, stands out as a standard that can and should effectively stimulate all the members of the Church to fulfil courageously the duties attached to their Christian vocation.[...] It manifests also more clearly to all believers the heavenly goods already present in this world; it bears a clearer witness to the new and eternal life which Christ's passion has won for us, and it foreshadows more directly the future resurrection and the glory of the heavenly kingdom.[...]

Thus, the state of life which is constituted by the profession of the evangelical counsels, though it is not part of the hierarchical structure of the Church, decidedly belongs to her life and holiness.

DECLARATION *DIGNITATIS HUMANAE* (1965)

(Object and foundation of religious liberty)

2048   2. This Vatican Council declares that the human person has a right to religious freedom. This freedom means that all are to be immune from coercion on the part of individuals or of social groups and of any human power, in such wise that in religious matters no one is to be forced to act against conscience, or is, within just limits, to be hindered from acting in conformity with conscience, whether privately or publicly, whether alone or in association with others. The Council further declares that the right ot religious freedom has its foundation in the very dignity of the human person, as this dignity is known through the revealed word of God and by reason itself. This right of the human person to religious freedom must be recognised in the constitutional law governing society in such a way that it becomes a civil right.

(Freedom of external religious practice).

2049   3. [...]The practice of religion, of its very nature, consists above all in those internal, voluntary and free acts whereby one sets the course of one's life towards God; such acts can be neither commanded nor forbidden by any merely human authority. But the social nature of human beings requires them to give external expression to their internal acts of religion, to communicate with others in religious matters and profess their religion in community.

Injury is done, therefore, to the human person and to the very order established by God for human beigns, if the free exercise of religion is denied to them in society when the just preservation of public order does not so require.[...]

(Freedom of religious groups)

2050   4. The freedom or immunity from coercion in religious matters, which is the endowment of persons as individuals, is also to be recognised as their right when they act in community. For religious communities are a requirement of the social nature both of the human being and of religion itself.

Hence, provided the just demands of public order are observed, immunity is due by right to these communities in order that they may govern themselves according to their own norms, honour the Supreme Being in public worship, assist their members in the practice of their religious life, strengthen them by instruction, and promote institutions in which they may work together for the purpose of ordering their own lives in accordance with their religious principles.[...]

PASTORAL CONSTITUTION *GAUDIUM ET SPES* (1965)

(Dignity of the human person made in God's image)

2051 12. Believers and non-believers alike generally agree to say that all things on earth must be ordained to the human person as their centre and crown.[...] Sacred Scripture teaches that the human being was created "in God's image", capable of knowing and loving the Creator, appointed by him Lord of all creatures on earth [*cf. Gen 1:26; Wis 2:23*], to rule over them and use them while giving glory to God [*cf. Sir 17:3-10*].[...] But God did not create the human person as a solitary being; from the beginning "male and female he created them" [*Gen 1:27*]; their companionship constitutes the primary expression of interpersonal communion. For one is in the depth of one's nature a social being: one can neither live nor develop one's talents except through relationships with others.[...]

(Dignity of the moral conscience)

2052 16. In the depths of their conscience human beings detect a law which they do not make for themselves but which they must obey. Its voice always summons them to love and to do what is good and to shun what is evil. At the right moment it resounds in the secrecy of the heart: do this, avoid that. For there is in one's heart a law written by God. The dignity of the human person lies in obeying it; and according to this law one will be judged [*cf. Rom 2:14-16*]. Conscience is the most secret core and sanctuary of the person. There one is alone with God, there in one's innermost self one perceives God's voice. Through conscience the person comes to know, in a wonderful manner, that law whose fulfilment consists in the love of God and neighbour [*cf. Mt 22:37-40; Gal 5:14*]. In loyalty to their conscience, Christians join with the rest of human beings in the search for truth and for a true solution to the many moral problems arising in the life of both individuals and society. The more a right conscience holds sway, the more do persons and groups abandon arbitrary decisions and endeavour to conform to the objective norms of morality. However, it often happens that conscience errs through invincible ignorance; yet it does not on that score lose its dignity. This, however, cannot be said when one cares little to seek for what is true and good, and when, through a habit of sin, one's conscience little by little becomes practically blind.

(Excellence of freedom)

2053   17. But it is only as a free being that the human person can turn to what is good. Our contemporaries set a high store on this freedom and pursue it eagerly; and rightly so, to be sure. Often, however, they foster it in a perverse manner, as a licence to do anything they please, even what is evil. But genuine freedom is a striking sign of God's image in human persons; for God was pleased to "leave the human being in the hand of one's own counsel" [*cf. Sir 15:14*], so that one may seek one's Creator of one's own accord, and by adhering to him reach in freedom to full perfection and happiness. The dignity of human persons, then, demands that they should act with deliberate and free choice. They must be led and guided from within by a personal decision, and not by a blind inner impulse or by mere external pleasure. They attain this dignity when, freeing themselves from all slavery of passion, they pursue their goal by the free choice of what is good and with intelligent application effectively procure for themselves the means to that goal. However, as their freedom is wounded by sin, they can make their Godward orientation fully effective only with the help of God's grace. And before the judgment seat of God each one will have to render an account of one's life, of the good and of the evil one has done [*cf. 2 Cor 5:10*].

(The community of human beings: interdependence of person and society)

2054   25. The social nature of the human being makes it evident that the development of the person and the progress of society are mutually dependent. The principle, subject and goal of all social institution is and must be the human person who, by one's very nature, has an absolute need of social life. Life in society is not something accidental to human beings; hence, by their dealings with other persons, by mutual services and by brotherly and sisterly dialogue, they develop all their personal gifts and are enabled to respond to their calling.

Among the social ties which human persons need for their development some, like the family and the political community, answer more immediately their intimate nature, while others originate rather from their own free will.

(Promoting the common good)

2055 26. Human interdependence is increasing daily and is gradually spreading to the entire world. Hence it follows that the common good—or the sum total of those conditions of social life which allow groups and each of their members as well to attain their own perfection more fully and more readily—is today taking on a more universal dimension, involving rights and duties with regard to the whole of humankind. Every group has to take into account the needs and lawful aspirations of other groups and even the common good of the entire human family.

At the same time, however, there is a growing awareness of the exalted dignity of the human person, who is superior to all things and whose rights and duties are universal and inviolable. There must, therefore, be made available to each all that one is in need of to live a truly human life.[...]

The social order and its development must result unceasingly in the good of the persons, since the order of things must be made subject to the order of persons, and not inversely.[...]

(Respect for the human person)

2056 27. To come now to practical and particularly urgent applications, the Council insists on respect for the human person: everyone should consider one's neighbours, no one excepted, as 'another self', take into account first of all their existence and the means necessary for them to live their life worthily, and beware not to imitate the rich man who did not care for the poor Lazarus [*cf. Lk 16:19-31*].

In our days especially, the duty is more binding than ever to make ourselves neighbours to absolutely every person and give active help to anyone crossing our path.[...]

(Essential equality of persons)

2057   29. All human persons, endowed with a rational soul
            and created in the image of God, have the same nature
and the same origin; redeemed by Christ, they all enjoy the same
divine calling and divine destiny. Hence the basic equality of all
must increasingly be recognised.

(Going beyond an individualistic ethics)

2058   30. The profound and rapid changes now taking place
            demand more urgently than ever that no one should rest
content with merely individualistic ethics for lack of attention
to present day trends or out of inertia. Nowadays justice and
charity demand more and more that every person contribute to
the common good, according to one's own abilities and taking
into account the needs of others, and that one promote and help
public or private institutions which serve to improve the living
conditions of people. But there are people who, while making
profession of lofty and generous ideas, continue to live as if they
did not care at all for the needs of society. [...] Let all consider it
a sacred duty to count social obligations among their primary
duties today and to heed to them.

(Norm of human activity)

2059   35. This, therefore, is the norm of human activity:
            according to God's design and will, it must be in
conformity with the genuine good of humankind and allow each,
both as indivudual and as a member of society, to pursue and
fulfil one's total vocation.

(Human activity brought to perfection in the Paschal Mystery)

2060   38. For the Word of God, through whom all things were
            made, was himself made flesh and dwelt on the earth of
human beings [*cf. Jn 1:3, 14*]. Thus he entered the world's history
as the perfect man, taking up into himself and recapitulating
that history [*cf. Eph 1:10*]. He it is who reveals to us that "God
is love" [*1 Jn 4:8*] and who teaches us at the same time that the
basic law of our perfection and hence of the transformation of
the world is the new commandment of love. To those who believe
in God's love, he thus brings the certainty that the way of love
lies open to all and that the efforts made to built up a universal

kinship are not wasted. [...] Constituted Lord by his resurrection and having been given all power in heaven and on earth [*cf. Acts 2:36; Mt 28:18*], Christ is now at work in the hearts of people through the power of his Spirit.

(The laity called to exercise moral responsibility)

2061   43. It pertains to their [the laity's] conscience, properly formed, to write the law of God into the life of the earthly city. From priests, the laity should look for light and spiritual energy. However, they should not imagine that their pastors are always such experts that they can give an immediate and concrete answer for every problem, however complicated, that arises, or even that such is their mission. Rather, enlightened by Christian wisdom and paying careful attention to the authoritative teaching of the Church, lay persons should assume their own responsibilities.

PAUL VI

DECLARATION *DE PERSONA HUMANA* OF THE S. CONGREGATION FOR THE DOCTRINE OF THE FAITH
(29 December, 1975)

For the first time, in this Declaration on Sexual Ethics, the concept of 'fundamental option' is adopted by the magisterium, although its excesses are rejected. Mortal sin is described as the violation of the order of love which is equivalent to a change in the fundamental option. The text is found in AAS 68 (1976) 77-96.

(Fundamental option and particular acts)

2062   10. In reality, it is precisely the fundamental option which in the last resort defines a person's moral disposition. But it can be completely changed by particular acts, especially when, as it happens, these have been prepared for by previous more superficial acts.

(Mortal sin, serious violation of the order of love)

2063   10. Persons, therefore, sin mortally not only when their actions come from direct contempt for love of God and neighbour, but also when they consciously and freely, for whatever reason, choose something which is seriously disordered. For in this choice,[...] there is already included contempt for the divine comandment: the person turns oneself away from God and loses charity.

JOHN PAUL II
ENCYCLICAL LETTER *REDEMPTOR HOMINIS* (1979)

In his first Encyclical Letter on Christ, Redeemer of the human person, Pope John Paul II shows the value which one acquires in the eyes of God through the mystery of redemption; see n. 2172i. In this context he stresses the values of love and freedom based on truth. The text is found in AAS 71 (1979) 280-281.

(Freedom founded on truth)

2064 12. Jesus Christ meets the human person of every age, including our own, with the same words: "You will know the truth and the truth will make you free" *[Jn 8:32]*. These words contain both a fundamental requirement and a warning: the requirement of an honest relationship with regard to truth as a condition for authentic freedom and the warning to avoid every kind of illusory freedom, every freedom that fails to enter into the whole truth about human beings and the world. Today also, even after two thousand years, we see Christ as the one who brings people freedom based on truth, frees them from what curtails, diminishes and as it were breaks off this freedom at its root, in their soul, their heart and their conscience.

APOSTOLIC CONSTITUTION *SACRAE DISCIPLINAE LEGES*
(25 January, 1983)

In the document promulgating the New Code of Canon Law, the Pope explains its purpose and scope. The text is found in the Codex Iuris Canonici, *1983.*

(The purpose of the Code)

2065 [...] It is sufficiently clear that the purpose of the Code is not in any way to replace faith, grace, charisms and above all charity in the life of the Chruch or of Christ's faithful. On the contrary, the Code rather looks towards the achievement of order in the ecclesial society, so that while attributing primacy to love, grace and charisms, it may facilitate at the same time an orderly development in the life both of the ecclesial society and of the individual persons who belong to it.

An instrument, such as the Code is, fully accords with the nature of the Church, particularly as presented in the authentic teaching of the Second Vatican Council, seen as a whole, and especially in its ecclesiological doctrine. In fact, in a certain sense, the new Code can be viewed as a great effort to translate the conciliar ecclesiological teaching into canonical terms. If it is impossible perfectly to transpose the image of the Church described by conciliar doctrine into canonical language, nevertheless the Code must always be related to that image as to its primary pattern, whose outline, given its nature, the Code must express as far as possible.

And in fact a Code of Canon Law is absolutely necessary for the Church. Since the Church is established in the form of a social and visible unit, it needs rules, so that its hierarchical and organic structure may be visible, that its exercise of the functions divinely entrusted to it, particularly of sacred power and of the administration of the sacraments, be properly ordered; that the mutual relationships of Christ's faithful be reconciled in justice based on charity, with the rights of each safeguarded and defended; and lastly, that the common initiatives which are undertaken so that the Christian life may ever be more perfectly carried out, be supported and strengthened by canonical laws.

DISCOURSE TO OFFICIALS OF THE ROMAN ROTA
(26 January, 1984)

In this discourse the Pope outlines the principles of interpretation of the New Code of Canon Law in the spirit of Vatican II. The text is found in AAS 76 (1984) 643-649.

(Interpretation of the Code)

2066   This knowledge [of the New Code] presumes an assiduous, scientific, deep study which is not limited to pointing out the possible variations with respect to the previous laws, or to establishing its purely literal or philological meaning, but which can also take into consideration the mind of the legislator and the reason of the law, so as to give you a global view which enables you to penetrate the spirit of the law, because, in substance, the matter is this: The code is a new law and it is to be evaluated primarily in the perspective of the Second Vatican Council, to which it is intended to conform fully.

APOSTOLIC EXHORTATION *RECONCILIATIO ET PAENITENTIA*

(2 December, 1984)

The Apostolic Exhortation speaks of the mystery of sin, personal and social, in its different dimensions. While sin in the proper sense is always said to be personal, the importance of social sin in its various meanings is brought out. For an introduction to the document, see n. 1673i. The text is found in AAS 77 (1985) 185-275.

(Rupture with God, within oneself and in human relationships)

2067a 15. As a rupture with God, sin is an act of disobedience by the creature who rejects, at least implicitly, the very one from whom one came and who sustains one in life. It is therefore a suicidal act. Since by sinning one refuses to submit to God, one's internal balance is also destroyed and it is precisely within oneself that contradictions and conflicts arise. Wounded in this way, the person almost inevitably causes damage to the fabric of relationships with others and with the created world. This is an objective law and an objective reality, verified in many ways in the human psyche and in the spiritual life, as well as in society, where it is easy to see the signs and effects of internal disorder.

(Personal sin and social sin)

2067b 16. Sin in the proper sense, is always a personal act, since it is an act of freedom on the part of an individual person, and not properly of a group or community. This individual may be conditioned, incited and influenced by numerous and powerful external factors. One may also be subjected to tendencies, defects and habits linked with one's personal conditions. In not a few cases such external and internal factors may attenuate, to a greater or lesser degree, the person's freedom and therefore the responsibility and guilt. But it is a truth of faith, also confirmed by our experience and reason, that the human person is free. This truth cannot be disregarded in order to place the blame for individuals' sins on external factors such as structures, systems or other people.

2067c To speak of *social sin* means in the first place to recognise that, by virtue of a human solidarity which is as mysterious and intangible as it is real and concrete, each individual's sin in some way affects others. This is the other aspect of that solidarity which on the religious level is developed in the profound and magnificent mystery of the Communion of Saints.[...] *To this law of ascent* there unfortunately corresponds the *law of descent.* Consequently, one can speak of a *communion of sin,* whereby a soul that lowers itself through sin drags down with itself the Church and, in some way, the whole world. In other words, there is no sin, not even the most intimate and secret one, that exclusively concerns the person committing it.

Some sins, however, by their very matter constitute a direct attack on one's neighbour and, more exactly, in the language of the Gospel, against one's brother or sister. They are offences against God because they are offences against one's neighbour. These sins are usually called social *sins,* and this is the second meaning of the term.[...]

The third meaning of *social sin* refers to the relationship between the various human communities. These relationships are not always in accordance with the plan of God, who intends that there be justice in the world, and freedom and peace between individuals, groups and peoples.[...]

Having said this in the clearest and most unequivocal way, one must add at once that there is one meaning sometimes given to *social sin* that is not legitimate or acceptable, even though it is very common in certain quarters. This usage contrasts *social sin* and *personal sin,* not without ambiguity, in a way that leads more or less consciously to the watering down and almost the abolition of *personal sin,* with the recognition only of *social* guilt and responsibilities.[...]

Whenever the Church speaks of situations of sin, or when she condemns as *social sins* certain situations or the collective behaviour of certain groups, big or small, or even of whole nations or blocs of nations, she knows and she proclaims that such cases of *social sin* are the result of the accumulation and concentration of many *personal sins.* It is the case of the very personal sins of those who cause or support evil or who exploit it; of those who are in a position to avoid, eliminate or at least limit certain social evils but who fail to do so out of laziness, fear or the conspiracy of silence, through secret complicity or indifference; of those who take refuge in the supposed impossibility of changing the world, and also of those who sidestep the effort and sacrifice required, producing specious reasons of a higher order. The real responsibility, then, lies with individuals.

(Mortal sin and venial sin)

2067d 17. Now sin is a disorder perpetrated by the human being against this life-principle. And when "through sin, the soul commits a disorder that reaches the point of turning away from its ultimate end—God—to which it is bound by charity, then the sin is mortal; on the other hand, whenever the disorder does not reach the point of a turning away from God, the sin is venial."[1] For this reason venial sin does not deprive the sinner of sanctifying grace, friendship with God, charity, and therefore eternal happiness, whereas just such a deprivation is precisely the consequence of mortal sin.[...]

Considering sin from the point of view of its *matter,* the ideas of death, rupture with God the supreme good, of deviation from the path that leads to God or interruption of the journey towards him (which are all ways of defining mortal sin) are linked with the idea of the gravity of sin's objective content. Hence in the Church's doctrine and pastoral action, *grave* sin is in practice identified with *mortal* sin.[...]

It must be added—as was likewise done at the Synod—that some sins are *intrinsically* grave and mortal by reason of their matter. That is, there exist acts which, *per se* and in themselves, independently of circumstances, are always seriously wrong by reason of their object. These acts, if carried out with sufficient awareness and freedom, are always gravely sinful [*cf. n. 1945*].

(Loss of the sense of sin)

2067e 18. This sense is rooted in the human person's moral conscience and is as it were its thermometer. It is linked to the *sense of God,* since it derives from one's conscious relationship with God as Creator, Lord and Father. Hence, just as it is impossible to eradicate completely the sense of God or to silence the conscience completely, so the sense of sin is never completely eliminated.

Nevertheless, it happens not infrequently in history, for more or less lengthy periods and under the influence of many different

---

1. Cf. St. Augustinie. *De spiritu et littera*, XXVIII: *CSEL* 60, 202sq.

factors, that the moral conscience of many people becomes seriously clouded.[...] When the conscience is weakened *the sense of God* is also obscured, and as a result, with the loss of this decisive inner point of reference, the sense of sin is also lost.[...]

The sense of sin also easily declines as a result of a system of ethics deriving from a certain historical relativism. This may take the form of an ethical system which relativizes the moral norm, denying its absolute and unconditional value, and as a consequence denying that there can be intrinsically illicit acts, independent of the circumstances in which they are performed by the subject.[...]

The restoration of the *proper sense of sin* is the first way of facing the grave spiritual crisis looming over human beings today. But the sense of sin can only be restored through a *clear reminder of the unchangeable principles of reason and faith* which the moral teaching of the Church has always upheld.

ADDRESS TO CONGRESS OF MORAL THEOLOGIANS
(10 April, 1986)

The Pope upholds the concept of absolute norms and intrinsically evil acts as following from the very dignity of the human person. The text is found in AAS 78 (1986) 1098-1103.

(There exist intrinsically evil acts...)

2068   3. To reduce the moral quality of our actions regarding creatures, to attempt to improve reality in its nonethical content would be equivalent, in the last analysis, to destroying the very concept of morality. The first consequence, indeed, of this reduction is the denial that, in the context of such actions, there exist acts which are always and everywhere in themselves illicit.

(...and absolute norms)

2069   4. Called, as a person, to immediate communion with God; the object, as a person, of an entirely singular Providence, the human being bears a law written in one's heart that one has not given to oneself, but which expresses the immutable demands of one's personal *being* created by God, granted a finality by God; and in itself endowed with a dignity that is infinitely superior to that of things. This law is not merely made up of general guidelines, whose specific extent is in their respective context conditioned by different and changeable historical situations. There are moral norms that have a precise content which is immutable and unconditional—for example the norm that prohibits contraception or that which forbids the direct killing of an innocent person. To deny the existence of norms having such a value can be done only by one who denies the existence of a *truth* above the person, of an immutable nature in the person based ultimately on the creative wisdom which is the measure of all reality. It is necessary, therefore, that ethical reflection be founded and rooted even more deeply in true anthropology, and this, ultimately, on the metaphysics of creation, which is at the centre of all Christian thinking.

S.. CONGREGATION FOR THE DOCTRINE OF THE FAITH INSTRUCTION *DONUM VITAE* (22 February, 1987)

In this instruction on Respect for Human Life (for introduction, cf. n. 2244i), the relationship between science and morality is explained. The text is found in AAS 80 (1988) 70-102.

(Role of the magisterium)

2070   Intr., 1. The Church's magisterium does not intervene on the basis of a particular competence in the area of the experimental sciences; but having taken account of the data of research and technology, it intends to put forward, by virtue of its evangelical mission and apostolic duty, the moral teaching corresponding to the dignity of the person and to his or her integral vocation. It intends to do so by expanding the criteria of moral judgment as regards the application of scientific research and technology, especially in relation to human life and its beginnings. These criteria are the respect, defence and promotion of the human person, with the "primary and fundamental right" to life, and dignity as a person who is endowed with a spiritual soul and with moral responsibility and who is called to beatific communion with God.

(Science and technology at the service of the human person)

2071   Intr., 2. Science and technology are valuable resources for human beings when placed at their service and when they promote their integral development for the benefit of all; but they cannot of themselves show the meaning of existence and of human progress. Being ordered to the human being, who initiates and develops them, they draw from the person and the person's moral values the indication of their purpose and the awareness of their limits.

It would on the one hand be illusory to claim that scientific research and its application are morally neutral; on the other hand one cannot derive criteria for guidance from mere technical efficiency, from research's possible usefulness to some at the expense of others, or, worse still, from prevailing ideologies. Thus science and technology require, for their own intrinsic meaning, an unconditional respect for the fundamental criteria of the moral law; that is to say, they must be at the service of the human persons, of their inalienable rights and their true and integral good according to the design and will of God.

The rapid development of technological discoveries gives greater urgency to this need to respect the criteria just mentioned; science without conscience can only lead to the human being's ruin. "Our era needs such wisdom more than bygone ages if the discoveries made by human persons are to be further humanised. For the future of the world stands in peril unless wiser people are forthcoming" [GS 15].

JOHN PAUL II
ENCYCLICAL LETTER *VERITATIS SPLENDOR*
(6 August, 1993)

In this encyclical Pope John Paul II treats certain fundamental aspects of Catholic moral doctrine. The enyclical is addressed specifically to Bishops, who have special responsibilities of vigilance in this matter. It is the first time that the magisterium has presented in detail the foundations and principles of this teaching. Thus many of the matters treated have not appeared in earlier documents. The Pope speaks more explicitly than his predecessors of development within the moral tradition. The document recognizes that there have been positive and praiseworthy endeavours to renew moral theology after the Second Vatican Council and moral theologians are encouraged to continue their work. However, doubts and objections have been raised with regard to some points of the Church's moral teaching. The encyclical interprets this as more than limited and occasional dissent, and judges it to be a general and systematic calling into question of traditional moral doctrine. This doctrine it restates and defends. While the encyclical rejects a number of serious errors, it does not name their authors. A prudent reserve is appropriate in identifying the descriptions of erroneous theories with the opinions of particular scholars. The text is found in AAS 85 (1993) 1133-1228.

(Development within tradition)

2072a 27. Within tradition, the authentic interpretation of the
           Lord's law develops with the help of the Holy Spirit.
The same Holy Spirit who is at the origin of the revelation of
Jesus' commandments and teachings guarantees that they will
be reverently preserved, faithfully expounded and correctly
applied in different times and places. This constant "putting into
practice" of the commandments is the sign and fruit of a deeper
insight into revelation and of an understanding in the light of
faith of new historical and cultural situations. Nevertheless, it
can only confirm the permanent validity of revelation and follow
in the line of the interpretaion given to it by the great tradition
of the Church's teaching and life, as witnessed by the teaching
of the fathers, the lives of the saints, the church's liturgy and the
teaching of the magisterium.

(Difference between truth and manner of expression)

2072b 29. The council also encouraged theologians, "while
           respecting the methods and requirements of theological
science, to look for a more appropriate way of communicating
doctrine to the people of their time; since there is a difference
between the deposit or the truths of faith and the manner in
which they are expressed, keeping the same meaning and the
same judgment" [*cf. GS 62*].

(The magisterium does not impose a particular system)

2072c 29. Certainly the Church's magisterium does not intend
           to impose upon the faithful any particular theological
system, still less a philosophical one. Nevertheless, in order to
"reverently preserve and faithfully expound" the word of God
[*cf. DV 10*], the magisterium has the duty to state that some
trends of theological thinking and certain philosophical
affirmations are incompatible with revealed truth [*cf. n. 134*].

(The role of conscience correctly understood)

2073   32. Conscience is no longer considered in its primordial
           role as an act of a person's intelligence, the function of
which is to apply the universal knowledge of the good in a
specific situation and thus to express a judgment about the right
conduct to be chosen here and now. Instead, there is a tendency

to grant to the individual conscience the prerogative of independently determining the criteria of good and evil and then acting accordingly.

(Freedom and law)

2074   35. God's law does not reduce, much less do away with human freedom; rather, it protects and promotes that freedom. In contrast, however, some present day cultural tendencies have given rise to several currents of thought in ethics which centre upon an alleged conflict between freedom and law. These doctrines would grant to individuals or social groups the right to determine what is good or evil.

(Critique of the theory of autonomous ethical reason)

2075a   37. The word of God would be limited to proposing an exhortation, a generic paraenesis, which the autonomous reason alone would then have the task of completing with normative directives which are truly "objective," that is adapted to the concrete historical situation.[...] No one can fail to see that such an interpretation of the autonomy of human reason involves positions incompatible with Catholic teaching.

(Reason, creativity, autonomy and eternal law)

2075b   40. The teaching of the council emphasises, on the one hand, the role of human reason in discovering and applying the moral law: the moral life calls for that creativity and originality typical of the person, the source and cause of one's own deliberate acts. On the other hand, reason draws its own truth and authority from the eternal law, which is none other than divine wisdom itself [*cf. nn. 2124-2126*]. At the heart of the moral life we thus find the principle of a "rightful autonomy" [*cf. GS 41*] of man and woman, the personal subjects of their actions.

(The new law is the law of the Spirit)

2076   45. [...] The Church receives the gift of the new law, which is the "fulfilment" of God's law in Jesus Christ and in his Spirit. This is an "interior law" [*cf. Jer 31:31-33*], "written not with ink but with the Spirit of the living God, not on tablets of stone but on tablets of human hearts" [*2 Cor 3:3*] a law of perfection and of freedom [*cf. 2 Cor 3:17*], "the law of the Spirit of life in Christ Jesus" [*Rom 8:2*].

(The unity of the human person)

2077　48. The spiritual and immortal soul is the principle of unity of the human being, whereby it exists as a whole—*corpore et anima unus*—*[cf. GS 14]* as a person. These definitions not only point out that the body, which has been promised the resurrection, will also share in glory. They also remind us that reason and free will are linked with all the bodily and sense faculties. The person, including the body, is completely entrusted to self, and it is in the unity of body and soul that the person is the subject of one's own moral acts. The person, by the light of reason and the support of virtue, discovers in the body the anticipatory signs, the expression and the promise of the gift of self, in conformity with the wise plan of the Creator.

(False dissociation of morality from bodily aspects)

2078　49. A doctrine which dissociates the moral act from the bodily dimensions of its exercise is contrary to the teaching of Scripture and tradition. Such a doctrine revives in new forms certain ancient errors which have always been opposed by the Church, inasmuch as they reduce the human person to a "spiritual" and purely formal freedom. This reduction misunderstands the moral meaning of the body and of kinds of behaviour involving it *[cf. 1 Cor 6:19]*.

(The nature of the human person as norm)

2079　50. At this point the true meaning of the natural law can be understood: It refers to the human being's proper and primordial nature, the "nature of the human person," *[cf. GS 51]* which is the very person in the unity of soul and body, in the unity of spiritual and biological inclinations and of all other specific characteristics necessary for the pursuit of one's end.

[...] Indeed, natural inclinations take on moral relevance only insofar as they refer to the human person and the person's authentic fulfilment, a fulfilment which for that matter can take place always and only in human nature. By rejecting all manipulations of corporeity which alter its human meaning, the Church serves the human person and shows one the path of true love, the only path on which one can find the true God.

(Creative conscience: an incorrect and correct understanding)

2080a 56. [...] An attempt is made to legitimize so-called "pastoral" solutions contrary to the teaching of the magisterium and to justify a "creative" hermeneutic according to which the moral conscience is in no way obliged, in every case, by a particular negative precept. [...] Only the clarification made earlier with regard to the relationship, based on truth, between freedom and law makes possible a discernment concerning this "creative" understanding of conscience.

(The judgment of conscience)

2080b 59. The judgment of conscience is a practical judgment, a judgment which makes known what one must do or not do, or which assesses an act already performed by one. It is a judgment which applies to a concrete situation the rational conviction that one must love and do good and avoid evil. [...] Conscience thus formulates moral obligation in the light of the natural law: It is the obligation to do what the individual, through the workings of conscience, knows to be a good one is called to do here and now. The universality of the law and its obligation are acknowledged, not suppressed, once reason has established the law's application in concrete present circumstances [*cf. nn.* 2022-2025].

(The judgment of conscience and the hope of forgiveness)

2080c 61. [...]But the verdict of conscience remains in the person also as a pledge of hope and mercy: While bearing witness to the evil one has done, it also reminds one of the need, with the help of God's grace, to ask forgiveness, to do good and to cultivate virtue constantly.

(Erroneous conscience)

2080d 62. Conscience, as the judgment of an act, is not exempt from the possibility of error. As the council puts it, "not infrequently conscience can be mistaken as a result of invincible ignorance, although it does not on that account forfeit its dignity; but this cannot be said when a person shows little concern for seeking what is true and good, and conscience gradually becomes almost blind from being accustomed to sin" [*cf. n. 2052*]. In these brief words the council sums up the doctrine which the Church down through the centuries has developed with regard to the erroneous conscience.

(Fundamental choice)

2081a 66. There is no doubt that Christian moral teaching, even in its biblical roots, acknowledges the specific importance of a fundamental choice which qualifies the moral life and engages freedom on a radical level before God. It is a question of the decision of faith, of the obedience of faith [*cf.* Rom 16:26].

(False separation of choice from concrete behaviour)

2081b 67. To separate the fundamental option from concrete kinds of behaviour means to contradict the substantial integrity or personal unity of the moral agent in one's body and soul.

(Denial of the doctrine on mortal sin)

2081c 70. The separation of fundamental option from deliberate choices of particular kinds of behaviour disordered in themselves or in their circumstances, which would not engage that option, thus involves a denial of Catholic doctrine on mortal sin [*cf. n. 2067d*].[...]

(Criticism of proportionalism and consequentialism)

2082a 75. The teleological ethical theories (proportionalism, consequentialism), while acknowledging that moral values are indicated by reason and revelation, maintain that it is never possible to formulate an absolute prohibition of particular kinds of behaviour which would be in conflict, in every circumstance and in every culture, with those values. The acting subject would indeed be responsible for attaining the values pursued, but in two ways: the values or goods involved in a human act would be, from one viewpoint, of the moral order (in relation to properly moral values such as love of God and neighbour, justice, etc.) and, from another viewpoint, of the premoral order, which some term *nonmoral, physical,* or *ontic* (in relation to the advantages and disadvantages accruing both to the agent and to all other persons possibly involved, such as, for example, health or its endangerment, physical integrity, life, death, loss of material goods, etc.)

2082b   75. In this view, deliberate consent to certain kinds of
behaviour declared illicit by traditional moral theology
would not imply an objective moral evil.

2082c   76. Such theories, however, are not faithful to the
Church's teaching when they believe they can justify, as
morally good, deliberate choices of kinds of behaviour contrary
to the commandments of the divine and natural law. These
theories cannot claim to be grounded in the Catholic moral
tradition.

2082d   79. One must therefore reject the thesis, characteristic of
teleological and proportionalist theories, which holds that
it is impossible to qualify as morally evil according to its
species—its 'object'—the deliberate choice of certain kinds of
behaviour or specific acts apart from a consideration of the
intention for which the choice is made or the totality of the
foreseeable consequences of that act for all persons concerned.

(Intrinsically evil acts)

2082e   80. Reason attests that there are objects of the human
act which are by their nature "incapable of being
ordered" to God, because they radically contradict the good of
the person made in God's image. These are acts which, in the
Church's moral tradition, have been termed "intrinsically evil"
(intrinsece malum). They are such always and *per se*, in other
words, on account of their very object and quite apart from the
ulterior intentions of the one acting and the circumstances [*cf. n.*
2067d].

(Need for heroic commitment)

2083   93. Indeed, faced with the many difficulties which fidelity
to the moral order can demand even in the most ordinary
circumstances, the Christian is called, with the grace of God
invoked in prayer, to a sometimes heroic commitment.

(Moral norms do not depend on empirical surveys)

2084a   112. [...] The fact that some believers act without
following the teachings of the magisterium or
erroneously consider as morally correct a kind of behaviour
declared by their pastors as contrary to the law of God cannot
be a valid argument for rejecting the truth of the moral norms

taught by the Church. The affirmation of moral principles is not within the competence of formal empirical methods.

(Morality is not decided by democratic processes)

2084b 113. While exchanges and conflict of opinion may constitute normal expressions of public life in a representative democracy, moral teaching certainly cannot depend simply upon respect for a process: indeed, it is in no way established by following the rules and deliberative procedures typical of a democracy.

(Dissent)

2085 113. Dissent in the form of carefully orchestrated protests and polemics carried on in the media, is opposed to ecclesial communion and to a correct understanding of the hierarchical constitution of the people of God.

(Responsibility of Bishops)

2086 116. A particular responsibility is incumbent upon bishops with regard to Catholic institutions. [...] It falls to them, in communion with the Holy See, both to grant the title *Catholic* to church-related schools, universities, health-care facilities and counselling services, and, in cases of serious failure to live up to that title, to take it away.

ENCYLICAL LETTER *FIDES AT RATIO*
(14 September 1998)

The encyclical deals with the relationship between reason and faith, and in particular with the role of philosophy in theology. The text is found in AAS 91 (1999) 5-88.

(Moral theology needs philosophy)

2087 66.[...] Moral theology has perhaps an even greater need of philosophy's contribution. In the New Testament, human life is much less governed by prescriptions than in the Old Testament. Life in the Spirit leads believers to a freedom and responsibility which surpass the Law. Yet the Gospel and the Apostolic writings still set forth both general principles of Christian conduct and specific teachings and precepts. In order to apply these to the particular circumstances of individual and communal life, Christians must be able fully to engage their conscience and the power of their reason. In other words, moral theology requires a sound philosophical vision of human nature and society, as well as of the general principles of ethical decision-making.

(Moral theology needs a metaphysics of the true good)

2088   [...] Throughout the Encyclical *(Veritatis Splendor)* I underscored clearly the fundamental role of truth in the moral field. In the case of the more pressing ethical problems, this truth demands of moral theology a careful enquiry rooted unambiguously in the word of God. In order to fulfil its mission, moral theology must turn to a philosophical ethics which looks to the truth of the good, to an ethics which is neither subjectivist nor utilitarian. Such an ethics implies and presupposes a philosophical anthropology and a metaphysics of the good.

CHAPTER XXI

THE SOCIAL DOCTRINE OF THE CHURCH

There has never been a time when the moral teaching of the Church has not included a social aspect. The Old Testament injunctions on care for the orphan, widow, and stranger, and the New Testament parable of the Good Samaritan, the Sermon on the Mount, the warning that "those who do not love a brother or a sister whom they have seen, cannot love God whom they have not seen" (1 Jn 4:20), "You shall love your neighbour as yourself" (Mt 23:39), "[...] as you did it to one of these the least of my brethren, you did it to me", and countless others do not permit the Christian to interpret his or her vocation and salvation as merely a private, individual affair. In the medieval period there developed a teaching and practice associated with the problems of slavery, war (Truce of God, pax, tregua Dei, just war, military service), and usury, among others. Nonetheless, the social order (in particular the economic and political aspects thereof) in which the Christian had to live out his or her vocation had undergone such radical changes by modern times that the Church did find it necessary to formulate in the late nineteenth century a "'social doctrine', 'social teaching,' or even 'social magisterium.'" (Centesimus Annus, 2).

Leo XIII's Rerum Novarum *(1891) is usually considered the official beginning of this social doctrine. Drawing on insights within the tradition, it was a response to a new situation in Europe collectively referred to as the "social question". The industrial revolution had resulted in urban-dwelling, industrial workers who had no "property" to their name other than their labour. Pope Leo condemned the conditions they were forced to live in, which were a threat to the moral development of women, children, and family life. Against the critique of socialism, he defended the right to private property; yet he warned that liberal capitalism was inhuman and destructive of persons if it recognised no laws other than those of the marketplace. Pope Leo's analysis is not limited to pointing out and condemning injustice. It is also an intellectually sophisticated analysis of the new economic and political theories being advanced at the time. Opposed to the Church's teleological understanding of nature and her natural law tradition, new political and economic theories presupposed a quasi-mechanical understanding of nature, and offered new theories of political authority and legitimacy (social contract, 'state of nature', natural rights) and economic activity (classical capitalism and socialism).*

The twentieth century produced two "world wars", the most destructive the world has seen to date. In their wake there followed a cold war and arms race in the developed world, and a decolonisation of the so-called Third World. These newly independent countries were also affected by the East-West political tension: what was a cold war in Europe was often enough hot for them. Increasingly since the end of World War II, the Church's social teaching has addressed such problems on an international level, appealing to governments and "people of good will" as well as Christians. She has pointed out the need for supranational organisations like the United Nations for preserving peace, protecting human rights, helping refugees, and aiding the developing countries.

The Church has pointed out that it is not within her teaching competence to recommend a specific political or economic theory. But she does have a divinely imposed duty to speak out against the injustices some systems do produce, and to speak the truth about human nature, our divine vocation, the true basis of our dignity and to defend the same when it is threatened by political or economic systems that deny this truth about the human person.

The Church has always recognised the legitimate autonomy of the political and economic order, but has also cautioned that the "political" and the "economic" are not ultimate categories. When they become so, the resulting structures and systems begin to oppress rather than serve people.

The church has presented her social teaching in a way that makes much of it accessible to those who do not share the Christian faith. She has appealed to natural law principles, which are available to all those of good will. More recently the term "natural rights" or "human rights" has been used, but the term "natural law" has recently reappeared (e.g., Veritatis Splendor*). Despite this appeal to natural reason, the Church does consider her social teaching to be theological in nature; her appeal to natural law is ultimately based on a Christian anthropology which recognises the person as created in God's image, saved by Jesus Christ, and called to eternal beatitude with his or her creator and saviour. The common good of humanity is God. The Church's social doctrine, therefore, is a part of her moral theology* (Centesimus Annus, 55). *The Church has also had to correct* *periodically a misperception about her social doctrine. The Church does not advocate "a third way " (cf. nn. 2191, 2192a-b) between collectivist socialism and individualist, liberal capitalism, as if the "common good' were to be found at some neutral mid-point between the political left and right and the economic systems associated with them.*

More so than other official documents of the Church, those concerning her social doctrine must be read with an awareness of their historical context. The vast and rich material of these documents should be studied by reading the complete texts themselves, each of which is a response to changing particular concrete circumstances; here only some key texts are cited, in which the main elements of the doctrine are found.

*   *   *   *

The Texts are listed in chronological order, but the development of the doctrine can be discerned by also reading them thematically, as a response to the perduring problems of justice in light of the principles listed under (A), and the themes listed under (B).

(A) General Principles

Natural Law: 2012-13, 2020, 2023, 2029-30, 2107, 2119, 2132.
The Common good: 2013, 2019, 2055, 2107, 2111/3, 2115, 2125, 2129-2130, 2135-2137, 2153, 2190, 2196a, 2198a, 2198b, 2198c.
Subsidiarity: 2113, 2121-2122, 2148, 2150-2151, 2138, 2184, 2190.
Solidarity : 2184, 2122, 2133, 2184, 2193, 2199b.
Mutual rights and duties: 2027, 2040, 2130, 2133, 2135.
Dignity of human person: 2027, 2131, 2133, 2140/1.
Social justice : 2116-2117/1, 2150, 2152, 2174.
Ecology: 2189c, 2195c.

(B) Human Society

The Social teaching of the Church recognizes the complexity of the concrete situation: 2153a.
It is based on evangelical discernment: 2191, 2192a, 2192b.
The just social order has its ultimate source in God: 2124.
Authentic development not merely economic: 2145.
Primacy of persons over structures must be recognized: 2185.
This must be achieved in society and must respect the scale of human value : 2146, 2174.
Social progress must accompany economic development: 2116.
The goal is an integral humanism open to God: 2146, 2149.

Women have equal dignity and rights: 2153b, 2179, 2181.
Racial discrimination is to be condemned: 2153c.
The rights of migrants must be defended : 2153d.
Mass media are to be used responsibly: 2153e.
The nature of society requires authority: 2125.
Authority is ultimately based on God: 2126
Civil authority must respect the moral order : 2127.
People have a right to choose their form of government: 2128.
Civil authority must promote the common good in its entirety: 2129
*In particular, it must defend and promote the rights and duties of the
     human person:* 2130f, 2173.
*The principle of subsidiarity between State and private initiative must
     regulate the economic order :* 2113, 2184.
Wider sharing of responsibility is to be fostered: 2156d.

Right of Ownership

The universal destination of earthly goods is primary: 2141, 2147.
Ownership has a double character, individual and social: 2106,
     2110.
The right to private ownership is a natural right: 2101, 2119.
*It is subordinated to the fundamental right of each person to use the
     goods of the earth:* 2112, 2147, 2147a, 2189c.
Radical reforms are needed to ensure this fundamental right: 2148.
Rules for the use of private ownership: 2103, 2108.
*The limits in the use of ownership must be defined by the State in
     view of the common good:* 2107, 2147a.
The right of the State to possess productive goods: 2121.
The Church condemns "unchecked capitalism" and total collectivism:
     2147b.

Labour and Wages

Work is sharing in the creation and redemption in Christ: 2180.
Labour has a personal and necessary character: 2104.
The subjective meaning of work has primacy over the objective: 2175.
Labour has primacy over capital: 2176.
Work founds a right to ownership: 2177.
It has a double aspect, individual and social: 2106, 2210.
Both aspects must be considered in fixing wages: 2111/1-3.
Norms of a just wage: 2105, 2115, 2178.
Wage-contracts should be qualified by contracts of partnership:
     2109.

Shared responsibility must be granted to workers: 2117/1-3, 2177.

Relations between States

*They must be governed by respect of right and acknowledgment of
    equality:* 2132-2133, 2198f.
War of self-defence can be justified as a last resort: 2142.
In war international laws and agreements must be observed: 2142.
Total warfare is condemned: 2143.
Arms race is to be abandoned and disarmament to be fostered: 2134,
    2144, 2198e, 2199c.
Development is the new name for peace: 2153.
Monetary imperialism is to be condemned: 2147b, 2160.

World Community

*Complete development of the person includes the development of all
    humanity:* 2150.
Developing countries have a right to full development: 2160.
Solidarity and interdependence between rich and poor nations is needed:
    2122, 2150, 2184, 2190, 2198d.
It must be expressed in help given to poorer nations: 2151.
This help must be disinterested and given in mutual appreciation: 2123,
    2133.
In international transactions justice and charity are required: 2150,
    2152.
The world community requires a supra-national authority: 2135-2137.
*The principle of subsidiarity must regulate the relations between world
    authority and State Governments:* 2138.
*Developing nations should not be drawn into the conflicts of richer
    countries:* 2188.

Duties of Catholics in Public Life

Catholics must take an active part in it: 2061, 2139, 2157.
*Their collaboration with movements originating in non-Christian
    ideologies is subject to conditions:* 2140/1-2, 2154-2156, 2158.
The Church has a specific role to play in bringing about justice: 2159,
    2161.
*Action for the liberation of the human person is part of the Church's
    mission:* 2159, 2161, 2166, 2167, 2168.
The Church must witness to justice in her own life: 2162.
The Church's mission can not be reduced to a temporal project: 2170

Development and Liberation

The Christian vision of integral development: 2145.

Evangelisation is necessarily linked with human development : 2169.

The contribution of human sciences is to be positively evaluated: 2156a.

There is need for total, not mere economic, development: 2156b, 2172, 2189a-2189b, 2199d.

Preferential love is to be shown to the poor: 2153f, 2183.

The Gospel is a message of liberation : 2167, 2168.

The Church carries on a liberating mission : 2182a-2182b.

True liberation requires conversion: 2171.

The obstacles to the right development of nations must be overcome: 2160.

Revolution is legitimate only in the most extreme cases : 2147c, 2156c, 2186a-2186b.

There is need for education to justice: 2163.

Liturgy helps form just persons: 2164.

The Holy Year is the year of the poor, of a redistribution of goods: 2165.

Justice must be imbued with mercy: 2174.

LEO XIII
ENCYCLICAL LETTER *RERUM NOVARUM* (1891)

This is the first in the series of the great Encyclical Letters on social questions. Confronted with the phenomenon of growing industrialisation, it is mostly concerned with the problems of ownership and wages. The right to private ownership is founded both at the individual and at the family level. The social aspect of the question manifests itself in the use one must make of one's property. In the determination of just wage the personal and the necessary character of labour must be taken into account: this determination should not be left to the mere play of economic laws.

(Right and use of private property)

2101
3265
Every person has by nature the right to possess property as his or her own.[...] For God has granted the earth to humankind in general, not in the sense that all without distinction can deal with it as they like, but rather that no part of it was assigned to anyone in particular, and that the limits of private possession have been left to be fixed by our own industry and by the laws of individual races[...] Truly, that which is required for the preservation of life and for its well-being is produced in great abundance from the soil, but not until human beings have brought it into cultivation and exercised upon it their solicitude and skill. Now, when they thus turn the activity of their mind and the strength of their body towards procuring the fruits of nature, by such industry they make their own that portion of nature's field which they cultivate—that portion on which they leave, as it were, the impress of their individuality; and it cannot but be just that they should possess that portion as their own, and have the right to hold it—a right which no one is justified in violating.

2102
3266
The rights here spoken of, belonging to each individual person are seen in a much stronger light when considered in relation to one's social and domestic obligations.[...] That right to property, therefore, which has been proved to belong naturally to individual persons, must likewise belong to man in his capacity of head of a family; nay, that right is all the more valid in proportion as human personality in the life of the family takes various forms. For it is a most sacred law of nature that a father should provide food and all necessities for those whom he has begotten, and, similarly, it is natural that

he should wish that his children, who reproduce, so to speak, and prolong his personality, should be by him provided with all that is needed to enable them to keep themselves decently from want and misery amid the uncertainties of this mortal life. Now, in no other way can a father effect this except by the ownership of productive property, which he can transmit to his children by inheritance.[...]

2103   It is one thing to have a right to the possession of money,
3267   another to use one's money rightly. Private ownership, as we have seen, is the natural right of the person; and to exercise that right, especially as members of society, is not only lawful, but absolutely necessary.[...] But if the question be asked: How must one's possession be used?, the Church replies without hesitation in the words of St. Thomas Aquinas: "One should not consider one's material possessions as one's own, but as common to all, so as to share them without hesitation when others are in need. Hence the apostle says: 'As for the rich of this world, charge them[...]to be generous and willing to share' [*1 Tim 6:17*]."[1] True, no one is commanded to distribute to others that which is required for one's own needs and those of one's household; nor even to give away what is reasonably required to keep up becomingly one's condition in life.[...]But when what necessity demands has been supplied and one's standing fairly provided for, it becomes a duty to give to the needy out of what remains over. "Of that which remains, give alms" [*Lk 11:41 Vulg.*]. It is a duty, not of justice (save in extreme cases), but of Christian charity— a duty not to be enforced by law. But the laws and judgment of people must yield to the law and judgment of Christ our God, who in many ways urges on his followers the practice of almsgiving.[...]

(Rights arising from labour: A just wage)

2104   To labour is to exert oneself for the sake of procuring
what is necessary for the various purposes of life, and above all for self-preservation.

3268   [...]Hence a person's labour necessarily bears two notes or characters. First of all, it is personal, inasmuch as the force which acts is bound up with the personality and is the

---

1. *Summa theologica*, II, II, 66, 2.

exclusive property of the one who acts, and further, was given to that person for his or her benefit. Secondly, one's labour is necessary; for without the result of labour one cannot live, and self-preservation is a law of nature, which it is wrong to disobey.

2105 Now, were we to consider labour merely in so far as it
3269 is personal, doubtless it would be within the worker's
right to accept any rate of wages whatsoever; for in the same way as one is free to work or not, so is one free to accept a small wage or even no wage at all.

3270 But our conclusion must be very different if together with the personal element in a person's work we consider the fact that work is also necessary for a person to live; these two aspects of work are separable in theory, but not in reality. The preservation of life is the bounded duty of one and all, and to be wanting therein is a crime. It necessarily follows that each one has a natural right to procure for oneself what is required in order to live; and the poor can procure that in no other way than by what they earn through their work. Let then the workers and the employer make free agreements, and in particular let them agree freely as to the wages; nevertheless, underlying such agreements there is always a dictate of natural justice more imperious and ancient than any bargain between persons, namely, that wages ought not to be insufficient to support a frugal and well-behaved wage earner. If through necessity or fear of a worse evil the workers accept harder conditions, forced on them against their will, because an employer or contractor will give them no better, they are made the victims of force and injustice.[...]

PIUS XI
ENCYCLICAL LETTER *QUADRAGESIMO ANNO* (1931)

In this encyclical which celebrates the fortieth anniversary of Rerum Novarum *the social aspect is stressed more than in the previous document, both as regards the question of ownership and in the matter of wages. To attain a more perfect balance and social harmony, the Pope says, it is advisable to add to the wage contract a contract of partnership.*

(Ownership or right of property: individual and social character)

2106 The right to own private property has been given
3726 to the human person by nature, or rather by the Creator himself, not only in order that individuals may be able

to provide for their own needs and those of their families, but also that, by means of it, the goods which the Creator has destined for the human race may truly serve this purpose. Now these ends cannot be secured, unless some definite and stable order is maintained. There is therefore a double danger to be avoided. On the one hand, if the social and public aspect of ownership be denied or minimised, the logical consequence is what is called "individualism" or something approaching it; on the other hand, the rejection or toning down of its private and individual character necessarily leads to "collectivism" or at least to some of its tenets.[...]

(The State and ownership)

2107   It follows from the twofold character of ownership
3728   which we have termed individual and social, that
           individuals must take into account in this matter, not only their own advantage, but also the common good. To define in detail these duties, when the need occurs and when the natural law does not do so, is the function of the Government. Provided that the natural and divine law be observed, the public authority, in view of the common good, may specify more accurately what is licit and what is illicit for property owners in the use of their possessions.[...]

(Use of superfluous income)

2108   At the same time a person's superfluous income
3729   is not left entirely to one's own discretion.[...] On the
           contrary, the grave obligations of charity, beneficence and liberality, which rest upon the wealthy are constantly insisted upon in telling words by Holy Scripture and the Fathers of the Church.

However, the investment of superfluous income in securing favourable opportunities for employment, provided such employment be directed to the production of useful goods, is to be considered, according to the teaching of the angelic Doctor,[1] an act of real liberality, particularly appropriate to the needs of our time.

---

1. St. Thomas Aquinas, *Summa theologica*, II, II, 134, 3.

(A just wage)

2109 First of all, those who hold that the wage-contract
3733 is essentially unjust, and that in its place must be
           introduced a contract of partnership, are certainly in
error.[...] In the present state of human society, however, we deem
it advisable that the wage-contract should, when possible, be
qualified somewhat by a contract of partnership, as is already
being tried in various ways with no small gain both to the wage-
earners and to the employers. In this way wage-earners and
employers participate in the ownership or the management, or
in some way share in the profits.

In estimating a just wage, not one consideration alone but
many must be taken into account.[...]

(Labour's double aspect)

2110 The obvious truth is that in labour, especially hired
3734 labour, as in ownership, there is a social as well as a
           personal or individual aspect to be considered. For unless
human society forms a truly social and organic body; unless
labour be protected in the social and juridical order; unless the
various forms of human endeavour, dependent one upon the
other, are united in mutual harmony and mutual support; unless,
above all, intelligence, capital and labour combine together for a
common effort, one's toil cannot produce due fruit. Hence, if the
social and individual character of labour be overlooked, it can
neither be justly valued nor equitably remunerated.

From this double aspect, growing out of the very notion of
human labour, follow important conclusions for the regulation
and fixing of wages.

(a. Support of workers and their family)

2111/1 In the first place, the wage paid to workers must
3735   be sufficient for their own support and that of their
            family.[...] Every effort must therefore be made that
fathers of families receive a wage sufficient to meet adequately
ordinary domestic needs. If in the present state of society this is
not always feasible, social justice demands that reforms be
introduced without delay which will guarantee such a wage to
every adult working man.[...]

(b. State of business)

2111/2 The condition of any particular business and of its
3736 owner must also come into consideration for setting the
scale of wages; for it is unjust to demand wages so high
that an employer cannot pay them without ruin, and without
consequent distress amongst the working people themselves. If
the business makes too little profit on account of bad
management, want of enterprise or out-of-date methods, this is
not a just reason for reducing the workers' wages. If, however,
the business does not make enough money to pay the workers a
just wage, either because it is overwhelmed with unjust burdens,
or because it is compelled to sell its products at an unjustly low
price, those who thus injure it are guilty of grievous wrong; for
it is they who deprive the workers of the just wage, and force
them to accept lower terms.[...]

(c. Demands of the common good)

2111/3 Finally, the wage-scale must be regulated with a
3737 view to the economic welfare of the whole people. We
have already shown how conducive it is to the common
good that wage-earners of all kinds be enabled, by economising
that portion of their wage which remains after necessary expenses
have been met, to attain to the possession of a certain modest
fortune. Another point, however, of no less importance must not
be overlooked, in these our days especially, namely, that
opportunities for work be provided for those who are willing
and able to work. This depends in large measure upon the scale
of wages which multiplies opportunities for work as long as it
remains within proper limits, and reduces them if allowed to
depart from these limits.[...]To lower or raise wages unduly, with
a view to private profit and with no consideration for the common
good, is contrary to social justice, which demands that, by union
of effort and good will, such a scale of wages be set up, if possible,
so as to offer to the greatest number opportunities of employment
and of securing for themselves suitable means of livelihood.[...]

PIUS XII

DISCOURSE ON THE FIFTIETH ANNIVERSARY OF
RERUM NOVARUM (1941)

In this discourse Pope Pius XII clearly states the primacy of everyone's

right to make use of the goods of the earth. The text is found in AAS 33
(1941) 195ff.

(Use of material goods)

2112   [...] Every person, as a living being gifted with reason,
has in fact from nature the fundamental right to make
use of the material goods of the earth, while it is left to the
human will and to the juridical statutes of nations to regulate in
greater detail the exercise of this right. This individual right
cannot in any way be suppressed, even by other clear and
undisputed rights over material goods. Undoubtedly the natural
order, deriving from God, also demands private property and
the free reciprocal commerce of goods by interchange and gift,
as well as the function of the State to control both of these
institutions. But all this remains subordinated to the natural end
of material goods and cannot be emancipated from the first and
fundamental right which concedes their use to all; it should rather
serve to make possible the exercise of this right in conformity
with its end.[...]

JOHN XXIII

ENCYCLICAL LETTER *MATER ET MAGISTRA* (1961)

*In the last decades the socio-economic conditions have changed
considerably. We are involved in complex social structures as a result of the
development of social legislation and independent bodies, such as insurance
societies, etc. In many countries the status of industrial workers has improved
considerably while agricultural workers are often handicapped. The social
problem has also acquired world-wide dimensions due to the vastly different
conditions in prosperous and developing countries. This encyclical touches on
all these problems. On the question of private ownership a new note is struck.
It is not so much the question of subsistence that is stressed—this is often
sufficiently provided for by the various social securities—but the element of
freedom and the exercise of personal responsibility.*

(Private initiative, State intervention, and subsidiarity)

2113   [...] It should be affirmed that in the economy
3943   the first place must be given to the personal initiative
of private citizens, working as individuals or in various
associations for the pursuit of common interests.

But in this area, for reasons pointed out by our predecessors,
authorities also must play an active role in duly promoting
increased productivity with a view to social progress and the

welfare of all citizens. This activity of public authority, which encourages, stimulates, co-ordinates, supplements and completes, is based on the principle of subsidiarity.[...]

[...]This principal must always be retained: that Sate activity in the economic field, no matter what its reach or extent may be, ought not to be exercised in such a way as to curtail an individual's freedom of action, but rather to increase it, provided the essential rights of each individual person are duly safeguarded.[...]

(Socialisation)

2114 One of the characteristic features of our epoch is socialisation. By this term is meant the growing interdependence of human persons in society, giving rise to various patterns of group life and activity and in many instances to social institutions established on a juridical basis.[...]

It is clear that many benefits and advantages flow from socialisation thus understood.[...] At the same time, however, it multiplies institutional structures and extends more and more to minute details the juridical control of human relations in every walk of life.[...] We consider that socialisation can and ought to be brought about in such a way as to maximise its advantages and eliminate or minimise its negative consequences.

(Remuneration of work: standards of justice and equity)

2115 [...]It not infrequently happens that in economically advanced countries great, and sometimes very great, reward is paid for the performance of some small task, or one of doubtful value. At the same time, however, the diligent and profitable toil of whole classes of decent, hard-working persons receives a recompense that is too small, or even totally insufficient. Moreover, it may in no way correspond to their contribution to the good of the community, to the profit of the enterprises they are employed in or to the national economy.

3944 We judge it, therefore, to be our duty to reaffirm that just as the remuneration of work cannot be left entirely to the laws of the market, so too it cannot be fixed by an arbitrary decision. It must rather be determined according to justice and equity. This requires that workers should be paid a wage which allows them to live a truly human life and requires, too, that in the assessment of a fair wage for labour regard be had for the following: the contribution of individual workers to production; the economic health of the enterprise in which they are engaged; the demands of the national interest, especially with regard to any impact on employment of the total labour force; and finally the requirements of the universal common good, that is, of international communities of different nature and scope.

It is clear that these standards of judgment are valid always and everywhere. However, the degree to which they are applicable to concrete cases cannot be determined without reference to the available wealth.[...]

(Balancing economic development and social progress)

2116 Since the economies of various nations are evolving rapidly, [...] we consider it opportune to call attention to a fundamental principle of social justice, namely, that social progress should accompany and be adjusted to economic development in such a way that all classes of citizens can participate in the increased productivity.

(Shared responsibility)

2117/1
3947 Justice is to be observed not only in the distribution of wealth acquired by production but also the respect to the conditions under which production is achieved. For there is an innate demand in human nature that when people engage in productive activity, they should have the opportunity of exercising responsibility and of perfecting their personalities.[...]

2117/2
3948 [...] We uphold the desire of employees to participate actively in the management of enterprises in which they are employed.[...]

2117/3 [...]We cannot fail to emphasise how imperative it is or at least highly opportune that the workers should be able freely to make their voices heard, and listened to, beyond the confines of their individual productive units and at every level of society.[...] It is not the decisions made within each individual productive unit which have the greatest bearing [on the economic and social complex]; instead it is those made by public authorities or by institutions that function on a worldwide or national scale in regard to some economic sector or category of production.[...]

(Private property: changed conditions)

2118   [...] There are many citizens today—and their number
3949   is on the increase—who through belonging to insurance
         groups or through social security, can afford to face the
future with serenity. Formerly such serenity depended on the
ownership of property, however modest.[...] It is noted that today
people strive to acquire professional skills rather than to become
owners of property. They have greater confidence in income
derived from work or rights founded on work than in income
derived from capital or rights founded on capital.[...]

The aspects of the economy just alluded to have certainly
contributed to spreading a doubt whether, in the present state of
affairs, a principle of the socio-economic order consistently taught
and defended by our predecessors has diminished in or lost
its importance. The principle in question is that of the natural
right of private ownership, including ownership of productive
goods.

(Natural law and the right of private ownership)

2119   There is no reason for such a doubt to persist.The right
         of private ownership of goods, including productive
goods, has a permanent validity. This is so because it is a part of
the natural law, which teaches us that individuals are prior to
society and that society has as its purpose the service of the
human person.

Moreover, it would be useless to insist on free, private
initiative in the economic field, if the same initiative did not
include the power to dispose freely of the means indispensable
to its exercise. Further, history and experience testify that where
governments fail to recognize the right to private ownership of
goods, productive goods included, the fundamental
manifestations of freedom are suppressed or stifled. Hence one
may justifiably conclude that the exercise of freedom finds in
the right of ownership both a guarantee and an incentive.

(Right to property to be extended)

2120   It is not enough to assert the natural character
3951   of the right of private property, including productive
         property; strenuous efforts must be made to see that the
ability to exercise this is extended to all social classes.

(Public ownership, subsidiarity and the common good)

2121   The doctrine that has been set forth above obviously
          does not prohibit the State and other public agencies from
lawfully possessing productive goods, particularly when they
carry with them an opportunity for domination that is so great
that it cannot be left in the hands of private individuals without
injury to the community at large.[...] But in this matter also the
principle of subsidiarity stated above is to be faithfully observed.
Accordingly, the State and other agencies of public law should
not extend their ownership except where evident and real needs
of the common good dictate it; and they should be on their guard
against extending it to the point where private property is
excessively reduced or, even worse, abolished.

*(Just relations between nations in different stages of economic
development based on solidarity)*

2122   One of the most difficult problems facing the modern
          world concerns the relations between nations that are
economically advanced and those in the earlier stages of
development.[...] The solidarity which binds all persons and
makes them, as it were, members of the same family requires
that nations enjoying an abundance of material goods should
not remain indifferent to those nations whose citizens suffer from
internal problems that result in poverty, hunger and an inability
to enjoy even the more elementary human rights. This obligation
is all the more urgent since, given the growing interdependence
among nations, it is impossible to preserve a lasting and beneficial
peace while glaring socio-economic inequalities persist between
them.[...]

     [...]Emergency aid, though a duty imposed by humanity and
justice, will not suffice to eliminate or even reduce the permanent
factors which in not a few nations bring about misery, hunger
and want.[...] Part of the answer is to make available the capital
needed to step up the economic development of these nations
with the help of modern methods and techniques.

(Disinterested aid and cooperation on a world scale)

2123   [...]The more highly developed nations face one very
          great temptation. They must take care lest, while giving
technical and financial help to less developed nations, they turn

the political situation that prevails there to their own profit or imperialistic aggrandizement.[...] Necessity and justice alike demand that technical and financial aid be given with sincere political disinterestedness and for the purpose of bringing those nations on the way to economic development, to the point where they can achieve themselves their economic and social growth.[...]

[...] It can be said that contemporary problems of any importance, whatever their object may be—scientific, technical, economic, social, political or cultural—today commonly present supranational and often world dimensions.[...] Hence, mutual understanding and cooperation are a prime necessity. Individuals, and even all people, grow more and more convinced of this everyday. Nevertheless, it seems that people, especially those entrusted with greater responsibility, are unable to achieve the understanding and cooperation which the general public desires. The root of such inability is not to be sought in any shortage of scientific knowledge, technical skill or economic proficiency, but in the absence of mutual trust.[...] As a consequence, vast human energies and gigantic resources are employed for destructive rather than constructive purposes.[...]

Mutual trust among persons and among states cannot stand firm and become deep-rooted without initial recognition of and respect for a just moral order on both sides. The moral order, however, cannot be built except on God.

ENCYCLICAL LETTER *PACEM IN TERRIS* (1963)

The first part of this other encyclical of Pope John XXIII treats of the rights and duties of the human person; it has been dealt with in the chapter on the principles of the Christian life (cf. nn. 2028-2042). From this part, only one quotation is given here, which is more directly relevant to the social order (n. 2124). The other passages are taken from parts two, three and four, which deal with the relations between persons and State, between States, and finally between States and the world community. In the pastoral directives given at the end of the encyclical, the Pope encourages Catholics to work in harmony with other groups; he points out that a distinction must be made between error and the person who professes it, as well as between philosophical theories and the social movements that have arisen from them. This open and positive attitude, characteristic of Pope John, has paved the way for the Church's new approach to the modern world, officially stated in the Pastoral Constitution Gaudium et Spes *of the Second Vatican Council.*

(God and the moral order of society)

2124 The right order in human society is by nature spiritual.
3973   Founded as it is in truth, it must function according to
       the norms of justice; it should be inspired and perfected
by mutual love; and, finally, while preserving freedom, it should
be brought to an ever more humane equitableness. This order,
the principles of which are universal, absolute and unchangeable,
has its ultimate source in the one true God, who is personal and
transcends human nature. Inasmuch as God is the first truth and
the supreme good, he alone is the deepest source from which
society can draw its vitality.[...]

(The citizen and the State: State authority)

2125 Human society would not be well ordered and
3979   prosperous without persons lawfully vested with
       authority, who safeguard its institutions and see to the
common good. They derive their authority from God, as St. Paul
teaches: "For there is no authority except from God" *[Rom
13:1]*.[...] This authority, not less than society itself, has its source
in nature, and has, consequently, God for its author.

2126 Authority, however, is not without its own law. Being
3980   the power to command according to right reason, it
       derives its binding force from the moral order and from
God.[...] Thus, human authority can bind people in conscience
only when it rests upon and shares in the authority of God.

2127 [...]Since the right to command is required by the
3981   moral order and has its source in God, it follows that, if
       civil authorities make laws or command anything
contrary to that order and, therefore, contrary to the will of God,
neither the laws made nor the powers granted can be binding
on the consciences of the citizens, since "we must obey God
rather than human beings" *[Acts 5:29]*.[...]

2128 At the same time, the divine origin of authority
3982   does not take away from people the right to choose their
       rulers and form of government, and to determine both
the way in which authority is to be exercised and its limits. This
doctrine, then, is consonant with every form of truly democratic
regime.

(The common good)

2129 [...] Since the civil authority is entirely ordained to the
3983 common good of all, its holders while pursuing the
common good, must respect its true nature; they must
also adapt the exercise of their authority to present conditions.[...]

3984 Besides, the very nature of the common good requires
that all citizens should share in it, in different ways
according to each one's task, merits and circumstances.[...] The
common good concerns the whole person, the needs both of body
and soul. Hence it follows that the civil authorities must
undertake to procure it by ways and means proportionate to it:
while respecting the hierarchy of values, they should promote
simultaneously both the material and the spiritual welfare of the
citizens.

(Responsibilities of the public authority)

2130 Contemporary thought holds that the common
3985 good lies chiefly in maintaining the rights and duties of
the human person. Civil authorities therefore must ensure
that these rights be acknowledged and respected, mutually
coordinated, defended and promoted; then each one will be able
to carry out one's duties more easily.[...] When civil authorities
disown or violate the rights of the human person, they not only
fail in their duty, but their orders are without binding force.

One of the fundamental duties of civil authorities, therefore,
is to coordinate social relations in such fashion that the exercise
of one person's rights does not threaten others in the exercise of
their own rights nor hinder them in the fulfilment of their duties.
Finally, the rights of all should be effectively safeguarded and, if
they have been violated, completely restored.

(Participation of citizens in public life)

2131 Citizens have the right, by virtue of their dignity as
persons, to take an active part in government, although
the manner in which they share in it will depend on the level of
development of the political community.[...]

(Relations between States: Mutual rights and duties)

2132 States have mutual rights and duties, as our predecessors
taught repeatedly and we here reaffirm. Their

relationship must be harmonised in truth, in justice, in active solidarity, and in liberty. The same natural law which governs the relations between person and person must also rule the relations between State and State.[...]

2133 Truth must govern the relations between nations. This calls for the elimination of every trace of racism and for the recognition of the principle that all nations are by nature equal in human dignity. Each of them accordingly is vested with the right to existence, to self-development, to the means necessary to achieve that development, and to the primary responsibility for that achievement. Each one may rightfully claim due consideration and respect.[...] Dealings between States must also be ruled by justice. This requires the recognition of their mutual rights and the fulfilment of their respective duties.[...] Relations between nations should further be animated by an active solidarity shown by mutual cooperation in many spheres, such as, in our times, has already taken place with laudable results in the economic, social, political and educational spheres, in health and sport.[...]

(Disarmament)

2134
3991 Justice, right reason and humanity urgently demand that the arms race should cease; that the stockpiles which exist in various countries should be reduced equally and simultaneously; that nuclear arms should be banned, and a general agreement reached for a progressive disarmament with an effective method of control.[...] All must realise that there is no hope of putting an end to the building up of armaments,[...] unless the process is complete and thorough and unless it proceeds from an inner conviction; unless, that is, everyone sincerely cooperates to banish the fear and anxious expectations of war with which people are oppressed.[...]

People are becoming more and more convinced that conflicts which arise between States should not be resolved by recourse to arms, but rather through negotiation.[...]

(The World Community: Interdependence of political communities)

2135
3992 Recent progress in science and technology has deeply affected human persons; it has determined a world-wide movement for cooperation and union.[...] The

unity of the human family can never be destroyed, because it is made of members sharing with equal right in their same natural dignity. Hence it will always be a pressing need, arising from human nature itself, to attend seriously to the universal good, which bears on the entire human family.[...]

As a result of the far-reaching changes which have taken place in the relations within the human community, the universal common good gives rise to problems that are very grave, complex and extremely urgent, especially as regards world security and peace. On the other hand, the public authorities of the individual nations—all of whom have equal rights—no matter how often they meet and how much ingenuity they display in an effort to draw up new and more adequate juridical instruments, do not find satisfactory solutions.[...]

Yet, if serious consideration is given to the nature of the common good on the one hand, and, on the other, to the nature and function of public authority, it is clear that there exists between both a necessary connection.

(Universal common good and political authority)

2136 Today the universal common good poses problems of
3993   world-wide dimensions, which cannot adequately be
        tackled or solved except by a public authority with adequate power, juridical status and proportionate means enabling it to operate in an effective manner on a world-wide basis. It follows then that the moral order itself demands that such a universal public authority be established.

This universal authority, with world-wide power and endowed with the proper means to pursue the universal common good, must be set up by the common agreement of all nations, and not imposed by force.[...]

(Universal common good and personal rights)

2137 Because the universal common good, just as the national
3994   common good, is to be determined with reference to
        human persons, the world public authority must have as its fundamental objective the recognition, due respect, safeguarding and promotion of the rights of the human person.[...]

(Principle of subsidiarity and world authority)

2138 Within each country, relations between the government

3995   and the citizens, families and intermediate societies, are governed by the principle of subsidiarity. The same principle must rule the relations between the world public authority and the State governments. It belongs to the world authority to tackle and solve problems posed by the universal common good in the economic, social, political and cultural fields, which State governments are not equipped to solve adequately by themselves because of their complexity, vastness or urgency.

The world authority is not intended to curtail the sphere of action proper to the State governments or to replace them. Rather, it must aim at the creation in all countries of such conditions as will facilitate, not only for the governments, but also for the citizens and the intermediate societies, the fulfilment of their duties and the exercise of their rights.

(Pastoral directives)

2139   [...] We deem it opportune to remind our children of their duty to take an active part in public life and to contribute towards the attainment of the common good of the entire human family and of their own country.[...]

3996   [These social principles] provide Catholics, therefore, with a vast field in which they can collaborate both with Christians separated from the apostolic See and with people alien to the Christian faith who are perceptive and whose dispositions are morally upright. "On such occasions those who make profession of Catholicism must take special care to be consistent and not to compromise in matters wherein the integrity of religion or morals would suffer harm.[...]"[1]

2140/1   Moreover, one must always distinguish error and the person who errs, even, in the case of persons falling into error or lacking sufficient knowledge in matters pertaining to the religious and moral fields. The person who errs always remains a human being and retains in every case the dignity of a human person; this dignity must always be taken into account.[...]

2140/2   Similarly, one must clearly distinguish false
3997   philosophical theories on the nature, origin and destiny of the world and of the human being, from historical

---

1. JOHN XXIII, *Encyclical Letter Mater et Magistra*, AAS 53 (1961) 456.

movements with economic or social, cultural or political objectives, even if the latter owe their origin and inspiration to the former. For, while a doctrine, once fixed and definitively formulated, does not change, movements, concerned as they are with concrete and changing conditions, cannot but be influenced by that change.[...].

THE SECOND VATICAN GENERAL COUNCIL
PASTORAL CONSTITUTION *GAUDIUM ET SPES* (1965)

The general moral teaching of the first part of the Constitution has been dealt with in the previous chapter (cf. nn. 2051ff). In its second part the Constitution turns its attention to urgent problems of the present time (cf. n. 2043i). Among these the topics relevant to this chapter are "the socio-economic and political life, the solidarity of the family of nations, and peace" (46). The Constitution reaffirms the principles laid down in the previous encyclicals, notably in Mater et Magistra and Pacem in Terris. It takes a clear stand on the matter of war and especially of total warfare. It also gives directives for the cooperation between rich and developing nations.

The main doctrinal points are as follows. Chapter III on "the socio-economic life" shows that economic development is at the service of the whole person(64). It explains the meaning of work, affirms the person's right to work, treats of just wages and working conditions and of the opportunities due to people to develop their talents (67). It defends participation by the workers in management and their right to form labour unions (68). It completely reverses the perspective regarding earthly goods, first stressing the patristic doctrine of the universal destination of property (69), and only in this context affirming the right to private ownership (71). Chapter IV on "the life of the political community" explains its nature and goal (74) and advocates cooperation of all in public life (75). Chapter V on "fostering peace and building the community of nations" affirms that the pursuit of the universal common good requires that the community of nations be organised (84). It stresses international cooperation in the economic field (85) and lays down norms for this cooperation (86).

(Universal destination of created goods)

2141   69. God has intended the earth and all that it contains for the use of all people and all peoples. Hence justice, accompanied by charity, must so regulate the distribution of created goods that they are actually available to all in an equitable measure. Whatever may be the different forms of ownership, adapted to the legitimate local usages according to diverse and changeable circumstances, this universal destination of earthly goods must always be heeded. Therefore, in using them everyone should consider legitimate possessions not only as their own but also as common property, in the sense that they should be able to profit not only themselves but other people as well. Moreover, all have the right to possess a share of earthly goods sufficient for themselves and their families. This is what the Fathers and Doctors of the Church had in mind when teaching that people are obliged to come to the aid of the poor, and to do so not merely out of their superfluous goods. Someone who is in extreme necessity has the right to procure for oneself what is necessary from the riches of other people.

(Avoidance of war: Curbing the savagery of war)

2142 79. [...] The Council intends before all else to recall the permanent binding force of the natural rights of nations and of their universal principles.[...] Actions that deliberately violate them, and orders that command such actions are criminal; nor can blind obedience excuse people who carry out such orders. Among these actions must be reckoned first of all those which, for whatever reason or by whatever method, tend to the extermination of an entire people, nation or ethnic minority; such actions must be vehemently condemned as heinous crimes.[...]

In matters of war, there exist various international agreements which a number of nations have signed, aimed at making military action and its consequences less inhuman.[...] Agreements of this kind must be observed.[...] Moreover, it seems right that laws should make humane provisions for the case of those who for reasons of conscience refuse to bear arms, provided they agree to serve the human community in some other way.

Certainly, war has not been eradicated from human affairs. And, as long as the danger of war remains and there is no competent international authority with sufficient forces at its disposal, governments cannot be denied the right of legitimate self-defence, once every means for a peaceful settlement has been exhausted.[...] But it is one thing to go to war in just defense of the people, and another to seek to subjugate other nations. The possession of armaments does not make every military or political use of them lawful. Neither does the mere fact that war has unfortunately already broken out render everything permissible between the warring camps.

(Total warfare)

2143   80. [...]The Sacred Synod makes its own the condemnations of total warfare pronounced already by recent Popes, and issues the following declaration:

Every act of war tending to indiscriminate destruction of entire towns or large areas along with their population is a crime against God and against human beings themselves, which must be condemned with firmness and without hesitation.

(The arms race)

2144   81. To be sure, scientific weapons are not being stocked for the sole purpose of using them in time of war. Since the defensive strength of each party is held to depend on its capacity for immediate retaliation against an adversary, the accumulation of arms, which increases year by year, serves as an unprecedented deterrent to possible enemy attack.[...]

Whatever be the case with this method of deterrence, people should be convinced that the arms race, in which quite a considerable number of nations are now engaged, is not a safe way to preserve a steady peace, and the so-called balance resulting from it is neither a stable nor a true peace. The causes of war are thereby far from being eliminated. Rather they threaten to be gradually aggravated. While extravagant sums are being spent in preparing ever new weapons, no adequate remedy can be found for so many present-day miseries in the world.[...]

For that reason it must be stated again: the arms race is a most grievous plague for humankind, and it wrongs the poor in an intolerable manner. It is much to be feared that, if this race persists, it may some day spawn all the deadly disasters the means for which it is now making ready.[...]

PAUL VI

ENCYCLICAL LETTER *POPULORUM PROGRESSIO* (1967)

The Pope proposes a Christian vision of development. He reaffirms more strongly the universal destination of created goods (cf. n. 2141) and severely condemns "unchecked capitalism". He notes that, though it is every person's right to make use of the goods of the earth, the gap is widening between the wealth of the privileged and the misery of others. To remedy this situation is a pressing need. But the true welfare of the human person extends far beyond economic needs: it includes all values inherent in its personality. The problem of human progress has world-wide dimensions. Private initiative is not enough; the question has to be dealt with on an international basis; it is the strict duty of prosperous nations to help developing nations. Peace can only be obtained through a social order based on universal justice. The Pope warns against the temptation to violence, but concedes its possibility in extreme cases. The text is found in AAS 59 (1967) 257ff.

(Christian vision of development)

2145   14. Development cannot be limited to mere economic growth. In order to be authentic, it must be complete, integral; that is, it has to promote the good of every person and of the whole person.

15. In the design of God, all are called upon to develop and fulfil themselves, for every life is a vocation.[...] Endowed with intelligence and freedom, they are responsible for their fulfilment as they are for their salvation. They are aided, or sometimes impeded, by those who educate them and those with whom they live, but each one remains, whatever be those influences affecting them, the principal agent of their own success or failure.

(Communal responsibility and scale of values)

2146   17. But each person is a member of society, and is part of the whole of humankind. It is not just individuals, but all human beings who are called to this fulness of development.

18. This personal and communal development would be threatened if the true scale of values were undermined. The desire for necessities is legitimate and work undertaken to obtain them is a duty.[...] But the acquiring of temporal goods can lead to greed, to the insatiable desire for more, and can make increased power a tempting objective.

19. Increased possession is not the ultimate goal of nations nor individuals. All growth is ambivalent, It is essential if one is to develop as a person, but in a way it imprisons one if one considers it the supreme good and restricts one's vision.[...] Both for nations and for individual persons, avarice is the most evident form of the moral underdevelopment.

20. If further development calls for the work of more and more technicians, even more necessary is the deep thought and reflection of wise people in search of a new humanism which will enable modern men and women to find themselves anew

by embracing the higher values of love and friendship, of prayer and contemplation.This is what will permit the fullness of authentic development, a development which is for each and all the transition from less human conditions to those which are more human.

(The universal purpose of created things and right of property)

2147 22. "Fill the earth and subdue it" *[Gen 1:28]:* the Bible, from the first page on, teaches us that the whole of creation is for human beings, that it is their responsibility to develop it by intelligent effort and by means of their labour to perfect it, so to speak, for their use. If the world is made to furnish each individual with the means of livelihood and the instruments for growth and progress, each one has therefore the right to find in the world what is necessary for oneself.[...]All other rights whatsoever, including those of property and of free commerce, are to be subordinated to this principle. They should not hinder but on the contrary favour its application. It is a grave and urgent social duty to redirect them to their primary finality.

(Right to private property not absolute)

2147a 23. "How does God's love abide in anyone who has the world's goods and sees a brother or sister in need, and yet refuses help?" *[1 Jn 3:17]*. It is well known how strong were the words used by the Fathers of the Church to describe the proper attitude of persons who possess anything towards persons in need. To quote Saint Ambrose: "You are not making a gift of your possessions to poor persons. You are handing over to them what is theirs. For what has been given in common for the use of all, you have arrogated to yourself. The world is given to all, and not only to the rich."[1] That is, private property does not constitute for anyone an absolute and unconditional right. No one is justified in keeping for one's exclusive use what one does not need, when others lack necessities.[...] If there should arise a conflict between acquired private rights and primary community exigencies, it is the responsibility of public authorities to look for a solution, with the active participation of individuals and social groups.

---

1. *De Nabuthe*, c. 12, n. 53.

24. If certain landed estates impede the general prosperity because they are extensive, unused or poorly used, or because they bring hardship to people or are detrimental to the interests of the country, the common good sometimes demands their expropriation. [...] It is unacceptable that citizens with abundant incomes from the resources and activity of their country should transfer a considerable part of this income abroad purely for their own advantage, without care for the manifest wrong they inflict on their country by doing so.

(Liberal capitalism severely condemned)

2147b 26. [...] It is unfortunate that on these new conditions of society a system has been constructed which considers profit as the key motive for economic progress, competition as the supreme law of economics, and private ownership of means of production as an absolute right that has no limits and carries no corresponding social obligation. This unchecked liberalism leads to the dictatorship rightly denounced by Pius XI as producing "the international imperialism of money".[1] One cannot condemn such abuses too strongly by solemnly recalling once again that the economy is at the service of the person.

(Revolution legitimate only in the most extreme cases)

2147c c. There are certainly situations whose injustice cries to heaven. When whole populations, destitute of necessities, live in a state of dependence, barring them from all initiative and responsibility, and from all opportunity to advance culturally and share in social and political life, recourses to violence, as a means to right these wrongs to human dignity, is a grave temptation.

31. We know, however, that a revolutionary uprising—save where there is manifest, long-standing tyranny which would do great damage to fundamental personal rights and dangerous harm to the common good of the country—produces new injustices, throws more elements out of balance and brings new disasters. A real evil should not be fought at the cost of greater misery.

---

1. *Quadragesimo Anno, AAS* 23 (1931) 212.

(Planning for reform)

2148 32. We want to be clearly understood: the present situation must be faced with courage and the injustices linked with it must be fought against and overcome. Development demands bold transformations, far-reaching innovations. Urgent reforms should be undertaken without delay. It is for each one to take one's share in them with generosity, particularly those whose education, position and opportunities afford them wide scope for action.[...]Individual initiative alone and the mere free play of competition could never assure successful development.[...]

33. Hence programmes are necessary in order to encourage, stimulate, coordinate, supplement and integrate the activity of individuals and of intermediate societies. It pertains to the public authorities to choose, even to lay down the objectives to be pursued, the ends to be achieved, and the means for attaining these, and it is for them to stimulate all the forces engaged in this common action. But let them take care to associate private initiative and intermediate societies with this work. They will thus avoid the danger of complete collectivisation or of arbitrary planning, which, by denying liberty, would prevent the exercise of the fundamental rights of the human person.

(The aim is integral humanism)

2149 42. What must be aimed at is integral humanism. And what is that if not the fully-rounded development of the whole person and of all persons? A humanism closed in on itself, and not open to the values of the spirit and to God who is their origin and source, can only achieve apparent success. It is true that people can organise the world apart from God; but without God they can organise it in the end only to their own detriment. An isolated humanism inevitably becomes inhuman. There is no true humanism but that which is open to the Absolute and is conscious of a vocation which gives human life its true meaning.[...]

(The development of the human race in a spirit of solidarity)

2150 43. There can be no progress towards the complete development of the person without the simultaneous development of all humanity in a spirit of solidarity.[...]

44. This duty is the concern especially of the prosperous nations. Their obligations stem from a kinship that is at once human and supernatural, and take on a threefold aspect: the duty of human solidarity—the aid that rich nations must give to developing countries; the duty of social justice—the rectification of inequitable trade relations between powerful nations and weak nations; the duty of universal charity—the effort to bring about a world that is more human towards all, where all will be able to give and receive, without one group making progress at the expense of the other. The question is urgent, for on it depends the future of the civlisation of the world.

(The duty of human solidarity binding on nations)

2151   48. The same duty of solidarity that rests on individuals exists also for nations.[...] Given the increasing needs of the developing countries, it should be considered quite normal for an advanced country to devote a part of its production to meet their needs, and to train teachers, engineers, technicians and scholars prepared to put their knowledge and their skill at the disposal of less fortunate peoples.

49. We must repeat once more that the superfluous wealth of rich countries should be placed at the service of poor nations.[...]

50. In order to be fully effective, these efforts ought not to remain scattered or isolated, much less be in competition with one another for reasons of power or prestige; the present situation calls for concerted planning.[...]

(Equity in trade relations)

2152   The teaching of our predecessor Leo XIII in his Encyclical Letter *Rerum Novarum* is always valid: if the position of the contracting parties are too unequal, the consent of the parties does not suffice to guarantee the justice of their contract, and the rule of free agreement remains subservient to the demands of the natural law.[1] What was true of the just wage for the individual is also true of international contracts: An economy of exchange can no longer be based solely on the law of free competition, a law which, in its turn, too often creates an

---

1. Leo XIII, *Acta* XI (1892) 131.

economic dictatorship. Freedom of trade is fair only if it is subject to the demands of social justice.

(Development is the new name for peace)

2153 Excessive economic, social and cultural inequalities among people arouse tensions and conflicts, and are a danger to peace.[...] To wage war on misery and to struggle against injustice is to promote, along with improved conditions, the human and spiritual progress of all persons, and therefore the common good of humanity. Peace cannot be limited to a mere absence of war, the result of an ever precarious balance of forces. No, peace is something that is built up day after day, in the pursuit of an order intended by God, which implies a more perfect form of justice among people.

APOSTOLIC LETTER *OCTOGESIMA ADVENIENS* (1971)

On the occasion of the eightieth anniversary of the encyclical Rerum Novarum *the Pope addressed an apostolic letter to Cardinal Maurice Roy, president of the Council of the Laity and of the Pontifical Commission for Justice and Peace.*

The letter stresses the new dimensions and applications of social justice in the world today (3-7). Some of the problems mentioned are: urbanisation, youth, women, workers' unions, strikes, immigration, and the impact of mass media (8-21). In a following section, the Pope, while insisting on the duty of Christians to take part in political activities (24), states the limits within which they may collaborate with movements which have their origin in secular ideologies but are in part distinct from them (26-41). The letter then restates the Christian principles that must guide people in their social and political attitudes (42-47). It ends with a call to action addressed to all Christians (48-52). The text is found in AAS 63(1971) 401ff.

(Social teaching recognizes complexity of particular situations)

2153a 4. In the face of such widely varying situations it is difficult for us to utter a unified message and to put forward a solution which has universal validity. Such is not our ambition, nor is it our mission. It is up to the Christian communities to analyse with objectivity the situation which is proper to their own country, to shed on it the light of the Gospel's unalterable words and to draw principles of reflection, norms of judgment and directives for action from the social teaching of Church.

(Role of women)

2153b 13. [...] In many countries a charter for women which would put an end to an actual discrimination and would establish relationships of equality in rights and of respect for their dignity is the object of study and at times of lively demands. We do not have in mind that false equality which would deny the distinction laid down by the Creator himself and which would be in contradiction with woman's proper role, which is of such capital importance, at the heart of the family as well as within society. Developments in legislation should on the contrary be directed to protecting her proper vocation and at the same time recognizing her independence as a person, and her equal rights to participate in cultural, economic, social and political life.

(Racial discrimination condemned)

2153c 16. Racial discrimination possesses at the moment a character of very great relevance by reason of the tension which it stirs up both within certain countries and on the international level. People rightly consider unjustifiable and reject as inadmissible the tendency to maintain or introduce legislation or behaviour systematically inspired by racist prejudice. The members of humankind share the same basic rights and duties, as well as the same supernatural destiny. Within a country which belongs to each one, all should be equal before the law, find equal admittance to economic, civic, and social life and benefit from a fair sharing of the nation's riches.

(Right of migrants)

2153d 17. We are thinking also of the precarious situation of a great number of emigrant workers whose condition as foreigners makes it all the more difficult for them to make any sort of social vindication, in spite of their real participation in the economic effort of the country that receives them. It is urgently necessary for people to go beyond a narrowly nationalist attitude in their regard and to give them a charter which will assure them a right to emigrate, favour their integration, facilitate their professional advancement and give them access to decent housing where, if such is the case, their families can join them.

(Responsible use of the mass media)

2153e 20. Among the major changes of our times, we do not wish to forget to emphasise the growing role being assumed by the media of social communication and their influence on the transformation of mentalities, of knowledge, of organizations and of society itself. Certainly they have many positive aspects. Thanks to them, news from the entire world reaches us practically in an instant, establishing contacts which supersede distances and creating elements of unity among all people. A greater spread of education and culture is becoming possible. Nevertheless, by this very action the media of social communication are reaching the point of representing as it were a new power. One cannot but ask about those who really hold this power, the aims that they pursue and the means they use, and finally, about the effect of their activity on the exercise of individual liberty, both in the political and ideological spheres and in social, economic and cultural life. The persons who hold this power have a grave moral responsibility with respect to the truth of the information that they spread, the needs and the reactions that they generate and the values which they put forward.

(Preferential respect for the poor)

2153f 23. In teaching us charity, the Gospel instructs us in the preferential respect for the poor and the special situation they have in society: the more fortunate should renounce some of their rights so as to place their goods more generously at the service of others. If, beyond legal rules, there is really no deeper feeling of respect and service of others, then even equality before the law can serve as an alibi for flagrant discrimination, continued exploitation and actual contempt.

(Attraction of socialist currents)

2154 31. Some Christians are today attracted by socialist currents and their various developments. They try to recognise therein some of the aspirations which they carry within themselves in the name of their faith. They feel that they are inserted in that historical current and wish to play a part within it. Now this historical current takes on, under the same name, different forms according to different continents and cultures, even if it drew its inspiration, and still does in many cases, from ideologies incompatible with the faith. Careful judgment is called for. Too often Christians attracted by socialism tend to idealise it, in general and without restriction, as a perfect good; socialism then simply means a will for justice, solidarity and equality. They refuse to recognise the limitations of the historical socialist movements, which remain conditioned by the ideologies from which they originated. Distinctions must be made to guide concrete choices between the various levels of expression of socialism: a generous aspiration and a seeking for a more just society; historical movements with a political organisation and aim; an ideology which claims to give a complete and self-sufficient picture of the person. Nevertheless, these distinctions must not lead one to consider such levels as completely separated and independent. The concrete link which, according to circumstances, exists between them must be clearly marked out. This insight will enable Christians to see the degree of commitment possible along these lines, while safeguarding the values, especially those of liberty, responsibility and openness to the spiritual, which guarantee the integral development of people.

(Historical evolution of Marxism)

2155 32. Other Christians even ask whether a historical development of Marxism might not authorise certain concrete rapprochements. They note in fact a certain splintering of Marxism, which until now appeared as a unitary ideology claiming to offer an explanation of the totality of the person and the world in its process of development, and consequently atheistic. Apart from the ideological confrontation officially separating the various champions of Marxism-Leninism in their individual interpretations of the thought of its founders, and apart from the open opposition between the political systems which make use of its name today, some people lay down distinctions between various levels of expression of Marxism.[...]

2156 34. While, in the doctrine of Marxism as concretely put in practice, one can distinguish these various aspects and the questions they pose for the reflection and activity of Christians, it would be illusory and dangerous to reach the point of forgetting the intimate link which radically binds them together, to accept the elements of Marxist analysis without recognising their relationship with ideology, and to enter into the practice of class struggle and its Marxist interpretations, while failing to take note of the kind of totalitarian and violent society to which this process leads.

(Value of human sciences)

2156a 38. In the world dominated by scientific and technological change, which threatens to drag it towards a new positivism, another more fundamental doubt is raised. Having subdued nature by using reason, human beings now find that themselves are as it were imprisoned within their own rationality; in turn they become the object of science. The 'human sciences' are today enjoying a significant flowering. On the one hand, they are subjecting to critical and rational examination the hitherto accepted knowledge about the human being, on the grounds that this knowledge seems either too empirical or too theoretical. On the other hand, methodological necessity and ideological presuppositions too often lead the human sciences to isolate, in the various situations, certain aspects of the human person, and yet to give these an explanation which claims to be complete, or at least an interpretation which is meant to be all-embracing, from a quantitative or phenomenological point of view. This scientific reduction betrays a dangerous presumption. To give a privileged position in this way to such an aspect of analysis is to mutilate persons and, under the pretext of a scientific procedure, to make it impossible to understand them in their totality.

39. One must be no less attentive to the action which the human sciences can instigate, giving rise to the elaboration of models of society to be subsequently imposed on people as scientifically tested types of behaviour. The person can then become the object of manipulations directing its desires and needs and modifying its behaviour and even its system of values.

40. [However], as in the case of the natural sciences, the Church has confidence in this research also and urges Christians to play an active part in it. Prompted by the same scientific demands and the desire to know the human person better, but at the same time enlightened by their faith, Christians who devote

themselves to the human sciences will begin a dialogue which promises to be fruitful.

(Ambiguous nature of progress)

2156b 41. Since the nineteenth century, Western societies and, as a result, many others have put their hopes in ceaselessly renewed and indefinite progress.[...] Yet a doubt arises today regarding both its value and its result.[...] The quality and the truth of human relations, the degree of participation and of responsibility, are no less significant and important for the future of society than the quantity and variety of the goods produced and consumed.[...]

Is not genuine progress to be found in the development of moral consciousness, which will lead human beings to exercise a wider solidarity and to open themselves freely to others and to God?

(Renouncing force)

2156c 43. In international exchanges there is need to go beyond relationships based on force in order to arrive at agreements reached with the good of all in mind. Relationships based on force have never in fact established justice in a true and lasting manner, even if at times the alternation of positions can often make it possible to find easier conditions for dialogue. The use of force, moreover, leads to the setting in motion of opposing forces, and from this springs a climate of struggle which opens the way to situations of extreme violence and to abuses.

(Wider sharing of responsibility)

2156d 47. The passing to the political dimension also expresses a demand made by people today: a greater sharing in responsibility and in decision-making. This legitimate aspiration becomes more evident as the cultural level rises, as the sense of freedom develops and as one becomes more aware of how, in a world facing an uncertain future, the choices of today are already the condition of life for tomorrow.[...] In order to counterbalance increasing technocracy, modern forms of democracy must be devised, not only making it possible for each one to become informed and to express oneself, but also by involving one in a shared responsibility.

(Need to become involved in action)

2157   48. Let each one examine oneself, to see what he or she has done up to now, and what he/she ought to do. It is not enough to recall principles, state intentions, point to crying injustice and utter prophetic denunciations; these words will lack real weight unless they are accompanied in each individual by a livelier awareness of his or her personal responsibility and by effective action. It is too easy to throw back on others the responsibility for injustice, if at the same time one does not realise how one shares in it personally, and how personal conversion is needed first. This basic humility will rid action of all inflexibility and sectarianism; it will preclude discouragement in the face of a task which seems limitless in size.[...]

2158   49. Thus, amid the diversity of situations, functions and organisations, each one must recognise his or her own responsibility and discern in his or her conscience what kind of action one should take part in. Surrounded by various currents into which, besides legitimate aspirations, there insinuate themselves more ambiguous tendencies, the Christian must make a wise and vigilant choice and avoid involving oneself in an unconditional collaboration which would be contrary to the principles of a true humanism, even in the name of a genuinely felt solidarity.[...]

THE THIRD SYNOD OF BISHOPS IN ROME
DE IUSTITIA IN MUNDO (1971)

After its discussion on the priestly ministry, regarded as the primary problem posed to the Church's inner life (cf. n. 1745i), the third Synod of bishops turned its attention to the question of justice in the world, which is the most crucial problem of humankind today. The official Synodal document, submitted to the Pope for his consideration, was published by him in Dec. 1971, together with the document on the priestly ministry. The text is made up of three parts: justice and world society; the Gospel message and the mission of the Church; the practice of justice. It looks realistically at the situation of a world in which, due to the present character of society, many are "silent, indeed voiceless, victims of injustice". It confronts this situation with the Gospel message, reflects on the role of the Church in the struggle against injustice, proposes lines of action as regards the Church's own witness, education for justice, and cooperation between Churches and international action.

The document stresses the right of nations to full development. It shows that action on behalf of justice and for the liberation of people is part of the Church's mission. The text is found in AAS 63 (1971) 923ff.

(*Action for the human being's liberation is part of the mission of the Church*)

2159 5. [...]We shared our awareness of the Church's vocation to be present at the heart of the world by proclaiming the good news to the poor, freedom to the oppressed, and joy to the afflicted.[...]

6. Action on behalf of justice and participation in the transformation of the world fully appear to us a constitutive dimension of the preaching of the Gospel, or, in other words, of the Church's mission for the redemption of the human race and its liberation from every oppressive situation.

(*Overcoming obstacles to right development of nations*)

2160 15. The right to development must be seen as a dynamic interpretation of all those fundamental human rights upon which the aspirations of individuals and nations are based.

16. This desire, however, will not satisfy the expectations of our time if it ignores the objective obstacles which social structures place in the way of a conversion of hearts, or even of the realisation of the ideal of charity. It demands on the contrary that the general condition of being marginal in society be overcome, so that an end will be put to the systematic barriers and vicious circles which oppose the collective advance towards enjoyment of adequate remuneration of the factors of production, and which strengthen the situation of discrimination with regard to access to opportunities and collective services from which a great part of the people are now excluded. If the developing nations and regions do not attain liberation through development, there is a real danger that the conditions of life created especially by colonial domination may evolve into a new form of colonialism in which the developing nations will be the victims of the interplay of international forces.

17. By taking their future into their own hands through a determined will for progress, the developing people—even if they do not achieve the final goal—will authentically manifest their own personalisation. And in order that they may cope with the unequal relationships within the present world complex, a certain

responsible nationalism gives them the impetus needed to acquire an identity of their own.

(Justice and liberation in the work of Christ and in the Church's mission)

2161   31. By his action and teaching Christ united in an indivisible way the relationship of each person to God and the relationship of each to others. Christ lived his life in the world as a total giving of himself to God for the salvation and liberation of human persons.[...]

34. One's [...] response to the love of God, saving us through Christ, is shown to be effective in one's love and service of others. Christian love of the neighbour, however, cannot be separated from justice. For love implies an absolute demand for justice, namely a recognition of the dignity and rights of one's neighbour. Justice attains its inner fullness only in love.[...]

35. [...] The mission of preaching the Gospel dictates at the present time that we should dedicate ourselves to the liberation of the person even in its present existence in this world.[...]

36. The Church has received from Christ the mission of preaching the Gospel message, which contains a call to people to turn away from sin to the love of the Father, universal brotherhood/ sisterhood and a consequent demand for justice in the world. This is the reason why the Church has the right, indeed the duty, to proclaim justice on the social, national and international levels, and to denounce instances of injustice, when the fundamental rights of people and their very salvation demand it. The Church, indeed, is not alone responsible for justice in the world; however, she has a proper and specific responsibility which is identified with her mission of giving witness before the world of the need for love and justice contained in the Gospel message.[...]

Of itself it does not belong to the Church, in so far as she is a religious and hierarchical community, to offer concrete solutions in the social, economic and political spheres for justice in the world. Her mission involves defending and promoting the dignity and fundamental rights of the human person.

(Witness of justice in the life of the Church)

2162   40. While the Church is bound to give witness to justice, she recognises that anyone who ventures to speak to people about justice must first be just in their eyes. Hence we must undertake an examination of the modes of acting and of the possessions and life style found within the Church herself.

41. Within the Church rights must be preserved.[...] Those who serve the Church by their labour, including priests and religious, should receive a sufficient livelihood and enjoy that social security which is customary in the region. Lay people should be given fair wages and a system of promotion. We reiterate the recommendation that lay people should exercise more important functions with regard to Church property and should share in its administration.

(Education to justice)

2163   49. [...]Educational method must be such as to teach people to live their life in its entire reality and in accord with the evangelical principles of personal and social morality which are expressed in the vital Christian witness of life.

50. [...] The method of education very frequently still in use today encourages narrow individualism. Part of the human family lives immersed in a mentality which exalts possessions. The School and the communications media, which are often obstructed by the established order, allow the formation only of persons desired by that order, that is to say, persons in its image, not new persons but copies of persons as they are.

51. But education demands a renewal of heart, a renewal based on the recognition of sin in its individual and social manifestations. It will also inculcate a truly and entirely human way of life in justice, love and simplicity. It will likewise awaken a critical sense, which will lead us to reflect on the society in which we live and on its values; it will make people ready to renounce these values when they cease to promote justice for all. In the developing countries, the principal aim of this education for justice consists in an attempt to awaken consciences to a knowledge of the concrete situation and in a call to secure a total improvement.[...]

52. Since this education makes people decidedly more human, it will help them to be no longer the object of manipulation by communications media or political forces. It will instead enable them to take in hand their own destinies and bring about communities which are truly human.

(Liturgy and formation for justice)

2164 58. The liturgy, [...] which is the heart of the Church's life, can greatly serve education for justice. For it is a thanksgiving to the Father in Christ, which through its communitarian form places before our eyes the bonds of our brotherhood/sisterhood and again and again reminds us of the Church's mission. The liturgy of the word, catechesis and the celebration of the sacraments, have the power to help us to discover the teaching of the prophets, the Lord and the Apostles on the subject of justice. The preparation of baptism is the beginning of the formation of the Christian conscience. The practice of penance should emphasise the social dimension of sin and of the sacrament. Finally, the Eucharist forms the community and places it at the service of others.

PAUL VI

BULL OF INDUCTION OF THE HOLY YEAR 1975
(23 May, 1974)

The Pope wanted the ensuing holy year to be an opportunity for universal spiritual renewal and reconciliation that would imply a commitment to social justice according to biblical tradition. The text is found in AAS 66 (1974) 289ff.

(The Jubilee calls for a new and just ordering of things)

2165 34. The ancient origins of the Jubilee as seen in the laws and institutions of Israel clearly show that this social dimension is part of its very nature. In fact, as we read in the book of Leviticus *[25: 8ff]*, the Jubilee Year, precisely because it was dedicated in a special way to God, involved a new ordering of all things that were recognised as belonging to God: the land which was allowed to lie fallow and was given back to its former owners; economic goods, in so far as debts were remitted; and, above all, the person, whose dignity and freedom were reaffirmed in a special way by the manumission of slaves. The year of God, then, was also the Year of the Human Being, the Year of the Earth, the year of the poor.

THE FOURTH SYNOD OF BISHOPS IN ROME
DE EVANGELIZATIONE MUNDI HODIERNI (1974)

In its concluding message to the Church, the Synod confirms that the mandate to evangelise all people constitutes the essential mission of the Church. However, it also points out that the salvation that Christ came to bring implies the complete liberation of human beings from every bondage, including unjust social structures.

(The evangelising mission of the Church includes the full liberation of people)

2166 12. Prompted by the love of Christ and illumined by the light of the Gospel, let us nurture the hope that the Church, in more faithfully fulfilling the work of evangelisation, will announce the total salvation of the human person or rather its complete liberation, and from now on will start to bring this about. The Church[...] must conform to Christ who explained his own mission in these words: "The spirit of the Lord is upon me, because he has anointed me to preach good news to the poor. He has sent me to proclaim release to the captives and sight to the blind, to set at liberty those who are oppressed" *[Lk 4:18].*

13. Faithful to her evangelising mission, the Church, as a truly poor, praying and brotherly/sisterly community, can do much to bring about the integral salvation or the full liberation of human beings. She can draw from the Gospel the most profound reasons and ever new incentives to promote generous dedication to the service of all human beings—the poor especially, the weak and the oppressed—and to eliminate the social consequences of sin which are translated into unjust social and political structures.[...] The Church does not remain within purely social and political limits[...] but leads towards freedom under all its forms—liberation from sin, from individual or collective selfishness—and to full communion with God and with human beings who are like brothers and sisters. In this way, the Church, in her evangelical way, promotes the true and complete liberation of all individuals, groups and peoples.

PAUL VI

APOSTOLIC EXHORTATION *EVANGELII NUNTIANDI* (1975)

Elaborating the theme of the fourth Synod of Bishops, the Pope renews the commitment of the Church to evangelisation which means "bringing the good news into all the strata of humanity, and through its influence transforming humanity from within and making it new" (cf. nn. 1149-1152). Hence it is essentially linked with justice, liberation and human development.

However, the mission of the Church cannot be reduced "to the dimensions of a simply temporal project". The Pope here condemns violence without the nuance of Populorum Progressio *(cf. n. 2147c). He declares that the specific contribution of the Church towards liberation is the inspiration of faith and the motivation of love. The text is found in* AAS 68(1976) 5ff.

(The Gospel message touches life as a whole)

2167   29.[...] Evangelisation would not be complete if it did not take account of the unceasing interplay of the Gospel and of the person's concrete life, both personal and social. This is why evangelisation involves an explicit message, adapted to the different situations constantly being realised, about the rights and duties of every human being, about family life without which personal growth and development is hardly possible, about life in society, about international life, peace, justice and development—a message especially energetic today of liberation.

(A message of liberation)

2168   30. [..]Numerous bishops from all continents, especially the bishops from the Third World, spoke at the last Synod[...] of people[...] engaged with all their energy in the effort and struggle to overcome everything which condemns them to remain on the margin of life: famine, chronic disease, illiteracy, poverty, injustices in international relations and especially commercial exchanges, situations of economic and cultural neo-colonialism, sometimes as cruel as the old political colonialism.The Church [...] has the duty to proclaim the liberation of millions of human beings—many of whom are her own children—the duty of assisting the birth of this liberation, of giving witness to it, of ensuring that it is complete. This is not foreign to evangelisation.

(Evangelisation necessarily linked with human advancement)

2169   31. Between evangelisation and human advancement—development and liberation—there are in fact profound links. These include links of an anthropological order, because the person who is to be evangelised is not an abstract being but is subject to social and economic questions. They also include links in the theological order, since one cannot dissociate the plan of Creation from the plan of Redemption. The latter plan touches the very concrete situations of injustice to be combatted and justice to be restored. They include links of the eminently evangelical order, which is that of charity: how in fact can one proclaim the new commandment without promoting in justice and peace the true, authentic advancement of the person?

(Church's mission not to be reduced to a temporal project)

2170   32. [....]Many, even generous Christians who are sensitive to the dramatic questions involved in the problem of liberation, in their wish to commit the Church to the liberation effort, are frequently tempted to reduce her mission to the dimensions of a simply temporal project.[...] Her activity, forgetful of all spiritual and religious preoccupations, would become initiatives of the political or social order. But if this were so, the Church would lose her fundamental meaning. Her message of liberation would no longer have any originality and would easily be open to manipulation by ideological systems and political parties. She would have no more authority to proclaim freedom in the name of God.

(True liberation involves a necessary conversion)

2171   36. The Church considers it undoubtedly important to build up structures which are more human, more just, more respectful of the rights of the person and less oppressive and less enslaving, but she is conscious that the best structures and the most idealized systems soon become inhuman if the inhuman inclinations of the human heart are not made wholesome, if those who live in these structures or who rule them do not undergo a conversion of heart and outlook.

JOHN PAUL II

ENCYCLICAL LETTER *REDEMPTOR HOMINIS* (1979)

In his first encyclical, the Pope states that the redemption of human persons accomplished in Jesus Christ is the centre of the Church's proclamation and the main spring of her activity. Redemption is understood as elevation of the human person to special communion with God (cf. n. 677); thereby each person takes on a special value (cf .n.678) which is the deepest foundation of human rights and true human progress. The Pope particularly stresses the values of love, truth and freedom(cf n. 2064). He vividly describes the threat one suffers from one's own works when one is alienated from God. He points out that even the so-called human rights can become oppressive if they are sought only in the 'letter' and not also the 'spirit' The text is found in AAS (1979) 257 ff.

(Progress or threat?)

2172   15. The people of today seem ever to be under threat from what they produce.[...] All too soon, often in an unforeseeable way, what this manifold activity of the person yields is not only subjected to 'alienation', in the sense that it is simply taken away from the person who produces it, but rather it turns against the person itself.[...] One therefore lives increasingly in fear.[...] Exploitation of the earth not only for industrial but also military purposes and the uncontrolled development of technology outside the framework of a long range authentically humanistic plan often bring with them a threat to the human being's natural environment, alienate it in its relations with nature.[...] The development of technology and the development of contemporary civilization, which is marked by the ascendancy of technology, demand a proportional development of morals.[...]

16. If therefore our time[...] shows itself a time of progress, it is also seen as a time of threat in many forms for human beings.[...] Their situation in the modern world seems indeed to be far removed from the objective demands of the moral order, from the requirements of justice, and even more of social love.[...] They cannot relinquish themselves or the place in the visible world that belongs to them; they cannot become the slave of things, the slave of economic systems, the slave of their own products.[...] [The] difficult road of the indispensable transformation of the structures of economic life is one on which it will not be easy to go forward without the intervention of a true conversion of mind, will and heart.

(Exercise of power must respect human rights)

2173   17. [...] The rights of power can only be understood on the basis of respect for the objective inviolable rights of the human person. The common good that authority in the State serves is brought to full realisation only when all the citizens are sure of their rights. The lack of this leads to the dissolution of society, opposition by citizens to authority, or a situation of oppression, intimidation, violence, and terrorism of which many examples have been provided by the totalitarianisms of this century. Thus the principle of human rights is of profound concern to the area of social justice and is the measure by which it can be tested in the life of political bodies.

ENCYCLICAL LETTER *DIVES IN MISERICORDIA* (1980)

As Jesus is the revelation of God's mercy, the Church is called upon to bring a message of mercy to the world. The Pope points out that justice, without the deeper power of love manifested in mercy, can deviate from its goal. The text is found in AAS 72 (1980) 1215 -1216.

(Justice needs to be imbued with mercy)

2174 12. The Church shares with the people of our time this profound and ardent desire for a life which is just in every aspect.[...] And yet, it would be difficult not to notice that very often programmes which start from the idea of justice[...] in practice suffer from distortions. Although they continue to appeal to the idea of justice, nevertheless experience shows that other negative forces have gained the upper hand over justice, such as spite, hatred and even cruelty. In such cases, the desire to annihilate the enemy, limit freedom, or even force human beings into total dependence, becomes the fundamental motive for action, and this contrasts with the essence of justice which by its nature tends to establish equality and harmony between the parties in conflict.[...] The experience of the past and of our time demonstrates that justice alone is not enough, that it can even lead to its own negation and destruction, if that deeper power, which is love, is not allowed to shape human life in all its dimensions.

ENCYCLICAL LETTER *LABOREM EXERCENS* (1981)

The encyclical develops the human aspect of work which it calls the fundamental dimension of human existence on earth. It stresses the primacy of the subjective meaning of work over the objective; it is an activity of the human person and not a mere factor of production. Work has a personal, familial and communitarian dimension. The document brings out the clear priority of work over capital which itself is the fruit of work. Once again it distinguishes the Church's stand on ownership from that of Marxist collectivism and "rigid captialism". It asks that the rights of workers be preserved in any system of ownership. The encyclical touches on the questions of employment, wages, unions, rights of agricultural workers, the disabled and migrant workers. Finally it outlines a spiritualily of work in the light of creation and redemption in Christ. The text is found in AAS 73 (1981) 577-647.

(The subjective meaning of work has primacy over the objective)

2175   6.[...] The basis for determining the value of work is not primarily the kind of work being done but the fact that the one who is doing it is a person.The sources of the dignity of work are to be sought primarily in the subjective dimension, not in the objective one.

Such a concept practically does away with the very basis of the ancient differentiation of people into classes according to the kind of work done.[...] This leads immediately to a very important conclusion of an ethical nature; however true it may be that the person is destined for work and called to it, in the first place work is 'for the person' and not the person, 'for work'.[...] Independently of the work that every one does, and presupposing that this work constitutes a purpose—at times a very demanding one—of one's activity, this purpose does not possess a definitive meaning in itself. In fact, in the final analysis it is always the person who is the purpose of the work, whatever work it is that is done by one—even if the common scale of values rates it as the merest 'service', as the most monotonous, even the most alienating work.

(Priority of labour over capital)

2176   12. The structure of the present-day situation is deeply marked by many conflicts caused by human beings, and the technological means produced by human work play a primary role in it.[...] In view of this situation we must first of all recall a principle that has always been taught by the Church: *the principle of the priority of labour over capital.* This principle directly concerns the means of production; in this process labour is always a primary *efficient cause,* while capital, the whole collection of means of production, remains a mere *instrument* or instrumental cause.

[...] Since the concept of capital includes not only the natural resources placed at people's disposal but also the whole collection of means by which they appropriate natural resources and transform them in accordance with their needs (and thus in a sense humanise them), it must immediately be noted that *all these means are the result of the historical heritage of human labour.*

(Work founds a right to ownership)

2177   14. From this point of view the position of 'rigid' capitalism continues to remain unacceptable, namely the position that defends the exclusive right to private ownership of the means of production as an untouchable 'dogma' of economic life.[...]

In the light of the above, the many proposals put forward by experts in Catholic social teaching and by the highest magisterium of the Church take on special significance: proposals for *joint ownership of the means of work,* sharing by the workers in the management and/or profits of business, so-called share holding by labour, etc.

[...] While the position of 'rigid' capitalism must undergo continual revision,[...] it must be stated that, from the same point of view, these many deeply desired reforms cannot be achieved by an *a priori elimination of private ownership of the means of production.*[...]

[...] Merely converting the means of production into State property in the collectivist system is by no means equivalent to 'socialising' that property. We can speak of socialising only when the subject character of society is ensured, that is to say, when on the basis of one's work each person is fully entitled to consider oneself a part-owner of the great work-bench at which he/she is working with everyone else.

(Just wage as criterion of justice in a socio-economic system)

2178 19. It should also be noted that the justice of a socio-economic system, and in each case, its just functioning, deserve in the final analysis to be evaluated by the way in which one's work is properly remunerated in the system. Here we return once more to the first principle of the whole ethical and social order, namely, *the principle of the common use of goods.* In every system, regardless of the fundamental relationships within it between capital and labour, wages, that is to say *remuneration for work,* are still a *practical means* whereby the vast majority of people have access to those goods which are intended for common use: both the goods of nature and manufactured goods.

(No discrimination against women)

2179 19.[...] The whole labour process must be organised and adapted in such a way as to respect the requirements of the person and his or her forms of life, above all life in the home, taking into account the individual's age and sex. It is a fact that in many societies women work in nearly every sector in life. But it is fitting that they should be able to fulfill their tasks in *accordance with their own nature*, without being discriminated against and without being excluded from jobs for which they are capable, but also without lack of respect for their family aspirations and for their specific role in contributing, together with men, to the good of society. The *true advancement of women* requires that labour should be structured in such a way that women do not have to pay for their advancement by abandoning what is specific to them and at the expense of the family, in which women as mothers have an irreplaceable role.

(Work as sharing in creation and redemption in Christ)

2180   25. The word of God's revelation is profoundly marked by the fundamental truth that the human being, created in the image of God, *shares by one's work in the activity of the Creator* and that, within the limits of one's own human capabilities, one in a sense continues to develop that activity, and perfects it as one advances further in the whole of creation.[...]

26. The truth that by means of work the human person participates in the activity of God himself, its Creator, was *given particular prominence by Jesus Christ*.[...]For Jesus not only proclaimed but first and foremost fulfilled by his deeds the 'Gospel', the word of eternal Wisdom, that had been entrusted to him. Therefore this was also 'the gospel of work', because *he who proclaimed it was himself a man of work*, a craftsman like Joseph of Nazareth.[...] It can indeed be said that *he looks with love upon human work* and the different forms that it takes, seeing in each one of these forms a particular facet of the human being's likeness with God, the Creator and Father.[...]

27. The Christian finds in human work a small part of the Cross of Christ and accepts it in the same spirit of redemption in which Christ accepted his Cross for us. In work, thanks to the light that penetrates us from the resurrection of Christ, we always find a *glimmer* of new life, of the *new good*, as if it were an announcement of "the new heavens and the new earth"*[cf. 2 Pet 3:13; Rev 21;1].*[...] On the one hand, this confirms the indispensability of the Cross in the spirituality of human work; on the other hand, the Cross which this toil constitutes reveals a new good springing from work itself, from work understood in depth and in all its aspects and never apart from work.

APOSTOLIC EXHORTATION *FAMILIARIS CONSORTIO*
(1981)

While describing marriage as communion of persons, the Pope again upholds the dignity and rights of women. For an introduction to the document, see n. 1843i.

(Dignity and rights of women)

2181   22. Above all it is important to underline the equal dignity and responsibility of women with men. This equality is realised in a unique manner in that reciprocal self-giving by each one to the other and by both to the children, which is proper to marriage and the family. What human reason intuitively perceives and acknowledges is fully revealed by the word of God: the history of salvation, in fact, is a continuous and luminous testimony to the dignity of women.

23. There is no doubt that the equal dignity and responsibility of men and women fully justifies women's access to public functions. On the other hand, the true advancement of women requires that clear recognition be given to the value of their maternal and family role, by comparison with all other public roles and all other professions. Furthermore, these roles and professions should be harmoniously combined if we wish the evolution of society and culture to be truly and fully human.

With due respect to the different vocations of men and women, the Church must in her own life promote as far as possible their equality of rights and dignity; and this for the good of all, the family, the Church and society.

But clearly all of this does not mean for women a renunciation of their feminity or an imitation of the male role, but the fullness of true feminine humanity which should be expressed in their activity, whether in the family or outside of it, without disregarding the differences of customs and cultures in this sphere.

S. CONGREGATION FOR THE DOCTRINE OF THE FAITH
INSTRUCTION *LIBERTATIS CONSCIENTIA*
(22 March, 1986)

In 1984, the Congregation had issued an Instruction, Libertatis Nuntius, *on certain aspects of "Liberation Theology". This was meant to be a warning against certain one-sided positions. In a new Instruction on Christian freedom and liberation, there is a critical, but positive evaluation of liberation theology. The text is found in* AAS *79 (1987) 554-559.*

(Liberating mission of the Church)

2182a 61. The Church is firmly determined to respond to the anxiety of contemporary people as they endure oppression and yearn for freedom. The political and economic running of society is not a direct part of her mission. But the Lord Jesus has entrusted to her the word of truth which is capable of enlightening consciences. Divine love, which is her life, impels her to a solidarity with everyone who suffers. If her members remain faithful to this mission, the Holy Spirit, the source of freedom, will dwell in them and they will bring forth fruits of justice and peace in their families and in the places where they work and live.

2182b 63. The Church's essential mission, following that of Christ, is a mission of evangelisation and salvation. She draws her zeal from the divine love.[...]

In this mission, the Church teaches the way which the human being must follow in this world in order to enter the Kingdom of God. Her teaching, therefore, extends to the whole moral order, and notably to the justice which must regulate human relations. This is part of the preaching of the Gospel.

But the love which impels the Church to communicate to all people a sharing in the grace of divine life also causes her, through the effective action of her members, to pursue people's true temporal good, help them in their needs, provide for their education and promote an integral liberation from everything that hinders the development of individuals. The Church desires the good of the human being in all its dimensions, first of all as a member of the City of God, and then as a member of the earthly city.

(Preferential love for the poor)

2183 68. In its various forms—material deprivation, unjust oppression, physical and psychological illness, and finally death—human misery is the obvious sign of the natural condition of weakness in which the human being finds itself since original sin and the sign of its need for salvation. Hence it drew the compassion of Christ the Saviour to take it upon himself and to be identified with the least of his brothers and sisters [cf. Mt 25:40, 45]. Hence also those who are oppressed by poverty are the object of a love of preference on the part of the Church, which since her origin and inspite of the failings of many of her members has not ceased to work for their relief, defence and liberation.[...]

The special option for the poor, far from being a sign of particularism, manifests the universality of the Church's being and mission. The option excludes no one.[...]

This is the reason why the Church cannot express this option by means of reductive sociological and ideological categories which would make this preference a partisan choice and a source of conflict.

(Solidarity and subsidiarity)

2184   73. Intimately linked to the *foundation*, which is the human person's dignity, are the *principle of solidarity* and the *principle of subsidiarity*.

By virtue of the first, each with one's brothers and sisters is obliged to contribute to the common good of society, at all levels.[1] Hence the Church's doctrine is opposed to all the forms of social and political individualism.

By virtue of the second, neither the State nor any society must ever substitute itself for the initiative and responsibility of individuals and of intermediate communities at the level of which they function, nor must they take away the room necessary for freedom. Hence the Church's social doctrine is opposed to all forms of collectivism.

(Primacy of persons over structures)

2185   75. The priority given to structures and technical organisation over the person and the requirements of its dignity is the expression of a materialistic anthropology and is contrary to the construction of a just social order. [cf. EN 18].

On the other hand, the recognised priority of freedom and of conversion of heart in no way eliminates the need for unjust structures to be changed. It is, therefore, perfectly legitimate that those who suffer oppression on the part of the wealthy or of the

---

1. JOHN XXIII, Encyclical *Mater et Magistra*, 131-133: *AAS* 53 (1961) 437.

politically powerful should take action, through morally licit means, in order to secure structures and institutions in which their rights will be truly respected.

(Violence can only be a last resort)

2186a   76. Systematic recourse to violence put forward as the necessary path to liberation has to be condemned as a destructive illusion and one that opens the way to new forms of servitude. One must condemn with equal vigour violence exercised by the powerful against the poor, arbitrary action by the police, and any form of violence established as a system of government.[...]

Nor can one accept the culpable passivity of the public powers in those democracies where the social situation of a large number of men and women is far from corresponding to the demands of constitutionally guaranteed individual and social rights.

2186b   79. These principles must be especially applied in the extreme case where there is recourse to armed struggle, which the Church's magisterium admits as a last resort to put an end to an obvious and prolonged tyranny which is gravely damaging the fundamental rights of individuals and the common good *[cf. n. 2147c].* Nevertheless, the concrete application of this means cannot be contemplated until there has been a very rigorous analysis of the situation. Indeed, because of the continual development of the technology of violence and the increasingly serious dangers implied in this recourse, that which today is termed "passive resistance" shows a way more conformable to moral principles and having no less prospects for success. One can never approve, whether perpetrated by established power or insurgents, crimes such as reprisals against the general population, torture, or methods of terrorism and deliberate provocation aimed at causing deaths during popular demonstrations. Equally unacceptable are detestable smear campaigns capable of destroying a person psychologically of morally.

(Inculturation and liberation)

2187   96. The Church, which is a communion which unites diversity and unity through its presence in the whole world, takes from every culture the positive elements which she finds there. But inculturation is not simply an outward adaptation; it is an intimate transformation of authentic cultural values by their integration into Christianity and the planting of Christianity in the different human cultures. Separation between the Gospel and culture is a tragedy of which the problems mentioned are a sad illustration. A generous effort to evangelize cultures is therefore necessary. These cultures will be given fresh life by their encounter with the Gospel. But this encounter presupposes that the Gospel is truly proclaimed [*cf. n. 1152*]. Enlightened by the Second Vatican Council, the Church wishes to devote all her energies to this task, so as to evoke an immense liberating effort.

ENCYCLICAL LETTER *SOLLICITUDO REI SOCIALIS*
(30 December, 1987)

On the twentieth anniversary of Populorum Progressio, *the Pope stresses the enduring value of the document and elaborates on the themes contained in it. He highlights the ethical and cultural character of the problems connected with development. He stresses the interdependence of the various regions of the world, as opposed to power blocs. He asks for a transcending of a mere economic notion of development and for seeking an authentic human development that is total, includes faith, and is based on human solidarity. He explicitly accepts the concept of social sin or "structures of sin" which, however, are the fruit of personal sin (cf. n. 2067b-c). The text is found in AAS 80 (1988)513-586.*

(Developing countries drawn into the conflicts of richer countries)

2188   21. Countries which have recently achieved independence, and which are trying to establish a cultural and political identity of their own, and effective and impartial aid from all the richer and more developed nations, find themselves involved in, and sometimes overwhelmed by, ideological conflicts, which inevitably create internal divisions, to the extent in some cases of provoking full civil war. This is also because investments and aid for development are often diverted from their proper purpose and used to sustain conflicts, apart from and in opposition to the interests of the countries which ought to benefit from them.

(Growing awareness of interdependence)

2189   26. In a world divided and beset with every type of conflict, the *conviction* is growing of a *radical* *interdependence* and consequently of the need for a solidarity which will take up interdependence and transfer it to the moral plane. Today perhaps more than in the past, people are realising that they are linked together in a *common destiny,* which is to be constructed together, if catastrophe for all is to be avoided. From the depth of anguish, fear and escapist phenomena like drugs, *typical of the contemporary world,* the idea is slowly emerging that the good to which we aspire cannot be obtained without an *effort and commitment on the part of all,* nobody excluded, and the consequent renouncing of personal selfishness.

(Need for total, not merely economic, development)

2189a   28. The "economic" concept itself linked to the world development, has entered into crisis. In fact there is a better understanding today that the *mere accumulation* of goods and services, is not enough for the realisation of human happiness. Nor, in consequence, does the availability of the many *real benefits* provided in recent times by science, bring freedom from every form of slavery. On the contrary, the experience of recent years shows that unless all the considerable body of resources and potential at people's disposal is guided by a *moral responsibility* and by an orientation towards the true good of the human race, it easily turns against the person to oppress it.

2189b   33. *People* or *nations* too have a right to their own full development which, while including[...] the economic and social aspects, should also include individual cultural identity and openness to the transcendent. Not even the need for development can be used as an excuse for imposing on others one's way of life or one's religious belief.

(Respect for creation. Interdependence determining relationship)

2189c   34. The moral character of development cannot exclude respect for the beings which constitute the natural world[...]called the cosmos. Such realities also demand respect, by virtue of a threefold consideration which it is useful to reflect upon carefully.

The first consideration is the appropriateness of acquiring a growing awareness of the fact that one cannot use with impunity the different categories of beings, whether living or inanimate—animals, plants, the natural elements—simply as one wishes, according to one's economic needs. On the contrary, one must take into account the nature of each being and of its mutual connection in an ordered system, which is precisely the cosmos.

The second consideration is based on the realization [...] that natural resources are limited; some are not, as it is said, renewable. Using them as if they were inexhaustible, with absolute dominion, seriously endangers their availability not only for the present generation but above all for generations to come.

The third consideration refers directly to the consequences of a certain type of development on the quality of life in industrialized zones. We all know that the direct or indirect result of industrialization is, even more frequently, the pollution of the environment, with serious consequences for the health of the population.

Once again it is evident that development, the planning which governs it and the way in which resources are used must include respect for moral demands. One of the latter undoubtedly imposes limits on the use of the natural world; [...] we are subject not only to biological laws but also to moral ones, which cannot be violated with impunity.

A true concept of development cannot ignore the use of the elements of nature, the renewability of resources and the consequences of haphazard industrialization,—three considerations which alert our consciences to the moral dimension of development.

(Interdependence determining relationships)

2190   38. It is above all a question of *interdependence,* sensed as a *system determining relationships* in the contemporary world, in its economic, cultural, political and religious elements, and accepted as *moral category.* When interdependence becomes recognised in this way , the correlative response as a moral and social attitude, as a "virtue", is *solidarity.* This then is not a feeling of vague compassion or shallow distress at the misfortunes of so many people, both near and far. On the contrary, it is a *firm and persevering determination* to commit oneself to the *common good;* that is to say, to the good of all and of each individual, because we are *all* responsible for *all*. The determination is based on the *solid* conviction that what is hindering full development is that desire for profit and that thirst for power already mentioned.

These attitudes and "structures of sin" are only conquered—presupposing the help of divine grace—by a *diametrically opposed attitude:* a commitment to the good of one's neighbour with the readiness, in the Gospel sense, to "lose oneself" for the sake of the other instead of exploiting the other for one's own advantage [*cf. Mt 10:40-41; 20:25; Mk 10: 42-45; Lk 22:25-27].*

(*Nature of Church's social doctrine*)

2191 41. The Church's social doctrine is not a *"third way"* between *liberal capitalism and Marxist collectivism,* nor even a possible alternative to other solutions less radically opposed to one another; rather, it constitutes a *category of its own.* Nor is it an *ideology,* but rather the *accurate formulation* of the results of a careful reflection on the complex realities of human existence, in society and in the international order, in the light of faith and of the Church's tradition. Its main aim is to *interpret* these realities, determining their conformity with or divergence from the lines of the Gospel teaching on the human person and its vocation, which is at once earthly and transcendent; its aim is thus to *guide* Christian behaviour. It therefore belongs to the field[...] of *theology,* and particularly moral theology.

CONGREGATION FOR CATHOLIC EDUCATION GUIDELINES FOR THE STUDY AND TEACHING OF THE CHURCH'S SOCIAL DOCTRINE IN PRIESTLY FORMATION (30 December, 1988)

In this document the Congregation for Catholic Education returns with further precisions to the question of the nature of the Church's social doctrine and indicates the function played in it by the social sciences. The text is found in Origins, *3 August, 1989, pp. 169-187.*

(*Nature of Social Doctrine*)

2192a 3. [...]The social teaching of the Church draws its origin from the encounter of the evangelical message and its ethical requirements with the problems that arise in the life of society. The needs that emerge from this encounter become the subject of moral reflection which matures in the Church through scientific research, but also through the experience of the Christian community which must measure itself every day against the various situations of misery and, above all, with the problems created by the appearance and development of the phenomenon of industrialisation and the socio-economic systems related to it.

6. Social doctrine includes a threefold dimension: theoretical, historical and practical. These dimensions make up its basic structure and are inter-related and inseparable.

First of all, there is a "theoretical dimension" because the magisterium of the Church has explicitly formulated an organic and systematic reflection in its social documents. The magisterium indicates the sure path for building relations of co-existence in a new social order according to universal criteria which can be accepted by all. These are permanent ethical principles, not changeable historical judgments or "technical matters, for which [the magisterium] has neither the equipment nor the mission"[1].

Next, there is a "historical dimension" in the social doctrine of the Church, because, in it the use of principles is framed in a real view of society and inspired by an awareness of its problems.

Lastly, there is a "practical dimension" because social doctrine does not end only with a statement of permanent principles for reflection, or with the mere interpretation of the historical conditions of society. It also proposes the effective application of these principles in practice by translating them concretely into the ways and to the extent that circumstances permit or require it.[2]

(Discernment of choices between systems)

2192b 51. The saving mission of the Church, that springs from the teachings, witness and the life of Jesus Christ, the Saviour, implies two unavoidable choices: one for the person according to the Gospel, and another for the evangelical image of society. Without hypothesising a "third way" *[cf. n. 2191]* with regard to the "liberal utopia" and the "socialist utopia", believers must always opt for the humanising model of socio-economic relations which are in harmony with the above-mentioned scale of values. In this perspective, the pillars of every truly human model—that is, one in harmony with the dignity of the person—are: truth, freedom, justice, love, responsibility, solidarity, and

---

1. Pius XI, *Quadragesimo Anno: AAS* 23 (1971) 190.
2. John XXIII, *Mater et Magistra: AAS* 53 (1961) 453.

peace. The attainment of these values in the society's structure implies the primacy of the person over things, the priority of work over capital, and overcoming the antinomy between labour and capital [cf. nn. 2176, 2177]. These choices in themselves are not political, but they concern the political sphere and especially the relationship between Church and politics. They are not socio-economic either, but they also involve this dimension in the individual society and Church-society relationship. Therefore it is clear that one cannot do without the ethical judgment of the Church regarding the foundations of the social system to be built, and the concrete plans and programmes of coexistence in which the image of the human being and of society offered by the gospel must also come together.

(Ideology and the role of the social sciences)

2192c 68. [...] Thus social doctrine of the Church cannot do without the social sciences if it wants to stay in contact with the life of society and effectively influence pastoral reality.[...] The human sciences in fact are an important instrument for evaluating the changing situations and setting up a dialogue with the world and with people of all opinions [GS 43; OT 19]. They offer the social teaching in the empirical context in which the fundamental principles can and should be applied; they make abundant material for analysis available for the evaluation and judgment of social situations and structures; they aid orientation in the concrete choices to be made. Undoubtedly, in study and interest in the social sciences, the danger must be avoided of falling into the snares of ideologies that manipulate the interpretation of data, or into positivism which over-evaluates empirical data to the detriment of an overall understanding of the human being and the world.

JOHN PAUL II
ENCYCLICAL LETTER *CENTESIMUS ANNUS*
(1 May, 1991)

The encyclical commemorates the one hundredth anniversary of Rerum Novarum. *The Pope uses this occasion to propose a "rereading" of Pope Leo's encyclical in light of political, social, and economic developments during the last century. It includes an invitation to "look back" at Leo's text itself, to "look around" at the "new things" of our own day, and to "look to the future" as we find ourselves able to "glimpse the third millennium of the Christian* era". *The Pope also offers an analysis of recent events, in particular those toward the end of 1989 and the beginning of 1990 in Central and Eastern Europe. He cautions, however, that "such an analysis is not meant to pass definitive judgments, since this does not fall per se within the magisterium's specific domain" (3).*

The collapse of Marxist totalitarianism in Europe has had world-wide as well as European consequences. In some parts of the Third World the condition of workers is little better than it was when Pope Leo wrote. In other areas, although workers might not be exploited outright, they are often marginalised by being deprived of the training and education that would allow them to participate fully in the economic and political process. Such countries are looking for new models of true human development, and the richer industrialised countries have duties of justice toward them.

In the industrialised countries of the so-called First and Second world, some are only now beginning the post war period (28). There are also new forms of alienation that threaten human beings: consumerism, terrorism, 'systematic anti-childbearing campaigns', abortion, a 'culture of death', drug addiction, atheism in the name of 'political realism' (24-25), and the destruction of the environment. At the heart of these problems lies an "anthropological error" concerning the human person's true nature (37). Atheism, whether theoretical or practical, both denies and threatens the person's true dignity.

The common basis for genuine development, the development of a "human ecology" (39), is recognition of the right to life, freedom of religion, and work toward the common good guided by the principles of justice, solidarity, and subsidiarity. Some problems (foreign debt of poor countries, threats of war and peace, ecological problems) are by their very nature so vast that international cooperation among nations and with international organisations will be necessary to address them.

The encyclical is the Pope's ninth, his third social encyclical. It was promulgated on 1 May, 1991, after the collapse of socialism in most of Eastern Europe and the end of the Persian Gulf War, but before the collapse of the Communist Party in the Soviet Union. It figures prominently in the sections of the New Catechism of the Catholic Church in the sections dealing with the Church's social teaching. The text is found in Origins, *5 January, 1995.*

(Solidarity)

2193   10. [...] What we nowadays call the principle of solidarity [...] is clearly seen to be one of the fundamental principles of the Christian view of social and political organisation. This principle is frequently stated by Pope Leo XIII, who uses the term *friendship*, a concept already found in Greek philosophy. Pope Pius XI refers to it with the equally meaningful term of *social charity*. Pope Paul VI, expanding the concept to cover the many modern aspects of the social question, speaks of a *civilisation of love.*

(Politics and the hermeneutic of original sin)

2194a 25. [...] Human beings, who are created for freedom, bear within themselves the wound of original sin, which constantly draws them toward evil and puts them in need of redemption. Not only is this doctrine an integral part of Christian revelation, it also has great hermeneutical value insofar as it helps one to understand human reality. They tend towards good, but they are also capable of evil. They can transcend their immediate interest and still remain bound to it. The social order will be all the more stable, the more it takes this fact into account and does not place in opposition personal interest and the interests of society as a whole, but rather seeks ways to bring them into fruitful harmony.[...] Where self-interest is violently suppressed, it is replaced by a burdensome system of bureaucratic control which dries up the wellsprings of initiative and creativity. When people think they possess the secret of a perfect social organisation which makes evil impossible, they also think they can use any means, including violence and deceit, in order to bring that organisation into being. Politics then becomes a "secular religion" which operates under the illusion of creating paradise in this world. But no political society—which possesses its own autonomy and laws—can ever be confused with the kingdom of God.

(The poor not a burden)

2194b 28. [...]It will be necessary above all to abandon a mentality in which the poor—as individuals and as people—are considered a burden, as irksome intruders trying to consume what others have produced.[...] The advancement of the poor constitutes a great opportunity for the moral, cultural and even economic growth of all humanity.

(True development, religious freedom, and political order)

2194c 29. [...] Development must not be understood solely in economic terms, but in a way that is fully human.[...] The apex of development is the exercise of the right and duty to seek God, to know him and to live in accordance with that knowledge.[...] Total recognition must be given to the rights of the human conscience, which is bound only to the truth, both natural and revealed. The recognition of these rights represents the primary foundation of authentically free political order.

(New types of property)

2194d   32. In our time in particular there exists another form of ownership which is becoming no less important than land; the possession of know-how, technology and skill. The wealth of the industrialised nations is based much more on this kind of ownership than on natural resources.

(Marginalisation of the poor)

2194e   33.[...] The risks and problems connected with this kind of process [modern business economy] should be pointed out [...] [for] many people [...] have no possibility of acquiring the basic knowledge which would enable them to express their creativity and develop their potential. They have no way of entering the network of knowledge and intercommunication which would enable them to see their qualities appreciated and utilized. Thus, if not actually exploited, they are to a great extent marginalised; economic development takes place over their heads, so to speak, when it does not actually reduce the already narrow scope of their old subsistence economies. They are unable to compete against the goods which are produced in ways which are new and which properly respond to needs, needs which they had previously been accustomed to meeting through traditional forms of organisation. Allured by the dazzle of an opulence which is beyond their reach and at the same time driven by necessity, these people crowd the cities of the Third World where they are often exposed to situations of violent uncertainty without the possibility of becoming integrated.

(Capitalism, knowledge, and the Third World)

2194f   33. [...]In spite of the great changes which have taken place in the more advanced societies, the human inadequacies of capitalism and the resulting domination of things over people are far from disappearing. In fact, for the poor, to the lack of material goods has been added a lack of knowledge and training which prevents them from escaping their state of humiliating subjection.[..] Unfortunately, the great majority of people in the Third World still live in such conditions. It would be a mistake, however, to understand this "world" in purely geographic terms

(Free market economy and the Third World)

2194g 34. It would appear that on the level of individual nations and of international relations the free market is the most efficient instrument for utilising resources and effectively responding to need. But this is true only for those needs which are "solvent" insofar as they are endowed with purchasing power and for those resources which are "marketable" insofar as they are capable of obtaining a satisfactory price. But there are many human needs which find no place in the market. It is a strict duty of justice and truth not to allow fundamental human needs to remain unsatisfied and not to allow those burdened by such needs to perish. It is also necessary to help these needy people to acquire expertise, to enter the circle of exchange and to develop their skills in order to make the best use of their capacities and resources.[...] In Third World contexts, certain objectives stated by *Rerum Novarum* remain valid and in some cases still constitute a goal yet to be reached, if the human person's work and its very being are not to be reduced to the level of a mere commodity. These objectives include a sufficient wage for the support of the family, social insurance for old age and unemployment, and adequate protections for the conditions of employment.

(Business profit and human dignity)

2194h 35. [...]The Church acknowledges the legitimate role of profit as an indication that a business is functioning well.[...] But profitability is not the only indicator of a firm's condition. It is possible for the financial accounts to be in order and yet for the people—who make up the firm's most valuable asset—to be humiliated and their dignity offended.[...] The purpose of a business firm is not simply to make a profit, but is to be found in its very existence as a community of persons who in various ways are endeavouring to satisfy their basic needs and who form a particular group at the service of the whole of society. Profit is a regulator of the life of a business, but it is not the only one; other human and moral factors must also be considered.[...] It is unacceptable to say that the defeat of so-called "real socialism" leaves capitalism as the only model of economic organisation. It is necessary to break down the barriers and monopolies which leave so many countries on the margins of development and to provide all individuals and nations with the basic conditions which will enable them to share in development.

(Consumerism, drug use, social dysfunction)

2195a 36. [...] Of itself, an economic system does not possess criteria for correctly distinguishing new and higher forms of satisfying human needs from artificial new needs which hinder the formation of a mature personality.[...] A striking example of artificial consumption contrary to the health and dignity of the human person [...] is the use of drugs. Widespread drug use is a sign of a serious malfunction in the social system; it also implies a materialistic and in a certain sense destructive "reading" of human needs.

(Having vs. being)

2195b 36. [...]It is not wrong to want to live better; what is wrong is a style of life which is presumed to be better when it is directed to "having" rather than "being" and which wants more not in order to be more, but in order to spend life in enjoyment as an end in itself.

(Ecology, natural and human)

2195c 37.[...]At the root of the senseless destruction of the natural environment lies an anthropological error.[...] Human beings, who discover their capacity to transform and in a certain sense create the world through their own work, forget that this is always based on God's prior and original gift of the things that are.[...] Instead of carrying out their role as cooperators with God in the work of creation, they set themselves up in place of God and thus end up provoking a rebellion on the part of nature, which is more tyrannised than governed by them.[...]

38. [...] Too little effort is made to safeguard the moral conditions for an authentic "human ecology". Not only has God given the earth to human beings, who must use it with respect for the original good purpose for which it was given to them, but we too are God's gift to ourselves.[...]

39. The first and fundamental structure for "human ecology" is the family, in which one receives one's first formative ideas about truth and goodness, and learns what it means to love and to be loved, and thus what it means to be a person.

(Failure of Marxism, danger of capitalist ideology)

2195d 42. The Marxist solution has failed, but the realities of marginalisation and exploitation remain in the world, especially in the Third World, as does the reality of human alienation, especially in the more advanced countries.[...]There is a risk that a radical capitalistic ideology could spread which refuses even to consider these problems in the *a priori* belief that any attempt to solve them is doomed to failure, and which blindly entrusts their solution to the free development of market forces.

(Role of Church's social teaching)

2196a 43. The Church has no models to present; models that are real and truly effective can only arise within the framework of different historical situations through the efforts of all those who responsibly confront concrete problems in all their social, economic, political and cultural aspects as these interact with one another. For such a task the Church offers her social teaching as an indispensable and ideal orientation, a teaching which[...] recognises the positive value of the market and of enterprise, but which at the same time points out that these need to be oriented toward the common good.

(Church's evaluation of democratic systems)

2196b 46. The Church values the democratic system inasmuch as it ensures the participation of citizens in making political choices, guarantees to the governed the possibility both of electing and holding accountable those who govern them and of replacing them through peaceful means when appropriate.[...] Authentic democracy is possible only in a state ruled by law and on the basis of a correct conception of the human person.[...] Nowadays there is a tendency to claim that agnosticism and sceptical relativism are the philosophy and the basic attitude which correspond to democratic forms of political life. Those who are convinced that they know the truth and firmly adhere to it are considered unreliable from a democratic point of view, since they do not accept that truth is determined by the majority or that it is subject to variation according to different political trends. It must be observed in this regard that if there is no ultimate truth to guide and direct political activity, then ideas and convictions can easily be manipulated for reason of power. As history demonstrates, a democracy without values easily turns into open or thinly disguised totalitarianism.

(The Church and the autonomy of the political order)

2196c   47.[...]The Church respects the legitimate autonomy of the democratic order and is not entitled to express preferences for this or that institutional or constitutional solution. Her contribution to the political order is precisely her vision of the dignity of the person revealed in all its fulness in the mystery of the incarnate Word.

(Limited but necessary intervention of State in economy)

2196d   48.[...] The State could not directly ensure the right to work for all its citizens unless it controlled every aspect of economic life and restricted the free initiative of individuals. This does not mean, however, that the state has no competence in this domain.[...]The State has a duty to sustain business activities by creating conditions which will ensure job opportunities, by stimulating those activities where they are lacking or by supporting them in moments of crisis.

(Social teaching and Christian anthropology)

2197a   55. The Church receives "the meaning of the human person" from divine revelation.[...] Christian anthropology therefore is really a chapter of theology, and for this reason, the Church's social doctrine by its concern for persons and by its interest in the way they conduct themselves in the world "belongs to the field [...] of *theology*, and particularly of moral theology" *[cf. n. 2191]*.

(Gospel message not a theory)

2197b   57. As far as the Church is concerned, the social message of the Gospel must not be considered a theory, but above all else a basis and motivation for action .

(Justice and love for the poor)

2197c   58. Love for others, and in the first place love for the poor, in whom the Church sees Christ himself, is made concrete in the promotion of justice. Justice will never be fully attained unless people see in the poor person, who is asking for help to survive, not an annoyance or a burden, but an opportunity for showing kindness and a chance for greater enrichment. Only such an awareness can give the courage needed to face the risk and the change involved in every authentic attempt to come to the aid of another. It is not merely a matter of "giving from one's surplus", but of helping entire people which are presently excluded or marginalised to enter into the sphere of economic and human development.

CATHOLIC BISHOPS' CONFERENCE OF ENGLAND AND WALES ON THE CATHOLIC CHURCH'S SOCIAL TEACHING
(October 1996)

The Catholic Bishops' Conference of England and Wales has issued a statement : The Common Good and the Catholic Social Teaching, *in which they adapt the social teaching of the Church as the conditions have changed. The text has been edited by the Conference itself in a booklet (London 1996, p. 33).*

(Democracy and human rights are necessary for the common good; but neither of them can be considered for granted)

2198a 34. The Church has been able to make its own contribution to political theory by exploring the limitations of the democratic process, for instance by warning that democracy can never be a self-fulfilling justification for policies that are intrinsically immoral. Democracy is not a self-sufficient moral system; [...] it requires the presence of a system of common values.

36 . Human rights are sometimes advanced to support claims to individual autonomy which are morally inappropriate. Not everything said to be a "right" really is one.[...] However, that reservation must not be allowed to destroy the value of the principle itself : that individuals have a claim on each other and on society for certain basic minimum conditions without which the value of human life is diminished or even negated. These rights are inalienable.[...] [They] derive from the nature of the human person made in the image of God, and are in no way dependent for their existence on recognition by the State by way of public legislation.

37. These rights are universal; [...] they all flow from the one fundamental right : the right to life. From this derives the right to these conditions which made the life more truly human :

religious liberty, decent work, housing, health care, freedom of speech, education and the right to raise and to provide for a family. [...] Every member of the community has a duty to the common good in order that the rights of others can be satisfied and their freedoms respected. Those whose rights are being denied should be helped to claim them.

39. Catholic social teaching sees an intimate relationship between social and political liberation on the one hand, and on the other, the salvation to which the Church calls us in the name of Jesus Christ. The spreading of this message of salvation is the task of evangelisation. Evangelisation means bringing the good news of the Gospel into every stratum of humanity, and through its influence transforming humanity from within and making it new.

40. That must include liberating humanity from all forces and structures which oppress it, though political liberation cannot be an end in itself.[...] All Catholics who engage in the political life of the nation are entitled to regard themselves as engaging in evangelisation, providing they do so in accordance with the principles of Catholic teaching. One of the most important steps in evangelisation of the social order is the freeing of individuals from the inertia and passivity that comes from oppression, hopelessness or cynicism, so that they can discover they can exert greater control over their own destinies and contribute to the well-being of the others.

(Definition of the common good)

2198b 48. That common good is the whole network of social conditions which enables individuals and groups to flourish and live a fully, genuinely human life, otherwise described as "integral human development". All are responsible for all, collectively, at the level of the society or nation, not only as individuals.

(There is a connection between subsidiarity and solidarity)

2198c 53. Subsidiarity and solidarity [are] two fundamental principles of this body of teaching [the social doctrine of the Church]. Subsidiarity should never be made an excuse for selfishness nor promoted at the expense of the common good or to the detriment of the poorest and more vulnerable sections of the community. Pope John-Paul II defined the concept of solidarity in *Sollicitudo Rei socialis*.

PONTIFICAL COUNCIL *COR UNUM*
WORLD HUNGER
(24 October 1996)

The Pontifical Council Cor Unum *is the Holy See agency for promoting and coordinating charity and development aid. It said in the present document that continued high level of world hunger does not mean that too little food is produced but is due to the structural problems and inequitable access to it. One of the points in the discussion is the care for the earth [Libreria Editrice Vaticana 1996].*

(Linking ecology with economy)

2198d 31. It is urgently necessary to manage this planet in an ecologically sustainable manner. From the viewpoint of the agrifood production [...] there are two elements to consider.

First of all, this sort of environmentally friendly management will have a cost which needs to be incorporated into economic activity. We should ask ourselves whether it will always be those living in poverty who have to bear this burden in the detriment of their nutrition.

Second, of concern is the gaining of a better understanding of the linkage of ecology and economy within the current notion of sustainable development. But this objective must not distract from the need to put even greater effort into promoting equitable development.

In the end, the development cannot be sustainable unless equitable. Otherwise it is likely that the present distortions will be compounded by new ones.

JOHN PAUL II
ADDRESS TO THE DIPLOMATIC CORPS
(January 13, 1997)

Pope John Paul II has used the opportunity offered by his annual address to the Diplomatic Corps to propose an evaluation of the international situation in a Christian perspective. He especially insisted on the meaning of Peace and the danger caused by the proliferation of nuclear weapons. He renews his support for the Treaty on Non Proliferation of which the Holy See is a party. The English version is in Origins, *January 30, 1997, vol. 26 N.32, pp. 521-525.*

(Disarmament)

2198e 2. In the sphere of Nuclear weapons, the banning of tests and the further development of these weapons, disarmament and non proliferation are closely linked and must be achieved as quickly as possible under effective international controls. These are steps towards a general and total disarmament which the international community as a whole should accomplish without delay.

(The meaning of peace)

2198f   3. Peace cannot be just nor can it long endure unless it rests upon sincere dialogue between equal partners, with respect for each other's identity and history; unless it rests on the right of peoples to the free determination of their own destiny, upon their independence and security. There can be no exception.

4. What the international community perhaps lacks most of all today is not written conventions or forums for self expression—there is a profusion of these—but a moral law and the courage to abide by it. The community of nations, like every human society, cannot escape this basic principle: it must be regulated by a rule of law valid for all of them without exception. Every juridical system, as we know, has as its foundation and end the common good. And this implies to the international community as well : the good of all and the good of the whole. This is what makes possible equitable solutions in which gain is not made at the expense of the others, even when those who benefit are the majority. Justice is for all, without injustice being inflicted on anyone. The function of law is to give each person his due, to give what is owed to him in justice. Law therefore has a strong moral implication.

PONTIFICAL COUNCIL FOR JUSTICE AND PEACE

TOWARD A BETTER DISTRIBUTION OF LAND

THE CHALLENGE OF AGRARIAN REFORM

(23 November, 1997)

The Pontifical Council for Justice and Peace makes public a document on agrarian reform which "is not only a question of distributive justice and economic growth but also of great political wisdom". The document stresses that agrarian reform must not be confined to land redistribution but offer a response to the practical problems of the agricultural sector in developing countries; it proposes an ecological vision of creation. See also n. 1674.

(Care of creation)

2199a 22. The first page of the Bible tells us of the creation of the world and the human person *[Gen 1:27]* [...]. Solemn words describe the task that God entrusts to them *[Gen 1:28]* [...]. The first task that God gives them—clearly a fundamental one—concerns the attitude that they should have toward the earth and all creatures. *Subject* and *dominion* are too easily understood concepts and can, in fact, seem to justify the type of despotic and unbridled domination that takes no care of the earth and its fruit, but despoils it for personal advantage. However, in Biblical language they are used to describe the rule of a wise king who cares for the wellbeing of all subjects. Man and woman must care for creation so that it will serve them and remain at the disposition of all, not just a few.

23. The underlying nature of creation is that of being a gift of God, a gift for all, and God wants it to remain so. God's first command is therefore to preserve the earth in its nature as gift and blessing, not to transform it in an instrument of power or motive for division. The right and duty of the human person to have dominion over the earth is derived from being the image of God. All, and not a few, are responsible for creation [...]. Work is for the realization of the person.

SPECIAL ASSEMBLY OF THE SYNOD OF BISHOPS FOR ASIA. MESSAGE TO THE PEOPLE OF GOD
(23 May, 1998)

The Synod encourages the theologians to continue studying inculturation. Professing that Christ is the only Saviour, the message considers special points as the massive poverty, the nuclear race, the cancellation of the debts for the Asian nations.... (Text in Origins, *May 28 1998, vol. 28 N. 2, pp. 16-22).*

(Demand for justice, democracy and solidarity)

2199b We could not help but feel deeply concerned when hearing of the hardships people have to undergo in several countries of Asia on account of recurring violence, internal strife, tensions and wars between countries. [...] When considering the suffering of the people of Irak, especially women and children, we strongly urge that steps be taken to lift the embargo against that country. Elsewhere in Asia people are suffering under political regimes that pay no heed to their legitimate claims for legitimate freedom and greater respect for their basic rights. Others are struggling to regain sovereignty or greater autonomy. We need to create a greater awareness of the danger of the development and expansion of the armaments industry. These trends serve to suppress the people's demand for justice and democracy. [...] We call on the particular churches of the First World to be in solidarity with the poor in Asia and to be their advocates with their own governments and with world economic institutions such as the World Bank, the International Monetary Fund and the World Trade Organization so as to bring about what Pope John Paul II called for in his World Day of Peace Message: "Globalization without marginalization. Globalization with solidarity".

CATHOLIC BISHOPS' CONFERENCE OF INDIA

PLEA FOR UNIVERSAL DISARMAMENT
(11 June, 1998)

Both India and Pakistan conducted nuclear weapons tests in May 1998. The Catholic Bishops' Conference of India has urged the government to insist on a peace policy by actions for development (Text in Origins, *August 13, 1998, vol. 28 N.10, pp. 161-163).*

2199c Now that the nuclear weapons race on the subcontinent of South Asia is a reality, the most urgent need is to restore mutual confidence between the countries of the region. [...] The most urgent and pressing need is to de-escalate the tension through diplomatic and political discussions in an atmosphere of mutual understanding and respect for life and cultural heritage. [...] The resources of India and of all nations of the sub-continent must be dedicated singularly to the welfare of the people of the region. [...] Nuclear energy must be used only in the service of the people's development and peace; nuclear research and technology must have the single objective of fighting disease and improving the quality of life.

JOHN PAUL II

APOSTOLIC EXHORTATION *ECCLESIA IN AMERICA*
(January 22, 1999)

The Apostolic Exhortation Ecclesia in America *was signed by Pope John-Paul II the day he arrived in Mexico for a five days visit, January 22, 1999.*

This document responds to the questions raised during the Special Assembly for America of the Synod of Bishops in 1997, November 16-December 12. While the Pope's document focuses on evangelisation, it insists also on social questions, among which the globalization and the debt phenomenon. [English Text in Origins, *February 4, 1999, vol. 28:N.33, pp. 565-592].*

(Globalization, its cultural aspect)

2199d 20. There is an economic globalization which brings some positive consequences.[...] However, if globalization is ruled merely by the laws of the market applied to suit the powerful, the consequences cannot but be negative. [...] While aknowledging the positive values which come with globalization, the Church considers with concern the negative aspects which follow in its wake. And what should we say about the cultural globalization produced by the power of the media? Everywhere the media impose new scales of values which are often arbitrary and basically materialistic, in the face of which it is difficult to maintain a lively commitment to the values of the Gospel.

22. Among the causes which have helped to create massive external debt are not only massive interests rates, caused by speculative financial policies, but also the irresponsibility of people in government who, in incurring debts, have given too little thought to the real possibility of repaying it. This has been aggravated by the fact that huge sums obtained through international loans sometimes go to enrich individuals instead of being used to pay for the changes needed for the country's development. At the same time, it would be unjust to impose the burden resulting from these irresponsible decisions upon those who did not make them.

CHAPTER XXII

SEXUAL ORDER AND RESPECT FOR LIFE

God has created the human race in the complementarity of the sexes so that man and woman may find their fulfilment through a mutual union ordained by the Creator to the generation of new human life. It is in this complementarity that they are created as the image of God. Human sexuality is not only a biological drive, but an emotional and spiritual potentiality which calls for free decision and personal commitment. In the Christian context, virginity and marriage, chastity and the sexual order, take on new dimensions: all are related to the mystery of Christ and of the Church.

Chastity is the progressive integration of human sexuality with love according to one's state, married or celibate; it implies a gradual spiritualisation of the sex instinct by true charity. Respect for the sexual order established by God and confirmed by Christ is part of the Christian's conformity to the ideal of Christian love.

The Church has been especially concerned with the respect due to the sexual order because of the important personal, social and Christian values involved in it. The earlier documents principally dealt with the right use of sexual pleasure and defended its legitimacy within the boundaries of that order. The moral teaching of the Church sought to avoid the excesses of rigorism on the one hand and hedonism on the other. The Christian attitude to sex has been reaffirmed in recent years in opposition to the strong erotic currents pervading modern society. While taking a firm stand against these currents which depersonalise the use of sex, the Church has stressed the potentiality of sexual intercourse in marriage for preserving and promoting conjugal love, provided its full significance as an act open to procreation be not contradicted.

New moral problems have arisen in recent years in the procreative sphere because of the discovery of new means of controlling the generative process. The Church has reacted against practices that seem to be a sub-human manipulation of human procreation. The documents stress the close link between conjugal love with its specific act and procreation.

On this basis, are condemned contraception, on the one hand, and the practice of artificial insemination and in-vitro fertilization, on the other. At the same time, in view of the population problem in many areas, the Church recommends responsible parenthood through natural means in order that the offspring may have the guarantee of such human conditions as are conducive to their full development. The Church warns against the danger of indiscriminate genetic manipulation.

Human life is held sacred, whatever its stage of development or condition. As it is the most basic value upon which all other human values depend, the Church strongly condemns any violation of the right to life for any cause, by abortion, infanticide or euthanasia.

* * *

The doctrinal aspects of marriage have been treated in Chapter XVIII. The moral aspects of sex and the respect for life, considered in this chapter, fall under the following headings:

Right ordering of Sexuality

A right order in the use of sex is needed: 2201/9, 2201/48, 2201/50, 2228.

Premarital intercourse is never justified: 2229.

In marriage, the enjoyment of sexual pleasure is legitimate: 2211; but just moderation is needed: 2212.

Sexual intimacy plays an important role in fostering marital love: 2204, 2215, 2217, 2219.

Masturbation is forbidden by the law of nature: 2201/49, 2231.

Homosexuals deserve understanding, but homosexual activity cannot be condoned: 2230, 2243a-2243d.

There is need for proper sex education: 2232, 2239, 2240.

Responsible Parenthood

Parenthood must be responsible and generous: 2214, 2220.

The decision regarding the number of children ultimately belongs to the spouses: 2214, 2219.

Conjugal love and respect for life are to be harmonized: 1841, 2215, 2247.

The divine plan for transmission of human life must be observed: 2220, 2236, 2244.

The morality of family planning methods is determined by objective criteria: 2217.

The use of infertile periods is licit: 2204, 2225, 2236.
Positive interference with the procreative effect is an intrinsic disorder: 2202, 2209, 2222, 2223, 2236.
Direct sterilization is unlawful: 2222.
Indirect sterilization may be licit: 2224.
Artificial insemination does not fully accord with the personal nature of human procreation: 2210, 2213, 2244.
Artificial fertilization and surrogate motherhood are also against God's plan: 2247-2249.
Even the simple case of homologous in-vitro fertilization is illicit: 2250.
There is no true and proper right to have a child: 2252.
Grave dangers of indiscriminate genetic manipulation should be noted: 2238.
The State has a role in population control provided personal rights are respected: 2218, 2219, 2264.
It has no right to impose sterilization or a eugenic programme: 2207, 2208.
Population education and family planning information are needed: 2219.
In areas relating to responsible parenthood, confessors are to follow certain traditional rules of pastoral practice, as well as the more recently proposed principle of gradualness: 2266, 2267.

Respect for Human Life

Human life is inviolable from the moment of conception: 2244a, 2245-2246b.
Abortion is always a grave evil: 2205, 2216, 2221, 2226, 2227, 2257.
Pre-natal diagnosis and experimentation should not expose the foetus to harm: 2246, 2258.
Euthanasia is a grave violation of human life: 2233-2235, 2259.
Its deepest causes need to be tackled: 2241.
There is no obligation to use disproportionate means of saving or prolonging life: 2235.
Drug addicts need rehabilitation: 2242.
Autonomy and personal dignity of patients must be respected: 2237.
At present there is a "structure of sin" which is a "culture of death": 2253.
The choice for life has its full moral meaning when formed by faith: 2254.
The circumstances where the death penalty may be used are practically non-existent: 2255, 2269.

Direct, voluntary killing of the innocent is always gravely immoral: 2256.

"Tyrannical" decisions concerning the defenceless: 2260.

No law can legitimize abortion and euthanasia: conscientious objection is required: 2261a.

Obeying or supporting unjust laws is prohibited: 2261b.

Support for restrictive laws could be justified: 2262.

Democratic means should be used to seek realistic changes of law: 2263.

Women who have had an abortion can seek forgiveness and peace: 2265.

INNOCENT XI

ERRORS OF LAXIST MORALITY CONDEMNED BY THE HOLY OFFICE (1679)

Among the errors of laxist morality condemned in this decree of the Holy Office (cf. nn. 2006/1 ff), some are related to the sexual order. Pending further decision (cf. n. 2006/1 i), the propositions are condemned as causing scandal and harmful in practice. It must be noted that the ninth proposition is condemned only in the sense given to it by laxist morality; this condemnation has wrongly been made use of by the rigorists to defend their own position.

[2201/9]
2109
The marriage act performed for pleasure alone is entirely free of all fault and venial defect.

[2201/48]
2148
It seems clear that fornication by itself implies no malice and is evil solely because it is forbidden, so that the contrary seems entirely in disagreement with reason.

[2201/49]
2149
Masturbation is not forbidden by natural law. Hence, if God had not forbidden it, it would often be good and at times even an obligation under pain of mortal sin.

[2201/50]
2150
Intercourse with a married woman, with the consent of the husband, is not adultery.

PIUS XI

ENCYCLICAL LETTER *CASTI CONNUBII* (1930)

After exposing the doctrine on Christian marriage (cf. nn. 1824-1833) the Pope condemns certain abuses which were becoming widespread. These include hedonism, trial marriage, marital infidelity and divorce. The condemnation is particularly firm as regards 'Onanism'. Perhaps the Pope had directly in mind only interrupted intercourse, though the document generally received a stricter interpretation, later favoured by Pius XII.[1] But the encyclical recognises the lawfulness of choosing the sterile period for intercourse, since the marital act is meant for fostering mutual love besides achieving the end of procreation. Sterilisation is condemned in particular when it is imposed by civil authority for eugenic reasons, in violation of the natural right to marry and beget children. Destruction of unborn life is condemned as a grave crime.

---

1. Cf J.T. NOONAN, *Contraception* (Cambridge 1966) 429.

(Interference with the procreative effect of intercourse is always illicit)

2202 [...]No reason whatever, even the gravest, can make what
3716   is intrinsically against nature become conformable with
        nature and morally good. The conjugal act is of its very
nature designed for the procreation of offspring; and, therefore,
those who in performing it deliberately deprive it of its natural
power and efficacy, act against nature and do something which
is shameful and intrinsically immoral[...].

3717   Wherefore, [...]the Catholic Church, to whom God has
        committed the task of teaching and preserving morality
and right conduct in their integrity, standing firm amidst this
moral ruin, raises her voice in sign of her divine mission to keep
the chastity of the marriage contract unsullied by this ugly stain,
and through our voice proclaims anew that any use of marriage
in the exercise of which the act is deprived, by human
interference, of its natural power to procreate, is an offence
against the law of God and nature, and those who commit it are
guilty of grave sin[...].

(The innocent partner is excused)

2203 Holy Church is also well aware that in many cases one
3718   of the partners is more sinned against than sinning,
        reluctantly allowing a violation of the right order for a
truly grave reason. Such a partner is not guilty, so long as the
law of charity even then is remembered and every effort made
to dissuade and prevent the other partner from sinning.

(The use of infertile period is licit)

2204 Nor are husband and wife to be accused of acting
3718   against nature if they make use of their right in the
        proper and natural manner, even though natural causes,
either circumstances of time or certain defects, render the origin
of new life impossible. Both marriage and the use of marital
rights have secondary ends—such as mutual help, the fostering
of reciprocal love, and the abatement of concupiscence—which
husband and wife are quite entitled to have in view, so long as
the intrinsic nature of that act, and, therefore, its due ordination
to its primary end, is safeguarded.[...]

(Abortion is not justified on any ground)

2205 Another very grave crime is to be noted [...] which

3719   consists in the taking of the life of the offspring hidden
          in the mother's womb. Some want it to be allowed and
left to the will of the father or mother; others say that it is lawful
when there are weighty reasons which they call medical, social,
or eugenic "indications". [...]

2206   As for what they call "medical and therapeutic
3720   indications", we have much pity for the mother whose
          health and even life is gravely imperilled in the
performance of the duty allotted to her by nature; nevertheless,
what valid reason could there be for excusing in any way the
direct killing of the innocent? This is precisely what we are
dealing with here. Whether inflicted upon the mother or upon
the child, it is against the precept of God and the law of nature:
"You shall not kill" [Ex 20:13]. The life of both is equally sacred,
and no one, not even public authority, can ever have the power
to destroy it. It is no use to appeal to the right of taking away
life in punishment; for here we are dealing with the innocent,
whereas that right applies only with regard to the guilty. Nor
does the right to use violence in self-defence against an unjust
aggressor apply here; for who would call the innocent child an
unjust aggressor? Again, there is no question here of what is
called the "law of extreme necessity", as though this could extend
even to the direct killing of the innocent. Upright and skillful
doctors are, therefore, most praiseworthy for striving to safeguard
and preserve the lives of both mother and child; on the contrary,
those show themselves most unworthy of the noble medical
profession who bring about the death of one or the other, under
the pretence of practicing medicine or out of misguided pity.[...]

(Eugenics through legislation is not justified)

2207   There are some who, in their excessive preoccupation
3722   with eugenic considerations are not content to give
          salutary advice for the improvement of the unborn child's
health and strength, which is certainly quite reasonable. They
want to set these considerations above all other ends, even those
of a higher order, and would have the public authority forbid
marriage to any persons, who, in the light of the laws and
conjectures of eugenic science, are deemed likely, because of their
heredity, to beget defective offspring, even though in themselves
they are fit to marry. They even demand that legislation be passed

to deprive such persons of that natural faculty by medical action, even against their will. [...]

(The State has no right to impose sterilisation)

2208
3722
Public authorities have no direct power over the bodily members of the citizens and, therefore, in the absence of any crime or any cause calling for corporal punishment, they can never directly injure or attack the integrity of the body on any ground whatever, eugenic or otherwise.[...]

PIUS XII

ALLOCATION TO MIDWIVES (1951)

In this allocution, meant to exhort midwives to live up to their noble calling, Pius XII strongly reaffirms the Church's condemnation of contraception and points out the need for self-control in marriage. The text is found in AAS 43 (1951) 835ff.

2209
Our predecessor, Pius XI, of happy memory, in his encyclical *Casti Connubii* of December 31, 1930, once again solemnly proclaimed the fundamental law of conjugal relations; every attempt of either husband or wife in the performance of the conjugal act or in the development of its natural consequences which aims at depriving it of its inherent force and hinders the procreation of new life is immoral *[cf n. 2202]*; and no "indication" or need can turn an act which is intrinsically immoral into a moral and lawful one *[cf. nn. 2205f]*. The precept is in full force today as in the past, and it will be so in the future as well and always, because it is not due to a simple human fancy but is the expression of a natural and divine law.

(Artificial insemination contradicts the personal nature of human procreation)

2210
To reduce the common life of husband and wife and the conjugal act to a mere organic function for the transmission of seed would be to convert the domestic hearth, the family sanctuary, into a biological laboratory.[...] The conjugal act, in its natural structure, is a personal action, in which husband and wife simultaneously and immediately cooperate; the very nature of the agents and the quality of the act make it to be the expression of a reciprocal gift, which, according to holy scripture,

effects union "in one flesh" [cf. Gen 2:24]. This is more than the union of two genes, which can be effected even by artificial means, that is, without the natural action of husband and wife. The conjugal act, ordained and desired by nature, is a personal cooperation, the right to which husband and wife confer on each other when contracting marriage.

(Just moderation in seeking pleasure)

2211 The same Creator, who in his bounty and widsom willed to make use of the work of man and woman, by uniting them in matrimony, for the preservation and propagation of the human race, has also decreed that in this function the partners should experience pleasure and happiness of body and spirit. Husband and wife, therefore, by seeking and enjoying this pleasure, do no wrong. They accept what the Creator has destined for them.

2212 Nevertheless, here also, husband and wife must know how to keep themselves within the limits of just moderation. As with the pleasure of food and drink, so with the sexual pleasure, they must not abandon themselves without restraint to the impulse of the senses. The correct rule is this: the use of the natural procreative process is morally lawful in marriage only, and in the service of, and in accordance with the ends of marriage itself. Hence it follows that only in marriage and in submission to this rule is the desire and enjoyment of this pleasure and satisfaction lawful. For the pleasure is subordinate to the law of the action whence it is derived, and not vice versa the action to the pleasure. Moreover, this law, so very reasonable, concerns not only the substance but also the circumstances of the action, so that, even when the substance of the act remains morally right, it is possible to sin in the way it is performed.

ALLOCUTION TO THE SECOND WORLD CONGRESS OF FERTILITY AND STERILITY (1956)

Pope Pius XII again takes a stand against artificial insemination by bringing out the personal aspect of human generation according to the divine plan. The text is found in Pius XII, Discorsi Radiomessagi, *vol. 18, pp. 211-221.*

2213 The Church has likewise rejected the opposite attitude which pretended to separate, in procreation, the biological activity from the personal relations of husband and wife. The child is the fruit of the marriage union, when this union finds its full expression in the setting into motion of the functional organs, of the sensible emotions related to them, and of the spiritual and disinterested love which animates such a union. It is within the unity of this human act that the biological conditions of procreation must be viewed. It is never permitted to separate these different aspects to the point of excluding positively either the ordination to procreation or the conjugal relation.

THE SECOND VATICAN GENERAL COUNCIL
PASTORAL CONSTITUTION *GAUDIUM ET SPES* (1965)

In this Constitution the Council stresses the personal values of Christian marriage and conjugal life (cf.nn.1834-840). It declares that well ordered sexual intercourse is an important factor in fostering marital love. The parents are called upon to cooperate with the love of the Creator and Saviour, with a sense of human and Christian responsibility which takes into account the interest of the family, of society and of the Church (50).

Because of the demographic pressure and other sociological factors of our time, the Council had to deal with the problem of reconciling marital love with the respect for life. It clearly states the need for responsible parenthood. In planning the size of the family, dishonourable practices like abortion and infanticide are excluded. The morality of the means employed does not depend only on subjective motivation, but must be determined by objective standards, based on the nature of the human persons and of their actions. The full meaning of mutual self-giving and of human procreation in the context of true love render the use of some methods unlawful according to objective criteria followed by the Church's doctrine (51). But the Council has deliberately refrained from making a definitive pronouncement on the morality of specific methods of birth. regulation since the matter was being studied by a papal commission. Nevertheless, it states several principles which must guide the solution of specific questions.

The Council calls for a vigorous programme to promote the family which is the foundation of society (52). It also sets the limits of the competence of the public authorities with regard to population problems (87).

The Council upholds the values of life from the moment of conception. Abortion is considered an abominable crime.

(Responsible parenthood)

2214 50. In their function of transmitting life and bringing up children, which must be regarded as their proper mission, the spouses know that they are cooperators with the love of God the Creator and, so to speak, its interpreters. Therefore, they will discharge their task with a sense of human and Christian responsibility; and, with docile reverence towards God, by common counsel and effort, they will endeavour to form a right judgment. In doing so, they will take into account their own good and that of the children already born or to be born; they will consider carefully the material and spiritual conditions of their times and of their own situation, and, finally, they will consult the interests of their own family, of the temporal society, and of the Church herself. It is the spouses themselves who ultimately must make this judgment in the sight of God. In their way of acting, Christian spouses should be aware that they cannot proceed arbitrarily but must always be guided by their conscience, a conscience duly conformed to the divine law itself; and let them be docile towards the teaching authority of the Church which interprets the law authentically in the light of the Gospel. That divine law shows the full meaning of conjugal love; it protects this love and leads it to its true human fulfilment. When Christian spouses, trusting in divine Providence and fostering in themselves a spirit of sacrifice, assume their function of procreating children with a generous, human and Christian sense of responsibility, they give glory to the Creator and grow towards perfection in Christ. Among the spouses who thus fulfil their God-given task, those merit a special mention who, after prudent and common deliberation, magnanimously accept to bring up, as far as their means allow, even a large number of children.

(Conjugal intimacy and respect for human life)

2215 51. The Council realises that couples who wish to organise their married life harmoniously are often hindered by certain modern conditions of life, and that they may happen to be in circumstances in which they cannot increase the number of their children, at least for the time being. As a result, the faithful exercise of love and full community of life are difficult for them to maintain. But when the intimacy of married life is broken off, faithfulness can often be imperilled and the offspring can suffer: for, then, the education of the children and the courage to accept more children are both in danger.

There are people who venture to offer to these problems dishonourable solutions and who do not even draw back from the taking of life. But the Church reminds them that there can be no real contradiction between the divine law of transmitting life and that of fostering genuine conjugal love.

(Abortion is immoral)

2216 51. For God, the Master of life, has entrusted to human beings the noble ministry of safeguarding life—a ministry to be discharged in a manner worthy of them. Therefore, life must be guarded with great care from the moment of conception; abortion and infanticide are heinous crimes.

(The morality of methods of birth regulation is based on objective criteria)

2217 51. Human sexuality and the human person's faculty of generating surpass in a wonderful way all that is found in the lower degrees of life; hence the acts proper to married life, when performed in keeping with the true human dignity, must be surrounded with great reverence. Therefore, when there is question of harmonising conjugal love with a responsible transmission of life, the morality of any way of acting does not depend only on the sincerity of the intention and on the evaluation of the motives; it must be determined by objective criteria, based on the nature of the person and of human acts. Such criteria respect the full meaning of mutual self-gift and human procreation, in a context of true love. This is impossible unless the virtue of conjugal chastity is sincerely practised. On the strength of these principles, the children of the Church are not allowed, in the matter of regulating procreation, to adopt methods which are reproved by the teaching authority of the Church interpreting the divine law.

(The role of the State in the population problem)

2218 87. [...] Within the limits of their competence, governments have rights and duties with regard to the population problem in their own nation, for instance, in the matter of social and family legislation, of migration of rural people to the cities, of information concerning the situation and needs of the country.[...]

2219 Many people assert that the growth of the world population, or at least that of some countries, must be radically reduced, by every means and by every kind of government intervention. Hence this Council exhorts all to beware of solutions, advocated privately or publicly, and sometimes even imposed, which are contrary to the moral law. For, in view of the human person's inalienable right to marry and to beget children, the decision concerning the number of children they should have depends on the honest judgment of the parents, and may not be committed in any way to the decision of public authority. As this judgment presupposes a rightly formed conscience, it is important that all should be given the possibility of exercising their responsibility in an upright and truly human manner which, while taking into account the circumstances and times, is ever mindful of the law of God. This requires that education and social conditions in various places be improved, and especially that the possibility be offered of a religious formation or at least a complete moral training. Furthermore, people should be judiciously informed of the progress of science in the study of the methods by which married people can be helped in regulating births, when the reliability of these methods has been adequately tested and their harmony with the moral law established.

PAUL VI

ENCYCLICAL LETTER *HUMANAE VITAE* (1968)

Since 1965 the difficult question of birth-regulation was studied, on the Pope's request, by a commission of experts. The Second Vatican Council left it to the Pope to pronounce on the legitimacy of methods of birth-control in the light of the findings of this special commission (cf. n 2214i). Having personally examined the data contained in the report of the commission, the Pope took position in 1968.

The encyclical first exposes the positive values attached to the conjugal love as cooperation with the Creator in the transmission of new life. It calls for responsible parenthood in the light of an integral vision of the human person's vocation (cf.n. 1841i), along the lines of the teaching of Vatican II (cf.n.2214). It shows the intimate connection which exists between the two aspects of the conjugal act (n. 1841), whose finality must be respected. On the strength of these doctrinal principles, the encyclical declares that "each and every marriage act" (quilibet matrimonii usus) must be open to the transmission of life (11). Various means of birth-regulation are therefore excluded, notably those by which the working of the natural process of generation would be prevented. Contraception and direct sterilisation are an intrinsic disorder, while recourse to infecund periods is always licit. The principle of totality according to which a conjugal act in which conception is voluntarily prevented could be considered lawful in the context of the totality of a fecund marital life is declared erroneous. After considering the serious consequences deriving from artificial birth-control, the encyclical ends with a pastoral exhortation: married couples are called to generosity and trust in God; educators are asked to create an atmosphere favourable to chastity; pastors are invited to expound the Church's teaching faithfully, and at the same time to treat people with kindness and understanding.

Though the encyclical is a clear papal statement, commanding a corresponding assent, it is not an infallible document. While explaining it, several national hierarchies have introduced nuances in its teaching and made suggestions for its pastoral application. Thus, the French bishops do not exclude a recourse to other means, considered as a lesser evil, when periodic continence is not possible and a person is in a 'perplexed conscience' or faced with a conflict of duties.[1] The text is found in AAS 60 (1968)481ff.

(The divine plan for the transmission of human life)

2220   13. It is in fact justly observed that a conjugal act imposed upon one's partner without regard for his or her condition and lawful desires is not a true act of love, and, therefore, denies an exigency of right moral order in the relationship between husband and wife. Hence, one who reflects well must also recognise that a reciprocal act of love, which jeopardises the potentiality to transmit life which God the creator, according to particular laws, inserted therein, is in contradiction with the innate design of marriage, and with the will of the Author of life. To use this divine gift while destroying, even if only partially, its true meaning and its purpose is to contradict the nature both of man and woman and of their most intimate relationship, and, therefore, it is to contradict also the plan of God and his will. On the other hand, to make use of the gift of conjugal love while respecting the laws of the generative process means to acknowledge oneself not to be the arbiter of the sources of human life, but rather the minister of the design established by the Creator. In fact, just as one does not have unlimited dominion over one's body in general, so also, with particular reason, one has no such dominion over one's generative faculties as such, because of their intrinsic ordination towards raising up life, of which God is the principle.[...]

---

1. Cf. *The Catholic Mind*, 1969, 47ff.

(Contraception is intrinsically a disorder)

2221 14. In conformity with these landmarks in the human and Christian vision of marriage, we must once again declare that the direct interruption of the generative process already begun, and above all, directly willed and procured abortion, even if for therapeutic reasons, are to be absolutely excluded as licit means of regulating birth.

2222 Equally to be excluded, as the teaching authority of the Church has frequently declared, is direct sterilisation, whether permanent or temporary, whether of the man or of the woman. Similarly excluded is every action which either in anticipation of the conjugal act, or in its accomplishment, or in the development of its natural consequences, proposes, whether as an end or as a means, to render procreation impossible.

2223 To justify conjugal acts made intentionally infecund, one cannot invoke as valid reasons the lesser evil, or the fact that such acts would constitute a totality together with the fecund acts already performed or to follow later, and hence would share in one and the same moral goodness. In truth, if it is something licit to tolerate a lesser evil in order to avoid a greater evil or to promote a greater good, it is not licit, even for the gravest reasons, to do evil so that good may follow therefrom; that is, to make into the object of a positive act of the will something which is intrinsically a disorder, and hence unworthy of the human person, even when the intention is to safeguard or promote individual, family or social well-being. Consequently it is an error to think that a conjugal act which is deliberately made infecund and so is intrinsically dishonest could be made honest and right by the ensemble of a fecund conjugal life.

(Indirect sterilisation is not unlawful)

2224 15. The Church, on the contrary, does not at all consider illicit the use of therapeutic means truly necessary to cure diseases of the organism, even if an impediment to procreation, which may be foreseen, should result therefrom, provided such impediment is not, for whatever motive, directly willed.

(The use of the sterile period is permissible)

2225 16. [...] If there are serious motives to space out births, which are derived from the physical or psychological conditions of husband and wife, or from external conditions, the Church teaches that it is then licit to take into account the natural rhythms immanent in the generative functions, for the use of marital rights in the infecund periods only, and in this way to regulate birth without offending against the moral principles which we have recalled earlier.

The Church is coherent with herself when she considers recourse to the infecund periods to be licit, while at the same time condemning, as being always illicit, the use of means directly contrary to fecundation, even if such use is inspired by reasons which may appear honest and serious. In reality, there are essential differences between the two cases: in the former, the married couple make legitimate use of natural disposition; in the latter, they impede the development of natural processes.

DECLARATION *DE ABORTU PROCURATO* OF THE S. CONGREGATION FOR THE DOCTRINE OF THE FAITH
(28 June, 1974)

The widespread evil of abortion, the increasing permissive attitude towards it and the trend to its legalization have prompted the S. Congregation to recall the essential elements of the Church's doctrine in the matter. This doctrine is primarily based on the value and respect due to human life in the light of reason and of faith. The Document explicitly grants that the moment of animation is under dispute. But even when the presence of the soul is only probable, the taking of life would involve incurring the risk of killing a human person. As life is the most basic value, procured abortion would never be justified by the intention of protecting any other value. The right of the unborn person to live calls for protection on the part of society and public authority. The Document also declares: "Never, under any pretext, may abortion be resorted to, either by a family or political authority, as a legitimate means of regulating births" (cf. n. 2221). The Document points out that it is not enough to condemn abortion, but there is also the need for tackling the causes that lead to it. However, it does not answer questions like: 1) what would be the moral evaluation of expelling the zygote before nidation if the absence of human personhood could be shown with moral certainty at that stage?; 2) when the death of the mother would also entail the death of the foetus, would not intervention be a lesser evil? The text is found in AAS 66 (1974) 730-747.

(Abortion never licit)

2226 12. Any discrimination based on the various stages of life is no more justified that any other discrimination. The right to life remains complete in an old person, even one greatly weakened; it is not lost by one who is incurably sick. The right to life is no less to be respected in the small infant just born than in the mature person. In reality, respect for human life is called for from the time that the process of generation begins. From the time that the ovum is fertilized, a life is begun which is neither that of the father nor of the mother; it is rather the life of a human being with its own growth. It would never be made human if it were not human already.

13. To this perpetual evidence—perfectly independent of the discussions on the moment of animation—modern genetic science brings valuable confirmation. It has demonstrated that, from the first instant, there is established the programme of what this living being will be: this individual with one's characteristic aspects already well determined.[...] Moreover, it is not up to biological sciences to make a definitive judgment on questions which are properly philosophical and moral such as the moment when a human person is constituted or the legitimacy of abortion. From a moral point of view this is certain: even if a doubt existed concerning whether the fruit of conception is already a human person, it is objectively a grave sin to dare to risk murder.

(Combatting the causes of abortion)

2227 26.[...] One can never approve of abortion; but it is above all necessary to combat its causes. This includes political action, which will be in particular the task of the law. But it is necessary at the same time to influence morality and to do everything possible to help families, mothers and children. Considerable progress in the service of life has been accomplished by medicine. One can hope that such progress will continue, in accordance with the vocation of doctors, which is not to suppress life but to care for it and favour it as much as possible. It is equally desirable that, in suitable institutions, or, in their absence, in the outpouring of Christian generosity and charity, every form of assistance should be developed.

DECLARATION *DE PERSONA HUMANA* OF THE S. CONGREGATION FOR THE DOCTRINE OF THE FAITH
(29 December, 1975)

The increasing breakdown of sexual morality as well as questioning of the traditional doctrine of the Church on the matter has led the S. Congregation to reaffirm the basic principles of sexual ethics.

Although the doctrine is presented in the traditional natural law perspective, there are some new openings. There is emphasis on the dignity and values of the human person as well as on relationships. The basic principle that every genital act must be within the marital framework is defended by an appeal to the meaning of sexuality as an expression of inter-personal relationship. At the same time, the need for pastoral understanding is stressed. Modern psychology is credited with much value in formulating a more equitable judgment on moral responsibility and in orienting pastoral action. Although it is reaffirmed that masturbatory acts are in the objective order seriously evil, the importance of considering the totality of the individuals' practice of charity and justice or their fundamental option (cf. n. 2062) is also recognised. The Document also calls for a healthy sex education in the context of total education. The text is found in AAS 68 (1976) 77-96.

(Basic principle of sexual ethics)

2228   5. This same principle which the Church holds from divine Revelation and from her authentic interpretation of the natural law, is also the basis of her traditional doctrine, which states that the use of the sexual function has its true meaning and moral rectitude only in true marriage.

(Premarital intercourse never justified)

2229   7. However firm the intention of those who practice such premature sexual relations may be, the fact remains that these relations cannot ensure, in sincerity and fidelity, the interpersonal relationship between a man and a woman, nor especially can they protect this relationship from whims and caprices.

Experience teaches us that love must find its safeguard in the stability of marriage, if sexual intercourse is truly to respond to the requirements of its own finality and to those of human dignity. These requirements call for a conjugal contract sanctioned and guaranteed by society—a contract which establishes a state of life of capital importance both for the exclusive union of man and woman and for the good of their family and of the human community. Most often, in fact, premarital relations exclude the possibility of children. What is represented to be conjugal love is not able to develop into paternal and maternal love. Or, if it does happen to do so, this will be to the detriment of the children, who will be deprived of the stable environment in which they ought to develop in order to find in it the ways and means of their insertion into society as a whole.

(Homosexual acts always illicit)

2230   8. In the pastoral field, these homosexuals must certainly
be treated with understanding and sustained in the hope
of overcoming their personal difficulties and their inability to fit
into society. Their culpability will be judged with prudence. But
no pastoral method can be employed which would give moral
justification to these acts, on the ground that they would be
consonant with the condition of such people. For according to
the objective moral order, homosexual relations are acts which
lack an essential and indispensable finality. In sacred scripture
they are condemned as a depravity and even presented as the
sad consequence of rejecting God. This judgment of Scripture
does not of course permit us to conclude that all those who suffer
from this anomaly are personally responsible for it, but it does
attest to the fact that homosexual acts are intrinsically disordered
and can in no case be approved of.

(Masturbation intrinsically evil)

2231   9. Whatever the force of certain arguments of a biological
and philosophical nature, which have sometimes been
used by theologians, in fact both the magisterium of the Church—
in the constant tradition—and the moral sense of the faithful
have declared without hesitation that masturbation is an
intrinsically and seriously disordered act. The main reason is that,
whatever the motive for acting in this way, the deliberate use of
the sexual faculty outside normal conjugal relations essentially
contradicts the finality of the faculty. For it lacks the sexual
relationship called for by the normal order, namely the relationship
which realises "the full communion of mutual self-giving and
human procreation in the context of true love" [GS 51].

In the pastoral ministry, in order to form an adequate
judgment in concrete cases, the habitual behaviour of people will
be considered in its totality, not only with regard to the
individual's practice of charity and of justice, but also with regard
to the individual's care in observing the particular precepts of
chastity. In particular one will have to examine whether the
individual is using the necessary means, both natural and
supernatural, which Christian asceticism from its long experience
recommends for overcoming the passions and progressing in
virtue.

(Need for sex education)

2232 13. Parents, in the first place, and also teachers of the young must endeavour to lead their children and their pupils by way of a complete education, to the psychological, emotional and moral maturity befitting their age. They will therefore prudently give them information suited to their age; and they will assiduously form their wills in accordance with Christian morals, not only by advice but above all by the example of their own lives, relying on God's help, which they will obtain in prayer. They will likewise protect the young from many dangers of which they are quite unaware.

DECLARATION ON EUTHANASIA OF THE S. CONGREGATION FOR THE DOCTRINE OF THE FAITH
(5 May, 1980)

As a sequel to the document on Procured Abortion (cf. nn. 2226-2227), in which the principle of the inviolability of human life at any stage or in any condition was upheld, this document again clarifies that the right to life extends to all, whether the aged, the sick or the unborn. Recent advances in medicine have increased immensely the capacity to prolong life, which gives rise to a double problem: a) would it be permissible at some stage to provide an 'easy death' in order to put an end to the suffering of the patient and anxiety of the family?; b) to what extent is one obliged to use the life prolonging procedures now available? While the Declaration answers a resolute 'no' to the first question, it adopts a new way of speaking regarding the use of therapeutic means in terminal illness, namely the distinction between 'proportionate' and 'disproportionate' means. It clarifies the meaning of 'right to die' and explains the Christian meaning of suffering and death. The text is found in AAS 72 (1980) 542-552.

(Direct killing of an innocent never permissible)

2233 It is necessary to state firmly once more that nothing and no one can in any way permit the killing of an innocent human being, whether a foetus or an embryo, an infant or an adult, an old person or one suffering from an incurable disease, or a person who is dying. Furthermore, no one is permitted to ask for this act of killing, either for oneself or for another person entrusted to his or her care, nor can he or she consent to it, either explicitly or implicitly; nor can any authority legitimately recommend or permit such an action. For it is a question of the violation of the divine law, an offence against the dignity of the human person, a crime against life and an attack on humanity.

The pleas of gravely ill people who sometimes ask for death are not to be understood as implying a true desire for euthanasia; in fact, it is almost always a case of an anguished plea for help and love. What a sick person needs, besides medical care, is love, the human and supernatural warmth with which the sick person can and ought to be surrounded by all those close to him or her, parents and children, doctors and nurses.

(Right to die with dignity)

2234   Today it is very important to protect, at the moment of death, both the dignity of the human person and the Christian concept of life, against a technological attitude that threatens to become an abuse. Thus some people speak of a 'right to die', which is an expression that does not mean the right to procure death either by one's own hand or by means of someone else's as one pleases, but rather the right to die peacefully with human and Christian dignity.

(No obligation to use 'disproportionate' means)

2235   However, is it necessary in all circumstances to have recourse to all possible remedies?

In the past, moralists replied that one is never obliged to use 'extraordinary' means. This reply, which as a principle still holds good, is perhaps less clear today, by reason of the imprecision of the term and the rapid progress made in the treatment of sickness. Thus, some people prefer to speak of 'proportionate' means. In any case, it will be possible to make a correct judgment as to the means by studying the type of treatment to be used, its degree of complexity or risks, its cost and the possibilities of using it, and comparing these elements with the result that can be expected, taking into account the state of the sick person and his or her physical and moral resources.

JOHN PAUL II

APOSTOLIC EXHORTATION *FAMILIARIS CONSORTIO*
(1981)

While reaffirming the basic stand of Humanae Vitae *(nn. 2220-2225), the Pope brings out more clearly the ethical differences between suppression of fertility and respecting the same through natural family planning. As was the case in* Humanae Vitae, *here too the Pope does not say how one should proceed in conflict situations. For an introduction to the document, see n. 1843i.*

(Ethical differences between contraception and natural family planning)

2236   32. When couples, by means of recourse to contraception separate these two meanings [unitive and procreative, of the conjugal act] which God the Creator has inscribed in the being of man and woman, and in the dynamism of their sexual communion, they act as 'arbiters' of the divine plan and they 'manipulate' and degrade human sexuality—and with it themselves and their married partner—by altering its value of 'total' self-giving. Thus the innate language that expresses the total reciprocal self-giving of husband and wife is overlaid, through contraception, by an objectively contradictory language, namely, that of not giving oneself totally to the other. This leads not only to a positive refusal to be open to life but also to a falsification of the inner truth of conjugal love, which is called upon to give itself in personal totality.

When, instead, by means of recourse to periods of infertility, the couple respect the inseparable connection between the unitive and procreative meanings of human sexuality, they are acting as 'ministers' of God's plan and they 'benefit from' their sexuality according to the original dynamism of 'total' self-giving, without manipulation or alteration.

In the light of the experience of many couples and of the data provided by the different human sciences, theological reflection is able to perceive and is called to study further *the difference, both anthropological and moral,* between contraception and recourse to the rhythm of the cycle: it is a difference which is much wider and deeper than is usually thought, one which involves in the final analysis two irreconcilable concepts of the human person and of human sexuality. The choice of the natural rhythms involves accepting the cycle of the person, that is the woman, and thereby accepting dialogue, reciprocal respect, shared responsibility and self-control.

ADDRESS TO CATHOLIC DOCTORS
(3 October, 1982)

The pope exhorts physicians to respect the autonomy and personal dignity

of the patient. The text is found in Osservatore Romano *(English Edition),*
25 October, 1982, pp. 9-10.

(Humanising the medical profession)

2237   4. Your commitment cannot be limited to only
professional correctness, but must be sustained by that
interior attitude which is fittingly called "spirit of service". In
fact, the patient to whom you dedicate your care and your studies
is not a nameless individual to whom the fruit of your knowledge
is applied but a responsible person who must be called upon to
participate in the improvement of one's health and the
achievement of one's cure. The patient must be put in the position
of being able to make personal choices and not have to submit
to the decisions and choices of others.

The appeal to "humanise" the doctor's work and the place
where it is practiced is placed in these terms. Humanising means
the proclamation of the dignity of the human person, respect for
his or her corporality, for his or her spirit and culture. It is your
task to seek to discover ever more deeply the biological
mechanisms which control life so as to be able to intervene in
them, on the strength of a power over things which the Lord
has given to human persons.

In so doing, it is also your commitment to constantly keep
within the perspective of the human person and of the
requirements which spring from his or her dignity. In more
concrete terms: no one of you can limit yourself to being a doctor
of an organ or apparatus, but must treat the whole person, and
what is more, the interpersonal relationships which contribute
to the person's well-being.

ADDRESS TO WORLD MEDICAL ASSOCIATION
(29 October, 1983)

The Pope warns against the dangers of indiscriminate genetic
manipulation. The text is found in AAS 76 (1984)   389-395.

(Dangers of indiscriminate genetic manipulation)

2238   6. The biological nature of each person is untouchable
in the sense that it is constitutive of the personal identity
of the individual throughout the whole course of his or her history.
Each human person, in one's absolutely unique singularity, is
constituted not only by a spirit, but by a body as well. Thus, in

the body and through the body, one touches persons themselves in their concrete reality. To respect the dignity of the human person, consequently, amounts to safeguarding this identity of the person *corpore et anima unus,* as Vatican II says *[GS 14].*

It is on the basis of this anthropological vision that one should find the fundamental criteria for decision-making in the case of not strictly therapeutic interventions, for example, those aimed at the human biological condition.

Moreover, the fundamental attitudes that inspire the interventions of which we are speaking should not flow from a racist or materialist mentality aimed at a human well-being that is, in reality, reductionist. The dignity of the human person transcends one's biological condition.

Genetic manipulation becomes arbitrary and unjust when it reduces life to an object, when it forgets that it is dealing with a human subject, capable of intelligence and freedom, worthy of respect, whatever may be its limitations; or when it treats this person in terms of criteria not founded on the integral reality of the human person, at the risk of infringing upon one's dignity. In this case, it exposes the individual to the caprice of others, thus depriving the person of one's autonomy.

S. CONGREGATION FOR CATHOLIC EDUCATION
EDUCATIONAL GUIDANCE ON HUMAN LOVE
(1 November, 1983)

The document provides positive guidance on sex education in the context of personality development and education to human love. As a basis for proper sex education, the Christian concept of sexuality in the vision of Pope John Paul II is presented. The text is found in Osservatore Romano *(English Edition), 5 December, 1983, pp. 5-9.*

(Christian concept of sexuality)

2239a 22. In the Christian vision of man and woman, a particular function of the body is recognised, because it contributes to the revealing of the meaning of life and of the human vocation. Corporeality is, in fact, a specific mode of existing and operating proper to the human spirit. This significance is first of all of an anthropological nature: the body reveals the person, "expresses the person"[1] and is, therefore, the

---

1. JOHN PAUL II, General Audience, 14 November, 1979

first message of God to the same man and woman, almost a kind of "primordial sacrament, understood as a sign which efficaciously transmits in the visible world the invisible mystery hidden in God from all eternity."[1]

2239b 23. There is a second significance of a theological nature; the body contributes to revealing God and his creative love, inasmuch as it manifests the creatureliness of man and woman, whose dependence bestows a fundamental gift, which is the gift of love.

2239c 24. The body, inasmuch as it is sexual, expresses the vocation of man and woman to reciprocity, which is to love and to the mutual gift of self. The body, in short, calls man and woman to the constitutive vocation to fecundity as one of the fundamental meanings of their being sexual.

2239d 26. Man and woman constitute two modes of releasing, on the part of the human creature, a determined participation in the Divine Being; they are created in the "image and likeness of God" [cf. Gen 2:26] and they fully accomplish such vocation not only as single persons, but also as couples, which are communities of love. Oriented to unity and fecundity, the married man and woman participate in the creative love of God, living in communion with him through the other.

(Nature, purpose and means of sex education)

2240a 34. A fundamental objective of this education is an adequate knowledge of the nature and importance of sexuality and of the harmonious and integral development of the person toward psychological maturity, with full spiritual maturity in view, to which all believers are called.

2240b 35. In the Christian anthropological perspective, affective sex education must consider the totality of the person and insist, therefore, on the integration of the biological, psycho-affective, social and spiritual elements. This integration has become more difficult because the believer also bears the consequences of sin from the beginning.

A true formation is not limited to the informing of the intellect, but must pay particular attention to the will, to feelings

---

2. JOHN PAUL II, General Audience, 20 February, 1980.

and emotions. In fact, in order to move to maturation in affective sexual life, self-control is necessary, which presupposes such virtues as modesty, temperance, respect for self and for others, openness to one's neighbour.

2240c   36. Also if the modes are diverse which sexuality assumes in single people, education must first of all promote that maturity which "entails not only accepting the value of sexuality integrated in the totality of human values, but also seeing it as giving a possibility for offering, that is, a capacity for giving, for altruistic love. When such a capacity is sufficiently acquired, an individual becomes capable of spontaneous contacts, emotional self-control and commitment of one's free will."[1]

2240d   42. Educators will have to bear in mind the fundamental stages of such an evolution: the primitive instinct, which in the beginning is manifested in a rudimentary state, meets in its turn the ambivalence of good and evil. Then with the help of education, the feelings are stabilized and at the same time augment the sense of responsibility. Gradually selfishness is eliminated, a certain asceticism is stabilized, others are accepted and loved for themselves, the elements of sexuality are integrated: genitality, eroticism, love and charity. Also if the result is not always attained, they are more numerous than may be thought who come near the goal to which they aspire.

ADDRESS TO A CULTURAL RENEWAL COURSE ON OPPOSING EUTHANASIA
(6 September, 1984)

In this address to the Catholic University of the Sacred Heart in Rome, the Pope uncovers the roots of the increasing acceptance of euthanasia. The text is found in The Pope Speaks *29 (1984) 352-355.*

(Euthanasia against the Christian concept of life)

2241   3. But the real problem to be confronted in the growing social acceptance of euthanasia seems to be elsewhere. As has already been seen in the case of abortion, the moral condemnation of euthanasia goes unheard by and is incomprehensible to those who are imbued, perhaps

---

1. S. Congregation for Catholic Education, Guidelines for Formation to Priestly Celibacy, 11 April, 1974, no. 22.

unconsciously, with a conception of life that is irreconcilable with the Christian message and with the very dignity of the human person, correctly understood.

To find proof of this, it is sufficient to consider some of the negative characteristics in vogue in the culture that abstracts from the transcendent:

- the habit of disposing of human life at its source;
- the tendency of appreciating personal life only to the degree that it can provide riches and pleasure;
- regarding material well-being and pleasure as supreme good, and thus, viewing suffering as an absolute evil to be avoided at all costs and by every means;
- viewing death as an absurd end to a life that could have given further pleasures, or as liberation from a life "deprived of meaning", because it was destined for further suffering.

With God out of the picture, it follows that one is responsible solely to oneself and the freely established laws of society.

Paradoxically, where these attitudes have taken root among persons and social groups, it can appear logical and "humane" to "gently" put an end to one's or another's life when that life holds only suffering or serious impairment. But in reality, this is absurd and inhuman.

ADDRESS AT INAUGURATION OF
ITALIAN SOLIDARITY CENTRE
(21 June, 1986)

The Pope deals with the problem of drug addiction and the approach to rehabilitation of drug addicts. The text is found in AAS 79 (1987) 34-38.

(Dealing with drug addiction)

2242   The drug problem cannot be dealt with merely through the use of other drugs, because drug addiction is more a disease of the mind than of the body. It is not a matter here of substituting a less dangerous poison for a moral harmful one, but of changing the quality of life itself. This is a task that requires the effort of each of you as persons who have at heart the true values that dwell in the heart of every creature made in the image of God. The "Project Person" that you intend to realise in this centre aims above all at helping the drug addict to know and face one's own problems, and this within the context of a prolonged and effective community experience in which one can recover and return to social life as an active and finally free person. This type of programme, born from the collaboration of former drug addicts and professionals in the social and psychological sciences, places the emphasis on the personal responsibility of the drug user, because in the last analysis, it is he or she who chose the path of those experiences and is thus the one who must first of all make the decision to stop, while accepting the assistance of others in his or her recovery.

S. CONGREGATION FOR THE DOCTRINE OF THE FAITH LETTER TO THE BISHOPS OF THE CATHOLIC CHURCH ON THE PASTORAL CARE OF HOMOSEXUAL PERSONS
(1 October, 1986)

The document insists on the stand that homosexual activity is always objectively disordered. But it asks the pastors of the Church to show compassion to those afflicted with a homosexual orientation. The text is found in AAS 79 (1987) 543-554.

(Church's condemnation of homosexual activity based on scripture)

2243a 5. What should be noticed is that, in the presence of a remarkable diversity, there is nevertheless a clear consistency within the scriptures themselves on the moral issue of homosexual behaviour. The Church's doctrine regarding this issue is thus based, not on isolated phrases for facile theological argument, but on the solid foundation of a constant biblical testimony. The community of faith today, in unbroken continuity with Jewish and Christian communities within which the ancient scriptures were written, continues to be nourished by those same scriptures and by the spirit of Truth whose word they are.

(Attacks against homosexual persons are to be deplored but this does not mean the activity is to be condoned)

2243b 10. It is deplorable that homosexual persons have been and are the object of violent malice in speech or in action. Such treatment deserves condemnation from the Church's pastors wherever it occurs. It reveals a kind of disregard for others which endangers the most fundamental principles of a healthy society. This intrinsic dignity of each person must always be respected in word, in action and in law.

But the proper reaction to crimes committed against homosexual persons should not be a claim that the homosexual condition is not disordered. When such a claim is made and when the homosexual activity is consequently condoned, or when civil legislation is introduced to protect behaviour to which no one has any conceivable right, neither the Church nor society at large should be surprised when other distorted notions and practices gain ground, and irrational and violent reactions increase.

(Culpability may be reduced, but is not always absent)

2243c   11. In fact, circumstances may exist, or may have existed in the past which would reduce or remove culpability of the individual in a given instance; or other circumstances may increase it. What is at all costs to be avoided is the unfounded and demeaning assumption that the sexual behaviour of homosexual persons is totally compulsive and therefore inculpable. What is essential is that the fundamental liberty which characterises and gives dignity to the human person be recognised as belonging to the homosexual person as well. As in every conversion from evil, the abandonment of homosexual activity will require a profound collaboration of the individual with God's liberating grace.

(Person-centred approach needed)

2243d   16. The human person, made in the image of God, can hardly be adequately described by a reductionist reference to his or her sexual orientation. Everyone living on the face of the earth has personal problems and difficulties, but challenges to growth, strengths, talents and gifts as well. Today, the Church provides a badly needed context for the care of the human person when she refuses to consider the person as a "homosexual" or a "heterosexual" and insists that every person has a fundamental identity: the creature of God, and by grace, his child and heir to eternal life.

S. CONGREGATION FOR THE DOCTRINE OF THE FAITH
INSTRUCTION *DONUM VITAE*
(22 February, 1987)

This Instruction on respect for human life in its origins and on the dignity of procreation replies to certain questions raised by recent advances in bio-technology. The unconditional respect for human life from the moment of conception and respect for the God-given character of the transmission of human life are stressed. The document seems to go further than preceding ones in asking that the human being be respected and treated as a person from the time of conception. Regarding transmission of new human life, even the 'simple case' of in-vitro fertilization is excluded. The text is found in AAS 80 (1988) 70-102.

(Fundamental criteria for a moral judgment)

2244a Intr., 4. The fundamental values connected with the techniques of artificial human procreation are two: the life of the human being called into existence and the special nature of the transmission of human life in marriage. The moral judgment on such methods of artificial procreation must therefore be formulated in reference to these values.

Physical life, with which the course of human life in the world begins, certainly does not itself contain the whole of the person's value, nor does it represent the supreme good of the person who is called to eternal life. However, it does constitute in a certain way the fundamental value of life, precisely because upon one's physical life all other values of the person are based and developed. The inviolability of the innocent human being's right to life "from the moment of conception to death" is a sign and requirement of the very inviolability of the person to whom the Creator has given the gift of life.

By comparison with the transmission of other forms of life in the universe, the transmission of human life has a special character of its own, which derives from the special nature of the human person. "The transmission of human life is entrusted by nature to a personal and conscious act and as such is subject to the all-holy laws of God: immutable and inviolable laws, which must be recognised and observed. For this reason one cannot use means and follow methods which could be licit in the transmission of life of the plants and animals."[1]

2244b Intr., 5. Human procreation requires on the part of the spouses responsible collaboration with the fruitful love of God; the gift of human life must be actualised in marriage through the specific and exclusive acts of husband and wife, in accordance with the law inscribed in their persons and in their union.

---

1. JOHN XXIII, Encyclical Letter *Mater et Magistra*, III: *AAS* 53 (1961) 447.

(Respect for human embryos)

2245 1,1. Thus the fruit of human generation from the first moment of its existence, that is to say, from the moment the zygote has been formed, demands the unconditional respect that is morally due to the human being in its bodily and spiritual totality. The human being is to be respected and treated as a person from the moment of conception; and therefore from that same moment one's rights as a person must be recognized, among which in the first place is the inviolable right of every innocent human being to life.

This doctrinal reminder provides the fundamental criterion for the solution of the various problems posed by the development of the bio-medical sciences in this field: since the embryo must be treated as a person, it must also be defended in its integrity, tended and cared for, to the extent possible, in the same way as any other human being as far as medical assistance is concerned.

(Pre-natal diagnosis and experimentation)

2246a 1.2. Pre-natal diagnosis is permissible, with the consent of the parents after they have been adequately informed of the methods employed if the methods safeguard the life and integrity of the embryo and the mother without subjecting them to disproportionate risks. But this diagnosis is gravely opposed to the moral law when it is done with the thought to possibly inducing an abortion depending upon the results; a diagnosis which shows the existence of malformation or a hereditary illness must not be equivalent to a death-sentence. Thus a woman would be committing a gravely illicit act if she were to request such a diagnosis with the deliberate intention of having an abortion should the result confirm the existence of a malformation or abnormality. The spouse or relatives or anyone else would similarly be acting in a manner contrary to the moral law if they were to counsel or impose such a diagnostic procedure on the expectant mother with the same intention.

2246b I,4. As regards experimentation, and presupposing the general distinction between experimentation for purposes which are not directly therapeutic and experimentation which is clearly therapeutic for the subject, in the case in point one must also distinguish between experimentation carried out on embryos which are still alive and experimentation carried out on embryos which are dead. If the embryos are living, whether viable or not, they must be respected just like any other human person; experimentation on embryos which is not directly therapeutic is illicit.

No objective, even though noble in itself, such as a foreseeable advantage to science, to other human beings or to society, can in any way justify experimentation on living human embryos or foetuses, whether viable or not, either inside or outside the mother's womb. The informed consent ordinarily required for clinical experimentation on adults cannot be granted by the parents, who may not freely dispose of the physical integrity of life of the unborn child. Moreover, experimentation on embryos and foetuses always involves risk, and in most cases it involves the certain expectation of harm to their physical integrity or even their death.

(Heterologous artificial fertilization)

2247 II,2. Respect for the unity of marriage and for conjugal fidelity demands that the child be conceived in marriage: the bond existing between the husband and wife accords the spouses, in an objective and inalienable manner, the exclusive right to become father and mother solely through each other. Recourse to the gametes of a third person, in order to have sperm or ovum available, constitutes a violation of the reciprocal commitment of the spouses and a grave lack in regard to that essential property of marriage which is its unity.

Heterologous artificial fertilization violates the right of the child; it deprives the child of its filial relationship with its parental origins and can hinder the maturing of its personal identity. Furthermore it offends the common vocation of the spouses who are called to fatherhood and motherhood: it objectively deprives conjugal fruitfulness of its unity and integrity; it brings about and manifests a rupture between genetic parenthood and responsibility for upbringing. Such damage to the personal relationships within the family has repercussions on civil society: what threatens the unity and stability of the family is a source of dissension, disorder and injustice in the whole of social life.

(Surrogate motherhood)

2248 II,3. Surrogate motherhood represents an objective failure to meet obligations of maternal love, of conjugal fidelity and of responsible motherhood; it offends the dignity and the right of the child to be conceived, carried in the womb, brought into the world and brought up by its parents; it sets up, to the detriment of families, a division between the physical, psychological and moral elements which constitute those families.

(Homologous artificial fertilization)

2249 II,4. The conjugal act by which the couple mutually expresses openness to their self-gift at the same time expresses openness to the gift of life. It is an act that is inseparably corporal and spiritual. It is in their bodies and through their bodies that the spouses consummate their marriage and are able to become father and mother. In order to respect the language of their bodies and their natural generosity, the conjugal union must take place with respect for its openness to procreation; and the procreation of a person must be the fruit and the result of married love.[...] Fertilization achieved outside the bodies of the couples remains by this fact deprived of the meanings and values which are expressed in the language of the body and in the union of persons.

Only respect for the link between the meanings of the conjugal act and respect for the unity of the human being make possible procreation in conformity with the dignity of the person. In this unique and unrepeatable origin, the child must be respected and recognised as equal in personal dignity to those who give it life. The human person must be accepted in the parental act of union and love; the generation of the child must therefore be the fruit of that mutual self-giving which is realised in the conjugal act wherein the spouses cooperate as servants and not masters in the work of the Creator who is Love.

(Homologous in vitro fertilization)

2250 II,5. Conception *in vitro* is the result of the technical action which presides over fertilization. Such fertilization is neither in fact achieved nor positively willed as the expression and fruit of the specific act of conjugal union. In homologous "in vitro" fertilization and embryo transfer, therefore, even if it is considered in the context of "de facto" existing sexual relations, the generation of the human person is objectively deprived of its proper perfection: namely, that of being the result and fruit of a conjugal act in which the spouses can become "cooperators with God for giving life to a new person".[1]

These reasons enable us to understand why the act of conjugal love is considered in the teaching of the Church as the only setting worthy of human procreation. For the same reasons the so-called "simple case", i.e., a homologous *in vitro* fertilization and embryo transfer procedure that is free of any compromise with the abortive practice of destroying embryos and with masturbation, remains a technique which is morally illicit because it deprives human procreation of the dignity which is proper and connatural to it.

(Homologous artificial insemination)

2251   II,6. Homologous artificial insemination within marriage cannot be admitted except for those cases in which the technical means is not a substitute for the conjugal act but serves to facilitate and to help so that the act attains its natural end.

(No true and proper right to have a child)

2252   II,8. On the part of the spouses, the desire for a child is natural: it expresses the vocation to fatherhood and motherhood inscribed in conjugal love. Nevertheless, marriage does not confer upon the spouses the right to have a child, but only the right to perform those natural acts which are *per se* ordered to procreation.

A true and proper right to a child would be contrary to the child's dignity and nature. The child is not an object to which one has a right, nor can the child be considered as an object of ownership: rather, a child is a gift, "the supreme gift" and the most gratuitous gift of marriage, and is a living testimony of the mutual giving of the parents. For this reason, the child has the right, as already mentioned, to be the fruit of the specific act of the conjugal love of the parents; and it also has the right to be respected as a person from the moment of conception.

ENCYCLICAL LETTER *EVANGELIUM VITAE*
(25 March, 1995)

The encyclical gathers together and reaffirms the teaching of the Catholic Church on the inviolability of human life. While there is nothing here that is really new, there are three novel aspects that are noteworthy. Firstly, the Pope

---

1. *Familiaris Consortio*, 14: *AAS* 74 (1982) 96

includes many issues in a unified and coherent ethic of respect for life. Secondly, while not setting aside the natural law, he develops a theological argument, drawn from revelation, for the value of human life. Thirdly, on the level of specific norms he takes a more restrictive position on the death penalty than previous official teaching, for example in the Catechism of the Catholic Church *(but, cf. n. 2269). While the Pope does not invoke infallibility, he has used language indicating that these are teachings of the ordinary, universal magisterium which are true and definitive. The most controversial features may well be the Pope's condemnation of the legal justification of attacks on life, the tyrannical decision not to protect life, and his rejection of such as unjust laws. The text can be found in* Origins 24 *(1995) 689-727.*

(Structure of sin—culture of death)

2253 12.[...] We are confronted by an even larger reality, which can be described as veritable structure of sin. This reality is characterised by the emergence of a culture which denies solidarity and in many cases takes the form of a veritable "culture of death".

(Revelation as the basis for the value of life)

2254 28. The unconditional choice for life reaches its full religious and moral meaning when it flows from, is formed by and nourished by faith in Christ. Nothing helps us so much to face positively the conflict between death and life in which we are engaged as faith in the Son of God who became man and dwelt among human beings so "that they may have life, and have it abundantly" *[Jn 10:10]*. It is a matter of faith in the risen Lord, who has conquered death; faith in the blood of Christ "that speaks more graciously than the blood of Abel" *[Heb 12:24]*.

(The death penalty)

2255 56.[...] The nature and extent of the punishment must be carefully evaluated and decided upon, and ought not go to the extreme of executing the offender except in cases of absolute necessity: In other words, when it would not be possible otherwise to defend society. Today however, as a result of steady improvements in the organisation of the penal system, such cases are very rare, if not practically nonexistent.

(Authoritative rejection of direct killing of the innocent)

2256 57.[...] By the authority which Christ conferred upon Peter and his successors, and in communion with the bishops of the Catholic Church, *I confirm that the direct and voluntary killing of an innocent human being is always gravely immoral.* This doctrine, based upon that unwritten law which the human person, in the light of reason, finds in one's own heart [*cf. Rom 2:14-15*], is reaffirmed by Sacred Scripture, transmitted by the tradition of the Church and taught by the ordinary and universal magisterium [*cf. LG 25*].

(Authoritative rejection of abortion)

2257   62.[...] By the authority which Christ conferred upon Peter and his successors, in communion with the bishops—who on various occasions have condemned abortion and who in the aforementioned consultation, albeit dispersed throughout the world, have shown unanimous agreement concerning this doctrine—*I declare that direct abortion, that is, abortion willed as an end or as a means, always constitutes a grave moral disorder,* since it is the deliberate killing of an innocent human being [*cf. nn. 2216, 2221*]. This doctrine is based upon the natural law and upon the written Word of God, is transmitted by the Church's tradition and taught by the ordinary and universal magisterium [*cf. LG 25*].

(Human embryos not to be objects of experimentation)

2258   63.[...] The use of human embryos or foetuses as an object of experimentation constitutes a crime against their dignity as human beings who have a right to the same respect owed to a child once born, just as to every person.

(Authoritative rejection of euthanasia)

2259   65.[...] In harmony with the magisterium of my predecessors [*cf. GS 27*] and in communion with the bishops of the Catholic Church, *I confirm that euthanasia is a grave violation of the law of God,* since it is the deliberate and morally unacceptable killing of a human person. This doctrine is based upon the natural law and upon the written word of God, is transmitted by the Church's tradition and taught by the ordinary and universal magisterium [*cf. LG 25*].

(Tyrannical decisions against the weakest)

2260   70. When a parliamentary or social majority decrees that it is legal, at least under certain conditions, to kill unborn human life, is it not really making a "tyrannical" decision with regard to the weakest and most defenceless of human beings?

(Unjust laws and conscientious objection)

2261a 73. Abortion and euthanasia are thus crimes which no human law can claim to legitimise. There is no obligation in conscience to obey such laws; instead there is a grave and clear obligation to oppose them by conscientious objection.

2261b 73. In the case of an intrinsically unjust law, such as a law permitting abortion or euthanasia, it is therefore never licit to obey it, or to "take part in a propaganda campaign in favour of such a law, or vote for it".

(Conscience and voting for a more restrictive law)

2262 73. A particular problem of conscience can arise in cases where a legislative vote would be decisive for the passage of a more restrictive law, aimed at limiting the number of authorised abortions, in place of a more permissive law already passed or ready to be voted on. [...] In a case like the one just mentioned, when it is not possible to overturn or completely abrogate a pro-abortion law, an elected official, whose absolute personal opposition to procured abortion was well known, could licitly support proposals aimed at limiting the harm done by such a law and at lessening its negative consequences at the level of general opinion and public morality. This does not in fact represent an illicit cooperation with an unjust law, but rather a legitimate and proper attempt to limit its evil aspects.

(Democratic means for realistically attainable change)

2263 90.[...] All have a responsibility for shaping society and developing cultural, economic, political and legislative projects which, with respect for all and in keeping with democratic principles, will contribute to the building of a society in which the dignity of each person is recognized and protected and the lives of all are defended and enhanced.

[...] The Church encourages political leaders, starting with those who are Christians, not to give in, but to make those choices which, taking into account what is realistically attainable, will lead to the re-establishment of a just order in the defence and promotion of the value of life.

(Public authorities and population questions)

2264 91. Certainly public authorities have a responsibility to "intervene to orient the demography of the population." But such interventions must always take into account and respect the primary and inalienable responsibility of married couples and families, and cannot employ methods which fail to respect the person and fundamental human rights, beginning with the right to life of every human being.

(To women who have had an abortion)

2265 99. The Church is aware of the many factors which may have influenced your decision, and she does not doubt that in many cases it was a painful and even shattering decision. The wound in your heart may not yet have healed. Certainly what happened was and remains terribly wrong. But do not give in to discouragement and do not lose hope. [...] You will come to understand that nothing is definitively lost and you will also be able to ask forgiveness from your child, who is now living in the Lord.

PONTIFICAL COUNCIL FOR THE FAMILY
VADEMECUM FOR CONFESSORS CONCERNING SOME
ASPECTS OF THE MORALITY OF CONJUGAL LIFE
(12 February, 1997)

This document presents a summary of traditional pastoral guidelines for confessors in relation to contraception and other problems that may arise in married life. The text is found in Origins 26 (1997) 617-625.

2266 1. In dealing with penitents on the matter of responsible procreation, the confessor should keep four aspects in mind: a) the example of the Lord who "is capable of reaching down to every prodigal son, to every human misery, and above all to every form of moral misery, to sin"; b) a prudent reserve in inquiring into these sins; c) help and encouragement to the penitents so that they may be able to reach sufficient repentance and accuse themselves fully of grave sins; d) advice which inspire all, in a gradual way, to embrace the path of holiness.

2267 9. The pastoral "law of gradualness", not to be confused with the "gradualness of the law" which would tend to diminish the demands it places on us, consists in requiring a decisive break with sin together with a progressive path towards total union with the will of God and with his loving demands. [...] It is part of the church's pedagogy that husbands and wives would first recognize clearly the teaching of *Humanae Vitae* as indicating the norm for the exercise of their sexuality, and that they should endeavour to establish the conditions necessary for observing the norm [*cf. Familiaris Consortio, 34*].

2268   13. Special difficulties are presented by cases of cooperation in the sin of a spouse who voluntarily renders the unitive act infecund. In the first place, it is necessary to distinguish cooperation in the proper sense, from violence or unjust imposition on the part of one of the spouses, which the other spouse in fact cannot resist. This cooperation can be licit when the three following conditions are jointly met:

1. when the action of the cooperating spouse is not already illicit in itself;
2. when proportionally grave reasons exist for cooperating in the sin of the other spouse;
3. when one is seeking to help the other spouse to desist from such conduct (patiently, with prayer, charity and dialogue; although not necessarily in that moment, nor on every single occasion).

CATECHISM OF THE CATHOLIC CHURCH
(Definitive text, 8 September, 1997)

(The definitive text includes an important change to the statement on the death penalty of the original text of 1992. The text is found in Origins 27 *(1997) 257.*

(On death penalty)

2269   2267. Assuming that the guilty party's identity and responsibility have been fully determined, the traditional teaching of the Church does not exclude recourse to the death penalty, if this is the only possible way of effectively defending human lives against the unjust aggressor.

If, however, non-lethal means are sufficient to defend and protect people's safety from the aggressor, authority will limit itself to such means, as these are more in keeping with the concrete conditions of the common good and are more in conformity to the dignity of the human person.

Today, in fact, as a consequence of the possibilities which the state has for effectively preventing crime, by rendering one who has committed an offense incapable of doing harm—without definitely taking away from him the possibility of redeeming himself—the cases in which the execution of the offender is an absolute necessity are very rare, if not practically nonexistent. [cf. n. 2255].

CHAPTER XXIII

CHRISTIAN FULFILMENT

God—throughout the span of time—desires to bring his creative plan to completion and mysteriously guides the whole of creation towards fulfilment. The Paschal Mystery, already foretold in the Exodus experience that inaugurated the Sinaitic covenant, represents the peak expression of God's desire that humanity—and the whole of creation—move steadily forward toward the full actualization of all they hope for (Rom 8:19-25).

After God's self-manifestation at creation (Gen 1 and 2) reached its climax in the incarnation of the Word, it still envisions its full scope in the final glorification of that same Word. Consequently, the timeframe between the Incarnation and the Second Coming of Jesus Christ as the Lord of all things constitutes the time of the Church, the new people of God, "a sign and instrument [...] of communion with God and of unity among all human beings" (LG 1).

The Church itself, as God's pilgrim people, advances in Christ through the Spirit towards the Father. At the parousia, the 'last day' when Christ "delivers the kingdom to God the Father", God will "be everything to every one" (I Cor 15:24.28). The time of the Church, hence, is one of hope and transformation, desire and anticipation, poverty and expectation, nascent solidarity and shared communion. Believers savour the full communion they already enjoy, in faith, with God and one another. At the same time, in hope and love, they await the day when Christ "appears", when "we shall be like him, for we shall see him as he is" (I Jn 3:2).

At the end of time, the Second Coming of the Lord in glory will therefore usher in the definitive revelation of creation's total renewal in God: whatever God offered in promise to our forefathers and mysteriously extends to us in Christ, will manifest itself fully when all God's family will be one and the whole universe will attain maturity. The Church's doctrine on human destiny is totally centred on Jesus Christ, the Eschaton in person: in him, God blesses our human condition with holiness and righteousness, perfection and glory.

The Church has constantly believed that, at the end of one's life, when one sees God face to face (cf. 1 Cor 13:12), every person must measure oneself with the ultimate expression of the Father's love, in Christ, through the Spirit.

The just, in their final encounter with God's loving mercy, appease their longing; conformed once for all to the Mystery of Christ, their life of grace has led them to correspond—as well as they could—to God's holiness. God himself welcomes them—purified from sin and its effects—into the eternal glory of the blessed, calling them to partake of his light and joy. In and through them, the Kingdom of God reaches its fulness and the pilgrim Church finally arrives at the communion of saints, to share fully God's banquet.

On the other hand, the Church has always held that God himself respects the choice of those who might deliberately and intentionally opt against his saving love. They close themselves definitely to his love and place themselves beyond the sway of his mercy. Every human being faces one of the following alternatives: either to live with the Lord in eternal beatitude, or to remain far from his presence.

The teaching authority of the Church, in the course of history, addresses mainly two issues: millenarism, and purification from sin after death.

In certain circumstances, some may feel the end approaching, while others even preach the end is near. The Church dwells on humanity's role in the construction of God's Kingdom, that the latter may grow and be operative in history, as it avoids, at all costs, any apocalyptic calls: "It is not for you to know the times or seasons which the Father has fixed by his own authority" (Acts 1: 7). Still less can the believer assent to millenaristic tendencies that limit to a select few the realization of the Father's desire that humankind enter into communion with him.

During the Middle Ages, the magisterium pondered the events that accompany death: purification (purgatory) as the person's ultimate encounter with the love of Christ that overcomes the imperfection of sin; the intercession on behalf of the dead as a participation in the saving mission of Christ; the resurrection of individual bodies and the vision of God as entering into full communion with the three divine Persons. Throughout, the Church insisted on the virtue of Christian hope.

Overruling individualistic and intimistic approaches to eschatology, the Second Vatican Council accentuates (a) the ecclesial dimension of the things hoped for, (b) the understanding of human existence as a pilgrimage to the Father of all, and (c) the end as the completion of God's "plan for the fulness of time, to unite all things in him, things in heaven and things on earth" (Eph 1:10). Within this perspective,

Mary's Assumption proclaims her as "the beginning and the pattern of the Church in its perfection, and a sign of hope and comfort for" the people of God "on their pilgrim way" (Preface for August 15, Missal of Paul VI; cf. nn. 713- 715).

* * *

These, then, are the doctrinal points contained in the following documents:

The Pilgrim People of God

The Church is the eschatological community, awaiting Christ's second coming and the fulfilment of all creation: 2311, 2316, 2325a-b, 2327.

Time—in need of sanctification—is of fundamental importance to the believer: 2326b, 2327.

The communion of saints comprises the pilgrim Church, those who are being purified, and the blessed in heaven: 39/23, 2312, (2313f).

The 'Last' Things

Death, as we experience it, is a punishment for sin and will be destroyed in Christ's second coming: 39/21, 508-509, 2312, 2315, 2316, 2319a-c.

Reincarnation is completely foreign to our faith: 2326a.

Those who depart from this life free from sin go to eternal happiness: 5, 10, 17, 20, 25, 26, 39/21, (2303) 2305, 2309, 2317, 2321a.

Heaven consists in the vision of God: 39/22, 1997, 2305f, 2309, 2321a-c.

Those who are subject to temporal punishment are to be purified: 26, 35, 1548, 1557, 1685/22, 1689, (2304), 2308, 2310, 2317, 2322a-b.

They are helped by the acts of intercession and the good works of the faithful: 26, 35, 1548, 1557, 1685/22, 1689, (2304), 2308, 2310, 2317.

Those who die in mortal sin condemn themselves: 17, 20, 26, 506, (2303), 2307, 2317, 2323a-c.

Their punishment is eternal: 17, 20, 506, 2301, (2303), 2317, 2323a.

The 'Last' Day

In the end of times, all will rise in their bodies: 5, 10, 12, 17, 20, 25, 27, 2302, (2303), 2307, 2317, 2318a-d, 2324a-b.

They will be judged by Christ: 5, 7, 10, 12, 17, 20, 23, 27, 2302, (2303), 2307, 2320.

THE COUNCIL OF CONSTANTINOPLE
ANATHEMAS AGAINST THE ORIGENISTS (543)

Emperor Justinian drew up a series of canons against the Origenists which were subsequently promulgated at the Provincial Council of Constantinople in 543. On the basis of Platonic philosophy the Origenists attempted to explain the creation and the end of the world by laws of inner necessity. According to them human souls pre-existed to their infusion in the body (cf. n. 401), and all would one day be freed from the imprisonment of the body to recover their pristine spiritual state. Consequently, the punishment of hell was only temporary; it was to be followed by the general restoration of all souls to their former state (apokatastasis). This document of condemnation seems to have been signed by all the Eastern Patriarchs and possibly was confirmed by Pope Vigilius.

2301 9. If anyone says or holds that the punishment of the
411 demons and of impious human beings is temporary, and
that it will have an end at some time, or that there will be a complete restoration *(apokatasasis)* of demons and impious human beings, *anathema sit.*

THE ELEVENTH COUNCIL OF TOLEDO
SYMBOL OF FAITH (675)

A Creed or profession of faith, prepared by Quiricius, archbishop of Toledo, was approved at the beginning of this provincial Council by the seventeen bishops present. Besides a long elaboration on the mystery of the Trinity (cf. nn. 308ff) and of the Incarnation and Redemption (cf. nn. 628ff), it contains a much shorter treatment of Christian eschatology. Though never approved by a Pope, this document, always held in high regard by the Church, is among the important formulas of doctrine: most of its contents belong to the doctrine of faith (cf. n. 18). Its doctrine is partly inspired by the Pseudo-Athanasian Symbol Quicumque (cf. nn. 16f), partly by the great Latin doctors, especially St. Augustine and St. Hilary.

(On the fate of the human being after death)

2302 Thus, according to the example of our Head, we confess
540 that there is a true resurrection of the body for all the
dead. And we do not believe that we shall rise in an ethereal body or in any other body, as some foolishly imagine, but in this very body in which we live and are and move. After having given an example of this holy resurrection, our Lord and Saviour by his ascension returned to the throne of his Father from which in his divine nature he had never departed. There,

seated at the right hand of the Father, he is awaited till the end time as judge of all living and the dead. From there he shall come with all the holy [angels and human beings] to pass judgment and to render to each one the reward due to one, according to what each one has done while in the body, whether good or evil [cf. 2 Cor 5:10].

We believe that the holy Catholic Church, which he purchased at the price of his own blood, will reign with him forever. Taken up into her bosom, we believe in and profess one baptism for the remission of all sins. By this faith we truly believe in the resurrection of the dead and look forward to the joys of the world to come. This only must we pray and beg for, that when the Son, having completed the judgment, will have delivered the Kingdom to God the Father [cf. 1 Cor 15:24], he may make us share in his Kingdom, so that through this faith by which we have adhered to him, we may reign with him forever.

THE FOURTH LATERAN GENERAL COUNCIL
SYMBOL OF LATERAN (1215)

(2303) *The twelfth general Council was held at the Lateran in 1215, under Pope Innocent III. Before the decrees concerning the recovery of the Holy Land and the general reform of the Church, the Council issued a profession of the Catholic faith directly intended against the errors of the Albigensians and the Cathars(cf.n.19i). The Albigensian system was in certain respects the upshot of the previous Manichaean heresy, which held matter to be intrinsically evil as proceeding from an eternal evil principle. Imprisoned in the bodies, human souls were to undergo a gradual purification through a process of transmigration till their final restoration to their original heavenly state; consequently the punishment of hell was not considered as eternal. Against these heretical tendencies, the Council's profession of faith declares the Catholic doctrine of creation according to which all things, spiritual and corporeal, are created by God, and naturally good (cf. n. 19). It goes on to express the Christian faith as regards the resurrection of the bodies, the judgment of all according to their deeds, and the subsequent eternal reward or punishment. The text is found in n.20.*

THE SECOND GENERAL COUNCIL OF LYONS
"PROFESSION OF FAITH OF MICHAEL PALAEOLOGUS"
(1274)

(2304) *Among the points of dissent between the Latin and the Greek Churches which the Second General Council of Lyons attempted to settle, several were related to Christian eschatology. The profession of faith* *proposed by Pope Clement IV to Emperor Michael Palaeologus as early as 1267 as pre-required condition for union was read at the Council convened by Pope Gregory X in 1274, but was neither discussed at the Council nor accepted by the Greeks as a basis for a doctrinal agreement with the Latins (cf.n.22i).The eschatological doctrine is treated in the second part of the "Profession of Faith of Michael Palaeologus" In the context of a complete doctrine of individual eschatology, which will be taken up later by the Council of Florence (cf.nn.2308f), it lays stress on the immediate retribution and on purgatory, the two main points on which Latins and Greeks were at variance in current controversies; it also affirms the efficacy of prayer for the dead. A clause on the general judgment is added to mark the agreement between Greeks and Latins on this point. The text is found under nn.25-27.*

BENEDICT XII
CONSTITUTION *BENEDICTUS DEUS* (1336)

The common teaching of the Church on immediate retribution after death held that the blessed on entering the heavenly state were introduced to the immediate and eternal vision of God. Departing from this traditional opinion, Pope John XXII, in a series of sermons preached in 1331, asserted, as a private theologian, that soon after death the blessed enjoy only the vision of Christ's glorified humanity, while the access to the vision of the Triune God will be opened to them only after the resurrection, on the day of judgment. The following year, he adapted this opinion of a progressive retribution to the condition of the damned. The Pope's opinion led to a fierce controversy, notably between the Franciscans who supported the Pope and the Dominicans who opposed him.The university of Paris requested the Pope to settle the dispute authoritatively. Though he intended to heed the request, John XXII was able only to retract his own former opinion on the eve of his death and to submit personally to the traditional doctrine of the Church.His successor Benedict XII, after a thorough enquiry, issued in 1336 the Constitution Benedictus Deus by which he meant to bring the controversy to an end. According to this Constitution the souls of the blessed departed see the Triune God face to face immediately after death and prior to the resurrection. But the nature of their intermediate state between death and resurrection, which is conceived as that of bodiless souls, is presupposed by the Constitution rather than directly taught.

(On the beatific vision of God)

2305
1000
By this Constitution which is to remain in force for ever, we with apostolic authority, define the following:
According to the general disposition of God, the souls of all the saints who departed from this world before the passion of our Lord Jesus Christ and also of the holy apostles, martyrs, confessors, virgins and other faithful who died after receiving the holy baptism of Christ—provided they were not in need of any

purification when they died, or will not be in need of any when they die in the future, or else, if they then needed or will need some purification, after they have been purified after death—and again the souls of children who have been reborn by the same baptism of Christ or will be when baptism is conferred on them, if they die before attaining the use of free will: all these souls, immediately *(mox)* after death and, in the case of those in need of purification, after the purification mentioned above, since the ascension of our Lord and Saviour Jesus Christ into heaven, already before they take up their bodies again and before the general judgment, have been, are and will be with Christ in heaven, in the heavenly kingdom and paradise, joined to the company of the holy angels. Since the passion and death of the Lord Jesus Christ, these souls have seen and see the divine essence with an intuitive vision and even face to face, without the mediation of any creature by way of object of vision; rather the divine essence immediately manifests itself to them, plainly, clearly and openly, and in this vision they enjoy the divine essence. Moreover, by this vision and enjoyment the souls of those who have already died are truly blessed and have eternal life and rest. Also the souls of those who will die in the future will see the same divine essence and will enjoy it before the general judgment.

2306 Such a vision and enjoyment of the divine essence do
1001 away with the acts of faith and hope in these souls, inasmuch as faith and hope are properly theological virtues. And after such intuitive and face-to-face vision and enjoyment has or will have begun for these souls, the same vision and enjoyment has continued and will continue without any interruption and without end until the last Judgment and from then on forever.

(On hell and the general judgment)

2307 Moreover we define that according to the general
1002 disposition of God, the souls of those who die in actual mortal sin go down into hell immediately *(mox)* after death and there suffer the pain of hell. Nevertheless, on the day of judgment all will appear with their bodies "before the judgment seat of Christ" to give an account of their personal deeds, "so that each one may receive good or evil, according to what one has done in the body" [2 Cor 5:10].

THE GENERAL COUNCIL OF FLORENCE
DECREE FOR THE GREEKS (1439)

The reunion with the Orientals, attempted by the second Council of Lyons in 1274, did not materialise in practice. A new and more successful attempt at reconciliation, the results of which, however, were also short-lived, was made at the Council of Florence under Pope Eugene IV. Besides the sections on the procession of the Holy Spirit (cf. 322 ff), on the Eucharist (cf.n.1508), and on the Roman primacy (cf. n. 809), the Decree for the Greeks contains a section on Christian eschatology. As regards the doctrine of purgatory the Orientals admitted its existence as well as the efficacy of prayers offered for the dead. But, while the Latin Church explained its nature with the help of the juridical concept of satisfaction, the East conceived it in a more mystical manner, as a process of maturation and spiritual growth. With regard to the beatific vision, the Orientals denied its immediate possibility and held that it would begin only after the general resurrection. In settling this double issue, the Council repeats almost verbatim *the previous decree of Lyons (cf. nn. 26-27), with an important addition, however, concerning the various degrees of intensity of the vision which depend on the diversity of merits. The section on purgatory strikes a careful balance between the Western conception of satisfaction-expiation and the Oriental insistence on purification. Moreover, out of consideration for the Oriental position, the Council deliberately omits all allusion to fire and carefully avoids whatever could lead to the concept of purgatory as a place.*

(On the eternal fate of the dead)

2308   And, if they are truly penitent and die in God's love
1304   before having satisfied by worthy fruits of penance for
their sins of commission and omission, their souls are cleansed after death by purgatorial penalties. In order that they be relieved from such penalties, the acts of intercession *(suffragia)* of the living faithful benefit them, namely the sacrifices of the Mass, prayers, alms and other works of piety which the faithful are wont to do for the other faithful according to the Church's practice.

2309   The souls of these who, after having received baptism,
1305   have incurred no stain of sin whatever, and those souls
who, after having contracted the stain of sin, have been cleansed, either while in their bodies or after having been divested of them as stated above, are received immediately *(mox)* into heaven, and see clearly God himself, one and three, as he is, though some more perfectly than others, according to the diversity of merits.

1306   As for the souls of those who die in actual mortal sin or
        with original sin only, they go down immediately *(mox)*
to hell *(in infernum)*,to be punished however with different
punishments.

THE GENERAL COUNCIL OF TRENT
TWENTY FIFTH SESSION
DECREE ON PURGATORY (1563)

Luther had rejected the doctrine of indulgences in 1517. Soon after, he took objection to the doctrine of purgatory. In his first writings, however, he attacked this doctrine only indirectly, denying its scriptural foundation and raising doubts as regards the state of souls in purgatory and the possibility for them of expiation for sins. This first position of Luther is reflected in four propositions condemned by Pope Leo X in the Bull Exsurge Domine *(1520) (cf.DS 1487-1490). Later on, as his position gradually hardened, Luther denied the existence of purgatory. This denial was in the logic of the system; expiation for sins contradicted the fundamental principles of the Reformation on salvation* sola gratia.*

The question of purgatory was on the agenda of the Council already in 1547. It was touched upon during the sixth session in the decree on justification (cf.n.1980), and again during the twenty-second session in the doctrine on the sacrifice of the Mass (cf. nn. 1548, 1557). But its explicit discussion was postponed till the last session which took place in 1563. At that moment, various reasons forced the Council fathers to wind up hurriedly the Council work. Several questions left pending were thus examined more at the disciplinary than at the doctrinal level. Before treating of the cult of saints (cf. nn. 1255 ff) and indulgences (cf. n. 1686), the twenty-fifth session devoted a decree to the question of purgatory, based on the Council's previous doctrine on the subject. This decree is notable for its sobriety. Though disciplinary rather than doctrinal in nature, it teaches again the existence of purgatory and the usefulness of prayers offered for the dead, as belonging to the Catholic faith; but it remains silent as regards the nature of purgatory.*

2310   The Catholic Church, instructed by the Holy Spirit and
1820   in accordance with sacred Scripture and the ancient
        tradition of the Fathers, has taught in the holy Councils
and most recently in this ecumenical Council that there is a
purgatory *[cf.n.1980]*, and that the souls detained there are helped
by the acts of intercession *(suffragia)* of the faithful, and especially
by the acceptable sacrifice of the altar *[cf. nn. 1548, 1557]*. Therefore
this holy Council commands the bishops to strive diligently that
the sound doctrine of purgatory, handed down by the holy fathers
and the sacred councils, be believed by the faithful and that it be

adhered to, taught and preached everywhere. But let the more difficult and subtle questions which do not make for edification and, for the most part, are not conducive to an increase of piety [cf. 1 Tim. 1:4] be excluded from the popular sermons to uneducated people. Likewise they should not permit opinions that are doubtful and tainted with error to be spread and exposed. As for those things that belong to the realm of curiosity or superstition, or smack of dishonourable gain, they should forbid them as scandalous and injurious to the faithful.

THE SECOND VATICAN GENERAL COUNCIL

The eschatological character of the Church comes to the foreground in the Second Vatican Council more than in earlier documents. This is due to the fact that the Church is conceived no longer primarily as an institution with static structures, but as the pilgrim People of God moving towards its heavenly destiny, and as the sacrament of salvation (LG 1,9,48), containing already and effectively communicating God's saving grace, while still awaiting its last manifestation.

According to Vatican II, the human person can be understood only in relation to the final destiny of one's whole being: made up of a body which "is to be raised again on the last day" and of a "spiritual and immortal" soul, the human being is one (GS 14) (cf. n. 421). Similarly, the whole of human history is considered as tending to its final goal which it will reach "in the Holy City, whose light shall be the glory of God, when the nations will walk in his light"(NA 1) (cf. n. 1019). Again, human solidarity and all human activity will attain their final destiny in Christ's heavenly Kingdom (GS 32,39). For Christ is not only the Alpha, but also the Omega, the fulfilment of all creation (GS 45) (cf. n. 669). It is in this cosmic perspective that the life of the Church herself is viewed as oriented towards the Kingdom. The main eschatological text of the Council is chapter VIII of the Constitution Lumen Gentium *on the eschatological nature of the Church (48-51) .Unlike the original draft which was more individualistic the final text is fully ecclesial. It pictures the entire pilgrim Church on its way to its final consummation. Other texts corroborate the same approach. The earthly liturgy makes the Church "share in foretaste in that heavenly liturgy which is celebrated in the Holy City of Jerusalem" (SC 8). The time of her missionary activity "lies between the first coming of the Lord and the second" and "tends towards the eschatological fulfilment"(AG 9). Thus the eschatological doctrine of Vatican II opens up for the world and the Church the grandiose horizon of a final transfiguration into Christ's glory.*

Symptomatic of the Council's approach is the meaning given to the mystery of death in the Constitution Gaudium et Spes. *Death is the most anguishing question that is put to people: "It is in the face of death that the riddle of human existence becomes most acute"(GS 18). But when the Council explains its meaning in the plan of God, it does not merely repeat the traditional doctrine of death as the punishment for sin (GS 18), but rather insists on its positive significance: in the light of the word of God death is for us the decisive conformation to Christ's Paschal Mystery, associating us intimately with Christ's own death and resurrection (GS 22). Already defeated by Christ on the cross, the last enemy will be definitively vanquished by him in the end of times (GS 39: cf. LG 49).*

DOGMATIC CONSTITUTION *LUMEN GENTIUM* (1964)

(Eschatological character of our vocation in the Church)

2311 48. The Church to which all of us are called in Christ Jesus and in which, through God's grace, we acquire holiness, will reach her consummation only in the glory of heaven, when the time will come for the restoration of all things *[cf. Acts 3:21]*, when, along with humankind, the whole universe—which is intimately related to human beings and achieves its goal through them—will be established in Christ *[cf Eph 1:10; Col 1:20; 2 Pet 3:10-13]*.

[...] The promised restoration which we are awaiting has already begun in Christ; it is carried forward in the mission of the Holy Spirit and through him it continues in the Church in which faith teaches us the meaning also of our temporal existence.[...]

Therefore, the final stage of time has already come upon us *[cf. 1 Cor 10:11]*. The renewal of the world is irrevocably determined and, in some real manner, it is anticipated in the present era.[...] However, until there will be the new heavens and the new earth in which justice will dwell *[cf. 2 Pet 3:13]*, the pilgrim Church, in her sacraments and institutions, which belong to the present era, bears the image of this world which is passing away, and she has her abode among the creatures who groan and are still in travail, awaiting the manifestation of the children of God *[cf.Rom 8:19-22]*.

(Communion between the Church of heaven and the Church on earth)

2312 49.[...] Until the Lord shall come in his majesty, and all his angels with him *[cf. Mt 25:31]*, and death having been destroyed, all things shall be subject to him *[cf. 1 Cor 15:26-27]*, some of his disciples are pilgrims on earth, while others have died and are being purified, and still others are glorified, seeing "clearly God himself, one and three, as he is"*[cf.n.2309]*. We all, however, in various ways and degrees share in the same love of God and neighbour, and we all sing the same hymn of glory to our God.

(The text continues as under n. 1689)

(Relations between the pilgrim Church and the heavenly Church)

(2313) *50. (In the life of the Church on earth the communion of saints is expressed by the intercessory prayers for the dead and in the veneration of the saints. The Church prays for the intercession of the saints, proposes them to imitation of the faithful, derives from their lives, which show a secure path to perfect union with Christ, new inspiration for seeking the City that is to come. The veneration of the saints by the Church on earth and their intercession in heaven for the wayfarers manifests the bond of charity that unites all in Christ. This communion finds expression primarily in the sacred liturgy.)*

(Pastoral directives)

(2314) *51.(The cult of the saints should be fostered according to the ancient tradition; yet, abuses and excesses must be avoided. The true cult of the saints consists not so much in the multiplicity of external acts, but rather in the intensity of an active love.]*

PASTORAL CONSTITUTION *GAUDIUM ET SPES* (1965)

(Death according to Christian faith)

2315 18. While in the face of death all imagination fails, the Church, taught by divine revelation, states that the human being was created by God for a happy goal beyond the reach of the miseries of this earthly life. In addition, our Christian faith teaches that bodily death—from which humankind would have been preserved had it not sinned *[cf. Wis 1:13, 2:23f; Rom 5:21, 6;23 James 1:15]* will be overcome by the all-powerful mercy of the Saviour, when human beings will be restored to the salvation lost through their own fault. God has called and still calls them to be united to him with their whole being by an everlasting sharing in a divine life beyond all decay. Christ achieved this victory when, liberating the human beings from death, he rose again to life *[cf. 1 Cor 15:56f]*. Thus, to any thoughtful person, the faith, when presented with its solid foundations, offers an answer to one's anxiety about what the future holds for one. At the same time it offers one the possibility of beings united in Christ with one's loved ones who have already died, and gives one hope that they have already attained to true life with God.

(New earth and new heaven)

2316   39. We do not know the time for the consummation of the earth and of humankind *[cf. Acts 1:7]*, nor do we know the manner in which the universe will be transformed. The form of this world, deformed by sin, passes away *[cf. 1 Cor 7:31]*; but we are taught that God is preparing a new dwelling place and a new earth, where justice will reign *[cf.2 Cor 5:2; 2 Pet 3:13]* and whose happiness will fulfill and surpass all the longings for peace that arise in the hearts of people *[cf. 1 Cor 2:9 Rew 21:4-5]*. Then, with death defeated, the children of God will be raised up in Christ. What had been sown in weakness and corruption will be clothed with incorruptibility *[cf. 1 Cor 15:42, 53]*; charity and its works will remain *[cf. 1 Cor 13:8, 3:14]*, and this whole creation made by God for our sake will be freed from the bondage of vanity *[cf Rom 8:9-21][...]*.

For those values of human dignity, brotherly/sisterly fellowship and freedom, all these noble fruits of nature and of our effort, which we shall have spread over the earth in the Spirit of the Lord and according to his command, we shall find again later, cleansed of all stain, illuminated and transfigured, when Christ will hand over to the Father an eternal and universal Kingdom, "a Kingdom of truth and life, of holiness and grace, of justice, love and peace."[1] Here on earth the Kingdom is present already in mystery; at the coming of the Lord it will be brought to completion.

LETTER OF THE S. CONGREGATION FOR THE DOCTRINE OF THE FAITH ON CERTAIN QUESTIONS CONCERNING ESCHATOLOGY
(17 May, 1979)

This document is concerned with the problems of eschatology arising mostly from new anthropological perspectives. While firmly insisting on the substance of the Christian doctrine on life after death, the resurrection of the whole person, the purification of the elect, and eternal reward or punishment,

---

1. *Roman Missal*, Preface of the feast of Christ the King.

the document remains silent about modern controversies, e.g., the possibility of purification of the human being at the moment of death or the eventual salvation of all out of God's infinite mercy.

There is a noteworthy discrepancy between the text of the Osservatore Romano *(23 July, 1979, pp.7-8) and of the* Acta Apostolicae Sedis 71 *(1979) 939. N.3 speaks about the personal subsistence of the "soul" after death, leaving open, according to the text in O.R., the possibility of an immediate "resurrection" of the whole person. The official text in AAS, however, qualifies the "human self" that lives on beyond death as "deprived for the present of the complement of its body" (interim tamen complemento sui corporis carens), thus maintaining the traditional view that the wholeness of the person after death, which includes the bodily existence, is delayed presumably till the end of time. This change in the official text may point to an insecurity about the degree to which modern anthropology should be allowed to affect traditional theological thinking.*

(Condition of the human person after death)

2317 The Sacred Congregation, whose task is to advance and protect the doctrine of the faith, here wishes to recall what the Church teaches in the name Christ, especially concerning what happens between the death of the Christian and the general resurrection.

1. The Church believes (cf. the Creed) in the resurrection of the dead.

2. The Church understands this resurrection as referring to the whole person; for the elect it is nothing other than the extension to human beings of the resurrection of Christ himself.

3. The Church affirms that a spiritual element survives and subsists after death, an element endowed with consciousness and will, so that the "human self" subsists, though deprived for the present of the complement of its body. To designate this element, the Church uses the word "soul", the accepted term in the usage of scripture and tradition. Although not unaware that this term has various meanings in the Bible, the Church thinks that there is no valid reason for rejecting it; moreover she considers that the use of some word as a vehicle is absolutely indispensable in order to support the faith of Christians.

4. The Church excludes every way of thinking or speaking that would render meaningless or unintelligible her prayers, her funeral rites and religious acts offered for the dead. All these are, in their substance, *loci theologici.*

5. In accordance with the Scriptures, the Church looks for

"the glorious manifestation of our Lord Jesus Chris t"(*DV* 4), believing it to be distinct and deferred with respect to the situation of people immediately after death.

6. In teaching her doctrine about the human person's destiny after death, the Church excludes any explanation that would deprive the assumption of the Virgin Mary of its unique meaning, namely the fact that the bodily glorification of the virgin is an anticipation of the glorification that is the destiny of all the other elect.

7. In fidelity to the New Testament and tradition, the Church believes in the happiness of the just who will one day be with Christ. She believes that there will be eternal punishment for the sinner, who will be deprived of the sight of God, and that this punishment will have a repercussion on the whole being of the sinner. She believes in the possibility of a purification for the elect before they see God, a purification altogether different from the punishment of the damned. This is what the Church means when speaking of hell and purgatory.

When dealing with the situation of the human being after death, one must especially beware of arbitrary imaginative representations; excess of this kind is a major cause of the difficulties that Christian faith often encounters. Respect must, however, be given to the images employed in the Scriptures. Their profound meaning must be discerned, while avoiding the risk of over-attenuating them, since this often empties of substance the realities designated by the images.

Neither Scripture nor theology provides sufficient light for a proper picture of life after death. Christians must firmly hold the two following essential points: on the one hand, they must believe in the fundamental continuity, thanks to the power of the Holy Spirit, between our present life in Christ and the future life (charity is the law of the Kingdom of God and our charity on earth will be the measure of our sharing in God's glory in heaven); on the other hand, they must be clearly aware of the radical difference between the present life and the future one, due to the fact that the economy of faith will be replaced by the economy of fulness of life; we shall be with Christ and "we shall see God" [cf. 1 Jn 3:2], and it is in these promises and marvellous mysteries that our hope essentially consists. Our imagination may be incapable of reaching these heights, but our heart does so instinctively and completely.

CATECHISM OF THE CATHOLIC CHURCH
(7 December 1992)

The following paragraphs of the Catechism illustrate the way the Church is reformulating its understanding of the so-called "last things". The current emphasis of the magisterium is threefold: (a) it reinterprets tradition, so as to centre it clearly and unequivocally on Christ and the Paschal Mystery; (b) it insists on the 'relational', positive character of anything that has to do with the end of our earthly existence; and (c) it rereads in the light of the Eucharist the whole body of the Church's teaching on the final destiny of humanity.

All the subtitles that follow are taken directly from the Catechism, with the exception of the first.

(Resurrection of the flesh)

2318a 990. The term "flesh" refers to the human being in its state of weakness and mortality *[Gen 6:3; Ps 56:5; Is 40:6]*. The "resurrection of the flesh" (the literal formulation of the Apostles' Creed) means not only that the immortal soul will live on after death, but that even our "mortal body" will come to life again *[Rom 8:11]*.

(How do the dead rise?)

2318b 997. What is "rising"? In death, the separation of the soul from the body, the human body decays and the soul goes to meet God, while awaiting its reunion with its glorified body. God, in his almighty power, will definitively grant incorruptible life to our bodies by reuniting them with our souls, through the power of Jesus' Resurrection.

2318c 999. How? Christ is raised with his own body: [...] [Lk 24:39]; but he did not return to an earthly life. So, in him, "all of them will rise again with their own bodies which they now bear," but Christ "will change our lowly body to be like his glorious body," into a "spiritual body": *[Lateran Council IV: cf. n. 20; Phil 3:21; 2 Cor 15:44]*.

But someone will ask, "How are the dead raised? With what kind of body do they come?" You foolish man! What you sow does not come to life unless it dies. And what you sow is not the body which is to be, but a bare kernel [...].What is sown is perishable, what is raised is imperishable.[...] The dead will be raised imperishable [...]. For this perishable nature must put on the imperishable, and this mortal nature must put on immortality *[I Cor 15:35-37.42.52.53]*.

2318d 1000. This "how" exceeds our imagination and understanding; it is accessible only to faith. Yet our participation in the Eucharist already gives us a foretaste of Christ's transfiguration of our bodies:

"Just as bread that comes from the earth, after God's blessing has been invoked upon it, is no longer ordinary bread, but Eucharist, formed of two things, the one earthly and the other heavenly: so too our bodies, which partake of the Eucharist, are no longer corruptible, but possess the hope of resurrection" [St Irenaeus, *Adv. Haeres.* 4, 18, 4-5: PG 7/1, 1028-1029].

2318e 1003. United with Christ by Baptism, believers already truly participate in the heavenly life of the risen Christ, but this life remains "hidden with Christ in God" [Col 3:3; cf. Phil 3:20]. The Father has already "raised us up with him, and made us sit with him in the heavenly places in Christ Jesus" [Eph 2:6]. Nourished with his body in the Eucharist, we already belong to the Body of Christ. When we rise on the last day we "also will appear with him in glory" [Col 3:4].

(Death)

2319a 1008. Death is a consequence of sin. The Church's magisterium, as authentic interpreter of the affirmations of Scripture and Tradition, teaches that death entered the world on account of man's sin [cf. Gen 2:17; 3:3; 3:19; Wis 1: 13; Rom 5:12; 6:23; DS 1511]. Even though the human beings' nature is mortal God had destined it not to die. Death was therefore contrary to the plans of God the Creator and entered the world as a consequence of sin [cf. Wis 2:23-24]. "Bodily death, from which man would have been immune had he not sinned" is thus "the last enemy" of the human being left to be conquered [GS 18/2; cf. I Cor 15:26].

2319b 1009. Death is transformed by Christ. Jesus, the Son of God, also himself suffered the death that is part of the human condition. Yet, despite his anguish as he faced death, he accepted it in an act of complete and free submission to his Father's will [cf. Mk 14:33-34; Heb 5:7-8]. The obedience of Jesus has transformed the curse of death into a blessing [cf. Rom 5:19-21].

2319c 1013. Death is the end of the human person's earthly pilgrimage, of the time of grace and mercy which God offers one so as to work out one's earthly life in keeping with the divine plan, and to decide one's ultimate destiny. When "the single course of our earthly life" is completed [LG 48/3], we shall not return to other earthly lives: "It is appointed for people to die once" [Heb 9:27]. There is no "reincarnation" after death.

(The Particular Judgment)

2320   1022. Each person receives one's eternal retribution in one's immortal soul at the very moment of death, in a particular judgment that refers one's life to Christ: either entrance into the blessedness of heaven—through a purification [cf. *Council of Lyons II, n. 2304; Council of Florence, nn. 2308-2309; Council of Trent, n. 2310]* or immediately [cf. Benedict XII, *Benedictus Deus,* nn. 2305-2306; John XXII, *Ne super his: DS* 990],—or immediate and everlasting damnation [cf. Benedict XII, *Benedictus Deus,* n. 2307].

At the evening of life, we shall be judged on our love [St. John of the Cross, *Dichos 64].*

(Heaven)

2321a   1024. This perfect life with the Most Holy Trinity—this communion of life and love with the Trinity, with the Virgin Mary, the angels and all the blessed—is called "heaven." Heaven is the ultimate end and fulfilment of the deepest human longings, the state of supreme, definitive happiness.

2321b   1025. To live in heaven is "to be with Christ." The elect live "in Christ" [Phil 1:23; cf. Jn 14:3; 1 Thess 4:17], but they retain, or rather find, their true identity, their own name [cf. Rev 2:17].

For life is to be with Christ; where Christ is, there is life, there is the kingdom [St Ambrose, *In Luc.*, 10, 121: PL 15, 1834A].

2321c   1028. Because of his transcendence, God cannot be seen as he is, unless he himself opens up his mystery to the human person's immediate contemplation and gives one the capacity for it. The Church calls this contemplation of God in his heavenly glory "the beatific vision". [...]

(The final purification, or purgatory)

2322a   1030. All who die in God's grace and friendship, but still imperfectly purified, are indeed assured of their eternal salvation; but after death they undergo purification, so as to achieve the holiness necessary to enter the joy of heaven.

2322b 1031. The Church gives the name Purgatory to this final purification of the elect, which is entirely different from the punishment of the damned [cf. Council of Florence: n. 2308; Council of Trent: n. 2310 and n. 1980; see also Benedict XII, Benedictus Deus: n. 2305]. The Church formulated her doctrine of faith on Purgatory especially at the Councils of Florence and Trent. The tradition of the Church, by reference to certain texts of Scripture, speaks of a cleansing fire [cf. I Cor 3:15; 1 Pet 1:7]

(Hell)

2323a 1035. The teaching of the Church affirms the existence of hell and its eternity. Immediately after death the souls of those who die in a state of mortal sin descend into hell, where they suffer the punishments of hell, "eternal fire" [cf. nn. 17, 20, 26/4, 810, 2301, 2307; DS 409, 1575; Paul VI, Credo, n. 39/12]. The chief punishment of hell is eternal separation from God, in whom alone one can possess the life and happiness for which one was created and for which one longs.

2323b 1036. The affirmations of Sacred Scripture and the teachings of the Church on the subject of hell are a call to the responsibility incumbent upon the person to make use of one's freedom in view of one's eternal destiny. They are at the same time an urgent call to conversion: [...] [Mt 7:13-14]. [...]

2323c 1037. God predestines no one to go to hell [cf. Council of Orange II: n. 1922; Council of Trent: DS 1567]; for this, a willful turning away from God (a mortal sin) is necessary, and persistence in it until the end. In the Eucharistic liturgy and in the daily prayers of her faithful, the Church implores the mercy of God, who does not want "any to perish, but all to come to repentance" [2 Pt 3:9]: Father, accept this offering from your whole family. Grant us your peace in this life, save us from final damnation, and count us among those you have chosen [Roman Missal, Eucharistic Prayer I (Roman Canon), 88].

(The Last Judgment)

2324a 1040. The Last Judgment will come when Christ returns in glory. Only the Father knows the day and the hour;

only he determines the moment of its coming. Then through his Son Jesus Christ he will pronounce the final word on all history. We shall know the ultimate meaning of the whole work of creation and of the entire economy of salvation and understand the marvellous ways by which his Providence led everything towards its final end. The Last Judgment will reveal that God's justice triumphs over all the injustices committed by his creatures and that God's love is stronger than death [cf. Song 8:6].

2324b 1041. The message of the Last Judgment calls people to conversion while God is still giving them "the acceptable time, [...] the day of salvation" [2 Cor 6:2]. It inspires a holy fear of God and commits them to the justice of the Kingdom of God. It proclaims the "blessed hope" of the Lord's return, when he will come "to be glorified in his saints, and to be marvelled at in all who have believed." [Tit 2:13; 2 Thes 1: 10].

(The Hope of the New Heaven and the New Earth)

2325a 1045. For the human person, this consummation will be the final realization of the unity of the human race, which God willed from creation and of which the pilgrim Church has been "in the nature of sacrament" [cf. LG 1]. Those who are united with Christ will form the community of the redeemed, "the holy city" of God, "the Bride, the wife of the Lamb" [Rev 21:2, 9]. She will not be wounded any longer by sin, stains, self-love, that destroy or wound the earthly community [cf. Rev 21:27]. The beatific vision, in which God opens himself in an inexhaustible way to the elect, will be the ever-flowing well-spring of happiness, peace, and mutual communion.

2325b 1047. The visible universe, then, is itself destined to be transformed, "so that the world itself, restored to its original state, facing no further obstacles, should be at the service of the just," sharing their glorification in the risen Jesus Christ [St Irenaeus, *Adv. Haeres.* 5, 32, 1: PG 7/2, 210].

JOHN PAUL 11
APOSTOLIC LETTER *TERTIO MILLENNIO ADVENIENTE*
10 November, 1994

In view of the completion of the second millennium of Christianity, John Paul's Apostolic Letter expounds on the themes of the end and the fulfilment of time. He excludes any reading that can diminish or alter the positivity of time. The desire to prolong time indefinitely and the concept of reincarnation do not take properly into account the way the Incarnation transformed time and history. The Word made flesh sanctions the indissoluble unity of eternity and time, God and humanity. The sanctification of time is no pious exercise, nor something that God leaves to our initiative. It is the ultimate corollary of the central mystery of the Christian faith. The full text can be found in AAS 87 (1994), pp. 5-41; Origins 24 (1994), pp. 40]ff.

2326a   9. Speaking of the birth of the Son of God, Saint Paul places this event in the "fullness of time" *[cf. Gal 4:4]. Time is indeed fulfilled by the very fact that God, in the Incarnation, came down into human history.* Eternity entered into time: what "fulfilment" could be greater than this? What other "fulfilment" would be possible? Some have thought in terms of certain *mysterious cosmic cycles* in which the history of the universe, and of humankind in particular, would constantly repeat itself. True, the human person rises from the earth and returns to it *[cf. Gen 3:19]*: this is an immediately evident fact. Yet in the human person there is an irrepressible longing to live forever. How are we to imagine a life beyond death? Some have considered various forms of *reincarnation:* depending on one's previous life, one would receive a new life in either a higher or lower form, until full purification is attained. This belief, deeply rooted in some Eastern religions, itself indicates that the person rebels against the finality of death. One is convinced that one's nature is essentially spiritual and immortal.

Christian revelation excludes reincarnation, and speaks of a fulfilment which one is called to achieve in the course of a single earthly existence. One achieves this fulfilment of one's destiny through the sincere gift of self, a gift which is made possible only through one's encounter with God. It is in God that one finds full self-realization: *this is the truth revealed by Christ.* The human person fulfils oneself in God, who comes to meet one through his Eternal Son. Thanks to God's coming on earth, human time, which began at Creation, has reached its fullness. "The fullness of time" is in fact eternity, indeed, it is *the One who is eternal,* God himself. Thus, to enter into "the fullness of time" means to reach the end of time and to transcend its limits, in order to find time's fulfilment in the eternity of God.

2326b   10. *In Christianity time has a fundamental importance.* Within the dimension of time the world was created; within it the history of salvation unfolds, finding its culmination in the "fullness of time" of the Incarnation, and its goal in the glorious return of the Son of God at the end of time. *In Jesus Christ, the Word made flesh, time becomes a dimension of God,* who is himself eternal. With the coming of Christ there begin "the last days" [*cf. Heb 1: 2*], the "last hour" [*cf. 1 Jn 2:18*], and the time of the Church, which will last until the Parousia.

From this relationship of God with time there arises *the duty to sanctify time.* This is done, for example, when individual times, days or weeks, are dedicated to God, as once happened in the religion of the Old Covenant, and as happens still, though in a new way, in Christianity. In the liturgy of the Easter Vigil the celebrant, as he blesses the candle which symbolizes the Risen Christ, proclaims: "Christ yesterday and today, the beginning and the end, Alpha and Omega, all time belongs to him, and all the ages, to him be glory and power through every age for ever". He says these words as he inscribes on the candle the numerals of the current year. The meaning of this rite is clear: it emphasizes the fact that *Christ is the Lord of time;* he is its beginning and its end; every year, every day and every moment are embraced by his Incarnation and Resurrection, and thus become part of the "fullness of time". For this reason, the Church too lives and celebrates the liturgy in the span of a year. *The solar year is thus permeated by the liturgical year,* which in a certain way reproduces the whole mystery of the Incarnation and Redemption, beginning from the First Sunday of Advent and ending on the Solemnity of Christ the King, Lord of the Universe and Lord of History. Every Sunday commemorates the day of the Lord's Resurrection.

APOSTOLIC LETTER *DIES DOMINI*
(31 May 1998)

If Sunday is the first day of the week (cf. n. 440i), already from patristic times the Church professes it to be also the eight. The fact that the Lord's Day celebrates both the 'origin' and the 'fulfilment' of all there is, can only be encountered in the Christian faith. On this account the Pope can speak of 'the pilgrim and eschatological character of the people of God' as something that defines and characterizes the Christian's daily life. Each day's activity finds its roots in creation and its goal in the Lord's return. Christian existence is, according to St Augustine, an "exercise of desire". The full text is in Origins *28 (1998), pp. 133-151.*

2327   37. As the Church journeys through time, the reference to Christ's Resurrection and the weekly recurrence of this solemn memorial help to remind us of *the pilgrim and eschatological character of the People of God*. Sunday after Sunday the Church moves towards the final "Lord's Day", that Sunday which knows no end. The expectation of Christ's coming is inscribed in the very mystery of the Church *[cf. LG 48-51]* and is evidenced in every Eucharistic celebration. But, with its specific remembrance of the glory of the Risen Christ, the Lord's Day recalls with greater intensity the future glory of his "return". This makes Sunday the day on which the Church, showing forth more clearly her identity as "Bride", anticipates in some sense the eschatological reality of the heavenly Jerusalem. Gathering her children into the Eucharistic assembly and teaching them to wait for the "divine Bridegroom", she engages in a kind of "exercise of desire" *["Haec est vita nostra, ut desiderando exerceamur"*: Saint Augustine, *In Prima Ioan. Tract. 4, 6: SC 75, 232]*, receiving a foretaste of the joy of the new heavens and new earth, when the holy city, the new Jerusalem, will come down from God, "prepared as a bride adorned for her husband" *[Rev 21:2]*.

TABLES AND INDICES

CHRONOLOGICAL TABLE OF DOCUMENTS

(Figures refer to the numbers of the volume)

1832	GREGORY XVI, Encyclical Letter *Mirari Nos Arbitramur:* 1007
1844	Promise signed by L.E Bautain: 101-105
1846	PIUS IX, Encyclical Letter *Qui Pluribus:* 106-111,1008
1854	id., Bull *Ineffabilis Deus:* 709
1854	id., Allocution *Singulari Quadam:* 813,1009-1011
1855	The fourth proposition signed by A.Bonnetty: 105
1862	PIUS IX , Encyclical Letter *Amantissimus:* 1206
1863	id., Encyclical Letter *Quanto Conficiamur Moerore:* 814, 1012
1864	id., Encyclical Letter *Quanta Cura:* 815-816
1864	id., Syllabus of condemned errors: 112/2-11, 411/1-2 1013/15-79, 2010/56-63
1868	id., Letter *lam vos Omnes* to Protestants and other non Catholics: 901-902

THE FIRST VATICAN GENERAL COUNCIL

1870	Session III: Dogmatic Constitution *Dei Filius* on the Catholic faith: 113-140, 216-219, 327-331, 412-418, (817)
1870	Session IV: Dogmatic Constitution *Pastor Aeternus* on the Church of Christ: 818-840
1873	PIUS IX, Encyclical Letter *Quartus Supra* to the Armenians: 903
1875	Collective Declaration of the German Hierarchy: 841
1880	LEO XIII, Encyclical Letter *Arcanus Divinae Sapientiae:* 1820-1823
1885	id., Encyclical Letter *Mortale Dei:* 1014-1015
1887	Errors of A. Rosmini-Serbati condemned by the Holy Office: 141-142
1888	LEO XIII, Encyclical Letter *Libertas Praestantissimum:* 2011-2014
1891	id., Encyclical Letter *Rerum Novarum:* 2101-2105
1891	id., Encyclical Letter *Octobri Mense:* 710
1893	id., Encyclical Letter *Providentissimus Deus:* 220-227
1894	id., Encyclical Letter *Praeclara Gratulationis:* 904- 906
1894	id., Constitution *Orientalium Dignitas:* 1207
1896	id., Bull *Apostolicae Curae* on Anglican Ordinations: 1722-1728
1897	id., Encyclical Letter *Divinum Illud:* 1993-1994
1899	id., Letter *Testem Benevolentiae* to Cardinal Gibbons, archbishop of Baltimore: 2015-2018

BIBLICAL INDEX

(For the scriptural texts mentioned in the documents the references in ordinary characters indicate the marginal number of the documents. For scriptural texts, mentioned in the introductions, the references indicate the page numbers; these are printed in italics.)

ANALYTICAL AND ONOMASTIC INDEX

(For the main topics this Index refers in bold characters to the page numbers of the analytical tables of the various chapters. Italics indicate page numbers of the volume and ordinary characters its marginal numbers.)

CONCORDANCE WITH DENZINGER-SCHÖNMETZER

(This concordance leaves out the numbers referring to documents quoted elsewhere in the book. Figures between brackets indicate texts not quoted but summarised.)

ND	DS	ND	DS
1	2	146	3876
2	10	147-148	3882-3883
3	13		
4	16	(202)	213
5	30	(203)	179
6	40	205	517
7-8	125-126	206	609
9	41	207	685
10-11	42-43	208	1334
12-13	150-151	210-213	1501-1504
14-15	71-72	214-215	1506-1507
16-17	75-76	216-217	3006-3007
19-21	800-802	218	3029
22-25	851-855	219	3011
26-29	855-861	221-222	3283-3284
30-38	1862-1870	223-224	3286-3288
		225-227	3290-3293
101-104	2765-2768	228/1	3401
105	2814	228/4	3404
106	2775	228/9	3409
107-111	2776-2780	228/11	3411
112/2	2902	228/14-16	3414-3416
112/3-5	2903-2905	228/23-24	3423-3424
112/6-7	2906-2907	229	3650
112/8-9	2908-2909	230-231	3652-3653
112/10-11	2910-2911	233-234	3825-3826
113-114	3004-3005	235	3828
115-117	3026-3029	236	3830
118-122	3008-3012	237	3864
123	3013	238	3887
124	3014	239	3898
125-130	3031-3036	240-244	3999a-d
131-136	3015-3020		
137-139	3041-3043	301	112
140	3044-3045	302	113
141-142	3201-3205	303	115
143	3537	305	150
143/1-13	3538-3550	306/1-3	153-155
144-145	3875-3876	306/10-13	162-165

ND	DS	ND	DS
306/16-24	168-177	618/2-3	404-405
308-316	525-532	619/1-5	416-420
317	803	620/1-10	421-432
318-320	804-806	621-623	434-437
321	850	624-626	474-476
322-324	1300-1302	627/1-16	501-516
325-326	1330-1331	628-634	533-539
327	3001	635-637	556-558
328-331	3021-3024	638	610
		639	619
401/1	403	640	791
401/8	410	643	1025-1027
402/5	455	644-645	1337-1338
402/6	456	646	1347
402/7-8	457-458	647	1529
402/9	459	648	1880
402/11-13	461-463	649	2661
403	790	650/27-38	3427-3438
405	902	651/1-3	3645-3647
406/1-3	951-953	652	3675
406/26-27	976-977	653	3676
406/28	978	661	3812
407	1007	663	3905
408	1333	664	3922
409	1336	665-667	3924-3925
410	1440		
411/1-2	2901-2902	703	503
412-413	3002-3003	704	1400
414-418	3021-3025	705	1516
419-420	3896-3897	706	1573
		707	1880
501	222	708	1973
(502)	223	709	2803-2804
503	239	710	3274
504-505	371-372	712	3370
506	780	713	3902
507-513	1510-1516	715	3903-3904
514/26	1926		
514/46-49	1946-1949	801	217
		804	870-875
603/6-7	158-159	805/2-4	942-944
603/14	166	807/8	1158
604-605	250-251	807/37	1187
606/1-12	252-263	808/1	1201
607-608	272-273	808/3	1203
609-610	291-292	808/5-6	1205-1206
611-612	293-294	808/10	1210
613-616	300-303	808/13	1213
617	401	808/15	1215

ND	DS	ND	DS
809	1307-1308	1325	2328
810	1351	1326/39-41	3439-3441
813	2865i	1327	3489
814	2865-2867	1331	3840
815	2893	1333	3855
816	2895		
818-840	3050-3075	1401	110
841	3115	1402	120
846/6-7	3406-3407	1403	128
846/52-56	3452-3456	1404	183
848	3801	1405	184
849	3802	1406	215
850	3804	1408	741
851	3807	1409	780
852	3808	1410	781
854-857	3866-3872	1411	794
858-859	3885-3886	1412-1415	1314-1316
		1416-1418	1317-1319
901-902	2998-2999	1419	1349
		1420-1433	1614-1627
1003	1348	1434-1436	1628-1630
1004	1350	1437/42-43	3442-3443
1005	1351	1437/44	3444
1006	2720		
1007	2730	1501	700
1008	2785	1502-1503	782-783
1013/15-17	2915-2917	1504	794
1013/21	2921	1506	1199
1013/77-79	2977-2979	1507/16-17	1256-1257
1014-1015	3176-3177	1508	1303
		1509-1511	1320-1322
1209/1-4	3379-3382	1512-1520	1635-1643
1214-1215	3819-3820	1521-1522	1645-1646
1218	3841	1523-1525	1648-1650
1219-1220	3842-3843	1526-1536	1651-1661
1221	3844	(1537-1540)	1726-1730
1222	3846	1541-1544	1731-1734
1251-1252	600-6001	1545-1554	1738-1749
1253	653-654	1555-1563	1751-1759
1254	1269	1566	3848
1255-1257	1821-1823	1569	3853
		1570	3854
1301	793	1571	3891
1303	1154		
1304	1262	1601	127
1305-1308	1310-1313	1602	129
1309	1451	1603	216
1310-1323	1600-1613	1604	236
1324	1728	1605	308

ND	DS	ND	DS
1606	323	1829	3707
1608	812	1830	3710
1609	814	1831	3712
1610	1157	1832	3714
1611/20-21	1260-1261		
1611/25	1265	1901-1906	225-230
1612	1323	1907	238
1613	1324-1325	1908	240
1614/5-14	1455-1464	1909	241
1615-1626	1668-1680	1910-1914	243-249
1627-1629	1684-1686	1915-1918	373-376
1630-1632	1689-1691	1919-1920	377-378
1633-1635	1692-1693	1921-1922	396-397
1635-1637	1694-1696	1923/2-3	1452-1453
1638-1640	1697-1700	1923/31-32	1481-1482
1641-1655	1701-1715	1923/36	1486
1656-1659	1716-1719	1924-1983	1520-1583
1660/46-47	3446-3447	1984/21	1921
1660/48	3448	1984/23	1923
1681-1683	1025-1027	1984/55	1955
1684/26-27	1266-1267	1984/78	1978
1685/17-22	1467-1472	1984/79	1979
1686	1835	1985/13	1913
		1985/42	1942
1701	101	1985/63	1963
1702	478	1986/20	1920
1703	794	1986/50	1950
1704	1145	1986/54	1954
1705	1326	1986/67	1967
1706	1763	1986/74	1974
1707-1713	1764-1770	1987/27-28	1927-1928
1714-1721	1771-1778	1987/39	1939
1722-1724	3316-3317	1987/40	1940
1725-1726	3317ab	1987/41	1941
1727-1728	3318-3319	1987/66	1966
1729/49-50	3449-3450	1988/16	1916
1734-1736	3849-3852	1988/34	1934
1737	3858-3859	1988/38	1938
		1989/1-5	2001-2005
(1801)	755-756	1990/1	2401
1802	794	1990/38-41	2438-2441
1803	1327	1990/59	2459
1804-1807	1797-1800	1991/44-47	2444-2447
1808-1819	1801-1812	1992/10-11	2410-2411
1820	3142	1992/23	2423
1821	3144	1993	3329
1822-1823	3145-3146	1994	3330-3331
1824-1825	3700-3701	1995	3810-3813
1826-1828	3704-3706	1996/1997	3814-3815

ND	DS	ND	DS
2005	2048	2109-2111/3	3733-3737
2006/3	2103	2113	3943
2007/1-2	2201-2202	2115-2116	3944
2007/4-5	2204-2205	2117/1-3	3947-3948
2007/14	2214	2118-2119	3949
2008/2	2291	2120	3951
2009/2-3	2302-2303	2124	3973
2010/56	2956	2125-2130	3979-3985
2010/59	2959	2134-2140/2	3991-3997
2010/63	2963		
2011	3245	2201/9	2109
2012-2013	3247-3248	2201/48-50	2148-2150
2014	3251	2202	3716-3717
2015-2017	3343-3345	2203-2204	3718
2018	3346	2205-2206	3719-3720
2020	3780-3781	2207-2208	3722
2022-2025	3918-3921		
2026-2042	3956-3972	2301	411
		2302	540
2101-2105	3265-3270	2305-2307	1000-1002
2106	3726	2308-2309	1304-1306
2107-2108	3728-3729	2310	1820

CONCORDANCE OF DENZINGER-SCHÖNMETZER WITH NEUNER-DUPUIS

DS	ND	DS	ND
2	1	250-251	604-605
10	2	252-263	606/1-12
13	3	272-273	607-608
16	4	291-292	609-610
30	5	293-294	611-612
40	6	300-303	613-616
41	9	308	1605
42-43	10-11	323	1606
71-72	14-15	371-372	504-505
75-76	16-17	373-376	1915-1918
101	1701	377-378	1919-1920
110	1401	396-397	1921-1922
112	301	401	617
113	302	403	401/1
115	303	404-405	618/2-3
120	1402	410	401/8
125-126	7-8	411	2301
127	1601	416-420	619/1-5
128	1403	421-432	620/1-10
129	1602	434-437	621-623
150-151	12-13	455	402/5
150	305	456	402/6
153-155	306/1-3	457-458	402/7-8
158-159	603/6-7	459	402/9
162-165	306/10-13	461-463	402/11-13
166	603/14	474-476	624-626
168-177	306/16-24	478	1702
179	(203)	501-516	627/1-16
183	1404	503	703
184	1405	517	205
213	(202)	525-532	308-316
215	1406	533-539	628-634
216	1603	540	2302
217	801	556-558	635-637
222	501	600-601	1251-1252
223	(502)	609	206
225-230	1901-1906	610	638
236	1604	619	639
238	1907	653-654	1253
239	503	685	207
240	1908	700	1501
241	1909	741	1408
243-249	1910-1914	755-756	(1801)

DS	ND	DS	ND
780	506	1304-1306	2308-2309
780	1409	1307-1308	809
781	1410	1310-1313	1305-1308
782-783	1502-1503	1314-1316	1412-1415
790	403	1317-1319	1416-1418
791	640	1320-1322	1509-1511
793	1301	1323	1612
794	1411	1324-1325	1613
794	1504	1326	1705
794	1703	1327	1803
794	1802	1330-1331	325-326
800-802	19-21	1333	408
803	317	1334	208
804-806	318-320	1336	409
812	1608	1337-1338	644-645
814	1609	1347	646
850	321	1348	1003
851-855	22-25	1349	1419
855-861	26-29	1350	1004
870-875	804	1351	810, 1005
902	405	1400	704
942-944	805/2-4	1440	410
951-953	406/1-3	1451	1309
976-977	406/26-27	1452-1453	1923/2-3
978	406/28	1455-1464	1614/5-14
1000-1002	2305-2307	1467-1472	1685/17-22
1007	407	1481-1482	1923/31-32
1025-1027	643	1486	1923/36
1025-1027	1681-1683	1501-1504	210-213
1145	1704	1506-1507	214-215
1154	1303	1510-1516	507-513
1157	1610	1516	705
1158	807/8	1520-1583	1924-1983
1187	807/37	1529	647
1199	1506	1573	706
1201	808/1	1600-1613	1310-1323
1203	808/3	1614-1627	1420-1433
1205-1206	808/5-6	1628-1630	1434-1436
1210	808/10	1635-1643	1512-1520
1213	808/13	1645-1646	1521-1522
1215	808/15	1648-1650	1523-1525
1256-1257	1507/16-17	1651-1661	1526-1536
1260-1261	1611/20-21	1668-1680	1615-1626
1262	1304	1684-1686	1627-1629
1265	1611/25	1689-1691	1630-1632
1266-1267	1684/26-27	1692-1693	1633-1634
1269	1254	1694-1696	1635-1637
1300-1302	322-324	1697-1700	1638-1640
1303	1508	1701-1715	1641-1655

DS	ND	DS	ND
1716-1719	1656-1659	2291	2008/2
1726-1730	(1537-1540)	2302-2303	2009/2-3
1728	1324	2328	1325
1731-1734	1541-1544	2401	1990/1
1738-1749	1545-1554	2410-2411	1992/10-11
1751-1759	1555-1563	2433	1992/23
1763	1706	2438-2441	1990/38-41
1764-1770	1707-1713	2444-2447	1991/44-47
1771-1778	1714-1721	2459	1990/59
1797-1800	1804-1807	2661	649
1801-1812	1808-1819	2720	1006
1820	2310	2730	1007
1821-1823	1255-1257	2765-2768	101-104
1835	1686	2775	106
1862-1870	30-38	2776-2780	107-111
1880	648	2785	1008
1880	707	2803-2804	709
1913	1985/13	2814	105
1916	1988/16	2865i	813
1920	1986/20	2865-2867	814
1921	1984/21	2893	815
1923	1984/23	2895	816
1926	514/26	2901-2902	411/1-2
1927-1928	1987/27-28	2902	112/2
1934	1988/34	2903-2905	12/3-5
1938	1988/38	2906-2907	112/6-7
1939	1987/39	2908-2909	112/8-9
1940	1987/40	2910-2911	112/10-11
1941	1987/41	2915-2917	1013/15-17
1942	1985/42	2921	1013/21
1946-1949	514/46-49	2956	2010/56
1950	1986/50	2959	2010/59
1954	1986/54	2963	2010/63
1955	1984/55	2977-2979	1013/77-79
1963	1985/63	2998-2999	901-902
1966	1987/66	3001	327
1967	1986/67	3002-3003	412-413
1973	708	3004-3005	113-114
1974	1986/74	3006-3007	216-217
1978	1984/78	3008-3011	118-121
1979	1984/79	3011	219
2001-2005	1989/1-5	3012	122
2048	2005	3013	123
2103	2006/3	3014	124
2109	2201/9	3015-3020	131-136
2148-2150	2201/48-50	3021-3025	414-418
2201-2202	2007/1-3	3021-3024	328-331
2204-2205	2007/4-5	3026-3027	115-117
2214	2007/14	3029	218

DS	ND	DS	ND
3031-3036	125-130	3675	652
3041-3043	137-139	3676	653
3044-3045	140	3700-3701	1824-1825
3050-3075	818-840	3704-3706	1826-1828
3115	841	3707	1829
3142	1820	3710	1830
3144	1821	3712	1831
3145-3146	1822-1823	3714	1832
3176-3177	1014-1015	3716-3717	2202
3201	141	3718	2203-2204
3205	142	3719-3720	2205-2206
3245	2011	3722	2207-2208
3247-3248	2012-2013	3726	2106
3251	2014	3728-3729	2107-2108
3265-3270	2101-2105	3733-3737	2109-2111/3
3274	710	3780-3781	2020
3283-3284	221-222	3801	848
3286-3288	223-224	3802	849
3290-3293	225-227	3804	850
3316-3317	1722-1724	3807	851
3317ab	1725-1726	3808	852
3318-3319	1727-1728	3810-3813	1995
3329	1993	3812	661
3330-3331	1994	3814-3815	1996-1997
3343-3345	2015-2017	3819-3820	1214-1215
3346	2018	3825-3826	233-234
3370	712	3828	235
3379-3382	1209/1-4	3830	236
3401	228/1	3840	1331
3404	228/4	3841	1218
3406-3407	846/6-7	3842	1219-1220
3409	228/9	3844	1221
3411	228/11	3846	1222
3414-3416	228/14-16	3848	1566
3423-3424	228/23-24	3849-3852	1734-1736
3427-3438	650/27-38	3853	1569
3439-3441	1326/39-41	3854	1570
3442-3443	1437/42-43	3855	1333
3444	1437/44	3858-3859	1737
3446-3447	1660/46-47	3864	237
3448	1660/48	3866-3872	854-857
3449-3450	1729/49-50	3875	144
3452-3456	846/52-56	3876	145-146
3489	1327	3882-3883	147-148
3537	143	3885-3886	858-859
3538-3550	143/1-13	3887	238
3645-3647	651/1-3	3891	1571
3650	229	3896-3897	419-420
3652-3653	230-231	3898	239

DS	ND	DS	ND
3902	713	3947-3948	2117/1-3
3903-3904	715	3949	2118-2119
3905	663	3951	2120
3918-3921	2022-2025	3956-3972	2026-2042
3922	664	3973	2124
3924-3925	665-667	3979-3985	2125-2130
3943	2113	3991-3997	2134-2140/2
3944	2115-2116	3999a-d	241-244